Writing Analytically with Readings

David Rosenwasser
Jill Stephen

Muhlenberg College

THOMSON
WADSWORTH

Australia Brazil Canada Mexico Singapore Spain United Kingdom United States

Writing Analytically with Readings
Rosenwasser/Stephen

Editor in Chief: *PJ Boardman*
Publisher: *Lyn Uhl*
Senior Acquisitions Editor: *Aron Keesbury*
Development Editor: *Mary Beth Walden*
Assistant Editor: *Cheryl Forman*
Editorial Assistant: *Lindsey Veautour*
Senior Technology Project Manager: *Joe Gallagher*
Managing Marketing Manager: *Mandee Eckersley*
Marketing Assistant: *Kathleen Remsberg*
Senior Marketing Communications Manager: *Stacey Purviance*
Associate Content Project Manager: *Jennifer Kostka*
Senior Art Director: *Cate Rickard Barr*
Print Buyer: *Betsy Donaghey*

Permissions Manager: *Ron Montgomery*
Permissions Researcher: *Julie McBurney*
Production Service/Compositor: *GEX Publishing Services*
Text Designer: *Meral Dabcovich/GEX Publishing Services*
Photo Manager: *Sheri Blaney*
Photo Researcher: *Sharon Donahue*
Cover Designer: *Gina Petty*
Text/Cover Printer: *Courier Corporation/Westford*
Cover Art: *Photographer: 1937: Bill Hedrich. Hedrich-Blessing, HB-04414-D3, Edgar Kaufman residence, Fallingwater, Bear Run (Pa)-Chicago Historical Society; Architect: Frank Lloyd Wright. Alterations have been made to the original copy, including cropping, tinting, or detailing.*

Every effort has been made to verify the authenticity and sources of URLs listed in this book. All URLs were correctly linked to their websites at the time of publication. Due to the quickly evolving nature of the Internet, however, it is possible that a link may break or a URL may change or become obsolete. Should you discover any inconsistencies, please contact http://www.thomsonedu.com/support and a correction will be made for the next printing

Printed in the United States of America
1 2 3 4 5 6 7 10 09 08 07 06

Thomson Higher Education
25 Thomson Place
Boston, MA 02210-1202
USA

For more information about our products, contact us at:
Thomson Learning Academic Resource Center
1-800-423-0563
For permission to use material from this text or product, submit a request online at **http://www.thomsonrights.com**
Any additional questions about permissions can be submitted by e-mail to **thomsonrights@thomson.com**

Credits appear on pages C-1–C-4, which constitute a continuation of the copyright page.

Library of Congress Control Number:
2006909264

ISBN-13: 978-1-4130-1349-8
ISBN-10: 1-4130-1349-X

BRIEF CONTENTS

CONTENTS

CHAPTER 7 Recognizing and Fixing Weak Thesis Statements 197

CHAPTER 8 Introductions and Conclusions 219

Four Editorials 687

JAMES J. KILPATRICK: ***Justices Amended Constitution on Their Own ...*** 687

RICHARD A. EPSTEIN: ***... By Letting Redevelopers Take Little Guy's Property*** 688

JOHN F. GRIM: ***More than Abortion Is at Stake in Supreme Court Picks*** 689

PAUL KRUGMAN: ***Losing Our Country*** 691

GEORGE ORWELL: ***Politics and the English Language*** 694

"Political language—and with variations this is true of all political parties, from Conservatives to Anarchists—is designed to make lies sound truthful and murder respectable, and to give an appearance of solidity to pure wind."

DANTE CHINNI: ***Why Should We Trust This Man?*** 706

"[Frank Luntz is] possibly the best example of what we could call the pollster pundit: someone who both purports to scientifically poll the opinions of the public, and then also interpret that data to support his own—in Luntz's case, conservative—point of view."

FRANK LUNTZ: ***Interview*** 725

"The only thing I don't believe in is lying. Beyond that, you can use almost anything."

MATT BAI: ***The Framing Wars*** 725

"Conservative politicians, Lakoff suggests, operate under the frame of a strict father, who lays down inflexible rules and imbues his family with a strong moral order. Liberals, on the other hand, are best understood through a frame of the nurturant parent, who teaches his child to pursue personal happiness and care for those around him."

JAMES PECK: ***September 11th: A National Tragedy?*** 740

"To its credit, melodrama cares about questions of morality and takes seriously the evil that men do. But it also divides the world into stark, simplistic categories. It thrives on a politics of us and them. Since September 11th, I believe we've been living out a national melodrama."

For Further Research: The Language of Politics and the Politics of Language 747

Chapter 20 The Review as Cultural Analysis 749

About the Readings in This Chapter 749

ADAM GOPNIK: ***The Unreal Thing: What's Wrong with the Matrix?*** 752

"Although the movie was made in 1999, its strength as a metaphor has only increased in the years since. The monopolization of information by vast corporations; the substitution of an agreed-on fiction [...]; the sense that we have lost control not only of our fate but of our small sense of what's real—all these things can seem part of ordinary life now."

ADAM GOPNIK: ***American Electric: Did Franklin fly that kite?*** 762

"We are said to be living in an icon-smashing age, but the odd thing is how few shards can be found on the floor [...]. The Founding Fathers have been remade as Founding Brothers, our superior siblings."

MATT BAI: King of the Hill ***Democrats?*** 772

"There is more reality about American life in five minutes of *King of the Hill* than in a full season of watching Paris Hilton prance around a farm in high heels."

IMAGES

PREFACE

This edition of *Writing Analytically* is the first to be accompanied by readings and images—material for writers to write about and to use as models and lenses in doing their own writing about the world. This is two books in one. The first fourteen chapters are a self-standing rhetoric. The next six chapters are topic-centered units of readings and images, surrounded with an apparatus that overtly links these to pertinent parts of the rhetoric.

Our original book, *Writing Analytically* (now in its fourth edition), evolved out of our experience as directors of a Writing Across the Curriculum (WAC) program at a small liberal arts college and out of our writing workshops for faculty at our own and other colleges and universities. We learned from faculty across the curriculum that what they wanted from student writing was not passive summary, not personal narrative, not opinions and debate-style argument, but analysis.

What they did want was in-depth, non-evaluative reflection. They wanted writing aimed at understanding rather than at promoting a particular point of view. They wanted students to think on the page about what things mean—which is our primary definition of analysis.

Writing Analytically with Readings offers alternatives to oversimplified thinking of the like/dislike, agree/disagree variety. It argues that an idea is not the same thing as an opinion and demonstrates how to respect the complexity of subjects where there is no single right answer.

To best serve teachers of writing in various disciplines and in various kinds of first-year composition courses, we designed our rhetoric, *Writing Analytically*, so that it could be easily adapted to a range of course contents. We wanted teachers to be able to take from the book what they needed and in whatever order they needed it, rather than having the content and sequencing of their courses dictated by our book.

Given this rationale and our own professional histories, we were initially hesitant about producing an expanded edition of *Writing Analytically with Readings*. But many colleagues have told us that they would like a version of *Writing Analytically* that shows students how to apply its thinking and writing strategies to an expanded set of examples. Over the past two years, our interest in the project has continued to grow, for we have had to teach ourselves about the chapters that comprise the book, and we have had to appeal to our colleagues in other disciplines to become our teachers as well.

We here offer a map of *Writing Analytically with Readings.*

WHY YET ANOTHER ANTHOLOGY OF READINGS?

- To illustrate analytical writing—what it is—in a more sustained way
- To provide essays that would prompt students to respond with writing that is analytical rather than argumentative
- To provide readers with a better balance than currently exists of imitable academic writing and smart contemporary journalism aimed at educated audiences

The book is organized entirely around analytical writing. We acknowledge that analytical essays inevitably make arguments, but we think there is value in distinguishing between argument and analysis, and we think that students need to learn to analyze first. And so, rather than asking students to *produce* issue-oriented, pro-con arguments, the book teaches students how to *analyze* arguments by locating binaries, uncovering assumptions, and inferring implications (see Chapters 2 and 3).

The essays in each of the book's six topic chapters work as primary material for analytical summary, comparative analysis, and synthesis, and also as lenses and models for student application to other materials.

LINKS TO WRITING ACROSS THE CURRICULUM (WAC)

Although *Writing Analytically* developed from our backgrounds as WAC directors, the book is not a WAC text. That is, it does not aim primarily to introduce students to the academic disciplines as different discourse communities, each with its own characteristic vocabulary and epistemology. We think it an unreasonable expectation that a first-year writing text ought to be able to introduce students to the diverse vocabularies, protocols, and mindsets of the different academic disciplines. But it is possible for an anthology of readings to teach students the habits of mind that serious, intellectually stimulating academic writing across the disciplines shares.

We include readings from a number of disciplines—political science, history, communications, American studies, photography, film studies, and so on—but we do not emphasize these as disciplinary templates for writing. As evidenced by the Voices from Across the Curriculum sections of Part One, we hesitate to speak for other disciplines' ways of knowing. Instead, we have consulted colleagues, asking them in each case, what are the one or two readings that you would recommend for first-year students? What essays have your students responded to with active discussion and engaged writing?

In a few cases, we have chosen essays written by these colleagues, and two that appear here were written especially for this volume. One, an interview with a photography professor whose own work documents the almost vanished world of American steel-making, offers his historical and theoretical framework for understanding contemporary American photography. The other piece, by a political science professor who is also a well-known pollster, addresses the history, use, and abuse of political labels in contemporary culture.

A GUIDE TO PART ONE: THE RHETORIC

HAVING IDEAS

Writing Analytically with Readings is about how to have ideas and develop them in an academic setting and beyond. It offers a book-length treatment of analysis, a form of thinking and writing required in virtually all college courses but frequently overshadowed in writing texts and first-year composition courses by emphasis on argument (persuasion), expressive writing, or the traditional rhetorical modes.

The book proceeds on the assumption that there are certain elements of effective analytical writing common to all disciplines. Our experience teaching seminars to faculty across the curriculum has convinced us that the area of consensus about writing is larger and more significant than the differences. So, although the book respects disciplinary difference, it does not lead with difference. Instead, it attempts to forge a common language for talking about writing that does not over-rely on the technical jargon of any one discipline. In the many instances where discussion of disciplinary difference is clearly called for, we create spaces—labeled Voices from Across the Curriculum—for professors from various disciplines to write in their own words about their practices and preferences.

Writing Analytically with Readings is deeply committed to the concept of writing to learn—that is, to the notion that writing is a tool that can facilitate and enrich understanding. Thus, the book emphasizes ways of using writing to figure out what things mean. It encourages writers to assume an exploratory stance toward ideas and evidence: to delay their judgments in favor of understanding, to treat their ideas as hypotheses to be tested rather than as self-evident truths, and to share their thought processes with readers.

THE EVOLVING THESIS

The book most markedly differs from other writing texts in its treatment of the "thesis" (a paper's governing idea). Most textbooks about writing tend to present thesis statements as the finished products of an act of thinking—as inert statements that writers should march through their papers from beginning to end. In practice, though, the relationship between thesis and evidence is far more fluid and dynamic. In most good writing, the thesis grows and changes in response to evidence, even in final drafts. So we argue that the problem with much writing of the sort that people are taught to do in school is that it arrives *prematurely* at an idea that the writer then "proves" by attaching it to a number of examples (a pattern we call 1 on 10; see Chapter 5). For the best quick hit on what the book has to say about thesis statements, start with the sections in Chapter 1 called "What It Means to Have an Idea" and "Moving from Idea to Thesis Statement: What a Good Thesis Looks Like."

The book also differs from many textbooks in its approach to argument. We believe writers should learn to analyze before concentrating on persuasive writing. The best arguments start from the best ideas, which are arrived at through careful analysis. Much weak writing, in other words, is prematurely and too narrowly thesis-driven precisely because people try to formulate and argue the thesis before they have done much (or any) analyzing. For readers interested in argument, the methods the book offers in its first two chapters, and especially the third part of Chapter 3 ("Reformulating Binaries and Uncovering Assumptions"), are well suited to both analyzing and constructing arguments.

The way to better writing that this book recommends sounds easy but actually isn't. As writers and thinkers, we all need to SLOW DOWN—to dwell longer in the open-ended, exploratory, information-gathering stage. This requires specific tasks that will reduce the anxiety for answers, impede the reflex move to judgments, and encourage a more hands-on, less passive engagement with materials. *Writing Analytically with Readings* supplies these tasks for each phase of the writing and idea-generating process—making observations, inferring implications, and making the leap to possible conclusions.

Our three chapters on style (Chapters 10, 11, and 14), like the other chapters in the book, are about thinking. We use them early in our writing courses, inviting students to perceive a writer's characteristic sentence shapes and words as useful windows on that writer's mind, his or her way of approaching the world.

Past readers of the book have asked if we could include in one place a brief annotated list of the various observation and idea-generating strategies that the book recommends. These can be found in a brief glossary of these strategies—entitled The Book's Heuristics: An Overview—located near the end of this preface. Quick access to the book's perspective on writing can also be achieved by browsing the "Try this" exercises, the short sections at the beginning of the first fourteen chapters called "Quick Takes," as well as the Guidelines sections that end each of these chapters.

A GUIDE TO PART TWO: READINGS AND IMAGES

THE THREE LIVES OF A READING

At the heart of *Writing Analytically with Readings* is the notion that every reading can function in three ways in a writing course:

1. As an Object for Analysis (pursuing implication and complication)
2. As a Lens for Viewing Other Material (epistemology—how we come to know things)
3. As a Model for Imitating (organization)

To dilate briefly on each of these categories:

1. As Object: The reading offers interesting and relatively sophisticated primary material for students to analyze. Writing tasks attached to the readings teach readers to use writing in order to read more deeply and reflectively.
2. As Lens: The reading contains theories and analytical methods that readers can extract and use to view other materials, both verbal and nonverbal, in the "outside" world. Writing assignments related to the readings prompt ways of applying information and theoretical materials, which is a critical skill in college writing.
3. As Model: The reading offers a way of approaching a topic. Tasks linked to specific readings show writers how to emulate the ways that effective analytical writing operates.

PRINCIPLES OF SELECTION FOR ESSAYS

We kept asking ourselves as we read a range of possible materials to include, what would our students *do* with this reading? How could they *use* it? How could they turn it into a lens? Where might they locate a complication that would give them something to say about it—and not just repeat what it already says?

We think we have put together a collection of readings and images that are informative and interesting but, most important, thought-provoking and imitable. Each of the book's six topic categories contains essays of sufficient depth and complexity to comprise an interpretive context to guide readers' own analyses as they move from writing about the reading to applying the reading to other readings, and to their observations about the world. We have, in short, sought writing capable of helping readers become better able to navigate and understand the verbal environment all around them.

The selections are not ideological in the sense of essays chosen to move readers toward a particular or dogmatic point of view. Instead we have aimed for serious writing on matters of interest and importance now, such as

- changing habits of communication in a technological world
- public and private space in America today
- neighborhoods: the way we live now
- race, ethnicity, and the "melting pot"
- reading the labels: liberal, conservative, and other semantically challenging key words
- interpreting images

The selections are moderate in length and difficulty: not byte-sized but also not graduate school level pieces on cultural theory. We have kept in mind that the primary audience for the anthology is made up of reasonably engaged first-year students.

Most selections are fairly current—since 2000—though there are some classic essays, often serving as theoretical frames [e.g., Jane Jacobs (1962), John Berger (1972), Susan

Sontag (1976), and Margaret Visser (1991)]. In some cases the older pieces will offer writers the challenging opportunity to update these classic claims or to assess them from the perspective of the present. We have also included in a few cases several articles by a single writer, to encourage reading more deeply within and across a writer's work—for example, Matt Bai on politics, and Adam Gopnik on reviews as cultural analysis.

Like the original *Writing Analytically*, the anthology of readings is designed to be used in a variety of ways. It has stand-alone topic chapters from which writing professors could choose, but the chapters are also heavily cross-referenced. So, for example, the discourse of public and private that begins in Chapter 15 in the context of Manners, Communication, and Technology re-emerges in treatments of the New Urbanism in Chapter 16, Places and Spaces: Cities and Suburbs, and finds echoes in concerns about mass persuasion in Chapter 19, The Language of Politics and the Politics of Language.

The anthology does not try to provide all that a writing teacher might want in each topic area. Instead, it *samples* available readings on the topic, providing enough depth and breadth to introduce it. In Chapter 16, Places and Spaces: Cities and Suburbs, for example, there are readings on the culture of cities and how cities are being reshaped through commercial pressures. Such pieces attune readers to looking *at* the management of public and private space for its social implications, wherever the readers happen to be situated. At the end of the chapter, they will find a list of print and internet sources where they might pursue interestingly related topics such as the new urbanism. And given that "the new urbanism" is itself up for political grabs, these readers might profitably go to another of the book's available lenses, Chapter 19, The Language of Politics and the Politics of Language, to begin to untangle the conservative and liberal approaches to this new buzz phrase.

THE APPARATUS IN PART TWO

Each chapter has a brief introduction that funnels into an equally brief survey of the readings. Every reading selection is also briefly introduced and, following the selection, under the heading Things to Do with the Reading, are a series of thinking and writing tasks designed to encourage analysis. These all seek to encourage readers to tap into the Three Lives of A Reading—as an Object for Analysis (pursuing implication and complication), as a Lens for Viewing Other Material (epistemology), and as a Model for Imitating (organization).

Some of the items listed in Things to Do with the Reading are labeled as Applications (which involve using the reading as a lens) or as Links (which overtly connect the reading to another reading in the same chapter) or as Links Across Chapters. We have chosen not to specify which of the thinking and writing tasks should become exercises, which should become full-fledged papers, and so forth. The instructor's manual will, however, offer more concrete suggestions along these lines.

Finally, at the end of every chapter, there is a section entitled For Further Research. These sections were compiled by our invaluable colleague, reference librarian Kelly Cannon. (He also authored "Electronic Research: Finding Quality on the Web" in Chapter 13.) Essentially, he has provided a series of leads for readers (and teachers) to pursue if they were to extend the inquiry started by the chapter's actual selections. Each For Further Research is divided into Online and In Print sources, and for each of these sources, Cannon has provided a brief summary along with a possible writing task under the heading of Explore.

PEDAGOGICAL PRINCIPLES

The kinds of thinking and writing tasks that we have included for every reading selection in the Things to Do with the Readings sections share a set of principles. These tasks reject two fairly common pedagogical practices: the highly personal reaction and the guessing game. The problem with calling for a reader's immediate "reaction" to a reading is that such reactions tend to be unreflective, and in most cases, overgeneralizations or cultural clichés. For the same reason, we seek to avoid triggering a reader's like/dislike, agree/disagree switch (see pages 22–23 on Overpersonalizing).

Like the rhetoric *Writing Analytically*, the anthology is keenly interested in observational methods. We believe in reading to write but also in writing to read. Writing to read requires looking at the words, slowing down the process, in order to see more and to see better.

Collaborative versus teacher-centered models of instruction

Writing Analytically with Readings moves away from teacher-centered modes of instruction in which the teacher's job is to design a series of questions or work sheets (usually aimed at a predetermined end) and moves toward a mode of instruction in which teachers and students share the thinking and writing strategies and thus function more collaboratively—more collegially—in the classroom.

Looking at, not through, words

The book vigorously opposes "reading for the gist"—leaps to broad generalizations and judgments. It promotes "becoming conversant"—being able to speak the language of a piece by getting physical with its words.

Slowing down

The book provides readers and writers with methods for prolonging and systematizing the observation phase in order to lead them to more productive (less clichéd) conclusions.

Doing things with the reading

The book shows writers how to take the next step beyond summarizing and synthesizing readings. One of the biggest differences between high school and college reading practices is that college students are expected to understand fairly sophisticated theoretical frameworks and apply these to other materials. The goal is to learn how to do things with the readings rather than just passively registering the information contained in them.

Extracting a reading's analytical method

The book shows how to separate a reading's analytical method from the particular argument to which it leads. Not that the argument should be ignored, but our emphasis rests on educing an author's methodology and having readers apply it in their own writing projects to related phenomena, which these writers can observe in their own environments. One can, in other words, learn a lot about looking at spaces from an urban studies article on the relocation of the homeless in Los Angeles without necessarily focusing on either L.A. or the homeless (see Mike Davis's "Fortress Los Angeles" in Chapter 16). Most college campuses, for example, offer significant opportunities to observe the manipulation of public space either to encourage or deter use by certain populations.

Doing observational fieldwork

We are fond of sending students out, singly or in groups, to do what we call observational fieldwork (see Chapter 1). People need to be able to take the theory and method in the readings and "test drive" these, so to speak, in the world. There are opportunities for observational fieldwork in all of the chapters in Part Two, under the heading of "Application" in the apparatus that follows each reading selection. The book presses readers to become more aware of their verbal environments—the student newspaper, things overheard in the cafeteria, graffiti, the ever-changing language of courtship, and so forth.

THE BOOK'S HEURISTICS: AN OVERVIEW

As this book uses the term, a heuristic—from the Greek word for "discover"—is a formula for searching evidence to arrive at ideas. We think of the heuristics as "universal" topics because they can be applied to virtually any subject matter. They are topics of invention—fairly formulaic moves that you can make to notice more about a subject, to discover what you think about it, and to arrive at more sophisticated topics, which can then be developed further.

Here is a skeletal list of the book's primary heuristics, along with a brief description and a reference to the chapters in which they are discussed:

1. **Paraphrase × (times) 3** (see Chapters 1 and 4)

   Paraphrasing inevitably discloses that what is being paraphrased is more complicated than it first appeared. When you recast a sentence or two—finding the best synonyms you can think of for the original language, translating it into a parallel statement—you are thinking about what the words mean. Do it three times to open a range of meanings. Paraphrase is not summary; it's a mode of inquiry and the first step toward interpretation. It also gives writers something to do with the reading besides simply recording it or agreeing/disagreeing with it.

2. **Notice and Focus + Ranking** (see Chapter 1)

   The prompt here—What do you notice?—helpfully short-circuits the tendency to generalize. It redirects the writer's attention to the subject matter and thus delays the pressure to come up with answers prematurely. The second step has you focus by asking you to rank (create an order of importance for) the various features you have noticed about the subject.

3. **[What do you find most] "Interesting" or "Strange"?** (see Chapter 1)

   These prompts can be integrated into other heuristics or used to get you thinking on the page, as in, "What I find most strange about x is. ..." They offer alternatives to what we call the judgment reflex—a counterproductive habit of mind that approaches the world in terms of like/dislike, right/wrong, should/shouldn't. The prompts shift attention from pro/con argument to thinking aimed at understanding and theorizing about the nature of things. They invite writers to defamiliarize, rather than to normalize, things out of our range of notice.

4. **Looking for Patterns of Repetition and Contrast (aka the Method)** (see Chapters 2 and 3)

This is the book's primary heuristic for the observation stage of analysis. It consists of data gathering in response to three basic questions: What do you notice? What repeats? What is opposed to what? Here are the steps:

Step 1. List exact repetitions and the number of each (words, details).

Step 2. List strands—groupings of same or similar kinds of words, details (for example, *polite*, *courteous*, *mannerly*). Explain the strand's connecting logic with a label.

Step 3. List organizing contrasts—binary oppositions (for example, *open/closed*, *gray/brown*). Start with what's on the page; then move to implied terms.

Step 4. Select and list the two or three most significant repetitions, strands, and binaries.

Step 5: Locate anomalies: exceptions to the pattern, things that seem not to fit. Then compose one healthy paragraph explaining your choice of one repetition, strand, or binary as most significant.

5. **The Five Analytical Moves** (see Chapter 2)

These moves define the context within which Looking for Patterns and other heuristics operate. The moves establish the ground for having ideas.

Move 1: Suspend judgment (understand before you judge).

Move 2: Define significant parts and how they are related.

Move 3: Look for patterns of repetition and contrast and for anomalies (aka the Method).

Move 4: Make the implicit explicit (convert to direct statement meanings that are only suggested—make details "speak").

Move 5: Keep reformulating questions and explanations. (What other details seem significant? What else might they mean?)

6. **Asking So What?** (see Chapter 1)

This question is our universal prompt for spurring the leap to interpretation. It is shorthand for questions such as these:

Why does this observation matter? Where does it get us?

What ideas are implicit in it?

How can we begin to generalize from the observation to the larger subject?

Asking So what? presses writers to move beyond the patterns and emphases they've been observing in the data and make some kind of claim. The So what? question should be posed all of the time, not just at the end of the thinking process, and not just once about an observation.

7. **Freewriting & Passage-Based Focused Freewriting** (see Chapters 1 and 4)

The central question to ask in improving one's ability to read critically is What is the single sentence that I think is most important for us to discuss and why? This heuristic works on the assumption that readers will have a better appreciation of how the whole works when they've seen how a piece works. A freewrite should target key phrases and paraphrase them, ask So what? about the details, and address how the passage is representative of broader issues in the reading.

8. **Finding "Go To" Sentences** (see Chapter 11)

What are the two or three sentence structures that reveal the tendency any given writer has to shape his or her thought—the characteristic ways he or she uses language? Because the way that a sentence is structured reveals a way of thinking, identifying a writer's typical sentence structure—the form he or she tends to "go to"—can be revelatory. Then ask yourself in what ways this type of sentence reveals how the writer thinks.

9. **"Seems to Be about *X*, but Could Also Be (or Is 'Really') about *Y*"** (see Chapter 3)

This prompt is based on the conviction that understandings are rarely simple and overt, but rather, complexly embedded in particular contexts. Completing the formula by supplying key terms for *x* and *y*, writers get practice in making the implicit explicit and accepting the existence of multiple plausible meanings for something. (Note: The word *really* aims not to suggest a single hidden right answer but to prompt a range of less obvious landing sites for interpretive leaps.) "Seems to be about *x*" is especially useful when considering the rhetoric of a piece: its complex and various ways of targeting and appealing to an audience. It's also useful for "reading against the grain"—seeking out what something is about that it probably does not know it's about.

10. **Doing 10 on 1** (see Chapters 1 and 5)

This heuristic encourages analyzing in depth. The phrase 10 on 1 is shorthand for the principle that it is better to make ten observations or points about a single representative issue or example (10 on 1) than to make the same basic point about ten related issues or examples (1 on 10). (The number 10 is arbitrary, standing for "a lot.") Doing 10 on 1 helps writers narrow their focus and draw out as much meaning as possible from their best examples. It operates to locate a range of possible meanings suggested by the evidence. It will also prevent you from jumping to a thesis prematurely, while your thinking is still too general.

11. **A Template for Organizing Papers Using 10 on 1** (see Chapter 5)

Here is a pared-down version of a formula for organizing a paper by doing 10 on 1. It is an alternative to more rigid models, such as five-paragraph form, which tend to stunt rather than promote thinking.

1. In the introduction, note a pattern or tendency in the evidence and explain why you find it potentially significant and worth looking at (a working thesis about what this pattern might reveal or accomplish).
2. Zoom in on your representative example, some smaller part of the larger pattern. Argue for the example's representativeness and usefulness in coming to a better understanding of your subject.
3. Do 10 on 1 on this example, sharing your observations and tentative conclusions (answers to the So what? question). Then use complicating evidence to refine your claims.
4. In a short paper, move to conclusion, offering a qualified version of your thesis and brief commentary on the ways your analysis has illuminated the larger subject.

5. In a longer paper, begin "constellating"—that is, exploring the connections among several representative 10-on-1 examples. The first of these is used as a lens for examining the others; each example in turn further qualifies and develops the claim (with conclusion to follow).

12. Applying a Reading as a Lens (see Chapter 4)

This heuristic models how to compare two readings without just listing similarities and differences. It suggests how to focus on the way a reading uses its point of view as a lens—a way of looking at or understanding something else (another subject or another reading). The key move is for the reader to assume that the match between lens A and subject B won't be exact, and therefore he or she should focus on how A both fits and does not fit B. The writer then uses the differences to develop the analysis.

13. [Looking for] Difference Within Similarity and Similarity Despite Difference (see Chapter 5)

This heuristic seeks to make the standard "comparison and contrast" move more analytical—not just a mechanical matching exercise ("A does this; B does that," and so on). The formula is this:

- Identify fundamental similarity. Account for its significance by answering the question, So what that A and B have this similarity?
- Then, given the similarity, locate the most important difference, and again ask So what? When A and B are obviously similar, look for unexpected difference. When A and B are obviously different, look instead for unexpected similarity.

These steps will prevent a conclusion such as "Thus, we see there are many similarities and differences between A and B."

14. Six Steps for Making a Thesis Evolve (through Successive Complications) (see Chapter 6)

This heuristic offers the book's primary model for developing complex ideas on a subject and then organizing a paper around this process. It emphasizes using evidence that complicates the major claim, to make the claim more supple and accurate.

1. Formulate an idea about your subject—a working thesis.
2. See how far you can make this thesis go in accounting for (confirming) evidence.
3. Locate complicating evidence that is not adequately accounted for by the thesis.
4. Make explicit the apparent mismatch between the thesis and selected evidence, asking and answering So what?
5. Reshape your claim to accommodate the evidence that hasn't fit.
6. Repeat steps 2, 3, 4, and 5 several times.

In contrast to debate-style argument, this format has the advantage of trying neither to hide nor to ignore evidence that doesn't fit the claim. That is because it approaches evidence as more than "the stuff that proves I'm right." The evolving thesis seeks to account fully and accurately for what is there.

15. Conversing with Sources (see Chapter 12)

This is less a single heuristic than a governing idea for how to approach secondary materials in ways that get beyond using them as answers or disagreeing with the experts. The various ways of conversing share the approach of using the source as a point of departure. Here is a brief list of how to use sources in this way:

- Make as many points as you can about a single representative passage from your source, and then branch out from this center to analyze other passages that "speak" to it in some way.
- Build upon the source's point of view, extending its implications.
- Apply the idea in the source to another subject.
- Agree with most of what the source says but take issue with one small part that you want to modify.
- Identify a contradiction in the source and explore its implications, without necessarily arriving at a solution.

ACKNOWLEDGMENTS

For this edition of *Writing Analytically with Readings* first thanks go to the person who persuaded us to take on so daunting a task in the first place, Dickson Musslewhite, former acquisitions editor at Thomson. We are grateful to Dickson, who saw us through *Writing Analytically*'s third and fourth editions, fortifying us with his humor, intelligence, good will, and first-rate fiction. We are now fortunate to have Aron Keesbury, acquisitions editor (and poet), shepherding the book into the marketplace. Our profound gratitude goes to developmental editor extraordinaire, Mary Beth Walden, for her tireless efforts on our behalf—her confidence in our vision of the book and her understanding of what writers need in order to find their way through so large a project. Michael Rosenberg, publisher at Thomson, has been gracious with his ideas, both for this and for subsequent writing projects. We also appreciate Jennifer Kostka's guiding the text through the production process.

This book first came into being primarily because of the insight and patience of one person, our original developmental editor, Karl Yambert, then at Harcourt. We remain grateful to Karl for starting our education (still under way) on how to write a decent "how to" book for writers. Similar thanks go to his successor, Michell Phifer, who made the revision and production phases of the second and third editions a pleasure, and to our former acquisitions editors, John Meyers, who taught us about getting a book out of the hands of the publisher and into the hands of readers, and Julie McBurney, who brought the second edition into being and who journeyed through the wilderness of securing permissions for this edition. We had the good fortune to work with Karen R. Smith, former developmental editor at Thomson, who consistently offered her encouragement, patience, and good advice on the evolution of the fourth edition.

We are deeply grateful to our colleagues and students at Muhlenberg College for their many contributions to this first edition of *Writing Analytically with Readings*. Former students Sarah Kersh and Robbie Saenz de Viteri spent a summer gleaning cool readings to get us started. Kelly Cannon contributed all of the For Further Research sections, bringing his inimitable combination of skills as reference librarian, offbeat intellectual, and English PhD to the task. Jack Gambino, and Jim Peck, admired colleagues and friends, generously agreed to let us include their work among our reading selections. So did Mary Lawlor, whose essay on Edward Curtis fell victim to page constraints for this edition. For Chris Borick and Joe Elliott, who spent a semester producing pieces for us to include in key locations in the anthology, we reserve particular thanks. Thanks for taking the time to think with us and write for us, Chris; and thanks for those memorable Friday morning interviews, Joe, where you taught us how to look at photographs.

Our debts to our teaching and writing friends are very great. Christine Farris has been a great friend of the book since its early days. She and John Schilb and their colleagues at Indiana University (especially Matthew Johnson) keep us in touch with the ideas and problems that first brought the book into being. Ted Leahy, also of Indiana, merits special thanks for his willingness to take on the Instructor's Manual for this new version of the book. Our friend Dean Ward at Calvin College has been a source of inspiration and good conversation on writing for many years. Thanks as well to Georgina Hill, Matt Hollrah, and to our friends at the National Writing Project: Richard Louth and Lin Spence. Especially important to the fourth edition of the rhetoric, Wendy Hesford and Eddie Singleton of Ohio State University and their graduate students continue to affect the way we think about writing and writing pedagogy.

We are also, of course, deeply indebted to our students and colleagues at Muhlenberg College, who have shared their writing and their thinking about writing with us:

Students:

Rachel Breckman
Wendy Eichler
Pete Lankarge
Jake McNamara
Liz McNierney
Thomas Prevete
Kim Schmidt
Jessica Skrocki
Laura Sutherland

Colleagues:

Anna Adams
Karen Beck
Jim Bloom
Christopher Borick
Ted Conner
Karen Dearborn
Patrice DiQuinzio
Joseph Elliott
Jack Gambino
Barri Gold
Mary Lawlor
John Malsberger
James Marshall
Linda Miller
Robert Milligan
Rich Niesenbaum
Fred Norling
James Peck
Jeff Pooley
Mark Sciutto
Grant Scott
Scott Sherk
Laura Snodgrass
Jeremy Teissere
Alan Tjeltveit
Bruce Wightman

and our good friend and confidant, Alec Marsh. Carol Proctor in the English Department looks out for us and casts a sympathetic eye on our organizational deficiencies. We also thank Muhlenberg College for continuing to support our participation at national conferences.

Finally, last but certainly not least, we are grateful to the many reviewers who took the time to offer their input on Writing Analytically with Readings: Dan Albergotti, Elon University; Stephanie Almagno, Piedmont College; Joyce Anderson, Millersville University; Paul Aviles, Onondaga Community College; Dr. Diana Badur, Black Hawk College; Donna Bauerly, Loras College; Rebecca Baumann, Indiana University; Linda Bips, Muhlenberg College; Beau Black, Weatherford College; Margaret D. Bonesteel, Syracuse University; Margot Boyer, North Seattle Community College; Norman Boyer, Saint Xavier University; Melanie Brezniak, Indiana University Bloomington; Cheryl Brown, Towson University; Jessica Brown, City College of San Francisco; Robin Bryant,

Phillips Community College; Patricia Burdette, Ohio State-Mansfield; Melissa Burley, University of Miami; Susan Callaway, University of St. Thomas; Anita P. Chirco, Keuka College; Wayne Christensen, Florida Memorial University; J.C. Clapp, North Seattle Community College; Michelle Collins-Sibley, Mount Union College; Innam Dajany, North Country Community College; Susan Davis, Indiana University; Kate Dobson, McDaniel College; Victoria Dowling, University of Massachusetts; Jayme Duncan Eveland, Indiana University; Dr. Chitralekha Duttagupta, Arizona State University; Sharyn Emery, Indiana University; Mary Ertel, Medaille College; Rebecca Fast, The Ohio State University Mansfield; Dr. Patricia Feito, Barry University/ ACE; Karen Feldman, University of California, Berkeley; Fran Ferrante, University of San Francisco; Judy Fowler, Fayetteville State University; Sue Frankson, College of DuPage; Erica Frisicaro, University of St. Thomas; Ryan Futrell, Cedarville University; Greta Gard, Indiana University; Margaret V. Gardineer, Felician College; Jill Gatlin, University of Washington; Mary A. Gervin, Albany State University; Sue Granger-Dickson, Bakersfield College; Sally Green, University of Colorado at Boulder; Jane Hammons, University of California, Berkeley; Corliss Harmer, Antioch University; Suzanne Harper, Penn State Worthington; Jennifer Hellwarth, Allegheny College; Scott Hermanson, Dana College; Margaret Hermes, Indiana University; Lisa Hermsen, Rochester Institute of Technology; Nels P. Highberg, University of Hartford; Mica Hilson, Indiana University; Susan Isaac, Georgia Military College; Dawnelle A. Jager, Syracuse University; Jacqueline Jenkins-Glymph, Stanford University; Rick Johnston, Indiana University; Gail Jones, University of Texas at San Antonio; Jason B. Jones, Central Connecticut State University; Justin A. Joyce, University of Illinois at Chicago; Erick Kelemen, Columbia College; Karalyn Kendall, Indiana University, Bloomington; Jessica Ketcham, Louisiana State University; Melissa Korber, Las Positas College; Anne Langendorfer, The Ohio State University; Kathy Lattimore, SUNY Cortland; Melissa Lingle-Martin, Indiana University; Stephanie M. Loomis, Boston College; Michael Lueker, Our Lady of the Lake University; Sonja Lynch, Wartburg College; Renee Major, Louisiana State University; Ann Marshall, Weatherford College; David W. Marshall, Indiana University-Bloomington; Kim Martin, Fort Lewis College; David McAvoy, Indiana University, Bloomington; Laura McCracken, North Seattle Community College; Susanne Meslans, Edmonds Community College; Michael Moghtader, James Madison University; Deborah Montuori, Shippensburg University; Gwendolyn Morgan, Montana State University; Jane Mueller Ungari, Robert Morris College; Sean P. Murphy, College of Lake County; Debbie Olson, Central Washington University; Elizabeth Passmore, University of Connecticut; Velvet Pearson, Long Beach City College; Adrienne Peek, Modesto Junior College; Kate Pluta, Bakersfield College; Donna Qualley, Western Washington University; Deborah Renville, Kankakee Community College; Celia Rasmussen, Indiana University, Bloomington; Kathleen Riley, Ohio Dominican University; Rochelle Rodrigo, Mesa Community College; Cheryl Ronish, Lower Columbia College; Margaret Rozga, University of Wisconsin-Waukesha; Paul Sanchez, Fresno City College; Heather Schell, George Washington University; Dr. Laine Scott, LaGrange College; Rachella Sinclair, University of San Francisco; Virginia Skinner-Linnenberg, Nazareth College; Harvey Solganick, LeTourneau University; Jean Sorensen, Grayson County College; Randolph Splitter, De Anza College; Melissa Storms, North Seattle Community College; Karen J. Strewler, University of Wisconsin-Superior; Liz Stringer, East Mississippi Community College; Nicole Tobin, Indiana University; Dorothy Tsuruta, San Francisco State University; Joseph Viera, Nazareth College; Robin Vogelzang, Indiana University; Courtney Weikle, Ohio State University; Stephanie Wells, Orange Coast; Laura Wilder, SUNY Albany; April Witt, Indiana University; Sarah Wolf Newlands, Portland State University; Monica Zewe, Mercyhurst North East College.

PART I

THE RHETORIC

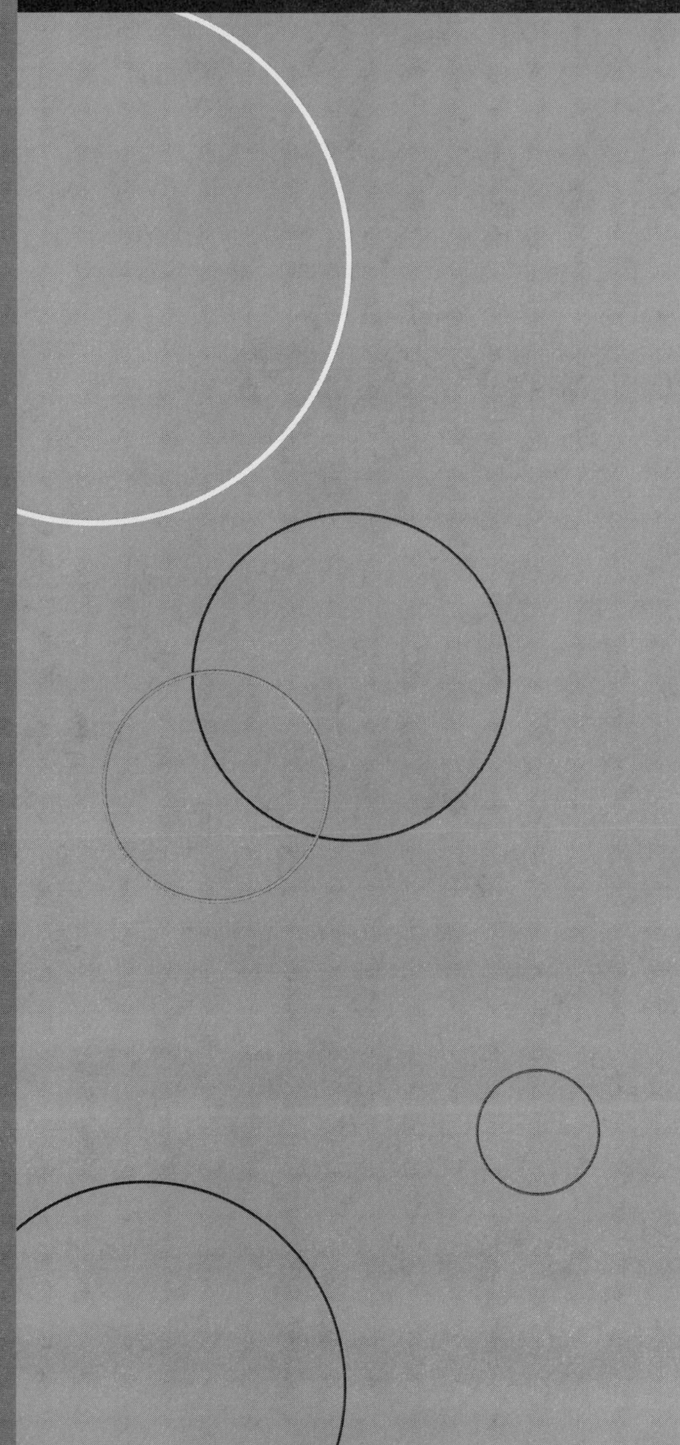

CHAPTER 1

Seeing Better: The Analytical Habit of Mind

"See better, Lear." – William Shakespeare

"Reserving judgements is a matter of infinite hope." – F. Scott Fitzgerald

Quick Take

This book is interested in ideas: what they are, how they operate in a piece of writing, and how they happen. Our primary claim about ideas is that they are the product of minds habituated to focusing sustained attention on details: the analytical habit of mind. Central to this habit of mind is a writer's willingness to use description as an analytical tool.

People who have ideas are not necessarily smarter or more creative than the rest of us, and they may not even work harder. People who are struck more often by the thing we call inspiration have method on their side, whether they are aware of this fact or not. This chapter introduces many of the book's idea-generating strategies, including Notice and focus, 10 on 1, paraphrase × 3, and asking "So what?"

The chapter is divided into four sections. The first section emphasizes description as an analytical tool—a means of attending more closely to evidence. It is all about learning to see more when we observe things.

The second section seeks to open things up in your writing. It proposes the value of tolerating uncertainty and of becoming more aware of counterproductive habits of mind that can close thinking down prematurely.

Those of you who wish to get to the heart of the book's analytical method could move directly to Sections 3 and 4 of this first chapter. These include "What It Means to Have an Idea" and the book's basic strategies for observing, uncovering implication, and pushing observations to conclusions. Section 4 is an extended example of student writing using these strategies. In Section 4 you will also learn how to mark up a draft to find opportunities for developing its ideas.

We hope that you find the book's writing exercises enjoyable as well as useful, and that they help you cultivate confidence in your own writing process. Writing, like most worthwhile human activities, works best if powered, at least in part, by joy.

SECTION 1: SEEING THE DETAILS

Although much of this first section is about description, and thus might seem to be geared more to the needs of the fiction or memoir writer than to people learning to write analytically, we believe that good analytical writing (and thinking) depends upon the same skills that energize all good writing: attention to concrete detail. If you can afford to spend some time on the description exercises, especially Hemingway's five finger exercise in this first section of the chapter, before you move on to more strictly analytical writing, your work will benefit.

NOTICING (AND THE DEADENING EFFECT OF HABIT)

Some people, perhaps especially the very young, are good at noticing details. They see things the rest of us don't see or have ceased to notice. But why is this? Is it just that people become duller as they get older? The poet William Wordsworth, among others, argued that we aren't the victims of declining intelligence but of habit. That is, as we organize our lives so that we can function more efficiently, we condition ourselves to see in more predictable ways and to screen out things that are not immediately relevant to our daily needs.

You can test this theory by considering what you did and did not notice this morning on the way to work or class. Getting where we need to go, following a routine for moving through the day, can be done with minimal engagement of either the brain or the senses. Our minds are often, as we say, "somewhere else." As we walk along, our eyes wander a few feet in front of our shoes or stare blankly in the direction of our destination. Moving along the roadway in cars, we periodically realize that miles have gone by while we were driving on automatic pilot, attending barely at all to the road or the car or the landscape. Arguably, even when we try to focus on something we want to consider, the habit of not really attending to things stays with us. We glide over the top. We go for rapidly acquired impressions and then relax our attention and forget the rest.

People tend to remember their reactions and impressions. The dinner was dull. The house was beautiful. The music was exciting. But they forget the specific, concrete causes of these impressions (if they ever fully noticed them). As a result, we deprive ourselves of material to think with—the data that might allow us to reconsider our initial impressions and to share them with others. A premise of this book is that frequent writing trains people to become more observant, better able to remember the details of an experience, and thus much more likely to have ideas.

People tend to remember their reactions but forget the cause.

The deadening effect of habit on seeing and thinking has long been a preoccupation of artists as well as philosophers and psychologists. Some people have even defined the aim of art as "defamiliarization." "The essential purpose of art," writes the novelist David Lodge, "is to overcome the deadening effects of habit by representing familiar things in unfamiliar ways." The man who coined the term *defamiliarization*, Victor Shklovsky, wrote, "Habitualization devours works, clothes, furniture, one's wife, and the fear of war. . . . And art exists that one may recover the sensation of life" (David Lodge, *The Art of Fiction*. New York: Penguin, 1992, p.53). This claim takes us to the chapter's first and most fundamental exercise, tracing impressions back to causes.

TRACING IMPRESSIONS BACK TO CAUSES

To become more aware—which is key to becoming a better writer—we have to train ourselves to notice more: both our impressions of things and how these impressions are formed. The single best piece of advice we know on this subject can be found in the counsel the writer Ernest Hemingway offered to a young man who had come to him for guidance on becoming a writer. You can try this advice yourself in the box below.

Try this 1.1: Hemingway's Five Finger Exercise

Read the passage by Ernest Hemingway below and then start practicing the five finger exercise that he recommends. Practice it at least once a day for a week in a notebook that you set aside for trying out the writing exercises in this book. Each five finger exercise will probably be about a paragraph, or at most a page in length. At the end of the week, type your two best five finger exercises. If possible, read them aloud to a class or smaller group of people who also have been doing the exercise.

Throughout the passage Hemingway refers to experiences on a day of deep sea fishing.

> Watch what happens today. If we get into a fish, see exactly what it is that everyone does. If you get a kick out of it while he is jumping, remember back until you see exactly what the action was that gave you the emotion. Whether it was the rising of the line from the water and the way it tightened like a fiddle string until drops started from it, or the way he smashed and threw water when he jumped. Remember what the noises were and what was said. Find what gave you the emotion; what the action was that gave you the excitement. Then write it down, making it clear so the reader will see it too and have the same feeling you had. That's a five finger exercise.

After you've done some writing, go back over what you have said and select the most significant details. A good description is not an undifferentiated catalogue, the verbal equivalent of a photograph. Good description is highly selective. Build a descriptive paragraph around these details. We like the term *telling details* for those you think are most revealing in sharing with readers the essential character and feel of an experience. Your goal is to cause a person who reads your paragraph to think and feel as you did. Achieve this without telling your readers how you thought and felt. Let the details do the telling. Show rather than tell.

WHAT WE DO WHEN WE DESCRIBE THINGS

The passage from Hemingway offers not only a useful exercise but also an opportunity to consider just what it is that we do—and why—when we describe things. Describing consists of a combination of three activities, all of which are illustrated in the following sentence, which describes a bullfighter's way of walking: "The gypsy was walking out toward the bull again, walking heel-and-toe, insultingly, like a ballroom dancer." Let's consider what this sentence does and then compare it with the way Hemingway handles description in the five finger exercise.

The three things that people typically do in description are

1. **offer concrete detail**—that is, details that allow others to share the writer's sensory experience ("walking heel-and-toe");
2. **make comparisons** that allow readers to understand something unfamiliar in terms of something they might be expected to know better ("like a ballroom dancer"); and
3. **name the experience** in some way (for example, happy, sad, confusing), often through the use of evaluative adjectives and adverbs ("insultingly").

A good description is not an undifferentiated catalogue, the verbal equivalent of a photograph. Good description is highly selective.

Try this 1.2: Looking at What We Do When We Describe

Look back at Hemingway's five finger exercise above and consider which of the three descriptive activities he relies on the most. Find the comparisons, the concrete detail, and any direct naming or evaluating of the experience of the sort that we see with the word *insultingly* in the sentence about the gypsy. Look also at the parts of speech Hemingway uses. Does he seem to prefer any particular parts of speech—nouns, for example, or adjectives, or verbs? What is the role of nouns relative to adjectives? You will notice that Hemingway doesn't use many adjectives. Why might this be, and what is the effect of leaving adjectives out?

EVALUATIVE AND ABSTRACT VERSUS CONCRETE WORDS

It is useful to consider that adjectives and adverbs can be divided into two basic types: those that offer concrete information, something we can actively imagine and visualize, such as walking heel-to-toe, and those that offer judgments (good, bad, pretty, ugly, depressing, exciting). Evaluative adjectives and adverbs don't actually tell readers very much about the subject itself, only about the impact that the subject had on the writer. Evaluative adjectives, the ones that offer judgments rather than concrete detail, don't really describe. Instead they simply label. They tell us how the writer responded, but they don't share the causes of that response with the reader. It is this problem, among others, that the five-finger exercise addresses.

Consider the difference for a reader in being told, "The lecture was boring" or being offered the following rendering of the same thing in concrete detail: "The professor leaned forward on the podium, fixing his eyes on his notes. As the minutes ticked by, the professor's eyes moved from the notes to some spot high on the ceiling at the back of the room and then back to the notes again. Sentence after sentence rolled out, with nothing more to mark its passing than these slight shifts in the professor's eyes, never once stopping to alight on his students."

You can best address the evaluative adjective problem by sharing with your readers the actual data, the concrete detail that made you respond as you did. This shift from evaluative adjectives and explicit statement to concrete detail is called showing versus telling. Concrete detail allows you to share your data—the grounds of your convictions—with your readers. Evaluative adjectives and abstractions shut the reader out of your thinking process.

A concrete detail is one that allows us to visualize (see in our mind's eye) or hear or touch or smell the particulars of an experience. The opposite of *concrete* is *abstract*. The word *democracy* is abstract. It is a concept—an idea. We know what it means, but we cannot see it, taste it, hear it, or smell it. The red handle on the lever that closes the curtain in a voting booth and the many little boxes with names next to them are concrete details, the stuff of democracy as an experience. (For an extended discussion of concrete versus abstract words, see Chapter 10, "Choosing Words.")

Try this 1.3: Distinguishing Abstract from Concrete Words

Make a list of the first ten words that come to mind and then arrange them from most concrete to most abstract. Then repeat the exercise by choosing key words from a page of something you have written recently.

Try this 1.4: Distinguishing Evaluative from Nonevaluative Words

The dividing line between evaluative and nonevaluative words is often much harder to see in practice than you might assume. Categorize each of the terms in the following list as judgmental or nonjudgmental, and be prepared to explain your reasoning: monstrous, delicate, authoritative, strong, muscular, automatic, vibrant, tedious, pungent, unrealistic, flexible, tart, pleasing, clever, and slow.

SHOWING VERSUS TELLING

The act of describing, of showing rather than telling, is just as important to analytical writing—in fact to all kinds of writing—as it is to the writing of poems or fiction. Browse through, for example, a history book—even a history textbook—the newspaper, or any collection of essays, including some on scientific subjects, and you will find description (and narrative as well, since the two so often go hand in hand). Description is essential to writing. We simply cannot think well without it. Although the various academic disciplines differ in the kinds of description they employ and in the ways that description may be used, they all call for keeping thinking in touch with telling detail.

Try this 1.5: Showing versus Telling: an Evocative Place

Pick a place, either from memory or from your current experience, that appeals to your senses, a place that makes you take notice of your surroundings. Describe this place in a way that will cause another person to experience it as you do. Avoid evaluative adjectives and descriptions of your feelings. Write the piece without telling your readers your reactions to the place or the reasons for them. Offer instead the concrete details that shape your response to the place. You can include action and people other than yourself in your description if you like.

As we have already noted, this kind of writing is not the sole province of short-story writers, novelists, and poets. All kinds of writing depend on the writer's ability to use words to re-create experience. Weak writing tends to offer the writer's conclusions without sharing his or her experience of the evidence with readers. Your goal as a writer is to let your readers think with you. This means that you have to give them the stuff that made you think as you do, to risk letting them think along with you rather than just imposing your views. Good writing offers not only a writer's conclusions, but the thinking about particulars that produced the conclusions.

Another piece of Hemingway's conversation with the young writer offers us some useful thinking on the relation between judgments (evaluation) and understanding.

> Then get in somebody else's head for a change. Don't just think who is right. . . . As a writer you should not judge. You should understand.
>
> When people talk, listen completely. Don't be thinking what you're going to say. Most people never listen. Nor do they observe. You should be able to go into a room and when you come out know everything that you saw there and not only that. If that room gave you any feeling, you should know exactly what it was that gave you that feeling. Try that for practice. When you're in town stand outside the theater and see how the people differ in the way they get out of taxis and motor cars. There are a thousand ways to practice.

Notice that in his advice here, Hemingway concentrates not only on activities—observing and remembering—but on habits of mind that get in the way of observing and remembering. Judging, as we discuss at more length later in this chapter, is the habit of mind most likely to shut down our powers of observation. This is so because once a judgment has been made, we tend to screen out anything that runs counter to it. Judgments cause us to fall back on evaluative adjectives rather than doing the more difficult job of tracing our judgments back to causes. When we don't trace our judgments back to causes, we deprive ourselves of the data necessary for reconsidering our response. It is through this process that our responses to the world harden into the kinds of automatic judgments that we call opinions.

Try this 1.6: Observation Fieldwork

Station yourself somewhere on campus, such as the entrance to the student union or any place where people tend to gather. Go there every day for at least five days and write a neutral description of what you see and hear. Don't include judgments or conclusions about your scene. Just collect detail that strikes you as particularly telling. You will find that it is surprisingly difficult to leave out your reactions, though you should recognize that the details you choose to record are already reactions because it is you and your orientation toward the world that have selected them.

When you are finished, put together a one- to two-page account that tells by showing—that is, your account should be made up entirely of telling detail rather than your interpretations of the significance of that detail. Your goal is to provide readers of your account with a window on the world, but one that is, of course, highly selective, because writing does not operate like a camera eye. Writing is inevitably and necessarily more selective. Keep revising your account until you have a rendering of your "data"—the observed details—that will cause your readers to think and feel as you do about the scene.

Description as a Form of Analysis Virtually all forms of description are implicitly analytical. When you choose what you take to be the three most telling details about your subject, you have selected significant parts and used them as a means of getting at what you take to be the character of the whole. This is what analysis does: it goes after an understanding of what something means, its nature, by zeroing in on the function of significant detail.

What follows are two short descriptive passages from personal essays written by students. Analyze the different kinds of descriptive work that goes on in each: explicit telling, especially with evaluative adjectives; showing, through the use of concrete detail; and making comparisons. What seems to you to be the most important telling detail in each? What does this detail "say"?

Notice, by the way, that the distinction between evaluative adjectives and concrete ones is not always entirely clear. *Blurry*, for example, as used in the second piece, is both an evaluation and a concrete detail. As an evaluation it means "not clear." As a concrete detail, it suggests the actual experience of memory in which images are present but are dim and jumbled and ill defined.

For your consideration of word choice in the passages, let us add another interesting category—the kind of adverbs known as intensifiers. Like adjectives and adverbs that merely name evaluative conclusions (such as *boring*), intensifiers offer little or no information about the subject. An intensifier is a verbal exclamation point. You can greatly improve your writing by systematically cutting out the intensifiers (*very*, *really*, *terribly*, etc.). Spot the intensifier in our last sentence. Sometimes intensifiers are good for purposes of emphasis—but a little bit goes a long way.

Two Examples of Description as a Form of Analysis

First student description

22 Green Hill Road was the most beautiful house I had ever seen. The bricks a light brown, and the ivy growing along the sides reflected the sun with such perfection every afternoon. Everything about it was magnificent, but the best part about it was how it never changed—even from the moment I moved in when I was three, the house itself had always been there for me to come back to.

It was junior year in high school and I was visiting 22 Green Hill Road to pick up a few things, when I noticed something different under the clock that wasn't there when I moved out with my mom months earlier. It was a frame filled with pictures of a woman in the process of rolling down a luscious light green hill. I couldn't stop staring at her: her hair was dark brown and her jeans were a size too big. I had never met her before, and she certainly did not belong in my kitchen—the kitchen that was once so familiar I could recall every detail on every wall. My father walked in.

I turned to him. "Who . . . is this?" I asked him. It took him a while to figure out what to say. He sighed and answered, "That's my friend Beth." He had an ultimate innocence in his voice that never went away; I could never stay mad at him for long.

"Oh," I replied. Then I asked what I wished I had not for a long time afterward. "Did you take this?" He backed away from me.

Whenever I stopped by, from that moment on, he turned the frame around so I could not see the images of a strange yet now so familiar woman in what used to be my kitchen.

Second student description

I wish I could tell you more about that night, but it's kind of blurry. What do I remember? My father's voice, "Mommy passed away." I know I cried, but for how long I don't remember. My boyfriend was there; he only heard my end of the conversation. He drove me home from college. I guess that took a couple of hours. There was a box of tissues on my lap, but I didn't use any. He smoked a cigarette at one point, and opened up a window. The black air rushed in and settled on me like a heavy cloak.

Try this 1.7: Finding the Implicit Analysis in Description

In addition to noting the different kinds of descriptive activities and descriptive words that appear in the two passages above, you could think about what it is that each writer is analyzing through the use of description. Which sentences and which details reveal the implicit analysis contained in the description? Consider for example what thinking is implicit in the following two sentences: "It was a frame filled with pictures of a woman in the process of rolling down a luscious light green hill. I couldn't stop staring at her: her hair was dark brown and her jeans were a size too big." Why these details rather than others the writer might have selected? Why the word *luscious*? In the second descriptive passage, what implicit analysis does the sentence about the box of tissues reveal?

A NOTE ON MATCHING SENTENCE SHAPES TO SUBJECTS

The management of sentence style—syntax—is as important to the effect of both of these descriptive pieces, especially the second one, as the word choice is. In our chapter on sentence style (Chapter 11) we discuss a useful concept we learned from a colleague: the "go to" sentence. The "go to" sentence is the sentence type, the particular way of ordering words, that each of us habitually goes to. The "go to" sentence is actually a feature of who we are, because it embodies how we characteristically respond to the world.

All of us have "go to" sentences that we fall back on in daily life—in speaking as well as writing. Our choice of sentence shape is influenced by how we think, but it varies according to the subjects we are writing and talking about. The matching of sentence shape to subject matter is especially interesting in the second descriptive passage above.

The "go to" sentence is actually a feature of who we are, because it embodies how we characteristically respond to the world.

The second passage tends to go to sentences that offer flat, largely unembellished declarative statements, as in "He drove me home from college" or "He smoked a cigarette at one point, and opened up a window." If you know something about how to analyze the shapes of sentences, you might profitably spend a little time trying to figure out the relation between the kinds of sentences the writer typically uses in the second description and the content of that passage. It will help if you know the difference between coordinate sentences, in which everything is treated at one level of importance, and subordinate sentences, in which some things depend upon and are set up as less important than other things. (See the glossary in Chapter 14.)

WRITING THE SELF AS AN INTRODUCTION TO ANALYSIS

All writing is, in a sense, personal, since there is an "I" doing the thinking and selecting the details to consider. But most analytical writing done in the academic disciplines is about some subject other than the self. Writing about the self, about one's own memories and defining experiences, is, however, a useful way to stimulate our thinking about words (evaluative and abstract versus concrete, for example) and about the role of detail in shaping our ideas about things.

And so, we offer the following assignment for a personal essay. It treats the writer's self as the subject of an analysis and calls for the writer to conduct that analysis through the careful selection and arrangement of telling detail. It helps in thinking about this kind of writing to assume that we all have various versions of ourselves to offer to others—and to ourselves. In other words, writing the self inevitably means constructing a version of yourself, not just writing what "is."

Try this 1.8: Writing the Self

Write a brief (two-page) descriptive piece about yourself that you would be willing to read out loud to others engaged in the same exercise. Do this by offering a narrative of some revealing and representative "moment"—perhaps a kind of moment that tended to recur—in your life. Sometimes the most telling moments, those that play a significant role in how we come to be who we are, are subtle, small moments, rather than "big" life-changing experiences. Some of these small but significant moments are barely remembered until we start looking for them with writing. Thus, they engage readers in the writer's process of discovery, which is what good writing should do.

Your piece will necessarily be a blend of showing and telling, of description and more explicit analysis, but make sure not to substitute telling readers how you felt for re-creating the experience that made you feel as you did. Offer your experience of a revealing moment to your readers. Avoid evaluative (empty of detail, judgmental) adjectives. Insofar as judgments are being made in your piece, let them be implied rather than overtly stated, as the author of the descriptive piece on the picture of a strange woman in her kitchen does. We learn a lot in that piece about how the writer thinks and the kinds of judgments she was making, but she does not dwell on her thinking or her judgments. She lets us see these through her choice of detail.

One of us does a version of this assignment with the following direction: talk about a single event in your life that most people don't know about, and if we did, we'd understand you better.

Two Examples of Writing the Self

Here are two excerpts from longer personal essays that students eventually developed from this short assignment. The first is an opening paragraph. It offers less concrete detail than the other examples, but there is a lot of thought-provoking work and implicit analysis going on in the writer's word choice. The second is a paragraph from a piece in which we learn about the writer—as she learns about herself—in the context of her relationship with a best friend who was, in a way, her opposite.

Memoir 1

I was still young enough to be in elementary school, and my siblings were newly initiated teens, when my parents brought home one day, strapped to the back of my mother's GMC Suburban, a behemoth on wheels. Upon further inquisition and speculation, we discovered that this three-dimensional, trapezoidal structure was hospitable and meant to house individuals for lengths of time—a home on wheels. My family was from then on in possession of a trailer, one that had to be dragged across miles of circuitous highways and man-made, pothole-studded campgrounds before returning to the driveway of our little ranch house in the town my siblings and I refer to today as a branch of white-trash suburbia.

Memoir 2

She used to come to me for advice on relationships. She was the science geek and I was her public relations advisor. We were supposed to stick to our roles. After that night, though, we were playing her game. She was the referee just waiting for me to foul so she could blow the whistle. The more we saw of each other, the worse it got. Instead of sitting on our comfy pedestals, sizing up the rest of the world, now we were both at our own separate podiums, ready for debate.

SECTION 2: OPENING THINGS UP: NEGATIVE CAPABILITY, PARAPHRASE × 3, FREE-WRITING, AND COUNTERPRODUCTIVE HABITS OF MIND

This section of the chapter seeks to open things up in your writing. It proposes the value of tolerating uncertainty—a stance toward experience for which we like the poet John Keats's concept of "negative capability." We introduce two primary strategies for opening things up rather than closing them down: paraphrase × 3 and freewriting in its various forms. The section concludes with a more theoretical discussion of counterproductive habits of mind that cause us to short-circuit our thinking. These are judging, generalizing, personalizing, and confusing opinions with ideas. By becoming more self-conscious about the ways you think, you can become more comfortable with uncertainty and thus remain more open to evidence and the ideas it invites you to have.

NEGATIVE CAPABILITY: LOCATING AN AREA OF UNCERTAINTY

Most of us learn early in life to pretend that we understand things even when we don't. Rather than ask questions, and risk looking foolish, we nod our heads. Soon, we even come to believe that we understand things when really we don't, or not nearly as well as we think we do. This understandable but problematic human trait means that, to become better thinkers, most of us will have to cultivate a more positive attitude toward not knowing. Prepare to be surprised at how difficult this can be.

Start by trying to accept that uncertainty—even its more extreme version, confusion—is a productive state of mind, a precondition to allowing yourself to have ideas. The poet John Keats coined a memorable phrase for this productive habit of mind. He called it negative capability.

> I had not had a dispute but a disquisition with Dilke, on various subjects; several things dovetailed in my mind, & at once it struck me, what quality went to form a Man of Achievement especially in Literature & which Shakespeare possessed so enormously—I mean *Negative Capability*, that is when man is capable of being in uncertainties, Mysteries, doubts, without any irritable reaching after fact & reason.
>
> —Letter to George and Thomas Keats, December 1817

The key phrases here are "capable of being in uncertainties" and "without any irritable reaching." Keats is not saying that facts and reason are unnecessary and therefore can be safely ignored. But he does praise the kind of person who can remain calm (rather than becoming irritable) in a state of uncertainty. His is a praise for a way of being that is capable of staying open to possibilities for longer periods of time than most of us are comfortable with.

Try to accept that uncertainty is a productive state of mind, a precondition to allowing yourself to have ideas.

Another nineteenth-century poet, Emily Dickinson, writes in the same vein as Keats's concept of negative capability in her poem that begins "Perception of an object/Costs precise the object's loss." When we leap prematurely to our perceptions about a thing, we place a filter between ourselves and the "object," shrinking the amount and kinds of information that can get through to our minds and our senses. The point of the Dickinson poem is a paradox—that the ideas we arrive at actually deprive us of material with which to have more ideas. So we have to be careful about leaping to conclusions, about the ease with which we move to generalization, because if we are not careful, such moves will lead to a form of mental blindness—loss of the object.

By training yourself to be more comfortable with not knowing, you give yourself license to start working with your material, the data, *before* you try to decide what you think it means. The problem with convincing ourselves that we have the answers is that we are thus prevented from *seeing the questions*, which are usually much more interesting than the temporary stopping points we have initially elected as answers.

PARAPHRASE × 3: OPENING UP THE MEANING OF WORDS

Paraphrasing is an extremely valuable activity in analysis—and in all kinds of thinking. Our term for looking closely at evidence is *descriptive paraphrase.* What does this mean? Too often when people look at words they summarize—that is, they produce a general overview of what the words say. Paraphrasing stays much closer to the actual words than summarizing. The word *paraphrase* means to put one phrase next to ("para") another phrase. When you paraphrase a passage, you cast and recast its key terms into near synonyms.

Descriptive paraphrasing calls for careful restatement. We call it paraphrase × 3 because usually only one paraphrase—one synonym—is not enough. Take a sentence you want to understand better and recast it into other language three times. This will banish the problematic notion that the meaning of words is self-evident, and it will stimulate your thinking.

Why is paraphrasing useful? The answer has to do with words—what they are and what we do with them. When we read, it is easy to skip quickly over the words, assuming we know what they mean. Yet when people start talking about what they mean by particular words—the difference, for example, between *assertive* and *aggressive* or the meaning of ordinary words such as *polite* or *realistic* or *gentlemanly*—they usually find less agreement than they expected.

Most words mean more than one thing and mean different things to different people. Words matter. They are our primary means of negotiating the space between ourselves and others, and of figuring out our relation to the world. Yet most of us go through our days assuming that the meaning of the words we use—and those spoken to us by others—is obvious.

The next time you find yourself staring at something and saying to yourself, "I don't understand this" or "I don't know what I would say about this," try paraphrasing. Ideas will come.

Try this 1.9: Paraphrase versus the Transparent Theory of Language

Consider that meaning is not separable from the language in which it appears; what you say is inescapably a product of how you say it. This is to say that language doesn't merely "reflect" reality; in a sense, it invents it. What we see as reality is shaped by the words we use. This idea is known as the constitutive theory of language. It is opposed to the so-called "transparent" theory of language, which implies that we can see through words to some meaning that exists beyond and is independent of them.

In a famous essay called "Politics and the English Language," George Orwell points out that our ability to think clearly about important matters is greatly reduced by the human tendency to settle for abstractions, rather than more concrete words, and to unthinkingly plug in prefabricated—which is to say, clichéd—language in place of fresher words that still have the power to provoke thought. In this context, political conflicts can be seen as a war of words. This is nowhere more evident than in the language we use to talk about war. Consider, for example, the effect and possible purpose of referring to bombs as *ordinance*.

You might profitably spend a week noting the different words that two different political orientations—for example, Democrats and Republicans—use for the same thing. You might also spend a week collecting clichés. This too is useful for becoming more self-conscious about the relation between words and thinking. What is the problem with clichés, especially given that the ideas they offer are typically reasonable and even well said?

Try this 1.10: Looking at Gendered Language

Another excellent way to start looking at words and stop assuming that their meaning is self-evident is to consider the way our language encodes and quietly invites us to accept value assumptions about gender (masculinity and femininity—as opposed to the biological fact of being male or female). What words do we have in English for unmarried men, for example? What words do we use for unmarried women? What words do we use for men who are sexually active with more than one person? What words do we use for women who are sexually active with more than one person?

The words we use to describe men versus women change with social norms on what constitutes ideal male or female behavior. This process is often interestingly local, which is to say that it occurs inside particular discourse communities (groups sharing a common language). If you are reading this book on a college campus, you might spend a week collecting words that encode changing attitudes toward idealized forms of masculinity and femininity. What, for example, has happened to the word *geek* as a word for describing a particular kind of male? Is *geek* used as often to describe women? If not, why not?

THE IMPORTANCE OF EXPLORATORY WRITING

This book has a lot to say about exploratory writing. We believe that most writing courses and writing texts, although they advocate attention to the process rather than just to the products of writing, include way too little exploratory writing and practically no specific procedures for the exploration stage. A revealing feature of supposedly process-oriented writing texts is their use of the word *prewriting*. Exploratory writing is writing. Exploratory writing precedes a finished draft, but it is not something that comes *before* writing, nor is it something that the final form of the writing needs to entirely exclude.

The problem with convincing ourselves that we have the answers is that we are thus prevented from seeing the questions, which are usually much more interesting than the temporary stopping points we have initially elected as answers.

Among practiced writers, the similarities between exploratory writing and "finished" (revised and polished) writing are significant. This is not because writers stop doing exploratory writing and manage to go straight to finished drafts. Instead, the finished form of the writing behaves more in the meditative and searching way that good exploratory writing behaves.

This is not to say that we think writers should care only about process and not about product, or that they should substitute freewriting and inconclusive thinking for carefully organized finished drafts. Instead we argue that revising the final or next to final draft would be much easier if the writer had spent more time doing various kinds of exploratory writing before moving to the final draft stage. We also argue that good writing, at whatever stage, should have an exploratory feel, that it should share its discovery process with the reader. To a significant extent, especially in analytical writing, the final draft of an essay re-creates for the reader the writer's experience of arriving at his or her key ideas.

FREEWRITING: HOW TO DO IT AND WHAT IT'S GOOD FOR

The writer Anne Lamott writes eloquently (in *Bird by Bird*) about the internal censor we all hear as a nasty voice—actually a collection of nasty voices—in our heads that keep us from writing. These are the internalized voices of past critics whose comments have become magnified to suggest that we will never get it right. Freewriting allows us to tune out these voices long enough to discover what we might think.

In freewriting, you write *without stopping* for a predetermined period of time, usually ten or fifteen minutes. There aren't many rules to freewriting, just that it is important to keep your pen (or fingers on the keyboard) moving. Don't reread as you go. Don't pause to correct things. Don't cross things out. Just keep writing. To get to good writing, we first have to tolerate some chaos. In freewriting, especially if you engage in it frequently, you will often surprise yourself with the quality of your own thinking, with the ideas you didn't really know you had and the many details you hadn't really noticed until you started writing. For a good example of what can be done with a freewrite, see "Doing 10 on 1: An Example from Student Writing" near the end of this chapter.

Some Forms of Freewriting

There are many forms of freewriting, but they are all premised on the belief that the act of writing is not just a way of recording what you think, but of discovering what you think. Unlike a finished essay, in which the sentences follow logically as you unfold your central idea, freewriting encourages you to leap associatively from idea to idea as they arise.

One of the advantages of this less structured, less sequential kind of writing is that it effectively reduces anxiety. Rather than worrying about what you can find to say, you start saying things. Not everything you come up with will be worthy of developing into a paper, but you will often be surprised at the connections you make and the workable starting points you discover when prewriting.

1. *Freewrites* are the loosest form of exploratory writing, requiring only that you write more or less continuously—and usually without much premeditation—for a specified period of time (usually somewhere between ten and twenty minutes). Try to keep moving. Don't pause to edit or correct or bite your pen, or stare into space; just write.
2. *Focused freewrites* follow the same procedure as freewrites, except that you attempt to stay within a more narrowly defined subject. Often you will take your best idea from a previous freewrite and then explore it on the page for ten minutes or so without stopping. Or you might put a single word or idea at the top of the page and write continuously about that.
3. *Writer's notebooks* (*journals*) are unlike a personal diary in which you keep track of your days' activities and recount the feelings these occasioned; journals are for generating and collecting ideas and for keeping track of your ongoing interactions with course materials. A journal can be, in effect, a collection of focused freewrites that you develop in response to the reading and lectures in a course.

The best way to get a journal to work for you is to experiment. You might try, for example, copying and commenting on statements from your reading or class meetings that you found potentially illuminating. Use the journal to write down the ideas, reactions, and germs of ideas you had during a class discussion or that you found running around in your head after a late night's reading. Use the journal to retain your first impressions of books or films or music or performances or whatever, so that you can then look back at them and trace the development of your thinking.

If possible, write in your journal every day. As with freewriting, the best way to get started is just to start, see what happens, and take it from there. Also as with freewriting, the more you write, the more you'll find yourself noticing and thus the more you'll have to say.

Try this 1.11: Descriptions from Everyday Life

Descriptive freewriting is an especially fruitful activity for training thinking and observation skills. Spend a week describing things that you can observe in your everyday environment—whatever interests you on a particular day, or the same kind of thing over a period of days. Get the detail of what you are describing on the page. If judgments and generalizations come out, let them come, but don't stay on them long. Try to get back to the narration of detail as quickly as you can. At the end of the week you could write a piece called either "What I learned in a week of looking at . . ." or come up with your own shaping title. See if you can turn your freewrites into an essay—either descriptive or analytical.

COUNTERPRODUCTIVE HABITS OF MIND

We began this chapter with an emphasis on noticing details (our discussion of Hemingway's five finger exercise). We have been arguing that cultivating an attitude of uncertainty improves your ability to really see and think about the world: indeed, the best ideas often start with something puzzling rather than with something you are sure that you already understand. And we have spoken of the importance of tracing impressions back to causes, because people so readily remember how they felt but fail to register the details that caused them to feel that way. What follows is a glossary of counterproductive habits of mind.

Generalizing What it all boils down to is . . .What this adds up to is . . .The gist of her speech was . . . Generalizing is not always a bad habit. Reducing complex events or theories or books or speeches to a reasonably accurate summarizing statement requires practice and skill. We generalize from our experience because this is one way of arriving at ideas. The problem with generalizing as a habit of mind is that it deflects attention—usually much too swiftly—from the data that produced the generalization in the first place.

Generalizations are just as much a problem for readers and listeners as they are for writers. Consider for a moment what you are actually asking others to do when you offer them a generalization such as "His stories are very depressing." Unless the recipient of this observation asks a question—such as "Why do you think so?"—he or she is being required to take your word for it: the stories are depressing because you say so.

What happens instead if you offer a few details that caused you to think as you do? Clearly, you are on riskier ground. Your listener might think that the details you cite are actually not depressing or that this is not the most interesting or useful way to think about the stories. He or she might offer a different generalization, a different reading of the data, but at least conversation has become possible. There is something available to think with: the actual stuff of experience from which further generalizations can be made.

Vagueness and generality are major blocks to learning because, as habits of mind, they allow you to dismiss virtually everything you've read and heard except the general idea you've arrived at. Often the generalizations that come to mind are so broad that they tell us nothing. To say, for example, that a poem is about love or death or rebirth, or that the economy of a particular emerging nation is inefficient, accomplishes very little, since the generalizations could fit almost any poem or economy. In other words, your generalizations are often sites where you stopped thinking prematurely, not the "answers" you've thought they were.

The simplest antidote to the problem of generalizing is to train yourself to be more self-conscious about where your generalizations come from. Remember to trace your general impressions back to the particulars that caused them. This tracing of attitudes back to their concrete causes is the most basic—and most necessary—move in the analytical habit of mind. It will help you go through the world in less of a haze. Deciding to be more conscious of our own responses to the world and their causes is also an antidote to the inevitable numbing, the desensitizing, that takes place as habit takes control of our daily lives. Choose to notice more and to keep noticing.

Here's another strategy for bringing your thinking down from high levels of generality. Think of the words you use in terms of an *abstraction ladder.* The more general and vague the word, the higher its position on the abstraction ladder. "Mammal," for example, is higher on the abstraction ladder than "cow." You might try using "Level 3 Generality" as a convenient tag phrase reminding you to steer clear of the higher reaches of abstract generalization, some so high up the ladder from the concrete stuff that produced them that there is barely enough air to sustain the thought.

Why "Level 3" instead of "Level 2"? There aren't just two categories, abstract and concrete: the categories are the ends of a continuum, a sliding scale. And too often when writers try to concretize their generalizations, the results are still too general: they change "animal" to "mammal," but they need "cow" or, better, "black angus."

The Judgment Reflex Much of what passes for thinking—in the press, on television, in everyday conversation—is actually not thinking but reflex behavior, reaction rather than thinking: right/wrong, good/bad, loved it/hated it, couldn't relate to it, boring.

It would be impossible to overstate the mind-numbing effect that the judgment reflex has on thinking. Why? Consider what we do when we judge something and what we ask others to do when we offer them our judgments. "Ugly," "realistic," "pretty," "boring," "wonderful," "unfair," "crazy." Notice that the problem with such words is a version of the problem with all generalizations—lack of information. What have you actually told someone else if you say that X is ugly or boring or realistic?

FIGURE 1.1 The problem with generalizing diagram

THE PROBLEM

data (words, images, other detail) ---leaps to---> broad generalization

data ---leaps to---> evaluative claims (like/dislike; agree/disagree)

The Judgment Reflex

In its most primitive form—most automatic and least thoughtful—judging is like an on/off switch. When the switch gets thrown in one direction or the other—good/bad, right/wrong, positive/negative—the resulting judgment predetermines and overdirects any subsequent thinking we might do. Rather than thinking about what X is or how X operates, we lock ourselves prematurely into proving that we were right to think that X should be banned or supported.

The psychologist Carl Rogers has written at length on the problem of the judgment reflex. He claims that our habitual tendency as humans—virtually a programmed response—is to evaluate everything and to do so very quickly. Walking out of a movie, for example, most people will immediately voice their approval or disapproval, usually in either/or terms: I liked it *or* didn't like it; it was right/wrong, good/bad, interesting/boring. The other people in the conversation will then offer their own evaluations plus their judgments of the others' judgments: I think that it was a good movie and that you are wrong to think it was bad. And so on.

This kind of reflex move to evaluation closes off thinking with likes and dislikes and instant categories. The fact that you liked or didn't like a movie probably says more about you—your tastes, interests, biases, and experiences—than it does about the movie. What makes a movie boring? That it doesn't have enough car chases? That its plot resembles half the plots on cable channels? That the leading man is miscast or the dialogue too long-winded? At the least, in such cases, you'd need to share with readers your *criteria* for judgment—your reasons and your standards of evaluation.

When people leap to judgment, they usually land in the mental pathways they've grown accustomed to traveling, guided by family or friends or popular opinion. If you can break the evaluation reflex and press yourself to analyze before judging a subject, you will often be surprised at how much your initial responses change. As a general rule, you should seek to understand the subject you are analyzing before moving to a judgment about it. Try to figure out what your subject means before deciding how you feel about it.

Try to figure out what your subject means before deciding how you feel about it.

This is not to say that all judging should be avoided. Obviously, our thinking on many occasions must be applied to decision making—deciding whether we should or shouldn't vote for a particular candidate, should or shouldn't eat french fries, or should or shouldn't support a ban on cigarette advertising.

A writer needs to take into account how the judgment has been affected by the particular situation (context) and to acknowledge how thinking about these details has led to restricting (qualifying) the range of the judgment: X is *sometimes* true in these particular circumstances; Z is *probably* the right thing to do *but only when* A and B occur. Ultimately, in other words, analytical thinking does need to arrive at a point of view—which is a form of judgment—but analytical conclusions are usually not phrased in terms of like/dislike or good/bad. They disclose what a person has come to understand about X rather than how he or she imperiously rules on the worth of X.

In some ways, the rest of this book consists of a set of methods for blocking the ever-present judgment reflex in favor of more thoughtful responses. For now, here are two things to try in order to short-circuit the judgment reflex and begin replacing it with a more thoughtful, more patient, and more open-mindedly curious habit of mind. First, try the cure that Carl Rogers recommended to negotiators in industry and government. Do not assert an agreement or disagreement with another person's position until you can repeat that position in a way the other person would accept as fair and accurate. This is surprisingly hard to do because we are usually so busy calling up judgments of our own that we barely hear what the other person is saying.

Second, try eliminating the word "should" from your vocabulary for a while, since judgments so often take the form of recommendations. The analytical habit of mind is characterized by the words "why," "how," and "what." Analysis asks the following: What is the aim of the new law? Why do laws of this sort tend to get passed in some parts of the country rather than in others? How does this law compare with its predecessor? Judgments take the form of *should statements*. We *should* pass the law. We *should* not consider putting such foolish restrictions into law.

You might also try eliminating evaluative adjectives—those that offer judgments with no data. "Green" is a descriptive, concrete adjective. It offers something we can experience. "Beautiful" is an evaluative adjective. It offers only judgment.

Debate-Style Argument People are customarily introduced to writing arguments through the debate model. They are taught to argue pro *or* con on a given position or issue, with the aim of defeating an imagined opponent and convincing

VOICES FROM ACROSS THE CURRICULUM

Habits of Mind

Readers should not conclude that the "Counterproductive Habits of Mind" presented in this chapter are confined to writing. Psychologists who study the way we process information have established important links between the way we think and the way we feel. Some psychologists such as Aaron Beck have identified common "errors in thinking" that parallel the habits of mind discussed in this chapter. Beck and others have shown that falling prey to habits of mind is associated with a variety of negative outcomes. For instance, a tendency to engage in either/or thinking, overgeneralization, and personalization has been linked to higher levels of anger, anxiety, and depression. Failure to attend to these errors in thinking chokes off reflection and analysis. As a result, the person becomes more likely to "react" rather than think, which may prolong and exacerbate the negative emotions.

—*Mark Sciutto, Professor of Psychology*

an audience of the rightness of one side of the argument. To its credit, the debate model teaches writers to consider more than a single viewpoint, their opponent's as well as their own.

But unfortunately, it can also train them, even if inadvertently, to see the other side only as the opposition and to concentrate their energy only on winning the day. The problem with this approach is that it overemphasizes the bottom line—aggressively advancing a claim for *or* against some view—without *first* engaging in the exploratory interpretation of evidence that is so necessary to arriving at thoughtful arguments.

Thus, debate-style argument produces a frame of mind in which defending positions matters more than taking the necessary time to develop ideas worth defending. And, very possibly, it nourishes the mudslinging and opinionated mind-set—attack first—that proliferates in editorials and television talk shows, not to mention the conversations you overhear in going about your life. We are not saying that people should forget about making value and policy decisions and avoid the task of persuading others. We are saying that too many of the arguments we all read, hear, and participate in every day are based on insufficient analysis.

Debate-style argument produces a frame of mind in which defending positions matters more than taking the necessary time to develop ideas worth defending.

The remedy, we suggest, is the temporary suspension of the pro/con, debate-style habit of mind. Argument and analysis are profoundly connected, but their stances toward subject matter and audience differ so much that most people need to learn them separately before being able to put them back together. And because the argumentative habit of mind is so aggressively visible in our culture, most people never get around to experimenting with the more reflective and less combative approach that analysis embraces. Thus, this book asks you to turn off the argument switch, not forever, but for as long as it takes for you to cultivate other habits of mind that argument might otherwise overshadow.

Although analysis and argument proceed in essentially the same way, they differ in the kinds of questions they try to answer. Argument, at its most dispassionate, asks "What can be said with truth about X or Y?" In common practice, though, the kinds of questions that argument more often answers are more committed, directive, and should-centered, such as "Which is better, X or Y?," "How can we best achieve X or Y?," and "Why should we stop doing X or Y?"

Analysis, by contrast, asks "What does X or Y mean?" In analysis the evidence (your data) is something you wish to understand, and the claims are assertions about what that evidence means. The claim that an argument makes—for example, readers should or shouldn't vote for bans on smoking in public buildings, or they should or shouldn't believe that gays can function effectively in the military—is often an answer to a "should" question. The writer of an analysis is more concerned with discovering how each of these complex subjects might be defined and explained than with convincing readers to approve or disapprove of them.

Overpersonalizing (Naturalizing Our Assumptions) The assumption that what seems true to me must be obviously and self-evidently true to everybody else is known as naturalizing your assumptions. The word *naturalize* in this context means you are representing—and seeing—your own assumptions as part of the universal scheme of things. The term *common sense* often accompanies naturalized assumptions, as in, "Oh, that's just common sense"—which means that my point of view doesn't need defending or even explaining, because any sensible person would think in this way. What is common sense—"natural"—for one person and so not even in need of explaining can be quite uncommon and not so obviously sensible to someone else.

The problem with "the personal" really has to do with how that term is commonly (mis)understood. It is usually located as one half of a particularly vicious binary that might be schematized thus:

subjective	objective
personal expression	impersonal analysis
passionately engaged	detached
genuinely felt	heartless

Like most vicious binaries, the personal/impersonal, heart/head binary overstates the case and obscures the considerable overlap of the two sides.

Most effective analytical prose has a strong personal element—the writer's stake in the subject matter. As readers, we want the sense that a writer is engaged with the material, cares about what he or she says about it, and is sharing what he or she finds interesting about it.

But in another sense, no writing is strictly personal. As contemporary cultural theorists are fond of pointing out, the "I" is not a wholly autonomous free agent who writes from a unique point of view. Rather, the "I" is always affected by forces outside the self—social, cultural, educational, historical, and so forth—that shape the self. The extreme version of this position allots little space for what we like to think of as individuality at all: the self is a site through which dominant cultural ways of understanding the world (ideologies) circulate. That's a disarming notion, but one worth pondering.

From this perspective we are like actors who don't know that we're actors, reciting various cultural scripts that we don't realize are scripts. This is, of course, an extreme position. A person who believes that civil rights for all is an essential human right is not necessarily a victim of cultural brainwashing. The grounds of his or her belief, shaped by participation in a larger community of belief (ethnic, religious, family tradition, and so forth) are, however, not merely personal.

Try this 1.12: Looking for Naturalized Assumptions

Start listening to the things people say in everyday conversation. Read some newspaper editorials with your morning coffee (a pretty disturbing way to start the day in most cases). Watch for examples of people naturalizing their assumptions. You will find examples of this everywhere. Also, try paraphrasing the common complaint "I couldn't relate to it." What does being able to "relate" to something consist of? What problems would follow from accepting this idea as a standard of value?

One telltale sign of an overpersonalizing writer is his or her tendency to let personal narratives substitute for careful consideration of a subject. When we substitute personal narrative for analysis, our own experiences and prejudices tend to become an unquestioned standard of value. Your disastrous experience with a health maintenance organization (HMO), for example, may predispose you to dismiss a plan for nationalized health care, but your writing needs to examine in detail the holes in the plan, not simply evoke the three hours you lingered in some doctor's waiting room.

This is not to say that there is no learning or thinking value in telling our experiences. Storytelling has the virtue of offering concrete experience—not just the conclusions the experience may have led to. Personal narratives can take us back to the source of our convictions. The problem comes when "relating" to someone's story becomes a habitual substitute for thinking through the ideas and attitudes that the story suggests.

The antidote to the overpersonalizing habit of mind is to become more self-conscious about it. If we keep in mind that the "I" we tend to lead with is not simply a free agent but also a product of cultural influences, we will be more likely to notice our first responses and become curious about them. Ask yourself, Is this what I really believe? Asking that question is a healthy habit to cultivate and one that can often help you see the logic of other possible responses to the position you've initially taken.

Opinions (versus Ideas) Consider for a moment the often-heard claim "I'm entitled to my opinion." This claim is worth exploring. What is an opinion? How is it (or isn't it) different from a belief or an idea? If I say that I am entitled to my opinion, what am I asking you to do or not do?

Many of the opinions people fight about are actually clichés, pieces of much-repeated conventional wisdom. For example, "People are entitled to say what they want. That's just my opinion." But, of course, this assertion isn't a private and personal revelation. It is an exaggerated and overstated version of one of the items in the U.S. Bill of Rights, guaranteeing freedom of speech. Much public thinking has gone on about this private conviction, and it has thus been carefully qualified. A person can't, for example, say publicly whatever he or she pleases about other people if what he or she says is false and damages the reputation of another person—at least without threat of legal action.

Our opinions are learned. They are products of our culture and our upbringing—not personal possessions. It is okay to have opinions, but not to give too many of our views and opinions protected-species status, walling them off into a reserve, not to be touched by reasoning or evidence.

Our opinions are learned. They are products of our culture and our upbringing—not personal possessions.

Some things, of course, we have to take on faith. Religious convictions, for example, are more than opinions, though they operate in a similar way: we believe where we can't always prove. But even our most sacred convictions are not really harmed by thinking. The world's religions are constantly engaged in interpreting and reinterpreting what religious texts mean, what various traditional practices mean, and how they may or may not be adapted to the attitudes and practices of the world as it is today.

SECTION 3: THE BASIC ANALYTICAL STRATEGIES: FROM OBSERVATIONS TO IDEAS

This part of the chapter offers an observation exercise (Notice and focus, plus interesting and strange), another version of this exercise (10 on 1), and a verbal prompt for pushing observations to conclusions: the So what? question. This sequence of activities is our basic analytical formula. Spend some time practicing these moves and continue to use them with other exercises in this book.

THE DOGFISH PROBLEM: PREMATURE LEAPS TO THESIS

Often, it is not just carelessness or a judgmental cast of mind that closes down the information-gathering stage. People sometimes have unreasonable expectations of themselves when it comes to having ideas. They think that they should get to ideas right away, that arriving at a "thesis" is a necessary starting point for analysis. We like calling this "idea-first—look-later" anxiety *the dogfish problem* (a term coined by the writer Walker Percy in his essay about ways of knowing called "The Loss of the Creature"). For our purposes, the dogfish problem sets up an analogy between writing and other forms of analysis. A writer trying to start with a thesis before looking openly (with negative capability) at the evidence is like a scientist trying to theorize about the nature of dogfish with no more than a cursory look at one.

Our discussion of what it means to have an idea (below) is premised on avoidance of the dogfish problem in favor of negative capability (discussed in Section 2). Having ideas is dependent on allowing yourself to notice things in your subject that you want to better understand rather than glossing over things with a quick and too easy understanding. This relates, of course, to what we have said so far about how attending to conclusions but not their causes prevents us from thinking and seeing. The main point in the following discussion of ideas is that you need to start with something that is puzzling rather than with things that you think are clearly and obviously true.

WHAT IT MEANS TO HAVE AN IDEA

As a general rule, analytical topics privilege live questions over inert answers. Thinking, as opposed to reporting or reacting, should lead you to ideas. But what does it mean to have an idea? This question lies at the heart of our book.

Some years ago, while teaching a writing seminar for faculty in the writing across the curriculum program at our college, we were taken aback by faculty response to the suggestion that they should be expecting their students to arrive at ideas. "Ideas!" one professor of psychology exclaimed. "Do you mean like a PhD thesis?" We were unprepared for this reaction, because our seminars had taught us that faculty across the curriculum, regardless of discipline, shared similar expectations of their students' writing. Faculty told us they wanted not passive summary, not issue-oriented argument, and not personal "reaction" papers, but analysis. And yet they were dubious about accepting that their undergraduate students could arrive at ideas, which is the aim of analysis.

Clearly, a writer in the early stages of learning about a subject can't be expected to arrive at an idea so original that, like one in a PhD thesis, it revises complex concepts in a discipline. But the opposite expectation seems to us to be just as clearly wrong—that undergraduates are simply too inexperienced in the various academic disciplines to do anything but absorb information.

And so, we began looking at ideas—in our own writing, in our colleagues' writing, in our students' writing. Our primary discovery was that ideas are usually much smaller in scope, much less grand, than people seem to expect them to be. We also discovered that it is easiest to understand what ideas are by considering what ideas do and where they can be found. Here is a partial list:

- An idea answers a question; it explains something that needs to be explained or provides a way out of a difficulty that other people have had in understanding something.
- An idea usually starts with an observation that is puzzling, with something you want to figure out rather than something you think you already understand.
- An idea may be the discovery of a question where there seemed not to be one.
- An idea may make explicit and explore the meaning of something implicit—an unstated assumption upon which an argument rests, or a logical consequence of a given position.
- An idea may connect elements of a subject and explain the significance of that connection.
- An idea often accounts for some *dissonance*—that is, something that seems to not fit together.
- An idea provides direction; it helps you see what to do next.

Analysis places you in a situation where there are problems to resolve and competing ideas for you to bring into some kind of alignment. The starting point for analysis is a situation where there is something for you to negotiate, where you are required not just to list answers but to ask questions, make choices, and engage in reasoning about the meaning and significance of your evidence.

WHAT'S AN IDEA?

An idea usually starts with an observation that is puzzling, with something you want to figure out.

- Something *smaller* than most people suspect
- A subtle distinction
- A qualification
- An unearthed connection between two positions not previously linked
- Discovery of a question where there seemed not to be one
- *Something that accounts for some dissonance, what seemed not to fit together*

COMMON MISCONCEPTIONS ABOUT IDEAS

- Something large and global, and usually contentious
- Like a PhD thesis?

Try this 1.13: Researching Ideas Across the Curriculum

As you go through your education, you may find it interesting to think about how different disciplines seem to define what an idea is, what it does, and how you recognize one. Visit a professor in a discipline you find interesting and interview him or her about what constitutes an idea in that discipline. Ask for one or two single-sentence statements of ideas that the professor may have seen lately in a journal in his or her field, or may be working on in his or her research. You might also ask the professor to share with you a couple of good ideas that past students have arrived at in his or her courses. Write an account of your interview, including an example of what your interviewee considered a good idea and why.

MOVING FROM IDEA TO THESIS STATEMENT: WHAT A GOOD THESIS LOOKS LIKE

There are considerable misunderstandings about thesis statements among students—and among many teachers. The most disabling misunderstanding for students is that a writer needs to have a thesis before he or she begins writing. Good thesis statements are the product of writing, not its precursor. Worrying about having a thesis statement too early in the writing process will just about guarantee papers that support overly general and often obvious ideas. Arriving prematurely at claims also blinds writers to complicating evidence (that which runs counter to the thesis) and so—as we argue at length in Chapter 6, "Making a Thesis Evolve"—deprives writers of their best opportunities to arrive at better ideas.

Another disabling assumption is that good writing must include, preferably in the first or second paragraph, a single-sentence (at most, two-sentence) statement of a governing idea that the paper will go on to support. This sentence is typically meant to appear at the end of the introductory paragraph, although the location of a paper's primary claim differs across the academic disciplines and according to whether the paper is deductively or inductively organized.

The fact is that the main idea of most analytical writing is too complex to be asserted as a single-sentence claim—at least one that would be understood at the beginning of the paper. Nevertheless, it is also true that a writer has not moved from the exploratory writing phase to the writing of a paper until he or she has discovered an idea around which his or her thinking can cohere. Without a governing idea to hold on to, readers will not understand why you are telling them what you are telling them. For a paper to make sense to readers, a thesis, or, in the case of inductively organized papers, a thesis "trail" (some sense of the issues and questions that are generating the paper's forward momentum) must be evident.

The best way to learn about thesis statements is to look for them in published writing. When you start doing this, you will find that the single-sentence thesis statement as prescribed in writing textbooks is a rather rare specimen. It is most common in argument, wherein a writer has a proposition that he or she wants readers to either adopt or dismiss. In analytical writing, the thesis is more likely to become evident in phases. Sometimes, for example, as much as the first third of a paper will explore an idea that the rest of the paper will subsequently replace with a different, though not necessarily opposing, perspective. If you look closely, however, you will see the markers—the trail—that lets readers anticipate a shift from one possible way of seeing things to another.

This point—about the pressure of one way of seeing things against another—allows us to define what a good thesis in an analytical paper looks like. It is important to remember that a thesis is an idea. It is a thought that you have arrived at about your evidence, rather than something you can expect to find, ready-made, in whatever it is you are studying.

Good writing, especially good analytical writing, begins with something puzzling that the writer wishes to understand better. The pursuit of understanding is exploratory. "Good" thesis statements enable exploration. "Bad" thesis statements disable it by closing things down way too tightly at the outset.

A strong thesis comes from carefully examining and questioning your subject to arrive at a theory about its meaning and significance that would not have been immediately obvious to your readers. A weak thesis either makes no claim or makes a claim that doesn't need proving, such as a statement of fact or an opinion with which virtually all of your readers would most likely agree before reading your essay (for example, "Exercise is good for you").

"Good" thesis statements enable exploration. "Bad" thesis statements disable it by closing things down way too tightly at the outset.

Here are two characteristics that an idea needs to have to work as a thesis:

1. The thesis of an analytical paper is an idea about what some feature or features of your subject *means.*
2. A thesis should be an idea that is in need of argument, which is to say it should not be a statement of fact or an idea with which most readers would already agree.

Below are six examples of good thesis statements, which is to say good translations of ideas into forms that could direct the development of an essay. None of these appeared in the first paragraph of the paper for which they served as the "driver." But each was clearly led to by a "thesis trail," and each emerged fairly early in the essay as the writer's explanation of the particular phenomenon he or she had noticed that served as a launching pad for the essay.

Let's consider how these statements, as good examples of what a thesis should look like, relate to the defining characteristics of ideas as explained in the section above, "What It Means to Have an Idea." The first thing you should notice about all these thesis statements is *the presence of tension*—the pressure of one idea against another idea, of one potentially viable way of seeing things against another viable, but finally less satisfactory way of seeing things.

Try this 1.14: Spotting the Tension in Good Thesis Statements

A quick review of our list of things that ideas do will reveal that good ideas usually take place with the aid of some kind of back pressure, by which we mean that the idea takes shape by pushing against (so to speak) another way of seeing things. This is not the same as setting out to overturn and completely refute one idea in favor of another. More often what happens is that the thesis statement's primary idea emerges as some kind of clarification of another idea. Both ideas remain, but the forward momentum of the thesis comes from playing the newer idea off the older one, wherein the newer idea clarifies and builds upon the older one.

Look at the thesis statements below, all of which are taken from published analytical essays. Find the tension in each, which is to say the defining pressure of one idea against another possibility. In the first thesis sentence, for example, the primary idea is that the new advertising campaign for Dockers trousers is radical. The back pressure against which this idea takes shape is that this new campaign may not seem radical. The writer will demonstrate the truth of both of these claims, rather than overturning one and then championing the other. The same can be said of the parts of the second thesis statement. One part of the thesis makes claims for the benefits of cosmetic surgery. The forward momentum of the thesis statement comes from the back pressure of this idea against the idea that cosmetic surgery will also make life worse for everyone. Notice that the thesis statement does not simply say, "Cosmetic surgery is bad."

1. It may not seem like it, but "Nice Pants" is as radical a campaign as the original Dockers series.
2. If opponents of cosmetic surgery are too quick to dismiss those who claim great psychological benefits, protesters are far too willing to dismiss those who raise concerns. Cosmetic surgery might make individual people happier, but in the aggregate it makes life worse for everyone.
3. The history of thought in the modern era of history of thinking about the self may be an exaggeration, but the consequences of this vision of a self set apart have surely been felt in every field of inquiry.
4. We may join with the modern builders in justifying the violence of means—the sculptor's hammer and chisel—by appealing to ends that serve the greater good. Yet too often modern planners and engineers would justify the creative destruction of habitat as necessary for doubtful utopias.
5. The derogation of middlebrow, in short, has gone much too far. It's time to bring middlebrow out of its cultural closet, to hail its emollient properties, to trumpet its mending virtues. For middlebrow not only entertains, it educates—pleasurably training us to appreciate high art.
6. There is a connection between the idea of place and the reality of cellular telephones. It is not encouraging. Places are unique—or at least we like to believe they are—and we strive to experience them as a kind of engagement with particulars. Cell phones are precisely the opposite.

If you have been taught to write in five-paragraph form in school (which is just about the only place that this oversimplified organizational scheme can be found), you will initially have some difficulty writing thesis statements of the sort you have just seen. This is because the typical three-part thesis of five-paragraph form offers a short list of broadly stated topics (rather than well-defined claims about the topics) and then offers examples of each part in the body paragraphs. This form invites listing rather than the articulation of ideas.

There is nothing wrong with partitioning the development of a subject into manageable parts (the best thing about five-paragraph form). There is a lot wrong with a thesis that makes no claim or an overly general and obvious claim such as "Television causes adolescents to become violent, lazy, and ill read." All of these general claims may be true, but nothing much of substance can be said about them in a short paper that is trying to cover all three. And notice the lack of tension in this sample thesis statement. Try writing a better thesis statement—one that has tension—about the effect of some aspect of television on teenagers. (See Chapter 7 for more on good and bad thesis statements.)

NOTICE AND FOCUS (RANKING)

So far this chapter has offered three strategies for getting past generalizations—tracing impressions back to causes (Hemingway's five-finger exercise), freewriting (various forms of exploratory writing), and paraphrase × 3 (a means of fighting the tendency to think that the meaning of words is self-evident). The next technique—Notice and focus—is aimed at helping you dwell longer with the data before feeling compelled to decide what the data means. Observation and interpretation go hand in hand, but it helps greatly to allow yourself a distinct observation stage and to prolong this beyond what most people find comfortable. The more you allow yourself to notice—the longer you allow yourself to dwell with the data before searching after a "point" about it—the richer and more rewarding your interpretation of the evidence will ultimately be.

Notice and focus is governed by repeatedly returning to the question "What do you notice?" As we have been arguing in the chapter so far, most people's tendency is to generalize and thus to rapidly move away from whatever it is they are looking at. The question What do you notice? redirects attention to the subject matter itself and delays the pressure to come up with answers, with a closing off of the experience.

So, the **first step** is for you to repeatedly answer the question What do you notice? Be sure to cite actual details of the thing being observed rather than moving to more general observations about it. (Note that this is more difficult than it sounds.) This phase of the exercise should produce an extended and unordered list of details—features of the thing being observed—that call attention to themselves for one reason or another.

The **second step** is the focusing part in which you *rank* (create an order of importance for) the various features of your subject you have noticed. Answer the question "What three details (specific features of the subject matter) are most interesting (or significant or revealing or strange)?" The purpose of relying on *interesting* or one of the other suggested words is that these will help to deactivate the like/dislike switch of the judgment reflex, and replace it with a more analytical perspective.

The **third step** in this process is to say why the three things you selected struck you as the most interesting (or revealing or significant or strange). This prioritizing of your observations triggers interpretive leaps to the meaning of whatever it is that you find most interesting in your observations.

Remember to start by noticing as much as you can about whatever it is you are studying. Narrow your scope to a representative portion of your evidence, and then dwell with the data. Record what you see. Don't move to generalization, or worse, to judgment. What this procedure will begin to demonstrate is how useful description is as a tool for arriving at ideas. Stay at the description stage longer (in that attitude of uncertainty we recommend), and have better ideas. Training yourself to notice will improve your memory and your ability to think.

Try this 1.15: Doing Notice and Focus with Words and Places and Images

Begin practicing this technique with visual detail. List a number of details about a place, for example, or about a magazine advertisement or some other visual image. Once you have allowed yourself to notice a number of things about the place or the image, choose the details that you think are most important for understanding its character. In both the noticing and focusing stages, use the four words suggested above—*interesting, significant, revealing,* or *strange.* In our classes we invite student thinking by advising them to keep completing the sentence "What I find interesting about this is . . . ."

Next, try this exercise with other subjects—a photograph, a cartoon, an editorial, conversations overheard around campus, looking at people's shoes, political speeches, and so forth. Make Notice and focus a habit of mind.

PROMPTS: INTERESTING AND STRANGE

Consider the verbal prompts *interesting, strange, revealing,* and *significant.* What do these do? First, they offer alternatives to the judgment reflex (like/dislike, right/wrong, and should/shouldn't). The prompts shift attention from pro/con argument to thinking aimed at understanding, at theorizing about the nature of things. The same words also press you to notice more and to stay more aware of the connections between your responses and the particulars that gave rise to them.

What does it mean to find something "interesting"? Often we are interested by things that have captured our attention without our clearly knowing why. Interest and curiosity are near cousins. Interest is also related to negative capability. When you can allow yourself to think that you don't have to have all the answers immediately, you can trust yourself to dwell with questions, a primary characteristic of good thinking.

The word *strange* is a useful prompt because it gives us permission to notice oddities, the things we called anomalies. *Strange* invites us to *defamiliarize* (notice what is strange—unfamiliar) about things within our range of notice.

RULES OF NOTICE & HABITS OF MIND
WORDS MATTER

- Not "What do you think?" &
- Not "What do you like or dislike?"

but

- "What do you notice?"

A few prompts:

- What do you find most INTERESTING?
- What do you find most STRANGE?
- What do you find most REVEALING?

Strange, in this context, is not a judgmental term but one denoting features of a subject or situation that aren't readily explainable. Where you locate something strange, you have something to interpret—to figure out what makes it strange and why.

Along similar lines, the words *revealing* and *significant* work by requiring you to make choices that can lead to interpretive leaps. If something strikes you as revealing, even if you're not yet sure why, you will eventually have to produce some theories on what it reveals. If something strikes you as significant, you will motivate yourself to come up with some things that it might signify or "say."

Try this 1.16: A Noticing Exercise on Conversation

Listen in on some conversations, writing down as much seemingly relevant detail (exact words and probably the physical actions that accompany them) as you can. Don't worry about order. Just keep recording what you hear and asking yourself what you notice. You will be able to shape the piece later in a way that you think best represents what you heard. After you have done the work of recording, say to yourself, What did I learn? What was especially *interesting, or revealing, or strange* about what I heard? Respond to these questions with freewriting, preferably in more than one freewriting session. Then produce two pieces of revised (shaped and ordered) writing: One should be the show-versus-tell "recording" of what you heard, the one that you hope will communicate by re-creating—without your explicitly telling—the effect that the talk had on you. The other should be a blend of empirical detail (showing) and analysis (your interpretation). Analyze rather than judge. Don't tell your readers what you liked or disliked. Tell them instead what was interesting and revealing and why.

PUSHING OBSERVATIONS TO CONCLUSIONS: ASKING SO WHAT?

The prompt for making the move from observation to implication and ultimately interpretation is: So what? The question is shorthand for questions such as the following:

Why does this observation matter? What does it mean?

Where does this observation get us?

How can we begin to generalize about the subject?

Asking, So what? is a calling to account, which is why, in conversation, its force is potentially rude. That is, the question intervenes rather peremptorily with a "Why does *this* matter?" It is thus a challenge to make meaning through a creative leap—to move beyond the patterns and emphases you've been observing in the data to tentative conclusions on what these observations suggest.

The peremptoriness of the So what? question can, we think, be liberating. Okay, take the plunge, it says. Start laying out possible interpretations. And, when you are tempted to stop thinking too soon, asking So what? will press you onward.

At the least, consider asking and answering So what? at the ends of paragraphs. And then, if you ask So what? again of the first answer you've offered, you'll often tell yourself where your thinking needs to go next.

For example, let's say you make a number of observations about the nature of e-mail communication—it's cheap, informal, often grammatically incorrect, full of abbreviations ("IMHO"), and ephemeral (impermanent). You rank these and decide that its ephemerality is most interesting. So what? Well, that's why so many people use it, you speculate, because it doesn't last. So what that its popularity follows from its ephemerality? Well, apparently we like being released from the hard-and-fast rules of formal communication; e-mail frees us. So what? Well, . . .

The repeated asking of this question causes people to push on from and pursue the implications of their first responses; it prompts people to reason in a chain, rather than settling prematurely for a single link.

In Chapter 6, "Making a Thesis Evolve," we have more to say about what to do when your answer to So what? calls to mind conflicting data or an opposing idea, and thus interferes with the forward flow of your thinking. For now, start experimenting with asking So what?

Asking So What?: An Example The following is the opening paragraph of a talk given by a professor of Politial Science, Dr. Jack Gambino, at our college on the occasion of a gallery opening. Study this piece of writing for the various methods of observation and interpretation it uses. Start by noticing the particular details that the writer has chosen to notice. Then look for places where he goes after implication (makes the details speak) by deciding what is interesting or strange or revealing about particular details. Finally, try putting question marks at the places where it seems to you that the writer has asked himself So what?

If you look closely at Camilo Vergara's photo of Fern Street, Camden, 1988, you'll notice a sign on the side of a dilapidated building:

Danger: Men Working

W. Hargrove Demolition

Perhaps that warning captures the ominous atmosphere of these very different kinds of photographic documents by Camilo Vergara and Edward Burtynsky: "Danger: Men Working." Watch out—human beings are at work! But the work that is presented is not so much a building-up 'as it is a tearing-down—the work of demolition. Of course, demolition is often necessary in order to construct anew: old buildings are leveled for new projects, whether you are building a highway or bridge in an American city or a dam in the Chinese countryside. You might call modernity itself, as so many have, a process of creative destruction, a term used variously to describe modern art, capitalism, and technological innovation. The photographs in this exhibit, however, force us to pay attention to the "destructive" side of this modern equation. What both Burtynsky and Vergara do in their respective ways is to put up a warning sign—they question whether the reworking of our natural and social environment leads to a sustainable human future. And they wonder whether the process of creative destruction may not have spun recklessly out of control, producing places that are neither habitable nor sustainable. In fact, a common element connecting the two photographic versions is the near absence of people in the landscape. While we see the evidence of the transforming power of human production on the physical and social environment, neither Vergara's urban ruins nor Burtynsky's industrial sites actually show us "men working." Isolated figures peer suspiciously out back doors or pick through the rubble, but they appear out of place. It is this sense of displacement—of human beings alienated from the environments they themselves have created—that provides the most haunting aspect of the work of these two photographers.

NARROW YOUR SCOPE BY DOING 10 ON 1

One sure way to notice more is to narrow your scope. The wider your scope, and the more ground you try to cover, the less you will be able to say in any sort of depth about your subject.

The term *10 on 1* is shorthand for the principle that it is better to make ten observations or points about a single representative issue or example (10 on 1) than to make the same basic point about ten related issues or examples (1 on 10). Doing 10 on 1 teaches writers to narrow their focus and then analyze in depth, drawing out as much meaning as possible from their best examples.

Ten, in this case, is an arbitrary number. We offer it to you as a reminder that the best writing comes when writers engage in prolonged scrutiny of a single telling piece of evidence rather than shutting down their thinking with a premature leap to the first idea that might serve as a thesis (the tendency we labeled earlier as the dogfish problem). A paper that has evolved from detailed analysis of what the writer takes to be his or her single most telling example is far more likely to arrive at a good idea than a paper that settles prematurely for one idea and applies it mechanically to each piece of evidence it encounters.

What exactly are the "1" and the "10," and how do you go about finding them? In the case of 10 on 1, the 1 is a representative example, an opportunity to narrow your focus to the point where you could consider your subject in more detail, drawing out observations and implications (10). The 10 are the observations you make about your representative example—ten things you notice about it, some combination of observations and implications. The practice of doing 10 on 1 is the opposite of attaching a single observation or implication to ten examples.

The shift from making one observation about ten examples to making ten possible observations about your single best example is the aim of the exercise. If you can keep the number ten in mind, it will prod you to keep asking yourself questions rather than stopping the observation process too soon. What do I notice? What else do I notice? What might this imply? What else might it imply?

How then should you go about selecting the example that you will analyze in depth? In many cases, your thinking process will start with a version of 1 on 10 as a preliminary step—locating some single trait or set of traits that a number of examples in your subject seem to share. Then you can narrow your scope to one of these ten examples that seems interestingly representative, thereby creating a space for in-depth analysis.

For extended discussion of doing 10 on 1, see Chapter 5, "Linking Evidence and Claims: 10 on 1 versus 1 on 10." We include brief mention of 10 on 1 in this chapter in order to better integrate it with our other observational strategies, such as Notice and focus, which it builds upon.

SECTION 4: HOW TO MARK UP A DRAFT

This last section of the chapter opens with a student freewrite and then offers a technique for analyzing a freewrite to better see its thinking and how this thinking might be developed.

DOING 10 ON 1: AN EXAMPLE FROM STUDENT WRITING

Freewrite on a scene from the film *Good Bye Lenin!*

By Sarah Kersh

The movie shows us Alex and Lara's first date, which is to a sort of underground music club where the performers wear costumes made of plastic tubing and leather, and play loud hard-core rock music. At first, the musicians look surreal, as though they are part of a strange dream from which, at any moment, Alex will awake. The Western rock is real, though, as are the sci-fi costumes, and the scene moves forward to show Alex and Lara climbing a stairway out onto what looks like a fire escape and then through a window and into an apartment.

Here, Alex and Lara settle down into conversation. The young couple sits, hand in hand, and gazes together into the night sky; yet, as the camera pans away, we see that the apartment where the two have retreated is missing its façade. Inside, three walls are still decorated, complete with furniture, wallpaper, and even working lamps; yet, the two sit on the ledge of the fourth wall, which has crumbled away completely.

On the surface, I think the movie invites us to read this as a visual representation of the new lives Alex, Lara, and the other characters face now that the wall has fallen. As a Westerner, at first I read this scene as a representation of the new relationship between Lara and Alex. In other words, I imagined the movie's placement of the couple on the ledge of a domestic space as a representation of where their lives were going together—toward some shared domestic life, toward living together, toward becoming a family. I also thought this was a clever representation of the collapse of communism—this wall has also fallen down.

I don't think, however, that the movie lets us entertain this one romanticized reading of the scene for long—the image is too frightening. As the camera pans away, we see that this isn't a new Westernized apartment; this is an East German flat decorated in much the same way as Alex's home was only months before. The image is alarming; the wall here has been ripped down, and we are forced to ask, did the fall of communism violently blow apart domestic and daily living of East German people?

The movie allows us this dichotomy and, I think, fights to sustain it. On one hand, Alex and Lara would not be on this date if the wall hadn't come down, and yet the scene is more than just another representation of East Germany torn between Communism and the new Westernization. The movie tries hard to remind us that the rapid Westernization of East Germany devastated while it liberated in other ways. This scene uses space to represent Alex and Lara's (and East Germany's) dilemma: Alex and Lara gaze out at the night sky but only because the wall has been blown apart. The exposed apartment is uninhabitable and yet the lights still work, the pictures are still hung, and a young couple leans against one another inside.

HOW TO ANALYZE A FREEWRITE FOR IDEAS: AN EXAMPLE

The student freewrite on a scene from the film *Good Bye Lenin!* is an opportunity to practice some text marking and freewriting strategies that can help you make better use of your own freewriting. These strategies will also help you see that freewrites can be smart and thoughtful.

One of our colleagues invites her students to do their freewriting on the word processor and then to go back either in the same writing session or later—in a different type font—to places where the writer seems to have hit upon something interesting that he or she hadn't completely figured out. As an aid in finding such places in the freewrite, the sentence "The part I liked best was . . ." can serve to get things started. The result of these different-font insertions into the original freewrite is a form of what we call focused freewriting. Similar to but not the same as revising an essay draft, focused freewrites pick up at places where the original freewrite gave up too soon. In practice, a series of focused freewrites—each one starting from some promising but underdeveloped starting point in the previous freewrite—can lead to an essay draft.

Instructions: Look at the student freewrite on *Good Bye Lenin!* and nominate one place she might profitably return to for a different-font "look again/expansion."

The same colleague who uses this technique of focused freewriting also has students look at each other's freewrites in small groups to consider the movement and types of thinking that the freewrites contain. In the small groups, students collaboratively mark up each freewrite as follows:

- **Mark things that are interesting but not yet fully thought out with an asterisk in the margin.** These are potential sites for subsequent freewrites. Try to explain what has been left unsaid.
- **Mark claims—assertions made about the evidence—with the letter** *C.* Claims are ideas that the evidence seems to support. An example of a claim in the student freewrite is "I don't think, however, that the movie lets us entertain this one romanticized reading of the scene for long." Another claim is "I think the movie invites us to read this as a visual representation of the new lives Alex, Lara, and the other characters face now that the wall has fallen."
- **Underline evidence.** The evidence is the freewrite's pool of primary material (data)—details from the film, rather than the writer's ideas about it. An example of evidence in the freewrite is, "As the camera pans away, we see that this isn't a new Westernized apartment; this is an East German flat decorated in much the same way as Alex's home was only months before." Another example of evidence in the freewrite is "The young couple sits, hand in hand, and gazes together into the night sky; yet, as the camera pans away, we see that the apartment where the two have retreated is missing its façade." This second piece of evidence is the 1 of the 10 on 1 that this freewrite is. In effect, the whole freewrite goes after the range of possible implications that may be inferred from the image of the young couple sitting at the edge of an apartment that is missing one of its walls, presumably a result of war damage.
- **Circle complications.** Complications can be found both in the evidence a writer cites and in the claims a writer makes about it. Complicating evidence is evidence that does not fit the claims the writer has been making. The complication of a claim is a statement that qualifies and finds problems in (problematizes) the original claim.

An example of complicating evidence in the freewrite is "As the camera pans away, we see that this isn't a new Westernized apartment; this is an East German flat decorated in much the same way as Alex's home was only months before. The image is alarming; the wall here has been ripped down." This evidence causes the writer to reconsider her earlier claim: "I imagined the movie's placement of the couple on the ledge of a domestic space as a representation of where their lives were going together—toward some shared domestic life, toward living together, toward becoming a family."

We see the writer articulating the resulting complication of her claim when she writes, "and we are forced to ask, did the fall of communism violently blow apart domestic and daily living of East German people?" Notice that the writer doesn't just notice the complication, concede how it might complicate her thinking, and then go back to her claims about the scene as a sign of Lara and Alex's happy domestic future. She uses contradictory evidence to complicate her claim, but doesn't stop there. Look at the freewrite for places where the writer moves through successive complications—that is, where she complicates a previous claim that was itself a complication.

- **Mark potential thesis statements with a** ***Th*** **in the margin.** This freewrite seems to have arrived at what we call in Chapter 6 ("Making a Thesis Evolve") a working thesis. A working thesis is a claim of sufficient scope and significance to launch a paper's exploration process. The working thesis (in most academic disciplines) usually appears at or near the end of an essay's first paragraph. The potential thesis in the freewrite is "the scene is more than just another representation of East Germany torn between Communism and the new Westernization. The movie tries hard to remind us that the rapid Westernization of East Germany *devastated while it liberated* in other ways. This scene uses space to represent Alex and Lara's (and East Germany's) dilemma: Alex and Lara gaze out at the night sky but only because the wall has been blown apart."

Something really interesting has happened here. The phrase in italics is the heart of this potential working thesis. It meets all the requirements of a good analytical thesis. It is in need of argument (that is, its meaning is not self-evident); it is not a fact or something most readers would already agree with; and it has tension, that is, it has the necessary back pressure of one idea against a competing possibility that would give the essay forward momentum. Good thesis statements are often the result of qualifying (limiting, modifying) an overstated, insufficiently complicated claim, which is why tension is a defining characteristic of good thesis statements.

Overall, we see that the writer has succeeded in finding something puzzling rather than settling for her first response (happy domestic future). She has made the most important move in using writing to arrive at ideas—starting with questions, with something she wants to understand better, rather than with answers. When the writer arrives at tentative answers, she tests them rather than just adding more evidence to prove that she is right.

An exciting thing about this freewrite is that it contains fruitful starting points for a subsequent draft that the writer may not yet fully recognize. In studying her freewrite, she will enable herself to see them and follow through on where they might lead. Has the writer yet realized the implications of her own observations in the last sentence of the freewrite? What are the implications of that last sentence? What might the writer discover if she began her different-font freewrite there?

Rules of Thumb for Handling Complexity

1. **Reduce scope.** Whenever possible, drastically reduce the range of your inquiry. Resist the temptation to try to include too much information. Even when an assignment calls for broader coverage of a subject, you will usually do best by covering the ground up front and then analyzing one or two key points in greater depth.
2. **Don't trust your first responses.** If you settle for these, the result is likely to be superficial, obvious, and overly general. A better strategy is to examine your first responses for ways in which they are inaccurate and then develop the implications of these overstatements (or errors) into a new formulation. In many cases, writers go through this process of proposing and rejecting ideas ten times or more before they arrive at an angle or approach that will sustain an essay. A first response is okay for a start, as long as you don't stop there.
3. **Begin with questions, not answers.** You are usually better off to begin with something that you don't understand very well and want to understand better. Begin by asking what kinds of questions the material poses.

4. **Write all the time about what you are studying.** Don't wait to start writing until you think you have an idea you can organize a paper around. Ideally, you should be formulating possible topics long before an actual topic is assigned. By writing informally—as a matter of routine—about what you are studying, you can acquire the habits of mind necessary to having and developing ideas. Similarly, by reading as often and as attentively as you can, and writing spontaneously about what you read, you will accustom yourself to being a less passive consumer of ideas and information, and will have more ideas and information available to think actively with and about.
5. **Accept that interest is a product of writing—not a prerequisite.** The best way to get interested is to expect to become interested. Writing gives you the opportunity to cultivate your curiosity by thinking exploratively. Rather than approaching topics in a mechanical way, or putting them off to the last possible moment and doing the assignment grudgingly, try giving yourself and the topic the benefit of the doubt. If you can suspend judgment and start writing, you will often find yourself uncovering interests where you had not seen them before.
6. **Use the "back burner."** In restaurants, the back burner is the place that chefs leave their sauces and soup stocks to simmer while they are engaged in other, more immediately pressing, and faster operations on the front burners. Think of your brain as having a back burner—a place where you can set and temporarily forget (though not entirely) some piece of thinking that you are working on. A good way to use the back burner is to read through and take some notes on something you are writing about—or perhaps a recent draft of something you are having trouble finishing—just before you go to sleep at night.

   Writers who do this often wake up to find whole outlines and whole strings of useful words already formed in their heads. Keep a notebook by your bed and record these early-morning thoughts. If you do this over a period of days (which assumes, of course, that you will start your writing projects well in advance of deadlines), you will be surprised at how much thinking you can do when you didn't know you were doing it. The back burner keeps working during the day as well—periodically insisting that the front burner, your more conscious self, listen to what it has to say. Pretty soon, ideas start popping up all over the place.

ASSIGNMENT: Doing 10 on 1: A Sample Assignment

As we discuss at more length in Chapter 5, "Linking Evidence and Claims: 10 on 1 versus 1 on 10," doing 10 on 1 is a productive alternative to the shallow analysis of evidence encouraged by organizational schemes such as five-paragraph form, which typically attach evidence to predetermined ideas and provide very little analysis of either. When you do 10 on 1, you have the space to analyze your evidence and to pursue a range of possible implications. If you were writing a short paper about a film, for example, you might spend most of your paper laying out the implications of telling details in a scene that you find especially interesting and revealing, as in the student freewrite on *Good Bye Lenin!* In a longer paper, you would then use your analysis of this scene to open up interestingly related moments from elsewhere in the film and arrive at some conclusions.

- Pick a single scene from a film (or a single photograph from a collection of a photographer's photographs, or some other single example that is interestingly representative of a larger subject). Do 10 on 1 with your scene or other representative example. Notice as much as you can about it. What details repeat? What is opposed to what? (See the heuristic "Looking for Patterns of Repetition and Contrast" in Chapter 2.)
- Make details speak. What do the details "say"? What are some of the things that the film seems to say in this way? Do 10 on 1 in pursuit of implications.
- If time and space allow, pick another scene that is interestingly related to the first one and do 10 on 1 with it. How are the two scenes related, and so what?

We use the word *constellating* to describe a paper that is organized by drawing connections among interestingly related examples, each of which is analyzed using 10 on 1. This strategy works well as an organizational scheme in both exploratory and more polished drafts. For a fuller discussion of constellating as an organizational strategy for papers employing 10 on 1, see the template on pg. 160 in Chapter 5, "Linking Evidence and Claims: 10 on 1 versus 1 on 10." ◗

GUIDELINES FOR SEEING BETTER

1. Trace impressions back to causes.
2. Attend to details; most of us aren't in the habit of noticing details.
3. Narrow your scope in order to notice more.
4. Notice at least ten things in your evidence before you start to have ideas; keep your mind open longer to detail before deciding what it means.
5. Pay attention to the words you choose to describe your evidence; description leads to interpretation because claims are implicit in what you notice.
6. Push yourself to interpretive leaps by asking yourself, So what? This question is shorthand for What are we to make of this? Another version of the same question would be And so?
7. Keep taking your ideas (answers to the repeated application of the So what? question) back to their causes, the details that made you think as you do. Good thinking stays grounded in the evidence.
8. In sum, to have better ideas stay open longer to the data and to a range of possible ideas about the data.

CHAPTER 2

What Is Analysis and How Does It Work?

Quick Take

To analyze something is to ask what that something means. It asks how something does what it does or why it is as it is. Analysis is a form of detective work that begins not with the views you already have, but with something you are seeking to understand. As we said in the discussion of "What It Means to Have an Idea" in Chapter 1, analysis typically pursues something puzzling; it finds questions where there seemed not to be any; and it makes connections that might not have been evident at first.

People analyze all the time, but they don't always realize that this is what they're doing. A first step, then, toward becoming a better analytical thinker and writer is to become more aware of your own thinking processes, building on skills you already possess and eliminating habits that get in the way. Toward this end, here are five moves to practice, five activities people engage in when they analyze. The remainder of the chapter explains and offers examples of these moves as analytical activities.

- Move 1: Suspend Judgment (understand before you judge)
- Move 2: Define Significant Parts and How They're Related
- Move 3: Look for Patterns of Repetition and Contrast and for Anomaly
- Move 4: Make the Implicit Explicit (convert to direct statement meanings that are suggested indirectly)
- Move 5: Keep Reformulating Questions and Explanations

The first of these five moves, *suspending judgment*, is really more a precondition than an actual activity, but because it takes an act of will to suspend judgment and substitute other ways of thinking, we include it as an analytical move.

The second two activities—*defining significant parts and how they're related*, and *looking for patterns of repetition and contrast*—are the primary ways of looking at evidence analytically. The two are related. Looking for patterns is your best means of deciding which parts of a subject to focus on and how best to relate these to each other and to your subject as a whole.

The last two moves, *making the implicit explicit* and *repeatedly reformulating questions and explanations*, are the steps that push observations toward conclusions (the "So what?" part of the process, as explained in Chapter 1).

This chapter has a lot to say about implication, because a primary definition of analysis is that it makes the implicit explicit. The chapter offers exercises for recognizing the difference between an implication and a hidden meaning. The hidden meaning theory of interpretation ("reading *between* the lines") misinterprets analysis as a fanciful imposition of a writer's feelings and opinions onto a subject ("reading *into* the subject"). Analysis, the chapter argues, is a systematic and logical way of reading the lines themselves rather than the white space that lies between them.

The chapter ends by illustrating the importance of selecting and defending the appropriateness of an *interpretive context* as a means of legitimizing a writer's theory about what something means. We illustrate the concept of interpretive context with two short examples and one longer one—a student paper analyzing a perfume advertisement. Chapter 3 offers three more examples of analytical writing, each illustrating the role of the five analytical moves and the concept of interpretive context.

A. FIVE ANALYTICAL MOVES

Analysis is the search for meaningful pattern. In Chapter 1 we talked about the analytical habit of mind: the habit of attending to detail, of tracing impressions back to causes, of searching out questions rather than rushing to answers. That chapter, you'll recall, recommended locating yourself in an area of uncertainty, where there is something to figure out. Overall, the chapter defined the analytical habit of mind as an exploratory stance toward experience.

The first chapter's various thinking and writing practices—Hemingway's five-finger exercise, showing versus telling, freewriting, paraphrase × 3, Notice and focus, asking So what?, and 10 on 1—all share the goal of opening up rather than closing down a subject and the writer's thinking about it.

This chapter, in addition to offering further definitions of analysis—as a process—will provide you with an additional technique for making observations about evidence. This technique, looking for patterns of repetition and contrast ("the Method"), is a sequence of steps for noticing meaningful patterns in whatever it is you are studying.

MOVE 1: SUSPEND JUDGMENT

We discussed this essential move in some detail in Chapter 1, so we'll just restate it briefly here. Suspending judgment is a necessary precursor to thinking analytically because our habitual tendency to evaluate tends to shut down our ability to see and to think. It takes considerable effort to break the habit of responding to everything with likes and dislikes, with agreeing and disagreeing. Just listen in on a few conversations to be reminded of how pervasive this phenomenon really is. Even when you try to suppress them, judgments tend to come.

In the last chapter we suggested that you could get around this reflex move to judgment in several ways. One is to trace impressions back to causes, rather than just settling into and accepting the judgment. Another is to remember that judgments usually say more about the person doing the judging than they do about the subject. The determination that something is "boring" is especially revealing in this regard. Yet people typically roll their eyes and call things boring, as if this assertion clearly said something about the thing they are reacting to but not about the mind of the beholder.

Judgments usually say more about the person doing the judging than they do about the subject. The determination that something is "boring" is especially revealing in this regard.

Consciously leading with the word *interesting* (as in "What I find most interesting about this is . . .") tends to deflect the judgment response into a more exploratory state of mind, one that is motivated by curiosity and thus better able to steer clear of approval and disapproval. The phrase *naturalizing your own assumptions* helps too. It can be used as a kind of mantra to help you notice when you are slipping into the assumption that what feels right and "natural" for you is self-evidently true, right, and natural for others too.

MOVE 2: DEFINE SIGNIFICANT PARTS AND HOW THEY'RE RELATED

Whether you are analyzing an awkward social situation, an economic problem, a painting, a substance in a chemistry lab, or your chances of succeeding in a job interview, the process of analysis is the same:

- divide the subject into its defining parts, its main elements or ingredients, and
- consider how these parts are related, both to each other and to the subject as a whole.

One common denominator of all effective analytical writing is that it pays close attention to detail. We analyze because our global responses—to a play, for example, or a speech or a social problem—are too general. The move from generalization to analysis, from the larger subject to its key components, is characteristic of good thinking. To understand a subject, we need to get past our first, generic, evaluative response to discover what the subject is "made of," the particulars that contribute most strongly to the character of the whole.

If all analysis did, however, was take subjects apart, leaving them broken and scattered, the activity would not be worth very much. The student who presents a draft of a paper to his or her professor with the words, "Go ahead; rip it apart," reveals a disabling misconception about analysis—that, like dissecting a frog in a biology lab, analysis takes the life out of its subjects. Clearly, analysis means more than breaking a subject into its parts. When you analyze a subject, you ask not just what it is made of, but also how the parts contribute to the meaning of the subject as a whole.

VOICES FROM ACROSS THE CURRICULUM

Science as a Process of Argument

I find it ironic that the discipline of science, which is so inherently analytical, is so difficult for students to think about analytically. Much of this comes from the prevailing view of society that science is somehow factual. Science students come to college to learn the facts. I think many find it comforting to think that everything they learn will be objective. None of the wishy-washy subjectivity that many perceive in other disciplines. There is no need to argue, synthesize, or even have a good idea. But this view is dead wrong.

Anyone who has ever done science knows that nothing could be further from the truth. Just like other academics, scientists spend endless hours patiently arguing over evidence that seems obscure or irrelevant to laypeople. There is rarely an absolute consensus. In reality, science is an endless process of argument, obtaining evidence, analyzing evidence, and reformulating arguments. To be sure, we all accept gravity as a "fact." To not do so would be intellectually bankrupt, because all reasonable people agree to the truth of gravity. But to Newton, gravity was an argument for which evidence needed to be produced, analyzed, and discussed. It's important to remember that a significant fraction of his intellectual contemporaries were not swayed by his argument. Equally important is that many good scientific ideas of today will eventually be significantly modified or shown to be wrong.

—Bruce Wightman, Professor of Biology

MOVE 3: LOOK FOR PATTERNS OF REPETITION AND CONTRAST AND FOR ANOMALY (THE METHOD)

We have been defining analysis as understanding parts in relation to each other and to a whole. But how do you know which parts to attend to? What makes some details in the material you are studying more worthy of your attention than others? Here are three procedures for selecting significant parts of the whole. First, we'll briefly discuss the three procedures. Then we will restate them in the form of an observation strategy (the Method) for locating meaningful patterns.

Look for a pattern of repetition (exact repetitions and strands). In virtually all subjects, repetition is a sign of emphasis. In a symphony, for example, certain patterns of notes repeat throughout, announcing themselves as major themes. In a legal document, such as a warranty or lease, a reader quickly becomes aware of words that are part of a particular idea or pattern of thinking, as in, for instance, disclaimers of accountability.

The repetition may not be exact. In Shakespeare's play *King Lear*, for example, references to seeing and eyes call attention to themselves through repetition. A reader of the play would do well to look for various occurrences of words and other details that might be part of this pattern. Let's say you notice that references to seeing and eyes almost always occur along with another strand of language having to do with the concept of proof. How might noticing these two strands lead to an idea? You might start by inferring from the two patterns that the play is concerned with ways of knowing (proving) and with seeing as opposed to other ways of knowing, such as faith or intuition.

Look for binary oppositions and organizing contrasts. Repetition of the same or similar type of word or detail (strands) almost always causes you to notice contrasts (opposing words and details) as well. A strand having to do with eyes and seeing may be contrasted with another strand having to do with its opposite: blindness and ways of accessing experience other than through the eyes. You will find a number of oppositions in virtually anything you study. These usually appear as what are called binary oppositions.

A binary opposition is a pair of elements (words, details, concepts, etc.) in which the two members of the pair are more or less direct opposites. The word *binary* means "consisting of two." We say more below and in subsequent chapters (especially the last section of Chapter 3, "Analyzing an Argument by Reformulating Binaries and Uncovering Assumptions") about the value of searching out binary oppositions. For now, we ask you to begin noticing the oppositions that occur in things that you look at and read.

Through noticing binaries and then casting and recasting the words you use to name them, you enable yourself to discover what is at stake in whatever you are looking at or reading. Writing, as we argue in more detail in our chapter on reading, is virtually always attempting to address some problem or issue. Until you can find the problem, until you can see how the issue is defined, you will not fully understand what you are reading. This is why the process of noticing binaries is valuable.

Look for anomalies—things that seem unusual, that seem not to fit. An anomaly (*a* = not, and *nom* = name) is something that is hard to name, what the dictionary defines as a deviation from the normal order. Along with looking for pattern, it is fruitful to attend to anomalous details—those that seem not to fit the pattern. Anomalies help us revise our stereotypical assumptions. A recent TV commercial for a baseball team, for example, featured its star player reading a novel by Dostoyevsky in the dugout during a game. In this case, the anomaly, a baseball player who reads serious literature, is being used to subvert (question, unsettle) the stereotypical assumption that sports and intellect don't belong together.

Anomalies are important because noticing them often leads to new and better ideas. Most advances in scientific thought, for example, have arisen when a scientist has observed some phenomenon that does not fit with a prevailing theory. Just as people tend to leap to evaluative judgments, they also tend to avoid information that challenges (by not conforming to) opinions they already hold. The result is that they ignore the evidence that might lead them to a better theory. (For much more on this process of using potentially contradictory and seemingly anomalous evidence to evolve an essay's main idea, see Chapter 6, "Making a Thesis Evolve.")

We will now recast the process of looking for repetition and contrast into a series of steps that we call the Method (for short).

Looking for Patterns of Repetition and Contrast (The Method) Looking for patterns of repetition and contrast (the Method) is a universal assignment, by which we mean that it works with all kinds of materials—a political speech, an essay, a film or scene from a film, a place, a book of poems, a photograph, your own essay drafts that you seek to revise—and with a wide range of purposes. The method of looking for patterns works through a series of steps. Hold yourself initially to doing the steps one at a time and in order. List what you notice for each step as thoroughly as you can before moving on. As you get adept at using this procedure, you will be able to record your answers under each of the three steps simultaneously. This analytical method can be applied to virtually anything.

Step 1. *Locate exact repetitions*—identical or nearly identical words or details—and note the number of times each repeats.

For example, if the word *seems* repeats three times, write "seems × 3." Consider different forms of the same word—*seemed*, *seem*—as exact repetitions. Similarly, if you are working with images rather than words, the repeated appearance of high foreheads would constitute an exact repetition.

Concentrate on substantive words, although sometimes seemingly unimportant words such as *and* become interesting when they begin to repeat a lot. If you are working with a longer text, such as an essay or book chapter or short story, limit yourself to recording the half-dozen or so words that call attention to themselves through repetition.

Step 2. *Locate repetition of the same or similar kind of detail or word (strands) and name the connecting logic.* A strand is a grouping of the same or similar kinds of words or details. (For example, *polite, courteous, mannerly* and *accuse, defense, justice, witness* are strands.)

Simply listing the various strands that you find in your evidence will go a long way toward helping you discover what is most interesting and important for you to address. But to use the discovery of strands as an analytical tool, you have to do more than list. You have to name the common denominators that make the words or details in your list identifiable as a strand. Naming and renaming your strands will trigger ideas; it is itself an analytical move. And again, when working with longer pieces, try to locate the half-dozen strands that seem to you most important.

Step 3. *Locate details or words that form or suggest binary oppositions, and select from these the most important ones, which function as organizing contrasts.*

Sometimes patterns of repetition that you begin to notice in a particular subject matter will be significant because they are part of a contrast—a basic opposition—around which the subject matter is structured. To find these oppositions, ask yourself, *What is opposed to what?*

When looking for binary oppositions, start with what's on the page. List words and details that are set in opposition to other words and details. Gradually move to implied binaries, but keep these close to the data. Images of rocks and water, for example, might suggest the implied binary permanence/impermanence or the binary unchanging/changing.

One advantage of detecting binary oppositions and elements of them that repeat is that this process will lead you to discover *organizing contrasts*, which are key in helping you locate central issues and concerns in the material you are studying. Organizing contrasts unify and give structure to the whole. Some examples that we encounter frequently are nature/civilization, city/country, public/private, organic/inorganic, and voluntary/involuntary.

Step 4. *List what you take to be the **two** most important exact repetitions, **two** most important strands, and **two** most important binaries.* Usually you will find that strands work in opposition to other strands.

At this point you are ready to use *ranking* (selecting some items from your lists as more important, more interesting than others) as a means of moving toward interpretive leaps. We ask you to choose the two most important kinds of repetition from each of your three kinds of lists so that you don't cut out too much data too soon. Your most important binaries might be a pair of opposed terms and/or ideas, but each might also be a strand that is opposed to another strand.

Step 5. *Write one healthy paragraph—half a page or so—in which you explain your choice of one repetition or one strand or one binary as most important for understanding whatever it is that you have been observing.*

Anomaly

After you have produced your three lists, selected the most important items from each, and written a paragraph explaining your ranking, you are ready to add a step to the process of looking for patterns. Along with looking for patterns, it is fruitful to attend to anomalous details—those that seem not to fit the pattern.

Like searching out binary oppositions, searching out anomalies often takes you to those places in your subject matter where something is going on—where some kind of breaking out of an old pattern or some attempt at "re-seeing" is beginning.

Why add anomalies as a separate activity? Anomalies become evident only after you have begun to discern a pattern, so it is best to locate repetitions, strands, and organizing contrasts—things that fit together in some way—before looking for things that seem not to fit. Once you see an anomaly, you will often find that it is part of a strand you had not detected, a strand that may be the other side of a previously unseen binary. In this respect, looking for anomalies is great for shaking yourself out of potentially limited ways of looking at your evidence and getting you to consider other possible interpretations. See an example of the use of anomaly in the essay on Ovid later in the chapter, as well as in the student essay on a dance performance toward the end of the chapter.

"The Method": What It Is and Why It Works

Think of this method of analysis as a form of mental doodling, which is actually what it is. The major advantage of this kind of doodling is that it encourages the attitude of *negative capability* that we spoke of in Chapter 1. Rather than worrying about what you are going to say, or about whether or not you understand, you instead get out a pencil and start tallying up what you see. Engaged in this process, you'll soon find yourself gaining entry to the logic of your subject matter.

While you are involved in the kinds of observing and listing activities that this method involves, you will be allowing your mind to range freely over the data. The activities of circling, underlining, and listing cause you to get physical with your data, and thus to come down from abstractions into the realm of concrete detail.

The Method shares aims with the observation strategies introduced in Chapter 1, but its approach to evidence differs in interesting ways. The primary observation strategy of Chapter 1, Notice and focus, tends to cut through to individual details. It acts like a laser beam to target something interesting and often anomalous (strange) that allows a writer to economically capture the character of the whole through a representative part. Because it relies on what you happen to notice or find interesting, Notice and focus is more intuitive and more reliant on fortuitous discoveries than the method of looking for patterns.

Looking for patterns, by contrast, is more comprehensive. It goes for the whole picture, involving methodical application of a matrix or grid of observational moves upon a subject. Although these are separate moves, they also work together and build cumulatively to the discovery of an infrastructure, a blueprint of the whole.

Strands, Binaries, and the Writing (and Revision) Process

What is the value of looking for strands—groups of the same or similar kinds of details (or words)? The presence of strands in written or visual texts has much to do with the way we arrive at ideas, the way we go about finding out what we think. When you write a paper or a letter or a story or a poem, or when you compose some kind of picture, your thinking (at the semiconscious and subconscious, as well as the conscious levels) moves not just forward, in a straight line, but sideways and in circles.

LOOKING FOR PATTERNS OF REPETITION AND CONTRAST (THE METHOD)

- Do the steps (in writing) one at a time and in order.
- Resist the urge to leap to conclusions; dwell with the data first.

Step 1. List all details (or words) that repeat exactly and the number of repetitions of each.

Step 2. List strands—groupings of the same or similar kinds of words, details.

(for example: *polite, courteous, mannerly*)

Be able to explain the strand's connecting logic; name it.

Think carefully about what goes with what.

Step 3. List organizing contrasts—binary oppositions.

(for example, open/closed, round/pointed)

Start with what's on the page.

Gradually move to implied binaries but stay close to the data.

List as many binaries as you can.

Step 4. Select and list the two most significant repetitions, the two most significant strands, and the two most significant binaries.

Step 5. Select and list the one repeated detail, *or* one strand, *or* one binary that you take to be the most significant for arriving at ideas about what the image communicates. Write one paragraph explaining your choice.

This is to say that much of the thinking that we do as we write and as we read happens through a process of association, which is, by its very nature, repetitive. In associative thinking, thoughts develop as words, and details suggest other words and details that are like them. As you habituate yourself to looking for patterns of repetition and contrast, you will be surprised at how much repetition (of various kinds) goes on in any piece of communication.

When you write a paper or a letter or a story or a poem, or when you compose some kind of picture, your thinking (at the semiconscious and subconscious, as well as the conscious levels) moves not just forward, in a straight line, but sideways and in circles.

Revision is the process of consciously recognizing and clarifying patterns of repetition and contrast in your drafts. Recognizing patterns of repetition and contrast helps writers and artists come to see what they wish to say; the same process of recognition produces readers' and viewers' understanding of the things they read and see. In this sense, writing (making something out of words) and reading (arriving at an understanding of someone else's words) operate in much the same way.

Try this 2.1: Doing the Method on a Poem

Use the Method on the following student poem. Write up the lists called for in steps 1–4 of the Method, and then write the healthy paragraph called for in step 5 in which you explain your choice of one exact repetition, one strand, or one binary as most significant. We have done this for you below in the section called "Doing the Method: An Example." If you can make up your own lists and write your own paragraph before looking at ours, you'll learn more. There is, however, another "Try this" later in this chapter that we do not analyze for you.

Brooklyn Heights, 4:00 A.M.
Dana Ferrelli

sipping a warm forty oz.
Coors Light on a stoop in
Brooklyn Heights. I look
across the street, in the open window;
Blonde bobbing heads, the
smack of a jump rope, laughter

of my friends breaking
beer bottles. Putting out their
burning filters on the #5 of
a hopscotch court.
We reminisce of days when we were
Fat, pimple faced—

look how far we've come. But tomorrow
a little blonde girl will
pick up a Marlboro Light filter, just to play.
And I'll buy another forty, because
that's how I play now.

Reminiscing about how far I've come

Doing the Method on a Poem: Our Analysis

1. *Words that repeat exactly*: forty × 2, blonde × 2, how far we've (I've) come × 2, light × 2, reminisce, reminiscing × 2, filter, filters × 2, Brooklyn Heights × 2
2. *Strands:* jump rope, laughter, play, hopscotch (connecting logic: childhood games representing the carefree worldview of childhood)

   Coors Light, Marlboro Light filters, beer bottles (drugs, adult "games," escapism?)
   Smack, burning, breaking (violent actions and powerful emotion: burning)
3. *Binary oppositions:* how far we've come/how far I've come (a move from plural to singular, from a sense of group identity to isolation, from group values to a more individual consideration)

   Blonde bobbing heads/little blonde girl
   Burning/putting out
   Coors Light, Marlboro Lights/jump rope, hopscotch
   How far I've come (two meanings of *far*?, one positive, one not)
   Heights/stoop
   Present/past
4. *Two most important repetitions:* forty, how far we've/I've come

   Two most important strands: jump rope, laughter, play, hopscotch
   Coors Light, Marlboro Light filters, beer bottles
   Two most important binaries: jump rope, laughter, play, hopscotch versus
   Coors Light, Marlboro Light filters, beer bottles;
   Burning/putting out
5. *Write one healthy paragraph in which you explain your choice of* ***one*** *repetition or* ***one*** *strand or* ***one*** *binary as most important for understanding whatever it is that you have been observing.*

This is a poem about growing up—or failing to grow up, both being subjects about which the poem expresses mixed emotions. The repetition of *forty* (forty-ounce beer, forty cigarettes) is interesting in this context. It signals a certain weariness—perhaps with a kind of pun on forty to suggest middle age and thus the speaker's concern about moving toward being older in a way that seems stale and flat. The beer, after all, is warm—which is not the best state for a beer to be in, once opened, if it is to retain its taste and character. Forty cigarettes, forty ounces of beer—"supersizing"—suggest excess.

This reading of forty as excess along with the possible allusion to middle age takes us to what is, in our reading of the poem, the most important (or at least most interesting) binary opposition: *burning versus putting out*. We are attracted to this binary because it seems to be part of a more intense strand in the poem, one that runs counter to the weary prospect of moving on toward a perhaps lonely ("how far *I've* come") middle-aged feeling. Burning goes with breaking and the smack of the jump rope, and even putting out, if we visualize putting out not just as fire extinguished but in terms of putting a cigarette out by pushing the burning end of it into something (the number 5 on the Hopscotch court). The poem's language has a violent and passionate edge to it, even though the violent words are not always in a violent context (for example, the smack of the jump rope).

This is a rather melancholy poem in which, perhaps, the poetic voice is mourning the passing, the "putting out" of the passion of youth ("burning"). In the poem's more obvious binary—the opposition of childhood games to more "adult" ones—the same melancholy plays itself out, making the poem's refrain-like repetition of "how far I've come" ring with unhappy irony. The little blonde girl is an image of the speaker's own past self (since the poem talks about reminiscing), and the speaker mourns that little girl's (her own) passing into a more uncertain and less carefree state. It is 4:00 A.M. in Brooklyn Heights—just about the end of night, the darkest point perhaps before the beginning of morning, and windows in the poem are open, so things are not all bad. The friends make noise together, break bottles together, revisit hopscotch square 5 together, and contemplate moving on.

Analysis of Our Analysis The point of tallying repetitions and strands and binaries and then selecting the most important and interesting ones is to trigger ideas. The hope is that the discipline of having to look closely at and notice patterns in the language will produce more specific, more carefully grounded conclusions than you otherwise might notice.

Virtually everything in our three paragraphs moves from the repeated words and patterns we noticed in the evidence. We didn't go outside the poem to generalities, nor did we take some single item out of context (looking for pattern helps prevent you from doing that) and produce an interpretation that might not be true to the rest of the poem.

We couldn't, by the way, find any anomalies in the poem—things that seemed not to fit. Of course, it is often the case that what at first seems to be an anomaly is actually part of a pattern you haven't yet fully noticed. For good examples of writers making use of anomalies in their evidence, see the Ovid example and the student paper on dance later in the chapter.

Try this 2.2: Doing the Method on a Speech

Here is a speech that no doubt all readers of this book will know. Many of you may even have committed it to memory at some point. Try looking for patterns of repetition and contrast in it. See what this method allows you to notice about what is already a familiar piece of prose. Later, after you read our chapter on sentence style, you could come back to this speech and see what you notice in it if you look for pattern in terms of Lincoln's syntactical choices. This exercise could also serve as a model for further practice in looking for patterns of repetition and contrast in speeches. Speeches by various presidents, for example, are easy to find on the Internet. Your aim in doing the Method on speeches is to arrive at conclusions about the speech that get beyond the obvious and the general. What does doing the Method on this speech cause you to notice that you may not have noticed before?

The Gettysburg Address
Nov. 19, 1863

Fourscore and seven years ago our fathers brought forth on this continent a new nation, conceived in liberty and dedicated to the proposition that all men are created equal.

Now we are engaged in a great civil war, testing whether that nation or any nation so conceived and so dedicated can long endure. We are met on a great battlefield of that war. We have come to dedicate a portion of it as a final resting place for those who died here that the nation might live. This we may, in all propriety do. But in a larger sense, we cannot dedicate, we cannot consecrate, we cannot hallow this ground. The brave men, living and dead who struggled here have hallowed it far above our poor power to add or detract. The world will little note nor long remember what we say here, but it can never forget what they did here.

It is rather for us the living, we here be dedicated to the great task remaining before us—that from these honored dead we take increased devotion to that cause for which they here gave the last full measure of devotion—that we here highly resolve that these dead shall not have died in vain, that this nation shall have a new birth of freedom, and that government of the people, by the people, for the people shall not perish from the earth.

Start by listing words that repeat exactly. Then list repetitions of the same or similar kinds of words (strands). Then list words that fall into opposition to each other—binary oppositions. As you start listing, you will find that strands begin to suggest other strands that are in opposition to them. And you may find that words you first took to be parts of a single strand are actually parts of different strands and are, perhaps, in opposition. This process of noticing and then relocating words and details into different patterns is the part of doing the Method that pushes your analysis to possible interpretations.

A Note on the Importance of Finding Binaries

Let's think further about what binaries are and what they reveal. Binaries are deeply engrained in the ways that we think. Thinking is not possible without them. But the discovery of binaries is not an end unto itself. Why is it useful to find binary oppositions (binaries)? And why isn't this search for binaries a problem, like approaching the world as though everything in it could be divided into only two possibilities (either/or thinking)?

When you run into a binary opposition in your thinking, it is like a fork in the road, a place where two paths going in different directions present themselves and you pause to choose the direction you will take. Binary oppositions are sites of uncertainty, places where there is struggle among various points of view. As such, binaries are the breeding ground of ideas.

Binary oppositions are sites of uncertainty, places where there is struggle among various points of view.

When you find a binary opposition in an essay, a film, or a political campaign, you locate the argument that the film, essay, or campaign is having with itself, the place where something is at issue. You avoid the rigidifying and reductive habit of mind called either/or thinking when you allow yourself to notice binaries, but immediately begin to ask questions about and complicate them. To "complicate" a binary is to discover evidence that unsettles it and to formulate alternatively worded binaries that more accurately describe what is at issue in the evidence.

As a general rule, analysis favors live questions—where something remains to be resolved—over inert answers, places where things are already pretty much nailed down and don't leave much space for further thinking. Finding binaries will help you find the questions around which almost anything is organized. This is why we ask you to select those binary oppositions in your subject matter that seem to you to be "organizing contrasts." Much analytical thinking, whether you are aware of doing it or not, involves determining which of a number of opposing elements is the most fundamental, the most important for understanding how something operates as a whole. Think of an organizing contrast as the structural beam that gives conceptual shape to a piece. (See Chapter 3, Section C).

There is usually no single "right" answer about which of a number of binary oppositions is the primary organizing contrast. This is because analytical thinking involves interpretation. Interpretive conclusions are not matters of fact, but theories. It is in the nature of theories to be tentative and open to alternative readings of the same information. This is why good analytical thinking takes time and is inevitably open-ended.

Analysis at Work: An Example (a Student Draft on Ovid's **Metamorphoses*)***

This preliminary draft of a paper on Ovid's *Metamorphoses*, a collection of short mythological tales dating from ancient Rome, exemplifies a writer in the process of discovering a workable idea. She begins with a list of similar examples. As the examples accumulate, the writer begins to make connections and formulate trial explanations. We have not included enough of this excerpt to get to the tentative thesis the draft is working toward, although it is already beginning to emerge. What we want to emphasize here is the writer's willingness to accumulate data and to locate it in various patterns of similarity and contrast.

The draft begins with two loosely connected observations about Ovid's stories: that males dominate females, and that many characters in the stories lose the ability to speak and thus become submissive and dominated. In the excerpt, the writer begins to connect these two observations and speculate about what this connection means.

We have included annotations in the draft to suggest how the writer's ideas evolve as she looks for pattern, contrast, and anomaly. Notice in particular how the writer manages to remain open to reformulation.

> There are many other examples in Ovid's *Metamorphoses* that show the dominance of man over woman through speech control. In the Daphne and Apollo story, Daphne becomes a tree to escape Apollo, but her ability to speak is destroyed. Likewise, in the Syrinx and Pan story, Syrinx becomes a marsh reed, also a life form that cannot talk, although Pan can make it talk by playing it. [The writer establishes a pattern of similar detail.]
>
> Pygmalion and Galatea is a story in which the male creates his rendition of the perfect female. The female does not speak once; she is completely silent. Also, Galatea is referred to as *she* and never given a real name. This lack of a name renders her identity more silent. [Here the writer begins to link the contrasts of speech/silence with the absence/presence of identity.]
>
> Ocyrhoe is a female character who could tell the future, but was changed into a mare so that she could not speak. One may explain this transformation by saying it was an attempt by the gods to keep the future unknown. [Notice how the writer's thinking expands as she sustains her investigation of the overall pattern of men silencing women: here she tests her theory by adding another variable: prophecy.]
>
> However, there is a male character, Tiresias, who is also a seer of the future and is allowed to speak of his foreknowledge, thereby becoming a famous figure. (Interestingly, Tiresias during his lifetime has experienced being both a male and a female.) [Notice how the Ocyrhoe example has spawned a contrast based on gender in the Tiresias example. The pairing of the two examples demonstrates that the ability to tell the future is not the sole cause of silencing, since male characters who can do it are not silenced—though the writer pauses to note that Tiresias is not entirely male.]
>
> Finally, in the story of Mercury and Herse, Herse's sister, Aglauros, tries to prevent Mercury from marrying Herse. Mercury turns her into a statue; the male directly silences the female's speech.
>
> The woman silences the man in only two stories studied. [Here the writer searches out an anomaly—women silencing men—that grows in the rest of the paragraph into an organizing contrast.] In the first, "The Death of Orpheus," the women make use of "clamorous shouting, Phrygian flutes with curving horns, tambourines, the beating of breasts, and Bacchic howlings" (246) to drown out the male's songs, dominating his speech in terms of volume. In this way, the quality of power within speech is demonstrated: "for the first time, his words had no effect, and he failed to move them [the women] in any way by

his voice" (247). Next the women kill him, thereby rendering him silent. However, the male soon regains his temporarily destroyed power of expression: "the lyre uttered a plaintive melody and the lifeless tongue made a piteous murmur" (247). Even after death, Orpheus is able to communicate. The women were not able to destroy his power completely, yet they were able to severely reduce his power of speech and expression. [The writer learns, among other things, that men are harder to silence; Orpheus's lyre and his severed head continue to sing after his death.]

The second story in which a woman silences a man is the story of Actaeon, in which the male sees Diana naked, and she transforms him into a stag so that he cannot speak of it: "he tried to say 'Alas!' but no words came" (79). This loss of speech leads to Actaeon's inability to inform his own hunting team of his true identity; his loss of speech leads ultimately to his death. [This example reinforces the pattern that the writer had begun to notice in the Orpheus example.]

Thinking Recursively: Reformulating Binaries

For the purposes of using the Method, recursive thinking is essential. Working with strands is an inherently recursive activity because you'll tend to first think that one set of words or details fits together as a strand and then you'll find yourself regrouping—reformulating your strands as new patterns begin to strike you. As you begin to notice repetitions, they tend to suggest strands, and strands tend to beget organizing contrasts.

Thinking is not simply linear and progressive, moving from point A to point B to point C like stops on a train. Careful thinkers are always retracing their steps, questioning their first—and second—impressions, assuming that they've missed something. All good thinking is *recursive*—that is, it repeatedly goes over the same ground, reformulating ideas and rethinking connections.

Nowhere is it more important to *reformulate* than in working with organizing contrasts. This is because the habit of mind called binary (either/or) thinking can retard thought through oversimplification—through a tendency toward rigidly dichotomized points of view. But finding binary oppositions as a means of locating what is at issue and then using the binaries to *start* rather than end your thinking process is not reductive. Notice how in the Ovid example the writer keeps reformulating her ways of categorizing her data.

Let's consider a brief example in which a writer starts with the binary: was the poet Emily Dickinson psychotic, or was she a poetic genius? This is a useful, if overstated, starting point for prompting thinking. Going over the same ground, the writer might next decide that the opposing terms *insanity* and *poetic genius* don't accurately name the issue. He or she might decide, as the poet Adrienne Rich did, that poetic genius is often perceived as insanity by the culture at large and, thus, it's not a viable either/or formulation. This move, by the way, is known as *collapsing the binary:* coming to see that what had appeared to be an opposition is really two parts of one complex phenomenon.

Perhaps the insanity/poetic genius binary would be better reformulated in terms of conventionality/unconventionality—a binary that might lead the writer to start reappraising the ways in which Dickinson is not as eccentric as she at first appears to be.

Regrouping Strands and Binaries as a Method of Analysis: An Example

Although the steps of the Method are discrete and modular, they are also consecutive; they entail a kind of narrative logic. Each step leads logically to the next and then to various kinds of regrouping (which is actually rethinking). Let's run through a hypothetical example of this way of thinking with repetition, strands, and binaries.

The first step, the discovery of repetition, reveals what a piece of writing is about. If, for example, a piece of reading reveals numerous repetitions of the word *duty*, you would then know that (whatever the piece might think about duty) it is clearly, at the most factual level, *about* duty.

The repetition of *duty* might alert you to look for other related words that will begin to suggest themselves as part of a strand—at which point you would begin to educe and construct a *discourse* of duty, a strand of related words that your observation of repetitions of the word *duty* illuminated. You might then notice *guilt, responsibility, shame, obligation, task*, and so on as a *discursive strand* that further reveals what the piece is about. At this point of strand formation, you have already made an interpretive leap (observation has blended into interpretation). You would need to follow this up consciously by *articulating the logic of the strand*. In this case, it might be "words that suggest the writer's worries about performing certain acts."

Note that what the text thinks of the duty strand—what it is inviting us to think of duty, and how it resolves the problem or issue or question associated with duty—requires a step beyond noticing that the text is about duty because that word repeats. The formulation of a primary strand, which reveals what the text is about and interested in, usually leads to a next step: what the text is worried about, anxious about, trying to resolve. The formulation of a strand is thus usually one half of an organizing contrast.

The formulation of a primary strand, which reveals what the text is about and interested in, usually leads to a next step: what the text is worried about, anxious about, trying to resolve.

So we should ask ourselves, What is duty in tension with here? To what is it opposed? Often the answer will turn out to be another term in the strand—let's say *shame*. And so we come to see, as our analysis evolves, that two words we had first grouped together, and rightly so, can also be separated into an organizing contrast, with each as the key term in its own strand. If you look back at our analysis of the poem above, you can see this happening.

The *duty* strand might retain *task, responsibility, work, reward*, and others from the original strand, which would now be "the upside of doing what is expected." The opposing *shame* strand might include *guilt* and other words that the discovery of this new strand would start to illuminate, say, *fear, humble, revulsion*. If the *duty* strand is the "upside," then the *shame* and *guilt* strand is the "downside," that which the text is worried and potentially anxious about.

The writer's consideration of how the text mediates the tension made apparent by this reward/revulsion, duty/guilt contrast would be the primary culminating business of the analysis, which might issue in a thesis such as "Although the American tobacco industry repeatedly pays lip service to the guilt it feels for making a profit on the lungs of its citizenry, ultimately it flees the shame in the name of corporate responsibility to serving its shareholders their slice of the American dream."

Try this 2.3: Apply the Method to Something You Are Reading

Try the Method on a piece of reading that you wish to understand better, perhaps a series of editorials on the same subject, an essay, one or more poems by the same author (since the Method is useful for reading across texts for common denominators), a collection of stories, a political speech, and so on. You can work with as little as a few paragraphs or as much as an entire article or chapter or book. By focusing on repetition (exact repetitions and strands), contrast (binary oppositions), and anomalies, you press yourself to get closer to your data—to become more aware of what the subject is made of, rather than generalizing broadly about it.

This exercise can produce fruitful results with almost any kind of material. It offers, for example, a very useful way of accessing and characterizing the mental habits of particular authors. It is also particularly useful with complex theoretical arguments, as it allows you to gradually discover what the argument is made of rather than allowing yourself to become daunted by the scope and difficulty of the material. For more suggestions on working with difficult theoretical readings, see the sections on paraphrase × 3 in Chapter 1, "the pitch and the complaint" in Chapter 4, and our example of uncovering assumptions in a reading, which appears at the end of Chapter 3.

MOVE 4: MAKE THE IMPLICIT EXPLICIT

A definition of analytical writing to which this book repeatedly returns is that it makes explicit (overtly stated) what is implicit (suggested but not directly stated) in both your subject and your own thinking. This process of converting suggestions into direct statements is essential to analysis, but it is also the feature of analyzing that is least understood by inexperienced writers. They fear that, like the emperor's new clothes, implications aren't really "there," but are instead the phantasms of an overactive imagination. "Reading between the lines" is the common and telling phrase that expresses this anxiety. The implication is that analysis makes something out of nothing—the spaces between the lines—rather than what is there in black and white. Another version of this anxiety is implied by the term *hidden meanings.*

Some people fear that, like the emperor's new clothes, implications aren't really "there," but are instead the phantasms of an overactive imagination. "Reading between the lines" is the common and telling phrase that expresses this anxiety.

Implication versus Hidden Meanings

The problem some people have with this analytical move—making the implicit explicit—is that it focuses on a "part" of the whole that is not overtly (materially) present, but rather is something that some part of the whole suggests. Making the implicit explicit is an interpretive move and not simply a matter of observation. This aspect of analytical thinking is the least understood by people who are easily put off by analysis. Such people invariably jeer at analysis for allegedly picking things apart (which we call defining significant parts in relation to the whole) and finding "hidden meanings" (which we call making the implicit explicit).

Implications are not hidden, but neither are they completely spelled out so that they can be simply extracted. The word *implication* comes from the Latin *implicare*, which means "folded in." The word *explicit* is in opposition to the idea of implication. It means "folded out."

This etymology of the two words, *implicit* and *explicit*, suggests that meanings aren't actually "hidden," but neither are they opened to full view. An act of mind is required to take what is folded in and fold it out for all to see. What follows is a brief exercise on implication consisting of a series of observations for which you are asked to supply implications. On the basis of this activity, we then ask you to theorize the difference between an implication and a hidden meaning.

Try this 2.4: Inferring Implications from Observations

Do this exercise along with other people if you can, because part of its aim is to determine the extent to which different people infer the same implications. Write a list of as many plausible implications as you can think of for each of the items below.

1. The sidewalk is disappearing as a feature of the American residential landscape. New housing developments have them only if a township requires them of the developer.
2. New house designs are tending increasingly toward open plans in which the kitchen is not separated from the rest of the house. New house designs continue to have a room called the living room, usually a space at the front of the house near the front door, but many (not all) also have a separate space called the family room, which is usually in some part of the house farther removed from the front door and closer to the kitchen.
3. "Good fences make good neighbors."—Robert Frost
4. In the female brain, there are more connections between the right hemisphere (emotions, spatial reasoning) and the left hemisphere (verbal facility). In the male brain, these two hemispheres remain more separate.
5. An increasing number of juveniles—people under the age of eighteen—are being tried and convicted as adults, rather than as minors, in America, with the result that more minors are serving adult sentences for crimes they committed while still in their teens.
6. Neuroscientists tell us that the frontal cortex of the brain, the part that is responsible for judgment and especially for impulse control, is not fully developed in humans until roughly the age of twenty-one. What are the implications of this observation relative to observation 5?

7. Linguists have long commented on the tendency of women's speech to use rising inflection at the end of statements as if the statements were questions. An actual command form—Be home by midnight!—thus becomes a question instead. What are we to make of the fact that in recent years younger men (under 30) have begun to end declarative statements and command forms with rising inflections?
8. Shopping malls and grocery stores rarely have clocks.

After you have made your list of implications for each item, consider how you arrived at them. On the basis of this experience, how would you answer the following questions? What is the difference between an idea being "hidden" and an idea being implied? What, in other words, is an implication? To what extent do you think most people would arrive at the same implications that you did?

Having done the preceding exercise with inferring implications, you could now make up your own list of observations and pursue implications. Make some observations, for example, about the following, and then suggest the possible implications of your observations.

- changing trends in automobiles today
- what your local newspaper chooses to put on its front page (or editorial page) over the course of a week
- shows (or advertisements) that appear on network television (as opposed to cable) during one hour of evening prime time
- advertisements for scotch whiskey in highbrow magazines

We end this discussion of the fourth analytical move, making the implicit explicit, with a quick summary of the steps that analysis typically takes from observations to conclusions. These steps may be charted as follows:

Observation (description) → Implications → Conclusions (So what?)

In *step 1* of this process, you describe your evidence, paraphrasing key language and looking for interesting patterns of repetition and contrast.

In *step 2* you begin querying your own observations by making what is implicit explicit.

In the *final step* you push your observations and statements of implications to interpretive conclusions by asking, So what?

As we have argued in this chapter and in Chapter 1, the analytical process requires certain critical shifts in your attention. In Chapter 1, with the exercise called Notice and focus, we noted that writers need to start by asking themselves not "What do I think?" but "What do I notice?"

A similar shift that is conducive to inferring implication is:

***Not** What do I think?*

but

What does it say?

MOVE 5: KEEP REFORMULATING QUESTIONS AND EXPLANATIONS

Analysis, like all forms of writing, requires a lot of experimenting. Because the purpose of analytical writing is to figure something out, you shouldn't expect to know at the outset exactly where you are going, how all your subject's parts fit together, and to what end. The key is to be patient and to know that there are procedures—in this case, questions—you can rely on to take you from uncertainty to understanding.

The following groups of questions (organized according to the analytical moves they're derived from) are typical of what goes on in an analytical writer's head as he or she attempts to understand a subject. These questions will work with almost anything you want to think about. As you will see, they are geared toward helping you locate and try on explanations for the meaning of various patterns of details.

Which details seem significant? Why?
What does the detail mean?
What else might it mean?
(Moves: Define Significant Parts; Make the Implicit Explicit)

How do the details fit together? What do they have in common?
What does this pattern of details mean?
What else might this same pattern of details mean? How else could it be explained?
(Move: Look for Patterns of Repetition and Contrast)

What details don't seem to fit? How might they be connected with other details to form a different pattern?
What does this new pattern mean? How might it cause me to read the meaning of individual details differently?
(Moves: Look for Anomalies, Keep Reformulating Questions)

The process of posing and answering such questions—the analytical process—is one of trial and error. Learning to write well is largely a matter of learning how to frame questions. One of the main things you acquire in the study of an academic discipline is knowledge of the kinds of questions that the discipline typically asks. For example, an economics professor and a sociology professor might observe the same phenomenon, such as a sharp decline in health benefits for the elderly, and analyze its causes and significance in different ways. The economist might consider how such benefits are financed and how changes in government policy and the country's population patterns might explain the declining supply of funds for the elderly. The sociologist might ask about attitudes toward the elderly and about the social structures that the elderly rely on for support.

Whatever questions you ask, the answers you propose will often produce more questions. Like signposts on a trail, details (data) that initially seem to point in one direction may, on closer examination, lead you someplace else. Dealing with these realities of analytical writing requires patience, but it will also make you a more confident thinker, because you'll come to know that your uncertainty is a normal and necessary part of writing.

Using Exploratory Writing to Find Workable Questions

The process of having ideas rarely moves steadily forward, traveling in an uninterrupted line from point to point like a connect-the-dots picture. Instead, thinking and writing are *recursive* activities, which means that we move forward by looking backward, by repeatedly going over the same ground, looking for wrong turns, uncovering signposts we may have missed, and reinterpreting signposts passed earlier because of what we later discovered.

A good paper is essentially the answer to a good question, an explanation of some feature or features of your subject that need explaining. If you don't take the time to look for questions, you might end up writing a tidy but relatively pointless paper. Spend some time simply recording what you notice about your subject without worrying about where these observations might lead. By opening up your thinking in this way, you will discover more data to think with, more possible starting points from which to develop an idea. And you will be less likely to get trapped into seeing only those features of your subject that support the first conclusion you come to.

A good paper is essentially the answer to a good question, an explanation of some feature or features of your subject that need explaining. If you don't take the time to look for questions, you might end up writing a tidy but relatively pointless paper.

When you shift from exploratory writing to writing a first draft, you may not—and most likely will not—have all the answers, but you will waste significantly less time chasing ill-focused and inadequately considered ideas than might otherwise have been the case. Even as you write this draft, however, a good phrase to keep in mind is *Share your thought processes with the reader*. If readers can't see how you got to the position you are offering them, they have little reason to accept it, no matter how smooth the sentence style, grammar, paragraphing, and organization may be.

B. SOME COMMON CHARGES AGAINST ANALYSIS

Once you accept the challenge of thinking and writing analytically—the careful, recursive, and nonjudgmental observation of your subject and of your own thoughts—you can expect to encounter another obstacle. Although analysis is an activity we call on constantly in our everyday lives, many people are deeply suspicious of it. "Why can't you just enjoy the movie rather than picking it apart?" they'll say. Or, "Oh, you're just making that up!" You may even be accused of being unfeeling if you adopt an analytical stance, because it is typical of the anti-intellectual position to insist that feeling and thinking are separate and essentially incompatible activities. Some people fear that trusting our intellects will make us less feeling and sensitive. With this fear goes the opposite one—that trusting our feelings will necessarily render us incapable of thinking. Both of these suspicions about analysis have long histories.

Though among the most astutely analytical of thinkers, the famous nineteenth-century English Romantic poet William Wordsworth wrote that "we murder to dissect," thus giving voice to the still common anxiety that analysis takes the life out of things. This attitude arose in reaction against an equally extreme position from the eighteenth century (the so-called Age of Reason or Enlightenment), known for its indictment of emotion as the enemy of rationality.

In response to the eighteenth century's elevation of reason over all other human faculties, the nineteenth century sought to correct the imbalance by elevating the faculties of feeling and imagination. Few thinkers of either century really adhered to these positions in such extreme forms, but suffice it to say that analysts of human beings seem always to have been perplexed about how our various capacities fit together into a functional whole. One aim of this book is to demonstrate that taking refuge in either side of the opposition between thinking and feeling is not only counterproductive but unnecessarily reductive.

CHARGE 1: "ANALYSIS KILLS ENJOYMENT"

Why should enjoyment and understanding be incompatible? At the root of the analysis-kills-the-fun complaint is the idea that analysis is critical—in the sense of disapproving and negative. From this point of view, the basic activity of analysis (asking questions), along with its deliberate delaying of evaluation, seems skeptical, uncommitted, and uncaring. But raising questions and working out the possible meanings of significant details is not necessarily negative, nor does it require a complete absence of feeling.

In fact, analytical thinkers tend to be more dedicated than most people to understanding, and thus to being sensitive to rather than attacking a subject. Understanding is not the enemy of enjoyment, at least not for people who enjoy thinking. In any case, the global "I like it/I don't like it" move is less common to people who have learned to think analytically because they are more likely to make careful distinctions—deciding to like some features of a subject (for well-explained reasons) while disliking others.

CHARGE 2: "ANALYSIS FINDS MEANINGS THAT ARE NOT THERE"

What about the charge that analysis "reads into" a subject things that aren't there ("reading between the lines")? What does the charge mean, and why do people make it? The phrase *reading between the lines*, as we noted in our discussion of making the implicit explicit, implies that we are actually reading not the words on the page but the white space between the sentences. This implication suggests that analytical conclusions are merely fanciful and "made up," because white space offers evidence, presumably, of nothing.

The related term, *hidden meaning*, implies an act of conspiracy on the part of either an author, who chooses to deliberately obscure his or her meaning, or on the part of readers, who conspire to "find" things lurking below the surface that other readers don't know about and are unable to see. People who think it a good idea to look for "hidden meanings" assume that such meanings are there and are worth looking for. People who use the term derisively assume either that such meanings are not "there" (not real, but imagined) or that, if they are "there," they should not be hidden, thus sparing readers the trouble of looking for them. A further assumption is that people probably know what they mean most of the time but, for some perverse reason, are unwilling to come out and say so.

Proponents of these views of analysis are, in effect, committing themselves to the position that everything in life means what it says and says what it means. This position posits another related one: that meanings are always obvious and understood in the same way by everyone, and thus don't require interpretation (which is an example of "naturalizing our own assumptions" as discussed in Chapter 1). People who use the expressions *hidden meanings* and *reading between the lines* generally don't recognize that these phrases imply theories of interpretation, but they do.

It is probably safe to assume that most writers try to write what they mean and mean what they say. That is, they try to control the range of possible interpretations that their words could give rise to, but there is always more going on in a piece of writing (as in our everyday conversation) than can easily be pinned down and controlled. It is, in fact, an inherent property of language that it always means more than and thus other than it says. (See further discussion of this matter in the section "Reading With and Against the Grain" in Chapter 4.)

The hidden meaning theory is an exaggeration, an overextension of the idea of implication and a denial of the possibility that the implications of, say, a campaign slogan or a new fashion trend or a new tax law can be worked out rationally. The fact that ideas can be suggested rather than directly stated doesn't make such ideas "hidden."

Meanings and Social Context

You can easily test some of these assertions as you go through an ordinary day. What, for example, does the choice of wearing a baseball cap to a staff meeting or to a class "say"? Note, by the way, that a communicative gesture such as the wearing of a hat need not be premeditated to communicate something to other people. The hat is still "there" and available to be "read" by others as a sign of certain attitudes and a culturally defined sense of identity—with or without your intention. Things communicate meaning to others whether we wish them to or not, which is to say that the meanings of most things are socially determined.

Berets and baseball caps, for example, carry different associations because they come from different social contexts. Baseball caps convey a set of attitudes associated with the piece of American culture they come from. They suggest, for example, popular rather than high culture, casual rather than formal, young—perhaps defiantly so, especially if worn backward—rather than old, and so on. The social contexts that make gestures like our choice of hats carry particular meanings are always shifting, but some such context is always present.

We can, of course, protest that the "real" reason for turning our baseball cap backward is to allow more light in, making it easier to see than when the bill of the cap shields our faces. This practical rationale makes sense, but it does not explain away the social statement that the hat and a particular way of wearing it might make. As a certain practice becomes increasingly common, its character as a social signal becomes less pronounced. Like all complex social behaviors, our choices in clothing and the messages they send are constantly changing.

Because meaning is, to a significant extent, socially determined, we can't entirely control what our clothing, our manners, our language, or even our way of walking communicates to others. This is one of the reasons that analysis makes some people suspicious and uneasy. They don't want to acknowledge that they are sending messages in spite of themselves, messages they haven't deliberately and overtly chosen.

It helps to remember that interpretive leaps—conclusions arrived at through analysis—about what some gesture or word choice or clothing combination or scene in a film means, follow certain established rules of evidence. One such rule is that the conclusions of a good analysis do not rest on details taken out of context, but instead test and support claims about the details' significance by locating them in a pattern of similar detail. (See the previous section on the five analytical moves.) In other words, analytical thinkers are not really free to say whatever they think, as those who are made uneasy by analysis sometimes fear.

Reading What's Left Out

We should acknowledge, with respect to the reading-between-the-lines charge, that analysis sometimes does draw out the implications of things that are not there, because they have been deliberately omitted. Usually we recognize such omissions because we have been led to expect something that we are not given, making its absence conspicuous.

An analysis of the Nancy Drew mysteries, for example, might attach significance to the absence of a mother in the books, particularly in light of the fact that biological mothers, as opposed to wicked stepmothers, are pretty rare in many kinds of stories, such as fairy tales, that involve female protagonists (for example, "Hansel and Gretel," "Cinderella," and "Snow White"). Taking note of the absent mothers as a potentially significant omission could lead to a series of analytical questions, such as the following: How might this common denominator of certain kinds of children's stories be explained? What features of the stories' social, psychological, historical, economic, and other possible contexts might offer an explanation? As this example suggests, things are often left out for a reason, and a good analysis should therefore be alert to potentially meaningful omissions.

Try this 2.5: Reading What's Missing

Consider what you might make of a cigarette advertisement that includes a line of laughing young men and women in unisex attire holding one of their number across their outstretched arms, but does not include cigarettes or any sign of smoking. What might the omission of smoking in the picture mean, since its sponsor no doubt wishes to encourage the activity? What does this omission imply about the nature of the advertisement's message and its means of influencing viewers?

Try doing the same exercise with a political speech or a piece of public relations writing or coverage of the same situation in two different newspapers or magazines (in which case you would consider the implications of one periodical leaving out what the other chose to include). In what other kinds of communication might attention to what has been left out be especially revealing?

CHARGE 3: "SOME SUBJECTS WEREN'T MEANT TO BE ANALYZED"

The preceding examples, Nancy Drew mysteries and cigarette ads, raise the argument that it is foolish to analyze subjects that were meant only to entertain (like science-fiction movies) or to serve some practical need (like shopping malls or blue jeans). Should analytical thinkers steer clear of subjects that supposedly weren't meant to be analyzed, such as bowling and late-night television? This is a complex question because it runs into people's prejudices about so-called "highbrow" versus "lowbrow" activities. If asked to name highbrow subjects, most of us would come up with the same kind of list. Mozart's string quartets, for example, or foreign movies with subtitles are highbrow. The World Wrestling Entertainment (as seen on TV) is lowbrow. Highbrows are meant to stick to their own turf. To the extent that analytical thinking is labeled a highbrow activity, people are offended by its presuming to intrude on lowbrow terrain. It's okay to analyze Mozart or art films but not romance novels or popular entertainments.

The question of intention—what was and what wasn't "meant" to be analyzed—is, at least in part, an extension of the highbrow/lowbrow divide. The makers of tough-guy movies may not have intended to promote the value of rugged individualism and may even have produced completely different statements of their intentions. What the makers of a particular product or idea intend, however, is only a part of what their work means; intention does not finally control the implications that a work possesses.

A Sample Student Paper: A Close Reading of a Performance

The following student paper is an example of a close reading, which is the kind of attention to evidence this book is inviting you to make habitual. A close reading

VOICES FROM ACROSS THE CURRICULUM

Taking the Pressure Off

When writing about dance, the primary evidence is the dance itself and the theatrical accompaniments enhancing the work (sets, costumes, music, narrative, lights, etc.). Seeing and understanding how and what dance communicates is the main task of the dance writer. Because dance is often abstract and purposely open to multiple interpretations, students are usually terrified at the prospect of finding and interpreting evidence in support of a thesis. Typical first responses to analysis include

> "I enjoy watching dance, but I have never looked for meaning or message."
>
> "I don't know enough about dance to understand it."

My responses include, "Sit back, relax, and enjoy the dance—save analysis for later. Start your analysis by pretending you are discussing the performance with a friend who did not see it. As you tell him or her about the performance, you will naturally begin to gather evidence and analyze."

—*Karen Dearborn, Professor of Dance*

explicates; that is, it unfolds an interpretation by making explicit selected features of a subject that otherwise might not be readily recognized or understood. A close reading moves beyond the obvious, but it does not leap to some hidden meaning that is unconnected to the evidence. Rather, it stays close to and follows logically from the evidence: the meaning is implicit in the details, waiting to be brought out by the writer careful enough to look closely and questioningly.

Try this 2.6: Tracking the Moves in a Student Paper

The student paper exemplifies the five analytical moves around which this chapter is organized: suspending judgment, defining parts and how they are related, looking for patterns of repetition and for anomaly, making the implicit explicit, and asking questions. It also should prompt you to further consider the common charges against analysis, especially the charge that analysis finds meanings that are not there.

As you read the student paper, look for the five moves and how the writer uses evidence.

- What elements of the paper seem to be factual reporting—that is, description rather than interpretation of details in the dance?
- Locate those places in the paper where the student writer arrives at conclusions about what the details of the dance mean.
- Where has the writer made the move from implicit to explicit?
- This paper makes interesting use of anomaly. Find the anomaly.
- Look for places where the writer specifies one or more interpretive contexts. Consider, for example, the paper's opening sentence. We'll have more to say about interpretive contexts in the chapter's final two examples.

Hua dan: The Dance of Values in the Beijing Opera

[1] Lanfang says in his autobiography that "The beautiful dance movements created by past artists are all based on gestures in real life, synthesized and accentuated to become art ..." (36). In this quote Lanfang emphasizes a representation of life through "beautiful" movement. As he is a product of his culture, he is describing what his culture deems "beautiful." The female roles in the Beijing Opera, particularly the *Hua dan*, convey their own set of cultural values about femininity in Chinese culture.

[2] There is much posing and holding of shapes within the *Hua dan* role. There is a gentle, poised focus in these moments. This allows the viewers time to take in the elegance of the shape, costumes, makeup, music, and artistry of the performer. The fruit of these efforts becomes evident and framed by the pausing. The work the performers put in is valued in the pause.

[3] All the movements are very clear in their choices between making angles and using the full extension of the limbs, particularly the arms. The angular shapes give a sharp contrast to the extension of the arms

and legs. Circular formations of the arms are seamlessly round and often repeated to emphasize their distinctness. This exactness and clarity emphasizes the importance and power of the body. By paying such attention to particulars it gives greater emphasis to the powers held in making these shapes.

[4] There is much repetition and opening and closing in the movement. Repetition can represent the large amount of time females spend on such activities. It can also give a sense of the time it actually takes for such actions in real life, such as sewing. The women do spend much time sewing, and this time is represented. It also takes consistency and dedication to complete such tasks multiple times, so these become valued characteristics.

[5] Rhythm is also an element of the very controlled female walking consisting of small, even, steps. The feet barely leave the floor and don't extend into kicks or jumps, as do some of the male roles. Even in the *Hua dan* demonstration in the "Aspects of Peking Opera" video when a bounce was in the character's step and the eyes were alive, the flow of the walk remained consistent. The smallness of the steps could represent the female's place in society. They are petite and not flashy in their maneuvers. They complete their tasks without much fanfare. Keeping the feet low also limits the opening of the legs. Such protection and withholding represents a value in itself—the absence of overt sexual suggestion. Although the male characters may be more likely to overtly demonstrate their strength and power, it takes a great amount of control and focus for the women to execute their walks, so this convention is demonstrating the value of women keeping their struggles and work hidden.

[6] Although my viewing of Peking Opera is limited, it caught my eye to see the *Hua dan*'s shoulders finally move in a flirtation demonstration in the "Aspects" video. This isolation and interruption of flow seemed out of character to all other demonstrated acts. All other actions were focused on creating lines and full range of motion. Breaking typically occurs only at the elbows and wrists. These shoulder shrugs break not only the lines but the flowing rhythm. Making flirtation stand out suggests that in the context of the opera, such coquettish moments are important for the audience both in terms of character and life off the stage. It also reminds the viewers that there are even more areas of the body that have not been used but are present within the character and performer.

[7] What are the recurring themes in all these observations? They lie in control, value of movement, and repetition. The "beauty" lies not only in the quality of the movement but in what it represents. The dainty representation of females, their modesty and strong work ethic, and care in their activities are of great importance, but so too is the slight pleasure in restricted flirtation. When combined, these qualities of movement create a carefully crafted portrayal of a polished female. It serves to represent not only a clear character but a beautiful and desirable female figure.

Try this 2.7: Casting a New Thesis Using Anomaly

The student paper on dance is a promising draft. Let's consider what she might do to make it even better by taking better advantage of some seemingly anomalous details. At one point the writer notes features of the dance that she describes as seeming "out of character." In Chapter 1 in the section called "What It Means to Have an Idea," we said that ideas often try to account for some kind of dissonance. We have also said that anomaly is useful for prompting good thinking because it causes you to complicate your initial formulations and evolve them into more carefully qualified, better-developed ideas.

Look at the anomaly paragraph ([6]) and then at the paper's concluding paragraph. Then try casting a thesis statement that takes the anomaly more fully into account. See the section called "Moving from Idea to Thesis Statement" in Chapter 1.

Specifying an Interpretive Context

We spoke earlier in this chapter about things that seemingly are or are not "meant" to be analyzed. Writers sometimes resist analysis on the grounds that some things were not intended to mean anything outside a limited context, such as entertainment, and so should not be analyzed from any other point of view. Barbie dolls are toys intended for young girls. Should the fact that the makers of Barbie intended to entertain children rule out analysis of Barbie's characteristics (built-in earrings and high-heeled feet), and thus what the doll "says" about different ideals of femininity?

What the makers of a particular product or idea intend is only part of what that product or idea communicates. The urge to cordon off certain subjects from analysis on the grounds that they weren't meant to be analyzed unnecessarily excludes a wealth of information—and meaning—from your range of vision. It is, however, right to be careful about the interpretive contexts we bring to our experience. Looking to an author's statements of intention as a key to the meaning of his or her work is not necessarily wrong. It is, in fact, a useful and interesting thing to do. But it can be limiting and misleading. What you want to avoid is defining your choice of interpretive contexts too narrowly.

Notice how in the following analysis the student writer's interpretation relies on his choice of a particular interpretive context, post–World War II Japan. Had he selected another context, he might have arrived at some different conclusions about the same details. Notice also how the writer perceives a pattern in the details and queries his own observations (asking So what?) to arrive at an interpretation.

"Kamaitachi" in Post-war Japan

The series entitled "Kamaitachi" is a journal of [Japanese photographer Eikoh] Hosoe's desolate childhood and wartime evacuation in the Tokyo countryside. He returns years later to the areas where he grew up, a stranger to his native land, perhaps likening himself to the legendary Kamaitachi, an invisible sickle-toothed weasel, intertwined with the soil and its unrealized fertility.

"Kamaitachi #8" (1956), a platinum palladium print, stands alone to best capture Hosoe's alienation from and troubled expectation of the future of Japan. [Here the writer chooses a biographical approach as his interpretive context.]

The image is that of a tall fence of stark horizontal and vertical rough wood lashed together, looming above the barren rice fields. Straddling the fence, half-crouched and half-clinging, is a solitary male figure, gazing in profile to the horizon. Oblivious to the sky above of dark and churning thunderclouds, the figure instead focuses his attentions and concentrations elsewhere. [The writer selects and describes significant detail.]

It is exactly this *elsewhere* that makes the image successful, for in studying the man we are to turn our attention toward him and away from the print. He hangs curiously between heaven and earth, suspended on a makeshift man-made structure, in a purgatorial limbo awaiting the future. He waits with anticipation—perhaps dread?—for a time that has not yet come; he is directed away from the present, and it is this sensitivity to time that sets this print apart from the others in the series. One could argue that in effect this man, clothed in common garb, has become Japan itself, indicative of the post-war uncertainty of a country once-dominant and now destroyed. What will the future (dark storm clouds) hold for this newly humbled nation? [Here the writer notices a pattern of "in-between-ness" and locates it in a historical context to make his interpretive leap.]

Remember that regardless of the subject you select for your analysis, you should directly address not just What does this say? but also, as this writer has done, What are we invited to make of it, and in what context? Here is yet another shift that can help you prompt analytical thinking:

Not *What do I think about it?* **but** *What am I being invited to think and by what means?*

When you consider how your response is being shaped by whatever it is you are looking at, you are engaged in *rhetorical analysis*.

C. RHETORICAL ANALYSIS

We will end this chapter with discussion of a particular kind of analysis—rhetorical analysis. To analyze the rhetoric of something is to determine how that something persuades and positions its readers or viewers or listeners. Rhetorical analysis is an essential skill because it reveals how particular pieces of communication seek to enlist our support and shape our behavior. Only then can we decide whether or not we should be persuaded to respond as we have been invited to respond.

Everything has a rhetoric: classrooms, churches, speeches, supermarkets, department store windows, Starbucks, photographs, magazine covers, your bedroom, this book. Intention, by the way, is not the issue. It doesn't matter whether the effect of a place or a piece of writing on its viewers (or readers) is deliberate and planned or not. What matters is that you can notice how the details of the thing itself encourage or discourage certain kinds of responses in the "consumers" of whatever it is you are studying. What, for example, does the high ceiling of a Gothic cathedral invite in the way of response from people who enter it? What do the raised platform at the front of a classroom and the tidy rows of desks secured to the floor say to the students who enter there?

Everything has a rhetoric: classrooms, churches, speeches, supermarkets, department store windows, Starbucks, photographs, magazine covers, your bedroom, this book.

If you are reading this book in a first-year college writing course, you may be asked to write a rhetorical analysis, often of a visual image of some kind, early in the semester. What follows is an exercise in rhetorical analysis that will help you better understand the aims and methods of this kind of analysis. We think it is easiest to start with analysis of visual rhetoric—the rhetoric, for example, of a typical classroom.

Try this 2.8: Rhetorical Analysis of a Place

Go someplace: the foyer of a campus building, the center of a campus quadrangle, a classroom, a coffee shop, a waiting room, someone's office or workstation (other than your own) at work, a courthouse or town hall, or any other place that you find interesting or frequent regularly. Study the details of the place and make a list of what you see. Description, as we repeatedly argue in this book, is essential to analysis and actively encourages interpretive leaps. Want to know more about something you are studying? Write a description of it and see what happens in the process. Description is the best antidote to writer's block.

After you gather your data, ask yourself the questions below. These questions overlap somewhat, which is to say that they go after the same kind of thinking in slightly different ways. Concentrate on the question or questions that work best for you.

- In what ways and by what means does this space shape the way I feel and think and behave?
- What does this space say to its occupants about how they should think and feel and behave in the space?
- What assumptions did the makers of this space seem to have about the people who would occupy it?

RHETORICAL ANALYSIS OF A PLACE: A BRIEF EXAMPLE

To get you started on a rhetorical analysis of a place, here is the beginning of one on the layout of our college campus. It was written as a freewrite and could serve as the basis for further observation.

> The campus is laid out in several rows and quadrangles. It is interesting to observe where the different academic buildings are, relative to the academic

departments they house. It is also interesting to see how the campus positions student housing. In a way, the campus is set up as a series of quadrangles—areas of space with four sides. One of the dormitories, for example, forms a quadrangle. Quadrangles invite people to look in—rather than out. They are enclosed spaces, the center of which is a kind of blank. The center serves as a shared space, a safely walled-off area for the development of a separate community. The academic buildings also form a quadrangle of sorts, with an open green space in the center. On one side of the quadrangle are the buildings that house the natural and social sciences. Opposite these—on the other side of a street that runs through the center of campus—is the modern brick and glass structures that house the arts and the humanities....

RHETORICAL ANALYSIS OF AN ADVERTISEMENT: AN EXAMPLE

Our final example is a student's rhetorical analysis of a perfume advertisement that appeared in a magazine aimed at young women. The analysis, which offers the writer's thinking on secondary sources as well as on the advertisement itself, was written in a course called Introduction to Communication. The writer's aim is not only to tell her readers what the advertisement "says," but to locate it in a social context. The student uses her secondary sources to provide an interpretive context (a lens) through which to see the rhetoric of the ad—its means of persuasion.

The visual imagery of advertisements offers instructive opportunities for rhetorical analysis because advertising is a form of persuasion. Advertisers attend carefully to rhetoric by carefully targeting their audiences. This means advertisements are well suited to the questions that rhetorical analysis typically asks: How is the audience being invited to respond and by what means (in what context)? You'll notice that in the rhetorical analysis of the magazine ad, the writer occasionally extends her analysis to evaluative conclusions about the aims and possible effects (on American culture) of the advertisement.

Marketing the Girl Next Door: A Declaration of Independence?

[1] Found in *Seventeen* magazine, the advertisement for "tommy girl," the perfume manufactured by Tommy Hilfiger, sells the most basic American ideal of independence. Various visual images and text suggest that purchasing tommy girl buys freedom and liberation for the mind and body. This image appeals to young women striving to establish themselves as unbound individuals. Ironically, the advertisement uses traditional American icons as vehicles for marketing to the modern woman. Overall, the message is simple: American individualism can be found in a spray or nonspray bottle.

[2] Easily, the young woman dominates the advertisement. She has the look of the all-American "girl next door." Her appeal is a natural one, as she does not rely on makeup or a runway model's cheekbones for her beauty. Freckles frame her eyes that ambitiously gaze skyward; there are no limits restricting women in capitalist America. Her flowing brown hair freely rides a stirring breeze. Unconcerned with the order of a particular hairstyle, she smiles and enjoys the looseness of her spirit. The ad tells us how wearing this perfume allows women to achieve the look of self-assured and liberated indifference without appearing vain.

[3] The second most prevalent image in the advertisement is the American flag, which neatly matches the size of the young woman's head. The placement and size of the flag suggest that if anything is on her cloudless mind, it is fundamental American beliefs that allow for such self-determination. The half-concealed flag is seemingly continued in the young woman's hair. According to the ad, American ideals reside well within the girl as well as the perfume.

[4] It is also noticeable that there is a relative absence of all land surrounding the young woman. We can see glimpses of "fruited plains" flanking the girl's shoulders. This young woman is barely bound to earth, as free as the clouds that float beneath her head. It is this liberated image Americans proudly carry that is being sold in the product.

[5] The final image promoting patriotism can be found in the young woman's clothing. The young woman is draped in the blue jean jacket, a classic symbol of American ruggedness and originality. As far as we can see, the jacket is spread open, supporting the earlier claim of the young women's free and independent spirit. These are the very same ideals that embody American pride and patriotism. The ad clearly employs the association principle in linking the tommy girl fragrance with emotionally compelling yet essentially unrelated images of American nationalism and patriotism.

[6] A final obvious appeal to American nationalism is the tagline of the advertisement, the underlying message being "a declaration of independence." The young woman has already declared her independence, and now it is your turn. Doesn't every young woman want to be in that green field, hair blowing in the wind, wearing a confident look outlined against an American flag and clean, carefree, endless blue sky?

[7] Lastly, the advertisement utilizes several implicit arrows that point to the actual product of tommy girl perfume. The white writing against the dark blue jean jacket catches the eye first, encouraging the reader to continue in the traditional, left to right order. When the writing stops, we are naturally pointed toward the product. In addition, the young woman's hair, seen earlier as an extension of the American flag, is flurrying out and somewhat downward. We follow the hair to its end, where it seemingly kisses the product's cap. All visual indications of direction in the advertisement lead the viewer to an inevitable end: the irresistible scent of tommy girl perfume.

[8] But we might also look beyond the ad's overt messages, and examine its effects on the viewer and our society as a whole. Returning to the ad's portrayal of the young woman, we are shown a girl with a natural beauty, free of worries or cares about conforming to the pressures of society as a female. Jean Kilbourne (2003) argues that countless ads tell women to search for freedom and independence through being thin, as echoed in the ad's skinny and attractive young woman. Kilbourne actually refers to another tommy girl ad that uses the same tagline: "'A declaration of independence,' proclaims an ad

for perfume that features an emaciated model, but in fact the quest for a body as thin as the model's becomes a prison for many women and girls" (p. 263). She argues that ads encouraging a search for feminine independence often promote the worship of the thinness ideal, as well as the dilemma of being a successful and powerful woman while remaining "feminine" and unthreatening (pp. 262–264).

[9] Additionally, the ad for tommy girl perfume is also effective because it "takes on the trappings of a movement for social justice," according to Thomas Frank (1997, p. 187). Frank describes how advertisers constantly link products with the rebellious, revolutionary political and social movements of the past in order to conjure the vehement emotions associated with their resounding emotional content. The tommy girl ad emphasizes typical patriotic American images—like the American flag and denim clothing—as well as the phrase *a declaration of independence,* which explicitly creates a connection between the perfume and the American colonists' revolutionary pursuit of liberty in their beliefs and behavior during the American Revolution.

[10] Yet in reality, this marketing of liberation is paradoxical; although this freeing message promotes rebellion and nonconformity, it actually supports the market economy and feeds into capitalism and conformity. When advertisers employ political protest messages to be associated with products, they imply that buying the product is a form of political action.

[11] But lastly, the ad gives another paradoxical message with the portrayal of the beauty of the American, unspoiled, natural environment. Another typical American image is of the untouched landscapes, green pastures, and cloudless blue skies of the open frontier, which serves as the ad's backdrop. The ad's clear blue sky with the American flag flying freely in the wind encourages the viewer to link the beauty of the natural American landscape with the purchase of tommy girl. Sut Jhally, editor of the video *Advertising and the End of the World* (1998), would argue that the ad's purpose—the consumption of the product—is paradoxically putting the environment at risk. Our "freedom" to buy all of what we need (and especially, what we don't need) is essentially spoiling the natural surroundings that we romanticize. And so the viewers are simply left to decide: Does this tommy girl ad truly portray a declaration of independence, or of *dependence?*

References

Frank, T. (1997). Liberation marketing and the culture trust. In E. Barnouw et al. (Ed.), *Conglomerates and the media* (pp. 173–190). New York: The New Press.

Jhally, S. (Ed.). (1998). *Advertising and the end of the world* [Videotape]. Northampton, MA: Media Education Foundation.

Kilbourne, J. (2003). The more you subtract, the more you add: Cutting girls down to size. In G. Dines & J. Humez (Eds.), *Gender, race and class in media* (pp. 258–267). Thousand Oaks, CA: Sage.

Try this 2.9: Commenting on a Draft

Throughout this book we provide discussions of student texts in bracketed comments located at the ends of paragraphs. Usually these perform descriptive paraphrasing of what the piece of writing *does* (rather than what it says), along with pointing out how it exemplifies general procedures of analytical writing that we have been discussing. Do these two tasks for "Marketing the Girl Next Door: A Declaration of Independence?" Describe what the writer does paragraph by paragraph and locate her use of the various analytical moves presented in this chapter. (For an example, see "'Kamaitachi' in Postwar Japan" at the end of the previous section.)

ASSIGNMENT: Making the Implicit Explicit and Pushing Observations to Conclusions

1. Locate any magazine ad that you find interesting. Ask yourself, What is this a picture of? Use the preceding paper as a kind of model for rendering the implicit explicit. Don't settle for just one or even three answers. Keep answering the question in different ways, letting your answers grow in length as they identify and begin to interpret the significance of telling details. Attend to your choice of language, because your word choice as you summarize details will begin to suggest to you the ad's range of implication.

   If you find yourself getting stuck, rephrase the question as, "What is this ad really about, and why did the advertiser choose this particular image or set of images? Your repeated answering of the first question should eventually lead you to answer the second question.

2. Write an essay in which you make observations about some cultural phenomenon, some place and its social significance, or an event (in terms of its significance in some context of your choice) and then push these observations to tentative conclusions by repeatedly asking, So what?

   Be sure to query your initial answers to the So what? question with further So what? questions, trying to push further into your own thinking and into the meaning of whatever it is you have chosen to analyze. Trends of some sort are good to work with. Marketing trend? So what? Trends in movies about unmarried women or married men or . . . So what? And so forth.

   Since the chapter offers sample analyses of paintings and advertisements, you might choose one of these. Cartoons are interesting subjects too. Here you would really have to think a lot about your choice of interpretive context. Gender? Politics? Humor? Family life? American stereotypes? Remember that the guiding questions of rhetorical analysis are What are we invited to make of this, by what means, and in what context?

GUIDELINES FOR HOW ANALYSIS WORKS

1. As you analyze a subject, ask not just "What are its defining parts?" but also "How do these parts help me to understand the meaning of the subject as a whole?"
2. When you describe and summarize, attend carefully to the language you choose, since the words themselves will usually contain the germs of ideas.
3. Always note repetitions in your subject. There is no surer means of discovering what it is about.
4. Simply listing the various strands that you find in your evidence will go a long way toward helping you discover what is most interesting and important for you to address. Then make sure to name each strand. Naming and renaming strands is itself an analytical move that will trigger further ideas.
5. Finding binaries will help you find the questions around which a film or an essay or a speech or a poem—almost anything—is organized. Through noticing binaries and then casting and recasting the words you use to name them, you enable yourself to discover what is at stake in whatever you are looking at or reading. To find these oppositions, ask yourself, *What is opposed to what?*
6. Always keep an eye out for anomalous details—those that seem not to fit the pattern. Anomalies help us revise our stereotypical assumptions.
7. Don't assume that all meanings are overt and ready-made, waiting to be found. Most of the time, they are implicit—not the same as *hidden*—and an act of mind is required to take what is folded in and convert the suggested meanings of particular details into overt statements.
8. Remember that regardless of the subject you select for your analysis, you should directly address not just What does this say? but also, What are we invited to make of it, and in what *context*?
9. As a general rule, analysis favors live questions—where something remains to be resolved—over inert answers, places where things are already pretty much nailed down and don't leave much space for further thinking.
10. The process of posing and answering questions—the analytical process—is one of trial and error. Learning to write well is largely a matter of learning how to frame questions. Whatever questions you ask, the answers you propose will often produce more questions.

CHAPTER 3

Putting Analysis to Work: Three Extended Examples

Quick Take

This chapter applies and further explores the approaches to analytical writing offered in Chapters 1 and 2. The first two extended examples—an analysis of a painting and an analysis of a magazine cover—illustrate the move from description to interpretation. The third extended example—analysis of an argument—illustrates the processes of reformulating binaries and uncovering unstated assumptions (reasoning back to premises).

The first of the extended examples, the analysis of a painting, differentiates summary from analysis, applies the five analytical moves detailed in Chapter 2, and takes up the issue of what we call the *fortune cookie* versus the *anything goes* theories of interpretation.

The second example, an analysis of a magazine cover, applies one of the five analytical moves—looking for patterns of repetition and contrast (the Method)—and then addresses the issue of multiple meanings by demonstrating the *process of choosing and applying multiple interpretive contexts.*

The third extended example—an editorial that analyzes other editorials on a social issue (a set of guidelines governing sexual conduct at Antioch College)—picks up Chapter 2's discussion of *binary oppositions* and adds to it the process of *locating unstated assumptions in an argument.* This section of the chapter is our best advice on analyzing and constructing arguments.

A. EXTENDED EXAMPLE 1: MOVING FROM DESCRIPTION TO INTERPRETATION

What is the difference between a description or a summary and analysis? And, at what point does analysis become interpretation? What we have suggested thus far is that analysis implies a search for meaning, and that analysis and interpretation are inseparable. The process of noticing, of recording selected details and patterns of detail (analysis) is already the beginning of interpretation. But, once the move from observation to conclusions begins, writers need to make explicit and defend the appropriateness of the interpretive context in which this leap takes place.

DIFFERENTIATING ANALYSIS FROM SUMMARY

Summary differs from analysis, because the aim of summary is to recount—in effect, to reproduce someone else's ideas. But summary and analysis are also clearly related and usually operate together. Summary is important to analysis, since you can't analyze a subject without laying out its significant parts for your reader. Similarly, analysis is important to summary, because summarizing is more than just copying someone else's words. We offer both our description/summary and our analysis of a painting—*Whistler's Mother*—to demonstrate the difference between the two ways of approaching subjects. You will see, however, that our analysis would not be possible without the description that allowed us to see which patterns of detail in the painting to attend to.

FIGURE 3.1 *Arrangement in Grey and Black: The Artist's Mother* by James Abbott McNeill Whistler, 1871.

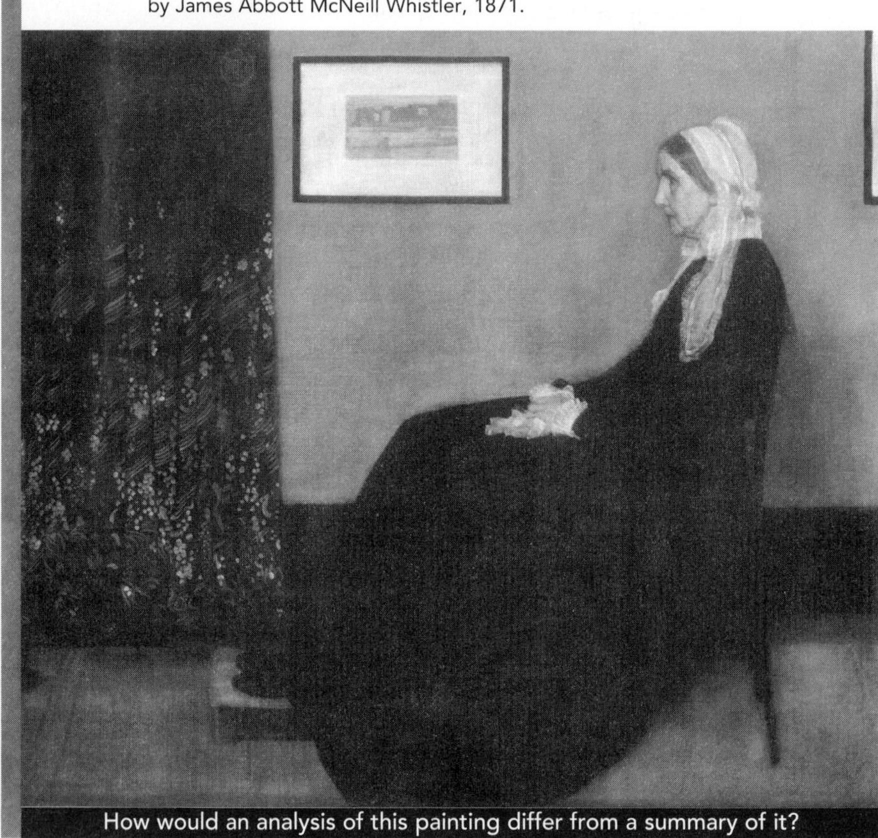

How would an analysis of this painting differ from a summary of it?

Try this 3.1: Analyzing *Whistler's Mother*

You will be better able to make use of our analysis of the picture if you try to do your own analysis of it first. Start with the steps of the observational strategy "looking for patterns of repetition and contrast" (the Method). What details repeat in the picture? What patterns of similar detail (strands) can you find? What details and patterns of detail seem to fall into organizing contrasts? Compile your three lists in writing; then rank the top two in each category, and write a paragraph on why you would choose one of these as most important.

A primary aim of this book's observation strategies, as you will recall, is to shift your attention from premature generalizing about a subject to recording detail that actually appears in it. Description is the best antidote to what we call in Chapter 1 the dogfish problem—trying to start with an idea about your subject without first really looking at it. This book's basic formula can be stated as follows:

- **What do you notice?**
- **What repeats?**
- **What is opposed to what?**
- **So what?**

Try applying this formula to the painting.

Summary, like analysis, is a tool of understanding and not just a mechanical task. But a summary stops short of analysis because summary typically makes much smaller interpretive leaps. A summary of the painting popularly known as *Whistler's Mother*, for example, would tell readers what the painting includes, which details are the most prominent, and even what the overall effect of the painting seems to be. A summary might say that the painting possesses a certain serenity, and that it is somewhat spare, almost austere. This kind of language still falls into the category of focused description, which is what a summary is.

An analysis would include more of the writer's interpretive thinking. It might tell us, for instance, that the painter's choice to portray his subject in profile contributes to our sense of her separateness from us and of her nonconfrontational passivity. We look at her, but she does not look back at us. Her black dress and the fitted lace cap that obscures her hair are not only emblems of her *self-effacement*, disguising her identity like her expressionless face, but also the tools of her *self-containment* and thus of her power to remain aloof from prying eyes. What is the attraction of this painting (this being one of the questions that an analysis might ask)? What might draw a viewer to the sight of this austere, drably attired woman, sitting alone in the center of a mostly blank space? Perhaps it is the very starkness of the painting, and the mystery of self-sufficiency at its center, that attracts us. (See Figure 3.1.)

Observations of this sort go beyond describing what the painting contains and enter into the writer's ideas about what its details imply, what the painting invites us to make of it and by what means.

Notice in our analysis of the painting how intertwined the description (summary) is with the analysis. Laying out the data is key to any kind of analysis, not simply because it keeps the analysis accurate but because, crucially, it is in the act of carefully describing a subject that analytical writers often have their best ideas.

You may not agree with the terms by which we have summarized the picture, and thus you may not agree with such conclusions as "the mystery of self-sufficiency." Nor is it necessary that you agree, because *there is no single, right answer to what the painting is about*. The absence of a single right answer does not, however, mean that anything goes.

As we discuss in more detail below (under the heading "The Limits on Interpretation"), your readers' willingness to accept an analytical conclusion is powerfully connected to their ability to see its *plausibility*—that is, how it follows from both the supporting details that you have selected and the language you have used in characterizing those details. The writer who can offer a plausible (not necessarily or obviously true, but believable) description of a subject's key features is likely to arrive at conclusions about possible meanings that others would share. Often the best that you can hope for with analytical conclusions is not that others will say, "Yes, that is obviously right," but "Yes, I can see where it might be possible and reasonable to think as you do."

FIGURE 3.2 Summary and analysis of *Whistler's Mother* diagram

Data		Method of Analysis		Interpretive Leaps
subject in profile, not looking at us	→	make implicit explicit (speculate about what the detail might suggest)	→	figure strikes us as separate, nonconfrontational, passive.
folded hands, fitted lace cap, contained hair, expressionless face	→	locate pattern of same or similar detail; make what is implicit in pattern of details explicit	→	figure strikes us as self-contained, powerful in her separateness and self-enclosure self-sufficient?
pattered curtain and picture versus still figure and blank wall; slightly frilled lace cuffs and ties on cap versus plain black dress	→	locate organizing contrast; make what is implicit in the contrast explicit	→	austerity and containment of the figure made more pronounced by slight contrast with busier, more lively, and more ornate elements and with little picture showing world outside.
slightly slouched body position and presence of support for feet	→	anomalies; make what is implicit in the anomalies explicit	→	These details destabilize the serenity of the figure, adding some tension to the picture in the form of slightly uneasy posture and figure's need for support: she looks too long, drooped in on her own spine.

Summary and Analysis of *Whistler's Mother*

Here are two general rules to be drawn from this discussion of analysis and summary:

1. **Describe with care.** The words you choose to summarize your data will contain the germs of your ideas about what the subject means.
2. **In moving from summary to analysis**, look consciously at the language you have chosen, asking, "Why did I choose this word? What ideas are implicit in the language I have used?"

DIFFERENTIATING ANALYSIS FROM EXPRESSIVE WRITING

In expressive writing, your primary subject is yourself, with other subjects serving as a means of evoking greater self-understanding. In analytical writing, your reasoning may derive from personal experience, but it is your reasoning and not you or your experiences that matter. Analysis asks not just the expressive question, "What do I think?" but "How good is my thinking? How well does it fit the subject I am trying to explain?"

We don't mean to suggest that expressive writing cannot be analytical or that analytical writing cannot be expressive. Expressive (writer-centered) writing is analytical in its attempts to define and explain a writer's feelings, reactions, and experiences. And analysis is a form of self-expression, since it inevitably reflects the ways a writer's experiences have taught him or her to think about the world.

Although observations like those offered in the preceding interpretive leaps column go beyond simple description, they don't move from the picture into autobiography. They stay with the task of explaining the painting, rather than moving to private associations that the painting might prompt, such as effusions about old age, or rocking chairs, or the character and situation of the writer's own grandmother. Such associations could well be valuable unto themselves as a means of prompting a searching piece of expressive writing. They might also help a writer interpret some feature of the painting that he or she was working to understand. But the writer would not be free to use pieces of his or her personal history as conclusions about what the painting communicates unless these conclusions could also be reasonably inferred from the painting itself.

Let's say, for example, that a writer believed that the woman is mourning the death of a son or is patiently waiting to die. In support of these theories, the writer might cite the black dress, the woman's somber expression, and the relative darkness of the painting. This selection of details might be sufficient to support some kind of interpretation concerning sadness or loss, but would clearly not support a leap to an implied narrative about a dead son. To make such a leap would be to substitute a personal narrative for analysis, to arrive at implications that are not sufficiently grounded in the evidence.

Because darkness and dark clothing need not operate as symbols of death, and because the woman's expression is not unquestionably grief-stricken (she looks expressionless to us), a writer might well need more evidence to jump to a narrative about the feelings and situation of the mother (a kind of jump that personal/expressive writing can be quick to make because it typically seeks shared feeling and experience). If, for example, part of a coffin were showing from behind the curtain, or if there were an hourglass somewhere in the painting, a reader might more plausibly conclude that mourning and mortality are governing contexts.

A few rules are worth highlighting here:

1. The range of associations for explaining a given detail or word must be governed by context.
2. It's fine to use your personal reactions as a way to explore what a subject means, but take care not to make an interpretive leap stretch further than the actual details will support.
3. Because the tendency to transfer meanings from your own life onto a subject can lead you to ignore the details of the subject itself, you need always to be asking yourself, "What other explanations might plausibly account for this same pattern of detail?"

THE LIMITS ON INTERPRETATION

Where do meanings come from? The first thing to understand about meanings is that they are *made*, not ready-made in the subject matter. They are the product of a transaction between a mind and the world, between a reader and a text or texts. That is, the making of meaning is a process to which the observer and the thing observed both contribute. It is not a product of either alone.

If meanings aren't ready-made, there to be found in the subject matter, what's to prevent people from making things mean whatever they want them to—say, for example, that *Whistler's Mother* is a painting about death, with the black-clad mother mourning the death of a loved one, perhaps a person who lived in the house represented in the painting on the wall? There are in fact limits on the meaning-making process.

- Meanings must be reasoned from sufficient evidence if they are to be judged plausible. Meanings can always be refuted by people who find fault with your reasoning or can cite conflicting evidence.
- Meanings, to have value outside one's own private realm of experience, have to make sense to other people. The assertion that Whistler's mother is an alien astronaut, for example, her long black dress concealing a third leg, is unlikely to be deemed acceptable by enough people to give it currency. This is to say that the relative value of interpretive meanings is socially (culturally) determined. Although people are free to say that things mean whatever they want them to mean, saying doesn't make it so.

MULTIPLE MEANINGS AND INTERPRETIVE CONTEXTS

In the last section we demonstrated that there are certain limits on interpretation, chiefly that interpretation has to follow the rules of evidence. It is useful and reassuring to know that a person can't just make up meanings and say they are true simply because he or she says so. But it is also necessary to recognize that meanings are multiple. Very few things in life are so simple as to communicate only one thing.

Evidence usually will support more than one plausible interpretation. Consider, for example, a reading of *Whistler's Mother* that a person might produce if he or she began with noticing the actual title, *Arrangement in Grey and Black: The Artist's Mother.* From this starting point, a person might focus observation on the disposition of color exclusively and arrive at an interpretation that *Arrangement* is a painting about painting (which might then explain why there is also a painting on the wall). The figure of the mother then would have meaning only insofar as it contained the two colors mentioned in the painting's title, black and gray, and the painting's representational content (the aspects of life that it shows us) would be ignored. This is a promising and plausible idea for an interpretation. It makes use of different details from previous interpretations we've suggested, but it would also address some of the details already targeted (the dress, the curtain) from an entirely different context, focusing on the use and arrangement of color.

To generalize: two equally plausible interpretations can be made of the same thing. It is not the case that our first reading, focusing on the profile view of the mother and suggesting the painting's concern with mysterious separateness, is right, whereas the aesthetic view, building from the clue in the title, is wrong. They operate within different contexts. An interpretive context is a lens. Depending on the context you choose—preferably a context suggested by the evidence itself—you will see different things.

An interpretive context is a lens. Depending on the context you choose—preferably a context suggested by the evidence itself—you will see different things.

Regardless of how the context is arrived at, an important part of getting an interpretation accepted as plausible is to *argue for the appropriateness of the interpretive context you use*, not just the interpretation it takes you to.

AUTHOR'S INTENTION AS AN INTERPRETIVE CONTEXT

Let's turn now to an interpretive context that frequently creates problems in analysis: authorial intention. People relying on authorial intention as their interpretive context typically assert that the author—not the work itself—is the ultimate and correct source of interpretations. The work means what its author says it means, and even without his or her explicit interpretation, we are expected to guess at it.

Let's say that an enterprising person discovered that after Whistler did the painting, he wrote a letter to a friend in which he commented upon his intention, saying that because his mother had been needling him about painters never amounting to anything, he had deliberately painted her unflatteringly in somber puritanical tones as an act of revenge.

Armed with such a statement of the artist's intention, an interpretation of the painting as an act of revenge might be considered plausible, but the artist's stated intention would not necessarily require us to give this interpretation privileged status over the others we have suggested. Whatever an author thinks he or she is doing is often a significant part of the meaning of what he or she creates, but it

FIGURE 3.3 *The Dancers* by Sarah Kersh. Pen-and-ink drawing, 6" x 13.75".

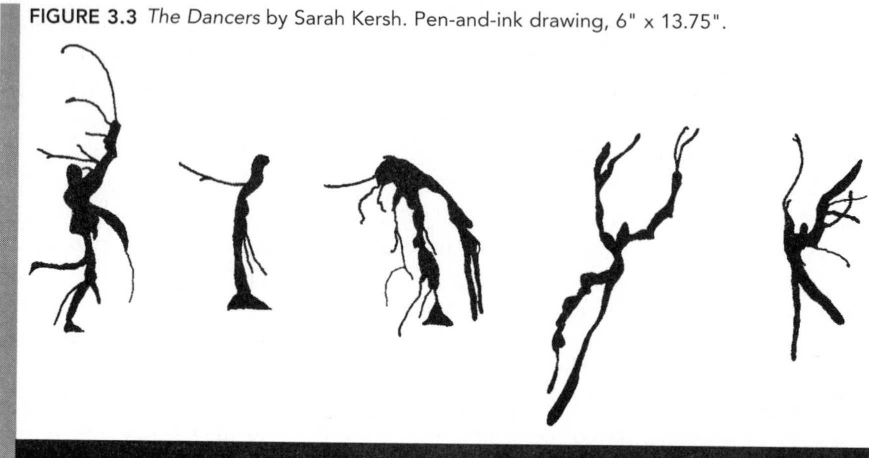

does not outrank or exclude other interpretations. It is simply another context for understanding.

Why is this so? In our earlier discussion of personalizing ("Naturalizing Your Own Assumptions" in Chapter 1), we suggested that people are not entirely free agents, immune to the effects of the culture they inhabit. It follows that when people produce writing and works of art, they are inevitably affected by the culture, sometimes in ways they are aware of and sometimes in ways they don't stop to think about.

It is interesting and useful to try to determine from something you are analyzing what its makers might have intended. But, by and large, you are best off concentrating on what the thing itself communicates as opposed to what someone might have wanted it to communicate. As a rule, intention does not finally control the implications that an event, a text, or anything else possesses. (For a fuller discussion of this issue see "Reading with and against the Grain" in Chapter 4, our chapter on reading.)

Look at the drawing titled *The Dancers* above. What follows is the artist's statement about how the drawing came about and what it came to mean to her.

> This piece was created completely unintentionally. I poured some ink onto paper and blew on it through a straw. The ink took the form of what looked like little people in movement. I recopied the figures I liked, touched up the rough edges, and ended with this gathering of fairy-like creatures. I love how in art something abstract can so suddenly become recognizable.

In this case, interestingly, the artist initially had no intentions beyond experimenting with materials. As the work evolved, she began to arrive at her own interpretation of what the drawing might suggest. Most viewers would probably find the artist's interpretation plausible, but this is not to say that the artist must have the last word and that it is somehow an infraction for others to produce alternative interpretations.

But suppose the artist had stopped with her first two sentences. Even this explicit statement of her lack of intention would not prohibit people from interpreting the drawing in some of the ways that the she later goes on to suggest. The artist's initial absence of a plan doesn't require viewers to interpret *The Dancers* as only ink on paper.

Where do meanings come from? In the maker? In the thing itself? Although it is interesting and useful to infer from the material itself what a creator might have been trying to accomplish, the maker's personal intentions don't control meaning.

Where do meanings come from? In the maker? In the thing itself?

THE FORTUNE COOKIE SCHOOL OF INTERPRETATION

The theory of interpretation that we call the Fortune Cookie School believes that things have a single, hidden, "right" meaning, and that if a person can only "crack" the thing, it will yield an extractable and self-contained "message." There are several problems with this conception of the interpretive process.

First, the assumption that things have single hidden meanings interferes with open-minded and dispassionate observation. The thinker looks solely for clues pointing to *the* hidden message and, having found these clues, discards the rest, like the cookie in a Chinese restaurant once the fortune has been extracted. The fortune cookie approach forecloses on the possibility of multiple plausible meanings, each within its own context. When you assume that there is only one right answer, you are also assuming that there is only one proper context for understanding and, by extension, that anybody who happens to select a different starting point or context and who thus arrives at a different answer is necessarily wrong.

Most of the time, practitioners of the fortune cookie approach aren't even aware that they are assuming the correctness of a single context, because they don't realize a fundamental truth about interpretations: they are always limited by contexts. In other words, we are suggesting that claims to universal truths are always problematic. Things don't just mean in some simple and clear way for all people in all situations; they always mean within a network of beliefs, from a particular point of view. The person who claims to have access to some universal truth, beyond context and point of view, is either naïve (unaware) or, worse, a bully—insisting that his or her view of the world is obviously correct and must be accepted by everyone.

Things don't just mean in some simple and clear way for all people in all situations; they always mean within a network of beliefs, from a particular point of view.

THE "ANYTHING GOES" SCHOOL OF INTERPRETATION

At the opposite extreme from the single-right-answer Fortune Cookie School lies the completely relativist Anything Goes School. The problem with the anything goes approach is that it tends to assume that *all* interpretations are equally viable, that meanings are simply a matter of individual choice, irrespective of evidence or plausibility. Put another way, it overextends the creative aspect of interpretation to absurdity, arriving at the position that you can see in a subject whatever you want to see.

As we suggest throughout this book, it is simply not the case that meaning is entirely up to the individual. Some readings are clearly better than others: the aesthetic or separateness readings of *Whistler's Mother* are better than the mourning or, especially, alien astronaut interpretations. The better interpretations have more evidence and rational explanation of how the evidence supports the interpretive claims—qualities that make these meanings more public and negotiable.

In the field of logic there is a principle known as parsimony. This principle holds that "no more forces or causes should be assumed than are necessary to account for the facts" *(The Oxford English Dictionary)*. In other words, the explanation that both explains the largest amount of evidence (accounts for facts) and is the simplest (no more than necessary) is the best. There are limits to this rule as well: sometimes focusing on what appears to be an insignificant detail as a starting point can provide a revelatory perspective on a subject. But as rules go, parsimony is a useful one to keep in mind as you start sifting through your various interpretive leaps about a subject.

SEEMS TO BE ABOUT *X* BUT COULD ALSO BE (IS "REALLY") ABOUT *Y*

This book's opening chapters have focused your attention on three prerequisites to becoming a more perceptive analytical thinker:

- Training yourself to observe more fully and more systematically—dwelling longer with the data before leaping to generalizations, using Notice and focus (ranking), the Method, looking for anomalies, and reformulating binaries.
- Pushing yourself to make interpretive leaps by describing carefully and then querying your own observations by repeatedly asking, So what?
- Getting beyond common misconceptions about where meanings come from—that meanings are hidden, that they are "read into" something but are really "not there" (reading between the lines), that there are single right answers or that anything goes, that meanings ought to be controlled by a maker's intentions, that some things should not be analyzed because they weren't meant to be, and so forth.

A useful verbal prompt for acting on these principles is Seems to be about *x* but could also be (or is "really") about *y*. Here's why the formula works. Frequently, the nominal (in name only) subject matter—what a book or speech *appears* to be about, what it says it is about—is not what the book or speech *is actually most interested in*. The nominal subject, in other words, is a means to some other end; it creates an opportunity for some less overtly designated matter to be put forward.

Consider the following example:

A recent highly successful television ad campaign for Nike Freestyle shoes contains sixty seconds of famous basketball players dribbling and passing and otherwise handling the ball in dexterous ways to the accompaniment of court noises and hip-hop music. The ad seems to be about *x* (basketball or shoes) but could also be about *y*. Once you've made this assertion, a rapid-fire (brainstormed) list might follow in which you keep filling in the blanks (*x* and *y*) with different possibilities. Alternatively, you might find that filling in the blanks (*x* and *y*) leads to a more sustained exploration of a single point. This is your eventual goal, but doing a little brainstorming first would keep you from shutting down the interpretive process too soon.

Here is one version of a rapid-fire list, any item of which might be expanded:

Seems to be about basketball but is "really" about dance.

Seems to be about selling shoes but is "really" about artistry.

Seems to be about artistry but is "really" about selling shoes.

Seems to be about basketball but is "really" about race.

Seems to be about basketball but is "really" about the greater acceptance of black culture in American media and society.

Seems to be about the greater acceptance of black culture in American media but is "really" about targeting black basketball players as performing seals or freaks.

Seems to be about individual expertise but is "really" about working as a group.

Here is one version of a more sustained exploration of a single seems-to-be-about-*x* statement.

The Nike Freestyle commercial seems to be about basketball but is really about the greater acceptance of black culture in American media. Of course it is a shoe commercial and so aims to sell a product, but the same could be said about any commercial.

What makes the Nike commercial distinctive is its seeming embrace of African-American culture. The hip-hop sound track, for example, which coincides with the rhythmic dribbling of the basketball, places music and sport on a par, and the dexterity with which the players (actual NBA stars) move with the ball—moonwalking, doing 360s on it, balancing it on their fingers, heads, and backs—is nothing short of dance.

The intrinsic cool of the commercial suggests that Nike is targeting an audience of basketball lovers, not just African-Americans. If I am right, then it is selling blackness to white as well as black audiences. Of course, the idea that blacks are cooler than whites goes back at least as far as the early days of jazz and might be seen as its own strange form of prejudice. . . . In that case, maybe there is something a little disturbing in the commercial, in the way that it relegates the athletes to the status of trained seals. I'll have to think more about this.

Note: Don't be misled by our use of the word *really* in this formula, ("Seems to be about *x*, is really about *y*") into thinking that there should be some single, hidden, right answer. Rather, the aim of the formula is to prompt you to think recursively, to come up, initially, with a range of landing sites for your interpretive leap, rather than just one. The prompt serves to get you beyond the obvious—for example, that the ad appears to be about basketball but is really about selling shoes. Both basketball and shoe sales are the ad's nominal subjects, what it is overtly about. But nominal subjects allow for the expression of other, less immediately obvious ideas and attitudes.

Try this 3.2: Apply the Formula "Seems to Be About x, But Could Also Be About *y*"

As we have been saying, this formula is useful for quickly getting past your first responses. An alternative version of this formula is "Initially I thought x about the reading, but now I think *y*." Take any reading assignment you have been given for class, and write either formula at the top of a page, fill in the blanks, and then explain the statement in a few paragraphs. You might also try these formulas when you find yourself getting stuck while drafting a paper.

B. EXTENDED EXAMPLE 2: SELECTING AN INTERPRETIVE CONTEXT

This extended example offers in more detail than the previous chapter a writer's decision-making process in choosing an interpretive context and working through the evidence to the conclusions it suggests. A major point of this section is that interpretive contexts are suggested by the material you are studying; they aren't simply imposed. Explaining why you think a subject should be seen through a particular interpretive "lens" is an important part of making interpretations reasonable and plausible. Our discussion will illustrate how, once an interpretive context is selected, a writer goes about analyzing evidence to test as well as support the usefulness of that context.

The example upon which we are focusing is a description of a visual image, a cover from *The New Yorker* magazine. Because we were not able to get permission to reprint the image, you will need to rely on the description, assimilating the details as we list them. Given our emphasis on interpretive context, however, the absence of the actual visual details is not critical. And in any event, producing a close verbal description of anything you are analyzing is one of the best ways to begin.

Description of a *The New Yorker* cover, dated October 9, 2000

The picture contains four women, visible from the waist up, standing in a row in semi-profile, staring out at some audience other than us, since their eyes look off to the side. All four gaze in the same direction. Each woman is dressed in a bathing suit and wears a banner draped over one shoulder in the manner of those worn in the swimsuit competition at beauty pageants. Three of the women are virtually identical. The banners worn by these three women show the letters *gia, rnia,* and *rida,* the remainder of the letters being cut off by the other women's shoulders, so that we have to fill in the missing letters to see which state each woman represents.

The fourth woman, who stands third from the left in line, tucked in among the others who look very much alike, wears a banner reading *york.* This woman's appearance is different in just about every respect from the other three. Whereas they are blonde with long flowing hair, she is dark with her hair up in a tight bun. Whereas their mouths are wide open, revealing a wall of very white teeth, her mouth is closed, lips drawn together. Whereas their eyes are wide open and staring, hers, like her mouth, are nearly closed, under deeply arched eyebrows. The dark woman's lips and eyes and hair are dark. She wears dark eye makeup and has a pronounced dark beauty mark on her cheek. Whereas the other three women's cheeks are high and round, hers are sharply angular. The three blonde women wear one-piece bathing suits in a nondescript gray color. The dark-haired woman, whose skin stands out in stark contrast to her hair, wears a two-piece bathing suit, exposing her midriff. Like her face, the dark-haired woman's breast, sticking out in half profile in her bathing suit, is pointed and angular. The other three women's breasts are round and quietly contained in their high-necked gray bathing suits.

LOOKING FOR PATTERNS OF REPETITION AND CONTRAST: AN EXAMPLE

As we discussed in Chapter 2, looking for repetition is your best means of getting at the essential character of a subject. It will prevent you from generalizing, instead involving you in hands-on engagement with the details of your evidence. Our formula for looking for patterns, the Method, has five steps, which you should try to do one at a time so as not to rush to conclusions. You will find, however, that step 1, looking for things that repeat exactly, tends to suggest items for step 2, repetition of the same or similar kinds of words or details (strands), and that step 2 leads naturally to step 3, looking for binary oppositions and organizing contrasts. And so, in practice, noticing and listing the elements of strands tend to coincide with the discovery of binary oppositions.

Here are our partial lists of exact repetitions and strands and binary oppositions in *The New Yorker* cover:

Some Details that Repeat Exactly

Large, wide open, round eyes (3 pairs)

Long, blonde, face-framing hair (3)

Small, straight eyebrows (3 pairs)

Wide-open (smiling?) mouths with expanses of white teeth (3)

(but individual teeth not indicated)

banners (4) but each with different lettering

round breasts (3)

states that end in *a* (3)

Some Strands (groups of the same or similar kinds of details)

Lots of loose and flowing blonde hair/large, fully open, round eyes/large, open, rather round (curved) mouths:

Connecting logic = open, round

Skin uniformly shaded on three of the figures/minimal color and shading contrasts/mouths full of teeth but just a mass of white without individual teeth showing:

Connecting logic = homogenous, undifferentiated, indistinct

Binary Oppositions

Blonde hair/black hair

Open mouths/closed mouth

Straight eyebrows/slanted (arched) eyebrows

Round breasts/pointed breast

Covered midriff/uncovered midriff

Notice that we have tried hard to stick with "the facts" here—concrete details in the picture. If we were to try, for example, to name the expression on the three blonde women's faces and the one on the black-haired woman (expressionless versus knowing? vapid versus shrewd? trusting versus suspicious? and so on), we would move from data gathering—direct observation of detail—into interpretation. The longer you delay interpretation in favor of noticing patterns of like and unlike detail, the more thoughtful and better grounded your eventual interpretation will be.

PUSHING OBSERVATIONS TO CONCLUSIONS: SELECTING AN INTERPRETIVE CONTEXT

As we argued in the first extended example of this chapter, the move from observations to conclusions depends on context. You would, for example, come up with different ideas about the significance of particular patterns of detail in *The New Yorker* cover if you were analyzing them in the context of the history of *The New Yorker* cover art than you might if your interpretive context was other art done by the cover's artist. Both of these possibilities suggest themselves, the first by the fact that the title of the magazine, *The New Yorker*, stands above the women's heads, and the second by the fact that the artist's name, Falconer, runs across two of the women.

What other interpretive contexts might one plausibly and fairly choose, based on what the cover itself offers us? Consider the cover's date, for example—October 9, 2000. Some quick research into what was going on in the country in the early fall of 2000 might provide some clues about how to read the cover in a *historical context*. November 2000 was the month of a presidential election. At the time the cover was published, the long round of presidential primaries, with presidential hopefuls courting various key states for their votes, had ended, but the last month of campaigning by the presidential nominees—Al Gore and George W. Bush—was in full swing.

You might wish to consider whether and how the cover speaks to the country's political climate during the Gore/Bush competition for the presidency. The banners and the bathing suits and the fact that the women stand in a line staring out at some implied audience of viewers, perhaps judges, reminds us that the picture's narrative context is a beauty pageant, a competition in which women representing each of the states compete to be chosen the most beautiful of them all. Choosing to consider the cover in the context of the presidential campaign would be reasonable; you would not have to think you were imposing a context on the picture in an arbitrary and ungrounded way.

Clearly there is other information on the cover that might allow you to interpret the picture in some kind of political and or more broadly cultural context. A significant binary opposition is New York versus Georgia, California, and Florida. The three states having names ending in the same letter are represented by look-alike, virtually identical blondes. The anomalous state, New York, is represented by a woman, who, despite standing in line with the others, is about as different from them as a figure could be. *So what* that the woman representing New York looks so unlike the women from the other states? And why those states?

If you continued to pursue this interpretive context, you might want more information. Which presidential candidate won the primary in each of the states pictured? How were each of these states expected to vote in the election in November? When is the Miss America pageant held? Which state won the Miss America title in the time period before the cover was published? Since timing would matter in the case of a topical interpretive context, it would also be interesting to know when the cover art was actually produced and when the magazine accepted it. If possible, you could also try to discover whether other of the cover artist's work was in a similar vein.

MAKING AN INTERPRETATION PLAUSIBLE

As we have been arguing, the picture will "mean" differently, depending on whether we understand it in terms of American presidential politics in the year 2000, or in terms of American identity politics at the same point, specifically attitudes of and about New Yorkers, and *The New Yorker* magazine's place among these attitudes—and influence on them. As we have already observed, analytical thinking involves interpretation, and interpretive conclusions are tentative and open to alternative possibilities. An interpretive conclusion is not a fact, but a theory. Interpretive conclusions stand or fall not so much on whether they can be proved right or wrong (or some combination of the two), but on whether they are demonstrably plausible.

An interpretive conclusion is not a fact, but a theory.

What makes an interpretation plausible? We might choose not to accept your interpretation for a number of reasons. We might, for example, be New Yorkers and, further, inclined to think that New Yorkers are cool and that this is what the picture "says." You might be from one of the states depicted on the cover in terms of look-alike blondes and, further, inclined to think that New Yorkers are full of themselves and forever portraying the rest of the country as shallowly conformist and uncultured.

But none of these personal influences ultimately matters. What matters is that you share your data, show your reasons for believing that it means what you say it means, and do this well enough for a reader to find your interpretation reasonable (whether he or she actually believes it or not). Then you will have passed the plausibility test. Your interpretation will stand until another person offers an analysis with interpretive conclusions that seems more plausible than yours, pointing to more or better evidence, and arguing for the meaning of that evidence more convincingly.

ARRIVING AT AN INTERPRETIVE CONCLUSION: MAKING CHOICES

Let's try on one final interpretive context, and then see which of the various contexts (lenses) through which we have viewed the cover produces the most credible interpretation, the one that seems to best account for the patterns of detail in the evidence. Different interpretations will account better for some details than others—which is why it enriches our view of the world to try on different interpretations. Ultimately, you will have to decide which possible interpretation, as seen through which plausible interpretive context, best accounts for what you think is most important and interesting to notice about your subject.

We will try to push our own interpretive process to a choice by selecting one interpretive context as the most revealing: *The New Yorker* magazine itself. The dark-haired figure wearing the New York banner is, in a sense, the magazine or, at least, a potential reader—a representative New Yorker. What, then, does the cover "say" to and about New Yorkers and to and about the magazine and its readers?

Throughout this book we use the question "So what?" to prompt interpretive leaps. *So what* that the woman representing New York is dark when the other women are light, is closed (narrowed eyes, closed mouth, hair tightly pulled up and back) when the others are open (wide-open eyes and mouths, loosely flowing hair), is pointed and angular when the others are round, sports a bared midriff when the others are covered?

As with our earlier attempt to interpret the cover in the context of the 2000 presidential campaign, interpreting it in the context of other *The New Yorker* covers would require a little research. How do *The New Yorker* covers characteristically represent New Yorkers? What might you discover by looking for patterns of repetition and contrast in a set of *The New Yorker* covers rather than just this one?

We are willing to bet that you would soon discover the magazine's droll awareness of its own heralding of New Yorkers as sophisticated, cultured, and cosmopolitan: it at once embraces and sends up the stereotype. How does the cover read in the context, for example, of various jokes about how New Yorkers think of themselves relative to the rest of the country, such as the cover depicting the United States as two large coastlines, east and west, connected by an almost nonexistent middle?

Armed with the knowledge that the covers are not only characteristically laughing at the rest of the country but also at New Yorkers themselves, you might begin to *make explicit what is implicit* in the cover (one of the analytical moves listed in Chapter 2).

Here are some attempts at making the cover speak. Does the cover "say" that New Yorkers are shrewder, less naïve (less open), warier than other Americans, but largely because they are also more worldly and smarter? Is the cover in some way a "dumb blonde" joke in which the dark woman with the pronounced beauty mark and calculating gaze participates but also sets herself apart from some kind of national "beauty" contest? Are we being invited (intentionally or not) to invert the conventional value hierarchy of dark and light so that the dark woman—the sort that gets represented as the evil stepmother in fairy tales such as "Snow White"—becomes "the fairest of them all," and nobody's fool?

Let's end this sample analysis and interpretation with two possibilities—somewhat opposed to each other, but probably both "true" of what the cover communicates, at least to certain audiences (East and West Coast Americans, and readers of *The New Yorker*). At its most serious, *The New Yorker* cover may speak to American history in which New York has been the point of entry for generations of immigrants, the "dark" (literally and figuratively) in the face of America's blonde northern European legacy.

Within the context of other *The New Yorker* covers, however, we might find ourselves gravitating to a less serious and perhaps equally plausible interpretive conclusion: that the cover is a complex joke. It appears to be saying, yes, America, we do think that we're cooler and more individual and less plastic than the rest of you, but we also know that we shouldn't be so smug about it.

C. EXTENDED EXAMPLE 3: ANALYZING AN ARGUMENT BY REFORMULATING BINARIES AND UNCOVERING ASSUMPTIONS

Our most direct advice on analyzing arguments and thus on learning to write them more effectively can be found in this section. Here you will see how to unearth the essentially binary structure of arguments and how to uncover the unstated assumptions upon which arguments typically rest. The technique of locating, assessing the accuracy of, and recasting binaries is a very effective way of meeting other people's arguments—and revising your own. Arguing with someone else's argument is usually as much a matter of addressing what is left unsaid—the assumptions "underneath" the argument that the arguer takes to be "givens" (obvious truths)—as confronting what gets argued overtly.

THINKING WITH AND ABOUT BINARIES

In human—and computerized—thinking, a binary is a pair of elements, usually in opposition to each other, as in off/on, yes/no, right/wrong, agree/disagree, and so on. Many ideas begin with a writer's noticing some kind of opposition or tension or choice within a subject—capital punishment either does or does not deter crime; a character in a novel is either a courageous rebel or a fool; a new environmental policy is either visionary or blind. A major advantage of looking for and using binaries is that they help you determine what issues are at stake in your subject, because binaries position you among competing choices.

There is an old joke to the effect that there are two kinds of people: those who like binary thinking and those who do not. Part of the humor here seems to lie in the recognition that we cannot help but think in binary terms. As the philosopher Herbert Marcuse says, "We understand that which is in terms of that which is not": light is that which is not dark; masculine is that which is not feminine; civilized is that which is not primitive. Creating opposing categories is fundamental to defining things. But as these examples may suggest, binaries are also dangerous because they can perpetuate what is called reductive thinking, especially if applied uncritically.

If you restrict yourself to thinking in binary terms, you can run into two problems. First, most subjects cannot be adequately considered in terms of only two options—either this or that, with nothing in between. Second, binaries often conceal value judgments: the category "primitive," as opposed to "civilized," is not a neutral description but a devaluation. In sum, it is useful and necessary to construct binaries, but it is dangerous to ignore the gray areas in between and the value judgments that binaries tend to conceal.

It is dangerous to ignore the gray areas in between and the value judgments that binaries tend to conceal.

Often the trouble starts with the ways binaries are phrased. Two of the most common and potentially counterproductive ways of phrasing binaries are *either/or* and *agree/disagree.* In the vast majority of cases, there are more than two alternatives, but the either/or or agree/disagree phrasing prevents you from looking for them. And it does not acknowledge that both alternatives may have some truth to them. A new environmental policy may be both visionary and blind. And there may be more accurate categories than visionary and blind for considering the merits and demerits of the policy.

Framing an issue in either/or terms can be useful for stimulating a chain of thought, but it is usually not a good way to end one. Consider the either/or binary, "Was the Civil War fought over slavery or economics?" You could begin this way, but if you're not careful—conscious of the all-or-nothing force of binary formulations—you could easily get trapped in an overly dichotomized position; in this case, that economics caused the war and that slavery had nothing to do with it, or vice versa.

You can't analyze without binaries, but you need to be wary of putting everything into big, undifferentiated categories, labeled all black or all white, with nothing in between.

A Procedure for Using Binaries Analytically

Strategy 1: Locate a Range of Opposing Categories

The first step in using binaries analytically is to locate and distinguish them carefully. Consider, for example, the binaries contained in the following question: Does the model of management known as Total Quality Management (TQM) that is widely used in Japan work in the American automotive industry? The most obvious binary in this question is work versus not work. But there are also other binaries in the question—Japanese versus American, for example, and TQM versus more traditional and more traditionally American models of management. These binaries imply further binaries. Insofar as TQM is acknowledged to be a team-oriented, collaborative management model, the question requires a writer to consider the accuracy and relative suitability of particular traits commonly ascribed to Japanese versus American workers, such as communal and cooperative versus individualistic and competitive.

Strategy 2: Analyze and Define the Key Terms

Having located the various binaries, you should begin to analyze and define terms. What, for example, does it mean to ask whether TQM *works* in the American automotive industry? Does work mean "make a substantial profit"? Does work mean "produce more cars more quickly"? Does work mean "improving employee morale"? You would probably find yourself drowning in vagueness unless you carefully argued for the appropriateness of your definition of this key term.

Strategy 3: Question the Accuracy of the Binary

Having begun to analyze and define your terms, you would next need to determine how accurately they define the issues raised by your subject. You might consider, for example, the extent to which American management styles actually differ from the Japanese version of TQM. In the process of trying to determine if there are significant differences, you could start to locate particular traits in these management styles and in Japanese versus American culture that might help you formulate your binary more precisely. Think of the binary as a starting point—a kind of deliberate overgeneralization—that allows you to set up positions you can then test in order to refine.

Strategy 4: Substitute "To What Extent?" for "Either/Or"

The best strategy in using binaries productively is usually to locate arguments on both sides of the either/or choice that the binary poses and then choose a position somewhere between the two extremes. Once you have arrived at what you consider the most accurate phrasing of the binary, you can rephrase the original either/or question in the more qualified terms that asking "To what extent?" allows. Making this move does not release you from the responsibility of taking a stand and arguing for it.

So, in answer to a question such as "Was the Civil War fought over slavery or economics?" you would attempt to determine *the extent to which* each side of the binary—slavery and economics—could reasonably be credited as the cause of the war. To do so, you would first rephrase the question thus: To what extent did economics, rather than slavery, cause the Civil War? Rephrasing in this way might also enable you to see problems with the original binary formulation.

By analyzing the terms of the binary, you would come to question them and ultimately arrive at a more complex and qualified position to write about. Admittedly, in reorienting your thinking from the obvious and clear-cut choices that either/or formulations provide to the murkier waters of asking "To what extent?" your decision process will be made more difficult. The gain, however, is that the to-what-extent mind-set, by predisposing you to assess multiple and potentially conflicting points of view, will enable you to address more fairly and accurately the issues raised by your subject.

Applying these steps will usually cause you to do one or more of the following:

1. Discover that you have not adequately named the binary and that another opposition would be more accurate.
2. Weight one side of your binary more heavily than the other, rather than seeing the issue as all or nothing.
3. Discover that the two terms of your binary are not really so separate and opposed after all but are actually parts of one complex phenomenon or issue (collapsing the binary).

Where might you end up if you approached our earlier sample topic (whether or not TQM works in the American automotive industry) by asking *to what extent* one side of the binary better suits available evidence, rather than arguing that one side is clearly the right choice and the other entirely wrong? You would still be arguing that one position on TQM in American industry is more accurate than the other, but you would inevitably arrive at more carefully qualified conclusions than the question might otherwise have led you to. You would most likely take care, for example, to suggest the danger of assuming that all American workers are rugged individualists and all Japanese workers are communal bees.

Try this 3.3: Applying the Strategies for Using Binaries Analytically

Apply the strategies to analyze the assumptions and issues in the statements below, doing with them what we did in our TQM example. This does not mean you must proceed step-by-step through the strategies, but at the least, for each thesis statement or question you should do the following:

- List all the binaries you can find, both implicit and explicit, in each example.
- Isolate the one or two key terms that reveal what is at issue for each writer, and determine what they mean. You should write out the implied definitions.

In number 2, for example, the key binary appears to be "first-world" versus "third-world," but even more important for defining the writer's thinking is arguably what he or she means by "good."

- Even if the original formulation looks okay to you, assume that it is an overgeneralization that needs to be refined and rephrased. On the basis of your list of oppositions and definitions of key terms, rewrite each statement in a more qualified and more accurate form.

In proposing your revised statements, you might try substituting "to what extent" for "either/or" (which will press you to limit the claims that binary formulations are prone to overstate).

1. It is important to understand why leaders act in a leadership role. What is the driving force? Is it an internal drive for the business or group to succeed, or is it an internal drive for the leader to dominate over others?
2. Is nationalism good for emerging third-world countries?
3. The private lives of public figures should not matter in the way they are assessed by the public. What matters is how competently they do their jobs.
4. The Seattle sound of rock 'n' roll known as grunge is not original; it's just a rehash of punk and New Wave elements.

Try this 3.4: Writing an Analysis from Organizing Contrasts

Locate some organizing contrasts in anything—something you are studying, something you've just written, something you saw on television last night, something on the front page of the newspaper, something going on at your campus or workplace, and so forth. As we've said, binaries are pervasive in the way we think; therefore, you can expect to find them everywhere. Consider, for example, the binaries suggested by current trends in contemporary music or by the representation of women in birthday cards. Having selected the binaries you want to work with, pick one and try out the four steps we suggest for working with binaries.

UNCOVERING ASSUMPTIONS (REASONING BACK TO PREMISES)

All arguments ultimately rest on fundamental assumptions called givens—positions not in need of argument because you assume the reader will "give" them to you as true. Often, however, these assumptions need first to be acknowledged and then argued, or at least tested. You cannot assume that their truth is self-evident. The failure to locate and examine unacknowledged assumptions (premises) is the downfall of many essays. The problem occurs because our categories—the mental boxes we've created over time—have become so fixed, so unquestioned, that we cease to be fully aware of them.

Everything you read has basic assumptions that underlie it. What are assumptions in this context? They are the basic ground of beliefs from which a position springs, its starting points or givens, its basic operating premises. *The Oxford*

English Dictionary defines a premise—from a Latin word meaning "to put before"—as "a previous statement or proposition from which another statement is inferred or follows as a conclusion."

All arguments or articulations of point of view have premises—that is, they are based in a given set of assumptions, which are built upon to arrive at conclusions. A lot of the time, though, the assumptions are not visible; they're implicit (which is why they need to be inferred). They're usually not actively concealed by writers—writers hiding from readers the subterranean bases of their outlooks—which might be considered unethical. Rather, many writers (especially inexperienced ones) remain unaware of the premises that underlie their points of view—probably because they were never taught to be aware of them. Similarly, most readers don't know that they should search out the starting points of what they read, so of course they also don't know how.

Most readers tend to credit what they read as true, or at least relatively neutral, especially if it's in a book. In other words, most people aren't aware that everything they read (and write) comes from given sets of assumptions. It follows that the ability to uncover assumptions is a powerful analytical procedure to learn—it gives you insight into the roots, the basic givens that a piece of writing (or a speaker) has assumed are true.

When you locate assumptions in a text, you understand the text better—where it's coming from and what else it believes that is more fundamental than what it is overtly declaring. You also find things to write about; uncovering assumptions offers one of the best ways of developing and revising your own work. Uncovering assumptions can help you understand why you believe *x*, or may reveal to you that two of your givens are in conflict with each other.

To uncover assumptions, you need to read "backward"—to ask what a reading must also already believe, given that it believes what it overtly claims. In other words, you need to imagine or reinvent the process of thinking by which a writer has arrived at a position.

To uncover assumptions, you need to read "backward"—to ask what a reading must also already believe, given that it believes what it overtly claims.

Say you read a piece that praises a television show for being realistic but faults it for setting a bad example for the kids who watch it. What assumptions might we infer from such a piece?

- Television should attempt to depict life accurately (realistically).
- Television should produce shows that set good examples.
- Kids imitate or at least have their attitudes shaped by what they watch on television.
- Good and bad examples are clear and easily recognizable by everyone.

Note that none of these assumptions is self-evidently true—each would need to be argued for. And some of the assumptions conflict with others—for example, that shows should be both morally uplifting and realistic, given that in "real life" those who do wrong often go unpunished. These are subjects an analytical response to the piece (or a revision of it) could bring out.

Try this 3.5: Uncover Assumptions in Statements

You can practice uncovering assumptions with all kinds of material—newspaper editorials, statements you see on billboards, ideas you are studying in your courses, jokes, and so forth. You could try the kind of fieldwork assignment that we recommend in Chapter 1. Spend a week jotting down in your notebook interesting statements you overhear. Choose the most interesting of these from the standpoint of the implied (but unstated) premises upon which each statement seems to rest. Make a list of the uncovered assumptions.

Uncovering Assumptions (Reasoning Back to Premises): A Brief Example

Consider the assertion "Tax laws benefit the wealthy." No matter how you might develop this claim (moving it forward), you would get into trouble if you didn't also move backward to uncover the premises embedded in this thesis about the purpose of tax laws. The wording of this claim seems to conceal an egalitarian premise: the assumption that tax laws should not benefit anyone, or, at least, that they should benefit everyone equally. But what is the purpose of tax laws? Should they redress economic inequities? Should they spur the economy by rewarding those who generate capital? You might go to the U.S. Constitution and/or legal precedents to resolve such questions, but our point here is that you would need to move your thesis back to this point and test the validity of the assumptions upon which it rests.

Regardless of the position you might adopt—attacking tax laws, defending them, showing how they actually benefit everyone, or whatever—you would risk arguing blindly if you failed to question what the purpose of tax law is in the first place. This testing of assumptions would, at the least, cause you to qualify and refine your thesis.

A Step-by-Step Procedure for Uncovering Assumptions How do you actually go about uncovering assumptions? Here's a fairly flexible procedure, which we will apply step-by-step to the claim "Tax laws benefit the wealthy."

1. **Paraphrase the explicit claim.** This activity will get you started interpreting the claim, and it may begin to suggest the claim's underlying assumptions. We might paraphrase the claim as "The rules for paying income tax give rich people monetary advantages" or "The rules for paying income tax help the rich get richer."
2. **List the implicit ideas that the claim seems to assume to be true.** Here are two: "Tax laws shouldn't benefit anybody" and "Tax laws should benefit those who need the benefit, those with the least money."
3. **Determine the various ways that the key terms of the claim might be defined, as well as how the writer of the claim has defined them.** This process of definition will help you see the key concepts upon which

the claim depends. How does the writer intend "benefit"? Does he or she mean that tax laws benefit only the wealthy and presumably harm those who are not wealthy? Where does the line between wealthy and not wealthy get drawn?

4. **Try on an oppositional stance to the claim to see if this unearths more underlying assumptions.** Regardless of your view on the subject, suppose for the sake of argument that the writer is wrong. This step allows you to think comparatively, helping you to see the claim more clearly, to see what it apparently *excludes* from its fundamental beliefs.

   Knowing what the underlying assumption leaves out helps us see the narrowness upon which the claim may rest; we understand better its limits. Two positions that the claim appears to exclude are "Tax laws benefit the poor" and "Tax laws do not benefit the wealthy."

A Sample Essay: Analyzing an Argument by Reasoning Back to Premises

Because the following essay originally appeared (in 1993) as a newspaper editorial (in *The New York Times*), it is less expository (explanatory) than much academic analytical writing. We have included it because it so clearly illustrates how a writer reasons forward to conclusions by reasoning backward to premises. The essay also illustrates how the strategies of refocusing binaries and qualifying claims operate in a finished piece of writing. As we noted above, these strategies, which are so useful for recognizing and fixing problems in writing, are equally useful for producing ideas.

As you read this editorial on the controversial rules established at Antioch College to govern sexual conduct among its students, try to focus not only on the content of the argument, but also on its form; that is, how the writer moves from one phase of his thinking to the next. Toward this end, we have added our own summaries of what each paragraph of the editorial accomplishes. At the end of the editorial we sum up the writer's primary developmental strategies in a form you can apply to your own writing.

"Playing by the Antioch Rules"

by Eric Fassin

[1] A good consensus is hard to find, especially on sexual politics. But the infamous rules instituted last year by Antioch College, which require students to obtain explicit verbal consent before so much as a kiss is exchanged, have created just that. They have provoked indignation (this is a serious threat to individual freedom!) as well as ridicule (can this be serious?). Sexual correctness thus proves a worthy successor to political correctness as a target of public debate. [The writer names the issue: the complaint that Antioch's rules threaten individual freedom.]

[2] Yet this consensus against the rules reveals shared assumptions among liberals, conservatives and even radicals about the nature of sex in our culture. [The writer identifies members of an unlikely consensus and focuses on a surprising similarity.]

[3] The new definition of consent at Antioch is based on a "liberal" premise: it assumes that sexual partners are free agents and that they mean what they say—yes means yes, and no means no. But the initiator must now obtain prior consent, step by step, which in practice shifts the burden of clarification from the woman to the man. The question is no longer "Did she say no?" but "Did she say yes?" Silence does not indicate consent, and it becomes his responsibility to dispel any ambiguity. [The writer identifies assumption of freedom underlying the rules.]

[4] The novelty of the rules, however, is not as great as it seems. Antioch will not exert more control over its students; there are no sexual police. In practice, you still do what you want—as long as your partner does not complain . . . the morning after. If this is censorship, it intervenes *ex post facto*, not *a priori*. [The writer questions the premise that rules will actually control individual freedom more than current norms do.]

[5] In fact, the "threat" to individual freedom for most critics is not the invasion of privacy through the imposition of sexual codes, but the very existence of rules. Hence the success of polemicists like Katie Roiphe or Camille Paglia, who argue that feminism in recent years has betrayed its origins by embracing old-style regulations, paradoxically choosing the rigid 1950s over the liberating 1960s. Their advice is simply to let women manage on their own, and individuals devise their own rules. This individualist critique of feminism finds resonance with liberals, but also, strangely, with conservatives, who belatedly discover the perils of regulating sexuality. [The writer locates an antiregulatory (laissez-faire) premise beneath the freedom premise.]

[6] But sexual laissez-faire, with its own implicit set of rules, does not seem to have worked very well recently. Since the collapse of established social codes, people play the same game with different rules. If more women are complaining of sexual violence, while more men are worrying that their words and actions might be misconstrued, who benefits from the absence of regulation? [The writer attacks the laissez-faire premise for ineffectiveness.]

[7] A laissez-faire philosophy toward relationships assumes that sexuality is a game that can (and must) be played without rules, or rather that the invention of rules should be left to individual spontaneity and creativity, despite rising evidence that the rule of one's own often leads to misunderstandings. When acted out, individual fantasy always plays within preordained social rules. These rules conflict with the assumption in this culture that sex is subject to the reign of nature, not artifice, that it is the province of the individual, not of society. [The writer uncovers an assumption beneath the laissez-faire premise: sex is natural and thus outside social rules.]

[8] Those who believe that society's constraints should have nothing to do with sex also agree that sex should not be bound by the social conventions of language. Indeed, this rebellion against the idea of social constraints probably accounts for the controversy over explicit verbal consent—from George Will, deriding "sex amidst semicolons," to Camille Paglia railing, "As if sex occurs in the verbal realm." As if sexuality were incompatible with words. As if the only language of sex were silence. For *The New Yorker*, "the [Antioch] rules don't get rid of the problem of unwanted sex at all; they just shift the advantage from the muscle-bound frat boy to the honey-tongued French major." [The writer develops the linguistic implications of the natural premise and questions the assumption that sex is incompatible with language.]

[9] This is not very different from the radical feminist position, which holds that verbal persuasion is no better than physical coercion. In this view, sexuality cannot be entrusted to rhetoric. The seduction of words is inherently violent, and seduction itself is an object of suspicion. (If this is true, Marvell's invitation "To His Coy Mistress" is indeed a form of sexual harassment, as some campus feminists have claimed.) [The writer develops a further implication: that the attack on rules masks a fear of language's power to seduce—and questions the equation of seduction with harassment.]

[10] What the consensus against the Antioch rules betrays is a common vision of sexuality which crosses the lines dividing conservatives, liberals and radicals. So many of the arguments start from a conventional situation, perceived and presented as natural: a heterosexual encounter with the man as the initiator, and the woman as gatekeeper—hence the focus on consent. [The writer redefines consensus as sharing the unacknowledged premise that conventional sex roles are natural.]

[11] The outcry largely results from the fact that the rules undermine this traditional erotic model. Not so much by proscribing (legally), but by prescribing (socially). The new model, in which language becomes a normal form of erotic communication, underlines the conventional nature of the old one. [The writer reformulates the claim about the antirules consensus: rules undermine attempts to pass off traditional sex roles as natural.]

[12] By encouraging women out of their "natural" reserve, these rules point to a new definition of sexual roles. "Yes" could be more than a way to make explicit the absence of "no"; "yes" can also be a cry of desire. Women may express demands, and not only grant favors. If the legal "yes" opened the ground for an erotic "yes," if the contract gave way to desire and if consent led to demand, we would indeed enter a brave new erotic world. [The writer extends the implication of the claim: rules could make sex more erotic rather than less free.]

[13] New rules are like new shoes: they hurt a little at first, but they may fit tomorrow. The only question about the Antioch rules is not really whether we like them, but whether they improve the situation between men and women. All rules are artificial, but, in the absence of generally agreed-upon social conventions, any new prescription must feel artificial. And isn't regulation needed precisely when there is an absence of cultural consensus? [The writer questions the standard by which we evaluate rules; the writer proposes reformulating the binary from artificial versus natural to whether or not rules will improve gender relations.]

[14] Whether we support or oppose the Antioch rules, at least they force us to acknowledge that the choice is not between regulation and freedom, but between different sets of rules, implicit or explicit. They help dispel the illusion that sexuality is a state of nature individuals must experience outside the social contract, and that eroticism cannot exist within the conventions of language. As Antioch reminds us, there is more in eroticism and sexuality than is dreamt of in this culture. [The writer culminates with his own idea: rules are good because they force us to acknowledge as a harmful illusion the idea that sex operates outside social conventions.]

Despite its brevity, this editorial covers a daunting amount of ground—an examination of "shared assumptions among liberals, conservatives and even radicals about the nature of sex in our culture" (paragraph 2). The writer, given his audience (readers of the Sunday *New York Times*), allows himself more breadth in both his topic and his claims than he would if he were writing an article on the same subject in an academic setting, where he would narrow his focus to supply more analysis of issues and evidence. The aim of editorials like this one is not only to inform or persuade but also to provoke and entertain. Nevertheless, the strategies that direct the thinking in this piece are, with some minor exceptions, the same as they would be in a more extended analytical piece. They are central strategies that you can apply to many sorts of writing situations, such as analyzing arguments and as a means of finding and developing your own ideas.

Strategies for Writing an Argument by Reasoning Back to Premises The strategies that direct the thinking in this editorial offer a model for uncovering assumptions in the service of arriving at ideas. If you examine what the writer has done—not just what he has said—you might arrive at the following primary moves, which can be phrased as general guidelines.

1. **Paraphrase the explicit claims; search out the meanings of key terms.** The writer does not begin by offering his own conclusion on whether the views he has thus far described are right or wrong. Instead, he slows down the forward momentum toward judgment and begins to analyze what the consensus against the Antioch rules might mean (liberals,

conservatives, and radicals) with respect to the nature of sex in our culture." In fact, the author spends the first three-quarters of the essay trying on various answers to this question of meaning.

Note: A careful reader would recognize by tonal signals such as the exclamation point after "serious threat to individual freedom!" that the opening paragraph has, in fact, begun to announce its position, albeit not overtly, by subtly overstating its opposite. It is not until later in the editorial, however, that we can clearly recognize that the writer is employing a common introductory strategy—defining the position you plan to argue against.

2. **Uncover assumptions to decide what is really at issue.** Rather than proceeding directly to a judgment on whether or not the rules threaten individual freedom, the writer carefully searches out the assumptions—the premises and the givens—underlying the attacks on the rules. He proposes, for example, that underneath the attack by the consensus on the rules and its defense of individual freedom lies a basic assumption about sex and society, that sexuality should not be governed by rules because it is natural rather than cultural: "These rules conflict with the assumption in this culture that sex is subject to the reign of nature, not artifice, that it is the province of the individual, not of society" (paragraph 7).
3. **Attend to organizing contrasts, but be alert to the possibility that they may be false dichotomies, and reformulate them as necessary.** A false dichotomy (sometimes called a false binary) inaccurately divides possible views on a subject into two opposing camps, forcing a choice between black and white when some shade of gray might be fairer and more accurate. It is always a good strategy to question any either/or dichotomy. Consider the extent to which its opposing terms define the issue fairly and accurately before accepting an argument in favor of one side or the other.

   Consider, too, how you might reject *both* choices offered by an either/or opposition to construct an alternative approach that is truer to the issues at hand. This is what the author of the editorial does. He outlines and then rejects as a false dichotomy the assumption he has uncovered that is held by the consensus view—that sexual behavior is either a province of individual freedom or is regulated by society:

   False Dichotomies
   freedom versus regulation
   natural versus artificial
   no rules versus rules

Reasoning back to premises and reformulating binaries has led the writer to his primary idea. He argues that much of what we perceive to be natural, such as the notion of men as sexual initiators and women as nay-sayers and gatekeepers, is in fact governed by social rules and conventions. He proposes that what is really at stake—the root assumption shared by the anti-rules consensus—is a different dichotomy, a choice between two sets of rules, one implicit and one explicit. If you look for patterns of repetition and contrast in the editorial (see Chapter 2), new organizing contrasts emerge:

Reformulated Dichotomies
rules versus rules
implicit versus explicit
not working versus might work
based on "no" versus based on "yes"

The editorial concludes that we need to decide questions of sexual behavior—at Antioch and in the culture at large—by recognizing and evaluating the relative merits of the two sets of rules rather than by creating a false dichotomy between rules and no rules, between regulation and freedom: "The choice is not between regulation and freedom, but between different sets of rules" (paragraph 14).

4. **When you write your analysis of the reading, rehearse for your readers the thinking process by which you have uncovered the assumptions—not just the conclusions to which the process has led you.** Notice that virtually the entire editorial has consisted of uncovering assumptions as a way of arriving at new ways of thinking.

Try this 3.6: Uncovering Assumptions in an Argument

In the paragraph below the writer has made her premises quite clear but has not acknowledged the possible validity of competing premises. (It is this same neglect of other possible positions that Fassin makes the substance of his editorial against the detractors of the Antioch Rules—use him as a model). If she could become more self-conscious of reasoning back to premises, she would be more likely to discover these competing claims and either qualify her argument or overtly counter these competing claims.

Field hockey is a sport that can be played by either men or women. All sports should be made available for members of both sexes. As long as women are allowed to participate on male teams in sports such as football and wrestling, men should be allowed to participate on female teams in sports such as field hockey and lacrosse. If females press for and receive equal opportunity in all sports, then it is only fair that men be given the same opportunities. If women object to this type of equal opportunity, then they are promoting reverse discrimination.

First, examine the paragraph and lay out her premises in your own words. That is, find at least two key assumptions that she wishes us to accept. Hint: The writer assumes, for example, that fairness ought t precedence over other possible values in the selection of athletic More generally, think about how she is defining other key terms

Then lay out at least two competing premises—the basis which a counterargument might be built.

ASSIGNMENT: Analyzing an Editorial or Other Argument by Locating Binaries and Reasoning Back to Premises

Locate the binaries in an editorial or other position piece and explain the extent to which these are adequate and/or inadequate ways of defining the subject. You might want to try the formula "This article/argument/point of view/work appears to be about *x*, but could also be (or is really) about *y*." This formula will impel you to reason back to premises, redefine key terms, and reformulate binaries.

Alternatively, you might write a paper in which you reason back to the premises that underlie some idea or attitude of your own, preferably one that has undergone some kind of change in recent years (for example, your attitude toward the world of work, toward marriage, toward family life, toward community, toward religion, and so on).

ASSIGNMENT: Analyzing a Portrait from Description to Interpretation

Locate any portrait, preferably a good reproduction from an art book or magazine, one that shows detail clearly. Then do a version of what we've done with Whistler in Figure 3.2.

Your goal is to produce an analysis of the portrait with the steps we included in analyzing *Whistler's Mother*. First, summarize the portrait, describing accurately its significant details. Do not go beyond a recounting of what the portrait includes; avoid interpreting what these details suggest.

Then use the various methods offered in this chapter to analyze the data. What repetitions (patterns of same or similar detail) do you see? What organizing contrasts suggest themselves? In light of these patterns of similarity and difference, what anomalies do you then begin to detect? Move from the data to interpretive conclusions by making the implicit explicit (one of the five analytical moves) and by repeatedly asking So what?

This process will produce a set of interpretive leaps, which you should then try to assemble into a more coherent claim of some sort—about what the portrait "says" or reveals within some specified interpretive context.

ASSIGNMENT: Analyzing a Magazine Cover by Researching an Interpretive Context

Choose a magazine that, like *The New Yorker*, has interesting covers. Write an analysis of one such cover by studying other covers from the same magazine. The analysis of *The New Yorker* cover in the middle third of the chapter offers a model for how to do this. You will almost certainly need to do the following:

1. Apply the Method—looking for patterns of repetition and contrast—to the cover itself, so that you arrive at key repetitions, strands, and organizing contrasts and begin to ponder a range of possible interpretive leaps to what they signify.

2. Use these data to suggest plausible interpretive contexts for the cover. Remember that interpretive contexts are not simply imposed from without; they're suggested by the evidence.
3. Then move to the other covers. Perform similar operations on them to arrive at an awareness of common denominators among the covers, and to analyze what those shared traits might reveal or make more evident in the particular cover you are studying. You will be trying to figure out how the magazine conceives of itself and its audience by the way that it characteristically represents its "face."

GUIDELINES FOR PUTTING ANALYSIS TO WORK

1. Look for a range of plausible interpretations rather than assuming that there will be only one right answer. Control the range of possible interpretations by attending carefully to context.
2. Laying out the data is key to any kind of analysis, not simply because it keeps the analysis accurate but because, crucially, it is in the act of carefully describing a subject that analytical writers often have their best ideas. The words you choose to summarize your data will contain the germs of your ideas about what the subject means.
3. All explanations and interpretations occur in a context, which functions like a lens for focusing your subject. An important part of getting an interpretation accepted as plausible is to *argue for the appropriateness of the interpretive context you use*, not just the interpretation it takes you to.
4. It is interesting and sometimes useful to try to determine from something you are analyzing what its makers might have intended. But, by and large, you are best off concentrating on what the thing itself communicates as opposed to what someone might have wanted it to communicate. Besides, intentions can rarely be known with much accuracy.
5. Arguing with someone else's argument is usually as much a matter of addressing what is left unsaid—the assumptions "underneath" the argument that the arguer takes to be "givens" (obvious truths)—as confronting what gets argued overtly.
6. A major advantage of looking for and using binaries is that they help you determine what issues are at stake in your subject; binaries position you among competing choices.
7. Think of the binary as a starting point—a kind of deliberate overgeneralization—that allows you to set up positions you can then test in order to refine. Although framing an issue in either/or terms can be useful for stimulating a chain of thought, it is usually not a good way to end one. Let *either/or* become *the extent to which*.

GUIDELINES FOR PUTTING ANALYSIS TO WORK (CONTINUED)

8. Uncovering assumptions underneath a given position is a powerful analytical tool. To uncover assumptions, you need to read "backward"—to ask *what a reading must also already believe*, given its overt claims. In other words, you need to imagine or reinvent the process of thinking by which a writer has arrived at a position.

CHAPTER 4

Reading: How to Do It and What to Do with It

Quick Take

This chapter concentrates on how to get better ideas from and about what you read. In a phrase, it endorses "active reading": concrete strategies for questioning and marking and writing about readings more acutely.

These strategies aim to make you more conscious as a reader. For instance, the chapter advocates most strongly the practice of selecting a passage (even a single sentence) from whatever you are reading that you think it is most important to discuss.

What do you do with this passage once you've selected it? If you want to better understand something that you're reading—or revising in your own writing—ask yourself what certain key words mean, even if you think you know what they mean, and start paraphrasing.

The chapter also suggests methods of finding "good" passages, expanding the ways you think about a reading. There's a section of the chapter, for example, on recognizing what a reading *does*, rather than concentrating solely on what it *says*. We talk about how to describe the way a reading behaves—and once you can do that, it is much easier to imitate as a model or apply to another reading.

Other sections discuss how to freewrite about, summarize, compare and contrast, and locate definitions in readings. The latter two are among the original topics of invention in classical rhetoric—the traditional ways of finding and accessing ideas. (They still work.) We approach all these forms from the point of view of both reader and writer, as ways of both accessing readings and exploring primary data in your own writing.

One more thing: many of the skills taught in this chapter are also treated in the first two chapters, so if you are beginning the book here, you might find it beneficial to follow the cross-references to the appropriate sections of those chapters.

A. HOW TO READ: WORDS MATTER

A well-known twentieth-century philosopher, Ludwig Wittgenstein, noted in a famous saying that we cannot make a proposition about the world; we can only make a proposition about another proposition about the world. The statement implies that we live in a world of language. This is not to say that everything is words, that words are the only reality. But to an enormous extent, we understand the world and our relation to it by working through language, by "reading."

As you have probably noticed, this book has been using the word *reading* to mean "interpreting." This usage hearkens back to the idea of the world as a text. The idea wasn't new with Wittgenstein, by the way. The Puritans also envisioned the world as a text in which God read their lives, and so, predictably, they started reading their lives too, reflecting on events that befell them, and querying whether those events were signs of salvation or damnation. (The stakes for being a good reader couldn't have been higher!) In short, reading for them meant gathering evidence and analyzing it to arrive at ideas or conclusions.

We know the world through language; it's the medium in which we dwell.

Considering how central reading is in our lives, it's amazing how little we think about words themselves. We use words all the time, but often unthinkingly. We don't plan out our sentences before we utter them, for example, and the same goes for most of the ones we write. In previous chapters we put forth the notion that there are almost always multiple plausible interpretations. Similarly, all words have multiple meanings; check any dictionary, and you will find more than one definition for virtually every word.

Most of us live, however, as if there were a consensus about what words mean. Often—much more than you suspect—there isn't a consensus. We tend to assume that words (like life itself) have simple and single meanings. Don't believe it. Words are promiscuous; they won't stay put, won't stick to a single meaning. This is often a source of the comic. A posting on the Internet of memorably silly headlines included "Teacher Strikes Idle Kids," "Panda Mating Fails: Veterinarian Takes Over," "New Vaccines May Contain Rabies," "Local High School Drop-outs Cut in Half," and "Include Your Children When Baking Cookies" (or if you prefer, "Kids Make Nutritious Snacks"). Another posting included sentences such as "The bandage was wound around the wound" and "After a number of injections my jaw got number." It's often a nutty language, and we need to remember this whenever we start getting too complacent about the meanings of words being singular and obvious.

BECOMING CONVERSANT VERSUS READING FOR THE GIST

Many readers operate under the dubious impression that they are to "read for the gist"—for the main point that is to be gleaned through a glancing speed-reading. Quite simply, you cannot expect to demonstrate your control of the information without getting closer to it than generalizations allow. One of the most crippling and frustrating things for many students is to expect that if they read through something once and then look away, they should be able either to accurately and productively restate it or to have an idea about it. The vast majority of writing tasks that you will encounter require as a prerequisite your *conversancy* with material that you have read—not inert generalizations about it.

It is a reasonable expectation both in academic courses and in the workplace that you should become *conversant* with the material. To become conversant means that

1. after a significant amount of work with the material, you should be able to talk about it conversationally with other people and answer questions about it without having to look everything up.
2. you should be able to converse with the material—to be in some kind of dialogue with it, to see the questions the material asks, and to pose your own questions about it.

Few people are able to really understand things they read or see without making the language of that material their own in some way. We can learn, in other words, only by finding ways to actively engage material rather than moving passively through it. This is why working closely with the language that you are reading is essential to becoming conversant with that reading.

To become conversant with something you have read means that you can talk about it conversationally with other people and answer questions about it without having to look everything up.

Various reading-related writing tasks can enable you to become conversant with a written text. Among them, we have singled out three for particular concentration:

- passage-based focused freewriting
- paraphrasing
- summarizing

Along with note taking and outlining, these are not just empty mechanical tasks, but the mind's means of acquiring material, both the ideas and the language. The first part of this chapter takes up each of these tasks in turn, offering versions of them to use as heuristics (means of finding things out). First, however, we want to pause to introduce a frame for reading critically.

A FRAME FOR READING CRITICALLY: THE PITCH, THE COMPLAINT, AND THE MOMENT

So words matter; they are our primary means of negotiating our relation to the world. But when you actually sit down to read for more than the gist, what can you do to read more actively? What can you look for and make note of? If you set out to choose passages that are "most important," by what criteria can you make such selections?

A useful premise to start from is that information is virtually never neutral. There is, in much of the reading you will do, no such thing as "just information." Rather, most readings—at least those encountered in work and school settings—have the following three components:

- a **pitch**, what the piece wishes you to believe
- a **complaint**, what the piece is reacting to
- a **moment**, the historical context within which the piece is operating

Whether you are paraphrasing, summarizing, selecting a passage for a focused freewriting, or otherwise looking for ways to separate out what is important in a reading, seeking out these three components will always be a boon to reading critically. Here's a bit more on each:

The pitch: A reading is an argument, a presentation of information that makes a case of some sort, even if the argument is not explicitly stated. Look for language that reveals the position or positions the piece seems interested in having you adopt. As we say in the discussion of categorical thinking at the end of Chapter 7, it is not only debate-style argument that makes a case for things. Analysis, for example, argues for understanding a subject in a particular way.

The complaint: A reading is a reaction to some situation, some set of circumstances, that the piece has set out to address. An indispensable means of understanding someone else's writing is to figure out what seems to have caused the person to write the piece in the first place. Writers write, presumably, because they think something needs to be addressed. What? Look for language in the piece that reveals the writer's starting point. If you can find the position or situation he or she is worried about and possibly trying to correct, you will find it much easier to locate the argument, the position the piece asks you to accept.

If you can find the position a writer is worried about and possibly trying to correct, you will find it much easier to locate the position the piece asks you to accept.

The moment: A reading is a response to the world conditioned by the writer's particular moment in time. In your attempt to figure out not only what a piece says but where it is coming from (the causes of its having been written in the first place and the positions it works to establish), history is significant. When was the piece written? Where? What else was going on at the time that might have shaped the writer's ideas and attitudes? You don't necessarily have to run to a history book for every older text that you encounter, but neither do you want to ignore the extent to which writers are conditioned by their times.

One more thing: the more difficult the reading is to get through, the more this approach will help you. Complex, abstract theoretical pieces will get clearer once you have identified these three components; they can provide invaluable grounding for your reading.

Try this 4.1: Locating the Pitch and the Complaint

You can read more actively by trying to figure out from the language of the reading what its author is worried about and what he or she is trying to "fix." This is true even of textbooks: informational reading still has a point of view. *Whenever you can, find the position that the reading is trying to resist, revise, or replace.* Take a passage of anything you are reading for work or school, and look for language that reveals the position or positions the piece seems interested in having you adopt. It is easier to find the pitch if you first look for language that reveals the position or situation the writer is trying to correct. Type out the sentences that most fully articulate the pitch and the complaint. Then paraphrase them to enrich your sense of where the writer is coming from and where the piece is trying to take you.

Alternatively, you could tackle the following piece of dyspepsia:

> The World Series victory that was earned by the Boston Red Sox gratified legions of fans who had suffered for many years. If the media were to be believed, these fans had been mourning their unrequited fandom since 1918, when Babe Ruth was sold to the Yankees. But all of the media hoopla surrounding the Sox' victory could not obscure the fact that the 2004 World Series will *not* go down in history as one of the better ones. Aside from the first game, there were no close contests. And the usual components that go into making a series memorable—extra-inning games, spectacular rallies, seesaw battles—were sadly absent. Instead, we were left with an overdose of media hype. Because the games were not exciting, and the writers had to write something, we just got more and more and more tired rehearsals of the lifting of "the curse"—itself a media creation of a book written only a decade ago. So maybe the Red Sox lifted the so-called curse, but perhaps, rather than being exorcized, it was merely transferred to baseball fans everywhere.

PASSAGE-BASED FOCUSED FREEWRITING

Passage-based focused freewriting is one of the best analytical exercises you can do to get ideas about what you are reading. It brings together several of the writing strategies discussed earlier in the book, most notably focused freewriting and 10 on 1 (introduced in Chapter 1). Its aim is to prompt in-depth analysis of a representative example, on the assumption that you'll attain a better appreciation of how the whole works after you've explored how a piece works.

In general, freewriting is a method of arriving at ideas by writing continuously about a subject for a specified period (usually ten to twenty minutes) without pausing to edit or correct or bite your pen or stare into space. The rationale behind this activity can be understood through the well-known remark by the novelist E. M. Forster (in regard to the "tyranny" of prearranging everything) we have already quoted, but that bears repeating: "How do I know what I think until I see what I say?" Freewriting gives you the chance to see what you say.

In passage-based focused freewriting, you narrow the scope to a single passage, a brief piece of the reading (at least a sentence, at most a paragraph) to anchor your analysis. You might choose the passage in answer to the following question:

What is the one passage in the reading that needs to be discussed, that poses a question or a problem, or that seems (in some way perhaps difficult to pin down) anomalous or even just unclear?

You can vary this question by selecting the passage that you find most puzzling or most important or most dissonant or whatever. Alternatively, you might apply the strategy of looking for patterns to a piece of the text to help you locate a passage containing a repetition, strand, or organizing contrast you wish to explore further.

One advantage of focused freewriting is that its impromptu nature forces you to articulate what you notice as you notice it, not delaying—or, as is more common, simply avoiding—thinking in a relatively disciplined way about what you are reading. There is no set procedure for such writing, but it usually involves the following:

- It attends to *the context* surrounding the passage, summarizing the larger section of which the passage is a part.
- It selects and *paraphrases key phrases* or terms in the passage, teasing out the possible meanings of these words.
- It relentlessly *asks, So what? about the details*: so what that the passage uses this language, moves in this way, arrives at these points? and so forth.
- It addresses *how the passage is representative of broader issues* in the reading; perhaps it refers to another, similar passage.

Passage-based focused freewriting thus makes use of the other skills that we will discuss in this chapter as well: paraphrasing, summarizing, and narrowing the focus. It is an effective way of preparing for class discussion and of testing possible areas of concentration for a paper.

Try this 4.2: Doing a Passage-Based Focused Freewrite

Select a passage from any of the material that you are reading and copy it at the top of the page. Then do a twenty-minute focused freewrite on it. Strive by the end of the time allotted to make some kind of interpretive leap, some consolidation of what you have learned about the reading by doing the exercise.

Your primary aim is to generate ideas about the reading. You can do that almost formulaically by following the steps below. You needn't proceed in the numbered order, but you should probably include each of these steps.

1. **Seek to understand before you judge.** Keep your attention on the point of view advanced by the text, not your own agreement/disagreement or like/dislike. Get detached and scientific: focus on what the text is saying and doing and what it is inviting readers to think about various matters.

   Your point of view inevitably suffuses any analysis, since you are the one selecting the evidence and offering the observations about it, but your point of view (POV) should not be foregrounded—at least not as a like/dislike. Insofar as your POV does enter overtly as judgment, that should come after you've analyzed the data and come to a conclusion about what the text thinks or is "saying." In the case of a literary text or a film, your comments should address the work, not a character. Don't offer your POV on Hamlet as if he were a person (he's not); rather, offer your POV on the play's POV of Hamlet.
2. **Choose a limited piece of concrete evidence to focus on.** Select a passage that you find interesting, that you have questions about, probably one that you don't quite understand. That way the writing will have some work to do—to help you understand it by putting your thoughts into some kind of sustained analytical form. Always write out the quote and include the page number. The act of copying it will often induce you to notice more about it.
3. **Contextualize the evidence.** Where does it come from in the text? Who is saying what where to whom when about what? Briefly answering these questions will prevent you from taking things out of context. Identifying the source of the language—the speaker, the POV—is key here, because it always matters who is producing the language you are looking at.
4. **Make observations about the evidence:** stay close to the evidence; dwell with it—most writers leave it far too quickly to launch into generalizations that are often clichés. What words seem interesting and important to you, and why? Try to *paraphrase* parts of the passage; this is one of the best ways of beginning to define and question and get ideas about the evidence. Attend to the possibility of multiple meanings; ask yourself what key words mean; notice the metaphorical use of language as opposed to literal statements, and so forth.
5. **Share your reasoning about what the evidence means as you move from observation to implication.** Remember that evidence can never speak for itself; you need to explain how and why it means what you claim it means.
6. **Culminate your discussion by openly addressing the representativeness of your passage.** That is, move from your analysis of local details to address what, given your analysis, the work is "saying" about this or that issue or question. Even if you are running out of time, you should leap to this move—with a sentence like "I'm out of time, but my big point is . . ."—before you stop.

It is often productive to take the focused freewrite and type it, revising and further freewriting until you have filled the inevitable gaps in your thinking that the time limit has created. Eventually, you can build up, through a process of accretion, the thinking for an entire paper in this way.

Try this 4.3: Keeping a Reading Journal

Realistically, there probably isn't time (or at least enough discipline) to do a passage-based focused freewriting at the end of every extended reading session you do. A less labor-intensive alternative is to keep a reading journal, which can supply selections for the focused freewritings and has the added benefit, in an academic setting, of preparing you for class. (This is the standard preparatory assignment for all of our classes: to bring one sentence from the reading that you think it is important for the class to discuss, with some jotted reasons why.)

To keep a reading journal, simply copy key sentences from the reading. How many is up to you—say, at least three—and then briefly make a few informal comments about them: which words you think are key, what the passage leads you to think, how it connects to something else you are reading or thinking about, its anomalous relationship to most of the text, whatever strikes you. The reading journal will not only help make class discussion more substantive—that is, less windy, general, and prone to merely personal likes and dislikes—but more important, you will be compiling your own "book" of the course as you go along—an invaluable resource for writing papers and studying for exams.

In addition, the sheer act of copying (typing is fine) the quotes will sensitize you to the style of the writers you are reading. As chapters 10 and especially 11 discuss, style is essential knowledge, because it is the shape that thinking takes. You will be surprised at what you notice for the first time just in the act of copying.

PARAPHRASE × 3

The exercise we call Paraphrase × 3 offers the quickest means of seeing how a little writing about what you're reading can lead to having ideas about it. Paraphrasing is an activity we introduce in our overture of essential analytical skills in Chapter 1 as a tool for beginning to interpret because it tends to uncover areas of uncertainty and find questions.

Paraphrasing is commonly misunderstood as summary—a way of shrinking an idea you've read about—or perhaps as simply a way to avoid plagiarism by "putting it in your own words." Rather, *the goal of paraphrasing is to open up the possible meanings of the words*; it's a mode of inquiry.

Paraphrasing is particularly helpful in getting you beyond the problem of using secondary sources encountered in your reading as final answers, which can leave you with nothing to say on your own. By paraphrasing you can begin to work your way around a quotation, to see various ways it might be interpreted. (See Chapter 12.) Along the same lines, paraphrasing is essential in making evidence speak—that is, in not leaving it to speak for itself (because it won't do so adequately—see Chapter 5).

When you paraphrase, don't just go for the gist; replace all of the key words. The new words you come up with represent first stabs at interpretation, at having ideas about what you are reading.

If you paraphrase a key passage from a reading several (say, three) times, you will discover that it gets you working with the language. But you need to paraphrase *slavishly*. You can't let yourself just go for the gist; replace all of the key words. The new words you will be forced to come up with represent first stabs at interpretation, at having (small) ideas about what you are reading by unearthing a range of possible meanings embedded in the passage. Then, you will have *something to do* with your writing about the reading beyond simply recording it or agreeing/disagreeing with it.

Try this 4.4: Doing Paraphrase × 3

Recast the substantive language of something you are reading into other words that mean as close to the same thing as possible. Try not to make the language more general. Paraphrasing does not condense—that's the job of summary. Regardless of what you paraphrase, remember this key: it is in successive recastings that the meaning grows in depth and variousness.

You might begin with two of our favorite candidates for paraphrase × 3:

- *"I am entitled to my opinion."*
- *"We hold these truths to be self-evident."*

(It is interesting to note that Thomas Jefferson originally wrote the words "sacred and undeniable" in his draft of the Declaration of Independence, instead of "self-evident." So what?)

The productive power of the exercise is more evident when you shift to something more challenging—say, a passage you find central or difficult in any of your assigned reading, the kind of passage most likely to attract yellow highlighter.

SUMMARY

Summary is the standard way that reading—not just facts and figures but also other people's theories and observations—enters your writing. The aim of summarizing is to recount (in effect, to reproduce) someone else's ideas, to achieve sufficient understanding of them to converse productively with what you have been reading.

Summary and analysis go hand in hand. Neither aims to approve or disapprove of its subject; the goal for both is to understand rather than evaluate.

Summary is a necessary early step in analysis because it provides *perspective* on the subject as a whole by explaining the meaning and function of each of that subject's parts. Within larger analyses—papers or reports—summary performs the essential function of *contextualizing* your subject accurately. It creates a fair picture of what's there. If you don't take the time to get your whole subject in perspective, you will be more prone to misrepresenting it in your analysis.

But summarizing isn't simply the unanalytical reporting of information; it's more than just shrinking someone else's words. To write an accurate summary, you have to ask analytical questions, such as the following:

- Which of the ideas in the reading are most significant? Why?
- How do these ideas fit together?
- What do the key passages in the reading mean?

Summarizing is, then, like paraphrasing, a tool of understanding and not just a mechanical task. But a summary stops short of in-depth analysis because summarizing typically makes much smaller interpretive leaps.

When summaries go wrong, they are just lists. At best, they do very little logical connecting among the parts beyond "next."

STRATEGIES FOR MAKING SUMMARIES MORE ANALYTICAL

What information should be included and what excluded? This is the perennial question that summarizing raises. When summaries go wrong, they are just lists. A list is a simple "this and then this and then this" sequence. Sometimes lists are random, as in a shopping list compiled from the first thing you thought of to the last. Sometimes they are organized: fruit and vegetables here, dried goods there. At best, they do very little logical connecting among the parts beyond "next."

Summaries that are just lists tend to dollop out the information monotonously. They omit the *thinking* that the piece is doing—the ways it is connecting the information, the contexts it establishes, and the implicit slant or point of view. Be aware that the thinking the piece is doing is not necessarily the same as the ideas it may contain. Two articles on European attitudes toward the younger Bush's presidency, for example, may contain essentially the same information but vary widely in how they assemble it, how they connect the dots. Writing analytical summaries can teach you how to read for the connections, the lines that connect the dots. And when you're operating at that level, you are much more likely to have ideas about what you are summarizing. Here are five strategies for seeing and connecting the dots in what you are reading and, by extension, for deciding what to include and exclude in your summaries.

1. **Look for the underlying structure.** Use the strategy of looking for patterns of repetition and contrast. (See Chapter 2.) Even if you apply it to just a few selected paragraphs, it will provide you with the terms that get repeated, and these will almost always suggest strands, which in turn make up the organizing contrasts. This tool, in other words, works to

categorize and then further organize information and, in so doing, to bring out the underlying structure of the reading you are summarizing.

2. **Select the information that you wish to discuss on some principle other than general coverage (usually "and-then" lists) of the material.** Use the Notice-and-focus strategy to *rank* these items in some order of importance. (See Chapter 1.) Let's say that you are writing a paper on major changes in the tax law or on recent developments in U.S. policy toward Eastern Europe. Rather than simply collecting the information, try to arrange it into hierarchies. What are the least or most significant changes or developments, and why? Which are most overlooked or most overrated or most controversial or most practical, and why? All of these terms—*significant*, *overlooked*, and so forth—have the effect of focusing the summary. In other words, they will guide your decisions about what to include and exclude. As you rank, however, it is important to distinguish between the rankings that are implicit within the piece (for a strict summary) and your own rankings of the material (for beginning to use the summary in a context of your own).
3. **Reduce the scope of what you choose to summarize, and say more about less.** Both the looking-for-pattern and Notice-and-focus strategies inevitably involve some loss of breadth; you won't be able to cover everything. But this is usually a trade-off worth making. Your ability to rank parts of your subject or choose a particularly revealing feature or pattern to focus on will give you surer control of the material than if you just reproduce what is in the text. You can still begin with a brief survey of major points to provide context, before narrowing the focus.

   Reducing scope is an especially efficient and productive strategy when you are trying to understand a reading you find difficult or perplexing. It will move you beyond passive summarizing and toward having ideas about the reading. If, for example, you are reading Chaucer's *Canterbury Tales* and start cataloguing what makes it funny, you are likely to end up with unanalyzed plot summary—a list that arranges its elements in no particular order. But narrowing the question to "How does Chaucer's use of religious commentary contribute to the humor of 'The Wife of Bath's Tale'?" reduces the scope to a single tale and the humor to a single aspect of humor. Describe those as accurately as you can, and you will begin to notice things.
4. **Get some detachment: shift your focus from *what?* to *how?* and *why?*** Most readers tend to get too single-minded about absorbing the information. That is, they attend only to the *what:* what the reading is saying or is about. They take it all in passively. But through an act of will, as a tool in your repertoire, you can deliberately shift your focus to *how* it says what it says, and *why*. If, for example, you were asked to discuss the major discoveries that Darwin made on *The Beagle*, you could avoid simply listing his conclusions by redirecting your attention to *how* he proceeds. You could choose to focus, for example, on Darwin's use of the scientific method, examining how he builds and, in some cases, discards hypotheses. Or you might select several passages that illustrate how

Darwin proceeded from evidence to conclusion and then *rank* them in order of importance to the overall theory. Notice that in shifting the emphasis to Darwin's thinking—the *how* and *why*—you would not be excluding the *what* (the information component) from your discussion.

Let's take one more example. If you were studying the reasons the American colonies rebelled against England, so broad a subject would tend to produce passive summary—a list of standard generalizations about the American Revolution. But what if you narrowed the focus to the Boston Tea Party and considered how American and British history textbooks differ in their treatment of this crucial event? Note that this question would still enable you to address, though in much more focused form, the broader question of why the colonies rebelled.

Try this 4.5: Coverage versus Ranking

Write two summaries of the same article or book chapter. Make the first one consecutive—that is, try to cover the piece by essentially listing the key points as they appear. Limit yourself to a typed page. Then rewrite the summary, doing the following:

- rank the items in order of importance according to some principle that you designate, explaining your rationale;
- eliminate the last few items on the list, or at most, give each a single sentence; and
- use the space you have saved to include more detail about the most important item or two.

The second half of this assignment will probably require closer to two pages.

B. WHAT TO DO WITH THE READING: AVOIDING THE MATCHING EXERCISE

What does it mean "to do something with the reading"? Obviously, you can paraphrase, summarize, or do a focused freewrite with it, but these exercises aim primarily to establish a more accurate, active, and rich understanding of what the reading is doing and saying. That's why they are included under the heading "How to Read: Words Matter." When, by contrast, you *do* something with the reading, you use it for purposes that are different from the aims of the reading itself. This distinction holds for all kinds of reading, not just the academic or literary varieties. In a guide to bike repair, you might paraphrase the directions for replacing the brakes to make sure your understanding of this complex procedure is sufficiently clear. But if you use the knowledge you've gained to fix the brakes on some other machine, adapting what you've learned, you'll be doing something with the reading.

Much of the rest of this book suggests ways of negotiating what you read. In Chapter 12, for example, we concentrate on how to use secondary research. For now, we will discuss four basic approaches to doing things with the reading:

- applying a reading as a lens for examining something else
- comparing one reading with another
- using a reading as a model for writing
- uncovering the assumptions in a reading—where the piece is "coming from"

APPLYING A READING AS A LENS

Problem: A matching exercise, a mere demonstration of applicability.

Solution: Emphasize the shift in context, and then seek out areas of dissonance to analyze.

We apply what we read all the time. It's a standard academic assignment. You read an article on gender and blue jeans and then connect its ideas to something else—how, for example, magazine ads represent jeans-wearing with respect to gender. Or you study Freud's *The Interpretation of Dreams* and then analyze a dream of your own or a friend's as you project what Freud would have done. Or you apply his theory of repression to the behavior of a character in a novel or to some newfound realization about your mother's occasional bouts of frenzied housecleaning or your father's zealous weeding when he's upset. Freud thus becomes a *lens* for seeing the subject.

But what about taking an article on liberation theology as practiced by certain Catholic priests in Latin America and applying it to the rise of Islamic fundamentalism in the Middle East? Or for that matter, what about applying the directions for fixing the brakes on a bicycle to the analogous task on a car? Obviously, the original texts may be somewhat useful, but there are also significant differences between the two religious movements and between the two kinds of brakes.

So what should you do? When using a reading as a lens for better seeing what is going on in something you are studying, assume that the match between the lens and your subject will never be exact. It is often in the area where things don't match up exactly that you will find your best opportunity for having ideas.

Think about how lens A both fits and does not fit subject B: use the differences to develop your analysis.

The big problem with the way most people apply a reading is that they do so too indiscriminately, too generally. They essentially construct a *matching exercise* in which each of a set of ideas drawn from text A is made to equate with a corresponding element (an idea or a fact) from subject B, often in virtual list-like fashion. Matching exercises are more useful in some contexts than in others (great for fixing your bike's brakes, less so for analyzing your parents). At their worst, matching exercises are static, mechanical, and inaccurate. This is because they concentrate on similarities and forget the rest. As a result, the lens screens out what it cannot bring into focus, and the writer applying it distorts what he or she sees. Like an optometrist figuring out the new prescription for your glasses, you need to constantly adjust the lens whenever you bring it to new material. Don't just slap on A: really think about how it both fits *and* doesn't fit B.

Remember that whenever you apply lens A to a new subject B, you are taking A from its original context and using its ideas in at least somewhat different circumstances for at least somewhat different purposes. How does this shift change things, and thus, how may it require you to refocus the lens? Freud's theory of repression wasn't actually talking about your father, after all. The goal is not to dismiss Freud but to adjust his thinking to the particular case. There's always the danger that the reading you're applying will become a club to bludgeon your subject into submission.

Applying a Reading as a Lens: An Example Here is an excerpted version of a student paper that uses the theoretical lens of racial difference to examine Shakespeare's *The Tempest*. The writer considers the way the fatherly power figure and sorcerer Prospero, the ruler of the island where he has been shipwrecked, treats the creature Caliban, whom he finds there and enslaves. We have put inside brackets some commentary on how the writer applies the lens. Brackets and ellipses [. . .] indicate where we have abridged the essay.

> In their *Introduction to Literature, Criticism, and Theory*, Andrew Bennett and Nicholas Royle devote one chapter to the theme of "Racial Difference." They begin this chapter with a reference to Charlotte Bronte's novel *Jane Eyre*, and from this standpoint, they discuss a character in the book named Bertha, a West Indian Creole bound by chains in her white husband's attic. Of a scene in the narrative—told by the white female narrator—wherein Bertha's appearance is described, they write: "No longer a woman, Bertha is the other of humanity, unrecognizable as human, a beast with a purely animal physiognomy. Almost invisible, Bertha cannot be seen. Invisibility, as this suggests [. . .] is the condition of racial otherness" (199). [The writer begins by introducing the theoretical lens.]

> It is in such a way that Prospero's narrative portrays Caliban. As *The Tempest* was initially performed in seventeenth-century England, the audience to whom Prospero delivers his epilogue is primarily, if not fully, white—thus, racially homogeneous. And as Bennett and Royle further remind us, "Western humanism necessarily defines itself through racial otherness, by constructing a racial other which then stands in opposition to the humanity of the racially homogeneous" (201). Taking this into account, we begin to see how the construction of Caliban as his nonhuman other, by blatant contrast, could make Prospero seem all the more human to his racially alike audience. [Here the writer applies the theory. Note how he takes care to differentiate the context, suggesting a particularly seventeenth-century reading of the racism.]

> The narrative achieves this end by utilizing the speech of several characters in the play to represent Caliban's behavior, nature, and physiognomy as decisively nonhuman. This narratological effect is carried out in several ways,

mostly through appeals to a colonialist audience: by the portrayal of Caliban as verbally belligerent; by asserting that he once tried to rape Prospero's virgin daughter Miranda; by having nearly every character he encounters regard him as a monster on account of his appearance; and by scripting nearly every character, including Caliban himself, to believe that his nature is naturally that of a slave for the colonialist project. [The writer now moves confidently beyond the theoretical reading into his own analysis of Shakespeare's text.]

[. . .] Thus, Caliban's physiognomy in this colony is that of a monster. Such a reference is made numerous times throughout the narrative. In the second scene of the second act, we find several malicious racial slurs referring to Caliban, which in Prospero's narrative are delivered humorously by the drunken butler and jester, Stephano and Trinculo respectively. When Trinculo encounters Caliban lying motionless upon the ground, he observes: "What have we here, a man or a fish? Dead or alive? A fish, he smells like a fish, a very ancient and fishlike smell" (II, ii, 24–26). Soon thereafter, both Trinculo and Stephano refer to Caliban as a "mooncalf" (II, ii, 101, 106); by this they are referring to him as monstrous or as a freak. [As the essay nears its end, the writer has begun to focus on the details for making his case about the play's incorporation of Elizabethan racism.]

This is an effective application of a theoretical lens to open up a text to analysis from a particular interpretive context. The next step the writer might take if he were to extend the discussion would be to ponder the ways that subject B does *not* fit lens A. So what, for example, that Caliban is not "invisible" (199)? And does the play in any way contradict the quote from page 201 by, say, humanizing Caliban despite Prospero's attempts to dehumanize him? Nonetheless, the writer has done very well to recognize and then develop the implications of the different historical context.

Try this 4.6: Using a Quotation as a Lens

Using the preceding paper excerpt as a model, apply the following generalization about talk shows to a talk show of your choice: "These shows obviously offer a distorted vision of America, thrive on feeling rather than thought, and worship the sound-byte rather than the art of conversation" (Stark 243). Alternatively, take any general claim you find in your reading and apply it to some other text or subject. Either way, strive to produce several paragraphs in which you avoid the matching exercise and instead probe both lens A and subject B.

COMPARING AND CONTRASTING ONE READING WITH ANOTHER

Problem: Stopping too soon, with only a list of similarities and differences.

Solution: Look for difference within similarity or for similarity despite difference.

Comparing and contrasting is another traditional assignment done with readings that falls flat when it turns into a mechanical matching exercise. Comparing readings resembles applying a reading as a lens. These activities are not intended as ends in themselves; they almost always contribute to some larger process of understanding.

The rationale for working comparatively is that you can usually discover ideas about a reading much more easily when you are not viewing it in isolation. You can observe it from a different perspective, in relation to something else. When used in this way, the comparison is usually not a 50-50 split; you've moved to a comparison of A with B because you want to better understand A.

In short, a good comparison should open up a reading, not close it down. It does more than demonstrate that you've "done the reading." We're all completely familiar with the formulaic conclusions to the comparisons produced by the matching-exercise mentality: "Thus, we see there are many similarities and differences between A and B." Perfunctory, pointless, and inert lists: that's what you get if you stop the process of comparing and contrasting too soon, before you've focused and explored something interesting that you notice.

A good comparison should open up a reading, not close it down.

How do you avoid the ubiquitous matching-exercise habit? Here are three guidelines for productively comparing A with B:

1. **Focus the comparison to give it a point.** A comparison won't have a point inherently—you need to consciously give it one. It's often useful to assume that what you have originally taken for a point has not yet gone far enough and is still too close to summary. Rather than sticking with a range of broad comparisons, try to focus on a key comparison, one that you find interesting or revealing. (Looking for patterns, Notice and focus, and other tools can help you select your focus.) Although narrowing the focus in this way might seem to eliminate other important areas of consideration, in fact it usually allows you to incorporate at least some of these other areas in a more tightly connected, less list-like fashion.

   If, to return to an earlier example, you were to compare the representations of the Boston Tea Party in British and American history texts, you would *begin but not stop* with identifying similarities and differences. The goal of your reading would be to focus on some particular matches that seem especially revealing—for example, that British and American texts trace the economic background of the incident in different ways. Then, in response to the So what? question, you could attempt to develop some explanation of what these differences reveal and why they are significant. You might, for example, decide that the British texts view the matter from a more global economic perspective, whereas American texts emphasize nationalism.

2. **Look for significant difference between A and B, given their similarity.** One of the best ways to arrive at a meaningful and interesting focus is to follow a principle that we call *looking for difference within similarity*. The procedure is simple but virtually guaranteed to produce a focused idea.
   - **a.** First, deal with the similarity. Identify what you take to be the essential similarity and then ask and answer, So what? Why is this similarity significant?
   - **b.** Then, in this context, identify the differences that you notice.
   - **c.** Choose one difference you find particularly revealing or interesting, and again ask, So what? What is the significance of this difference?

   You can repeat this procedure with a range of key similarities and differences. Can you think of ways that the various differences are connected?

   The phrase *difference within similarity* is to remind you that once you have started your thinking by locating apparent similarities, you can usually refine that thinking by pursuing significant, though often less obvious, distinctions among the similar things. In Irish studies, for example, scholars characteristically acknowledge the extent to which contemporary Irish culture is the product of colonization. To this extent, Irish culture shares certain traits with other former colonies in Africa, Asia, Latin America, and elsewhere. But instead of simply demonstrating how Irish culture fits the general pattern of colonialism, these scholars also isolate the ways that Ireland *does not fit* the model. They focus, for example, on how its close geographical proximity and racial similarity to England, its colonizer, have distinguished the kinds of problems it encounters today from those characteristic of the more generalized model of colonialism. In effect, looking for difference within similarity has led them to locate and analyze the anomalies. (See the end of the next chapter for an extended example of looking for difference within similarity.)
3. **Look for unexpected similarity between A and B, given their difference.** A corollary of the preceding principle is that you should focus on *unexpected similarity rather than obvious difference*. The fact that in the Bush presidency Republicans differ from Democrats on environmental policy is probably a less promising focal point than their surprising agreement on violating the so-called lockbox policy against tapping Social Security funds to finance government programs. Most readers would expect the political parties to differ on the environment, and a comparison of their positions could lead you to do little more than summarizing. But a surprising similarity, like an unexpected difference, necessarily raises questions for you to pursue: do the parties' shared positions against the lockbox policy, for example, share the same motives?

Try this 4.7: Looking for Significant Difference or Unexpected Similarity

This exercise is based on those strategies that aim at getting you to rank your comparisons and contrasts by some principle—as the "Try this" on summary invited you to do—as a means of getting beyond a pointless matching exercise.

Choose any item from the list that follows, and practice reading comparatively. After you've done the research necessary to locate material to read and analyze, list as many similarities and differences as you can: go for coverage. Then, review your list, and select the two or three most revealing similarities and the two or three most revealing differences. At this point, you are ready to write a few paragraphs in which you argue for the significance of a key difference or similarity. In so doing, you may find it interesting to focus on an *unexpected* similarity or difference—one that others might not initially notice. (We recommend trying the "unexpected" gambit.)

1. accounts of the same event from two different newspapers or magazines or textbooks
2. two CDs (or even songs) by the same artist or group
3. two ads for the same kind of product
4. graffiti in men's bathrooms versus graffiti in women's bathrooms
5. the political campaigns of two opponents running for the same or similar office
6. courtship behavior as practiced by men and by women
7. two breeds of dog
8. two clothing styles as emblematic of socioeconomic class or a subgroup in your school, town, or workplace

Obviously, these paragraphs could also easily grow into a full-fledged paper.

READING AND WRITING DEFINITIONS

Before leaving comparison/contrast, we would like to pause briefly to consider a common kind of reading-based writing assignment: the definition. Like comparison/contrast, definition can easily fall prey to pointlessness, unless you can give it a point. In other words, definition is meaningful only within some context: you define "rhythm and blues" because it is essential to any further discussion of the evolution of rock 'n' roll music; or because you need that definition to discuss the British Invasion spearheaded by groups such as The Beatles, The Rolling Stones, and The Yardbirds in the late 1960s; or because you cannot classify John Lennon or Mick Jagger or Eric Clapton without it. When you construct a summary of existing definitions with no clear sense of purpose, you tend to list definitions indiscriminately. As a result, you are likely to overlook conflicts among the various definitions and overemphasize their surface similarities.

It is usually effective whenever you need to define a key term to sample a range of definitions. This will enable you to achieve some perspective on the term, to understand its richness of implication. In such cases, you can simply list definitions from a range of sources by exploring competing parts or versions of the definition. The definition of capitalism that you might take from Karl Marx, for example, will differ in its emphases from Adam Smith's. In this case, you would not only isolate the most important of these differences but also try to account for the fact that Marx's villain is Smith's hero. Such an accounting would probably lead you to consider how the definition has been shaped by each of these writers' political philosophies or by the culture in which each theory was composed.

Notice that proceeding in this way also makes use of the strategy called "The Pitch, the Complaint, and the Moment." Many exercises in definition involve attempts to correct or find a problem with the way someone else has defined a term. They exploit difference. Others, it should be noted, look for unexpected similarity among apparently disparate definitions.

Try this 4.8: Defining in Depth

This chapter has been suggesting in different contexts that analytical acts require productive tension. The simple application of a lens as a matching exercise too easily becomes mechanical and directionless. A paper on alcoholism, for example, would lose focus if a writer were to use all of the definitions available. If, instead, she could convert the act of definition into a comparison and contrast of competing definitions, her writing would have more analytical edge, and it would more easily achieve a point and purpose for the definition. With an eye to the pitch, the complaint, and the moment, she would also be able to query whether the reading was defining alcoholism as primarily moral or physiological or psychological.

Using this example as a model, write a comparative definition in which you seek out different and potentially competing definitions of the same term or terms. Begin with a dictionary such as the *Oxford English Dictionary* (popularly known as the *OED*, available in most library reference rooms) that contains both historically based definitions that track the term's evolution over time and etymological definitions that identify the linguistic origins of the term—what the words from which it came (in older languages) mean. Locate both the etymology and the historical evolution of the term or terms.

Then look up the term in one, or preferably several, specialized dictionaries. We offer a list of some of these in Chapter 13, "Finding and Citing Sources," but you can also ask your reference librarian for pertinent titles. Summarize key differences and similarities among the ways the dictionaries have defined your term or terms. Then write several paragraphs—or even a comparative essay in which you argue for the significance of a key similarity or difference, or an unexpected one.

Here is the list of words: *hysteria, ecstasy, enthusiasm, witchcraft, leisure, gossip, bachelor, spinster, romantic, instinct, punk, thug, pundit, dream, alcoholism, aristocracy, atom, ego, pornography, conservative, liberal, entropy, election, tariff.* Some of these words are interesting to look at together, such as *ecstasy/enthusiasm* or *liberal/conservative* or *bachelor/spinster.* Feel free to write on a pair instead of a single word.

READING, BINARY THINKING, AND AVOIDING AGREE/DISAGREE

Binary thinking looms large in this chapter's approach to reading critically. As we have seen, binary thinking is a form implicit in our treatment of comparison and contrast. It also informs the solution we offer to energizing writing definitions—to exploit the tension among competing versions of what a word means.

Most important, readings can be mapped in terms of a primary binary of pitch versus complaint. In terms of readings, this binary marks pivotal sites of anxiety or concern, an index of what the reading is grappling with.

Creating opposing categories (binary oppositions) is fundamental to defining things. But binaries are also dangerous because they can invite reductive thinking—oversimplifying a subject by eliminating alternatives between the two extremes. This is the danger posed by the agree/disagree move. Often it is invited by a paper assignment that involves reading comparatively, asking writers to take sides between two positions or to agree or disagree with a given position. This wording is potentially misleading, as you are rarely being asked for as *unqualified* an opinion as agree or disagree. In such cases, beware agreeing or disagreeing 100% with almost any position. The wiser move is usually to locate something you agree with and something you may wish to qualify.

Seek alternatives to agreeing and disagreeing with readings. Look instead for the binaries that inform the reader and observe how the writer qualifies and recasts them.

Your best strategy in dealing with agree/disagree questions is to start not by choosing one side or the other and arguing for it, but with some more expository (explanatory) mode, such as comparison and contrast or definition, that will help you understand what is at stake on each side of the opposition. In most cases, if you take time to analyze the agree/disagree issue, you will come to question its terms and ultimately to arrive at a more complex and qualified position to write about. You should aim, in other words, at using the binary split to organize the issue, but then move beyond the generally oversimplified either/or format to discuss how both sides of the issue are related.

USING A READING AS A MODEL

Most of the critical activities that people do with readings involve assimilating and thinking about the information that is being conveyed to them. But to use a reading as a model is to *focus instead on presentation*. This represents a change in orientation for most readers, and it takes a little practice to learn how to do it. A useful guideline to remember is *look beyond content* (or subject matter).

We are, for the most part, "seduced" by the content of what we read, so we do not see how the piece is "behaving"—how it sets us up, how it repeats certain phrases, how it is patterned. This is the analytical function of focusing on presentation. To focus on presentation is to focus on what a piece of writing *does* rather than on what it *says*. It involves *describing*, as closely as you can, how the piece of writing proceeds—what it does first, then what, then what, and so forth. Consider, for example, what the following sentence does: "Time flies like an arrow; fruit flies like a banana." The first half of the sentence is an old proverb that compares the passage of time to the flight of an arrow. The second half appears to be another comparison presented in exactly the same way. But it's actually a set-up designed to trick readers into misreading, giving us an image of flying fruit rather than of fruit-eating insects. *Flies* is a verb in the first half of the sentence but a noun in the second half. *Like* is a comparative in the first half but a verb in the second half.

Concentrating on presentation—on what the writing is doing—is necessary when you are using a reading as a model. Using a reading as a lens can often come close to adopting it as a model, if we are, say, using the same key terms, the same interpretive context, and perhaps, the same general subject as our model reading. If you were to do an analysis of programs designed to help smokers quit by using an analysis of programs designed to help drinkers quit, the latter might be used as a model for the former. If the drinking cessation piece began with a long anecdote to phrase some central problem in program design, and you then began your piece with an analogous problem serving the same aim for your piece, that would represent a use of a reading as a model.

Consider the following essay opening in regard to presentation. Try to look beyond content to focus on how it behaves, on what it does.

> Why is something comic? Philosophers and social commentators and literary artists have spent millennia trying to answer that question definitively—and failing. At least there still is no consensus, no one theory to which most people subscribe.
>
> The comic is often thought of in opposition to the serious. Consider that often-heard phrase "I was just kidding." When do we hear it uttered? Almost always it's when the kidding has gone too far, and the one thing we know for sure is that the speaker, though he or she may have *also* been kidding, was not *just* kidding. He or she was using humor as a way of speaking the truth.
>
> This suggests at least two ideas about the comic: (1) that it is a way of being serious. And (2) that it is a way of using language that operates under different rules from "normal," non-kidding speech. So the serious/comic opposition is dubious at best, and probably downright false. What lies underneath "I was just

> kidding" is the notion that we cannot easily speak what we take to be a truth about another person without pretending not to mean it. What might we conclude from these two ideas? The term we need to oppose to *the comic* is not *serious* but *solemn* or *sober;* for, far from being trivial and unserious, the comic is a rhetoric for voicing matters that are profoundly serious.

How would we describe this piece as a model? Here's one version of how the behavior of the opening paragraph might be described, sentence by sentence:

- It opens by asking a rhetorical question about an abstract subject (the comic).
- It then locates the question in a broad cultural and historical context (it mentions different kinds of thinkers and a long range of time) and concludes anti-climactically—that is, it frustrates the expectation that the question can be answered, but not until the end of the sentence *(failing).*
- It then qualifies this rather bold assertion (of no consensus), shrinking the claim that there is no definitive answer to the question to suggest that there may be a range of answers.

The second paragraph of the example then immediately picks up one approach to defining the comic, offers an example, and begins to analyze it. And so forth.

The larger point that we wish to illustrate here is that a reading can be understood as a series of rhetorical moves—a shift from what something says to what it invites us to think and by what means. (See "The Psychology of Form" in Chapter 9 for more on this.) Moreover, to view a reading in this way is to gain privileged knowledge about it, to understand it more actively and with surer control than is available just from memorizing the information it contains.

When you read try detaching from the pure information-assimilation mode to observe *how* the reading says *what* it says. Where does it make claims? What kind of evidence does it provide? Does the writer overtly reveal his or her premises? How and when does she use metaphors or analogies?

Not all reading proceeds in a straight narrative line from A to B to C. Some pieces are organized like quilts, a series of patches or vignettes operating as variations on a theme.

And what about the overall organization of the piece you are reading? Not all reading proceeds in a straight narrative line from A to B to C. Some pieces are organized like quilts, a series of patches or vignettes operating as variations on a theme. Others favor a radial organization—locating some central issue or example in the center, and then spiraling out to connect it to other matters, then returning to it again and spiraling out again. A 10-on-1 analysis often takes this form, with the writer returning to the 1 for more details to explore.

Inexperienced writers sometimes resist using readings as models because they fear that imitation will suppress their ability to think for themselves. In practice this fear usually proves ungrounded. Learning to see how other writers organize their thinking expands rather than closes down your range as both a reader and a writer.

WAYS TO MARK WHAT A READING DOES (RATHER THAN SAYS)

There is no single way to mark what a reading does. How you describe its behavior will probably depend on the context within which you are studying it. If your goal is to use it as a model for imitation, it would probably make sense to proceed like the essay on comedy, focusing on the writer's rhetorical moves. To some extent that would also entail identifying how the writer uses evidence *(E)*, claim *(C)*, complication *(CL)*, transition *(TR)*, and restatement *(R)*. These initials might be used to mark up any reading to discern what it is doing. And obviously, others could be added (*TOP* for a topic sentence, *M* for a metaphor, *TH* for thesis, and so forth). Transitions are, by the way, particularly useful sites for readers attempting to use a reading as a model. Because transitions typically reach backward to what has already been said before they look forward, they offer us quick reviews and reassessments of the writer's lines of thought.

Even if you do not intend to imitate a reading as a model, there is abundant reason to mark up the readings that you are studying for what that practice can reveal. Close engagement with the text is next to impossible unless you mark it up. If you don't like writing in books, photocopy the relevant pages so that you can free yourself to do the on-the-page sketch work that is essential to careful thinking about the reading. The heuristic Looking for patterns of repetition and contrast (the Method) suggests another vocabulary for marking a reading—less for imitation of its interpretive moves than for analysis of its verbal underpinnings. In this case, you could

- circle repeated words and keep track of how often they repeat
- mark strands—words that repeat as part of a pattern of the same or similar kinds of language—and connect them with lines (aka strands)
- designate in the margins key organizing contrasts, writing the terms next to a +/- sign
- star anomalies

In addition, make use of *marginalia*—brief notes to yourself about what you notice or your response to it. If your reading is marked with these signs and notes, you will inevitably become more conversant with it and better able to find your way around in it. More important, though, the reading will begin to reveal its structure and concerns. Often it will disclose secrets of which it (or its author) may be unaware. See, in this context, the discussion at the end of this chapter on reading with and against the grain.

Try this 4.9: Describing and Marking What a Reading Does

Describe the final two paragraphs of the excerpt from the comedy essay, along the lines that the first paragraph has been described. Where are the claims *(C)*? Where are the qualifications of the claims *(Q)*? How does the discussion progress? Then try marking the essay, using either the claim-evidence language or the repetition-strand-contrast language. What do you learn?

UNCOVERING THE ASSUMPTIONS IN A READING

Uncovering assumptions is a primary and powerful move in reading analytically. We have devoted an extended analysis to it at the end of Chapter 3. Since this move—also known as "reasoning back to premises"—is such an important tool in a reader's arsenal, we will briefly revisit the topic here.

An assumption is the basic ground of belief from which a position springs, its starting points or "givens." All arguments or articulations of point of view have underlying assumptions. All readings are built on assumptions. A lot of the time, assumptions are not visible; they are *implicit*, which is why they need to be inferred as a discrete critical act.

Sometimes a text hides its premises (a pro-Nazi website, for example, that is ostensibly concerned with the increasing disorder of society). Sometimes a source just doesn't divulge its premises and perhaps does not know them. In any case, when you locate assumptions in a text, you understand the text better—where it's coming from and what else it believes that is more fundamental than what it is overtly declaring.

Chapter 3 offers a step-by-step procedure for uncovering assumptions. The essential move is to ask, "Given its overt claim, what must this reading also already believe?" To answer this question you need to make inferences from the primary claims to the ideas that underlie them. In effect, you are working backward, reinventing the chain of thinking that led the writer to the position you are analyzing.

Try this 4.10: What Must the Writer Also Already Believe?

Here's a prime example of a statement that conceals a wealth of assumptions. In the reference application sent to professors for students who are seeking to enter a student-teaching program, the professor is asked to rank the student from one to four (unacceptable to acceptable) on the following criterion: "The student uses his/her sense of humor appropriately."

What must the writers of the recommendation form also already believe? Compile a list of their assumptions. Here are two strategies that can help you do this:

- Do Paraphrase x 3 on the quotation (the explicit claim) to help you see the range of implicit ideas attached to it.
- Articulate what the claim is *not* saying, because understanding that will often bring into relief the underlying positions that it is saying.

For more practice, locate a statement from anything you are reading that you find interesting or challenging. Paraphrase it. Then uncover assumptions, asking what the text must also already believe, given that it believes this. List at least three assumptions. Or uncover the assumptions in the following enigmatic statement: "Telling others about oneself is, then, no simple matter. It depends on what *we* think *they* think we ought to be like—or what selves in general ought to be like" (Jerome Bruner, *Making Stories: Law, Literature, Life* [Cambridge: Harvard UP, 2002, 66]).

Try this 4.11: Uncovering Assumptions in a Reading

Uncover the assumptions in the following brief excerpt from a student paper. You may choose to apply the procedure for uncovering assumptions given in Chapter 3: (1) paraphrase the explicit claim, (2) list the implicit assumptions (the ideas that the claim assumes to be true), (3) define key terms, and (4) try on an oppositional stance to see if this unearths more underlying assumptions. The result of this process should be a list of the premises upon which the writer's argument operates that the paragraph has not made sufficiently clear. At this point, you might write a page about the paragraph, providing the results of your analytical reading.

> In all levels of trade, including individual, local, domestic, and international, both buyers and sellers are essentially concerned with their own welfare. This self-interest, however, actually contributes to the health and growth of the economy as a whole. Each country benefits by exporting those goods in which it has an advantage and importing goods in which it does not. Importing and exporting allow countries to focus on producing those goods that they can generate most efficiently. As a result of specializing in certain products and then trading them, self-interest leads to efficient trade, which leads to consumer satisfaction.

READING WITH AND AGAINST THE GRAIN

It is useful to think of both written and visual works as independent entities; independent, that is, of their authors, produced by authors but not ultimately controlled by them. The poet Emily Dickinson expresses this idea in a poem about an author sending his or her words into the world. Dickinson writes, "A word is dead / When it is said, / Some say. / I say it just / Begins to live / That day."

If we allow ourselves to think in this way—that writing, once committed to the page and released into the world by its author, comes to have a life of its own—then we are at liberty to see what is going on in that "life" that may or may not have been part of the author's original intention. If we take this writing-as-a-living-creature analogy a step further, we might reasonably grant that a piece of writing (say, a book), like a person, has an unconscious. In other words, we can ask not only what the book knows, what it seems fully aware of, but also what the book is saying that it seems not to know it is saying.

You might now be saying to yourself, "Doesn't this strategy for thinking about writing take us back to the hidden meaning theory that you debunked in Chapter 2?" Well, not really. Surely you have had the experience of looking back on something really good that you have written and wondering where it came from. You hadn't planned to say it that way ahead of time; it just "came out." This suggests that writers and artists are never fully in control of what they communicate, that words and images always, inescapably, communicate more than we intend. So it does not necessarily follow that writers and artists deliberately hide anything from us.

Instead, their work has revealed meanings that they may not have intended to reveal and that they probably didn't know they were revealing. Any of us who has had what we thought to be a perfectly clear and well-intentioned letter misinterpreted (or so we thought) by its recipient can understand this idea. When we look at the letter again, we usually see what it said that we hadn't realized (at least not consciously) we were saying.

When we ask ourselves what a work (and, by implication, an author) might not be aware of communicating, we are doing what is called reading against the grain. When we ask ourselves what a work seems aware of, what its (and, by implication, its author's) conscious intentions are, we are "reading with the grain."

Most good reading starts by reading with the grain, with trying to determine what the work and its author intend. This doesn't mean, as we discussed in Chapter 2, that an author's stated intentions get the last word on what his or her work can be taken to mean. But if we appreciate what authors and artists have to offer us, and if we respect them and the creative process, then we owe it to them and to ourselves to try to determine what they wished to say to us.

A philosophy professor at our college communicates this idea in his lectures when he tries to impersonate whatever philosopher the class is reading by responding to questions as he thinks this philosopher might. In this way, he elicits a *sympathetic reading*, which he argues must always come first.

Both reading with the grain and reading against the grain require us to attend to implication (a concept discussed at length in Chapter 2). Sometimes, what readers might reasonably infer fits less easily with what the piece seems to want to tell us. In this case, we are put in the position of reading against the grain—following something other than the dominant pattern in the writer's thinking.

You can ask not only what the book knows, what it seems fully aware of, but also what the book is saying that it seems not to know it is saying.

For example, in the classic novel *Jane Eyre*, the narrator, Jane, repeatedly remarks on her own plain appearance, with the implication that physical beauty is transient and relatively insignificant. The text is in fact obsessed with her plainness; it is almost obligatory for every new character entering the novel to reflect at some point on Jane's unattractiveness. Not that they don't like Jane—on the contrary, they esteem her greatly even as they acknowledge her lack of physical charms. Are we then to conclude that Jane and the novel believe that physical appearance does not matter? Probably not. Reading against the grain, we'd see the novel's very obsession with plainness as a symptom of how worried it is about the subject, how much it actually believes (but won't admit) that looks matter.

Is reading against the grain—looking for what a work is saying that it might not know it is saying, that it might not mean to say—a hostile and potentially destructive activity? Some authors think so, because writers naturally seek to control the range of meanings their writing communicates. Inquiring into intention can make these writers nervous. They tend to think that the fewer questions asked about their creative process the less likely they will become paralyzed through self-consciousness. Other authors freely admit that writing is a somewhat scary as well as exhilarating process over which they have only tenuous control. Writers in this second camp are more likely to agree that there will be things in their writing—probably things worth finding—that they were not aware of.

In any case, when we seek to uncover assumptions in a reading, we are speculating (making inferences) that may run both with and against the grain. One of the best ways to do this is to use the looking-for-patterns heuristic, which often discovers revealing patterns of repetition of which the author may not be aware.

We can end this discussion of reading with and against the grain by returning to Dickinson's observation that the meaning of words is not fixed when they get put on paper. Her saying that words only begin to live that day is an author's generous acknowledgment that a writer's works belong not just to the writer but also to his or her readers. We cannot make of them what we will (as we argued in opposing the "anything goes" school of interpretation in Chapter 3), but it is part of reading well to uncover ideas and assumptions that are not clearly and obviously evident as part of a writer's stated aims.

Try this 4.12: Appears to Be about X but Is Really about Y

For obvious reasons, this heuristic, introduced in Chapter 3, deserves another try here, in the context of reading with (that is, "about x") and against (that is, "really about y") the grain. You might apply the looking-for-patterns strategy to the passage of your choice to see if it will yield up any implicit, indirect clues to meanings that run counter to the overtly stated ones.

ASSIGNMENT: Writing about Reading

These exercises and essay project apply the concepts offered in this chapter. Many of the "Try this" assignments can be expanded into papers as well.

1. Write a summary of a piece of writing using one or more of the following methods:
   - **a.** Paraphrase × 3
   - **b.** Ranking and reducing scope
   - **c.** Finding the underlying structure
   - **d.** Attending to the pitch, the complaint, and the moment
   - **e.** Passage-based focused freewriting
2. Use a reading as a lens for examining a subject. For example, look at a piece of music or a film through the lens of a review that does not discuss the particular piece or film you are writing about. Or you might read about a particular theory of humor and use that as a lens for examining a comic play, film, story, television show, or stand-up routine.

3. Compare and contrast two readings on the same or similar subjects by looking for significant difference, given their similarities, or unexpected similarity, given their differences.
4. Write an essay in which you develop a position by uncovering the assumptions in a reading or set of related readings. You might try this with an editorial or a batch of editorials on the same subject. Reviews are often a good target for this assignment, because they tend to offer judgments. You could also uncover the assumptions of a policy decision at your school or place of work. This will work best if you have not just the policy but some kind of written manifesto on it. (Policies relating to student life are often quite revealing of what the institution actually thinks of its students.)

GUIDELINES FOR READING ANALYTICALLY

1. Get beyond reading for the gist. Always mark a few key passages in whatever you read.
2. Whenever you read critically, look for the pitch and the complaint—what the writer wants to convince you of, and the position that he or she is reacting against. Also be aware of the moment—how the historical context qualifies the way we interpret the reading.
3. Experiment with passage-based focused freewriting. Find out what you think by seeing what you say.
4. Keep a reading journal. The act of copying key sentences from a reading and jotting a few notes will inevitably lead you to remember more and discover more about what you are reading.
5. Paraphrase key passages to open up the language and reveal complexities you may not have noticed. Paraphrasing three times is sure to help get you started interpreting a reading, moving you beyond just repeating pieces of it as answers.
6. Summarize analytically with ranking, not just coverage. Narrow the scope.
7. In applying a reading as a lens, think about how lens A both fits *and* does not fit subject B: use the differences to develop your analysis.
8. Avoid turning comparisons into pointless matching exercises. Set up similarities and differences to discuss the significance of that comparison.
9. Uncover unstated assumptions by asking, Given its overt claim, what must this reading also already believe?
10. A provocative way to open up interpretation is to try reading against the grain of a text. Ask, What does this piece believe that it does not know it believes? Using the method to uncover repetitions will sometimes provide the evidence to formulate against-the-grain claims.

CHAPTER 5

Linking Evidence and Claims: 10 on 1 versus 1 on 10

Quick Take

This chapter is about evidence—what it is, what it is meant to do, and how to recognize when you are using it well. The chapter's overall argument is that you should use evidence to test, refine, and develop your ideas, rather than just to prove that they are correct. The chapter begins by analyzing two common problems—claims without evidence (unsubstantiated claims), and evidence without claims (pointless evidence). It then moves to a discussion of strategies for analyzing evidence in depth. These include the following:

- 10 on 1, a heuristic discussed in Chapter 1 but developed here in the context of organization and evidence
- pan, track, and zoom: organizing a paper like a film
- looking for difference within similarity as a way of developing comparisons beyond matching exercises

The chapter suggests these three heuristics as alternatives to five-paragraph form, a popular organizational model that generally blocks writers from engaging in more sustained, subtle, and revelatory thinking.

By way of definition, a *claim* is an assertion that you make about your evidence—an idea that you believe the evidence supports. The primary claim in a paper is the *thesis.* In analytical writing, the thesis is a theory that explains what some feature or features of a subject mean. The subject itself, the pool of primary material (data) being analyzed, is known as *evidence.*

A. LINKING EVIDENCE AND CLAIMS

THE FUNCTION OF EVIDENCE

A common assumption about evidence is that it is "the stuff that proves I'm right." Although this way of thinking about evidence is not wrong, it is much too limited. Corroboration (proving the validity of a claim) is one of the functions of evidence, but not the only one.

It helps to remember that the word *prove* actually comes from a Latin verb meaning "to test." The noun form of prove, *proof*, has two meanings: (1) evidence sufficient to establish a thing as true or believable, and (2) the act of testing for truth or believability. When you operate on the first definition of proof alone, you are far more likely to seek out evidence that supports only your point of view, ignoring or dismissing other evidence that could lead to a different and possibly better idea. You might also assume that you can't begin writing until you have arrived at an idea you're convinced is right, since only then could you decide which evidence to include. Both of these practices close down your thinking instead of leading you to a more open process of formulating and testing ideas.

Beginning with the goal of establishing an idea as believable and true can interfere with the need to examine the idea. Moreover, this approach can lead to an unnecessarily combative debate style of argument in which the aim is to win the game and defeat one's opponents. In debate style, convincing others that you're right is more important than arriving at a fair and accurate assessment of your subject. By contrast, the advantage to following the second definition of the word proof—in the sense of testing—is that you will be better able to negotiate among competing points of view. In addition, this practice will predispose your readers to consider what you have to say, because you are offering them not only the thoughts a person has had, but also a person in the act of thinking.

THE FALLACY THAT FACTS CAN SPEAK FOR THEMSELVES

Evidence rarely, if ever, can be left to speak for itself. The word *evident* comes from a Latin verb meaning "to see." To say that the truth of a statement is "self-evident" means that it does not need proving because its truth can be plainly seen by all. When a writer leaves evidence to speak for itself, he or she is assuming that it can be interpreted in only one way, and that readers necessarily will think as the writer does.

But the relationship between evidence and claims is rarely self-evident: that relationship virtually *always* needs to be explained. One of the key analytical moves of Chapter 2 was making the implicit explicit. That is also the rule in the domain of evidence. Perhaps the single most important lesson about using evidence that this chapter has to teach is that the thought connections that have occurred to you will not automatically occur to others. Persuasive writing always makes the connections between evidence and claim overt.

The thought connections that have occurred to you will not automatically occur to others.

Writers who think that evidence speaks for itself often do very little with their evidence except put it next to their claims: "The party was terrible: there was no alcohol"—or, alternatively, "The party was great: there was no alcohol." Just juxtaposing the evidence with the claim leaves out the thinking that connects them, thereby implying that the logic of the connection is obvious. But even for readers prone to agreeing with a given claim, simply pointing to the evidence is not enough.

It should be acknowledged, however, that the types and amounts of evidence necessary for persuading readers and building authority also vary from one discipline to another, as does the manner in which the evidence is presented. Although some disciplines—the natural sciences, for example—require writers to present evidence first and then interpret it, others (the humanities and some social sciences) expect interpretation of the evidence as it is presented. In all disciplines—and virtually any writing situation—it is important to support claims with evidence, to make evidence lead to claims, and especially to be explicit about how you've arrived at the connection between your evidence and your claims (see Figure 5.1).

Of course, before you can attend to the relationship between evidence and claims, you first have to make sure to include both of them. Let's pause to take a look at how to remedy the problems posed by leaving one out: unsubstantiated claims and pointless evidence.

SUPPORTING UNSUBSTANTIATED CLAIMS: PROVIDING EVIDENCE

Problem: Making claims that lack supporting evidence.

Solution: Learn to recognize and support unsubstantiated assertions.

Unsubstantiated claims occur when a writer concentrates only on conclusions, omitting the evidence that led to them. At the opposite extreme, pointless evidence results when a writer offers a mass of detail attached to an overly general claim. Both of these problems can be solved by offering readers the evidence that led to the claim and explaining how the evidence led there. The word *unsubstantiated* means "without substance." An unsubstantiated claim is not necessarily false; it just offers none of the concrete "stuff" upon which the claim is based. When a writer makes an unsubstantiated claim, he or she has assumed that readers will believe it just because the writer put it out there.

Perhaps more important, unsubstantiated claims deprive you of details. As Chapter 1 has argued, without details you're left with nothing concrete to think about. If you lack some actual "stuff" to analyze, you can easily get stuck in a set of abstractions, which tend to overstate your position and leave your readers wondering exactly what you mean. The further away your language gets from the concrete, from references to physical detail—things that you can see, hear, count, taste, smell, and touch—the more abstract it becomes. An aircraft carrier anchored outside a foreign harbor is concrete; the phrase *intervening in the name of democracy* is abstract.

FIGURE 5.1 Linking Evidence and Claims

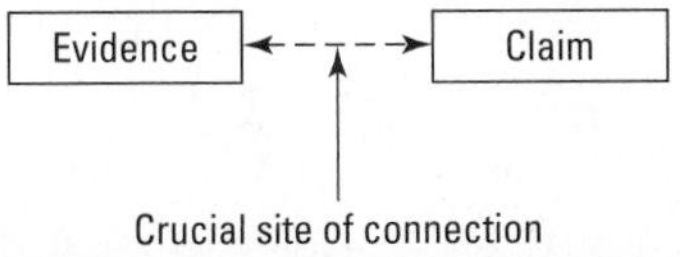

DISTINGUISHING EVIDENCE FROM CLAIMS

To check your drafts for unsubstantiated assertions, you first have to know how to recognize them. A fundamental skill to possess is the ability to *distinguish* evidence from claims. It is sometimes difficult to separate facts from judgments, data from interpretations of the data. Writers who aren't practiced in this skill can believe that they are offering evidence when they are really offering only unsubstantiated claims. In your own reading and writing, pause once in a while to label the sentences of a paragraph as either evidence *(E)* or claims *(C)*. What happens if we try to categorize the sentences of the following paragraph in this way?

> The owners are ruining baseball in America. Although they claim they are losing money, they are really just being greedy. A few years ago, they even fired the commissioner, Fay Vincent, because he took the players' side. Baseball is a sport, not a business, and it is a sad fact that it is being threatened by greedy businessmen.

The first and last sentences of the paragraph are claims. They draw conclusions about as yet unstated evidence that the writer will need to provide. The middle two sentences are harder to classify. If particular owners have said publicly that they are losing money, the existence of the owners' statements is a fact. But the writer moves from evidence to unsubstantiated claims when he suggests that the owners are lying about their financial situation and are doing so because of their greed. Similarly, it is a fact that commissioner Fay Vincent was fired, but only an assertion that he was fired "because he took the players' side." Although many of us might be inclined to accept some version of the writer's claim as true, we should not be asked to accept his opinion as self-evident truth. What is the evidence in support of the claim? What are the reasons for believing that the evidence means what he says it does?

Try this 5.1: Distinguishing Evidence from Claims

Take an excerpt from your own writing, at least two paragraphs in length—perhaps from a paper you have already written or a draft you are working on—and at the end of every sentence label the sentence as either evidence *(E)* or claim *(C)*. For sentences that appear to offer both, determine which parts of the sentence are evidence and which are claim, and then decide which one, *E* or *C*, predominates. What is the ratio of evidence to claim, especially in particularly effective or weak paragraphs?

As an alternative or a preface to the above exercise, mark the following paragraph with *C*s and *E*s. We have numbered the sentences for easier isolation and discussion. A few of them—1 and 7, for example—are arguably quite tricky to decide about: which part of the sentence is a claim, and which part evidence? Keep in mind that you are making your decisions on the basis of the writer's use of the sentences, not simply on their content. Is a secondary source's judgment that is imported into an essay as *support* for the writer's point of view ultimately *C* or *E*, for example?

(1) Though many current historians would argue that Andrew Jackson's treatment of the Native Americans was contrary to the ideals and precepts of the American Revolution, one must consider the legal and moral context of both Jackson and the time period in which he lived. (2) Jackson, both as a general and as a president, had no real love for the Native American populations in the southern and western United States. (3) As a military general he had defended the borders of the United States many times against Indian attacks and negotiated treaties with some of the tribes during the term of President James Monroe. (4) However, Jackson was also the archetype of the general American view of the Native Americans. (5) He described the Indians as barbarians and cruel savages in a letter to a fellow politician (Hollitz 172) and tried to convince President Monroe, during his negotiations with the Creek Indians, that Native Americans "are the subjects of the United States, inhabiting its territory and acknowledging its sovereignty" (Hollitz 174). (6) He subsequently argued that it was "absurd for the sovereign to negotiate with the subjects" (Hollitz 174). (7) Jackson and many of his contemporaries also saw the Indians only as a hindrance to America's exploitation of southern and western farmland and that they should be removed to facilitate American expansion. (8) This is clearly seen in a letter Jackson wrote to his wife in which he describes removing the natives of Alabama in terms of the fertile lands and wealth it will bring the United States as well as a secure southern border (Hollitz 173). (9) They were subjects of American sovereignty. (10) In this sense, Jackson's policy of Indian removal was in line with the best wishes of the people that the ideals of the American Revolution were set aside for, the American citizens who wished for more fertile lands and safe borders. (11) Jackson was indeed providing for the citizens that he believed the Declaration of Independence encompassed.

GIVING EVIDENCE A POINT: MAKING DETAILS SPEAK

Problem: Presenting a mass of evidence without explaining how it relates to the claims.

Solution: Make details speak. Explain how evidence confirms and qualifies the claim.

Your thinking emerges in the way that you follow through on the implications of the evidence you have selected. You need to interpret it for your readers. You have to make the details speak, conveying to your readers *why* they mean what you claim they mean.

The following example illustrates what happens when a writer leaves the evidence to speak for itself.

> Baseball is a sport, not a business, and it is a sad fact that it is being threatened by greedy businessmen. For example, Eli Jacobs, the previous owner of the Baltimore Orioles, recently sold the team to Peter Angelos for one hundred million dollars more than he had spent ten years earlier when he purchased it. Also, a new generation of baseball stadiums have been built in the last decade—in Baltimore, Chicago, Arlington (Texas), Cleveland, and most recently, in San Francisco, Milwaukee, Houston, and Philadelphia. These parks are enormously expensive and include elaborate scoreboards and luxury boxes. The average baseball players, meanwhile, now earn more than a million dollars a year, and they all have agents to represent them. Alex Rodriguez, the shortstop for the New York Yankees, is paid more than twenty million dollars a season. Sure, he set a record for most homers in a season by a shortstop, but is any ballplayer worth that much money?

Unlike the previous example, which was virtually all claims, this paragraph, except for the opening claim and the closing question, is all evidence. The paragraph presents what we might call an "evidence sandwich": it encloses a series of facts between two claims. (The opening statement blames "greedy businessmen," presumably owners, and the closing statement appears to indict greedy, or at least overpaid, players.) Readers are left with two problems. First, the mismatch between the opening and concluding claims leaves it not altogether clear what the writer is saying that the evidence suggests. And second, he has not told readers why they should believe that the evidence means what he says it does. Instead, he leaves it to speak for itself.

If readers are to accept the writer's implicit claims—that the spending is too much and that it is ruining baseball—he will have to show *how* and *why* the evidence supports these conclusions. The rule that applies here is that *evidence can almost always be interpreted in more than one way.*

We might, for instance, formulate at least three conclusions from the evidence offered in the baseball paragraph. We might decide that the writer believes baseball will be ruined by going broke or that its spirit will be ruined by becoming too commercial. Worst of all, we might disagree with his claim and conclude that baseball is not really being ruined, since the evidence could be read as signs of health rather than decay. The profitable resale of the Orioles, the expensive new ballparks (which, the writer neglects to mention, have drawn record crowds), and the skyrocketing salaries all could testify to the growing popularity rather than the decline of the sport.

How to Make Details Speak: An Example The best way to begin making the details speak is to take the time to look at them, asking questions about what they imply.

1. Say explicitly what you take the details to mean.
2. State exactly how the evidence supports your claims.
3. Consider how the evidence complicates (qualifies) your claims.

The writer of the baseball paragraph leaves some of his claims and virtually all of his reasoning about the evidence implicit. What, for example, bothers him about the special luxury seating areas? Attempting to uncover his assumptions, we might speculate that he intends it to demonstrate how economic interests are taking baseball away from its traditional fans because these new seats cost more than the average person can afford. This interpretation could be used to support the writer's governing claim, but *he would need to spell out the connection, to reason back to his own premises*. He might say, for example, that baseball's time-honored role as the all-American sport—democratic and grass-roots—is being displaced by the tendency of baseball as a business to attract higher box office receipts and wealthier fans.

The writer could then make explicit what his whole paragraph implies, that baseball's image as a popular pastime in which all Americans can participate is being tarnished by players and owners alike, whose primary concerns appear to be making money. In making his evidence speak in this way, the writer would be practicing step 3 above—using the evidence to complicate and *refine* his ideas. He would discover which specific aspect of baseball he thinks is being ruined, clarifying that the "greedy businessmen" to whom he refers include both owners and players.

Let's emphasize the final lesson gleaned from this example. When you focus on tightening the links between evidence and claim, the result is almost always a "smaller" claim than the one you set out to prove. This is what evidence characteristically does to a claim: it shrinks and restricts its scope. This process, also known as qualifying a claim, is the means by which a thesis develops (or as we call it in Chapter 6, evolves).

Sometimes it is hard to give up on the large, general assertions that were your first response to your subject. But your sacrifices in scope are exchanged for greater accuracy and validity. The sweeping claims you lose ("Greedy businessmen are ruining baseball") give way to less resounding but also more informed, more incisive, and less judgmental ideas ("Market pressures may not bring the end of baseball, but they are certainly changing the image and nature of the game").

B. DEVELOPING A THESIS IS MORE THAN REPEATING AN IDEA ("1 ON 10")

When the time comes to compose a formal paper with a thesis, it is very common for writers to abandon the wealth of data and ideas they have accumulated in the exploratory writing stage, panic, and revert to old habits: "Now I better have my one idea and be able to prove to everybody that I'm right." Out goes careful attention to detail. Out goes any evidence that doesn't fit. Instead of analysis, they substitute the kind of paper we call a demonstration. That is, they cite evidence to prove that a generalization is generally true. The problem with the demonstration lies with its too limited notions of what a thesis and evidence can do in a piece of analytical thinking.

Demonstrations are the result of two primary mistaken assumptions about what an analytical paper is—that the thesis doesn't change and that evidence exists solely to confirm the general validity of the thesis. For these notions we'd like to substitute the following two:

- A strong thesis *evolves:* it changes as a paper progresses. The changes in the thesis are galvanized by its repeated encounters with evidence.
- Evidence has a second function beyond corroborating claims: to test and develop and evolve the thesis, making the thesis account more accurately for the evidence.

The absence of change is the primary trait of a weak thesis. Like an *inert* (unreactive) material, a weak thesis neither affects nor is affected by the evidence that surrounds it. A paper produced by repeating a single idea generally follows the form we call 1 on 10: the writer makes a single and usually very general claim ("History repeats itself," "Exercise is good for you," and so forth) and then proceeds to affix it to ten examples. (See Figure 5.2 "Doing 1 on 10.") As we discuss in Chapter 1 under "Narrow Your Scope by Doing 10 on 1," a writer who reasserts the same idea about each example is going to produce a list, not a piece of developed thinking. By contrast, in nearly all good writing the thesis evolves by *gaining in complexity* and, thus, in accuracy as the paper progresses.

The absence of change is the primary trait of a weak thesis. Like an inert (unreactive) material, a weak thesis neither affects nor is affected by the evidence that surrounds it.

Where do writers get the idea in the first place that a thesis should be static? In most cases they learned it early in their writing careers as part of a stubbornly inflexible organizational scheme known as five-paragraph form.

WHAT'S WRONG WITH FIVE-PARAGRAPH FORM?

Perhaps the best introduction to what's wrong with five-paragraph form can be found in Greek mythology. On his way to Athens, the hero Theseus encounters a

FIGURE 5.2

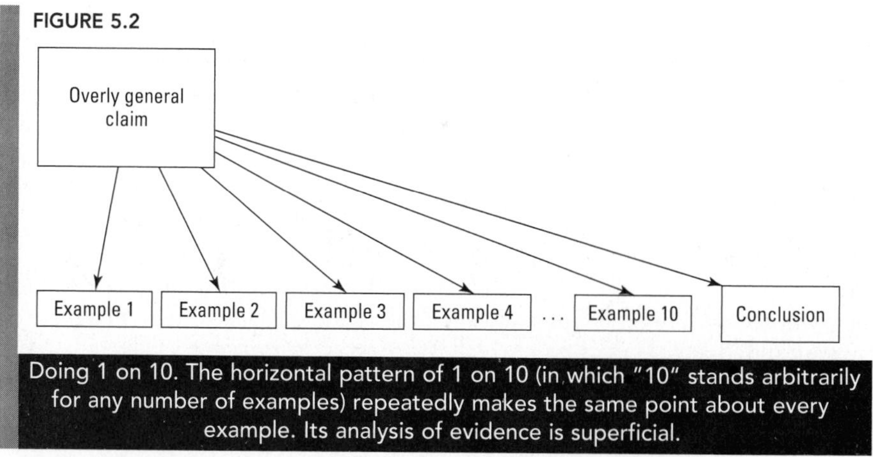

Doing 1 on 10. The horizontal pattern of 1 on 10 (in which "10" stands arbitrarily for any number of examples) repeatedly makes the same point about every example. Its analysis of evidence is superficial.

particularly surly host, Procrustes, who offers wayfarers a bed for the night but with a catch. If they do not fit his bed exactly, he either stretches them or lops off their extremities until they do. This story has given us the word "procrustean," which the dictionary defines as "tending to produce conformity by violent or arbitrary means." Five-paragraph form is a procrustean formula that most students learn in high school. Although it has the advantage of providing a mechanical format that will give virtually any subject the appearance of order, it usually lops off a writer's ideas before they have the chance to form or stretches a single idea to the breaking point. In other words, this simplistic scheme blocks writers' abilities to think deeply or logically, restricting rather than encouraging the development of complex ideas.

A complex idea is one that has many sides. To treat such ideas intelligently, writers need a form that will not require them to cut off all of those sides except the one that most easily fits the bed. Most of you will find the basic five-paragraph form familiar:

1. An introduction that announces the writer's main idea, about which he or she will make three points
2. Three paragraphs, each on one of the three points
3. A conclusion beginning "Thus, we see" or "In conclusion" that essentially repeats the introduction.

Here is an example in outline form:

Introduction: The food in the school cafeteria is bad. It lacks variety, it's unhealthy, and it is always overcooked. In this essay I will discuss these three characteristics.

Paragraph 2: The first reason cafeteria food is bad is that there is no variety. (Plus one or two examples—no salad bar, mostly fried food, and so forth)

Paragraph 3: Another reason cafeteria food is bad is that it is not healthy. (Plus a few reasons—high cholesterol, too many hot dogs, too much sugar, and so forth)

Paragraph 4: In addition, the food is always overcooked. (Plus some examples—the vegetables are mushy, the "mystery" meat is tough to recognize, and so forth)

Conclusion: Thus, we see . . . (Plus a restatement of the introductory paragraph)

Most high school students write dozens of themes using this basic formula. They are taught to use five-paragraph form because it seems to provide the greatest good—a certain minimal clarity—for the greatest number of students. But the form does not promote logically tight and intellectually aggressive writing. It is a meat grinder that can turn any content into sausage.

At the root of the problem with five-paragraph form is its most distinctive characteristic—the classic tripartite (three-part) thesis, which generates the organizational format ("The economy of Bolivia is characterized by *x*, *y*, *z*"). The problem with this thesis shape is that it is not really a thesis. It offers a list in place of an idea. It tells the writer that he or she will have to write a paragraph on each of the items in the list, but it doesn't let the reader (or the writer) know why this might be worth doing.

When you are in a pinch, as, for example, when you are trying to write the essay section of the new SAT exam where five-paragraph form *seemingly* still reigns, the form's partitioning aspect can be useful. Partitioning your subject into sections will at least split your thinking tasks into three or more smaller portions. But you need to try to make the thesis and its supporting body paragraphs do more than listing.

As we make clear at various points in the book, a good thesis must have tension in it, the pressure of one possible idea against another. Simply saying that the economy today has three problems, and then listing them, isn't really a thesis. Such a statement might get you by in a standardized essay exam (even though it shouldn't), but in the rest of your writing you want to do more than make lists of broad generalizations. A thesis that says, "There are three reasons for our being bogged down in the war with Iraq today" will direct you to an orderly development of your points, but not to much analysis of them. Good analysis requires narrower scope; its products are more carefully defined idea.

WHAT FIVE-PARAGRAPH FORM LOOKS LIKE

If you have been taught to write in five-paragraph form, you have come to expect your thinking to be tidily packaged. The thesis of a paper in five-paragraph form lists three elements of some kind at the end of the first paragraph: three reasons, three causes, three effects, three characteristics, and so forth. The paper then follows like a paint-by-number picture with a paragraph devoted to each of the three elements in the thesis. Then the paper comes to rest, wearily, with restatement (often exact repetition) of the three-part thesis in the first sentence of the concluding paragraph.

The problem with this orderly scheme is that it doesn't leave much room for thinking. In fact, it actually discourages thinking because it makes writers afraid to look closely at the evidence. If they look too closely, they might find something that doesn't fit. But it is precisely the something that doesn't seem to fit, the thing writers call a *complication*, that triggers good ideas. The tidy packaging of five-paragraph form keeps complications at a safe distance. When complications do force their way onto the scene, five-paragraph form swiftly seeks to dismiss them. It tends to locate them as concessions and refutations—things to be gotten through in an obligatory way so that the writer can return to the main business at hand: reciting his or her idea as if the complication had never been.

But it is precisely the something that doesn't seem to fit, the thing writers call a complication, that triggers good ideas. The tidy packaging of five-paragraph form keeps complications at a safe distance.

The three elements get marched through the paper with no questions asked, and the paper ends the way it began—with a list. This is all quite comforting to some writers, because five-paragraph form papers virtually write themselves. Just come up with a list of three things, preferably things that can be stated in single words, as in "*Dr. Faustus* is a play about lust, greed, and ambition," and then produce an example or two of each in your three body paragraphs. Nothing to it.

The fact that there is almost "nothing to it" is the problem. Ideas that come too easily, that seem to write themselves, are sometimes the worthwhile products of inspiration. More often they are unexamined first responses, exercises in the exposition of the obvious, prefabricated and unreflective recitations of conventional ideas. If one definition of analysis is that it locates significant parts in order to arrive at a better understanding of the whole, then five-paragraph form is a too-mechanical form of analysis.

Here is a short list of the bad mental habits taught by five-paragraph form:

1. that papers need only repeat (rather than develop) their main ideas
2. that an introduction is a conclusion, and thus that nothing need happen to the thesis on the way from the beginning of the paper to the end
3. that a thesis is essentially inert, unaffected by what it passes through
4. that a paper need only provide evidence in support of its thesis, rather than using evidence to test and evolve the main idea; complicating evidence may get acknowledged in the form of concessions and refutations, but such evidence remains too inert to have any effect on the writer's thinking
5. that all body paragraphs are essentially the same—a single claim at the beginning (one of the three elements of the thesis turned into a sentence, as in "We also see that *Dr. Faustus* is a play about greed.") followed by a short list of reasons or examples
6. that a thesis consists of generalities and broadly stated themes, usually ones that no one would be likely to disagree with

Try this 5.2: Identifying Five-Paragraph Form

Take a minute to examine the introductory paragraph below. What evidence do you find there to suggest that it is setting up a five-paragraph form essay?

Throughout the film *The Tempest*, a version of Shakespeare's play *The Tempest*, there were a total of nine characters. These characters were Calibano, Alonso, Antonio, Aretha, Freddy, the doctor, and Dolores. Each character in the film represented a person in Shakespeare's play, but there were four people who were greatly similar to those in Shakespeare, and who played a role in symbolizing aspects of forgiveness, love, and power.

Predict the organization of this essay, paragraph by paragraph. Can you discern any possible openings where the writer might locate and develop an idea? (There are some.)

Here are two *quick checks* to see whether a paper of yours has closed down your thinking through a scheme such as five-paragraph form:

1. *Look at the paragraph openings.* If these read like a list, each beginning with an additive transition such as *another* followed by repetition of your central point ("Once again we see . . . " or "Yet another example is . . ."), you are probably not developing your ideas sufficiently.
2. *Compare the wording in the last statement of the paper's thesis (in the conclusion) with the first statement of it in the introduction.* If the wording at these two locations is virtually the same, you'll know that your thesis has not responded adequately to your evidence.

C. BUILDING A PAPER BY ANALYZING EVIDENCE IN DEPTH: "10 ON 1"

How do you move from making details speak and explaining how evidence confirms and qualifies the claim to actually composing a paper? One way is through the practice we call 10 on 1*:* a focused analysis of a representative example. (See Figure 5.3.) We first introduced this term near the end of Chapter 1, where it is presented as a heuristic for focusing observation and asking So what? We return to it now in the context of linking evidence and claims in composing an analytical essay.

FIGURE 5.3

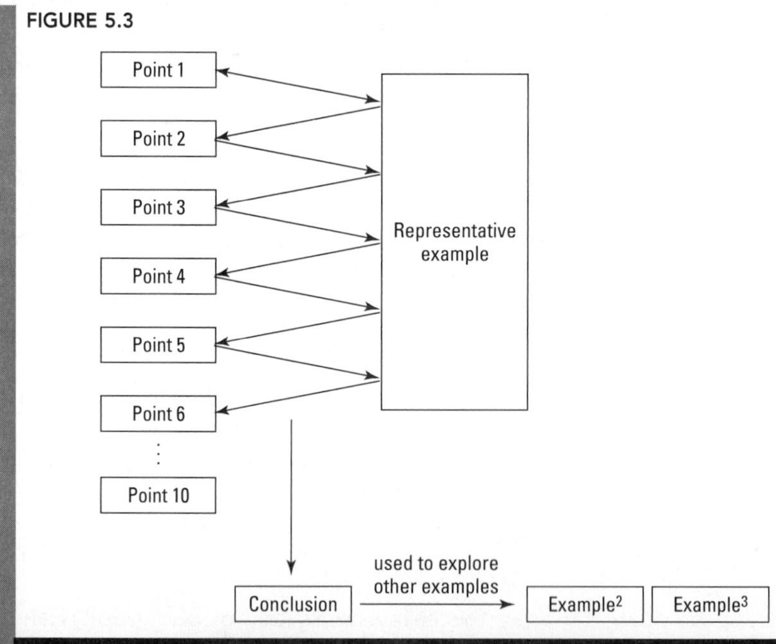

Doing 10 on 1. The pattern of 10 on 1 (in which "10" stands arbitrarily for any number of points) successively develops a series of points about a single representative example. Its analysis of evidence is in depth.

To repeat the general rule of 10 on 1, it is better to make ten observations or points about a single representative issue or example than to make the same basic point about ten related issues or examples (as in the static demonstration we call 1 on 10, which repeats the same "answer" ten times). As a guideline, 10 on 1 will lead you to draw out as much meaning as possible from your best examples. It depends upon narrowing the focus and then analyzing in depth.

You can use 10 on 1 to accomplish various ends: (1) to locate the range of possible meanings your evidence suggests, (2) to make you less inclined to cling to your first claim, (3) to open the way for you to discover the complexity of your subject, and (4) to slow down the rush to generalization and thus help to ensure that when you arrive at a working thesis, it will be more specific and better able to account for your evidence.

WHAT THE "1" IS

The "1" is a representative example, what you have narrowed your focus to. How do you select the "1"? One of the best ways is to use the looking-for-patterns heuristic (the Method) to identify a strand or pattern and then to choose the example of it you find most interesting, strange, revealing, and so forth. Here, in effect, you do 1 on 10 as a preliminary step—locating ten examples that share a trait—and then focus on one of these for in-depth analysis.

Proceeding in this way would guarantee that your example was representative, which is essential, because in doing 10 on 1 you are taking one part of the whole, putting it under a microscope, and then generalizing about the whole on the basis of analyzing a single part. In the preceding section we used the baseball example in this way, doing 10 on 1 with the student's paragraph as a way of anchoring our generalizations about giving evidence a point. (See pages 142–143.)

WHAT THE "10" ARE

The "10" comprise both observations and interpretive leaps that you make about the "1," both what you notice about the evidence and what you make of what you notice. To get the "10"—to analyze in depth—use the various tools, prompts, and procedures that have been introduced in this book thus far:

- Look at the example and ask yourself what you notice.
- Use Looking for Patterns of Repetition and Contrast to uncover and organize data.
- Locate anomalies and query them.
- Locate, name, and reformulate binaries.
- Try "seems to be about x but is *also* about y."
- Employ Paraphrase × 3 on key sentences or phrases if your evidence has a verbal component.
- Uncover the assumptions in your example.
- As you try on different interpretations, repeatedly ask, So what? to develop the implications of your thinking.
- As a major claim begins to emerge (and it will), seek out conflicting evidence to enable you to qualify the claim still further.

PAN, TRACK, AND ZOOM: THE FILM ANALOGY

To understand how 10 on 1 can generate the form of a paper, let's turn to an analogy. The language of filmmaking offers a useful way for understanding the different ways that a writer can focus evidence. The writer, like the director of a film, controls the focus through different kinds of shots.

The pan—The camera pivots around a stable axis, giving the viewer the big picture. Using a pan, we see everything from a distance. Pans provide a context, some larger pattern, the "forest" within which the writer can also examine particular "trees." Pans establish the representativeness of the example the writer later examines in more detail, showing that it is not an isolated instance.

The track—The camera no longer stays in one place but follows some sequence of action. For example, whereas a pan might survey a room full of guests at a cocktail party, a track would pick up a particular guest and follow along as she walks across the room, picks up a photograph, proceeds through the door, and throws the photo in a trash can. Analogously, a writer tracks by moving in on selected pieces of the larger picture and following them to make telling connections among them.

The zoom—The camera moves in even closer on a selected piece of the scene, allowing us to notice more of its details. For example, a zoom might focus in on the woman's hand as she crumples the photograph she's about to throw away or on her face as she slams the lid on the trash can. A writer zooms in by giving us more detail on a particular part of his or her evidence and making the details say more. The zoom is the shot that enables you to do 10 on 1.

In a short paper (three to five pages), you might devote as much as 90 percent of your writing to exploring what one example (the "1"—your zoom) reveals about the larger subject. Even in a paper that uses several examples, however, as much as 50 percent might still be devoted to analysis of and generalization from a single case. The remaining portion of the paper would make connections with other examples, testing and applying the ideas you arrived at from your single case. In-depth analysis of your best example thus creates a center from which you can move in two directions: (1) toward generalizations about the larger subject and (2) toward other examples, using your primary example as a tool of exploration.

This same model, applicable across a wide variety of writing situations, can be reduced to a series of steps:

1. Use the Method to find a revealing pattern or tendency in your evidence. (See Chapter 2.)
2. Select a representative example.
3. Do 10 on 1 to produce an in-depth analysis of your example.
4. Test your results in similar cases.

An analysis of the representation of females on television, for example, would fare better if you focused on one show—say, *Buffy, the Vampire Slayer*—narrowed the focus to teenage girls, and tested your results against other shows with teenage girl characters, such as *Felicity*, *Gilmore Girls*, and *Seventh Heaven*. Similarly, a study of the national debt might focus on Social Security, analyzing it in order to arrive at generalizations to be tested and refined in the context of, say, health care or military spending.

A close look at virtually anything will reveal its complexity, and you can bring that complex understanding to other examples for further testing and refining. We call this process of using the "1" as a lens through which to analyze other examples "constellating the evidence." Like the imaginary lines that connect real stars into a recognizable shape, your thinking configures the examples into some larger meaning. This practice often supplies the backbone for longer essays in both exploratory and more polished drafts.

It is, of course, important to let your readers know that you are using the one primary example in this generalizable way. Note how the writer of the following discussion of the people's revolt in China in 1989 sets up his analysis. He first explains how his chosen example—a single photograph (shown in Figure 5.4) from the media coverage of the event—illuminates his larger subject. The image is of a Chinese man in a white shirt who temporarily halted a line of tanks on their way to quell a demonstration in Tiananmen Square in Beijing.

> The tank image provided a miniature, simplified version of a larger, more complex revolution. The conflict between man and tank embodied the same tension found in the conflict between student demonstrators and the Peoples' Army. The man in the white shirt, like the students, displayed courage, defiance, and rebellious individuality in the face of power. Initially, the peaceful revolution succeeded: the state allowed the students to protest; likewise, the tank spared the man's life. Empowered, the students' demands for democracy grew louder. Likewise, the man boldly jumped onto the tank and addressed the soldiers. The state's formerly unshakable dominance appeared weak next to the strength of the individual. However, the state asserted its power: the Peoples' Army marched into the square, and the tanks roared past the man into Beijing.

FIGURE 5.4 Tiananmen Square, Beijing, 1989.

The image appeals to American ideology. The man in the white shirt personifies the strength of the American individual. His rugged courage draws on contemporary heroes such as Rambo. His defiant gestures resemble the demonstrations of Martin Luther King Jr. and his followers. American history predisposes us to identify strongly with the Chinese demonstrators: we have rebelled against the establishment, we have fought for freedom and democracy, and we have defended the rights of the individual. For example, *The New York Times* reported that President George [H. W.] Bush watched the tank incident on television and said, "I'm convinced that the forces of democracy are going to overcome these unfortunate events in Tiananmen Square." Bush represents the popular American perspective of the Chinese rebellion; we support the student demonstrators.

This analysis is a striking example of doing 10 on 1. In the first paragraph, the writer constructs a detailed analogy between the particular image and the larger subject of which it was a part. The analogy allows the writer not just to describe but also to interpret the event. In the second paragraph, he develops his focus on the image as an image, a photographic representation tailor-made to appeal to American viewing audiences. Rather than generalizing about why Americans might find the image appealing, he establishes a number of explicit connections (does 10 on 1) between the details of the image and typical American heroes. By drawing out the implications of particular details, he manages to say more about the significance of the American response to the demonstrations in China than a broader survey of those events would have allowed.

The rule of thumb here is to say more about less (rather than less about more) to allow a carefully analyzed part of your subject to provide perspective on the whole. In the following 10 on 1 draft, what does the writer focus on, and *not* focus on? How does the perspective emerge?

The rule of thumb here is to say more about less (rather than less about more).

The thing about comic strips is that people always appear to be talking at the same time. Their words hang above them in bubbles—attached loosely to their mouths or the tops of their heads. The words seem to grow from their speakers and then just float there above them—untethered somehow but also fixed—black letters (usually) against a white ground. Another thing about comic strips is that they have a clear end and beginning. They move across the page in a relentless order—one thing following the next. But the beginning remains in full view when we get to the end. We can see how we got to where we end up even though the characters can't—as they are stuck in their individual frames, each a separate moment in time.

I remember the cartoons the artist Andy Warhol used to draw—or paintings, rather, based on cartoons. The faces—usually of a famous person who was already a cartoon of sorts in life (like Marilyn Monroe)—were unusually large and very brightly colored, especially the lips. The texture of the faces was made up of many dots, clearly visible, to remind us that we were looking at a painting of a person rather than, say, a photograph. Perhaps the dots also remind us of how thinly held together we are—not one solid being, but a collection of parts.

Cartoons are flat. When we look at them we imagine the people (or animals) in them to be round, like ourselves. As the reader of a comic strip you are always free to start over when you get to the end—or to start at the end and read back to the beginning. In the second reading, you might find yourself saying to the characters in the first frame, "Wait! You are going to regret saying that!"

Note how the writer has defamiliarized her subject in the opening paragraph, looking at rather than through the conventions of comic strips. As she observes one technical element of the form—the speech bubble—she begins to see other formal elements, such as the printing and the order of the frames. This focus leads her to a digression in the second paragraph, but that is an opportunity rather than a problem, for the Warhol example gets her to think about how stylized human figures are in comics, and by implication, in all representations. She brings this insight back with her in the final paragraph as her gaze returns to the comic strip. Sure, the piece is still in the draft stage, but the writer's use of 10 on 1 has already generated a focus capable of sustaining a paper with a refreshingly offbeat focus on the conventions of its subject.

Try this 5.3: Doing 10 on 1 with Newspaper Visuals

Search out photographs in the newspaper and do 10 on 1. Or alternatively, spend some time doing 10 on 1 on a comic strip. What perspectives emerge once you have restricted the focus? List details, but also list multiple implications. Remember to ask not just What do I notice? but What else do I notice? And not just What does it imply? but What else might it imply?

DEMONSTRATING THE REPRESENTATIVENESS OF YOUR EXAMPLE

Problem: Generalizing on the basis of too little and unrepresentative evidence.

Solution: Survey the available evidence and argue overtly for the representativeness of the examples on which you focus.

Focusing on your single best example has the advantage of economy, cutting to the heart of the subject, but it runs the risk that the example you select might not in fact be representative. Thus, to be safe, you need to demonstrate its representativeness overtly. This means showing that your example is part of a larger pattern of similar evidence and not just an isolated instance.

In terms of logic, the problem of generalizing from too little and unrepresentative evidence is known as an *unwarranted inductive leap*. The writer leaps from one or two instances to a broad claim about an entire class or category. Just because you see an economics professor and a biology professor wearing corduroy jackets, for example, you would not want to leap to the conclusion that all professors wear corduroy jackets.

The surest way you can guard against this problem is by reviewing the range of possible examples to make certain that the ones you choose to focus on are representative. By looking for patterns of repetition and contrast (the Method) you could identify the strand to which your example belongs, which could then be included as a pan in the introductory paragraph. If you were writing about faith as it is portrayed in the book of Exodus, for example, you might suggest the general trend by briefly panning across instances in which the Israelites have difficulty believing in an unseen God. Then, you could concentrate (zoom in) on the best example.

Most of the time, unwarranted leaps result from making too large a claim and avoiding examples that might contradict it. A good check is *deliberately to seek out the single piece of evidence that might most effectively oppose your point of view and address it.* Doing so will prompt you to test the representativeness of your evidence and often to qualify the claims you have made for it.

Try this 5.4: Doing 10 on 1 with a Reading

Take a piece of reading—a representative example—from something you are studying and do 10 on 1. The key to doing 10 on 1 successfully is to slow down the rush to conclusions so that you can allow yourself to notice more about the evidence and make the details speak. The more observations you assemble about your data *before* settling on your main idea, the better that idea is likely to be. Remember that a single, well-developed paragraph from something you are reading can be enough to practice on, especially because you are working on saying more about less rather than less about more.

10 ON 1 AND DISCIPLINARY CONVENTIONS

In some cases, the conventions of a discipline appear to discourage doing 10 on 1. The social sciences in particular tend to require a larger set of analogous examples to prove a hypothesis. Especially in certain kinds of research, the focus of inquiry rests on discerning broad statistical trends over a wide range of evidence. But some trends deserve more attention than others, and some statistics similarly merit more interpretation than others. The best writers learn to choose examples carefully—each one for a reason—and to concentrate on developing the most revealing ones in depth; the interpretive and statistical models for analyzing evidence are not necessarily opposed to one another.

For instance, proving that tax laws are prejudiced in particularly subtle ways against unmarried people might require a number of analogous cases along with a statistical summary of the evidence. But even with a subject such as this, you could still concentrate on some examples more than others. Rather than moving through each example as a separate case, you could use your analyses of these primary examples as *lenses* for investigating other evidence.

CONVERTING A 1-ON-10 PAPER INTO A 10-ON-1 PAPER: AN EXTENDED EXAMPLE

The following student paper, about the recurrence of flood stories in religious texts and myth, shows what happens when a writer falls into doing 1 on 10. That is, rather than zooming in on representative examples to test and refine his ideas, he attaches the same underdeveloped point to each of his examples. Typical of the 1-on-10 pattern, the flood paper views everything from the same relatively unrevealing distance.

The point is a promising one, however, and the writer has taken some productive steps analytically. As you will see, for example, he locates a pattern of like detail and begins to make the implications of his observations overt. He also offers evidence for his claims rather than leaving them unsupported.

We are using the essay as an extended example because of the way that diagnosing its strengths and weaknesses and contemplating revision strategies allow us to demonstrate several of the analytical moves discussed in this chapter and the previous one:

1. Doing 10 on 1: zooming in more closely on evidence (10 on 1), drawing out more of its possible meanings
2. Using the film analogy: thinking and talking about a piece of writing in regard to the way the writer adjusts the focus and observational distance as the essay progresses
3. Looking for difference within similarity (see Chapter 4): emphasizing contrasts and anomalies, deliberately attending to things that seem not to fit the pattern of like detail
4. Constellating the evidence: organizing the paper by drawing connections among interestingly related examples, each of which is analyzed using 10 on 1

As you may recall from Chapter 4, the phrase *difference within similarity* suggests that once you have started your thinking by locating apparent similarities, you can usually refine that thinking by pursuing significant, though often less obvious distinctions among the similar things. As the revision suggestions for the following paper illustrate, this heuristic is also a way of getting beyond 1 on 10.

In the essay that follows, we have used boldface to track the "one" point—the as-yet-underdeveloped thesis idea—that the writer has attached to each of his examples (1 on 10). Brackets and ellipses [. . .] indicate where we have abridged the essay.

Flood Stories

[1] **The role of people**, as reflected in Genesis, Ovid's *Metamorphoses,* and the *Epic of Gilgamesh,* **is solely to please the gods**. Men, as the gods' subordinates, exist to do right in the gods' eyes **and make them feel more like gods**; for without men, whom could the gods be gods of? [. . .]

[2] In Genesis, for example, God created humans in his own image or likeness, and **when they displeased Him, He destroyed them**. If God

could see wickedness in his creations, perhaps it was like seeing wickedness in himself. Further, the idea of having evidence of God being able to create an imperfect, "wicked" race of humans may have been a point God wasn't willing to deal with. The Lord saw that the wickedness of man was great in the earth, and that every imagination of the thoughts of his heart was only evil continually. And the Lord was sorry that he had made man on the earth and it grieved him to his heart. It seems as though **God had become unhappy with his creations** so they were to be destroyed. Like a toy a child no longer has use for, humankind was to be wasted.

[3] Similarly, in Ovid's *Metamorphoses*, God made humanity and "fashioned it into the image of the all-governing gods." Again here, humans were made in the gods' image to serve as an everlasting monument of their glorification, to honor them and do good by them. In other words, **humans spent less time making the gods happy** and therefore made them unhappy. Some men even questioned the reality of the gods' existence and the strength of their power. Lyacon, for example, had a driving tendency to try to belittle the gods and make them look like fools. **The gods were very displeased** with this trend, and now the entire race had to be destroyed. A flood would be sent to wipe out the race of men. [The writer then summarizes several examples in which the wicked are destroyed and a few upstanding citizens are preserved and arrives at the following conclusion:] Thus, the justification of yet another flood **to appease the gods' egos**.

[4] Further evidence of **humans as being a mere whim of the gods to make them happy** lies in the flood story in the *Epic of Gilgamesh*. It is obvious **the gods weren't concerned with humankind, but rather with their own comfort**. As the story goes, Enlil, the god of earth, wind, and air, couldn't bear the noise humans were making while he tried to sleep, so he gathered all the gods together, and thus they jointly decided to get rid of their grief of having all the humans around by destroying them. Ea [the god of wisdom], however, warned one man (Utnapishtim) of the flood to come. He told him to build a boat for himself and his wife and for the "seeds of all living creatures." [. . .]

[5] Enlil later repented the harshness of his actions, deified Utnapishtim and his wife and then had the two live far away "on the distance of the rivers' mouths." It possibly **could have been belittling** to have Utnapishtim and his wife speaking to the new race of humans in terms of how rash and mindlessly the gods were capable of acting, so he immortalized them and had them live far out of the reach of human ears—"the secret of the gods."

[6] It seems that the **main objective of the gods was to remain gods; for that is what made them happy. And humanity's role, then, was as the gods' stepping-stone to their happiness.** [. . .] Witnessing the fall of humankind, for the gods, was like witnessing imperfection in

> themselves, and thus their fall; anything causing these feelings didn't do the gods any good and therefore could be terminated without a second thought. **It was the job of human beings to make the gods happy**, and upon failure at this task, they could be "fired" (death), only to be replaced later—it wasn't a position which the gods could hold vacant for long. Thus were the great flood stories.

An Analysis of the Draft in the Context of the Film Analogy and Looking for Difference within Similarity The writer of this essay has already accomplished a lot. In terms of the film analogy, he starts with a pan on the "big picture." Panning on all three stories has allowed him to discover similarities among his blocks of evidence and to demonstrate that the examples he has chosen are representative of his generalization—his claim—that in all three flood stories men exist "solely to please the gods." The writer then constructs a series of tracks, summaries of each of the three stories that isolate some interesting parallels for readers to ponder. The problem is that, rather than allowing his tracks to set up zooms, the writer returns again and again to versions of his original pan. The result is a 1-on-10 paper in which the writer sees, in effect, only what he wants to see: opportunities to repeatedly match the evidence to his one governing claim.

What's wrong, one might ask, with showing how the evidence fits the claim? Isn't this what writers are supposed to do? The answer is that writers do want to use evidence to show that their claims have validity, but not in so general and redundant a way. As the final sentence of the essay demonstrates ("Thus were the great flood stories"), the writer never really arrives at a conclusion. To develop his central claim, the writer needs to devote much less space to repeating that claim, and (much) more to actually looking at key pieces of evidence, zooming in on significant variations within the general pattern.

In his second paragraph, for example, the writer makes a claim about the God of Genesis that overlooks significant evidence. The claim is as follows:

> God had become unhappy with his creations so they were to be destroyed. Like a toy a child no longer has use for, humankind was to be wasted.

It is here that the writer allows the 1-on-10 pattern to rush his thinking and distract him from his evidence. The depiction of God as one who treats humans like toys may accurately describe Enlil, the god in Gilgamesh who, as we are later told, decides to get rid of humans because they make too much noise. But it does not so easily fit the God of Genesis, about whom the writer has just told us that "the wickedness of man . . . grieved him to his heart." Doesn't the grief that this evidence mentions suggest that God's decision to flood the earth was possibly ethical rather than childishly selfish and rash? And the statement from Genesis that "every imagination of the thoughts of [man's] heart was only evil continually" would seem to indicate that humans were not simply victims of divine prerogative, but rather that they deserved punishment.

The writer doesn't consider these other possible interpretations because his reliance on pans—the general pattern—has predisposed him to see his evidence only as another sign of the gods' egotism, their desire to remain "happy" at any cost. Pressed by the desire to "match" examples to his one governing idea, the writer is not allowing himself to really examine his evidence. Instead, he has attempted to squeeze that evidence into a pattern he has apparently superimposed from Gilgamesh, thereby neglecting potentially significant differences among his examples. Thus, he is not prepared to deal with potentially significant differences among his examples.

Ways to Revise the Draft Using 10 on 1 and Looking for Difference within Similarity How might the writer make better use of the evidence he has collected, using the principle of looking for difference within similarity?

Revision Strategy 1:
Assume that the essay's "answer"—its conclusion about the evidence—does not yet go far enough. Rather than having to throw out his thinking, the writer should consider, as is almost always the case in revision, that he hasn't refined his initial idea enough. As an interpretation of the evidence, it leaves too much unaccounted for.

Revision Strategy 2:
Find a "1" to use with 10 on 1—a piece of the evidence sufficiently revealing to be analyzed in more detail; then zoom in on it. In the case of the writer of "Flood Stories," that 1 might be a single story, which he could examine in more detail. He could then test his claims about this story through comparison and contrast with the other stories. In the existing draft, the writer has not used comparison and contrast to refine his conclusion; he has just imposed the same conclusion on the other stories. Alternatively, the 1 might be the single most interesting feature that the three stories share.

Revision Strategy 3:
To find the most revealing piece or feature of the evidence, keep asking, What can be said with some certainty about the evidence? This question will induce a writer to rehearse the facts to keep them fresh, so that his or her first impressions don't "contaminate" or distort consideration of subsequent evidence.

If the writer of the flood paper were to apply these strategies, he might have a conversation with himself that sounded something like this:

> "What can I say with some certainty about my evidence?"
>
> "In all three of these stories, a first civilization created by a god is destroyed by the same means—a flood."

Notice that this is a factual *description* of the evidence rather than a speculation about it. You are always better off to report the facts in your evidence carefully and fully before moving to conclusions. (This is harder to do than you might think.)

> "What else is certain about the evidence?"

> "In each case the gods leave a surviving pair to rebuild the civilization rather than just wiping everybody out and inventing a new kind of being. Interestingly, the gods begin again by choosing from the same stock that failed the first time around."

Mulling over the evidence in this way, taking care to lay out the facts and distinguish them from speculation, can help you decide what evidence to zoom in on. One of the chief advantages of zooms is that they get you in close enough to your evidence to see the questions its details imply.

Revision Strategy 4:
Examine the evidence closely enough to see what questions the details imply and what other patterns they reveal. So far, the writer of the flood paper has worked mostly from two quite general questions: Why did the gods decide to wipe out their creations? And why do the gods need human beings? But there are other questions his evidence might prompt him to ask. In each story, for example, the gods are disappointed by humankind, yet they don't invent submissive robots who will dedicate their lives to making the deities feel good about themselves. Why not? This question might cause the writer to uncover a shared feature of his examples (a pattern) that he has thus far not considered—the surviving pairs.

Revision Strategy 5:
Use zooms to uncover implications that can develop your interpretation further. Having selected the surviving pairs for more detailed examination, what might the writer conclude about them? One interesting fact that the surviving pairs reveal is that the flood stories are not only descriptions of the end of a world but also creation accounts, because they also tell us how a new civilization, the existing one, got started.

At this point, the writer might apply the principle of looking for difference within similarity to the survival pairs. Given the recurrence of the survival pairs in the three stories, where might the writer locate a significant difference? One potentially significant difference involves the survival pair in the story of Gilgamesh, who are segregated from the new world and granted immortality. Perhaps this separation suggests that the new civilization will not be haunted by the painful memory of a higher power's intervention, leaving humans less fearful of what might happen in the future. This distinction could focus the argument in the essay; it does not distract from the writer's overall generalization but rather develops it.

Notice how the hypothetical revision we've been producing has made use of looking for difference within similarity to constellate the zooms on a limited set of details. Instead of repeatedly concluding that the gods destroy humans when humans fail to make them happy, the writer might be on his way to a thesis about the relative optimism or skepticism of the way the flood stories represent change. Such a thesis might posit, for example, that the flood stories propose the view that real change is necessarily apocalyptic rather than evolutionary. Or, the thesis might be that the flood stories present qualified optimism about the possibility of new starts. And so forth.

Try this 5.5: Describing Evidence

Have a conversation with yourself (on paper) about some piece of evidence you are studying. Start with the question we proposed for the student writer of the flood stories essay: What can be said with some certainty about this evidence? What, in other words, is clearly true of the data? What can be reported about it as fact without going on to interpretation of the facts?

This distinction between fact and interpretation can be a tricky one, but it is also essential, because, if you can't keep your data separate from what you've begun to think about them, you risk losing sight of the data altogether. Press yourself to keep answering the same question—What can be said with some certainty about this evidence? or a variant of the question, such as What's clearly true of this evidence is. . . .

You may find it helpful to do this exercise with a partner or in a small group. If you work in a small group, have one member record the results as these emerge. You might also try this exercise as a freewrite and then share your results with others by reading aloud your list of facts or putting them on a blackboard along with other people's results. Once you've assembled a list of what can fairly be stated as fact about your evidence, you are ready to start on some version of the question, What do these facts suggest? or What features of these data seem most to invite/require interpretation?

A TEMPLATE FOR ORGANIZING PAPERS USING 10 ON 1

Here is a template for writing papers to be used with doing 10 on 1. It brings together much of the key terminology introduced in this chapter. Think of it not as a rigid format but as an outline for moving from one phase of your paper to the next.

1. In your introduction, start by noting (panning on) an interesting pattern or tendency you have found in your evidence. Explain what attracted you to it—why you find it potentially significant and worth looking at. This paragraph would end with a tentative theory (working thesis) about what this pattern or tendency might reveal or accomplish.
2. Zoom in on your representative example, some smaller part of the larger pattern.
3. Argue for the example's representativeness and usefulness in coming to a better understanding of your subject.
4. Do 10 on 1—analyze your representative example—sharing with your readers your observations (what you notice) and your tentative conclusions (answers to the So what? question). Then use complicating evidence to refine your claims.
5. In a short paper you might at this point move to your conclusion, with its qualified, refined version of your thesis and brief commentary on what

you've accomplished—that is, the ways in which your analysis has illuminated the larger subject.

6. In a longer paper you would begin constellating—organizing the essay by exploring and elaborating the connections among your representative examples analyzed via 10 on 1. In the language of the film analogy, you would move from your initial zoom to another zoom on a similar case, to see the extent to which the thesis you evolved with your representative example needed further adjusting to better reflect the nature of your subject as a whole. This last move is a primary topic of our next chapter.

ASSIGNMENT: Writing a Paper Using 10 on 1

Write a paper in which you do 10 on 1 with a single, representative example of something you are trying to think more carefully about. This could be a representative passage from a story or a representative story from a volume of stories by a single author. It could be a representative poem from a short volume of poetry or a representative passage from a nonfiction book or article. It could be a passage from a favorite columnist or a single representative song from a CD. It could be a single scene or moment or character from a film or play or other performance. It could be one picture or work of art that is representative of a larger exhibit.

Brainstorm your "1" on the page, making observations and asking, So what? Draw out as much meaning as possible from your representative example. Go for depth. Then use this example as a lens for viewing similar examples. Use the template in the previous section as a model for organizing the paper.

GUIDELINES FOR ANALYZING EVIDENCE

1. Learn to recognize unsubstantiated assertions, rather than treating claims as self-evident truths. Whenever you make a claim, offer your readers the evidence that led you to it.
2. Make details speak. Explain how evidence confirms or qualifies your claim, and offer your reasons for believing the evidence means what you say it does.
3. Say more about less rather than less about more, allowing a carefully analyzed part of your subject to provide perspective on the whole.
4. It is generally better to make ten points on a representative issue or example than to make the same basic point about ten related issues or examples; this axiom we call 10 on 1.
5. Argue overtly that the evidence on which you choose to focus is representative. Be careful not to generalize on the basis of too little or unrepresentative evidence.

GUIDELINES FOR ANALYZING EVIDENCE (CONTINUED)

6. Use your best example as a lens through which to examine other evidence. Analyze subsequent examples to test and develop your conclusions, rather than just confirming that you are right.
7. Look for difference within similarity as a way of doing 10 on 1. Rather than repeating the same overly general claim (i.e., doing 1 on 10), use significant variation within the general pattern to better develop your claim.
8. To find the most revealing piece or feature of the evidence, keep asking yourself, What can I say with some certainty about the evidence? If you continually rehearse the facts, you are less likely to let an early idea blind you to subsequent evidence.
9. Whatever kind of evidence you're using, the emphasis rests on how you use what you have: on articulating what the evidence means, and carefully linking it to your claims.

CHAPTER 6

Making a Thesis Evolve

Quick Take

In a good piece of writing, the thesis—the primary claim—operates as a powerful tool of discovery. Its function is to examine and question your subject to arrive at some point about its meaning that would not have been immediately obvious to your readers. The paper itself records the refining of the thesis, its central idea.

This view of the thesis as fluid and dynamic, growing and changing as it encounters evidence, goes against the way most textbooks present the thesis. They see the thesis as the finished product of an act of thinking: an inert assertion to be marched through a paper from beginning to end. But if you actually study how a thesis behaves in a piece of writing—if you track its recurrences through an essay—you'll see that a strong thesis *evolves*; it is not static.

This chapter will show you ways of querying your own thesis formulations and using evidence to make your thesis evolve. The payoff is that your claims will become more specific, more qualified, more true. But you'll need to get past the idea that what we call complicating evidence—data for which your thesis does not completely account—is a problem that needs to be avoided in favor of a new and simpler claim. Here's the mantra: *the complications you encounter are an opportunity to make your thesis evolve*, not a problem. Formulating a claim, seeking out conflicting evidence, and then using these conflicts to revise the claim is a primary movement of mind in analytical writing. The savvy writer will take advantage of opportunities to make apparent complications overt in order to make his or her claim respond more fully to the evidence.

The chapter contains one heuristic, Six Steps for Making a Thesis Evolve through Successive Complications, which offers a skeletal version of this process.

Before we go further, here's a quick look at the difference between good and bad thesis statements. It summarizes where we've been and points to where we're headed.

WHAT A GOOD WORKING THESIS DOES

Promotes thinking: leads you to greater precision about what things mean
Reduces scope: separates useful evidence from the welter of details
Provides direction: helps you decide what to talk about and what to talk about next
Contains tension: balances *this* against *that* in a form such as "although x, nevertheless *y* . . ."

WHAT A BAD THESIS DOES

Addicts you too early to a too-large idea, so that you stop actually seeing the evidence in its real-life complexity or thinking about the idea itself
Produces a demonstration rather than discovery of new ideas by making the same overly general point again and again about a range of evidence
Includes too much possible data without helping you see what's most important to talk about

WHAT'S WRONG WITH A STATIC THESIS?

Basically, a static thesis is imprecise, overly general, and redundant. It asserts a meaning that is applied again and again as an answer, using different but similar pieces of evidence. Usually this answer is simple and single. It needs to be, because it is being asked to explain a lot, to contain so much evidence. The truth, though, is rarely either simple or single.

The static thesis—a broad label slapped on a bunch of examples—tends to produce *demonstrations*. Demonstrations point at something—"See?"—and then they're done with it. They're not interested in seeing *into* things, only looking at them from a distance to confirm a point so broad, such as "Exercise is good for you," that it was probably not worth offering as a thesis in the first place.

The staple of the demonstration form of paper writing is the five-paragraph form, which we critiqued earlier. The form predisposes the writer to begin with a BIG claim, such as "Environmentalism prevents economic growth," and then offer a paragraph on three examples (say, statutes that protect endangered wildlife, inhibit drilling for oil, and levy excessive fines on violators). Then the big claim simply gets repeated again, after a "Thus, we see . . ."

At the least, such a thesis is inaccurate. It's too easy to find exceptions to the claim and also to question what its key words actually mean. Mightn't environmentalism also promote economic growth by, say, promoting tourism? And is the meaning of economic growth self-evident? Couldn't a short-term economic boon be a long-term disaster, as might be the case for oil exploration in the polar regions?

In sum, most of what typically goes wrong in using a thesis is the result of a writer leaping too quickly to a generalization that would do as a thesis, and then treating evidence *only* as something to be mustered in support of that idea. Simply repeating the same big idea keeps things too superficial. In papers that contain a static thesis, nothing happens to the claim itself: it doesn't grow, add to our knowledge, or generate new ideas.

*Most of what typically goes wrong in using a thesis is the result of a writer leaping too quickly to a generalization that would do as a thesis, and then treating evidence **only** as something to be mustered in support of that idea.*

A. EVOLVING A THESIS

THE RECIPROCAL RELATIONSHIP BETWEEN WORKING THESIS AND EVIDENCE: THE THESIS AS A CAMERA LENS

It's useful to think of the thesis as a camera lens that affects how we see the subject, what evidence we select, and what questions we ask about that evidence. But it's essential to understand that the subject being viewed also affects the lens. In good analytical writing, the analysis of evidence should also focus and refocus (bring about revision of) the thesis. Even in a final draft, writers are usually fine-tuning their governing idea in response to their analysis of evidence. The relationship between thesis and subject is thus *reciprocal* (see Figure 6.1).

In the terms of this analogy, very broad thesis statements, made up of imprecise (fuzzy) terms, make bad camera lenses. If your lens is insufficiently sharp, you are not likely to see much in your evidence. If you say, for example, that "the economic situation today is bad," you will at least have some sense of direction, but the imprecise terms *bad* and *economic situation* don't provide you with a focus

FIGURE 6.1 The Reciprocal Relationship Between Thesis and Evidence.

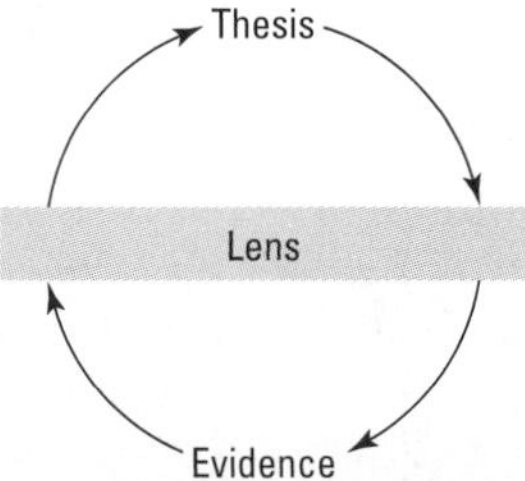

Like a lens, the thesis affects the way a writer sees evidence. Evidence should also require the writer to readjust the lens.

clear enough to distinguish significant detail in your evidence. Without significant detail to analyze, you can't develop your thesis, either by showing readers what the thesis is good for (what it allows us to understand and explain) or by clarifying its terms.

Let's take one more brief example of a fuzzy-lens thesis and lay out a few basic moves for evolving it. Say that you're looking for a trend (or strand) in contemporary films you've seen and, as a working thesis, you claim that "Women in contemporary films are represented as being more sensitive than men." To avoid a mere demonstration and instead make this thesis evolve, you would need to

- query its key terms, asking yourself what these actually mean, and
- search for data that not only matched your claim but also didn't match it.

You'd more or less be assuming that you had overstated things, and you'd be looking for ways to press yourself to make further distinctions in your initial formulation, to make it less fuzzy.

Having claimed that the films show women as more sensitive than men, ask yourself what *sensitive* means, and by what criteria you are assessing its presence and absence. Is the overt expression of tender feelings the only acceptable evidence for being sensitive? Couldn't men have less demonstrative ways of being sensitive? What is the best piece or two of evidence that men do show something like sensitivity in the films you're considering?

And surely you could also complicate that claim by locating it within a richer *context*. It's not enough to assert that women are represented as sensitive in the films. What are these films inviting us to think about their sensitivity? Are the women punished for it in the plots? Are they rewarded with being liked (approved of) by the films, even if this trait causes them problems?

Such considerations as these would require significant *reformulation* of the thesis. This procedure will normally be repeated several times, with each new discussion of significant evidence. For this reason you may find it useful to think of the claim-making aspect of a piece of writing not simply as a thesis, which implies that it is a settled thing, but rather as *a working thesis*, which suggests that the claim is in process, metamorphosing through a series of contexts within the paper.

The term working thesis suggests that the claim is in process, not static.

By the end of the paper, the claim that "women are more sensitive than men" should have evolved into a more carefully defined and qualified statement that reflects the thinking you have done in your analysis of evidence. This is what good concluding paragraphs do; they reflect back on and reformulate your paper's initial position in light of the thinking you have done about it (see Figure 6.2).

You might ask, Isn't this reformulating of the thesis something a writer does *before* he or she writes the essay? Certainly some of it is accomplished in your exploratory drafting and note taking, and your revision process should weed out

FIGURE 6.2 Evolving thesis diagram

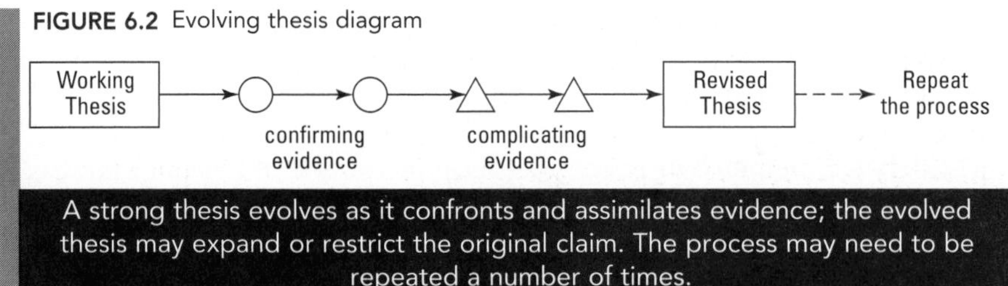

A strong thesis evolves as it confronts and assimilates evidence; the evolved thesis may expand or restrict the original claim. The process may need to be repeated a number of times.

various false starts and dead ends. But your finished paper should include the evolutions of your thesis. To an extent, all good writing re-creates the chains of thought that lead writers to their conclusions. If you just listed your conclusions, your readers might rightly question how you arrived at them. The main routes of your movement from a tentative idea to a refined and substantiated theory should remain visible for readers to follow. (See "The Evolving Thesis in a Final Draft" later in this chapter for further discussion of how much thesis evolution to include in your final draft.)

A FIRST NOTE ON THE SHAPE OF THESIS STATEMENTS

Before we move on to concentrated applications of the procedure for making a thesis evolve, take a look back at the shape of the imprecise thesis statements used as examples in this chapter:

> Environmentalism prevents economic growth.
>
> The economic situation today is bad.
>
> Women in contemporary films are represented as being more sensitive than men.

All three are simple, declarative sentences that offer very abstract assertions. That is, they are both grammatically and conceptually simple. More than that, they're *slack*—especially the first two, which stand alone, not in relation to anything else.

The very *shape* of these weak thesis statements is a warning sign. Most effective working theses, though they may begin more simply, achieve both grammatical and conceptual complexity as they evolve. Such theses contain tension, the balance of this against that; this degree, with that qualification. Often they begin with *although* or incorporate *however* or use an *appears to be about* x *but is actually about* y kind of formulation. Here, by contrast to the weak theses above, are three possible evolutions of the "sensitivity" thesis:

> Although women cry more readily in contemporary films, the men, by not crying, seem to win the audience's favor.
>
> The complications that fuel the plots in today's romantic comedies arise because women and men express their sensitivity so differently; the resolutions, however, rarely require the men to capitulate.
>
> A spate of recent films has witnessed the emergence of the new "womanly" man as hero, and not surprisingly, his tender qualities seem to be the reason he attracts the female love interest.

Try this 6.1: Qualifying Overstated Claims

Using as a model of inquiry the treatment of the example thesis "Women in contemporary films are represented as being more sensitive than men," seek out complications in one of the overstated claims in the following list. These complications might include conflicting evidence (which you should specify) and questions about the meaning or appropriateness of key terms (again, which you should exemplify). Illustrate a few of these complications, and then reformulate the claim in language that is more carefully qualified and accurate.

Welfare encourages recipients not to work.
Midwives are more caring than gynecologists.
Religious people are more moral than those who are not religious.
School gets in the way of education.
Herbal remedies are better than pharmaceutical ones.
The book is always better than the film.

PROCEDURE FOR MAKING THE THESIS EVOLVE THROUGH SUCCESSIVE COMPLICATIONS: THE EXAMPLE OF *EDUCATING RITA*

This section of the chapter presents an extended example that illustrates how the initial formulation of a thesis might evolve—through a series of complications—over the course of a draft. It closely follows in organization the "Six Steps for Making a Thesis Evolve."

Let's consider the stages you might go through within a more finished draft to evolve a thesis about a film. In *Educating Rita*, a working-class English hairdresser (Rita) wants to change her life by taking courses from a professor (Frank) at the local university, even though this move threatens her relationship with her husband (Denny), who burns her books and pressures her to quit school and get pregnant. Frank, she discovers, has his own problems: he's a divorced alcoholic who is bored with his life, bored with his privileged and complacent

SIX STEPS FOR MAKING A THESIS EVOLVE

1. Formulate an idea about your subject—a working thesis.
2. See how far you can make this thesis go in accounting for (confirming) evidence.
3. Locate complicating evidence that is not adequately accounted for by the thesis.
4. Make explicit the apparent mismatch between the thesis and selected evidence, asking and answering So what?
5. Reshape your claim to accommodate the evidence that hasn't fit.
6. Repeat steps 2, 3, 4, and 5 several times.

students, and bent on self-destruction. The film follows the growth of Frank and Rita's friendship and the changes it brings about in their lives. By the end of the film, each has left a limiting way of life behind and has set off in a seemingly more promising direction. She leaves her constricting marriage, passes her university examinations with honors, and begins to view her life in terms of choices; he stops drinking and sets off, determined but sad, to make a new start as a teacher in Australia.

Formulate an idea about your subject, a working thesis (step 1).

Working thesis: *Educating Rita* celebrates the liberating potential of education.

The film's relatively happy ending and the presence of the word *educating* in the film's title make this thesis a reasonable opening claim.

See how far you can make this thesis go in accounting for evidence (step 2). The working thesis seems compatible, for example, with Rita's achievement of greater self-awareness and independence. You would go on to locate similar data that would support the idea that education is potentially liberating. She becomes more articulate, which allows her to free herself from otherwise disabling situations. She starts to think about other kinds of work she might do, rather than assuming that she must continue in the one job she has always done. She travels, first elsewhere in England and then to the Continent. So, the thesis checks out as viable: there is enough of a match with evidence to make it worth pursuing.

Locate evidence that is not adequately accounted for by the thesis and ask So what? about the apparent mismatch between the thesis and selected evidence (steps 3 and 4). Other evidence troubles the adequacy of the working thesis, however: Rita's education causes her to become alienated from her husband, her parents, and her social class; at the end of the film she is alone and unsure about her direction in life. In Frank's case, the thesis runs into even more problems. His boredom, drinking, and alienation seem to have been caused, at least in part, by his education rather than by his lack of it. He sees his book-lined study as a prison. Moreover, his profound knowledge of literature has not helped him control his life: he comes to class drunk, fails to notice or care that his girlfriend is having an affair with one of his colleagues, and asks his classes whether it is worth gaining all of literature if it means losing one's soul.

Reshape your claim to accommodate the evidence that hasn't fit (step 5). *Question: What are you to do?* You cannot convincingly argue that the film celebrates the liberating potential of education, because that thesis ignores such a significant amount of the evidence. Nor can you "switch sides" and argue that the film attacks education as life-denying and disabling, because this thesis is also only partially true.

What not to do. Faced with evidence that complicates your thesis, you should not assume that it is worthless and that you need to start over from scratch. View the "problem" you have discovered as an opportunity to modify your thesis rather than abandon it. After all, the thesis still fits a lot of significant evidence. Rita is arguably better off at the end of the film than at the beginning: we are not left to believe that she should have remained resistant to education, like her husband, Denny, whose world doesn't extend much beyond the corner pub.

What to do. Make apparent complications explicit—the film's seemingly contradictory attitudes about education—and then modify the wording of your thesis in a way that might resolve or explain these contradictions. You might, for example, be able to resolve an apparent contradiction between your initial thesis (the film celebrates the liberating potential of education) and the evidence by proposing that there is more than one version of education depicted in the film. You would, in short, start qualifying and clarifying the meaning of key terms in your thesis.

In this case, you could divide education as represented by the film into two kinds: enabling and stultifying. The next step in the development of your thesis would be to elaborate on how the film seeks to distinguish true and enabling forms of education from false and debilitating ones (as represented by the self-satisfied and status-conscious behavior of the supposedly educated people at Frank's university).

> **Revised thesis:** *Educating Rita* celebrates the liberating potential of enabling—in contrast to stultifying—education.

Repeat steps 2, 3, 4, and 5 (step 6). Having refined your thesis in this way, you would then repeat the step of seeing what the new wording allows you to account for in your evidence. The revised thesis might, for example, explain Frank's problems as being less a product of his education than of the cynical and pretentious versions of education that surround him in his university life. You could posit further that, with Rita as inspiration, Frank rediscovers at least some of his idealism about education.

What about Frank's emigration to Australia? If we can take Australia to stand for a newer world, one where education would be less likely to become the stale and exclusive property of a self-satisfied elite, then the refined version of the thesis would seem to be working well. In fact, given the possible thematic connection between Rita's working-class identity and Australia (associated, as a former frontier and English penal colony, with lower-class vitality as opposed to the complacency bred of class privilege), the thesis about the film's celebration of the contrast between enabling and stultifying forms of education could be sharpened further. You might propose, for example, that the film presents institutional education as desperately in need of frequent doses of "real life" (as represented by Rita and Australia)—infusions of working-class pragmatism, energy, and optimism—if it is to remain healthy and open, as opposed to becoming the oppressive property of a privileged social class. This is to say that the film arguably exploits stereotypical assumptions about social class.

> **Revised thesis:** *Educating Rita* celebrates the liberating potential of enabling education, defined as that which remains open to healthy doses of working-class, real-world infusions.

Similarly, you can make your supporting ideas (those on which your thesis depends) more accurate and less susceptible to oversimplification by seeking evidence that might challenge their key terms. Sharpening the language of your supporting assertions will help you develop your thesis.

Consider, for example, the wording of the supporting idea that *Educating Rita* has a happy ending. Some qualification of this idea through consideration of possibly conflicting evidence could produce an adjustment in the first part of the working thesis, that the film celebrates education and presents it as liberating. At the end of the film, Frank and Rita walk off in opposite directions down long, empty airport corridors. Though promising to remain friends, the two do not become a couple. This closing emphasis on Frank's and Rita's alienation from their respective cultures, and the film's apparent insistence on the necessity of each going on alone, significantly qualifies the happiness of the "happy ending."

Once you have complicated your interpretation of the ending, you will again need to modify your thesis in accord with your new observations. Does the film simply celebrate education if it also presents it as being, to some degree, incompatible with conventional forms of happiness? By emphasizing the necessity of having Frank and Rita each go on alone, the film may be suggesting that to be truly liberating, education—as opposed to its less honest and more comfortable substitutes—inevitably produces and even requires a certain amount of loneliness and alienation. Shown in Figure 6.3 are the successive revisions of the thesis.

Final version of thesis: *Educating Rita* celebrates the liberating potential of enabling education (kept open to real-world, working-class energy) but also acknowledges its potential costs in loneliness and alienation.

Try this 6.2: Tracking a Thesis

As should be clear now, various versions of the thesis recur throughout a piece of writing, usually with increasing specificity, complication, and grammatical complexity. The four thesis statements on *Educating Rita* illustrate this pattern of recurrence clearly. One of the best ways to teach yourself how and where to locate statements of the thesis in your own writing is to track the thesis in a piece of reading. Ideally you should choose an essay or article used in one of your courses, because this exercise will also powerfully increase your understanding of the reading. Use a highlighter to mark the evolutions. Where in the essay do you find the thesis? How has it changed in each recurrence? In response to what complication?

B. USING THE EVOLVING THESIS TO ORGANIZE THE FINAL DRAFT

Having achieved a final version of a thesis, *what next?* Why wouldn't a writer just offer the last and fullest statement of the thesis in his or her first paragraph and then prove it?

Usually it's neither possible nor desirable to encapsulate in the opening sentences what it will actually take the whole paper to explain. The position articulated in the fully evolved thesis is typically too complex to be stated intelligibly and concisely in the introduction. But more, if you think of an essay as an

FIGURE 6.3 Successive Revisions of a Thesis.

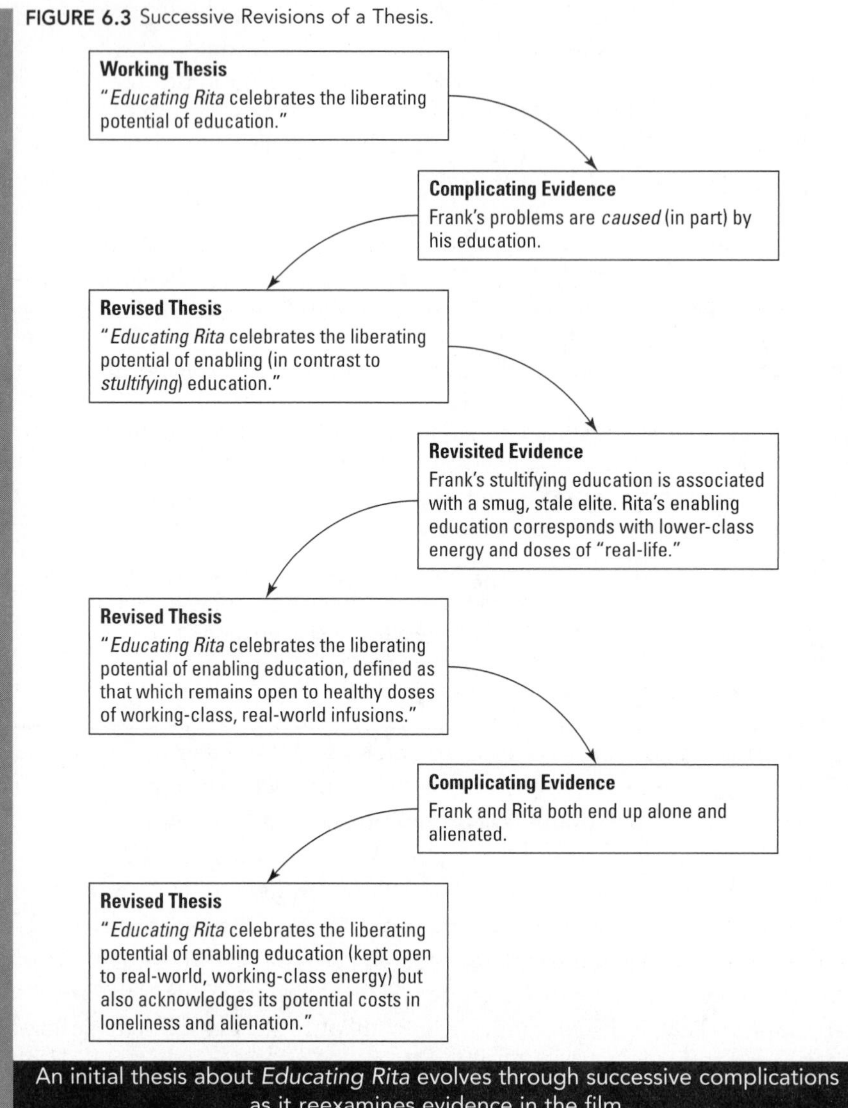

Working Thesis
"*Educating Rita* celebrates the liberating potential of education."
Complicating Evidence
Frank's problems are *caused* (in part) by his education.
Revised Thesis
"*Educating Rita* celebrates the liberating potential of enabling (in contrast to *stultifying*) education."
Revisited Evidence
Frank's stultifying education is associated with a smug, stale elite. Rita's enabling education corresponds with lower-class energy and doses of "real-life."
Revised Thesis
"*Educating Rita* celebrates the liberating potential of enabling education, defined as that which remains open to healthy doses of working-class, real-world infusions."
Complicating Evidence
Frank and Rita both end up alone and alienated.
Revised Thesis
"*Educating Rita* celebrates the liberating potential of enabling education (kept open to real-world, working-class energy) but also acknowledges its potential costs in loneliness and alienation."

An initial thesis about *Educating Rita* evolves through successive complications as it reexamines evidence in the film.

act of thinking, then the evolutions of the thesis record the history of your various changes in thinking as you confronted evidence. If your readers get to see these, they are far more likely to go along with you, literally to follow your trains of thought.

Before treating these matters in more detail, however, let us nail down a general answer to the question of thesis locations.

- The first articulation of the working thesis almost always occurs late in the opening paragraph or early in the second paragraph of a piece, after the writer has presented the problem or question that establishes the tension the thesis aims to resolve, and given some kind of context for it.

- Subsequent articulations of the thesis usually occur at points of transition, typically at paragraph openings following the analysis of complicating evidence. These thesis evolutions are often overtly marked as such—the writer tells readers that on the basis of this analysis, it is necessary to amend the governing claim. This kind of explicit updating has the added benefit of providing unity to the essay, using the thesis as a kind of spine.
- The final statement of the thesis occurs in the concluding paragraph, or perhaps the penultimate one. It is usually offered in clear relationship to the terms offered in the introduction, so the reader is offered a last vision of where the essay has traveled.

If you think of an essay as an act of thinking, then the evolutions of the thesis record the history of your various changes in thinking as you confronted evidence.

A more complete answer to the questions of where and how to locate versions of the thesis in a final draft involves two related issues: (1) the location of the thesis statement in relation to the conventional shapes of argument—induction and deduction—and (2) the customary location of the thesis according to the protocols (ways of proceeding) of different disciplines. We will treat each of these in its turn.

THE EVOLVING THESIS AND COMMON THOUGHT PATTERNS: DEDUCTION AND INDUCTION

Put simply, in a deductive paper a fairly full-fledged version of the thesis appears at the beginning; in an inductive paper, it appears at the end (see Figure 6.4, A and B).

As a thought process, deduction reasons from a general principle (assumed to be true) to the particular case. It introduces this principle up front and then uses it to select and interpret evidence. For example, a deductive paper might state in its first paragraph that attitudes toward and rules governing sexuality in a given culture can be seen, at least in part, to have economic causes. The paper might then apply this principle, already assumed to be true, to the codes governing sexual behavior in several cultures or several kinds of sexual behavior in a single culture.

A good deductive argument is, however, more than a mechanical application or matching exercise of general claim and specific details that are explained by it. Deductive reasoning uses the evidence to draw out the implications—what logicians term *inferring the consequences*—of the claim. The general principle explains selected features of particular cases, and *reciprocally*, the evidence brings out implications in the principle.

Thus, the general principle stated at the beginning of the paper and the idea stated as the paper's conclusion are not the same. Rather, the conclusion presents the (evolved) idea that the writer has arrived at through the application of the principle.

FIGURE 6.4 Deduction and Induction.

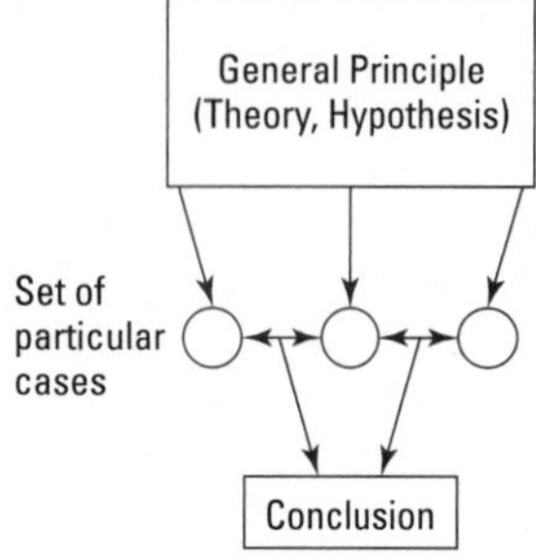

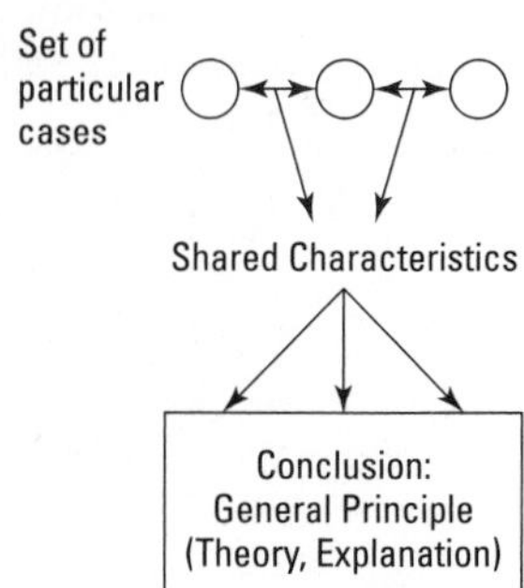

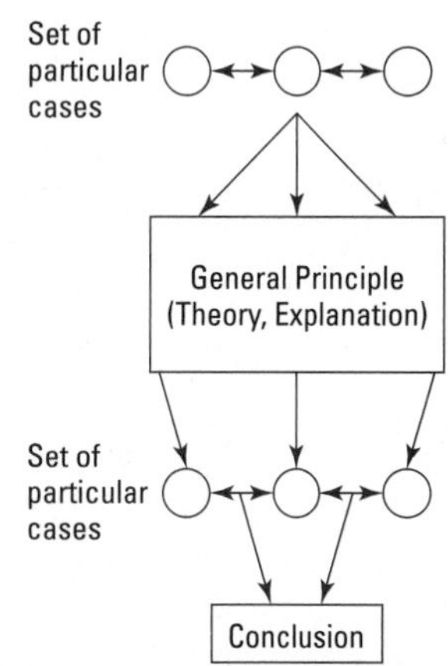

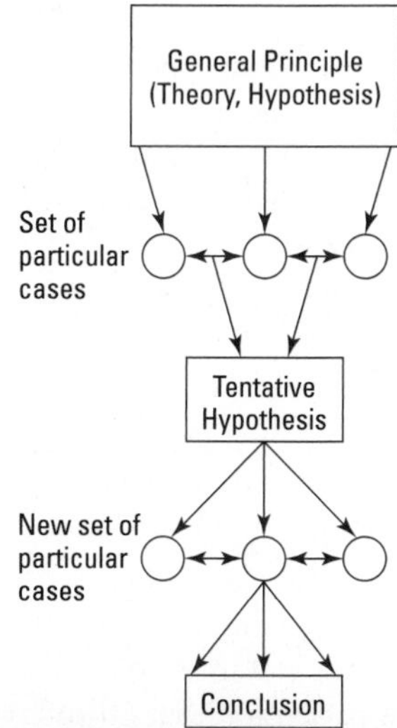

Deduction (A) uses particular cases to exemplify general principles and analyze their implications. Induction (B) constructs general principles from the analysis of particular cases. In practice, analytical thinking and writing blend deduction and induction and start either with particular cases (C) or a general principle (D).

An inductively organized paper typically begins not with a principle already accepted as true but with particular data for which it seeks to generate some explanatory principle.

Whereas deduction moves by applying a generalization to particular cases, induction moves from the observation of individual cases to the formation of a general principle. Because all possible cases can obviously never be examined—every left-handed person, for example, if one wishes to theorize that left-handed people are better at spatial thinking than right-handers—the principle (or thesis) arrived at through inductive reasoning always remains open to doubt.

Nevertheless, the thesis of an inductive paper is generally deemed acceptable if a writer can demonstrate that the theory is based on a reasonably sized sampling of representative instances. (This matter of representativeness was taken up in our earlier discussion of 10 on 1.) Suffice it to say that a child who arrives at the thesis that all orange food tastes bad on the basis of squash and carrots has not based that theory on an adequate sampling of available evidence.

What we hope this discussion makes clear is that whether your analysis is primarily inductive or deductive, the thesis will undergo evolution as it confronts evidence. What still needs to be understood, though, is that in most cases induction and deduction operate in tandem (see Figure 6.4, C and D). It's true that in some disciplines (philosophy, for example) the deductive pattern of argument prevails, but not exclusively: the analysis of evidence, though clearly designed to reflect a general principle, will also lead to new formulations that will modify the general principle in various ways.

It is in the nature of analysis to move between the particular and the general, regardless of which comes first. Whether the overall shape of the analysis—its mode of progression—is primarily inductive or deductive, it will still *gain in complexity* from beginning to end. The statement with which you begin is not also the end (see Figure 6.4).

Try this 6.3: Formulating an Inductive Principle

Study a group of like things inductively. You might, for example, use greeting cards aimed at women versus greeting cards aimed at men, a group of poems by one author, or ads for one kind of product (jeans) or aimed at one target group (teenage girls).

Make use of the looking-for-patterns heuristic (see the Method in Chapter 2) to compile and organize a set of significant details about the data, and then leap to a general claim about the group that you think is interesting and reasonably accurate. This generalization is your inductive principle. Then use the principle to examine deductively more data of the same kind, exploring its implications as you evolve it more accurately.

THE EVOLVING THESIS AS HYPOTHESIS AND CONCLUSION IN THE NATURAL AND SOCIAL SCIENCES

A thesis functions differently depending on the academic discipline—whether it must be stated in full at the outset, for example, and what happens to it between the beginning of the paper and the end. The differences appear largest as you move back and forth between courses in the humanities and courses in the natural and certain of the social sciences.

VOICES FROM ACROSS THE CURRICULUM

The Hypothesis in the Sciences

It should go without saying that if the empirical evidence doesn't confirm your hypothesis, you rethink your hypothesis, but it's a complex issue. Researchers whose hypotheses are not confirmed in fact often question their *method* ("if I had more subjects," or "a better manipulation of the experimental group," or "a better test of intelligence," etc.) as much as their hypothesis. And that's often legitimate. Part of the challenge of psychological research is its reliance on a long array of assumptions. Failure to confirm a hypothesis could mean a problem in any of that long array of assumptions. So failure to confirm your hypothesis is often difficult to interpret.

–Alan Tjeltveit, Professor of Psychology

The thesis in Experimental Psychology papers is the statement of the hypothesis. It is always carefully and explicitly stated in the last few sentences of the introduction. The hypothesis is usually a deductive statement such as, If color does influence mood, then an ambiguous picture printed on different colors of paper should be interpreted differently, depending on the color of the paper. Specifically, based on the results of Jones (1997), the pink paper should cause participants to perceive the picture as a more calm and restful image, and the green paper should cause the picture to be interpreted as a more anxious image.

–Laura Snodgrass, Professor of Psychology

The thesis is usually presented in the abstract and then again at the end of the introduction. Probably the most frequent writing error is not providing a thesis at all. Sometimes this is because the student doesn't *have* a thesis; other times it is because the student wants to maintain a sense of mystery about the paper, as if driving toward a dramatic conclusion. This actually makes it harder to read. The best papers are clear and up front about what their point is, then use evidence and argument to support and evaluate the thesis. I encourage students to have a sentence immediately after their discussion of the background on the subject that can be as explicit as "In this paper I will argue that although research on toxic effects of methyl bromide provides troubling evidence for severe physiological effects, conclusive proof of a significant environmental hazard is lacking at this time."

I try to avoid the use of the term *hypothesis.* I think it gives the false sense that scientists always start with an idea about how something works. Frequently, that is not the case. Some of the best science has actually come from observation. Darwin's work on finches is a classic example. His ideas about adaptation probably derived *from* observation.

–Bruce Wightman, Professor of Biology

> Economists do make pretense to follow scientific methodology. Thus we are careful not to mix hypothesis and conclusion. I think it's important to distinguish between what is conjectured, the working hypothesis, and what ultimately emerges as a result of an examination of the evidence. Conclusions come only after some test has been passed.
>
> *–James Marshall, Professor of Economics*

Broadly speaking, papers in the humanities are inclined to begin inductively, and papers in the natural and social sciences deductively. The natural and social sciences generally use a pair of terms, *hypothesis* and *conclusion*, for the single term *thesis*. Because writing in the sciences is patterned according to the scientific method, writers in disciplines such as biology and psychology must report how the original thesis (hypothesis) was tested against empirical evidence and then conclude on this basis whether or not the hypothesis was confirmed.

The gap between this way of thinking about the thesis and the concept of an evolving thesis is not as large as it may seem. The scientific method is in sync with one of the chapter's main points, that something must happen to the thesis between the introduction and the conclusion, so that the conclusion does more than just reassert what was already asserted in the beginning.

Analogously, in a scientific paper, the hypothesis is tested against evidence, the results of which allow the writer to draw conclusions about the hypothesis's validity. Although the hypothesis does not change (or evolve), the testing of it and subsequent interpretation of those results produce commentary on and, often, qualifications of the paper's central claim.

In the natural and social sciences, successive reformulations of the thesis are less likely to be recorded and may not even be expressly articulated. But, as in all disciplines, the primary analytical activity in the sciences is to repeatedly reconsider the assumptions upon which a conclusion is based.

THE EVOLVING THESIS AND INTRODUCTORY AND CONCLUDING PARAGRAPHS

If you are not using the hypothesis/conclusion format, your final drafts could often begin by predicting the evolution of their theses. Thus, the *Educating Rita* paper might open by using a version of the seems-to-be-about-*x* gambit, claiming that at first glance the film seems to celebrate the liberating potential of education. You could then lay out the evidence for this view and proceed to complicate it in the ways we've discussed.

What typically happens is that you lead (usually at the end of the first paragraph or at the beginning of the second) with the best version of your thesis that you can come up with that will be understandable to your readers without a lengthy preamble. If you find yourself writing a page-long introductory paragraph to get to your initial statement of thesis, try settling for a simpler articulation of your central idea in its first appearance. As you move through the paper, substantiate, elaborate on, test, and qualify your paper's opening gambit.

VOICES FROM ACROSS THE CURRICULUM

Recognizing Your Thesis

For an analytical or interpretive historical essay, *thesis* is a conventional term and one of much value. The thesis usually is that point of departure from the surfaces of evidence to the underlying significance, or problems, a given set of sources reveal to the reader and writer. In most cases, the thesis is best positioned up front, so that the writer's audience has a sense of what lies ahead and why it is worth reading on. I say *usually* and *in most cases* because the hard and fast rule should not take precedence over the inspirational manner in which a thesis can be presented. But the inspiration is not to be sought after at the price of the thesis itself. It is my experience, in fact, that if inspiration strikes, one realizes it only after the fact.

Recognizing a thesis can be extremely difficult. It can often be a lot easier to talk "about" what one is writing than to say succinctly what the thrust of one's discussion is. I sometimes ask students to draw a line at the end of a paper after they have finished it, and then write one, at most two sentences, saying what they most want to tell their readers. My comment on that postscript frequently is "Great statement of your thesis. Just move it up to your first paragraph."

–Ellen Poteet, Professor of History

The most important thing to do in the introductory paragraph of an analytical paper is to lay out a genuine issue, which is to say, something that seems to be at stake in whatever you are studying. Ideally, you should select a complex issue—one not easily resolved, seeming to have some truth on both sides—and not an overly general one. Otherwise you run the risk of writing a paper that proves the obvious or radically oversimplifies.

Set up this issue as quickly and concretely as you can, avoiding generic (fits anything) comments, throat clearing, and review-style evaluations. As a general rule, you should assume that readers of your essay will need to know on page 1—preferably by the end of your first paragraph—what your paper is attempting to resolve or negotiate.

The first paragraph does not need to—and usually can't—offer your conclusion; it will take the body of your paper to accomplish that. It should, however, provide a quick look at particular details that set up the issue. Use these details to generate a theory, a *working hypothesis*, about whatever it is you think is at stake in the material. The rest of the paper will test and develop this theory.

Your concluding paragraph will offer the more carefully qualified and evolved version of your thesis that the body of your paper has allowed you to arrive at. Rather than just summarize and restate what you said in your introduction, the concluding paragraph should leave readers with what you take to be your single best insight, and it should put what you have had to say into some kind of perspective. See Chapter 8 for a more extended discussion of introductions and conclusions.

C. EVOLVING A THESIS IN AN EXPLORATORY DRAFT: *LAS MENINAS*

Now let's look at another extended example, this time using it to bring together the strategies that we have suggested so far for writing an analytical paper. The example is a student writer's exploratory draft on a painting called *Las Meninas* (Spanish for "the ladies-in-waiting") by the seventeenth-century painter Diego Velázquez. We have, by the way, selected a paper on a painting because all of the student's data (the painting) is on one page where you can keep referring back to it, trying to share in the writer's thought process.

Look at the painting in Figure 6.5, and then read the student's draft. As you read, you will notice that much of the essay is still unfocused with listlike description, but as we noted in Chapter 1, careful description is a necessary stage in moving toward interpretations of evidence, especially in an exploratory draft where the writer is not yet committed to any single position. Notice how the writer's word choice in her descriptions prompts various kinds of interpretive leaps. We have added in brackets our observations about how the writer is proceeding.

FIGURE 6.5 *Las Meninas* by Diego Velázquez, 1656.

Approximately 10'5" x 9'. Museo del Prado, Madrid.

Velázquez's Intentions in *Las Meninas*

[1] Velázquez has been noted as being one of the best Spanish artists of all time. It seems that as Velázquez got older, his paintings became better. Toward the end of his life, he painted his masterpiece, *Las Meninas*. Out of all his works, *Las Meninas* is the only known self-portrait of Velázquez. There is much to be said about *Las Meninas*. The painting is very complex, but some of the intentions that Velázquez had in painting *Las Meninas* are very clear. [The writer opens with background information and a broad working thesis (underlined).]

[2] First, we must look at the painting as a whole. The question that must be answered is, Who is in the painting? The people are all members of the Royal Court of the Spanish monarch Philip IV. In the center is the king's daughter, who eventually became Empress of Spain. Around her are her *meninas* or ladies-in-waiting. These *meninas* are all daughters of influential men. To the right of the *meninas* are dwarfs who are servants, and the family dog who looks fierce but is easily tamed by the foot of the little dwarf. The more unique people in the painting are Velázquez himself, who stands to the left in front of a large canvas; the king and queen, whose faces are captured in the obscure mirror; the man in the doorway; and the nun and man behind the *meninas*. To analyze this painting further, the relationship between characters must be understood. [The writer describes the evidence and arrives at an operating assumption—focusing on the relationship between characters.]

[3] Where is this scene occurring? Most likely it is in the palace. But why is there no visible furniture? Is it because Velázquez didn't want the viewers to become distracted from his true intentions? I believe it is to show that this is not just a painting of an actual event. This is an event out of his imagination. [The writer begins pushing observations to tentative conclusions by asking, So what?]

[4] Now, let us become better acquainted with the characters. The child in the center is the most visible. All the light is shining on her. Maybe Velázquez is suggesting that she is the next light for Spain and that even God has approved her by shining all the available light on her. Back in those days there was a belief in the divine right of kings, so this just might be what Velázquez is saying. [The writer starts ranking evidence for importance and continues to ask, So what?; she arrives at a possible interpretation of the painter's intention.]

[5] The next people of interest are the ones behind the *meninas*. The woman in the habit might be a nun and the man a priest.

[6] The king and queen are the next group of interesting people. They are in the mirror, which is to suggest they are present, but they are not as visible as they might be. Velázquez suggests that they are not always at the center where everyone would expect them to be. [The writer continues using Notice and focus plus asking So what?; the

writer has begun tackling evidence that might conflict with her first interpretation.]

[7] The last person and the most interesting is Velázquez. He dominates the painting along with the little girl. He takes up the whole left side along with his gigantic easel. But what is he painting? As I previously said, he might be painting the king and queen. But I also think he could be pretending to paint us, the viewers. The easel really gives this portrait an air of mystery because Velázquez knows that we, the viewers, want to know what he is painting. [The writer starts doing 10 on 1 with her selection of the most significant detail.]

[8] The appearance of Velázquez is also interesting. His eyes are focused outward here. They are not focused on what is going on around him. It is a steady stare. Also interesting is his confident stance. He was confident enough to place himself in the painting of the royal court. <u>I think that Velázquez wants the king to give him the recognition he deserves by including him in the "family</u>." And the symbol on his vest is the symbol given to a painter by the king to <u>show that his status and brilliance have been appreciated by the monarch</u>. It is unknown how it got there. It is unlikely that Velázquez put it there himself. That would be too outright, and Velázquez was the type to give his messages subtly. Some say that after Velázquez's death, King Philip IV himself painted it to finally <u>give Velázquez the credit he deserved for being a loyal friend and servant</u>. [The writer continues doing 10 on 1 and asking, So what?; she arrives at three tentative theses (underlined).]

[9] I believe that Velázquez was very ingenious by putting his thoughts and feelings into a painting. He didn't want to offend the king who had done so much for him. It paid off for Velázquez because he did finally get what he wanted, even if it was after he died. [The writer concludes and is now ready to redraft to tighten links between evidence and claims, formulate a better working thesis, and make this thesis evolve.]

DESCRIPTION TO ANALYSIS: THE EXPLORATORY DRAFT

There are a number of good things about this draft. The writer has, for example, used the *interesting* prompt to press herself to notice and emphasize particular details in her evidence. The purpose of the exploratory draft is to use writing as a means of arriving at a working thesis that your next draft can more fully evolve. Most writers find that potential theses emerge near the end of the exploratory draft—which is the case in the student draft (see the three claims that are underlined in paragraph 8).

As you can see, the writer has not wasted time trying for a polished introductory paragraph. She has instead crafted an opening that allows her to get started and to start fast—no rambling prefatory material. This introduction, with its overly broad working thesis, does its job. It provides enough direction to guide the writer in her initial examination of evidence, using the artist's intention as her *interpretive context.*

INTERPRETIVE LEAPS AND COMPLICATING EVIDENCE

Notice that as early as paragraphs 3 and 4, the writer has begun to push herself to tentative conclusions (interpretive leaps) about the meaning of selected features of her evidence. What is especially good about the draft is that it reveals the writer's willingness to push on from her first idea (reading the painting as an endorsement of the divine right of kings, expressed by the light shining on the princess) by seeking out *complicating evidence.*

The writer could have settled for the divine-right-of-kings idea, and then simply foregrounded details in the picture that would corroborate it, such as the deferential bowing of the *meninas* arranged in a circle with the princess at the center. But this potential thesis would not have accounted for enough of the evidence, especially evidence that clearly doesn't fit, such as the small size and decentering of the king and queen, and the large size and foregrounding of the painter himself.

Rather than ignoring these potentially troublesome details, the writer instead zooms in on them, making the painter's representation of himself and of his employers the 1 for doing 10 on 1 (making a number of observations about a single representative piece of evidence and analyzing it in depth). This analytical move produces a burst of interpretive thinking in the form of three related claims (underlined in paragraph 8 in the student's draft), all of which have thesis potential.

REVISING THE EXPLORATORY DRAFT

Now what? The writer is ready to rewrite the paper to more carefully formulate and evolve her thesis. What could she do better as she reviews her evidence in preparation for starting this next draft?

First, she could make more use of looking for **patterns of repetition and contrast** (see Chapter 2).

Examples of exact or nearly exact **repetitions**:

the pictures in the background
the fact that both the dwarf and the painter, each on his own side of the painting, stare confidently and directly at the viewer

Examples of **strands** (repetition of a similar kind of detail):

details having to do with family
servants (dwarf, *meninas*, dog? painter?)
details having to do with art and the making of art

Examples of **organizing contrasts**—binaries:

royalty/commoners
employers/servants
large/small
foreground/background
central (prominent)/marginalized (less prominent)

The writer also might make more productive use of the **So what?** question, asking it repeatedly about pieces of evidence and about her own claims. In this way she might press herself to arrive at a range of possible answers until she finds the one that seems to best fit the evidence.

So what that the king and queen are small, but the painter, princess, and dwarf are all large and fairly equal in size and prominence? So what that there are size differences in the painting? What might large or small size mean?

Here are some possible answers to these So what? questions:

- Perhaps the king and queen have been reduced so that Velázquez can showcase their daughter, the princess.
- Perhaps the size and physical prominence of the king and queen are relatively unimportant. In that case, what matters is that they are a presence, always overseeing events (an idea implied but not developed in paragraph 6).
- Perhaps the relative size and/or prominence of figures in the painting can be read as indicators of what the painter wants to say about their importance.
- Perhaps the painter is demonstrating his ability to make the king and queen any size—any level of importance—he chooses. Although the writer does not overtly say so, the king and queen are among the smallest and the least visible figures.

TESTING THE ADEQUACY OF THE THESIS

The evidence that the writer included in paragraphs 6 and 7 (the decentering of the king and queen and the prominence and confident stare of the painter) caused her to drop her initial thinking—that the primary intention was to endorse the divine right of kings. The direction that her thinking takes next is not, however, an entirely new idea. The shift she is apparently making (but not yet overtly articulating) is from the painting as showcase of royal power to the painting as showcase of the painter's own power.

Given the answers posed above to the So what? question about the relative size and importance of the king and queen versus the painter—parallel to if not greater in prominence than the princess herself—the writer should probably choose the second of the two potential theses arrived at in paragraph 8. That idea—that the painting is a bid for recognition of the painter's status and brilliance—explains more of the evidence than anything else she has come up with so far. It explains, for example, the painter's prominence and the relative insignificance of the monarchs; the painter, in effect, creates their stature (size, power) in the world through his paintings. Framed in a mirror and appearing to hang on the wall, the king and queen are, arguably, suspended among the painter's paintings, mere reflections of themselves—or, rather, the painter's reflection of them.

HOW THE NEXT DRAFT MIGHT GO

Let's see how well the status-and-brilliance idea accounts for details in the painting. This thesis seems useful in accounting for the presence of the large dwarf in the right-hand foreground. Positioned in a way that links him with the painter, the dwarf arguably furthers the painting's message and does so, like much else in the painting, in the form of a loaded joke: the small ("dwarfed" by the power of others) are brought forward and made big.

What other features of the painting might the thesis account for? How about the various ways that the painting seems to deny viewers' expectations? Both by decentering the monarchs and concealing what is on the easel, the painter again emphasizes his power, in this case, over the viewers (among whom might be the king and queen if their images on the back wall are mirrored reflections of them standing, like us, in front of the painting). He is not bound by anyone's expectations and in fact appears to take a certain pleasure in using viewers' expectations to manipulate them: he can make them wish to see something he has the power to withhold.

Does this mean that the status-and-brilliance thesis is adequately evolved? If (as the writer has said) the painter is demonstrating that he can make the members of the royal family any size he wants, then the painting is not only a bid for recognition but also a playful, though not so subtle, threat: be aware of my power and treat me well, or suffer the consequences. As artist, the painter decides how the royal family will be seen. The king and queen depend on the painter, as they do in a different way on the princess, with whom Velázquez makes himself equal in prominence, to extend and perpetuate their power.

Before leaving this example we want to emphasize that the version of the thesis that we have just proposed is not necessarily the "right" answer. Looked at in a different context, the painting might have been explained primarily as a demonstration of the painter's mastery of the tools of his trade—light, for example, and perspective. But our proposed revision of the thesis for the *Las Meninas* paper meets two important criteria for evaluating the adequacy of a thesis statement.

1. It unifies the observations the writer has made.
2. It is capable of accounting for a wide range of evidence.

Remember that the thesis develops through successive complications. Allowing your thesis to run up against potentially conflicting evidence ("But what about this?") enables you to build upon your initial idea, extending the range of evidence it can accurately account for by clarifying and qualifying its key terms. Although throwing out the old thesis and starting over may be what is needed, you should first try to use evidence that is not accounted for by your current thesis as a means of evolving the thesis further.

D. THE EVOLVING THESIS IN A FINAL DRAFT

It seems fitting, after the examples of papers in the planning *(Rita)* and drafting *(Meninas)* stages, that we conclude this chapter with an example of an evolving thesis in a final draft. Here is a piece analyzing a recent German film about an East German family around the time of the fall of the Berlin Wall in 1989. (Note: there is also a freewrite on this film at the end of Chapter 1.) Certainly there is more that could be done with this essay, but it is on balance a strong piece that illustrates a number of the features of effective analysis that we have been discussing. In addition, we have included within brackets brief descriptions of how the essay evolves and underlined versions of its thesis.

Good Bye Lenin! Before and After the Fall

[1] The recent German film *Good Bye Lenin!* directed by Wolfgang Becker is a comedy that appears to celebrate the freedom that comes with the tearing down of the Berlin Wall and the reunification of Germany in 1989. It follows the life of Alex Schäfer, who also provides voice-over narration interpreting events from before until after the wall falls. Before, he grows up dreaming of becoming a cosmonaut, but he ends up working in a TV repair shop in East Berlin. Afterward, he peddles satellite TV dishes as part of a joint East–West German venture and visits postmodern nightclubs with his Russian nurse girlfriend, Lara. But amidst the celebratory fireworks and the influx of Mercedes and Burger Kings, there is a bittersweet tone, for the film also appears to mourn the loss of a socialist version of what Alex calls "idealism"—a term that refers to his mother's utopian socialist ideals of social equality, innocent goodwill, and boundless possibility. [The writer establishes a working thesis evident in the tension between the two uses of *appears*, suggesting that the essay will negotiate the tension between celebration and mourning.]

[2] Clearly the film is interested in comparing life before unification with what comes afterward, because the central event of the plot presses Alex to restore the before. His ardent Communist mother, Kathrin, suffers a stroke and falls into a coma as she glimpses her son protesting the regime. When she suddenly awakens eight months later, Alex and his sister Ariane are told that any shocks, any changes in her environment, will threaten her life, and so Alex strives to conceal from her the fact that Germany has reunified while she has been asleep, and that the East has rapidly begun to become Westernized. By superimposing a faux view of the Communist past onto the capitalist present, director Becker is using *Good Bye Lenin!* to assess the change, to explore the profit and loss of both the before and the after. [The terms profit and loss keep this paragraph in touch with the celebrate/mourn binary of its working thesis. But the writer has come to recognize that the director complicates both the celebration of the fall of the wall and the mourning of the lost socialist "utopia."]

[3] Most of the action in the film concerns Alex's attempts to restore the appearance of the past and to preserve the illusion that the past is still present. We repeatedly see him filling old East German–labeled jars with new international products; it is an act of devotion, a sign of his love for his afflicted mother. Of course, complications arise—cracks in the façade that occur when his mother glimpses evidence of the change.

[4] As a repeated strategy—and a major source of the film's comedy—Alex and his coworker Denis conceive and make videotaped bogus television news accounts that explain these cracks. For example, when the mother sees a banner advertising Coca-Cola, the videotape announces the discovery that Coke is actually an East German formula stolen by the West and now returned to its rightful home. Here Alec and his friend have become comic versions of the old socialist state, reinterpreting the facts—and covering up the truth—in order to preserve old loyalties and the status quo. <u>The friends' attempts to reassure the mother by protecting her socialist dreams are comic but also poignant, and so the element of mourning remains</u>. [In this and the preceding paragraph the writer negotiates the tension between the comedy and the sense of mourning for the lost past. Does the mourning get cancelled, he wonders? No, he decides.]

[5] This comic pattern gets repeated several times throughout the film and culminates in the comic climax: one of the final faux news reports interprets footage of the wall being torn down as an act of disgruntled West Germans seeking solace from capitalist greed and competition in the peace and tranquility of the East. This is funny because it inverts the truth. The film actually shows us the East German youth becoming entranced by the outlandish décor (lamp shades of purple fur), rock music, cars, and money that invade from the West. Similarly, Alex's sister Ariane has given up her studies and gone to work at a Burger King managed by her eventual husband. The film focuses in this way on capitalist culture as seen from the socialist point of view.

[6] From this perspective, <u>there is little to celebrate</u>, as the invading western culture seems frivolous, fixated on material goods and inclined to sacrifice the long term good in favor of short term gain. We see Burger King uniforms everywhere; Becker is making it clear that in place of uniformity in the service of the state, there is now uniformity in the service of international fast food corporations. [The writer confronts evidence that causes him to qualify his claim that the film celebrates the fall of the wall.]

[7] The comedy feels good—there are many laugh-out-loud moments—but *Good Bye Lenin!* is not all good times, liberation, and rock 'n' roll. In a film in which videotapes are shown to be calculated deceptions, designed to pacify those too frail to accommodate change, we dare not accept the film itself as offering some uncomplicated vision of things.

[8] Interestingly, the comedy tends to drop out at disruptive moments. For example, we are shown the desperate emptiness of the lives of the older generation of East Germans who feel lost because of the changes, roaming around the apartment house, grumbling amidst the piles of

furniture and other detritus of the previous regime now abandoned to the street. We see the skirmishes between Alex and Ariane about the lengths to which they are going to preserve the illusion for their mother. [The writer notes a deepening of the mourning element called attention to in places in the film where the comedy drops out.]

[9] Surely one of the most important of such moments occurs near the end, when Alex's girlfriend, Lara, who has nursed his mother since she first fell ill, betrays the dream script that he has created for his mother, a script of the past as unchanged in the present, an East Germany intact and self-professedly superior to the West.

[10] It is a very brief scene, lasting only a few seconds, spliced into a longer narrative episode. The mother has suffered a relapse, and in response to her dying request, her son Alex has traveled to the West to retrieve his father, who had fled the Communist regime perhaps fifteen years before. As Alex is returning to the hospital with his father, the scene shifts to Lara telling Kathrin that the wall fell some months ago and that Alex has staged the unchanged present she has been inhabiting since awaking from her coma. Kathrin shakes her head in disbelief. The camera then cuts away and never returns to this conversation.

[11] The scene is, at the same time, a moment of truth-telling to the mother and betrayal of the son. It is not, strictly speaking, required by the plot: shortly thereafter the mother will die, and the film will end amidst fireworks celebrating the official reunification of Germany. So why does the film make the decision to include this moment? [The writer concludes the analysis by formulating a conclusion that follows the pattern of bringing together opposites—truth-telling and betrayal—and then asks So what?]

[12] Without this scene, Alex succeeds in his scheme—the hero achieves his goal. And his goal is humanitarian, surely, in preserving his mother's illusions. But from the outset Ariane opposes the scheme, and later Lara too confronts Alex about the extremity and impracticality of his position. We begin to see it as *his obsession,* and somehow, his need or desire to preserve the past, which his mother's infirmity conveniently enables. <u>The scheme of re-creating the past increasingly comes to appear to be an opportunity to create an idealized version of the past that never existed but has been associated with his mother almost from the beginning</u>. Alex admits as much in one of his voice-overs later in the film, speaking of the world his and his friend's videotapes have created as "an ideal socialism" like the one that he and his mother wished to believe in. [The writer uses evidence to shift his thinking on what it is that the film mourns—not the actual socialist state that is gone, but his and his mother's illusions and powerful desire to idealize the past.]

[13] And so ultimately *Good Bye Lenin!* is a film that is anxious about resisting change and accepting delusions, even beautiful illusions. It seems to insist that if we retain them, we must do so with the knowledge that they are false. Interestingly, the women are in solidarity here: Lara does not allow Kathrin to die deluded. Alex, on the other hand, apparently exits the film oblivious to the fact that his mother has been undeceived—but that is another matter. [The first two sentences of this paragraph represent a late evolution of the thesis as the writer continues to develop the implications of his conclusion. He then introduces a new complication, as he considers how the treatment of gender might bear on the film's critique of socialism.]

[14] The film is also anxious about simply acceding to change—specifically, the capitalism it represents as dominating the West, which the videotaped news report comically represents as a hell worth fleeing. Surely the film recognizes the greater liberties that the West makes possible; it does not confuse the "ideal socialism" in which Alex and Kathrin wish to believe with the somber political realities of East Germany. We learn, for instance, that Kathrin was removed from her beloved teaching job because of her too ardent idealism, and that her husband fled the country to escape the prejudice that was directed against him because he was not a member of the Communist Party. [The writer returns to his earlier claim about the film both celebrating and mourning the changes brought about the fall of the Berlin wall. The writer has discovered that the film is not really about capitalism and socialism so much as it is about the stories we tell ourselves and the ideals we have tried to live by.]

[15] In the end, it seems, *Good Bye Lenin!* wants to value the dream, the utopian vision of ideal socialism, especially because with the advent of Western capitalism into East Germany, one source of that dream has been desiccated. But the film takes great pains to qualify that dream—to distinguish it from East German Communist practice, and crucially, to insist that we recognize that it is only a dream and not the real thing. That is why Lara tells Kathrin the truth. In the spiraling success story of a newly reunited Germany, Wolfgang Becker has made a film that reminds us that the stories we tell others fill psychic needs not just for others but for ourselves, and that we need to be reminded that all stories, however necessary, in one way or another are false. [The writer concludes by returning to his essay's opening binary formulation and offering a more evolved version of his thesis as it pertains to the film's point of view, but that also beckons beyond it, to the constructed and inevitably partisan nature of all accounts of the world. The writer acknowledges the film's anxiety about embracing change but then presents further evidence for what has emerged as his major claim, that the film recognizes that ideal socialism never existed and that the East German version of real socialism may not warrant much mourning.]

RECAP OF THE EVOLVING THESIS IN *GOOD BYE LENIN!* BEFORE AND AFTER THE FALL

As we hope you can see, this essay's thesis evolution does not evolve in a straight line or into a single claim. There is a logic to the thesis development, but it is not a clear and predictable evolution. Rather, we can see that the basic terms of the thesis—celebrating the future versus mourning the past, the individual versus the collective, the dominant and accepted historical script versus the comic inversion of the script—get taken to different places, and impel different kinds of discoveries as the writer raises and revisits them.

The celebration/mourning binary in the essay begins a chain of analysis that allows the writer to discover what is for him a more important binary—between betrayal and truth-telling, evident in the moment Lara talks to Kathrin—that does not erase or replace the original contrast so much as grow out of it.

In the concluding phase of the essay, the writer becomes increasingly concerned with the problematic truth value of all motives and all representations of the past. This emphasis leads him to recognize the distinction the film makes between delusions and necessary but recognized illusions, and by the final paragraph he has arrived at the conclusion that the film impels us to see all representations as necessarily partisan.

And so finally, what might we conclude? Perhaps that the evolving thesis as a principle of development does not necessarily move toward greater truth, only toward new or additional truths, discoveries different from those with which it began. In this context, then, the thesis becomes a necessary constituent of analytical writing because it defines a field of play and allows a writer to go places. That is more than enough for writers who want to increase their understanding, and for their readers.

Try this 6.4: Tracking a Thesis in a Student Draft

Track the evolutions of the thesis in the draft printed below. It is a fairly early draft; the writer has not yet been expected to attend to organization, style, and so forth. In fact, one purpose of such idea-gathering drafts is to invite you to conduct an open-minded survey of the data, which with any luck will culminate in the discovery of one or more possible working theses.

Instructions: Locate significant repetition and contrast; then work with the relationship between thesis and evidence.

1. Circle or underline the paper's key words, its patterns of repetition, and organizing contrasts.
2. Briefly list the details you find most interesting in the draft, and in a sentence explain why.
3. Identify versions of the writer's thesis.
4. Go back through the paper and mark evidence that seems not to fit this thesis.
5. Play around with ranking and renaming the paper's various strands and organizing contrasts. What other possible theses or qualified version of the existing one might these data suggest?

Mall Cuisine Goes International

[1] At the outer reaches of a fantastic enclosed shopping mall near downtown Boston's Copley Square there is a truly unique restaurant named Bon Marche. The mall is huge, connecting several high-rise hotels, and it offers literally hundreds of upscale shops.

[2] My friend and I entered Bon Marche just to look around; we were hungry for some breakfast, and it looked interesting. Almost immediately a Latino guy about twenty wearing a green beret stopped us to give us a check. He told us that there was one for takeout and one for eating there, and then he explained how the restaurant worked. There were a number of different stations serving food, and you were supposed to give them your ticket to be stamped when they served you your food. The ticket, by the way, which was designed to look like a passport, included a comical warning that if you lost it, you would be required to wash dishes there for two days.

[3] The stations were scattered all over this enormous room, and each one offered a different kind of food. (We later learned that they had a market downstairs too, where they sold the food uncooked.) A lot of the foods were international in flavor. There was lots of seafood, especially shellfish of various kinds. Other stations offered omelettes, sushi, wood-oven-cooked pizza, fresh-squeezed juices (including carrot!), soups such as chowders and bouillabaisse, crepes, Oriental stir-fries, and various kinds of bread and pastries. I did notice, though, that there was no lox, though plenty of fresh salmon they would cook for you.

[4] I noticed that at a number of these stations, you could basically design your food choice. For example, you would choose what "innards" you wanted in your omelette from a variety of ingredients in silver bowls at the front of the station. The same went for the stir-fry station and the pizza station, where you chose among toppings. And most of the stations also offered vegetarian options.

[5] We decided to have breakfast, and that's when we discovered one drawback to this station idea. We had to wait in line for about fifteen minutes before we were able to order our omelettes. They looked and smelled great, and they came with hash browns, but when we asked for some bacon, the Latina girl who was cooking told us that we had to go to another station where they cook breakfast meats. That would mean waiting in line again, while our food was getting cold. And then we'd have to wait in line again if we wanted juice, which was at another station.

[6] Just as there is a great variety of exotic foods, there are a lot of diverse seating areas at Bon Marche. One area was glassed in, like a French bistro, with small white tables that had multicolored umbrellas in them. Another seemed Indonesian—rattan furniture and hay bales. We chose an area by the windows looking out over downtown Boston. It was decorated with lattices like a grape arbor at an Italian villa.

[7] Once we noticed the international character of Bon Marche's food and settings, we began to see it in other aspects of the place. First of all, there's the French name of the place. And virtually all of the staff were members of ethnic minorities—especially Latinos, African-Americans, and Asians. Plus the place was awash in the upbeat rhythms of Latino music—a kind of nouveau sound. Although most of the staff were young, the sushi counter proved an exception. That station featured two middle-aged Asian women, bent over their sushi mats, making mostly Boston rolls and California rolls, one after another after another. It was a pretty sad sight, and we were struck with how boring the job must be. How many omelettes was that woman cooking an hour, with the line getting longer every minute?

[8] Still, the food was tasty (and inexpensive!), and the atmosphere was really interesting. I had the overall impression that Bon Marche was all about youth and choice and feeling optimistic. Considering its great location and how busy it was, the staff must make pretty good money, and so they are getting to participate in the American dream of opportunity and freedom as well.

[9] That's when I realized that maybe what makes Bon Marche so great is that it embodies democracy. It has everything for everybody, and the individual gets to choose what he or she wants, down to the last detail. And the whole place was just bursting with food—there seemed to be abundance for all. It makes available to everyone the experience of international cuisines at affordable prices, whereas in the past you would have had to travel abroad or at least to expensive restaurants all over the city, to get this diversity. Mall culture offers the world in one convenient location, as Bon Marche exemplifies.

[10] As we were leaving, we saw more evidence for this democracy idea in the uniforms that the staff were wearing. They all had full-length aprons matching the color of their berets—the men all wore green berets and the women wore red ones. This uniform was bright and happy, and the berets seemed to symbolize that everyone was equal. Also the berets seem to go with the

restaurant's French name, except that the berets themselves had these fitted leather bases that made them seem stiffer than traditional French berets.

[11] The cashier was located at the front of the restaurant, and when she gave us our receipts, we also received what they called "exit visas" that we then had to hand to a guy standing about four feet away, just at the interface of the restaurant and the rest of the mall. It was as if were leaving this fantasy world behind.

[12] Maybe that's why we noticed the contrast in the store next door to Bon Marche. It was a bank—a large, glassed-in open space. There were about fifteen desks equipped with computer workstations, each with a swivel chair and file cabinets. We could see the workers from behind as they went about their business. I'm not sure exactly how this fits with my ideas about Bon Marche, but it was interesting. The bank was not a fantasy space, but it did convey a sense of openness just like the restaurant did. Maybe this openness is related to the democracy idea.

REVISION CHECKLIST FOR ORGANIZING AN ESSAY WITH AN EVOLVING THESIS

The following is a handout that our colleague Professor Barri Gold adapted largely from this chapter to distribute to her students.

I'm pretty sure I have a good idea, but I'm still not sure how to organize a paper . . .

The format of your paper should reflect a willingness to test your own thesis and to advance your thinking. A paper that begins and ends on the same idea, a paper that goes nowhere, suggests that you have closed yourself off to possibilities that don't fit neatly into your preconceived ideas.

The following is a useful though very general outline for structuring the bulk of your paper (does not include introductions and conclusions):

1. Clear statement of **working thesis**.
2. Confirming evidence—that is, evidence that supports your thesis. To a large extent, this is the most familiar part of your paper . . . the part in which you argue your case.

3. **Complicating evidence**—that is, evidence that does not readily support your thesis.

   Many people have trouble with this concept, so, more elaborately:

   Complicating evidence may (but need not) be contradictory (something that actually disproves or undermines your thesis). Such evidence is often quite useful for forcing you to rethink and advance your thesis.

   Complicating evidence may be something for which your thesis does not account. It may seem outside the scope of your thesis.

   As such, it may be used to test the limits of your thesis. It could force you to specify your thesis/categories.

   Complicating evidence may also add another element to your thinking. It may lead you to consider the significance of another theme, etc., on your current working thesis.
4. **Rethink/revise your thesis** in such a way that it incorporates this new, complicating evidence.
5. **Go to step 1.**

Yes. This structure is reiterative. You may go through this several times during the course of a paper. Your judgment should determine which iterations are interesting enough to be incorporated into your final draft. Begin with a working thesis that is neither too obvious nor too far-fetched to convince your reader(s) and work step-by-step through increasingly subtle, difficult, or complex ideas.

Some advice on **microstructure:**

- **Depth** is more useful than breadth. It is better to spend your time really exploring your best representative example than to accumulate many superficially treated examples intended to make the same point.
- **What you need to make your point:** At each moment, you should make it clear to your reader (1) what point you are making, (2) what evidence you are using to support that point, (3) how you read the evidence, (4) how it actually does support your local point, and (5) how it connects to your overall point or current working thesis.

A special note on item 3 above: Remember, different readers will understand any given quote differently. If you do not explain your reading/interpretation, you may lose your reader. If you think your quote does not need explanation, you are probably making a point that is too obvious and you should rethink your point, your working thesis, and/or your paper overall.

ASSIGNMENT: Evolving a Thesis on a Film or Painting

The chapter has already modeled this process with these forms. Alternatively, you might use an episode of a television show or an advertisement.

First, begin by formulating a variety of possible statements about the film or painting that could serve as a working thesis. These might be in answer to the question What is the film/painting about? or What does it "say"? Or you might begin with looking for patterns of repetition and contrast and formulate a thesis to explain a pattern of repetition or contrast you have observed. In any case, you shouldn't worry that these initial attempts will inevitably be overstated and thus only partially true—you have to start somewhere. At this point you will have completed step 1.

Next, follow the remainder of the procedure for making the thesis evolve, listed again here for convenience:

1. Formulate an idea about your subject, a working thesis.
2. See how far you can make this thesis go in accounting for confirming evidence.
3. Locate evidence that is not adequately accounted for by the thesis.
4. Make explicit the apparent mismatch between the thesis and selected evidence, asking and answering So what?
5. Reshape your claim to accommodate the evidence that hasn't fit.
6. Repeat steps 2, 3, 4, and 5 several times.

GUIDELINES FOR FINDING AND DEVELOPING A THESIS

1. A thesis is an idea that you formulate and reformulate about your subject. It should offer a theory about the meaning of evidence that would not have been immediately obvious to your readers.
2. Look for a thesis by focusing on an area of your subject that is open to opposing viewpoints or multiple interpretations. Rather than trying to locate a single right answer, search for something that raises questions.
3. Treat your thesis as a hypothesis to be tested rather than an obvious truth.
4. Most effective theses contain tension, the balance of this against that, this degree with that qualification. They are conceptually complex, and that is reflected in their grammatical shape—often they begin with *although* or incorporate *however.*
5. The body of your paper should serve not only to substantiate the thesis by demonstrating its value in selecting and explaining evidence, but also to bring the opening version of the thesis into better focus.
6. Evolve your thesis—move it forward—by seeing the questions that each new formulation of it prompts you to ask.

GUIDELINES FOR FINDING AND DEVELOPING A THESIS (CONTINUED)

7. Develop the implications of your evidence and of your observations as fully as you can by repeatedly asking, So what?
8. When you encounter potentially conflicting evidence (or interpretations of that evidence), don't simply abandon your thesis. Take advantage of the complications to expand, qualify, and refine your thesis until you arrive at the most accurate explanation of the evidence that you can manage.
9. Arrive at the final version of your thesis by returning to your initial formulation—the position you set out to explore—and restating it in the more carefully qualified way you have arrived at through the body of your paper.
10. To check that your thesis has evolved, locate and compare the various versions of it throughout the draft. Have you done more than demonstrate the general validity of an unqualified claim?

CHAPTER 7

Recognizing and Fixing Weak Thesis Statements

Quick Take

This chapter will teach you how to recognize the difference between good thesis statements—statements that make claims that need proving—and weak thesis statements. Weak thesis statements have in common the fact that they don't give the writer enough to do in his or her essay. Typically a weak thesis is an unproductive claim because it doesn't actually require further thinking or proof, as, for example, in the case of "The jeans industry targets its advertisements to appeal to young adults" (probably a statement of fact that doesn't need proving) or "An important part of one's college education is learning to better understand others' points of view" (a piece of conventional wisdom that most people would already accept as true, and thus not in need of arguing).

Solutions? Be suspicious of your first responses to a subject. Privilege live questions over inert answers. Find ways to bring out the complexity of your subject. Look again at "What It Means to Have an Idea" in Chapter 1, which tells you to start with something puzzling that you want to figure out rather than with something you already believe to be clearly and obviously true. When in doubt, do more exploratory writing to trigger better ideas.

A. FIVE KINDS OF WEAK THESES AND HOW TO FIX THEM

A *strong thesis* makes a claim that (1) requires analysis to support and evolve it and (2) offers some point about the significance of your evidence that would not have been immediately obvious to your readers. By contrast, a *weak thesis* either makes no claim or makes a claim that does not need proving. As a quick flash-forward, here are the five kinds of weak thesis statements—ones that

1. make no claim ("This paper will examine the pros and cons of . . .");
2. are obviously true or are a statement of fact ("Exercise is good for you");
3. restate conventional wisdom ("Love conquers all");
4. offer personal conviction as the basis for the claim ("Shopping malls are wonderful places"); and
5. make an overly broad claim ("Individualism is good").

WEAK THESIS TYPE 1: THE THESIS MAKES NO CLAIM

The following statements are not productive theses because they do not advance an idea about the topics the papers will explore.

Problem Examples

I'm going to write about Darwin's concerns with evolution in *The Origin of Species.*

This paper will address the characteristics of a good corporate manager.

Both problem examples name a subject and link it to the intention to write about it, but they don't make any claim about the subject. As a result, they direct neither the writer nor the reader toward some position or plan of attack. The second problem example begins to move toward a point of view through the use of the value judgment *good,* but this term is too broad to guide the analysis. The statement-of-intention thesis invites a list: one paragraph for each quality the writer chooses to call good. Even if the thesis were rephrased as "This paper will address why a good corporate manager needs to learn to delegate responsibility," the thesis would not adequately suggest why such a claim would need to be argued or defended. *There is, in short, nothing at stake, no issue to be resolved.* A writer who produces a thesis of this type is probably unduly controlled by a relatively passive, information in/information out approach to learning.

Solution Raise specific issues for the essay to explore.

Solution Examples

Darwin's concern with survival of the fittest in *The Origin of Species* initially leads him to neglect a potentially conflicting aspect of his theory of evolution—survival as a matter of interdependence.

The very trait that makes for an effective corporate manager—the drive to succeed—can also make the leader domineering and therefore ineffective.

Some disciplines expect writers to offer statements of method and/or intention in their papers' openings. Generally, however, these openings also make a claim: for example, "In this paper I will examine how congressional Republicans undermined the attempts of the Democratic administration to legislate a fiscally responsible health care policy for the elderly," *not* "In this paper I will discuss America's treatment of the elderly." (See Chapter 8, "Introductions and Conclusions," for further discussion of using overt statements of intention.)

WEAK THESIS TYPE 2: THE THESIS IS OBVIOUSLY TRUE OR IS A STATEMENT OF FACT

The following statements are not productive theses because they do not require proof. A thesis needs to be an assertion with which it would be possible for readers to disagree.

Problem Examples

The jeans industry targets its advertisements to appeal to young adults.

The flight from teaching to research and publishing in higher education is a controversial issue in the academic world. I will show different views and aspects concerning this problem.

If few people would disagree with the claim that a thesis makes, there is no point in writing an analytical paper on it. Though one might deliver an inspirational speech on a position that virtually everyone would support (such as the value of tolerance), endorsements and appreciations don't usually lead to analysis; they merely invite people to feel good about their convictions.

In the second problem example, few readers would disagree with the fact that the issue is "controversial." In the second sentence of that example, the writer has begun to identify a point of view—that the flight from teaching is a "problem"—but her next declaration, that she will "show different views and aspects," is a statement of fact, not an idea. The phrasing of the claim is noncommittal and so broad that it prevents the writer from formulating a workable thesis. If you find yourself writing theses of this type, review the discussion of the problems with generalizing in Chapter 1.

Solution Find some avenue of *inquiry*—a question about the facts or an issue raised by them. Make an assertion with which it would be possible for readers to disagree.

Solution Examples

By inventing new terms, such as *loose fit* and *relaxed fit,* the jeans industry has attempted to normalize, even glorify, its product for an older and fatter generation.

The "flight from teaching" to research and publishing in higher education is a controversial issue in the academic world. As I will attempt to show, the controversy is based to a significant degree on a false assumption, that doing research necessarily leads teachers away from the classroom.

WEAK THESIS TYPE 3: THE THESIS RESTATES CONVENTIONAL WISDOM

Restatement of one of the many clichés that constitute a culture's conventional wisdom is not a productive thesis unless you have something to say about it that hasn't been said many times before.

Problem Examples

An important part of one's college education is learning to better understand others' points of view.

From cartoons in the morning to adventure shows at night, there is too much violence on television.

"*I* was supposed to bring the coolers; *you* were supposed to bring the chips!" exclaimed ex-Beatle Ringo Starr, who appeared on TV commercials for Sun Country Wine Coolers a few years ago. By using rock music to sell a wide range of products, the advertising agencies, in league with corporate giants such as Pepsi, Michelob, and Ford, have corrupted the spirit of rock 'n' roll.

All of these examples say nothing worth proving because they are clichés. (Conventional wisdom is a polite term for cliché.) Most clichés were fresh ideas once, but over time they have become trite, prefabricated forms of nonthinking. Faced with a phenomenon that requires a response, many inexperienced writers rely on a knee-jerk reaction: they resort to a small set of culturally approved "answers." In this sense, clichés resemble statements of fact. So commonly accepted that most people nod to them without thinking, statements of conventional wisdom make people feel a comfortable sense of agreement with one another. The problem with this kind of packaged solution is that because conventional wisdom is so general and so conventional, it doesn't teach anybody—including the writer—anything. Worse, because the cliché appears to be an idea, it prevents the writer from engaging in a fresh, open-minded exploration of his or her subject.

There is some truth in all of the problem examples above, but none of them *complicates* its position. A thoughtful reader could, for example, respond to the claim that advertising has corrupted the spirit of rock 'n' roll by suggesting that rock 'n' roll was highly commercial long before it colonized the airwaves. The conventional wisdom that rock 'n' roll is somehow pure and honest whereas advertising is phony and exploitative invites the savvy writer to formulate a thesis that overturns these clichés. As our solution example demonstrates, one could argue that rock actually has improved advertising, not that ads have ruined rock—or, alternatively, that rock has shrewdly marketed idealism to a gullible populace. At the least, a writer deeply committed to the original thesis would do better to examine what Ringo was selling—what he stands for in this particular case—than to discuss rock and advertising in such general terms.

Solution Seek to complicate—see more than one point of view on—your subject. Avoid conventional wisdom unless you can qualify it or introduce a fresh perspective on it.

Solution Examples

Although an important part of one's college education is learning to better understand others' points of view, a persistent danger is that students will simply be required to substitute their teachers' answers for the ones they grew up believing uncritically.

Although some might argue that the presence of rock 'n' roll sound tracks in TV commercials has corrupted rock's spirit, this point of view not only falsifies the history of rock but also blinds us to the ways that the music has improved the quality of television advertising.

Try this 7.1: Revising Weak Thesis Statements

You can learn a lot about writing strong thesis statements by analyzing and rewriting weak ones. Rewrite the three weak theses that follow. As in the case of our solution examples, revising will require you to add information and thinking to the weak theses. Try, in other words, to come up with some interesting claims that most readers would not already have thought of to develop the subject of television violence. (The third thesis you will recognize as a problem example for which we offered no solution.)

1. In this paper I will discuss police procedures in recent domestic violence cases.
2. The way that the media portrayed the events of April 30, 1975, when Saigon fell, greatly influenced the final perspectives of the American people toward the end result of the Vietnam War.
3. From cartoons in the morning to adventure shows at night, there is too much violence on television.

WEAK THESIS TYPE 4: THE THESIS OFFERS PERSONAL CONVICTION AS THE BASIS FOR THE CLAIM

A statement of one's personal convictions or one's likes or dislikes does not alone supply sufficient grounds for a productive thesis.

Problem Examples

The songs of the punk rock group Minor Threat relate to the feelings of individuals who dare to be different. Their songs are just composed of pure emotion. Pure emotion is very important in music, because it serves as a vehicle to convey the important message of individuality. Minor Threat's songs are meaningful to me because I can identify with them.

Sir Thomas More's *Utopia* proposes an unworkable set of solutions to society's problems because, like communist Russia, it suppresses individualism.

Although I agree with Jeane Kirkpatrick's argument that environmentalists and business should work together to ensure the ecological future of the world, and that this cooperation is beneficial for both sides, the indisputable fact is that environmental considerations should always be a part of any decision that is made. Any individual, if he looks deeply enough into his soul, knows what is right and what is wrong. The environment should be protected because it is the right thing to do, not because someone is forcing you to do it.

Like conventional wisdom, personal likes and dislikes can lead inexperienced writers into knee-jerk reactions of approval or disapproval, often expressed in a moralistic tone. The writers of the problem examples above assume that their primary job is to judge their subjects or testify to their worth, not to evaluate them analytically. As a result, such writers lack critical detachment not only from their topics but, crucially, from their own assumptions and biases. They have *taken personal opinions for self-evident truths*. You can test a thesis for this problem by asking if the writer's response to questions about the thesis would be "because I think so."

The most blatant version of this tendency occurs in the third problem example, which asserts, "Any individual, if he looks deeply enough into his soul, knows what is right and what is wrong. The environment should be protected because it is the right thing to do." Translation (only slightly exaggerated): "Any individual who thinks about the subject will obviously agree with me because my feelings and convictions feel right to me, and therefore they must be universally and self-evidently true." The problem is that this writer is not distinguishing between his own likes and dislikes (or private convictions) and what he takes to be right, real, or true for everyone else. Testing an idea against your own feelings and experience is not an adequate means of establishing whether something is accurate or true.

Solution Try on other points of view honestly and dispassionately; treat your ideas as hypotheses to be tested rather than obvious truths. In the following solution examples, we have replaced opinions (in the form of self-evident truths) with ideas—theories about the meaning and significance of the subjects that could be supported and qualified with evidence.

Treat your ideas as hypotheses to be tested rather than obvious truths.

Solution Examples

Sir Thomas More's *Utopia* treats individualism as a serious but remediable social problem. His radical treatment of what we might now call "socialization" attempts to redefine the meaning and origin of individual identity.

Although I agree with Jeane Kirkpatrick's argument that environmentalists and business should work together to ensure the ecological future of the world, her argument undervalues the necessity of pressuring businesses to attend to environmental concerns that may not benefit them in the short run.

It is fine, of course, to write about what you believe and to consult your feelings as you formulate an idea. But the risk you run by arguing from your unexamined feelings and convictions is that you will prematurely dismiss from consideration anything that is unfamiliar or does not immediately conform to what you already believe. The less willing you are to test these established and habitual convictions, the less chance you will have to refine or expand the ways in which you think. You will continue to play the same small set of tunes in response to everything you hear. And without the ability to think from multiple perspectives, you will be less able to defend your convictions against the ideas that challenge them, because you won't really have examined the logic of your own beliefs—you just believe them.

At the root of this problem lurks an anti-analytical bias that predisposes many writers to see any challenge to their habitual ways of thinking as the enemy and to view those who would raise this challenge as cynics who don't believe in anything. Such writers often feel personally attacked, when in fact the conviction they are defending is not really so personal after all. Consider, for example, the first two problem examples above, in which both writers take individualism to be an incontestable value. Where does this conviction come from? Neither of the writers arrived at the thesis independent of the particular culture in which they were raised, permeated as it is by the "rugged individualism" of John Wayne and Sylvester Stallone movies.

In other words, *individualism* as an undefined blanket term verges on *cultural cliché.* That it is always good or positive is a piece of conventional wisdom. But part of becoming educated is to take a look at such global and undefined ideas that one has uncritically assimilated. Clearly, the needs and rights of the individual in contemporary American culture are consistently being weighed and balanced against the rights of other individuals and the necessity of cooperation in groups. Look at the recent nationwide concerns with health maintenance organizations (HMOs), which control health costs but constrain the individual prerogative of the physician, or with the rights of crime victims who are banding together to seek support from a government they believe is protecting the individual rights of the criminal at the expense of the individual rights of the victim.

In light of these considerations, the writers of the first two problem examples would have to question *to what extent* they should attack a book or support a rock band merely on the basis of whether or not each honors individualism. If the author of the second problem example had been willing to explore how Thomas More conceives of and critiques individualism, he or she might have been able to arrive at a revealing analysis of the tension between the individual and the collective rather than merely dismissing the entire book.

This is not to say that the first requirement of analytical writing is that you abandon all conviction or argue for a position you do not believe. But we are suggesting that the risk of remaining trapped within a limited set of culturally inherited opinions is greater than the risk that you will run by submerging your personal likes or dislikes and instead honestly and dispassionately trying on different points of view. The energy of analytical writing comes not from rehearsing your convictions but from treating them as hypotheses to be tested, as scientists do—from finding the boundaries of your ideas, reshaping parts of them, and seeing connections you have not seen before.

When a writing assignment asks for your ideas about a subject, it is usually not asking for your opinion, what you think *of* the subject, but for your reasoning on what the subject means. As we discussed in the first chapter, *an idea is not the same thing as an opinion.* The two are closely related, because both, in theory, are based on reasoning. Opinions, however, often take the form of judgments, the reflections of our personal attitudes and beliefs. Although having ideas necessarily involves your attitudes and beliefs, it is a more disinterested process than opinion making. The formulation of ideas, which is one of the primary aims of analysis, involves questioning. By contrast, opinions are often habitual responses, mental reflexes that kick in automatically when an answer seems to be called for. (The discussions of personalizing, judging, and opinions in Chapter 1 explain more fully how placing too much emphasis on yourself can interfere with your thinking.)

VOICES FROM ACROSS THE CURRICULUM

Ideas Versus Opinions

Writers need to be aware of the distinction between an argument that seeks support from evidence, and mere opinions and assertions. Many students taking political science courses often come with the assumption that in politics one opinion is as good as another. (Tocqueville thought this was a peculiarly democratic disease.) From this perspective any position a political science professor may take on controversial issues is simply his or her opinion to be accepted or rejected by students according to their own beliefs/prejudices. The key task, therefore, is not so much the substitution of knowledge for opinions, but substituting well-constructed arguments for unexamined opinions.

What is an argument and how might it be distinguished from opinions? Several things need to be stressed: (1) The thesis should be linked to evidence drawn from relevant sources: polling data, interviews, historical material, and so forth. (2) The thesis should make as explicit as possible its own ideological assumptions. (3) A thesis, in contrast to mere statement of opinion, is committed to making an argument, which means that it presupposes a willingness to engage with others. To the extent that writers operate on the assumption that everything is in the end an opinion, they have no reason to construct arguments; they are locked into an opinion.

—*Jack Gambino, Professor of Political Science*

WEAK THESIS TYPE 5: THE THESIS MAKES AN OVERLY BROAD CLAIM

An overly general claim is not a productive thesis because it oversimplifies and is too broad to direct development. Such statements usually lead either to say-nothing theses or to reductive either/or thinking. (See "Working with Categorical Thinking" later in the chapter.)

Problem Examples

Violent revolutions have had both positive and negative results for man.

There are many similarities and differences between the Carolingian and the Burgundian Renaissances.

Othello is a play about love and jealousy.

It is important to understand why leaders act in a leadership role. What is the driving force? Is it an internal drive for the business or group to succeed, or is it an internal drive for the leader to dominate others?

Overly generalized theses avoid complexity. (See the discussion of generalizing in Chapter 1.) At their worst, as in our first three examples, they settle for assertions broad enough to fit almost any subject and thus say nothing in particular about the subject at hand. A writer in the early stages of his or her drafting process might begin working from a general idea, such as what is positive and negative about violent revolutions or how two historical periods are like and unlike, but these formulations are not specific enough to guide the development of a paper. Such broad categories are likely to generate listing, not thinking. We can, for example, predict that the third thesis will prompt the writer to produce a couple of paragraphs demonstrating that *Othello* is about love and then a couple of paragraphs demonstrating that *Othello* is about jealousy, without analyzing what the play says about either.

Our fourth problem example, inquiring into the motivation of leaders in business, demonstrates how the desire to generalize can drive writers into logical errors. Because this thesis overtly offers readers two possible answers to its central question, it appears to avoid the problem of oversimplifying a complex subject. But this appearance of complexity is deceptive, because the writer has reduced the possibilities to only two answers—an either/or choice: is "the driving force" of leadership a desire for group success or a desire to dominate others? Readers can only be frustrated by being asked to choose between two such options when the more logical answer probably lies somewhere in between or somewhere else altogether. (See the discussion of binaries in Chapters 2 and 3.)

The best way to avoid the problem evident in the first three examples is to sensitize yourself to the characteristic phrasing of such theses: "both positive and negative," "many similarities and differences," or "both pros and cons." Virtually everything from meat loaf to taxes can be both positive and negative.

Solution Convert broad categories and generic (fits anything) claims to more specific, more qualified assertions; find ways to bring out the complexity of your subject.

Solution Examples

Although violent revolutions begin to redress long-standing social inequities, they often do so at the cost of long-term economic dysfunction and the suffering that attends it.

The differences between the Carolingian and Burgundian Renaissances outweigh the similarities.

Although *Othello* appears to attack jealousy, it also supports the skepticism of the jealous characters over the naïveté of the lovers.

B. HOW TO REPHRASE THESIS STATEMENTS: SPECIFY AND SUBORDINATE

Clear symptoms of an overly generalized thesis can be found by looking at its grammar. Each of the first three problem examples for Weak Thesis Type 5, for example, relies mostly on nouns rather than verbs; the nouns announce a broad heading, but the verbs don't do anything with or to the nouns. In grammatical terms, these thesis statements don't *predicate* (affirm or assert something about the subject of a proposition). Instead, they rely on anemic verbs such as *is* or *are*, which function as equal signs that link general nouns with general adjectives rather than specify more complex relationships.

By replacing the equal sign with a more active verb, you can force yourself to advance some sort of claim, as in one of our solutions; for example, "The differences between the Carolingian and Burgundian Renaissances *outweigh* the similarities." Although this reformulation remains quite general, it at least begins to direct the writer along a more particular line of argument. Replacing the *is* or *are* equal signs with stronger verbs will usually impel you to rank ideas in some order of importance and to assert some conceptual relation among them.

In other words, the best way to remedy the problem of overgeneralization is to move toward specificity in word choice, in sentence structure, and in idea. If you find yourself writing "The economic situation is bad," consider revising it to "The tax policies of the current administration threaten to reduce the tax burden on the middle class by sacrificing education and health-care programs for everyone."

Here's the problem/solution in schematic form:

Broad Noun	+	**Weak Verb**	+	**Vague, Evaluative Modifier**
The economic situation		is		bad
Specific Noun	+	**Active Verb**	+	**Specific Modifier**
(The) tax policies (of the current administration)		threaten to reduce (the tax burden on the middle class)		by sacrificing education and health-care programs for everyone

By eliminating the weak thesis formula—broad noun plus *is* plus vague evaluative adjective—a writer is compelled to qualify, or define carefully, each of the terms in the original proposition, arriving at a more particular and conceptually rich assertion.

A second way to rephrase overly broad thesis statements, in tandem with adding specificity, is to subordinate one part of the statement to another. The both-positive-and-negative and both-similarity-and-difference formulas are recipes for say-nothing theses because they encourage pointless comparisons. Given that it is worthwhile to notice both strengths and weaknesses—that your subject is not all one way or all another—what can you do to convert the thesis from a say-nothing to a say-something claim? Generally, there are two strategies for this purpose that operate together. The first we have already discussed.

1. *Specify*—Replace the overly abstract terms—terms such as *positive* and *negative* (or *similar* and *different*)—with something specific; *name* something that is positive and something that is negative instead.
2. *Subordinate*—Rank one of the two items in the pairing underneath the other. When you subordinate, you put the most important, pressing, or revealing side of the comparison in what is known as the main clause and the less important side in what is known as the subordinate clause, introducing it with a word such as *although*. (See Chapter 11 for the definitions of main and subordinate clauses.)

In short, specify to focus the claim, and subordinate to qualify (further focus) the claim still more. This strategy produces the remedies to both the *Othello* and the violent revolution examples in "Weak Thesis Type 5: The Thesis Makes an Overly Broad Claim." As evidence of the refocusing work that fairly simple rephrasing accomplishes, consider the following version of the violent revolution example, in which we merely invert the ranking of the two items in the pair.

> Although violent revolutions often cause long-term economic dysfunction and the suffering that attends it, such revolutions at least begin to redress long-standing social inequities.

Also see the section titled "A First Note on the Shape of Thesis Statements" in Chapter 6.

VOICES FROM ACROSS THE CURRICULUM

Making the Thesis Specific

Good thesis: "Although Graham and Wigman seem different, their ideas on inner expression (specifically subjectivism versus objectivism) and the incorporation of their respective countries' surge of nationalism bring them much closer than they appear."

Not-so-good thesis/question: "What were Humphrey's and Weidman's reasons behind the setting of *With My Red Fires*, and of what importance were the set and costume design to the piece as a whole?"

What I like about the good thesis is that it moves beyond the standard "they are different, but alike" (which can be said about anything) to actually tell the reader what specific areas the paper will explore. I can also tell that the subject is narrow enough for a fairly thorough examination of one small slice of these two major choreographers' work rather than some overgeneralized treatment of these two historic figures. I would probably encourage the writer of the not-so-good thesis to search for a better thesis with the question, How does the costume design of *With My Red Fires* support this story of young lovers and their revolt against the family matriarch?

—Karen Dearborn, Professor of Dance

ANOTHER NOTE ON THE PHRASING OF THESIS STATEMENTS: QUESTIONS

The following question is frequently asked about thesis statements: is it okay to phrase a thesis as a question? The answer is both yes and no. Phrasing a thesis as a question makes it more difficult for both the writer and the reader to be sure of the direction the paper will take, because a question doesn't make an overt claim. Questions, however, can clearly imply claims. And many writers, especially in the early, exploratory stages of drafting, begin with a question. As we note in the discussion "What It Means to Have an Idea" in Chapter 1, an idea answers a question; it explains something that needs to be explained. Also, an idea may result from the discovery of a question where there seemed not to be one. Ideas start with something you want to figure out rather than with something that you and possibly most of your readers already understand.

As a general rule, use thesis questions cautiously, especially in final drafts. Although a thesis question often functions well to spark a writer's thinking, it can too often muddy the thinking by leaving the area of consideration too broad. Just make sure you do not let the thesis-question approach allow you to evade the responsibility of making some kind of claim.

Try this 7.2: Determining What the Thesis Requires You to Do Next

Learning to diagnose the strengths and weaknesses of thesis statements is a skill that comes in handy as you read the claims of others and revise your own. A good question for diagnosing a thesis is, What does the thesis require the writer to do next? This question should help you figure out what the thesis actually wants to claim, which can then direct you to possible rephrasings that would better direct your thinking. Using this question as a prompt, list the strengths and weaknesses of the two thesis statements below, and then rewrite them. In the first statement, rewrite just the last sentence (the other sentences have been included to provide context).

1. Many economists and politicians agree that, along with the Environmental Protection Agency's newest regulations, a global-warming treaty could damage the American economy. Because of the great expense that such environmental standards require, domestic industries would financially suffer. Others argue, however, that severe regulatory steps must be taken to prevent global warming, regardless of cost. Despite both legitimate claims, the issue of protecting the environment while still securing our global competitiveness remains critical.
2. Regarding the promotion of women into executive positions, they are continually losing the race because of a corporate view that women are too compassionate to keep up with the competitiveness of a powerful firm.

C. WORKING WITH CATEGORICAL THINKING

Categorical thinking is an unavoidable and distinctive feature of how all human beings go about analyzing a subject. It is also extremely useful: to generalize from particular experiences, we try to put them into meaningful categories. When we contract an illness, doctors diagnose it by type. When we study personality theory, different behaviors are grouped by personality type. Subject areas in school are categorized into divisions: the natural sciences, the social sciences, the humanities. Analytical thought is quite unthinkable without categories.

But categorical thinking can also be dangerous. It can mislead us into oversimplification when the categories are too broad or too simply connected. This is especially the case with the either/or choices to which categorical thinking is prone: approve/disapprove, real/unreal, accurate/inaccurate, believable/unbelievable. Such either/or thinking often provokes thinkers into a premature and overly narrow decision either to support the subject or to denounce it. This rush to value judgment can so dominate a writer's attention that he or she fails to examine not only the values upon which the judgment is based, but also the subject itself.

If you look back over the examples in "Five Kinds of Weak Theses," you will notice that a number of them engage in the dangerous side of categorical thinking. That is, they are overly global—inclined to all-or-nothing claims. The writer who evaluates leadership in terms of its selflessness/selfishness, for example, needs to pause to consider why we should evaluate leadership in those terms in the first place.

Many weak theses are the result of oversimplified categorical thinking. The writer puts everything into big, undifferentiated categories, labeled all black or all white, with nothing in between. The trick is to use categorical thinking in a way that allows you to make careful distinctions.

TWO WAYS TO IMPROVE THE LOGIC OF YOUR THESIS STATEMENTS

We will refer to the following two examples to illustrate two key ways to strengthen the logic of your thesis statements: (1) by qualifying your claims and (2) by checking for the unstated assumptions upon which your claims depend.

> ***Example I:*** I think there are many things shown on TV that are damaging for people to see. But there is no need for censorship. No network is going to show violence without the approval of the public, obviously for financial reasons. What must be remembered is that the public majority will see what it wants to see in our mass society.

> ***Example II:*** Some members of our society feel that [the televised cartoon series] *The Simpsons* promotes wrong morals and values for our society. Other members find it funny and entertaining. I feel that *The Simpsons* has a more positive effect than a negative one. In relation to a real-life marriage, Marge and Homer's marriage is pretty accurate. The problems they deal with are not very large or intense. As for the family relationships, the Simpsons are very close and love each other.

Qualifying Overextended Claims The main problem with Example I is the writer's failure to qualify his ideas, a problem that causes him to generalize to the point of oversimplification. Note the writer's habit of stating his claims absolutely (we have italicized the words that make these claims unqualified):

> "there is *no* need for censorship"
> "*no* network is going to show violence without"
> "*obviously* for financial reasons"
> "what *must* be remembered"
> "the majority *will* see"

Broad, pronouncement-like claims are difficult to support fairly. The solution is for the writer to limit his claims more carefully, especially his key premise about public approval. The assertion that a commercial television industry will, for financial reasons, give the public "what it wants" is true *to an extent*. But, as with the "extent to which" strategy for refocusing binaries (see Chapter 3), the solution here is to modify this claim as well as consider other possibilities.

Couldn't it also be argued, for example, that given the power of television to shape people's tastes and opinions, the public sees not just what it wants but what it has been taught to want? This necessary complication of the writer's argument about public approval seriously undermines the credibility of his global assertion that "there is no need for censorship." The remedy lies with qualifying his thesis. Simply reversing it to "there is a need for censorship" would not solve the problem, because the need for defining and limiting the writer's position will be just as great on the other side of the issue.

Example II appears to be more qualified than Example I (because it acknowledges the possibility of at least two points of view). The writer opens by attempting to acknowledge the existence of more than one point of view on the show, and rather than broadly asserting that the show is positive and accurate, she tempers these claims (as italics show): "I *feel* that *The Simpsons* has a *more* positive effect *than* a negative one"; Marge and Homer's marriage is *pretty* accurate." These qualifications, however, are superficial. The writer does not explore what *accurate* means. Instead, she assumes the standard of accuracy (that an accurate show is a good show) as a given.

Checking for Unstated Assumptions Before she could persuade us to approve of *The Simpsons* for its accuracy in depicting marriage, the writer of Example II would have to convince us that accuracy is a reasonable criterion for evaluating TV shows (especially cartoons) rather than simply accepting it as an unstated assumption. Would an accurate depiction of the life of a serial killer, for example, necessarily make for a "positive" show? Similarly, if a fantasy show has no interest in accuracy, is it necessarily "negative" and without moral value?

When writers present a debatable premise as if it were self-evidently true, the conclusions built upon it cannot stand. At the least, the writer of Example II needs to recognize her debatable premise, articulate it, and make an argument in support of it. She might also precede her judgment about the show with more analysis. Before deciding that the show is "more positive than negative" and thus does not promote "wrong morals and values for our society," she could convey what the show has to say about marriage, how it goes about making this statement, and why (in response to what).

When writers present a debatable premise as if it were self-evidently true, the conclusions built upon it cannot stand.

Likewise, if the writer of Example I had looked at his own claims rather than rushing to argue an absolute position on censorship, he would have noticed how much of the thinking that underlies them remains unarticulated and thus unexamined. His argument that "there is no need for censorship," for example, depends on the validity of another of his assertions, that "no network is going to show violence without the approval of the public, obviously for financial reasons." The writer's argument depends on readers' accepting a position that he asserts ("obviously") as though it were too clearly true to need defending.

Spelling out the issue of the networks' financial dependence on public approval would help this writer clarify and qualify his thesis. It would also allow him to sort out the logical contradiction with his opening claim that "there are many things shown on TV that are damaging for people to see." If television networks will broadcast only what the public approves of, then apparently the public must approve of being damaged or fail to notice that it is being damaged. If the public either fails to notice it is being damaged or approves of it, aren't these credible arguments for, rather than against, censorship?

CLOSE READING VERSUS DEBATE-STYLE ARGUMENT

To formulate a revealing and insightful idea—an effective thesis—you may have to alter some of your conceptions of what writing is supposed to do. The agree/disagree mode of writing and thinking that you will often see in editorials, hear in the media, and even practice sometimes in school may incline you to focus all your energy on the bottom line—aggressively advancing a claim either for or against some view—without first engaging in the exploratory interpretation of evidence that is so necessary to arriving at thoughtful arguments.

Writing, especially as it is used in school, is often divided into kinds. And clearly, the kind of writing this book addresses—analysis—differs in both method and aim from, say, descriptive writing or narration. Those of you who have been taught to write arguments may find that some of the prescriptions we offer on analytical writing seem to run counter to what you've learned. Our aim in this section is to break down unnecessary divisions between argument and analysis, proposing that the interpretive skill called close reading is essential to both.

A close reading explicates (unfolds) an interpretation by making selected features of your subject explicit that otherwise might not be readily recognized or understood. A close reading moves beyond the obvious, but it does not leap to some hidden meaning that is unconnected to the evidence. Rather, it follows logically from the evidence; the meaning is implicit in the details, waiting to be brought out by the writer who is careful enough to look closely and questioningly.

It is, we believe, a common misconception that interpretation (close reading) goes on only in art or literature courses, whereas science, social science, and philosophy courses require a different kind of writing called argument. Many of you will have been introduced to writing arguments through the debate-model—writing pro or con on a given position, with the aim of defeating an imagined opponent and convincing your readers of the rightness of your position. But as the *American College Dictionary* says, "to argue implies reasoning or trying to understand; it does not necessarily imply opposition." It is this more exploratory, tentative, and dispassionate mode of argument that this book encourages you to practice.

Adhering to the more restrictive, debate-style definition of argument can create a number of problems for careful analytical writers:

1. By requiring writers to be oppositional, it inclines them to discount or dismiss problems in the side or position they have chosen; they cling to the same static position rather than testing it as a way of allowing it to evolve.
2. It inclines writers to either/or thinking rather than encouraging them to formulate more qualified positions that integrate apparently opposing viewpoints.
3. It overvalues convincing someone else at the expense of developing understanding.

Too often interpretation and argument are treated as essentially different kinds of writing, each with a particular purpose. In practice, interpretation and argument are inseparable. As our examples in Chapter 6 show, even the most tentative and cautiously evolving interpretation is ultimately an argument; it asks readers to accept a particular interpretation of a set of data. And like argument, interpretation carefully connects evidence with claims; it does not, as it is sometimes misconceived, incline the writer toward undirected and purposeless impressionism.

Similarly, even the most passionately committed argument is an interpretation; its credibility rests on the plausibility of its reading of evidence. You cannot argue from evidence unless you are first sure that you know what that evidence means. Most illogical argument occurs when writers assume that the meaning of their data is self-evident. In other words, you need to analyze your subject dispassionately before you can fairly argue a position about it.

Analysis is an important corrective to narrow and needlessly oppositional thinking. A writer who is skeptical of global generalizations and of unexamined value judgments may sound timid and even confused compared with the insistent pronouncements of daytime talk shows and televised political debates. But the effort you put into carefully formulating your ideas by qualifying them, checking for unstated assumptions, and acknowledging rather than ignoring problems in your position will make you a stronger writer and thinker. For more discussion of debate-style argument see the "Counterproductive Habits of Mind" section in Chapter 1.

D. COMMON LOGICAL ERRORS IN CONSTRUCTING A THESIS

In further service to our project of giving you ways of avoiding weak thesis statements, this section will move briefly to the field of logic, which has given us terms that are shorthand for certain common thinking errors. We will treat six errors, all of which involve the root problem of oversimplification in the way the thesis explains the meaning of evidence.

1. **Simple cause–complex effect**—One of the most common problems of thinking, the fallacy of simple cause–complex effect, involves assigning a simple cause to a complex phenomenon that cannot be so easily explained. A widespread version of this fallacy is seen in arguments that blame individual figures for broad historical events. For example, "Eisenhower caused America to be involved in the Vietnam War." This claim ignores the cold war ethos, the long history of colonialism in Southeast Asia, and a multitude of other factors. When you reduce a complex sequence of events to a simple and single cause—or assign a simple effect to a complex cause—you will virtually always be wrong.
2. **False cause**—Another common cause/effect thinking error, false cause, is produced by assuming that two events are causally connected when such a connection does not necessarily exist. One of the most common forms of this fallacy—known as *post hoc, ergo propter hoc* (Latin for "after this, therefore because of this")—assumes that because *A* precedes *B*, *A* causes *B*. For example, it was once thought that the sun shining on a pile of garbage caused the garbage to conceive flies.

   This error is the stuff that superstition is made of. "I walked under a ladder, and then I got hit by a car" becomes "Because I walked under a ladder, I got hit by a car." Because one action precedes a second one, the first action is assumed to be the cause of the second. A more dangerous form of this error goes like this:

Evidence: A new neighbor moved in downstairs on Saturday. My television disappeared on Sunday.
Conclusion: The new neighbor stole my TV.

As the examples illustrate, *typically in false cause some significant alternative has not been considered*, such as the presence of flies' eggs in the garbage. Similarly, it does not follow that if a person watches television and then commits a crime, television watching necessarily causes crime; there are other causes to be considered.

Try this 7.3: Identifying Logical Errors and Formulating Alternative Explanations

Predictably, instances of simple cause/complex effect and false cause are harder to spot when we encounter them in published settings. Identify possible sites of simple cause/complex effect and false cause in the following real-life example. Then formulate a few alternative explanations that one might offer to the theory that television watching is the primary cause of the increased risk of starting drinking. What cause-and-effect explanations might there be for the decreased risk of drinking that corresponds with adolescents watching movies on a VCR?

A newspaper article on a study conducted at Stanford University about the connection between adolescents' television-viewing habits and drinking reports that high school students who watch a lot of television and music videos are more likely to start drinking than are other students. In the study of 1,553 ninth graders, with each increase of one hour per day of watching music videos there was a 31 percent greater risk of starting to drink. Each hour increase of watching other kinds of television corresponded with a 9 percent greater risk. Each hour spent watching movies in a video cassette recorder corresponded to an 11 percent *decreased* risk of starting to drink alcohol. Computer and video games had no effect either way, and among those who already drank, watching television and videos made no difference. Because these data were reported in the newspaper in very abbreviated form, there was little interpretation of the evidence except for the observations that alcohol is the most common beverage shown on television and that drinking on television is done by attractive people, often in association with sexually suggestive content.

3. **Analogy and false analogy**—An analogy is a device for understanding something that is relatively foreign in terms of something that is more familiar. When you argue by analogy, you are saying that what is true for one thing is also true for something else that it in some way resembles. The famous poetic line "my love is like a red, red rose" is actually an argument by analogy. At first glance, this clichéd comparison seems too far-fetched to be reasonable. But is it a false analogy, or a potentially

enabling one? Past users of this analogy have thought the thorns, the early fading, the beauty, and so forth sufficient to argue from the comparison. Similarly, glance back to the first paragraph of the Tiananmen Square essay on page 151 in Chapter 5 in which the writer's deft use of an extended analogy opens up his subject analytically. Analogies, in short, are not bad or illogical in themselves. In fact, they can be incredibly useful, depending on how you handle them.

The danger that arguing analogically can pose is that an *inaccurate* comparison (usually one that oversimplifies) prevents you from looking at the evidence. Flying to the moon is like flying a kite? Well, it's a little like that, but this kind of oversimplification is essentially falsifying. In most ways that matter, sending a rocket to the moon does not resemble sending a kite into the air.

Another way that an analogy can become false is when it becomes overextended: there is a point of resemblance at one juncture, but the writer then goes on to assume that the two items being compared necessarily resemble each other in most other respects. To what extent is balancing your checkbook really like juggling? On the other hand, an analogy that first appears overextended may not be. How far, for example, could you reasonably go in comparing a presidential election to a sales campaign or an enclosed shopping mall to a village main street?

Let's examine one more false analogy, from a recent ad campaign: "You choose the president; why not choose your cable company?" What's wrong with this comparison? For one thing, each of us is not entitled to our choice of president. If we were, there would be a lot of presidents. And, second, the rules and circumstances covering what is best in the nation's communication network are not necessarily the same as the rules and circumstances guiding the structure of our federal government. So the analogy doesn't work very well. What is true for one side of the comparison is not necessarily true for the other side; the differences are greater than the similarities.

When you find yourself reasoning by analogy, ask yourself two questions: (1) are the basic similarities greater and more significant than the obvious differences? and (2) am I overrelying on surface similarities and ignoring more essential differences?

Try this 7.4: Observing Analogies

We observed at the beginning of this book that one of the best ways of improving your thinking is to become more aware of yourself doing it. To put this observation into practice, here's something you might try. Keep a record during the course of a single day of the number of times you or others around you (in conversation, in the newspaper, on the radio, at work, in the classroom, and so forth) make use of analogy. In some cases a single word will reveal that a common phrase, such as *nuclear family* is actually an analogy. At the end of the day, look over your list and isolate the most appropriate and insightful analogy as well as the most distorting one. If possible, share them with someone else (or a small group) who has been doing the same thing.

You might profitably spend another day doing this same exercise looking for examples of simple cause/complex effect and *post hoc ergo propter hoc*. (If you don't find an astonishing number of these, listen harder!)

4. **Equivocation**—Equivocation is the first of three logical errors that deal with matters of phrasing. As Chapter 6 and this chapter show, finding and developing a thesis emphasizes the importance of word choice—of carefully casting and recasting the language with which you categorize and name your ideas.

   Equivocation—slipping between two meanings for a single word or phrase—confuses an argument. An example would be "Only man is capable of religious faith. No woman is a man. Therefore, no woman is capable of religious faith." Here the first use of *man* is generic, intended to be gender neutral, whereas the second use is decidedly masculine. One specialized form of equivocation results from what are sometimes called *weasel words*. A weasel word is one that has been used so loosely that it ceases to have much (or any) meaning. (The term derives from the weasel's reputed practice of sucking the contents from an egg without destroying the shell.) The word *natural*, for example, can mean "good, pure, and unsullied," but it can also refer to the ways of nature (flora and fauna). Such terms (*love*, *reality*, and *experience* are others) invite equivocation because they mean so many different things to different people.
5. **Begging the question**—To beg the question is to argue in a circle by asking readers to accept without argument a point that is actually at stake. This kind of fallacious argument hides its conclusion among its assumptions. For example, "*Huckleberry Finn* should be banned from school libraries as obscene because it uses obscene language" begs the question by presenting as obviously true issues that are actually in question: the definition of obscenity and the assumption that the obscene should be banned because it is obscene.
6. **Overgeneralization**—An overgeneralization is an inadequately qualified claim. It may be true that some heavy drinkers are alcoholics, but it would not be fair to claim that all heavy drinking indicates or leads to alcoholism. As a rule, be wary of "totalizing" or making global pronouncements; the bigger the generalization, the more likely it will admit of exceptions. See for examples the process of qualifying a claim we illustrate in the discussion of *Educating Rita* in Chapter 6 and in the solutions in "Weak Thesis Type 5" in this chapter.

   One particular form of overgeneralization, the *sweeping generalization*, occurs when a writer overextends the reach of the claim. The claim itself may be adequately qualified, but the problem comes in an overly broad application of that generalization, suggesting that it applies in every case, whereas it applies only in some.

When you move prematurely from too little evidence to a broad conclusion, you have fallen into *hasty generalization*. Much of this book addresses ways of avoiding this problem, also known as an unwarranted inductive leap. See "Demonstrating the Representativeness of Your Example" in Chapter 5.

There are, of course, other common logical errors that can undermine the construction of valid claims. For one more example, see the section called "Strategy 3: Put Your Sources into Conversation with One Another" in Chapter 12 for a discussion of the problem in an argument called *straw man*, in which a writer builds his or her case on a misrepresentation of an opponent's argument.

ASSIGNMENT: "Love Is the Answer"—Analyzing Clichés

It's not necessarily that clichés are untrue, just that they are not worth saying (even if you're John Lennon, who offered this sodden truism in one of his more forgettable tunes).

One of the best ways to inoculate yourself against habitually resorting to clichés to provide easy and safe answers to all the problems of the planet—easy because they fit so many situations generically, and safe because, being so common, they *must* be true—is to go out and collect them, and then use this data gathering to generate a thesis. Spend a day doing this, listening and looking for clichés—from overheard conversations (or your own), from reading matter, from anywhere (talk radio and TV are exceptionally rich resources) that is part of your daily round.

Compile a list, making sure to write down not only each cliché but the context in which it is used. From this data, and applying what you have learned from the two thesis chapters, formulate a thesis and write a paper about one or more of the clichés that infect some aspect of your daily life. You might find it useful to use the reading-for-pattern heuristic to identify key shared traits among the clichés and/or among the contexts in which you have discovered them. And you might apply the advice provided under "Weak Thesis Type 3" to work out alternative formulations to certain clichés to discover what that might teach us about the ways clichés function in given situations—how, for example, they do and don't fit the facts of the situation. If you can find a copy of Paul Muldoon's short poem "Symposium," that might anchor an analysis—what is that poem telling us about cliché?—or provide a lens for uncovering aspects of your data.

GUIDELINES FOR RECOGNIZING AND FIXING WEAK THESIS STATEMENTS

1. Your thesis should make a claim with which it would be possible for readers to disagree. In other words, move beyond defending statements that your readers would accept as obviously true.
2. Be skeptical of your first (often semiautomatic) response to a subject: it will often be a cliché (however unintentional). Avoid conventional wisdom unless you introduce a fresh perspective on it.
3. Convert broad categories and generic (fits anything) claims to more specific assertions. Find ways to bring out the complexity of your subject.
4. Submit the wording of your thesis to this grammatical test: if it follows the "abstract noun + is + evaluative adjective" formula ("The economic situation is bad"), substitute a more specific noun and an active verb that will force you to predicate something about a focused subject ("Tax laws benefit the rich").
5. Routinely examine and question your own key terms and categories rather than simply accepting them. Assume that they mean more than you first thought.
6. Always work to uncover and make explicit the unstated assumptions (premises) underlying your thesis. Don't treat debatable premises as givens.
7. As a rule, be suspicious of thesis statements that depend on words such as *real*, *accurate*, *believable*, *right*, and *good*. These words usually signal that you are offering personal opinions—what "feels" right to you—as self-evident truths for everybody.
8. One way to assess the adequacy of a thesis statement is to ask yourself where the writer would need to go next to develop his or her idea. If you can't answer that question, the thesis is still too weak.
9. Qualify your claims; you will avoid the global pronouncements—typical of the dangers of overly categorical thinking—that are too broad to be of much use (or true).

CHAPTER 8
Introductions and Conclusions

Quick Take

This chapter addresses two perennial trouble-spots in all kinds of writing: introductions and conclusions. Because disciplinary formats often control the final form of beginnings and endings, more than a third of this chapter consists of "Voices from Across the Curriculum" boxes. Nonetheless, the chapter emphasizes the common elements that characterize introductions and conclusions across the curriculum.

The chapter gives special attention to strategies for solving two particular problems: trying to do too much in the introduction and not doing enough in the conclusion.

As with other aspects of writing analytically, there are no absolute rules for writing introductions and conclusions, but there does seem to be a consensus across the disciplines that introductions should raise issues rather than settle them, and conclusions should go beyond merely restating what has already been said. Or, in mantra form, insofar as disciplinary conventions permit, *In introductions, play an ace but not your whole hand; and in conclusions, don't just summarize—culminate.*

Play an ace, establishing your authority with your readers, without having to play your whole hand. Raise the issue; don't settle it.

A. INTRODUCTIONS AND CONCLUSIONS AS SOCIAL SITES

When you read, you enter a world created with written language—a textual world—and to varying degrees, you leave the world "out there." Even if other people are around, we all read in relative isolation; our attention is diverted from the social and physical world upon which the full range of our senses normally operates.

In this context, place yourself in the position of the writer, rather than a reader, and consider the functions that the introduction and conclusion provide for a piece of writing. Your introduction takes the reader from a sensory world and submerges him or her into a textual one. And your conclusion returns the reader to his or her nonwritten reality. Introductions and conclusions *mediate*—they carry the reader from one way of being to another. They function as the most social parts of any written communication, the passageways in which you need to be most keenly aware of your reader.

At both sites, there is a lot at stake. The introduction gives the reader his or her first impression, and we all know how indelible that can be. The conclusion leaves the reader with a last—and potentially lasting—impression of the written world you have constructed.

B. THE FUNCTION OF INTRODUCTIONS

As the Latin roots of the word suggest—*intro,* meaning "within," and *ducere,* meaning "to lead or bring"—an introduction brings the reader into a subject. Its length varies, depending on the scope of the writing project. An introduction may take a paragraph, a few paragraphs, a few pages, a chapter, or even a book. In most academic writing that you will do, one or two paragraphs is a standard length. In that space you should try to accomplish some or all of the following objectives:

- Define your topic—the issue, question, or problem—and say why it matters.
- Indicate your method of approach to the topic.
- Provide necessary background or context.
- Offer the working thesis (hypothesis) that your paper will develop.

An objective missing from this list that you might expect to find there is the admonition to engage the reader. Clearly, all introductions need to engage the reader, but this admonition is too often misinterpreted as a directive to be entertaining or cute. In academic writing, you don't need a gimmick to engage your readers; you can assume they care about the subject. You will engage them if you can articulate why your topic matters, doing so in terms of existing thinking in the field. Especially in a first draft, the objectives just listed are not so easily achieved, which is why many writers defer writing the polished version of the introduction until they have completed at least one draft of the paper. At that point, you will usually have a clearer notion of why your subject matters and which aspect of your thesis to place first. Often the conclusion of a first draft becomes the introduction to the second draft.

Other writers find that they can't proceed on a draft until they have arrived at an introduction that clearly defines the question or problem they plan to write about and its significance. For these writers, crafting an approach to the topic in the introduction is a key part of the planning phase, even though they also expect to revise the introduction based on what happens in the initial draft.

In any case, the standard shape of an introduction is a *funnel.* It starts wide, providing background and generalization, and then narrows the subject to a particular issue or topic. Here is a typical example from a student paper.

> People have a way of making the most important obligations perfunctory, even trivial, by the steps they take to observe them. For many people traditions and rituals become actuality; the form overshadows the substance. They lose sight of the underlying truths and what these should mean in their lives, and they tend to believe that observing the formalities fulfills their obligation. This is true of professional ethics as they relate to the practice of examining and reporting on financial data—the primary role of the auditor.

The paragraph begins with a generalization in the first sentence (about making even important obligations perfunctory) and funnels down in the last sentence to a working thesis (about the ethics of an auditor's report on financial data).

PUTTING AN ISSUE OR QUESTION IN CONTEXT

In the accompanying "Voices from Across the Curriculum" boxes, notice that implicit in all of the professors' accounts is some concept of the funnel. Rather than leaping immediately to the paper's issue, question, or problem, most effective introductions provide some broader context to indicate why the issue matters.

Although the various models we offer here differ in small ways from discipline to discipline, the essential characteristics that they share suggest that most professors across the curriculum want the same things in an introduction: *the locating of a problem or question within a context that provides background and rationale, culminating in a working thesis.*

USING PROCEDURAL OPENINGS

In the interests of clear organization, some professors require students to include in the introduction an explanation of how the paper will proceed. Such a general statement of method and/or intention is known as *procedural openings.* Among the disciplines in which you are most likely to find this format are philosophy, political science, and sociology.

The procedural opening is particularly useful in longer papers, where it can provide a condensed version of what's to come as a guide for readers. Also note that he advises placing it early in the essay but not in the first paragraph, which he reserves for "presenting anomalies." In other words, he seems to value the introduction primarily as a site for the writer's idea, for "stating the specific point of departure," and, that taken care of, only secondarily as a place for forecasting the plan of the paper. These priorities bear mentioning because they imply *a potential danger in relying too heavily on procedural openings—that the writer will avoid making a claim at all.*

The statement of a paper's plan is not the same thing as its thesis. As Chapter 7 discussed, one kind of weak thesis offers a general plan *in place of* supplying an idea about the topic that the paper will explore and defend. Consider the deficiencies of the following procedural opening.

> In this paper I will first discuss the strong points and weak points in America's treatment of the elderly. Then I will compare this treatment with that in other industrial nations in the West. Finally, I will evaluate the various proposals for reform that have been advanced here and abroad.

This paragraph does not fare well in fulfilling the four functional objectives of an introduction listed at the beginning of this chapter. It identifies the subject, but it neither addresses why the subject matters nor suggests the writer's approach. Nor does it provide background to the topic or suggest a hypothesis that the paper will pursue. Even though a procedural opening is built into the conventions of report writing, these conventions also stipulate that the writer include some clear statement of the hypothesis, which counteracts the danger that the writer won't make any claim at all.

VOICES FROM ACROSS THE CURRICULUM

Providing an Introductory Context

Although some expression of the main idea should find its way into the opening paragraph, that paragraph is also an opportunity to draw the reader in, to convince the reader to read on. What's the point of your paper? Why is the issue important? Is it a theoretical issue? A policy issue? What's the historical context? Is this a question that represents a part of a larger question?

–James Marshall, Professor of Economics

I think it is important to understand that an introduction is not simply the statement of a thesis but also the place where the student needs to set a context, a framework that makes such a thesis statement interesting, timely, or in some other way important. It is common to see papers in political science begin by pointing out a discrepancy between conventional wisdom (what the pundits say) and recent political developments, between popular opinion and empirical evidence, or between theoretical frameworks and particular test cases. Papers, in other words, often begin by presenting *anomalies.*

I encourage students to write opening paragraphs that attempt to elucidate such anomalies by:

1. Stating the specific point of departure: are they taking issue with a bit of conventional wisdom? Popular opinions? A theoretical perspective? This provides the context in which a student is able to "frame" a particular problem, issue, and so forth. Students then need to indicate:
2. Why the wisdom/opinion/theory has become problematic or controversial by focusing on a particular issue, event, test case, or empirical evidence. (Here the students' choice of topic becomes important, because topics must be both relevant to the specific point of departure as well as to some degree controversial.) I would also expect the following in the opening paragraph(s):
3. A brief statement of the tentative thesis/position to be pursued in the paper. This can take several forms, including the revising of conventional wisdom/theory/opinion, discarding it in favor of alternative conceptions, or calling for redefinition of an issue and question. In papers directed toward current political practices (for instance, an analysis of a particular environmental policy or of a proposal to reform political parties), the thesis statement may be stated by indicating (a) hidden or flawed assumptions in current practices or (b) alternative reforms and/or policy proposals.

–Jack Gambino, Professor of Political Science

VOICES FROM ACROSS THE CURRICULUM

Procedural Openings

I encourage students to provide a "road map" paragraph early in the paper, perhaps the second or third paragraph. (This is a common practice in the professional journals.) The "road map" tells the reader the basic outline of the argument. Something like the following: "In the first part of my paper I will present a brief history of the issue. . . . This will be followed by an account of the current controversy. . . . Part III will spell out my alternative account and evidence. . . . I then conclude. . . . " I think such a paragraph becomes more necessary with longer papers.

–Jack Gambino, Professor of Political Science

I address the issue of an opening paragraph by having the students conceive of an opening section (or introduction) that tells the uninformed reader what's about to happen. I'll say, "Assume I know next to nothing about what lies ahead; so let me, the reader, know. 'My paper's about boom. In it, I'll do boom, boom. I chose this topic for the following reasons: boom, boom, boom.' Then get on with it."

–Frederick Norling, Professor of Business

C. HOW MUCH TO INTRODUCE UP FRONT

Introductions need to do a lot in a limited space. To specify a thesis and locate it within a larger context, to suggest the plan or outline of the entire paper, and to negotiate first relations with a reader—that's plenty to pack into a paragraph or two. In deciding how much to introduce up front, you must make a series of difficult choices. We list some of these choices next, phrased as questions you can ask yourself:

- How much can I assume my readers know about my subject?
- Which parts of the research and/or the background are sufficiently pertinent to warrant inclusion?
- How much of my thesis do I include, and which particular part or parts should I begin with?
- What is the proper balance between background and foreground?
- Which are the essential parts of my plan or road map to include?

TYPICAL PROBLEMS THAT ARE SYMPTOMS OF DOING TOO MUCH

If you ponder the preceding questions, you can avoid writing introductions that try to turn an introduction into a miniature essay. Consider the three problems discussed next as symptoms of *overcompression*, telltale signs that you need to reconceive, and probably reduce, your introduction.

Digression *Digression* results when you try to include too much background. If, for example, you plan to write about a recent innovation in video technology, you'll need to monitor the amount and kind of technical information you include in your opening paragraphs. You'll also want to avoid starting at a point that is too far away from your immediate concerns, as in "From the beginning of time humans have needed to communicate."

The standardized formats that govern procedural openings in some disciplines can help you to avoid digressing endlessly. There is a given sequence of steps to follow for a psychology report of an empirical study, for instance. Nonetheless, these disciplinary conventions leave plenty of room for you to lose your focus. You still need to be selective about which contexts are sufficiently relevant to be included up front.

In disciplines that do not stipulate a specific format for contextualizing, the number of choices is greater, and so is the danger that you will get sidetracked into paragraphs of background that bury your thesis and frustrate your readers. One reason that many writers fall into this kind of digression in introductions is that they misjudge how much their audience needs to know. As a general rule in academic writing, *don't assume that your readers know little or nothing about the subject.* Instead, use the social potential of the introduction to negotiate your audience, setting up your relationship with your readers and making clear what you are assuming they do and do not know.

Incoherence *Incoherence* results when you try to preview too much of your paper's conclusion. Incoherent introductions move in too many directions at once, usually because the writer is trying to conclude before going through the discussion that will make the conclusion comprehensible. The language you are compelled to use in such cases tends to be too dense, and the connections between the sentences tend to get left out, because there isn't enough room to include them. After having read the entire paper, your readers may be able to make sense of the introduction, but in that case, the introduction has not done its job.

The following introductory paragraph is incoherent, primarily because it tries to include too much. It neither adequately connects its ideas nor defines its terms.

> Twinship is a symbol in many religious traditions. The significance of twinship will be discussed and explored in the Native American, Japanese Shinto, and Christian religions. Twinship can be either in opposing or common forces in the form of deities or mortals. There are several forms of twinship that show duality of order versus chaos, good versus evil, and creation versus destruction. The significance of twinship is to set moral codes for society and to explain the inexplicable.

Prejudgment *Prejudgment* results when you appear to have already settled the question to be pursued in the rest of the paper. The problem here is logical. In the effort to preview your paper's conclusion at the outset, you risk appearing to assume something as true that your paper will in fact need to test. In most papers in the humanities and social sciences, where the thesis evolves in specificity and complexity between the introduction and conclusion, writers and readers can find such assumptions prejudicial. Opening in this way, at any event, can make the rest of the paper seem redundant. Even in the sciences, where a concise statement of objectives, plan of attack, and hypothesis are usually required up front, a separate "Results" section is reserved for the conclusion.

The following introductory paragraph *prejudges*: it offers a series of conclusions already assumed to be true without introducing the necessary background issues and questions that would allow the writer to adequately explore these conclusions.

> Field hockey is a sport that can be played by either men or women. All sports should be made available for members of both sexes. As long as women are allowed to participate on male teams in sports such as football and wrestling, men should be allowed to participate on female teams in sports such as field hockey and lacrosse. If women press for and receive equal opportunity in all sports, then it is only fair that men be given the same opportunity. If women object to this type of equal opportunity, then they are promoting reverse discrimination.

This paragraph also exemplifies the type of weak thesis that can result when its assumptions are left unstated (and so earlier in the book we invited you to ferret out unstated assumptions in this passage). Prejudgment is in fact a case of assuming too much up front. Read what an economics professor says on the same subject.

VOICES FROM ACROSS THE CURRICULUM

Avoiding Strong Claims in the Introduction

I might be careful about how tentative conclusions should play in the opening paragraph, because this can easily slide into a prejudging of the question at hand. I would be more comfortable with a clear statement of the prevailing views held by others. For example, a student could write on the question, "Was Franklin Delano Roosevelt a Keynesian?" What purpose would it serve in an opening paragraph to reveal without any supporting discussion that FDR was or was not a Keynesian?

What might be better would be to say that in the public mind FDR is regarded as the original big spender, that some people commonly associate New Deal policies with general conceptions of Keynesianism, but that there may be some surprises in store as that common notion is examined.

In sum, I would discourage students from making strong claims at or near the beginning of a paper. Let's see the evidence first. We should all have respect for the evidence. Strong assertions, bordering on conclusions, too early on are inappropriate.

–James Marshall, Professor of Economics

Try this 8.1: Introductions and Audience

Compare and contrast introductory paragraphs from a popular magazine with those from an academic journal aimed at a more specialized audience. Select one of each and analyze them to determine what each author assumes the audience knows. Where in each paragraph are these assumptions most evident? If you write out your analysis, it should probably take about a page, but this exercise can also be done productively with others in a small group.

D. OPENING GAMBITS: FIVE GOOD WAYS TO BEGIN

The primary challenge in writing introductions, it should now be evident, lies in occupying the middle ground between overassertive prejudgment and avoidance of taking a position. There are a number of fairly common opening gambits that can help you to stake out an effective middle ground. An opening gambit in games such as chess is the initial move—not an announcement of the entire game plan.

GAMBIT 1: CHALLENGE A COMMONLY HELD VIEW

One of the best opening gambits is to challenge a commonly held view. This is what the economics professor advises when he suggests that rather than announcing up front the answer to the question at which the paper arrives, you convey that "there may be some surprises in store as that common notion is examined." This move has several advantages. Most important, it provides you with a framework *against* which to respond; it allows you to begin by reacting. Moreover, because you are responding to a known position, you have a ready way of integrating context into your paper. As the economics professor notes of the FDR example, until we understand why it matters whether or not FDR was a Keynesian, it is pointless to answer the question.

GAMBIT 2: BEGIN WITH A DEFINITION

In the case of the FDR example, a writer would probably include another common introductory gambit, *defining* "Keynesianism." Beginning with a definition is a reliable way to introduce a topic, so long as that definition has some significance for the discussion to follow. If the definition doesn't do any conceptual work in the introduction, the definition gambit becomes a pointless cliché.

You are most likely to avoid a cliché if you cite a source other than a standard dictionary for your definition. The reference collection of any academic library contains a range of discipline-specific lexicons that provide more precise and authoritative definitions than Webster ever could. A useful alternative is to quote a particular author's definition of a key term (such as Keynesianism) because you want to make a point about his or her particular definition: for example, "Although the *Dictionary of Economics* defines Keynesianism as *XYZ*, Smith treats only *X* and *Y* (or substitutes *A* for *Z*, and so forth)."

GAMBIT 3: OFFER A WORKING HYPOTHESIS

But, you may be wondering, where is the thesis in the FDR example? As the economics professor proposes, you are often better off introducing a working hypothesis—an opening claim that stimulates the analytical process—instead of offering some full declaration of the conclusion. The introduction he envisions, for example, would first suggest that the question of FDR's Keynesianism is not as simple as is commonly thought and then imply further that the common association of "New Deal policies with general conceptions of Keynesianism" is, to some extent, false.

GAMBIT 4: LEAD WITH YOUR SECOND-BEST EXAMPLE

Another versatile opening gambit, where disciplinary conventions allow, is to use your *second-best example* to set up the issue or question that you later develop in depth with your best example. This gambit is especially useful in papers that proceed inductively on the strength of representative examples. As you are assembling evidence in the outlining and prewriting stage, in many cases you will accumulate a number of examples that illustrate the same basic point. For example, several battles might illustrate a particular general's military strategy; several primaries might exemplify how a particular candidate tailors his or her speeches to appeal to the religious right; several scenes might show how a particular playwright romanticizes the working class; and so on.

Save the best example to receive the most analytical attention in your paper. If you were to present this example in the introduction, you would risk making the rest of the essay vaguely repetitive. A quick close-up of another example will strengthen your argument or interpretation. By using a different example to raise the issues, you suggest that the phenomenon exemplified is not an isolated case and that the major example you will eventually concentrate upon is indeed representative.

What kind of example should you choose? By calling it second best, we mean to suggest only that it should be another resonant instance of whatever issue or question you have chosen to focus upon. Given its location up front and its function to introduce the larger issues to which it points, you should handle it more simply than subsequent examples. That way your readers can get their bearings before you take them into a more in-depth analysis of your best example in the body of your paper.

GAMBIT 5: EXEMPLIFY THE TOPIC WITH A NARRATIVE

A common gambit in the humanities and social sciences, the narrative opening introduces a short, pertinent, and vivid story or anecdote that exemplifies a key aspect of a topic. Although generally not permissible in the formal reports assigned in the natural and social sciences, narrative openings turn up in virtually all other kinds of writing across the curriculum. Here is an example from a student paper in psychology.

> In the past fifteen years, issues surrounding AIDS have incited many people to examine their thoughts and feelings about homosexuality. As a result, instances of prejudice and discrimination toward gays, lesbians, and bisexuals

have risen recently (Herek 1989). Although some instances are sufficiently damaging to warrant criminal charges, other less serious instances of prejudice occur every day. Nonetheless, they demonstrate a problem with our society that needs to be addressed. I witnessed one of these subtle demonstrations of prejudice in a social psychology class. The topic of the class was love and relationships, how they develop, endure, and deteriorate. Although the professor had not specifically stated it previously, the information being presented was relevant to homosexual relationships as well as heterosexual ones. At one point during her lecture, the professor was presenting an example using a hypothetical sorority member. The professor, in passing, referred to the sorority member's love relationship partner as a "she." This reference to a homosexual relationship did not seem intentional on the professor's part. However, many in the class noticed and reacted with silence at first, then glances at neighbors, which led finally to nervous laughter. After this disruption ended, a student explained to the professor what had been said that caused the disruption. And in response the professor promptly explained that the theories for love and relationships also apply to homosexual relationships.

In that moment of nervous laughter, many in the class displayed prejudice against homosexual relationships. In particular, they were displaying a commonly held belief that homosexual relationships are not founded on the same emotions, thoughts, and feelings that heterosexual relationships are. The main causes of prejudice displayed in class against homosexuality include social categorization and social learning.

As this introduction funnels to its thesis, the readers receive a graphic sense of the issue that the writer will now develop nonnarratively. Such nonnarrative treatment is usually necessary because by itself anecdotal evidence can be seen as merely personal. Storytelling is suggestive but usually does not constitute sufficient proof; it needs to be corroborated. In the preceding paragraph the writer has strengthened his credibility by focusing not on his personal responses but rather on the lesson to be drawn from his experience—a lesson that other people might also draw from it.

Like challenging a commonly held view or using a second-best example, a narrative opening will also help to safeguard you from trying to do too much up front. All three of these gambits enable you to play an ace, establishing your authority with your readers, without having to play your whole hand. They offer a starting position rather than a miniaturized version of the entire paper. As a general rule (disciplinary conventions permitting), use your introduction to pose one problem and offer one enigmatic example—seeking in some way to engage readers in the thought process that you are beginning to unfold. Raise the issue; don't settle it.

Try this 8.2: Analyzing Introduction

One of the best ways to learn about introductions is to gather some sample introductory paragraphs and, working on your own or in a small group, figure out how each one works, what it accomplishes.

Here are some particular questions you might pose:

- Why does the writer start in this way—what is accomplished?
- What kind of relationship does this opening establish with the audience and to what ends?
- How does the writer let readers know why the writing they are about to read is called for, useful, and necessary?
- Where and by what logic does the introduction funnel?

E. THE FUNCTION OF CONCLUSIONS

Like the introduction, the conclusion has a key social function: it escorts the readers out of the paper, just as the introduction has escorted them in. What do readers want as they leave the textual world you have taken them through? Although the form and length of the conclusion depend on the purpose and disciplinary conventions of the particular paper, it is possible to generalize a set of shared expectations for the conclusion across the curriculum. In some combination most readers want three things: a judgment, a culmination, and a send-off.

Judgment—The conclusion is the site for final judgment on whatever question or issue or problem the paper has focused upon. In most cases, this judgment occurs in overt connection with the introduction, often repeating some of its key terms. The conclusion normally reconsiders the question raised by the opening hypothesis and, however tentatively, rules yea or nay. It also explicitly revisits the introductory claim for why the topic matters.

Culmination—More than simply summarizing what has preceded or reasserting your main point, the conclusion needs to culminate. The word "culminate" is derived from the Latin "*columen,*" meaning "top or summit." To culminate is to reach the highest point, and it implies a mountain (in this case, of information and analysis) that you have scaled. When you culminate a paper in a conclusion, you bring things together and ascend to one final statement of your thinking.

When you culminate a paper in a conclusion, you bring things together and ascend to one final statement of your thinking.

Send-Off—The climactic effects of judgment and culmination provide the basis for the send-off. The send-off is both social and conceptual, a final opening outward of the topic that leads the reader out of the paper with something further to think about. As is suggested by most of the professors in the accompanying "Voices from Across the Curriculum" boxes, the conclusion needs to move beyond the close analysis of data that has occupied the body of the paper into a kind of speculation that the writer has earned the right to formulate.

Here is an example of a conclusion that contains a final judgment, a culmination, and a send-off. The paper, a student's account of what she learned about science from doing research in biology, opens by claiming that, to the apprentice, "science assumes an impressive air of complete reliability, especially to its distant human acquaintances." Having been attracted to science by the popular view that it proceeds infallibly, she arrives at quite a different final assessment:

> All I truly know from my research is that the infinite number of factors that can cause an experiment to go wrong make tinkering a lab skill just as necessary as reading a buret. A scientist can eventually figure out a way to collect the data she wants if she has the patience to repeatedly recombine her materials and tools in slightly different ways. A researcher's success, then, often depends largely on her being lucky enough to locate, among all the possibilities, the one procedure that works.
>
> Aided more by persistence and fortune than by formal training, I evolved a method that produced credible results. But, like the tests from which it derived, the success of that method is probably also highly specific to a certain experimental environment and so is valid only for research involving borosilicate melts treated with hydrofluoric and boric acids. I've discovered a principle, but it's hardly a universal one: reality is too complex to allow much scientific generalization. Science may appear to sit firmly on all-encompassing truths, but the bulk of its weight actually rests on countless little rules tailored for particular situations.

This writer deftly interweaves the original claim from her introduction—that "science assumes an impressive air of complete reliability"—into a final *judgment* of her topic, delivered in the last sentence. This judgment is also a *culmination*, as it moves from her account of doing borosilicate melts to the small but acute generalization that "little rules tailored for particular situations" rather than "all-encompassing truths" provide the mainstay of scientific research. Notice that *a culmination does not need to make a grand claim in order to be effective.* In fact, the relative smallness of the final claim, especially in contrast to the sweeping introductory position about scientific infallibility, ultimately provides a *send-off* made effective by its unexpected understatement.

VOICES FROM ACROSS THE CURRICULUM

Expanding Possibilities in the Conclusion

I tell my students that too many papers "just end," as if the last page or so were missing. I tell them the importance of ending a work. One could summarize main points, but I tell them this is not heavy lifting. They could raise issues not addressed (but hinted at) in the main body: "given this, one could consider that." I tell them that a good place for reflection might be a concluding section in which they take the ball and run: react, critique, agree, disagree, recommend, suggest, or predict.

I help them by asking, "Where does the paper seem to go *after* it ends on paper?" That is, I want the paper to live on even though the five pages are filled. I don't want to suddenly stop thinking or reacting just because I've read the last word on the bottom of page 5. I want an experience, as if the paper is still with me.

I believe the ending should be an expansion on or explosion of possibilities, sort of like an introduction to some much larger "mental" paper out there. I sometimes encourage students to see the concluding section as an option to introduce ideas that can't be dealt with now. Sort of a "Having done this, I would want to explore boom, boom, boom if I were to continue further." Here the students can critique and recommend ("Having seen 'this,' one wonders 'that'").

–Frederick Norling, Professor of Business

There must be a summation. What part did the stock market crash of 1929 play in the onset of the Great Depression? Let's hear that conclusion one more time. Again, but now in an abbreviated form, what's the evidence? What are the main ambiguities that remain? Has your paper raised any new questions for future research? Are there any other broader ramifications following in the wake of your paper?

–James Marshall, Professor of Economics

VOICES FROM ACROSS THE CURRICULUM

Limiting Claims in the Conclusion

In the professional journals, conclusions typically appear as a refined version of a paper's thesis—that is, as a more qualified statement of the main claim. An author might take pains to point out how this claim is limited or problematic, given the adequacy of available evidence (particularly in the case of papers dependent on current empirical research, opinion polls, etc.). The conclusion also may indicate the implications of current or new evidence on conventional wisdom/theory—how the theory needs to be revised, discarded, and so forth. Conclusions of papers that deal with contemporary issues or trends usually consider the practical consequences or the expectations for the future.

The conclusion does not appear simply as a restatement of a thesis, but rather as an attempt to draw out its implications and significance (the "So what?"). This is what I usually try to impress upon students. For instance, if a student is writing on a particular proposal for party reform, I would expect the concluding paragraph to consider both the significance of the reform and its practicality.

I should note that professional papers often indicate the tentativeness of their conclusions by stressing the need for future research and indicating what these research needs might be. Although I haven't tried this, maybe it would be useful to have students conclude papers with a section entitled "For Further Consideration" in which they would indicate those things that they would have liked to have known but couldn't, given their time constraints, the availability of information, and lack of methodological sophistication. This would serve as a reminder of the tentativeness of conclusions and the need to revisit and revise arguments in the future (which, after all, is a good scholarly habit).

–Jack Gambino, Professor of Political Science

WAYS OF CONCLUDING

The three professors quoted on pages 230–232 all advise some version of the judgment/ culmination/send-off combination. The first professor stresses the send-off.

Although it is true that the conclusion is the place for "broader ramifications," this phrase should not be understood as a call for a global generalization. As the professor in the "Voices from Across the Curriculum" box suggests, often the culmination represents a final limiting of a paper's original claim.

THREE STRATEGIES FOR WRITING EFFECTIVE CONCLUSIONS

There is striking overlap in the advice offered in the cross-disciplinary "voices." All caution that the conclusion should provide more than a restatement of what you've already said. All suggest that the conclusion should, in effect, serve as the introduction to some "larger 'mental' paper out there" (as one professor puts it) beyond the confines of your own paper. By consensus, the professors make three recommendations for conclusions:

1. *Pursue implications.* Reason inductively from your particular study to consider broader issues, such as the study's practical consequences or applications, or future-oriented issues, such as avenues for further research. To unfold implications in this way is to broaden the view from the here and now of your paper by looking outward to the wider world and forward to the future.
2. *Come full circle.* Unify your paper by interpreting the results of your analysis in light of the context you established in your introduction.
3. *Identify limitations.* Acknowledge restrictions of method or focus in your analysis, and qualify your conclusion (and its implications) accordingly.

Try this 8.3: Analyzing a Sample Conclusion

Consider the following example, which supplies the concluding paragraphs to the paper whose introduction we analyzed earlier as an example of a narrative opening on pages 227–228. That opening anecdote, you may recall, introduced the problems of social categorization and social learning as causes of homophobia in the academic environment.

First reread the writer's introduction (under Gambit 5). Then determine how his conclusion has implemented the three strategies for concluding effectively—unfolding implications, coming full circle, and limiting claims. Jot answers to the following questions: What does he repeat of the claims made in the introduction? How does he change the context in which these claims are now to be viewed? What words does he use to qualify both the final summary of evidence and his concluding claim?

There are many other instances of prejudice, stereotyping, and discrimination against homosexuals. These range from beliefs that homosexual partners cannot be adequate parents, to exclusion from the military, to bias (hate) crimes resulting in murder. But in recent decades, attempts have been made to help end these discriminations. One of the first occurred in 1973 when the American Psychological Association changed its policy so that homosexuals were no longer regarded as mentally ill (Melton, 1989). Thus the stigma that homosexuals are not able to fully contribute to society was partially lifted.

Other ways that have been suggested to reduce prejudice regarding homosexuals include increasing intergroup contact. In this way, each group may come to recognize similarities and encounter counterstereotypical information. Herek (1989) also suggests that education in elementary through high schools about diversity and tolerance of it—for students as well as teachers—may help prevent stereotypes, prejudice, and hate crimes. And if people are made aware of their schemas and stereotypes, they may consider information they would have ignored based on their schemas. We may never be able to eliminate the process of social categorization, but perhaps we may be able to teach that all out-groups are not necessarily "bad."

F. SOLVING TYPICAL PROBLEMS IN CONCLUSIONS

The primary challenge in writing conclusions, it should now be evident, lies in finding a way to culminate your analysis without claiming either too little or too much. There are a number of fairly common problems to guard against if you are to avoid either of these two extremes.

REDUNDANCY

In Chapter 5 we lampooned an exaggerated example of the five-paragraph form for constructing its conclusion by stating "Thus, we see" and then repeating the introduction verbatim. The result is *redundancy*. As you've seen, it's a good idea to refer back to the opening, but it's a bad idea just to reinsert it mechanically. Instead, reevaluate what you said there in light of where you've ended up, repeating only key words or phrases from the introduction. This kind of *selective repetition* is a desirable way of achieving unity and will keep you from making one of two opposite mistakes—either repeating too much or bringing up a totally new point in the conclusion.

RAISING A TOTALLY NEW POINT

Raising a totally new point can distract or bewilder a reader. This problem often arises out of a writer's praiseworthy desire to avoid repetition. As a rule, you can guard against the problem by making sure that you have clearly expressed the conceptual link between your central conclusion and any implications you may draw. *An implication is not a totally new point but rather one that follows from the position you have been analyzing.*

Similarly, although a capping judgment or send-off may appear for the first time in your concluding paragraph, it should have been *anticipated* by the body of your paper. Conclusions often indicate where you think you (or an interested reader) may need to go next, but you don't actually go there. In a paper on the economist Milton Friedman, for example, if you think that another economist offers a useful way of critiquing him, you probably should not introduce this person for the first time in your conclusion.

OVERSTATEMENT

Many writers are confused over how much they should claim in the conclusion. Out of the understandable (but mistaken) desire for a grand (rather than a modest and qualified) culmination, writers sometimes *overstate* the case. That is, they assert more than their evidence has proven or even suggested. Must a conclusion arrive at some comprehensive and final answer to the question that your paper has analyzed? Depending on the question and the disciplinary conventions, you may need to come down exclusively on one side or another. In a great many cases, however, the answers with which you conclude can be more moderate. Especially in the humanities, good analytical writing seeks to unfold successive layers of implication, so it's not even reasonable for you to expect neat closure. In such cases, you are usually better off qualifying your final judgments, drawing the line at points of relative stability.

Must a conclusion arrive at some final answer? You are usually better off qualifying your final judgments, drawing the line at points of relative stability.

ANTICLIMAX

It makes a difference precisely where in the final paragraph(s) you qualify your concluding claim. The end of the conclusion is a "charged" site, because it gives the reader a last impression of your paper. As the next chapter on formats will discuss in more detail, if you end with a concession—an acknowledgement of a rival position at odds with your thesis—you risk leaving the reader unsettled and possibly confused. The term for this kind of letdown from the significant to the inconsequential is "anticlimax." In most cases, you will flub the send-off if you depart the paper on an anticlimax.

There are many forms of anticlimax besides ending with a concession. If your conclusion peters out in a random list or an apparent afterthought or a last-minute qualification of your claims, the effect is anticlimactic. And for many readers, *if your final answer comes from quoting an authority in place of establishing your own, that, too, is an anticlimax.*

At the beginning of this section we suggested that a useful rule for the introduction is to play an ace but not your whole hand. In the context of this card-game analogy, it is similarly effective to *save an ace for the conclusion.* In most cases, this high card will provide an answer to some culminating "So what?" question—a last view of the implications or consequences of your analysis.

Save an ace for the conclusion—a high card that answers some culminating "So what?" question or offers a last view of the implications or consequences of your analysis.

G. SCIENTIFIC FORMAT: INTRODUCTIONS AND CONCLUSIONS

Formats control fairly strictly the form of standard writing projects in the natural sciences and psychology.

INTRODUCTIONS OF REPORTS IN THE SCIENCES

The professors quoted in the "Voices from Across the Curriculum" boxes in the remainder of this chapter emphasize the importance of isolating a specific question or issue and locating it within a wider context. Notice, as you read these voices, how *little* the model for an introduction changes in moving from a social science (psychology) to the natural sciences of biology and physics.

In the sciences, the introduction is an especially important and also somewhat challenging section of the report to compose because it requires a writer *not merely to assemble but also to assimilate* the background of information and ideas that frame his or her hypothesis.

VOICES FROM ACROSS THE CURRICULUM

Introductions in the Sciences

A paper usually starts by making some general observation or a description of known phenomena and by providing the reader with some background information. The first paragraphs should illustrate an understanding of the issues at hand and should present an argument for why the research should be done. In other words, a context or framework is established for the entire paper. This background information must lead to a clear statement of the objectives of the paper and the hypothesis that will be experimentally tested. This movement from broad ideas and observations to a specific question or test starts the deductive scientific process.

–Richard Niesenbaum, Professor of Biology

VOICES FROM ACROSS THE CURRICULUM

Assimilating Prior Research

The introduction is one of the hardest sections to write. In the introduction, students must summarize, analyze, and integrate the work of numerous other authors and use that to build their own argument.

Students frequently have trouble writing the introduction. They tend to just list the conclusions of previous authors. So-and-So said this, and So-and-So said this, and on and on in a list format. Usually, they *quote* the concluding statements from an article. But the task is really to read the article and *summarize* it in your own words. The key is to analyze rather than just repeat material from the articles so as to make clear the connections among them. (It is important to note that experimental psychologists almost never use direct quotes in their writing. Many of my students have been trained to use direct quotation for their other classes, and so I have to spend time explaining how to summarize without directly quoting or plagiarizing the work that they have read.)

Finally, in the introduction the students must show explicitly how the articles they have summarized lead to the hypothesis they have devised. Many times the students see the connection as implicitly obvious, but I require that they explicitly state the relationships between what they read and what they plan to do.

–*Laura Snodgrass, Professor of Psychology*

One distinctive feature of scientific papers is that a separate prefatory section called the *abstract* precedes the introduction. Authors also produce abstracts for papers in many other disciplines, but these are usually published separately—for example, in a bibliography, in a journal's table of contents, and so forth. (See the end of Chapter 13 for further discussion of abstracts.)

VOICES FROM ACROSS THE CURRICULUM

Writing Abstracts

The publishable paper in physics begins with an abstract, which briefly describes the experiment, gives the conclusion, and the significance of the work, all in three or four sentences. In the opening paragraph of the main body of the paper, the writer tries to put the work to be described into some larger context. This context usually includes reference to the following:

- similar experiments, which may, or may not, have shown similar results; and
- theoretical work suggesting the importance of the experiment, the scientific or technological significance of the work.

–*Robert Milligan, Professor of Physics*

VOICES FROM ACROSS THE CURRICULUM

Writing Conclusions in the Sciences

The conclusion occurs in a section labeled "Discussion" and, as quoted from the *Publication Manual of the American Psychological Association* (4th ed., Washington, DC, 1994), is guided by the following questions:

- What have I contributed here?
- How has my study helped to resolve the original problem?
- What conclusions and theoretical implications can I draw from my study? (p. 19)

In a broad sense, one particular research report should be seen as but one moment in a broader research tradition that *preceded* the particular study being written about and that will *continue after* this study is published. And so the conclusion should tie this particular study into both previous research considering implications for the theory guiding this study and (when applicable) practical implications of this study. One of the great challenges of writing a research report is thus to place this particular study within that broader research tradition. That's an analytical task.

–Alan Tjeltveit, Professor of Psychology

Papers are concluded with a "Discussion" section in which conclusions are analyzed and qualified and in which ultimately their implications for the "bigger picture" are presented. The conclusion of the paper often represents the move from the deductive to the inductive aspect of science. The specific results first are interpreted (but not restated), and their implications and limitations are then discussed. The original question should be rephrased and discussed in light of the results presented. Conclusions should be qualified, and alternative explanations should be considered. Finally, conservative generalizations and new questions are posed.

–Richard Niesenbaum, Professor of Biology

In the "Discussion" section, students must critically evaluate the extent to which the empirical evidence they have collected supports the hypothesis they put forth in the introduction. If the data does not support their hypothesis, they need to explain why. The reasons typically are either that there was something wrong with the hypothesis or something wrong with the experiment. Interestingly, students usually find it easier to write the "Discussion" section if their hypothesis was not supported than if it was—to guess what went wrong—because it is difficult to integrate new results into existing theory.

–Laura Snodgrass, Professor of Psychology

DISCUSSION SECTIONS OF REPORTS IN THE SCIENCES

As is the case with introductions, the conclusions of reports written in the natural sciences and psychology are regulated by formalized disciplinary formats.

Conclusions, for example, occur in a section entitled "Discussion." As the voices in the "Voices from Across the Curriculum" box on page 237 demonstrate, the organization and contents of discussion sections vary little from discipline to discipline. For that matter, the imperatives that guide discussion sections share essential traits with conclusions across the curriculum. Look for these similarities in the three comments in the box.

ASSIGNMENT: Revising the Introduction and Conclusion of a Previous Paper

Select one of your previous papers and entirely rewrite the introductory and concluding paragraphs. Your revisions should be guided by the chapter's overarching points: *Introductions should raise issues rather than settle them, and conclusions should culminate, going beyond restating what has already been said.* As you plan your revisions, consciously apply the concrete suggestions contained in the chapter's lists of gambits and discussion of strategies. How might the introduction be rewritten to use one of the opening gambits? Which of the opening gambits would be most appropriate? Experiment with at least two. Then rewrite your conclusion in explicit conversation with your introduction, qualifying your opening claims and pushing to answer one culminating but qualified "So what?" at which the original ending never arrived.

GUIDELINES FOR WRITING INTRODUCTIONS AND CONCLUSIONS

Introductions

1. The introduction seeks to raise the issue, not settle it. Articulate why, in the context of existing thinking on the subject, your topic matters.
2. Don't try to do too much. Offer only the most relevant context, the most essential parts of your road map, and (disciplinary conventions permitting) a first rather than last claim.
3. Always introduce a working (hypo)thesis, frame it with (appropriately cited) background or other context, and specify your method or angle of approach.
4. Especially in longer papers, you can use a procedural opening to forecast the organization clearly, but don't let it distract you from also stating your claim.
5. Experiment with opening gambits: challenge a common view, use your second-best example to set up the issue, or exemplify the problem with a narrative opening.

Conclusions

6. Culminate—don't just summarize. Offer your most fully evolved and qualified statement of the thesis or your final judgment on the question posed in the introduction.

GUIDELINES FOR WRITING INTRODUCTIONS AND CONCLUSIONS (CONTINUED)

7. Come full circle: revisit the introductory hypothesis and context. This strategy will unify your paper and locate it within an ongoing conversation on your topic.
8. Your conclusion should not unqualifiedly claim more than your evidence has established, but it should leave the reader with further implications or speculations to ponder (a send-off).
9. Let your conclusion gradually escort the reader out of the paper. Like the introduction, it is a social site, so try to leave the reader with a positive last impression.

CHAPTER 9

Organization: Forms and Formats

Quick Take

This is a chapter about organization, about the forms and formats writers use to give structure to their ideas. The first half of the chapter concentrates on *disciplinary formats*—the rules governing the forms of finished papers in the various disciplines. More specifically, it argues for recognizing the *heuristic value* of these formats—that is, their function as tools of invention, offering writers means for finding things out. The second half of the chapter broadens the focus beyond formats to consider *rhetoric:* how a writer's awareness of an audience's attitudes and needs affects the shape of her or his writing.

What the chapter does not focus on are the various models of overall organization treated earlier in the book as alternatives to five-paragraph form. See the sections titled "Pan, Track, and Zoom: The Film Analogy" in Chapter 5 (on evidence) as well as the "Procedure for Making the Thesis Evolve through Successive Complications" in Chapter 6 (on the evolving thesis). Both of these offer flexible wide-scale models for organization.

This chapter is less concerned with teaching you particular formats than with teaching you ways of thinking about and putting to best use whatever formats you are asked to write in. As you will see, academic disciplines differ in the extent to which they adhere to prescribed organizational schemes. In biology and psychology, for example, formal papers and reports generally follow an explicitly prescribed pattern of presentation. Some other disciplines are less uniform and less explicit about their reliance on formats, but writers in these fields—economics, for example, or political science—usually operate within fairly established forms as well.

The second half of the chapter, titled "The Psychology of Form," raises rhetorical issues as a lead-in to discussion of such topics as how to organize comparisons, how to situate concessions and refutations, how to use thesis shape to determine the shape of a paper, and how to use transitions and paragraphing in the overall organization of an essay.

A. THE TWO FUNCTIONS OF FORMATS: PRODUCT AND PROCESS

Most of the writing (and thinking) we do is generated by some kind of format, even if we are not aware of it. Writers virtually never write in the absence of conventions. Accordingly, you should not regard most of the formats that you encounter simply as *prescriptive* (that is, strictly required) sets of artificial rules. Rather, try to think of them as descriptive accounts of the various *heuristics*—sets of questions and categories—that humans typically use to guide and stimulate their thinking.

The first step in learning to use formats productively is to recognize that they have two related but separate functions: product and process.

- *As sets of rules for organizing a final product,* formats make communication among members of a discipline easier and more efficient. By standardizing the means of displaying thinking in a discipline, the format enables readers to compare more readily one writer's work with that of others in the field, because readers will know where to look for particular kinds of information—the writer's methodology, for example, or his or her hypothesis or conclusions.
- *As guides and stimulants to the writing process,* formats offer writers a means of finding and exploring ideas. The procedures that formats contain seek to guide the writer's thinking process in a disciplined manner, prompting systematic and efficient examination of a subject. The notion of formats functioning as aids to invention—idea generation—goes back at least as far as Aristotle, whose *Rhetoric* defined twenty-eight general "topics" (such as considering causes and effects or dividing a subject into parts) that speakers might pursue to invent arguments.

Perhaps the biggest problem that formats can create for writers is *a premature emphasis on product*—on the form of the finished paper at the expense of process. When this happens, they tend to lose sight of *the logic* that formats provide for dividing the subject into parts, arranged in a particular order. The conventional format of the scientific paper, for example, stipulates the inclusion of a review of prior research to induce writers to arrive at thoughtful connections between their own work and earlier experiments.

USING FORMATS HEURISTICALLY: AN EXAMPLE

To lose sight of the heuristic value of formats is to become preoccupied with formats as disciplinary etiquette. The solution to this problem probably sounds easier than it is: you need to *find the spaces in a format that will allow it to work as a heuristic.* Consider how you might go about using even a highly specified organizational scheme like the following:

1. State the problem.
2. Develop criteria of adequacy for a solution.
3. Explore at least two inadequate solutions.
4. Explicate the proposed solution.
5. Evaluate the proposed solution.
6. Reply to anticipated criticisms.

The best reason not to ignore any of the six steps in this problem/solution format is that the format does have a logic, although it leaves that logic unstated. The purpose of including at least two inadequate solutions (step 3), for example, is to protect the writer against moving to a conclusion too quickly on the basis of too little evidence. The requirements that the writer evaluate the solution and reply to criticisms (steps 5 and 6) press the writer toward complexity, to prevent a one-sided and uncritical answer. In short, heuristic value in the format is there for a writer to use if he or she doesn't allow a premature concern with matters of form to take precedence over thinking. It would be a mistake, in other words, to assume that one must move through the six steps consecutively; the writer would need to arrange his or her thinking in that order only when putting together the final product.

FORMATS IN THE NATURAL AND SOCIAL SCIENCES

In some disciplines, especially in the natural sciences and psychology, the pattern of presentation for formal papers and reports is explicitly prescribed and usually mandatory. As noted in Chapter 13, for example, the American Psychological Association (APA) issues a disciplinary style guide (now in its fifth edition) to which all writers seeking to publish in the field must adhere. In other disciplines, particularly in the humanities and other of the social sciences, the accepted patterns of organization are less rigidly defined. Nonetheless, writers in these fields also operate to a significant extent within established forms, such as those set forth by the Modern Language Association (MLA) handbook.

Because formats offer a means not only of displaying thinking in a discipline but also of shaping it, the format that a discipline tacitly or overtly requires conditions its members to think in particular ways. Learning to use the format that scientists use predisposes you to think like a scientist. Learning the differences among the various disciplines' formats can help you recognize differences in *epistemology* (ways of knowing). As we stress elsewhere in this book, how you say something is always a part of what you say; the two can't be easily separated. Although knowing the required steps of a discipline's writing format won't write your papers for you, not knowing how writers in that discipline characteristically proceed can keep you from being read.

Nonetheless, the various formats across the disciplines, the skeletons that both shape and display thinking in those disciplines, are actually quite similar. They usually contain most of the same elements, although these elements may be called by different names and arranged in slightly different orders. A science paper and a history paper, for example, both advance a hypothesis, provide context for it, specify methodology, and support their claims by carefully weighing the evidence.

The various formats across the disciplines are actually quite similar. A science paper and a history paper both advance a hypothesis, provide context for it, specify methodology, and support their claims by carefully weighing the evidence.

VOICES FROM ACROSS THE CURRICULUM

Using the Scientific Format

There are firm rules in organizing scientific writing. Papers are usually divided into four major sections: (1) Introduction: provides context and states the question asked and the hypothesis tested in the study; (2) Methodology: describes experimental procedure; (3) Results: states the results obtained; and (4) Discussion: analyzes and interprets results with respect to the original hypothesis, and discusses implications of the results. As this organizational model should make clear, scientific papers are largely deductive, with a shift to inductive reasoning in the discussion when the writer usually attempts to generalize or extend conclusions to broader circumstances.

Scientific papers also include an abstract, which is placed on the page after the title page. The abstract summarizes the question being investigated in the paper, the methods used in the experiment, the results, and the conclusions drawn. The reader should be able to determine the major topics in the paper without reading the entire paper. Compose the abstract after the paper is completed.

–Richard Niesenbaum, Professor of Biology

In writing in the social sciences, there is a standard plot with three alternative endings. The Introduction (a standard section of APA style) sets forth the problem, which the Methods section promises to address. The Results section "factually" reports the outcome of the study, with the Discussion section interpreting the results. The data are given the starring role in determining which ending is discussed in the Discussion section: hypothesis confirmed, hypothesis rejected, or hard to say. (I would say "which ending the author chooses" versus "which ending is discussed," but the data are supposed to be determinative, and the role of the author/investigator neutral.) Analytical thinking comes in setting up the problem and making sense of the results in conjunction with existing literature on the subject.

–Alan Tjeltveit, Professor of Psychology

Experimental Psychology uses a very rigid format. I explain to the students the functions of the different sections for the reader. Once students start to read journal articles themselves, the functions of the sections become clear. Readers do not always want to read or reread the whole article. If I want to replicate someone's research, I may read just the Methods section to get the technical details I need. I may read just the Results section to get a sense of the numerical results I might expect. On the other hand, I may not care about the details of how the experiment was run. I might just want to know if it worked, in which case I would read the first few sentences of the Discussion section. The format lets me know exactly where to find whatever I might be looking for, without having to read through the whole article.

–Laura Snodgrass, Professor of Psychology

VOICES FROM ACROSS THE CURRICULUM

Treating the Format Flexibly

Scientific format appears highly formulaic at first glance. Papers are generally broken into four sections: Introduction (What is this all about, What do we already know, Why do we care?), Experimental Procedures (What did you actually do?), Results (What happened in your experiments?), and Discussion (What do you think it means? What are the remaining questions?). This breakdown is useful because it emphasizes the process of argument (introduction and results), providing evidence (results) and analysis (discussion). However, although this may seem different from writing in other disciplines, I think of it as a codification of basic analytical writing that is common in most disciplines.

A common mistake made by beginning and intermediate students is taking this breakdown too literally. To be comprehensible, the rules must be broken periodically. For example, results frequently must be referred to in the Experimental Procedures section to understand *why* the next procedure was performed. Similarly, the Results section frequently must include some discussion, so that the reader understands the immediate significance of the results, if not the broader implications. For example, the following sentences might appear in a Results section: "These data suggest that the p53 protein may function in repressing cell division in potential cancer cells. To test this possibility, we overexpressed p53 protein in a transformed cell line." The first sentence provides an interpretation of the results that is necessary to understand why the next experiment was performed.

–Bruce Wightman, Professor of Biology

You should note that the observations in the preceding "Voices from Across the Curriculum" boxes apply to much, but certainly not all, of the writing that goes on in the sciences. In the last box, a professor of biology concentrates on the logic of the scientific format, but he also stresses its relative *flexibility*. That is, the distinctions among the various parts are not always as clear-cut as some students may think they are.

B. THE PSYCHOLOGY OF FORM

Thus far in this book we have talked about form primarily in relation to the search for meaning. We've demonstrated that some forms of arranging ideas (five-paragraph form, for example) interfere with a writer's ability to have ideas in the first place. Whatever form one uses, we've argued, has to be flexible enough to allow ideas to evolve. The point is that various factors influence a writer's decisions about forms and formats. These include both the demands of the subject itself and those of the discourse community within which the writing seeks to communicate.

We now wish to expand upon the role that a writer's sense of his or her *audience* plays in determining the formal presentation of ideas. We have titled this section "The Psychology of Form" to emphasize the effects that a chosen form has on an audience—on its receptiveness to a writer's ideas, for example.

Since classical times, there have been numerous studies of this subject, known as *rhetoric.* The study of rhetoric is primarily concerned with the various means at a writer's (or speaker's) disposal for influencing the views of an audience. In early rhetorics, Greek and Roman writers divided these means into three large categories: *ethos*, *logos*, and *pathos.* We'll use these categories for organizing what we wish to say about the relationship between formal structures and audience.

1. ***Ethos.*** The category of ethos has to do with the character of the speaker or writer. The basic idea of ethos is that if an audience perceives a speaker to be ethical and rational, it will be inclined to perceive her or his argument as ethical and rational too. Thus, writers attend to the kind of *persona* they become on the page, the personality conveyed by the words and the tone of the words. In classical orations—the grandparent of virtually all speech and essay formats—the first section was always allotted to particular means of establishing an appealing persona, one that an audience would want to listen to and believe.

   Although there are many ways of talking about ethos, throughout this book we implicitly recommend essentially the same kind of writer's persona—one that is primarily interested in understanding a subject and conveying that understanding. Such a persona assumes a relationship of mutual interest with his or her audience and avoids a defensive posture toward the material or the audience.
2. ***Logos.*** This category has to do with the character of the thinking itself, which has been our emphasis throughout this book—the rational component, evident in the presence and development of the ideas.
3. ***Pathos.*** This category includes appeals to the audience's emotions—which writing does all of the time, whether a writer wants it to or not. It is possible to think of the form of a paper in terms of how it might negotiate, for example, the likes and dislikes, the hopes and fears, of its assumed audience. If, for instance, you were to present an argument in favor of a position with which you knew in advance that your audience was predisposed to disagree, you would probably choose to delay making a case for it until you had found various ways of earning that audience's trust. By contrast, when presenting an argument to an audience of like-minded people, you would be much more likely to start out with the position you planned to advance.

In any piece of writing, there are always issues of authority. As a writer you need to concern yourself with using language in a way that will incline readers to credit what you say. We have been advancing as the best source of authority your ability to show others why and how you take the evidence to mean what you say it does. A premise of this book is that rather than spend a lot of time cultivating a set of rhetorical strategies for defeating opponents, writers should find ways to make their thinking about evidence clear and convincing in its clarity. Moreover, we have generally supported a more Rogerian approach to argument, whereby a writer seeks to negotiate among competing possibilities and invite collaboration from readers. (See the discussion of Carl Rogers in Chapter 1.)

HOW TO LOCATE CONCESSIONS AND REFUTATIONS

In the language of argument you *concede* whenever you acknowledge that a position at odds with your own does indeed have merit, even though you continue to believe that your position overall is the more reasonable one. A central idea of Chapter 6, "Making a Thesis Evolve," in fact, is that one option for dealing with views that conflict with your own is to use them to evolve your own position, thereby assimilating them. Another option is to argue against these views so as to *refute* their reasonableness.

There are several guidelines for locating concessions and refutations in an argument. It is a rule of thumb, for example, not to make your readers wait too long before you either concede or refute a view that you can assume will already have occurred to them. If you delay too long, you may inadvertently suggest either that you are unaware of the competing view or that you are afraid to bring it up.

You can often house short and easily managed concessions and refutations within the first several paragraphs and, in this way, clear a space for the position you wish to promote. In the case of more complicated and potentially more threatening alternative arguments, you may need to express your own position clearly and convincingly first. But to avoid the rhetorical problem of appearing to ignore the threat, you will probably need to give it a nod, telling readers that you will return to a full discussion of it later, once you have laid out your own position in some detail.

Here are some more specific guidelines:

- Don't end on a concession. If you do include a concession in your concluding paragraph, be sure to return to your own position in the final sentences.
- If you state an opposing argument in your introduction, you should be sure that it can be accurately presented in the brief form that introductory paragraphs require. The danger here is turning the opposing view into a straw man—an easily knocked-down version of the opposing view. (See Chapter 12 for a discussion of straw man.)
- One way of making sure you don't treat an opposing argument unfairly, but also don't inadvertently convince your readers that this argument is better than your own, is to concede the merits of this opposing view but then argue that, in the particular context you are addressing, your argument is more important, more appropriate, and so forth.
- The placement of arguments has much to do with their relative complexity. Reasonably straightforward and easily explained concessions and refutations can often be grouped in one place, perhaps as early as the second or third paragraph of a paper. The approach to concession and refutation in more complex arguments does not allow for such grouping. For each part of your argument, you will probably need to concede and refute as necessary, before moving to the next part of your argument and repeating the procedure.

To qualify as a concession, a writer needs to represent the competing point of view as genuinely creditable—rather than only seemingly creditable until he or she lays out a means of opposing it. Refutations typically operate not just by revealing poor thinking or inadequate evidence in a competing point of view, but also by proposing the greater value of adopting another position. Refutations often concede an opposing argument's genuine merits but then refute its importance in favor of a position that holds more promise under a given set of circumstances.

Try this 9.1: Locating Concessions and Refutations

The following passage from a student essay on the relation between gender inequality and language makes skillful use of concessions and refutations. The excerpt is part of an introductory paragraph, after the writer has set up the issue: whether or not the elimination of sexism in language (the use of male pronouns and words such as *mankind,* for example, in circumstances applying to both men and women) through the use of generic pronouns (those that do not indicate gender, such as *they* rather than *he*) can help eliminate gender exclusion in the culture. The paragraph names the two sides of the issue and moves from there to a tentative thesis.

Study the paragraph to answer the following questions: (1) What language functions as concession? (2) What language functions as refutation? (3) What part of the competing argument does the refutation still appear willing to concede? (4) How is the refutation that the writer offers different from the position to which he concedes?

Gender Inequality and Linguistic Bias

The more conservative side on this issue questions whether the elimination of generic pronouns can, in fact, change attitudes, and whether intentionally changing language is even possible. The reformist side believes that the elimination of generic pronouns is necessary for women's liberation from oppression and that reshaping the use of male pronouns as generic is both possible and effective. Although the answer to the debate over the direct link between a change in language and a change in society is not certain, it is certain that the attitudes and behaviors of societies are inseparable from language. Language conditions what we feel and think. The act of using *they* to refer to all people rather than the generic *he* will not automatically change collective attitudes toward women. These generic pronouns should be changed, however, because (1) the struggle itself increases awareness and discussion of the sexual inequalities in society, and subsequently, this awareness will transform attitudes and language, and (2) the power of linguistic usage has been mainly controlled by and reserved for men. Solely by participating in linguistic reform, women have begun to appropriate some of the power for themselves.

ORGANIZING COMPARISONS AND CONTRASTS

Chapter 4 discusses reading comparatively as a means of arriving at ideas. Here we address this subject from the perspective of organizing a paper. The first decision a writer has to make when arranging comparisons and contrasts is whether to address the two items being compared and contrasted *sequentially* in blocks or *point by point.* For example, if you are comparing subject A with subject B, you might first make all the points you wish to make about A and then make points about B by explicitly referring to A as you go. The advantage of this format is that it will allow you to use comparing and contrasting to figure out what you wish to say as you are drafting.

The disadvantage of this subject-A-then-subject-B format is that it can easily lose focus. If you don't manage to keep the points you raise about each side of your comparison parallel, you may end up with a paper comprising two loosely connected halves. The solution is to make your comparisons and contrasts in the second half of the paper connect explicitly with what you said in the first half. What you say about subject A, in other words, should set the subtopics and terms for discussion of subject B.

The alternative pattern of organization for comparisons and contrasts is to organize by topic—not A and then B but A1 and B1, A2 and B2, A3 and B3, and so forth. That is, you talk about both A and B under a series of subtopics. If, for example, you were comparing two films, you might organize your work under such headings as directing, script, acting, special effects, and so forth.

The advantage of this format is that it better focuses the comparisons, pressing you to use them to think with. The disadvantage is that organizing in this way is sometimes difficult to manage until you've already done quite a bit of thinking about the two items you're comparing. The solution, particularly in longer papers, is sometimes to use both formats. You begin by looking at each of your subjects separately to make the big links and distinctions apparent and then focus what you've said by further pursuing selected comparisons one topic at a time.

Regardless of which format you adopt, the comparisons and contrasts will not really begin to take shape until you have done enough preliminary drafting to discover what the most significant similarities and differences are and, beyond that, whether the similarities or the differences are most important—whether, that is, your primary goal is to compare or to contrast. At this point, you can begin to operate according to the principle we discuss next: climactic order.

CLIMACTIC ORDER

Climactic order has to do with arranging the elements in a list from least important to most important. The idea is to build to your best points, rather than leading with them and thereby allowing the paper to trail off from your more minor and less interesting observations.

Build to your best points, rather than leading with them and thereby allowing the paper to trail off.

But what are your best points? A frequent mistake that writers commit in arranging their points climactically—and one that has much to do with the psychology of form—is to assume that the best point is the most obvious, the one with the most data attached to it and the one least likely to produce disagreement with readers. Such writers end up giving more space than they should to ideas that really don't need much development because they are already evident to most readers.

A better strategy is to define as your best points those that the Notice-and-focus strategy locates as the *most revealing, most thought-provoking, and often, at first glance, least obvious.* In this case, if you followed the principle of climactic order, you would begin with the most obvious and predictable points—and ones that, psychologically speaking, would get readers assenting—and then build to the more revealing and less obvious ones. For example, if the comparisons between film A and film B are fairly mundane but the contrasts are really provocative, you'd get the comparisons out of the way first and build to the contrasts, exploiting difference within similarity. (See Chapter 4.)

Note that the principle of climactic order works with all kinds of organizational schemes, not just with comparison and contrast. If, for example, there are three important reasons for banning snowmobiling in your town, you might choose to place the most compelling one last. If you were to put it first, you might draw your readers in quickly (a principle used by news stories) but then lose them as your argument seemed to trail off into less interesting rationales. Similarly, if you have four examples for a point you wish to make, you might use a pan to cover the first three to pave the way for a zoom on the one you think is the best and most revealing.

HOW THESIS SHAPES PREDICT THE SHAPE OF THE PAPER

Early in Chapter 6 we noted that a strong thesis usually contains tension, the balance of this against that, this degree with that qualification. This tension is often evident in the actual sentence structure of the thesis statement. Many thesis statements begin with a grammatically subordinate idea that they go on to replace or outweigh with a more pressing claim: "Although *x* appears to account for *z*, *y* accounts for it better." (You will probably recognize this sentence structure as a version of one of the earlier prompts to interpretation: saying something "seems to be about *x*, but is really or could also be about *y*.") This formula can also organize a paper, which proceeds by following the pattern predicted by the order of clauses in the thesis statement. The first part of the paper deals with the claims for *x* and then moves to a fuller embrace of *y* (usually in overt relation to *x*). (See Chapter 11 for a discussion of grammatical subordination.)

The advantage of this subordinate construction (and the reason that so many theses are set up this way) is that the subordinate idea helps you define your own position by giving you something to define it against. As should be evident at this point, both the thesis shape containing subordination and the paper that follows from it are versions of climactic order.

In practice, using this shape will often lead you to arrive at some compromise position between the claims of both *x* and *y*. What appeared to be a binary opposition—"not *x* but *y*"—emerges as a complex combination of the two. (See Chapter 2 on refocusing binaries.)

Sometimes this combination is already evident in a thesis shape related to the subordination model: "*not only* x *but also* y." Here the emphasis predicts that you will make *additional* claims, probably less obvious ones *(y)*, after you have discussed *x*.

As is evident in the previous chapter's discussion of introductory paragraphs, one of the most important things to accomplish in an introduction is to locate an issue, question, or problem—something that is at stake—and then place it in an explanatory context. The subordinate clause of a thesis helps you demonstrate that there is in fact an issue involved—that is, more than one possible explanation for the evidence you are considering—and thus a reason to write the paper in the first place.

Another thesis shape that can predict the shape of a paper is the *list.* This shape, in which a writer might offer three points and then devote a section to each, often leads to sloppier thinking than one having a thesis statement containing both subordinate and independent clauses, because the list often does not sufficiently specify the connections among its various components. As a result, it fails to assert a relationship among ideas. The list is in fact the shape used by five-paragraph form—a form that does (we'll concede!) achieve considerable clarity of organization but at the (very high) cost of oversimplifying and derailing analysis.

Try this 9.2: Predicting Thesis Shapes

It is a useful skill, both in reading and writing, to predict paper shapes from thesis shapes. Unlike the multiple parts of the thesis that merely lists, productive thesis statements arrange the parts in some sort of overt relation to each other. For each of the theses below, what shape is predicted? That is, what will probably be discussed first, what second, and why? Which words in the thesis are especially predictive of the shape the paper will take?

1. The reforms in education, created to alleviate the problems of previous reforms, have served only to magnify the very problems they were meant to solve.
2. Joinville paints, though indirectly, a picture of military, social, and political gain having very little to do with religion and more to do with race hatred and the acquisition of material wealth.
3. Although women more readily cry in contemporary films, the men, by not crying, seem to win the audience's favor.
4. The complications that fuel the plots in today's romantic comedies arise because women and men express their sensitivity so differently; the resolutions, however, rarely require the men to capitulate.

THE SHAPING FORCE OF TRANSITIONS

A list, we have said, is a slack form of organization: overly loose, not identifying how *this* is related to *that* with the tension necessary to give a paper tensile strength. The same criticism applies to the *connective tissue* among the parts of an essay. Although transitional wording such as *another example of* or *also* at the beginning of paragraphs does tell readers that a related point or example will follow, it does not specify that relationship beyond piling on another *and.* The organizational model at work in this sort of additive scheme is again the list—the most diffuse and potentially illogical form of organization. (For additional analysis of the shortcomings of listing, see "Strategies for Making Summaries More Analytical" in Chapter 4.)

If you find yourself relying on *another* and *also* at points of transition, force yourself to substitute other transitional wording that indicates *more precisely* the nature of the relationship with what has gone before in the paper. Language such as *similarly* and *by contrast* can sometimes serve this purpose. In many cases, however, some restatement of what has been said and its relation to what will come next is called for. Don't underestimate the amount of productive restating that goes on in papers—it's not necessarily redundant. It can also be a "saying again" in different language for the purpose of advancing the writer's thinking further. *A good transition reaches backward, telling where you've been, as the grounds for making a subsequent move forward.*

The linkage between where you've been and where you're going is usually a point in your writing at which thinking is taking place. Often this kind of transitional thinking will require you to concentrate on articulating *how* what has preceded connects to what will follow—the logical links. This is especially the case in the evolving rather than the static model of thesis development, in which the writer continually updates the thesis as it moves through evidence. It follows that thinking tends to occur at points of transition. If it doesn't, you're far more likely to run into problems in organization.

Thinking tends to occur at points of transition.

The first step toward improving your use of transitions (and thereby, the organization of your writing) is to become *conscious* of them. If you notice that you are beginning successive paragraphs with *Another reason,* for example, you can probably conclude that you are listing rather than developing your ideas.

Try this 9.3: Tracking Transitions

To see how the transitions work as a skeleton for something you are reading (or have written), search out words that function as *directional indicators,* especially at the beginnings of paragraphs but also within them. *And,* for example, is a plus sign. It indicates that the writer will add something, essentially continuing in the same direction. The words *but, yet, nevertheless,* and *however* are among the many transitional words that alert readers to changes in the direction of the writer's thinking. They might indicate, for example, the introduction of a qualification, a potentially contradictory piece of evidence, an alternative point of view, and so forth. Note as well that some additive transitions do more work than *also* or *another.* The word *moreover* is an additive transition, but it adds emphasis to the added point. The transitional sequence *not only . . . but also* restates and then adds information in a way that clarifies what has gone before.

As an exercise in becoming more conscious of how transitions shape the thinking—the advancing and connecting of ideas—in a piece of writing, track the transitions. Take a few pages of something you are reading (preferably a complete piece, such as a short article) and circle or underline all the directional indicators. Remember to check not only the beginnings of paragraphs but within them. Then, survey your markings. What do you notice now about the shape of the piece? Describe the shape. This exercise is also a splendid way to expand your repertoire of transitional words to use in your own writing.

THE VIRTUES OF PARAGRAPHING

Be sure to paragraph, both for your own and for your readers' benefit. Paragraphing is a kindness to your reader because it divides your thinking into manageable bites. If you find a paragraph growing longer than half a page—particularly if it is your opening or second paragraph—search out a place to make a paragraph break. More frequent paragraphing provides readers with convenient resting points from which to relaunch themselves into your thinking.

Long paragraphs are daunting—rather like mountains are—and they are easy to get lost in, for both readers and writers. When writers try to do too much in a single paragraph, they often lose the focus and lose contact with the larger purpose or point that got them into the paragraph in the first place. Remember that old high school rule about one idea to a paragraph? Well, it's not a bad rule, though it isn't exactly right, because sometimes you need more space than a single paragraph can provide to lay out a complicated phase of your overall argument. In that case, just break wherever it seems reasonable to do so to keep your paragraphs from becoming ungainly.

Long paragraphs are daunting—rather like mountains are—and they are easy to get lost in.

When you draft, start a new paragraph whenever you feel yourself getting stuck—it's the promise of a fresh start. When you revise, use paragraphs as a way of cleaning up your thinking, dividing it into its most logical parts.

When you draft, start a new paragraph whenever you feel yourself getting stuck—it's the promise of a fresh start.

A short paragraph always provides emphasis, for which most readers will thank you.

ASSIGNMENT: Inferring the Format of a Published Article

Often the format governing the organization of a published piece is not immediately evident. That is, it is not subdivided according to conventional disciplinary categories that all members of a given discourse community obey. Especially if you are studying a discipline in which the writing does not follow an explicitly prescribed format, such as history, literature, or economics, you may find it illuminating to examine representative articles or essays in that discipline, looking for an implicit format. In other words, you can usually discern some underlying pattern of organization: the formal conventions, the rules that are being followed even when these are not highlighted.

The following assignment works well whether you tackle it individually or in a group. It can lead to a paper, an oral report, or both. First, you need to assemble several articles from the same or a similar kind of journal or magazine. *Journal* is the name given to publications aimed at specialized, usually scholarly, audiences, as opposed to general or popular audiences. *Time*, *Newsweek*, and *The New Yorker* are called magazines rather than journals because they are aimed at a broader general audience. *Shakespeare Quarterly* is a journal; *Psychology Today* is a magazine.

Having found at least three journal or magazine articles, study them to focus on the following question: Insofar as there appears to be a format that articles in this journal or magazine adhere to, what are its parts?

How, for example, does an article in this journal or magazine typically begin and end? Does there seem to be a relatively uniform place in which these articles include opposing arguments? You will, in other words, be analyzing the articles inductively (reasoning from particular details to general principles). Begin with the product and reason backward to the skeleton beneath the skin.

Note that if your professor directs you to work with magazines rather than journals, you should probably further narrow the focus—to a *Time* cover story, to *The New Yorker*'s "Letter from [the name of a city]," or another such recurring feature. Even gossip columns and letters of advice to the lovelorn in teen magazines adhere to certain visible though not explicitly marked formats.

Write up your results. Cite particular language from at least two articles in support of your claims about the implicit format. In presenting your evidence, keep the focus on the underlying form, showing how the different articles proceed in the same or similar ways. Don't let yourself get too distracted by the articles' content, even though there may be similarities here as well. Instead, work toward formulating a rationale for the format—what you take to be its psychology of form. You will need (for example) both to lay out the typical form of the introduction and to account for its taking that typical form. Devote several paragraphs to this rationale, either at the end of your report or integrated within it.

GUIDELINES FOR ORGANIZATION: FORMS AND FORMATS

1. Find the space in a format that will allow it to work as a heuristic, a set of steps designed not just to organize but to stimulate and guide your thinking. Avoid the slot-filler mentality.
2. Look for and expect to find the common denominators among the various formats you learn to use across the curriculum. You can master—and benefit from—virtually any format if you approach it not as a set of arbitrary and rigid rules, but as a formalized guide to having ideas.
3. Don't make your readers wait too long before you concede or refute a view that you can assume will already have occurred to them. Otherwise, they may assume you are unaware of the competing view or afraid to bring it up.
4. Always treat opposing views fairly. A good strategy is to concede their merits but argue that, in the particular context you are addressing, your position is more important or appropriate.
5. Use climactic order to organize your points, building to your best ones. The best ones are usually the most revealing and thought-provoking, not the most obvious or commonly agreed upon.
6. Phrasing your thesis to include a subordinate construction—"although *x* appears to account for *z*, *y* accounts for it better"—will give your paper a ready-made organizational shape, along with giving you something to define your own position against.
7. A good transition reaches backward, telling where you've been, as the grounds for making a subsequent move forward. Opt for *similarly* and *by contrast*, for example, which specify connections for your readers, rather than merely additive transitions such as *another* and *also*.
8. Half a page is a healthy length for most paragraphs, long enough to launch an idea but short enough to give your reader time to rest.

CHAPTER 10

Style: Choosing Words

Quick Take

Style, loosely defined, refers to the choices a writer makes among linguistic options. Each time this book has undergone revision, its two style chapters have been moved farther forward, and pieces of them have been located still earlier. This is because we have become increasingly convinced of the importance of style to *how* a writer thinks and to *what* a writer thinks.

This first chapter on style addresses word choice, also known as **diction**, and its effect on style. As an overarching aim, the chapter seeks to make you more self-conscious about the kinds of words you habitually use, and to expand the range of choices. Chapter 11 attempts to do the same with respect to sentence shapes, also known as **syntax**.

This chapter takes as a premise that most people simply don't pay attention to words. That is, they use words as if their sounds and shapes were invisible and their meanings were single and self-evident. One goal of this chapter is to interest you in words themselves—as *things* with particularized qualities, complex histories, and varied shades of meaning.

The two chapters have three primary lessons to teach, which we have boldfaced as objectives, followed by a little commentary:

1. **Understanding that style is not merely decorative.** It is often mistakenly assumed that style is separate from meaning and in that sense largely decorative. From this perspective, paying close attention to style seems finicky, or worse, cynical—a way of dressing up the content to sell it to readers or listeners. The problem with this perspective is that it subscribes to what linguistic philosophers call *the transparent theory of language*. This is the idea that meaning exists outside of language—that we somehow see *through* words to meaning and can then address that meaning without addressing the words that embody it. In the transparent theory of language, words are merely pointers to get past.

These chapters seek to persuade you to adopt the perspective that words *constitute* meaning; that is, that words are the medium in which we dwell. How something is phrased is an integral part of what it says, not subtractable. If you say something in another way, you are saying something else. (This position, known as *the constitutive theory of language*, has been embraced by virtually all contemporary rhetoricians.) In practical terms, this means that *how things are said profoundly affects what they say.*

2. **Seeing style as a matter of choices.** You may have been taught that you should always avoid the first-person *I* in academic writing, steer clear of jargon, and never start a sentence with *and* or *but.* These are matters of usage, not hard-and-fast rules of grammar. There are occasions when all three rules, and others like them, should be rejected. This chapter seeks to persuade you that all writing is *contextual*, its appropriateness dependent on the rhetorical situation.
3. **Learning that simplicity does not equal clarity.** This chapter targets the unexamined cultural bias in favor of "straight talk." The assumption seems to be that people who use too many words, especially big ones, are needlessly complicating what would otherwise be obvious to anyone's common sense. *Not so.* (The previous sentence intends to illustrate that those imperious arbiters of style, Strunk and White, are sometimes correct—"Never use six words when three will do," they say in *The Elements of Style*—but not always.) Of course, simplicity is sometimes preferable, and Chapter 11 devotes considerable attention to ways of reducing excess verbiage.

A. NOT JUST ICING ON THE CAKE

It is commonly assumed that "getting the style right" is a task that begins at the editing stage of producing a paper, as part of polishing the final draft. This assumption is only partly true. You probably should delay a full-fledged stylistic revision until a late stage of drafting, but that doesn't mean that you should totally ignore stylistic questions as you draft, because the decisions you make about how to phrase your meaning inevitably exert a powerful influence on the meaning you make.

And what is style? Well, it's not just icing on the cake—cosmetic, a matter of polishing the surface. Broadly defined, *style refers to all of a writer's decisions in selecting, arranging, and expressing what he or she has to say.* Many factors affect your style: your aim and sense of audience, the ways you approach and develop a topic, the kinds of evidence you choose, and, particularly, the kinds of syntax and diction you characteristically select.

Getting the style right is not as simple as proofreading for errors in grammar or punctuation. Proofreading occurs in the relatively comfortable linguistic world of simple right and wrong. Stylistic considerations, by contrast, take place in the more exploratory terrain of *making choices* among more and less effective ways of formulating and communicating your meaning.

In this sense, style is personal. The foundations of your style emerge in the dialogue you have with yourself about your topic. When you revise for style, you consciously reorient yourself toward communicating the results of that dialogue to your audience. Stylistic decisions, then, are a mix of the unconscious and conscious, of chance and choice. You don't simply impose style onto your prose; it's not a mask you don or your way of icing the cake. Revising for style is more like sculpting. As a sculptor uses a chisel to "bring out" a shape from a block of walnut or marble, a writer uses style to "bring out" the shape of the conceptual connections in a draft of an essay. As the two style chapters will suggest in various ways, this "bringing out" demands a certain *detachment from your own language.* It requires that you *become aware of your words as words and of your sentences as sentences.*

If stylistic considerations are not merely cosmetic, then it follows that rethinking the way you have said something can lead you to rethink the substance of what you have said. This point is sufficiently important to illustrate here for both syntax and diction, before this chapter narrows its focus to diction alone.

How does the difference in sentence structure affect the meaning of the following two sentences?

> **Draft:** The history of Indochina is marked by colonial exploitation as well as international cooperation.

> **Revision:** The history of Indochina, *although* marked by colonial exploitation, testifies to the possibility of international cooperation.

In the draft, the claim that Indochina has experienced colonial exploitation is equal in weight to the claim that it has also experienced international cooperation. But the revision ranks the two claims. The "although" clause makes the claim of exploitation secondary to the claim of cooperation. The first version of the sentence would probably lead you to a broad survey of foreign intervention in Indochina. The result would likely be a static list in which you judged some interventions to be "beneficial" and others "not beneficial." The revised sentence redirects your thinking, tightens your paper's focus to prioritize evidence of cooperation, and presses you to make decisions, such as whether the positive consequences of cooperation outweigh the negative consequences of colonialism. In short, the revision leads you to examine the dynamic relations between your two initial claims.

Rethinking what you mean is just as likely to occur when you attend to word choice. Notice how the change of a single word in the following sentences could change the entire paper.

> **Draft:** The president's attitude toward military spending is ambiguous.

> **Revision:** The president's attitude toward military spending is ambivalent.

In the draft, the use of the word "ambiguous" (meaning "open to many interpretations") would likely lead to a paper on ways that the president's decisions are unclear. The choice of "ambiguous" might also signal that the writer and not the president is unclear on what the president's actions could be taken to mean. If the president's policies aren't unclear—hard to interpret—but are divided, conflicted over competing ways of thinking, then the writer would want the word "ambivalent." This recognition would lead not only to reorganizing the final draft but also to refocusing the argument, building to the significance of this ambivalence (that the president is torn between adopting one of two stances) rather than to the previous conclusion (that presidential policy is incoherent).

B. TONE

Tone is the *implied attitude* of a piece of language toward its subject and audience. Whenever you revise for style, your choices in syntax and diction will affect the tone. There are no hard and fast rules to govern matters of tone, and your control of it will depend upon your sensitivity to the particular context—your understanding of your own intentions and your readers' expectations.

Let's consider, for example, the tonal implications of the warning signs in the subways of London and New York.

London: Leaning out of the window may cause harm.

New York: Do not lean out of the window.

Initially, you may find the English injunction laughably indirect and verbose in comparison with the shoot-from-the-hip clarity of the American sign. But that is to ignore the very thing we are calling *style*. The American version appeals to authority, commanding readers what not to do without telling them why. The English version, by contrast, appeals to logic; it is more collegial toward its readers and assumes they are rational beings rather than children prone to misbehave.

In revising for tone, you need to ask yourself if the attitude suggested by your language is appropriate to the aim of your message and to your audience. Your goal is to keep the tone *consistent* with your rhetorical intentions. The following paragraph, from a college catalogue, offers a classic mismatch between the overtly stated aim and the tonal implications:

> The student affairs staff believes that the college years provide a growth and development process for students. Students need to learn about themselves and others and to learn how to relate to individuals and groups of individuals with vastly different backgrounds, interests, attitudes and values. Not only is the tolerance of differences expected, but also an appreciation and a celebration of these differences must be an outcome of the student's experience. In addition, the student must progress toward self-reliance and independence tempered by a concern for the social order.

The explicit content of this passage—*what* it says—concerns tolerance. The professed point of view is student-friendly, asserting that the college exists to allow students "to learn about themselves and others" and to support the individual in accord with the "appreciation . . . of . . . differences." But note that the implicit tone—*how* the passage goes about saying *what* it says—is condescending and intolerant. Look at the verbs. An imperious authority lectures students about what they "*need* to learn," that tolerance is "*expected*," that "celebration . . . *must* be an outcome," and that "the student *must* progress" along these lines. Presumably, the paragraph does not intend to adopt this high-handed manner, but its deafness to tone subverts its desired meaning.

Try this 10.1: Analyzing Tone-Deaf Prose

Using the example from the college catalogue as a model, locate and bring to class examples of tonal inconsistency or inappropriateness that you encounter in your daily life. If you have difficulty finding examples, try memos from those in authority at your school or workplace, which often contain excruciating examples of officialese. Type one of your passages, and underneath it compose a paragraph of analysis in which you single out particular words and phrases and explain how the tone is inappropriate. Then rewrite the passage to remedy the problem.

LEVELS OF STYLE: WHO'S WRITING TO WHOM, AND WHY DOES IT MATTER?

How you say something is always a significant part of *what* you say. To look at words as words is to focus on the *how* as well as the *what*. Imagine that you call your friend on the phone, and a voice you don't recognize answers. You ask to speak with your friend, and the voice responds, "With whom have I the pleasure of speaking?" By contrast, what if the voice instead responds, "Who's this?" What information do these two versions of the question convey, beyond the obvious request for your name?

How something is phrased is an integral part of what it says. If you say something in another way, you are saying something else.

The first response—"With whom have I the pleasure of speaking?"—tells you that the speaker is formal and polite. He is also probably fastidiously well educated: he not only knows the difference between "who" and "whom" but also obeys the etiquette that outlaws ending a sentence with a preposition ("Whom have I the pleasure of speaking *with?*"). The very formality of the utterance, however, might lead you to label the speaker pretentious. His assumption that conversing with you is a "pleasure" suggests empty flattery. On the other hand, the second version—"Who's this?"—while also grammatically correct, is less formal. It is more direct but also terse to a fault; the speaker does not seem particularly interested in treating you politely.

The two hypothetical responses represent two different levels of style. Formal English obeys the basic conventions of standard written prose, and most academic writing is fairly formal. An informal style—one that is conversational and full of slang—can have severe limitations in an academic setting. The syntax and vocabulary of written prose aren't the same as those of speech, and attempts to import the language of speech into academic writing can result in your communicating less meaning with less precision.

Let's take one brief example:

> Internecine quarrels within the corporation destroyed morale and sent the value of the stock plummeting.

The phrase "internecine quarrels" may strike some readers as a pretentious display of formal language, but consider how difficult it is to communicate this concept economically. "Fights that go on between people related to each other" is awkward; "brother against brother" is sexist and a cliché; and "mutually destructive disputes" is acceptable but long-winded.

It is arguably a part of our national culture to value the simple and the direct as more genuine and democratic than the sophisticated, which is supposedly more aristocratic and pretentious. This "plain-speaking" style, however, can hinder your ability to develop and communicate your ideas. In the case of "internecine," the more formal diction choice actually communicates more, and more effectively, than the less formal equivalents.

Our national culture values the simple and the direct as more genuine and democratic than the sophisticated, but the plain-speaking style can hinder your ability to communicate your ideas.

When in doubt about how your readers will respond to the formality or informality of your style, you are usually better off opting for some version of "With whom have I the pleasure of speaking?" rather than "Who's this?" The best solution will usually lie somewhere in between: "May I ask who's calling?" would protect you against the imputation of either priggishness or piggishness.

What generalizations about style do these examples suggest?

- There are many ways of conveying a message.
- The way you phrase a message constitutes a significant part of its meaning.
- Your phrasing gives your reader cues that suggest your attitude and your ways of thinking.
- There are no transparent (absolutely neutral) delivery systems.
- All stylistic decisions depend on your sensitivity to context—who's talking to whom about what subject and with what aims.

The last of these generalizations concerns what is called the *rhetorical situation. Rhetoric* is the subject that deals with how writers and speakers behave in given situations and, more specifically, how they can generate language that produces the effects they desire on a particular audience. Obviously, as you make stylistic choices, you need to be aware of the possible consequences of making certain statements to a certain audience in a certain fashion.

Try this 10.2: Analyzing Effective Tone

Find an example of tone that you think is just about perfect for the message and audience. Type it, and underneath discuss why it succeeds. Be as specific as you can about how the passage functions stylistically. Talk about particular phrasings and the match between what is being said and how it is said. Factor into your discussion the relationship between levels of style in the example and its presumed audience.

C. THE PERSON QUESTION

"The person question" concerns which of the three basic forms of the pronoun you should use when you write. Here are the three forms, with brief examples.

First person: I believe Heraclitus is an underrated philosopher.

Second person: You should believe that Heraclitus is an underrated philosopher.

Third person: He or she believes that Heraclitus is an underrated philosopher.

Which person to use is a stylistic concern, since it involves a writer's *choices* as regards to level of formality, the varying expectations of different audiences, and overall tone.

As a general rule, in academic writing you should discuss your subject matter in the third person and avoid the first and second person. There is logic to this rule: most academic analysis focuses on the subject matter rather than on you as you respond to it. If you use the third person, you will keep the attention where it belongs.

THE FIRST-PERSON PRONOUN "I": PRO AND CON

Using the first-person "I" can throw the emphasis on the wrong place. Repeated assertions of "in my opinion" actually distract your readers from what you have to say. Omit them except in the most informal cases. You might, however, consider using the first person in the drafting stage if you are having trouble bringing your own point of view to the forefront. In this situation, the "I" becomes a strategy for loosening up and saying what you really think about a subject rather than adopting conventional and faceless positions. In the final analysis, though, most analytical prose will be more precise and straightforward in the third person. When you cut "I am convinced that" from the beginning of any claim, what you lose in personal conviction, you gain in concision and directness by keeping the focus on the main idea in a main clause.

Are there cases when you should use "I"? Contrary to the general rule, some professors actually prefer the first-person pronoun in particular contexts, as noted in the accompanying "Voices from Across the Curriculum" box.

VOICES FROM ACROSS THE CURRICULUM

Using the First-Person *I* in Academic Writing

Avoid phrases like "*The author* believes (or will discuss) . . ." Except in the paper's abstract, "*I* believe (or will discuss)" is okay, and often best.

–Alan Tjeltveit, Professor of Psychology

I prefer that personal opinion or voice (for example, "I this," or "I that") appear throughout. I like the first person. No "the author feels" or "this author found that," please! Who is the author? Hey, it's you!

–Frederick Norling, Professor of Business

The biggest stylistic problem is that students tend to be too personal or colloquial in their writing, using phrases such as the following: "*Scientists all agree . . .*"; "*I find it amazing that . . .*"; "*The thing that I find most interesting . . .*" Students are urged to present data and existing information in their own words, but in an objective way. My preference in writing is to use the active voice in the past tense. I feel this is the most direct and least wordy approach: *I asked this . . . ; I found out that . . . ; These data show. . . .*

–Richard Niesenbaum, Professor of Biology

Note that these are not blanket endorsements; they specify a limited context within which "I" is preferred. The biology professor's cautioning against using an overly personal and colloquial tone is also probably the consensus view.

Although a majority of professors may prefer the first-person "I think" to the more awkward "the writer (or 'one') thinks," we would point out that, in the service of reducing wordiness, you can often avoid both options. For example, in certain contexts and disciplines, the first-person-plural "we" is acceptable usage: "The president's speech assumes that *we* are all dutiful but disgruntled taxpayers." The one case in which the first person is particularly appropriate occurs when you are citing an example from your own experience. Otherwise, if you are in doubt about using "I" or "we," avoid these first-person pronouns.

THE SECOND-PERSON PRONOUN "YOU" AND THE IMPERATIVE MOOD

As for the second person, proceed with caution. Using "you" is a fairly assertive gesture. Many readers will be annoyed, for example, by a paper about advertising that states, "When you read about a sale at the mall, you know it's hard to resist." Most readers resent having a writer airily making assumptions about them or telling them what to do. Some rhetorical situations, however, call for the use of "you." Textbooks, for example, use "you" frequently because it creates a more direct relationship between authors and readers. Yet, even in appropriate situations, directly addressing readers as "you" may alienate them by ascribing to them attitudes and needs they may not have.

The readiest alternative to "you," the imperative mood, requires careful handling for similar reasons. The *imperative mood* of a verb expresses a direct request or command, leaving "you" understood, as in the following instance: "Don't [you] dismiss the European perspective too quickly." Such a sentence, though, runs the same kind of risk as the previous example: readers might resent your assumption that they would dismiss the European perspective or, at any rate, dislike being told so forcefully how to think about it. On the other hand, in certain writing situations the imperative mood is both appropriate and useful: when you are giving a set of step-by-step instructions ("*Take* a right on 12th Street and then turn left at the light onto Vine") or politely soliciting your readers' attention ("*Consider* the plight of Afghan refugees"). In both cases, the imperative engages readers more unobtrusively than would inserting an awkward "you should" or "one should" before the verbs.

The conventional argument for using the first and second person is that "I" and "you" are personal and engage readers. It is not necessarily the case, however, that the third person is therefore impersonal. Just as film directors put their stamps on films by the way they organize the images, move among camera viewpoints, and orchestrate the sound tracks, so writers, even when writing in the third person, have a wide variety of resources at their disposal for making the writing more personal and accessible for their audiences. See, for example, the discussion of the passive voice in the next chapter.

D. SHADES OF MEANING: CHOOSING THE BEST WORD

The nineteenth-century English statesman Benjamin Disraeli once differentiated between "misfortune" and "calamity" by commenting on his political rival William Gladstone: "If Mr. Gladstone fell into the Thames, it would be a misfortune; but if someone dragged him out, it would be a calamity." "Misfortune" and "calamity" might mean the same thing to some people, but in fact the two words allow a careful writer to discriminate fine shades of meaning.

One of the best ways to get yourself to pay attention to words as words is to practice making subtle distinctions among related words. The "right" word contributes accuracy and precision to your meaning. The "wrong" word, it follows, is inaccurate or imprecise. The most reliable guide to choosing the right word and avoiding the wrong word is a dictionary that includes not only concise definitions but also the origin of words (known as their *etymology*). A dicey alternative is a thesaurus (a dictionary of synonyms, now included in most word processing software): it can offer you a host of choices, but you run a fairly high risk of choosing an inappropriate word. If you go the thesaurus route, check the word you select in the dictionary. The best dictionary for the job, by the way, is the *Oxford English Dictionary*, which commonly goes by its initials, *OED*. Available in every library reference collection and usually online at colleges and universities as well, it provides historical examples of how every word has been used over time.

Frankly, many of the most common diction errors are caused by ignorance. The writer has not learned the difference between similar terms that actually have different meanings. If you confuse "then" and "than," or "infer" and "imply," you will not convey the meaning that you intend, and you will probably confuse your readers and invite them to question your control of language. Getting the wrong word is, of course, not limited to pairs of words that are spelled similarly. A *notorious* figure is widely but unfavorably known, whereas a *famous* person is usually recognized for accomplishments that are praiseworthy. Referring to a famous person as notorious—a rather comic error—could be an embarrassing mistake. Take the time to learn the differences among seemingly similar words.

A slightly less severe version of getting the wrong word occurs when a writer uses a word with a shade of meaning that is inappropriate or inaccurate in a particular context. Take, for example, the words "assertive" and "aggressive." Often used interchangeably, they don't really mean the same thing—and the difference matters. Loosely defined, both terms mean "forceful." But "assertive" suggests being "bold and self-confident," whereas "aggressive" suggests being "eager to attack." In most cases, you compliment the person you call assertive but raise doubts about the person you call aggressive (whether you are giving a compliment depends on the situation: "aggressive" is a term of praise on the football field but less so if used to describe an acquaintance's behavior during conversation at the dinner table).

One particularly charged context in which shades of meaning matter to many readers involves the potentially sexist implications of using one term for women and another for men. If, for example, in describing a woman and a man up for the same job, we referred to the woman as *aggressive* but the man as *assertive*, our diction would deservedly be considered sexist. It would reveal that what is perceived as poised and a sign of leadership potential in a man is being construed as unseemly belligerence in a woman. The sexism enters when word choice suggests that what is assertive in a man is aggressive in a woman.

In choosing the right shade of meaning, you will get a sharper sense for the word by knowing its etymological history—the word or words from which it evolved. In the preceding example, "aggressive" derives from the Latin "*aggressus*," meaning "to go to or approach"; and "*aggressus*" is itself a combination of "*ad*," a prefix expressing motion, and "*gradus*," meaning "a step." An aggressive person, then, is "coming at you." "Assertive," on the other hand, comes from the Latin "*asserere*," combining "*ad*" and "*serere*," meaning "to join or bind together." An assertive person is "coming to build or put things together"—certainly not to threaten.

Try this 10.3: Playing with Etymology

One of the best ways to get yourself to pay attention to words as words is to practice making fine distinctions among related words, as we did with "aggressive" and "assertive." The following exercise will not only increase your vocabulary but also acquaint you with that indispensable reference work for etymology, the *Oxford English Dictionary* (*OED*).

Look up one of the following pairs of words in the *OED*. Write down the etymology of each word in the pair, and then, in a paragraph for each, summarize the words' linguistic histories—how their meanings have evolved across time. (The *OED*'s examples of how the word has been used over time will be helpful here.)

ordinal/ordinary	explicate/implicate
tenacious/stubborn	induce/conducive
enthusiasm/ecstasy	adhere/inhere
monarchy/oligarchy	overt/covert

Alternatively, select a pair of similar words or, for that matter, any key words from your reading for a course, and submit them to this exercise.

WHAT'S BAD ABOUT "GOOD" AND "BAD" (AND OTHER BROAD, JUDGMENTAL TERMS)

Vague evaluative terms such as "good" and "bad" can seduce you into stopping your thinking while it is still too general and ill-defined—a matter discussed at length in Chapter 1 in the section entitled "The Judgment Reflex." If you train yourself to select more precise words whenever you encounter "good" and "bad" in your drafts, not only will your prose become clearer but also the search for new words will probably start you thinking again, sharpening your ideas. If, for example, you find yourself writing a sentence such as "The subcommittee made a *bad* decision," ask yourself *why* you called it a bad decision. A revision to "The subcommittee made a shortsighted decision" indicates what in fact is bad about the decision and sets you up to discuss why the decision was myopic, further developing the idea.

Be aware that often these evaluative terms are disguised as neutrally descriptive ones—"natural," for instance, and "realistic." Realistic according to whom, and defined by what criteria? Something is natural according to a given idea about nature—an assumption—and the same goes for "moral." These are not terms that mean separately from a particular context or ideology (that is, an assumed hierarchy of value). Similarly, in a sentence such as "Society disapproves of interracial marriage," the broad and apparently neutral term "society" can blind you to a host of important distinctions about social class, about a particular culture, and so on.

CONCRETE AND ABSTRACT DICTION

At its best, effective analytical prose uses both concrete and abstract words. Simply defined, *concrete diction* evokes: it brings things to life by offering your readers words that they can use their senses upon. "Telephone," "eggshell," "crystalline," "azure," "striped," "kneel," "flare," and "burp" are examples of concrete diction. In academic writing, there is no substitute for concrete language whenever you are describing what happens or what something looks like—in a laboratory experiment, in a military action, in a painting or film sequence. In short, the language of evidence and of detail usually consists of concrete diction.

Concrete diction evokes: it brings things to life by offering your readers words they can use their senses upon.

By contrast, *abstract diction* refers to words that designate concepts and categories. "Virility," "ideology," "love," "definitive," "desultory," "conscientious," "classify," and "ameliorate" are examples of abstract diction. So are "democracy," "fascism," "benevolence," and "sentimentality." In academic writing, by and large, this is the language of ideas. We cannot do without abstract terms, and yet writing made up only of such words loses contact with experience, with the world that we can apprehend through our senses.

The line between abstract and concrete is not always as clear as these examples may suggest. You may recall the concept of the ladder of abstraction that we discuss in the section entitled "Generalizing" in the first chapter. There we propose that abstract and concrete are not hard-and-fast categories so much as a continuum, a sliding scale. Word A (for example, "machine") may be more abstract than word B ("computer") but more concrete than word C ("technology").

Just as evidence needs to be organized by a thesis and a thesis needs to be developed by evidence, so concrete and abstract diction need each other. Use concrete diction to illustrate and anchor the generalizations that abstract diction expresses. Note the concrete language used to define the abstraction "provinciality" in this example.

> There is no cure for *provinciality* like traveling abroad. In America the waiter who fails to bring the check promptly at the end of the meal we rightly convict for not being watchful. But in England, after waiting interminably for the check and becoming increasingly irate, we learn that only an ill-mannered waiter would bring it without being asked. We have been rude, not he.

In the following example, the abstract terms "causality," "fiction," and "conjunction" are integrated with concrete diction in the second sentence.

> According to the philosopher David Hume, *causality* is a kind of *fiction* that we ascribe to what he called "the constant *conjunction* of observed events." If a person gets hit in the eye and a black semicircle develops underneath it, that does not necessarily mean the blow caused the black eye.

A style that omits concrete language can leave readers lost in a fog of abstraction that only tangible details can illuminate. The concrete language helps readers see what you mean, much in the way that examples help them understand your ideas. Without the shaping power of abstract diction, however, concrete evocation can leave you with a list of graphic but ultimately pointless facts. The best writing integrates concrete and abstract diction.

Try this 10.4: Recasting the Diction

Compose a paragraph using only concrete diction and then one using only abstract diction. Compare results with another person who has done the same task, as this can lead to an interesting discussion of kinds of words, where they reside on the ladder of abstraction, and why.

Try this 10.5: Replacing Abstract Assertions with Concrete Details

Rewrite the sentences listed below, substituting more concrete language and/or more precise abstractions. Support any abstractions you retain with appropriate detail. Just for the challenge, try to rewrite so that your sentences include no abstract claims; that is, use only concrete details to convey the points.

It was a great party; everybody had fun.
It was a lousy party; everybody disliked it.
The book was really boring.
The film was very interesting.
His morals were questionable.
Social Security is not an entitlement.
He became extraordinarily angry.

LATINATE DICTION

One of the best ways to sensitize yourself to the difference between abstract and concrete diction is to understand that many abstract words are examples of what is known as Latinate diction. This term describes words in English that derive from Latin roots, words with such endings as "–tion," "–ive," "–ity," "–ate," and "–ent." (Such words will be designated by an *L* in the etymological section of dictionary definitions.) Taken to an extreme, Latinate diction can leave your meaning vague and your readers confused. Note how impenetrable the Latinate terms make the following example:

> The examination of different perspectives on the representations of sociopolitical anarchy in media coverage of revolutions can be revelatory of the invisible biases that afflict television news.

This sentence actually makes sense, but the demands it makes upon readers will surely drive off most of them before they have gotten through it. Reducing the amount of Latinate diction can make it more readable.

> Because we tend to believe what we see, the political biases that afflict television news coverage of revolutions are largely invisible. We can begin to see these biases when we focus on how the medium reports events, studying the kinds of footage used, for example, or finding facts from other sources that the news has left out.

Although the preceding revision retains a lot of Latinate words, it provides a ballast of concrete, sensory details that allows readers to follow the idea. Although many textbooks on writing argue against using Latinate terms where shorter, concrete terms (usually of Anglo-Saxon origin) might be used instead, such an argument seems needlessly limiting in comparison with the advantages offered by a thorough mixture of the two levels of diction. It's fine to use Latinate diction; just don't make it the sole staple of your verbal diet.

Try this 10.6: Distinguishing Latinate from Anglo-Saxon Diction

Select a paragraph or two from one of your papers and identify the Latin and Anglo-Saxon diction. Actually mark the draft—with an *L* or an *A*, with a circle around one kind of word and a square around the other. Then find Anglo-Saxon substitutes for Latinate terms and Latinate substitutes for Anglo-Saxon terms if you can (with the help of a dictionary and perhaps a thesaurus). Ideally, you might then do a final revision in which you synthesize the best from both paragraphs to arrive at a consummate revision of your original paragraph.

USING AND AVOIDING JARGON

Many people assume that all jargon—the specialized vocabulary of a particular group—is bad: pretentious language designed to make most readers feel inferior. Many writing textbooks attack jargon in similar terms, calling it either polysyllabic balderdash or a specialized, gatekeeping language designed by an in-group to keep others out.

In many academic contexts, jargon is downright essential. It is conceptual shorthand.

Yet, in many academic contexts, jargon is downright essential. It is conceptual shorthand, a technical vocabulary that allows the members of a group (or a discipline) to converse with one another more clearly and efficiently. Certain words that may seem odd to outsiders in fact function as connective tissue for a way of thought shared by insiders. The following sentence, for example, although full of botanical jargon, is also admirably cogent:

> In angiosperm reproduction, if the number of pollen grains deposited on the stigma exceeds the number of ovules in the ovary, then pollen tubes may compete for access to ovules, which results in fertilization by the fastest growing pollen tubes.

We would label this use of jargon acceptable, because it is written, clearly, *by* insiders *for* fellow insiders. It might not be acceptable language for an article intended for readers who are not botanists, or at least not scientists.

The problem with jargon comes when this insiders' language is ostensibly directed at outsiders as well. The language of contracts offers a prime example of such jargon at work.

> The Author hereby indemnifies and agrees to hold the Publisher, its licensees, and any seller of the Work harmless from any liability, damage, cost, and expense, including reasonable attorney's fees and costs of settlement, for or in connection with any claim, action, or proceeding inconsistent with the Author's warranties or representations herein, or based upon or arising out of any contribution of the Author to the Work.

Run for the lawyer! What does it mean to "hold the Publisher . . . harmless"? To what do "the Author's warranties or representations" refer? What exactly is the author being asked to do here—release the publisher from all possible lawsuits that the author might bring? We might label this use of jargon *obfuscating;* although it may aim at precision, it leaves most readers bewildered. Although average readers are asked to sign them, such documents are really written by lawyers for other lawyers.

As the botanical and legal examples suggest, the line between *acceptable* and *obfuscating* jargon has far more to do with the audience to whom the words are addressed than with the actual content of the language. Because most academic writing is addressed to insiders, students studying a particular area need to learn its jargon. Using the technical language of the discipline is a necessary skill for conversing with others in that discipline. Moreover, by demonstrating that you can "talk the talk," you will validate your authority to pronounce an opinion on matters in the discipline.

Here are two guidelines that can help you in your use of jargon: (1) when addressing *insiders*, use jargon accurately ("talk the talk"); and (2) when addressing *outsiders*—the general public or members of another discipline—either define the jargon carefully or replace it with a more generally known term, preferably one operating at the same level of formality (which is to say that you would not substitute "gut" for "abdominal cavity").

As the anecdote in the accompanying "Voices from Across the Curriculum" box illustrates, questions of jargon—which are also questions of tone—are best resolved by considering the particular contexts for given writing tasks.

VOICES FROM ACROSS THE CURRICULUM

When to Use and Not Use Jargon

I worked for the Feds for many years before seeking the doctorate. My job required immense amounts of writing: reports, directives, correspondence, and so forth. But, on a day-to-day basis for almost seven years I had to write short "write-ups" assessing the qualifications of young people for the Peace Corps and VISTA programs. I'd generate "list-like," "bullet-like" assessments: "Looks good with farm machinery, has wonderful volunteer experience, would be best in a rural setting, speaks French." But I had to conclude each of these assessments with a one-page narrative. Here I tended to reject officious governmentese for a more personal style. I'd write as I spoke. Rather than "Has an inclination for a direction in the facilitation of regulation," I'd write "Would be very good directing people on projects." I'd drop the "-tion" stuff and write in "speak form," not incomplete sentences, but in what I call "candid, personal" style. I carry this with me today.

–Frederick Norling, Professor of Business

THE POLITICS OF LANGUAGE

We cannot leave the domain of style without reflecting on its place in what we might label the culture of inattention and cliché that surrounds us. To make this move is to acknowledge that style has political and ethical implications. A little over a half-century ago, in his famous essay "Politics and the English Language," George Orwell warns of the "invasion of one's mind by ready-made phrases . . . [which] can only be prevented if one is constantly on guard against them." The worst modern writing, he declares, "consists in gumming together long strips of words which have already been set in order by someone else, making the results presentable by sheer humbug."

Insofar as style is an expression of the writer's self, Orwell implies (1) we are under attack from broad cultural clichés and sentimental nostrums that do our thinking for us, and (2) it is thus a matter of personal integrity and civic responsibility to ask ourselves a series of questions about the sentences that we write.

> What am I trying to say? What words will express it? What image or idiom will make it clearer? Is this image fresh enough to have an effect? [. . .] Could I put it more shortly? Have I said anything that is avoidably ugly?"

Words matter. They matter in how we name things, in how we phrase meanings—but also in how we are shaped by the words we read and hear in the media. Words don't simply reflect a neutral world that is out there in some objectively hard way that offers self-evident meanings we can universally agree upon. Words don't reflect—they constitute; they call the world into being. They call us into being when we write them.

Earlier in this chapter we noted, for example, that the decision to call a woman "aggressive" as opposed to "assertive" matters. There are examples all around you of language creating rather than merely reflecting reality. Start looking for these on the front page of your newspaper, in political speeches, in advertising, even in everyday conversation. Does it matter, for instance, that there are no equivalents to the words "spinster" or "whore" for men? Does it change things to refer to a bombing mission as a "containment effort" or, by way of contrast, to call an enthusiastic person a "fanatic"?

An article a few years back in the journal *Foreign Affairs* by Peter van Ham (October 2001) offers one last dispatch from the frontier of the culture of inattention and cliché. The article is about the rise of the so-called brand state—about how nations market themselves not only to consumers but to other nations. A brand, defined as "a customer's idea about a product," is a powerful tool to replace what a thing is with what other people, for reasons of their own, would have you think it is. This is the world we inhabit, and style can be its adversary or its accomplice. In the last analysis, that's what's at stake in choosing to care about style.

ASSIGNMENT: Style Analysis

Write a paper that analyzes the style of a particular group or profession (for example, sports, advertising, bureaucracy, show business, or music reviewing). Or as an alternative, adopt the voice of a member of this group, and write a parody that critiques or analyzes the language practices of the group. If you choose (or are assigned) the latter, be aware that there is always a risk in parody of belittling in an unduly negative way a style that is not your own.

Obviously, you will first need to assemble and make observations about a number of samples of the style that you are analyzing or parodying. Use the Method to help you uncover the kinds of words that get repeated, the most common strands, and so forth. Look at the level of formality, the tone, the use of concrete and abstract diction, and the predilection for Latinate as opposed to Anglo-Saxon words. Who's writing to whom about what, and so what that the writing adopts this style?

Also, see the assignments at the end of Chapter 11.

GUIDELINES FOR CHOOSING WORDS

1. Remember that revision is not merely cosmetic: to change the words is to change the meaning.
2. Strive for distance on your own prose as you edit for diction: place yourself in the position of the audience. Is the tone appropriate to the rhetorical context?
3. There are always shades of meaning. Strive to choose the best—the most accurate and appropriate—word for the situation. When in doubt, consult etymology, the history of the word, as the most reliable guide to its usage.

GUIDELINES FOR CHOOSING WORDS (CONTINUED)

4. Avoid *good*, *bad*, *real*, and other broad, judgmental terms that prematurely close off analysis.
5. Blend concrete and abstract diction, which is generally the language of details and the language of abstractions, respectively. In particular, go easy on those Latinate *–tion* words.
6. In given contexts, jargon is useful shorthand, but there is always the danger of getting used by it. Make sure you know what the words mean, and don't overrely on them.

CHAPTER 11

Style: Shaping Sentences (and Cutting the Fat)

Quick Take

When you write, you build. Writing, after all, is also known as composition—from the Latin *compositio,* meaning "made up of parts." We speak of *constructing* sentences and paragraphs and essays. The fundamental unit of composition is the sentence. Every sentence has a shape, and learning to see that shape is essential to editing for style. Once you can recognize the shape of a sentence, you can recast it to make it more graceful or logical or emphatic.

A sentence is a pathway to having ideas. Recasting sentences is thus not just a stylistic practice, but a thinking practice. The way a sentence is structured reveals a way of thinking. Casting and recasting sentences in different words and in different shapes helps you experiment with the way you arrive at ideas, with the path you characteristically take.

Whether we recognize it or not, most of us have a "go to" sentence—the sentence shape we repeatedly go to as we write and talk. If a person's "go to" sentence takes the form "Although _______, the fact is that _______," we might see that person as inclined to qualify his or her thoughts ("Although") and as someone who is disinclined to immediately impose his or her ideas on others ("the fact that" comes in the second half of the sentence, where it gets a lot of emphasis but is also delayed and qualified by the sentence's opening observation).

When you read something, you should be looking for the writer's "go to" sentence and considering what it might reveal about his or her characteristic ways of thinking. As a regular practice, select one sentence in whatever you are reading that you think is typical of that writer's way of putting sentences together. Then ask yourself why this type of sentence is appropriate to the kind of thinking going on in the reading, how it can be seen as doing what it describes.

Then find your own "go to" sentence. What does it reveal to you about how you think?

A. HOW TO RECOGNIZE THE FOUR BASIC SENTENCE SHAPES

Style, defined in Chapter 10, has to do with choices—the choices a writer makes about how to express something. But these decisions can be realized only if you can recognize and use the basic building blocks of composition. Although many of these building blocks are named in the rest of the chapter, you may encounter some terms you're not sure about. If that happens, consult the "Glossary of Grammatical Terms" at the end of Chapter 14. (In particular, see entries for the following terms: *clause*, *conjunction*, *conjunctive adverb*, *coordination*, *direct object*, *phrase*, *preposition*, *subject*, *subordination*, and *verbals*.)

Every sentence is built upon the skeleton of its independent clause(s), the subject and verb combination that can stand alone. Consider the following four sentences:

> Consumers shop.
>
> Consumers shop; producers manufacture.
>
> Consumers shop in predictable ways, so producers manufacture with different target groups in mind.
>
> Consumers shop in ways that can be predicted by such determinants as income level, sex, and age; consequently, producers use market research to identify different target groups for their products.

Certainly these four sentences become progressively longer, and the information they contain becomes increasingly detailed, but they also differ in their structure—specifically, in the number of independent and dependent clauses they contain. Given that the sentence is the fundamental unit of composition, you will benefit immensely, both in composing and in revising your sentences, if you can identify and construct the four basic sentence types.

THE SIMPLE SENTENCE

The *simple sentence* consists of a single independent clause. At its simplest, it contains a single subject and verb.

> Consumers shop.

Other words and phrases can be added to this sentence, but it will remain simple so long as "Consumers shop" is the only clause.

> Most consumers shop unwisely.

Even if the sentence contains more than one grammatical subject or more than one verb, it remains simple in structure.

> Most consumers *shop* unwisely and *spend* more than they can afford. [two verbs]
>
> Both female consumers and their husbands shop unwisely. [two subjects]

The sentence structure in the example that uses two verbs ("shop" and "spend") is known as a *compound predicate*. The sentence structure in the example that uses two subjects ("consumers" and "husbands") is known as a *compound subject*. If, however, you were to add both another subject and another verb to the original simple sentence, you would have the next sentence type, a compound sentence.

THE COMPOUND SENTENCE

The *compound sentence* consists of at least two independent clauses and no subordinate clauses. The information conveyed in these clauses should be of roughly equal importance.

> Producers manufacture, and consumers shop.

> Producers manufacture, marketers sell, and consumers shop.

As with the simple sentence, you can also add qualifying phrases to the compound sentence, and it will remain compound, as long as no dependent clauses are added.

> Consumers shop in predictable ways, so producers manufacture with different target groups in mind.

> Consumers shop recklessly during holidays; marketers are keenly aware of this fact.

Note that a compound sentence can connect its independent clauses with either a coordinate conjunction or a semicolon. (The primary use of the semicolon is as a substitute for a coordinate conjunction, separating two independent clauses.) If you were to substitute a subordinating conjunction for either of these connectors, however, you would have a sentence with one independent clause and one dependent clause. For example:

> *Because* consumers shop in predictable ways, producers manufacture with different target groups in mind.

This revision changes the compound sentence into the next sentence type, the complex sentence.

THE COMPLEX SENTENCE

The *complex sentence* consists of a single independent clause and one or more dependent clauses. The information conveyed in the dependent clause is subordinated to the more important independent clause (a matter we take up in more detail momentarily under subordination). In the following example, the subject and verb of the main clause are underlined, and the subordinating conjunctions are italicized:

> *Although* mail-order merchandising—*which* generally saves shoppers money—has increased, most consumers still shop unwisely, buying on impulse rather than deliberation.

This sentence contains one independent clause ("consumers shop"). Hanging upon it are two introductory dependent clauses ("although merchandising has increased" and "which saves") and a participial phrase ("buying on impulse"). If you converted either of these dependent clauses into an independent clause, you would have a sentence with two independent clauses (a compound sentence) and a dependent clause. In the following example, the subjects and verbs of the two main clauses are underlined, and the conjunctions are italicized:

> Mail-order merchandising—*which* generally saves shoppers money—has increased, *but* consumers still shop unwisely, buying on impulse rather than deliberation.

This revision changes the complex sentence into the next sentence type, the compound-complex sentence.

THE COMPOUND-COMPLEX SENTENCE

The *compound-complex sentence* consists of two or more independent clauses and one or more dependent clauses.

> Consumers shop in ways that can be predicted by such determinants as income level, sex, and age; consequently, producers use market research that aims to identify different target groups for their products.

This sentence contains two independent clauses ("consumers shop" and "producers use") and two dependent clauses ("that can be predicted" and "that aims").

Try this 11.1: Composing the Four Sentence Shapes

As we have done with the consumers-shop example, compose a simple sentence and then a variety of expansions: a compound subject, a compound predicate, a compound sentence, a complex sentence, and a compound-complex sentence.

To prevent this exercise from becoming merely mechanical, keep in mind how different sentence shapes accomplish different ends. In other words, make sure your compound sentence balances two items of information, that your complex sentence emphasizes one thing (in the main clause) over another (in the subordinate clause), and that your compound-complex sentence is capable of handling and organizing complexity.

B. COORDINATION, SUBORDINATION, AND EMPHASIS

A *clause* is a group of words containing a subject and a predicate. The syntax of a sentence can give your readers cues about whether the idea in one clause is equal to (coordinate) or subordinate to the idea in another clause. In this context, grammar operates as a form of implicit logic, defining relationships among the clauses in a sentence according to the choices that you make about coordination, subordination, and the order of clauses. In revising your sentences, think of coordination and subordination as tools of logic and emphasis, helping to rank your meanings.

COORDINATION

Coordination uses grammatically equivalent constructions to link ideas. These ideas should carry roughly equal weight as well. Sentences that use coordination connect clauses with coordinating conjunctions (such as *and*, *but*, and *or*). Here are two examples.

> Historians organize the past, *and* they can never do so with absolute neutrality.

> Homegrown corn is incredibly sweet, *and* it is very difficult to grow.

If you ponder these sentences, you may begin to detect the danger of the word *and*. It does not specify a precise logical relationship between the things it connects but instead simply adds them.

Notice that the sentences get more precise if we substitute *but* for *and*.

> Historians organize the past, *but* they can never do so with absolute neutrality.
>
> Homegrown corn is incredibly sweet, *but* it is very difficult to grow.

These sentences are still coordinate in structure; they are still the sentence type known as compound. But they achieve more emphasis than the *and* versions. In both cases, the *but* clause carries more weight, because *but* always introduces information that qualifies or contradicts what precedes it.

REVERSING THE ORDER OF COORDINATE CLAUSES

In both the *and* and *but* examples, the second clause tends to be stressed. The reason is simple: *the end is usually a position of emphasis*.

You can see the effect of clause order more starkly if we reverse the clauses in our examples.

> Historians are never absolutely neutral, but they organize the past.
>
> Homegrown corn is very difficult to grow, but it is incredibly sweet.

Note how the meanings have changed in these versions by emphasizing what now comes last. Rather than simply having their objectivity undermined ("Historians are never absolutely neutral"), historians are now credited with at least providing organization ("they organize the past"). Similarly, whereas the previous version of the sentence about corn was likely to dissuade a gardener from trying to grow it ("it is very difficult to grow"), the new sentence is more likely to lure him or her to nurture corn ("it is incredibly sweet").

Nonetheless, all of these sentences are examples of coordination because the clauses are grammatically equal. As you revise, notice when you use coordinate syntax, and think about whether you really intend to give the ideas equal weight. Consider as well whether reversing the order of clauses will more accurately convey your desired emphasis to your readers.

Try this 11.2: Rearranging Coordinate Clauses

Rearrange the parts of the following coordinate sentence, which is composed of four sections, separated by commas. Construct at least three versions, and jot down how the meaning changes in each version.

> I asked her to marry me, two years ago, in a shop on Tremont Street, late in the fall.

Then subject two sentences of your own, perhaps taken from your papers, to the same treatment. Make sure to describe how the meaning changes in each case, because it will get you accustomed to seeing the effects of the rearrangings.

SUBORDINATION

In sentences that contain *subordination*, there are two "levels" of grammar—the main clause and the subordinate clause—that create two levels of meaning. When you put something in a main clause, you emphasize its significance. When you put something in a subordinate clause, you make it less important than what is in the main clause.

As noted in the discussion of complex sentences, a subordinate clause is linked to a main clause by words known as *subordinating conjunctions.* Here is a list of the most common ones: *after, although, as, as if, as long as, because, before, if, rather than, since, than, that, though, unless, until, when, where, whether,* and *while.* All of these words define something *in relation to* something else:

If you study hard, you will continue to do well.

You will continue to do well, *if* you study hard.

In both of these examples, *if* subordinates "you study hard" to "you will continue to do well," regardless of whether the *if* clause comes first or last in the sentence.

REVERSING MAIN AND SUBORDINATE CLAUSES

Unlike the situation with coordinate clauses, the emphasis in sentences that use subordination virtually always rests on the main clause, regardless of the clause order. Nevertheless, the principle of end-position emphasis still applies, though to a lesser extent than among coordinate clauses. Let's compare two versions of the same sentence.

Although the art of the people was crude, it was original.

The art of the people was original, although it was crude.

Both sentences emphasize the idea in the main clause ("original"). Because the second version locates the "although" clause at the end, however, the subordinated idea ("crude") has more emphasis than it does in the first version.

The end is a site of maximum emphasis in a sentence: if it matters a lot, put it last.

You can experiment with the meaning and style of virtually any sentence you write by reversing the clauses. Here, taken almost at random, is an earlier sentence from this chapter, followed by two such transformations.

When you put something in a subordinate clause, you make it less important than what is in the main clause.

Put information in a subordinate clause if you want to make it less important than what is in the main clause.

If you want to make information less important than what is in the main clause, put it in a subordinate clause.

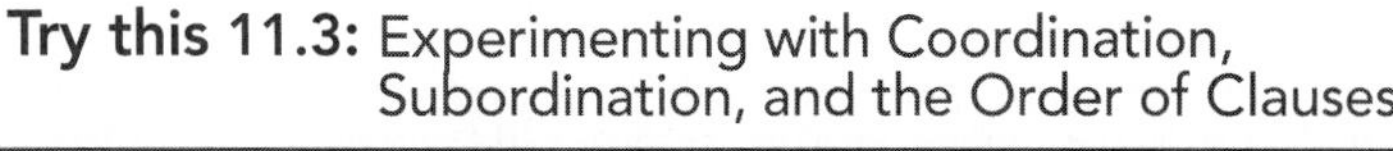

Try this 11.3: Experimenting with Coordination, Subordination, and the Order of Clauses

Do two rewrites of the following sentence, changing the order of clauses and subordinating or coordinating as you wish. We recommend that you make one of them end with the word *friendly.*

Faculty members came to speak at the forum, and they were friendly, but they were met with hostility, and this hostility was almost paranoid.

How does each of your revisions change the meaning and emphasis?

PARALLEL STRUCTURE

One of the most important and useful devices for shaping sentences is *parallel structure* or, as it is also known, *parallelism.* Parallelism is a form of symmetry: it involves placing sentence elements that correspond in some way into the same (that is, parallel) grammatical form. Consider the following examples, in which the parallel items are underlined or italicized:

> The three kinds of partners in a law firm who receive money from a case are popularly known as finders, binders, and grinders.

> The Beatles acknowledged their musical debts to American rhythm and blues, to English music hall ballads and ditties, and later to classical Indian ragas.

> There was no way that the president could gain the support of party regulars *without alienating* the Congress, and no way that he could appeal to the electorate at large *without alienating* both of these groups.

> In the entertainment industry, the money that goes out to hire *film stars* or *sports stars* comes back in increased ticket sales and video or television rights.

As all of these examples illustrate, at the core of parallelism lies repetition—of a word, a phrase, or a grammatical structure. *Parallelism uses repetition to organize and emphasize certain elements in a sentence, so that readers can perceive more clearly the shape of your thought.* In the Beatles example, each of the prepositional phrases beginning with *to* contains a musical debt. In the president example, the repetition of the phrase *no way that* emphasizes his entrapment.

Parallelism has the added advantage of *economy*: each of the musical debts or presidential problems might have had its own sentence, but in that case the prose would have been wordier and the relationships among the parallel items more obscure. Along with this economy come *balance* and *emphasis.* The trio of rhyming words (*finders*, *binders*, and *grinders*) that concludes the law-firm example gives each item equal weight; in the entertainment-industry example, "comes back" answers "goes out" in a way that accentuates their symmetry.

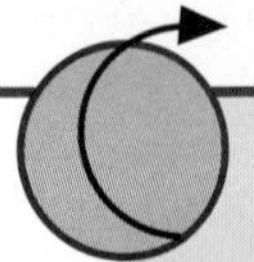

Try this 11.4: Finding Parallelisms

List all of the parallelisms in the following famous passage from the beginning of the Declaration of Independence:

> We hold these truths to be self-evident: that all men are created equal; that they are endowed by their Creator with certain inalienable rights; that, among these, are life, liberty, and the pursuit of happiness.

Remember that parallelism can occur with clauses, phrases, and prepositional phrases. You might find it useful to review the entries for these terms in the glossary in Chapter 14. After you have completed your list, what do you notice about the way that the parallel structures accumulate? And what is the effect of the placement and phrasing of these parallelisms? In other words, try to describe how this famous passage develops stylistically.

One particularly useful form of balance that parallel structure accommodates is known as *antithesis* (from the Greek word for "opposition"), a conjoining of contrasting ideas. Here the pattern sets one thing against another thing, as in the following example:

> Where bravura failed to settle the negotiations, tact and patience succeeded.

"Failed" is balanced antithetically against "succeeded," as "bravura" against "tact and patience." Antithesis commonly takes the form of "if not *x*, at least *y*" or "not *x*, but *y*."

When you employ parallelism in revising for style, there is one grammatical rule you should obey. It is important to avoid what is known as *faulty parallelism*, which occurs when the items that are parallel in content are not placed in the same grammatical form.

> **Faulty:** *To study* hard for four years and then *getting* ignored once they enter the job market is a hard thing for many recent college graduates to accept.

> **Revised:** *To study* hard for four years and then *to get* ignored once they enter the job market is a hard thing for many recent college graduates to accept.

As you revise your draft for style, search for opportunities to place sentence elements in parallel structure. Try this consciously: include and underline three uses of it in a draft of your next writing assignment. Remember that parallelism can occur with *clauses*, *phrases*, and *prepositional phrases*. Often the parallels will be hidden in the sentences of your draft, but they can be brought out with a minimum of labor. After you've acquired the habit of casting your thinking in parallel structures, they will rapidly become a staple of your stylistic repertoire, making your prose more graceful, clear, and logically connected.

Try this 11.5: Correcting Errors in Parallelism

Rewrite the following examples of faulty parallelism using correct parallel structure. In the last of these sentences you will need to contemplate the thinking behind it as well as its form.

1. The problems with fast food restaurants include the way workers are exploited, eating transfatty acids, and that the food can damage your liver.
2. Venus likes to play tennis and also watching baseball games.
3. In the 1960s the use of drugs and being a hippie was a way for some people to let society know their political views and that they were alienated from the mainstream.

C. PERIODIC AND CUMULATIVE SENTENCES: ADDING SHAPES TO THE MAIN CLAUSE

The shape of a sentence governs the way it delivers information. The order of clauses, especially the placement of the main clause, affects what the sentence means.

There are two common sentence shapes defined by the location of their main clauses; these are known as *periodic* and *cumulative* sentences.

The shape of a sentence governs the way it delivers information.

THE PERIODIC SENTENCE: SNAPPING SHUT

The main clause in a periodic sentence builds to a climax that is not completed until the end. Often, a piece of the main clause (such as the subject) is located early in the sentence, as in the following example.

> The *way* that beverage companies market health—"No Preservatives," "No Artificial Colors," "All Natural," "Real Brewed"—*is* often, because the product also contains a high percentage of sugar or fructose, *misleading*.

We have italicized the main clause to clarify how various modifiers interrupt it. The effect is suspenseful: not until the final word does the sentence consummate its fundamental idea. Pieces of the main clause are spread out across the sentence. (The term *periodic* originates in classical rhetoric to refer to the length of such units within a sentence.)

Another version of the periodic sentence locates the entire main clause at the end, after introductory modifiers.

> Using labels that market health—such as "No Preservatives," "No Artificial Colors," "All Natural," and "Real Brewed"—while producing drinks that contain a high percentage of sugar or fructose, *beverage companies are misleading*.

As was previously discussed, the end of a sentence normally receives emphasis. When you use a periodic construction, the pressure on the end intensifies because the sentence needs the end to complete its grammatical sense. In both of the preceding examples, the sentences "snap shut." They string readers along, delaying *grammatical closure*—the point at which the sentences can stand alone independently—until they arrive at climactic ends. (Periodic sentences are also known as *climactic sentences.*)

If you are revising and want to underscore some point, try letting the sentence snap shut upon it.

You should be aware of one risk that accompanies periodic constructions. If the delay lasts too long because there are too many "interrupters" before the main clause gets completed, your readers may forget the subject that is being predicated. To illustrate, let's add more subordinated material to one of the preceding examples.

> The way that beverage companies market health—"No Preservatives," "No Artificial Colors," "All Natural," "Real Brewed"—is often, because the product also contains a high percentage of sugar or fructose, not just what New Agers would probably term "immoral" and "misleading" but what a government agency such as the Food and Drug Administration should find illegal.

Arguably, the additions (the "not just" and "but" clauses after "fructose") push the sentence into incoherence. The main clause has been stretched past the breaking point. If readers don't get lost in such a sentence, they are at least likely to get irritated and wish the writer would finally get to the point.

Nonetheless, with a little care, periodic sentences can be extraordinarily useful in giving emphasis. If you are revising and want to underscore some point, try letting the sentence snap shut upon it. Often the periodic *potential* will already be present in the draft, and stylistic editing can bring it out more forcefully. Note how minor the revisions are in the following example:

> **Draft:** The novelist Virginia Woolf suffered from acute anxieties for most of her life. She had several breakdowns and finally committed suicide on the eve of World War II.

> **Revision:** Suffering from acute anxieties for most of her life, the novelist Virginia *Woolf* not only *had* several *breakdowns but,* finally, on the eve of World War II, *committed suicide.*

This revision has made two primary changes. It has combined two short sentences into a longer sentence, and it has made the sentence periodic by stringing out the main clause (italicized). What is the effect of this revision? Stylistically speaking, the revision radiates a greater sense of its writer's authority. The information has been arranged for us. After the opening dependent clause ("Suffering . . ."), the subject of the main clause ("Woolf") is introduced, and the predicate is protracted in a *not only/but* parallelism. The interrupters that follow "had several breakdowns" ("finally, on the eve of World War II") increase the suspense, before the sentence snaps shut with "committed suicide."

In general, when you construct a periodic sentence with care, you can give readers the sense that you are in control of your material. You do not seem to be writing off the top of your head, but rather from a position of greater detachment, rationally composing your meaning.

THE CUMULATIVE SENTENCE: STARTING FAST

The cumulative sentence is in many respects the opposite of the periodic. Rather than delaying the main clause or its final piece, the cumulative sentence begins by presenting the independent clause as a foundation and then *accumulates* a number of modifications and qualifications. As the following examples illustrate, the independent clause provides quick grammatical closure, freeing the rest of the sentence to amplify and develop the main idea.

> *Robert F. Kennedy was assassinated* by Sirhan B. Sirhan, a twenty-four-year-old Palestinian immigrant, prone to occultism and unsophisticated left-wing politics and sociopathically devoted to leaving his mark in history, even if as a notorious figure.

> *There are two piano concerti* composed solely for the left hand, one by Serge Prokofiev and one by Maurice Ravel, and both commissioned by Paul Wittgenstein, a concert pianist (and the brother of the famous philosopher Ludwig Wittgenstein) who had lost his right hand in combat during World War I.

Anchored by the main clause, a cumulative sentence moves serially through one thing and another thing and the next thing, close to the associative manner in which people think. To an extent, then, cumulative sentences can convey more immediacy and a more conversational tone than can other sentence shapes. Look at the following example:

> The film version of *Lady Chatterley's Lover* changed D. H. Lawrence's famous novel a lot, omitting the heroine's adolescent experience in Germany, making her husband much older than she, leaving out her father and sister, including a lot more lovemaking, and virtually eliminating all of the philosophizing about sex and marriage.

Here we get the impression of a mind in the act of thinking. Using the generalization of changes in the film as a base, the sentence then appends a series of parallel participial phrases ("omitting," "making," "leaving," "including," "eliminating") that moves forward associatively, gathering a range of information and laying out possibilities. Cumulative sentences perform this outlining and prospecting function very effectively. On the other hand, if we were to add four or five more changes to the sentence, readers would likely find it tedious, or worse, directionless. As with periodic sentences, overloading the shape can short-circuit its desired effect.

Try this 11.6: Writing Periodic and Cumulative Sentences

If you consciously practice using periodic and cumulative constructions, you will be surprised how quickly you can learn to produce their respective effects in your own writing. You will also discover that both of these sentence shapes are already present in your prose in some undiscovered and thus unrefined way. It is often simply a case of bringing out what is already there. Try including at least one of each in the next paper you write.

Toward that end, compose a simple sentence on any subject, preferably one with a direct object. Then construct two variations expanding it, one periodic and one cumulative. Here, as a model, is an example using the core sentence "James Joyce was a gifted singer."

Periodic: Although known primarily as one of the greatest novelists of the twentieth century, James Joyce, the son of a local political functionary who loved to tip a few too many at the pub, was also a gifted—and prizewinning—singer.

Cumulative: James Joyce was a gifted singer, having listened at his father's knee to the ballads sung in pubs, having won an all-Ireland prize in his early teens, and having possessed a miraculous ear for the inflections of common speech that was to serve him throughout the career for which he is justly famous, that of a novelist.

Can't think of a core sentence? Okay, here are a few:

Why do airlines show such mediocre films?
The Abu Ghraib prison scandal rocked the nation.
Manny Ramirez and friends lifted the curse of the Bambino.
Every senator is a millionaire.

D. CUTTING THE FAT

If you can reduce verbiage, your prose will communicate more directly and effectively.

In cutting the fat, you need to consider both the diction and the syntax. When it comes to diction, the way to eliminate superfluous words is deceptively simple: ask yourself if you need all of the words you've included to say what you want to say. Such revision requires an aggressive attitude. *Expect* to find unnecessary restatements or intensifiers such as "quite" and "very" that add words but not significance.

In terms of syntax, there are a few technical operations that you can perform—particularly on the *verbs* in your sentences—to reduce the number of words. The remainder of the chapter discusses these matters in more depth, but here's a preview.

- Convert sentences from the passive into the active voice. Writing "He read the book" reduces by a third "The book was read by him," and eliminating the prepositional phrase ("by him") clarifies the relationships within the sentence.
- Replace anemic forms of the verb "to be" with vigorous verbs and direct subject–verb–object syntax. Often you will find such verbs lurking in the original sentence, and once you've recognized them, conversion is easy: "The Watergate *scandal* was an event whose effects were felt across the nation" becomes "Watergate *scandalized* people across the nation."

- Avoid unnecessary subordination. It is illogical to write, "*It is true that* more government services mean higher taxes." If "it is true," then just write, "More government services mean higher taxes"—don't muffle your meaning in a subordinate "that" clause.

Writing "He read the book" reduces by a third "The book was read by him."

Beyond these technical operations, perhaps the most useful way to cut the fat is to have confidence in your position on a subject and state it clearly in your paper. A lot of fat in essays consists of "throat clearings," attempts to avoid stating a position. Move quickly to an example that raises the question or issue you wish to analyze.

EXPLETIVE CONSTRUCTIONS

The syntactic pattern for "It is true *that* more government services mean higher taxes" is known as an *expletive* construction. The term *expletive* comes from a Latin word that means "serving to fill out." The most common expletives are *it* and *there*. Consider how the expletives function in the following examples.

> *There* are several prototypes for the artificial heart.
>
> *It* is obvious that the American West exerted a profound influence on the photography of Ansel Adams.

Compare these with versions that simply eliminate the expletives.

> The artificial heart has several prototypes.
>
> The American West exerted a profound influence on the photography of Ansel Adams.

As the revisions demonstrate, most of the time you can streamline your prose by getting rid of expletive constructions. The "It is obvious" opening, for example, causes the grammar of the sentence to subordinate its real emphasis. In some cases, however, an expletive can provide a useful way of emphasizing, as in the following example: "There are three primary reasons that you should avoid litigation." Although this sentence subordinates its real content (avoiding litigation), the expletive provides a useful frame for what is to follow.

STATIC (INTRANSITIVE) VERSUS ACTIVE (TRANSITIVE) VERBS: "TO BE" OR "NOT TO BE"

Verbs energize a sentence. They do the work, connecting the parts of the sentence with each other. In a sentence of the subject–verb–direct object pattern, the verb—known as a *transitive verb*—functions as a kind of engine, driving the subject into the predicate, as in the following examples.

> John F. Kennedy effectively *manipulated* his image in the media.
>
> Thomas Jefferson *embraced* the idea of America as a country of yeoman farmers.

Verbs energize a sentence. A transitive verb functions as an engine, driving the subject into the predicate.

By contrast, "is" and other forms of the verb "to be" provide an equal sign between the subject and the predicate but otherwise tell us nothing about the relationship between them. "To be" is an *intransitive* verb; it cannot take a direct object. Compare the two preceding transitive examples with the following versions of the same sentences using forms of the verb "to be."

John F. Kennedy *was* effective at the manipulation of his image in the media.

Thomas Jefferson's idea *was* for America to be a country of yeoman farmers.

Rather than making things happen through an active transitive verb, these sentences let everything just hang around in a state of being. In the first version, Kennedy did something—*manipulated* his image—but in the second he just *is* (or *was*), and the energy of the original verb has been siphoned into an abstract noun, "manipulation." The revised Jefferson example suffers from a similar lack of momentum compared with the original version: the syntax doesn't help the sentence get anywhere.

Certain situations, however, dictate the use of forms of "to be." For definitions in particular, the equal sign that an "is" provides works well. For instance, "Organic gardening *is* a method of growing crops without using synthetic fertilizers or pesticides." As with choosing between active and passive voices, the decision to use "to be" or not should be just that—a conscious decision on your part.

If you can train yourself to eliminate every unnecessary use of "to be" in a draft, you will make your prose more vital and direct. In most cases, you will find

TABLE 11.1 Static and Active Verbs

Action Hidden in Nouns and "to be" Verbs	Action Emphasized in Verbs
The cost of the book *is* ten dollars.	The book *costs* ten dollars.
The acknowledgment of the fact *is* increasingly widespread that television *is* a replacement for reading in American culture.	People increasingly *acknowledge* that television *has replaced* reading in American culture.
A computer *is* ostensibly a labor–saving_ device—until the hard drive *is* the victim of a crash.	A computer ostensibly *saves labor*—until the hard drive *crashes*.
In the laying of a flagstone patio, the important preliminary steps to remember *are* the excavating and the leveling of the area and then the filling of it with a fine grade of gravel.	To *lay* a flagstone patio, first *excavate* and *level* the area and then *fill* it with a fine grade of gravel.

the verb that you need to substitute for "is" lurking somewhere in the sentence in some other grammatical form. In the preceding sentence about Kennedy, "manipulate" is implicit in "manipulation." In Table 11.1, each of the examples in the left-hand column uses a form of "to be" for its verb (italicized) and contains a potentially strong active verb lurking in the sentence in some other form (underlined). These "lurkers" have been converted into active verbs (italicized) in the revisions in the right-hand column.

If you can eliminate every unnecessary use of "to be" in a draft, you will make your prose more vital and direct.

Clearly, the examples in the left-hand column have problems other than their reliance on forms of "to be"—notably wordiness. "To be" syntax tends to encourage this circumlocution and verbosity.

Try this 11.7: Finding the Active Verb

Take a paper you've written and circle the sentences that rely on forms of "to be." Then, examine the other words in these sentences, looking for "lurkers." Rewrite the sentences, converting the lurkers into vigorous verbs. You will probably discover many lurkers, and your revisions will acquire more energy and directness.

ACTIVE AND PASSIVE VOICES: DOING AND BEING DONE TO

In the *active voice*, the grammatical subject acts; in the *passive voice*, the subject is acted upon. Here are two examples.

Active: Adam Smith wrote *The Wealth of Nations* in 1776.

Passive: *The Wealth of Nations* was written by Adam Smith in 1776.

The two sentences convey identical information, but the emphasis differs—the first focuses on the author, the second on the book. As the examples illustrate, using the passive normally results in a longer sentence than using the active. If we consider how to convert the passive into the active, you can see why. In the passive, the verb requires a form of "to be" plus a past participle. (For more on participles, see the "Glossary of Grammatical Terms" in Chapter 14.) In this case, the active verb "wrote" becomes the passive verb "was written," the grammatical subject ("Smith") becomes the object of the preposition "by," and the direct object ("*The Wealth of Nations*") becomes the grammatical subject.

Now consider the activity being described in the two versions of this example: a man wrote a book. That's what happened in life. The grammar of the active version captures that action most clearly: the grammatical subject ("Smith") performs the action, and the direct object *("The Wealth of Nations")* receives it, just as in life. By contrast, the passive version alters the close link between the syntax and the event: the object of the action in life *("The Wealth of Nations")* has become the grammatical subject, whereas the doer in life ("Smith") has become the grammatical object of a prepositional phrase.

Note, too, that the passive would allow us to omit "Smith" altogether: "*The Wealth of Nations* was written in 1776." A reader who desired to know more and was not aware of the author would not appreciate this sentence. More troubling, the passive can also be used to conceal the doer of an action—not "I made a mistake" (active) but rather "A mistake has been made" (passive).

In sum, there are three reasons for avoiding the passive voice when you can: (1) it's longer, (2) its grammatical relationships often reverse what happened in life, and (3) it can omit the performer responsible for the action.

On the other hand, sometimes there are good reasons for using the passive. If you want to emphasize the object or recipient of the action rather than the performer, the passive will do that for you: "*The Wealth of Nations* was written in 1776 by Adam Smith" places the stress on the book. The passive is also preferable when the doer remains unknown: "The president has been shot!" is probably a better sentence than "Some unknown assailant has shot the president!"

Try this 11.8: Identifying Different Verb Forms

Circle and identify every verb in the paragraph below. Use the abbreviations *VA* = active voice, *VP* = passive voice, *VB* = verb of being. This exercise will give you helpful training in identifying the forms of verbs, so that you can see what the different forms do as well as manipulate them more easily.

> The 2004 World Series victory that was earned by the Boston Red Sox gratified legions of fans who had suffered for many years. Indeed, if the media were to be believed, these fans had been mourning their unrequited fandom since 1918, when Babe Ruth was sold to the Yankees. But all of the media hoopla about the fact that the Sox had been victorious could not obscure the fact that the series will not go down in history as one of the better ones. Aside from the first game, there were no close contests. And the usual components that go into making a series memorable—extra-inning games, spectacular rallies, seesaw battles—were sadly absent. Instead, we were left with an overdose of media hype. Because the games were lousy, and the writers had to write something, we just got more and more and more tired rehearsals of the lifting of the curse. So maybe the Sox lifted the curse, but perhaps it was laid upon the fans.

Alternatively, you might use a passage from a book you are reading or from one of your own drafts.

Especially in the natural sciences, the use of the passive voice is a standard practice. There are sound reasons for this disciplinary convention: science tends to focus on what happens to something in a given experiment, rather than on the actions of that something. Compare the following sentences.

Passive: Separation of the protein was achieved by using an electrophoretic gel.

Active: The researcher used an electrophoretic gel to separate the protein.

If you opted for the active version, the emphasis would rest, illogically, on the agent of the action (the researcher) rather than on what happened and how (electrophoretic separation of the protein).

More generally, the passive voice can provide a way to avoid using the pronoun "I," whether for reasons of convention, as indicated earlier, or for other reasons. For example, the following passive sentence begins a business memo from a supervisor to the staff in her office.

The Inventory and Reprint departments have recently been restructured and merged.

Like many passive sentences, this one names no actor; we do not know for sure who did the restructuring and merging, though we might imagine that the author of the memo is the responsible party. The supervisor might, then, have written the sentence in the active voice.

I have recently restructured and merged the Inventory and Reprint departments.

But the active version is less satisfactory than the passive one for two reasons: one of practical emphasis and one of sensitivity to the audience (tone). First, the fact of the changes is more important for the memo's readers than is the announcement of who made the changes. The passive sentence appropriately emphasizes the changes; the active sentence inappropriately emphasizes the person who made the changes. Second, the emphasis of the active sentence on "I" (the supervisor) risks alienating the readers by taking an autocratic tone and by seeming to exclude all others from possible credit for the presumably worthwhile reorganization.

On balance, "consider" is the operative term when you choose between passive and active as you revise the syntax of your drafts. Recognize that you do have choices—in emphasis, in relative directness, and in economy. All things being equal and disciplinary conventions permitting, the active is usually the better choice.

Try this 11.9: Converting Passive to Active

Identify all of the sentences that use the passive voice in one of your papers. Then, rewrite these sentences, converting passive into active wherever appropriate. Finally, count the total number of words, the total number of prepositions, and the average sentence length (words per sentence) in each version. What do you discover? Alternatively, you could do this with the World Series example in the previous "Try this" exercise.

For more practice, here's another exercise. Compose a paragraph of at least half a page in which you use only the passive voice and verbs of being, followed by a paragraph in which you use only the active voice. Then, rewrite the first paragraph using only active voice, if possible, and rewrite the second paragraph using only passive voice and verbs of being as much as possible. How do the paragraphs differ in shape, length, and coherence?

EXPERIMENT!

A key idea of this chapter is that there are not necessarily right and wrong choices when it comes to sentence style but instead better and best choices for particular situations. The from-the-hip plain style of a memo or a set of operating instructions for your lawn mower is very likely not the best style choice for a good-bye letter to a best friend, a diplomatic talk on a sensitive political situation, or an analysis of guitar styles in contemporary jazz.

Is style a function of character and personality? Is it, in short, personal, and thus something to be preserved in the face of would-be meddlers carrying style manuals and grammar guides? Well, as you might guess at this point in the book, the answer is yes and no. We all need to find ways of using words that do not succumb to the mind-numbing environment of verbal cliché in which we dwell. It helps then, to become more self-conscious about style and not assume that it is inborn. Staying locked into one way of writing because that is "your style" is as limiting as remaining locked into only one way of thinking.

This chapter has presented some terms and techniques for experimenting with sentence styles. Equipped with these, you might profitably begin to read and listen for style more self-consciously. Find models. When a style appeals to you, figure out what makes it work. Copy sentences you like. Try imitating them. Know, by the way, that imitation will not erase your own style—it will allow you to experiment with new moves, new shapes into which to cast your words.

Try this 11.10: Finding the Representative Sentence in a Reading

As we discussed in the Quick Take for this chapter, the ability to isolate a characteristic stylistic passage in any writing and then analyze it can yield privileged insights into how the writer makes meanings and by extension, what those meanings are. Try this with any writer whose work you are studying. Talk about particular stylistic features of diction and syntax. How is the passage representative? What is the significance of these representative characteristics?

VOICES FROM ACROSS THE CURRICULUM

Reading Attentively to Improve One's Style

Aside from the usual basic writing errors, the stylistic problems I most frequently encounter in students' papers are odd word selection and awkward sentence structure. I think both problems find their genesis in the same broader problem. You learn how to make telling use of the vocabulary you've been forced to memorize only by reading. You fashion an appealing sentence based on what you've read others doing.

—James Marshall, Professor of Economics

Try this 11.11: Finding Your "Go To" Sentence

Bring it all back home. Examine your own stylistic habits in diction but particularly in syntax. What is the favored shape with which you compose the world when you write? And once you have it, ask and answer, So what?

ASSIGNMENTS: Stylistic Analysis

1. Analyze the style—the syntax but also the diction—of two writers doing a similar kind of writing; for example, two sportswriters, two rock music reviewers, or two presidents. Study first the similarities. What style characteristics does this type of writing seem to invite? Then study the differences. How is one writer (Bush, Reagan, or Clinton, for example) recognizable through his or her style?
2. Analyze your own style, past and present. Assemble some pieces you have written, preferably of a similar type, and study them for style. Do you have some favorite stylistic moves? What sentence shapes (simple, compound, complex, compound-complex, highly parallel, periodic, or cumulative) dominate in your writing? What verbs? Do you use forms of "to be" a lot, and so forth?
3. For many people, Lincoln's Gettysburg Address (see p. 52) is one of the best examples of the careful matching of style to situation. Delivered after a long talk by a previous speaker at the dedication of a Civil War battlefield on a rainy day, the speech composed by Abraham Lincoln (some say on the back of an envelope) is a masterpiece of style. Analyze its sentence structure, such as its use of parallelism, antithesis, and other kinds of repetition. Which features of Lincoln's style seem to you to be most important in creating the overall effect of the piece? (Or do this with any popular journalist whom you read regularly and who you

think has an especially effective style. Or look for another inspirational speech and see if such occasional writing has anything in common.)

4. Do a full-fledged stylistic revision of a paper. The best choice might well be an essay you already have revised, resubmitted, and had returned, because in that case, you will be less likely to get distracted by conceptual revision and so can concentrate on stylistic issues. As you revise, try to accomplish each of the following:

   a. Sharpen the diction.

   b. Blend concrete and abstract diction.

   c. Experiment with the order of and relation among subordinate and coordinate clauses.

   d. Choose more knowingly between active and passive voice.

   e. Cut the fat, especially by eliminating unnecessary "to be" constructions.

   f. Vary sentence length and shape.

   g. Use parallelism.

   h. Experiment with periodic and cumulative sentences.

   i. Fine-tune the tone.

GUIDELINES FOR SHAPING SENTENCES

1. Revise sentences to clarify their meaning by revealing the organization of thought. Align like with like, set difference against difference, and in general use form to emphasize what's important and demote what is not.
2. Become aware of your own syntactic habits. What is your "go-to sentence," and how might you build upon it to extend your range and force?
3. Cut the fat. Don't use five words ("due to the fact that") when one will do ("because"). Root out expletives that needlessly subordinate ("It is true that . . ."). Avoid redundancy.
4. Tighten the syntax of your sentences by energizing the verbs. The active voice generally achieves directness and economy; it will promote clarity and cut fat.
5. Look for potentially strong active verbs "lurking" in sentences that use a form of "to be." Beware habitual use of "to be" and passives, since these forms tend to blur or submerge the action, omit its performers, and generally lack momentum.
6. Look at the order and arrangement of clauses. Are ideas of equal importance in coordinate constructions? Have you used subordination to rank ideas? Have your sentences exploited the end as a position of emphasis?
7. Look at the shapes of your sentences. Do they use parallelism to keep your ideas clear? Where do you find opportunities for composing periodic and cumulative sentences that revision can bring out?

CHAPTER 12
Writing the Researched Paper

Quick Take

This chapter is about how to integrate secondary sources into your writing. That is often a daunting task, because it requires you to negotiate with authorities who generally know more than you do about the subject at hand. Simply ignoring sources is a head-in-the-sand attitude, and besides, you miss out on learning what people interested in your subject are talking about. But what role can you invent for yourself when the experts are talking? Just agreeing with a source is an abdication of your responsibility to present your thinking on the subject, but taking the opposite tack by disagreeing with some professor who has studied your subject and written books about it would also appear to be a fool's game. So what are you to do?

This chapter attempts to answer that question. It lays out the primary trouble spots that arise when writers use secondary materials, and it suggests remedies—for the most part, ways of using sources as points of departure for your own thinking rather than using them as either The Answer or a whipping boy. We call this concept *conversing with sources.*

In demonstrating ways of conversing with sources, the chapter also makes use of specialized applications of the tools introduced in the earlier chapter (4) on reading. That chapter addresses skills such as paraphrasing, summarizing, applying a reading as a lens, comparing readings, and uncovering assumptions in readings. Those same skills can be applied to secondary materials to raise issues and questions rather than just plugging them in as the conventional solution to the clichéd problem—what a colleague of ours calls Plug 'n' Chug.

Here's a short list of the chapter's chief strategies by name:

Strategy 1: Make Your Sources Speak

Strategy 2: Use Your Sources to Ask Questions, Not Just to Provide Answers

Strategy 3: Put Your Sources into Conversation with One Another

Strategy 4: Find Your Own Role in the Conversation

Strategy 5: Supply Ongoing Analysis of Sources (Don't Wait until the End)

Strategy 6: Attend Carefully to the Language of Your Sources by Quoting or Paraphrasing Them

This is, by the way, the first of two chapters on using sources. The next chapter treats such practical matters as finding and evaluating sources in print and electronic media, integrating quotations into one's own prose, and citing sources.

A. WHAT TO DO WITH SECONDARY SOURCES

First, by way of definition, we use the terms *source* and *secondary source* interchangeably to designate ideas and information about your subject that you find in the work of other writers. Secondary sources allow you to gain a richer, more informed, and complex vantage point on your *primary sources.* Here's how primary and secondary sources can be distinguished: if you were writing a paper on the philosopher Nietzsche, his writing would be your primary source, and critical commentaries on his work would be your secondary sources. If, however, you were writing on the poet Yeats, who read and was influenced by Nietzsche, a work of Nietzsche's philosophy would become a secondary source of yours on your primary source, Yeats's poetry.

"SOURCE ANXIETY" AND WHAT TO DO ABOUT IT

Typically, inexperienced writers either use sources as "answers"—they let the sources do too much of their thinking—or ignore them altogether as a way of avoiding "losing their own ideas." Both of these approaches are understandable but inadequate. We will take up the first of these in some detail in a moment, but for now let's concentrate on the second, ignoring sources altogether.

Typically, inexperienced writers either use sources as "answers"—they let the sources do too much of their thinking—or ignore them altogether as a way of avoiding "losing their own ideas."

Confronted with the seasoned views of experts in a discipline, you may well feel that there is nothing left for you to say because it has all been said before or, at least, it has been said by people who greatly outweigh you in reputation and experience. This anxiety explains why so many writers surrender to the role of conduit for the voices of the experts, providing conjunctions between quotations. So why not avoid what other people have said? Won't this avoidance ensure that your ideas will be original and that, at the same time, you will be free from the danger of getting brainwashed by some "expert"?

The answer is "no." If you don't consult what others have said, you run at least two risks: you will waste your time reinventing the wheel, and you will undermine your analysis (or at least leave it incomplete) by not considering information or acknowledging positions that are commonly discussed in the field.

If you don't consult what others have said, you run the risk of reinventing the wheel.

By remaining unaware of existing thinking, you choose, in effect, to stand outside of the conversation that others interested in the subject are having. Standing in this sort of intellectual vacuum sometimes appeals to writers who fear that consulting sources will leave them with nothing to say. But it is possible, as this chapter shows, to find a *middle ground* between developing an idea that is entirely independent of what experts have written on a subject and producing a paper that does nothing but repeat other people's ideas. A little research—even if it's only an hour's browse in the reference collection of the library—will virtually always raise the level of what you have to say above what it would have been if you had consulted only the information and opinions that you carry around in your head.

By remaining unaware of existing thinking, you choose, in effect, to stand outside of the conversation that others interested in the subject are having.

A good rule of thumb for coping with "source anxiety" is to formulate a tentative position on your topic before you consult secondary sources. In other words, give yourself time to do some preliminary thinking. Try writing informally about your topic, analyzing some piece of pertinent information already at your disposal. That way you will have your initial responses written down to weigh in relation to what others have said. Writing of this sort can also help you to select what to look at in the sources you eventually consult.

THE CONVERSATION ANALOGY

Now, let's turn to *the major problem in using sources—a writer leaving the experts he or she cites to speak for themselves.* In this situation, the writer characteristically makes a generalization in his or her own words, juxtaposes it to a quotation or other reference from a secondary source, and assumes that the meaning of the reference will be self-evident. This practice not only leaves the connection between the writer's thinking and his or her source material unstated but also substitutes mere repetition of someone else's viewpoint for a more active interpretation. The source has been allowed to have the final word, with the effect that it stops the discussion and the writer's thinking.

First and foremost, then, you need to do something with the reading. Clarify the meaning of the material you have quoted, paraphrased, or summarized and explain its significance in light of your evolving thesis.

It follows that the first step in using sources effectively is to reject the assumption that sources provide final and complete answers. If they did, there would be no reason for others to continue writing on the subject. As in conversation, we raise ideas for others to respond to. Accepting that no source has the final word does not mean, however, that you should shift from unquestioning approval to the opposite pole and necessarily assume an antagonistic position toward all sources. Indeed, a habitually antagonistic response to others' ideas is just as likely to bring your conversation with your sources to a halt as is the habit of always assuming that the source must have the final word.

Most people would probably agree on the attributes of a really good conversation. There is room for agreement and disagreement, for give and take, among a variety of viewpoints. Generally, people don't deliberately misunderstand each other, but a significant amount of the discussion may go into clarifying one's own as well as others' positions. Such conversations construct a genuinely collaborative *chain* of thinking: Karl builds on what David has said, which induces Jill to respond to Karl's comment, and so forth.

There are, of course, obvious differences between conversing aloud with friends and conversing on paper with sources. As a writer, you need to construct the chain of thinking, orchestrate the exchange of views with and among your sources, and give the conversation direction. A good place to begin in using sources is to recognize that you need not respond to everything another writer says, nor do you need to come up with an entirely original point of view—one that completely revises or refutes the source. You are using sources analytically, for example, when you note that two experiments (or historical accounts, or whatever) are similar but have different priorities or that they ask similar questions in different ways. Building from this kind of observation, you can then analyze what these differences imply.

WAYS TO USE A SOURCE AS A POINT OF DEPARTURE

There are, in any case, many ways of approaching secondary sources, but these ways generally share a common goal: to use the source as a point of departure. Here is a partial list of ways to do that.

- Make as many points as you can about a single representative passage from your source, and then branch out from this center to analyze other passages that "speak" to it in some way. (See "Building a Paper by Analyzing Evidence in Depth: '10 on 1'" in Chapter 5.)
- Use Notice and focus to identify what you find most strange in the source (see Chapter 1); this will help you cultivate your curiosity about the source and find the critical distance necessary to thinking about it.
- Use Looking for Patterns of Repetition and Contrast to identify the most significant organizing contrast in the source (see Chapter 2); this will help you see what the source itself is wrestling with, what is at stake in it.
- Apply an idea in the source to another subject. (See "Applying a Reading as a Lens" in Chapter 4.)
- Uncover the assumptions in the source, and then build upon the source's point of view, extending its implications. (See "Uncovering the Assumptions in a Reading" in Chapter 4.)
- Agree with most of what the source says, but take issue with one small part that you want to modify.
- Identify a contradiction in the source, and explore its implications, without necessarily arriving at a solution.

In using a source as a point of departure you are in effect using it as a stimulus to have an idea. As you may recall from the discussion of what it means to have an idea in Chapter 1, most strong analytical ideas launch you into a process of resolving problems and bringing competing positions into some kind of alignment. They locate you where there is something to negotiate, where you are required not just to list answers but also to ask questions, make choices, and engage in reasoning about the significance of your evidence.

If you quote with the aim of conversing with your sources rather than allowing them to do your thinking for you, you will discover that sources can promote rather than stifle your ability to have ideas. So try to think of sources not as answers but as voices inviting you into a community of interpretation, discussion, and debate. As the discussion of reporting versus analyzing in the "Voices from Across the Curriculum" box demonstrates, this practice is common to different academic disciplines.

Try to think of sources not as answers but as voices inviting you into a community of interpretation, discussion, and debate.

VOICES FROM ACROSS THE CURRICULUM

Reporting Versus Analyzing in Scientific Experiments

There is a big difference between simply reporting on what has been done in a scientific venture and analyzing and evaluating the venture. One of the problems with trying to *read* critical analyses of scientific work is that few scientists want to be in print criticizing their colleagues. That is, for political reasons scientists who write reviews are likely to soften their criticism or even avoid it entirely by reporting the findings of others simply and directly. However, by definition such a review is not critical. That author stakes out no particular point of view and thus does not have to defend anything.

What I want from students in molecular biology is a critical analysis of the work they have researched. This can take several forms.

First, *analyze* what was done. What were the assumptions (hypotheses) going into the experiment? What was the logic of the experimental design? What were the results?

Second, *evaluate* the results and conclusions. Here, it's even appropriate to use the first person. *You* are commenting on the field. Foremost, how well do the results support the conclusions? What alternative interpretations are there? What additional experiments could be done to strengthen or refute the argument? This is hard, no doubt, but it is what you should be doing every time you read anything in science or otherwise.

Third, *synthesize* the results and interpretations of a given experiment in the context of the field. How does this study inform other studies? Even though practicing scientists are hesitant to do this in print, everyone does it informally in journal clubs held usually on a weekly basis in every lab all over the world.

–Bruce Wightman, Professor of Biology

B. SIX STRATEGIES FOR ANALYZING SOURCES

Many people never get beyond like/dislike responses with secondary materials. If they agree with what a source says, they say it's "good," and they cut and paste the part they can use as an answer. If the source somehow disagrees with what they already believe, they say it's "bad," and they attack it or—along with readings they find "hard" or "boring"—discard it. As readers they have been conditioned to develop a point of view on a subject without first figuring out the conversation (the various points of view) that their subject attracts. They assume, in other words, that their subject probably has a single meaning—a gist—disclosed by experts, who mostly agree. The six strategies that follow offer ways to avoid this trap.

STRATEGY 1: MAKE YOUR SOURCES SPEAK

Quote, paraphrase, or summarize *in order to* analyze—not *in place of* analyzing. Don't assume that either the meaning of the source material or your reason for including it is self-evident. Stop yourself from the habit of just stringing together citations for which you provide little more than conjunctions. Instead, explain to your readers what the quotation or paraphrase or summary of the source means. What elements of it do you find interesting or revealing or strange? Emphasize how those affect your evolving thesis.

Make your sources speak. Quote, paraphrase, or summarize in order to analyze—not in place of analyzing. Don't assume that either the meaning of the source material or your reason for including it is self-evident.

In making a source speak, focus on articulating how the source has led to the conclusion you draw from it. Beware of simply putting a generalization and a quotation next to each other (juxtaposing them) without explaining the connection. Instead fill the crucial site between claim and evidence (see Figure 5.1) with your *thinking*. Consider this problem in the following paragraph from a student's paper on political conservatism.

> Edmund Burke's philosophy evolved into contemporary American conservative ideology. There is an important distinction between philosophy and political ideology: philosophy is "the knowledge of general principles that explain facts and existences." Political ideology, on the other hand, is "an overarching conception of society, a stance that is reflected in numerous sectors of social life" (Edwards 22). Therefore, conservatism should be regarded as an ideology rather than a philosophy.

The final sentence offers the writer's conclusion—what the source information has led him to—but how did it get him there? The writer's choice of the word "therefore" indicates to the reader that the idea following it is the result of a process of logical reasoning, but this reasoning has been omitted. Instead, the writer assumes that the reader will be able to connect the quotations with his conclusion. The writer needs to *make the quotation speak* by analyzing its key terms more closely. What is "an overarching conception of society," and how does it differ from "knowledge of general principles"? More important, what is the rationale for categorizing conservatism as either an ideology or a philosophy?

Here, by contrast, is a writer who makes her sources speak. Focus on how she integrates analysis with quotation.

> Stephen Greenblatt uses the phrase "self-fashioning" to refer to an idea he believes developed during the Renaissance—the idea that one's identity is not created or born but rather shaped, both by one's self and by others. The idea of self-fashioning is incorporated into an attitude toward literature that has as its ideal what Greenblatt calls "poetics of culture." A text is examined with three elements in mind: the author's own self, the cultural self-fashioning process that created that self, and the author's reaction to that process. Because our selves, like texts, are "fashioned," an author's life is just as open to interpretation as that of a literary character.
>
> If this is so, then biography does not provide a repository of unshakeable facts from which to interpret an author's work. Greenblatt criticizes the fact that the methods of literary interpretation are applied just to art and not to life. As he observes, "We wall off literary symbolism from the symbolic structures operative elsewhere, as if art alone were a human creation" (Begley 37). If the line between art and life is indeed blurred, then we need a more complex model for understanding the relationship between the life and work of an author.

In this example, the writer shows us how her thinking has been stimulated by the source. At the end of the first paragraph and the beginning of the second, for example, she not only specifies what she takes to be the meaning of the quotation but also draws a conclusion about its implications (that the facts of an author's life, like his or her art, require interpretation). And this manner of proceeding is habitual: the writer repeats the pattern in the second paragraph, *moving beyond what the quotation says to explore what its logic suggests.*

STRATEGY 2: USE YOUR SOURCES TO ASK QUESTIONS, NOT JUST TO PROVIDE ANSWERS

Use your selections from sources as a means of raising issues and questions. Avoid the temptation to plug in such selections as answers that require no further commentary or elaboration. You will no doubt find viewpoints you believe to be valid, but it is not enough to drop these answers from the source into your own writing at the appropriate spots. You need to *do* something with the reading, even with those sources that seem to have said what you want to say.

As long as you consider only the source in isolation, you may not discover much to say about it. Once you begin considering it in other contexts and with other sources, you may begin to see aspects of your subject that your source does not adequately address. Having recognized that the source does not answer all questions, you should not conclude that the source is "wrong"—only that it is limited in some ways. Discovering such limitations is in fact advantageous, because it can lead you to identify a place from which to launch your own analysis.

It does not necessarily follow that your analysis will culminate in an answer to replace those offered by your sources. Often—in fact, far more often than many writers suspect—it is enough to discover issues or problems and raise them clearly. Phrasing *explicitly* the issues and questions that remain *implicit* in a source is an important part of what analytical writers do, especially with cases in which there is no solution, or at least none that can be presented in a relatively short paper. Here, for example, is how the writer on Stephen Greenblatt's concept of self-fashioning concludes her essay:

> It is not only the author whose role is complicated by New Historicism; the critic also is subject to some of the same qualifications and restrictions. According to Adam Begley, "it is the essence of the new-historicist project to uncover the moments at which works of art absorb and refashion social energy, an endless process of circulation and exchange" (39). In other words, the work is both affected by and affects the culture. But if this is so, how then can we decide which elements of culture (and text) are causes and which are effects? If we add the critic to this picture, the process does indeed appear endless. The New Historicists' relationship with their culture infuses itself into their assessment of the Renaissance, and this assessment may in turn become part of their own self-fashioning process, which will affect their interpretations, and so forth... .

Notice that this writer *incorporates the quotation into her own chain of thinking.* By paraphrasing the quotation ("In other words"), she arrives at a question ("how then") that follows as a logical consequence of accepting its position ("but if this is so"). Note, however, that she does not then label the quotation right or wrong. Instead, she tries to figure out *to what position it might lead* and to what possible problems.

By contrast, the writer of the following excerpt, from a paper comparing two films aimed at teenagers, settles for plugging in sources as answers and consequently does not pursue the questions implicit in her quotations.

> In both films, the adults are one-dimensional caricatures, evil beings whose only goal in life is to make the kids' lives a living hell. In *Risky Business,* director Paul Brickman's solution to all of Joel's problems is to have him hire a prostitute and then turn his house into a whorehouse. Of course, as one critic observes, "the prostitutes who make themselves available to his pimply faced buddies are all centerfold beauties: elegant, svelte, benign and unquestionably healthy (after all, what does V.D. have to do with prostitutes?)" (Gould 41)—not exactly a realistic or legal solution. Allan Moyle, the director of *Pump Up the Volume,* provides an equally unrealistic solution to Mark's problem. According to David Denby, Moyle "offers self-expression as the cure to adolescent funk. Everyone should start his own radio station and talk about his feelings" (59). Like Brickman, Moyle offers solutions that are neither realistic nor legal.

This writer is having a hard time figuring out what to do with sources that offer well-phrased and seemingly accurate answers (such as "self-expression is the cure to adolescent funk"). Her analysis of both quotations leads her to settle for the bland

and undeveloped conclusion that films aimed at teenagers are not "realistic"—an observation that most readers would already recognize as true. But unlike the writer of the previous example, she does not ask herself, "*If this is true, then what follows?*" Had she asked some such version of the So what? question, she might have inquired how the illegality of the solutions is related to their unrealistic quality. So what, for example, that the main characters in both films are not marginalized as criminals and made to suffer for their illegal actions, but rather are celebrated as heroes? What different kinds of illegality do the two films apparently condone, and how might these be related to the different decades in which each film was produced? Rather than use her sources to think with, in order to clarify or complicate the issues, the writer has used them to confirm a fairly obvious generalization.

STRATEGY 3: PUT YOUR SOURCES INTO CONVERSATION WITH ONE ANOTHER

Rather than limiting yourself to agreeing or disagreeing with your sources, aim for conversation with and among them. Although it is not wrong to agree or disagree with your sources, it is wrong to see these as your only possible moves. It is sometimes useful and perhaps even necessary to agree or disagree, but these judgments should (1) always be *qualified* and (2) occur only *in certain contexts.*

Rather than limiting yourself to agreeing or disagreeing with your sources, aim for conversation with and among them.

Selective analytical summarizing of a position with which you essentially agree or disagree, especially if located early in a final draft (after you've figured out what to think in your previous drafts), can be extraordinarily helpful in orienting your readers for the discussion to follow. This practice of *framing the discussion* typically locates you either for or against some well-known point of view or frame of reference; it's a way of sharing your assumptions with the reader. You introduce the source, in other words, to succinctly summarize a position that you plan to develop or challenge in a qualified way. This latter strategy—sometimes known as **straw man**, because you construct a "dummy" position specifically in order to knock it down—can stimulate you to formulate a point of view, especially if you are not accustomed to responding critically to sources.

As this boxing analogy suggests, however, setting up a straw man can be a dangerous game. If you do not fairly represent and put into context the straw man's argument, you risk encouraging readers to dismiss your counterargument as a cheap shot and to dismiss you for being *reductive.* On the other hand, if you spend a great deal of time detailing the straw man's position, you risk losing momentum in developing your own point of view.

In any case, if you are citing a source in order to frame the discussion, the more reasonable move is both to agree *and* disagree with it. First, identify shared premises; give the source some credit. Then distinguish the part of what you have cited that you intend to develop or complicate or dispute. This method of proceeding is obviously less combative than the typically blunt straw man approach; it verges on conversation.

In the following passage from a student's paper on Darwin's theory of evolution, the student clearly recognizes that he needs to do more than summarize what Darwin says, but he seems not to know any way of conversing with his source other than indicating his agreement and disagreement with it.

> The struggle for existence also includes the dependence of one being on another being to survive. Darwin also believes that all organic beings tend to increase. I do not fully agree with Darwin's belief here. I cannot conceive of the fact of all beings increasing in number. Darwin goes on to explain that food, competition, climate, and the location of a certain species contribute to its survival and existence in nature. I believe that this statement is very valid and that it could be very easily understood through experimentation in nature.

This writer's use of the word "here" in his third sentence is revealing. He is tagging summaries of Darwin with what he seems to feel is an obligatory response—a polite shake or nod of the head: "I can't fully agree with you there, Darwin, but here I think you might have a point." The writer's tentative language lets us see how uncomfortable, even embarrassed, he feels about venturing these judgments on a subject that is too complex for this kind of response. It's as though the writer moves along, talking about Darwin's theory for a while, and then says to himself, "Time for a response," and lets a particular summary sentence trigger a yes/no switch. Having pressed that switch, which he does periodically, the writer resumes his summary, having registered but not analyzed his own interjections. There is no reasoning in a chain from his own observations, just random insertions of unanalyzed agree/disagree responses.

Here, by contrast, is the introduction of an essay that uses summary to frame the conversation that the writer is preparing to have with her source.

> In *Renaissance Thought: The Classic, Scholastic and Humanist Strains,* Paul Kristeller responds to two problems that he perceives in Renaissance scholarship. The first is the haze of cultural meaning surrounding the word "humanism": he seeks to clarify the word and its origins, as well as to explain the apparent lack of religious concern in humanism. Kristeller also reacts to the notion of humanism as an improvement upon medieval Aristotelian scholasticism.

Rather than leading with her own beliefs about the source, the writer emphasizes the issues and problems she believes are central in it. Although the writer's position on her source is apparently neutral, she is not summarizing passively. In addition to making choices about what is especially significant in the source, she has also located it within the conversation that its author, Kristeller, was having with his own sources—the works of other scholars whose view of humanism he wants to revise ("Kristeller responds to two problems").

As an alternative to formulating your opinion of the sources, try constructing the conversation that you think the author of one of your sources might have with the author of another. *How might they recast each other's ideas, as opposed to merely agreeing or disagreeing with those ideas?* Notice how, farther on in the paper, the writer uses this strategy to achieve a clearer picture of Kristeller's point of view:

> Unlike Kristeller, Tillyard [in *The Elizabethan World Picture*] also tries to place the seeds of individualism in the minds of the medievals. "Those who

know most about the Middle Ages," he claims, "now assure us that humanism and a belief in the present life were powerful by the 12th century" (30). Kristeller would undoubtedly reply that it was scholasticism, lacking the humanist emphasis on individualism that was powerful in the Middle Ages. True humanism was not evident in the Middle Ages.

In Kristeller's view, Tillyard's attempts to assign humanism to medievals are not only unwarranted, but also counterproductive. Kristeller ends his chapter on "Humanism and Scholasticism" with an exhortation to "develop a kind of historical pluralism. It is easy to praise everything in the past that appears to resemble certain favorable ideas of our own time, or to ridicule and minimize everything that disagrees with them. This method is neither fair nor helpful" (174). Tillyard, in trying to locate humanism within the medieval world, allows the value of humanism to supersede the worth of medieval scholarship. Kristeller argues that there is inherent worth in every intellectual movement, not simply in the ones that we find most agreeable.

Kristeller's work is valuable to us primarily for its forthright definition of humanism. Tillyard has cleverly avoided this undertaking: he provides many textual references, usually with the companion comment that "this is an example of Renaissance humanism," but he never overtly and fully formulates the definition in the way that Kristeller does.

As this excerpt makes evident, the writer has found something to say about her source by putting it into conversation with another source with which she believes her source, Kristeller, would disagree ("Kristeller would undoubtedly reply"). Although it seems obvious that the writer prefers Kristeller to Tillyard, her agreement with him is not the main point of her analysis. She focuses instead on foregrounding the problem that Kristeller is trying to solve and on relating that problem to different attitudes toward history. In so doing, she is deftly orchestrating the conversation between her sources. Her next step would be to distinguish her position from Kristeller's. Having used Kristeller to get perspective on Tillyard, she now needs somehow to get perspective on Kristeller. The next strategy addresses this issue.

Try this 12.1: Making One Source Speak to Another

This exercise requires you to filter one source through another, speculating (imagining) how each source would respond to the other's position. Choose two articles or book chapters by different authors or by the same author at different points in his or her career. The overriding aim of the exercise is to give you practice in getting beyond merely reacting and generalizing, and instead, participating in your sources' thinking.

As a kind of model for this exercise, you might look again at the preceding example in which the student writer compares and contrasts two historical scholars on the nature of Renaissance humanism. This example demonstrates the difference between having an idea about someone else's idea and simply reacting to someone else's idea.

Keep in mind that your aim in this exercise is not to arrive at your opinion of the sources, but to construct the conversation that you think the author of one of your sources might have with the author of another. How might they recast each other's ideas, as opposed to merely agreeing or disagreeing with those ideas? It's useful to confine yourself to thinking as impartially as you can about the ideas found in your two sources.

STRATEGY 4: FIND YOUR OWN ROLE IN THE CONVERSATION

Even in cases in which you find a source's position entirely congenial, it is not enough simply to agree with it. In order to converse with a source, you need to find some way of having a distinct voice in that conversation. This does not mean that you should feel compelled to attack the source but rather that you need to find something of your own to say about it.

In general, you have two options when you find yourself strongly in agreement with a source. You can (1) apply it in another context to qualify or expand its implications. Or you can (2) seek out other perspectives on the source in order to break the spell it has cast upon you. "To break the spell" means that you will necessarily become somewhat disillusioned but not that you will then need to dismiss everything you previously believed.

How, in the first option, do you take a source somewhere else? Rather than focusing solely on what you believe your source finds most important, *locate a lesser point, not emphasized by the reading, that you find especially interesting and develop it further.* This strategy will lead you to uncover new implications that depend upon your source but lie outside its own governing preoccupations. In the preceding humanism example, the writer might apply Kristeller's principles to new geographic (rather than theoretical) areas, such as Germany instead of Italy.

The second option, researching new perspectives on the source, can also lead to uncovering new implications. Your aim need not be simply to find a source that disagrees with the one that has convinced you and then switch your allegiance, because this move would perpetuate the problem from which you are trying to escape. Instead, you would use additional perspectives to gain some critical distance from your source. An ideal way of sampling possible critical approaches to a source is to consult book reviews on it found in scholarly journals. Once the original source is taken down from the pedestal through additional reading, there is a greater likelihood that you will see how to distinguish your views from those it offers.

You may think, for example, that another source's critique of your original source is partly valid and that both sources miss things that you could point out; in effect, you *referee* the conversation between them. The writer on Kristeller might play this role by asking herself: "So what that subsequent historians have viewed his objective—a disinterested historical pluralism—as not necessarily desirable and in any case impossible? How might Kristeller respond to this charge, and how has he responded already in ways that his critics have failed to notice?" Using additional research in this way can lead you to *situate* your source more fully and fairly, acknowledging its limits as well as its strengths.

VOICES FROM ACROSS THE CURRICULUM

Bringing Sources Together

Avoid serial citation summaries; that is, rather than discussing what Author A found, then what Author B found, then what Author C found, and so forth, *integrate* material from all of your sources. For instance, if writing about the cause and treatment of a disorder, discuss what all authors say about cause, then what all authors say about treatment, and so forth, addressing any contradictions or tensions among authors.

–Alan Tjeltveit, Professor of Psychology

In other words, this writer, in using Kristeller to critique Tillyard, has arrived less at a conclusion than at her next point of departure. A good rule to follow, especially when you find a source entirely persuasive, is that if you can't find a perspective on your source, you haven't done enough research.

STRATEGY 5: SUPPLY ONGOING ANALYSIS OF SOURCES (DON'T WAIT UNTIL THE END)

Unless disciplinary conventions dictate otherwise, analyze *as* you quote or paraphrase a source, rather than summarizing everything first and leaving your analysis for the end. A good conversation does not consist of long monologues alternating among the speakers. Participants exchange views, query, and modify what other speakers have said. Similarly, when you orchestrate conversations with and among your sources, you need to *integrate your analysis into your presentation* of them.

In supplying ongoing analysis, you are much more likely to explain how the information in the sources fits into your unfolding presentation, and your readers will be more likely to follow your train of thought and grasp the logic of your organization. You will also prevent yourself from using the sources simply as an answer. A good rule of thumb in this regard is to *force yourself to ask and answer "So what?" at the ends of paragraphs.* In laying out your analysis, however, take special care to distinguish your voice from the sources'. (For further discussion of integrating analysis into your presentation of sources, see the commentary on the research paper later in this chapter.)

STRATEGY 6: ATTEND CAREFULLY TO THE LANGUAGE OF YOUR SOURCES BY QUOTING OR PARAPHRASING THEM

Rather than generalizing broadly about ideas in your sources, you should spell out what you think is significant about their key words. In those disciplines in which it is permissible, *quote sources if the actual language that they use is important to your point.* This practice will help you to represent the view of your source fairly and accurately. In situations where quoting is not allowed—such as in the report format in psychology—you still need to attend carefully to the meaning of key words in order to arrive at a paraphrase that is not overly general. As we have suggested repeatedly, paraphrasing provides an ideal way to begin interpreting, since the act of careful rephrasing usually illuminates attitudes and assumptions implicit in a text. It is almost impossible not to have ideas and not to see the questions when you start paraphrasing.

Another reason that quoting and paraphrasing are important is that your analysis of a source will nearly always benefit from attention to the way the source represents its position (not just from dwelling on the position itself). Although focusing on the manner of presentation matters more with some sources than with others—more with a poem or scholarly article in political science than with a paper in the natural sciences—the information is never wholly separable from how it is expressed. If you are going to quote *Newsweek* on Pakistan, for example, you will be encountering not "the truth" about American involvement in this Asian nation but rather one particular representation of the situation—in this case, one crafted to meet or shape the expectations of mainstream popular culture. Similarly, if you quote President Bush on terrorism, what probably matters most is that the president chose particular words to represent—and promote—the government's position. *It is not neutral information.* The person speaking and the kind of source in which his or her words appear usually acquire added significance when you make note of these words rather than just summarizing them.

Try this 12.2: Using Passage-Based Freewriting to Converse with Sources

Select a passage from a secondary source that appears important to your evolving thinking about a subject you are studying, and try doing a passage-based focused freewrite on it. You might choose the passage in answer to the question "What is the one passage in the source that I need to discuss, that poses a question or a problem or that seems, in some way perhaps difficult to pin down, anomalous or even just unclear?" Copy the passage at the top of the page, and go for 20 minutes. As noted in the discussion of freewriting in Chapter 4, try to isolate and paraphrase key terms as you relentlessly ask "So what?" about the details. Also, remember to consider how the passage is representative of broader issues in the source; you may wish to refer to a similar passage for this purpose.

Try this 12.3: Freewriting by Applying a Secondary Source to a Primary Source

As a variation on the preceding exercise, *apply a brief passage from a secondary source to a brief passage from a primary source.* Choose the secondary source passage first—one that you find particularly interesting, revealing, or problematic. Then locate a corresponding passage from the primary source to which the sentence from the first passage can be connected in some way. Copy both passages at the top of the page, and then write for 20 minutes. You should probably include paraphrases of key phrases in both—not just the primary text—but your primary goal is to think about the two together, to allow them to interact.

C. MAKING THE RESEARCH PAPER MORE ANALYTICAL: A SAMPLE ESSAY

The following is an example of a typical college research paper. We offer a brief analysis of each paragraph with an eye to diagnosing what typically goes wrong in writing a research paper and how applying a version of the six strategies for analyzing sources can be used to remedy the problems.

The Flight from Teaching

[1] The "flight from teaching" (Smith 6) in higher education is a controversial issue of the academic world. The amount of importance placed on research and publishing is the major cause of this flight. I will show different views and aspects concerning the problem plaguing our colleges and universities, through the authors whom I have consulted. [The introductory paragraph needs to be revised to eliminate prejudgment. Calling the issue "controversial" implies that there are different points of view on the subject. The writer, however, offers only one and words it in a way that suggests she has already leaped to a premature and oversimplified conclusion. Instead, she needs to better frame the issue and then replace the procedural opening (see Chapter 8) with a more hypothetical working thesis that will enable her to explore the subject.]

[2] Page Smith takes an in-depth look at the "flight from teaching" in *Killing the Spirit*. Smith's views on this subject are interesting, because he is a professor with tenure at UCLA. Throughout the book, Smith stresses the sentiment of the student being the enemy, as expressed by many of his colleagues. Some professors resent the fact that the students take up their precious time—time that could be better used for research. Smith goes on about how much some of his colleagues go out of their way to avoid their students. They go as far as making strange office hours to avoid contact. Smith disagrees with the hands-off approach being taken by the professors: "There is no decent, adequate, respectable education, in the proper sense of that much-abused word, without personal involvement by a teacher with the needs and concerns, academic and personal, of his/her students. All the rest is 'instruction' or 'information transferal,' 'communication technique,' or some other impersonal and antiseptic phrase, but it is not teaching and the student is not truly learning" (7). [The writer summarizes and quotes one of her sources but does not analyze or offer any perspective on it.]

[3] Page Smith devotes a chapter to the ideal of "publish or perish," "since teaching is shunned in the name of research." Smith refutes the idea that "research enhances teaching" and that there is a "direct relationship between research and teaching" (178). In actuality, research inhibits teaching. The research that is being done, in most cases, is too specialized for the student. As with teaching and research, Smith believes there is not necessarily a relationship between research and publication. Unfortunately those professors who are devoted to teaching find themselves without a job and/or tenure unless they conform to the requirements of publishing. Smith asks, "Is not the atmosphere hopelessly polluted when professors are forced to do research in order to validate themselves, in order to make a living, in order to avoid being humiliated (and terminated)?" (197). Not only are the students and the professors suffering, but also as a whole, "Under the publish-or-perish standard, the university is perishing" (180). [The writer continues her summary of her source, using language that implies but does not make explicit her apparent agreement with it. She appears to use the source to speak for her but has not clearly distinguished her voice from that of her source. See, for example, the third sentence and the last sentence of the paragraph. Is the writer only reporting what Smith says or appropriating his view as her own?]

[4] Charles J. Sykes looks at the "flight from teaching" in *Profscam: Professors and the Demise of Higher Education.* Sykes cites statistics to show the results of the reduction of professors' teaching loads enabling them time for more research. The call to research is the cause of many problems. The reduced number of professors actually teaching increases both the size of classes and the likelihood that students will find at registration that their courses are closed. Students will also find they do not have to write papers, and often exams are multiple choice, because of the large classes. Consequently, the effects of the "flight from teaching" have "had dramatic ramifications for the way undergraduates are taught" (40). [The writer summarizes another of her sources without analysis of its reasoning and again blurs the distinction between the source's position and her own.]

[5] E. Peter Volpe, in his chapter "Teaching, Research, and Service: Union or Coexistence?" in the book *Whose Goals for American Higher Education?*, disagrees strongly that there is an overemphasis on research. Volpe believes that only the research scholar can provide the best form of teaching because "Teaching and research are as inseparable as the two faces of the same coin" (80). The whole idea of education is to increase the student's curiosity. When the enthusiasm of the professor, because of his or her research, is brought into the classroom, it intensifies that curiosity and therefore provides "the deepest kind of intellectual enjoyment" (80). Volpe provides suggestions for

solving the rift between students and professors, such as "replacing formal discourse by informal seminars and independent study programs" (81). He feels that this will get students to think for themselves and professors to learn to communicate with students again. Another suggestion is that the government provide funding for "research programs that are related to the education function" (82). This would allow students the opportunity to share in the research. In conclusion, Volpe states his thesis to be, "A professor in any discipline stays alive when he carries his enthusiasm for discovery into the classroom. The professor is academically dead when the spark of inquiry is extinguished within him. It is then that he betrays his student. The student becomes merely an acquirer of knowledge rather than an inquirer into knowledge" (80). [Here the writer summarizes a source that offers an opposing point of view. It is good that she has begun to represent multiple perspectives, but as with the preceding summaries, there is not yet enough analysis. If she could put Volpe's argument into active conversation with those of Sykes and Smith, she might be able to articulate more clearly the assumptions her sources share and to distinguish their key differences. How, for example, do the three sources differ in their definitions of research and of teaching?]

[6] The "flight from teaching" is certainly a problem in colleges and universities. When beginning to research this topic, I had some very definite opinions. I believed that research and publication should not play any role in teaching. Through the authors utilized in this paper and other sources, I have determined that there is a need for some "research" but not to the extent that teaching is pushed aside. College and universities exist to provide an education; therefore, their first responsibility is to the student. [Here the writer begins to offer her opinion of the material, which she does, in effect, by choosing sides. She appears to be compromising—"there is a need for some 'research' but not to the extent that teaching is pushed aside"—but as her last sentence shows, she has in fact dismissed the way that Volpe complicates the relationship between teaching and research.]

[7] I agree with Smith that research, such as reading in the professor's field, is beneficial to his or her teaching. But requiring research to the extent of publication in order to secure a tenured position is actually denying education to both the professors and their students. I understand that some of the pressure stems from the fact that it is easier to decide tenure by the "tangible" evidence of research and publication. The emphasis on "publish or perish" should revert to "teach or perish" (Smith 6). If more of an effort is required to base tenure upon teaching, then that effort should be made. After all, it is the education of the people of our nation that is at risk. [The writer continues to align herself with one side of the issue, which she continues to summarize but not to raise questions about.]

[8] In conclusion, I believe that the problem of the "flight from teaching" can and must be addressed. The continuation of the problem will lead to greater damage in the academic community. The leaders of our colleges and universities will need to take the first steps toward a solution. [The writer concludes with a more strongly worded version of her endorsement of the position of Smith and Sykes on the threat of research to teaching. Notice that the paper has not really evolved from the unanalyzed position it articulated in paragraph 2.]

D. STRATEGIES FOR WRITING AND REVISING RESEARCH PAPERS

Here we offer some general strategies gleaned from and keyed to our analysis of a typical paper, "The Flight from Teaching," that can be applied to any research project.

1. **Be sure to make clear who is talking.** When, for example, the writer refers to the professors' concern for their "precious time" in paragraph 2 or when she writes that "In actuality, research inhibits teaching" in paragraph 3, is she simply summarizing Smith or endorsing his position? You can easily clarify who's saying what by inserting attributive tag phrases such as "in Smith's view" or "in response to Smith, one might argue that." Remember that your role is to provide explanation of and perspective on the ideas in your source—not, especially early on, to cheerlead for it or attack it.
2. **Analyze as you go along rather than saving analysis for the end (disciplinary conventions permitting).** It is no coincidence that a research paper that summarizes its sources and delays discussing them, as "The Flight from Teaching" does, should have difficulty constructing a logically coherent and analytically revealing point of view. The *organization* of this research paper interferes with the writer's ability to have ideas about her material because the gap is too wide between the presentation and analysis of her sources. As a result, readers are left unsure how to interpret the positions she initially summarizes, and her analysis, by the time she finally gets to it, is too general.
3. **Quote *in order to* analyze: make your sources speak.** Even if the language you quote or paraphrase seems clear in what it means to you, the aim of your analysis is to put what you have quoted or paraphrased into some kind of frame or perspective. Quoting is a powerful form of evidence, but recognize that you can quote *very* selectively—a sentence or even a phrase will often suffice. After you quote, you will usually need to paraphrase in order to discover and articulate the implications of the quotation's key terms. *As a general rule, you should not end a discussion with a quotation but rather with some point you want to make about the quotation.*

   The following sentence from the second paragraph of "The Flight from Teaching" demonstrates the missed opportunities for analysis that occur when a quotation is allowed to speak for itself.

> Smith disagrees with the hands-off approach being taken by the professors: "There is no decent, adequate, respectable education, in the proper sense of that much-abused word, without personal involvement by a teacher with the needs and concerns, academic and personal, of his/her students" (7).

This sentence is offered as part of a neutral summary of Smith's position, which, the writer informs us "disagrees with the hands-off approach." But notice how Smith's word choices convey additional information about his point of view. The repetition of "personal" and the quarrelsome tone of "much-abused" suggest that Smith is writing a polemic—that he is so preoccupied with the personal that he wishes to restrict the definition of education to it. The writer may agree with Smith's extreme position, but the point is that if she attends to his actual language, she will be able to characterize that position much more accurately.

By contrast, notice how the writer in the following example quotes *in order to* analyze the implications of the source's language:

> If allegations that top levels of U.S. and British governments acted covertly to shape foreign policy are truthful, then this scandal, according to Friedman, poses serious questions concerning American democracy. Friedman explains, "The government's lack of accountability, either to Congress or to the public, was so egregious as to pose a silent threat to the principles of American democracy" (286). The word "principles" is especially important. In Friedman's view, without fundamental ideals such as a democracy based on rule by elected representatives *and* the people, where does the average citizen stand? What will happen to faith in the government, Friedman seems to be asking, if elected representatives such as the president sully that respected office?

By emphasizing Friedman's word choice ("principles"), this writer uses quotation not only to convey information but also to frame it, making a point about the source's point of view.

4. **Try converting key assertions in the source into questions.** When you are under the spell of a source, its claims sound more final and unquestionably true than they actually are. So, a useful habit of mind is to experiment with rewording selected assertions as questions. Consider, for example, what the writer of "The Flight from Teaching" might have discovered had she tried converting the following conclusions (in paragraph 4) drawn from one of her sources into questions.

> The call to research is the cause of many problems. The reduced number of professors actually teaching increases both the size of classes and the likelihood that students will find at registration that their courses are closed. Students will also find they do not have to write papers, and often exams are multiple choice, because of the large classes.

Some questions: Is it only professors' desire to be off doing their own research that explains closed courses, large class sizes, and multiple-choice tests? What about other causes for these problems, such as the cost of hiring additional professors or the pressure universities put on professors to publish in order to increase the status of the institution? We are not suggesting that the writer should have detected these particular problems in the passage but rather that she needs, somewhere in the paper, to *raise questions about the reasoning implicit in her sources.*

By *querying how your sources are defining, implicitly and explicitly, their key terms*, you can gain perspective on the sources, uncovering their assumptions. Consider in this context the writer's own fullest statement of her thesis.

> Through the authors utilized in this paper and other sources, I have determined that there is a need for some 'research' but not to the extent that teaching is pushed aside. Colleges and universities exist to provide an education; therefore, their first responsibility is to the student (paragraph 6).

More questions: What do she and her sources mean by "research" and what do they mean by "teaching"? To what extent can the writer fairly assume that the primary purpose of universities is and should be "to provide an education"? Can't an education include being mentored in the skills that university teachers practice in their own research? And isn't teaching only one of a variety of contributions that universities make to the cultures they serve?

5. **Get your sources to converse with one another, and actively referee the conflicts among them.** By doing so, you will often find the means to reorganize your paper around issues rather than leave readers to locate these issues for themselves as you move from source to source. Both looking for difference within similarity and looking for similarity despite difference are useful for this purpose. (See Chapter 4.)

   The organizing contrast that drives "The Flight from Teaching" is obviously that between teaching and research, but what if the writer actively sought out an unexpected similarity that spanned this binary? For example, Smith asserts that "research inhibits teaching" (paragraph 3), whereas Volpe contends that "only the research scholar can provide the best form of teaching because 'teaching and research are as inseparable as the two faces of the same coin'" (paragraph 5). But both sides *agree* that educating students is the "first responsibility" of colleges and universities, despite differing radically on how this responsibility is best fulfilled. Given this unexpected similarity, the writer could then explore the significance of the difference—that Smith believes professors' research gets in the way of excellent teaching, whereas Volpe believes research is essential to it. If the writer had brought these sources into dialogue, she could have discovered that the assertion she offers as her conclusion is, in fact, inaccurate, even an evasion.

   By way of conclusion, we would like to emphasize that these five strategies share a common aim: to get you off the hot seat of judging the experts when you are not an expert. Most of us are more comfortable in situations in which we can converse amicably rather than judge and be judged. Think of that as you embark on research projects, and you will be far more likely to learn and to have a good time doing it.

AN ANALYTICAL RESEARCH PAPER: A GOOD EXAMPLE

What does an effective analytical research paper look like? Look at the following piece, which demonstrates the analytical skills we discuss in this chapter. We include brief commentary at the ends of selected paragraphs, but for the most part, you should notice how the writer uses her sources to focus questions, analyzing as she goes along. Also, note her habitual use of complicating evidence to evolve the conversation she is having with her sources.

Horizontal & Vertical Mergers Within the Healthcare Industry

[1] The United States healthcare industry is constantly changing, as new ideas and strategies are developed to make healthcare more accessible and affordable for a greater number of people. Mergers within the industry are one of the new influential methods of altering the relationship between buyers and sellers of healthcare. Mergers distort the traditional roles of physicians, hospitals, and patients, but do so with an emphasis on cost-cutting, more efficient management, and better quality of care. Whether these mergers actually succeed in their outward goals is debatable; many studies have shown that these acquisitions seldom fully meet their objectives. Mergers are business deals, occurring in every market. But the healthcare market is unique in that its product, a necessity, often becomes an economic luxury—not everyone can afford the costs of medical coverage or care. [The introduction opens with a clear premise—constant change—and rapidly limits the focus to mergers as one cause of change. The writer raises but does not prematurely resolve the question of mergers' successes and ends the paragraph by distinguishing what is at stake in her topic.]

[2] The first distinct type of acquisition is known as a horizontal merger. It describes the joining of two hospital systems into one. Some simple examples of horizontal mergers include the transaction between Memorial Health System and Adventist Health System, both located in Florida: the four-hospital Memorial purchased the thirty-two-hospital Adventist in late August, 2000. Another example is the purchase of St. Mary Medical Hospital by Trinity Health, in separate parts of Michigan, completed in July 2000. In this case, the new hospital system was renamed St. Mary Mercy Hospital.[1] There are advantages and disadvantages to horizontal mergers, which will be explored, but a hospital system's main objectives in merging include reducing managerial costs, combining marketing efforts, pooling capital, and reducing excess equipment. [Having used a panning shot to establish context in the first paragraph, the writer now tracks one kind of merger and suggests that further debate is to come.]

[1] "Mergers & Acquisitions," *Business Watch*: July 2000, p. 63.

[3] A vertical merger, however, is one in which a company is bought by another company within the same "supply chain" – that is, a firm might purchase its merchandise supplier.[2] In healthcare economies, this applies to suppliers and buyers of healthcare services, such as hospitals and HMO's, or hospitals and physicians. There are several complications to vertical mergers, especially apparent when the level of competition between the two merging entities is explored. Esther Gal-Or's article, "The Profitability of Vertical Mergers Between Hospitals and Physician Practices," will be used to illustrate these complications. [The writer begins to foreground a complication that she will develop into an organizing contrast in the next paragraph, that between private profit and public good.]

[4] The selling point for all horizontal and vertical mergers is the expected increase in efficiency under the new system. But mergers benefit the merging parties immensely; are their public goals of efficiency and, in turn, lowered costs, really being achieved? In their article, "Are Multihospital Systems More Efficient?" economists Dranove, Durkac, and Shanley write that although "the conventional wisdom is that [horizontal mergers] will generate efficiencies in the production of services, surprisingly little systematic evidence exists to support this view."[3] By studying local Californian hospital systems in the 1980's and 1990's, the three researchers found that "the benefits of horizontal integration stem from greater efficiencies in marketing hospital systems . . . than from efficiencies in the production of services." [The writer uses sources to frame questions. She then cites sources offering slightly different answers to the question of efficiency.]

[5] Using data from the California Office of Statewide Health Planning and Development, the researchers selected eleven hospital systems that met their requirements for inclusion in the study. After investigating costs per admission, administrative costs, price/cost margins, and limitations, the research "[challenged the idea] that horizontally integrated hospitals generate production efficiencies." More specifically, the study showed that the multihospital systems did not consistently reduce high-tech services, or have lower patient costs. In fact, the study concluded that "integrated hospital systems are more likely than their nonintegrated hospital counterparts to have unusually high administrative costs" and that they had "unusually high price/cost margins and operating profits."[4] These findings raise questions as to why hospitals merge if a merger does not provide a substantial increase in the method of operation's efficiency. If it actually results in higher costs for consumers in certain instances, what benefit does a

[2] Ibid, 1.

[3] Dranove, Durkac, Shanley. "Are Multihospital Systems More Efficient?" *Health Affairs*: Volume 15, 1996.

[4] Ibid, 102.

merger bring? [The writer again uses her sources to focus relevant questions. Notice how she moves beyond what one of her sources says to query what it suggests.]

[6] The instance is similar with vertical mergers. Many times, the joining of a hospital and HMO plan or hospital and physician practice does not result in the expected lowered costs and higher quality care for consumers. In her article "The Profitability of Vertical Mergers Between Hospitals and Physician Practices," Esther Gal-Or outlines her complex and thorough study of vertical mergers. Gal-Or details several different facets of the vertical merger: there are possible restrictions that these new systems face, all of which jeopardize their original intent for efficiency. She also notes the importance of the competition between the two, writing

> When the degree of competitiveness [between the hospital and physician practice] is comparable, a vertical merger enhances the bargaining position of both merging parties vis-à-vis insurers. In contrast, when one provider's market is much more competitive than the other a vertical merger may reduce the joint profits of the merged entity.[5]

Therefore, the success of a vertical merger depends upon the relationship between the two merging parties. [Here the writer leads with similarity despite difference to get her to her next source, which she briefly summarizes before zooming on a selected piece. Her final sentence draws a conclusion from the quotation, though more analysis of it might have enriched the conversation.]

[7] Two examples noted in Gal-Or's study show the types of vertical mergers that are changing U.S. healthcare today. One of these is Allina Health System, a Minnesota-based system that covers over 25% of the state's residents through its HMO and PPO plans. A 1994 merger between a hospital chain and a health plan, Allina is continuing to acquire more hospitals and physician practices. Blue Cross of Western Pennsylvania, another example in the article, has also been purchasing physician practices.[6] Gal-Or's study eventually finds that when "two providers' markets are characterized by comparable degrees of competitiveness . . . both the merging hospital and the merging physician can negotiate higher rates with insurers . . . . Consumers are obviously worse off, as a result, since the higher rates translate to higher premia charged by insurers."[7] This offers a major criticism of vertical mergers because consumers are surely not looking to raise the cost of their premiums. These mergers, especially with the

[5] Gal-Or, Esther. "The Profitability of Vertical Mergers Between Hospitals and Physician Practices. *Journal of Health Economics*: October 1999, p.623.
[6] Ibid, 624.
[7] Ibid, 625.

evidence provided in this article, seem to benefit the suppliers of healthcare but only at the financial expense of the patients. [Using representative examples from her source, the writer interprets significant detail to draw a conclusion.]

[8] By contrast, in a study entitled "What Types of Hospital Mergers Save Consumers Money," four researchers studied 3,500 United States hospitals from 1986–1994, including 122 horizontal mergers. Their study found that the mergers saved consumers by approximately 7%, which may show that vertical mergers (which also accounted for a large section of the systems studied) do reduce costs to consumers.[8] [The paper pauses here to introduce complicating evidence, which leads to a brief concession (see Chapter 9). Note how the writer qualifies it with her choice of the word "may."]

[9] Mergers, especially between hospitals, also provoke an interesting ethical dilemma. Special interest groups like Planned Parenthood and the American Civil Liberties Union (ACLU) have recently argued that these mergers are being treated as business contracts between two "sellers" and that the emphasis on providing better coverage for all has been disregarded. They argue that mergers aim not to help consumers, but to reduce internal costs and therefore raise profits for the hospitals. There are two aspects of hospital mergers that most concern these groups: first, the acquisition between religious and non-religious health facilities, resulting in religiously restrictive hospital systems, and, second, the possibility of a system becoming the only option for patients in rural communities. The ACLU recently released the following:

> Many nonsectarian hospitals have recently been merging with religiously controlled hospitals. As a condition of the merger . . . these hospitals observe religious prohibitions against providing certain health services. The most publicized and significant prohibitions are found in the *Ethical and Religious Directives for Catholic Health Care Services*. . . . The *Directives* bar Catholic health care facilities from providing tubal ligation, vasectomy, abortion, in vitro fertilization, contraception, and emergency contraception in the case of rape.[9]

[Notice the evolving conversation, as the writer shifts from economic issues to the ethics these issues entail. Also note her habitual focus on complication, citing the "aspects that most concern."]

[10] In many instances, even when a Catholic hospital is acquired by a nonreligious facility, the terms of the agreement include the system's

[8] "Which Types of Hospital Mergers Save Consumers Money?" *Health Affairs:* Volume 16, p. 62–74.

[9] "Hospital Mergers: The Threat to Reproductive Health Services." www.aclu.org.

adherence to these Catholic provisions. A statement from Planned Parenthood notes, "a Catholic hospital, or an HMO contracted with a Catholic hospital, is a community's only provider—leaving women with little or no access to reproductive health services."[10] For some, the decision to choose a hospital is religiously motivated; for others, especially women, they believe it is a personal right to have access to these reproductive health services. The ACLU and Planned Parenthood, however, feel strongly that it is a patient's right to choose whether or not to use these specific services. They also feel that mergers between hospitals jeopardize that right by creating a system in which certain services may not be available, regardless of patient preference. [The conversation continues to evolve as the writer introduces new complicating evidence ("the second ethical issue") and analyzes its implications. Notice as well the diverse range of sources she has brought to bear.]

[11] This argument is closely related to the second ethical issue against horizontal hospital mergers. In more rural communities, where there may be few options from which medical care consumers can choose, mergers create a monopolistic environment. The ACLU states that "low-income women and women in rural areas with few choices in medical care are the most vulnerable . . . Women who live in rural communities frequently have little choice . . . ."[11] This is detrimental to consumer choice because mergers in rural communities most likely create only one hospital system. A dissatisfied consumer in this situation does not have the power to switch medical suppliers; the power is taken away from the consumer and the seller has the ultimate control over the cost, type, and quality of care. Mergers in rural communities greatly resemble a monopolistic market force, and for this reason, are often the targets of antitrust cases against the new hospital system.

[12] The issue of antitrust violations frequently arises regarding mergers in the healthcare industry. This, too, is a criticism of the acquisitions. The majority of the antitrust cases in the United States involve horizontal mergers because, often, they produce one hospital system that borders closely on the definition of a monopoly. But there have also been antitrust questions raised regarding vertical mergers. The Marshfield Clinic case, from 1996, shows some of the questions. The Marshfield Clinic was a physician-owned clinic in Wisconsin that had vertically integrated with its HMO. But in the merger, the clinic had also excluded Blue Cross/Blue Shield HMO coverage from its services. Eventually, the courts found in favor of the Marshfield Clinic because its HMO obviously did not have the power to eliminate Blue Cross/Blue Shield from the healthcare market. [As has been the case

[10] "Opposing Dangerous Hospital Mergers." www.plannedparenthood.org.
[11] "Hospital Mergers: The Threat to Reproductive Health Services." www.aclu.org.

throughout the paper, the writer continues to focus on the important questions raised by her representative examples.]

[13] The most recent development in the antitrust cases of hospital mergers is the influential lobby groups, petitioning state governments on behalf of the hospital systems to exempt mergers within the medical industry from antitrust laws. The state of Maine lately encountered such a request. The 565-bed Maine Medical Center, in an effort to merge with two other hospitals, successfully lobbied the state government in 1996 to pass legislation exempting hospitals from state antitrust laws. Since the enactment of the Maine law, nearly twelve other states have also passed laws to free multihospital systems from antitrust regulations.[12] These laws have significant implications for the future of horizontal hospital mergers. They create a safer environment for mergers to occur: without antitrust laws, hospitals can freely merge and even assume a monopolistic form that jeopardizes the market of healthcare. [As the paper approaches its end, the writer cites the "most recent" developments and opens out the conversation to "significant implications for the future."]

[14] The advantages for horizontal and vertical mergers seem clear – by combining efforts, and creating one system, a multihospital facility should manage its administrative duties more efficiently, provide a higher level of care, and lower costs for its patients. Mergers should make the healthcare industry more successfully directed. The ultimate aim of any improvement or change in the industry should be to make better healthcare more accessible to a broader number of Americans. It appears as though horizontal and vertical mergers have the opposite effect on the industry. Their failure to provide a more efficient means of business and the way multihospital systems capitalize on reduced costs by simply earning a larger profit show that these mergers serve the providers, not the consumers. Additionally, multihospital systems jeopardize choices in care for those patients who would want specific services (which might not be available from a large system, religiously controlled). They also create a monopoly for consumers geographically distant from other choices. The horizontal and vertical mergers within the medical care market have not met expectations; instead, they reduce medical choices for consumers, do not guarantee increased efficiency, and create additional profits for the hospitals, physicians, and insurance companies involved. [The paper concludes by coming full circle—back to change—and focusing on an unexpected similarity between horizontal and vertical mergers that leads her to take a stand in the debate that the paper's sources have been staging.]

---

[12] "Smaller Hospitals Quicker to Use Maine Merger Law." *Modern Healthcare*: October 7, 1996.

ASSIGNMENTS: Exercises in Researched Writing

At the end of the next chapter, we place a research sequence that makes use of the skills discussed in both chapters.

1. Here are a series of exercises organized in ascending order of complexity that go into writing a researched paper. You can practice these one at a time, and then learn to put them together.
   - **a.** Compose an analytical summary of a single source (try ranking).
   - **b.** Write about a primary source using a single secondary source as a lens.
   - **c.** Compose a comparative analytical summary of two sources (try difference within similarity or similarity despite difference).
   - **d.** Write a synthesis that brings together three or more sources, using them to raise questions and allowing each to help you complicate positions in the others (as the paper on mergers in healthcare does).

2. Here are a set of writing assignments, each using a strategy discussed in the chapter. The skills called for in the following sequence are also discussed in Chapter 4, "Reading: How to Do It and What to Do with It."
   - **a.** Practice making quotations speak by using paraphrase as a means of uncovering assumptions and bringing out implications. Use this method to zoom in on how sources define key terms.
   - **b.** Practice putting two or more sources in conversation with each other: figure out how each source might see and recast the other's ideas. Construct and referee a conversation among your sources.
   - **c.** Practice finding your voice in the conversation: take a source and apply it to another context, or locate a point it makes but does not dwell on and develop it further.
   - **d.** Repeatedly do the two "Try this" exercises on passage-based focused freewriting contained in this chapter (12.2 and 12.3). Make these into regular exercises—habits of mind. Also apply the heuristic "Looking for Patterns of Repetition and Contrast" (see Chapter 2) as a means of developing a more detailed and in-depth knowledge of your source and what is at stake in it.

GUIDELINES FOR WRITING THE RESEARCHED PAPER

1. Avoid the temptation to plug in sources as answers. Aim for a *conversation* with them. Think of sources as voices inviting you into a community of interpretation, discussion, and debate.
2. Quote, paraphrase, or summarize *in order to* analyze. Explain what you take the source to mean, showing the reasoning that has led to the conclusion you draw from it.

GUIDELINES FOR WRITING THE RESEARCHED PAPER (CONTINUED)

3. Quote sparingly. You are usually better off centering your analysis on a few quotations, analyzing their key terms, and branching out to aspects of your subject that the quotations illuminate.
4. Don't underestimate the value of close paraphrasing. You will almost invariably begin to interpret a source once you start paraphrasing its key language.
5. Locate and highlight what is at stake in your source. Which of its points does the source find most important? What positions does it want to modify or refute, and why?
6. Look for ways to develop, modify, or apply what a source has said, rather than simply agreeing or disagreeing with it.
7. If you challenge a position found in a source, be sure to represent it fairly. First, give the source some credit by identifying assumptions you share with it. Then, isolate the part that you intend to complicate or dispute.
8. Look for sources that address your subject from different perspectives. Avoid relying too heavily on any one source.
9. When your sources disagree, consider playing mediator. Instead of immediately agreeing with one or the other, clarify areas of agreement and disagreement among them.

CHAPTER 13

Finding and Citing Sources

Quick Take

This chapter shifts attention to more technical matters associated with writing the researched paper, including finding and citing sources. Although doing conventional library research has obviously changed a lot since the advent of computers, many of the basic strategies remain the same. More than just mechanically gathering information, research continues to be a primary means of discovering the ongoing conflicts about a subject and having ideas about it. Engaging the information sparks thinking, not just arranging.

The core of this chapter is a discussion of research methodologies written by a reference librarian. It offers a wealth of insider's tips for making more productive use of your research time, especially online and with databases. Among the featured topics are the following:

- **How to assess a web page, including how to find out more about its author's credentials**
- **How to search databases by subject heading in addition to keyword**
- **Where to find full-text databases in different disciplines**
- **The best subject-specific databases by discipline**
- **A "Fool-Proof Recipe for Great Research—Every Time"**
- **Where to find citation guides on the web**

The chapter also offers sections on the following topics:

- How to cite secondary sources in MLA and APA style
- How to integrate source material smoothly into your own prose while clearly distinguishing it from your comments about it
- What plagiarism is and isn't, and how to avoid it
- How to compose abstracts of sources

A. GETTING STARTED

The problem with doing research in the Information Age is that there is so much information available. How do you know which information is considered respectable in a particular discipline and which isn't? How can you avoid wasting time with source materials that have been effectively refuted and replaced by subsequent thinking? A short answer to these questions is that you should start not in the stacks but in the reference room of your library or with its electronic equivalent.

If you start with specialized dictionaries, abstracts, and bibliographies, you can rapidly gain both a broad perspective on your subject and a summary of what particular sources contain. This is the purpose of the reference room: it offers sources that review and summarize material for you in shorthand forms. In any case, you should take care not to get bogged down in one author's book-length argument until you've achieved a wider view of how other sources treat your subject.

You should be aware that reference sources use agreed-upon keywords for different subjects. Thus, don't be surprised if the subject headings you enter initially yield nothing. Always check first at the reference desk for the *Library of Congress Subject Headings* to see what headings might be appropriate for your subject. It will tell you, for example, that fraternities and sororities are listed not under "fraternities and sororities" but rather under "Greek letter organizations."

Ask your reference librarian to direct you to the printed and online *indexes*, *bibliographies*, *specialized dictionaries*, and compilations of *abstracts* that are pertinent to your subject or discipline. An index offers a list of titles directing you to scholarly journals; often this list is sufficient to give you a clearer idea of the kinds of topics about which writers in the field are conversing. Here are a few index titles, indicating the range of what's available: *Applied Science and Technology Index*, *Art Index*, *Biography Index*, *Business Periodicals Index*, *Education Index*, *General Science Index*, *Humanities Index*, *Literary Criticism Index*, *New York Times Index*, *Philosopher's Index*, *Religion Index*, *Reader's Guide to Periodical Literature*, and *Social Sciences Index*.

A half-hour spent with a reference librarian can save you a half a day wandering randomly though the stacks.

Compilations of abstracts and annotated bibliographies provide more information—anywhere from a few sentences to a few pages that summarize each source. (See the section on abstracts and how to write them at the end of this chapter.) Here are a few commonly used titles: *Abstracts of English Studies*, *Chemical Abstracts*, *Communication Abstracts*, *Dissertation Abstracts*, *Historical Abstracts*, *MLA (Modern Language Association) International Bibliography*, *Psychological Abstracts*, *Monthly Catalog of United States Government Publications*, *Sociological Abstracts*.

Specialized dictionaries and encyclopedias are sometimes extraordinarily useful in sketching the general terrain for a subject, and they often include bibliographical leads as well. Here are some titles, ranging from the expected to the eccentric: *Dictionary of the History of Ideas*, *Dictionary of Literary Biography*, *Encyclopedia of American History*, *Encyclopedia of Bioethics*, *Encyclopedia of Crime and Justice*, *Encyclopedia of Economics*, *Encyclopedia of Native American Religions*, *Encyclopedia of Philosophy*, *Encyclopedia of Psychology*, *Encyclopedia of Unbelief*, *Encyclopedia of World Art*, *Encyclopedic Dictionary of Mathematics*, *Macmillan Encyclopedia of Computers*, *Encyclopedia of Medical History*, *McGraw Hill Encyclopedia of Science and Technology*, *New Grove Dictionary of Music and Musicians*, *Oxford English Dictionary*.

Most of the indexes just listed also include book reviews. The *Reader's Guide to Periodical Literature* will locate reviews as well as articles in popular—general audience—publications such as *Time* and *Newsweek*. For a broader range of titles, you might also consult *Book Review Index*, *Book Review Digest*, and *Subject Guide to Books in Print*. Indexes organized by discipline are more likely to take you to sources reviewed in academic journals; consult with your reference librarian for the indexes most pertinent to your subject.

Periodicals and journals offer an effective next step in finding sources once you've surveyed your topic in digest form. These are generally more up to date than either reference materials or books. Most library reference rooms have either a booklet that lists all of the periodicals and journals to which the library subscribes or a means of accessing a list of such holdings through the electronic catalogue. There are thousands of specialized journals available. If an index or bibliography refers you to a journal that your library does not hold, the library can usually get it for you (sometimes for a small fee) through a service known as interlibrary loan. Now, many articles and reviews can be downloaded electronically; see the next section entitled "Electronic Research: Finding Quality on the Web."

A FEW RULES OF THUMB FOR GETTING STARTED

We might generalize a rule voiced by the psychology professor on the next page: Start in the present and work backward. Usually the most current materials will include bibliographical citations that can help you identify the most important sources in the past. Along the same lines, you are usually better off starting with journal articles rather than books, because they are more current.

Start in the present and work backward. The most current materials include citations that identify the most important sources in the past.

As a second rule of thumb, the reliability of the source is always an issue, but what's most important is knowing its slant. For example, *Newsweek* can be a useful source if you want evidence about popular understanding of a subject or issue, but in this case, the fact that the material comes from *Newsweek* and thus represents a position aimed at a mainstream, nonacademic audience provides the central reason for citing it. The evidence is *always* qualified by the frame.

The reliability of the source is always an issue, but what's most important is knowing its slant. There is no such thing as neutral information; it's always framed, and so it always has, at least implicity, a point of view.

The matter of deciding what kinds of sources are best suited to your topic and how to discern their point of view is the subject of the following section, written by a reference librarian, on using and evaluating sources via the computer. And let us say here that as a final rule of thumb for doing research economically, a half-hour spent with a reference librarian in the reference collection before you go randomly through the stacks collecting books is always time well spent.

VOICES FROM ACROSS THE CURRICULUM

Tips for Starting Your Research

A useful research technique is to begin with indexes that will take you to specialized periodicals rather than beginning with books. Most scholarly journals have an index in the last issue for each year. Listed alphabetically by author, subject, or title are articles for a given year. Also, you may want to use any number of indexes. Here you look up a key word or phrase (of your choosing), and the index tells you when, what, where, and so forth for the word/phrase. Some of the key indexes are: *Social Science Index, Wall Street Journal Index* (for *WSJ* stories), *New York Times Index* (for *NYT* stories), and the *Public Affairs Information Service.*

A critical part of the bibliographic effort is to find a topic on which there are materials. Most topics can be researched. The key is to choose a flexible keyword/phrase and then try out different versions of it. For example, a bibliography on "women in management" might lead you to look up *women, females, business* (women in), *business* (females in), *gender in the workplace, sexism and the workplace, careers* (of men, of women, in business), *women and CEOs, women in management, affirmative action and women, women in corporations, female accountants,* and so forth. Be imaginative and flexible. A little bit of time with some of the indexes, listed earlier, will provide you with a wealth of sources.

—Frederick Norling, Professor of Business

Use quality psychological references. That is, use references that professional psychologists use and regard highly. *Psychology Today* is not a good reference; *Newsweek* and *Reader's Digest* are worse. And don't even think about the *National Enquirer.* APA journals, such as the *Journal of Abnormal Psychology,* on the other hand, are excellent.

In looking for reference material, be sure to search under several headings. For example, look under *depression, affective disorders,* and *mood disorders.*

Books (e.g., *The Handbook of Affective Disorders*) are often very helpful, especially for giving a general overview of a topic. Books addressing a professional audience are generally preferable to those addressing a general, popular audience.

Finally, references should be reasonably current. In general, the newer, the better. For example, with rare exceptions (classic articles), articles from before 1970 are outdated and so should not be used.

—Alan Tjeltveit, Professor of Psychology

B. ELECTRONIC RESEARCH: FINDING QUALITY ON THE WEB

By Kelly Cannon, Reference Librarian

The Internet has dramatically altered public access to information. But the quality of information has also changed; it is almost as easy to publish on the web as it is to surf it. A general caveat might well be Reader Beware.

Take as an example *Martinlutherking.org* (http://www.martinlutherking.org). This site appears prominently in any web search for information about Martin Luther King, Jr. The website is visually appealing, claiming to include "essays, speeches, sermons, and more." But who created the site? As it turns out, after a little digging (see Tips #1 and #2 later in the chapter), the site is sponsored by Stormfront, Inc. (http://stormfront.org/), an organization out of West Palm Beach, Florida, serving "those courageous men and women fighting to preserve their White Western culture, ideals and freedom of speech." This author is concealed behind the work, a ghost writer of sorts. While the site is at one's fingertips, identifying the author is a challenge, more so than in the world of print publications, where author and publisher are located on the same pages as the title. For those websites with no visible author, no publishing house, no recognized journal title, no peer-review process, and no library selection process (the touchstones of scholarship in the print world), seemingly easy Internet research is now more problematic: the user must discern for him- or herself what is and is not authoritative information.

UNDERSTANDING DOMAIN NAMES

But how is the user to begin evaluating a web document? Fortunately, there are several clues to assist you through the Internet labyrinth. One clue is in the web address itself. For example, the *Internet Movie Database* has http://imdb.com as its web address (also known as URL, or uniform resource locator). One clue lies at the very end of the URL, in what is known as the domain name, in this case the abbreviation ".com." Websites ending in ".com" are commercial, often with the purpose of marketing a product. Sites ending in ".org" generally signal nonprofits, but many have a veiled agenda, whether it is marketing or politics. Like the ".coms," ".org" addresses are sold first-come first-served. (The organization that oversees the many vendors of ".com" and ".org" domain names is The Internet Corporation for Assigned Names and Numbers, or ICANN [http://www.icann.org/].)

On the other hand, ".edu" and ".gov" sites may indicate less bias, as they are ostensibly limited exclusively to educational and government institutions, and they are often the producers of bonafide research. In particular, ".gov" sites contain some of the best information on the Internet. This is in part because the U.S. government is required by an act of Congress to disseminate to the general public a large portion of its research. The U.S. government, floated as it is by tax dollars, provides the high-quality, free websites reminiscent of the precommercial Internet era. This means that government sites offer high-quality data, particularly of a statistical nature. Scholars in the areas of business, law, and the social sciences can benefit tremendously, without subscription fees, from a variety of government databases. Prime examples are the legislative site known as *Thomas* (http://thomas.loc.gov) and data gathered at the website of the Census Bureau (http://www.census.gov).

PRINT COROLLARIES

But a domain name can be misleading; it is simply one clue in the process of evaluation. Another clue, perhaps more significant, is the correlation between a website and the print world. Many websites offer print corollaries, and some have print equivalents. For example, Johns Hopkins University Press now publishes all its journals, known and respected for years by scholars, in both print and electronic formats. Many college and university libraries subscribe to these Johns Hopkins journals electronically, collectively known as *Project Muse* (http://muse.jhu.edu/). In this case, the scholar can assume that the electronic form of the journal undergoes the same editorial rigor as the print publication, because they are identical in content.

WEB CLASSICS

Building a reputation of high quality takes time. But the Internet has been around long enough now that some publications with no pre-web history have caught the attention of scholars who turn to these sites regularly for reliable commentary on a variety of subject areas.

These high-quality sites can best be found by tapping into scholarly web directories such as the *Librarians' Index to the Internet* (http://lii.org/), which work like mini search engines but are managed by humans who sift through the chaff, including in these directories only what they deem to be gems.

The student looking specifically for free, peer-reviewed journals original to the web can visit a highly specific directory called the *Directory of Open Access Journals* (http://www.doaj.org/), listing nothing more or less than several hundred journals in a variety of subject areas. Many libraries have begun to link to these journals to promote their use by students and faculty.

Then there are gems that compare better to highbrow magazines or newspapers such as *The New Yorker*. Two celebrated examples are *Salon.com* (http://salon.com), and *Slate* (http://slate.com), both online literary reviews. Once tapped into, these sites do a good job of recommending other high-quality websites. Scholars are beginning to cite from these web-based publications just as they would from any print publication of long-standing reputation.

ASKING THE RIGHT QUESTIONS

In the end, it is up to the individual user to evaluate each website independently. Here are some critical questions to consider:

Question: Who is the author?

Response: Check the website's home page, probably near the bottom of the page.

Question: Is the author affiliated with any institution?

Response: Check the URL to see who sponsors the page.

Question: What are the author's credentials?

Response: Check an online database like *Academic Search* (http://www.epnet.com) or LexisNexis Academic (http://www.lexis-nexis.com) to see if this person is published in journals or books.

Question: Has the information been reviewed or peer-edited before posting?

Response: Probably not, unless the posting is part of a larger publication; if so, the submission process for publication can be verified at the publication home page.

Question: Is the page part of a larger publication?

Response: Try the various links on the page to see if there is an access point to the home page of the publication. Or try the "backspacing" technique mentioned later in the chapter.

Question: Is the information documented properly?

Response: Check for footnotes or methodology.

Question: Is the information current?

Response: Check the "last update," usually printed at the bottom of the page.

Question: What is the purpose of the page?

Response: Examine content and marginalia.

Question: Does the website suit your purposes?

Response: Review what the purpose of your project is. Review your information needs: primary vs. secondary, academic vs. popular. And always consult with your instructor.

FOR SUBSCRIBERS ONLY

An organized and indexed collection of discreet pieces of information is called a *database*. Two examples of databases are a library's card catalogue and online catalogue. The World Wide web is full of databases, though they are often restricted to subscribers. Subscription fees can be prohibitive, but fortunately for the average researcher, most college and university libraries foot the bill. The names of these databases are now well known, and arguably contain the most thoroughly reviewed (i.e., scholarly) full text available on the web: *Academic Search* from Ebsco (http://www.epnet.com), *Expanded Academic* from Thomson Gale (http://www.galegroup.com/), *Proquest Direct* from ProQuest (http://www.proquest.com), and *Omnifile* from Wilson (http://www.hwwilson.com). Inquire at your library to see if you have access to these databases.

Each of these databases contains its own proprietary search engine, allowing refinement of searches to a degree unmatched by search engines on the Internet at large. Why? For one, these databases are exclusive rather than inclusive, as the Internet is. More is not better in an information age. The fact that information is at your fingertips, and sometimes "in your face," can be a problem. Well-organized databases are shaped and limited by human hands and minds, covering only certain media types or subject areas.

More is not better in an information age.

Secondly, *databases allow searching by subject heading, in addition to keyword searching*. This means that a human has defined the main subject areas of each entry, consequently allowing the user much greater manipulation of the search. For example, if I enter the words "New York City" in a simple keyword search, I will retrieve everything that simply mentions New York City even once; the relevance will vary tremendously. On the other hand, if subject headings have been assigned, I can do a subject search on New York City and find only records that are devoted to my subject. This may sound trivial, but in the age of information overload, precision searching is a precious commodity.

In the age of information overload, precision searching is a precision commodity.

While there is no foolproof way to a perfect database search, here is a point that will save you hours of frustration: consult with the most frequent users of research databases—reference librarians. Ask them (a) which databases they would use for your research topic and (b) how they would construct a search.

BIBLIOGRAPHIC RESEARCH

Up until now, we've only addressed electronic information that is full text. There may come a time when most secondary information needed for research is available online and as full text, but because of copyright and other restrictions, much scholarly information is still available only in print. This almost always implies a slight delay in retrieving the information: where full-text databases and the Internet promise instant gratification, more traditional modes of research necessitate either document delivery (fax or mail) or a visit to the library or other holding institution where a copy of the item can be retrieved. As individual journals begin to publish online (bypassing print altogether), the access to scholarly material may improve, but for now print copies remain the norm.

What has improved tremendously—with few exceptions—is the *indexing* of scholarly journals. Even if the journals themselves are not readily available in an electronic format, the indexing is available electronically. These electronic indexes provide basic bibliographic information and sometimes an abstract (summary) of the article or book chapter. When professors refer to bibliographic research, they probably mean research done with indexes. These indexes are available in any of three formats—print, CD-ROM, or online—depending on the academic institution. Inquire at your library about index availability.

Many academic institutions now subscribe to the following indexes online: *MLA* (literary criticism), *ERIC* (education), *PsycInfo* (psychology), *Historical Abstracts* (non-U.S. history), *Sociological Abstracts* (sociology), *Biological Abstracts* (biology), and a host of others. Note that these indexes are specific to particular subject areas. Their coverage is not broad, but deep and scholarly. *These are the indexes to watch for when seeking the most scholarly information in your area of study.* If a professor asks students to support their papers with scholarly secondary research, these indexes provide that kind of information. While the full text is often not included, the indexing will provide information sufficient to track down the complete article, whether it is in the library or available through interlibrary loan or other document delivery service.

These indexes are a great aid in evaluating the scholarly merit of a publication, as they usually eliminate any reference that isn't considered scholarly by the academy. For example, *MLA* only indexes literary criticism that appears in peer-reviewed journals and academically affiliated books. So, consider the publications that appear in these indexes to have the academic "Good Housekeeping" seal of approval.

TUNING IN TO YOUR ENVIRONMENT

Every university and college is different, each with its own points of access to information. Below are some exercises to help you familiarize yourself with your own scholarly environment.

Exercise #1: Go to your library's reference desk and get a list of all the scholarly journal indexes that are available electronically at your school. Then get a list of all online, full-text databases that are available to you.

Exercise #2: Go to your library's reference desk and get a list of all the journals that the library subscribes to electronically. Then get a list of all journals that are available at your library either in print or electronically in your major area of study.

Exercise #3: Ask the reference librarian about web access in general for your major area of study. What tips can the library give you about doing electronic research at your academic institution? Are there any special databases, web search engines/directories, or indexes that you should consult in your research?

Exercise #4: Try out some or all of the full-text databases available on your campus. Now try the same searches in a scholarly index. What differences do you see in the quality/scope of the information?

Search Tips

Tip #1: Backspacing

"Backspacing" a URL can be an effective way to evaluate a website. It may reveal authorship or institutional affiliation. To do this, place the cursor at the end of the URL and then backspace to the last slash and press Enter. Continue backspacing to each preceding slash, examining each level as you go.

Tip #2: Using WHOIS

WHOIS (http://www.networksolutions.com/en_US/whois/) is an Internet service that allows anyone to find out who's behind a website.

Tip #3: Beware of the ~ in a Web Address

Many educational institutions allow the creation of personal home pages by students and faculty. While the domain name remains ".edu" in these cases, the fact that they are personal means that pretty much anything can be posted, and so cannot assure academic quality.

Tip #4: Phrase Searching

Not finding relevant information? Trying using quotation marks around key phrases in your search string. For example, search in *Google* for this phrase, enclosed in quotation marks: "whose woods these are I think I know."

Tip #5: Title Searching

Still finding irrelevant information? Limit your search to the titles of web documents. A title search is an option in several search engines, among them *Altavista* (advanced search) (http://www.altavista.com) and *Google* (advanced search) (http://www.google.com).

Tip #6: Full Text

The widest selection of previously published full text (newspapers, magazines, journals, book chapters) is available in subscription databases via the web. Inquire at your library to see if you have access to *LexisNexis Academic* (http://www.lexis-nexis.com), *Omnifile* (http://www.hwwilson.com), *Academic Search* (http://www.epnet.com), *ProQuest Direct* (http://www.proquest.com), *Expanded Academic* (http://www.galegroup.com), or other full-text databases.

The leading *free* full-text site is *LookSmart's FindArticles* (http://www.findarticles.com). This database of "hundreds of thousands of articles from more than 300 magazines and journals, dating back to 1998" can be searched by all magazines, magazines within categories, or specific magazine.

For the full text of books, try the *IPL Online Texts* directory (http://www.ipl.org/div/subject/browse/hum60.60.00/), pointing to the major digital text archives.

For more of the best full-text sites on the web, search on the term "full-text" in the *Librarians' Index to the Internet* (http://lii.org).

Tip #7: Archives of Older Published Materials

Full text for newspapers, magazines, and journals published prior to 1990 is difficult to find on the Internet. One subscription site that your library may offer is *JSTOR* (http://www.jstor.org), an archive of scholarly full-text journal articles dating back in some cases into the late 1800s. *LexisNexis Academic* (http://www.lexis-nexis.com), also a subscription service, includes the full text of popular periodicals such as the *New York Times* as far back as 1980.

Two free sites offer the full text of eighteenth- and nineteenth-century periodicals from Great Britain and the U.S. respectively: *Internet Library of Early Journals* (http://www.bodley.ox.ac.uk/ilej/) and *Nineteenth Century in Print* (http://memory.loc.gov/ammem/ndlpcoop/moahtml/snchome.html).

Use interlibrary loan or another document delivery service like *Ingenta* (http://www.ingenta.com) to have a copy of the print version of older titles sent to you. Electronic indexing (no full text) for older materials is readily available, back as early as 1900, sometimes earlier. Inquire at your library.

Tip #8: Best Sites, Free or Subscription, for Quantity and Quality of Scholarly Information Across the Disciplines

Below are a few of the sites most relied upon by academic librarians. For the subscription databases, you will need to inquire at your library for local availability.

A FOOLPROOF RECIPE FOR GREAT RESEARCH—EVERY TIME

First, search at least one of these multidisciplinary subscription databases; check your library's website for availability.

- *Academic Search Elite/Premier* (EBSCOhost) for journals
- *Expanded Academic* (Thomson Gale) for journals
- *Omnifile* (WilsonWeb) for journals
- *Proquest* for journals
- *WorldCat* (OCLC FirstSearch) for books

Second, search subject-specific databases. These too are mostly subscription databases; check your library's website for availability.

- Anthropology: *Anthropological Abstracts*
- Art: *Art Abstracts*
- Biology: *Biological Abstracts, Biosis*
- Business: *ABI Inform, Business Source Elite/Premier, Business & Company Resource Center, Dow Jones, LexisNexis*
- Chemistry: *SciFinder Scholar, Science Citation Index Expanded (ISI)*
- Communication: *Communication and Mass Media, Communication Abstracts*
- Computer Science: *INSPEC*
- Economics: *EconLit*
- Education: *ERIC* (free)
- Film Studies: *MLA*
- Geography/Geology: *GeoBase*
- History: *America History and Life, Historical Abstracts*
- Language, Literature: *MLA, LION (Literature Online)*
- Law: *LexisNexis, WestLaw*
- Mathematics: *MathSciNet*
- Medicine: *PubMed* (free)
- Music: *RILM*
- Philosophy: *Philosopher's Index*
- Physics: *INSPEC*
- Political Science: *PAIS*
- Psychology: *PsycInfo*
- Religion: *ATLA Religion*
- Sociology: *Sociological Abstracts*

Third, visit these not-to-be-missed free websites and meta-sites:

- Anthropology: *Anthropological Index Online* http://aio.anthropology.org.uk/cgi-bin/uncgi/search_bib_ai/anthind, *Anthropology Resources on the Internet* http://www.archeodroit.net/anthro/
- Art: *ArtCyclopedia* http://www.artcyclopedia.com/
- Biology: *Biology Browser* http://www.biologybrowser.org/, *Agricola* http://agricola.nal.usda.gov/
- Business: *EDGAR* http://www.sec.gov/edgar.shtml, *Hoover's Online* http://hoovers.com/free
- Chemistry: *Chemdex.org* http://www.chemdex.org/, *World of Chemistry* http://scienceworld.wolfram.com/chemistry/
- Communication: *ACA Communication Studies Center* http://www.americancomm.org/
- Computer Science: *CompInfo* http://www.compinfo-center.com/
- Economics: *Social Science Information Gateway (SOSIG)* http://sosig.esrc.bris.ac.uk/
- Education: *Educator's Reference Desk* http://eduref.org/
- Film Studies: *Film Studies Resources* http://www.lib.berkeley.edu/MRC/filmstudies/index.html
- Geography/Geology: *GeoSource* http://www.library.uu.nl/geosource/
- History: *American Memory* http://memory.loc.gov/ammem/amhome.html

- Language, Literature: *Online Literary Criticism Collection* http://www.ipl.org/div/litcrit/
- Law: *FindLaw* http://www.findlaw.com/
- Mathematics: Mathworld http://www.mathworld.wolfram.com/, *MathSearch* http://www.maths.usyd.edu.au:8000/MathSearch.html
- Medicine: *BioMed Central* http://www.biomedcentral.com/
- Music: *Internet Resources for Music Scholars* http://hcl.harvard.edu/loebmusic/online-ir-intro.html
- Philosophy: *Stanford Encyclopedia of Philosophy* http://plato.stanford.edu/contents.html
- Physics: *World of Physics* http://scienceworld.wolfram.com/physics/
- Political Science: *Social Science Information Gateway (SOSIG)* http://sosig.esrc.bris.ac.uk/, THOMAS http://thomas.loc.gov/
- Psychology: *Social Science Information Gateway (SOSIG)* http://sosig.esrc.bris.ac.uk/
- Religion: *Religion Online* http://www.religion-online.org/, *Hartford Institute for Religion Research* http://www.hartfordinstitute.org/
- Sociology: *Social Science Information Gateway (SOSIG)* http://sosig.esrc.bris.ac.uk/

CITATION GUIDES ON THE WEB

The two most common styles of documentation are those established by the Modern Language Association (MLA) and the American Psychological Association (APA). These associations each provide examples of basic citations of electronic and print resources at their websites; you will find the MLA at http://www.mla.org/publications/style and APA at http://www.apastyle.org.

Also, many writing centers have made available citation guides at their websites. One recommended site is by the writing center of Purdue University (http://owl.english.purdue.edu/handouts/research/index.html).

For citation examples not given at these websites, it is advisable to consult the associations' printed manuals—*Publication Manual of the American Psychological Association* or the *MLA Handbook for Writers of Research Papers*—in their most recent editions.

A LIBRARIAN'S GUIDELINES TO SUCCESSFUL RESEARCH

1. Consult with your professor to determine what types of resources will be most appropriate for the project at hand.
2. Consider whether you need scholarly or popular sources or a mixture of both.
3. Consider whether you need primary or secondary works or a mixture of both.
4. With the assistance of a reference librarian, find which search tools will direct you to the most relevant resources.
5. Range widely. Try a new search tool with each new research project.
6. Begin early, in case interlibrary loan is needed to obtain research owned only by other libraries.
7. Examine bibliographies at the end of the articles and books you've already found. Remember that one quality source can, in its bibliography, point to many other resources.

C. PLAGIARISM AND THE LOGIC OF CITATION

It is impossible to discuss the rationale for citing sources without reference to plagiarism, even though the primary reason for including citations is not to prove that you haven't cheated. It's essential that you give credit where it's due as a courtesy to your readers. Along with educating readers about who has said what, citations enable them to find out more about a given position and to pursue other discussions on the subject. Nonetheless, plagiarism is an important issue: academic integrity matters. And because the stakes are very high if you are caught plagiarizing, we think it necessary to pause in order to discuss how to avoid it.

In recent years there has been a significant rise in the number of plagiarism cases nationally. Many commentators blame the Internet, with its easily accessible, easy to cut-and-paste information, for increasing the likelihood of plagiarism. Others cite a lack of clarity about what plagiarism is and why it is a serious problem. So, let's start by clarifying.

Most people have some idea of what plagiarism is. You already know that it's against the rules to buy a paper from an Internet "paper mill" or to download others' words verbatim and hand them in as your own thinking. And you probably know that even if you change a few words and rearrange the sentence structure, you still need to acknowledge the source. By way of formal definition, plagiarism (as one handbook puts it) gives "the impression that you have written or thought something that you have in fact borrowed from someone else" (Joseph Gibaldi, *MLA Handbook for Writers of Research Papers*, Fifth edition. New York: MLA, 1999, p. 30). It is a form of theft and fraud. Borrowing from someone else, by the way, also includes taking and not acknowledging words and ideas from your friends or your parents. Put another way, any assignment with your name on it signifies that you are the author—that the words and ideas are yours—with any exceptions indicated by source citations and, if you're quoting, by quotation marks.

Knowing what plagiarism is, however, doesn't guarantee that you'll know how to avoid it. Is it okay, for example, to cobble together a series of summaries and paraphrases in a paragraph, provided you include the authors in a bibliography at the end of the paper? Or how about if you insert a single footnote at the end of the paragraph? The answer is that both are still plagiarism, because your reader can't tell where your thinking starts and others' thinking stops. As a basic rule of thumb, "*Readers must be able to tell as they are reading your paper exactly what information came from which source and what information is your contribution to the paper*" (Christine A. Hult, *Researching and Writing Across the Curriculum*. Boston: Allyn and Bacon, 1996, p. 203). More on this later.

WHY DOES PLAGIARISM MATTER?

A recent survey indicated that 53 percent of Who's Who High Schoolers thought that plagiarism was no big deal (Sally Cole and Elizabeth Kiss, "What Can We Do About Student Cheating?" *About Campus*, May–June 2000, p. 6). So why should institutions of higher learning care about it? Here are two great reasons:

- Plagiarism poisons the environment. Students who don't cheat get alienated by students who do and get away with it, and faculty can become distrustful of students and even disillusioned about teaching when constantly driven to track down students' sources. It's a lot easier, by the way, than most students think for faculty to recognize language and ideas that are not the student's own. And now there are all those search engines provided by firms like Turnitin.com that have been generated in response to the Internet paper-mill boom. Who wants another cold war?

- Plagiarism defeats the purpose of going to college, which is learning how to think. You can't learn to think by just copying others' ideas; you need to learn to trust your own intelligence. Students' panic about deadlines and their misunderstandings about assignments sometimes spur plagiarism. It's a good bet that your professors would much rather take requests for help and give extra time on assignments than have to go through the anguish of confronting students about plagiarized work.

So, plagiarism gets in the way of trust, fairness, intellectual development, and, ultimately, the attitude toward learning that sets the tone for a college or university community.

FREQUENTLY ASKED QUESTIONS (FAQS) ABOUT PLAGIARISM

Is it still plagiarism if I didn't intentionally copy someone else's work and present it as my own; that is, if I plagiarized it by accident?
Yes, it is still plagiarism. Colleges and universities put the burden of responsibility on students for knowing what plagiarism is and then making the effort necessary to avoid it. Leaving out the quotation marks around someone else's words or omitting the attribution after a summary of someone else's theory may be just a mistake—a matter of inadequate documentation—but faculty can only judge what you turn in to them, not what you intended.

If I include a list of works consulted at the end of my paper, doesn't that cover it?
No. A works-cited list (bibliography) tells your readers what you read but leaves them in the dark about how and where this material has been used in your paper. Putting one or more references at the end of a paragraph containing source material is a version of the same problem. The solution is to cite the source at the point that you quote or paraphrase or summarize it. To be even clearer about what comes from where, also use what are called in-text attributions. See the next FAQ on these.

What is the best way to help my readers distinguish between what my sources are saying and what I'm saying?
Be overt. Tell your readers in the text of your paper, not just in citations, when you are drawing on someone else's words, ideas, or information. Do this with phrases like "According to X . . ." or "As noted in X . . ."—so-called in-text attributions.

Be overt. Tell your readers in the text of your paper, not just in citations, when you are drawing on someone else's words, ideas, or information.

Are there some kinds of information that I do not need to document?
Yes. Common knowledge and facts you can find in almost any encyclopedia or basic reference text generally don't need to be documented (that is, John F. Kennedy became president of the United States in 1960). This distinction can get a little tricky because it isn't always obvious what is and is not common knowledge. Often, you need to spend some time in a discipline before you discover what others take to be known to all. When in doubt, cite the source.

When in doubt, cite the source.

If I put the information from my sources into my own words, do I still need to include citations?
Yes. Sorry, but rewording someone else's idea doesn't make it your idea. Paraphrasing is a useful activity because it helps you to better understand what you are reading, but paraphrases and summaries have to be documented and carefully distinguished from ideas and information you are representing as your own.

If I don't actually know anything about the subject, is it okay to hand in a paper that is taken entirely from various sources?
It's okay if (1) you document the borrowings and (2) the assignment called for summary. Properly documented summarizing is better than plagiarizing, but most assignments call for something more. Often comparing and contrasting your sources will begin to give you ideas, so that you can have something to contribute. If you're really stumped, go see the professor.

You will also reduce the risk of plagiarism if you consult sources after—not before—you have done some preliminary thinking on the subject. If you have become somewhat invested in your own thoughts on the matter, you will be able to use the sources in a more active way, in effect, making them part of a dialogue.

Is it plagiarism if I include things in my paper that I thought of with another student or a member of my family?
Most academic behavior codes, under the category called "collusion," allow for students' cooperative efforts only with the explicit consent of the instructor. The same general rule goes for plagiarizing yourself—that is, for submitting the same paper in more than one class. If you have questions about what constitutes collusion in a particular class, be sure to ask your professor.

What about looking at secondary sources when my professor hasn't asked me to? Is this a form of cheating?
It can be a form of cheating if the intent of the assignment was to get you to develop a particular kind of thinking skill. In this case, looking at others' ideas may actually retard your learning process and leave you feeling that you couldn't possibly learn to arrive at ideas on your own.

Professors usually look favorably on students who are willing to take the time to do extra reading on a subject, but it is essential that, even in class discussion, you make it clear that you have consulted outside sources. To conceal that fact is to present others' ideas as your own. Even in class discussion, if you bring up an idea you picked up on the Internet, be sure to say so explicitly.

HOW TO CITE SOURCES

In general, you will be expected to follow a formalized style of documentation. The two most common are the MLA style, which uses the author-work format, and the APA style, which uses the author-date format. Most writing handbooks (compilations of the rules of grammar and punctuation, available at most bookstores) contain detailed accounts of documentation styles. In addition, you can access various websites that will provide most (though not all) of this information. (See "Citations Guides on the Web" earlier in this chapter.)

The various styles differ in the specific ways that they organize the bibliographical information, but all of them share the following characteristics:

1. They place an extended citation for each source, including the author, the title, the date, and the place of publication, at the end of the paper. These end-of-text citations are organized in a list, usually alphabetically.
2. They insert an abbreviated citation within the text, located within parentheses directly following every use of the source. Usually this in-text citation consists of the author's name and either the page (in MLA) or date (in APA). In-text citations indicate in shorthand form in the body of your paper the source you are using and direct your readers to the complete citation located in a list of references at the end of the paper or report.
3. They distinguish among different kinds of sources—providing slightly differing formulas for citing books, articles, encyclopedias, government documents, interviews, and so forth.
4. They have particular formats for citing electronic sources of various kinds, such as CD-ROMs, the Internet, and online journals and databases. These citations replace the publication information typically provided for text references to printed material with what is called an *availability statement*, which provides the method of accessing the source. This statement should provide the information sufficient to retrieve the source.

You have probably already discovered that some professors are more concerned than others that students obey the particulars of a given documentation style. Virtually all faculty across the curriculum agree, however, that *the most important rule for writers to follow in documenting sources is formal consistency*. That is, all of your in-text citations should follow the same abbreviated format, and all of your end-of-text citations should follow the same extended format.

Once you begin doing most of your writing in a particular discipline, you may want to purchase or access on the Internet the more detailed style guide adhered to by that discipline. Because documentation styles differ not only from discipline to discipline but also even from journal to journal within a discipline, you should consult your professor about which documentation format he or she wishes you to use in a given course.

Here are a few basic examples of in-text and end-of-text citations in both MLA and APA form, followed by a brief discussion of the rules that apply.

1. **Single author, MLA style**

In-text citation: The influence of Seamus Heaney on younger poets in Northern Ireland has been widely acknowledged, but Patrick Kavanagh's "plain-speaking, pastoral" influence on him is "less recognized" (Smith 74).

"(Smith 74)" indicates the author's last name and the page number on which the cited passage appears. If the author's name had been mentioned in the sentence—had the sentence begun "According to Smith"—you would include only the page number in the citation. Note that there is no abbreviation for "page," that there is no intervening punctuation between name and page, and that the parentheses precede the period or other punctuation. If the sentence ends with a direct quotation, the parentheses come after the quotation marks but still before the closing period. Also note that no punctuation occurs between the last word of the quotation ("recognized") and the closing quotation mark.

End-of-text book citation: Douglas, Ann. *Terrible Honesty: Mongrel Manhattan in the 1920s*. New York: Farrar, Straus, and Giroux, 1995.

End-of-text article citation: Cressy, David. "Foucault, Stone, Shakespeare and Social History." *English Literary Renaissance* 21 (1991): 121–33.

MLA style stipulates an alphabetical list of references (by author's last name, which keys the reference to the in-text citation). This list is located at the end of the paper on a separate page and entitled "Works Cited."

Each entry in the "Works Cited" list is divided into three parts: author, title, and publication data. Each of these parts is separated by a period from the others. Titles of book-length works are italicized, unless your instructor prefers underlining. (Underlining is a means of indicating italics.) Journal citations differ slightly: article names go inside quotations, no punctuation follows the titles of journals, and a colon precedes the page numbers.

2. **Single author, APA style**

In-text citation: Studies of students' changing attitudes towards the small colleges that they attend suggest that their loyalty to the institution declines steadily over a four-year period, whereas their loyalty to individual professors or departments increases "markedly, by as much as twenty-five percent over the last two years" (Brown, 1994, p. 41).

For both books and articles, include the author's last name, followed by a comma, and then the date of publication. If you are quoting or referring to a specific passage, include the page number as well, separated from the date by a comma and the abbreviation "p." (or "pp.") followed by a space. If the author's name has been mentioned in the sentence, include only the date in the parentheses immediately following the author's name.

In-text citation: Brown (1992) documents the decline in students' institutional loyalty.
End-of-text book citation: Tannen, D. (1991). *You just don't understand: Women and men in conversation.* New York: Ballantine Books.
End-of-text article citation: Baumeister, R. (1987). How the self became a problem: A psychological review of historical research. *Journal of Personality and Psychology, 52,* 163–176.

APA style requires an alphabetical list of references (by author's last name, which keys the reference to the in-text citation). This list is located at the end of the paper on a separate page and entitled "References." Regarding manuscript form, the first line of each reference is not indented, but all subsequent lines are indented three spaces.

In alphabetizing the references list, place entries for a single author before entries that he or she has co-authored, and arrange multiple entries by a single author by beginning with the earliest work. If there are two or more works by the same author in the same year, designate the second with an "a," the third a "b," and so forth, directly after the year. For all subsequent entries by an author after the first, substitute three hyphens followed by a period [---.] for his or her name. For articles by two or more authors, use commas to connect the authors, and precede the last one with a comma and an ampersand [&].

The APA style divides individual entries into the following parts: author (using initials only for first and middle names), year of publication (in parentheses), title, and publication data. Each part is separated by a period from the others. Note that only the first letter of the title and subtitle of books is capitalized (although proper nouns would be capitalized as necessary).

Journal citations differ from those for books in a number of small ways. The title of a journal article is neither italicized (nor underlined) nor enclosed in quotation marks, and only the first word in the title and subtitle is capitalized. The name of the journal is italicized (or underlined), however, and the first word and all significant words are capitalized. Also, notice that the volume number (which is separated by a comma from the title of the journal) is italicized (or underlined) to distinguish it from the page reference. Page numbers for the entire article are included, with no "p." or "pp.," and are separated by a comma from the preceding volume number. If the journal does not use volume numbers, then "p." or "pp." is included.

HOW TO INTEGRATE QUOTATIONS INTO YOUR PAPER

An enormous number of writers lose authority and readability because they have never learned how to correctly integrate quotations into their own writing. The following guidelines should help.

1. **Acknowledge sources in your text, not just in citations.** *When you incorporate material from a source, attribute it to the source explicitly in your text—not just in a citation.* In other words, when you introduce the material, *frame* it with a phrase such as "according to Marsh" or "as Cartelli argues."

Although it is not required, you are usually much better off making the attribution overtly, even if you have also cited the source within parentheses or with a footnote at the end of the last sentence quoted, paraphrased, or summarized. If a passage does not contain an attribution, your readers will not know that it comes from a source until they reach the citation at the end. Attributing up-front clearly distinguishes what one source says from what another says and, perhaps more important, what your sources say from what you say. Useful verbs for introducing attributions include the following: notes, observes, argues, comments, writes, says, reports, suggests, and claims. Generally speaking, by the way, you should cite the author by last name only—as "Cartelli," not as "Thomas Cartelli" or "Mr. Cartelli."

2. **Splice quotations onto your own words.** *Always attach quotations to some of your own language; don't let them sit in your text as independent sentences with quotation marks around them.* You can normally satisfy this rule with an attributive phrase—commonly known as a tag phrase—that introduces the quotation.

Always attach quotations to some of your own language; don't let them sit in your text as independent sentences with quotation marks around them.

> According to Paul McCartney, "All you need is love."

Note that the tag phrase takes a comma before the quote.

Alternatively you can splice quotations into your text with a setup: a statement followed by a colon.

> Patrick Henry's famous phrase is one of the first that American schoolchildren memorize: "Give me liberty, or give me death."

The colon, you should notice, usually comes at the end of an independent clause (that is, a subject plus verb that can stand alone), at the spot where a period normally goes. It would be incorrect to write "Patrick Henry is known for: 'Give me liberty, or give me death.'"

The rationale for this guideline is essentially the same as that for the previous one: if you are going to move to quotation, you first need to identify its author so that your readers will be able to put it in context quickly.

Spliced quotations frequently create problems in grammar or punctuation for writers. Whether you include an entire sentence (or passage) of quotation or just a few phrases, you need to take care to integrate them into the grammar of your own sentence.

One of the most common mistaken assumptions is that a comma should always precede a quotation, as in "A spokesperson for the public defender's office demanded, 'an immediate response from the mayor.'" The sentence structure does not call for any punctuation after "demanded."

3. **Cite sources after quotations.** *Locate citations in parentheses after the quotation and before the final period.* The information about the source appears at the end of the sentence, with the final period following the closing parenthesis.

> A recent article on the best selling albums in America claimed that "Ever since Elvis, it has been pop music's job to challenge the mores of the older generation" (Hornby 168).

Note that there is normally *no punctuation* at the end of the quotation itself, either before or after the closing quotation mark. A quotation that ends either in a question mark or an exclamation mark is an exception to this rule, because the sign is an integral part of the quotation's meaning.

> As Hamlet says to Rosencrantz and Guildenstern, "And yet to me what is this quintessence of dust?" (2.2.304-05).

See the section entitled "How to Cite Sources" earlier in this chapter for the appropriate formats for in-text citations.

4. **Use ellipses to shorten quotations.** *Add ellipsis points to indicate that you have omitted some of the language from within the quotation.* Form ellipses by entering three dots (periods) with spaces in between them, or use four dots to indicate that the deletion continues to the end of the sentence (the last dot becomes the period). Suppose you wanted to shorten the following quotation from a recent article about Radiohead by Alex Ross:

> The album "OK Computer," with titles like "Paranoid Android," "Karma Police," and "Climbing Up the Walls," pictured the onslaught of the information age and a young person's panicky embrace of it (Ross 85).

Using ellipses, you could emphasize the source's claim by omitting the song titles from the middle of the sentence:

> The album "OK Computer" . . . pictured the onslaught of the information age and a young person's panicky embrace of it (Ross 85).

In most cases, the gap between quoted passages should be short, and in any case, you should be careful to preserve the sense of the original. The standard joke about ellipses is apposite here: A reviewer writes that a film "will delight no one and appeal to the intelligence of invertebrates only, but not average viewers." An unethical advertiser cobbles together pieces of the review to say that the film "will delight . . . and appeal to the intelligence of . . . viewers."

5. **Use square brackets to alter or add information within a quotation.** Sometimes it is necessary to change the wording slightly inside a quotation in order to maintain fluency. Square brackets indicate that you are altering the original quotation. Brackets are also used when you insert explanatory information, such as a definition or example, within a quotation. Here are a few examples that alter the original quotations cited above.

> According to one music critic, the cultural relevance of Radiohead is evident in "the album 'OK Computer' . . . [which] pictured the onslaught of the information age and a young person's panicky embrace of it" (Ross 85).
>
> Popular music has always "[challenged] the mores of the older generation," according to Nick Hornby (168).

Note that both examples respect the original sense of the quotation; they have changed the wording only to integrate the quotations gracefully within the writer's own sentence structure.

D. HOW TO PREPARE AN ABSTRACT

There is one more skill essential to research-based writing that we need to discuss: how to prepare an abstract. The aim of the nonevaluative summary of a source known as an abstract is to represent a source's arguments as fairly and accurately as possible, not to critique them. Learning how to compose an abstract according to the conventions of a given discipline is a necessary skill for academic researched writing. Because abstracts differ in format and length among disciplines, you should sample some in the reference section of your library or via the Internet to provide you with models to imitate. Some abstracts, such as those in *Dissertation Abstracts*, are very brief—less than 250 words. Others may run as long as two pages.

Despite disciplinary differences, abstracts by and large follow a generalizable format. The abstract should begin with a clear and specific explanation of the work's governing thesis (or argument). In this opening paragraph, you should also define the work's purpose, and possibly include established positions that it tries to refine, qualify, or argue against. What kind of critical approach does it adopt? What are its aims? On what assumptions does it rest? Why did the author feel it necessary to write the work—that is, what does he or she believe the work offers that other sources don't? What shortcomings or misrepresentations in other criticism does the work seek to correct?

You won't be able to produce detailed answers to all of these questions in your opening paragraph, but in trying to answer some of them in your note taking and drafting, you should find it easier to arrive at the kind of concise, substantive, and focused overview that the first paragraph of your abstract should provide. Also, be careful not to settle for bland, all-purpose generalities in this opening paragraph. And if you quote there, keep the selections short, and remember that quotations don't speak for themselves.

In sum, your aim in the first paragraph is to define the source's particular angle of vision and articulate its main point or points, including the definition of key terms used in its title or elsewhere in its argument.

Once you've set up this overview of the source's central position(s), you should devote a paragraph or so to the source's *organization* (how it divides its subject into parts) and its *method* (how it goes about substantiating its argument). What kind of secondary material does the source use? That is, how do its own bibliographic citations cue you to its school of thought, its point of view, its research traditions?

Your concluding paragraph should briefly recount some of the source's conclusions (as related to, but not necessarily the same as, its thesis). In what way does it go about culminating its argument? What kind of significance does it claim for its position? What final qualifications does it raise?

Here, as a model, is a good example of an abstract:

Abstract of "William Carlos Williams," an essay

by Christopher MacGowan

in *The Columbia History of American Poetry,*

pp. 395–418, Columbia University Press, 1993.

MacGowan's is a chronologically organized account of Williams' poetic career and of his relation to both modernism as an international movement and modernism as it affected the development of poetry in America. MacGowan is at some pains both to differentiate Williams from some features of modernism (such as the tendency of American writers to write as well as live away from their own cultural roots) and to link Williams to modernism. MacGowan argues, for example, that an essential feature of Williams's commitment as a poet was to "the local—to the clear presentation of what was under his nose and in front of his eyes" (385).

But he also takes care to remind us that Williams was in no way narrowly provincial, having studied in Europe as a young man (at Leipzig), having had a Spanish mother and an English father, having become friendly with the poets Ezra Pound and H. D. while getting his medical degree at the University of Pennsylvania, and having continued to meet important figures in the literary and art worlds by making frequent visits to New York and by traveling on more than one occasion to Europe (where Pound introduced him to W. B. Yeats, among others). Williams corresponded with Marianne Moore, he continued to write to Pound and to show Pound some of his work, and he wrote critical essays on the works of other modernists. MacGowan reminds us that Williams also translated Spanish works (ballads) and so was not out of contact with European influences.

Williams had a long publishing career—beginning in 1909 with a self-published volume called *Poems* and ending more than fifty years later with *Pictures from Brueghel* in 1962. What MacGowan emphasizes about this career is not only the consistently high quality of work, but also its great influence on other artists (he names those who actually corresponded with Williams and visited with him, including Charles Olson, Robert Creeley, Robert Lowell, Allen Ginsberg, and Denise Levertov). MacGowan observes that Williams defined himself "against" T. S. Eliot—the more rewarded and internationally recognized of the two poets, especially during their lifetimes—searching for "alternatives to the prevailing mode of a complex, highly allusive poetics," which Williams saw as Eliot's legacy (395). MacGowan depicts Williams as setting himself "against the international school of Eliot and Pound—Americans he felt wrote about rootlessness and searched an alien past because of their failure to write about and live within their own culture" (397).

ASSIGNMENT: A Research Sequence

The traditional sequence of steps for building a research paper—or for any writing that relies on secondary materials—is summary, comparative analysis, and synthesis. The following sequence of four exercises addresses the first two steps as discrete activities. (You might, of course, choose to do only some of these exercises.)

1. *Compose a relatively informal prospectus,* in which you formulate your initial thinking on a subject before you do more research. Include what you already know about the topic, especially what you find interesting, particularly significant, or strange. This exercise will help to deter you from being overwhelmed by and absorbed into the sources you will later encounter.
2. *Conduct a "what's going on in the field" search, and create a preliminary list of sources.* This exercise is ideal for helping you to find a topic or, if you already have one, to narrow it. The kinds of bibliographic materials you consult for this portion of the research project will depend on the discipline within which you are writing. Whatever the discipline, start in the reference room of your library with specialized indexes (such as the *Social Sciences Index* or the *New York Times Index*), book review indexes, specialized encyclopedias and dictionaries, and bibliographies (print version or CD-ROM) that will give you an overview of your subject or topic. If you have access to databases through your school or library, you should also search them. (See the section in this chapter entitled "Electronic Research: Finding Quality on the Web.")

   The "what's going on in the field" search has two aims:

   - To survey materials in order to identify trends—the kinds of issues and questions that others in the field are talking about (and, thus, find important)
   - To compile a bibliography that includes a range of titles that interest you, that could be relevant to your prospective topic, and that seem to you representative of research trends associated with your subject (or topic)

   You will not be committed at this point to pursuing all of these sources but rather to reporting what is being talked about. You might also compose a list of keywords (such as Library of Congress headings) that you have used in conducting your search. If you try this exercise, you will be surprised how much value there is in exploring indexes *just for titles,* to see the kinds of topics people are currently conversing about. And you will almost surely discover how *narrowly* focused most research is (which will get you away from global questions).

   Append to your list of sources (a very preliminary bibliography) a few paragraphs of informal discussion of how the information you have encountered (the titles, summaries, abstracts, etc.) has affected your thinking and plans for your paper. These paragraphs might respond to the following questions:

   a. In what ways has your "what's going on in the field" search led you to narrow or shift direction in or focus your thinking about your subject?

b. How might you use one or more of these sources in your paper?

c. What has this phase of your research suggested you might need to look for next?

3. *Write an abstract of an article (or book chapter)* from your "what's going on" exercise that you think you might use in your final paper. Use the procedure offered in the preceding section, "How to Prepare an Abstract." Aim for two pages in length. If other members of your class are working on the same or similar subjects, it is often extremely useful for everyone to share copies of their abstracts. Remember that your primary concern should lie with representing the argument and point of view of the source as fairly and accurately as possible.

   Append to the end of the abstract a paragraph or two that addresses the question, "How has this exercise affected your thinking about your topic?" Objectifying your own research process in this way will help to move you away from the cut-and-paste–provide-only-the-transitions mode of writing research papers.

4. *Write a comparative summary of two reviews of a single source.* Most writers, before they invest the significant time and energy required to study a book-length source, take the much smaller amount of time and energy required to find out more about the book. Although you should always include in your final paper your own analytical summary of books you consult on your topic, it's extremely useful also to find out what experts in the field have to say about the source.

   Select from your "what's going on" list one book-length source that you've discovered is vital to your subject or topic. As a general rule, if a number of your indexes, bibliographies, and so forth, refer you to the same book, it's a good bet that this source merits consulting.

   Locate two book reviews on the book, and write a summary that compares the two reviews. Ideally, you should locate two reviews that diverge in their points of view or in what they choose to emphasize. Depending on the length and complexity of the reviews, your comparative summary should require two or three pages.

   In most cases, you will find that reviews are less neutral in their points of view than are abstracts, but they always do more than simply judge. A good review, like a good abstract, should communicate the essential ideas contained in the source. It is the reviewer's aim also to locate the source in some larger context, by, for example, comparing it to other works on the same subject and to the research tradition the book seeks to extend, modify, and so forth. Thus, your summary should try to encompass how the book contributes to the ongoing conversation on a given topic in the field.

   Append to your comparative summary a paragraph or two answering the question "How has this exercise affected your thinking about your topic?"

   Obviously, you could choose to do a comparative summary of two articles, two book chapters, and so forth, rather than of two book reviews. But in any event, if you use books in your research, you should always find a means of determining how these books are received in the relevant critical community.

The next step, if you were writing a research paper, would involve the task known as *synthesis*, in which you essentially write a comparative discussion that includes more than two sources. Many research papers start with an opening paragraph that synthesizes prevailing, perhaps competing, interpretations of the topic being addressed. Few good research papers consist only of such synthesis, however. Instead, writers use synthesis to frame their ideas and to provide perspective on their own arguments; the synthesis provides a platform or foundation for their own subsequent analysis.

It is probably worth adding that bad research papers fail to use synthesis as a point of departure. Instead, they line up their sources and agree or disagree with them. To inoculate you against this unfortunate reflex, review the sections entitled "Six Strategies for Analyzing Sources" (especially "Strategy 4: Find Your Own Role in the Conversation") and "Strategies for Writing and Revising Research Papers" in Chapter 12. ◗

GUIDELINES FOR FINDING AND CITING SOURCES

1. Citing sources isn't just about acknowledging intellectual or informational debts; it's also a courtesy to your readers, directing them how to find out more about the subjected cited.
2. Before you settle in with one author's book-length argument, use indexes and bibliographies and other resources to achieve a broader view.
3. Given that the accessibility of Internet research had made it more difficult to distinguish reliable and authoritative information from fraudulent initiations, domain named ending in ".edu" and ".gov" usually offer more reliable choices than the standard ".com."
4. When professors direct you to do bibliographic research, they usually are referring to research done with indexes; these are available in print, online, and CD-ROM formats.
5. In evaluating a website about which you don't know much, try "backspacing" a URL to trace back to its authorship or institutional affiliation. Place the cursor at the end of the URL, backspace to the last slash, and press enter.
6. Avoid sacrificing your authority by incorrectly splicing quotation into your own discussions. For example, always attach a quotation to some of your own language; never let it stand as its own sentence in your text. Attribution — "According to Dickson" — before the quote fulfills this function nicely.
7. One of the best ways of getting to know an important source during the research process is to compose an abstract of it, from 250 words to two pages. A good abstract aims to summarize the governing argument, organization and method as fairly and accurately as possible.

CHAPTER 14

Nine Basic Writing Errors and How to Fix Them

Quick Take

This chapter appears at the end of the book not because grammar is unimportant, but because the end of the book is a convenient place for you to consult when you have questions about correctness and the so-called rules of writing.

There is more to thinking about grammar than the quest for error-free writing, as Chapter 11 on sentence style demonstrates, with its emphasis on how to analyze writers' syntactical choices and how to think about the relationship between a writer's style and his or her characteristic ways of thinking. Studying the nine basic writing errors one at a time, whether in a class or on your own, will enable you to find your way around in a sentence more easily, and thus, to build better sentences yourself.

The first part of this chapter, "Why Correctness Matters," makes the case for learning to recognize a pattern of error in your drafts and learning to prioritize the most serious problems, creating a hierarchy of error, rather than treating (and worrying about) all errors equally and all at the same time. Achieving grammatical correctness is a matter of both knowledge—how to recognize and avoid errors—and timing: when to focus on possible errors.

Thereafter, the chapter offers a quick-hit guide to punctuation—the five basic signs covered in two pages—followed by discussion of the nine most important grammar errors to avoid:

- **Sentence fragments**
- **Comma splices and fused (run-on) sentences**
- **Errors in subject–verb agreement**
- **Shifts in sentence structure (faulty predication)**
- **Errors in pronoun reference**
- **Misplaced modifiers and dangling participles**
- **Errors in using possessive apostrophes**
- **Comma errors**
- **Spelling/diction errors that interfere with meaning**

For each of these, the chapter offers a definition with examples, and then talks you through how to fix it—with a little "test yourself" section at the end.

As the chapter nears its end, you will find a brief "Glossary of Grammatical Terms" (four pages long) that defines and illustrates many of the key terms we have used earlier in the chapter and throughout the book. Do you know the difference between a clause and a phrase? It's a useful distinction to know when you're building sentences to last.

The chapter concludes with a grammar and style quiz, followed by chapter review guidelines and an answer key.

A. WHY CORRECTNESS MATTERS

This chapter addresses the issue of grammatical correctness and offers ways of recognizing and fixing (or avoiding) the most important errors. The first guideline in editing for correctness is to *wait* to do it until you have arrived at a reasonably complete conceptual draft. We have delayed until the end of the book our consideration of technical revisions precisely because if you get too focused on producing polished copy right up front, you may never explore the subject enough to learn how to have ideas about it. In other words, it doesn't make sense for you to let your worries about proper form or persuasive phrasing prematurely distract you from the more important matter of having something substantial to polish in the first place. Writers need a stage in which they are allowed to make mistakes and use writing to help them discover what they want to say. But at the appropriate time—the later stages of the writing process—editing for correctness becomes very important.

When a paper obeys the rules of grammar, punctuation, and spelling, it has achieved *correctness*. Unlike editing for style, which involves you in making choices between more and less effective ways of phrasing, editing for correctness locates you in the domain of right or wrong. As you will see, there are usually a number of ways to correct an error, so you are still concerned with making choices, but leaving the error uncorrected is not really a viable option.

Correctness matters deeply because your prose may be unreadable without it. If your prose is ungrammatical, not only will you risk incoherence (in which case your readers will not be able to follow what you are saying) but also you will inadvertently invite readers to dismiss you. Is it fair of readers to reject your ideas because of the way you've phrased them? Perhaps not, but the fact is they often will. A great many readers regard technical errors as an inattention to detail that also signals sloppiness at more important levels of thinking. If you produce writing that contains such errors, you risk not only distracting readers from your message but also *undermining your authority* to deliver the message in the first place.

B. THE CONCEPT OF BASIC WRITING ERRORS (BWEs)

You get a paper back, and it's a sea of red ink. But if you look more closely, you'll often find that you haven't made a million mistakes—you've made only a few, but over and over in various forms. This phenomenon is what the rhetorician Mina Shaughnessy addressed in creating the category of "basic writing errors," or BWEs. Shaughnessy argues that in order to improve your writing for style and correctness, you need to do two things:

- Look for a *pattern of error,* which will require you to understand your own logic in the mistakes you typically make.
- Recognize that not all errors are created equal, which means that you need to *address errors in some order of importance*—beginning with those most likely to interfere with your readers' understanding.

Not all errors are created equal: begin with those most likely to interfere with your readers' understanding.

The following BWE guide, "Nine Basic Writing Errors and How to Fix Them," that we have composed reflects Shaughnessy's view. First, it aims to teach you how to recognize and correct the basic kinds of errors that are potentially the most damaging to the clarity of your writing and to your credibility with readers. Second, the discussions in the guide seek to help you become aware of the patterns of error in your writing and discover the logic that has misled you into making them. If you can learn to see the pattern and then look for it in your editing and proofreading—expecting to find it—you will get in the habit of avoiding the error. In short, you will learn that your problem is not that you can't write correctly but simply that you have to remember, for example, to check for possessive apostrophes.

Our BWE guide does not, as we've mentioned, cover *all* of the rules of grammar, punctuation, diction, and usage, such as where to place the comma or period when you close a quotation or whether or not to write out numerals. For comprehensive coverage of the conventions of standard written English, you can consult one of the many handbooks available for this purpose. Our purpose is to provide a short guide to grammar—one that identifies the most common errors, provides remedies, and offers the logic that underlies them. This chapter's coverage of nine basic writing errors and how to fix them will help you eliminate most of the problems that routinely occur. We have arranged the error types in a hierarchy, moving in descending order of severity (from most to least problematic).

WHAT PUNCTUATION MARKS SAY: A "QUICK-HIT" GUIDE

These little signs really aren't that hard to use correctly, folks. A few of them will be treated in more specific contexts in the upcoming discussion of BWEs, but here are the basic rules of punctuation for the five basic signs.

The **period** [.] marks the end of a sentence. Make sure that what precedes it is an independent clause; that is, a subject plus verb that can stand alone.

The period says to a reader, "This is the end of this particular statement. I'm a mark of closure."

Example: Lennon rules.

The **comma** [,] separates the main (independent) clause from dependent elements that modify the main clause. It also separates two main clauses joined by a conjunction—known as a compound sentence. Information that is not central to the main clause is set off in a comma sandwich. The comma does *not* signify a pause.

The comma says to the reader, "Here is where the main clause begins (or ends)," or "Here is a break in the main clause." In the case of compound sentences (containing two or more independent clauses), the comma says, "Here is where one main clause ends, and after the conjunction that follows me, another main clause begins."

Examples: Lennon rules, and McCartney is cute.

Lennon rules, although McCartney is arguably more tuneful.

The **semicolon** [;] separates two independent clauses that are not joined by a conjunction. Secondarily, the semicolon can separate two independent clauses that are joined by a conjunction if either of the clauses already contains commas. In either case, the semicolon both shows a close relationship between the two independent clauses that it connects and distinguishes where one ends and the other begins. It is also the easiest way to fix comma splices (see "BWE 2" on page 356).

The semicolon says to the reader, "What precedes and what follows me are conceptually close but grammatically independent and thus equal statements."

Example: Lennon's lyrics show deep sympathy for the legions of "Nowhere Men" who inhabit the "Strawberry Fields" of their imaginations; McCartney's lyrics, on the other hand, are more upbeat, forever bidding "Good Day, Sunshine" to the world at large and "Michelle" in particular.

The **colon** [:] marks the end of a setup for something coming next. It provides a frame, pointing beyond itself, like a spotlight. The colon is quite dramatic, and unlike the semicolon, it links what precedes and follows it formally and tightly rather than loosely and associatively. It usually operates with dramatic force. It can frame a list to follow, separate cause and effect, or divide a brief claim from a more expanded version of the claim. The language on at least one side of the colon must be an independent clause, though both sides can be.

The colon says to the reader, "Concentrate on what follows me for a more detailed explanation of what preceded me" or "What follows me is logically bound with what preceded me."

Examples: *Rubber Soul* marked a change in The Beatles' song-writing: the sentimentality of earlier efforts gave way to a new complexity, both in the range of their subjects and the sophistication of their poetic devices.

Nowhere is this change more evident than in a sequence of songs near the album's end: "I'm Looking Through You," "In My Life," "Wait," and "If I Needed Someone."

The **dash** [—] provides an informal alternative to the colon for adding information to a sentence. Its effect is sudden, of the moment—what springs up impulsively to disrupt and extend in some new way the ongoing train of thought. A **pair of dashes** provides an invaluable resource to writers for inserting information within a sentence. In this usage, the rule is that the sentence must read coherently if the inserted information is left out. (Note that to type a dash, type two hyphens with no space between, before, or after. This distinguishes the dash from a hyphen [-], which is the mark used for connecting two words into one.)

The dash says to the reader, "This too!" or, in the case of a pair of them, "Remember the thought in the beginning of this sentence because we're jumping to something else before we come back to finish that thought."

Examples: For all their loveliness, the songs on *Rubber Soul* are not without menace—"I'd rather see you dead little girl than to see you with another man."

In addition to the usual lead, rhythm, and bass guitar ensemble, *Rubber Soul* introduced new instruments—notably, the harpsichord interlude in "In My Life," the sitar spiraling though "Norwegian Wood"—that had not previously been heard in rock'n'roll.

NINE BASIC WRITING ERRORS AND HOW TO FIX THEM

If you're unsure about some of the terms you encounter in the discussions of BWEs, see the "Glossary of Grammatical Terms" at the end of this chapter. You'll also find brief "Test Yourself" questions interspersed throughout this section. Do them: it's easy to conclude that you understand a problem when you are shown the correction, but understanding is not the same thing as actively practicing. There's an appendix to this chapter that contains answers to these sections, along with explanations.

BWE 1: Sentence Fragments The most basic of writing errors, a *sentence fragment*, is a group of words punctuated like a complete sentence but lacking the necessary structure: it is only part of a sentence. Typically, a sentence fragment occurs when the group of words in question (1) lacks a subject, (2) lacks a predicate, or (3) is a subordinate (or dependent) clause.

To fix a sentence fragment, either turn it into an independent clause by providing whatever is missing—a subject or a predicate—or attach it to an independent clause upon which it can depend.

Noun Clause (No Predicate) As a Fragment

A world where imagination takes over and sorrow is left behind.

This fragment is not a sentence but rather a noun clause—a sentence subject with no predicate. The fragment lacks a verb that would assert something about the subject. (The verbs "takes over" and "is left" are in a dependent clause created by the subordinating conjunction "where.")

Corrections

A world *arose* where imagination takes over and sorrow is left behind. [new verb matched to "a world"]

She entered a world where imagination takes over and sorrow is left behind. [new subject and verb added]

The first correction adds a new verb ("arose"). The second introduces a new subject and verb, converting the fragment into the direct object of "she entered."

Verbal As a Fragment

Falling into debt for the fourth consecutive year.

"Falling" in the preceding fragment is not a verb. Depending on the correction, "falling" is either a verbal or part of a verb phrase.

Corrections

The company was falling into debt for the fourth consecutive year. [subject and helping verb added]

Falling into debt for the fourth consecutive year *led the company to consider relocating.* [new predicate added]

Falling into debt for the fourth consecutive year, *the company considered relocating.* [new subject and verb added]

In the first correction, the addition of a subject and the helping verb "was" converts the fragment into a sentence. The second correction turns the fragment into a gerund phrase functioning as the subject of a new sentence. The third correction converts the fragment into a participial phrase attached to a new independent clause. (See the section entitled "Glossary of Grammatical Terms" and look under "verbal" for definitions of "gerund" and "participle.")

Subordinate Clause As a Fragment

I had an appointment for 11:00 and was still waiting at 11:30. Although I did get to see the dean before lunch.

"Although" is a subordinating conjunction that calls for some kind of completion. Like "if," "when," "because," "whereas," and other subordinating conjunctions (see the "Glossary of Grammatical Terms"), "although" *always* makes the clause that it introduces dependent.

Corrections

I had an appointment for 11:00 and was still waiting at *11:30, although* I did get to see the dean before lunch. [fragment attached to preceding sentence]

As the correction demonstrates, the remedy lies in attaching the fragment to an independent clause on which it can depend (or, alternatively, making the fragment into a sentence by dropping the conjunction).

Sometimes writers use sentence fragments deliberately, usually for rhythm and emphasis or to create a conversational tone. In less formal contexts, they are generally permissible, but you run the risk that the fragment will not be perceived as intentional. In formal writing assignments, it is safer to avoid intentional fragments.

TEST YOURSELF: FRAGMENTS

There are fragments in each of the following three examples, probably the result of their proximity to legitimate sentences. What's the problem in each case, and how would you fix it?

1. Like many other anthropologists, Margaret Mead studied non-Western cultures in such works as *Coming of Age in Samoa*. And influenced theories of childhood development in America.
2. The catastrophe resulted from an engineering flaw. Because the bridge lacked sufficient support.
3. In the 1840s the potato famine decimated Ireland. It being a country with poor soil and antiquated methods of agriculture.

A Note on Dashes and Colons

One way to correct a fragment is to replace the period with a dash: "The campaign required commitment. Not just money." becomes "The campaign required commitment—not just money." The dash offers you one way of attaching a phrase or dependent clause to a sentence without having to construct another independent clause. In short, it's succinct. (Compare the correction that uses the dash with another possible correction: "The campaign required commitment. It also required money.") Moreover, with the air of sudden interruption that the dash conveys, it can capture the informality and immediacy that the intentional fragment offers a writer.

You should be wary of overusing the dash as the slightly more presentable cousin of the intentional fragment. The energy it carries can clash with the decorum of formal writing contexts; for some readers, its staccato effect quickly becomes too much of a good thing.

One alternative to this usage of the dash is the colon. It can substitute because it also can be followed by a phrase, a list, or a clause. As with the dash, it must be preceded by an independent clause. And it, too, carries dramatic force because it abruptly halts the flow of the sentence.

The colon, however, does not convey informality. In place of a slapdash effect, it trains a light on what is to follow it. Hence, as in this sentence you are reading, it is especially appropriate for setting up certain kinds of information: explanations, lists, or results. In the case of results, the cause or action precedes the colon; the effect or reaction follows it.

Let us quickly review the other legitimate use of the dash: to enclose information within a sentence. In this use, dashes precede and follow the information, taking the role usually assigned to commas. Consider the following example:

> Shortly before the election—timing its disclosures for maximal destructive effect—the candidate's campaign staff levied a series of charges against the incumbent.

Note that if the information within the dashes is omitted, the sentence still reads grammatically.

BWE 2: Comma Splices and Fused (or Run-On) Sentences A comma splice consists of two independent clauses connected ("spliced") with a comma; a fused (or run-on) sentence combines two such clauses with no conjunction or punctuation. The solutions for both comma splices and fused sentences are the same.

1. Place a conjunction (such as "and" or "because") between the clauses.
2. Place a semicolon between the clauses.
3. Make the clauses into separate sentences.

All of these solutions solve the same logical problem: they clarify the boundaries of the independent clauses for your readers.

Comma Splice

He disliked discipline, he avoided anything demanding.

Correction

Because he disliked discipline, he avoided anything demanding. [subordinating conjunction added]

Comma Splice

Today most TV programs are violent, almost every program is about cops and detectives.

Correction

Today most TV programs are violent; almost every program is about cops and detectives. [semicolon replaces comma]

Because the two independent clauses in the first example contain ideas that are closely connected logically, the most effective of the three comma-splice solutions is to add a subordinating conjunction ("because") to the first of the two clauses, making it depend on the second. For the same reason—close conceptual connection—the best solution for the next comma splice is to substitute a semicolon for the comma. The semicolon signals that the two independent clauses are closely linked in meaning. In general, you can use a semicolon where you could also use a period.

The best cures for the perpetual comma splicer: recognize the difference between independent and dependent clauses and get rid of the "pause theory" of punctuation.

The best cures for the perpetual comma splicer are to learn to recognize the difference between independent and dependent clauses and to get rid of the "pause theory" of punctuation. All of the clauses in our two examples are independent. As written, each of these should be punctuated not with a comma but rather with a period or a semicolon. Instead, the perpetual comma splicer, as usual, acts on the "pause theory": because the ideas in the independent clauses are closely connected, the writer hesitates to separate them with a period. And so the writer inserts what he or she takes to be a shorter pause—the comma. But a comma is not a "breath" mark; it provides readers with specific grammatical information, in each of these cases mistakenly suggesting there is only one independent clause separated by the comma from modifying information. In the corrections, by contrast, the semicolon sends the appropriate signal to the reader: the message that it is joining two associated but independent statements. (Adding a coordinating conjunction such as "and" would also be grammatically correct, though possibly awkward.)

A comma is not a "breath" mark; it provides readers with specific grammatical information about where independent and dependent clauses are.

Fused Sentence

The Indo-European language family includes many groups most languages in Europe belong to it.

Correction

The Indo-European language family includes many groups. Most languages in Europe belong to it. [period inserted after first independent clause]

You could also fix this fused sentence with a comma plus the coordinating conjunction "and." Alternatively, you might condense the whole into a single independent clause.

Most languages in Europe belong to the Indo-European language family.

Comma Splices with Conjunctive Adverbs

Quantitative methods of data collection show broad trends, however, they ignore specific cases.

Sociobiology poses a threat to traditional ethics, for example, it asserts that human behavior is genetically motivated by the "selfish gene" to perpetuate itself.

Corrections

Quantitative methods of data collection show broad trends; however, they ignore specific cases. [semicolon replaces comma before "however"]

Sociobiology poses a threat to traditional ethics; for example, it asserts that human behavior is genetically motivated by the "selfish gene" to perpetuate itself. [semicolon replaces comma before "for example"]

Both of these examples contain one of the most common forms of comma splices. Both of them are compound sentences—that is, they contain two independent clauses. (See the section entitled "The Compound Sentence" in Chapter 11.) Normally, connecting the clauses with a comma and a conjunction would be correct; for example, "Most hawks hunt alone, but osprey hunt in pairs." In the preceding two comma splices, however, the independent clauses are joined by transitional expressions known as conjunctive adverbs. (See the "Glossary of Grammatical Terms.") When a conjunctive adverb is used to link two independent clauses, it *always* requires a semicolon. By contrast, when a coordinating conjunction links the two clauses of a compound sentence, it is *always* preceded by a comma.

In most cases, depending on the sense of the sentence, the semicolon precedes the conjunctive adverb and has the effect of clarifying the division between the two clauses. There are exceptions to this general rule, though, as in the following sentence:

> The lazy boy did finally read a *book, however;* it was the least he could do.

Here "however" is a part of the first independent clause and qualifies its claim. The sentence thus suggests that the boy was not totally lazy, because he did get around to reading a book. Note how the meaning changes when "however" becomes the introductory word for the second independent clause.

> The lazy boy did finally read a *book; however,* it was the least he could do.

Here the restricting force of "however" suggests that reading the book was not much of an accomplishment.

TEST YOURSELF: COMMA SPLICES

What makes each of the following sentences a comma splice? Determine the best way to fix each one and why, and then make the correction.

1. "Virtual reality" is a new buzzword, so is "hyperspace."
2. Many popular cures for cancer have been discredited, nevertheless, many people continue to buy them.
3. Elvis Presley's home, Graceland, attracts many musicians as a kind of shrine, even Paul Simon has been there.
4. She didn't play well with others, she sat on the bench and watched.

BWE 3: Errors in Subject–Verb Agreement The subject and the verb must agree in number, a singular subject taking a singular verb and a plural subject taking a plural verb. Errors in subject–verb agreement usually occur when a writer misidentifies the subject or verb of a clause.

Agreement Problem

> Various kinds of vandalism has been rapidly increasing.

Correction

> Various kinds of vandalism *have* been rapidly increasing. [verb made plural to match "kinds"]

When you isolate the grammatical subject ("kinds") and the verb ("has") of the original sentence, you can tell that they do not agree. Although "vandalism" might seem to be the subject because it is closest to the verb, it is actually the object of the preposition "of." The majority of agreement problems arise from mistaking the object of a preposition for the actual subject of a sentence. If you habitually make this mistake, you can begin to remedy it by familiarizing yourself with the most common prepositions. (See the "Glossary of Grammatical Terms," which contains a list of these.)

Agreement Problem

Another aspect of territoriality that differentiates humans from animals are their possession of ideas and objects.

Correction

Another aspect of territoriality that differentiates humans from animals *is* their possession of ideas and objects. [verb made singular to match subject "aspect"]

The subject of the sentence is "aspect." The two plural nouns ("humans" and "animals") probably encourage the mistake of using a plural verb ("are"), but "humans" is part of the "that" clause modifying "aspect," and "animals" is the object of the preposition "from."

Agreement Problem

The Republican and the Democrat both believe in doing what's best for America, but each believe that the other doesn't understand what's best.

Correction

The Republican and the Democrat both believe in doing what's best for America, but each *believes* that the other doesn't understand what's best. [verb made singular to agree with subject "each"]

The word "each" is *always* singular, so the verb ("believes") must be singular as well. The presence of a plural subject and verb in the sentence's first independent clause ("the Republican and the Democrat both believe") has probably encouraged the error.

TEST YOURSELF: SUBJECT–VERB AGREEMENT

Diagnose and correct the error in the following example.

The controversies surrounding the placement of Arthur Ashe's statue in Richmond was difficult for the various factions to resolve.

A Note on Nonstandard English

The term "standard written English" refers to language that conforms to the rules and conventions adhered to by the majority of English-speaking writers. The fact is, however, that not all speakers of English grow up hearing, reading, and writing standard written English. Some linguistic cultures in America follow, for example, a different set of conventions for subject–verb agreement. Their speakers do not differentiate singular from plural verb forms with a terminal "–s," as in standard English.

She walks home after work.

They walk home after work.

Some speakers of English do not observe this distinction, so that the first sentence becomes:

She walk home after work.

These two ways of handling subject–verb agreement are recognized by linguists not in terms of right versus wrong but rather in terms of dialect difference. A *dialect* is a variety of a language that is characteristic of a region or culture and is sometimes unintelligible to outsiders. The problem for speakers of a dialect that differs from the norm is that they can't always rely on the ear—on what sounds right—when they are editing according to the rules of standard written English. Such speakers need, in effect, to learn to speak more than one dialect so that they can edit according to the rules of standard written English in situations where this would be expected. This often requires adding a separate proofreading stage for particular errors, like subject–verb agreement, rather than relying on what sounds right.

BWE 4: Shifts in Sentence Structure (Faulty Predication) This error involves an illogical mismatch between subject and predicate. If you continually run afoul of faulty predication, you might use the exercises in a handbook to drill you on isolating the grammatical subjects and verbs of sentences, because that is the first move you need to make in fixing the problem.

Shift

In 1987, the release of more information became available.

Correction

In 1987, more *information* became available *for release.* [new subject]

It was the "information," not the "release," that "became available." The correction relocates "information" from its position as object of the preposition "of" to the subject position in the sentence; it also moves "release" into a prepositional phrase.

Shift

The busing controversy was intended to rectify the inequality of educational opportunities.

Correction

Busing was intended to rectify the inequality of educational opportunities. [new subject formulated to match verb]

The *controversy* wasn't intended to rectify, but busing was.

TEST YOURSELF: FAULTY PREDICATION

Identify and correct the faulty predication in this example:

The subject of learning disabilities is difficult to identify accurately.

BWE 5: Errors in Pronoun Reference There are at least three forms of this problem. All of them involve a lack of clarity about whom or what a pronoun (a word that substitutes for a noun) refers to. The surest way to avoid difficulties is to make certain that the pronoun relates back unambiguously to a specific word, known as the antecedent. In the sentence "Nowadays appliances don't last as long as they once did," the noun "appliances" is the antecedent of the pronoun "they."

Pronoun–Antecedent Agreement

A pronoun must agree in number (and gender) with the noun or noun phrase that it refers to.

Pronoun Error

It can be dangerous if a child, after watching TV, decides to practice what they saw.

Corrections

It can be dangerous if *children*, after watching TV, *decide* to practice what *they* saw. [antecedent (and verb) made plural to agree with pronouns]

It can be dangerous if a child, after watching TV, decides to practice what *he or she* saw. [singular pronouns substituted to match singular antecedent "child"]

The error occurs because "child" is singular, but its antecedent pronoun, "they," is plural. The first correction makes both singular; the second makes both plural. You might also observe in the first word of the example—the impersonal "it"—an exception to the rule that pronouns must have antecedents.

TEST YOURSELF: PRONOUN–ANTECEDENT AGREEMENT

What is wrong with the following sentence, and how would you fix it?

Every dog has its day, but all too often when that day happens, they can be found barking up the wrong tree.

Ambiguous Reference

A pronoun should have only one possible antecedent. The possibility of two or more confuses relationships within the sentence.

Pronoun Error

Children like comedians because they have a sense of humor.

Corrections

Because children have a sense of humor, *they* like comedians. [subordinate "because" clause placed first, and relationship between noun "children" and pronoun "they" tightened]

Children like comedians because *comedians* have a sense of humor. [pronoun eliminated and replaced by repetition of noun]

Does "they" in the original example refer to "children" or "comedians"? The rule in such cases of ambiguity is that the pronoun refers to the nearest possible antecedent, so here "comedians" possess the sense of humor, regardless of what the writer may intend. As the corrections demonstrate, either reordering the sentence or repeating the noun can remove the ambiguity.

TEST YOURSELF: AMBIGUOUS REFERENCE

As you proofread, it's a good idea to target your pronouns to make sure that they cannot conceivably refer to more than one noun. What's wrong with the following sentences?

1. Alexander the Great's father, Philip of Macedon, died when he was twenty-six.
2. The committee could not look into the problem because it was too involved.

Broad Reference

Broad reference occurs when a pronoun refers loosely to a number of ideas expressed in preceding clauses or sentences. It causes confusion because the reader cannot be sure which of the ideas the pronoun refers to.

Pronoun Error

As a number of scholars have noted, Sigmund Freud and Karl Marx offered competing but also at times complementary critiques of the dehumanizing tendencies of Western capitalist society. We see this in Christopher Lasch's analysis of conspicuous consumption in *The Culture of Narcissism.*

Correction

As a number of scholars have noted, Sigmund Freud and Karl Marx offered competing but also at times complementary critiques of the dehumanizing tendencies of Western capitalist society. We see *this complementary view* in Christopher Lasch's analysis of conspicuous consumption in *The Culture of Narcissism.* [broad "this" clarified by addition of noun phrase]

The word "this" in the second sentence of the uncorrected example could refer to the fact that "a number of scholars have noted" the relationship between Freud and Marx, to the competition between Freud's and Marx's critiques of capitalism, or to the complementary nature of the two men's critiques.

Beware "this" as a pronoun: it's the most common source of broad reference. The remedy is generally to avoid using the word as a pronoun. Instead, convert "this" into an adjective, and let it modify some noun that more clearly specifies the referent: "this complementary view," as in the correction or, alternatively, "this competition" or "this scholarly perspective."

TEST YOURSELF: BROAD REFERENCE

Locate the errors in the following examples, and provide a remedy for each.

1. Regardless of whether the film is foreign or domestic, they can be found in your neighborhood video store.
2. Many experts now claim that dogs and other higher mammals dream; for those who don't own such pets, this is often difficult to believe.

A Note on Sexism and Pronoun Usage

Errors in pronoun reference sometimes occur because of a writer's praiseworthy desire to avoid sexism. In most circles, the following correction of the preceding example would be considered sexist.

> It can be dangerous if a child, after watching TV, decides to practice what *he* saw.

Though the writer of such a sentence may intend "he" to function as a gender-neutral impersonal pronoun, it in fact excludes girls on the basis of gender. Implicitly, it also conveys sexual stereotypes (for example, that only boys are violent, or perhaps stupid, enough to confuse TV with reality).

The easiest way to avoid the problem of sexism in pronoun usage usually lies in putting things into the plural form, because plural pronouns ("we," "you," "they") have no gender. (See the use of "children" in the first correction of the pronoun–antecedent agreement example.) Alternatively, you can use the phrase "he or she." Many readers, however, find this phrase and its variant, "s/he," to be awkward constructions. Another remedy lies in rewriting the sentence to avoid pronouns altogether, as in the following revision.

> It can be dangerous if a child, after watching TV, decides to practice *some violent activity portrayed on the screen.*

BWE 6: Misplaced Modifiers and Dangling Participles Modifiers are words or groups of words used to qualify, limit, intensify, or explain some other element in a sentence. A misplaced modifier is a word or phrase that appears to modify the wrong word or words.

Misplaced Modifier

> At the age of three he caught a fish with a broken arm.

Correction

> At the age of three *the boy with a broken arm* caught a fish. [noun replaces pronoun; prepositional phrase revised and relocated]

The original sentence mistakenly implies that the fish had a broken arm. Modification errors often occur in sentences with one or more prepositional phrases, as in this case.

Misplaced Modifier

> According to legend, General George Washington crossed the Delaware and celebrated Christmas in a small boat.

Correction

> According to legend, General George Washington crossed the Delaware *in a small boat* and *then* celebrated Christmas *on shore.* [prepositional phrase relocated; modifiers added to second verb]

As a general rule, you can avoid misplacing a modifier by keeping it as close as possible to what it modifies. Thus, the second correction removes the implication that Washington celebrated Christmas in a small boat. When you cannot relocate the modifier, separate it from the rest of the sentence with a comma to prevent readers from connecting it to the nearest noun.

You can avoid misplacing a modifier by keeping it as close as possible to what it modifies.

A dangling participle creates a particular kind of problem in modification: the noun or pronoun that the writer intends the participial phrase to modify is not actually present in the sentence. Thus, we have the name dangling participle: the participle has been left dangling because the word or phrase it is meant to modify is not there.

Dangling Participle

After debating the issue of tax credits for the elderly, the bill passed in a close vote.

Correction

After debating the issue of tax credits for the elderly, *the Senate passed the bill* in a close vote. [appropriate noun added for participle to modify]

The bill did not debate the issue, as the original example implies. As the correction demonstrates, fixing a dangling participle involves tightening the link between the activity implied by the participle ("debating") and the entity performing that activity ("the Senate").

TEST YOURSELF: MODIFICATION ERRORS

Find the modification errors in the following examples and correct them.

1. After eating their sandwiches, the steamboat left the dock.
2. The social workers saw an elderly woman on a bus with a cane standing up.
3. Crossing the street, a car hit the pedestrian.

BWE 7: Errors in Using Possessive Apostrophes Adding *'s* to most singular nouns will make them show possession, for example, the plant*'s* roots, the accountant*'s* ledger. You can add the apostrophe alone, without the "s," for example, to make plural nouns that already end with "s" show possession: the flower*s*' fragrances, the ship*s*' berths (although you may also add an additional "s").

Apostrophe Error

The loyal opposition scorned the committees decisions.

Corrections

The loyal opposition scorned the *committee's* decisions.

The loyal opposition scorned the *committees'* decisions. [possessive apostrophe added]

The first correction assumes there was one committee; the second assumes there were two or more.

Apostrophe Error

The advisory board swiftly transacted it's business.

Correction

The advisory board swiftly transacted *its* business. [apostrophe dropped]

Unlike possessive nouns, possessive pronouns ("my," "your," "yours," "her," "hers," "his," "its," "our," "ours," "their," "theirs") *never* take an apostrophe.

TEST YOURSELF: POSSESSIVE APOSTROPHES

Find and correct any errors in the following sentence.

The womens movement has been misunderstood by many of its detractors.

BWE 8: Comma Errors As with other rules of punctuation and grammar, the many that pertain to comma usage share an underlying aim: to clarify the relationships among the parts of a sentence. Commas separate the parts of a sentence grammatically. One of their primary uses, then, is to help your readers distinguish the main clause from dependent elements, such as subordinate clauses and long prepositional phrases. They do not signify a pause, as was discussed under "BWE 2."

Comma Error

After eating the couple went home.

Correction

After *eating,* the couple went home. [comma added before independent clause]

The comma after "eating" is needed to keep the main clause "visible" or separate; it marks the point at which the prepositional phrase ends and the independent clause begins. Without this separation, readers would be invited to contemplate cannibalism as they move across the sentence.

Comma Error

In the absence of rhetoric study teachers and students lack a vocabulary for talking about their prose.

Correction

In the absence of rhetoric *study,* teachers and students lack a vocabulary for talking about their prose. [comma added to separate prepositional phrase from main clause]

Without the comma, readers would have to read the sentence twice to find out where the prepositional phrase ends—with "study"—in order to figure out where the main clause begins.

Comma Error

Dog owners, despite their many objections will have to obey the new law.

Correction

Dog owners, despite their many *objections,* will have to obey the new law. [single comma converted to a pair of commas]

A comma is needed after "objections" in order to isolate the phrase in the middle of the sentence ("despite their many objections") from the main clause. The phrase needs to be set off with commas because it contains additional information that is not essential to the meaning of what it modifies. (Dog owners must obey the law whether they object or not.) Phrases and clauses that function in this way are called *nonrestrictive.*

The test of nonrestrictive phrases and clauses is to see if they can be omitted without substantially changing the message that a sentence conveys ("Dog owners will have to obey the new law," for example). Nonrestrictive elements always take two commas—a comma "sandwich"—to set them off. Using only one comma illogically separates the sentence's subject ("dog owners") from its predicate ("will have to obey"). This problem is easier to see in a shorter sentence. You wouldn't, for example, write "I, fell down." As a rule, commas virtually never separate the subject from the verb of a sentence. (Here's an exception: "Ms. Taloora, a high fashion model, watches her diet scrupulously.")

Comma Error

Most people regardless of age like to spend money.

Correction

Most *people,* regardless of *age,* like to spend money. [comma sandwich added]

Here commas enclose the nonrestrictive elements; you could omit this information without significantly affecting the sense. Such is not the case in the following two examples.

Comma Error

People, who live in glass houses, should not throw stones.

Correction

People *who live in glass houses* should not throw stones. [commas omitted]

Comma Error

Please return the library book, that I left on the table.

Correction

Please return the library *book that* I left on the table. [comma omitted]

It is incorrect to place commas around "who live in glass houses" or a comma before "that I left on the table." Each of these is a *restrictive clause*—that is, it contains information that is an essential part of what it modifies. In the first sentence, for example, if "who live in glass houses" is left out, the fundamental meaning of the sentence is lost: "People should not throw stones." The word "who" is defined by restricting it to "people" in the category of glass-house dwellers. Similarly, in the second example the "that" clause contributes an essential meaning to "book"; the sentence is referring to not just any book but to a particular one, the one "on the table."

So remember the general rule: if the information in a phrase or clause can be omitted—if it is nonessential and therefore nonrestrictive—it needs to be separated by commas from the rest of the sentence. Moreover, note that nonrestrictive clauses are generally introduced by the word "which," so a "which" clause interpolated into a sentence takes a comma sandwich. ("The dinner, which I bought for $20, made me sick.") By contrast, a restrictive clause is introduced by the word "that" and takes no commas.

TEST YOURSELF: COMMA ERRORS

Consider the following examples as a pair. Punctuate them as necessary, and then briefly articulate how the meanings of the two sentences differ.

1. The book which I had read a few years ago contained a lot of outdated data.
2. The book that I had read a few years ago contained a lot of outdated data.

BWE 9: Spelling/Diction Errors That Interfere with Meaning Misspellings are always a problem in a final draft, insofar as they undermine your authority by inviting readers to perceive you as careless (at best). If you make a habit of using the spellchecker of a word processor, you will take care of most misspellings. But the problems that a spellchecker won't catch are the ones that can often hurt you most. These are actually diction errors—incorrect word choices in which you have confused one word with another that it closely resembles. In such cases, you have spelled the word correctly, but it's the wrong word. Because it means something other than what you've intended, you end up misleading your readers. (See "Shades of Meaning" in Chapter 10.)

The best way to avoid this problem is to memorize the differences between pairs of words that are commonly confused with each other but that have distinct meanings. The following examples illustrate a few of the most common and serious of these errors. Most handbooks contain a glossary of usage that *cites* more of these *sites* of confusion.

Spelling/Diction Error: "It's" Versus "Its"

Although you can't tell a book by its' cover, its fairly easy to get the general idea from the introduction.

Correction

Although you can't tell a book by *its* cover, *it's* fairly easy to get the general idea from the introduction. [apostrophe dropped from possessive and added to contraction]

"It's" is a contraction for "it is." "Its" is a possessive pronoun meaning "belonging to it." If you confuse the two, *it's* likely that your sentence will mislead *its* readers.

Spelling/Diction Error: "Their" Versus "There" Versus "They're"

Their are ways of learning about the cuisine of northern India besides going their to watch the master chefs and learn there secrets—assuming their willing to share them.

Correction

There are ways of learning about the cuisine of northern India besides going *there* to watch the master chefs and learn *their* secrets—assuming *they're* willing to share them. [expletive "there," adverb "there," possessive pronoun "their," and contraction "they're" inserted appropriately]

"There" as an adverb normally refers to a place; "there" can also be used as an expletive to introduce a clause, as in the first usage of the correction. (See the discussion of expletives under "Cutting the Fat" in Chapter 11.) "Their" is a possessive pronoun meaning "belonging to them." "They're" is a contraction for "they are."

Spelling/Diction Error: "Then" Versus "Than"

If a person would rather break a law then obey it, than he or she must be willing to face the consequences.

Correction

If a person would rather break a law *than* obey it, *then* he or she must be willing to face the consequences. [comparative "than" distinguished from temporal "then"]

"Than" is a conjunction used with a comparison, for example, "rather X than Y." "Then" is an adverb used to indicate what comes next in relation to time, for example, "first X, then Y."

Spelling/Diction Error: "Effect" Versus "Affect"

It is simply the case that BWEs adversely effect the way that readers judge what a writer has to say. It follows that writers who include lots of BWEs in their prose may not have calculated the disastrous affects of these mistakes.

Correction

It is simply the case that BWEs adversely *affect* the way that readers judge what a writer has to say. It follows that writers who include lots of BWEs in their prose may not have calculated the disastrous *effects* of these mistakes. [verb "affect" and noun "effects" inserted appropriately]

In their most common usages, "affect" is a verb meaning "to influence," and "effect" is a noun meaning "the result of an action or cause." The confusion of "affect" and "effect" is enlarged by the fact that both of these words have secondary meanings: the verb "to effect" means "to cause or bring about"; the noun "affect" is used in psychology to mean "emotion or feeling." Thus, if you confuse these two words, you will inadvertently make a meaning radically different from the one you intend.

TEST YOURSELF: SPELLING/DICTION ERRORS

Make corrections as necessary in the following paragraph.

> Its not sufficiently acknowledged that the behavior of public officials is not just an ethical issue but one that effects the sale of newspapers and commercial bytes in television news. When public officials don't do what their supposed to do, than their sure to face the affects of public opinion—if they get caught—because there are dollars to be made. Its that simple: money more then morality is calling the tune in the way that the press treats it's superstars.

C. GLOSSARY OF GRAMMATICAL TERMS

adjective An adjective is a part of speech that usually modifies a noun or pronoun, for example, *blue*, *boring*, *boisterous*.

adverb An adverb is a part of speech that modifies an adjective, adverb, or verb, for example, *heavily*, *habitually*, *very*. The adverbial form generally differs from the adjectival form via the addition of the ending "–ly"; for example, *happy* is an adjective, and *happily* is an adverb.

clause (independent and dependent) A clause is any group of words that contains both a **subject** and a **predicate**. An **independent clause** (also known as a **main clause**) can stand alone as a sentence. For example,

> The most famous revolutionaries of this century have all, in one way or another, offered a vision of a classless society.

The subject of this independent clause is "revolutionaries," the verb is "have offered," and the direct object is "vision." By contrast, a **dependent** (or **subordinate**) **clause** is any group of words containing a subject and verb that cannot stand alone as a separate sentence because it depends on an independent clause to complete its meaning. The following sentence adds two dependent clauses to our previous example:

> The most famous revolutionaries of this century have all, in one way or another, offered a vision of a classless society, *although* most historians would agree *that* this ideal has never been achieved.

The origin of the word "depend" is "to hang": a dependent clause literally hangs on the independent clause. In the preceding example, neither "although most historians would agree" nor "that this ideal has never been achieved" can stand independently. The "that" clause relies on the "although" clause, which in turn relies on the main clause. "That" and "although" function as **subordinating conjunctions**; by eliminating them, we could rewrite the sentence to contain three independent clauses:

> The most famous revolutionaries of this century have all, in one way or another, offered a vision of a classless society. Most historians would agree on one judgment about this vision: it has never been achieved.

comma splice A comma splice consists of two independent clauses incorrectly connected (spliced) with a comma. See "BWE 2."

conjunction (coordinating and subordinating) A conjunction is a part of speech that connects words, phrases, or clauses, for example, *and, but, although*. The conjunction in some way defines that connection: for example, *and* links; *but* separates. All conjunctions define connections in one of two basic ways. Coordinating conjunctions connect words or groups of words that have equal grammatical importance. The coordinating conjunctions are *and, but, or, nor, for, so,* and *yet.* Subordinating conjunctions introduce a dependent clause and connect it to a main clause. Here is a partial list of the most common subordinating conjunctions: *after, although, as, as if, as long as, because, before, if, rather than, since, than, that, though, unless, until, when, where, whether,* and *while.*

conjunctive adverb A conjunctive adverb is a word that links two independent clauses (as a conjunction) but that also modifies the clause it introduces (as an adverb). Some of the most common conjunctive adverbs are *consequently, furthermore, however, moreover, nevertheless, similarly, therefore,* and *thus.* Phrases can also serve this function, such as *for example* and *on the other hand.* When conjunctive adverbs are used to link two independent clauses, they always require a semicolon:

> Many pharmaceutical chains now offer their own generic versions of common drugs; however, many consumers continue to spend more for name brands that contain the same active ingredients as the generics.

When conjunctive adverbs occur within an independent clause, however, they are enclosed in a pair of commas, as is the case with the use of *however* earlier in this sentence.

coordination Coordination refers to grammatically equal words, phrases, or clauses. Coordinate constructions are used to give elements in a sentence equal weight or importance. In the sentence "The tall, thin lawyer badgered the witness, but the judge interceded," the clauses "The tall, thin lawyer badgered the witness" and "but the judge interceded" are coordinate clauses; "tall" and "thin" are coordinate adjectives.

***dependent clause* (see *clause*)**

direct object The direct object is a noun or pronoun that receives the action carried by the verb and performed by the subject. In the sentence, "Certain mushrooms can kill you," "you" is the direct object.

***gerund* (see *verbals*)**

fused* (*or run-on*) *sentence A fused sentence incorrectly combines two independent clauses with no conjunction or punctuation. See "BWE 2."

***independent clause* (see *clause*)**

***infinitive* (see *verbals*)**

***main clause* (see *clause*)**

noun A noun is a part of speech that names a person (*woman*), place (*town*), thing (*book*), idea (*justice*), quality (*irony*), or action (*betrayal*).

***object of the preposition* (see *preposition*)**

***participle and participial phrase* (see *verbals*)**

phrase A phrase is a group of words occurring in a meaningful sequence that lacks either a subject or a predicate. This absence distinguishes it from a clause, which contains both a subject and a predicate. Phrases function in sentences as adjectives, adverbs, nouns, or verbs. They are customarily classified according to the part of speech of their key word: "over the mountain" is a **prepositional phrase**; "running for office" is a **participial phrase**; "had been disciplined" is a **verb phrase**; "desktop graphics" is a **noun phrase**; and so forth.

predicate The predicate contains the verb of a sentence or clause, making some kind of statement about the subject. The predicate of the preceding sentence is "contains the verb, making some kind of statement about the subject." The simple predicate—the verb to which the other words in the sentence are attached—is "contains."

preposition, prepositional phrase A preposition is a part of speech that links a noun or pronoun to some other word in the sentence. Prepositions usually express a relationship of time (after) or space (above) or direction (toward). The noun to which the preposition is attached is known as the object of the preposition. A preposition, its object, and any modifiers comprise a prepositional phrase. "*With* love *from* me *to* you" strings together three prepositional phrases. Here is a partial list of the most common prepositions: *about, above, across, after, among, at, before, behind, between, by, during, for, from, in, into, like, of, on, out, over, since, through, to, toward, under, until, up, upon, with, within*, and *without*.

pronoun A pronoun is a part of speech that substitutes for a noun, such as *I, you, he, she, it, we*, and *they*.

run-on (or fused) sentence A run-on sentence incorrectly combines two independent clauses with no conjunction or punctuation. See "BWE 2."

sentence A sentence is a unit of expression that can stand independently. It contains two parts, a **subject** and a **predicate**. The shortest sentence in the Bible, for example, is "Jesus wept." "Jesus" is the subject; "wept" is the predicate.

sentence fragment A sentence fragment is a group of words incorrectly punctuated like a complete sentence but lacking the necessary structure; it is only a part of a sentence. "Walking down the road" and "the origin of the problem" are both fragments because neither contains a **predicate**. See "BWE 1."

subject The subject, in most cases a noun or pronoun, names the doer of the action in a sentence or identifies what the predicate is about. The subject of the previous sentence, for example, is "the subject, in most cases a noun or pronoun." The simple subject of that sentence—the noun to which the other words in the sentence are attached—is "subject."

subordination, subordinating conjunctions "Subordination" refers to the placement of certain grammatical units, particularly phrases and clauses, at a lower, less important structural level than other elements. As with coordination, the grammatical ranking carries conceptual significance as well: whatever is grammatically subordinated appears less important than the information carried in the main clause. In the following example, the 486-based personal computer is subordinated both grammatically and conceptually to the Pentium-based PC:

> Although 486-based personal computers continue to improve in speed, the new Pentium-based PC systems have thoroughly outclassed them.

Here "although" is a **subordinating conjunction** that introduces a subordinate clause, also known as a **dependent clause**.

verb A verb is a part of speech that describes an action (*goes*), states how something was affected by an action (*became angered*), or expresses a state of being (*is*).

verbals (participles, gerunds, and infinitives) Verbals are words derived from verbs. They are verb forms that look like verbs but, as determined by the structure of the sentence they appear in, they function as nouns, adjectives, or adverbs. There are three forms of verbals.

An **infinitive**—composed of the root form of a verb plus *to* (*to be*, *to vote*)—becomes a verbal when it is used as a noun ("*To eat* is essential"), an adjective ("These are the books *to read*"), or an adverb ("He was too sick *to walk*").

Similarly, a **participle**—usually composed of the root form of a verb plus "–ing" (present participle) or "–ed" (past participle)—becomes a verbal when used as an adjective. It can occur as a single word, modifying a noun, as in *faltering negotiations* or *finished business*. But it also can occur in a participial phrase, consisting of the participle, its object, and any modifiers. Here are two examples:

> *Having been tried and convicted,* the criminal was sentenced to life imprisonment.
>
> *Following the path of most resistance,* the masochist took deep pleasure in his frustration.

"Having been tried and convicted" is a participial phrase that modifies "criminal"; "Following the path of most resistance" is a participial phrase that modifies "masochist." In each case, the participial phrase functions as an adjective.

The third form of verbal, the **gerund**, resembles the participle. Like the participle, it is formed by adding "–ing" to the root form of the verb, but unlike the participle, it is used as a noun. In the sentence "Swimming is extraordinarily aerobic," the gerund "swimming" functions as the subject. Again like participles, gerunds can occur in phrases. The gerund phrases are italicized in the following example: "*Watching a film adaptation* takes less effort than *reading the book* from which it was made."

When using a verbal, remember that although it resembles a verb, it cannot function alone as the verb in a sentence: "Being a military genius" is a fragment, not a sentence.

ASSIGNMENT: Grammar and Style Quiz

Here is an error-laden paragraph to rewrite and correct by making changes in grammar and punctuation as necessary. You may need to add, drop, or rearrange words, but do not add any periods. That way, you will be able to test yourself on your ability to use commas plus conjunctions, semicolons, colons, and dashes rather than avoid these options by separating each independent clause into a simple sentence. The quiz also contains a few stylistic problems addressed in Chapters 10 and 11. A discussion of the errors and how to fix them can be found in the Appendix to this chapter.

It is a fact that fraternities and sororities are a major part of student life at the university, students are preoccupied with pledging. This is not approved of by most members of the faculty, however, they feel helpless about attacking them. Perceiving that the greek societies are attractive to the students but at the same time encouraging anti-intellectualism, it is not an issue that can be addressed easily. The student, who wants to be popular and cool feels that he should not talk in class, because interest in academics or having ideas outside class is uncool. Its more important to pledge the right house then being smart. If the administration would create alternatives to Greek life such as a honors program students lives would be more enriched. Although for now raising the cumulative grade point necessary to pledge and remain active would be a good start. Contrary to the Universitys stance against gender discrimination Greek life perpetuates gender stereotypes; for example, the dances at each house for freshman women but not men. Some of the best students agree with this but mistakenly believes that most faculty endorse the system.

GUIDELINES FOR REVISING FOR CORRECTNESS

1. In correcting grammar, seek to discover the patterns of error in your writing, and unlearn the logic that has led you to make certain kinds of errors recurrently.
2. Check the draft for errors that obscure the boundaries of sentences: fragments, comma splices, and run-ons. Begin by isolating the simple subject and predicate in the main clause(s) of every sentence (to make sure they exist); this check will also help you to spot faulty predication and errors in subject–verb agreement. Then, check to see that each independent clause is separated from others by a period, a comma plus coordinating conjunction, or a semicolon.
3. Check your sentences for ambiguity (the potential of being read in more than one way) by deliberately trying to misread them. If your sentence can be read to mean something other than what you intended, the most common causes are misplaced and dangling modifiers and errors in pronoun reference.
4. Fix errors in pronoun reference and misplaced modifiers by making sure that every pronoun has only one clear antecedent and that every modifying word or phrase is placed as close as possible to the part of the sentence it modifies.
5. Avoid dangling modifiers by being sure that the noun or pronoun being modified is actually present in the sentence. Avoid broad reference by adding the appropriate noun or noun phrase after the pronoun "this." (You can greatly improve the clarity of your prose just by avoiding use of the vague "this," especially at the beginnings of sentences.)
6. Check that commas are separating dependent clauses, long prepositional phrases, or other modifying elements from the main clause. A comma is not a pause; its function is to help readers locate your sentence's main (independent) clause(s).
7. Enclose nonrestrictive modifiers placed between the subject and predicate of a sentence in a pair of commas or—for more emphasis—in a pair of dashes. A nonrestrictive modifier is a phrase, often beginning with "which," that can be deleted from the sentence without changing the sentence's meaning.

Chapter 14 Appendix
Answer Key (with Discussion)

TEST YOURSELF SECTIONS

Test Yourself: Fragments

Original example: Like many other anthropologists, Margaret Mead studied non-Western cultures in such works as *Coming of Age in Samoa.* And influenced theories of childhood development in America.

Problem: The second sentence is actually a fragment, a predicate in need of a subject.

Possible correction: Like many other anthropologists, Margaret Mead studied non-Western cultures (in such works as *Coming of Age in Samoa*) in ways that influenced theories of childhood development in America.

Comment: There are many ways to fix this example, but its original form leaves ambiguous whether the fragment refers only to "Mead" or to "many other anthropologists" as well. The correction offered includes the other anthropologists in the referent and diminishes the emphasis on Mead's book by placing it within parentheses. Although the correction uses a subordinating "that" to incorporate the fragment into the first sentence, it keeps this information in an emphatic position at the end of the sentence.

Original example: The catastrophe resulted from an engineering flaw. Because the bridge lacked sufficient support.

Problem: The second sentence is actually a dependent clause; "because" always subordinates.

Possible correction: The catastrophe resulted from an engineering flaw: the bridge lacked sufficient support.

Comment: Because the colon has causal force, this is an ideal spot to use one, identifying the "flaw."

Original example: In the 1840s the potato famine decimated Ireland. It being a country with poor soil and antiquated methods of agriculture.

Problem: The second sentence is actually a fragment, a subject plus a long participial phrase.

Possible correction: In the 1840s the potato famine decimated Ireland, a country with poor and antiquated methods of agriculture.

Comment: The cause of this kind of fragment is usually that the writer mistakenly believes that "being" is a verb rather than a participle that introduces a long phrase (modifying "Ireland" in this case). It would also be correct simply to change the period to a comma in the original sentence.

Test Yourself: Comma Splices

Original example: "Virtual reality" is a new buzzword, so is "hyperspace."

Problem: This is a comma splice—both clauses are independent, yet they are joined with a comma.

Possible correction: "Virtual reality" is a new buzzword; so is "hyperspace."

Comment: Because the clauses are linked by association—both naming buzzwords—a semicolon would show that association. A writer could also condense the clauses into a simple sentence with a compound subject, for example, "Both 'virtual reality' and 'hyperspace' are new buzzwords."

Original example: Many popular cures for cancer have been discredited, nevertheless, many people continue to buy them.

Problem: A comma splice results from the incorrectly punctuated conjunctive adverb "nevertheless."

Possible correction: Many popular cures for cancer have been discredited; nevertheless, many people continue to buy them.

Comment: Without the semicolon to separate the independent clauses, the conjunctive adverb could conceivably modify either the preceding or the following clause. This problem is usually worse with "however."

Original example: Elvis Presley's home, Graceland, attracts many musicians as a kind of shrine, even Paul Simon has been there.

Problem: This is a comma splice—the two independent clauses are linked by a comma without a conjunction. The problem is exacerbated by the number of commas in the sentence; the reader cannot easily tell which one is used to separate the clauses.

Possible correction: Elvis Presley's home, Graceland, attracts many musicians as a kind of shrine—even Paul Simon has been there.

Comment: Although one could justly use a semicolon here, the dash conveys the impromptu effect of an afterthought.

Original example: She didn't play well with others, she sat on the bench and watched.

Problem: Because the second clause develops the first one, a writer might think that it is dependent on the first; conceptually, yes, but grammatically, no.

Possible correction: She didn't play well with others; she sat on the bench and watched.

Comment: If the writer wanted to link the two clauses more tightly, a colon would be appropriate instead of the semicolon.

Test Yourself: Subject–Verb Agreement

Original example: The controversies surrounding the placement of Arthur Ashe's statue in Richmond was difficult for the various factions to resolve.

Problem: The grammatical subject of the main clause ("controversies") is plural; the verb ("was") is singular.

Possible corrections: The controversies surrounding the placement of Arthur Ashe's statue in Richmond were difficult for the various factions to resolve (or, The controversy . . . was).

Comment: An error of this kind is encouraged by two factors: the distance of the verb from the subject and the presence of intervening prepositional phrases that use singular objects, either of which a writer might mistake for the grammatical subject of the main clause.

Test Yourself: Faulty Predication

Original example: The subject of learning disabilities is difficult to identify accurately.

Problem: The predicate matches the object of the preposition ("learning disabilities") rather than the subject of the main clause ("subject").

Possible correction: Learning disabilities are difficult to identify accurately.

Comment: Omitting the abstract opening ("The subject of") enables the predicate ("are") to fit the new grammatical subject ("disabilities").

Test Yourself: Pronoun–Antecedent Agreement

Original example: Every dog has its day, but all too often when that day happens, they can be found barking up the wrong tree.

Problem: The plural pronoun "they" that is the grammatical subject of the second clause does not have a plural antecedent in the sentence.

Possible correction: Every dog has its day, but all too often when that day happens, the dog can be found barking up the wrong tree.

Comment: If a writer vigilantly checks all pronouns, he or she will identify the intended antecedent of the pronoun "they" to be the singular "dog" and revise accordingly. The sentence would still be incorrect if the pronoun "it" were used instead of the repeated "dog," because "it" could refer to the nearest preceding noun, "day."

Test Yourself: Ambiguous Reference

Original example: Alexander the Great's father, Philip of Macedon, died when he was twenty-six.

Problem: A reader can't be sure whether "he" refers to Alexander or to Philip.

Possible correction: Alexander the Great's father, Philip of Macedon, died at the age of twenty-six.

Comment: The correction rewords to remove the ambiguous pronoun. This solution is less awkward than repeating "Philip" in place of "he," though that would also be correct.

Original example: The committee could not look into the problem because it was too involved.

Problem: A reader can't be sure whether "it" refers to "the committee" or to "the problem."

Possible correction: The committee was too involved with other matters to look into the problem.

Comment: As with the previous example, rewording to eliminate the ambiguous pronoun is usually the best solution.

Test Yourself: Broad Reference

Original example: Regardless of whether the film is foreign or domestic, they can be found in your neighborhood video store.

Problem: The plural pronoun "they" does not have a plural antecedent in the sentence.

Possible correction: Regardless of whether the film is foreign or domestic, it can be found in your neighborhood video store.

Comment: Although the sentence offers two options for films, the word "film" is singular and so, as antecedent, requires a singular pronoun ("it"). It is probably worth noting here that "it" would still be correct even if the original sentence began, "Regardless of whether the film is a foreign film or a domestic film." The rule for compound subjects that use an either/or construction is as follows: the number (singular or plural) of the noun or pronoun that follows *or* determines the number of the verb. Compare the following two examples: "Either several of his aides *or* the *candidate is* going to speak" and "Either the candidate *or* several of his *aides are* going to speak."

Original example: Many experts now claim that dogs and other higher mammals dream; for those who don't own such pets, this is often difficult to believe.

Problem: The referent of the pronoun "this" is unclear. Precisely what is "difficult to believe"—that mammals dream or that experts would make such a claim?

Possible correction: Many experts now claim that dogs and other higher mammals dream; for those who don't own such pets, this claim is often difficult to believe.

Comment: Often the best way to fix a problem with broad reference produced by use of "this" as a pronoun is to convert "this" to an adjective—a strategy that will require a writer to provide a specifying noun for "this" to modify. As a rule, when you find an isolated "this" in your draft, ask and answer the question "This what?"

Test Yourself: Modification Errors

Original example: After eating their sandwiches, the steamboat left the dock.

Problem: This is a dangling participle—the grammar of the sentence conveys that the steamboat ate their sandwiches.

Corrections: After the girls ate their sandwiches, the steamboat left the dock. Or, After eating their sandwiches, the girls boarded the steamboat, and it left the dock.

Comment: The two corrections model the two ways of remedying most dangling participles. Both provide an antecedent ("the girls") for the pronoun "their." The first correction eliminates the participial phrase and substitutes a subordinate clause. The second correction adds to the existing main clause ("steamboat left") another one ("girls boarded") for the participial phrase to modify appropriately.

Original example: The social workers saw an elderly woman on a bus with a cane standing up.

Problem: Misplaced modifiers create the problems in this sentence, which implies that the bus possessed a cane that was standing up. The problem exemplified here is produced from the series of prepositional phrases—"*on* a bus *with* a cane"—followed by the participial phrase "standing up," which is used as an adjective and intended to modify "woman."

Possible correction: The social workers saw an elderly woman on a bus. She was standing up with the help of a cane.

Comment: Writers often try to cram too much into sentences, piling on the prepositions. The best remedy is sometimes to break up the sentence, a move that usually involves eliminating prepositions, which possess a sludgy kind of movement, and adding verbs, which possess more distinct movement.

Original example: Crossing the street, a car hit the pedestrian.

Problem: The dangling participle ("Crossing the street") does not have a word to modify in the sentence. The sentence conveys that the car crossed the street.

Possible corrections: Crossing the street, the pedestrian was hit by a car. Or: As the pedestrian crossed the street, a car hit him.

Comment: The first solution brings the participial phrase closest to the noun it modifies ("pedestrian"). The second converts the participial into the verb ("crossed") of a dependent "as" clause and moves "pedestrian" into the clause as the subject for that verb. As in the "steamboat" example, one correction provides an appropriate noun for the participial phrase to modify, and the other eliminates the participle.

Test Yourself: Possessive Apostrophes

Original example: The womens movement has been misunderstood by many of its detractors.

Problem: The possessive apostrophe for "womens" is missing. The trickiness here in inserting the apostrophe is that this word is already plural.

Possible correction: The women's movement has been misunderstood by many of its detractors.

Comment: Because the word is already plural, it takes a simple "–'s" to indicate a movement belonging to women—not "–s'" (womens').

Test Yourself: Comma Errors

Original paired examples: The book which I had read a few years ago contained a lot of outdated data.

The book that I had read a few years ago contained a lot of outdated data.

Problem: In the first example, the modifying clause "which I had read a few years ago" is nonrestrictive: it could be omitted without changing the essential meaning of the sentence. Therefore, it needs to be enclosed in commas—as the "which" signals.

Possible correction: The book, which I had read a few years ago, contained a lot of outdated data.

Comment: The second example in the pair is correct as it stands. The restrictive clause, "that I had read a few years ago," does not take commas around it because the information it gives readers is an essential part of the meaning of "book." That is, it refers to not just any book read a few years ago, as in the first example in the pair, but rather specifies the one containing outdated data. "The book that I had read a few years ago" thus functions as what is known as a *noun phrase.*

Test Yourself: Spelling/Diction Errors

Original example: Its not sufficiently acknowledged that the behavior of public officials is not just an ethical issue but one that effects the sale of newspapers and commercial bytes in television news. When public officials don't do what their supposed to do, than their sure to face the affects of public opinion—if they get caught—because there are dollars to be made. Its that simple: money more then morality is calling the tune in the way that the press treats it's superstars.

Problems: The paragraph confuses the paired terms discussed under "BWE 9." It mistakes

"its" for "it's" before "not sufficiently."
"effects" for "affects" before "the sale."
"their" for "they're" before "supposed."
"than" for "then" before "their sure."
"they're" for "their" before "sure."
"affects" for "effects" before "of public opinion."
"its" for "it's" before "that simple."
"then" for "than" before "morality."
"it's" for "its" before "superstars."

Possible correction: It's not sufficiently acknowledged that the behavior of public officials is not just an ethical issue but one that affects the sale of newspapers and commercial bytes in television news. When public officials don't do what they're supposed to do, then they're sure to face the effects of public opinion—if they get caught—because there are dollars to be made. It's that simple: money more than morality is calling the tune in the way that the press treats its superstars.

Comment: If you confuse similar words, the only solution is to memorize the differences and consciously check your drafts for any problems until habit takes hold.

GRAMMAR AND STYLE QUIZ

The answers offered here are not exclusive—the only ways to correct the problems. In some cases, we have offered various satisfactory remedies, and as previously noted, a few of the suggested revisions—marked by a bullet—address editing for style (Chapters 10 and 11) rather than editing for correctness.

Line 1

- There are no grammatical errors per se, but "It is a fact that" is a wordy expletive that should be cut.

Line 2

- There is a comma splice between "university" and "students": insert a semicolon as the preferred option.
- "This," beginning the next sentence, is a broad reference and should be converted into an adjective, with a noun or noun phrase added, such as "This preoccupation" or "This dominance by Greek societies."
- In addition, a writer might recast the passive verb into the active: "Most faculty members do not approve of . . ."

Line 3

- There is a comma splice after "faculty": insert a semicolon.
- The antecedent of the pronoun "them" is ambiguous: substitute a noun such as "the Greeks."

Line 4

- "Perceiving" is a dangling participle: either recast to include a subject in a dependent clause (such as "Because most faculty members perceive") or insert "most faculty members" as a referent for the participle before "it" in Line 5.
- Capitalize "Greek."

Line 5

- Fix faulty parallelism: introduce the second item ("encouraging anti-intellectualism") with another "that" ("but at the same time that they encourage").
- The "it is" (an expletive) creates problems with broad reference. If Line 4 has been changed by eliminating the participle (using some version of the "Because most faculty members feel" option), recast the main clause. For example, following "anti-intellectualism," the sentence might read, "this issue cannot be addressed easily." If Line 4 has retained the participial phrase, then the revision would need to read something like "most faculty members believe that this issue cannot be addressed easily."

Line 6

- The "who" clause is restrictive: the comma must be dropped.
- The "he" is sexist: use "he or she," or change the number—to "Students who want ... feel that they."

Line 7

- Fix faulty parallelism: change "interest in" to "be*ing* interested in" so as to match "hav*ing* ideas."

Line 8

- Possessive "Its" should be the contraction "It's."
- Temporal "then" should be the comparative "than."
- Fix faulty parallelism: change "being" to "to be" to match "to pledge."

Line 9

- Change "a honors" to "an honors."
- Insert commas around the nonrestrictive modifying phrase "such as an honors program": these will separate it from both the long introductory dependent "if" clause that precedes it and the main clause that follows.

Line 10

- Make "students" a plural possessive: "students' lives."
- The "more enriched" is arguably wordy: "richer" is leaner.
- "Although" is a subordinating conjunction that creates a sentence fragment. The easiest solution is to cut it, though a writer could also attach the entire "although" clause to the previous sentence, using a comma or dash.

Line 11

- This is part of the fragment that began in Line 10.

Line 12

- Fix the possessive: make it "University's."
- Fix the case of the noun: make it "university's."
- Place a comma after "discrimination" to separate the long introductory modifying phrases from the main clause.

Line 13

- The semicolon is incorrect, because the sentence does not contain two independent clauses. A colon is better than a dash here, though both are technically correct.

Line 14

- Most rhetoricians consider “freshman” sexist: substitute “first-year.”
- The use of “this” is another egregious case of broad reference (ask, “Agree with *this what?*). The best solution is probably to rewrite this part of the sentence to clarify the meaning. For example, make it “Some of the best students object to Greek life in these terms and oppose the administration’s handling of the Greeks . . . ”

Line 15

- Fix subject–verb agreement: make it “some . . . believe.”

Here is how one corrected version of the quiz might look:

> Fraternities and sororities are a major part of student life at the university: students are preoccupied with pledging. Most faculty members do not approve of this dominance by Greek societies; however, they feel helpless about attacking the Greeks. Because faculty members perceive that the Greek societies are attractive to the students but at the same time that they encourage anti-intellectualism, this issue cannot be addressed easily. The student who wants to be popular and cool feels that he or she should not talk in class, because being interested in academics or having ideas outside class is uncool. It’s more important to pledge the right house than to be smart. If the administration would create alternatives to Greek life, such as an honors program, the students’ lives would be richer. For now, raising the cumulative grade point necessary to pledge and remain active would be a good start to solving the problem of Greek domination. Contrary to the university’s stance against gender discrimination, Greek life perpetuates gender stereotypes: for example, the dances at each house for first-year women but not men. Some of the best students object to Greek life in these terms and oppose the administration’s handling of the Greeks. But many of these same students mistakenly believe that most faculty members endorse the system.

PART 2

THE READINGS

CHAPTER 15

Manners, Communication, and Technology

Quick Take

One of our preliminary titles for this chapter was How We Live Now. All of the readings in this chapter focus on the relationships between the public and the private, with particular focus on how those relationships are affected by the technologies of the information age—technologies that have brought us closer together in some ways, and further estranged us from each other in other ways.

The writers in this chapter come from disparate backgrounds but they share a conviction that manners are anything but trivial—not simply a sign of your upbringing, the product of a parent's scolding about which fork to use, or how to answer the phone. Rather, manners have to do with the fundamental ways that people in the public sphere interact with one another; they have to do with the boundaries of civility. To understand manners is to understand how we live as social beings.

ABOUT THE READINGS IN THIS CHAPTER

The readings in this chapter explore the links among manners, communication, and technology. Christine Rosen starts things off with a historical piece (and position paper) on the cultural impact of the cell phone: "They encourage talk, not conversation." This focus leads her to voice the need for us to reclaim what she calls "social space." Paul Goldberger adopts a complementary view in his short piece on the tendency of cell phones to transport us "out of real space into a virtual realm."

Next, Jeffrey Rosen broadens the focus to consider how individuals today "brand" themselves as part of what he calls "America's culture of self-revelation." The proliferation of weblogs, for example, he interprets as a sign of how the internet complicates "our ability to negotiate the boundary between public and private." Geoffrey Nunberg does a variation on this theme in his short radio piece on the style of weblogs and the audiences they target and exclude.

Margaret Visser's analysis of table manners then offers a more detached, anthropological view of cultural practices and thus provides a lens for viewing all of the other selections in the chapter—the interpretive context of *ritual activity*, which provides collective order, especially in times of transition. Of all the pieces in the chapter, hers may provide the best model for doing your own primary research into how those around you behave, and what that behavior might mean.

The chapter then turns toward the personal essay in novelist Jonathan Franzen's witty discussion of the mismatch between the current outcry against the loss of privacy and the fact that we are "drowning" in it. He demonstrates how the concern with our private lives and those of public figures threatens to overwhelm the public sphere.

At the end of the chapter, Edward Tufte offers a brief and incisive satiric attack against what he claims is the stupidity of Microsoft PowerPoint. In light of the previous readings, Tufte's piece may provide a kind of test case, offering you the opportunity to apply the various lenses you've acquired—what would Christine Rosen, Visser, or Franzen say to Tufte?—as you pursue the implications of his analysis.

Christine Rosen

Our Cell Phones, Ourselves

A historian by training, Christine Rosen is a senior editor of *The New Atlantis: A Journal of Technology and Society,* where this piece first appeared in 2004. Rosen here offers a brief history of the cell phone and begins to chart the implications of its conquest of contemporary culture.

"Hell is other people," Sartre observed, but you need not be a misanthrope or a diminutive French existentialist to have experienced similar feelings during the course of a day. No matter where you live or what you do, in all likelihood you will eventually find yourself participating in that most familiar and exasperating of modern rituals: unwillingly listening to someone else's cell phone conversation. Like the switchboard operators of times past, we are now all privy to calls being put through, to the details of loved ones contacted, appointments made, arguments aired, and gossip exchanged. 1

Today, more people have cell phones than fixed telephone lines, both in the United States and internationally. There are more than one billion cell phone users worldwide, and as one wireless industry analyst recently told *Slate*, "some time between 2010 and 2020, everyone who wants and can afford a cell phone will have one." Americans spend, on average, about seven hours a month talking on their cell phones. Wireless phones have become such an important part of our everyday lives that in July, the country's major wireless industry organization featured the following "quick poll" on its website: "If you were stranded on a desert island and could have one thing with you, what would it be?" The choices: "Matches/Lighter," "Food/Water," "Another Person," "Wireless Phone." The World Health Organization has even launched an "International EMF Project" to study the possible health effects of the electromagnetic fields created by wireless technologies.

But if this ubiquitous technology is now a normal part of life, our adjustment to it has not been without consequences. Especially in the United States, where cell phone use still remains low compared to other countries, we are rapidly approaching a tipping point with this technology. How has it changed our behavior, and how might it continue to do so? What new rules ought we to impose on its use? Most importantly, how has the wireless telephone encouraged us to connect individually but disconnect socially, ceding, in the process, much that was civil and civilized about the use of public space?

Untethered

Connection has long served as a potent sign of power. In the era before cell phones, popular culture served up presidents, tin-pot dictators, and crime bosses who were never far from a prominently placed row of phones, demonstrating their importance at the hub of a vast nexus. Similarly, superheroes always owned special communications devices: Batman had the Batphone, Dick Tracy his wrist-phone, Maxwell Smart his shoe spy phone. (In the Flash comics of the 1940s, the hero simply outraces phone calls as they are made, avoiding altogether the need for special communication devices.) To be able to talk to anyone, at any time, without the mediator of the human messenger and without the messenger's attendant delays, is a thoroughly modern triumph of human engineering.

In 1983, Motorola introduced DynaTAC, now considered the first truly mobile telephone, and by the end of that year, the first commercial cellular phone systems were being used in Chicago and in the Baltimore/Washington, D.C. area. Nokia launched its own mobile phone, the cumbersome Cityman, in 1987. Americans were introduced to the glamour of mobile telephone communication that same year in a scene from the movie *Wall Street.* In it, the ruthless Gordon Gekko (played by Michael Douglas) self-importantly conducts his business on the beach using a large portable phone. These first-generation cell phones were hardly elegant—many people called them "luggables" rather than "portables," and as one reporter noted in *The Guardian*, "mobiles of that era are often compared to bricks, but this is unfair. Bricks are quite attractive and relatively light." But they made up in symbolic importance what they lacked in style; only the most powerful and wealthiest people owned them. Indeed, in the 1980s, the only other people besides the elite and medical professionals who had mobile technologies at all (such as pagers) were presumed to be using them for nefarious reasons. Who else but a roving drug dealer or prostitute would need to be accessible at all times?

This changed in the 1990s, when cell phones became cheaper, smaller, and more readily available. The technology spread rapidly, as did the various names given to it: in Japan it is *keitai*, in China it's *sho ji*, Germans call their cell phones *handy*, in France it is *le portable* or *le G*, and in Arabic, *el mobile, telephone makhmul*, or *telephone gowal.* In countries where cell phone use is still limited to the elite—such as Bulgaria, where only 2.5 percent of the population can afford a cell phone—its power as a symbol of wealth and prestige remains high. But in the rest of the world, it has become a technology for the masses. There were approximately 340,000 wireless subscribers in the United States in 1985, according to the Cellular Telecommunications and Internet Associate (CTIA); by 1995, that number had increased to more than 33 million, and by 2003, more than 158 million people in the country had gone wireless.

Why do people use cell phones? The most frequently cited reason is convenience, which can cover a rather wide range of behaviors. Writing in the *Wall Street Journal* this spring, an executive for a wireless company noted that "in Slovakia, people are using mobile phones to remotely switch on the heat before they return home," and in Norway, "1.5 million people can confirm their tax returns" using cell phone short text messaging services. Paramedics use camera phones to send ahead to hospitals pictures of the incoming injuries; "in Britain, it is now commonplace for wireless technology to allow companies to remotely access meters or gather diagnostic information." Construction workers on-site can use cell phones to send pictures to contractors off-site. Combined with the individual use of cell phones—to make appointments, locate a friend, check voicemail messages, or simply to check in at work—cell phones offer people a heretofore unknown level of convenience.

More than ninety percent of cell phone users also report that owning a cell phone makes them feel safer. The CTIA noted that in 2001, nearly 156,000 wireless emergency service calls were made every day—about 108 calls per minute. Technological Good Samaritans place calls to emergency personnel when they see traffic accidents or crimes-in-progress; individuals use their cell phones to call for assistance when a car breaks down or plans go awry. The safety rationale carries a particular poignancy after the terrorist attacks of September 11, 2001. On that day, many men and women used cell phones to speak their final words to family and loved ones. Passengers on hijacked airplanes called wives and husbands; rescue workers on the ground phoned in to report their whereabouts. As land lines in New York and Washington, D.C., became clogged, many of us made or received frantic phone calls on cell phones—to reassure others that we were safe or to make sure that our friends and family were accounted for. Many people who had never considered owning a cell phone bought one after September 11th. If the cultural image we had of the earliest cell phones was of a technology glamorously deployed by the elite, then the image of cell phones today has to include people using them for this final act of communication, as well as terrorists who used cell phones as detonators in the bombing of trains in Madrid.

Of course, the perceived need for a technological safety device can encourage distinctly irrational behavior and create new anxieties. Recently, when a professor at Rutgers University asked his students to experiment with turning off their cell phones for 48 hours, one young woman told *University Wire*, "I felt like I was going to get raped if I didn't have my cell phone in my hand. I carry it in case I need to call someone for help." Popular culture endorses this image of cell-phone-as-life-line. The trailer for a new suspense movie, *Cellular*, is currently making the rounds in theaters nationwide. In it, an attractive young man is shown doing what young men apparently do with their camera-enabled cell phones: taking pictures of women in bikinis and e-mailing the images to himself. When he receives a random but desperate phone call from a woman who claims to be the victim of a kidnapping, he finds himself drawn into a race to find and save her, all the while trying to maintain that tenuous cell phone connection. It is indicative of our near-fetishistic attachment to our cell phones that we can relate (and treat as a serious moment of suspense) a scene in the movie where the protagonist, desperately trying to locate a cell phone charger before his battery runs out, holds the patrons of an electronics store at gunpoint until the battery is rejuvenated. After scenes of high-speed car chases and large explosions, the trailer closes with a disembodied voice asking the hero, "How did you get involved?" His response? "I just answered my phone."

Many parents have responded to this perceived need for personal security by 10
purchasing cell phones for their children, but this, too, has had some unintended consequences. One sociologist has noted that parents who do this are implicitly commenting on their own sense of security or insecurity in society. "Claiming to care about their children's safety," Chantal de Gournay writes, "parents develop a 'paranoiac' vision of the community, reflecting a lack of trust in social institutions and in any environment other than the family." As a result, they choose surveillance technologies, such as cell phones, to monitor their children, rather than teaching them (and trusting them) to behave appropriately. James E. Katz, a communications professor at Rutgers who has written extensively about wireless communication, argues that parents who give children cell phones are actually

weakening the traditional bonds of authority; "parents think they can reach kids any time they want, and thus are more indulgent of their children's wanderings," Katz notes. Not surprisingly, "my cell phone battery died" has become a popular excuse among teenagers for failure to check in with their parents. And I suspect nearly everyone, at some point, has suffered hours of panic when a loved one who was supposed to be "reachable" failed to answer the cell phone.

Although cell phones are a technology with broad appeal, we do not all use our cell phones in the same way. In June 2004, Cingular announced that "for the fourth year in a row, men prove to be the more talkative sex in the wireless world," talking 16 percent more on their phones than women. Women, however, are more likely to use a cell phone "to talk to friends and family" while men use theirs for business—including, evidently, the business of mating. Researchers found that "men are using their mobile phones as peacocks use their immobilizing feathers and male bullfrogs use their immoderate croaks: To advertise to females their worth, status, and desirability," reported the *New York Times*. The researchers also discovered that many of the men they observed in pubs and nightclubs carried fake cell phones, likely one of the reasons they titled their paper "Mobile Phones as Lekking Devices Among Human Males," a lek being a "communal mating area where males gather to engage in flamboyant courtship displays." Or, as another observer of cell phone behavior succinctly put it: "the mobile is widely used for psychosexual purposes of performance and display."

The increasingly sophisticated accessories available on cell phones encourage such displays. One new phone hitting the market boasts video capture and playback, a 1.2 megapixel camera, a 256 color screen, speakerphone, removable memory, mp3 player, Internet access, and a global positioning system. The *Wall Street Journal* recently reported on cell phones that will feature radios, calculators, alarm clocks, flashlights, and mirrored compacts. Phones are "becoming your Swiss army knife," one product developer enthused. Hyperactive peacocking will also be abetted by the new walkie-talkie function available on many phones, which draws further attention to the user by broadcasting to anyone within hearing distance the conversation of the person on the other end of the phone.

With all these accoutrements, it is not surprising that one contributor to a discussion list about wireless technology recently compared cell phones and BlackBerrys to "electronic pets." Speaking to a group of business people, he reported, "you constantly see people taking their little pets out and stroking the scroll wheel, coddling them, basically 'petting' them." When confined to a basement conference room, he found that participants "were compelled to 'walk' their electronic pets on breaks" to check their messages. In parts of Asia, young women carry their phones in decorated pouches, worn like necklaces, or in pants with specially designed pockets that keep the phone within easy reach. We have become thigmophilic with our technology—touch-loving—a trait we share with rats, as it happens. We are constantly taking them out, fiddling with them, putting them away, taking them out again, reprogramming their directories, text messaging. And cell phone makers are always searching for new ways to exploit our attachments. Nokia offers "expression" phones that allow customization of faceplates and ring tones. Many companies, such as Modtones, sell song samples for cell phone ringers. In Asia, where cell phone use among the young is especially high, companies offer popular anime and manga cartoons as downloadable "wallpaper" for cell phones.

Cell phone technology is also creating new forms of social and political networking. "Moblogging," or mobile web logging, allows cell phone users to publish and update content to the World Wide Web. An increasing number of companies are offering cell phones with WiFi capability, and as Sadie Plant noted recently in a report she prepared for Motorola, "On the Mobile," "today, the smallest Motorola phone has as much computing power in it as the largest, most expensive computer did less than a generation ago." In his *Forbes* "Wireless Outlook" newsletter, Andrew Seybold predicted, "in twenty five years there aren't going to be any wired phones left and I think it might happen even much sooner than that—ten to fifteen years." As well, "the phone will be tied much more closely to the person. Since the phone is the person, the person will be the number." It isn't surprising that one of Seybold's favorite movies is the James Coburn paranoid comedy, *The Presidents' Analyst* (1967), whose premise "centered on attempts by the phone company to capture the president's psychoanalyst in order to further a plot to have phone devices implanted in people's brains at birth." Ma Bell meets *The Manchurian Candidate.*

Dodgeball.com, a new social-networking service, applies the principles of 15
websites such as Friendster to cell phones. "Tell us where you are and we'll tell you who and what is around you," Dodgeball promises. "We'll ping your friends with your whereabouts, let you know when friends-of-friends are within ten blocks, allow you to broadcast content to anyone within ten blocks of you or blast messages to your groups of friends." The service is now available in fifteen cities in the U.S., enabling a form of friendly pseudo-stalking. "I was at Welcome to the Johnson's and a girl came up behind me and gave a tap on the shoulder," one recent testimonial noted. " 'Are you this guy?' she inquired while holding up her cell phone to show my Dodgeball photo. I was indeed."

Political organizers have also found cell phone technology to be a valuable tool. Throughout 2000 in the Philippines, the country's many cell phone users were text-messaging derogatory slogans and commentary about then-President Joseph Estrada. With pressure on the Estrada administration mounting, activists organized large demonstrations against the president by activating cell phone "trees" to summon protesters to particular locations and to outmaneuver riot police. Estrada was forced from office in January 2001. Anti-globalization protesters in Seattle and elsewhere (using only non-corporate cell phones, surely) have employed the technology to stage and control movements during demonstrations.

Communication Delinquents

The ease of mobile communication does not guarantee positive results for all those who use it, of course, and the list of unintended negative consequences from cell phone use continues to grow. The BBC world service reported in 2001, "senior Islamic figures in Singapore have ruled that Muslim men cannot divorce their wives by sending text messages over their mobile phones." (Muslims can divorce their wives by saying the word "talaq," which means "I divorce you," three times).

Concerns about the dangers of cell phone use while driving have dominated public discussion of cell phone risks. A 2001 study by the National Highway Traffic Safety Administration estimated that "54 percent of drivers 'usually' have some type of wireless phone in their vehicle with them" and that this translates into approximately 600,000 drivers "actively using cell phones at any one time" on the road. Women and drivers in the suburbs were found to talk and drive more often, and "the highest national use rates were observed for drivers of vans and sport utility vehicles." New York, New Jersey, and Washington, D.C. all require drivers to use hands-free technology (headsets or speakerphones) when talking on the cell.

Cell phones can also play host to viruses, real and virtual. A 2003 study presented at the American Society for Microbiology's conference on infectious disease found that twelve percent of the cell phones used by medical personnel in an Israeli hospital were contaminated with bacteria. (Another recent cell phone-related health research result, purporting a link between cell phone use and decreased sperm counts, has been deemed inconclusive.) The first computer virus specifically targeting cell phones was found in late June. As *The Guardian* reported recently, anti-virus manufacturers believe that "the mobile phone now mirrors how the Net has developed over the past two or three years—blighted with viruses as people got faster connections and downloaded more information."

With technology comes addiction, and applicable neologisms have entered the 20
lexicon—such as "crackberry," which describes the dependence exhibited by some BlackBerry wireless users. In a 2001 article in *New York* magazine about feuding couples, one dueling duo, Dave and Brooke, traded barbs about her wireless addictions. "I use it when I'm walking down the street," Brooke said proudly. "She was checking her voice mail in the middle of a Seder!" was Dave's exasperated response. "Under the table!" Brooke clarified. A recent survey conducted by the Hospital of Seoul National University found that "3 out of 10 Korean high school students who carry mobile phones are reported to be addicted" to them. Many reported feeling anxious without their phones and many displayed symptoms of repetitive stress injury from obsessive text messaging.

The cell phone has also proven effective as a facilitator and alibi for adulterous behavior. "I heard someone (honest) talking about their 'shag phone' the other day," a visitor to a wireless technology blog recently noted. "He was a married man having an affair with a lady who was also married. It seems that one of the first heady rituals of the affair was to purchase a 'his and her' pair of prepay shag phones." A recent story in the *New York Times* documented the use of cell phone "alibi and excuse clubs" that function as an ethically challenged form of networking—Dodgeball for the delinquent. "Cell phone-based alibi clubs, which have sprung up in the United States, Europe, and Asia, allow people to send out mass text messages to thousands of potential collaborators asking for help. When a willing helper responds, the sender and the helper devise a lie, and the helper then calls the victim with the excuse," the report noted. One woman who started her own alibi club, which has helped spouses cheat on each other and workers mislead their bosses, "said she was not terribly concerned about lying," although she did concede: "You wouldn't really want your friends to know you're sparing people's feelings with these white lies." Websites such as

Kargo offer features like "Soundster," which allows users to "insert sounds into your call and control your environment." Car horns, sirens, the coughs and sniffles of the sick room—all can be simulated in order to fool the listener on the other end of the call. Technology, it seems, is allowing people to make instrumental use of anonymous strangers while maintaining the appearance of trustworthiness within their own social group.

Technology has also led to further incursions on personal privacy. Several websites now offer "candid pornography," peeping-Tom pictures taken in locker rooms, bathrooms, and dressing rooms by unscrupulous owners of cell phone cameras. Camera phones pose a potentially daunting challenge to privacy and security; unlike old-fashioned cameras, which could be confiscated and the film destroyed, digital cameras, including those on cell phones, allow users to send images instantaneously to any e-mail address. The images can be stored indefinitely, and the evidence that a picture was ever taken can be destroyed.

Will You Please Be Quiet, Please?

Certain public interactions carry with them certain unspoken rules of behavior. When approaching a grocery store checkout line, you queue behind the last person in line and wait your turn. On the subway, you make way for passengers entering and exiting the cars. Riding on the train, you expect the interruptions of the ticket taker and the periodic crackling blare of station announcements. What you never used to expect, but must now endure, is the auditory abrasion of a stranger arguing about how much he does, indeed, owe to his landlord. I've heard business deals, lovers' quarrels, and the most unsavory gossip. I've listened to strangers discuss in excruciating detail their own and others' embarrassing medical conditions; I've heard the details of recent real estate purchases, job triumphs, and awful dates. (The only thing I haven't heard is phone sex, but perhaps it is only a matter of time.) We are no longer *overhearing*, which implies accidentally stumbling upon a situation where two people are talking in presumed privacy. Now we are all simply *hearing*. The result is a world where social space is overtaken by anonymous, unavoidable background noise—a quotidian narration that even in its more interesting moments rarely rises above the tone of a penny dreadful. It seems almost cruel, in this context, that Motorola's trademarked slogan for its wireless products is "Intelligence Everywhere."

Why do these cell phone conversations bother us more than listening to two strangers chatter in person about their evening plans or listening to a parent scold a recalcitrant child? Those conversations are quantitatively greater, since we hear both sides of the discussion—so why are they nevertheless experienced as qualitatively different? Perhaps it is because cell phone users harbor illusions about being alone or assume a degree of privacy that the circumstances don't actually allow. Because cell phone talkers are not interacting with the world around them, they come to believe that the world around them isn't really there and surely shouldn't intrude. And when the cell phone user commandeers the space by talking, he or she sends a very clear message to others that they are powerless to insist on their own use of the space. It is a passive-aggressive but extremely effective tactic.

Such encounters can sometimes escalate into rude intransigence or even vio- 25
lence. In the past few years alone, men and women have been stabbed, escorted

off of airplanes by federal marshals, pepper-sprayed in movie theaters, ejected from concert halls, and deliberately rammed with cars as a result of their bad behavior on their cell phones. The *Zagat* restaurant guide reports that cell phone rudeness is now the number one complaint of diners, and *USA Today* notes that "fifty-nine percent of people would rather visit the dentist than sit next to someone using a cell phone."

The etiquette challenges posed by cell phones are universal, although different countries have responded in slightly different ways. Writing about the impact of cell phone technology in *The Guardian* in 2002, James Meek noted, with moderate horror, that cell phones now encourage British people to do what "British people aren't supposed to do: invite strangers, spontaneously, into our personal worlds. We let everyone know what our accent is, what we do for a living, what kind of stuff we do in our non-working hours." In France, cell phone companies were pressured by the public to censor the last four digits of phone numbers appearing on monthly statements, because so many French men and women were using them to confirm that their significant other was having an affair.

In Israel, where the average person is on a cell phone four times as much as the average American, and where cell phone technology boasts an impressive 76 percent penetration rate (the United States isn't projected to reach that level until 2009), the incursion of cell phones into daily life is even more dramatic. As sociologists Amit Schejter and Akiba Cohen found, there were no less than ten cell phone interruptions during a recent staging of *One Flew Over the Cuckoos' Nest* at Israel's National Theater, and "there has even been an anecdote reported of an undertaker's phone ringing inside a grave as the deceased was being put to rest." The authors explain this state of affairs with reference to the Israeli personality, which they judge to be more enthusiastic about technology and more forceful in exerting itself in public; the subtitle of their article is "chutzpah and chatter in the Holy Land."

In the U.S., mild regional differences in the use of cell phones are evident. Reporting on a survey by Cingular wireless, CNN noted that cell phone users in the South "are more likely to silence their phones in church," while Westerners "are most likely to turn a phone off in libraries, theaters, restaurants, and schools." But nationwide, cell phones still frequently interrupt movie screenings, theater performances, and concerts. Audience members are not the sole offenders, either. My sister, a professional musician, told me that during one performance, in the midst of a slow and quiet passage of Verdi's *Requiem*, the cell phone of one of the string players in the orchestra began ringing, much to the horror of his fellow musicians.

We cannot simply banish to Tartarus—the section of Hades reserved for punishment of the worst offenders—all those who violate the rules of social space. And the noise pollution generated by rude cell phone users is hardly the worst violation of social order; it is not the same as defacing a statue, for example. Other countries offer some reason for optimism: In societies that maintain more formality, such as Japan, loud public conversation is considered rude, and Japanese people will often cover their mouths and hide their phones from view when speaking into them.

Not surprisingly, Americans have turned to that most hallowed but least effec- 30
tive solution to social problems: public education. Cingular Wireless, for example,

has launched a public awareness campaign whose slogan is "Be Sensible." The program includes an advertisement shown in movie theaters about "Inconsiderate Cell Phone Guy," a parody of bad behavior that shows a man talking loudly into his cell phone at inappropriate times: during a date, in a movie, at a wedding, in the middle of a group therapy session. It is a miniature manners nickelodeon for the wireless age. July is now officially National Cell Phone Courtesy Month, and etiquette experts such as Jacqueline Whitmore of the Protocol School of Palm Beach advise companies such as Sprint about how to encourage better behavior in their subscribers. Whitmore is relentlessly positive: "Wireless technology is booming so quickly and wireless phones have become so popular, the rules on wireless etiquette are still evolving," she notes on her website. She cites hopeful statistics culled from public opinion surveys that say "98 percent of Americans say they move away from others when talking on a wireless phone in public" and "the vast majority (86 percent) say they 'never' or 'rarely' speak on wireless phones while conducting an entire public transaction with someone else such as a sales clerk or bank teller." If you are wondering where these examples of wireless rectitude reside, you might find them in the land of wishful thinking. There appears to be a rather large disconnect between people's actual behavior and their reports of their behavior.

Whitmore is correct to suggest that we are in the midst of a period of adjustment. We still have the memory of the old social rules, which remind us to be courteous towards others, especially in confined environments such as trains and elevators. But it is becoming increasingly clear that cell phone technology itself has disrupted our ability to insist on the enforcement of social rules. Etiquette experts urge us to adjust—be polite, don't return boorish behavior with boorish behavior, set a standard of probity in your own use of cell phones. But in doing so these experts tacitly concede that every conversation is important, and that we need only learn how and when to have them. This elides an older rule: when a conversation takes place in public, its merit must be judged in part by the standards of the other participants in the social situation. By relying solely on self-discipline and public education (or that ubiquitous modern state of "awareness"), the etiquette experts have given us a doomed manual. Human nature being what it is, individuals will spend more time rationalizing their own need to make cell phone calls than thinking about how that need might affect others. Worse, the etiquette experts offer diversions rather than standards, encouraging alternatives to calling that nevertheless still succeed in removing people from the social space. "Use text messaging," is number 7 on Whitmore's Ten Tips for the Cell Phone Savvy.

These attempts at etiquette training also evade another reality: the decline of accepted standards for social behavior. In each of us lurks the possibility of a Jekyll-and-Hyde-like transformation, its trigger the imposition of some arbitrary rule. The problem is that, in the twenty-first century, with the breakdown of hierarchies and manners, all social rules are arbitrary. "I don't think we have to worry about people being rude intentionally," Whitmore told *Wireless Week*. "Most of us simply haven't come to grips with the new responsibilities wireless technologies demand." But this seems foolishly optimistic. A psychologist quoted in a story by UPI recently noted the "baffling sense of entitlement" demonstrated by citizens in the wireless world. "They don't get sheepish when shushed," he marveled. "You're the rude one." And *contra* Ms. Whitmore, there is intention at work in this behavior, even if it is not intentional rudeness. It is the intentional removal of oneself from the social situation in public space. This removal, as sociologists have long shown, is something more serious than a mere manners lapse. It amounts to a radical disengagement from the public sphere.

Spectator Sport

We know that the reasons people give for owning cell phones are largely practical—convenience and safety. But the reason we answer them whenever they ring is a question better left to sociology and psychology. In works such as *Behavior in Public Spaces*, *Relations in Public*, and *Interaction Ritual*, the great sociologist Erving Goffman mapped the myriad possibilities of human interaction in social space, and his observations take on a new relevance in our cell phone world. Crucial to Goffman's analysis was the notion that in social situations where strangers must interact, "the individual is obliged to 'come into play' upon entering the situation and to stay 'in play' while in the situation." Failure to demonstrate this presence sends a clear message to others of one's hostility or disrespect for the social gathering. It effectively turns them into "non-persons." Like the piqued lover who rebuffs her partner's attempt to caress her, the person who removes himself from the social situation is sending a clear message to those around him: I don't need you.

Although Goffman wrote in the era before cell phones, he might have judged their use as a "subordinate activity," a way to pass the time such as reading or doodling that could and should be set aside when the dominant activity resumes. Within social space, we are allowed to perform a range of these secondary activities, but they must not impose upon the social group as a whole or require so much attention that they remove us from the social situation altogether. The opposite appears to be true today. The group is expected never to impinge upon—indeed, it is expected to tacitly endorse by enduring—the individual's right to withdraw from social space by whatever means he or she chooses: cell phones, BlackBerrys, iPods, DVDs screened on laptop computers. These devices are all used as a means to refuse to be "in" the social space; they are technological cold shoulders that are worse than older forms of subordinate activity in that they impose visually and auditorily on others. Cell phones are not the only culprits here. A member of my family, traveling recently on the Amtrak train from New York, was shocked to realize that the man sitting in front of her was watching a pornographic movie on his laptop computer—a movie whose raunchy scenes were reflected in the train window and thus clearly visible to her. We have allowed what should be subordinate activities in social space to become dominant.

One of the groups Goffman studied keenly were mental patients, many of them 35
residents at St. Elizabeth's Hospital in Washington, D.C., and his comparisons often draw on the remarkable disconnect between the behavior of people in normal society and those who had been institutionalized for mental illness. It is striking in revisiting Goffman's work how often people who use cell phones seem to be acting more like the people in the asylum than the ones in respectable society. Goffman describes "occult involvements," for example, as any activity that undermines others' ability to feel engaged in social space. "When an individual is perceived in an

occult involvement, observers may not only sense that they are not able to claim him at the moment," Goffman notes, "but also feel that the offender's complete activity up till then has been falsely taken as a sign of participation with them, that all along he has been alienated from their world." Who hasn't observed someone sitting quietly, apparently observing the rules of social space, only to launch into loud conversation as soon as the cell phone rings? This is the pretense of social participation Goffman observed in patients at St. Elizabeth's.

Goffman called those who declined to respond to social overtures as being "out of contact," and said "this state is often felt to be full evidence that he is very sick indeed, that he is, in fact, cut off from all contact with the world around him." To be accessible meant to be available in the particular social setting and to act appropriately. Today, of course, being accessible means answering your cell phone, which brings you in contact with your caller, but "out of contact" in the physical social situation, be it a crosstown bus, a train, an airplane, or simply walking down the street.

In terms of the rules of social space, cell phone use is a form of communications panhandling—forcing our conversations on others without first gaining their tacit approval. "The force that keeps people in their communication place in our middle-class society," Goffman observed, "seems to be the fear of being thought forward and pushy, or odd, the fear of forcing a relationship where none is desired." But middle class society itself has decided to upend such conventions in the service of greater accessibility and convenience. This is a dramatic shift that took place in a very short span of time, and it is worth at least considering the long-term implications of this subversion of norms. The behavioral rules Goffman so effectively mapped exist to protect everyone, even if we don't, individually, always need them. They are the social equivalent of fire extinguishers placed throughout public buildings. You hope not to have to use them too often, but they can ensure that a mere spark does not become an embarrassing conflagration. In a world that eschews such norms, we find ourselves plagued by the behavior that Goffman used to witness only among the denizens of the asylum: disembodied talk that renders all of us unwilling listeners.

We also use our cell phones to exert our status in social space, like the remnants of the entourage or train, which "led a worthy to demonstrate his status by the cluster of dependent supporters that accompanied him through a town or a house of parliament." Modern celebrities still have such escorts (a new cable television series, *Entourage*, tracks a fictional celebrity posse). But cell phones give all of us the unusual ability to simulate an entourage. My mother-in-law recently found herself sharing an elevator (in the apartment building she's lived in for forty years) with a man who was speaking very loudly into his cell phone. When she asked him to keep his voice down, he became enraged and began yelling at her; he was, he said, in the midst of an "important" conversation with his secretary. He acted, in other words, as if she'd trounced on the hem of his royal train. She might have had a secretary too, of course—for all he knew she might have a fleet of assistants at her disposal—but because she wasn't communicating with someone *at that moment* and he, thanks to his cell phone, was, her status in the social space was, in effect, demoted.

The language of wireless technology itself suggests its selfishness as a medium. One of the latest advances is the "Personal Area Network," a Bluetooth technology used in Palm Pilots and other personal digital assistants. The network is individualized, closed to unwelcome intruders, and totally dependent on the choices of the user. We now have our own technological assistants and networks, quite an impressive kingdom for ordinary mortals. In this kingdom, our cell phones reassure us by providing constant contact, and we become much like a child with a security blanket or Dumbo with his feather. Like a security blanket, which is also visible to observers, cell phones provide the "'publicization' of emotional fulfillment," as French sociologist Chantal de Gournay has argued. "At work, in town, while traveling—every call on the mobile phone secretly expresses a message to the public: 'Look how much I'm in demand, how full my life is.'" Unlike those transitional objects of childhood, however, few of us are eager to shed our cell phones.

Absent Without Leave

40 Our daily interactions with cell phone users often prompt heated exchanges and promises of furious retribution. When *New York Times* columnist Joe Sharkey asked readers to send in their cell phone horror stories, he was deluged with responses: "There is not enough time in the day to relay the daily torment I must endure from these cell-yellers," one woman said. "There's always some self-important jerk who must holler his business all the way into Manhattan," another commuter wearily noted. Rarely does one find a positive story about cell phone users who behaved politely, observing the common social space.

Then again, we all apparently have a cell phone *alter idem*, a second self that we endlessly excuse for making just such annoying cell phone calls. As a society, we are endlessly forgiving of our own personal "emergencies" that require cell phone conversation and easily apoplectic about having to listen to others'. At my local grocery store around 6:30 in the evening, it is not an uncommon sight to see a man in business attire, wandering the frozen food aisle, phone in hand, shouting, "Bird's Eye or Jolly Green Giant? What? Yes, I got the coffee filters already!" How rude, you think, until you remember that you left your own grocery list on the kitchen counter; in a split second you are fishing for your phone so that you can call home and get its particulars. This is the quintessential actor-observer paradox: as actors, we are always politely exercising our right to be connected, but as observers we are perpetually victimized by the boorish bad manners of other cell phone users.

A new generation of sociologists has begun to apply Goffman's insights to our use of cell phones in public. Kenneth J. Gergen, for example, has argued that one reason cell phones allow a peculiar form of diversion in public spaces is that they encourage "absent presence," a state where "one is physically present but is absorbed by a technologically mediated world of elsewhere." You can witness examples of absent presence everywhere: people in line at the bank or a retail store, phones to ear and deep into their own conversations—so unavailable they do not offer the most basic pleasantries to the salesperson or cashier. At my local playground, women deep in cell phone conversations are scattered on benches or distractedly pushing a child on a swing—physically present, to be sure, but "away" in their conversations, not fully engaged with those around them.

The first time you saw a person walking down the street having a conversation using a hands-free cell phone device you intuitively grasped this state. Wildly gesticulating, laughing, mumbling—to the person on the other end of the telephone, their street-walking conversation partner is engaged in normal conversation. To the outside observer, however, he looks like a deranged or slightly addled escapee from a psychiatric ward. Engaged with the ether, hooked up to an earpiece and dangling microphone, his animated voice and gestures are an anomaly in the social space. They violate our everyday sense of normal behavior.

The difficulty of harmonizing real and virtual presence isn't new. As Mark Caldwell noted in *A Short History of Rudeness* about the first telephones, "many early phone stories involved a bumpkin who nods silently in reply to a caller's increasingly agitated, 'Are you there?' " Even young children know Goffman's rules. When a parent is in front of a child but on the telephone (physically present but mentally "away"), a child will frequently protest—grabbing for the phone or vocalizing loudly to retrieve the parent's attention. They are expressing a need for recognition that, in a less direct and individualized way, we all require from strangers in public space. But the challenge is greater given the sheer number of wireless users, a reality that is prompting a new form of social criticism. As a "commentary on the potential of the mobile phone for disrupting and disturbing social interactions," the Interaction Design Institute Ivrea recently sponsored a project called "Mass Distraction." The project featured jackets and cell phones that only allowed participants to talk on their phones if the large hood of the jacket was closed completely over their head or if they continued to insert coins into the pocket of the jacket like an old fashioned pay phone. "In order to remain connected," the project notes, "the mobile phone user multitasks between the two communication channels. Whether disguised or not, this practice degrades the quality of the interaction with the people in his immediate presence."

Cocooned within our "Personal Area Networks" and wirelessly transported 45
to other spaces, we are becoming increasingly immune to the boundaries and realities of physical space. As one reporter for the *Los Angeles Times* said, in exasperation, "Go ahead, floss in the elevator. You're busy; you can't be expected to wait until you can find a bathroom. ... [T]he world out there? It's just a backdrop, as movable and transient as a fake skyline on a studio lot." No one is an outsider with a cell phone—that is why foreign cab drivers in places like New York and Washington are openly willing to ignore laws against driving-and-talking. Beyond the psychic benefits cell phone calls provide (cab driving is a lonely occupation), their use signals the cab driver's membership in a community apart from the ever-changing society that frequents his taxi. Our cell phones become our talismans against being perceived as (or feeling ourselves to be) outsiders.

Talk and Conversation

Recently, on a trip to China, I found myself standing on the Great Wall. One of the members of our small group had hiked ahead, and since the rest of us had decided it was time to get back down the mountain, we realized we would need to find him. Despite being in a remote location at high altitude, and having completely lost sight of him in the hazy late morning air, this proved to be the easiest of logistical tasks. One man pulled out his cell phone, called his wife back in the United States, and had her send an e-mail to the man who had walked ahead. Knowing that our lost companion religiously checked his BlackBerry wireless, we reasoned that he would surely notice an incoming message. Soon enough he reappeared, our wireless plea for his return having successfully traveled from China to Washington and back again to the Wall in mere minutes.

At the time, we were all caught up in the James Bond-like excitement of our mission. Would the cell phone work? (It did.) Would the wife's e-mail get through to our companion's BlackBerry? (No problem.) Only later, as we drove back to Beijing, did I experience a pang of doubt about our small communications triumph. There, at one of the Great Wonders of the World, a centuries-old example of human triumph over nature, we didn't hesitate to do something as mundane as make a cell phone call. It is surely true that wireless communication is its own wondrous triumph over nature. But cell phone conversation somehow inspires less awe than standing atop the Great Wall, perhaps because atop the Great Wall we are still rooted in the natural world that we have conquered. Or perhaps it is simply because cell phones have become everyday wonders—as unremarkable to us as the Great Wall is to those who see it everyday.

Christian Licoppe and Jean-Philippe Heurtin have argued that cell phone use must be understood in a broader context; they note that the central feature of the modern experience is the "deinstitutionalization of personal bonds." Deinstitutionalization spawns anxiety, and as a result we find ourselves working harder to build trust relationships. Cell phone calls "create a web of short, content-poor interactions through which bonds can be built and strengthened in an ongoing process."

But as trust is being built and bolstered moment by moment between individuals, public trust among strangers in social settings is eroding. We are strengthening and increasing our interactions with the people we already know at the expense of those who we do not. The result, according to Kenneth Gergen, is "the erosion of face-to-face community, a coherent and centered sense of self, moral bearings, depth of relationship, and the uprooting of meaning from material context: such are the dangers of absent presence."

No term captures this paradoxical state more ably than the word "roam," which 50
appears on your phone when you leave an area bristling with wireless towers and go into the wilds of the less well connected. The word appears when your cell phone is looking for a way to connect you, but the real definition of roam is "to go from place to place without purpose or direction," which has more suggestive implications. It suggests that we have allowed our phones to become the link to our purpose and the symbol of our status—without its signal we lack direction. Roaming was a word whose previous use was largely confined to describing the activities of herds of cattle. In her report on the use of mobile phones throughout the world, Sadie Plant noted, "according to the *Oxford English Dictionary*, one of the earliest uses of the word 'mobile' was in association with the Latin phrase *mobile vulgus*, the excitable crowd," whence comes our word "mob."

Convenience and safety—the two reasons people give for why they have (or "need") cell phones—are legitimate reasons for using wireless technology; but they are not neutral. Convenience is the major justification for fast food, but its overzealous consumption has something to do with our national obesity "epidemic." Safety spawned a bewildering range of anti-bacterial products and the overzealous prescription of antibiotics—which in turn led to disease-resistant bacteria.

One possible solution would be to treat cell phone use the way we now treat tobacco use. Public spaces in America were once littered with spittoons and the residue of the chewing tobacco that filled them, despite the disgust the practice fostered. Social norms eventually rendered public spitting déclassé. Similarly, it was not so long ago that cigarette smoking was something people did everywhere—in movie theaters, restaurants, trains, and airplanes. Non-smokers often had a hard time finding refuge from the clouds of nicotine. Today, we ban smoking in all but designated areas. Currently, cell phone users enjoy the same privileges smokers once enjoyed, but there is no reason we cannot reverse the trend. Yale University bans cell phones in some of its libraries, and Amtrak's introduction of "quiet cars" on some of its routes has been eagerly embraced by commuters. Perhaps one day we will exchange quiet cars for wireless cars, and the majority of public space will revert to the quietly disconnected. In doing so, we might partially reclaim something higher even than healthy lungs: civility.

This reclaiming of social space could have considerable consequences. As sociologist de Gournay has noted, "the telephone is a device ill suited to listening…it is more appropriate for exchanging information." Considering Americans' obsession with information—we are, after all, the "information society"—it is useful to draw the distinction. Just as there is a distinction between information and knowledge, there is a vast difference between conversation and talk.

Conversation (as opposed to "talk") is to genuine sociability what courtship (as opposed to "hooking up") is to romance. And the technologies that mediate these distinctions are important: the cell phone exchange of information is a distant relative of formal conversation, just as the Internet chat room is a far less compelling place to become intimate with another person than a formal date. In both cases, however, we have convinced ourselves as a culture that these alternatives are just as good as the formalities—that they are, in fact, improvements upon them.

"A conversation has a life of its own and makes demands on its own behalf," 55
Goffman wrote. "It is a little social system with its own boundary-making tendencies; it is a little patch of commitment and loyalty with its own heroes and its own villains." According to census data, the percentage of Americans who live alone is the highest it has ever been in our country's history, making a return to genuine sociability and conversation more important than ever. Cell phones provide us with a new, but not necessarily superior means of communicating with each other. They encourage talk, not conversation. They link us to those we know, but remove us from the strangers who surround us in public space. Our constant accessibility and frequent exchange of information is undeniably useful. But it would be a terrible irony if "being connected" required or encouraged a disconnection from community life—an erosion of the spontaneous encounters and everyday decencies that make society both civilized and tolerable.

THINGS TO DO WITH THE READING

1. Talk and conversation offer an organizing contrast (binary) in Rosen's essay. Track the strands attached to each of these key terms and write a paragraph or two about how they suggest what is at stake in this piece. What other binaries figure prominently?
2. Practice Paraphrase × 3 (see Chapters 1 and 4) as a way of more fully assimilating Rosen's position. Try paraphrasing paragraph 49, which begins "But as trust is being built." Or choose other paragraphs or single sentences that you think are key.
3. What is this essay assuming about the function of manners in a culture? In other words, reason back to the premises underlying Rosen's point of view. Rosen refers, for example, to something she calls "social space." What are some of Rosen's stated—and unstated—assumptions about this space? (See Chapter 3, Extended Example 3 on reasoning back to premises.)
4. Rosen's essay is a piece of research writing that makes use of a number of other writers and theorists, most notably the sociologist Erving Goffman. What use does Rosen make of this research?
5. **Application:** Near the end of the section "Will You Please Be Quiet, Please?", in paragraph 30 (which begins with "Not surprisingly"), Rosen cites an etiquette expert, Jacqueline Whitmore, who observes, "Wireless technology is booming so quickly and wireless phones are becoming so popular, the rules on wireless etiquette are still evolving." This idea is worth investigating. Spend a few days observing cell phone behavior; take careful notes. Your goal is to look for trends in cell phone etiquette. What is that etiquette? Where and how do you see it evolving? Write up your results.

   You might extend this project by exploring further the disagreement between Rosen and Whitmore on what Rosen calls "wireless rectitude." Rosen claims at the end of the paragraph that there is a mismatch between people's reports of their behavior and their actual behavior. Develop a few questions about cell phone use and ask them of your friends or peers. Compare the results with your actual observations.

Paul Goldberger

Disconnected Urbanism

Paul Goldberger is the architecture critic for *The New Yorker* and the dean of the Parsons School of Design, following a 25-year career at the *New York Times*, where he won a Pulitzer Prize in 1984 for his architecture criticism. His most recent book is entitled *Up From Zero: Architecture, Politics and the Rebuilding of New York* (2004). In this short piece, taken from Metropolismag.com (November 2003), Goldberger considers the impact of the cell phone on our sense of place.

There is a connection between the idea of place and the reality of cellular telephones. It is not encouraging. Places are unique—or at least we like to believe they are—and we strive to experience them as a kind of engagement with particulars. Cell phones are precisely the opposite. When a piece of geography is doing what it is supposed to do, it encourages you to feel a connection to it that, as in marriage, forsakes all others. When you are in Paris you expect to wallow in its Parisness, to feel that everyone walking up the Boulevard Montparnasse is as totally and completely there as the lampposts, the kiosks, the facade of the Brasserie Lipp—and that they could be no place else. So we want it to be in every city, in every kind of place. When you are in a forest, you want to experience its woodsiness; when you are on the beach, you want to feel connected to sand and surf. 1

This is getting harder to do, not because these special places don't exist or because urban places have come to look increasingly alike. They have, but this is not another rant about the monoculture and sameness of cities and the suburban landscape. Even when you are in a place that retains its intensity, its specialness, and its ability to confer a defining context on your life, it doesn't have the all-consuming effect these places used to. You no longer feel that being in one place cuts you off from other places. Technology has been doing this for a long time, of course—remember when people communicated with Europe by letter and it took a couple of weeks to get a reply? Now we're upset if we have to send a fax because it takes so much longer than e-mail.

But the cell phone has changed our sense of place more than faxes and computers and e-mail because of its ability to intrude into every moment in every possible place. When you walk along the street and talk on a cell phone, you are not on the street sharing the communal experience of urban life. You are in some other place—someplace at the other end of your phone conversation. You are there, but you are not there. It reminds me of the title of Lillian Ross's memoir of her life with William Shawn, *Here But Not Here*. Now that is increasingly true of almost every person on almost every street in almost every city. You are either on the phone or carrying one, and the moment it rings you will be transported out of real space into a virtual realm.

This matters because the street is the ultimate public space and walking along it is the defining urban experience. It is all of us—different people who lead different lives—coming together in the urban mixing chamber. But what if half of them are elsewhere, there in body but not in any other way? You are not on

Madison Avenue if you are holding a little object to your ear that pulls you toward a person in Omaha.

5 The great offense of the cell phone in public is not the intrusion of its ring, although that can be infuriating when it interrupts a tranquil moment. It is the fact that even when the phone does not ring at all, and is being used quietly and discreetly, it renders a public place less public. It turns the boulevardier into a sequestered individual, the flaneur into a figure of privacy. And suddenly the meaning of the street as a public place has been hugely diminished.

I don't know which is worse—the loss of the sense that walking along a great urban street is a glorious shared experience or the blurring of distinctions between different kinds of places. But these cultural losses are related, and the cell phone has played a major role in both. The other day I returned a phone call from a friend who lives in Hartford. He had left a voice-mail message saying he was visiting his son in New Orleans, and when I called him back on his cell phone—area code 860, Hartford—he picked up the call in Tallahassee. Once the area code actually meant something in terms of geography: it outlined a clearly defined piece of the earth; it became a form of identity. Your telephone number was a badge of place. Now the area code is really not much more than three digits; and if it has any connection to a place, it's just the telephone's home base. An area code today is more like a car's license plate. The downward spiral that began with the end of the old telephone exchanges that truly did connect to a place—RHinelander 4 and BUtterfield 8 for the Upper East Side, or CHelsea 3 downtown, or UNiversity 4 in Morningside Heights—surely culminates in the placeless area codes such as 917 and 347 that could be anywhere in New York—or anywhere at all.

It's increasingly common for cell-phone conversations to begin with the question, "Where are you?" and for the answer to be anything from "out by the pool" to "Madagascar." I don't miss the age when phone charges were based on distance, but that did have the beneficial effect of reinforcing a sense that places were distinguishable from one another. Now calling across the street and calling from New York to California or even Europe are precisely the same thing. They cost the same because to the phone they are the same. Every place is exactly the same as every other place. They are all just nodes on a network—and so, increasingly, are we.

THINGS TO DO WITH THE READING

1. Close read the final sentence of Goldberger's piece. Start by doing Paraphrase × 3 (see Chapters 1 and 4) to open the range of possible meanings. What is the *tone* of this remark? What point of view is Goldberger inviting readers to adopt? (See page 211 for an explanation of close reading and see page 260 for a definition of tone.)
2. **Link:** In "Our Cell Phones, Ourselves," Christine Rosen writes of the use of cell phones in public, "It is the intentional removal of oneself from the

social situation in public. This removal, as sociologists have long shown, is something more serious than a mere manners lapse. It amounts to a radical disengagement from the public sphere." Locate any statement in Goldberger's essay that connects in some interesting way with Rosen's remark. Then do a focused freewrite on the two together, getting them to interact. (See Try this 12.3 on pages 308–309 for the broader rationale.)

3. How is Goldberger using the term "public space"? The idea of a public sphere and of public space is one that connects not only the readings in this chapter but those in several other chapters as well, so you might wish to begin collecting the different ways that the readings define and value the idea of public space.
4. Obviously, this is a piece about cell phones. But it is also, arguably, using cell phones to discuss larger matters. In such cases, the writing prompt "Seems to be about *x* but could also be (is 'really') about *y*" (Chapter 3) can stimulate you to more fully register and develop the broader implications of the piece. Use the prompt to explore what the piece wishes to argue about the relationship between people and places. ("Seems to be about cell phones, but is really (or also) about *y*.")

Jeffrey Rosen

The Naked Crowd

"Why is it that American anxiety about identity has led us to value exposure over privacy? Why, in short, are we so eager to become members of the Naked Crowd, in which we have the illusion of belonging only when we are exposed?" This essay by a professor of law at George Washington University and legal affairs editor of the *New Republic* is excerpted from his recent book, *The Naked Crowd: Reclaiming Security and Freedom in an Anxious Age* (2004).

After 9/11, the most celebrated ritual of mourning was the *New York Times*'s Portraits of Grief. For months after the attack, the *New York Times* published more than 1,800 sketches of those who died in the collapse of the World Trade Centre. Not designed as obituaries in the traditional sense—at 200 words, there was no space for a full accounting of the lives that had been cut short—the Portraits were offered up as 'brief, informal, and impressionistic, often centred on a single story or idiosyncratic detail', intended not 'to recount a person's résumé, but rather to give a snapshot of each victim's personality, of a life lived'. 1

The Portraits were intended to be democratic—showing the personal lives of janitors as well as chief executives. Above all, they attempted to recognise the victims as distinctive individuals, each distinguished from the crowd. 'One felt, looking at those pages every day, that real lives were jumping out at you', said Paul Auster, the novelist, when interviewed by the *New York Times* about the profiles. 'We weren't mourning an anonymous mass of people, we were mourning thousands of individuals. And the more we knew about them, the more we could wrestle with our own grief.' (1)

Although public criticism of the Portraits of Grief was hard to detect during the months of their publication, a few dissident voices emerged after the series came to an end. More than 80 percent of the victims' families agreed to talk to the *New York Times*, but a handful of them later complained that the Portraits had failed to capture the people they had known. In an eloquent essay in the *American Scholar*, the literary critic Thomas Mallon echoed this criticism, arguing that in the process of trying to individualise their subjects, the Portraits of Grief had managed to homogenise them instead. 'To read the Portraits one would believe that work counted for next to nothing, that every hard charging bond trader and daredevil fireman preferred—and managed—to spend more time with his family than at the office', Mallon wrote.

American obituaries, to a certain extent, tend to obey the convention of speaking well of the dead (British obituaries are far nastier), but the Portraits of Grief were not successful on their own terms: instead of recognising the public achievements of lives that had reached some kind of fulfilment, the Portraits instead trivialised their subjects by emphasising one or two private hobbies or quirks. As a result, any genuine achievements or complexity of personality were airbrushed away in the narrative effort to reduce each person to a single, memorable, and democratically accessible detail. 'If Mayor Rudolph Giuliani had perished in the attacks, as he nearly did', Mallon concluded, 'he would be remembered in the Portraits as a rabid Yankee fan who sometimes liked to put on lipstick' (2).

5 The homogenising effects of the Portraits of Grief were inherent in the project itself. The *New York Times* instructed its reporters to convey a sense of the victims as distinct individuals by extracting from conversations with their families a single representative detail about their lives that would give readers the illusion of having known them. In each case, complexity and accuracy had to be sacrificed to the narrative imperative of finding a memorable quirk of personality with which the audience could quickly identify.

But the Portraits of Grief were not designed to do justice to the victims in all of their complexity. They were designed as a form of therapy for the families of the victims and as a source of emotional connection for the readers of the *New York Times.* They aspired to give all Americans the illusion of identifying with the victims, and therefore allowing them to feel that they themselves had somehow been touched by the horrific event. What was flattened out in this juggernaut of democratic connection was the individuality of the victims themselves.

This flattening resulted from a broader demand: the crowd's insistence on emotionally memorable images at the expense of genuine human individuality. The crowd, which thinks in terms of images rather than arguments, demands a sense of emotional connection with everyone who catches its fleeting attention. This means that everyone who is subject to the scrutiny of the crowd—from celebrities to political candidates to the families of terrorists' victims—will feel pressure to parcel out bits of personal information in order to allow unseen strangers to experience a sense of vicarious identification.

But revealing one or two personal details to strangers is inevitably a trivialising experience that leads us to be judged out of context. It's impossible to know someone on the basis of snippets of information; genuine knowledge is something that can only be achieved slowly, over time, behind a shield of privacy, with the handful of people to whom we've chosen to reveal ourselves whole.

The sociologist Thomas Mathiesen has contrasted Michel Foucault's Panopticon—a surveillance house in which the few watched the many—with what he called the 'Synopticon' created by modern television, in which the many watch the few. But in the age of the internet, we are experiencing something that might be called the 'Omnipticon' in which the many are watching the many, even though no one knows precisely who is watching or being watched at any given time. The homogenisation wrought by the Portraits of Grief is a symptom of the identity crisis that Americans are experiencing as they attempt to negotiate the challenges of the Omnipticon—a world in which more and more citizens are subject to the scrutiny of strangers. The challenges of interacting with strangers have increased the pressures on Americans to trade privacy for an illusory sense of security and connection, turning many of us into virtual portraits of grief.

Exposing Ourselves

10 The British sociologist Anthony Giddens has described the ways that citizens in a risk society can no longer rely on tradition or fixed hierarchies to establish their identity or to give them reliable guidance about whom to trust in a society of strangers. Confused and anxious about status in a world where status is constantly

shifting, we feel increasing pressure to expose details of our personal lives to strangers in order to win their trust, and we demand that they expose themselves in order to win our trust in return. 'Trust—in a person or in a system, such as a banking system—can be a means of coping with risk, while acceptance of risk can be a means of generating trust', Giddens writes (3).

In the past, intimate relationships of trust—such as marriage, friendship, and business associations—were based on rigidly controlled status hierarchies, which brought with them codes of expected behaviours: you could behave one way with your wife and another with your servant and another with your boss, because you had no doubt where you stood in relationship to each of them, and where they stood in relation to you. Today, by contrast, intimacy and trust are increasingly obtained not by shared experiences or fixed social status but by self-revelation: people try to prove their trustworthiness by revealing details of their personal lives to prove that they have nothing to hide before a crowd whose gaze is turned increasingly on all the individuals that compose it.

A world where individuals have to prove their trustworthiness and value every day before the crowd, choosing among an infinite range of lifestyles, behaviours, clothes, and values, is inevitably a world that creates great anxiety about identity. Rather than conforming to preexisting social roles, individuals are expected to find their true selves and constantly to market themselves to a sceptical world. In the 1950s, Eric Fromm wrote about the 'marketing orientation' of the American self, in which 'man experiences himself as a thing to be employed successfully on the market. ... His sense of value depends on his success: on whether he can sell himself favourably. ... If the individual fails in a profitable investment of himself, he feels that he is a failure; if he succeeds, *he* is a success.' (4) Fromm worried that the marketed personality, whose precarious sense of self-worth was entirely dependent on the fickle judgements of the market, would be wracked by alienation and anxiety.

The internet has vastly increased the opportunities for individuals to subject themselves to the demands of the personality market, resulting in ever increasing confusion and anxiety about how much of ourselves to reveal to strangers. The logic of Fromm's marketed self is being extended into a virtual world where the easiest way to attract the attention and winning the trust of strangers is to establish an emotional connection with them by projecting a consistent, memorable, and trustworthy image. In an ideal relationship of trust, self-revelation should be reciprocal. In the age of the internet, however, we are increasingly forced to interact with strangers whom we will never meet face-to-face. As a result, individuals find themselves in more and more situations where they feel pressure to reveal details of their personal lives without being able to gauge the audience's reaction. But the quest for attention from and emotional connection with strangers is fraught with peril (5).

In 2000, for example, Laurence Tribe, the constitutional scholar from Harvard Law School, posted a personal statement on his family's website. 'I'm Larry', Tribe wrote. 'I love brilliant magenta sunsets, unagi, Martin Amis' *Time's Arrow*, the fish tank at MGH, T.S. Eliot's 'Love Song of J Alfred Prufrock', eating, my stairmaster, looking at the ocean, dreaming about impossible things, *New Yorker* cartoons, the twist in a short story, *The Hotel New Hampshire*, good (and even not-so-good) movies, rereading *The Great Gatsby* and *Ethan Frome*, and Monet and Vermeer.' Several websites devoted to media gossip posted links mocking Tribe's statement for displaying the overly intimate tones of a personal ad. Embarrassed by the public reaction, Tribe tried to remove the statement, but one of the media gossip sites resurrected it from the archives of Google, the popular internet search engine. Tribe was then ridiculed more for his attempt to cover his tracks than for his initial act of self-exposure.

'The website itself was a thing our son helped Carolyn and me put together 15
one Christmas', Tribe emailed me later, reflecting on his experience. 'I was having fun letting my hair down, as it were, in just chatting about myself as unselfconsciously as I could, not giving much of a thought to who might read it but probably assuming, naively it now seems, that it wouldn't really be of interest to anybody. When I learned that people were finding it a source of public amusement, I do admit to being nonplussed and unsure of what to do.' Tribe's understandable error shows how hard it is to strike a decent balance between personal disclosure and the projection of a consistent image, especially on the internet.

Many citizens, of course, don't care if they embarrass themselves before strangers on the internet, as the proliferation of personal websites shows. It is now commonplace on a website to reveal hobbies, favourite foods and music, and pictures of children, in an effort to create an illusion of intimacy. Even the most intimate moments of life, such as a wedding, are now being posted on the web for public consumption. The private moments offered up for public consumption tend to be generic tropes of informality which, like the Portraits of Grief, have a homogenising effect. Instead of the beginning of a romantic partnership, one often has the impression of watching a particularly excruciating episode of *The Dating Game*. And then there are the reality TV shows, which represent the most absurd examples of the application of the values of the public opinion society to the most intimate activities of life.

One way of understanding privacy is not whether we choose to expose personal information in public—we all do at different times and places—but the ease with which we can return to being private. The internet, however, is complicating our ability to negotiate the boundary between public and private, making it hard to recover a private self that has been voluntarily exposed. Consider the proliferation of weblogs—personal internet journals that often combine political musings with intimate disclosures about daily life. There are more than half a million, according to a recent estimate (6). Some are devoted exclusively to public affairs, while others are nothing more than published diaries. A website called Diarist.net collects more than 5,000 journals from self-styled 'online exhibitionists' (7). Often, these diaries are virtually unreadable examples of self display, dreary accounts of daily navel gazing whose primary function seems to be therapeutic. But they reflect a common but treacherous error: that thoughts appropriate to reveal to friends and intimates are also appropriate to reveal to the world.

In a pluralistic society, people are and should be free to have different instincts about the proper balance between reticence and self-revelation. If exercises in personal exhibitionism give pleasure to the exhibitionists and an illusory sense of emotional connection for the virtual audience, there's no harm done except to the dignity of the individuals concerned, and that's nobody's business but their own.

But the growing pressure to expose ourselves in front of strangers has obvious and important consequences for a democracy's ability to strike a reasonable balance between liberty and security. The ease with which we reveal ourselves suggests that in the face of widespread anxiety about identity, people are more concerned with the feeling of connection than with the personal and social costs of exposure. Why is it that American anxiety about identity has led us to value exposure over privacy? Why, in short, are we so eager to become members of the Naked Crowd, in which we have the illusion of belonging only when we are exposed?

From Sincerity to Authenticity

Anxiety about how much of ourselves to reveal to strangers has always been a defining trait of the American character. But the form of the anxiety changed over the course of the nineteenth and twentieth centuries, reflecting changes in society and technology. In the late nineteenth century, conceptions of personal truthfulness changed in a way that the critic Lionel Trilling has described as a change from sincerity to authenticity (8).

20 By sincerity, Trilling meant the expectation that individuals should avoid duplicity in their dealings with each other: there should be an honest correlation between what is exposed in public and what is felt in private; but not everything that is felt has to be exposed. By authenticity, Trilling meant the expectation that instead of being honest with each other, individuals should be honest with themselves, and should have no compunction about directly exposing strangers to their most intimate emotions. Sincerity requires that whatever is exposed must be true; authenticity requires that everything must be exposed as long as it is deeply felt.

In an age of sincerity, the fine clothes and family crest of an aristocrat were the markers of the self; in an age of authenticity, as the sociologist Peter Berger has noted, 'the escutcheons hide the true self. It is precisely the naked man, and even more specifically the naked man expressing his sexuality, who represents himself more truthfully.' (9) The motto for the age of sincerity came from the Delphic Oracle: Know Thyself. The motto for the age of authenticity comes from the therapist: Be Thyself.

As self-disclosure became the yardstick of trustworthiness, individuals began to relate to strangers in psychological terms. Politicians, like actors on the stage, came to be judged as trustworthy only if they could convincingly dramatise their own emotions and motivations. 'The content of political belief recedes as in public, people become more interested in the content of the politician's life', Richard Sennett writes. 'The modern charismatic leader destroys any distance between his own sentiments and impulses and those of his audience, and so, focusing his followers on his motivations, deflects them from measuring him in terms of his acts.' (10) The earnest nod, the brow furrowed by concern, and the well-timed tear are now more important for politicians than traditional skills of oratory.

In *The Image*, Daniel Boorstin explored the way the growth of movies, radio, print, and television had transformed the nature of political authority, which came to be exercised not by distant and remote heroes but instead by celebrities, whom Boorstin defined as 'a person who is known for his well-knownness'. 'Neither good nor bad', a celebrity is 'morally neutral', 'the human pseudo-event', who has been 'fabricated on purpose to satisfy our exaggerated expectations of human greatness' (11). While the heroes of old exercised authority by being remote and mysterious, modern celebrities exercise authority by being familiar and intelligible, creating the impression—but not the reality—of emotional accessibility. Heroes were distinguished by their achievement, celebrities by their images or trademarks or 'name brands'.

In an age when images were becoming more important than reality, Boorstin lamented the fact that politicians were trying to hold the attention of the crowd by recasting themselves in the mould of celebrities, projecting an image of emotional authenticity through selective self-disclosure. He feared that as synthesised images took the place of complicated human reality, the result would be a proliferation of conformity: politicians would have to alter their personalities to fit with the images that the crowd expected them to present; and the believability of the image would become more important than the underlying human truth.

Boorstin wrote before the development of the internet. But as life increasingly 25
takes place in cyberspace, private citizens are now facing some of the same social pressures and technological opportunities as politicians to expose and market themselves to strangers, with similarly homogenising results. As the internet has increased the circumstances in which ordinary citizens are forced to present a coherent image to strangers, the methodology of public relations is increasingly being applied to the presentation of the self. Ordinary citizens are now being forced to market themselves like pseudo-events, using techniques that used to be reserved for politicians, corporations, and celebrities. In an eerie fulfilment of Boorstin's fears, business gurus today are urging individuals to project a consistent image to the crowd by creating a personal brand.

Personal Branding

The idea of selling people as products began to appear in magazines like *Ad Age* as early as the 1970s; but the idea of personal branding didn't proliferate until the 1990s, when a series of business books emerged with names like *Brand You*, *The Personal Branding Phenomenon*, and *Be Your Own Brand: A Breakthrough Formula for Standing Out from the Crowd*. To invent a successful brand you have to establish trust with strangers, argues the personal branding guru, Tom Peters. A brand is a 'trust mark' that 'reaches out with a powerful connecting experience'. To connect with colleagues and customers, you have to decide the one thing you want them to know about you and create an 'emotional context' by telling stories about yourself. Peters's nostrums are an example of the banalisation of Gustave Le Bon; and *Be Your Own Brand* is in the same vein. It defines a personal brand as 'a perception or emotion, maintained by somebody other than you, that describes the total experience of having a relationship with you.'

Like the brand of a corporation or product, personal brands are defined by whether people trust, like, remember, and value you: 'your brand, just like the brand of a product, exists on the basis of a set of perceptions and emotions stored in someone else's head'. To create a strong personal brand that makes and maintains an emotional connection with strangers, individuals are advised to be 'distinctive, relevant, and consistent'.

To achieve the goals of distinctiveness, relevance, and consistency, branded individuals are urged to simplify the complex characteristics that make up a genuine individual. Following the model of the Portraits of Grief, personal branders urge their clients to write down a list of the adjectives that best describe their personal style and values, and to incorporate three of them in a 'personal brand promise' that can easily be remembered. For example, a surgeon who says he is 'humble, collaborative, and friendly' promises 'the discipline to achieve world-class results'; a writer who claims to be 'enthusiastic, energetic, and professional' promises 'enthusiasm that will make your day'. These brand attributes are so abstract and banal that they are impossible to remember, which is why the entire enterprise seems dubious, even on its own terms; but they neatly achieve the goal of turning individuals into stereotypes, for the purpose of making them intelligible to strangers with short attention spans.

In *The Lonely Crowd*, his classic study of the American self in the 1950s, the sociologist David Riesman distinguished between the inner-directed individual, who derives his identity from an internal moral gyroscope, and the outer-directed individual, who derives his identity from the expectations of the crowd. By measuring individuals in terms of their success on the personality market, the personal branding strategy seems at first to be an apotheosis of outer-directedness. But the personal branding books deny this, emphasising that successfully branded individuals must first look inward, to discover their authentic selves, and then turn outward, attempting to market that self to the world.

'Trust is built faster and maintained longer when people believe you are being real, not putting on a false front to cover up what's really going on inside of you', the branding manual counsels. 'When it comes to relationships, authenticity is what others say they want most from us. We make the most lasting and vivid impressions when people witness us being true to our beliefs, staying in alignment with who and what we really are.' (12) The self constructed by the personal branders, then, is an anxious hybrid of Riesman's two types: a form of marketed authenticity in which the self is turned inside out, and then sold to the world.

Although the phenomenon of personal brand management is in its infancy, it represents the logical application of marketing technologies to the most intimate aspects of the self. But its hazards are already becoming evident; and they have to do with the substitution of image-making for genuine individuality. As early as 1997, the *New York Times* reported that an unhappy bachelor had convened a focus group of the single women who had rejected him. As he watched from behind a one-way mirror, they evaluated his dating performance, and offered advice for improvement. Meeting in the studios of a market research company called Focus Suites, where consumers usually gather to criticise soap or cereal, the women urged him to bolster his confidence and change his wardrobe. 'I think it's really alarming that we let a market economy dictate our human relationships', the head of the company told the *New York Times*. 'I think it's much more healthy for the human model to dictate to the business world than for the business model to inform human life.' (13)

Allowing public opinion to expand into the recesses of the soul, the entrepreneurs of the self insist that personal branding is a spiritual as well as an economic imperative. Nick Shore, the head of a New York advertising agency called the

Way Group, is writing a book called *Who Are You: The Search for Your Authentic Self in Business.* Over the phone, Shore told me that his personal 'brand DNA' was 'a punk rocker in a pinstripe suit—that's how I understand myself'. But when I met him at his stylish loft office in the Chelsea Market, he turned out to be a young British man in khakis and a sweater. 'The classical distinctions between personal life, professional life, what I do in my family, how I set up my business, how I plan my career' are breaking down, Shore said. 'It's this whole postmodern idea of the script to life just basically being thrown away and no one quite knows exactly what they're supposed to do in any given situation. … If I can't find true worth by looking to the corporation that I work for or by looking to the government or the queen, then ultimately you end up with yourself, you have to find your own truth.'

In the 1950s, the organisation man was told to find what the marketplace wants and supply it. But in a talent economy, Shore says, 'it's the other way around: find out what you are then go look for the space in the market place that needs that'. Successful brands must be authentic because 'the marketplace smells a rat', and consumers, in deciding whom to trust, are suspicious of any gaps between the image of the person or product being marked and the underlying reality. 'In the old days somebody would look at a business card and say, "oh, this guy's a vice president; I'll put him on a hierarchy". Now they look at your haircut and your shirt and a box of other stuff, and they say, "this is the box this guy fits in". And if what he's doing is not real, if he's only trying to protect an image, they notice.'

This leads to the phenomenon of marketed authenticity. 'Because consumers are sensitive to inauthenticity, you have to look inside out, not outside in: you have to start from the core and then move outward', Shore said. Only those whose public and private reality are aligned can sustain the attention of the marketplace. Far from trying to capture the authentic self in all of its complexities, however, branding is a technology for the simplification of identity, a response to the short attention spans of the audience. 'In marketing terms, it's always been about, strip away, strip away', Shore emphasised. 'People are troubled about thinking about more than one thing at once. If you're trying to project something and you try to be penetrative into people's consciousness you have to be absolutely simple and to the point about it all—otherwise people can't hold it.' In trying to excavate a person's 'brand DNA', Shore says that he is suspicious of long lists of abstract characteristics. 'It's too complicated, it's too generic. If I said, you are an "Individualistic Maverick", that can describe all people. But if I tell you that someone's a "Modern-Day Robin Hood", that's pointed. You'll remember "Modern-Day Robin Hood" for 10 years.' (A few hours later, when I tried to repeat this slogan to my wife, I had already managed to forget it.)

Although presented in the therapeutic language of self-actualisation, personal branding is ultimately a technology for the rigid control of personal identity. Personal branding claims to help individuals be distinctive, so that they can differentiate themselves from the crowd and become more successful competitors in the marketplace of the self. But in the process of seeking distinctiveness, personal branding is ultimately a recipe for a smothering conformity. Branding confuses distinctiveness and individuality.

Products can be differentiated from each other, with the techniques of advertising and public relations. But the application of branding technologies to the self is based on a category error: individuals can't distinguish themselves from the crowd by measuring their value to the crowd. All of the private attributes of human individuality change shape when they are turned outward and presented to the public: Eros becomes sex; sin becomes crime; guilt becomes shame.

When everything is exposed to the crowd, as John Stuart Mill recognised, individuality is impossible. 'As the various social eminences which enabled persons entrenched on them to disregard the opinion of the multitude, gradually become levelled; as the very idea of resisting the will of the public, when it is positively known that they have a will disappears more and more from the minds of practical politicians; there ceases to be any social support for nonconformity', Mill lamented. 'It is individuality we war against', he concluded, because of the 'ascendancy of public opinion in the State' (14).

We can now appreciate with special force the distinction between the individuality praised by Mill and the individualism lamented by Alexis de Tocqueville, which he defined as the tendency of citizens in a democracy to isolate themselves from each other and to focus obsessively on their own self-interest. Even more than the Victorian era, ours is an age of individualism rather than individuality. The growth of media technologies such as the internet and television have increased the overwhelming authority of public opinion, as citizens in the Omnipticon find more and more aspects of their personal and public lives observed and evaluated by strangers. These technologies tend to encourage citizens to be self-absorbed, as terrifying images from across the country or across the globe give them an exaggerated sense of personal vulnerability.

At the same time, by decreasing the distance between central authorities and individual citizens, these technologies lead people to expect personal protection from national leaders, rather than taking responsibility for their own freedom and security at a local level. The related feelings of personal anxiety and personal helplessness feed on themselves, and the technology now exists to bring about the conformity that Mill most feared.

The Comfort of Strangers?

The personal branding movement is based on the same fantasy that underlay the Portraits of Grief, which is the fantasy that people can achieve emotional intimacy with strangers. But there is no such thing as public intimacy. Intimacy can be achieved only with those who know us; and strangers cannot know us; they can only have information about us or impressions of us. To offer up personal information that has been taken out of context, in an effort to create the illusion of emotional connection with strangers, requires us to homogenise and standardise the very qualities that made the information personal in the first place. The family members of the 9/11 victims who offered up details of their mourning to the *New York Times* are not so different from the family members of the victim of a car crash who, moments after the accident, weep on cue for the local news. What is most alarming about these scenes is not the tears but the fact that, even at moments of tragedy, we instinctively look at the camera and talk into the microphone.

The personal branding phenomenon is a crude attempt to provide regulated forms of self-exposure, to maintain some kind of boundary between public and private in a world where self-revelation has become a social imperative. And of course most citizens will never resort to expert assistance in their efforts to present a coherent face to the world. But living in the Omnipticon, where we are increasingly unsure about who is observing us, individuals will have to worry more about acting consistently in public and private, in precisely the way the branding advisors prescribe.

In the 1980s, before the proliferation of the web, the sociologist Joshua Meyrowitz discussed the way the electronic media were changing what he called the 'situational geography' of social life (15). As television made us one large audience to performances that occurred in other places, the old walls that separated backstage areas, where people could let down their hair and rehearse for public performances, from the frontstage areas, where the formal performances occurred, began to collapse. Television made viewers aware of the discrepancy between front- and backstage behaviour (such as the woman who plays hard to get, or the fearful man who acts confident in a reality TV dating show), and it became increasingly hard for people to project different images in public and in private without appearing artificial or inauthentic.

Now that the internet is allowing strangers to observe us even as we observe them, ordinary citizens have to worry more about being caught off guard, like actors with their wigs off. As a form of self-defence, all citizens face the same pressures that confused Laurence Tribe: we will increasingly adopt what Meyrowitz called 'middle region' behaviour in public: a blend of the formal frontstage and informal backstage, with a bias toward self-conscious informality. As private concerns like sexual behaviour and depression, anxieties and doubts become harder to conceal, they have to be integrated into the public performance. The result can create an illusion of familiarity—the crazy heavy metal rock star Ozzy Osborne looked cuddlier (though still scatological) as MTV cameras recorded every moment of his domestic life for a reality TV show. But the cuddly domesticated Osborne was far less eccentric, and far less distinctive, than his onstage persona had led audiences to expect.

Like Boorstin, Meyrowitz worried that conformity and homogeneity would result as the electronic media expanded the middle region at the expense of front- and backstage behaviour. In addition to blurring the boundaries between political leaders and followers, Meyrowitz predicted that the electronic technologies of exposure would blur the boundaries between the behaviour of men and women, as well as children and adults. All of these groups speak and act differently when they are segregated from each other; and once the boundaries that separate the groups began to collapse, each of these groups would begin to act more like the others. Now the democratising technology of the internet is fulfilling Meyrowitz's fears: as more personal information about ourselves is available on the web, private figures are feeling the same pressure that public figures have long experienced to expose details of their personal lives as a form of self-defence; and men, women, and children are blurring into a indistinguishable cacophony of intimate exposure.

To the degree that self-revelation to strangers is a bid for relief from anxiety 45
about identity, however, it may not succeed. Social psychologists who have studied the therapeutic effects of emotional disclosure have discovered a consistent pattern: people who receive positive social support for their emotional disclosures tend to feel better as a result, while those who receive negative responses—from indifference to hostility—feel worse.

For example, a nationwide study of psychological responses to 9/11 found that those who sought social support and vented their anxieties without receiving positive reinforcement were more likely to feel greater distress during the six months after the attack than those who engaged in more social coping activities such as giving blood or attending memorial services (16). This is consistent with studies of Vietnam veterans and survivors of the California firestorms, who actually felt worse after sharing their feelings with strangers who made clear they didn't want to listen. ('Thank you for not sharing your earthquake story', read an especially wounding T-shirt.) Those who shared their pain with unreceptive audiences felt worse than those who didn't talk at all, although not as good as those who shared their pain with a receptive audience.

Studies of the benefits of writing as well as talking about emotional experiences confirm the same insight: emotional disclosure can have therapeutic effects when it helps people to become less isolated and more integrated with social networks, but it can have negative effects when it leads people to vent their feelings in a void, without the support of a receptive audience (17). This suggests that therapeutic venting on the internet to a faceless audience in an unreciprocated bid for attention and emotional support is unlikely to help, and may well make things worse.

In *The Book of Laughter and Forgetting*, Milan Kundera examines the phenomenon of graphomania—the pathological desire to express yourself in writing before a public of unknown readers. 'General isolation breeds graphomania, and generalised graphomania in turn intensifies and worsens isolation', Kundera writes. 'Everyone [is] surrounded by his own words as by a wall of mirrors, which allows no voice to filter through from outside.' Kundera contrasts the reticence of his heroine, who is mortified by the idea that anyone except for her beloved might read her love letters, with the graphomania of a writer like Johann Wolfgang von Goethe, who is convinced that his worth as a human being will be called into question if a single human being fails to read his words. The difference between the lover and Goethe, he says, 'is the difference between a human being and a writer'.

In an indifferent and socially atomised universe, 'everyone is pained by the thought of disappearing, unheard and unseen' as a result, everyone is tempted to become a writer, turning himself 'into a universe of words'. But 'when everyone wakes up as a writer', Kundera warns, 'the age of universal deafness and incomprehension will have arrived' (18). Now, we are living in an age of graphomania; we are experiencing the constant din of intimate typing—in email, in chatrooms, on the web and in the workplace. The clacking noise we hear in the air is the noise of endless personal disclosure. But as Kundera recognised, instead of forging emotional connections with strangers, personal exposure in a vacuum may increase social isolation, rather than alleviate it.

Many factors put tremendous pressure on individuals in the Naked Crowd, to 50
expose personal details of their lives and strip themselves bare. The crowd

demands exposure out of a combination of voyeurism, desire for emotional connection, fear of strangers, democratic suspicion of reticence as sign of elitism, demand for markers of trustworthiness, and an unwillingness to conceive of public events or to relate to public figures except in personal terms. From the perspective of the individual who is pursuing the attention of the crowd, there is, as Charles Derber has suggested, the hope of gaining a mass audience by self-exposure; the demands of a therapeutic culture, which rewards people who talk about intimate problems in public by casting them as victims and survivors; the narcissism that leads people obsessively to call attention to their own fears and insecurities about their identity, in a world where identity is always up for grabs; and the expansion of democratic technologies, which create so many new opportunities for individuals to expose themselves before the crowd (19). Above all, there is the desire to establish oneself as trustworthy in a risk society by proving—through exposure—that we have nothing to hide.

All this suggests little cause for optimism that, in the face of future terrorist threats, the crowd will strike the balance between personal security and personal exposure in a reasonable way. Individuals, as we've seen, don't care much about privacy in the aggregate at all: faced with a choice between privacy and exposure, many people would rather be exposed than be private, because the crowd demands no less. Concerned mainly about controlling the conditions of their own exposure, many people are only too happy to reveal themselves promiscuously if they have the illusion of control

Anxious exhibitionists, trained from the cradle to believe that there is no more valuable currency than personal exposure, are not likely to object when their neighbors demand that they strip themselves bare. But just as public intimacy is a kind of delusion, so is the hope of distinguishing ourselves from the crowd by catering to the crowd's insatiable demands for exposure. It is impossible to achieve genuine distinction without a certain heedlessness of public opinion. We can turn ourselves into Portraits of Grief only at the cost of looking more like each other. As both spectators and actors in the Naked Crowd, we are too willing to surrender privacy for an illusory sense of emotional connection and security. Perhaps we will realise what a poor bargain we have struck only after it is too late.

Notes

(1) 'Closing a Scrapbook Full of Life and Sorrow', Janny Scott, *New York Times*, 31 December 2001; (2) 'The Mourning Paper', Thomas Mallon, *The American Scholar*, Spring 2002, p6–7; (3) *Conversations with Anthony Giddens: Making Sense of Modernity*, Anthony Giddens and Christopher Pierson, Stanford University Press, 1998, p101; (4) *The Sane Society*, Erich Fromm, Reinhart, 1955, p141–42; (5) *The Pursuit of Attention: Power and Ego in Everyday Life*, Charles Derber, Oxford University Press, 2000, p81; (6) See 'Online Diary: Blog Nation', *New York Times*, 22 August 2002; (7) See the Diarist.net website; (8) *Sincerity and Authenticity*, Lionel Trilling, Harvard University Press, 1972; (9) *The Homeless Mind: Modernisation and Consciousness*, Peter L Berger, Brigitte Berger and Hansfried Kellner, Random House, 1973, p90; (10) *The Fall of Public Man*, Richard Sennett, WW Norton & Co, 1974, p196, 265; (11) *The Image: A Guide to Pseudo-Events in America*, Daniel J. Boorstin, Atheneum, 1977, p57–58; (12) *Be Your Own Brand: A Breakthrough Formula for Standing Out from the Crowd*, David McNally and Karl D Speak, Berrett-Koehler, 2002, p4, 7, 11, 13, 47; (13) 'Hold Me! Squeeze Me! Buy a Six-Pack!', Alex Kuczynski, *New York Times*, 16 November 1997; (14) *On Liberty*, in *On Liberty and Other Essays*, John Stuart Mill, Oxford University Press, 1998, p82, 79; (15) *No Sense of Place: The Impact of Electronic Media on Social Behaviour*, Joshua Meyrowitz, Oxford University Press, 1985, p6; (16) 'Nationwide Longitudinal Study of

Psychological Responses to September 11', Roxane Cohen Silver, E Alison Holman, Daniel N McIntosh, Michael Poulin, and Virginia Gil-Rivas, 288 *Journal of the American Medical Association* 1235, p1241–1242, 2002; (17) 'Patterns of Natural Language Use: Disclosure, Personality, and Social Integration', JW Pennebaker and A Graybeal, 10 *Current Directions In Psychological Science* 92, 2001; (18) *The Book of Laughter and Forgetting*, Milan Kundera, Perennial Classics, 1999, p127–28, 146, 147; (19) *The Pursuit of Attention: Power and Ego in Everyday Life*, Charles Derber, Oxford University Press, 2000, pxv–xviii

THINGS TO DO WITH THE READING

1. Binaries are usually a sign of what is at stake in a piece of writing. They are also the place where key terms and subtle distinctions among them tend to congregate. Consider the distinction that Rosen makes between "the individuality praised by Mill and the individualism lamented by Alexis de Tocqueville" (see paragraph 38). Define the difference, and then track the ways that the concept of individuality is used in the piece. What other key terms are aligned with it? And what are the various terms that are opposed to it? Make two lists.
2. Make a list of other significant binaries in the piece and write about the one that you think is most interesting or revealing. You might consider, for example, sincerity versus authenticity or "heroes of old" (see paragraph 23) versus modern celebrities.
3. This essay is very anxious about representations of self—about our burgeoning desire as a culture to "brand" the self in pursuit of "the fantasy that people can achieve emotional intimacy with strangers" (see paragraph 40). Why does Rosen call it a fantasy? Do a passage-based focused freewrite (see Chapter 4) on a single paragraph that would allow you to answer this question. An obvious prime candidate is the first paragraph under the subheading "The comfort of strangers?"
4. It is often productive to think about a piece of writing in terms of its hopes and its fears. In this piece, the fears are fairly clear. For example, the essay ends with a warning. Why does Rosen think that we have struck "a poor bargain" in exchanging "privacy" for "an illusory sense of emotional connection"? To answer this question is to get at what this piece is worried about. Less immediately accessible are its hopes. What are its hopes? Is there a better bargain he would have us strike?
5. Consider *to what extent* Jeffrey Rosen and Christine Rosen might agree on the place of private experience in public life. Imagine the conversation they might have on locating the line between public and private. What would be the primary thing they'd agree on? If it's fair to say that Jeffrey Rosen is concerned with the loss of what he calls "genuine individuality" (see paragraph 31), what is Christine Rosen's primary concern? (For discussion of "to what extent" questions, see page 95).
6. **Application—Using the Reading as a Lens:** Look at either the self-representation of a current politician (national or local) or a modern hero. In light of Rosen's claims (via Boorstin) in paragraph 23, what do you notice?

Geoffrey Nunberg

Blogging in the Global Lunchroom

Geoffrey Nunberg is the chair of the usage panel of the *American Heritage Dictionary*. He is also a professor of linguistics and author of a number of books and articles on the nature of contemporary language practices, as well as a contributor to the National Public Radio show "Fresh Air," where this piece originally appeared in 2004. Nunberg is interested in the stylistic differences between journalistic writing as it appears in newspapers and magazines, and the internet world of commentary known as the blogosphere.

1 Over the last couple of months, I've been posting on a group blog called languagelog.org, which was launched by a couple of linguists as a place where we could vent our comments on the passing linguistic scene.

Still, I don't quite have the hang of the form. The style that sounds perfectly normal in a public radio feature or an op-ed piece comes off as distant and pontifical when I use it in a blog entry. Reading over my own postings, I recall what Queen Victoria once said about Gladstone: "He speaks to me as if I were a public meeting."

I'm not the only one with this problem. A lot of newspapers have been encouraging or even requiring their writers to start blogs. But with some notable exceptions, most journalists have the same problems that I do. They do all the things you should do in a newspaper feature. They fashion engaging leads, they develop their arguments methodically, they give context and background, and tack helpful ID's onto the names they introduce—"New York Senator Charles E. Schumer (D)."

That makes for solid journalism, but it's not really blogging. Granted, that word can cover a lot of territory. A recent Pew Foundation study found that around three million Americans have tried their hands at blogging, and sometimes there seem to be almost that many variants of the form. Blogs can be news summaries, opinion columns, or collections of press releases, like the official blogs of the presidential candidates. But the vast majority are journals posted by college students, office workers, or stay-at-home moms, whose average readership is smaller than a family Christmas letter. (The blog hosting site livejournal.com reports that two-thirds of bloggers are women—I'm not sure what to make of that proportion.)

5 But when people puzzle over the significance of blogs nowadays, they usually have in mind a small number of A-List sites that traffic in commentary about politics, culture, or technology—blogs like Altercation, Instapundit, Matthew Yglesias, Talking Points or Doc Searls. It's true that bloggers like these have occasionally come up with news scoops, but in the end they're less about breaking stories than bending them. And their language is a kind of anti-journalese. It's informal, impertinent, and digressive, casting links in all directions. In fact one archetypal blog entry consists entirely of a cryptic comment that's linked to another blog or a news item—"Oh, please," or "He's married to her?"

That interconnectedness is what leads enthusiasts to talk about the blogosphere, as if this were all a single vast conversation—at some point in these discussions, somebody's likely to trot out the phrase "collective mind." But if there's a new public sphere assembling itself out there, you couldn't tell from the way bloggers address their readers—not as anonymous citizens, the way print columnists do, but as co-conspirators who are in on the joke.

Taken as a whole, in fact, the blogging world sounds a lot less like a public meeting than the lunchtime chatter in a high-school cafeteria, complete with snarky comments about the kids at the tables across the room. (Bloggers didn't invent the word snarky, but they've had a lot to do with turning it into the metrosexual equivalent of bitchy. On the Web, blogs account for more than three times as large a share of the total occurrences of snarky as of the occurrences of irony.)[1]

Some people say this all started with Mickey Kaus's column in *Slate*, though Kaus himself cites the old *San Francisco Chronicle* columns of Herb Caen. And Camille Paglia not surprisingly claims that her column in *Salon.com* was the first true blog, and adds that the genre has been going downhill ever since.

But blogs were around on the web well before Kaus or Paglia first logged in.[2] And if you're of a mind to, you can trace their print antecedents a lot further back than Caen or Hunter S. Thompson. That informal style recalls the colloquial voice that Addison and Steele devised when they invented the periodical essay in the early 18th century, even if few blogs come close to that in artfulness. Then too, those essays were written in the guise of fictive personae like Isaac Bickerstaff and Sir Roger de Coverly, who could be the predecessors of pseudonymous bloggers like Wonkette, Atrios, or Skippy the Bush Kangaroo, not to mention the mysterious conservative blogger who goes by the name of Edward Boyd.[3]

For that matter, my languagelog co-contributor Mark Liberman recalls that 10
Plato always had Socrates open his philosophical disquisitions with a little diary entry, the way bloggers like to do: "I went down yesterday to see the festival at the Peiraeus with Glaucon, the son of Ariston, and I ran into my old buddy Cephalus and we got to talking about old age ..."

Of course whenever a successful new genre emerges, it seems to have been implicit in everything that preceded it. But in the end, this is a mug's game, like asking whether the first SUV was a minivan, a station wagon, or an off-road vehicle.

The fact is that this is a genuinely new language of public discourse—and a paradoxical one. On the one hand, blogs are clearly a more democratic form of expression than anything the world of print has produced. But in some ways they're also more exclusionary, and not just because they only reach about a tenth of the people who use the web.[4] The high, formal style of the newspaper op-ed page may be nobody's native language, but at least it's a neutral voice that doesn't privilege the speech of any particular group or class. Whereas blogspeak is basically an adaptation of the table talk of the urban middle class—it isn't a language that everybody in the cafeteria is equally adept at speaking. Not that there's anything wrong with chewing over the events of the day with the other folks at the lunch table, but you hope that everybody in the room is at least reading the same newspapers at breakfast.[5]

Notes

[1] This is a rough estimate, arrived at by taking the proportion of total Google hits for a word that occurs in a document that also contains the word blog:

snarky: 87,700
snarky + blog: 32,600 (37%)
irony: 1,600,000
irony + blog: 168,000 (10.5%)

Of course the fact that the word blog appears in a page doesn't necessarily mean that it is a blog, but it turns out that more than 90 percent of the pages containing the word are blog pages, and in any case, the effect would be the same for both terms. And while some part of this variation no doubt reflects the status of snarky as a colloquial word that is less likely to show up in serious literary discussions and the like, the effect is nowhere near so marked when we look at the word bitchy:

bitchy: 250,000
bitchy + blog: 43,700 (17.5%)

That is, the specialization to blogs is more than twice as high for snarky as for bitchy, even though both are colloquial items.

[2] Many have given credit for inventing the genre to Dave Winer, whose *Scripting News* was one of the earliest weblogs, though Winer himself says that the first weblog was Tim Berners-Lee's page at CERN. But you could argue that blog has moved out from under the derivational shadow of its etymon—the word isn't just a truncation of weblog anymore. In which case, the identity of the first "real blog" is anybody's guess—and it almost certainly will be.

[3] James Wolcott makes a similar comparison in the current *Vanity Fair*, and goes so far as to suggest that "If Addison and Steele, the editors of *The Spectator* and *The Tatler*, were alive and holding court at Starbucks, they'd be WiFi-ing into a joint blog." That's cute, but I think it gets Addison and Steele wrong—the studied effusions of Isaac Bickertaff and Sir Roger de Coverly may have sounded like blogs, but they were fashioned with an eye towards a more enduring literary fame. Which is not to say that blogs couldn't become the basis for a genuine literary form. As I noted in a "Fresh Air" piece a few years ago that dealt more with blogs as personal journals:

> There's something very familiar about that accretion of diurnal detail. It's what the novel was trying to achieve when eighteenth-century writers cobbled it together out of subliterary genres like personal letters, journals, and newspapers, with the idea of reproducing the inner and outer experience that makes up daily life. You wonder whether anything as interesting could grow up in the intimate anonymity of cyberspace. (See "I Have Seen the Future, and It Blogs," in Going Nucular, *PublicAffairs*, May, 2004.)

So it's not surprising that a number of fictional blogs ("flogs"? "blictions"?) have begun to emerge, adapting the tradition of the fictional diary that runs from Robinson Crusoe to Bridget Jones' Diary. As to whether that will ultimately amount to "anything as interesting" as the novel, the jury is likely to be out for a while.

[4] The Pew study found that 11% of Internet users have read the blogs or diaries of other Internet users.

[5] For a diverting picture of the blogosphere-as-lunchroom, see Whitney Pastorek's recent piece in the *Village Voice*, "Blogging Off."

THINGS TO DO WITH THE READING

1. Given that this is a short radio piece, Nunberg doesn't have the time to develop the implications of his observations at much length. So, this piece would be useful for practicing one of the skills described in Chapter 12 for "using the source as a point of departure": "Uncover the assumptions in the source, and then build upon the source's point of view, extending its implications" (see page 298).

   First, determine what Nunberg's primary claims are in this piece. Locate sentences that you think best capture his main ideas about blogs. (One of these has to do with his analogy between blogs and high school lunch rooms, about which he says, "blogspeak is basically an adaptation of the table talk of the urban middle class: it isn't a language that everybody in the cafeteria is equally adept at speaking.")

   Then go after assumptions and implications. What are some of the implications of the thinking that Nunberg lays out in his final paragraph? And what assumption underlies his final sentence? Remember not to advance your own point of view on Nunberg's thinking, i.e., don't get sucked into agree/disagree mode. Instead, concentrate on laying out Nunberg's underlying assumptions and implications. See pages 97–100 for discussion of how to uncover assumptions.

2. **Link:** Put Nunberg's piece into conversation with one or more of the other essays in this chapter using the strategy called "Similarity within Difference" (Chapter 5). Goldberger's piece "Disconnected Urbanism" might be a good choice, and like Nunberg's essay, it's short. First develop the difference. Then, look past the difference to locate a point of contact, of similarity. Or, if you think the similarity between the two is more obvious than the difference, start with the similarity and then look past the similarity to what you consider a significant difference.

3. **Application:** Clearly, this piece could launch a more extended project in which you follow up some of Nunberg's leads and look for trends in blogspeak. With the definition of style from Chapter 10 in mind, you might explore to what extent there is a discernible blog style. You might check out the range of blogs listed on the website for Arts and Letters Daily, or alternatively, those listed on Nunberg's own website. Links to both can be found at www.thomsonedu.com/english/rosenwasser.

Margaret Visser

"Ritual," "Fingers," & "Knives, Forks, Spoons"

Born in South Africa and educated in Zambia, Zimbabwe, France, and Canada, Margaret Visser brings a cross-cultural view to the rituals of eating and to the role that manners play in sustaining public life. Before becoming an award-winning author, Visser was a professor of Greek and Latin in Canada for nearly 20 years, as well as a longtime broadcaster on a popular radio program. These selections from her book, *The Rituals of Dinner* (1991), offer an analysis of, in the words of her subtitle, *The Origins, Evolutions, Eccentricities, and Meaning of Table Manners.*

Ritual

A North American father, presumably initiating his son, aged fifteen, into the world of adult business affairs, took him out to what the boy described as "a big dinner meeting." When the company was served spaghetti, the boy ate it with his hands. "I would slurp it up and put it in my mouth," he admitted. "My dad took some grief about it." The October 1985 newspaper article does not describe the response of the rest of the company. The son was sent to a boarding school to learn how to behave. "When we have spaghetti," he announced later, "you roll it up real tightly on your fork and put it in your mouth with the fork." 1

What he described, after having learned it, is a dinner-table ritual—as automatic and unquestioned by every participant in it, as impossible to gainsay, as the artificial rules and preferences which every cannibal society has upheld. Practical reasons can be found for it, most of them having to do with neatness, cleanliness, and noiselessness. Because these three general principles are so warmly encouraged in our culture, having been arrived at, as ideals to be striven for, after centuries of struggle and constraint, we simply never doubt that everyone who is right-minded will find a spaghetti-eating companion disgusting and impossible to eat with where even one of them is lacking. Yet we know from paintings and early photographs of spaghetti-eaters in nineteenth-century Naples (where the modern version of spaghetti comes from) that their way of eating pasta was with their hands—not that the dish was likely to appear at a formal dinner. You had to raise the strings in your right hand, throw back your head, then lower the strings, dexterously, with dispatch, and *without slurping* (there are invariably "polite" and "rude" ways of eating), into your open mouth. The spaghetti in the pictures does not seem to have sauce on it.

Today, spaghetti-eating manners demand forks, and fistfuls of wet pasta are simply not acceptable at any "civilized" occasion. The son's ignorance cast a dark reflection upon his father: he had not been doing his duty, had not given his child a proper "upbringing." Even if the boy had not seen spaghetti before, he subsequently admitted that what he ought to have done was to look about him, watch how other people were eating this awkward food, and imitate them. In any case, the options were clear after this demonstration of ineptitude: either the boy learned his table manners, or he would not be asked to a "big dinner meeting" again, by anyone who had heard of his unfinished education.

He had offended not only against modern proprieties that limit the use of hands while eating, but also against ritual: he had done something *unexpected.* Ritual is action frequently repeated, in a form largely laid down in advance; it aims to get those actions right. Everyone present knows what should happen, and notices when it does not. Dinner too is habitual, and aims at order and communication, at satisfying both the appetite of the diners and their expectations as to how everybody present should behave. In this sense, a meal can be thought of as a ritual and a work of art, with limits laid down, desires aroused and fulfilled, enticements, variety, patterning, and plot. As in a work of art, not only the overall form but also the details matter intensely.

5 This pernicketiness has some of its basis in biology. Human beings, like animals, are extremely sensitive to small signs, to tiny noises in the night, to small discrepancies in the customary layout of their environment, for these may be the only warnings received before a hidden danger strikes. Alertness and sensitivity are normally essential for survival, especially in the wild. But being human, and depending as we do on knowing our way round our complex and perilous social world, it is entirely necessary to us that we should also react instinctively to very small signs given by other people in social contexts. No one in the group might even be conscious that such a sign has been given. But those of us with the best-attuned social sense will instantly and instinctively "know" what is afoot. Every person must be careful—or rather, drilled from an early age until automatically disposed—not only to notice signs, but also to *provide* them, as a reassurance that this person is what other members of the group hope he or she is; that this individual wishes to join in, play the game, and be civil.

It is equally understandable that mixing with people whose rituals differ from our own can be very trying. Innumerable travellers' tales involve the visiting hero being offered some horrendous "delicacy" which he has either to eat, or risk offending his host. But we can be put out just because some foreigner raises his eyebrows to mean yes, or asks us how much money we make, or stalks off in a rage because we folded our arms or failed to take our hands out of our pockets. The really dramatic "ethnic" behaviour we consciously apprehend at once, and so can "make allowances" for; everyone has heard of the chances of having to eat an eyeball, or smash glasses after the toast. But the smaller, less noticeable signs can catch us off our guard and rob us more insidiously of our sense of security. Most of the picturesque details that strike travellers as weird have to do with table manners. Tourists quite commonly visit marvels as mighty as the Pyramids of Egypt, but come home really jolted by, and unable to forget, the Egyptian manner of pouring tea into a glass until it slops into the saucer. When eating and drinking we are particularly sensitive and vigilant, and immediately react to the slightest deviation from what we have learned to regard as the proprieties.

Ritual, being both expected behaviour and correct, is a series of actions constantly repeated. Repetitiveness serves the meaning being expressed, for if the pattern is at least generally constant we can concentrate on the message embodied in the performance. (We do not have to think how to handle our knife and fork every time we are served, but can set to and enjoy the steak, while demonstrating effortless restraint and competence, and showing our desire to be communicative, sharing companions.) We also notice the slight *intentional* variations which always occur in ritual, and are therefore thrown into relief. (What fun, and how formally informal, to be served artichokes and be allowed to use our hands.) But this does not entirely account for our need constantly to repeat actions ritually. The repetition soothes us, apparently, in and by itself—inducing what James Joyce called "those here-we-are-again gaieties." Rituals survive because people want them to do so; they "work." Culture, not instinct, determines a good deal of what we do. Human beings rejoice in the action of patterning, in itself.

There is no etymological connection whatever between the words "man" (or "wo*man*" or "hu*man*") and "manners," but speakers of English have nonetheless found the presence of that common syllable fascinating. "Meat feeds, cloth cleeds, but manners make the man," went a sixteenth-century jingle: what you eat and what you wear are less important than how you do both. In our own time, Mae West assures us:

It's not what I share but the way that I share it—
That's all, brother, that's all.

The problem is: how much of the way we are *is* culture, and how much is not ours to control?

Ever since humankind began thinking (the word or syllable "man" very 10
possibly comes from a root word meaning "think"), at any rate since the age of the earliest cave paintings, we have speculated and worried about the difference between ourselves and animals. It has always been intensely important for us to grasp this difference as far as we are able to do so, especially since we cannot help noticing how much like animals we are. For animals have no culture in the human sense; animals are therefore not, as human beings are, free from some of the tyranny of natural law. Nothing could be more revealing about twentieth-century preoccupations and anxieties than the latest way of posing this forty-thousand-year-old problem. We now tend to ask not "How are people different from animals?" but "In what ways are we the same?" We are so terrified of our own power, our own clear *difference* from animals, that we desperately seek ways to assure ourselves of our affiliation with the rest of creation. We are trying to remind ourselves, among other things, how much we belong; and struggling to restrain our greed and control our power, which we now see as threatening the earth and everything living on it. We are especially fascinated to find correspondences in animals, not only with our physical nature and biological needs, but with our social behaviour as well.

It was with considerable excitement, therefore, that a longing to repeat a successful scenario was reputedly found among monkeys living on Koshima Islet in Japan. One day in 1953 a year-and-a-half-old female ape called Imo appears to have deeply impressed her fellows (and the watching Japanese scientists) by washing her sweet potato in water before she ate it. She repeated this action whenever she subsequently ate. She would hold the potato under the water with one hand and brush it, presumably trying to get the mud off, with the other. Other monkeys imitated her. The fashion spread, mainly among her kin and playmates. Within four or five years, potato-washing before eating had become *de rigueur* among most monkeys aged two to seven, and among some adults as well. All monkeys over five who took up washing potatoes were females.

Starting in 1958, a tradition had begun, as these females passed on potato-washing by example to their children. The salt taste on potatoes dipped in sea water seems to have resulted in a variant: some monkeys began dipping their potatoes in salt water in between bites; others kept on simply washing them first. It certainly is tempting to detect here not only an ability in a group of monkeys to adopt improvements once they have been discovered by a particularly gifted member, but also an obsessive delight in drama that "works," and a love of sticking to "the way it's done," even without the conscious perception of material benefits. We are reminded of human rituals, and the satisfactions we find in the constant re-enactment of routines, experiencing them as not merely useful but pleasantly repeatable.

Another of the reasons for "manners" is precisely that they pressure people to behave in a predictable fashion. When we all "know what to do" on a given occasion—say at a wedding, or a death—we are all enabled by convention to interrelate, to play our often preordained roles, just where having to make choices and think up scenarios would be most difficult and exhausting. This is why rules of politeness tend to cluster round moments of transition, of meeting others, making decisions, conferring, parting, commemorating. Rituals are there to make difficult passages easier. They include the gestures—waving, nodding, smiling, speaking set phrases—which daily smooth our meetings with other people; the attitudes and postures we adopt when standing or sitting in the presence of others, especially when we are talking to them; the muttering of "excuse me" when interrupting others or squeezing past them. Full-dress celebrations of coming together, of marking transitions and recollections, almost always require food, with all the ritual politeness implied in dining—the proof that we all know how eating should be managed. We eat whenever life becomes dramatic: at weddings, birthdays, funerals, at parting and at welcoming home, or at any moment which a group decides is worthy of remark. Festivals and feasts are solemn or holy days; they are so regularly celebrated by people meeting for meals that "having a feast" has actually come to mean "eating a lot."

Families meet for meals, too; the custom goes back 2 million years, to the daily return of protohominid hunters and foragers to divide food up with their fellows—whom they have usually, but by no means always, decided they would *not* eat. The extent to which we demand meals at regular times, mostly giving them specific names each with their own connotations (breakfast, lunch, supper), is as arbitrary as it can be solemnly binding. We even develop physical demands for food when food is "due"; the stomach contractions we experience at midday or in the evening, often quite painful ones, which signal mealtimes and which we call "hunger," are strictly speaking nothing of the kind. They are the result of habit and bodily rhythms only, and they result from a culturally induced custom of eating regular meals. It is often part of a society's manners code never to eat between meals, so that not only the meals but also the spaces between them are controlled. This turns every shared family dinner into a mini-feast or festival, so that it can, like a feast, celebrate both the interconnectedness and the self-control of the group's members. Family dinners are rituals too, even though the typical "plot" of a family meal might include the device of lowering the level of formality as compared with other ritual occasions.

15 The predictability of manners (if *this* is happening, then we must all do *that*) makes us interlock with each other, all act in concert. We connect, in addition, with events, dates, shared emotions, kinship and group ties, the life cycle, the world in general. Conventions, as the word suggests, are attitudes and patterns of behaviour we have in common: we "come together" (as in a business or political "convention") in accepting them, or at least in knowing what they are, as everybody else does—everybody, that is, with whom we are accustomed to associate. It is an extremely complex and time-consuming business, making all these customary links and celebrating all this understanding. But if we stop celebrating, we also soon cease to understand; the price for not taking the time and the trouble is loss of communication. And conversely, the moment communication is lost, "manners" drop away. *Li Chi*, the Chinese *Book of Rites*, compiled in the first century B.C., warns that "the ruin of states, the destruction of families, and the perishing of individuals are always preceded by their abandonment of the rules of propriety."

Today, whatever we eat is enormously controlled and limited by rules—we demand that it be so—and the conditions under which we live make food supplies necessarily impossible without artifice. We also, even when alone, keep rules of bodily propriety that are as strict as they are largely unconscious; other people are present to us in that they have formed our habits. And few of us willingly eat always alone. Food is still our ritual relaxation (a "break" in the working day), our chance to choose companions and talk to them, the excuse to recreate our humanity as well as our strength, and to renew our relationships.

Ritual is an expression of solidarity. Our own society is not one homogeneous mass: individuals in it belong not only to it and to their families, but often, in addition, to groups of people chosen for various reasons; one person may belong to many such groups. Each of these groups must "define" itself (literally, "place a boundary round" itself), or cease to exist as a group; it must declare itself to be *both* a single entity *and* marked off from the rest. Definitional enactment of togetherness and difference may include clothing style, bodily markings such as shaven heads or wild locks, and "in" language; nothing is as powerful, however, as ritual performance. People get together and enact what they hold in common. They might speak their agreement as part of the occasion, but more satisfactory still is the doing of an action together. The actual taking part establishes identity. It is obvious why the action of eating together—of *partaking* in a meal—suggests itself so immediately. An action comprises not only what is done, but how: the two are indissociable in the course of the action's performance. In ritual behaviour, the "how" as well as the "what" of the matter have been laid down in advance. The individual performs, but the group's conventions have decided the sequence, the spatial layout, and the manner. Table manners are rituals because they are the way in which it is commonly agreed that eating *should* be performed.

There is another kind of solidarity expressed by ritual, and this it shares with language. Language is a cultural construct inherited from the past. If we wish to speak and be understood, we have no choice but to learn the linguistic system. This necessity forces us to enter into relationship—whether we like it or not—with the past: we need, and willingly accept, the constraints of pre-ordained rules. Language is not only for communication with people our own age; it is something we have in common with people older than us, who may have spoken our language before we were born. (Writing and reading have been invented to permit the extension of this continuity into the past and the future.) When we are young, older people occupy the field; they are in charge and in power. We must learn their language in order to meet and communicate with them, and if we want one day to occupy their place. We must, similarly, learn their manners if we want to be asked to dinner by them.

The group which decides the “how” of ritual is composed not only of the present participants but also of the dead, insofar as we are prepared to entertain the ideas of people no longer living. Ritual is about *lasting* (which is one reason why ritual occasions are constantly repeated). Because it is pre-ordained, it always expresses order, and it predicts endurance; it links the present with the past, and it hopes also to link the present with the future. Ritual can be used, in its “continuity” function, to keep things going when energy flags and the members in a group cannot maintain their experience at the pitch they would like. People often say that “going through the motions” can help to remind them of past, more successful, experiences. It is possible to look about and see other people apparently rising to the occasion—so perhaps those less inspired might manage, too. Ritual can not only raise the emotional tone of the proceedings, but also lower it if necessary: for instance, ritual politeness can prevent rage from boiling over into action.

20 But what about ritual that is merely empty form? Animals can “pretend,” as a puppy does when playing with a ball instead of pursuing prey; but animals can never match the human capacity for performing a ritual without intending what it says. Ritual becomes meaningless to us, and finally destructive, if it is used for deception. Jesus participated in many social and religious rituals and objected to bad manners. He nevertheless condemned the false pretences to purity of soul which were expressed, for example, by pre-dinner ablutions, and pointed to Isaiah’s insight that God detests “lip-service” that covers up the truth. Self-aggrandizing ritual was to be replaced by actions expressing real love and humility: where rituals impede us, they must be changed.

In our own time, cataclysmic social revolutions have made large numbers of rules and conventions redundant, and many of them have not yet been replaced with new signs and voluntary constraints that are broadly recognized and accepted. This is a time of transition, when old manners are dying and new ones are still being forged. A good many of our uncertainties, discomforts, and disagreements stem from this state of flux. Sometimes we hold the terrifying conviction that the social fabric is breaking up altogether, and that human life is becoming brutish and ugly because of a general backsliding from previous social agreements that everyone should habitually behave with consideration for others. At other times a reaction against the social rituals of our own recent past leads us to lump all manners together as empty forms, to be rejected on principle. There is a shying away from elaboration, a preference for the bare bones of everything. We often seem, for instance, to prefer listening to incoherent speakers than to articulate ones, feeling that incoherence is “straight from the heart” while fluency must be a trick, or at least a method of hiding something. Apologies have almost gone out of style because they are hard to make, and being required by others to make them easily convinces us that they are merely insincere.

We do cling to the (largely unexamined) ideal that we should strive to be "natural." Spontaneity seems to be annihilated by anything resembling ritual: how can you be "natural" and still behave in predictable, because pre-ordained, patterns? (People rarely think of animal rituals, which are natural yet invariable, in this context.) We are also deceived, by our desire to reject ritual, into thinking that we are "freely choosing," from within each individual self, to act in ways that are often in fact decided in advance by cultural forces, or by unrecognized but nevertheless real social structures. Such structures, indeed, often govern us precisely insofar as we are unconscious of their existence.

The conventional prejudice against ritual assumes that rituals never change, and that individuals can have no influence upon ritual forms. In fact, individuals are just as important to ritual performance as the group and the rules are. It is only the individual who can personally *mean* what is going on. Each participant uses that ritual, plays with it, rings changes on it, subtly brings it into line with his or her present needs. Ritual is a process; it guides, but it also serves, and is guided. People do influence ritual—and they do so just because human rituals are not "natural." We made them, so we can adapt them to our present requirement. We can also bend the rules if necessary: ritual codes that last always make allowance for circumstance.

The fact is that our personalities are necessarily both individual and social, "natural" and "cultural": these aspects of us can be discussed separately, but they cannot exist alone. The life of the social and cultural "parts" of us is communication with others, and this is achieved and enhanced by means of shared patterns, routines, systems of signals, in a word the performance—whether conscious or not—of rituals. (Even a hermit is a socially conditioned being. Hermits react to society by deliberately leaving it. They normally live alone, and act differently, in ways their societies can "read" and understand.)

It might well seem to us at times, when we are disheartened by spectacles of 25
human error and iniquity, that "culture" is a thoroughly bad thing; that we should stick with plain sex and nutrients and try to get over the rest. But as long as we live in society, purely physical and individual needs and desires must be mediated by rituals and manners. Social forms become part of the environment; society cannot exist without them. None of us would want to live "by bread alone," even if it were possible. We are forced to create culture just because we are ourselves the building blocks of society. But that very condition makes society a human construct: if its manners deteriorate or become inappropriate, they can conceivably be changed, just because we ourselves collectively make and live by them. Therein lies our freedom.

Fingers

One of the more spectacular triumphs of human "culture" over "nature" is our own determination when eating to avoid touching food with anything but metal implements. Our self-satisfaction with this marvellous instance of artificiality, however, should not lead us to assume that people who habitually eat with their hands are any less determined than we are to behave "properly"; for they too overlay "animal" instincts with manners, and indulge in both the constraints and the ornamentations which characterize polite behaviour. Forks, like handkerchiefs, look dangerously grubby objects to many people encountering them for the first time. To people who eat with their fingers, hands seem cleaner, warmer, more agile than cutlery. Hands are silent, sensitive to texture and temperature, and graceful—provided, of course, that they have been properly trained.

Washing, as we have already remarked, tends to be ostentatious and frequent among polite eaters with their hands. Ancient Romans, like the modern Japanese, preferred to bath all over before dinner. The etiquette of hand-washing in the Middle Ages was very strict. During the washing ritual, precedence was observed as it was in the seating of diners at the table; the bows, genuflections, and ceremonial flourishes of the ewerers or hand-washers were carefully prescribed. It was often thought disgusting, as it is in India today, to dip one's hands into the basin of water: a servant had to pour scented water *over* the hands so that it was used only once. (The modern North American preference for showers over baths is similar.) In modern Egypt, the basin is sometimes provided with a perforated cover so that the dirty water disappears at once from view. Hand-washing rules always insist that one must not splash or swish the water; be careful to leave some dry towel for the person washing next; and above all touch as little as possible between washing and beginning to eat. If an Abbasid (ninth-century Arab) guest scratched his head or stroked his beard after washing, everyone present would wait before beginning to eat, so that he could wash again. An Abbasid, like a modern Egyptian, host would wash first, so that guests need not look as though they were anxious to start the meal; alternatively, washing was done outside, and the meal began directly after the seating, usually when the guest of honour stretched his hand out to take the first morsel.

Desert Arabs go outside the tent, both before and after the meal, to perform ablutions by rubbing their hands with sand; they often prefer to perform this ritual before washing, even when there is plenty of water available. It is thought very rude to perform one's final washing before everyone else has finished eating; it would be the equivalent of our leaving the table while the meal is in progress. The corollary of this is that people who eat with their hands usually try to finish the meal together, since it is uncomfortable, for one thing, to sit for long when one has finished eating, holding out one greasy hand. Where family eating is done from a shared pot, there are rules about leaving some food over for the children, who eat more slowly than adults do. A great deal of attention, forethought, and control is required in order to finish a meal together, or at a moment agreed on in advance; it is a manoeuvre few of us have been trained to perform.

A monstrously greedy Greco-Roman banqueter is said to have accustomed his hands to grasping hot things by plunging them into hot water at the baths; he also habitually gargled with hot water, to accustom his mouth to high temperatures. He would then bribe the cook to serve the meal straight from the stove, so that he could grab as much food as possible and eat it while it was still hot—before anyone else could touch it. The story reminds us that eating food while it is hot is a habit both culture-specific and modern; a taste for it has developed in us, a taste which is dependent both on technology and on the little brothers of technology, the knife, fork, and spoon. People who eat their food with their hands usually eat it warm rather than steaming, and they grow up preferring it that way. (It is often said that one of the cultural barriers that divide "developed" from "developing" peoples is this matter of preference in the temperature at which food is eaten.) Where hot drinks are served, on the other hand (an example is the Arab coffee-drinking habit at mealtimes), people tend to like them very hot, as a contrast, and because the cups or glasses, together with the saucers under them, protect their hands.

Delicacy and adroitness of gesture are drummed into people who eat with 30
their hands, from childhood. It might be considered polite, for example, to scoop food up, or it could be imperative to grasp each morsel from above. Politeness works by abjuring whole ranges of behaviour which the body could easily encompass—indeed, very often the easier movement is precisely what is out of bounds. It was once the mark of the utmost refinement in our own culture to deny oneself the use of the fourth and fifth fingers when eating: the thumb and first two fingers alone were allowed. Bones—provided they were small ones—could be taken up, but held between thumb and forefinger only. We hear of especially sophisticated people who used certain fingers only for one dish, so that they had other fingers, still unsticky and ungreasy, held in reserve for taking food or sauce from a different platter. This form of constraint was possible only if the food was carefully prepared so that no tugging was necessary: the meat must be extremely tender, cut up, or hashed and pressed into small cakes. None but the rich and those with plenty of servants were likely to manage such delicacy; it followed that only they could be truly "refined."

Distancing the fourth and fifth fingers from the operation of taking food can be performed by lifting them up, elegantly curled; the constraint has forced them to serve merely as ornament. A hand used in this manner becomes a dramatic expression of the economy of politeness. When a modern tea-drinker is laughed at for holding her cup-handle in three fingers, lifting the two unused digits in the air, we think it is because we find her ridiculously pretentious. What we really mean is that she is conservative to the point that her model of social success is completely out of date, and the constraints and ornaments with which she clothes her behaviour are now inappropriate—which is another way of saying that, although she is trying very hard to be correct, she succeeds merely in being improper. Modern constraints and ornaments are, quite simply, different. We should remember that snobbery has usually delighted in scorning what is passé.

Left hands are very commonly disqualified from touching food at dinner. The *Li Chi* tells us that ancient Chinese children were trained from infancy never to use their left hands when eating. Ancient Greeks and Romans leaned on their left elbows when reclining at meals, effectively withdrawing their left hands from use. You *had* to lean on the left elbow even if you were left-handed: if you did not, you ruined the configuration of the party by facing the wrong way. The same problem confronted, even more vitally, an ancient Greek hoplite soldier. He formed part of a phalanx of shields, all of which had to be held on left arms so that they could overlap; fighting was done with swords grasped in the right. A shield on the right arm would have created a gap in the closed phalanx. It must have been very difficult to be left-handed in the ancient world.

Abbasid Arabs used to hold bread in their left hands because this was the part of the meal not shared from a common dish, and even strict modern Middle Eastern manners permit the use of the left for operations such as peeling fruit;

the main thing is not to take from a communal dish with the left, and to avoid bringing the left hand to the mouth. The left hand is traditionally discouraged at table because it is the non-sacred hand, reserved for profane and polluting actions from which the right hand abstains. One example of these tasks is washing after excretion. Now it is invariably important for human beings both culturally and for health reasons to understand that food is one thing and excrement another: the fact that they are "the same thing," that is, different phases of the same process, merely makes it imperative that we should keep the distinction clear, and continually demonstrate to others that we are mindful of it.

Eating together is a potent expression of community. Food is sacred, and must also be pure, clean, and undefiled. It crosses the threshold of the mouth, enters, and either feeds or infects the individual who consumes it: anything presented to us as edible which is perceived as impure in any sense immediately revolts us. Homage is paid to the purity of what we eat, and precaution taken to preserve it, in many different ways: we have already considered washing, white cloths and napkins, dish covers, poison-tastings, prayers, and paper wrappings, and we shall see many more of these. In our culture, lavatories (literally, "wash places"—only euphemisms are permissible for this particular piece of furniture) are kept discreetly closeted, either alone or in a bathroom; a "washroom" or a "toilet" (literally, a "place where there is a towel") is nearly unthinkable without a door for shutting other people out. The lavatory bowl is covered (sometimes the cover is covered as well), usually white, wastefully water-flushed (people even like to tint this water an emphatically artificial blue), and hedged about with special paper rolls and hand-washings.

Our fascination when we learn that people exist who will not touch food with 35
their left hands is rather interesting. It begins with our conviction that "civilized" people (ourselves, of course) should eat with knives and forks in the first place—that is, try not to handle food at all. We do not like the reason left hands are most often said to be banned among certain "foreigners," fastening as we do upon one reason when it is only one from a whole category of "profane" actions, because our taboo about washrooms is so strong that we cannot bear to be reminded of excretion—which we are, by the prohibition. In other words, our taboo is even stronger than theirs. Moreover, left hands have in fact an "unclean" connotation in our own culture.

"Right," after all, means "correct" or "okay" in English. "Sinister" originally meant "left." In French, a just man is *droit*, meaning both "right" and "straight," while *gauche* ("left") describes one who lacks social assurance, as well as dexterity and adroitness (both of which literally mean "right-handedness"). We raise right hands to take oaths and extend them to shake hands: left-handed people just have to fall in with this. In fact, left-handed people, like left-handed ancient Greeks, have always been regarded as an awkward, wayward minority, to the point where left-handed children have been forced, against their best interests, to use their right hands rather than their left. When sets of opposites (curved and straight, down and up, dark and light, cold and hot, and so forth) are set out, our own cultural system invariably makes "left" go with down, dark, round, cold—and female. Males are straight, up, light, hot—and right. Our metal eating implements free us from denying the left hand—but most of us are right-handed anyway, and knives (quintessentially "male" weapons, by the way) are held in right hands. And as we shall see, North Americans still prefer not only to cut with the right, but to bring food to their mouths with the right hand as well.

Eating with the help of both hands at once is very often frowned upon. The Bedouin diner is not permitted to gnaw meat from the bone: he must tear it away and into morsels using only the right hand, and not raise the hand from the dish in order to do so. Sometimes right-handed eaters confronted with a large piece of meat, a chicken, for instance, will share the task of pulling it apart, each of two guests using his right hand and exercising deft coordination; no attention should be drawn to this operation by any movement resembling a wrench or a jerk. Even on formal occasions our own manners permit us, occasionally, to use our fingers—when eating asparagus, for example (this is an early twentieth-century dispensation), or radishes, or apricots. But all of these are taken to the mouth with one hand only. We are still advised that corn kernels should be cut off the cobs in the kitchen, or that corn should, better still, be avoided altogether unless the meal is a very intimate affair. One reason why this vegetable has never become quite respectable is that corn cobs demand to be held in two hands. (More important reasons are of course that teeth come too obviously into play when eating them, and cheeks and chins are apt to get greasy.) When we chew, we should also be careful to fill only one cheek—not too full, to be sure. Two hands and two cheeks both signify indecent enthusiasm; cramming either hands or mouth is invariably rude.

Knives, Forks, Spoons

The Chinese knife is a cleaver, useful, so the Andersons tell us, for "splitting firewood, gutting and scaling fish, slicing vegetables, mincing meat, crushing garlic (with the dull side of the blade), cutting one's nails, sharpening pencils, whittling new chopsticks, killing pigs, shaving (it is kept sharp enough, or supposedly is), and settling old and new scores with one's enemies." Keeping this all-purpose tool apart from the dining table shows a resolute preference, in the table manners of the societies which use chopsticks, for polite restraint.

Men in the West used always to carry knives about with them, finding them indispensable for hundreds of purposes—including that of slicing food at the table. St. Benedict's *Rule* (sixth century) requires monks to go to bed dressed and ready to rise the next morning, but advises them to detach their knives from their belts in case they cut themselves during the night. In the Middle Ages only the nobility had special food knives, which they took with them when travelling: hosts were not usually expected to provide cutlery for dinner guests. To this day in parts of France, men carry with them their own personal folding knives, which they take out of their pockets and use for preference at intimate gatherings for dinner. Small boys love being given folding pen-knives with many attachments; these are the descendants of this ancient male perquisite.

Women must also have owned knives, but they have almost invariably been 40
discouraged from being seen using them. Swords and knives are phallic and masculine. In ancient Greece, when women committed suicide, people hoped they would politely refrain from using knives and opt for poison or the noose instead. At many medieval dinner tables men and women ate in couples from a

bowl shared between them, and when they did, men were expected courteously to serve their female partners, cutting portions of meat for them with their knives.

Prevention of the violence which could so easily break out at table is, as we have seen, one of the principal aims of table manners. In the West, where knives have not been banished, we are especially sensitive and vigilant about the use of these potential weapons. "When in doubt, do not use your knife" is a good all-purpose rule. We must cut steaks and slices of roast with knives, but the edge of a fork will do for an omelette, or for boiled potatoes, carrots, and other vegetables, especially if no meat is being served with them. If a knife is needed, in a right-handed person it will be occupying the right hand. The American way is to put the knife down when it has done its work, and take up the fork in the right hand; the fork is now available for breaking vegetables as well as lifting what has been cut. Europeans hold on to the knife and have to cut vegetables with it, since the fork is kept in the less capable hand.

Fish may be gently slit down the side facing upwards and separated into portions with the help of a knife, and a knife-blade held flat is useful for lifting fish bones; but everything has been done to bypass knives, because they are not necessary for cutting, at the fish course. Cooked fish must not be cut into fillets, for instance, but lifted from the bones bit by bit. Being gentle with fish had its aesthetic aspect. "In helping fish," pleads a cookbook in 1807, "take care not to break the flakes, which in cod and salmon are large and contribute much to the beauty of its appearance."

Ever since the sixteenth century there has been a taboo against pointing a knife at our faces. It is rude, of course, to point at anybody with a knife or a fork, or even a spoon; it is also very bad form to hold knife and fork in the fists so that they stand upright. But pointing a knife at *ourselves* is viewed with special horror, as Norbert Elias has observed. I think that one reason for this is that we have learned only very recently not to use our knives for placing food in our mouths: we are still learning, and we therefore reinforce our decision by means of a taboo. We *think* we hate seeing people placing themselves in even the slightest jeopardy, but actually we fervently hope they will not spoil the new rule and let us all down by taking to eating with their knives again.

For the fact is that people have commonly eaten food impaled on the points of their knives, or carried it to their mouths balanced on blades; the fork is in this respect merely a variant of the knife. With the coming of forks, knife-points became far less useful than they had been; their potential danger soon began in consequence to seem positively barbaric. The first steps in the subduing of the dinner knife were taken when the two cutting edges of the dagger-like knife were reduced to one. The blunt side became an upper edge, which is not threatening to fingers when they are holding knives in the polite manner. According to Tallement des Réaux, Richelieu was so appalled by the sight of Chancellor Séguier picking his teeth with a knife, that he ordered all the knife-blades in his establishment to have their points ground down into innocuously rounded ends. It later became illegal in France for cutlers to make pointed dinner knives or for innkeepers to lay them on their tables: Other countries soon followed suit. Pointed knives for all diners were later to return to the dining-room table, but as "steak" knives, which have a special image, linked deliberately with red meat and "getting down to business" when hungry. They are still quite rustic in connotation.

Italy and Spain led the world into the adoption of forks. In 1611, the 45
Englishman Thomas Coryat announced that he had seen forks in Italy and had decided to adopt them and continue to use them on his return home. The reason for the Italian custom was, he explains, that these extremely fastidious, ultra-modern people considered that any fingering of the meat being carved at table was a transgression against the laws of good manners, "seeing all men's fingers are not alike cleane." Even Coryat, however, does not seem to think of forks as for eating with, but for holding the meat still while carving oneself a slice from the joint intended to be shared by everyone.

The use of individual forks began to spread as the seventeenth century progressed. People would often share forks with others as they would spoons, wiping them carefully on their napkins before passing them on. Antoine de Courtin, in the late 1600s, advised using the fork mainly for fatty, sauce-laden, or syrupy foods; otherwise, hands would do. It was in the course of the seventeenth century, again, that hard plates—prerequisites for the constant use of individual knives and forks—began to be provided for every diner at table. At medieval banquets, plates had been trenchers (from the French *trancher*, "to slice"), made of sliced bread: they were for receiving morsels of food taken from a central dish with the hand, and for soaking up any dripping sauces, not for holding portions which needed subsequently to be pierced and cut up. Trenchers started to receive pewter or wooden underplaques, also called trenchers, in the fourteenth century; cut-marks found on some of them show us that people were beginning occasionally to use them to slice food. The solid non-serving dishes at this time and later were bowls shared between couples, as was the platter of Jack Spratt and his wife in the nursery rhyme.

Eating in the "English" manner means that the fork, having just left off being an impaling instrument, must enter the mouth with the tines down if it is not to be awkwardly swivelled round in the left, or less capable, hand. Food must therefore be balanced on the *back* of the rounded tines. This has two advantages for polite behaviour. First, a fork thus held encourages the mouth to take the food off it quickly and close to the lips—it is quite difficult to push the fork, with its humped tines, far into the mouth. "Weapons" should not be plunged into mouths; we now keep this rule faithfully, hardly needing it to be enunciated. The second advantage is that denying a modern fork its possible spoonlike use is wantonly perverse: it forces us to take small mouthfuls and to leave some of the food, unliftable, on the plate. It is difficult to get the food onto the fork, and harder still to balance and raise it faultlessly. Managing to eat like this with grace is a triumph of practice and determination, and therefore an ideal mannerly accomplishment.

The former way of eating was not dislodged in North America as it was in the rest of the world. It has been suggested by James Deetz that the old way was more deeply entrenched in America because forks arrived there relatively late. According to this theory, Americans remained attached to eating with their spoons; they would cut food (probably holding it still, when necessary, with their fingers or their spoons), then lift it in the spoon, first shifting it if necessary to the right hand, to their mouths. Forks, imported from Europe, were certainly used sometimes not only for impaling food but for transporting it into the mouth. Charles Dickens visited America in the early 1840s and witnessed eating with both knife and straight, long-pronged fork: he says in *American Notes* that people "thrust the broad-bladed knives and the two-pronged forks further down their throats than I ever saw the same weapons go before, except in the hands of a skilled juggler." But soon forks took their modern spoonlike form, so that they could be treated, after the spearing and cutting was done, as though they were spoons. Europeans, meanwhile, kept eating food impaled on the tines.

Americans have been badgered and ridiculed about their eating habits for over a hundred years. They have refused so far to change, not seeing any need to do so, and out of patriotic pride in non-conformity. In any case, as Miss Manners (1982) says, "American table manners are, if anything, a more advanced form of civilized behavior than the European, because they are more complicated and further removed from the practical result, always a sign of refinement."

50 The spoon is the safest, most comfortable member of the cutlery set. It is the easiest implement to use—babies start with spoons—and the one with the most versatility, which is the reason why its employment is constantly being restricted. Spoons are for liquids, porridge, and puddings—even the last being often given over to forks. Insofar as spoons have an infantile image, they lack prestige. (A Freudian analysis of the knife, fork, and spoon gives the spoon the female role in the trio; the fork, if I understand the writer correctly, is a male child of the knife and the spoon, and, like a little Oedipus, resentful of the knife and jealous of the spoon.) Social historians are puzzled by medieval paintings of banquets, which show knives but seldom spoons, although we know that spoons were often used. It has been suggested (unconvincingly, I think) that knives might simply have impressed the painters more. Spoons seem, at any rate, not to have been laid down on the table's surface as knives were.

But spoons can inspire affection as knives and forks cannot; they are unthreatening, nurturing objects. Superstitions about them show that they are subconsciously regarded as little persons: two on one saucer means an imminent wedding; dropping one on the table means a visitor is coming; and so on. Spoon-handles, more than knife- or fork-handles, are made in the shape of human figures, as in the sets of twelve apostle spoons. The Welsh traditionally made love-spoons carved with the lovers' hands, which they gave to each other as tokens, and an old English custom at Christmas was for all the diners to hold up their spoons and wish health to absent friends (spoons were customarily classed with cups and bowls). Spoons have always been popular as presents and commemorations, whereas knives are often superstitiously avoided as gifts, and forks somehow fail, still, to stand on their own as spoons and knives can.

THINGS TO DO WITH THE READING

1. A number of words appear in quotation marks in Visser's essay: "natural," "freely choosing," etc. Find all of the terms that Visser encloses in quotation marks, arrange these into strands and binaries, and then determine the rhetoric of this stylistic tendency. (See pages 69–70, 246, and 262 for a discussion of rhetorical analysis.) What do the quotation marks indicate in each case, and generally?
2. **Link:** According to Visser, "Mixing with people whose rituals differ from our own can be very trying. [...] The really dramatic 'ethnic' behavior we consciously apprehend at once, and so can 'make allowances for'; everyone has heard of having to eat an eyeball, or smash glasses after the toast. [...] But the smaller, less noticeable signs [of ritual difference] can catch us off our guard and rob us more insidiously of our sense of security" (see paragraph 6). The word "security" figures centrally in both Visser's and Jeffrey Rosen's arguments. How do the two writers differ in the point of view they invite us to take of security?
3. **Link:** Near the end of her discussion in "Rituals," Margaret Visser discusses what happens when a ritual comes to be seen as losing its force, becoming a "merely empty form" (see paragraph 20). Summarize this passage—it's the two paragraphs beginning "But what about ritual" and "In our time, cataclysmic"—locating key terms and paraphrasing several times the two or three sentences you find most interesting or perplexing. This activity will help you to control Visser's meaning. Then use the passage as a lens to think anew about the other reading selections in this Manners, Communication, and Technology chapter. See pages 117–120 for a discussion of how to write analytical summaries.

   To what extent might Christine Rosen and Jeffrey Rosen (and Jonathan Franzen, the author of the next reading) be willing to see the problems they survey in terms of the following observation from Visser: "In our own time, cataclysmic social revolutions have made large numbers of rules and conventions redundant, and many of them have not yet been replaced with new signs and voluntary constraints that are broadly recognized and accepted" (see paragraph 21)?
4. **Application:** Go to paragraph 5, beginning, "This pernicketiness has some of its basis in biology." First, explicate the paragraph by finding its key terms (repeated words) and strands (for example, *instinctively*, *automatically*, *instantly*). Also paraphrase key sentences such as the one beginning "Every person must be careful." Then use your explication of Visser's thinking in this paragraph as a lens for examining one of the following:
   - a social situation you have participated in or observed wherein the people both have and have not noticed and provided the necessary signs
   - a family occasion involving eating wherein the relative success or failure of the event depended on people reacting instinctively to very small signs

5. **Application:** Visser observes that rituals are especially important at times of transition and "difficult passages" (see paragraph 13). Use this thinking as a lens for analyzing and exemplifying some small social behavior such as the various rituals people typically employ for getting into and out of conversations (meeting others and parting).
6. **Application:** Manners, Visser tells us, "pressure people to behave in a predictable fashion" (see paragraph 13). Rituals, as the discussion in paragraphs 4–14 makes clear, concern repetition and rules that ultimately serve some conservative social function, providing stability and order while also celebrating what Visser terms our "interconnectedness and self-control." Make a more comprehensive list of the characteristics of ritual as Visser presents it. Then analyze some ritual from your everyday life. Use her discussion of eating utensils as a model.

   Chances are your choice of ritual will be one that you had never really noticed as ritual before. It could be anything where systems of manners apply:

   - how the classroom behavior in a particular course you are taking functions (including the one in which you are using this book)
   - hygiene in your living space
   - eating cheese or some other problematic food
   - eating pizza with others
   - fast food restaurants

   There are countless other examples. Your goal will be to recognize the activity as a ritual, and then to lay out the codes of etiquette that govern it and explore their implications.

Jonathan Franzen

Imperial Bedroom

Jonathan Franzen is the author of three novels, including *The Corrections*, which won the National Book Award in 2001. In this essay, taken from his collection *How To Be Alone* (2002), Franzen meditates on the invasion of public space by the private and mourns the eroding of the distinction between the two. He is a gifted stylist and an agile thinker, full of surprising reversals. For example: "The real reason that Americans are apathetic about privacy is so big as to be almost invisible: we're flat-out *drowning* in privacy. What's threatened isn't the private sphere. It's the public sphere."

Privacy, privacy, the new American obsession: espoused as the most fundamental of rights, marketed as the most desirable of commodities, and pronounced dead twice a week. 1

Even before Linda Tripp pressed the "Record" button on her answering machine, commentators were warning us that "privacy is under siege," that "privacy is in a dreadful state," that "privacy as we now know it may not exist in the year 2000." They say that both Big Brother and his little brother, John Q. Public, are shadowing me through networks of computers. They tell me that security cameras no bigger than spiders are watching from every shaded corner, that dour feminists are monitoring bedroom behavior and water-cooler conversations, that genetic sleuths can decoct my entire being from a droplet of saliva, that voyeurs can retrofit ordinary camcorders with a filter that lets them *see through people's clothing*. Then comes the flood of dirty suds from the Office of the Independent Counsel, oozing forth through official and commercial channels to saturate the national consciousness. The Monica Lewinsky scandal marks, in the words of the philosopher Thomas Nagel, "the culmination of a disastrous erosion" of privacy; it represents, in the words of the author Wendy Kaminer, "the utter disregard for privacy and individual autonomy that exists in totalitarian regimes." In the person of Kenneth Starr, the "public sphere" has finally overwhelmed—shredded, gored, trampled, invaded, run roughshod over—"the private."

The panic about privacy has all the finger-pointing and paranoia of a good old American scare, but it's missing one vital ingredient: a genuinely alarmed public. Americans care about privacy mainly in the abstract. Sometimes a well-informed community unites to defend itself, as when Net users bombarded the White House with e-mails against the "clipper chip," and sometimes an especially outrageous piece of news provokes a national outcry, as when the Lotus Development Corporation tried to market a CD-ROM containing financial profiles of nearly half the people in the country. By and large, though, even in the face of wholesale infringements like the war on drugs, Americans remain curiously passive. I'm no exception. I read the editorials and try to get excited, but I can't. More often than not, I find myself feeling the opposite of what the privacy mavens want me to. It's happened twice in the last month alone.

On the Saturday morning when the *Times* came carrying the complete text of the Starr report, what I felt as I sat alone in my apartment and tried to eat my breakfast was that my own privacy—not Clinton's, not Lewinsky's—was being violated. I love the distant pageant of public life. I love both the pageantry and the distance. Now a President was facing impeachment, and as a good citizen I had a duty to stay informed about the evidence, but the evidence here consisted of two people's groping, sucking, and mutual self-deception. What I felt, when this evidence landed beside my toast and coffee, wasn't a pretend revulsion to camouflage a secret interest in the dirt; I wasn't offended by the sex qua sex; I wasn't worrying about a potential future erosion of my own rights; I didn't feel the President's pain in the empathic way he'd once claimed to feel mine; I wasn't repelled by the revelation that public officials do bad things; and, although I'm a registered Democrat, my disgust was of a different order from my partisan disgust at the news that the Giants have blown a fourth-quarter lead. What I felt I felt personally. I was being intruded on.

5 A couple of days later, I got a call from one of my credit-card providers, asking me to confirm two recent charges at a gas station and one at a hardware store. Queries like this are common nowadays, but this one was my first, and for a moment I felt eerily exposed. At the same time, I was perversely flattered that someone, somewhere, had taken an interest in me and had bothered to phone. Not that the young male operator seemed to care about me personally. He sounded like he was reading his lines from a laminated booklet. The strain of working hard at a job he almost certainly didn't enjoy seemed to thicken his tongue. He tried to rush his words out, to speed through them as if in embarrassment or vexation at how nearly worthless they were, but they kept bunching up in his teeth, and he had to stop and extract them with his lips, one by one. It was the computer, he said, the computer that routinely, ah, scans the, you know, the pattern of charges … and was there something else he could help me with tonight? I decided that if this young person wanted to scroll through my charges and ponder the significance of my two fill-ups and my gallon of latex paint, I was fine with it.

So here's the problem. On the Saturday morning the Starr Report came out, my privacy was, in the classic liberal view, absolute. I was alone in my home and unobserved, unbothered by neighbors, unmentioned in the news, and perfectly free, if I chose, to ignore the report and do the pleasantly *al dente* Saturday crossword; yet the report's mere existence so offended my sense of privacy that I could hardly bring myself to touch the thing. Two days later, I was disturbed in my home by a ringing phone, asked to cough up my mother's maiden name, and made aware that the digitized minutiae of my daily life were being scrutinized by strangers; and within five minutes I'd put the entire episode out of my mind. I felt encroached on when I was ostensibly safe, and I felt safe when I was ostensibly encroached on. And I didn't know why.

THE RIGHT to privacy—defined by Louis Brandeis and Samuel Warren, in 1890, as "the right to be let alone"—seems at first glance to be an elemental principle in American life. It's the rallying cry of activists fighting for reproductive rights, against stalkers, for the right to die, against a national health-care database, for stronger data-encryption standards, against paparazzi, for the sanctity of employee e-mail, and against employee drug testing. On closer examination, though, privacy proves to be the Cheshire cat of values: not much substance, but a very winning smile.

Legally, the concept is a mess. Privacy violation is the emotional core of many crimes, from stalking and rape to Peeping Tommery and trespass, but no criminal statute forbids it in the abstract. Civil law varies from state to state but generally follows a forty-year-old analysis by the legal scholar Dean William Prosser, who dissected the invasion of privacy into four torts: *intrusion* on my solitude, the publishing of *private facts* about me which are not of legitimate public concern, publicity that puts my character in a *false light*, and *appropriation* of my name or likeness without my consent. This is a crumbly set of torts. Intrusion looks a lot like criminal trespass, false light like defamation, and appropriation like theft; and the harm that remains when these extraneous offenses are subtracted is so admirably captured by the phrase "infliction of emotional distress" as to render the tort of privacy invasion all but superfluous. What really undergirds privacy is the classical liberal conception of personal autonomy or liberty. In the last few decades, many judges and scholars have chosen to speak of a "zone of privacy," rather than a "sphere of liberty," but this is a shift in emphasis, not in substance: not the making of a new doctrine but the repackaging and remarketing of an old one.

Whatever you're trying to sell, whether it's luxury real estate or Esperanto lessons, it helps to have the smiling word "private" on your side. Last winter, as the owner of a Bank One Platinum Visa Card, I was offered enrollment in a program called PrivacyGuard®, which, according to the literature promoting it, "*puts you in the know* about the very personal records available to your employer, insurers, credit card companies, and government agencies." The first three months of PrivacyGuard® were free, so I signed up. What came in the mail then was paperwork: envelopes and request forms for a Credit Record Search and other searches, also a disappointingly undeluxe logbook in which to jot down the search results. I realized immediately that I didn't care enough about, say, my driving records to wait a month to get them; it was only when I called PrivacyGuard® to cancel my membership, and was all but begged not to, that I realized that the whole point of this "service" was to harness my time and energy to the task of reducing Bank One Visa's fraud losses.

10 Even issues that legitimately touch on privacy are rarely concerned with the actual emotional harm of unwanted exposure or intrusion. A proposed national Genetic Privacy Act, for example, is premised on the idea that my DNA reveals more about my identity and future health than other medical data do. In fact, DNA is as yet no more intimately revealing than a heart murmur, a family history of diabetes, or an inordinate fondness for Buffalo chicken wings. As with any medical records, the potential for abuse of genetic information by employers and insurers is chilling, but this is only tangentially a privacy issue; the primary harm consists of things like job discrimination and higher insurance premiums.

In a similar way, the problem of online security is mainly about nuts and bolts. What American activists call "electronic privacy" their European counterparts call "data protection." Our term is exciting; theirs is accurate. If someone is out to steal your Amex number and expiration date, or if an evil ex-boyfriend is looking for your new address, you need the kind of hard-core secrecy that encryption seeks to guarantee. If you're talking to a friend on the phone, however, you need only a *feeling* of privacy.

The social drama of data protection goes something like this: a hacker or an insurance company or a telemarketer gains access to a sensitive database, public-interest watchdogs bark loudly, and new firewalls go up. Just as most people are moderately afraid of germs but leave virology to the Centers for Disease Control, most Americans take a reasonable interest in privacy issues but leave the serious custodial work to experts. Our problem now is that the custodians have started speaking a language of panic and treating privacy not as one of many competing values but as the one value that trumps all others.

The novelist Richard Powers recently declared in a *Times* op-ed piece that privacy is a "vanishing illusion" and that the struggle over the encryption of digital communications is therefore as "great with consequence" as the Cold War. Powers defines "the private" as "that part of life that goes unregistered," and he sees in the digital footprints we leave whenever we charge things the approach of "that moment when each person's every living day will become a Bloomsday, recorded in complete detail and reproducible with a few deft keystrokes." It is scary, of course, to think that the mystery of our identities might be reducible to finite data sequences. That Powers can seriously compare credit-card fraud and intercepted cell-phone calls to thermonuclear incineration, however, speaks mainly to the infectiousness of privacy panic. Where, after all, is it "registered" what Powers or anybody else is thinking, seeing, saying, wishing, planning, dreaming, and feeling ashamed of? A digital *Ulysses* consisting of nothing but a list of its hero's purchases and other recordable transactions might run, at most, to four pages: was there really nothing more to Bloom's day?

When Americans do genuinely sacrifice privacy, moreover, they do so for tangible gains in health or safety or efficiency. Most legalized infringements—HIV notification, airport X-rays, Megan's Law, Breathalyzer roadblocks, the drug-testing of student athletes, laws protecting fetuses, laws protecting the vegetative, remote monitoring of automobile emissions, county-jail strip searches, even Ken Starr's exposure of presidential corruption—are essentially public health measures. I resent the security cameras in Washington Square, but I appreciate the ones on a subway platform. The risk that someone is abusing my E-ZPass toll records seems to me comfortably low in comparison with my gain in convenience. Ditto the risk that some gossip rag will make me a victim of the First Amendment; with two hundred and seventy million people in the country, any individual's chances of being nationally exposed are next to nil.

The legal scholar Lawrence Lessig has characterized Americans as "bovine" 15
for making calculations like this and for thereby acquiescing in what he calls the "Sovietization" of personal life. The curious thing about privacy, though, is that simply by expecting it we can usually achieve it. One of my neighbors in the apartment building across the street spends a lot of time at her mirror examining her pores, and I can see her doing it, just as she can undoubtedly see me sometimes. But our respective privacies remain intact as long as neither of us *feels* seen. When I send a postcard through the U.S. mail, I'm aware in the abstract that mail handlers may be reading it, may be reading it aloud, may even be laughing at it, but I'm safe from all harm unless, by sheer bad luck, the one handler in the country whom I actually know sees the postcard and slaps his forehead and says, "Oh, jeez, I know this guy."

OUR PRIVACY panic isn't merely exaggerated. It's founded on a fallacy. Ellen Alderman and Caroline Kennedy, in *The Right to Privacy*, sum up the conventional wisdom of privacy advocates like this: "There is less privacy than there used to be." The claim has been made or implied so often, in so many books and editorials and talk-show dens, that Americans, no matter how passive they are in their behavior, now dutifully tell pollsters that they're very much worried about privacy. From almost any historical perspective, however, the claim seems bizarre.

In 1890, an American typically lived in a small town under conditions of near-panoptical surveillance. Not only did his every purchase "register," but it registered in the eyes and the memory of shopkeepers who knew him, his parents, his wife, and his children. He couldn't so much as walk to the post office without having his movements tracked and analyzed by neighbors. Probably he grew up sleeping in the same bed with his siblings and possibly with his parents, too. Unless he was well off, his transportation—a train, a horse, his own two feet—either was communal or exposed him to the public eye.

In the suburbs and exurbs where the typical American lives today, tiny nuclear families inhabit enormous houses, in which each person has his or her own bedroom and, sometimes, bathroom. Compared even with suburbs in the sixties and seventies, when I was growing up, the contemporary condominium development or gated community offers a striking degree of anonymity. It's no longer the rule that you know your neighbors. Communities increasingly tend to be virtual, the participants either faceless or firmly in control of the face they present. Transportation is largely private: the latest SUVs are the size of living rooms and come with onboard telephones, CD players, and TV screens; behind the tinted windows of one of these high-riding I-see-you-but-you-can't-see-me mobile PrivacyGuard® units, a person can be wearing pajamas or a licorice bikini, for all anybody knows or cares. Maybe the government intrudes on the family a little more than it did a hundred years ago (social workers look in on the old and the poor, health officials require inoculations, the police inquire about spousal battery), but these intrusions don't begin to make up for the small-town snooping they've replaced.

The "right to be left alone"? Far from disappearing, it's exploding. It's the *essence* of modern American architecture, landscape, transportation, communication, and mainstream political philosophy. The real reason that Americans are apathetic about privacy is so big as to be almost invisible: we're flat-out *drowning* in privacy.

What's threatened, then, isn't the private sphere. It's the public sphere. Much 20
has been made of the discouraging effect that the Starr investigation may have on future aspirants to public office (only zealots and zeros need apply), but that's just half of it. The public world of Washington, because it's public, belongs to everyone. We're all invited to participate with our votes, our patriotism, our campaigning, and our opinions. The collective weight of a population makes possible our faith in the public world as something larger and more enduring and more dignified than any messy individual can be in private. But, just as one sniper in a church tower can keep the streets of an entire town empty, one real gross-out scandal can undermine that faith.

If privacy depends upon an expectation of invisibility, the expectation of *visibility* is what defines a public space. My "sense of privacy" functions to keep the public out of the private *and* to keep the private out of the public. A kind of mental Border collie yelps in distress when I feel that the line between the two has been breached. This is why the violation of a public space is so similar, as an experience, to the violation of privacy. I walk past a man taking a leak on a sidewalk in broad daylight (delivery-truck drivers can be especially self-righteous in their "Ya gotta go, ya gotta go" philosophy of bladder management), and although the man with the yawning fly is ostensibly the one whose privacy is compromised by the leak, I'm the one who feels the impingement. Flashers and sexual harassers and fellators on the pier and self-explainers on the crosstown bus all similarly assault our sense of the "public" by exposing themselves.

Since really serious exposure in public today is assumed to be synonymous with being seen on television, it would seem to follow that televised space is the premier public space. Many things that people say to me on television, however, would never be tolerated in a genuine public space—in a jury box, for example, or even on a city sidewalk. TV is an enormous, ramified extension of the billion living rooms and bedrooms in which it's consumed. You rarely hear a person on the subway talking loudly about, say, incontinence, but on television it's been happening for years. TV is devoid of shame, and without shame there can be no distinction between public and private. Last winter, an anchorwoman looked me in the eye and, in the tone of a close female relative, referred to a litter of babies in Iowa as "America's seven little darlin's." It was strange enough, twenty-five years ago, to get Dan Rather's reports on Watergate between spots for Geritol and Bayer aspirin, as if Nixon's impending resignation were somehow located in my medicine chest. Now, shelved between ads for Promise margarine and Celebrity Cruises, the news itself is a soiled cocktail dress—TV the bedroom floor and nothing but.

Reticence, meanwhile, has become an obsolete virtue. People now readily name their diseases, rents, antidepressants. Sexual histories get spilled on first dates, Birkenstocks and cutoffs infiltrate the office on casual Fridays, telecommuting puts the boardroom in the bedroom, "softer" modern office design puts the bedroom in the boardroom, sales-people unilaterally address customers by their first name, waiters won't bring me food until I've established a personal relationship with them, voice-mail machinery stresses the "I" in "*I'm* sorry, but *I* don't understand what you dialed," and cyberenthusiasts, in a particularly grotesque misnomer, designate as "public forums" pieces of etched silicon with which a forum's unshaved "participant" may communicate while sitting cross-legged in tangled sheets. The networked world as a threat to privacy? It's the ugly spectacle of a privacy triumphant.

A genuine public space is a place where every citizen is welcome to be present and where the purely private is excluded or restricted. One reason that attendance at art museums has soared in recent years is that museums still feel public in this way. After those tangled sheets, how delicious the enforced decorum and the hush, the absence of in-your-face consumerism. How sweet the promenading, the seeing and being seen. Everybody needs a promenade sometimes—a place to go when you want to announce to the world (not the little world of friends and family but the big world, the real world) that you have a new suit, or that you're in love, or that you suddenly realize you stand a full inch taller when you don't hunch your shoulders.

25 Unfortunately, the fully public place is a nearly extinct category. We still have courtrooms and the jury pool, commuter trains and bus stations, here and there a small-town Main Street that really is a main street rather than a strip mall, certain coffee bars, and certain city sidewalks. Otherwise, for American adults, the only halfway public space is the world of work. Here, especially in the upper echelons of business, codes of dress and behavior are routinely enforced, personal disclosures are penalized, and formality is still the rule. But these rituals extend only to the employees of the firm, and even they, when they become old, disabled, obsolete, or outsourceable, are liable to be expelled and thereby relegated to the tangled sheets.

The last big, steep-walled bastion of public life in America is Washington, D.C. Hence the particular violation I felt when the Starr Report crashed in. Hence the feeling of being intruded on. It was privacy invasion, all right: private life brutally invading the most public of public spaces. I don't want to see sex on the news from Washington. There's sex everywhere else I look—on sitcoms, on the Web, on dust jackets, in car ads, on the billboards at Times Square. Can't there be one thing in the national landscape that isn't about the bedroom? We all know there's sex in the cloakrooms of power, sex behind the pomp and circumstance, sex beneath the robes of justice; but can't we act like grownups and pretend otherwise? Pretend not that "no one is looking" but that *everyone* is looking?

For two decades now, business leaders and politicians across much of the political spectrum, both Gingrich Republicans and Clinton Democrats, have extolled the virtues of privatizing public institutions. But what better word can there be for Lewinskygate and the ensuing irruption of disclosures (the infidelities of Helen Chenoweth, of Dan Burton, of Henry Hyde) than "privatization"? Anyone who wondered what a privatized presidency might look like may now, courtesy of Mr. Starr, behold one.

IN DENIS JOHNSON'S SHORT STORY "Beverly Home," the young narrator spends his days working at a nursing home for the hopelessly disabled, where there is a particularly unfortunate patient whom no one visits:

> A perpetual spasm forced him to perch sideways on his wheelchair and peer down along his nose at his knotted fingers. This condition had descended on him suddenly. He got no visitors. His wife was divorcing him. He was only thirty-three, I believe he said, but it was hard to guess what he told about himself because he really couldn't talk anymore, beyond clamping his lips repeatedly around his protruding tongue while groaning.
>
> No more pretending for him! He was completely and openly a mess. Meanwhile the rest of us go on trying to fool each other.

In a coast-to-coast, shag-carpeted imperial bedroom, we could all just be messes and save ourselves the trouble of pretending. But who wants to live in a pajama-party world? Privacy loses its value unless there's something it can be defined against. "Meanwhile the rest of us go on trying to fool each other"—and a good thing, too. The need to put on a public face is as basic as the need for the privacy in which to take it off. We need both a home that's not like a public space and a public space that's not like home.

Walking up Third Avenue on a Saturday night, I feel bereft. All around me, 30
attractive young people are hunched over their StarTacs and Nokias with preoccupied expressions, as if probing a sore tooth, or adjusting a hearing aid, or squeezing a pulled muscle; personal technology has begun to look like a personal handicap. All I really want from a sidewalk is that people see me and let themselves be seen, but even this modest ideal is thwarted by cell-phone users and their unwelcome privacy. They say things like "Should we have couscous with that?" and "I'm on my way to Blockbuster." They aren't breaking any law by broadcasting these breakfast-nook conversations. There's no PublicityGuard that I can buy, no expensive preserve of public life to which I can flee. Seclusion, whether in a suite at the Plaza or in a cabin in the Catskills, is comparatively effortless to achieve. Privacy is protected as both commodity and right; public forums are protected as neither. Like old-growth forests, they're few and irreplaceable and should be held in trust by everyone. The work of maintaining them gets only harder as the private sector grows ever more demanding, distracting, and disheartening. Who has the time and energy to stand up for the public sphere? What rhetoric can possibly compete with the American love of "privacy"?

When I return to my apartment after dark, I don't immediately turn my lights on. Over the years, it's become a reflexive precaution on my part not to risk spooking exposed neighbors by flooding my living room with light, although the only activity I ever seem to catch them at is watching TV.

My skin-conscious neighbor is home with her husband tonight, and they seem to be dressing for a party. The woman, a vertical strip of whom is visible between the Levelors and the window frame, is wearing a bathrobe and a barrette and sitting in front of a mirror. The man, slick-haired, wearing suit pants and a white T-shirt, stands by the sofa in the other room and watches television in a posture that I recognize as uncommitted. Finally the woman disappears into the bedroom. The man puts on a white shirt and a necktie and perches sidesaddle on the arm of the sofa, still watching television, more involved with it now. The woman returns wearing a strapless yellow dress and looking like a whole different species of being. Happy the transformation! Happy the distance between private and public! I see a rapid back-and-forth involving jewelry, jackets, and a clutch purse, and then the couple, dressed to the nines, ventures out into the world.

[1998]

THINGS TO DO WITH THE READING

1. Much of the effect of Franzen's piece has to do with its style, and one element of the style is the repetition of certain metaphors. These metaphors are themselves complex nodes of meaning—usually an image that has been introduced and laden with feeling and point of view. In music and in some literary study as well, the use of a repeated image that accumulates meaning as it recurs is known as a *leitmotif.* There are numerous examples of this technique in the essay, but two prominent ones are "tangled sheets" and the "skin-conscious neighbor." Take notes on

where and how any of these repeated terms are used in the essay. Then write about what these leitmotifs mean.

2. At the end of Chapter 6, we conclude that the thesis is "a necessary constituent of analytical writing because it defines a field of play and allows a writer to go places" (see page 189). The sinuous turns of thought in Franzen's essay—which is clearly inductive and does not start with a thesis—make it a rich candidate for analyzing how the thesis evolves in a piece of writing. Familiarize yourself with the discussion of the evolving thesis on pages 165–171 and then do Try this 6.2: "Tracking a Thesis" (see page 171) with Franzen's essay. List all of the different versions of his primary claims to arrive at a chart of how the thinking in the piece moves.
3. A primary point about conclusions is to culminate, not simply summarize (see pages 229–235). Study the way that Franzen concludes his essay. What do you notice about his final paragraph? How does it proceed? What key terms from the essay does it include? How does it provide judgment, culmination, and send-off (see page 229)?
4. Read the Quick Take on shaping sentences at the beginning of Chapter 11 and use this as a lens for thinking about the connection between Franzen's favored sentence shapes and his way of thinking. A striking and thus emphatic "Go to" sentence shape of Franzen's is called chiasmus. Here are some examples of chiasmus from his essay:
   - "I felt encroached on when I was ostensibly safe, and I felt safe when I was ostensibly encroached on" (see paragraph 6).
   - "My 'sense of privacy' functions to keep the public out of the private and to keep the private out of the public" (see paragraph 21).
   - "Telecommuting puts the boardroom in the bedroom, 'softer' modern office design puts the bedroom in the boardroom" (see paragraph 23).

   And here is a variant, not quite chiasmus:

   - "If privacy depends upon an expectation of invisibility, the expectation of visibility is what defines a public space" (see paragraph 21).

   From these examples, determine what chiasmus (from the Greek for the letter X) does.

   What do you notice about the structure of Franzen's thinking in the essay that might prompt him to shape his sentences in this way?
5. Style creates what rhetoricians call *persona*—a version of the writer that he or she creates for the purpose at hand. Describe Franzen's persona in this piece, the sort of person he comes off as being on the page and the kind of relationship he seeks to establish with the reader. Determine what features of Franzen's style (word choice, tone, sentence shape) are most significant in creating this persona. Once you have gotten to this point, ask yourself, Why might Franzen have developed this persona for this piece?
6. **Link:** In their essays, Christine Rosen and Paul Goldberger mourn the loss of public space, as does Franzen. How do Franzen's thinking and values compare with those of the other two writers in this regard? Find

sentences about public space from each of the three essays and put these into conversation with each other. How, for example, does each define key terms? Looking at all three writers' definitions, what similarities and differences do you find? Here, for example, is a relevant passage from Christine Rosen: "As trust is being built and bolstered moment by moment between individuals, public trust among strangers in social settings is eroding. We are strengthening and increasing our interactions with the people we already know at the expense of those who we do not" (see paragraph 49).

7. **Application:** Use the essay as a lens to locate interesting instances of what Franzen calls "the panic about privacy." Alternatively, locate examples from your experience of public spaces as Franzen defines the term. Or apply the following remark as a lens to any show on the airwaves: "TV is devoid of shame, and without shame there can be no distinction between public and private" (see paragraph 22). ◗

Edward Tufte

PowerPoint Is Evil

Edward Tufte is a former professor of political science, computer science and statistics, and graphic design at Yale. He is the author of seven books and is also a sculptor and printmaker. This piece, taken from a longer monograph entitled *The Cognitive Style of PowerPoint*, sent ripples through both the academic and the corporate communities when it was first published. This excerpt appeared in www.wired.com in September of 2003.

Imagine a widely used and expensive prescription drug that promised to make us 1
beautiful but didn't. Instead the drug had frequent, serious side effects: It induced stupidity, turned everyone into bores, wasted time, and degraded the quality and credibility of communication. These side effects would rightly lead to a worldwide product recall.

Yet slideware—computer programs for presentations—is everywhere: in corporate America, in government bureaucracies, even in our schools. Several hundred million copies of Microsoft PowerPoint are churning out trillions of slides each year. Slideware may help speakers outline their talks, but convenience for the speaker can be punishing to both content and audience. The standard PowerPoint presentation elevates format over content, betraying an attitude of commercialism that turns everything into a sales pitch.

Of course, data-driven meetings are nothing new. Years before today's slideware, presentations at companies such as IBM and in the military used bullet lists shown by overhead projectors. But the format has become ubiquitous under PowerPoint, which was created in 1984 and later acquired by Microsoft. PowerPoint's pushy style seeks to set up a speaker's dominance over the audience. The speaker, after all, is making power points with bullets to followers. Could any metaphor be worse? Voicemail menu systems? Billboards? Television? Stalin?

Particularly disturbing is the adoption of the PowerPoint cognitive style in our schools. Rather than learning to write a report using sentences, children are being taught how to formulate client pitches and infomercials. Elementary school PowerPoint exercises (as seen in teacher guides and in student work posted on the Internet) typically consist of 10 to 20 words and a piece of clip art on each slide in a presentation of three to six slides—a total of perhaps 80 words (15 seconds of silent reading) for a week of work. Students would be better off if the schools simply closed down on those days and everyone went to the Exploratorium or wrote an illustrated essay explaining something.

In a business setting, a PowerPoint slide typically shows 40 words, which is 5
about eight seconds' worth of silent reading material. With so little information per slide, many, many slides are needed. Audiences consequently endure a relentless sequentiality, one damn slide after another. When information is stacked in time, it is difficult to understand context and evaluate relationships. Visual reasoning usually works more effectively when relevant information is shown side by side. Often, the more intense the detail, the greater the clarity

and understanding. This is especially so for statistical data, where the fundamental analytical act is to make comparisons.

Consider an important and intriguing table of survival rates for those with cancer relative to those without cancer for the same time period. Some 196 numbers and 57 words describe survival rates and their standard errors for 24 cancers.

Applying the PowerPoint templates to this nice, straightforward table yields an analytical disaster. The data explodes into six separate chaotic slides, consuming 2.9 times the area of the table. Everything is wrong with these smarmy, incoherent graphs: the encoded legends, the meaningless color, the logo-type branding. They are uncomparative, indifferent to content and evidence, and so data-starved as to be almost pointless. Chartjunk is a clear sign of statistical stupidity. Poking a finger into the eye of thought, these data graphics would turn into a nasty travesty if used for a serious purpose, such as helping cancer patients assess their survival chances. To sell a product that messes up data with such systematic intensity, Microsoft abandons any pretense of statistical integrity and reasoning.

Presentations largely stand or fall on the quality, relevance, and integrity of the content. If your numbers are boring, then you've got the wrong numbers. If your words or images are not on point, making them dance in color won't make them relevant. Audience boredom is usually a content failure, not a decoration failure.

FIGURE 15.1 Military parade, Stalin Square, Budapest, April 4, 1956.

At a minimum, a presentation format should do no harm. Yet the PowerPoint style routinely disrupts, dominates, and trivializes content. Thus PowerPoint presentations too often resemble a school play—very loud, very slow, and very simple.

The practical conclusions are clear. PowerPoint is a competent slide manager 10
and projector. But rather than supplementing a presentation, it has become a substitute for it. Such misuse ignores the most important rule of speaking: Respect your audience.

THINGS TO DO WITH THE READING

1. Tufte's argument is, among other things, a rhetorical analysis; it analyzes the kind of relationship that PowerPoint's style establishes with its audience (see pages 69–70). Given what PowerPoint does with information, what can we assume that the makers of this program assume about the audiences at whom PowerPoint demonstrations are aimed? See pages 97–100 for discussion of how to uncover assumptions.
2. **Link:** Various writers in this chapter have cast a skeptical eye upon the effect of electronic communication on the culture. How would Christine Rosen or Jeffrey Rosen respond to Tufte's point of view? Alternatively, what would Visser have to say about the etiquette of Microsoft PowerPoint?
3. **Application:** Conduct a comic collaboration with Tufte by fashioning a PowerPoint presentation of his argument. This would be a tricky analytical task, because it would require you to select and arrange the information in ways that harmonize with Tufte's tone (see page 260) and at the same time, accurately present his position. You might want to begin by pondering what Tufte means by the phrase "the PowerPoint cognitive style."

FOR FURTHER RESEARCH: MANNERS, COMMUNICATION, AND TECHNOLOGY

By Kelly Cannon, Reference Librarian

The readings and activities below invite you to further explore the theme of Manners, Communication, and Technology. WARNING: Some essays are polemical; they are intended to promote insight and discussion (or a starting point for your next paper). To access the online readings, visit the *Writing Analytically with Readings* website at www.thomsonedu.com/english/rosenwasser.

Online

Coursey, David. "The Downside of Citizen Journalism." *Publish*. 13 December 2005.
Argues that "lack of editorial oversight" in blogs and other online journalism leads to "unfounded allegations that damage credibility, harm reputations and waste time."

> **Explore:** What evidence or other persuasive devices does Coursey use to convince the reader to agree with him?

Horrigan, John B. "Online Communities: Networks That Nurture Long-Distance Relationships and Local Ties." *Pew Internet and American Life Project*. 31 October 2001. Pew Research Center. 30 December 2005.
A think-tank report claiming that the online world is a vibrant social universe where many internet users enjoy serious and satisfying contact with online communities.

> **Explore:** To what extent does this report reflect your experience with online communication? How so?

"How to Blog Safely (About Work or Anything Else)." *Electronic Frontier Foundation*. 2005. 8 December 2005.
"Simple precautions to help you maintain control of your personal privacy so that you can express yourself without facing unjust retaliation."

> **Explore:** Set up your own blog, taking the precautions suggested in this article. What ethical conundrums are raised by anonymous blogging? Why?

Shea, Virginia. *Netiquette*. San Francisco: Albion, 1994. 8 December 2005.
Basic etiquette for online communication.

> **Explore:** Apply these rules of netiquette in the next online communication you send. Watch for breaches of netiquette in the communications you receive from others.

Tynan, Dan. "Gadgetiquette 101." *PC World* 23.1 (January 2005). 14 December 2005.
Basic etiquette for gadget lovers.

> **Explore:** Monitor for a day the gadget use (cell phones, laptops, etc.) of those around you, especially in public places. What breaches of etiquette, if any, do you observe? How bothered or unbothered are you by such breaches? Why?

In Print

(Ask your librarian about possible online access to items marked with **.)

****Humphreys, Lee. "Social Topography in a Wireless Era: the Negotiation of Public and Private Space." *Journal of Technical Writing and Communication* 35.4 (2005): 367–384.**
In this study, the author explores how callers and bystanders negotiate privacy.

Explore: This study is typical of "empirical research." What is empirical about it? In what section can the results of the research be found? What other elements make this article typical of research performed in the social sciences?

****Uslaner, Eric M. "Trust, Civic Engagement, and the Internet." *Political Communication* 21.2 (April–June 2004): 223–242.**
Does the internet promote or impede social connections and trust? Using surveys from the Pew Center for the Internet and American Life, Uslaner contends that internet users are not social isolates.

Explore: Check out the Pew Internet and American Life Project online. Try to locate the data sources employed by Uslaner.

****Valkenberg, Patti M. et al. "Adolescents' Identity Experiments on the Internet." *New Media and Society* 7.3 (June 2005): 383–402.**
This author and her colleagues studied 600 9- to 18-year-olds, asking how and why they engaged in "internet-based identity experiments."

Explore: According to the study, what are the major reasons young people engage in identity experimentation over the internet? To what extent does this reflect your experience?

Zhang, Xiaoni. "What Do Consumers Really Know about Spyware?" *Communications of the ACM* 48.8 (August 2005): 44–48.
Zhang argues that consumer education is the best combatant to the ubiquitous form of privacy invasion known as spyware.

Explore: Examine the list of references at the end of the article. See if you can distinguish between these types of references: government documents, popular magazines, trade publications, and academic journals. (See Chapter 13 for a discussion of these types of references.)

CHAPTER 16

Places and Spaces: Cities and Suburbs

Quick Take

The readings in this chapter call to mind a provocative definition of nostalgia offered by a character in Don Delillo's 1985 novel *White Noise*: "Nostalgia," says the Visiting Lecturer in Communications, Murray Jay Suskind, "is a product of dissatisfaction and rage; a settling of grievances between the present and the past" (258). All of the essays in this chapter cast a skeptical eye to the future of urban and suburban life in America, and, explicitly or implicitly, they look back with a certain degree of nostalgia to a lost past when life appeared more genuinely democratic—and livable.

The writers all converse in one way or another with what is known as the New Urbanism, a movement seeking to rethink the ways our cities have declined and our suburbs have expanded in the past half-century. There are obviously potent comparisons with the preceding chapter. The interest in public versus private life treated in Chapter 15 returns here in the concern with impersonal living spaces—barren suburbs fueled by the car culture and fortressed cities fraught with risk.

ABOUT THE READINGS IN THIS CHAPTER

"The United States is the wealthiest nation in the history of the world," begins the first essay in this chapter, by James Howard Kunstler, "yet its inhabitants are strikingly unhappy." Kunstler's is an ethical call to attention, a plea for us to become citizens rather than simply consumers, by rebuilding the material culture that surrounds us in the public realm, starting at the level of the neighborhood. Jack Gambino's discussion of the landscapes of two contemporary photographers provides graphic illustration of Kunstler's vision. Although the two photographers' work differs widely in focus and tone, it shares a fascination with "creative destruction" that Gambino sees as distinctively Modern, and it functions, in both cases, as a kind of visual cultural memory against a past too easily forgotten.

Next, Adam Gopnik makes his first of several appearances in this book, offering a wry history of the redevelopment of Times Square in New York City in a way that offers a lens for viewing redevelopment anywhere. Gopnik's piece provides insight into the actual jostlings for power that accompany redevelopment, in this case, wherein "a question of virtue had to be disguised as a necessity of commerce."

The chapter concludes with two classic essays on civic space that might be fruitfully compared. A chapter from Jane Jacobs's pioneering study of city life analyzes safe versus unsafe neighborhoods. One conclusion she draws about her late 1950s New York City neighborhood is that "thinning out a city does not insure safety from crime and fear of crime." This line rings ominously against Mike Davis's chilling account of the spatial imperatives militating against the urban poor and the homeless in 1990s Los Angeles.

James Howard Kunstler

The Public Realm and the Common Good

The author and journalist James Howard Kunstler is an eloquent advocate of what is known as the "New Urbanism"—an urban design movement that arose in the late 1980s. The New Urbanism supports walkable neighborhoods, mixed use and mixed income housing, and a restored sense of community feeling, and it vigorously opposes urban sprawl. The following piece is excerpted from his book *Home From Nowhere: Remaking Our Everyday World for the Twenty-first Century* (1996). In it, Kunstler argues that the development of American towns and cities since World War II has been marked by an absence of respect for what he terms the "public realm," defined as "the physical manifestation of the common good."

The United States is the wealthiest nation in the history of the world, yet its inhabitants are strikingly unhappy. Unhappiness is manifest at every level of the national scene. From big city to the remotest rural trailer court, our civic life is tattered and frayed. Unspeakable crimes occur in the most ordinary places. Government can't fulfill its most basic role in guaranteeing the public safety. Our schools, in many cases, barely function. The consensus of what constitutes decent behavior fractured with the social revolutions of the 1960s and has not been restored. Anything goes. 1

Community, as it once existed in the form of places worth caring about, supported by local economies, has been extirpated by an insidious corporate colonialism that doesn't care about the places from which it extracts its profits or the people subject to its operations.

The Public Realm and the Common Good

American cities are dismal. The majority of American small towns have become dismal. Of course, those two types of places represent America as it developed before World War Two, and their current state must be understood as one of abandonment and dereliction. The newer suburban subdivisions are dismal, too, in their own unique way, as are the commercial highway strips, the malls, the office parks, and the rest of the autocentric equipment of the human habitat. Their architectural shortcomings aside, these places are dismal because the public realm that binds them together is degraded, incoherent, ugly and meaningless. In case the term *public realm* seems vague or mystifying, I shall attempt to define it with some precision.

The public realm is the connective tissue of our everyday world. It is made of those pieces of terrain left between the private holdings. It exists in the form of streets, highways, town squares, parks, and even parking lots. It includes rural or wilderness landscape: stretches of the seacoast, national forests, most lakes and rivers, and even the sky (though "air rights" are sometimes bought and sold in the cities). The public realm exists mainly outdoors because most buildings belong to private individuals or corporations. Exceptions to this are public institutions such as libraries, museums, and town halls, which are closed some hours of the day, and airports and train stations, which may be open around the clock.

Some places, while technically private, function as quasi-public realm—for instance, college campuses, ballparks, restaurants, theaters, nightclubs, and, yes, shopping malls, at least the corridors between the private shops. Their owners retain the right to regulate behavior within, particularly the terms of access, and so the distinction must be made that they are only nominally public. The true public realm then, for the sake of this argument, is that portion of our everyday world which belongs to everybody and to which everybody ought to have access most of the time. The public realm is therefore a set of real places possessing physical form.

The public realm in America became so atrocious in the postwar decades that 5
the Disney Corporation was able to create an artificial substitute for it and successfully sell it as a commodity. That's what Disney World is really about. In France, where the public realm possesses a pretty high standard of design quality and is carefully maintained as well, there is much less need for artificial substitutes, so few people feel compelled to go to EuroDisney (it lost over $1 billion in its first two years of operation). The design quality of everything at EuroDisney is about five notches *beneath* that of the most mediocre French street corner. The quality of the park benches and street lamps in EuroDisney is recognizably inferior to the quality of the park benches and street lamps in ordinary French towns. Even the flower beds lack finesse. They look like berms designed for corporate parking lots. There are more interesting things to eat along nine linear yards of the Rue Buci on the Left Bank than in all the magic kingdoms of EuroDisney.

The design quality of Disney World in Orlando, on the other hand, is about 1.5 notches better than the average American suburban shopping mall or housing subdivision—so Americans love it. Forget about how cheap-looking the benches and lampposts might be—we don't even have sidewalks in most of suburbia (and besides, nobody walks there anyway)—so *any* benches and lampposts seem swell. Americans love Disney World, above all, because it is uncontaminated by cars, except for a few antique vehicles kept around as stage props. By and large, they do not know that this is the reason they love Disney World. Americans are amazingly unconscious of how destructive the automobile has been to their everyday world.

Main Street USA is America's obsolete model for development—we stopped assembling towns this way after 1945. The pattern of Main Street is pretty simple: mixed use, mixed income, apartments and offices over the stores, moderate density, scaled to pedestrians, vehicles permitted but not allowed to dominate, buildings detailed with care, all built to last (though we still trashed it). Altogether it was a pretty good development pattern. It produced places that people loved deeply. That is the reason Main Street persists in our cultural memory. Many people still alive remember the years before World War Two and what it felt like to live in integral towns modeled on this pattern. Physical remnants of the pattern still stand in parts of the country for people to see, though the majority of Americans have moved into the new model habitat called suburban sprawl.

For all its apparent success, Suburban Sprawl sorely lacks many things that make life worth living, particularly civic amenities, which Main Street offered in spades. Deep down, many Americans are dissatisfied with suburbia—though they have trouble understanding what's missing—which explains their nostalgia for the earlier model. Their dissatisfaction is literally a *dis-ease.* They feel vaguely and generally un-well where they are. Nostalgia in its original sense means homesickness. Americans essay to cure their homesickness with costly visits to Disney World. The crude, ineffective palliatives they get there in the form of brass bands and choo-choo train rides leave them more homesick and more baffled as to the nature of their disease than when they arrived—like selling chocolate bars to someone suffering from scurvy—and pathetically, of course, they must return afterward to the very places that induce the disease of homesickness.

Historically Americans have a low regard for the public realm, and this is very unfortunate because the public realm is the physical manifestation of the common good. When you degrade the public realm, as we have, you degrade the common good.

Civic life is what goes on in the public realm. Civic life refers to our relations 10
with our fellow human beings—in short, our roles as citizens. Sometime in the past forty years we ceased to speak of ourselves as citizens and labeled ourselves consumers. That's what we are today in the language of the evening news—*consumers*—in the language of the Sunday panel discussion shows—*consumers*—in the blizzard of statistics that blows out of the U.S. Department of Commerce every month. Consumers, unlike citizens, have no responsibilities, obligations, or duties to anything larger than their own needs and desires, certainly not to anything like the common good. How can this be construed as anything other than an infantile state of existence? In degrading the language of our public discussion this way—labeling ourselves consumers—have we not degraded our sense of who we are? And is it any wonder that we cannot solve any of our social problems, which are problems of the public realm and the common good?

Charm, Sanity, and Grace

During America's financially richest period, we put up almost nothing but the cheapest possible buildings, particularly civic buildings. Look at any richly embellished 1904 firehouse or post office and look at its dreary concrete box counterpart today. Compare the home of a small-town bank president dating from the 1890s, with its masonry walls and complex roof articulation, to the flimsy house of a 1990s business leader, made of two-by-fours, sheetrock, and fake fanlight windows. When we were a far less wealthy nation, we built things with the expectation that they would endure. To throw away money (painfully expended) on something guaranteed to fall apart in thirty years would have seemed immoral, if not insane, in our great-grandfathers' day.

The buildings they constructed paid homage to history in their design—including elegant solutions to age-old problems posed by the cycles of light and weather—and they paid respect to the future through the expectation that they would endure through the lifetimes of the people who built them. They therefore evinced a sense of chronological connectivity—one of the fundamental patterns of the universe—an understanding that time is a defining dimension of existence, particularly the existence of living things, such as human beings, who miraculously pass into life and then tragically pass out of it, perhaps forever—we do not know—our self-awareness of this fate making it tragic.

Chronological connectivity lends meaning and dignity to our little lives. It charges the present with a more vividly conscious validation of our own aliveness. It puts us in touch with the ages and the eternities, suggesting that we are part of a larger and more significant organism. It even suggests that the larger organism we are part of *cares* about us, and that, in turn, we should respect ourselves, our fellow creatures, and all those who will follow us in time, as those preceding us respected us who followed them. In short, chronological connectivity puts us in touch with the holy. It is at once humbling and exhilarating. I say this as someone who has never followed any formal religious practice. Connection with the past and the future is a pathway that literally charms us in the direction of sanity and grace.

The antithesis to this can be seen in the way we have built since 1945. We reject the past and the future, and it shows in our graceless constructions. Our houses, commercial, and civic buildings are constructed with the fully conscious certainty that they will disintegrate in a few decades. There is even a name for this condition: the *design life*. Strip malls and elementary schools have short design lives. They are not expected to endure through the span of a human life. In fact, they fall apart in under fifty years. Since there is not expectation that these things will last, nor that they will speak to any era but their own, we seem to believe that there is no point in putting any money or effort into their embellishment—except for the sort of cartoon decoration that serves to advertise whatever product is sold on the premises. Nor do we care about age-old solutions to the problems of weather and light, because we have technical artifacts to mitigate these problems, namely electricity and central heating. In especially bad buildings, like the average WalMart, there may be no windows. Yet this process of disconnection from the past and future, and from the organic patterns of weather and light, all done for the sake of expedience, ends up diminishing us spiritually, impoverishing us socially, and degrading the aggregate set of cultural patterns that we call civilization. We register these discontinuities as *ugliness*, or the absence of beauty.

Our streets used to be charming and beautiful. The public realm of the street 15
was understood to function as an outdoor room. Like any room, it required walls to define the essential *void* of the room itself. Where I live, Saratoga Springs, New York, there once existed a magnificent building called the Grand Union Hotel. It was enormous—the largest hotel in the world in the late nineteenth century—occupying a six-acre site in the heart of town. The hotel consisted of a set of rather narrow buildings which lined the outside of an unusually large superblock. Inside the block was a semipublic parklike courtyard. Any reasonably attired person could walk in off the street, pass through the hotel lobby, and enjoy the interior park. The sides of the hotel that faced the street incorporated a gigantic veranda twenty feet deep, with a roof three stories high supported by columns. This facade functioned as a marvelous street-wall. Its size—a central cupola reached seven stories—was appropriate to the scale of the town's main street, called Broadway. The facade, or street-wall, was active and permeable. The veranda that lined it was filled with people sitting perhaps eight feet above the sidewalk grade, talking to each other while they watched the pageant life of the street. These veranda sitters were protected from the weather by the roof, and protected from the sun by elm trees along the sidewalk. The orderly rows of

elm trees performed an additional architectural function. Their trunks were straight and round, like columns, reiterating and reinforcing the pattern of the hotel facade, while the crowns formed a vaulted canopy over the sidewalk, pleasantly filtering the sunlight for pedestrians as well as the hotel patrons. Notice that the integral soundness of all these patterns worked to enhance the lives of everybody in town, a common laborer on his way home as well as a railroad millionaire rocking on the hotel veranda. In doing so, they supported civic life as a general proposition. They nourished our civilization.

While nothing lasts forever, it was tragic that this magnificent building was destroyed less than a hundred years after it was built. In 1953 America stood at the brink of the greatest building spree in history, and the very qualities that made the Grand Union Hotel so wonderful were antithetical to all the new stuff that America was about to build. The town demolished it with a kind of mad glee. What replaced the hotel was a strip mall anchored by, of all things, a *Grand Union* supermarket. This Grand Union shopping plaza was prototypical of its time. Tens of thousands of strip malls like it have been built all over America since then. It is in absolutely all its details a perfect piece of junk. It is the anti-place.

What had been the heart and soul of the town was now converted into a kind of mini-Outer Mongolia. The strip mall buildings were set back from Broadway one hundred and fifty feet, the setback now comprising a parking lot. The street and the buildings commenced a non-relationship. Since the new buildings were one story high, their scale bore no relation to the scale of the town's most important street. They failed to create a street-wall. The perception of the street functioning as an outdoor room was lost. The space between the buildings and the street now had one function: automobile storage. The street, and consequently, the public realm in general, was degraded by the design of the new strip mall. As the street's importance as a public space declined, people ceased to care what happened in it. If it became jammed with cars, so much the better, because individual cars were understood not merely as "personal transportation" but as *personal home delivery vehicles*, enabling people to physically haul home enormous volumes of merchandise very efficiently, at no cost to the merchandizer—a great boon for business. That is why the citizens of Saratoga in 1953 were willing to sacrifice the town's most magnificent building. It was okay to simply throw away the past. The owners of the supermarket chain that anchored the strip mall didn't live in town. They didn't care what effect their style of doing business would have on the town. They certainly didn't care about the town's past, and their interest in the town's future was limited only to technicalities of selling dog food and soap flakes.

What has happened to the interrelation of healthy, living patterns of human ecology in the town where I live has happened all over the country. Almost everywhere, the larger patterns are in such a sorry state that the details seem almost irrelevant. When my town invested tens of thousands of dollars in Victorian-style street lamps in an effort to create instant charm, the gesture seemed pathetic, because there was no awareness of the larger design failures. It is hard to overstate how ridiculous these lampposts look in the context of our desolate streets and the cheap, inappropriate new buildings amid their parking lots in what remains of our downtown. The lamppost scheme was like putting Band-Aids on someone who had tripped and fallen on his chainsaw.

Burn Your Zoning Laws

It is literally against the law almost everywhere in the United States to build the kind of places that Americans themselves consider authentic and traditional. It's against the law to build places that human beings can feel good in, or afford to live in. It's against the law to build places that are worth caring about.

Is Main Street your idea of a nice business district? Sorry, your zoning laws 20
won't let you build it, or even extend it where it already exists. Is Elm Street your idea of a nice place to live—you know, the houses with the front porches on a tree-lined street? Sorry, that's against the law, too. All you can build where I live, in upstate New York, is another version of Los Angeles. The zoning laws say so.

This is not a gag. Our zoning laws comprise the basic manual of instruction for how we create the stuff of our communities. Most of these laws have only been in place since World War Two. For the previous 300-odd years of American history we didn't have zoning laws. We had a popular *consensus* about the right way to assemble a town, or a city. Our best Main Streets and Elm Streets were not created by municipal ordinances, but by cultural agreement. Everybody agreed that buildings on Main Street ought to be more than one story tall, that corner groceries were good to have in residential neighborhoods, that streets ought to intersect with other streets to facilitate movements, that sidewalks were necessary, and that orderly rows of trees planted along them made the sidewalks much more pleasant, that rooftops should be pitched to shed rain and snow, that doors should be conspicuous so you could easily find the entrance to a building, that windows should be vertical to dignify a house. Everybody agreed that communities needed different kinds of housing to meet the needs of different families and individuals, and the market was allowed to supply it. Our great-grandfathers didn't have to argue endlessly over these matters of civic design. Nor did they have to reinvent civic design every fifty years because everybody forgot what they agreed about.

Zoning began as a political response to the obnoxious effect of industry on human settlements. Originally, its intent was to keep factories away from houses, to create separate zones for industry to carry on its noisy and dirty activities. Over the twentieth century, the imposition of motor vehicles brought the obnoxious noise and danger of industry to virtually every doorstep, and so zoning became preoccupied with problems posed by the movement and storage of cars. The problem became so pervasive that zoning completely replaced civic art as the ordering principle of human settlement, especially in the years since 1945.

The place that results from zoning is suburban sprawl. It must be understood as the product of a particular set of institutions. Its chief characteristics are the strict separation of human activities (or *uses*), mandatory driving to get from one use to the other, and huge supplies of free parking. After all, it's called *zoning* because the basic idea is that every activity demands a separate zone of its own. You can't allow people to live around shopping. That would be harmful and indecent. Better not even allow them within walking distance of it. They'll need their cars to haul all that stuff home, anyway—in case you haven't noticed, most supermarkets don't deliver these days. While you're at it, let's separate the homes, too, by income gradients. Don't let the $75,000-a-year families live near the $200,000-a-year families—they'll bring down your *property values*—and, for Godsake, don't let some $25,000-a-year recent college graduate live near any of them, or a $19,000-a-year widowed grandmother on Social

Security. There goes the neighborhood! Now, put all the workplaces in a separate office "park" or industrial "park," and make sure nobody can walk to them either. As for nice public squares, parks, and the like—forget it, we can't afford them because we spent all our public funds paving the four-lane highways and collector roads and the parking lots, and laying sewer and water lines out to the housing subdivisions, and hiring traffic cops to regulate the movement of people in their cars going back and forth to these segregated areas.

It soon becomes obvious that the model of the human habitat dictated by zoning is a formless, soulless, centerless, demoralizing mess. It bankrupts families and townships. It causes mental illness. It disables whole classes of decent, normal citizens. It ruins the air we breathe. It corrupts and deadens our spirits.

In the absence of a new widespread consensus about how to build a better 25
everyday environment, we'll have to replace the old set of rules with an explicit new set of rules. Or, to put it a slightly different way, replace zoning laws with principles of civic art.

A Short Course in the General Principles of Civic Art

The pattern under discussion here has been called variously *neo-traditional planning*, *traditional neighborhood development* (or the *TND*), *low-density urbanism*, *Transit-Oriented Development* (or the *TOD*), *the New Urbanism*, or just plain *civic art*. Its principles produce a setting that resembles the American town prior to World War Two.[1]

The Neighborhood

The basic unit of planning is the neighborhood. A neighborhood standing alone can be a village or a town. A cluster of neighborhoods becomes a bigger town. Clusters of a great many neighborhoods become a city. The population of a neighborhood can vary, depending on local conditions.

The neighborhood is limited in physical size, with a well-defined edge and a focused center. Human scale is the standard for proportion in buildings and their accessories. Automobiles and other wheeled vehicles are permitted, but do not take precedence over human needs, including aesthetic needs. The neighborhood contains a public transit stop.

The size of a neighborhood is defined as a five-minute walking distance (or a quarter-mile) from the edge to the center, thus a ten-minute walk edge to edge, or one-half a square mile. Chores that may require many separate, tedious car trips in sprawl can be accomplished in a single outing on foot (shop owners may

[1] The principles outlined here are derived from a consensus among members of the Congress for the New Urbanism. Other lists of princiiplies exist and have been articulated in various formats by Elizabeth Plater-Zyberk and Andres Duany, Peter Calthorpe, Daniel Solomon, Peter Katz, and Anthony Nelesson. A complementary list, called the Ahwahnee Principles, was drawn up in a 1991 conference at the Ahwahnee Lodge in Yosemite Park. Among the participants were Duany and Plater-Zyberk, Katz, Stefanos Polyzoides, and Elizabeth Moule, architects and planners, and Michael Corbett, a former mayor of Davis, California. The book *Town Planning in Practice*, by Raymond Unwin (1863-1940) republished in 1994 by the Princeton Architectural Press, is also a classic source.

offer home delivery of bulky merchandise). Walking allows a person to visit many different types of shops—thereby promoting small-scale, locally owned businesses, which, in turn, promote manifold civic benefits from the support of local institutions to the physical caretaking of the street. Walking down the street permits casual socializing. Pedestrians make streets safer by their mere presence in numbers. Finally, walking down the street is spiritually elevating. When neighborhoods are used by pedestrians, a much finer detailing inevitably occurs. Building facades become more richly ornamented and interesting. Little gardens and windowboxes appear. Shop windows create a continuity of public spectacle, as do outdoor cafes, both for walkers and the sitters. There is much to engage the eye and heart. In such a setting, we feel more completely human. This is not trivial.

The boundaries between neighborhoods are formed by corridors, which both 30
connect and define them. Corridors can incorporate natural features like streams or canyons. They can take the form of parks, natural preserves, travel corridors, railroad lines, or some integral combination of all these things. In towns and cities, a neighborhood or parts of neighborhoods can comprise a district. Districts are composed of streets or ensembles of streets where special activities get preferential treatment. The French Quarter of New Orleans is an example of a district. It is a whole neighborhood dedicated to entertainment in which housing, shops, and offices are also integral. A corridor can also be a district—for instance, a major shopping avenue between adjoining neighborhoods.

The neighborhood is emphatically mixed-use and provides housing for people with different incomes. Commerce is integrated with residential, business, and even industrial use, though not necessarily on the same street in a given neighborhood. Apartments are permitted over stores. There is a mixture of housing types.

The Street

The street is understood to be the preeminent form of public space and buildings that define it are expected to honor and embellish it. In the absence of a consensus about the appropriate decoration of buildings, an architectural code may be devised to establish some fundamental unities of massing, fenestration, materials, and roof pitch, within which many variations may function harmoniously. Buildings also define parks and squares, which are distributed throughout the neighborhood and appropriately designated for recreation, repose, periodic commercial uses (e.g., farmers' markets), or special events such as political meetings, concerts, theatricals, exhibitions, and fairs.

The street pattern is conceived as a network in order to create the greatest number of alternative routes from one part of the neighborhood to another. This has the beneficial effect of relieving vehicular congestion. This network can be a grid. Networks based on a grid must be modified by parks, squares, diagonals, T-intersections, roundabouts, and other devices that relieve the grid's tendency to monotonous regularity. The streets exist in a hierarchy from broad boulevards to narrow lanes and alleys. In a town or city, limited access highways may exist only in a corridor, preferably in the form of parkways. Cul-de-sacs (dead ends) are strongly discouraged except under extraordinary circumstances—e.g., where rugged topography requires them. In the New Urbanism, the meaning of the street as the essential fabric of public life is restored.

Under the regime of Zoning, all streets were made as wide as possible because the specialist in charge—the zoning engineer—was concerned solely with the movement of cars and trucks. In the process, much of the traditional decor that made streets pleasant for people was gotten rid of. For instance, street trees were eliminated. It is hard to overstate how much orderly rows of mature trees can improve even the most dismal street by softening its hard edges and sun-blasted bleakness. Under zoning, street trees were deemed a hazard to motorists and chopped down in many American towns after World War Two.

35 The practice of maximizing car movement, at the expense of all other concerns, was applied with particular zeal to housing subdivisions. Suburban streets were given the speed characteristics of country highways, though children played in them. Suburbs notoriously lack parks. The spacious private lots were supposed to make up for the lack of parks, but children have an uncanny tendency to play in the street anyway—bicycles don't work too well on the lawn. In the suburbs, where street trees were expressly forbidden, we see those asinine exercises in romantic landscaping that attempt to recapitulate the North Woods in clumps of ornamental juniper. Sidewalks, in a setting so inimical to walking, were deemed a waste of money.

Parallel parking is emphatically permitted along the curbs of all streets, except under the most extraordinary conditions. Parallel parking is desirable for two reasons: (1) Parked cars create a physical barrier, and a psychological buffer, that protects pedestrians on the sidewalk from moving vehicles; and (2) a rich supply of parallel parking can eliminate the need for parking lots, which are extremely destructive of civic fabric. Anyone who thinks that parallel parking "ruins" a residential street should take a look at some of the most desirable real estate in America (as reflected by house prices): Georgetown, Beacon Hill, Nob Hill, Alexandria, Charleston, Savannah, Annapolis, Princeton, Greenwich Village, Marblehead, et cetera. All permit parallel parking.

Civic buildings (town halls, churches, schools, libraries, museums) are placed on preferential building sites such as the frontage of squares, neighborhood centers, and where street vistas terminate, in order to serve as landmarks and to reinforce their symbolic importance.

Can America Become Civilized?

I don't know if we will be able to reinstate a social contract that recognizes both rights and responsibilities in a civic context. It will certainly not be possible unless we restore that context, and I mean in bricks and mortar. There is a vital relationship between the character of our surroundings and the common good. Rights and responsibilities need a civic setting in which to dwell. Such a setting is identical with the physical setting of our lives, an actual place that must be worth caring about.

It is easy to be discouraged. The general political attitude among the suburban well-off is that they have been willing to try almost any expensive social experiment *except* returning to live in towns and cities. In the face of this shunning, the will to behave constructively has been rather conspicuously absent among the urban poor themselves. But the poor nevertheless have responsibilities and obligations too, beginning with civil behavior and extending to useful work. One of the unfortunate side effects of the psychology of entitlement is the notion both among the poor and government officials that jobs must be *given* to idle people, and that they must be *good* jobs—which I take to mean something like professional careers. Nothing could be further from the way the world really operates.

40 It may strike some readers as an unbelievable effrontery to state that the poor ought to work in menial jobs. I am not arguing that they ought to live in violence and squalor—just the opposite. Before World War Two this was a nation full of menial employments, and many people so employed lived more decently than today's poor do, particularly in the cities where, for all the cities' historic shortcomings, the poor at least had easy access to a great deal of cultural and civic equipment. Poor people may have lived in cramped tenements in 1911, but they had access to well-maintained parks, low-cost public transit, safe streets, free public schools, excellent public libraries, museums, baths, and infirmaries. Most important, this civic equipment was shared by everybody. People of all stations in life went to parks, museums, and libraries. The poor *saw* the middle class and the wealthy every day in the public realm of the streets. They observed their behavior, and were constrained in their own behavior by seeing them. The poor saw where the rich lived. A boy from Hell's Kitchen could walk ten minutes across town and stand within a few yards of William H. Vanderbilt's front door on Fifty-ninth Street and Fifth Avenue with no fear of being hassled by private security guards. In short, the poor lived in a civic context that included the entire range of social classes, so that many of the problems of the poor in the cities were also the problems of the middle class and the rich.

Today the poor in most American cities live only in the context of the poor. The only place they see the other America is on television, and then through a wildly distorting lens that stimulates the most narcissistic, nihilistic consumer fantasies. Since the poor, by definition, can't participate fully in consumer culture, the predictable result is rage at what appears to be a cruel tease, and this rage is commonly expressed in crime. What may be equally damaging is that the poor see very little in the way of ordinary polite conduct, very little civil behavior. They do not see people routinely going about honorable occupations. What they do see all around is mayhem, squalor, and disorder, and almost no evidence that it is possible to live a happy life without being a sports hero, a gangster, or a television star.

The problems of the cities are not going to be relieved unless the middle class and the wealthy return to live there. For the moment these classes are off in suburbia. All the evidence demonstrates that suburbia is becoming unaffordable and unsustainable. The economy makes them nervous. Companies are shedding employees. They feel anxious, trapped. For the first time in American history, there is nowhere else left to go, no place to escape to. What will they do?

I'm afraid they may misunderstand the crisis of the suburbs, particularly as it manifests itself in the personal catastrophes of lost jobs, declining incomes, falling property values, family breakups, and misbehavior. Poor people are not the only Americans afflicted by the psychology of entitlement. Middle-class suburbanites really believe that they are owed a package of goodies called *the American Dream*, and when they are suddenly deprived of it, they may get very angry and vote for political maniacs.

The Republicans are now in charge of things at many levels of government, and though they have been shouting the loudest about the crisis of "family values," they are also the chief boosters of suburbia, which is to say, a profoundly uncivil living arrangement. Their chosen way of life is therefore at odds with their most cherished wishes for a civil society, and so it is unlikely that they are going to be able to solve any of the social problems they deplore—even the problems of their own children's behavior.

Suburban Moms and Dads wonder why their fifteen-year-old children seem 45
so alienated. These kids are physically disconnected from the civic life of their towns. They have no access to the civic equipment. They have to be chauffeured absolutely everywhere, to football practice, to piano lessons, to their friends' houses, to the library, and, of course, to the mall. All they live for is the day that they can obtain a driver's license and use their environment. Except then, of course, another slight problem arises: they need several thousand dollars to buy a used car and pay for insurance, which is usually exorbitant for teens, often more than the price of their cars. Is it really any wonder that these kids view their situation as some kind of swindle?

Americans are convinced that suburbia is great for kids. The truth is, kids older than seven need more from their environment than a safe place to ride their bikes. They need at least the same things adults need. Dignified places to hang out. Shops. Eating establishments. Libraries, museums, and theaters. They need a public realm worthy of respect. All of which they need access to on their own, without our assistance—which only keeps them in an infantile state of dependency. In suburbia, as things presently stand, children have access only to television. That's their public realm. It's really a wonder that more American children are not completely psychotic.

In order to make American towns and cities habitable again, we will have to take the greater portion of public money now spent on subsidizing car use and redirect it into replacing the civic equipment of the cities that was allowed to be trashed over the past several decades. The cost of doing these things is, fortunately, apt to be less than the cost of continuing to subsidize the suburban automobile infrastructure. For instance, a single new freeway exchange can cost $600,000,000, which is the same cost as building and equipping an entire twenty-mile-long electric trolley line.[2]

Making our cities habitable again will take a rededication to forms of buildings that were largely abandoned in America after World War Two. It will call for devices of civic art that *never* really caught on here, but have always existed in older parts of the world—for instance, waterfronts that are integral with the rest of the city. The human scale will have to prevail over the needs of motor vehicles. There will have to be ample provision for green space of different kinds—neighborhood squares, wildlife corridors, parks—because people truly crave regular contact with nature, especially pockets of repose and tranquillity, and having many well cared-for parcels of it distributed equitably around town improves civic life tremendously.

The transformation I propose will not be possible unless Americans recognize the benefits of a well-designed public realm, and the civic life that comes with it, over the uncivil, politically toxic, socially impoverished, hyper-privatized realm of suburbia, however magnificent the kitchens and bathrooms may be there.

[2] Author's interview with Milwaukee Mayor John O. Norquist, June 1995.

I don't believe that we can be an advanced society without cities. Tragically, American cities have become unworthy of the American republic. Our task is to make them worthy, to reconstruct them in a physical form that is worth caring about, and to reinhabit them.

The common good demands a public realm in which to dwell. It can't sustain 50
itself merely in our hearts or memories. This is, finally, the sentimental fallacy of the suburban patriot: that hanging a cast-iron eagle over your garage door proves you care about your country.

THINGS TO DO WITH THE READING

1. Apply the heuristic known as the Method (aka "Look for Patterns of Repetition and Contrast"—see Chapter 2) to Kunstler's piece. Make a list in the margins of the key terms repeated, the strands in which they participate, and the binary oppositions into which they are aligned. Then choose what you consider to be the two most important repetitions, the two most interesting strands, and the two most significant binaries. Finally, choose any ONE of these and write a paragraph or two about what it means and why it matters to Kunstler's vision.
2. In Chapter 4, we offer as a frame for reading critically the notion of understanding a piece of writing in terms of "the pitch, the complaint, and the moment" (see pages 111–112). Locate Kunstler's piece in this context (see Try this 4.1, page 113).
3. Kunstler argues that "in the past forty years we ceased to speak of ourselves as citizens and labeled ourselves consumers" (see paragraph 10). He then builds an argument of the different implications of these two key terms, *citizen* and *consumer*. What are these implications?

   Note: the words *citizen*, *civic* (as in civic center), and *civilized* play a key role in Kunstler's piece. Look up the etymology (word history—see pages 265–267) of these terms: how might they enrich your understanding of his point of view?
4. **Application:** If you read this essay carefully, it might function like a new pair of glasses to enable you to refocus your surroundings in strikingly new ways. In offering "A Short Course in the General Principles of Civic Art," Kunstler is actually trying to get us to see aspects of our environment to which we were previously relatively blind. Kunstler asserts that "the basic unit of planning is the neighborhood" (see paragraph 27). Apply his perceptions to your neighborhood, or one close to you. How is it constructed? How does it locate parking? Public transportation? How does it set up housing—and in what relation to income levels? Where, if at all, does it attend to what Kunstler terms "human needs" and "aesthetic needs" (see paragraph 28)? What ultimately does Kunstler's lens allow you to discover about your neighborhood?

Jack Gambino

Demolition Zones: Contemporary Photography by Edward Burtynsky and Camilo Jose Vergara

A political scientist looks at two contemporary photographers' representations of urban landscapes as sites of "creative destruction," commenting, "It is this sense of displacement—of human beings alienated from the environments they have created—that provides the common theme that haunts these two very different photographers."

If you look closely at Camilo Jose Vergara's "Fern Street, Camden" (1988), you'll notice a sign on the side of a dilapidated building: 1

"Danger: Men Working
W. Hargrove Demolition"

Perhaps that warning captures the ominous atmosphere evoked in the human and natural landscapes of two very different kinds of photographers, Camilo Jose Vergara and Edward Burtynsky. "Danger: Men Working." Watch out—human beings are at work! But the work they present is not so much a building-up as it is a tearing-down—the work of demolition. Of course, demolition is often necessary in order to construct anew: old buildings are leveled for new projects, whether they are the highways and high rises that dominate the contemporary American city or the massive dams now transforming portions of the Chinese countryside. To destroy in order to create: that is a modern formula. Modernity is, after all, a process of "creative destruction," a term used variously to describe the dynamics of modern art, capitalism, and technological innovation. The photographs in this exhibit, however, force us to pay attention to the destructiveness, both deliberate and unintentional, at the very heart of modern creation. What both Burtynsky and Vergara do in their respective ways is to point to the warning signs already posted on the modern landscape. They compel us to wonder whether the process of creative-destruction may not have spun recklessly out of control, producing places that are not just unsustainable in the future, but uninhabitable in the present. Indeed, a common element connecting their photographic visions is the near absence of people in the landscape. While we see the evidence of the transforming power of human production on the physical and social environment, neither Vergara's urban ruins nor Burtynsky's industrial sites actually show us "men working." Isolated figures peer suspiciously out back doors or pick through the rubble, but they appear out-of-place. It is this sense of displacement—of human beings alienated from the environments they themselves have created—that provides the common theme that haunts the work of these two very different photographers.

The dominant theme in Burtynsky's work, as he puts it, is "nature transformed through industry." His photos are large industrial landscapes—quarries, oil refineries, mines, dams—mostly dedicated to the extraction and production of energy resources. Burtynsky's landscapes vividly portray what landscape historian J.B. Jackson called the "engineered landscape"—a landscape developed for "the production, conservation, and use of energy." The Three Gorges Dam is, of course, one of the latest and largest of the modern engineer's remaking of the social and physical environment. Highways are another, more familiar example, with their horizontal forms and parallel lines, similar to the shiny, sleek pipeline cutting its way through the forest in Burtynsky ("Oil Fields #22", 2001). [See Figure 16.1.] What better image of the triumph of precision, linearity, efficiency, and clarity? Even the forest appears as a controlled environment, an ecological monoculture made available for easy exploitation. "To the engineer (and the engineer-minded society)," Jackson wrote, "a landscape is beautiful when the energy-flow system is functioning with unimpeded efficiency." A well-engineered highway or pipeline aims for this kind of efficiency. So will Three Gorges Dam, which, when completed, is expected to generate 8.4 billion kilowatts-per-hour of unimpeded energy for China's exploding industrial cities (one ninth of its electricity needs, according to some estimates). This massive attempt at state enforced modernization will not only meet practical energy needs; it will fulfill China's socialist destiny, as proclaimed by former President Jiang Zemin in a 1997 celebration of the Three Gorges Dam. Yet that destiny—"the great feat of conquering, developing and exploiting nature", to quote President Zemin—is hardly an exclusively socialist dream: it's what modernization is all about in capitalist societies as well.

The fact that the process of energy extraction and transfer, once initiated, could be maintained with little direct human presence suggests all the more that the engineer's

FIGURE 16.1 "Oil Fields, Alberta" by Edward Burtynsky

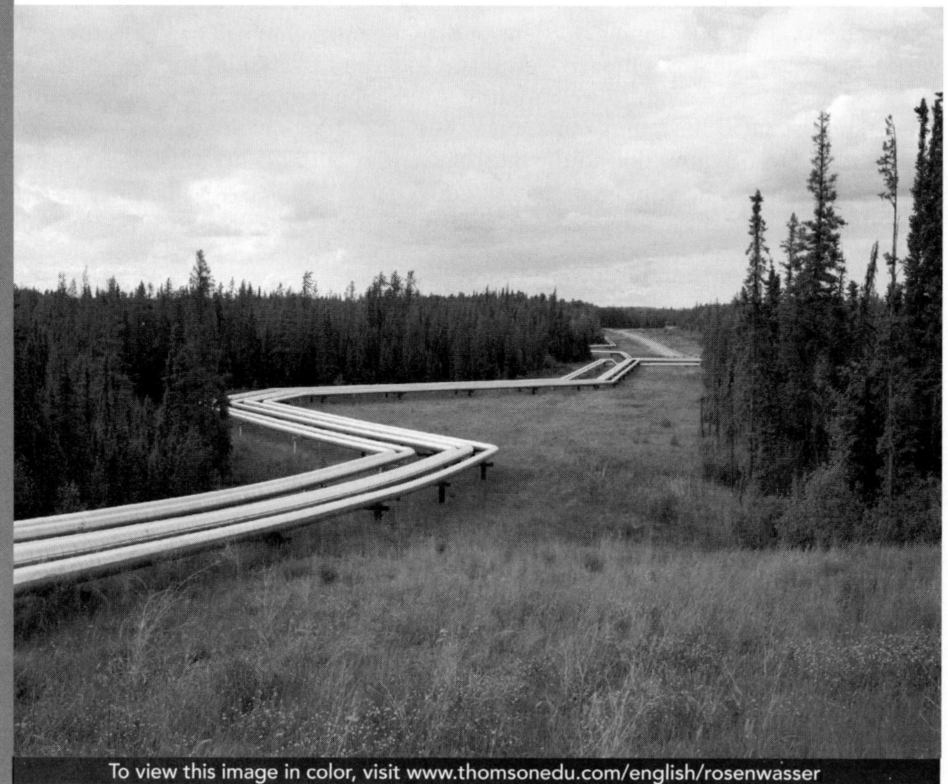

To view this image in color, visit www.thomsonedu.com/english/rosenwasser

quest for efficiency culminates in a kind of robotic automatism portrayed in "Oil Fields #13. Taft, California" (2002). [See Figure 16.2.] Earth-moving machines, cranes, and oil derricks largely occupy the industrial landscape Burtynsky portrays. But the engineer's ingenious instruments are not his real subject, as much as their unintentional and unexpected effects. Burtynsky is attracted to the awesome (awful) beauty of the industrial landscapes (something, one suspects, that the engineers may not have noticed), most notably in the chiseled shapes of the quarries of Utah and Vermont[1]. Yet whether they produce the effect of gigantic, abstract sculptures, as in the Vermont quarry, or the semblance of a classical amphitheatre, as in the Utah cooper mine, Burtynsky's photos remind us that the beauty of these landscapes cannot be separated from the industrial power that *forcefully cuts* them from the earth. Like all sculptures, they are creative works of violence—a form hammered and chiseled out of rock ("Rock of Ages," 1991). Here Burtynsky suggests a fascination with something deeper than the engineer's desire for efficiency—a fascination with the violence at the heart of the modern creative process. For the remnants of the violence are evident in the denuded forests, the pulverized concrete, the piles of rubble, the incisions in the earth, the jagged debris of partially demolished buildings. The sites of production are necessarily demolition zones.

FIGURE 16.2 "Oil Fields, Taft, California" by Edward Burtynsky

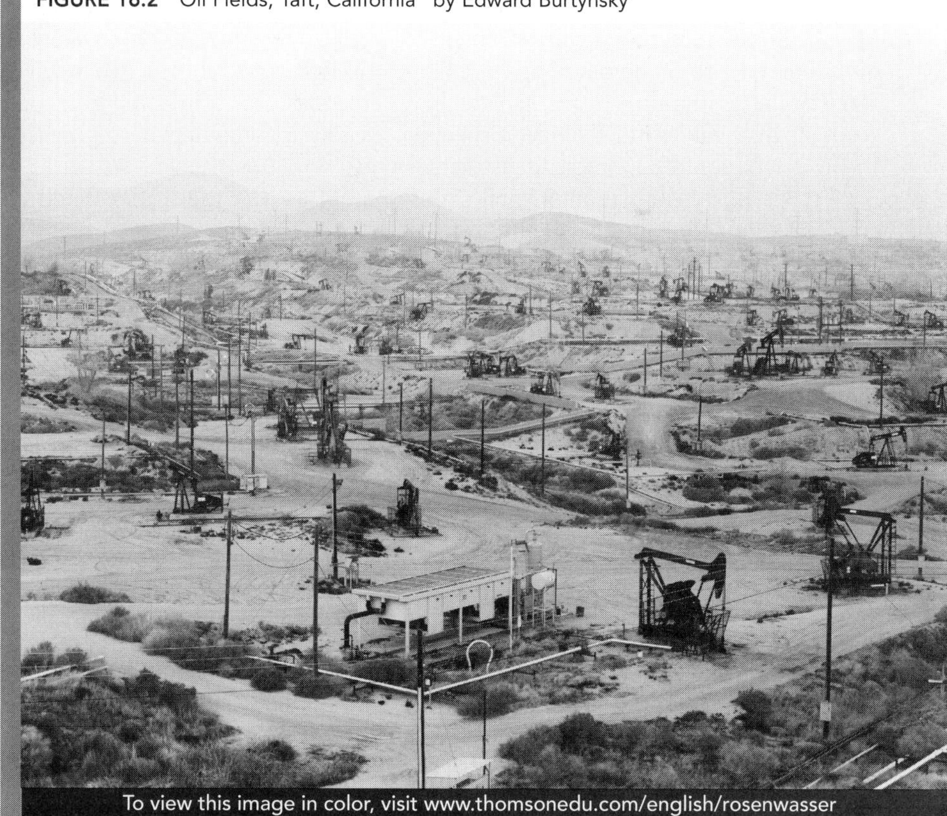

To view this image in color, visit www.thomsonedu.com/english/rosenwasser

[1] The unintended sculptured forms appear in other of Burtynsky's work, for example, in the series on ship breakers in Bangladesh.

To many modern architects, urban planners, and engineers, demolition is merely the prelude to a new construction, which, once completed, will cover over (and make us forget) both the physical scars to the land and the emotional scars of displaced people who found themselves in the way. We may join with the modern builders in justifying the violence of means—the sculptor's hammer and chisel—by applauding the greater goods these violent means serve. Sometimes the beauty of the end result does in fact conceal the violent incisions: we may still enjoy Paris' famed boulevard even after acknowledging that its designer, Baron Haussmann, under Louis Napoleon's authoritarian rule, had to *cut* through medieval streets of old Paris, uprooting tens of thousands of urban poor in the mid 19th century. Yet too often modern planners and engineers would justify the creative destruction of habitat as necessary for doubtful utopias: think of Le Corbusier who would have demolished those same 19th-century boulevards to create "a blank piece of paper" for an even more modern city of highways and skyscrapers! Stalin – whose displacement of Russian peasants through forced collectivization reached a level of unprecedented and perhaps unsurpassed brutality—bluntly insisted that "you can't make an omelet without breaking eggs." This was a maxim that Robert Moses, the master planner who ruthlessly leveled New York City neighborhoods to make way for expressways, loved to quote, adding his own: "When you operate in an overbuilt metropolis, you have to hack your way with a meat axe." Here the butcher's axe replaces the sculpture's chisel, but the point is the same—big modern projects require the demolition of existing structures and the displacement of people. The Three Gorges Dam also is a monument to modern ambition—a work in progress, which when completed, will literally *cut* the flow of the Yangtze River, causing it to form a 400 mile long reservoir that will eventually hide, it is hoped, the physical and human scars caused by the demolition of 11 cities and displacement of 1.2 million people.

Perhaps Burtynsky's monumental prints remind us that the scars created by 5
such modernization projects cannot be made-over by the engineers' sense of beauty in efficiency. He insists on keeping those scars exposed, even finding a seductive beauty in the jagged edges of demolished buildings and the raw incisions into the surface of the earth[2]. It seems to me, however, that it is a beauty we can only contemplate at a distance, by subtracting ourselves from the scene. We can be struck by the eerie surrealism of "Uranium Tailings" (2002), but we can't imagine human beings walking about in such a landscape. At the same time, he tells us that these inhuman places are part of the industrial infrastructure of a world dependent on energy extraction and consumption. We are made accomplices to those industrial processes and its byproducts: mountains of used tires, rusted hulks of ships, piles of rubble, demolished buildings. His landscapes are thus, as he understands them, a "metaphor for the dilemma of our modern existence: they

[2] While demolition is shown to be the underside of energy production in his Three Gorges Dam series, Burtynsky also points to another paradigmatic site of industrial modernization: the landfill. Mountains of used tires transform the landscape by "building it up", whereas energy extraction appears as a digging out (mines, quarries). The depletion of resources (abandoned mines) is thus coupled with the accumulation of waste. In his novel, *Underworld*, Don DeLillo also proposed the landfill—where the "waste stream ended"—as a paradigmatic site of industrial America.

search for a dialogue between attraction and repulsion, seduction and fear. We are drawn by desire—a chance at good living, yet we are consciously or unconsciously aware that the world is suffering for our success."[3] His images—especially the series on the Three Gorges Dam—not only bid us to gaze at the human and ecological costs of modernity's creative destructive process, but also warn us that these sites of demolition are never very far from our own safe places. [See Figure 16.3.]

If Burtynsky provokes questions about the seductive beauty of "nature transformed through industry," Camilo Vergara insists that we directly confront urban landscapes transformed by deindustrialization. Vergara's series on the hard luck city of Camden—which is part of a larger project documenting the "process of decline" of the American industrial city—invites us to move closer to inspect the details of places that few of us would call beautiful and most of us would like to avoid. Although we don't see them, the men working in Camden nowadays are doing the work of demolition. This is a bleak, harsh view with little to offer of the awesome industrial monuments found in Burtynsky's work. It is the view most suburbanites (now the majority of Americans) only catch glimpse of as they speed by on the highways and bridges to and from Philadelphia. Yet by placing us "among dereliction and destruction," Vergara calls on us to search for signs of resurgent life—what he calls "the energies of the outmoded."

FIGURE 16.3 "Three Gorges" by Edward Burtynsky

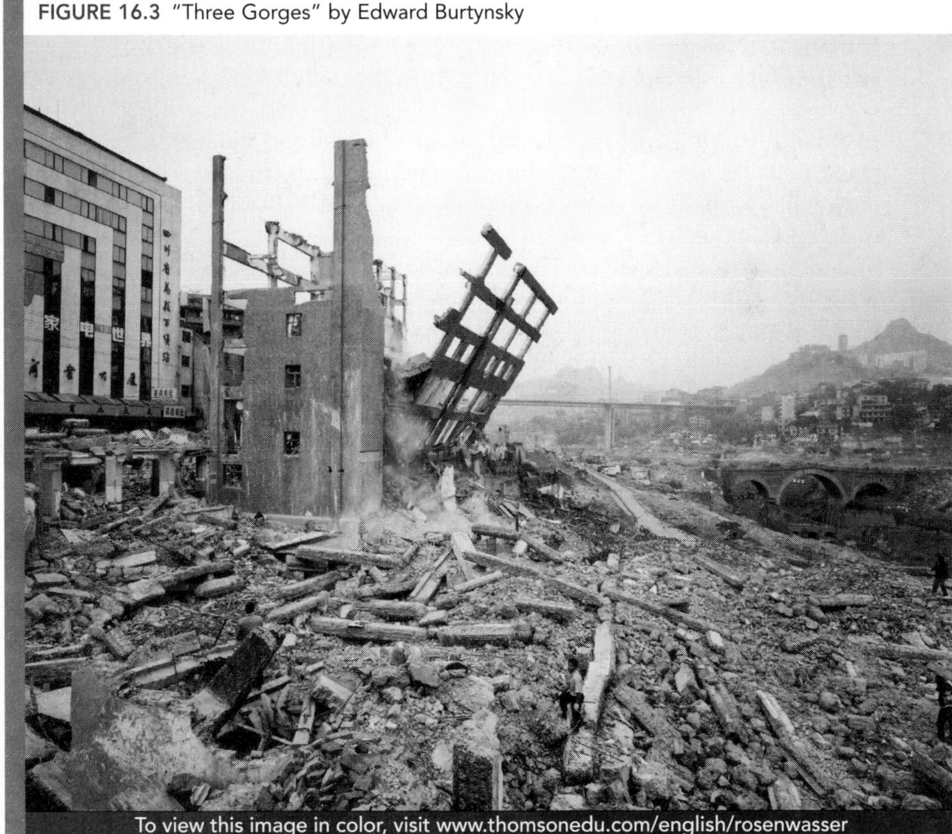

To view this image in color, visit www.thomsonedu.com/english/rosenwasser

[3] "Artist Statement." (http://www.edwardburtynsky.com/)

The Camden he documents is a site marked by a series of displacements. Once upon a time, the city was home to Walt Whitman and, later, Campbell Soups, and it could boast (despite W.C. Fields' joke that Camden is "the pimple on Philadelphia's ass") that it was "the biggest little city in the nation" making "everything from fountain pens to battleships." With over 105,000 people in the 1920's, it was home to thirteen downtown theatres, an opera company, a major shipbuilding port, an airport with flights to Europe, and a railroad terminus. The factories along the waterfront provided employment to large numbers of European immigrants and African-Americans. On Independence Day, 1926, when President Coolidge participated in the dedication ceremony for the Ben Franklin Bridge (called the Delaware River Bridge back then), the city notables could look forward to what they foresaw as an era of urban growth, with the new bridge making possible the city's "venture in progress."[4]

By now the story of urban decline of old industrial powerhouses like Camden, St. Louis, Detroit, and my hometown, Newark, is a familiar one. Factories moved to more spacious accommodations in the suburbs.[5] The Federal Housing Administration, which underwrote mortgages for families seeking to relocate in the suburbs, virtually wrote off loans to urban dwellers by "redlining" whole neighborhoods as too risky. Moreover, its misguided urban renewal projects during the 1950's and 1960's condemned and demolished entire neighborhoods, displacing thousands of urban families (one out of every 15 families in Camden). Low-income, high-rise apartments were built (the "projects" as they were called), which separated the poor both from the middle class and from places of employment. Many poor but settled neighborhoods were demolished only to be paved into parking lots. Along with the loss of jobs and the increasingly dilapidated housing, the exodus of the white middle class, the deterioration of the downtown commercial district, and mounting racial tensions and riots appeared to doom Camden by the early 1970s.

The irony is that the very structure that would lead to Camden's "venture in progress"—the Ben Franklin Bridge—helped facilitate its undoing. The construction of the bridge itself required the displacement of an entire neighborhood in the city. On and off ramps not only required the bulldozing of established neighborhoods in order to widen access roads, the roads themselves acted as a barrier effectively cutting the city into segments. Like Three Gorges Dam, the bridge was supposed to serve a larger public need by re-engineering the landscape for efficiency and ease of mobility. Such large-scale projects, which embodied the muscular industrial modernity of urban planners and engineers like Moses and Le Corbusier, actually replaced one icon of modernity, the bourgeois city, with another, the automobile. In the new city cars would displace pedestrians, and highways displace the street (Le Corbusier famously declared the "death of the street") as primary urban space. More than anything else, the

[4] Quotations from David L. Kirp, John P. Dwyer, Larry A. Rosenthal, *Our Town: Race, Housing, and the Soul of Suburbia*, (New Brunswick, N.J.: Rutgers University Press, 1997), pp. 15, 20.

[5] While manufacturing boomed in the outlying suburbs of Camden County during 1950-1970, the city of Camden lost half of its manufacturing jobs. Ibid.

car and highway transformed the American landscape. As urban problems became more intractable, more Americans fled to the suburbs fulfilling an early prophesy of no less a modernist than Henry Ford: "The ultimate solution [to urban problems everywhere] will be the abandonment of the city, its abandonment as a blunder."[6]

The process of urban decay was well underway when Vergara began his documentary project in the 1970s. What his time-series photos help us to see is the "process of decline" unfolding over many years, even decades.[7] The Fern Street series, for instance, shows the decay and eventual demolition of most of the houses on an urban residential street and their replacement by rubble strewn empty lots. [See Figure 16.4.] Abandoned buildings and vacant lots have become dead spaces, gaps in the urban fabric and depositories for all kinds of junk. It used to be that the city street was the scene of diversity and vitality—think of Jacob Riis' famous shot of Mulberry St. Bend in NY—life may have been tough, but it was teeming with energy. In a more optimistic vein, Jane Jacobs pointed out that the vitality of great American cities was always on the sidewalks where "a constant succession of eyes" of those passing by made the street both vitally interesting and safe.[8] In contrast, Vergara shows us urban scenes largely devoid of people; the isolated figures which emerge here and there only reinforce the sense of loneliness and exhaustion. In contrast, automobiles are present in virtually all of the photos, occupying not only the street, but empty lots and sidewalks as well. Vergara is haunted by the disappearance of a once vibrant "street life," so much so that he can't resist poking about the physical and psychic rubble for ghosts.

Anyone who has visited cities like Camden sees this strange process of the city "emptying out," becoming less densely populated (my hometown went from around 420, 000 when I was born, to about 250,000). Abandoned buildings decay, are demolished, and eventually paved into parking lots to accommodate suburban commuters. Many downtowns are nothing more than anonymous office buildings, surrounded by parking lots and a ring of run down houses. The parking lots erase the history of the place; the junk is gone, the buildings cleared, but so are the memories of the people who once lived there. But these empty spaces are for Vergara's lens not Le Corbusier's blank piece of paper; they are haunted places filled with fragmentary evidence of a former human presence. The exteriors of such places—which Vergara usually photographs directly from the street—go mostly unnoticed, both by those who live among them (notice the pedestrian in front of the dilapidated public library) and the suburban commuters. With his camera, he becomes the eyes on the empty streets that most of us overlook. More poignant are the images in which Vergara enters the interiors of dangerous buildings, an intruder who insists on exposing what is hidden inside those demolition zones, as in his eerie portrait of the Camden Public Library. [See Figure 16.5.]

[6] Ibid, 23.

[7] Vergara, *American Ruins* (New York: The Monacelli Press, 1999), p. 12.

[8] Jane Jacobs, *The Death and Life of Great American Cities.*

FIGURE 16.4 Collage of four color photographs, "Fern Street"—photographed by Camilo Jose Vergara in 1979, 1988, 1997, 2004

To view these four images in color, visit www.thomsonedu.com/english/rosenwasser

FIGURE 16.4 Continued

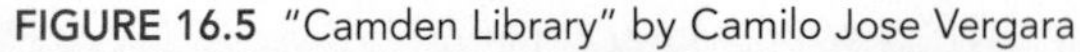

FIGURE 16.5 "Camden Library" by Camilo Jose Vergara

To view this image in color, visit www.thomsonedu.com/english/rosenwasser

Such photographic intrusion into unoccupied spaces (both physical and mental)—while often appearing merely as objective documentation—is in fact driven by his own sense of the "terrible loss" of urban decline, as he puts it.[9] His abandoned spaces are not only physical "gaps" in the urban fabric (representing the physical displacement of individuals and families), but interruptions in our collective memory and history. This points to an important feature of Vergara's work, and that which makes it more than a sociological record of the process of urban decline: he wants to meditate on the violent contradictions in modernity itself. Vergara, who grew up in a poor agricultural town in Chile and dreamed of a modern life of "Flash Gordon," came to America to study electrical engineering at Notre Dame: "I wanted to believe that science and technology would keep me from being poor."[10] What he discovered in America was not just the landscape of technical innovation and creativity but the contradictory underworld of decay and exhaustion. Modernity is not just about transforming nature and building an industrial civilization; it's about the violence that leaves the human habitat in fragments and a state of disrepair: "I became so attached to derelict buildings that sadness came not from seeing them overgrown and deteriorating—this often rendered them more picturesque—but from the violent destruction, which often left a big gap in the urban fabric."[11]

[9] American Ruins, 23.
[10] American Ruins, 22.
[11] American Ruins, 23.

Like Burtynsky, Vergara is intent on showing us demolition sites that contradict the more sanguine representations of the modern landscape. Both remind us that continuous innovation ("development," "modernization") of industrial civilization comes at a price: continuous demolition and displacement. But whereas Burtynsky bids us to keep a distant gaze on the monuments of creative-destruction in order to coolly resist the seduction of industrial power, Vergara wants us to join him as intruders into abandoned libraries and boarded-up houses, not just to expose the violent destruction in our midst, but, more importantly, to fill in the "gaps" in our collective memory. By photographing urban "ruins," Vergara hopes to search out and preserve traces of the "soul" "among the dereliction and destruction." What kind of soul might we find? Certainly not the "soul" in the machines that earlier modernists like Le Corbusier and Henry Ford celebrated. The automobile, of course, dominates the urban landscape, along with utility poles, garbage pails, barred windows and doors. But in Vergara's photos the presence of automobiles (often they, too, are left abandoned among the weeds) reminds us that the assumptions of the modern American dream—mobility based on cheap energy, prosperity defined as unlimited consumption, technology as the ever-expanding control over nature—have exacted a terrible price on the landscape.

But even among the ruins there remain signs of hope and redemption, evidenced by the many churches and religious symbols that fill Vergara's photos. Pentecostal churches have re-occupied numerous structures originally built for other purposes. (In my old Newark neighborhood, Hispanic Pentecostal churches have occupied what were once a delicatessen, a candy store, a firehouse, and a former go-go bar.) But unlike the stone-built churches—built to symbolize stability and permanence, not just of the church itself, but of the whole neighborhood in which it was located—these makeshift churches, whatever personal sense of salvation they provide their members, seem to be as temporary as the buildings surrounding them. They offer an enclave of survival in the urban landscape, but they are inward looking, often windowless structures seeking to defend themselves against the hostile world outside, just like the barred-pink fortress-house Vergara shows us on Fern Street.

Other signs of transcendence are scattered throughout Vergara's urbanscapes— 15
"Jesus" graffitied on a boarded-up house; a billboard advertising "detoxification" treatments ("Procedure Confidential"); a middle school sign proclaiming that "Everybody is Somebody and We Are Rising" (with several of its letters having already dropped to the ground). Christians might read spiritual significance in the mundane storefront sign of the "Penn Fish Co.," the fish as symbol of Christ, the fisher of men. [See Figure 16.6.] Yet, I don't see Vergara searching for a form of religious redemption in the urban wilderness he documents. His photographs fill in the "gaps" of historical memory by memorializing the fragmentary remains of a past. Abandoned buildings and empty lots become haunted ruins. "Penn Fish Co." thus evokes an era when the urban street formed the backdrop of a contemporary life—a scene of diversity, vitality, and permanence. Vergara knows he's playing with nostalgia in his photos: "I imagine Gary and Detroit as the noisy, dramatic cities they once were and I see myself photographing the ghosts left behind."[12] Like

[12] Op.Cit. 24.

FIGURE 16.6 "Penn Fish Co. (sign) Broadway, Camden, NJ" 2001 by Camilo Jose Vergara

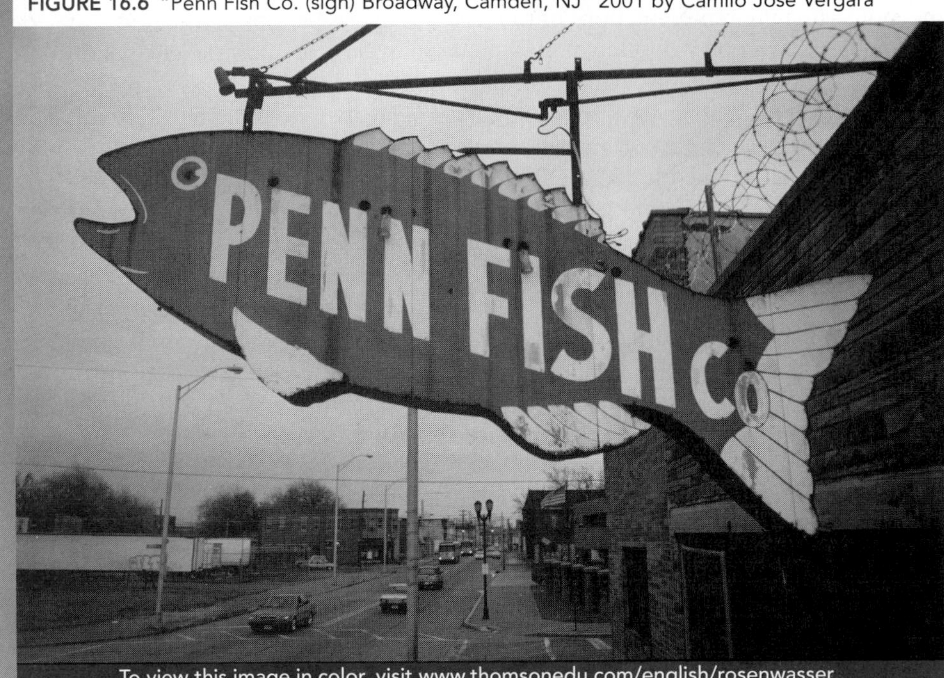

To view this image in color, visit www.thomsonedu.com/english/rosenwasser

Burtynsky's, there is nothing in Vergara's vision to suggest what we might do to control the creative-destructive processes of modernity; rather, his stark images call upon us to stop, look around us and think what we are doing. In a world that is obsessed with erasing the past, he would have us regain a sense of history by reflecting on the remnants of what we have lost.

THINGS TO DO WITH THE READING

1. **Link:** Locate a point of contact between Kunstler's essay and Gambino's—find a significant passage from each. Decide what Kunstler might say about one or more of the images that Gambino discusses and that is included with his essay. Consider, for example, Gambino's treatment of the Ben Franklin Bridge (see paragraph 9). See Try this 12.1: Making One Source Speak to Another (see page 305).
2. Gambino notes how often human figures are conspicuously absent in Burtynsky's and Vergara's photographs. But there are in fact some people in Burtynsky's "Three Gorges" (Figure 16.3) and in Vergara's "Fern Street" (Figure 16.4). What role do these human figures play in terms of how each photograph communicates?

3. As Chapter 6 attempts to convey, in much analytical writing the writer does not simply set out to prove a thesis but instead formulates a thesis in order to create a workable space in which a range of related claims might be made about the subject. Gambino's essay is a good place to observe this aspect of essay construction/organization in action.

   First find a sentence that serves as a thesis—the claim that causes the piece to cohere, to possess a sense of direction. (Note: you will find more than one version of this primary claim in an essay.) Then locate other interesting claims in the piece that the thesis seems to allow Gambino the space to produce. You'll notice these are connected to the thesis but not necessarily just another version of the same thing. Write down three or four of these, noting where you find them.

4. A handful of primary terms can cause a piece of writing to cohere, but also to define a space within which the writer can work. Two of these words in Gambino's essay are "gap" and "history." Determine how these words function in making the essay hold together, and write about that in a few sentences. Then find three or four other terms that operate in this manner, take one, and write about it.

5. Look at how Gambino uses the formula called "Seems to be about *x*, but could also be (is 'really') about *y*" (see pages 86–88) in paragraph 3. Here he says that the engineers' "ingenious instruments are not [Burtynsky's] real subject." As the paragraph progresses, Gambino complicates the essay's thinking, noting "Burtynsky's photos remind us that the beauty of these landscapes cannot be separated from the industrial power that *forcefully cuts* them from the earth." This is a symptom of the essay's fondness for paradox, also evident in the title of the photo, "Rock of Ages" (an old religious hymn about how some things can be relied on to last forever) and elsewhere in the piece. What do you make of these paradoxes? How do they function to organize the piece? What are the terms of the ambivalence that Gambino is investigating in this essay, and what point of view is he ultimately inviting us to take toward it?

6. **Application:** Imagine that Vergara and Burtynsky planned to spend a week taking photographs in the area in which you live. Where would each of them go to shoot, and why? Be as specific as you can. (Maybe you could take a point-and-shoot there yourself.)

   Note: You may wish to look ahead to the discussion of contemporary photography in the interview with Joseph Elliott, which opens Chapter 17. It will provide a crash course in thinking about photographs. In the interview Elliott discusses Vergara and Burtynsky overtly.

Adam Gopnik

Times Regained: How the Old Times Square Was Made New

Nominally a book review about two recent histories of the revitalization of Times Square in New York City, this essay also offers a resonant analysis of the patterns and politics of urban redevelopment. It is the first of several pieces by the essayist and cultural commentator Adam Gopnik, an award-winning journalist for *The New Yorker*.

This year marks the hundredth anniversary of the decision to take an hourglass-shaped traffic funnel between Forty-second Street and Forty-seventh Street on Broadway, which had been called Longacre Square, and rename it after the New York *Times*, which had just built its office there. This was less an honor than a consolation prize. The other, then bigger and brighter newspaper, the New York *Herald*, had claimed the other, then brighter and better square, eight blocks south, which still bears its ghostly name. Nine years later, in 1913, the *Times* scurried off to a prim side street and a Gothic Revival bishop's palace, where it has been lifting its skirts and shyly peeking around the corner at its old home ever since. 1

No other part of New York has had such a melodramatic, mood-ring sensitivity to the changes in the city's history, with an image for every decade. There was the turn-of-the-century Times Square, with its roof gardens and showgirls; the raffish twenties Times Square of Ziegfeld and Youmans tunes; the thirties Times Square of "42nd Street," all chorus lines and moxie; the forties, V-J "On the Town" Times Square, full of sailors kissing girls; the wizened black-and-white fifties Times Square of "Sweet Smell of Success," steaming hot dogs, and grungy beats; and then the sixties and the seventies Times Square of "Midnight Cowboy" and "Taxi Driver," where everything fell apart and Hell wafted up through the manhole covers. No other place in town has been quite so high and quite so low. Within a single half decade, it had Harpo Marx in the Marx Brothers' valedictory movie, "Love Happy," leaping ecstatically from sign to sign and riding away on the flying Mobilgas Pegasus, and, down below, the unforgettable image of James Dean, hunched in his black overcoat, bearing the weight of a generation on his shoulders.

Now, of course, we have the new Times Square, as fresh as a neon daisy, with a giant Gap and a Niketown and an Applebee's and an ESPN Zone and television announcers visible through tinted windows, all family retailing and national brands. In some ways, the Square has never looked better, with the diagonal sloping lines of the Reuters Building, the curving Deco zipper, even the giant mock dinosaur in the Toys R Us. There are, of course, people who miss the old Times Square, its picturesque squalor and violence and misery and exploitation. Those who pointed at the old Times Square as an instance of everything that capitalism can do wrong now point to the new Times Square as an instance of everything that capitalism can do worse. Where once Times Square was hot, it is now cold, where once varied, now uniform, where once alive, now dead. Which just proves, as with the old maxim about belief, that people who refuse to be sentimental about the normal things don't end up being sentimental about nothing; they end up being sentimental about anything, shedding tears about muggings and the shards of crack vials glittering like diamonds in the gutter.

And yet, whatever has been gained, something really is missing in the new Times Square. The forces that created it, and the mixed emotions that most of us have in its presence, are the subject of James Traub's "The Devil's Playground" (Random House; $25.95), which is both an engaged civics lesson and a work of social history. The book begins with an ironic moment—Traub takes his eleven-year-old son to the new Forty-second Street to see the old "42nd Street"—and then spirals back into history, moving decade by decade over the past century.

5 Traub, a writer for the *Times*, hates city myth but loves city history: on every page you learn something about how the city really happened, and how it really happens now. He is particularly good at wrestling complicated history into a few tight pages. He gives the best account we have of the original sin of New York: the birth, in 1811, of the iron street grid almost before there were any streets. The decision to lay a crisscross of numbers over the city without any breaks for public squares, plazas, or parks—a deliberately brutal nod to the governing principle of commerce—is why we still, sadly, call any awkward and accidental space created by the diagonal of Broadway intersecting an avenue a "square."

Traub also has a gift for filtering social history through a previously invisible individual agent. As always, the vast forces of mass culture turn out to be the idiosyncratic choices of a few key, mostly hidden players. The character of the signs in Times Square, for instance, was mostly the invention of O. J. Gude, the Sign King of Times Square. Gude, a true aesthete with a significant art collection, was the first to sense that the peculiar shape of Times Square—a triangle with sign-friendly "flats" at the base and the apex—made it the perfect place for big electric national-brand signs, or "spectaculars," as they were called, even before the First World War. In 1917, when Gude put up a two-hundred-foot-long spectacular, on the west side of Broadway between Forty-third and Forty-fourth, featuring twelve gleaming "spearmen" who went through spasmodic calisthenics, it was as big an event in American pop culture, in its way, as the opening of "The Jazz Singer," ten years later. Gude also had the bright idea of joining the Municipal Art Society, the leading opponent of big signs, and later helped shape the zoning ordinances that essentially eliminated big electric signs anywhere in midtown *except* in Times Square.

Times Square is famous for what used to be called its "denizens"—Damon Runyon, George S. Kaufman, Clifford Odets, A. J. Liebling—and Traub writes brief lives of a lot of them. But the history of the place isn't really a history of its illuminati; it's a history of its illuminations. Though social forces and neon signs flow out of individuals, they don't flow back into individuals so transparently. George S. Kaufman, to take one instance, was exclusively a creature of the theatre; if, like the galleries in SoHo in the nineteen-nineties, the Broadway theatre had in the thirties picked up and moved to Chelsea, Kaufman would have followed it blindly and would never have been seen on Forty-second Street again. Even Runyon has about as much to do with the history of Times Square as P. G. Wodehouse does with the history of Mayfair: his subject is language, not place, and in all of Runyon's stories it would be hard to find a single set-piece description of Times Square, a single bulb on a single sign. Individual artists help make cities, but cities don't make their artists in quite so neatly reciprocal a way. Dr. Johnson's "London" is a poem; "The London of Dr. Johnson" is a tour-bus ride.

Traub gives no false gloss to the decay of Times Square; it was really bad. The neighborhood declined to a point where, by the mid-seventies, the Times Square precincts placed first and second in New York in total felonies. (Harlem had a third as many.) These were crimes of violence, too: a rape or an armed robbery or a murder took place nearly every day and every night. Stevie Wonder's great 1973 song "Living for the City" has a spoken-word interlude in which the poor black kid from the South arrives on West Forty-second Street and in about five minutes is lured into the drug business. This was a song, but it was not a lie.

Traub's account of the area's transformation is lit from behind by another, still longer and larger one—Lynne B. Sagalyn's masterly "Times Square Roulette: Remaking the City Icon," just issued in paperback (M.I.T.; $29.95). Sagalyn teaches real estate at the University of Pennsylvania, and her book, the fruit of more than a decade of scholarly labor, is as mind-bendingly detailed an account of the relations of property and culture as one can find outside Galsworthy or Trollope.

It's full of eye-opening material, if one can keep one's eyes open long enough 10
to find it. Sagalyn's book is written, perhaps of necessity, in a prose so dense with city acronyms and cross-referential footnotes that it can defeat even the most earnest attention. Nonetheless, its material is the material of the city's existence. Reading it is like reading an advanced-biology textbook and then discovering that its sole subject is your own body.

Traub and Sagalyn agree in dispelling a myth and moving toward a history, and the myth irritates them both—Traub's usual tone of intelligent skepticism sometimes boils over here into exasperation. The myth they want to dispel is that the cleanup of Times Square in the nineties was an expression of Mayor Giuliani's campaign against crime and vice, and of his companion tendency to accept a sterilized environment if they could be removed, and that his key corporate partner in this was the mighty Disney, which led the remaking of West Forty-second Street as a theme park instead of an authentic urban street. As Traub and Sagalyn show, this is nearly the reverse of the truth. It was Mayor Koch who shaped the new Times Square, if anyone did, while the important private profit-makers and players were almost all purely local: the Old Oligarchs, the handful of rich, and mostly Jewish, real-estate families—the Rudins, Dursts, Roses, Resnicks, Fishers, Speyers, and Tishmans, as Sagalyn crisply enumerates them. Mayor Giuliani, basically, was there to cut the ribbon, and Disney to briefly lend its name.

The story follows, on a larger scale than usual, the familiar form of New York development, whose stages are as predictable as those of a professional wrestling match: first, the Sacrificial Plan; next, the Semi-Ridiculous Rhetorical Statement; then the Staged Intervention of the Professionals; and, at last, the Sorry Thing Itself. The Sacrificial Plan is the architectural plan or model put forward upon the announcement of the project, usually featuring some staggeringly obvious and controversial device—a jagged roof or a startling pediment—which even the architect knows will never be built, and whose purpose is not to attract investors so much as to get people used to the general idea that something is going to be built there. (Sometimes the Sacrificial Plan is known by all to be sacrificial, and sometimes, as in "The Lottery," known to everyone but the sacrifice.) The Semi-Ridiculous Rhetorical Statement usually accompanies, though it can precede, the Sacrificial Plan, and is intended to show that the plan is not as brutal and cynical as it looks but has been designed in accordance with the architectural mode of the moment. ("The three brass lambs that stand on the spires of Sheep's Meadow Tower reflect the historical context of the site ..." was the way it was done a decade ago; now it's more likely to be "In its hybrid façade, half mirror, half wool, Sheep's Meadow Tower captures the contradictions and deconstructs the flow of ...") The Staged Intervention marks the moment when common sense and common purpose, in the form of the Old Oligarchs and their architects—who were going to be in charge in the first place—return to rescue the project from itself. The Sorry Thing itself you've seen. (At Ground Zero, Daniel Libeskind supplied the sacrificial plan, and now he is pursuing all of the semi-ridiculous rhetoric, in the forlorn hope that, when the professionals stage their intervention, he will be the professional called on.)

The only difference in the Times Square project was that, because of its size, it all happened twice. (Actually, there were two dimensions to the remaking of Times Square—the West Forty-second Street projects, and the reclaiming of the Square itself—but each depended on the other, and, though administratively distinct, they were practically joined.) The first Sacrificial Plan appeared in the late seventies, and was called "the City at Forty-second Street." Presented by the developer Fred Papert, with the support of the Ford Foundation and with proposed backing from Paul Reichmann, of Olympia & York, it envisioned a climate-controlled indoor-mall Forty-second Street, with a five-hundred-thousand-square-foot "educational, entertainment, and exhibit center," and a 2.1-million-square-foot merchandise mart for the garment trade, all strung together with aerial walkways and, lovely period touch, equipped with a monorail. Mayor Koch wasn't happy about the plan; "We've got to make sure that they have seltzer"—that it's echt New York—"instead of orange juice," he said. But mostly he worried because someone else would be squeezing the oranges.

Still, the plan did what such plans are meant to do: establish the principle, civic-minded rather than commercial, that something had to be done here, and the larger principle that whatever was done should be done on a large scale—the old, outdoor theatre-and-arcade Forty-second Street could be turned into "a consumer-oriented exposition center with people moving across 42nd Street by means of pedestrian bridges," as one early draft of the rhetoric put it. As the initiative passed from the developers to the Koch administration, a further principle was established. The transformation could be made only by large-scale condemnation of what was already there, and the city and state together proposed a new way to link up private and public: the developers would get the right to build on condition that they paid directly for public improvements. The price of your tower on top was a cleaner subway station below.

Still more significant, and what should have been seen as a portent in the first 15
Sacrificial Plan, was the felt need to pull away from the street completely. This

was not simply snobbery but self-preservation; Forty-second Street wasn't dying but raving. The porno shops on West Forty-second Street weren't there because the middle class had fled. They were there because the middle class was there. The people who bought from the porn industry were the office workers who walked by the stores on the way to and from work, and the tourists who wanted to take back a little something not for the kids. The XXX video rooms and bookstores and grind-house theatres were going concerns, paying an average of thirty-two thousand dollars a year in rent; peep shows could gross five million a year. Though the retailers were obviously entangled with the Mafia, the buildings were owned by respectable real-estate families—for the most part, the same families who had owned the theatres since the thirties, the Brandts and the Shuberts. Times Square was Brechtville: a perfect demonstration of the principle that the market, left to itself, will produce an economy of crime as happily as an economy of virtue.

This—the crucial underlying reality in the Forty-second Street redevelopment—meant that the city, if it was to get the legal right to claim and condemn property in order to pass it over, had to be pointing toward some enormous, unquestioned commercial goal, larger or at least more concrete than the real goal, which was essentially ethical and "cultural." For once, the usual New York formula had to be turned right around: a question of virtue had to be disguised as a necessity of commerce. On Forty-second Street, a group of perfectly successful private businessmen in the movie-theatre business were being pushed aside in favor of a set of private businessmen in the tall-building business, and the legal argument for favoring the businessmen in the tall-building business was that they had promised that if you let them build a really tall building they would fix up the subway station.

This produced the Second Sacrificial Plan, of 1983: Philip Johnson and John Burgee's immense four towers straddling either side of Times Square on Forty-second, each with a slightly different pedimented top. The Semi-Ridiculous Rhetorical Statement invoked for this plan was that the pedimented tops "contextualized" the big buildings because they recalled the roofline of the old Astor Hotel, a victim of development twenty years before. They were by far the biggest and bulkiest buildings that had ever been proposed for midtown; Sagalyn gasps at the sheer zoning outrage of it. They had to be that big to establish their right to be at all. The Brandt family, which owned many of the theatres, sued and lost. "The Durst family interests put their name on five lawsuits," Sagalyn reports, "but the rumors of their financial backing of many more are legion." (The Dursts owned various individual lots along the street, which they intended to put together for their own giant building.) After ten years, they lost, too. Forty-seven suits were launched, and the plan withstood them all. The Johnson models, fortresses designed to withstand a siege of litigation, had triumphed. But nobody really wanted to build the buildings.

In the interim between the First Sacrificial Plan and the Second, however, something had changed in the ideology of architecture. A new orthodoxy had come into power, with an unapologetic emphasis on formal "delirium" and the chaotic surface of the city. In Rem Koolhaas's epoch-marking manifesto "Delirious New York" (1978), the buzz, confusion, danger, and weirdness of New

York were no longer things to worry about. In fact, they were pretty much all we had to boast of. To an increasing bias in favor of small-scale streetscapes and "organic" growth was added a neon zip of pop glamour. The new ideology was Jane Jacobs dressed in latex and leather.

By what turned out to be a happy accident, this previously academic, pop-perverse set of ideas had influenced minds at the Municipal Art Society—the very group that had fought against the idea of signs and signage in Times Square at the turn of the century. In 1985, after the appearance of the Johnson plan, the Municipal Art Society, under the impeccable direction of the white-shoed Hugh Hardy, took on as its cause the preservation of the "bowl of light" in Times Square and "the glitz of its commercial billboards and electronic signs." After being digested in various acronymic gullets, this campaign produced not only new zoning text (sections ZR81-832 and ZR81-85, as Sagalyn duly notes) but, as an enforcement mechanism, an entirely new unit of measurement: the LUTS, or "Light Unit Times Square." (Each sign had to produce a minimum LUTS reading; the lighting designer Paul Marantz gave it its name.)

20 And so the Municipal Art Society became the major apostle of a continuing chaotic commercial environment in Times Square, while the big developers had to make the old Beaux-Arts case for classical order, lucidity, and space—for "trees and clean streets ... museums and sidewalk cafés," in the plaintive words of the developer David Solomon. Eventually, in the early-nineties decline, Prudential, which had been holding on to the development on West Forty-second Street, was forced to sell its rights at a discount—to the Durst family, which had been leading the litigation against the plan all along but which, as everyone could have predicted, was there at the finale to develop and build, including 4 Times Square, the big building in which these words are being written.

None of this, however, could have created the new Times Square had it not been for other, unforeseeable changes. The first, and most important, was the still poorly explained decline in violent crime. (Traub tours the Eighth Avenue end of Forty-second with one of the district's privately financed security officers, who points out that there is still plenty of prostitution and drug-trafficking but very few muggings or assaults; even chain-snatching and petty theft are now rare.) This decline allowed for the emergence of the real hyperdrive of the new Square, the arrival of what every parent knows is the engine of American commerce: branded, television-based merchandise directed at "families" (that is, directed at getting children to torture their parents until they buy it). The critical demographic fact, as a few have pointed out, is the late onset of childbearing, delayed here until the habit of New York is set and the disposable income to spend on children is larger. When Damon Runyon was writing, the presence of Little Miss Marker in the Square was the material for a story. Now Little Miss Marker runs the place.

Of all the ironies of the Times Square redevelopment, the biggest is this: that the political right is, on the whole, happy with what has happened, and points to Times Square as an instance of how private enterprise can cure things that social engineering had previously destroyed, while the left points to Times Square as an instance of how market forces sterilize and drive out social forces of community and authenticity. But surely the ghosts of the old progressives in Union Square should be proudest of what has happened. It was, after all, the free market that produced the old Times Square: the porno stores were there because they made money, as part of a thriving market system. Times Square, and Forty-second Street, was saved by government decisions, made largely on civic grounds. Nothing would have caused more merriment on the conservative talk shows than the LUTS regulations—imagine some bureaucrat telling you how bright your sign should be—but it is those lights which light the desks of the guys at the offices of Clear Channel on Forty-second Street, and bring the crowds that make them safe. Civic-mindedness, once again, saved capitalism from itself.

And yet you don't have to have nostalgia for squalor and cruelty to feel that some vital chunk of New York experience has been replaced by something different, and less. Traub ends with the deconstructionist Mark Taylor, who trots out various depressions about the Society of Spectacle to explain the transformation, all of which are marvellously unilluminating. Times Square may be spectacular—that is what its signmakers have called their own signs for a century—but in the theoretical sense it's not a spectacle at all. It's not filled by media images that supplant the experience of real things. It's a tangible, physical, fully realized public square in which real people stare at things made by other people. The absence of spectacle, in that sense—the escape from the domination of isolated television viewing—is what still draws people on New Year's Eve, in the face of their own government's attempts to scare them away. (Dick Clark, of course, is a simulacrum, but he was born that way.)

Traub toys with the idea that the real problem lies in the replacement of an authentic "popular" culture, of arcades and Runyonesque song-pluggers, with a "mass" culture, of national brands and eager shoppers. But it's hard to see any principled way in which the twenty-foot-tall animatronic dinosaur at the new Toys R Us howls at the orders of mass culture, while O. J. Gude's dancing spearmen were purely Pop. The distinction between popular culture and mass culture is to our time what the distinction between true folk art and false folk art was to the age of Ruskin and Morris; we want passionately to define the difference because we know in our hearts that it doesn't exist. Even fairy tales turn out to be half manufactured by a commercial enterprise, half risen from the folkish ground. The idea that there is a good folkish culture that comes up from the streets and revivifies the arts and a bad mass culture imposed from above is an illusion, and anyone who has studied any piece of the history knows it.

25 All the same, there is something spooky about the contemporary Times Square. It wanders through you; you don't wander through it. One of the things that make for vitality in any city, and above all in New York, is the trinity of big buildings, bright lights, and weird stores. The big buildings and bright lights are there in the new Times Square, but the weird stores are not. By weird stores one means not simply small stores, mom-and-pop operations, but stores in which a peculiar and even obsessive entrepreneur caters to a peculiar and even an obsessive taste. (Art galleries and modestly ambitious restaurants are weird stores by definition. It's why they still feel very New York.) If the big buildings and the bright signs reflect the city's vitality and density, weird stores refract it; they imply that the city is so varied that someone can make a mundane living from one tiny obsessive thing. Poolrooms and boxing

clubs were visible instances of weird stores in the old Times Square; another, slightly less visible, was the thriving world of the independent film business, negative cutters, and camera-rental firms.

There is hardly a single weird store left on Broadway from Forty-second Street to Forty-sixth Street—hardly a single place in which a peculiar passion seems to have committed itself to a peculiar product. You have now, one more irony, to bend east, toward respectable Fifth Avenue, toward the diamond merchants and the Brazilian restaurants and the kosher cafeterias that still fill the side streets, to re-create something that feels a little like the old Times Square. (Wonderful Forty-fifth Street! With the Judaica candlesticks and the Japanese-film rental and the two-story shops selling cheap clothes and stereos, lit up bright.) Social historians like to talk about the Tragedy of the Commons, meaning the way that everybody loses when everybody overgrazes the village green, though it is in no individual's interest to stop. In New York, we suffer from a Tragedy of the Uncommons: weird things make the city worth living in, but though each individual wants them, no one individual wants to pay to keep them going. Times Square, as so often in the past, is responding, in typically heightened form, to the general state of the city: the loss of retail variety troubles us everywhere, as a new trinity of monotony—Starbucks, Duane Reade, and the Washington Mutual Bank—appears to dominate every block. We just feel it more on Broadway.

Do we overdraw Times Square history, make it more epic than it ought to be? Piccadilly and Soho, in London, and Place de Clichy, in Paris, are similar places, have known similar kinds of decline and similar kinds of pickup—but without gathering quite the same emotion. We make Times Square do more work than it ought to. Other great cities have public spaces and pleasure spaces, clearly marked, and with less confusion between them. When Diana died, it was Kensington Palace, not Piccadilly, that got the flowers, and in Paris it is the Champs-Élysées, not Place de Clichy, that gets the military parade on the fourteenth of July. Which returns us, with a certain sense of awe, to the spell still cast by the original sin of the 1811 grid plan. We make our accidental pleasure plazas do the work of the public squares we don't have. This is asking a lot of a sign, or even a bunch of bright ones lighting up the night.

THINGS TO DO WITH THE READING

1. This essay offers a number of models for how to analyze that are worthy of imitating. One is its use of the "Seems to be about *x*, but could also be (is 'really') about *y*" gambit (see page 86) to distinguish the "myths" about rebuilding from the "history." Make note of all of the too-easy answers—the misconceptions—that Gopnik points out. (Hint: reversals, surprises, and references to disguise are also signals of these misconceptions.) This will help you to assimilate the fairly complicated evolution of thinking in the piece and will in fact function as a kind of analytical summary (see pages 117–120).

2. **Link:** the reversals in this essay (mentioned above) also call to mind the fondness for paradox we pointed to in Gambino's piece. How does Gambino's treatment of such complicated notions as "creative destruction" resemble and differ from Gopnik's treatment of the tangled history of Times Square's redevelopment? You might note (and analyze) Gopnik's own fondness for verbal paradox, as in his discussion of the responses of the political left and right (see paragraph 22). A sentence in Gopnik that invites linkage to Gambino's perspective is "the transformation [of Times Square] could be made only by large-scale condemnation of what was already there" (see paragraph 14).
3. **Link:** In his essay, "The Public Realm and the Common Good," Kunstler has much to say about "civic" matters and about the commercial pressures that have shaped Americans' use of space. Look at Gopnik's essay using Kunstler as a lens. What, for example, might Kunstler say about the various plans for Times Square? Also consider how Gopnik's perspective might alter (complicate, qualify) Kunstler's. Useful sentences in Gopnik for this purpose are: "civic-mindedness, once again, saved capitalism from itself" and "Times Square, and Forty-second Street, were saved by government decisions, made largely on civic grounds" (see paragraph 22).
4. This essay is full of proper names. See, for example, paragraph 7: Damon Runyan (whose name coined the adjective "Runyonesque," which appears throughout the piece), P.G. Wodehouse, Sr., [Samuel] Johnson, among others. Make a list of names mentioned in Gopnik's piece and then Google them. How are these "allusions" functioning in this essay—what do they provide? Why does Gopnik do this? What does this way of proceeding suggest about his assumptions of his audience—readers of *The New Yorker*? (See the discussion of ethos in Chapter 9, page 246.)
5. **Application:** Don't let the witty way that Gopnik names the stages of redevelopment lead you to dismiss them as merely comic. The "familiar form" that he educes in four parts—the Sacrificial Plan, the Semi-Ridiculous Rhetorical Statement, the Staged Intervention of the Professionals, and the Sorry Thing Itself—offers a potent lens for examining redevelopment elsewhere. An obvious case in point as we write these words is New Orleans. How might we apply the four steps to the rebuilding efforts going on there? Do some research in the popular press (and/or Google) on the way this major project of urban rebuilding is being talked about and planned. Identify one or more Sacrificial Plans, Semi-Ridiculous Rhetorical Statements, and so forth. Then use your answers to fuel a few pages (or more) of analysis.

   You could also use Gopnik as a lens for examining something more local. Gopnik, like Kunstler, address the issue of zoning. Locate a zoning issue where you live and analyze it from Gopnik's and/or Kunstler's point of view. ◗

Jane Jacobs

The Uses of Sidewalks: Safety

This piece is excerpted from Jacobs's *The Death and Life of Great American Cities* (1961), a work commonly ranked among the most influential American books on urban planning. In a style of simple eloquence, Jacobs argues against the prevailing approach toward urban renewal in the 1950s, offering a point of view that remains pertinent today: "that the sight of people attracts still other people, is something that city planners and city architectural designers seem to find incomprehensible. They operate on the premise that city people seek the sight of emptiness, obvious order and quiet. Nothing could be less true."

Streets in cities serve many purposes besides carrying vehicles, and city sidewalks— 1
the pedestrian parts of the streets—serve many purposes besides carrying pedestrians. These uses are bound up with circulation but are not identical with it and in their own right they are at least as basic as circulation to the proper workings of cities.

A city sidewalk by itself is nothing. It is an abstraction. It means something only in conjunction with the buildings and other uses that border it, or border other sidewalks very near it. The same might be said of streets, in the sense that they serve other purposes besides carrying wheeled traffic in their middles. Streets and their sidewalks, the main public places of a city, are its most vital organs. Think of a city and what comes to mind? Its streets. If a city's streets look interesting, the city looks interesting; if they look dull, the city looks dull.

More than that, and here we get down to the first problem, if a city's streets are safe from barbarism and fear, the city is thereby tolerably safe from barbarism and fear. When people say that a city, or a part of it, is dangerous or is a jungle what they mean primarily is that they do not feel safe on the sidewalks.

But sidewalks and those who use them are not passive beneficiaries of safety or helpless victims of danger. Sidewalks, their bordering uses, and their users, are active participants in the drama of civilization versus barbarism in cities. To keep the city safe is a fundamental task of a city's streets and its sidewalks.

This task is totally unlike any service that sidewalks and streets in little towns 5
or true suburbs are called upon to do. Great cities are not like towns, only larger. They are not like suburbs, only denser. They differ from towns and suburbs in basic ways, and one of these is that cities are, by definition, full of strangers. To any one person, strangers are far more common in big cities than acquaintances. More common not just in places of public assembly, but more common at a man's own doorstep. Even residents who live near each other are strangers, and must be, because of the sheer number of people in small geographical compass.

The bedrock attribute of a successful city district is that a person must feel personally safe and secure on the street among all these strangers. He must not feel automatically menaced by them. A city district that fails in this respect also does badly in other ways and lays up for itself, and for its city at large, mountain on mountain of trouble.

Today barbarism has taken over many city streets, or people fear it has, which comes to much the same thing in the end. "I live in a lovely, quiet residential area," says a friend of mine who is hunting another place to live. "The only disturbing sound at night is the occasional scream of someone being mugged." It does not take many incidents of violence on a city street, or in a city district, to make people fear the streets. And as they fear them, they use them less, which makes the streets still more unsafe.

To be sure, there are people with hobgoblins in their heads, and such people will never feel safe no matter what the objective circumstances are. But this is a different matter from the fear that besets normally prudent, tolerant and cheerful people who show nothing more than common sense in refusing to venture after dark—or in a few places, by day—into streets where they may well be assaulted, unseen or unrescued until too late.

The barbarism and the real, not imagined, insecurity that gives rise to such fears cannot be tagged a problem of the slums. The problem is most serious, in fact, in genteel-looking "quiet residential areas" like that my friend was leaving.

10 It cannot be tagged as a problem of older parts of cities. The problem reaches its most baffling dimensions in some examples of rebuilt parts of cities, including supposedly the best examples of rebuilding, such as middle-income projects. The police precinct captain of a nationally admired project of this kind (admired by planners and lenders) has recently admonished residents not only about hanging around outdoors after dark but has urged them never to answer their doors without knowing the caller. Life here has much in common with life for the three little pigs or the seven little kids of the nursery thrillers. The problem of sidewalk and doorstep insecurity is as serious in cities which have made conscientious efforts at rebuilding as it is in those cities that have lagged. Nor is it illuminating to tag minority groups, or the poor, or the outcast with responsibility for city danger. There are immense variations in the degree of civilization and safety found among such groups and among the city areas where they live. Some of the safest sidewalks in New York City, for example, at any time of day or night, are those along which poor people or minority groups live. And some of the most dangerous are in streets occupied by the same kinds of people. All this can also be said of other cities.

Deep and complicated social ills must lie behind delinquency and crime, in suburbs and towns as well as in great cities. This book will not go into speculation on the deeper reasons. It is sufficient, at this point, to say that if we are to maintain a city society that can diagnose and keep abreast of deeper social problems, the starting point must be, in any case, to strengthen whatever workable forces for maintaining safety and civilization do exist—in the cities we do have. To build city districts that are custom made for easy crime is idiotic. Yet that is what we do.

The first thing to understand is that the public peace—the sidewalk and street peace—of cities is not kept primarily by the police, necessary as police are. It is kept primarily by an intricate, almost unconscious, network of voluntary controls and standards among the people themselves, and enforced by the people themselves. In some city areas—older public housing projects and streets with very high population turnover are often conspicuous examples—the keeping of public sidewalk law and order is left almost entirely to the police and special guards. Such places are jungles. No amount of police can enforce civilization where the normal, casual enforcement of it has broken down.

The second thing to understand is that the problem of insecurity cannot be solved by spreading people out more thinly, trading the characteristics of cities for the characteristics of suburbs. If this could solve danger on the city streets, then Los Angeles should be a safe city because superficially Los Angeles is almost all suburban. It has virtually no districts compact enough to qualify as dense city areas. Yet Los Angeles cannot, any more than any other great city, evade the truth that, being a city, it *is* composed of strangers not all of whom are nice. Los Angeles' crime figures are flabbergasting. Among the seventeen standard metropolitan areas with populations over a million, Los Angeles stands so pre-eminent in crime that it is in a category by itself. And this is markedly true of crimes associated with personal attack, the crimes that make people fear the streets.

Los Angeles, for example, has a forcible rape rate (1958 figures) of 31.9 per 100,000 population, more than twice as high as either of the next two cities, which happen to be St. Louis and Philadelphia; three times as high as the rate of 10.1 for Chicago, and more than four times as high as the rate of 7.4 for New York.

15 In aggravated assault, Los Angeles has a rate of 185, compared with 149.5 for Baltimore and 139.2 for St. Louis (the two next highest), and with 90.9 for New York and 79 for Chicago.

The overall Los Angeles rate for major crimes is 2,507.6 per 100,000 people, far ahead of St. Louis and Houston, which come next with 1,634.5 and 1,541.1, and of New York and Chicago, which have rates of 1,145.3 and 943.5.

The reasons for Los Angeles' high crime rates are undoubtedly complex, and at least in part obscure. But of this we can be sure: thinning out a city does not insure safety from crime and fear of crime. This is one of the conclusions that can be drawn within individual cities too, where pseudosuburbs or superannuated suburbs are ideally suited to rape, muggings, beatings, hold-ups and the like.

Here we come up against an all-important question about any city street: How much easy opportunity does it offer to crime? It may be that there is some absolute amount of crime in a given city, which will find an outlet somehow (I do not believe this). Whether this is so or not, different kinds of city streets garner radically different shares of barbarism and fear of barbarism.

Some city streets afford no opportunity to street barbarism. The streets of the North End of Boston are outstanding examples. They are probably as safe as any place on earth in this respect. Although most of the North End's residents are Italian or of Italian descent, the district's streets are also heavily and constantly used by people of every race and background. Some of the strangers from outside work in or close to the district; some come to shop and stroll; many, including members of minority groups who have inherited dangerous districts previously abandoned by others, make a point of cashing their paychecks in North End stores and immediately making their big weekly purchases in streets where they know they will not be parted from their money between the getting and the spending.

20 Frank Havey, director of the North End Union, the local settlement house, says, "I have been here in the North End twenty-eight years, and in all that time

I have never heard of a single case of rape, mugging, molestation of a child or other street crime of that sort in the district. And if there had been any, I would have heard of it even if it did not reach the papers." Half a dozen times or so in the past three decades, says Havey, would-be molesters have made an attempt at luring a child or, late at night, attacking a woman. In every such case the try was thwarted by passers-by, by kibitzers from windows, or shopkeepers.

Meantime, in the Elm Hill Avenue section of Roxbury, a part of inner Boston that is suburban in superficial character, street assaults and the ever present possibility of more street assaults with no kibitzers to protect the victims, induce prudent people to stay off the sidewalks at night. Not surprisingly, for this and other reasons that are related (dispiritedness and dullness), most of Roxbury has run down. It has become a place to leave.

I do not wish to single out Roxbury or its once fine Elm Hill Avenue section especially as a vulnerable area; its disabilities, and especially its Great Blight of Dullness, are all too common in other cities too. But differences like these in public safety within the same city are worth noting. The Elm Hill Avenue section's basic troubles are not owing to a criminal or a discriminated against or a poverty-stricken population. Its troubles stem from the fact that it is physically quite unable to function safely and with related vitality as a city district.

Even within supposedly similar parts of supposedly similar places, drastic differences in public safety exist. An incident at Washington Houses, a public housing project in New York, illustrates this point. A tenants' group at this project, struggling to establish itself, held some outdoor ceremonies in mid-December 1958, and put up three Christmas trees. The chief tree, so cumber-some it was a problem to transport, erect, and trim, went into the project's inner "street," a landscaped central mall and promenade. The other two trees, each less than six feet tall and easy to carry, went on two small fringe plots at the outer corners of the project where it abuts a busy avenue and lively cross streets of the old city. The first night, the large tree and all its trimmings were stolen. The two smaller trees remained intact, lights, ornaments and all, until they were taken down at New Year's. "The place where the tree was stolen, which is *theoretically* the most safe and sheltered place in the project, is the same place that is unsafe for people too, especially children," says a social worker who had been helping the tenants' group. "People are no safer in that mall than the Christmas tree. On the other hand, the place where the other trees were safe, where the project is just one corner out of four, happens to be safe for people."

This is something everyone already knows: A well-used city street is apt to be a safe street. A deserted city street is apt to be unsafe. But how does this work, really? And what makes a city street well used or shunned? Why is the sidewalk mall in Washington Houses, which is supposed to be an attraction, shunned? Why are the sidewalks of the old city just to its west not shunned? What about streets that are busy part of the time and then empty abruptly?

A city street equipped to handle strangers, and to make a safety asset, in itself, 25
out of the presence of strangers, as the streets of successful city neighborhoods always do, must have three main qualities:

First, there must be a clear demarcation between what is public space and what is private space. Public and private spaces cannot ooze into each other as they do typically in suburban settings or in projects.

Second, there must be eyes upon the street, eyes belonging to those we might call the natural proprietors of the street. The buildings on a street equipped to handle strangers and to insure the safety of both residents and strangers, must be oriented to the street. They cannot turn their backs or blank sides on it and leave it blind.

And third, the sidewalk must have users on it fairly continuously, both to add to the number of effective eyes on the street and to induce the people in buildings along the street to watch the sidewalks in sufficient numbers. Nobody enjoys sitting on a stoop or looking out a window at an empty street. Almost nobody does such a thing. Large numbers of people entertain themselves, off and on, by watching street activity.

In settlements that are smaller and simpler than big cities, controls on acceptable public behavior, if not on crime, seem to operate with greater or lesser success through a web of reputation, gossip, approval, disapproval and sanctions, all of which are powerful if people know each other and word travels. But a city's streets, which must control not only the behavior of the people of the city but also of visitors from suburbs and towns who want to have a big time away from the gossip and sanctions at home, have to operate by more direct, straightforward methods. It is a wonder cities have solved such an inherently difficult problem at all. And yet in many streets they do it magnificently.

It is futile to try to evade the issue of unsafe city streets by attempting to make some other features of a locality, say interior courtyards, or sheltered play spaces, safe instead. By definition again, the streets of a city must do most of the job of handling strangers for this is where strangers come and go. The streets must not only defend the city against predatory strangers, they must protect the many, many peaceable and well-meaning strangers who use them, insuring their safety too as they pass through. Moreover, no normal person can spend his life in some artificial haven, and this includes children. Everyone must use the streets.

On the surface, we seem to have here some simple aims: To try to secure streets where the public space is unequivocally public, physically unmixed with private or with nothing-at-all space, so that the area needing surveillance has clear and practicable limits; and to see that these public street spaces have eyes on them as continuously as possible.

But it is not so simple to achieve these objects, especially the latter. You can't make people use streets they have no reason to use. You can't make people watch streets they do not want to watch. Safety on the streets by surveillance and mutual policing of one another sounds grim, but in real life it is not grim. The safety of the street works best, most casually, and with least frequent taint of hostility or suspicion precisely where people are using and most enjoying the city streets voluntarily and are least conscious, normally, that they are policing.

The basic requisite for such surveillance is a substantial quantity of stores and other public places sprinkled along the sidewalks of a district; enterprises and public places that are used by evening and night must be among them especially. Stores, bars and restaurants, as the chief examples, work in several different and complex ways to abet sidewalk safety.

First, they give people—both residents and strangers—concrete reasons for using the sidewalks on which these enterprises face.

Second, they draw people along the sidewalks past places which have no attractions to public use in themselves but which become traveled and peopled as routes to somewhere else; this influence does not carry very far geographically, so enterprises must be frequent in a city district if they are to populate with walkers those other stretches of street that lack public places along the sidewalk. Moreover, there should be many different kinds of enterprises, to give people reasons for crisscrossing paths.

Third, storekeepers and other small businessmen are typically strong proponents of peace and order themselves; they hate broken windows and holdups; they hate having customers made nervous about safety. They are great street watchers and sidewalk guardians if present in sufficient numbers.

Fourth, the activity generated by people on errands, or people aiming for food or drink, is itself an attraction to still other people.

This last point, that the sight of people attracts still other people, is something that city planners and city architectural designers seem to find incomprehensible. They operate on the premise that city people seek the sight of emptiness, obvious order and quiet. Nothing could be less true. People's love of watching activity and other people is constantly evident in cities everywhere. This trait reaches an almost ludicrous extreme on upper Broadway in New York, where the street is divided by a narrow central mall, right in the middle of traffic. At the cross-street intersections of this long north-south mall, benches have been placed behind big concrete buffers and on any day when the weather is even barely tolerable these benches are filled with people at block after block after block, watching the pedestrians who cross the mall in front of them, watching the traffic, watching the people on the busy sidewalks, watching each other. Eventually Broadway reaches Columbia University and Barnard College, one to the right, the other to the left. Here all is obvious order and quiet. No more stores, no more activity generated by the stores, almost no more pedestrians crossing—and no more watchers. The benches are there but they go empty in even the finest weather. I have tried them and can see why. No place could be more boring. Even the students of these institutions shun the solitude. They are doing their outdoor loitering, outdoor homework and general street watching on the steps overlooking the busiest campus crossing.

It is just so on city streets elsewhere. A lively street always has both its users and pure watchers. Last year I was on such a street in the Lower East Side of Manhattan, waiting for a bus. I had not been there longer than a minute, barely long enough to begin taking in the street's activity of errand goers, children playing, and loiterers on the stoops, when my attention was attracted by a woman who opened a window on the third floor of a tenement across the street and vigorously yoo-hooed at me. When I caught on that she wanted my attention and responded, she shouted down, "The bus doesn't run here on Saturdays!" Then by a combination of shouts and pantomime she directed me around the corner. This woman was one of thousands upon thousands of people in New York who casually take care of the streets. They notice strangers. They observe everything going on. If they need to take action, whether to direct a stranger waiting in the wrong place or to call the police, they do so. Action usually requires, to be sure, a certain self-assurance about the actor's proprietorship of the street and the support he will get if necessary, matters which will be gone into later in this book. But even more fundamental than the action and necessary to the action, is the watching itself.

Not everyone in cities helps to take care of the streets, and many a city resi- 40
dent or city worker is unaware of why his neighborhood is safe. The other day an incident occurred on the street where I live, and it interested me because of this point.

My block of the street, I must explain, is a small one, but it contains a remarkable range of buildings, varying from several vintages of tenements to three- and four-story houses that have been converted into low-rent flats with stores on the ground floor, or returned to single-family use like ours. Across the street there used to be mostly four-story brick tenements with stores below. But twelve years ago several buildings, from the corner to the middle of the block, were converted into one building with elevator apartments of small size and high rents.

The incident that attracted my attention was a suppressed struggle going on between a man and a little girl of eight or nine years old. The man seemed to be trying to get the girl to go with him. By turns he was directing a cajoling attention to her, and then assuming an air of nonchalance. The girl was making herself rigid, as children do when they resist, against the wall of one of the tenements across the street.

As I watched from our second-floor window, making up my mind how to intervene if it seemed advisable, I saw it was not going to be necessary. From the butcher shop beneath the tenement had emerged the woman who, with her husband, runs the shop; she was standing within earshot of the man, her arms folded and a look of determination on her face. Joe Cornacchia, who with his sons-in-law keeps the delicatessen, emerged about the same moment and stood solidly to the other side. Several heads poked out of the tenement windows above, one was withdrawn quickly and its owner reappeared a moment later in the doorway behind the man. Two men from the bar next to the butcher shop came to the doorway and waited. On my side of the street, I saw that the locksmith, the fruit man and the laundry proprietor had all come out of their shops and that the scene was also being surveyed from a number of windows besides ours. That man did not know it, but he was surrounded. Nobody was going to allow a little girl to be dragged off, even if nobody knew who she was.

I am sorry—sorry purely for dramatic purposes—to have to report that the little girl turned out to be the man's daughter.

Throughout the duration of the little drama, perhaps five minutes in all, no 45
eyes appeared in the windows of the high-rent, small-apartment building. It was the only building of which this was true. When we first moved to our block, I used to anticipate happily that perhaps soon all the buildings would be rehabilitated like that one. I know better now, and can only anticipate with gloom and foreboding the recent news that exactly this transformation is scheduled for the rest of the block frontage adjoining the high-rent building. The high-rent tenants, most of whom are so transient we cannot even keep track of their faces,[1]

[1] Some, according to the storekeepers, live on beans and bread and spend their sojourn looking for a place to live where all their money will not go for rent.

have not the remotest idea of who takes care of their street, or how. A city neighborhood can absorb and protect a substantial number of these birds of passage, as our neighborhood does. But if and when the neighborhood finally *becomes* them, they will gradually find the streets less secure, they will be vaguely mystified about it, and if things get bad enough they will drift away to another neighborhood which is mysteriously safer.

In some rich city neighborhoods, where there is little do-it-yourself surveillance, such as residential Park Avenue or upper Fifth Avenue in New York, street watchers are hired. The monotonous sidewalks of residential Park Avenue, for example, are surprisingly little used; their putative users are populating, instead, the interesting store-, bar- and restaurant-filled sidewalks of Lexington Avenue and Madison Avenue to east and west, and the cross streets leading to these. A network of doormen and superintendents, of delivery boys and nursemaids, a form of hired neighborhood, keeps residential Park Avenue supplied with eyes. At night, with the security of the doormen as a bulwark, dog walkers safely venture forth and supplement the doormen. But this street is so blank of built-in eyes, so devoid of concrete reasons for using or watching it instead of turning the first corner off of it, that if its rents were to slip below the point where they could support a plentiful hired neighborhood of doormen and elevator men, it would undoubtedly become a woefully dangerous street.

Once a street is well equipped to handle strangers, once it has both a good, effective demarcation between private and public spaces and has a basic supply of activity and eyes, the more strangers the merrier.

Strangers become an enormous asset on the street on which I live, and the spurs off it, particularly at night when safety assets are most needed. We are fortunate enough, on the street, to be gifted not only with a locally supported bar and another around the corner, but also with a famous bar that draws continuous troops of strangers from adjoining neighborhoods and even from out of town. It is famous because the poet Dylan Thomas used to go there, and mentioned it in his writing. This bar, indeed, works two distinct shifts. In the morning and early afternoon it is a social gathering place for the old community of Irish longshoremen and other craftsmen in the area, as it always was. But beginning in midafternoon it takes on a different life, more like a college bull session with beer, combined with a literary cocktail party, and this continues until the early hours of the morning. On a cold winter's night, as you pass the White Horse, and the doors open, a solid wave of conversation and animation surges out and hits you; very warming. The comings and goings from this bar do much to keep our street reasonably populated until three in the morning, and it is a street always safe to come home to. The only instance I know of a beating in our street occurred in the dead hours between the closing of the bar and dawn. The beating was halted by one of our neighbors who saw it from his window and, unconsciously certain that even at night he was part of a web of strong street law and order, intervened.

A friend of mine lives on a street uptown where a church youth and community center, with many night dances and other activities, performs the same service for his street that the White Horse bar does for ours. Orthodox planning is much imbued with puritanical and Utopian conceptions of how people should spend their free time, and in planning, these moralisms on people's private lives are deeply confused with concepts about the workings of cities. In maintaining city street civilization, the White Horse bar and the church-sponsored youth center, different as they undoubtedly are, perform much the same public street civilizing service. There is not only room in cities for such differences and many more in taste, purpose and interest of occupation; cities also have a need for people with all these differences in taste and proclivity. The preferences of Utopians, and of other compulsive managers of other people's leisure, for one kind of legal enterprise over others is worse than irrelevant for cities. It is harmful. The greater and more plentiful the range of all legitimate interests (in the strictly legal sense) that city streets and their enterprises can satisfy, the better for the streets and for the safety and civilization of the city.

Bars, and indeed all commerce, have a bad name in many city districts pre- 50
cisely because they do draw strangers, and the strangers do not work out as an asset at all.

This sad circumstance is especially true in the dispirited gray belts of great cities and in once fashionable or at least once solid inner residential areas gone into decline. Because these neighborhoods are so dangerous, and the streets typically so dark, it is commonly believed that their trouble may be insufficient street lighting. Good lighting is important, but darkness alone does not account for the gray areas' deep, functional sickness, the Great Blight of Dullness.

Under the seeming disorder of the old city, wherever the old city is working successfully, is a marvelous order for maintaining the safety of the streets and the freedom of the city. It is a complex order. Its essence is intricacy of sidewalk use, bringing with it a constant succession of eyes. This order is all composed of movement and change, and although it is life, not art, we may fancifully call it the art form of the city and liken it to the dance—not to a simple-minded precision dance with everyone kicking up at the same time, twirling in unison and bowing off en masse, but to an intricate ballet in which the individual dancers and ensembles all have distinctive parts which miraculously reinforce each other and compose an orderly whole. The ballet of the good city sidewalk never repeats itself from place to place, and in any one place is always replete with new improvisations.

The stretch of Hudson Street where I live is each day the scene of an intricate sidewalk ballet. I make my own first entrance into it a little after eight when I put out the garbage can, surely aprosaic occupation, but I enjoy my part, my little clang, as the droves of junior high school students walk by the center of the stage dropping candy wrappers. (How do they eat so much candy so early in the morning?)

While I sweep up the wrappers I watch the other rituals of morning: Mr. Halpert unlocking the laundry's handcart from its mooring to a cellar door, Joe Cornacchia's son-in-law stacking out the empty crates from the delicatessen, the barber bringing out his sidewalk folding chair, Mr. Goldstein arranging the coils of wire which proclaim the hardware store is open, the wife of the tenement's superintendent depositing her chunky three-year-old with a toy mandolin on the stoop, the vantage point from which he is learning the English his mother cannot speak. Now the primary children, heading for St. Luke's, dribble through to the south; the children for St. Veronica's cross, heading to the west, and the children for P.S. 41, heading toward the east. Two new entrances are being made from the wings: well-dressed and even elegant women and men with brief cases emerge from doorways and side streets. Most of these are heading for the taxis are part of a wider morning ritual: having dropped passengers from midtown in the downtown financial district, they are now bringing downtowners up to midtown. Simultaneously, numbers of women in housedresses have emerged and as they crisscross with one another they pause for quick conversations that sound with either laughter or joint indignation, never, it seems, anything between. It is time for me to hurry to work too, and I exchange my ritual farewell with Mr. Lofaro, the short, thick-bodied, white-aproned fruit man who stands outside his doorway a little up the street, his arms folded, his feet planted, looking solid as earth itself. We nod; we each glance quickly up and down the street, then look back to each other and smile. We have done this many a morning for more than ten years, and we both know what it means: All is well.

55 The heart-of-the-day ballet I seldom see, because part of the nature of it is that working people who live there, like me, are mostly gone, filling the roles of strangers on other sidewalks. But from days off, I know enough of it to know that it becomes more and more intricate. Longshoremen who are not working that day gather at the White Horse or the Ideal or the International for beer and conversation. The executives and business lunchers from the industries just to the west throng the Dorgene restaurant and the Lion's Head coffee house; meat-market workers and communications scientists fill the bakery lunchroom. Character dancers come on, a strange old man with strings of old shoes over his shoulders, motor-scooter riders with big beards and girl friends who bounce on the back of the scooters and wear their hair long in front of their faces as well as behind, drunks who follow the advice of the Hat Council and are always turned out in hats, but not hats the Council would approve. Mr. Lacey, the locksmith, shuts up his shop for a while and goes to exchange the time of day with Mr. Slube at the cigar store. Mr. Koochagian, the tailor, waters the luxuriant jungle of plants in his window, gives them a critical look from the outside, accepts a compliment on them from two passers-by, fingers the leaves on the plane tree in front of our house with a thoughtful gardener's appraisal, and crosses the street for a bite at the Ideal where he can keep an eye on customers and wigwag across the message that he is coming. The baby carriages come out, and clusters of everyone from toddlers with dolls to teenagers with homework gather at the stoops.

When I get home after work, the ballet is reaching its crescendo. This is the time of roller skates and stilts and tricycles, and games in the lee of the stoop with bottletops and plastic cowboys; this is the time of bundles and packages, zigzagging from the drug store to the fruit stand and back over to the butcher's; this is the time when teen-agers, all dressed up, are pausing to ask if their slips show or their collars look right; this is the time when beautiful girls get out of MG's; this is the time when the fire engines go through; this is the time when anybody you know around Hudson Street will go by.

As darkness thickens and Mr. Halpert moors the laundry cart to the cellar door again, the ballet goes on under lights, eddying back and forth but intensifying at the bright spotlight pools of Joe's sidewalk pizza dispensary, the bars, the delicatessen, the restaurant and the drug store. The night workers stop now at the delicatessen, to pick up salami and a container of milk. Things have settled down for the evening but the street and its ballet have not come to a stop.

I know the deep night ballet and its seasons best from waking long after midnight to tend a baby and, sitting in the dark, seeing the shadows and hearing the sounds of the sidewalk. Mostly it is a sound like infinitely pattering snatches of party conversation and, about three in the morning, singing, very good singing. Sometimes there is sharpness and anger or sad, sad weeping, or a flurry of search for a string of beads broken. One night a young man came roaring along, bellowing terrible language at two girls whom he had apparently picked up and who were disappointing him. Doors opened, a wary semicircle formed around him, not too close, until the police came. Out came the heads, too, along Hudson Street, offering opinion, "Drunk … Crazy … A wild kid from the suburbs."[2]

Deep in the night, I am almost unaware how many people are on the street unless something calls them together, like the bagpipe. Who the piper was and why he favored our street I have no idea. The bagpipe just skirled out in the February night, and as if it were a signal the random, dwindled movements of the sidewalk took on direction. Swiftly, quietly, almost magically a little crowd was there, a crowd that evolved into a circle with a Highland fling inside it. The crowd could be seen on the shadowy sidewalk, the dancers could be seen, but the bagpiper himself was almost invisible because his bravura was all in his music. He was a very little man in a plain brown overcoat. When he finished and vanished, the dancers and watchers applauded, and applause came from the galleries too, half a dozen of the hundred windows on Hudson Street. Then the windows closed, and the little crowd dissolved into the random movements of the night street.

The strangers on Hudson Street, the allies whose eyes help us natives keep 60
the peace of the street, are so many that they always seem to be different people from one day to the next. That does not matter. Whether they are so many always-different people as they seem to be, I do not know. Likely they are. When Jimmy Rogan fell through a plate-glass window (he was separating some scuffling friends) and almost lost his arm, a stranger in an old T shirt emerged from the Ideal bar, swiftly applied an expert tourniquet and, according to the hospital's emergency staff, saved Jimmy's life. Nobody remembered seeing the man before and no one has seen him since. The hospital was called in this way: a woman sitting on the steps next to the accident ran over to the bus stop, wordlessly snatched the dime from the hand of a stranger who was waiting with his fifteen-cent fare ready, and raced into the Ideal's phone booth. The stranger raced after her to offer the nickel too. Nobody remembered seeing him before, and no one has seen him since. When you see the same stranger three or four times on Hudson Street, you begin to nod. This is almost getting to be an acquaintance, a public acquaintance, of course.

I have made the daily ballet of Hudson Street sound more frenetic than it is, because writing it telescopes it. In real life, it is not that way. In real life, to be sure, something is always going on, the ballet is never at a halt, but the general effect is peaceful and the general tenor even leisurely. People who know well such

[2] He turned out to be a wild kid from the suburbs. Sometimes, on Hudson Street, we are tempted to believe the suburbs must be a difficult place to bring up children.

animated city streets will know how it is. I am afraid people who do not will always have it a little wrong in their heads—like the old prints of rhinoceroses made from travelers' descriptions of rhinoceroses.

On Hudson Street, the same as in the North End of Boston or in any other animated neighborhoods of great cities, we are not innately more competent at keeping the sidewalks safe than are the people who try to live off the hostile truce of Turf in a blind-eyed city. We are the lucky possessors of a city order that makes it relatively simple to keep the peace because there are plenty of eyes on the street. But there is nothing simple about that order itself, or the bewildering number of components that go into it. Most of those components are specialized in one way or another. They unite in their joint effect upon the sidewalk, which is not specialized in the least. That is its strength.

THINGS TO DO WITH THE READING

1. Summarize Jacobs's argument with the technique called ranking (see pages 29, 117–120). Do this by locating all of the characteristics that Jacobs believes a neighborhood must have to remain safe. Concentrate on the one or two characteristics that Jacobs would say are most important.
2. Write a summary in which you focus on the mistakes that Jacobs says housing authorities and city planners make. Also focus on what Jacobs claims are mistaken assumptions about the causes of unsafe neighborhoods. How, for example, does she dispute the charge that the presence of poor people and minorities makes neighborhoods unsafe?
3. **Link:** Look at Kunstler's attack on the kind of segregation that zoning causes, and locate the common ground between Kunstler and Jacobs in this regard. It is interesting that Jacobs makes little mention of the impact of cars, except perhaps in her discussion of what she calls "pseudosuburbs" (see paragraph 17). Theoretically, both Kunstler and Jacobs would welcome the arrival of a restaurant in a residential area. How does the car culture complicate both writers' advocacy of mixed use (commercial and residential) areas?
4. **Link:** Now that you have read this essay, go back to the reference to Jane Jacobs in Gopnik's essay and explain it. Speaking of a change in architectural orthodoxy in New York, Gopnik writes, "The new ideology was Jane Jacobs dressed in latex and leather" (see paragraph 18).
5. **Link Across Chapters:** See the essays by Ishmael Reed and Marianna Torgovnick on neighborhoods in Chapter 18 and see the editorials by James J. Kilpatrick and Richard A. Epstein on uses of eminent domain in Chapter 19. Write an essay on interesting points of contact between Jacobs's argument and the experiences described by Reed and Torgovnick. Alternatively, consider how Jacobs might respond to the issue of eminent domain, and why.

6. **Application:** Use Jacobs's essay as a lens for observing and analyzing a neighborhood that you know. You might, for example, station yourself someplace in this neighborhood as Jacobs did: on the benches, on the median strip, on upper Broadway, or in front of the White Horse in the Village. What do you notice about the way people behave in this area? Gopnik notes that there is always a close relationship between property and culture. Consider how the neighborhood's architecture and the uses its buildings influence the absence or presence of what Jacobs calls "eyes on the street." You might also consider to what extent there is a "clear demarcation between what is public space and what is private space" (see paragraph 26). ◗

Mike Davis

Fortress Los Angeles

This piece is a *polemic* (from the Greek word for *warlike*) by Mike Davis: a former butcher, a longtime political activist, a professor, and the winner of a lucrative MacArthur Foundation grant—the so-called "genius" award given to the nation's most gifted creative minds. In the following excerpt from his most famous book, an urban study of contemporary Los Angeles entitled *City of Quartz* (1992), Davis examines how cultural attitudes and social class provide the actual material shape of urban design.

In Los Angeles—once a paradise of free beaches, luxurious parks, and "cruising strips"—genuinely democratic space is virtually extinct. The pleasure domes of the elite Westside rely upon the social imprisonment of a third-world service proletariat in increasingly repressive ghettos and barrios. In a city of several million aspiring immigrants (where Spanish-surname children are now almost two-thirds of the school-age population), public amenities are shrinking radically, libraries and playgrounds are closing, parks are falling derelict, and streets are growing ever more desolate and dangerous. 1

Here, as in other American cities, municipal policy has taken its lead from the security offensive and the middle-class demand for increased spatial and social insulation. Taxes previously targeted for traditional public spaces and recreational facilities have been redirected to support corporate redevelopment projects. A pliant city government—in the case of Los Angeles, one ironically professing to represent a liberal biracial coalition—has collaborated in privatizing public space and subsidizing new exclusive enclaves (benignly called "urban villages"). The celebratory language used to describe contemporary Los Angeles—"urban renaissance," "city of the future," and so on—is only a triumphal gloss laid over the brutalization of its inner-city neighborhoods and the stark divisions of class and race represented in its built environment. Urban form obediently follows repressive function. Los Angeles, as always in the vanguard, offers an especially disturbing guide to the emerging liaisons between urban architecture and the police state.

Forbidden City

Los Angeles's first spatial militarist was the legendary General Harrison Gray Otis, proprietor of the *Times* and implacable foe of organized labor. In the 1890s, after locking out his union printers and announcing a crusade for "industrial freedom," Otis retreated into a new *Times* building designed as a fortress with grim turrets and battlements crowned by a bellicose bronze eagle. To emphasize his truculence, he later had a small, functional cannon installed on the hood of his Packard touring car. Not surprisingly, this display of aggression produced a response in kind. On October 1, 1910, the heavily fortified *Times* headquarters—the command-post of the open shop on the West Coast—was destroyed in a catastrophic explosion, blamed on union saboteurs.

Eighty years later, the martial spirit of General Otis pervades the design of Los Angeles's new Downtown, whose skyscrapers march from Bunker Hill down the Figueroa corridor. Two billion dollars of public tax subsidies have enticed big banks and corporate headquarters back to a central city they almost abandoned in the 1960s. Into a waiting grid, cleared of tenement housing by the city's powerful and largely unaccountable redevelopment agency, local developers and offshore investors (increasingly Japanese) have planted a series of block-square complexes: Crocker Center, the Bonaventure Hotel and Shopping Mall, the World Trade Center, California Plaza, Arco Center, and so on. With an increasingly dense and self-contained circulation system linking these superblocks, the new financial district is best conceived as a single, self-referential hyperstructure, a Miesian skyscape of fantastic proportions.

5 Like similar megalomaniacal complexes tethered to fragmented and desolate downtowns—such as the Renaissance Center in Detroit and the Peachtree and Omni centers in Atlanta—Bunker Hill and the Figueroa corridor have provoked a storm of objections to their abuse of scale and composition, their denigration of street life, and their confiscation of the vital energy of the center, now sequestered within their subterranean concourses or privatized plazas. Sam Hall Kaplan, the former design critic of the *Times*, has vociferously denounced the antistreet bias of redevelopment; in his view, the superimposition of "hermetically sealed fortresses" and random "pieces of suburbia" onto Downtown has "killed the street" and "dammed the rivers of life."[1]

Yet Kaplan's vigorous defense of pedestrian democracy remains grounded in liberal complaints about "bland design" and "elitist planning practices." Like most architectural critics, he rails against the oversights of urban design without conceding a dimension of foresight, and even of deliberate repressive intent. For when Downtown's new "Gold Coast" is seen in relation to other social landscapes in the central city, the "fortress effect" emerges, not as an inadvertent failure of design, but as an explicit—and, in its own terms, successful—socio-spatial strategy.

The goals of this strategy may be summarized as a double repression: to obliterate all connection with Downtown's past and to prevent any dynamic association with the non-Anglo urbanism of its future. Los Angeles is unusual among major urban centers in having preserved, however negligently, most of its Beaux Arts commercial core. Yet the city chose to transplant—at immense public cost—the entire corporate and financial district from around Broadway and Spring Street to Bunker Hill, a half-dozen blocks further west.

Photographs of the old Downtown in its 1940s prime show crowds of Anglo, black, and Mexican shoppers of all ages and classes. The contemporary Downtown "renaissance" renders such heterogeneity virtually impossible. It is intended not just to "kill the street" as Kaplan feared, but to "kill the crowd," to eliminate that democratic mixture that Olmsted believed was America's antidote to European class polarization. The new Downtown is designed to ensure a seamless continuum of middle-class work, consumption, and recreation, insulated from the city's "unsavory" streets. Ramparts and battlements, reflective glass and elevated pedways, are tropes in an architectural language warning off the underclass Other. Although architectural critics are usually blind to this militarized syntax, urban pariah groups—whether young black men, poor Latino immigrants, or elderly homeless white females—read the signs immediately.

[1] *Los Angeles Times*, Nov. 4, 1978.

Finding the Analytical Lens

This strategic armoring of the city against the poor is especially obvious at street level. In his famous study of the "social life of small urban spaces," William Whyte points out that the quality of any urban environment can be measured, first of all, by whether there are convenient, comfortable places for pedestrians to sit. This maxim has been warmly taken to heart by designers of the high corporate precincts of Bunker Hill and its adjacent "urban villages." As part of the city's policy of subsidizing the white-collar residential colonization of Downtown, tens of millions of dollars of tax revenue have been invested in the creation of attractive, "soft" environments in favored areas. Planners envision a succession of opulent piazzas, fountains, public art, exotic shrubbery, and comfortable street furniture along a ten-block pedestrian corridor from Bunker Hill to South Park. Brochures sell Downtown's "livability" with idyllic representations of office workers and affluent tourists sipping cappuccino and listening to free jazz concerts in the terraced gardens of California Plaza and Grand Hope Park.

10 In stark contrast, a few blocks away, the city is engaged in a relentless struggle to make the streets as unlivable as possible for the homeless and the poor. The persistence of thousands of street people on the fringes of Bunker Hill and the Civic Center tarnishes the image of designer living Downtown and betrays the laboriously constructed illusion of an urban "renaissance." City Hall has retaliated with its own version of low-intensity warfare.

Although city leaders periodically propose schemes for removing indigents *en masse*—deporting them to a poor farm on the edge of the desert, confining them in camps in the mountains, or interning them on derelict ferries in the harbor—such "final solutions" have been blocked by council members' fears of the displacement of the homeless into their districts. Instead the city, self-consciously adopting the idiom of cold war, has promoted the "containment" (the official term) of the homeless in Skid Row, along Fifth Street, systematically transforming the neighborhood into an outdoor poorhouse. But this containment strategy breeds its own vicious cycle of contradiction. By condensing the mass of the desperate and helpless together in such a small space, and denying adequate housing, official policy has transformed Skid Row into probably the most dangerous ten square blocks in the world. Every night on Skid Row is Friday the 13th, and, unsurprisingly, many of the homeless seek to escape the area during the night at all costs, searching safer niches in other parts of Downtown. The city in turn tightens the noose with increased police harassment and ingenious design deterrents.

One of the simplest but most mean-spirited of these deterrents is the Rapid Transit District's new barrel-shaped bus bench, which offers a minimal surface for uncomfortable sitting while making sleeping impossible. Such "bumproof" benches are being widely introduced on the periphery of Skid Row. Another invention is the aggressive deployment of outdoor sprinklers. Several years ago the city opened a Skid Row Park; to ensure that the park could not be used for overnight camping, overhead sprinklers were programmed to drench unsuspecting sleepers at random times during the night. The system was immediately copied by local merchants to drive the homeless away from (public) storefront sidewalks.

Meanwhile Downtown restaurants and markets have built baroque enclosures to protect their refuse from the homeless. Although no one in Los Angeles has yet proposed adding cyanide to the garbage, as was suggested in Phoenix a few years back, one popular seafood restaurant has spent $12,000 to build the ultimate bag-lady-proof trash cage: three-quarter-inch steel rod with alloy locks and vicious out-turned spikes to safeguard moldering fishheads and stale french fries.

Public toilets, however, have become the real frontline of the city's war on the homeless. Los Angeles, as a matter of deliberate policy, has fewer public lavatories than any other major North American city. On the advice of the Los Angeles police, who now sit on the "design board" of at least one major Downtown project, the redevelopment agency bulldozed the few remaining public toilets on Skid Row. Agency planners then considered whether to include a "free-standing public toilet" in their design for the upscale South Park residential development; agency chairman Jim Wood later admitted that the decision not to build the toilet was a "policy decision and not a design decision." The agency preferred the alternative of "quasi-public restrooms"—toilets in restaurants, art galleries, and office buildings—which can be made available selectively to tourists and white-collar workers while being denied to vagrants and other unsuitables. The same logic has inspired the city's transportation planners to exclude toilets from their designs for Los Angeles's new subway system.[2]

Bereft of toilets, the Downtown badlands east of Hill Street also lack outside water sources for drinking or washing. A common and troubling sight these days is the homeless men—many of them young refugees from El Salvador—washing, swimming, even drinking from the sewer effluent that flows down the concrete channel of the Los Angeles River on the eastern edge of Downtown. The city's public health department has made no effort to post warning signs in Spanish or to mobilize alternative clean-water sources.

In those areas where Downtown professionals must cross paths with the 15
homeless or the working poor—such as the zone of gentrification along Broadway just south of the Civic Center—extraordinary precautions have been taken to ensure the physical separation of the different classes. The redevelopment agency, for example, again brought in the police to help design "twenty-four-hour, state-of-the-art security" for the two new parking structures that serve the *Los Angeles Times* headquarters and the Ronald Reagan State Office Building. In contrast to the mean streets outside, both parking structures incorporate beautifully landscaped microparks, and one even boasts a food court, picnic area, and historical exhibit. Both structures are intended to function as "confidence-building" circulation systems that allow white-collar workers to walk from car to office, or from car to boutique, with minimum exposure to the public street. The Broadway-Spring Center, in particular, which links the two local hubs of gentrification (the Reagan Building and the proposed Grand Central Square) has been warmly praised by architectural critics for adding greenery and art to parking. It also adds a considerable dose of menace—armed guards, locked gates, and ubiquitous security cameras—to scare away the homeless and the poor.

[2] Tom Chorneau, "Quandary Over a Park Restroom," *Downtown News*, Aug. 25, 1986.

The cold war on the streets of Downtown is ever escalating. The police, lobbied by Down-town merchants and developers, have broken up every attempt by the homeless and their allies to create safe havens or self-governed encampments. "Justiceville," founded by homeless activist Ted Hayes, was roughly dispersed; when its inhabitants attempted to find refuge at Venice Beach, they were arrested at the behest of the local council member (a renowned environmentalist) and sent back to Skid Row. The city's own brief experiment with legalized camping—a grudging response to a series of deaths from exposure during the cold winter of 1987—was abruptly terminated after only four months to make way for the construction of a transit maintenance yard. Current policy seems to involve perverse play upon the famous irony about the equal rights of the rich and poor to sleep in the rough. As the former head of the city planning commission explained, in the City of the Angels it is not against the law to sleep on the street per se—"only to erect any sort of protective shelter."[3] To enforce this proscription against "cardboard condos," the police periodically sweep the Nickel, tearing down shelters, confiscating possessions, and arresting resisters. Such cynical repression has turned the majority of the homeless into urban bedouins. They are visible all over Downtown, pushing their few pathetic possessions in stolen shopping carts, always fugitive, always in motion, pressed between the official policy of containment and the inhumanity of Downtown streets.

Sequestering the Poor

An insidious spatial logic also regulates the lives of Los Angeles's working poor. Just across the moat of the Harbor Freeway, west of Bunker Hill, lies the MacArthur Park district—once upon a time the city's wealthiest neighborhood. Although frequently characterized as a no-man's-land awaiting resurrection by developers, the district is, in fact, home to the largest Central American community in the United States. In the congested streets bordering the park, a hundred thousand Salvadorans and Guatemalans, including a large community of Mayan-speakers, crowd into tenements and boarding houses barely adequate for a fourth as many people. Every morning at 6 A.M. this Latino Bantustan dispatches armies of sewing *operadoras*, dishwashers, and janitors to turn the wheels of the Downtown economy. But because MacArthur Park is midway between Downtown and the famous Miracle Mile, it too will soon fall to redevelopment's bulldozers.

Hungry to exploit the lower land prices in the district, a powerful coterie of developers, represented by a famous ex-councilman and the former president of the planning commission, has won official approval for their vision of "Central City West": literally, a second Downtown comprising 25 million square feet of new office and retail space. Although local politicians have insisted upon a significant quota of low-income replacement housing, such a palliative will hardly compensate for the large-scale population displacement sure to follow the construction of the new skyscrapers and yuppified "urban villages." In the meantime,

[3] See "Cold Snap's Toll at 5 as Its Iciest Night Arrives," *Los Angeles Times*, Dec. 29, 1988.

Korean capital, seeking *lebensraum* for Los Angeles's burgeoning Koreatown, is also pushing into the MacArthur Park area, uprooting tenements to construct heavily fortified condominiums and office complexes. Other Asian and European speculators are counting on the new Metrorail station, across from the park, to become a magnet for new investment in the district.

The recent intrusion of so many powerful interests into the area has put increasing pressure upon the police to "take back the streets" from what is usually represented as an occupying army of drug-dealers, illegal immigrants, and homicidal homeboys. Thus in the summer of 1990 the LAPD announced a massive operation to "retake crime-plagued MacArthur Park" and surrounding neighborhoods "street by street, alley by alley." While the area is undoubtedly a major drug market, principally for drive-in Anglo commuters, the police have focused not only on addict-dealers and gang members, but also on the industrious sidewalk vendors who have made the circumference of the park an exuberant swap meet. Thus Mayan women selling such local staples as tropical fruit, baby clothes, and roach spray have been rounded up in the same sweeps as alleged "narcoterrorists."[4] (Similar dragnets in other Southern California communities have focused on Latino day-laborers congregated at streetcorner "slave markets.")

By criminalizing every attempt by the poor—whether the Skid Row homeless 20
or MacArthur Park venders—to use public space for survival purposes, law-enforcement agencies have abolished the last informal safety-net separating misery from catastrophe. (Few third-world cities are so pitiless.) At the same time, the police, encouraged by local businessmen and property owners, are taking the first, tentative steps toward criminalizing entire inner-city communities. The "war" on drugs and gangs again has been the pretext for the LAPD's novel, and disturbing, experiments with community blockades. A large section of the Pico-Union neighborhood, just south of MacArthur Park, has been quarantined since the summer of 1989; "Narcotics Enforcement Area" barriers restrict entry to residents "on legitimate business only." Inspired by the positive response of older residents and local politicians, the police have subsequently franchised "Operation Cul-de-Sac" to other low-income Latino and black neighborhoods.

Thus in November 1989 (as the Berlin Wall was being demolished), the Devonshire Division of the LAPD closed off a "drug-ridden" twelve-block section of the northern San Fernando Valley. To control circulation within this largely Latino neighborhood, the police convinced apartment owners to finance the construction of a permanent guard station. Twenty miles to the south, a square mile of the mixed black and Latino Central-Avalon community has also been converted into Narcotic Enforcement turf with concrete roadblocks. Given the popularity of these quarantines—save amongst the ghetto youth against whom they are directed—it is possible that a majority of the inner city may eventually be partitioned into police-regulated "no-go" areas.

The official rhetoric of the contemporary war against the urban underclasses resounds with comparisons to the War in Vietnam a generation ago. The LAPD's community blockades evoke the infamous policy of quarantining suspect

[4] *Los Angeles Times*, June 17, 1990.

populations in "strategic hamlets." But an even more ominous emulation is the reconstruction of Los Angeles's public housing projects as "defensible spaces." Deep in the Mekong Delta of the Watts-Willowbrook ghetto, for example, the Imperial Courts Housing Project has been fortified with chain-link fencing, restricted entry signs, obligatory identity passes—and a substation of the LAPD. Visitors are stopped and frisked, the police routinely order residents back into their apartments at night, and domestic life is subjected to constant police scrutiny. For public-housing tenants and inhabitants of narcotic-enforcement zones, the loss of freedom is the price of "security."

THINGS TO DO WITH THE READING

1. Apply the Method and Paraphrase × 3 to the reading (see pages 44–48 and 116–117). What significant words repeat? What strands do you find? What is opposed to what? And so what? How would you paraphrase the first sentence of paragraph 6?
2. Uncover assumptions in the piece, that is, reason back to its premises, the unstated givens upon which Davis's argument rests (see pages 132–133). First, list a few of the unstated assumptions. What, for example, are some of his unstated assumptions about the homeless and the poor in cities? Try reasoning back to premises with the first two sentences of the piece: if Davis believes this, what must he also already believe?
3. **Link:** Bring Davis and Jacobs together by locating difference within similarity (see pages 125–126). Jacobs and Davis have similar concerns, but they are writing at different points in time and about different places. Find the most significant point of contact between Davis's and Jacobs's ways of thinking about public spaces in cities. Given that similarity, what is the most revealing difference between the two arguments? Which of Davis's primary words does Jacobs's piece usefully illuminate? Consider, for example, the way the two writers use the word "street."
4. **Application:** Describe Davis's analytical method. List the key words that reveal his way of seeing a city. Then experiment with using his method as a lens for looking at a part of your campus or town. Is there, for example, a place where town or campus authorities have arranged things physically so as to encourage or discourage certain kinds of use and/or certain kinds of people? Note: You don't have to focus on homelessness or poverty. Make your priority thinking about public spaces and how they are managed.

FOR FURTHER RESEARCH: PLACES AND SPACES: CITIES AND SUBURBS

By Kelly Cannon, Reference Librarian

The readings and activities below invite you to further explore the theme of Places and Spaces: Cities and Suburbs. WARNING: Some essays are polemical; they are intended to promote insight and discussion (or a starting point for your next paper). To access the online readings, visit the *Writing Analytically with Readings* website at www.thomsonedu.com/english/rosenwasser.

Online

***American Factfinder*. 2005. United States Census Bureau. 3 November 2005.**
Graphical exploration of population density and other U.S. demographics based on U.S. census data.

Explore: Search on your community's name and then click on maps to get a visual of population density. Click on the maps themselves to get numerical data.

"Charter of the New Urbanism." *New Urbanism*. NewUrbanism.org. 3 November 2005.
Lists the basic tenets of NewUrbanism.org, a major not-for-profit concerned with remedies to urban blight and sprawl.

Explore: What, if anything, about the presentation of the website itself makes this organization's ideas more appealing?

Kirk, Patricia L. "Alternative Anchors." *Urban Land* (October 2003). 3 November 2005.
"With ambience becoming more important than ever, the [community] gathering place is beginning to replace the anchor."

Explore: How is the word "anchor" used here? Explore the website of the Urban Land Institute, the publishers of this article. Broadly conceived, what stance does this organization take on the subject of place and space in the United States?

Taylor, Jerry, and Peter Van Doren. "Sprawl for Me, But Not for Thee." *Heartland Institute*. 1 January 2001. 3 November 2005.
Contends that urban sprawl is loathed by the very people who cause it.

Explore: In further examination of the website, how does this one article on sprawl reflect the Heartland Institute's larger environmental views?

In Print

(Ask your librarian about possible online access to items marked with **.)

Hayden, Dolores. *A Field Guide to Sprawl*. New York: W.W. Norton, 2004.
Stunning aerial photographs of the history and effect of sprawl in the United States.

Explore: How do the images and text in this book work together to affect the audience? Can you think of a photograph you would take of your own community that would support or negate the author's stance on sprawl? What text would you write to accompany such a photograph?

****Lawlor, Julia. "Fighting the Battle of the Bungalow." *New York Times* (30 September 2005): F1–F7.**
Reports on the backlash against the coastal building boom nationwide, where mansions are replacing traditional cottages.

Explore: What are the differing views in this debate? To what extent does the writer of this article appear to take sides? How or how not?

****Maich, Steve. "Why Wal-Mart Is Good." *MacLean's* (25 September 2005): 26–33.**
Argues that Wal-Mart helps rather than hinders communities.

Explore: According to this article, what are the leading arguments against Wal-Mart? How does the author contend with these?

****Howell, Ocean. "The 'Creative Class' and the Gentrifying City." *Journal of Architectural Education* 59.2 (2005): 32–42.**
This study explores how Love Park in Philadelphia has been redesigned specifically to inhibit skateboarding. It argues that "bohemian" or "countercultural" lifestyles are becoming institutionalized agents of urban development.

Explore: What constitutes "bohemian" in this article? Have skateboarders or other "bohemians" affected any development in your community?

****Rappaport, Jordan. "The Shared Fortunes of Cities and Suburbs." *Economic Review (Federal Reserve Bank of Kansas City)* 90.3 (2005): 33–60.**
This study examines reasons for and patterns of urban sprawl and attempts to show how the success of a suburb is dependent on the health of its neighboring city.

Explore: What signs are there that this is a "scholarly" article? What types of evidence are used to support the author's conclusions? What type of evidence has the most impact? How so?

CHAPTER 17

Seeing

Quick Take

A recent article entitled "The Image Culture" by Christine Rosen (whose essay on cell phones opens Part 2: The Readings) begins by reflecting on the deluge of apocalyptic images that washed over us on the television and internet in the wake of Hurricane Katrina. Rosen goes on to consider the footage of the 9/11 attacks, citing our "saturation" by images. She quotes novelist Don DeLillo: "In our world we sleep and eat the image and pray to it and wear it too" (*The New Atlantis: A Journal of Technology and Society*, Fall 2005).

It has become a virtual cliché that in America the image has come to displace the word; and accordingly, in the schools and in the media, verbal literacy has lost ground to visual literacy. The aim of this chapter is not, however, to defend one side against the other. Rather, our overarching goal is to provide you with a vocabulary for seeing more acutely. This is a cultural as well as a perceptual matter. Inevitably, it involves attention to both the producing and the consuming ends of the so-called Image Culture: how images are created and for what ends, and how we have been conditioned to value and resist them.

ABOUT THE READINGS IN THIS CHAPTER

The interview that we conducted with photographer Joseph Elliott offers the primary lens for the selections in Seeing. Elliott distinguishes two primary ways of producing images—staging them and recording them. Attached to each of these approaches are assumptions that Elliott uncovers about how images communicate. Eventually, he evolves a series of qualified positions within the recorder/stager binary to arrive at a system for classifying a wide range of photographic approaches. Additionally, he offers specific technical advice for apprehending the formal elements of an image—what he refers to as "seeing the hand" of the photographer.

Next comes a classic and contentious piece entitled "In Plato's Cave" by philosopher and cultural critic Susan Sontag. Whereas Elliott values the photographer's role as a recorder of events, Sontag worries that the desire to record will supplant the desire to experience and become involved. Sontag worries that photography tends to appropriate (that is, "leach out") real life in a predatory fashion. And because photos tend to look recorded even though they all are staged, she argues, those in power exploit this fact to deceive us. Seeing, after all, tends to be believing.

Barry Lopez's "Learning to See" relocates the ethical discussion to the terrain of nature photography. He also returns the focus to some of the concerns with form discussed by Elliott. Lopez concentrates on the elusive photographic pursuit of light and spatial volume—of "the deep pattern of turbulence" and "indigenous time." The backbone of his essay is a narrative of how he came to give up his career as a photojournalist to concentrate on words rather than images. In the process of telling this story, he offers a striking comparison of the mindsets that go into capturing an event in words versus in pictures—and what each medium inevitably leaves out or keeps us from seeing.

The chapter concludes with John Berger's chapter on nudes from his famous book, *Ways of Seeing*. Like the other writers selected, he is interested in issues of spectatorship and power. His focus rests on the representation of the female form, and in particular, on how the nude functions as a category within which "women have been seen and judged as sights" and so, as Berger comments, "They do to themselves what men do to them. They survey, like men, their own femininity" (see paragraph 63). Following Berger's essay is an unconventional painting of a nude by Alice Neel and her full-frontal (clothed) portrait of a man. Readers are invited to use these as test cases for both the application and the limits of Berger's theories.

Finally, mention should be made of an essay included elsewhere in this book that easily could be incorporated here: Jack Gambino's "Demolition Zones: Contemporary Photography by Edward Burtynsky and Camilo Jose Vergara" (Chapter 16). Vergara is frequently mentioned in Elliott's interview as a representative "recorder."

Joseph Elliott, David Rosenwasser, and Jill Stephen

Looking at Photographs: Stagers and Recorders—an Interview with Joseph Elliott

Composed specifically for this book, this interview features Joseph Elliott, a noted photographer and a professor of art, on the subject of how photographers see. Elliott offers here a kind of short course on visual literacy from a photographer's point of view as he takes the authors through the two primary traditions of thinking about images: as recorded and as staged. In addition, he offers ways of analyzing the work of reigning art photographers in both traditions and suggests how we can expand our powers of observing the world that surrounds us. Since graduating with an M.F.A. from Pratt Institute, Elliott has had his photographs featured in 10 solo exhibits, 12 group exhibits, and many publications. He has also received 15 commissions from the Historic American Buildings Survey as well as numerous grants.

Note: the interviews that follow were conducted over a period of several months and are divided into seven meetings, each with its own title.

The First Meeting: 8/29/05 "The Two Camps"

David: Our book uses the metaphor of the lens to think about analyzing. Are 1
there primary lenses that you use when you think about photographers?

Joe: I see two camps: staging versus recording. Edward S. Curtis, the photographer of the American West, is a stager. He's not observing but staging. He's a romantic who fabricates a vision of the West. An interesting photographer to compare him to is Timothy H. O'Sullivan. If you Google-Image O'Sullivan, you'll see that he's a more dispassionate, severe recorder of the West.

David: So these approaches—staging and recording—are still present today?

Joe: Yes. Gregory Crewdson is a stager you might look at. His work has a cinematic feel. His point of view goes against the purist-observers, the ones who want to approach matters solely in the context of "Let's see what seeing is ..."

Another stager you might check out is Cindy Sherman, who has pho- 5
tographed herself for years in all manner of costumes and disguises (such as 1970s period dress). You might compare her with Diane Arbus, but with this difference: Arbus *found* the grotesque, but Sherman seems to say, "Let's just invent it." Sherman doesn't derive from Arbus; she draws on 1950's–60's popular culture, advertising images, movies and movie stills. In the current scene it seems as if films are getting more and more "still," and still photographers are getting more and more staged.

Jill: And contemporary recorders?

Joe: Andreas Gursky is an interesting recorder. His work seems to say, "Let's look at something clearly and make a giant print of it." Although he's a recorder most of the time, sometimes he digitally alters his images in subtle ways, perhaps in search of a more perfect banality. (For other straightforward types like Gursky, see Eggleston, Struth, Shore, and Sternfeld, who are replaying O'Sullivan. You could also think about my work and Vergara's.)

Jill: So you see yourself as a recorder, then?

Joe: I'm interested in a quality of seeing, with the aim to see things well and make a strong image. Then it is a matter of how to construct a frame and where to position the vantage point. I like to control frame and vantage point, as do all straight photographers, but not the object, so I'm not a fabricator. But like the fabricators, any photographer is clearly implicated by the process of taking photos. You are making an object, a photograph; you're creating, not just recording.

The Second Meeting: 10/21/05 "Burning Down the House"

The session begins with brief discussion of Alice in Wonderland *and the notion that that text is not simply words but a hybrid work of words and pictures—in which the pictures are integral— with a long history of illustration, starting with Lewis Carroll's own sketches (circa 1860) and famously followed by John Tenniel, whose illustrations are featured in the first edition.*

Joe: Carroll was also a well-known photographer of young girls in the early days 10
of photography as an art. Have you ever heard of Jock Sturges? Google-image him. He's a kind of modern-day Carroll who photographs children and adolescents, and who has been hounded by the authorities as morally suspicious.

Henry Peach Robinson and Oscar Rejlander were Carroll contemporaries, who we might term "Victorian fabricators."

Most photographers at this time were referred to as camera operators—recorders of images, trying to capture the real in some unmediated, unadulterated way, insofar as that is ever possible for a person with a camera. A photographer is inevitably selecting what to shoot and thus what not to shoot, and he or she is always framing the shot in various ways.

The Victorian fabricators saw themselves as artists. They embraced a belief in photography as an art form. The thought was, if you were going to produce a work of art, you had to make it entirely. You had to be seen as not just taking a picture of something out there and using factory-made materials to make the print. The audience had to be sure that the artist made the whole thing. From the 1870s–1890s the artist-photographer was a pictorialist—a person who had applied the emulsion and had made each photograph as its own object. The finished photos were often fabricated from many separate images, or were impressionistic, soft focused, subtly toned, resembling paintings and drawings.

Queen Victoria purchased a huge photo of the Last Supper done by Rejlander. A third key member of early Victorian photographic circles was Julia Margaret Cameron, who was well known in artistic and literary circles and was a friend of Tennyson.

The discussion moves to contemporary stagers and recorders in the world of art photography.

FIGURE 17.1 "Poling the Marsh Hay, England," 1886 by Peter Henry Emerson and Thomas Frederick Goodall

David: I saw in an interview with Gregory Crewdson, the stager you told me to Google, that he had traveled to various rust belt cities in the Northeast, and that Pittsfield, Massachusetts was eager to woo him, once he selected it as a possible site for his next project, Beneath the Roses. In a meeting with town officials, including the mayor and fire chief, he mentioned that he would like to burn down a house for one of his photographs, and "a few hours later they showed us up to 40 possible houses we were welcome to burn down. They were all owned by the city, on schedule for demolition" (See the link to "Desperate House Lives," available on the website for this book).

What's the difference between the photo that resulted and one of a house burning down here in Allentown? If he waited awhile listening to a police channel, he could have found many burning rust belt houses to photograph without employing 7 best boys and a huge production crew.

Joe: First of all, look at the context. Crewdson is a sophisticated Yale professor, top end. He sells in the most fashionable galleries in Chelsea. These factors in combination affect what he decides to shoot and how he decides to shoot it, the kind of art he decides to make. The image is designed in advance of the actual shooting, as it would be in filmmaking or advertising. Control is

FIGURE 17.2 Untitled (house fire) 1999 by Gregory Crewdson

To view this image in color, visit www.thomsonedu.com/english/rosenwasser

FIGURE 17.3 Untitled (pregnant woman) 2001 by Gregory Crewdson

To view this image in color, visit www.thomsonedu.com/english/rosenwasser

FIGURE 17.4 Untitled (ray of light) 2001 by Gregory Crewdson

To view this image in color, visit www.thomsonedu.com/english/rosenwasser

more complete that way. Racing to a real fire leaves too much to chance. Too much room for error. With such a huge production crew, Crewdson cannot afford to waste time. Crewdson isn't interested in making art using the real; his art isn't about the real.

David: Why burn a house down to make a picture?

Joe: It involves decadence, a level of decadence, the end of some period of American art. Decadence implies something that is over-ripe. It implies money, an affluence that is without striving. You see it in how carefully the water is spread on the ground to simulate recent rain in the photograph of the burning house, and in how big the image is, how lush the image is.

You can understand this better by comparing Crewdson to somebody like 20
Vergara. Vergara offers a counterpoint to this more fashionable art world. He actually photographs burnt out houses in Camden, New Jersey. [*See the Vergara photos in Jack Gambino's essay, "Demolition Zones: Contemporary Photography by Edward Burtynsky and Camilo Jose Vergara" in Chapter 16.*]

Crewdson is also attracted to burnt out rust belt cities, with a decayed past. But we need to focus on what he's looking at, and what world will receive his art.

The post-modern art world would say that Vergara, the more honest observer, doesn't get it. There is no irony in his work. He thinks real information matters. A gallery owner once told me, "You can't show documentary photographs (like Vergara's). It's not cool."

David: What is the "it" that Vergara doesn't get?

Joe: The idea that it's hopelessly romantic to think you can capture an image in real life, and bring it to people. But there's a step missing here. In the past there was a belief that you could shoot a picture of Omaha Beach as Robert Capa did, and the image would become vitally important to almost everyone. Spielberg's *Saving Private Ryan* fashions a long sequence of the D-Day invasion of Omaha beach based on this single Capa image.

Along these lines, Steichen's 1950s MOMA (Museum of Modern Art) exhibit, 25
The Family of Man, tried to show the universal commonalities of all world cultures in an effort to bring people together and promote world peace. Also see Lewis Hine, and the effect of his photos to motivate Congress to pass child labor protection laws.

Now that position gets discounted. It's seen as pretentious and as denying that the photographer is part of a world that oppresses anyway. So the thought is, if you cannot deny your complicity, maybe you just have to accept the construct, and make the biggest staged image you can and sell it to the wealthiest buyer you can find.

FIGURE 17.5 Portrait of a girl in mill (child labor) by Lewis Hine

Vergara, to return to our previous contrast, occupies a middle ground. His work won't tug at your heartstrings or show you the distended belly of a starving African child, but he'll show you picture after picture of Camden, and want you to *see* the setting as it is.

Another kind of straight photographer, less the anthropologist than Vergara, and more of what we might call a sensationalist, is the legendary Weegee, the 1940s photojournalist who listened to his police scanner in New York City and raced to position himself next to the guy who had jumped out of the window and splattered on the street. You might check out his famous book called *The Naked City*. Weegee anticipates Diane Arbus in some sense, and in another, Crewdson, who *aestheticizes* the crime scene. Arbus makes an art form out of the blunt, unflinching encounter. After we've seen Crewdson, Weegee's photos also seem staged.

David: You were speaking a few moments ago about the ethical position of the photographer, how he or she can get seen as contributing to some kind of oppression. Could you say more about that?

30 **Joe:** I have a friend, Bill Burke, who does what he calls "Docu-art": it looks like documentary investigation but is really an investigation of his own life choices and the resulting situations he finds himself in. In this case, Bill went to Vietnam and Cambodia to take photographs (he had skipped the actual war with a college deferment), and when he returned, he was attacked for "imaging the Other" (people of cultures and ethnicities unlike his own), using the "Other" as fodder for his work; he was accused of parasitism.

Burke's work fits the category of personal documentation, occupying a middle ground between the stagers and the recorders. His images are not staged, but are more consciously self-involved than the documentarians we have been discussing. Other members of this school are Larry Clark, *Tulsa* (teen age heroin addicts, his high school classmates), Sally Mann (her children), and Nan Goldin (street life in New York City in the 80s).

David: How do you categorize your own recent work in Costa Rica on the legacy of gold mining? Do your photos differ from the kind of documentary work that you've been talking about as more consciously self-involved?

Joe: The documentary, in the simplified sense of the word, means making the photographs that will become part of the history of a people or culture; you're trying to have as little influence as possible on the photographed subject. Of course, you do make decisions about what to shoot. You want it to last. You are "recording the site," which goes along with other methods of surveying, mapping, oral history, research, etc.—and otherwise, without the documenting, it could be lost. So you want to preserve it simply and cleanly, to be of use for the future. And the document itself also becomes part of the history.

We could apply this to Vergara's work. He'll have the map of Camden and drive up and down every street in his area of concentration to get total coverage. And he is not after some representative or iconic or symbolic images, but rather a density of images, a collecting.

35 **Jill:** Why does he record that space?

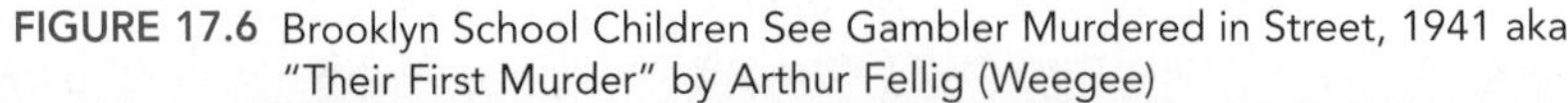

FIGURE 17.6 Brooklyn School Children See Gambler Murdered in Street, 1941 aka "Their First Murder" by Arthur Fellig (Weegee)

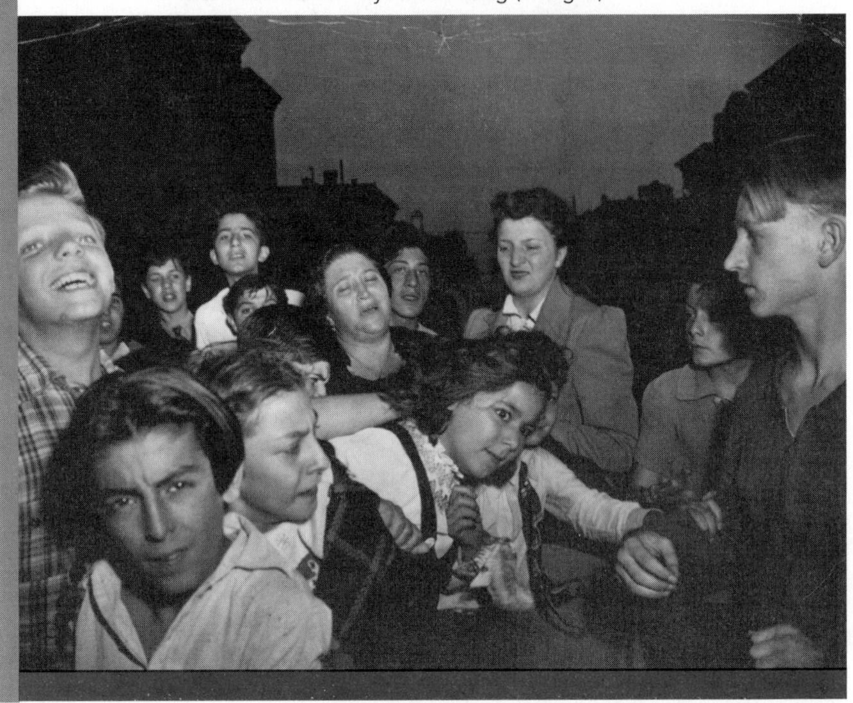

FIGURE 17.7 Untitled (Two men standing by car, Sumner, MS, ca. 1970) by William Eggleston

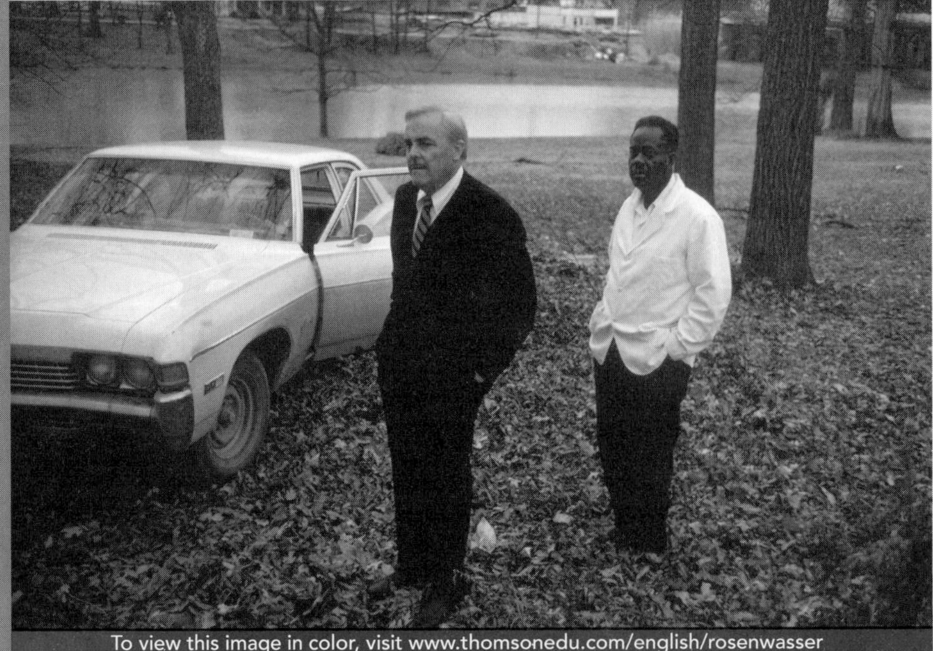

To view this image in color, visit www.thomsonedu.com/english/rosenwasser

Joe: Vergara wants to record change over time. He is interested in what happens to a place, the effects of politics, weather, crime, economic decline, etc. Only now, parts of Camden have become gentrified. What happens to the people? He doesn't follow them. (See the four Fern Street photos in Gambino's essay.)

Along these lines, you might look up Milton Rogovin, who returned to the same neighborhood in Buffalo over 20–30 years at regular intervals. He would find the same people and re-photograph them. Also you could look up Mark Klett's re-photographic surveys. He goes to sites that Timothy O'Sullivan, a documenter of the American West, had photographed and sets up his camera to see the site again but also to reveal how O'Sullivan had shaped the shot.

The Third Meeting: 10/28/05 "The Photographer's Hand"

David: At your direction, we've been spending a lot of time looking at books by John Szarkowski, the longtime director of photography at MOMA. How would you categorize him according to your Recorder/Stager categories?

Joe: Szarkowski was an advocate of the straight approach for many years. He seemed to ignore the fabricators. And so he essentially bypassed in his curatorship of MOMA's photographic collection the rise of the post-moderns (like Sherman and Wegman) who say all photographic representations are constructions, are contextualizations, are whatever the photographer makes of it, so let's make up the whole thing!

Szarkowski thus missed the boat when it came to including the fabricators in 40
the MOMA collection. And of course, this tradition had been producing work all along—e.g., Ray Metzger, Ralph Eugene Meatyard. In the 1970s Cindy Sherman would have given photos to MOMA for the asking. By the time MOMA came on board, five years ago, they paid a million dollars to catch up.

David: Szarkowski isn't still at MOMA, is he?

Joe: He has retired. Peter Galassi is now curator at MOMA. There is no one curator as influential as Szarkowski had been. But there are now many galleries in Chelsea that show photographers, whereas there were really only two in the mid 1970's, Witkin and Light galleries.

Szarkowski's choices are back in vogue, extolling the straightforward value of the big camera, showing meticulous details, as evident in certain photographers of the 1970s who are again becoming prominent. These include Stephen Shore, Joe Sternfeld, and William Eggleston, all color photographers.

Another change in the photography curatorial scene is that it has become more academy-oriented. Szarkowski was himself a photographer, as Stieglitz and Steichen before him had been. They were not trained in art programs or art history. Now the curators all have that training.

David: I've been meaning to ask you, how do the recorders view the stagers? And 45
how do the stagers, or, as you sometimes call them, the fabricators tend to view themselves?

Joe: The photo-art world is so diverse that there is a "live and let live" mentality now. The fabricators see themselves as being in some sense more honest, for admitting that they're making it up. This is the implicit argument in Crewdson's work. In his photo of the house on fire, the people on the train track on the other side of the frame are a competing focal point by design. Nothing is an accident in the photo. He wants it to be carefully observed, to invite a close reading. We may think of a photograph having an initial impact, but there's also something else going on, a counterpoint, a set of messages. A lot of this kind of work resembles film-making; the photograph is only a piece of it. The photograph is like a performance piece recorded by a camera that is being used in a straightforward way. Is it a photograph or an installation (or performance piece?) recorded in a photograph?

On the other hand, some of the recorders probably resent the success of the fashionable stagers for being driven by trend rather than the search for truth.

Jill: This reminds me of a remark that Szarkowski makes in *The Photographer's Eye*—that we tend to have faith in what we see in a photograph as real, but in fact the photographer is always "hiding his hand."

Joe: The question to ask beginning students is not, How does the photographer hide his hand? but Where is the photographer's hand? They assume there is no hand! In that famous Alfred Stieglitz photograph "Georgia Engelhard"–it's on the cover of Szarkowski's *Looking at Photographs*—we need to ask why Stieglitz included the edge, with the part of an urn and a rubber tree. *Where is the hand? is the question they need to lead with.* In Crewdson, by contrast, the hand is much easier to see. In the straightshooters it is less obvious.

The tradition of fabricators is full of other rich examples where we can easily 50
see the hand. Check out the work of Les Krims. His work was part of a 1970s phase in which photographers made little books. One is called "Making Chicken Soup," and features his mother doing exactly that in the kitchen—only she's naked. Another is called "The Incredible Stack'O'Wheat Murders" and features shots of murder scenes, but in each one there is a stack of pancakes. These are precedents for Crewdson.

O. Winston Link's photos of 1950's steam trains lit by hundreds of flash bulbs are another great precedent for Crewdson. Link in turn reminds us of the train motif in the surreal paintings of De Chirico and Magritte. In their paintings, though, the train, along with clocks, represents Modernism's rebellion against notions of Progress and clock time. But in Link's case the train represents the nostalgic past. The symbol has taken on a different meaning.

David: So in the kinds of photographs you've been talking about, the photographer tries to show his hand … ?

Joe: At the root of so much of the history of photography as a tradition is the question of where the art lies. Is the art in the making, the fabricating of the image? Is the art in the recording as cleanly and accurately as possible? Is the art an intellectual activity such as Duchamp's urinal, where naming it as art, framing it as art, makes it art? Szarkowski is most faithful to the second item in this list: if you take the machine and use it precisely and consciously, it will produce art. So, for example, he includes anonymous aerial shots taken from bombers in World War II in his book *Looking at Photographs*.

Photography became widely marketable in galleries when the whole process became detached from the hand of the photographer. Some prefer to be called "an artist who works with a camera" rather than "photographer." Photographers who make their own prints in the darkroom are now seen as hopelessly craftsy.

FIGURE 17.8 "Georgia Engelhard," 1921 by Alfred Stieglitz

To view this image in color, visit www.thomsonedu.com/english/rosenwasser

Jill: This whole discussion is making me think about the effects of digital technology. How does the rise of the computerized image affect the way you think about "the hand"? 55

Joe: Students who take beginning photography with me love to work in the dark room; it's all about the difference from producing digital images. Traditional photography is simpler, more tangible, more hands-on.

I also teach a course in digital photography. I can teach it coming out of the way I teach black and white—that there are certain roadblocks and limitations. But people don't normally think of it that way. The lens, the ability to capture light, too much or too little, these things are usually taken care of in automatic mode, but the digital camera can be taken back to a manual mode.

Manipulation of the image using Photoshop is not without precedent. Collage and montage, which the Modernists were famous for, anticipate the way a computer cuts and pastes. It's just easier now to amend the image, and it can be done so mindlessly.

Jill: So at least to some people, digitalization has to do with interfering somehow with the original recorded image?

Joe: For Vergara the photograph is evidence, with minimal "interference." It's 60
straight photography. This raises the question, how is evidence affected by "the hand" of the photographer? Photographs are of course all evidence, but evidence of what? And they are all inevitably constructs.

Vergara is coming from the surveyors, the Western survey photographers, a tradition of imperialist mapping. He is standing that tradition on its head by mapping the results of cultural and economic imperialism within American cities.

David: Can you tell us more about the tradition of survey photography? What made it imperialist?

Joe: The photographers—people like Carleton Watkins, O'Sullivan, and A.J. Russell—were hired by the U.S. Geological Survey and by the railroads in order to photograph all of the resources along new routes. Photographers were mapping the stuff that was ready to be taken by new investors. This was part of the exercise of Manifest Destiny in the opening of the West to commerce. So people argued that these new surveys of the West were needed to map our country, but one motivation was to discover the country's resources and know where they were. It's imperialist because you push the Native Americans out of the way.

Vergara comes at the other end of this tradition. His photographs say, well, this is what happened as a result of political and economic decisions that have shaped land use, property values, and people's lives.

Other documentarians were more sensationalist. In the tradition of news- 65
paper photography, for example, the photographs of Weegee convey the circumstances in which they were taken. This is unlike Vergara, whose work is much more distanced. Weegee is more of a raw sensationalist, an inverted Crewdson, almost a sentimentalist. When I look at Weegee's images, it's as if he's saying, "If you can't smell your subject, you're not close enough." They're taken with a big flash to produce that gritty light. There's a coarse tonal range, it's stark: the technology of the newspaper. The gritty light seems to fall off around the edges.

The Fourth Meeting: 11/10/05 Photographs and Paintings

Jill: Last time you were talking about the photographer's hand and the charge from some quarters that darkroom work has become quaint and nostalgic. Could you say more about that?

Joe: Fabricators tend to view the need for the dark room and the artist's hand as quaint—as too "craftsy," too absorbed in the making of "the thing itself." If you are Cindy Sherman and don't make it yourself, your art has moved to the realm of idea. For the postmodern photographer, the dark room is a waste of time. In this context, we might consider Crewdson as an impresario and director, who looks through the lens to make sure the shot is framed the right way but doesn't click the shutter. What the darkroom ace knows is just not that important. Crewdson hires darkroom aces (technicians) to work for him.

Jill: You've been telling us that there are different kinds of recorders and different schools of thought on fabrication. What at base *is* fabrication?

Joe: It is anything beyond point-and-shoot, whether the artist is building an elaborate set, like Crewdson, or cutting up and reassembling collages, like Metzger. You might also check out the work of Ralph Meatyard (an optometrist in Louisville). This collage process is also absorbed into painting, as in the "stuttering" Cubistic painting of *Nude Descending a Staircase* by Marcel Duchamp. Some people think that photography imitated Modernist painting, but the fact is that Modernist painters were influenced by photography. Cubism sees things from a lot of different angles at virtually the same time.

Jill: So the Cubists were influenced by photography? 70

Joe: At least by their knowledge of what the camera could do—how it sees.

Jill: Szarkowski points out that Edgar Degas, the French impressionist painter, was also an amateur photographer whose paintings were influenced by the structure of photographs.

Joe: Fabricators come from more than one tradition. One of these is the tradition of late 19th-century photographers like Henry Peach Robinson and Oscar Rejlander and Lewis Carroll, who dressed young girls in costumes. The other tradition comes out of European Modernism, and includes Bauhaus figures such as Moholy-Nagy, Hannah Hoch, and John Hartfield. This latter tradition features a combination of photography and print and drawing, in some cases reframing images from the popular press, as in Dada. You might want to check out Hans Belmer, who did grotesque, reconstructed dolls. His work is interesting in the context of the contemporary photographer Loretta Lux, a subtle fabricator who makes doll-like images of children. At the (Chicago) Institute of Design, Moholy-Nagy reinvents Bauhaus aesthetic, where Metzger is his student.

In the 1930s Bauhaus, there was the conviction that the machine should be used to make art—that intelligent art for the masses could be the product of the machine. But it is not art if no hand is involved (versus Szarkowski's assumption that you can make art without pretense, as in the aerial photographs). Multiple exposures like Metzger's make the constructedness of the image overt; they render the photographic process more self-conscious. If you have a machine and use it thoughtfully, it makes art.

FIGURE 17.9 *Nude Descending a Staircase #2* by Marcel Duchamp

To view this image in color, visit www.thomsonedu.com/english/rosenwasser

The Fifth Meeting: 11/18/05 On Portraiture

David: I spent some time Googling the photographers you mentioned last week. 75
In particular I was intrigued by Loretta Lux [*takes out copies—starting with the portrait of the girl in pigtails*]. What's the difference between this photograph and a snapshot? What do you notice about it?

Joe: First of all, the color. It's so flat; we could call it desaturated. Look at the tonal difference between the complexion of the face and the sky behind her. The difference is very slight. So the effect is to flatten the space. And the sky is straight out of Photoshop. This photograph is constructed in a computer. [*Note: please see copies of these photos online to apprehend the color.*]

It's interesting to compare Lux's work with Crewdson's. Hers is not like Crewdson's work, which operates in real space. He's limited to what the camera can record. But her work, with that spatial flattening, is comparatively unreal. Crewdson thinks of his art more as a film-maker would. You build a set; you control the lighting. If you went there and looked into the lens, it would look the way the photograph does.

But Lux, if you look at the heads in those portraits of the young boy set against the clouds, they're ever so slightly stretched ... it creates a kind of surrealist effect. The viewer says, "Oh, okay, wait a minute. The space is a little weird in this photograph, isn't it? Why are the colors this way? Why are the heads this way? Am I awake? Or am I dreaming?"

David: So what is Lux getting at?

Joe: Well, maybe it's something like this: we all like to have our kids have their 80
portraits taken at a studio. She's playing with and calling attention to our sense of what a portrait is. It's fabricated. And it's cheesey. "Why do we go to Wal-Mart and get these portraits made?," her work might be asking.

Her work is getting us to see that the typical child's portrait is staged. It's projecting an idealized image, a serene and perfect vision, not the messy room and screaming kid. The portrait represents what we think things should be like, not what they're really like.

And she's interested in this—our interest in portraits. Portraits and snapshots make up the vast majority of all photos made. People want to look at other people. In Lux, the children are idealized in a surreal way. The image is perfect in its own self-containment, but disorienting, off in ways that are hard to put your finger on.

David: Okay, so you're saying that these photos are satiric; they're sending up the conventions of portraiture. If you look at satire in literary terms, however, it's not only directed at certain targets; it's also coming from some relatively stable point of view. Where is Lux standing for her critique?

Joe: I think that the visual artist does not usually want to go that far. She's satisfied to point it out. What else is it? What is the surrealists' goal? Must it be an avant garde position, something never seen before? Or can her artist's role be that of a barometer, reflecting back to the culture what we are?

This can lead us to wonder, are artists really at the forefront of the culture, as 85
a lot of people like to think, or are they rather a barometer bringing out for the rest of us what is already happening, but which we may not be seeing? Maybe they're barometers rather than initiators.

I took a field trip with the senior art majors last Monday to the studio of a working sculptor. He made a powerful impression on them. The guy was a kind of living caricature of the self-involved, arrogant artist. He claimed that to make an impact you needed to create stuff that had never been seen before, and if he decided any of his own work was derivative, he'd throw it out. He was saying that the artist's role is to be the inventor of culture, not just a cultural analyst using the culture as material to work over.

This reminds me of another book by Szarkowski called *Mirrors and Windows*. The mirrors part suggests that photographs cause the viewer to see himself or herself. The windows help us to see what's out there more carefully, by framing it. In this context, Lux's portraits bounce us back to the conventions normally used to set up a portrait. But her work is twisting this and making us self-conscious of the conventions. But it's subtle, and things we think are natural—children's portraits—are really not natural; they're fabricated.

FIGURE 17.10 Portrait of a Girl #1 by Loretta Lux

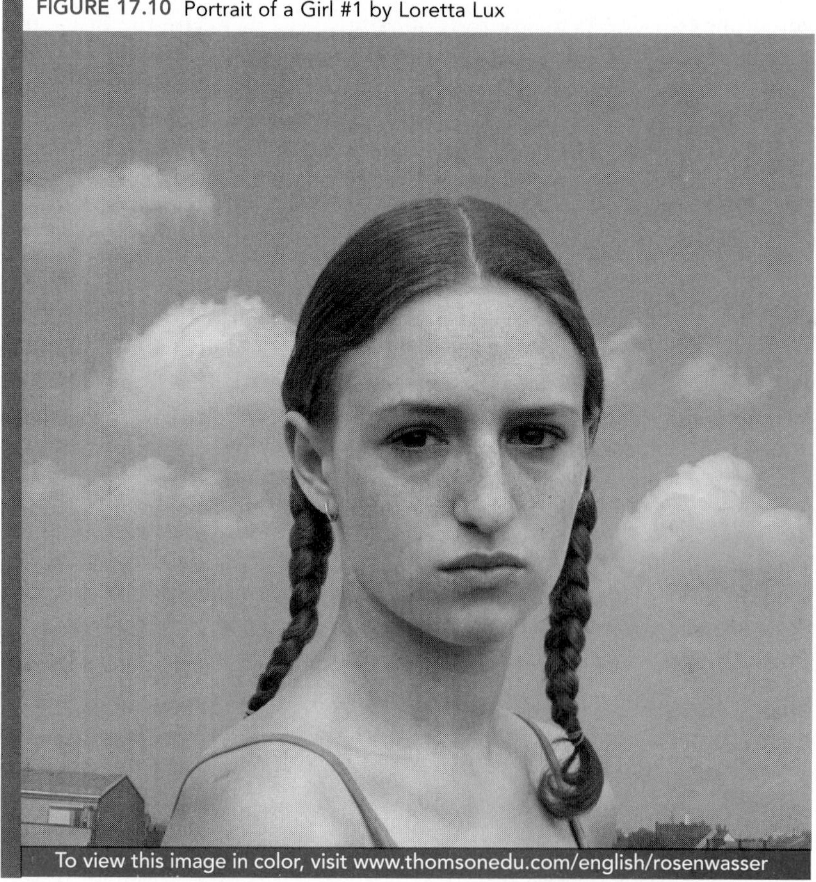

To view this image in color, visit www.thomsonedu.com/english/rosenwasser

FIGURE 17.11 Boy in a Blue Raincoat #2 by Loretta Lux

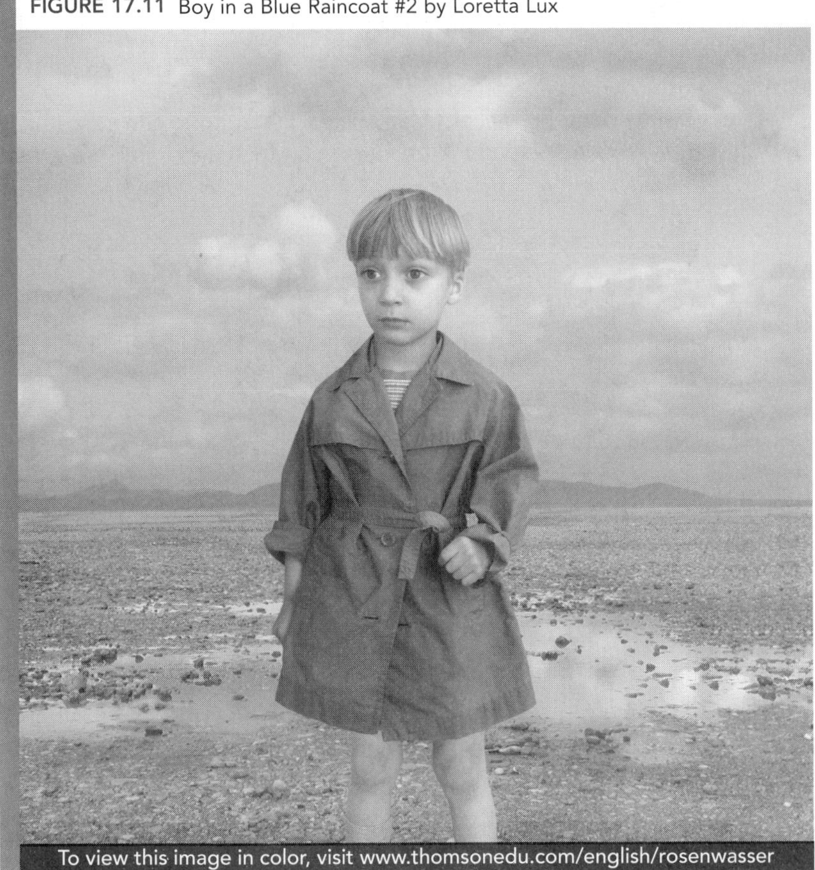

To view this image in color, visit www.thomsonedu.com/english/rosenwasser

David: Could you say more about the frame?

Joe: A frame requires a different kind of seeing, entirely different from the way we normally see. It makes us see and construct in a formal sense that has its own reasons for being; it's about conveying space, about balance, about traditional beauty in the relationship among the parts. Another way to look at it is that it forces us to examine everything inside the frame. Burtynski and the straightforward photographers induce us to look at what's inside the frame in some dispassionate way—all is equal inside the frame; things included are carefully chosen.

An illuminating comparison in this context might be between Lux and the work 90
of Eugene Smith. [*Joe turns to the portrait of the country doctor, which first appeared in the 1950s in* Life Magazine, *on page 150 of Szarkowski's* Looking at Photographs.] Smith's work has classical form—note how the figure of the doctor is centered, and thrust forward into the frame. He wants us to see a more heroic figure than the rest of us are. But framing gets us to examine carefully what's inside.

Jill: This reminds me of what the contemporary American poet Robert Pinsky has said about artistic truth: that it is not insistent but poised. Poise is a key word for him.

Joe: I would connect the word poise with the work of Walker Evans, Helen Levitt, and Roy deCarava as well as with Eugene Smith. Smith's work is so sculpturesque. It's like Michelangelo. He's a good example of romantic intensification. He's got a journalistic code to obey. But there is fabrication of a sort. "This is why people want to become doctors," his photograph is saying. Smith is interesting to contemplate, because he's so different from Crewdson or Lux.

FIGURE 17.12 Untitled (Dr. Ceriani with Injured Child, 1948)—black and white photo by W. Eugene Smith

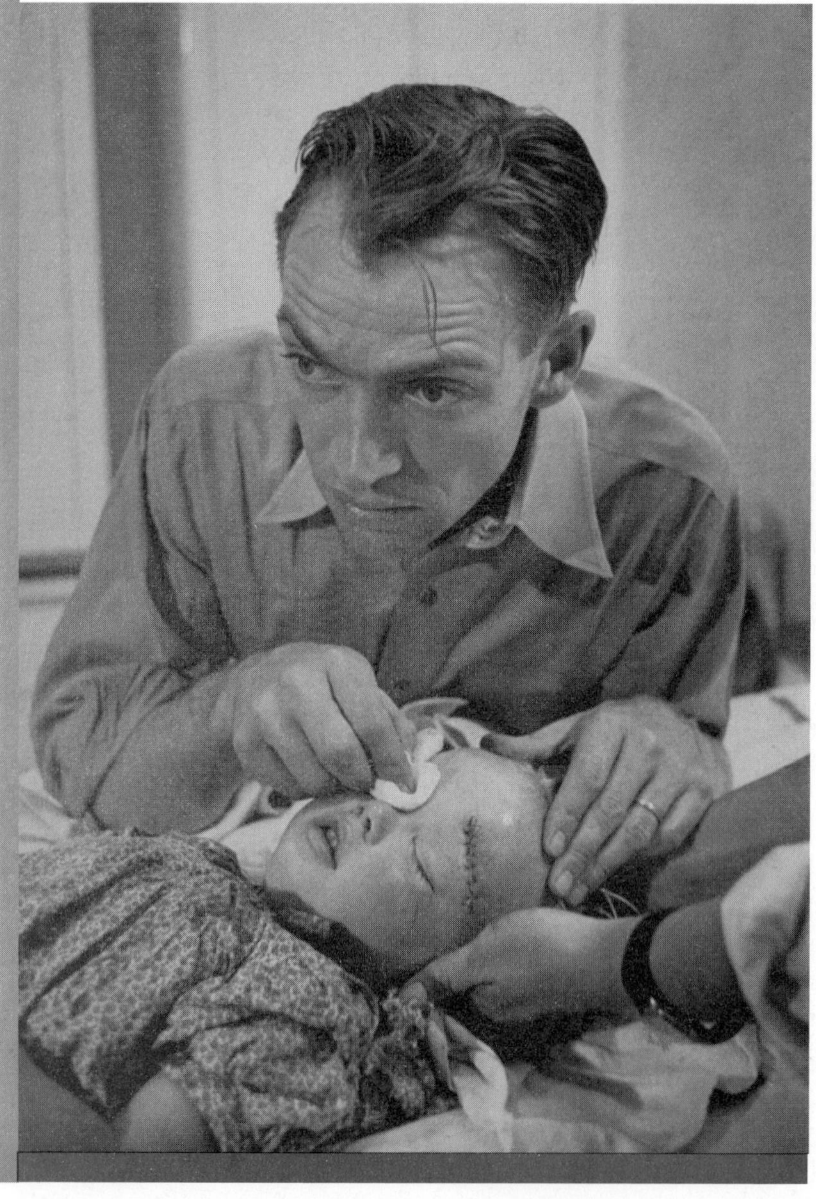

Jill: Some fabricators overdo romantic intensification on purpose, don't they?

Joe: Yes, like Lux, though I'm not sure that romantic is the correct word for Lux. Lux calls attention to this. Try to compare Lux to another photographer named Reineke Dijkstra, who compares with Gursky and Burtynsky—she's very straight.

[*Joe looks at the famous Andreas Gursky photograph of the candy and other food* 95
items, "99 Cent" (1999).] This photograph is huge—10' × 8'—and you can read the label on every Snickers bar, and all the things inside the frame are equal. He's showing us how we're surrounded with unending crappy stuff. The photograph is making a huge critique in a dispassionate way.

David: Well, who is doing romantic portraiture?

Joe: We have the clearly fabricated portraiture of Edward Curtis; he puts Native Americans up against a sylvan background in all their tribal gear and feathers. And while W. Eugene Smith has been out of fashion for all his romanticizing, at least he is doing it in a real context.

In thinking about portraits, it is interesting to think about the relationship between photographers and their subjects. In the famous Walker Evans' portraits of sharecroppers, the figure of the woman is tight-lipped. She does not want to be photographed, but she is allowing it. The husband is more accommodating, but he is still resisting. But Smith's figures do not resist the camera. They go along with it. They are part of the project.

The Sixth Meeting: 12/2/05 Varieties of Documentarians (Recorders)

Note: The photographers discussed in this interview later appear in a list of categories that Elliott has composed, which is included at the end of these interviews. The boldfaced labels in this interview are taken from that list.

Joe: In contemporary photography we want to be aware of the distance, that a photo is not just a piece of life; it's detached. One of the earlier assumptions was that a little camera could take you *into* life (for example: Brassai, Capa, Weegee).

From 1925 until recently, there was the assumption that the small, portable, 100
fast camera could bring us a slice of life, the essence of an event, a decisive moment. That slice of life, Salgado, Cartier-Bresson tradition has come to an end in art photography. And that may be because, why try to catch life in still form? Because it's superseded by video, by the videographers. But when things are moving, you can't meditate on them. We need the camera to stop time.

Jill: So is the small camera/slice of life approach always in the service of what you call recording?

Joe: In the documentary tradition, such as the photographs of W. Eugene Smith, *you are there*. As a photographer you bring the world to people with all the sweat attached. But Smith has also fabricated; he has framed the shot, controlling where we look, and so forth. And he has taken a lot of pictures of this guy. All in all, he has intensified the tools for making us see.

If you wanted to look at other comparable heroic photographs of this sort by Smith, check out the Albert Schweitzer picture, the white doctor in the jungle, bringing hope to these unfortunate lepers. Or there's a similar one of a Pittsburgh steel worker.

FIGURE 17.13 Andreas Gursky, "99 Cent," 1999

To view this image in color, visit www.thomsonedu.com/english/rosenwasser

Or if you wanted to move to more contemporary documentarians, try Sebastiao Salgado's *Workers* or Eugene Richards, who is grittier. These people are documentarians, but I call them **idea-driven documentarians** because they have a position that shapes the way they execute their photographs.

There is another interesting photographer in this category, Lauren 105
Greenfield, who is making a big splash. She focuses on girl culture. She's looking at suburban culture, not at Africa like Salgado or the ghetto, like Richards, who looks at crack addicts in Philly (and gets flak for exploiting their dire situation for his own benefit). She critiques young women's obsession with beauty in the culture. Is she saying this consumption is a bad thing? I don't know. See her image of teenagers in a convertible in California on the way to the beach, in swimsuits.

Jill: You also have a category that you call personal documentarians. How do they differ from the ones you call idea-driven?

Joe: Let's consider Nan Goldin. Her work is a cross between self-portraiture and the totally fabricated world of Cindy Sherman. But Goldin is a participant observer, as in anthropology. Whereas Eugene Smith is supposed to be a fly on the wall, Goldin turns the camera on herself as much as she does on the subcultures she documents. That's why I would call her a **personal documentarian**. The same goes for Sally Mann, who documents her own family. Her kids become actors in their own documentation, so she produces a documentary with the explicit cooperation of the subject.

Or consider Larry Sultan. He is a photographer of identity issues. He does "Pictures from Home," a series of his parents. He is a documentarian *and* a stager, doing photo essays about life in California. His colors and style anticipate Crewdson.

Jill: There are, then, documentarians who cross the line between the two camps, stagers and recorders?

Joe: Yes. And there are fabricators whose work comes out of the documentary 110
tradition of recorders, but in a clearly staged way. Consider Lorna Simpson, an African-American who photographs staged re-enactments of black women dressed in colonial costumes as slaves in the house. She is examining identity though these re-enactments—her work offers *pictures of representations: it's a framing of the representation.*

There is another interesting photographer in this context, An-My Le. She teaches at Bard, went to Yale. She photographs re-enactments of battles in Vietnam; this is a search for identity (she is Vietnamese). She does not use her own family history but someone else's fabrication of that history.

David: This leads to a problem common in post-modernism. Once you get rid of authenticity as a viable concept (since everything is a representation or role), it is extremely difficult to distinguish between kinds or degrees of fabrication in photographs, between Smith and Crewdson.

Joe: Do people no longer care where truth is located?

Jill: Your post-modernist would say it's all images on TV.

FIGURE 17.14 A community above Chimborazo, Ecuador, 1982 by Sebastiao Salgado

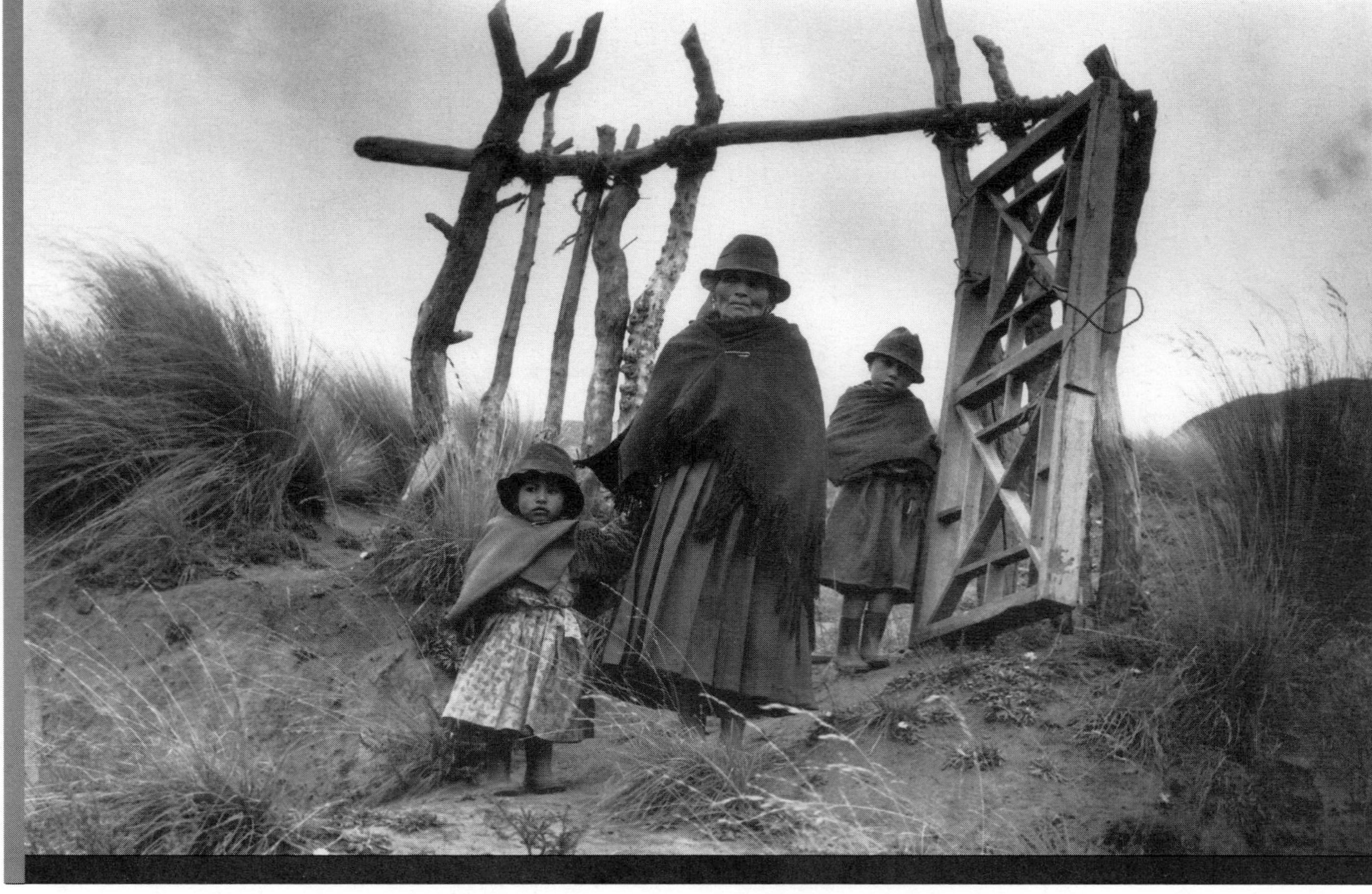

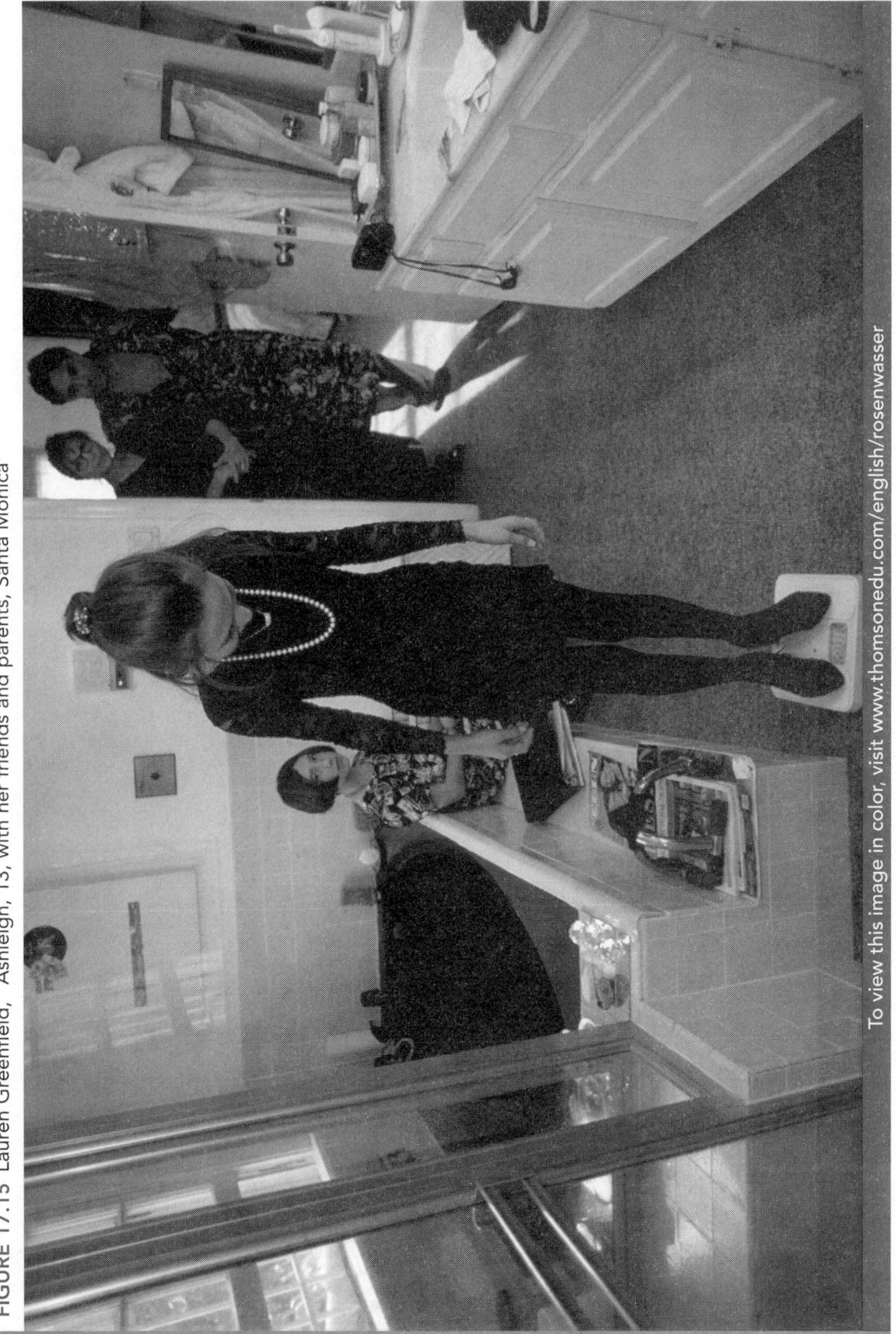

FIGURE 17.15 Lauren Greenfield, "Ashleigh, 13, with her friends and parents, Santa Monica"

To view this image in color, visit www.thomsonedu.com/english/rosenwasser

FIGURE 17.16 Girl with cigarette by Sally Mann

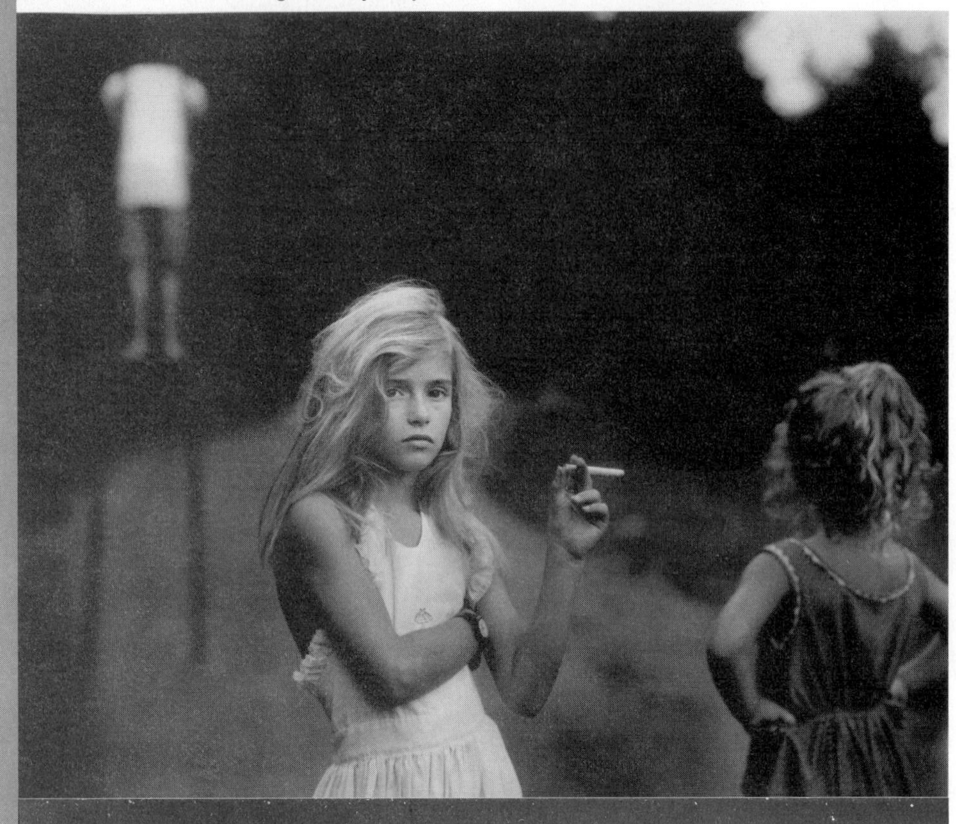

Joe: These images really are beautiful, technologically speaking—spectacular, if you choose to look at them.

Jill: How do we deal with those who are captivated by the televised image?

Joe: I pretend the TV world is not out there. The students have the camera, and within that context they'll explore and appreciate the world of black and white, learning to distinguish a good image from a bad one. It's simpler, quieter, bucolic, and they can claim ownership.

Jill: One of my students who is also taking your photography course mentioned that he was told to go shoot, and he started with guys in the middle of the frame and nothing else going on. But soon he learned how much more there was to think about in taking a good photograph.

Joe: Yeah, for example, I do not allow beginning students to crop their images. The frame of the image must be thought through by the artist. It would violate the art to crop; a photograph, they learn, is meticulously put together.

One of my models here is Eugene Smith, who was an anomaly in the world of 120
Life Magazine photographers. In the old days, the magazine would develop and select images from among all those submitted on film by its photographers. But Smith refused. He wanted to select and print the image himself. So he quit *Life*. He wanted the control to exhibit the maximum romantic values, as in the "Country Doctor" series.

David: On that note, what about photographers who are primarily interested in the medium itself?

Joe: I know this is a category we haven't discussed—the **Formalists**. It exists between the documentarians and the post-modern stagers. Formalists are mostly interested in how the image is framed and how photographic controls are used to form the image—its design. This category includes small camera explorers like Andre Kertesz and Lee Friedlander, but also artists who work on a more monumental scale, like Edward Weston, Aaron Siskind, and Hiroshi Sugimoto.

David: I've been looking at the photos in the *Blind Spot* magazines you gave me, especially from John Divola's "As Far As I Can Get" series. How would you locate his work?

Joe: His work is a form of fabrication. He is doing a kind of conceptual art move. You set up a lot of parameters with instructions in order to accomplish your art, and then you apply them. Sol Lewitt is an example. Divola does this. So does Ed Ruscha in his "26 Gasoline Stations" series. There is also his small fires series—it includes pictures of the flame on a glass ring, a cigarette, some pieces of paper burning. Another conceptual person is William Wegman, who established a basic collaboration with his dog, and he was determined to operate within that framework. My category for these artists is **Prescribed Process** (more commonly called Conceptual Art).

Jill: Oh, so the artist makes some rules to follow, and then the photographing 125
becomes a kind of controlled experiment?

Joe: Yes, it's not like Ruscha picked only certain gas stations to photograph because they were beautiful, or whatever, he had decided to photograph them all within a certain space—that was his rule.

The Seventh Meeting: 12/13/05 Writing about Photographs

David: One photographer you've said very little about is … you. We're sitting in this room across from one of the photographs that is part of your Bethlehem Steel series.

Joe: I began making photos at Bethlehem Steel in 1989 and continued until the plant closed in 1999. The motive was fascination with this gargantuan relic of the Machine Age. If I had to categorize the work, I would have to call myself a structural documentarian.

Jill: It's an interesting photograph. There's the protective clothing hanging on the wall. Is that a hat? Did you light the picture?

FIGURE 17.17 Portfolio of ten black and white gas station photos, 1962 by Ed Ruscha

FIGURE 17.18 Blast furnace rest area, Bethlehem, PA, 1992. 20" × 24" gelatin silver print by Joseph Elliott

Joe: No, the light came in from the window. I got that picture in less than minute. 130
The subject did not know he was being photographed. I just looked over and saw it, and I set up really quickly and took the shot. The foot of another man sneaks into the frame on the lower left. I only noticed this when I printed the photograph. The foot reminds us that there is a world going on outside the frame.

Jill: When I teach poetry-writing, we spend time thinking about how the details in most descriptive writing are implicitly metaphorical—that is, they are both literal and figurative.

David: What do you see as metaphorical in Joe's photograph?

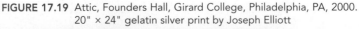

FIGURE 17.19 Attic, Founders Hall, Girard College, Philadelphia, PA, 2000. 20" × 24" gelatin silver print by Joseph Elliott

Jill: Well, the man is slightly out of focus, as if in motion; the image reminds us of the passage of time. He is in a box surrounded by his protective clothing, the hat, the gas mask. So the picture is all about containment and safety, but we also know it's a picture about something—the soon to be closed Bethlehem Steel—about to pass into oblivion.

Joe: Yes, I can see the containment, but if you look at it another way, it is hard to tell where the man is in relation to the space. We could be seeing a mirror reflection of him, or he could be inside the box.

Jill: As we talk I am thinking about how some people are inclined to look for 135
"messages" in photographs, which isn't exactly right. Others decide that they can make of the photograph whatever they wish, which isn't right either.

Joe: I have been reading a small book called *A Primer for Visual Literacy* by Donis A. Dondis. She says there are three levels on which we can look at a visual image: the representational, the formal, and the symbolic. People often want to jump to the symbolic. But we also need to deal with the other two levels whenever we discuss an image. The levels are not always equally important. As a practitioner I usually stay in the realms of the first two. When I teach beginning students we spend most of our time talking about the second.

Jill: In closing, could you talk to us a little bit about how you look at photographs, and how you teach your students to look at them?

David: How do you begin?

Joe: Well, first, I try to see everything that is in the frame. Too often we engage in unconscious cropping—we look at a piece of the photo instead of taking it all in. In a good photograph, you can't take a piece of it for the whole. It's all important.

One way to get inexperienced viewers to see more is to take a piece of paper 140
and slide it around, cutting off one side or another. Then you re-describe the work: what do you see now that you didn't see before? What does it feel like?

As for other moves, I sometimes give students a cardboard frame, and have them use it to frame the world—to think of the world in terms of framing shots.

Or a viewer can sometimes see more freshly by squinting at the image or turning it upside down. That has the effect of denaturalizing it, so you can see it freshly. Too often inexperienced viewers *get so stuck on the information that they can't see how it is put together.*

The more you look, the finer the distinctions you can learn to see.

Second, there is a kind of memory bank of images that I have access to in my brain when I look at photographs. This comes from a knowledge of the history of photography. I see photographs in the context of other photographs that I have seen.

Third, I try to fit the image roughly into one or more of the categories we 145
have been discussing. What is the cultural, conceptual, political basis for the image? What mode did the photographer choose to express the work?

Jill: Any favorite questions?

Joe: One question I really encourage asking is "Why is this art?" Note that the question is *not* "Is this art?" The implication is that these images are all art. We are looking for what makes them art. It is not our job to judge.

Try asking this question with Ed Ruscha's work, who in "26 Gasoline Stations" does 1950s Americana in canvases 7' × 30' long, featuring smoking rabbits, dogs' heads, phone poles, and other iconic images.

David: Thanks so much for talking to us, Joe.

Jill: Yes, and we'll be sure to call you before we burn down any houses.

Joseph Elliott's Photo-Categories

Note: Some artists fall into more than one category.

Stagers (Fabricators)

Prescribed Process

Edward Muybridge
Sol LeWitt
Bernd and Hilla Becher
Ed Ruscha
John Divola
William Wegman

Tableaux, Constructed in front of the camera or in the computer

Julia Cameron
Peter Henry Emerson
Edward Curtis
Gregory Crewdson
Cindy Sherman
Loretta Lux
Philip Lorca di Corcia
Jeff Wall
Almost all advertising images (GAP and Apple have used existing images of famous personalities, re-contextualizing them)
John Heartfield
An-My Le
Lorna Simpson (records other people's tableaux)
Larry Fink
David LaChapelle

Recorders (Observers)

Detached Documentarians

Timothy O'Sullivan
Eugene Atget
August Sander
Walker Evans
Alfred Stieglitz
Joel Sternfeld
Edward Burtynsky
Camilo Jose Vergara
William Eggleston
Joseph Elliott
An-My Le

Idea-driven Documentarians, lead with ideological frame

Eugene Smith
Dorothea Lange
Weegee
Larry Fink
Sebastio Salgado

Diane Arbus
Lauren Greenfield (Girl Culture)
Arlene Gottfred
Eugene Richards

Personal Documentarians

Nan Goldin
Larry Sultan
Robin Schwartz
Bill Burke
Sally Mann

Formalists

Walker Evans
Edward Weston
Ray Metzger
Hiroshi Sugimoto
Lee Friedlander

Works Cited or Recommended

Robert Adams, *On Beauty in Photography*
Roland Barthes, *Camera Lucida: Reflections on Photography*
Vicki Goldberg, *Photographers on Photography*
Lincoln Kirsten, *American Photographs: The 1939 Walker Evans MOMA Exhibition Catalogue*
Janet Malcolm, *Diana & Nikon: Essays on the Aesthetic of Photography*
October Magazine, "The Judgment Seat of Photography" (on Szarkowski's influence)
Aaron Scharf, *Art and Photography*
John Szarkowski, *American Landscapes: Photographs from the Collection of the Museum of Modern Art*
John Szarkowski, *Looking at Photographs*
John Szarkowski, *Mirrors and Windows*
John Szarkowski *The Photographer's Eye*
Alan Trachtenberg, *Reading American Photographs: Images as History: Mathew Brady to Walker Evans*

Things to Do with the Reading

1. Experiment with applying Elliott's primary categories—stagers versus recorders—to the photograph by Eggleston (see page 524). Which features of this photograph might cause you to see it as staged, and why? Which features might cause you to see it as essentially documentary (recorded), and why? You might also try this experiment with Lauren Greenfield's photograph, "Ashleigh, 13, with her friend and parents, Santa Monica" (see page 539).

2. Like all good thinkers and writers, Elliott not only creates categories but qualifies them and doesn't allow the categorizing process to cause him to gloss over photographers who don't neatly fit. So, for example, in one of his two primary categories, fabricators (aka stagers), he notes that the works of Gregory Crewdson and Loretta Lux are staged but with interesting differences. Locate this section of the interview (in the Fifth Meeting), choose relevant quotations, and paraphrase them (see page 13) in order to articulate and develop this difference. You should also, of course, study examples of the photographs themselves, or others by Crewdson and Lux.
3. In the Third Meeting, "The Photographer's Hand," Elliott comments,

    In [Crewdson's] photo of the house on fire, the people on the train track on the other side of the frame are a competing focal point by design. Nothing is an accident in the photo. He wants it to be carefully observed, to invite a close reading. We may think of a photograph having an initial impact, but there's also something else going on, a counterpoint, a set of messages (see paragraph 46).

    Use these observations as a lens for analyzing this photograph. Produce a close reading (see pages 65–66 and 211–212 on close reading). If the photo has competing focal points by design, what is achieved in this way? If the photo has an initial impact but also a counterpoint—more than one, potentially opposed, "messages"—what would you say these are? Make sure to share your reasoning about the evidence: why you think particular details mean what you claim they mean (see pages 138–139 on making evidence speak).

    Now try this with another Crewdson photograph—either the other ones in this book or one that you locate on the internet.
4. Elliott talks in the Third Meeting, "The Photographer's Hand," about looking for the photographer's hand in the Alfred Stieglitz photograph of "Georgia Engelhard." He asks, for example, why Stieglitz included the edge with the part of an urn and a rubber tree. Where is there evidence of the presence of the photographer's shaping influence—his "hand"—in the photograph?

    At the end of the Seventh Meeting, Elliott describes an exercise in which he has viewers take a piece of paper and slide it around on a photograph, blocking one side or another. He then asks them to re-describe the work each time: "what do you see now that you didn't see before"? Apply this procedure to the Stieglitz photo, and be sure not only to answer Elliott's question but also to ask and answer "so what?" about the difference. (See page 32 on the "So what?" question. Also see the next writing project for an extension of this one.)
5. In his famous book *Camera Lucida: Reflections on Photography*, Roland Barthes speaks of the punctum, which he defines as the single detail in a photograph that "arouses greatest sympathy" and is primarily responsible for the impact of the image on a viewer. In the previous exercise, you were asked to notice as much as you could about the details Stieglitz chooses to frame in his photograph. Barthes' approach is like the technique we call ranking, choosing and arguing for the importance of

a single element as a means of prompting an interpretive leap about the whole photograph (see pages 29–30 on ranking and interpretive leap). Select a punctum for Stieglitz's "Georgia Englehard" and use it to anchor an interpretation.

6. In the Third Meeting Elliott says that "Photographs are of course all evidence, but evidence of what?" (see paragraph 60). Use this remark to prompt an analysis of the photographs by Lauren Greenfield and Sally Mann. Elliott categorizes Greenfield as an "opinionated documentarian" and Mann as a "personal documentarian." His point is that both photographers are using their photographs to develop a point of view on their subjects. For what point of view (idea about the subject) does each photograph seem to serve as "evidence"?

7. In the Seventh Meeting, Elliott refers to a book entitled *A Primer for Visual Literacy* by Donis A. Dondis in which the author claims that there are three levels on which we can look at a visual image: the representational, the formal, and the symbolic. Elliott asserts that people too often leap to the symbolic before considering the other two levels. In other words, they leap to some larger (symbolic) meaning that they ascribe to the photo before they have dwelled with the representational details (what it is a picture of) or the formal way that shapes and perspectives are arranged inside the frame.

   Use description as an analytical tool for thinking about the William Eggleston photograph of two men by a car. First describe the photograph as a representation. What is it a picture of? You might wish to use Elliott's method of sliding a piece of paper around the photograph to make sure you don't leave important details out of your description.

   Next write a second description in which you attend to the formal level—the arrangement of elements in the frame, including various kinds of shapes and patterns of light and dark (this will require you to "see past the content").

   Finally, use these descriptions to prompt some interpretive leaps about the way the photograph operates symbolically. Which details of the photograph seem to invite a symbolic reading? Why? What unstated claims or positions might this photograph be voicing? (See pages 17–20 on the problem with premature leaps to generalization.)

8. **Application:** Look for trends in advertising photography. To what extent do you find evidence of documentary style photography in the world of print advertising? How is it being used, and for what purposes? You might also look for at least one clearly staged advertising photo that you think is representative of staging among advertising photos. And can you find an example of a hybrid, an image that seems to combine staging and recording in the services of advertising some product?

9. **Application:** Elliott discusses the work of Loretta Lux as a commentary on the conventions of portraiture, inviting us to think about what portraits are and why all of us (not just professional photographers) take portraits of people. Elliott refers to these conventions as "idealizing." Apply Elliott's discussion to other portraits—of your own (or family photographs), or of other photographers mentioned in the interview. As you study the portraits

you've assembled, try to make a list of what you think the conventions of portraiture actually *are*. Then work out the implications of these conventions, the meanings attached to them (see page 32, "Pushing Observations to Conclusions"). Your goal will be to arrive at what the photographer of your choice seems to be saying about portraiture. Keep in mind that in Elliott's terms, portraits can be to varying degrees both recorded and staged.

10. **Application:** Near the end of the Sixth Meeting, Elliott discusses those photographers he labels Prescribed Processors—that is, those who "set up a lot of parameters, with instructions to accomplish [their] art" (see paragraph 124). John Divola (not included here) photographs a lone runner against a variety of settings in his "As Far as I Can Get" series; Ed Ruscha trains his camera on "26 Gasoline Stations." Try the following experiment with prescribed processing: get a point-and-shoot camera and then select an object (or subject) and shoot the first 26 that you see. Use the photographs as a subject for analysis. What did you learn about your subject by repeatedly photographing it? How do you see this subject differently now? What did you learn about seeing by doing this project?

    You may wish to use one or more of the following heuristics to sharpen your observations. Look for anomalies—things that seem unusual or seem not to fit (see page 45). Use "Notice and Focus (Ranking)" (see pages 29–30, especially Try this 1.15).

11. **Link across Chapters:** In Chapter 16, James Howard Kunstler writes (in "The Public Realm and the Common Good") that public space has been seriously eroded by contemporary zoning and construction practices. Be a documentarian and try to record in both writing and images what you consider evidence for the degeneration of what he terms the "public realm," defined as "the physical manifestation of the common good."

    The famous documentary photographer Walker Evans shot a series of photographs of working class homes—usually houses built by particular industries for their workers. Locate these on the internet or in a book by Walker Evans (photographs) and Lincoln Kirstein (text) entitled *American Photographs* (the exhibition catalogue for Evans' 1938 exhibit at MOMA). Use these photographs as models for your own "portraits" of lower income housing in a locale near you. You can use both images and verbal depictions to capture what you think to be the essence of the place.

12. **Link across Chapters:** In Chapter 16, read Jack Gambino's "Demolition Zones: Contemporary Photography by Edward Burtynsky and Camilo Jose Vergara"—a political scientist's analysis of these two photographers' work as sites of "creative destruction." Take the Burtynsky photo of the pipeline (or any other photo of your choice), and do a reading of it on the three levels nominated by Dondis (see the Seventh Meeting of the Elliott interview). How would Elliott discuss Burtynsky's work? (He comments frequently on Vergara.)

Susan Sontag

In Plato's Cave

This essay from the influential cultural critic Susan Sontag first appeared as a chapter in her 1977 essay collection *On Photography*, which won the National Book Critics' Circle Award for Criticism in 1977. The art establishment initially regarded the book with horror, though over time many citizens of the art world have come to acknowledge its stimulating and disturbing discussion of the role of photography in contemporary culture. In an article commemorating the twentieth anniversary of its publication, Michael Starenko claimed that "Perhaps no photography book [. . .] has been analyzed and discussed with more intensity, from so many different and competing perspectives. [. . .] Sontag's claims about photography as well as her mode of argument have become part of the rhetorical 'tool kit' that photography theorists and critics carry around in their heads" ("Sontag's *On Photography* at 20," *Afterimage*, March–April 1998).

Humankind lingers unregenerately in Plato's cave, still revelling, its age-old habit, 1
in mere images of the truth. But being educated by photographs is not like being educated by older, more artisanal images. For one thing, there are a great many more images around, claiming our attention. The inventory started in 1839 and since then just about everything has been photographed, or so it seems. This very insatiability of the photographing eye changes the terms of confinement in the cave, our world. In teaching us a new visual code, photographs alter and enlarge our notions of what is worth looking at and what we have a right to observe. They are a grammar and, even more importantly, an ethics of seeing. Finally, the most grandiose result of the photographic enterprise is to give us the sense that we can hold the whole world in our heads—as an anthology of images.

To collect photographs is to collect the world. Movies and television programmes light up walls, flicker, and go out; but with still photographs the image is also an object, lightweight, cheap to produce, easy to carry about, accumulate, store. In Godard's *Les Carabiniers* (1963), two sluggish lumpen-peasants are lured into joining the King's Army by the promise that they will be able to loot, rape, kill, or do whatever else they please to the enemy, and get rich. But the suitcase of booty that Michel-Ange and Ulysse triumphantly bring home, years later, to their wives turns out to contain only picture postcards, hundreds of them, of Monuments, Department Stores, Mammals, Wonders of Nature, Methods of Transport, Works of Art, and other classified treasures from around the globe. Godard's gag vividly parodies the equivocal magic of the photographic image. Photographs are perhaps the most mysterious of all the objects that make up, and thicken, the environment we recognise as modern. Photographs really are experience captured, and the camera is the ideal arm of consciousness in its acquisitive mood.

To photograph is to appropriate the thing photographed. It means putting oneself into a certain relation to the world that feels like knowledge—and, therefore, like power. A now notorious first fall into alienation, habituating people to abstract the world into printed words, is supposed to have engendered that surplus of Faustian energy and psychic damage needed to build modern, inorganic societies. But print seems a less treacherous form of leaching out the world, of turning it into a mental object, than photographic images, which now provide most of the knowledge people have about the look of the past and the reach of the present. What is written about a person or an event is frankly an interpretation, as are handmade visual statements, like paintings and drawings. Photographed images do not seem to be statements about the world so much as pieces of it, miniatures of reality that anyone can make or acquire.

Photographs, which fiddle with the scale of the world, themselves get reduced, blown up, cropped, retouched, doctored, tricked out. They age, plagued by the usual ills of paper objects; they disappear; they become valuable, and get bought and sold; they are reproduced. Photographs, which package the world, seem to invite packaging. They are stuck in albums, framed and set on tables, tacked on walls, projected as slides. Newspapers and magazines feature them; cops alphabetise them; museums exhibit them; publishers compile them.

5 For many decades the book has been the most influential way of arranging (and usually miniaturising) photographs, thereby guaranteeing them longevity, if not immortality—photographs are fragile objects, easily torn or mislaid—and a wider public. The photograph in a book is, obviously, the image of an image. But since it is, to begin with, a printed, smooth object, a photograph loses much less of its essential quality when reproduced in a book than a painting does. Still, the book is not a wholly satisfactory scheme for putting groups of photographs into general circulation. The sequence in which the photographs are to be looked at is proposed by the order of pages, but nothing holds readers to the recommended order or indicates the amount of time to be spent on each photograph. Chris Marker's film, *Si j'avais quatre dromadaires* (1966), a brilliantly orchestrated meditation on photographs of all sorts and themes, suggests a subtler and more rigorous way of packaging (and enlarging) still photographs. Both the order and the exact time for looking at each photograph are imposed; and there is a gain in visual legibility and emotional impact. But photographs transcribed in a film cease to be collectable objects, as they still are when served up in books.

Photographs furnish evidence. Something we hear about, but doubt, seems proven when we're shown a photograph of it. In one version of its utility, the camera record incriminates. Starting with their use by the Paris police in the murderous roundup of Communards in June 1871, photographs became a useful tool of modern states in the surveillance and control of their increasingly mobile populations. In another version of its utility, the camera record justifies. A photograph passes for incontrovertible proof that a given thing happened. The picture may distort; but there is always a presumption that something exists, or did exist, which is like what's in the picture. Whatever the limitations (through amateurism) or pretensions (through artistry) of the individual photographer, a photograph—any photograph—seems to have a more innocent, and therefore more accurate, relation to visible reality than do other mimetic objects. Virtuosi of the noble image like Alfred Stieglitz and Paul Strand, composing mighty, unforgettable photographs decade after decade, still want, first of all, to show something 'out there', just like the Polaroid owner for whom photographs are a handy, fast form of note-taking, or the shutterbug with a Brownie who takes snapshots as souvenirs of daily life.

While a painting or a prose description can never be other than a narrowly selective interpretation, a photograph can be treated as a narrowly selective transparency. But despite the presumption of veracity that gives all photographs authority, interest, seductiveness, the work that photographers do is no generic exception to the usually shady commerce between art and truth. Even when photographers are most concerned with mirroring reality, they are still haunted by tacit imperatives of taste and conscience. The immensely gifted members of the Farm Security Administration photographic project of the late 1930s (among them Walker Evans, Dorothea Lange, Ben Shahn, Russell Lee) would take dozens of frontal pictures of one of their sharecropper subjects until satisfied that they had gotten just the right look on film—the precise expression on the subject's face that supported their own notions about poverty, light, dignity, texture, exploitation, and geometry. In deciding how a picture should look, in preferring one exposure to another, photographers are always imposing standards on their subjects. Although there is a sense in which the camera does indeed capture reality, not just interpret it, photographs are as much an interpretation of the world as paintings and drawings are. Those occasions when the taking of photographs is relatively undiscriminating, promiscuous, or self-effacing do not lessen the didacticism of the whole enterprise. This very passivity—and ubiquity—of the photographic record is photography's 'message', its aggression.

Images which idealise (like most fashion and animal photography) are no less aggressive than work which makes a virtue of plainness (like class pictures, still lifes of the bleaker sort, and mug shots). There is an aggression implicit in every use of the camera. This is as evident in the 1840s and 1850s, photography's glorious first two decades, as in all the succeeding decades, during which technology made possible an ever increasing spread of that mentality which looks at the world as a set of potential photographs. Even for such early masters as David Octavius Hill and Julia Margaret Cameron who used the camera as a means of getting painterly images, the point of taking photographs was a vast departure from the aims of painters. From its start, photography implied the capture of the largest possible number of subjects. Painting never had so imperial a scope. The subsequent industrialisation of camera technology only carried out a promise inherent in photography from its very beginning: to democratise all experiences by translating them into images.

That age when taking photographs required a cumbersome and expensive contraption—the toy of the clever, the wealthy, and the obsessed—seems remote indeed from the era of sleek pocket cameras that invite anyone to take pictures. The first cameras, made in France and England in the early 1840s, had only inventors and buffs to operate them. Since there were then no professional photographers, there could not be amateurs either, and taking photographs had no clear social use; it was a gratuitous, that is, an artistic activity, though with few pretensions to being an art. It was only with its industrialisation that photography came into its own as art. As industrialisation provided social uses for the operations of the photographer, so the reaction against these uses reinforced the self-consciousness of photography-as-art.

Recently, photography has become almost as widely practised an amusement as 10
sex and dancing—which means that, like every mass art form, photography is not practised by most people as an art. It is mainly a social rite, a defence against anxiety, and a tool of power.

Memorialising the achievements of individuals considered as members of families (as well as of other groups) is the earliest popular use of photography. For at least a century, the wedding photograph has been as much a part of the ceremony as the prescribed verbal formulae. Cameras go with family life. According to a sociological study done in France, most households have a camera, but a household with children is twice as likely to have at least one camera as a household in which there are no children. Not to take pictures of one's children, particularly when they are small, is a sign of parental indifference, just as not turning up for one's graduation picture is a gesture of adolescent rebellion.

Through photographs, each family constructs a portrait-chronicle of itself—a portable kit of images that bears witness to its connectedness. It hardly matters what activities are photographed so long as photographs get taken and are cherished. Photography becomes a rite of family life just when, in the industrialising countries of Europe and America, the very institution of the family starts undergoing radical surgery. As that claustrophobic unit, the nuclear family, was being carved out of a much larger family aggregate, photography came along to memorialise, to restate symbolically, the imperilled continuity and vanishing extendedness of family life. Those ghostly traces, photographs, supply the token presence of the dispersed relatives. A family's photograph album is generally about the extended family—and, often, is all that remains of it.

As photographs give people an imaginary possession of a past that is unreal, they also help people to take possession of space in which they are insecure. Thus, photography develops in tandem with one of the most characteristic of modern activities: tourism. For the first time in history, large numbers of people regularly travel out of their habitual environments for short periods of time. It seems positively unnatural to travel for pleasure without taking a camera along. Photographs will offer indisputable evidence that the trip was made, that the programme was carried out, that fun was had. Photographs document sequences of consumption carried on outside the view of family, friends, neighbours. But dependence on the camera, as the device that makes real what one is experiencing, doesn't fade when people travel more. Taking photographs fills the same need for the cosmopolitans accumulating photograph-trophies of their boat trip up the Albert Nile or their fourteen days in China as it does for lower-middle-class vacationers taking snapshots of the Eiffel Tower or Niagara Falls.

A way of certifying experience, taking photographs is also a way of refusing it—by limiting experience to a search for the photogenic, by converting experience into an image, a souvenir. Travel becomes a strategy for accumulating photographs. The very activity of taking pictures is soothing, and assuages general feelings of disorientation that are likely to be exacerbated by travel. Most tourists feel compelled to put the camera between themselves and whatever is remarkable that they encounter. Unsure of other responses, they take a picture. This gives shape to experience: stop, take a photograph, and move on. The method especially appeals to people handicapped by a ruthless work ethic—Germans, Japanese, and Americans. Using a camera appeases the anxiety which the work-driven feel about not working when they are on vacation and supposed to be having fun. They have something to do that is like a friendly imitation of work: they can take pictures.

People robbed of their past seem to make the most fervent picture takers, at 15
home and abroad. Everyone who lives in an industrialised society is obliged

gradually to give up the past, but in certain countries, such as the United States and Japan, the break with the past has been particularly traumatic. In the early 1970s, the fable of the brash American tourist of the 1950s and 1960s, rich with dollars and Babbittry, was replaced by the mystery of the group-minded Japanese tourist, newly released from his island prison by the miracle of overvalued yen, who is generally armed with two cameras, one on each hip.

Photography has become one of the principal devices for experiencing something, for giving an appearance of participation. One full-page ad shows a small group of people standing pressed together, peering out of the photograph, all but one looking stunned, excited, upset. The one who wears a different expression holds a camera to his eye; he seems self-possessed, is almost smiling. While the others are passive, clearly alarmed spectators, having a camera has transformed one person into something active, a voyeur: only he has mastered the situation. What do these people see? We don't know. And it doesn't matter. It is an Event: something worth seeing—and therefore worth photographing. The adcopy, white letters across the dark lower third of the photograph like news coming over a teletype machine, consists of just six words: '… Prague … Woodstock … Vietnam … Sapporo … Londonderry … LEICA'. Crushed hopes, youth antics, colonial wars, and winter sports are alike—are equalised by the camera. Taking photographs has set up a chronic voyeuristic relation to the world which levels the meaning of all events.

A photograph is not just the result of an encounter between an event and a photographer; picture-taking is an event in itself, and one with ever more peremptory rights—to interfere with, to invade, or to ignore whatever is going on. Our very sense of situation is now articulated by the camera's interventions. The omnipresence of cameras persuasively suggests that time consists of interesting events, events worth photographing. This, in turn, makes it easy to feel that any event, once underway, and whatever its moral character, should be allowed to complete itself—so that something else can be brought into the world, the photograph. After the event has ended, the picture will still exist, conferring on the event a kind of immortality (and importance) it would never otherwise have enjoyed. While real people are out there killing themselves or other real people, the photographer stays behind his or her camera, creating a tiny element of another world: the imagine-world that bids to outlast us all.

Photographing is essentially an act of non-intervention. Part of the horror of such memorable coups of contemporary photojournalism as the pictures of a Vietnamese bonze reaching for the gasoline can, of a Bengali guerrilla in the act of bayoneting a trussed-up collaborator, comes from the awareness of how plausible it has become, in situations where the photographer has the choice between a photograph and a life, to choose the photograph. The person who intervenes cannot record; the person who is recording cannot intervene. Dziga Vertov's great film, *Man with a Movie Camera* (1929), gives the ideal image of the photographer as someone in perpetual movement, someone moving through a panorama of disparate events with such agility and speed that any intervention is out of the question. Hitchcock's *Rear Window* (1954) gives the complementary image: the photographer played by James Stewart has an intensified relation to one event, through his camera, precisely because he has a broken leg and is confined to a wheelchair; being temporarily immobilised prevents him from acting on what he sees, and makes it even more important to take pictures. Even if incompatible with intervention in a physical sense, using a camera is still a form of participation. Although the camera is an observation station, the act of photographing is more than passive observing. Like sexual voyeurism, it is a way of at least tacitly, often explicitly, encouraging whatever is going on to keep on happening. To take a picture is to have an interest in things as they are, in the status quo remaining unchanged (at least for as long as it takes to get a 'good' picture), to be in complicity with whatever makes a subject interesting, worth photographing—including, when that is the interest, another person's pain or misfortune.

'I always thought of photography as a naughty thing to do—that was one of my favourite things about it', Diane Arbus wrote, 'and when I first did it I felt very perverse.' Being a professional photographer can be thought of as naughty, to use Arbus's pop word, if the photographer seeks out subjects considered to be disreputable, taboo, marginal. But naughty subjects are harder to find these days. And what exactly is the perverse aspect of picture-taking? If professional photographers often have sexual fantasies when they are behind the camera, perhaps the perversion lies in the fact that these fantasies are both plausible and so inappropriate. In *Blowup* (1966), Antonioni has the fashion photographer hovering convulsively over Verushka's body with his camera clicking. Naughtiness, indeed! In fact, using a camera is not a very good way of getting at someone sexually. Between photographer and subject, there has to be distance. The camera doesn't rape, or even possess, though it may presume, intrude, trespass, distort, exploit, and, at the farthest reach of metaphor, assassinate—all activities that, unlike the sexual push and shove, can be conducted from a distance, and with some detachment.

There is a much stronger sexual fantasy in Michael Powell's extraordinary 20
movie *Peeping Tom* (1960), which is not about a Peeping Tom but about a psychopath who kills women with a weapon concealed in his camera, while photographing them. Not once does he touch his subjects. He doesn't desire their bodies; he wants their presence in the form of filmed images—those showing them experiencing their own death—which he screens at home for his solitary pleasure. The movie assumes connections between impotence and aggression, professionalised looking and cruelty, which point to the central fantasy connected with the camera. The camera as phallus is, at most, a flimsy variant of the inescapable metaphor that everyone unselfconsciously employs. However hazy our awareness of this fantasy, it is named without subtlety whenever we talk about 'loading' and 'aiming' a camera, about 'shooting' a film.

The old-fashioned camera was clumsier and harder to reload than a brown Bess musket. The modern camera is trying to be a ray gun. One ad reads:

> The Yashica Electro-35 GT is the spaceage camera your family will love. Take beautiful pictures day or night. Automatically. Without any nonsense. Just aim, focus and shoot. The GT's computer brain and electronic shutter will do the rest.

Like a car, a camera is sold as a predatory weapon—one that's as automated as possible, ready to spring. Popular taste expects an easy, an invisible technology. Manufacturers reassure their customers that taking pictures demands no skill or expert knowledge, that the machine is all-knowing, and responds to the slightest pressure of the will. It's as simple as turning the ignition key or pulling the trigger.

Like guns and cars, cameras are fantasy-machines whose use is addictive. However, despite the extravagances of ordinary language and advertising, they are not lethal. In the hyperbole that markets cars like guns, there is at least this much truth: except in wartime, cars kill more people than guns do. The camera/gun does not kill, so the ominous metaphor seems to be all bluff—like a man's fantasy of having a gun, knife, or tool between his legs. Still, there is something predatory in the act of taking a picture. To photograph people is to violate them, by seeing them as they never see themselves, by having knowledge of them they can never have; it turns people into objects that can be symbolically possessed. Just as the camera is a sublimation of the gun, to photograph someone is a sublimated murder—a soft murder, appropriate to a sad, frightened time.

Eventually, people might learn to act out more of their aggressions with cameras and fewer with guns, with the price being an even more image-choked world. One situation where people are switching from bullets to film is the photographic safari that is replacing the gun safari in East Africa. The hunters have Hasselblads instead of Winchesters; instead of looking through a telescopic sight to aim a rifle, they look through a viewfinder to frame a picture. In end-of-the-century London, Samuel Butler complained that 'there is a photographer in every bush, going about like a roaring lion seeking whom he may devour'. The photographer is now charging real beasts, beleaguered and too rare to kill. Guns have metamorphosed into cameras in this earnest comedy, the ecology safari, because nature has ceased to be what it always had been—what people needed protection from. Now nature—tamed, endangered, mortal—needs to be protected from people. When we are afraid, we shoot. But when we are nostalgic, we take pictures.

It is a nostalgic time right now, and photographs actively promote nostalgia. Photography is an elegiac art, a twilight art. Most subjects photographed are, just by virtue of being photographed, touched with pathos. An ugly or grotesque subject may be moving because it has been dignified by the attention of the photographer. A beautiful subject can be the object of rueful feelings, because it has aged or decayed or no longer exists. All photographs are *memento mori*. To take a photograph is to participate in another person's (or thing's) mortality, vulnerability, mutability. Precisely by slicing out this moment and freezing it, all photographs testify to time's relentless melt.

Cameras began duplicating the world at that moment when the human land- 25
scape started to undergo a vertiginous rate of change: while an untold number of forms of biological and social life are being destroyed in a brief span of time, a device is available to record what is disappearing. The moody, intricately textured Paris of Atget and Brassaï is mostly gone. Like the dead relatives and friends preserved in the family album, whose presence in photographs exorcises some of the anxiety and remorse prompted by their disappearance, so the photographs of neighbourhoods now torn down, rural places disfigured and made barren, supply our pocket relation to the past.

A photograph is both a pseudo-presence and a token of absence. Like a wood fire in a room, photographs—especially those of people, of distant landscapes and faraway cities, of the vanished past—are incitements to reverie. The sense of the unattainable that can be evoked by photographs feeds directly into the erotic feelings of those for whom desirability is enhanced by distance. The lover's photograph hidden in a married woman's wallet, the poster photograph of a rock star tacked up over an adolescent's bed, the campaign-button image of a politician's face pinned on a voter's coat, the snapshots of a cabdriver's children clipped to the visor—all such talismanic uses of photographs express a feeling both sentimental and implicitly magical: they are attempts to contact or lay claim to another reality.

Photographs can abet desire in the most direct, utilitarian way—as when someone collects photographs of anonymous examples of the desirable as an aid to masturbation. The matter is more complex when photographs are used to stimulate the moral impulse. Desire has no history—at least, it is experienced in each instance as all foreground, immediacy. It is aroused by archetypes and is, in that sense, abstract. But moral feelings are embedded in history, whose personae are concrete, whose situations are always specific. Thus, almost opposite rules hold true for the use of the photograph to awaken desire and to awaken conscience. The images that mobilise conscience are always linked to a given historical situation. The more general they are, the less likely they are to be effective.

A photograph that brings news of some unsuspected zone of misery cannot make a dent in public opinion unless there is an appropriate context of feeling and attitude. The photographs Mathew Brady and his colleagues took of the horrors of the battlefields did not make people any less keen to go on with the Civil War. The photographs of ill-clad, skeletal prisoners held at Andersonville inflamed Northern public opinion—against the South. (The effect of the Andersonville photographs must have been partly due to the very novelty, at that time, of seeing photographs.) The political understanding that many Americans came to in the 1960s would allow them, looking at the photographs Dorothea Lange took of Nisei on the West Coast being transported to internment camps in 1942, to recognise their subject for what it was—a crime committed by the government against a large group of American citizens. Few people who saw those photographs in the 1940s could have had so unequivocal a reaction; the grounds for such a judgment were covered over by the pro-war consensus. Photographs cannot create a moral position, but they can reinforce one—and can help build a nascent one.

Photographs may be more memorable than moving images, because they are a neat slice of time, not a flow. Television is a stream of underselected images, each of which cancels its predecessor. Each still photograph is a privileged moment, turned into a slim object that one can keep and look at again. Photographs like the one that made the front page of most newspapers in the world in 1972—a naked South Vietnamese child just sprayed by American napalm, running down a highway toward the camera, her arms open, screaming with pain—probably did more to increase the public revulsion against the war than a hundred hours of televised barbarities.

One would like to imagine that the American public would not have been so 30
unanimous in its acquiescence to the Korean War if it had been confronted with photographic evidence of the devastation of Korea, an ecocide and genocide in

some respects even more thorough than those inflicted on Vietnam a decade later. But the supposition is trivial. The public did not see such photographs because there was, ideologically, no space for them. No one brought back photographs of daily life in Pyongyang, to show that the enemy had a human face, as Felix Greene and Marc Riboud brought back photographs of Hanoi. Americans did have access to photographs of the suffering of the Vietnamese (many of which came from military sources and were taken with quite a different use in mind) because journalists felt backed in their efforts to obtain those photographs, the event having been defined by a significant number of people as a savage colonialist war. The Korean War was understood differently—as part of the just struggle of the Free World against the Soviet Union and China—and, given that characterisation, photographs of the cruelty of unlimited American firepower would have been irrelevant.

Though an event has come to mean, precisely, something worth photographing, it is still ideology (in the broadest sense) that determines what constitutes an event. There can be no evidence, photographic or otherwise, of an event until the event itself has been named and characterised. And it is never photographic evidence which can construct—more properly, identify—events; the contribution of photography always follows the naming of the event. What determines the possibility of being affected morally by photographs is the existence of a relevant political consciousness. Without a politics, photographs of the slaughter-bench of history will most likely be experienced as, simply, unreal or as a demoralising emotional blow.

The quality of feeling, including moral outrage, that people can muster in response to photographs of the oppressed, the exploited, the starving, and the massacred also depends on the degree of their familiarity with these images. Don McCullin's photographs of emaciated Biafrans in the early 1970s had less impact for some people than Werner Bischof's photographs of Indian famine victims in the early 1950s because those images had become banal, and the photographs of Tuareg families dying of starvation in the sub-Sahara that appeared in magazines everywhere in 1973 must have seemed to many like an unbearable replay of a now familiar atrocity exhibition.

Photographs shock insofar as they show something novel. Unfortunately, the ante keeps getting raised—partly through the very proliferation of such images of horror. One's first encounter with the photographic inventory of ultimate horror is a kind of revelation, the prototypically modern revelation, a negative epiphany. For me, it was photographs of Bergen-Belsen and Dachau which I came across by chance in a bookstore in Santa Monica in July 1945. Nothing I have seen—in photographs or in real life—ever cut me as sharply, deeply, instantaneously. Indeed, it seems plausible to me to divide my life into two parts, before I saw those photographs (I was twelve) and after, though it was several years before I understood fully what they were about. What good was served by seeing them? They were only photographs—of an event I had scarcely heard of and could do nothing to affect, of suffering I could hardly imagine and could do nothing to relieve. When I looked at those photographs, something broke. Some limit had been reached, and not only that of horror; I felt irrevocably grieved, wounded, but a part of my feelings started to tighten; something went dead; something is still crying.

To suffer is one thing; another thing is living with the photographed images of suffering, which does not necessarily strengthen conscience and the ability to be compassionate. It can also corrupt them. Once one has seen such images, one has started down the road of seeing more—and more. Images transfix. Images anaesthetise. An event known through photographs certainly becomes more real than it would have been if one had never seen the photographs—think of the Vietnam War. (For a counter-example, think of the Gulag Archipelago, of which we have no photographs.) But after repeated exposure to images it also becomes less real.

The same law holds for evil as for pornography. The shock of photographed atrocities wears off with repeated viewings, just as the surprise and bemusement felt the first time one sees a pornographic movie wear off after one sees a few more. The sense of taboo which makes us indignant and sorrowful is not much sturdier than the sense of taboo that regulates the definition of what is obscene. And both have been sorely tried in recent years. The vast photographic catalogue of misery and injustice throughout the world has given everyone a certain familiarity with atrocity, making the horrible seem more ordinary—making it appear familiar, remote ('it's only a photograph'), inevitable. At the time of the first photographs of the Nazi camps, there was nothing banal about these images. After thirty years, a saturation point may have been reached. In these last decades, 'concerned' photography has done at least as much to deaden conscience as to arouse it.

The ethical content of photographs is fragile. With the possible exception of photographs of those horrors, like the Nazi camps, that have gained the status of ethical reference points, most photographs do not keep their emotional charge. A photograph of 1900 that was affecting then because of its subject would, today, be more likely to move us because it is a photograph taken in 1900. The particular qualities and intentions of photographs tend to be swallowed up in the generalised pathos of time past. Aesthetic distance seems built into the very experience of looking at photographs, if not right away, then certainly with the passage of time. Time eventually positions most photographs, even the most amateurish, at the level of art.

The industrialisation of photography permitted its rapid absorption into rational—that is, bureaucratic—ways of running society. No longer toy images, photographs became part of the general furniture of the environment—touchstones and confirmations of that reductive approach to reality which is considered realistic. Photographs were enrolled in the service of important institutions of control, notably the family and the police, as symbolic objects and as pieces of information. Thus, in the bureaucratic cataloguing of the world, many important documents are not valid unless they have, affixed to them, a photograph-token of the citizen's face.

The 'realistic' view of the world compatible with bureaucracy redefines knowledge—as techniques and information. Photographs are valued because they give information. They tell one what there is; they make an inventory. To spies, meteorologists, coroners, archaeologists, and other information professionals, their value is inestimable. But in the situations in which most people use photographs, their value as information is of the same order as fiction. The information that photographs can give starts to seem very important at that moment in cultural history when everyone is thought to have a right to something called news. Photographs were seen as a way of giving information to people who do not take easily to reading. The *Daily News* still calls itself 'New York's Picture Newspaper', its bid for populist identity. At the opposite end of the scale, *Le Monde*, a newspaper designed for skilled, well-informed readers, runs no photographs at all. The presumption is that, for such readers, a photograph could only illustrate the analysis contained in an article.

A new sense of the notion of information has been constructed around the photographic image. The photograph is a thin slice of space as well as time. In a world ruled by photographic images, all borders ('framing') seem arbitrary. Anything can be separated, can be made discontinuous, from anything else. All that is necessary is to frame the subject differently. (Conversely, anything can be made adjacent to anything else.) Photography reinforces a nominalist view of social reality as consisting of small units of an apparently infinite number—as the number of photographs that could be taken of anything is unlimited. Through photographs, the world becomes a series of unrelated, freestanding particles; and history, past and present, a set of anecdotes and *faits divers*. The camera makes reality atomic, manageable, and opaque. It is a view of the world which denies interconnectedness, continuity, but which confers on each moment the character of a mystery. Any photograph has multiple meanings; indeed, to see something in the form of a photograph is to encounter a potential object of fascination. The ultimate wisdom of the photographic image is to say: 'There is the surface. Now think—or rather feel, intuit—what is beyond it, what the reality must be like if it looks this way.' Photographs, which cannot themselves explain anything, are inexhaustible invitations to deduction, speculation, and fantasy.

Photography implies that we know about the world if we accept it as the 40
camera records it. But this is the opposite of understanding, which starts from *not* accepting the world as it looks. All possibility of understanding is rooted in the ability to say no. Strictly speaking, one never understands anything from a photograph. Of course, photographs fill in blanks in our mental pictures of the present and the past: for example, Jacob Riis's images of New York squalor in the 1880s are sharply instructive to those unaware that urban poverty in late-nineteenth-century America was really that Dickensian. Nevertheless, the camera's rendering of reality must always hide more than it discloses. As Brecht points out, a photograph of the Krupp works reveals virtually nothing about that organisation. In contrast to the amorous relation, which is based on how something looks, understanding is based on how it functions. And functioning takes place in time, and must be explained in time. Only that which narrates can make us understand.

The limit of photographic knowledge of the world is that, while it can goad conscience, it can, finally, never be ethical or political knowledge. The knowledge gained through still photographs will always be some kind of sentimentalism, whether cynical or humanist. It will be a knowledge at bargain prices—a semblance of knowledge, a semblance of wisdom; as the act of taking pictures is a semblance of appropriation, a semblance of rape. The very muteness of what is, hypothetically, comprehensible in photographs is what constitutes their attraction and provocativeness. The omnipresence of photographs has an incalculable effect on our ethical sensibility. By furnishing this already crowded world with a duplicate one of images, photography makes us feel that the world is more available than it really is.

Needing to have reality confirmed and experience enhanced by photographs is an aesthetic consumerism to which everyone is now addicted. Industrial societies turn their citizens into image-junkies; it is the most irresistible form of mental pollution. Poignant longings for beauty, for an end to probing below the surface, for a redemption and celebration of the body of the world—all these elements of erotic feeling are affirmed in the pleasure we take in photographs. But other, less liberating feelings are expressed as well. It would not be wrong to speak of people having a *compulsion* to photograph: to turn experience itself into a way of seeing. Ultimately, having an experience becomes identical with taking a photograph of it, and participating in a public event comes more and more to be equivalent to looking at it in photographed form. That most logical of nineteenth-century aesthetes, Mallarmé, said that everything in the world exists in order to end in a book. Today everything exists to end in a photograph.

THINGS TO DO WITH THE READING

1. This essay is a complex analysis conducted in a number of contexts—moral, political, psychological, and philosophical. The essay's first paragraph and its title, which reference the Greek philosopher Plato's famous Allegory of the Cave, announce Sontag's interest in locating photography in the context of the philosophy of art. Use Paraphrase × 3 (see pages 116–117) on the substantive language of the essay's third paragraph in order to produce a cogent typed page explaining the relationship Sontag says that photographic images and the act of photographing have on "the world." Query the language: why "treacherous," for example?

   Then extend your close examination to paragraphs 6 and 7. Here you will need to look up Plato's Allegory of the Cave and the word "mimetic"—a theory of art claiming that art is a reflection (or copy, imitation) of reality. Locate in the three paragraphs specific language that clarifies why it would be wrong to say that Sontag sees photography as mimetic. Remember that Paraphrase × 3 is a thinking tool. Write a number of paraphrases of key sentences in order to discover what you think are your clearest and most accurate restatements of Sontag's argument, and then turn these into a cogent analytical summary (see pages 117–120 on analytical summary).

2. The novelist and critic William Gass wrote of *On Photography* that

   > No simple summary of the views contained in Susan Sontag's brief but brilliant work on photography is possible, first because there are too many, and second because the book is a thoughtful meditation, not a treatise, and its ideas are grouped more nearly like a gang of keys upon a ring than a run of onions on a string.

The same might be said of just the essay "In Plato's Cave"—that it is too conceptually rich and meditative to allow simple summary. And yet, we can probably improve our ability to understand this densely idea-laden essay if we make a list of the most important statements or claims that Sontag makes. Copy out the five sentences you find most arresting in the piece, each from a different paragraph. Then use these to generate a focused freewrite—an opportunity for your own meditation.

Here are three possible ways of proceeding. (1) You might write about the single sentence you find most compelling, beginning by paraphrasing it. (2) You might look for some repeated element or contrast that figures in several of your sentences. (3) You might pair any of the sentences with one of the images included in this book in the essays by Elliott, Berger, or Gambino (see pages 113–116 on passage-based focused freewriting).

3. As the essay progresses, Sontag's thinking turns to the moral, ethical, and psychological effects of photography. In these contexts Sontag talks both about photography as an activity (with moral, ethical, and psychological consequences) and photographs as objects that have (or fail to have) some supposed impact on the world. Study paragraphs 29–36 of the essay, which deal with the impact and ethics of photographs that record atrocities—"the vast catalogue of misery and injustice throughout the world." In what terms does Sontag reject the often-made defense of photographs of atrocities and exploitation—that they call people's attention to problems and thus inspire people to address them? You might wish to include in your thinking the brief biographical account that Sontag provides in paragraph 33 of her first experience at age 12 with photographs of the Holocaust. (It is worth noting in this context that Sontag was a noted human rights activist for more than two decades, serving for several years as president of the American Center of PEN, the international writers' organization dedicated to freedom of expression and the advancement of literature.)

4. **Application:** Sontag, in her role of provocateur, loves to make bold claims—for example, that people take photos to opt out of life and to construct a family album of the ever-vanishing extended family. Use your own experience to engage these volatile notions.

Locate either some family photographs or photographs that you have taken as a tourist, select five or six, and then write a brief account of what you think the photographer (possibly you) was trying to accomplish in taking them. Be sure to include your reasoning. Then consider a few single sentences you've selected from Sontag's commentary on family photographs and vacation photographs (see paragraphs 10–18) and use these as a springboard for some sustained reflection on photography as an activity.

Warning: Don't turn this into an agree-disagree exercise. Use Sontag's thinking as a starting point for your thinking about the topic, not *primarily* as the impetus to support or refute her position. (See pages 18–21 on "The Judgment Reflex" and "Debate-Style Argument" for a discussion of the problem with agree-disagree response.)

5. **Application:** On the matter of the ethics of photography and its potential to effect social change, you could do some research on the life and work of one of the photographers that Joseph Elliot describes at the end of the interview as an Opinionated Documentarian or a Personal Documentarian. Try Nan Goldin, Lauren Greenfield, Sally Mann, or Sebastiao Salgado. Find claims in the Sontag essay that you think are interesting and illuminating in the context of your chosen photographer. See, for example, the discussion of photography as "an act of non-intervention" in paragraph 18, or the repeated references to sexual voyeurism and predation. Also try to find not only a range of images by the photographer of your choice but perhaps artistic statements by him or her, as well as short biographies and exhibition reviews.

   What might Sontag praise about this photographer's work? What might make her anxious about it? How might the photographer respond? Stage a conversation. (See pages 303–306, "Put Your Sources into Conversation with One Another" and Try this 12.1.)

6. **Link:** Both Elliott and Sontag consider the extent to which photographic images can bring about positive change in the world. Reread the Second Meeting in the Elliott interview and put it into conversation with Sontag's observations on the power of photographs to contribute to social change. What single sentence in the Sontag piece seems the furthest removed from Elliott's position on (for example) what documentary photographers do? What single sentence in the Second Meeting of the Elliott interview most closely resembles Sontag's position on the ethical situation of the photographer? Be sure to share your reasoning behind the sentence selections. (See pages 125–126 on Looking for Significant Difference or Unexpected Similarity.)

Barry Lopez

Learning to See

Barry Lopez is an award-winning writer of both nonfiction and fiction. In this essay, he provides an account of his decision to stop pursuing his "other" career, as a landscape photographer. In the process of telling this story, Lopez focuses astutely on an area of photography that neither Joseph Elliott nor Susan Sontag directly addresses: nature photography. His photographic career (which he decided to end in 1981) focused on subjects that included only the land. No people. For the most part, no animals. But as you will see, the land for Lopez is no inert entity, but the home of small miracles of physics.

1 In June 1989, I received a puzzling letter from the Amon Carter Museum in Fort Worth, Texas, an invitation to speak at the opening of a retrospective of the work of Robert Adams. The show, "To Make It Home: Photographs of the American West, 1965–1985," had been organized by the Philadelphia Museum of Art and would travel to the Los Angeles County Museum and the Corcoran Gallery of Art in Washington, D.C., before being installed at the Amon Carter, an institution renowned for its photographic collections, in the spring of 1990.

Robert Adams, an un-self-promoting man who has published no commercially prominent book of photographs, is routinely réferred to as one of the most important landscape photographers in America, by both art critics and his colleagues. His black-and-white images are intelligently composed and morally engaged. They're also hopeful, despite their sometimes depressing subject matter—brutalized landscapes and the venality of the American Dream as revealed in suburban life. Adams doesn't hold himself apart from what he indicts. He photographs with compassion and he doesn't scold. His pictures are also accessible, to such a degree that many of them seem casual. In 1981 he published *Beauty in Photography: Essays in Defense of Traditional Values*, one of the clearest statements of artistic responsibility ever written by a photographer.

If there is such a thing as an ideal of stance, technique, vision, and social contribution toward which young photographers might aspire, it's embodied in this man.

I suspected the Amon Carter had inadvertently invited the wrong person to speak. I'd no knowledge of the history of American photography sufficient to situate Robert Adams in it. I couldn't speak to the technical perfection of his prints. I'd no credentials as an art critic. As an admirer of the work, of course, I'd have something to say, but it could only be that, the words of an amateur who admired Adams's accomplishment.

5 I wondered for days what prompted the invitation. For about fifteen years, before putting my cameras down on September 13, 1981, never to pick them up again, I'd worked as a landscape photographer, but it was unlikely anyone at the Amon Carter knew this. I'd visited the museum in the fall of 1986 to see some of their luminist paintings and had met several of the curators, but our conversations could not have left anyone with the impression that I had the background to speak about Adams's work.

I finally decided to say yes. I wrote and told the person coordinating the program, Mary Lampe, that though I didn't feel qualified to speak I admired Mr. Adams's work, and further, I presumed an affinity with his pursuits and ideals as set forth in *Beauty in Photography.* And I told her I intended to go back and study the work of Paul Strand, Wynn Bullock, Minor White, Harry Callahan, and others who'd been an influence on my own work and thought, in order to prepare my lecture.

Months later, when I arrived at the museum, I asked Ms. Lampe how they had come to invite me and not someone more qualified. She said Mr. Adams had asked them to do so. I sensed she believed Robert Adams and I were good friends and I had to tell her I didn't know him at all. We'd never met, never corresponded, had not spoken on the phone. I was unaware, even, that it was "Bob" Adams, as Ms. Lampe called him.

"But why did you agree to come?" she asked.

"Out of respect for the work," I said. "Out of enthusiasm for the work." I also explained that I was intimidated by the prospect, and that sometimes I felt it was good to act on things like that.

Ms. Lampe subsequently sent Robert Adams a tape of my talk. He and I later 10
met and we now correspond and speak on the phone regularly. He set the course of our friendship in the first sentence of a letter he wrote me after hearing my presentation. "Your willingness to speak in my behalf," he wrote, "confirms my belief in the community of artists."

He believed from work of mine that he'd read that we shared a sensibility, that we asked similar questions about the relationship between culture and landscape, and that our ethical leanings and our sense of an artist's social responsibility were similar. He later told me that for these reasons he'd given my name, hopefully but somewhat facetiously, to Ms. Lampe, not knowing the curators and I were acquainted and that they would write me.

I've long been attracted to the way visual artists like Robert Adams imagine the world. The emotional impact of their composition of space and light is as clarifying for me as immersion in a beautifully made story. As with the work of a small group of poets I read regularly—Robert Hass, Pattiann Rogers, Garrett Hongo—I find healing in their expressions. I find reasons not to give up.

Though I no longer photograph, I have maintained since 1981 a connection with photographers and I keep up a sort of running conversation with several of them. We talk about the fate of photography in the United States, where of course art is increasingly more commodified and where, with the advent of computer manipulation, photography is the art most likely to mislead. Its history as a purveyor of objective reality, the idea that "the camera never lies," is specious, certainly; but with some artistic endeavors, say those of Cartier-Bresson, Aaron Siskind, or W. Eugene Smith, and in the fields of documentary photography, which would include some news photography, and nature photography, one can assert that the authority of the image lies with the subject. With the modern emphasis on the genius of the individual artist, however, and with the arrival of computer imaging, authority in these areas now more often lies with the photographer. This has become true to such an extent that the reversal that's occurred—the photographer, not the subject, is in charge—has caused the rules of evidence to be changed in courts of law; and it has foisted upon an unwitting public a steady stream, for example, of fabricated images of wildlife.

As a beginning photographer I was most attracted to color and form, to the emotional consequence of line. It is no wonder, looking back now, that I pored over the images of someone like Edward Weston, or that I felt isolated in some of my pursuits because at the time few serious photographers outside Ernst Haas and Eliot Porter worked as I did in color. I wanted to photograph the streaming of light. For a long while it made no difference whether that light was falling down the stone walls of a building in New York or lambent on the corrugations of a wheat field. Ansel Adams was suggested to me early on as a model, but he seemed to my eye inclined to overstate. I wanted the sort of subtlety I would later come to admire in Bob Adams's work and in the aerial photographs of Emmet Gowin.

15 The more I gravitated as a writer toward landscape as a context in which to work out what I was thinking as a young man about issues like justice, tolerance, ambiguity, and compassion, the more I came to concentrate on landforms as a photographer. I valued in particular the work of one or two wildlife photographers shooting *in situ*, in the bush. (I remember enthusiastically contacting friends about John Dominis's groundbreaking portfolio of African cat photographs, which appeared in three successive issues of *Life* in January 1967.) But I was not inclined toward mastering the kind of technical skill it took to make such photographs. More fundamentally, I had misgivings about what I regarded as invasions of the privacy of wild animals. The latter notion I thought so personal an idea I kept it mostly to myself; today, of course, it's a central concern of wildlife photographers, especially for a contingent that includes Frans Lanting, the late Michio Hoshino, Gary Braasch, Tui De Roy, and the team of Susan Middleton and David Liittschwager.

I began photographing in a conscientious way in the summer of 1965. I was soon concentrating on landscapes, and in the mid-1970s, with a small list of publication credits behind me, I made an appointment to see Joe Scherschel, an assistant director of the photographic staff at *National Geographic.* He told me frankly that though my landscape portfolio was up to the standards of the magazine, the paucity of wildlife images and human subjects made it unlikely that he could offer me any assignments. In response I remember thinking this was unlikely to change, for either of us. Discouraged, I started to scale back the effort to market my photographs and to make part of my living that way. I continued to make pictures, and I was glad that much of this work was still effectively represented by a stock agency in New York; but by 1978 I knew photography for me was becoming more a conscious exercise in awareness, a technique for paying attention. It would finally turn into a sequestered exploration of light and spatial volume.

Three events in the late 1970s changed the way I understood myself as a photographer. One summer afternoon I left the house for an appointment with an art director in a nearby city. Strapped to the seat of my motorcycle was a box of photographs, perhaps three hundred images representative of the best work I had done. The two-lane road I traveled winds gently through steep mountainous country. When I got to town the photographs were gone. I never found a trace of them, though I searched every foot of the road for two days. The loss dismantled my enthusiasm for photography so thoroughly that I took it for a message to do something else.

In the summer of 1976 my mother was dying of cancer. To ease her burden, and to brighten the sterile room in Lenox Hill Hospital in New York where she lay dying, I made a set of large Cibachrome prints from some of my 35-mm Kodachrome images—a white horse standing in a field of tall wild grasses bounded by a white post-and-plank fence; a faded pink boat trailer from the 1940s, abandoned in the woods; a small copse of quaking aspen, their leaves turning bright yellow on the far side of a remote mountain swamp. It was the only set of prints I would ever make. As good as they were, the change in color balance and the loss of transparency and contrast when compared with the originals, the reduction in sharpness, created a deep doubt about ever wanting to do such a thing again. I hung the images in a few shows, then put them away. I knew if I didn't start developing and printing my own images, I wouldn't be entering any more shows.

I winced whenever I saw my photographs reproduced in magazines and books, but I made my peace with that. Time-Life Books was publishing a series then called *American Wilderness*, each volume of which was devoted to a different landscape—the Maine woods, the Cascade Mountains, the Grand Canyon. I was pleased to see my work included in these volumes, but I realized that just as the distance between what I saw and what I was able to record was huge, so was that between what I recorded and what people saw. Seeing the printed images on the page was like finding one's haiku published as nineteen-syllable poems.

The third event occurred around the first serious choice I made as a photographer 20
to concentrate on a limited subject. The subject was always light, but I wanted to explore a single form, which turned out to be the flow of water in creeks and rivers near my home. I photographed in every season, when the water was high in February and March, when it was low in August, when it was transparent in July, when it was an opaque jade in December. In 1980 I began to photograph moving water in moonlight, exposures of twenty-five or thirty minutes. These images suffered from reciprocity failure—the color balance in them collapsed—but they also recorded something extraordinary, a pattern of flow we cannot actually see. They revealed the organizing principle logicians would one day call a strange attractor.

The streaming of water around a rock is one of the most complex motions of which human beings are aware. The change from a laminar, more or less uniform flow to turbulent flow around a single rock is so abstruse a transition mathematically that even the most sophisticated Cray computer cannot make it through to a satisfactory description.

Aesthetically, of course, no such difficulty exists. The eye dotes on the shift, delights in the scintillating sheeting, the roll-off of light around a rock, like hair responding to the stroke of a brush. Sometimes I photographed the flow of water in sunshine at 1/2000 of a second and then later I'd photograph the same rock in moonlight. Putting the photos side by side, I could see something hidden beneath the dazzle of the high-speed image that compared with our renderings of the Milky Way from space: the random pin-dot infernos of our own and every other sun form a spiraling, geometrical shape motionless to our eyes. In the moonlit photographs, the stray streaks from errant water splashes were eliminated (in light that weak, they occur too quickly to be recorded); what was etched on the film instead were orderly, fundamental lines of flow, created by particle after illuminated particle of gleaming water, as if each were a tracer bullet. (Years later, reading *Chaos*, James Gleick's lucid report on chaos theory, I would sit bolt upright in my chair. What I'd photographed was the deep pattern in turbulence, the clothing, as it were, of the strange attractor.)

In the months I worked at making these photographs, I came to realize I actually had two subjects as a photographer. First, these still images of a moving thing, a living thing—as close as I would probably ever come to fully photographing an animal. Second, natural light falling on orchards, images of a subject routinely understood as a still life. The orchards near me were mostly filbert orchards. In their change of color and form through the seasons, in the rain and snow that fell through them, in crows that sat on their winter branches, in leaves accumulated under them on bare dark ground, in the wind that coursed them, in the labyrinths of their limbs, ramulose within the imposed order of the orchard plot, I saw the same profundity of life I found in literature.

This was all work I was eager to do, but I would never get to it.

25 In September 1981 I was working in the Beaufort Sea off the north coast of Alaska with several marine biologists. We were conducting a food-chain survey intended to provide baseline data to guide offshore oil drilling, an impulsive and politically motivated development program funded by the Bureau of Land Management and pushed hard at the time by the Reagan government. On September 12, three of us rendezvoused at Point Barrow with a National Oceanic and Atmospheric Administration research vessel, the *Oceanographer*. They hoisted us, our gear, and our twenty-foot Boston Whaler aboard and we sailed west into pack ice in the northern Chukchi Sea.

Scientific field research is sometimes a literally bloody business. In our study we were trying to determine the flow of energy through various "levels" (artificially determined) of the marine food web. To gather data we retrieved plankton and caught fish with different sorts of traps and trawls, and we examined the contents of bearded seal, ringed seal, and spotted seal stomachs. To accomplish the latter, we shot and killed the animals. Shooting seals located us squarely in the moral dilemma of our work, and it occasioned talk aboard the *Oceanographer* about the barbarousness of science. The irony here was that without these data creatures like the ringed seal could not be afforded legal protection against oil development. The killings were a manifestation of the perversions in our age, our Kafkaesque predicaments.

I was disturbed by the fatal aspects of our work, as were my companions, but I willingly participated. I would later write an essay about the killing, but something else happened during that trip, less dramatic and more profound in its consequences for me.

Late one afternoon, working our way back to the *Oceanographer* through a snow squall, the three of us came upon a polar bear. We decided to follow him for a few minutes and I got out my cameras. The bear, swimming through loose pack ice, was clearly annoyed by our presence, though in our view we were maintaining a reasonable distance. He very soon climbed out on an ice floe, crossed it, and dropped into open water on the far side. We had to go the long way around in the workboat, but we caught up. He hissed at us and otherwise conveyed his irritation, but we continued idling along beside him.

Eventually we backed off. The bear disappeared in gauze curtains of blowing snow. We returned to the *Oceanographer*, to a warm meal and dry clothes.

30 Once the boat was secure and our scientific samples squared away in the lab, I went to my cabin. I dropped my pack on the floor, stripped off my heavy clothes, showered, and lay down in my bunk. I tried to recall every detail of the encounter with the bear. What had he been doing when we first saw him? Did he change direction then? How had he proceeded? Exactly how did he climb out of the water onto the ice floe? What were the mechanics of it? When he shook off seawater, how was it different from a dog shucking water? When he hissed, what color was the inside of his mouth?

I don't know how long I lay there, a half hour perhaps, but when I was through, when I'd answered these questions and was satisfied that I'd recalled the sequence of events precisely and in sufficient detail, I got up, dressed, and went to dinner. Remembering what happened in an encounter was crucial to my work as a writer, and attending to my cameras during our time with the bear had altered and shrunk my memory of it. While the polar bear was doing something, I was checking f-stops and attempting to frame and focus from a moving boat.

I regarded the meeting as a warning to me as a writer. Having successfully recovered details from each minute, I believed, of that encounter, having disciplined myself to do that, I sensed I wouldn't pick up a camera ever again.

It was not solely contact with this lone bear a hundred miles off the northwest coast of Alaska, of course, that ended my active involvement with photography. The change had been coming for a while. The power of the polar bear's presence, his emergence from the snow squall and his subsequent disappearance, had created an atmosphere in which I could grasp more easily a complex misgiving that had been building in me. I view any encounter with a wild animal in its own territory as a gift, an opportunity to sense the real animal, not the zoo creature, the TV creature, the advertising creature. But this gift had been more overwhelming. In some way the bear had grabbed me by the shirtfront and said, Think about this. Think about what these cameras in your hands are doing.

Years later, I'm still thinking about it. Some of what culminated for me that day is easy to understand. As a writer, I had begun to feel I was missing critical details in situations such as this one because I was distracted. I was also starting to feel uncomfortable about the way photographs tend to collapse events into a single moment, about how much they leave out. (Archeologists face a similar problem when they save only what they recognize from a dig. Years afterward, the context long having been destroyed, the archeologist might wonder what was present that he or she didn't recognize at the time. So begins a reevaluation of the meaning of the entire site.)

35 I was also disturbed about how nature and landscape photographs, my own and others', were coming to be used, not in advertising where you took your chances (some photographers at that time began labeling their images explicitly: NO TOBACCO, NO ALCOHOL), but in the editorial pages of national magazines. It is a polite fiction of our era that the average person, including the average art

director, is more informed about natural history than an educated person was in Columbus's age. Because this is not true, the majority of nature photographers who work out in the field have felt a peculiar burden to record accurately the great range of habitat and animal behavior they see, including nature's "dark" side. (Photographers accepted the fact back then that magazines in the United States, generally speaking, were not interested in photographs of mating animals—unless they were chaste or cute—or in predatory encounters if they were bloody or harrowing, as many were.)

What happened as a result of this convention was that people looking at magazines in the 1970s increasingly came to think of wild animals as vivacious and decorative in the natural world. Promoted as elegant, brave, graceful, sinister, wise, etc., according to their species, animals were deprived of personality and the capacity to be innovative. Every wildlife photographer I know can recount a story of confrontation with an art director in which he or she argued unsuccessfully for an image that told a fuller or a truer story about a particular species of animal in a layout. It was the noble lion, the thieving hyena, and the mischievous monkey, however, who routinely triumphed. A female wolf killing one of her pups, or a male bonobo approaching a female with a prominent erection, was not anything magazine editors were comfortable with.

In the late seventies, I asked around among several publishers to see whether they might have any interest in a series of disturbing photographs made in a zoo by a woman named Ilya. She'd taken them on assignment for *Life*, but very few of them were ever published because she'd concentrated on depicting animals apparently driven insane by their incarceration. I remember as particularly unsettling the look of psychosis in the face of a male lion, its mane twisted into knots. I could develop no interest in publishing her work. An eccentric view, people felt. Too distressing.

So, along with a growing political awareness of endangered landscapes and their indigenous animals in the 1970s came, ironically, a more and more dazzling presentation of those creatures in incomplete and prejudicial ways. Photo editors made them look not like what they were but the way editors wanted them to appear—well-groomed, appropriate to stereotype, and living safely apart from the machinations of human enterprise. To my mind there was little difference then between a *Playboy* calendar and a wildlife calendar. Both celebrated the conventionally gorgeous, the overly endowed, the seductive. I and many other photographers at the time were apprehensive about the implications of this trend.

Another concern I had that September afternoon, a more complicated one, was what was happening to memory in my generation. The advertising injunction to preserve family memories by taking photographs had become so shrill a demand, and the practice had become so compulsive, that recording the event was more important for some than participating in it. The inculcated rationale which grew up around this practice was that to take and preserve family photos was to act in a socially responsible way. The assumption seemed specious to me. My generation was the first to have ready access to inexpensive tape recorders and cameras. Far from recording memories of these talks and events, what we seemed to be doing was storing memories that would never be retrieved, that would never form a coherent narrative. In the same way that our desk drawers and cabinet shelves slowly filled with these "personal" sounds and images, we were beginning, it seemed to me, to live our lives in dissociated bits and places. The narrative spine of an individual life was disappearing. The order of events was becoming increasingly meaningless.

This worry, together with the increasingly commercial use to which the work 40
of photographers like myself was being put and the preference for an entertaining but not necessarily coherent landscape of wild animals (images that essentially lied to children), made me more and more reluctant to stay involved. Some of the contemporary photographers I most respect—Lanting, Hoshino, Braasch, De Roy, Jim Brandenburg, Flip Nicklin, Sam Abell, Nick Nichols, Galen Rowell—have managed through the strength of their work and their personal integrity to overcome some of these problems, which are part and parcel of working in a world dominated more and more by commercial interests pursuing business strategies. But I knew I had no gift here to persevere. That realization, and my reluctance to photograph animals in the first place, may have precipitated my decision that day in the Chukchi.

As a writer, I had yet other concerns, peculiar to that discipline. I had begun to wonder whether my searching for the telling photographic image in a situation was beginning to interfere with my writing about what happened. I was someone who took a long time to let a story settle. I'd began to suspect that the photographs made while I was in a note-taking stage were starting to lock my words into a pattern, and that the pattern was being determined too early. Photographs, in some way, were introducing preconceptions into a process I wanted to keep fluid. I often have no clear idea of what I'm doing. I just act. I pitch in, I try to stay alert to everything around me. I don't want to stop and focus on a finished image, which I'm inclined to do as a photographer. I want, instead, to see a sentence fragment scrawled in my notebook, smeared by rain. I don't want the clean, fixed image right away.

An attentive mind, I'm sure, can see the flaws in my reasoning. Some photographers are doing no more than taking notes when they click the shutter. It's only after a shoot that they discover what the story is. But by trying to both photograph and write, I'd begun to feel I was attempting to create two parallel but independent stories. The effort had become confusing and draining. I let go of photography partly because its defining process, to my mind, was less congruent with the way I wanted to work.

On June 16, 1979, forty-one sperm whales beached themselves at the mouth of the Siuslaw River on the Oregon coast, about one hundred miles from my home. I wrote a long essay about the stranding but didn't start work on it until after I'd spent two days photographing the eclipse of these beasts' lives and the aftermath of their deaths. That was the last time I attempted to do both things.

Perhaps the most rarefied of my concerns about photography that day in the Chukchi was one that lay for me at the heart of photography: recording a fleeting pattern of light in a defined volume of space. Light always attracted me. Indeed, twenty-five years after the fact, I can still vividly recall the light falling at dusk on a windbreak of trees in Mitchell, Oregon. It rendered me speechless when I saw it, and by some magic I managed to get it down on film. The problem of rendering volume in photography, however, was one I never solved beyond employing the conventional solutions of perspective and depth of field. I could recognize spatial volume successfully addressed in the work of other photographers—in Adams's work, for example, partly because so many of his photographs do not have an object as a subject. Finding some way myself to render volume successfully in a photograph would mean, I believed, walking too far away from my work as a writer. And, ultimately, it was as a writer that I felt more comfortable.

45 I miss making photographs. A short while ago I received a call from a curator at the Whitney Museum in New York named May Castleberry. She had just mounted a show called "Perpetual Mirage: Photographic Narratives of the Desert West" and I had been able to provide some minor assistance with it. She was calling now to pursue a conversation we'd begun at the time about Rockwell Kent, an illustrator, painter, and socialist widely known in the thirties, forties, and fifties. She wanted to hang a selection of his "nocturnes," prints and drawings Kent had made of people under starlit night skies. She was calling to see what I could suggest about his motivation.

Given Kent's leanings toward Nordic myth and legend and his espousal of Teddy Roosevelt's "strenuous life," it seemed obvious to me that he would want to portray his heroic (mostly male) figures against the vault of the heavens. But there were at least two other things at work here, I believed. First, Kent was strongly drawn to high latitudes, like Greenland, where in winter one can view the deep night sky for weeks on end. It was not really the "night" sky, however, he was drawing; it was the sunless sky of a winter day. Quotidian life assumes mythic proportions here not because it's heroic, but because it's carried out beneath the stars.

Secondly, I conjectured, because Kent was an artist working on flat surfaces, he sought, like every such artist, ways to suggest volume, to make the third dimension apparent. Beyond what clouds provide, the daytime sky has no depth; it's the night sky that gives an artist volume. While it takes an extraordinary person—the light and space artist James Turrell, say—to make the celestial vault visible in sunshine, many artists have successfully conveyed a sense of the sky's volume by painting it at night.

The conceit can easily grow up in a photographer that he or she has pretty much seen all the large things—the range of possible emotion to be evoked with light, the contrasts to be made by arranging objects in different scales, problems in the third and fourth dimension. But every serious photographer, I believe, has encountered at some point ideas unanticipated and dumbfounding. The shock causes you to reexamine all you've assumed about your own work and the work of others, especially the work of people you've never particularly understood. This happened most recently for me in seeing the photography of Linda Connor. While working on a story about international air freight, I became so disoriented, flying every day from one spot on the globe to another thousands of miles away, I did not know what time I was living in. Whatever time it was, it was out of phase with the sun, a time not to be dialed up on a watch, mine or anyone else's.

At a pause in this international hurtling, during a six-hour layover in Cape Town, I went for a ride with an acquaintance. He drove us out to Clifton Bay on the west side of Table Mountain. I was so dazed by my abuse of time that I was open to thoughts I might otherwise never have had. One of those thoughts was that I could recognize the physicality of time. We can discern the physical nature of space in a picture, grasp the way, for example, Robert Adams is able to photograph the air itself, making it visible like a plein air painter. In Cape Town that day I saw what I came to call indigenous time. It clung to the flanks of Table Mountain. It resisted being absorbed into my helter-skelter time. It seemed not yet to have been subjugated by Dutch and British colonial expansion, as the physical landscape so clearly had been. It was time apparent to the senses, palpable. What made me believe I was correct in this perception was that, only a month before, I'd examined a collection of Linda Connor's work, a book called *Luminance.* I realized there at Table Mountain that she'd photographed what I was looking at. She'd photographed indigenous time.

I'd grasped Ms. Connor's photographs in some fashion after an initial pass, but 50
I hadn't sensed their depth, their power, what Gerard Manley Hopkins called "the achieve of the thing." With this new insight I wrote her an excited note, an attempt to thank her for work that opened the door to a room I'd never explored.

One of the great blessings of our modern age, a kind of redemption for its cruelties and unmitigated greed, is that one can walk down to a corner book-store and find a copy of Ms. Connor's book. Or of Robert Adams's *What We Brought: The New World,* or Frans Lanting's *Bonobo: The Forgotten Ape,* or, say, Mary Peck's *Chaco Canyon: A Center and Its World,* and then be knocked across the room by a truth one had not, until that moment, clearly discerned.

It is more than illumination, though, more than a confirmation of one's intuition, aesthetics, or beliefs that comes out of the perusal of such a photographer's images. It's regaining the feeling that one is not cut off from the wellsprings of intelligence and goodwill, of sympathy for human plight.

I do not know, of course, why the photographers I admire, even the ones I know, photograph, but I am acutely aware that without the infusion of their images hope would wither in me. I feel an allegiance to their work more as a writer than as someone who once tried to see in this way, perhaps because I presume we share certain principles related to the effort to imagine or explain.

It is correct, I think, as Robert Adams wrote me that day, to believe in a community of artists stimulated by and respectful of one another's work. But it's also true that without an audience (of which we're all a part) the work remains unfinished, unfulfilled. A photographer seeks intimacy with the world and then endeavors to share it. Inherent in that desire to share is a love of humanity. In different media, and from time to time, we have succeeded, I believe, in helping one another understand what is going on. We have come to see that, in some way, this is our purpose with each other.

THINGS TO DO WITH THE READING

1. Like Sontag, Lopez has anxieties about the artistic, psychological, and ethical impact of photography—both as product and as activity. But he also testifies to the importance of photography in his life in strong terms: "I do not know, of course, why the photographers I admire, even the ones I know, photograph, but I am acutely aware that without the infusion of their images hope would wither in me" (see paragraph 53). Reflect and write on Lopez's anxieties about photography, especially in relation to his work as a writer. Then try to negotiate the gap between this anxiety and Lopez's powerful praise for photography as a source of hope.

   You might want to Google images from the photographers Lopez feels most strongly about (Linda Connors and Robert Adams) and make your analysis of these part of your essay. On the relationship between photography and writing, see paragraphs 31–34, Lopez's account of the aftermath of his encounter with the polar bear; also see the thinking in paragraph 34 about the way that "photographs tend to collapse events into a single moment."
2. **Link:** It is interesting to consider what Lopez thinks a photograph—at least his idea of photographs—is. Summarize and reflect on Lopez's various accounts of what he was trying to photograph, and then locate him in the context of the ideas in the Elliott interview. What, for example, does Lopez mean when he says "The subject was always light" (see paragraph 20)?
3. **Link:** The moral and psychological dimension that was central in the Sontag essay is central in Lopez's essay as well. Although Lopez finds things to worry about in landscape and nature photography, he also offers powerful praise of its recuperative and moral value, as is evident in the following statement: "The more I gravitated as a writer toward landscape as a context in which to work out what I was thinking as a young man about issues like justice, tolerance, ambiguity, and compassion, the more I came to concentrate on landforms as a photographer" (see paragraph 15). Summarize and reflect on this strand of thinking in the Lopez essay, and then put it into conversation with comparable strands in the Sontag essay and the Elliott interview.
4. **Link:** In his interview piece, Elliott argues that photography can be a form of historical research and historical archiving. See his comments in paragraph 33 on the documentary as supplying raw material "to be of use for the future." Sontag, by contrast, is inclined to think that photographers see only what they want to see and what the culture has already given them permission to see, and so theirs is a spurious form of history. Where does Lopez stand on this issue? Write an essay on what Lopez says photographers can achieve relative to what Elliott and Sontag say photography can (and can't) do.

5. **Application:** There is an interesting moment in paragraph 23 in which Lopez offers the verbal equivalent of something that he repeatedly tried to photograph (the natural light falling on orchards). This is a form of writing called *ekphrasis*. An ekphrastic piece of writing tries to be the verbal equivalent of a photograph. It strives to create the same mental images and the same emotional/psychological effect as a photograph or painting of the same thing might produce. Much ekphrastic writing takes the form of verbal re-enactments of paintings or photographs. Ekphrasis offers an illuminating exercise for thinking about visual images. Experiment with ekphrasis in one or both of the following ways:
   - Go somewhere that might inspire you to take a picture. Write a verbal equivalent of the picture that you would like to take. Take a photograph of the same subject. Write a short essay on what you learned by comparing and contrasting the two. Note: Avoid talking about which was better; concentrate instead on describing and reflecting on the differences.
   - Start with a photograph, preferably one of the type that you think Lopez would want to take. This can be a photograph of your own or one that you find by Googling some of the photographers that Lopez cites in his essay. Write a verbal equivalent of the photograph and then reflect (in writing) on what you learned in the process. ◗

John Berger

Images of Women in European Art

Originally produced for television in England, John Berger's book *Ways of Seeing* (1972), from which this essay is taken, focuses on the relationship between the implied spectator or viewer and a work of art. Interested especially in the history of the nude in European painting, Berger demonstrates the ways that these paintings were designed to flatter and enhance the power of male viewers, while inducing the women to see themselves as males would see them. Berger's chapter on nudes is part of an extended cultural and aesthetic discourse on what is called "the gaze." This concept originates with French theorists Jacques Lacan and Michel Foucault and has been extended and applied by other writers, such as the film theorist Teresa de Lauretis. Besides being an art critic, Berger is also an essayist, painter, and novelist.

According to usage and conventions which are at last being questioned but have 1
by no means been overcome, the social presence of a woman is different in kind from that of a man. A man's presence is dependent upon the promise of power which he embodies. If the promise is large and credible, his presence is striking. If it is small or incredible, he is found to have little presence. The promised power may be moral, physical, temperamental, economic, social, sexual—but its object is always exterior to the man. A man's presence suggests what he is capable of doing to you or for you. His presence may be fabricated, in the sense that he pretends to be capable of what he is not. But the pretense is always toward a power which he exercises on others.

By contrast, a woman's presence expresses her own attitude to herself, and defines what can and cannot be done to her. Her presence is manifest in her gestures, voice, opinions, expressions, clothes, chosen surroundings, taste—indeed there is nothing she can do which does not contribute to her presence. Presence, for a woman, is so intrinsic to her person that men tend to think of it as an almost physical emanation, a kind of heat or smell or aura.

To be born a woman has been to be born, within an allotted and confined space, into the keeping of men. The social presence of women has developed as a result of their ingenuity in living under such tutelage within such a limited space. But this has been at the cost of a woman's self being split into two. A woman must continually watch herself. She is almost continually accompanied by her own image of herself. Whilst she is walking across a room or whilst she is weeping at the death of her father, she can scarcely avoid envisaging herself walking or weeping. From earliest childhood she has been taught and persuaded to survey herself continually.

And so she comes to consider the *surveyor* and the *surveyed* within her as the two constituent yet always distinct elements of her identity as a woman.

She has to survey everything she is and everything she does because how she 5
appears to others, and ultimately how she appears to men, is of crucial importance for what is normally thought of as the success of her life. Her own sense of being in herself is supplanted by a sense of being appreciated as herself by another.

Men survey women before treating them. Consequently how a woman appears to a man can determine how she will be treated. To acquire some control over this process, women must contain it and interiorize it. That part of a woman's self which is the surveyor treats the part which is the surveyed so as to demonstrate to others how her whole self would like to be treated. And this exemplary treatment of herself by herself constitutes her presence. Every woman's presence regulates what is and is not "permissible" within her presence. Every one of her actions—whatever its direct purpose or motivation—is also read as an indication of how she would like to be treated. If a woman throws a glass on the floor, this is an example of how she treats her own emotion of anger and so of how she would wish it to be treated by others. If a man does the same, his action is only read as an expression of his anger. If a woman makes a good joke, this is an example of how she treats the joker in herself and accordingly of how she as a joker-woman would like to be treated by others. Only a man can make a good joke for its own sake.

One might simplify this by saying: *Men act* and *women appear*. Men look at women. Women watch themselves being looked at. This determines not only most relations between men and women but also the relation of women to themselves. The surveyor of woman in herself is male: the surveyed female. Thus she turns herself into an object—and most particularly an object of vision: a sight.

In one category of European oil painting women were the principal, ever-recurring subject. That category is the nude. In the nudes of European painting we can discover some of the criteria and conventions by which women have been seen and judged as sights.

The first nudes in the tradition depicted Adam and Eve. It is worth referring to the story as told in Genesis:

> And when the woman saw that the tree was good for food, and that it was a delight to the eyes, and that the tree was to be desired to make one wise, she took of the fruit thereof and did eat; and she gave also unto her husband with her, and he did eat.
>
> And the eyes of them both were opened, and they knew that they were naked; and they sewed fig-leaves together and made themselves aprons. … And the Lord God called unto the man and said unto him, "Where are thou?" And he said, "I heard thy voice in the garden, and I was afraid, because I was naked; and I hid myself. …"
>
> Unto the woman God said, "I will greatly multiply thy sorrow and thy conception; in sorrow thou shalt bring forth children; and thy desire shall be to thy husband and he shall rule over thee."

What is striking about this story? They became aware of being naked because, 10
as a result of eating the apple, each saw the other differently. Nakedness was created in the mind of the beholder.

The second striking fact is that the woman is blamed and is punished by being made subservient to the man. In relation to the woman, the man becomes the agent of God.

In the medieval tradition the story was often illustrated, scene following scene, as in a strip cartoon.

During the Renaissance the narrative sequence disappeared, and the single moment depicted became the moment of shame. The couple wear fig leaves or make a modest gesture with their hands. But now their shame is not so much in relation to one another as to the spectator.

Later the shame becomes a kind of display.

15 When the tradition of painting became more secular, other themes also offered the opportunity of painting nudes. But in them all there remains the implication that the subject (a woman) is aware of being seen by a spectator.

She is not naked as she is.

She is naked as the spectator sees her.

Often—as with the favourite subject of Susannah and the Elders—this is the actual theme of the picture. We join the Elders to spy on Susannah taking her bath. She looks back at us looking at her.

In another version of the subject by Tintoretto, Susannah is looking at herself in a mirror. Thus she joins the spectators of herself.

20 The mirror was often used as a symbol of the vanity of woman. The moralizing, however, was mostly hypocritical.

You painted a naked woman because you enjoyed looking at her, you put a mirror in her hand and you called the painting *Vanity*, thus morally condemning the woman whose nakedness you had depicted for your own pleasure.

The real function of the mirror was otherwise. It was to make the woman connive in treating herself as, first and foremost, a sight.

The judgment of Paris was another theme with the same inwritten idea of a man or men looking at naked women.

But a further element is now added. The element of judgment. Paris awards the apple to the woman he finds most beautiful. Thus Beauty becomes competitive. (Today The Judgment of Paris has become the Beauty Contest.) Those who are not judged beautiful are *not beautiful.* Those who are, are given the prize.

25 The prize is to be owned by a judge—that is to say to be available for him. Charles the Second commissioned a secret painting from Lely. It is a highly typical image of the tradition. Nominally it might be a *Venus and Cupid.* In fact it is a portrait of one of the King's mistresses, Nell Gwynne. It shows her passively looking at the spectator staring at her naked. [See Figure 17.26.]

This nakedness is not, however, an expression of her own feelings; it is a sign of her submission to the owner's feelings or demands. (The owner of both woman and painting.) The painting, when the King showed it to others, demonstrated this submission and his guests envied him.

It is worth noticing that in other non-European traditions—in Indian art, Persian art, African art, Pre-Columbian art—nakedness is never supine in this way. And if, in these traditions, the theme of a work is sexual attraction, it is likely to show active sexual love as between two people, the woman as active as the man, the actions of each absorbing the other. [See Figures 17.27 and 17.28.]

We can now begin to see the difference between nakedness and nudity in the European tradition. In his book *The Nude*, Kenneth Clark maintains that to be naked is simply to be without clothes, whereas the nude is a form of art. According to him, a nude is not the starting point of a painting but a way of seeing which the painting achieves. To some degree, this is true—although the way of seeing "a nude" is not necessarily confined to art. There are also nude photographs, nude poses, nude gestures. What is true is that the nude is always conventionalized—and the authority for its conventions derives from a certain tradition of art.

FIGURE 17.20 *Adam and Eve in the Garden of Eden; Fall and Expulsion* miniature from *Les Tres Riches Heures du Duc de Berry* by Pol de Limbourg

To view this image in color, visit www.thomsonedu.com/english/rosenwasser

FIGURE 17.21 *Fall of Man*, ca. 1525 by Jan Gossaert called Mabuse. Oil on oak, 170 × 114 cm

To view this image in color, visit www.thomsonedu.com/english/rosenwasser

FIGURE 17.22 *Susannah in Her Bath.* Canvas, 167 × 238 cm by Jacopo Robusti Tintoretto

To view this image in color, visit www.thomsonedu.com/english/rosenwasser

What do these conventions mean? What does a nude signify? It is not sufficient to answer these questions merely in terms of the art form, for it is quite clear that the nude also relates to lived sexuality.

To be naked is to be oneself. 30

To be nude is to be seen naked by others and yet not recognized for oneself. A naked body has to be seen as an object in order to become a nude. (The sight of it as an object stimulates the use of it as an object.) Nakedness reveals itself. Nudity is placed on display.

To be naked is to be without disguise.

To be on display is to have the surface of one's own skin, the hairs of one's own body, turned into a disguise which, in that situation, can never be discarded. The nude is condemned to never being naked. Nudity is a form of dress.

In the average European oil painting of the nude, the principal protagonist is never painted. He is the spectator in front of the picture, and he is presumed to be a man. Everything is addressed to him. Everything must appear to be the result of his being there. It is for him that the figures have assumed their nudity. But he, by definition, is a stranger—with his clothes still on.

Consider the *Allegory of Time and Love* by Bronzino. The complicated symbol- 35
ism which lies behind this painting need not concern us now, because it does not affect its sexual appeal—at the first degree. Before it is anything else, this is a painting of sexual provocation. [See Figure 17.29.]

FIGURE 17.23 *Susannah Bathing*. Oil on canvas (after 1560) by Jacopo Robusti Tintoretto

To view this image in color, visit www.thomsonedu.com/english/rosenwasser

The painting was sent as a present from the Grand Duke of Florence to the King of France. The boy kneeling on the cushion and kissing the woman is Cupid. She is Venus. But the way her body is arranged has nothing to do with their kissing. Her body is arranged in the way it is, to display it to the man looking at the picture. This picture is made to appeal to *his* sexuality. It has nothing to do with her sexuality. (Here and in the European tradition generally, the convention of not painting the hair on a woman's body helps towards the same end. Hair is associated with sexual power, with passion. The woman's sexual passion needs to be minimized so that the spectator may feel that he has the monopoly of such passion.) Women are there to feed an appetite, not to have any of their own. [...]

It is true that sometimes a painting includes a male lover.

But the woman's attention is very rarely directed towards him. Often she looks away from him, or she looks out of the picture toward the one who considers himself her true lover—the spectator-owner.

There was a special category of private pornographic paintings (especially in the eighteenth century) in which couples making love make an appearance. But even in front of these it is clear that the spectator-owner will in fantasy oust the other man, or else identify with him. By contrast the image of the couple in non-European traditions provokes the notion of many couples making love. "We all have a thousand hands, a thousand feet and will never go alone."

FIGURE 17.24 *Vanity*, central panel from the *Triptych of Earthly Vanity and Divine Salvation*, c. 1485 by Hans Memling

To view this image in color, visit www.thomsonedu.com/english/rosenwasser

FIGURE 17.25 *The Judgement of Paris*, 1639 (oil on canvas) by Peter Paul Rubens

To view this image in color, visit www.thomsonedu.com/english/rosenwasser

FIGURE 17.26 *Portrait of Nell Gwynne as Venus with her son as Cupid* by Sir Peter Lely

To view this image in color, visit www.thomsonedu.com/english/rosenwasser

FIGURE 17.27 Detail of 11th century sculpture of Vishnu and Lakeshmi, Parsavantha Temple, Khajuraho

To view this image in color, visit www.thomsonedu.com/english/rosenwasser

FIGURE 17.28 Moche vase with family group, 7th or 8th century AD

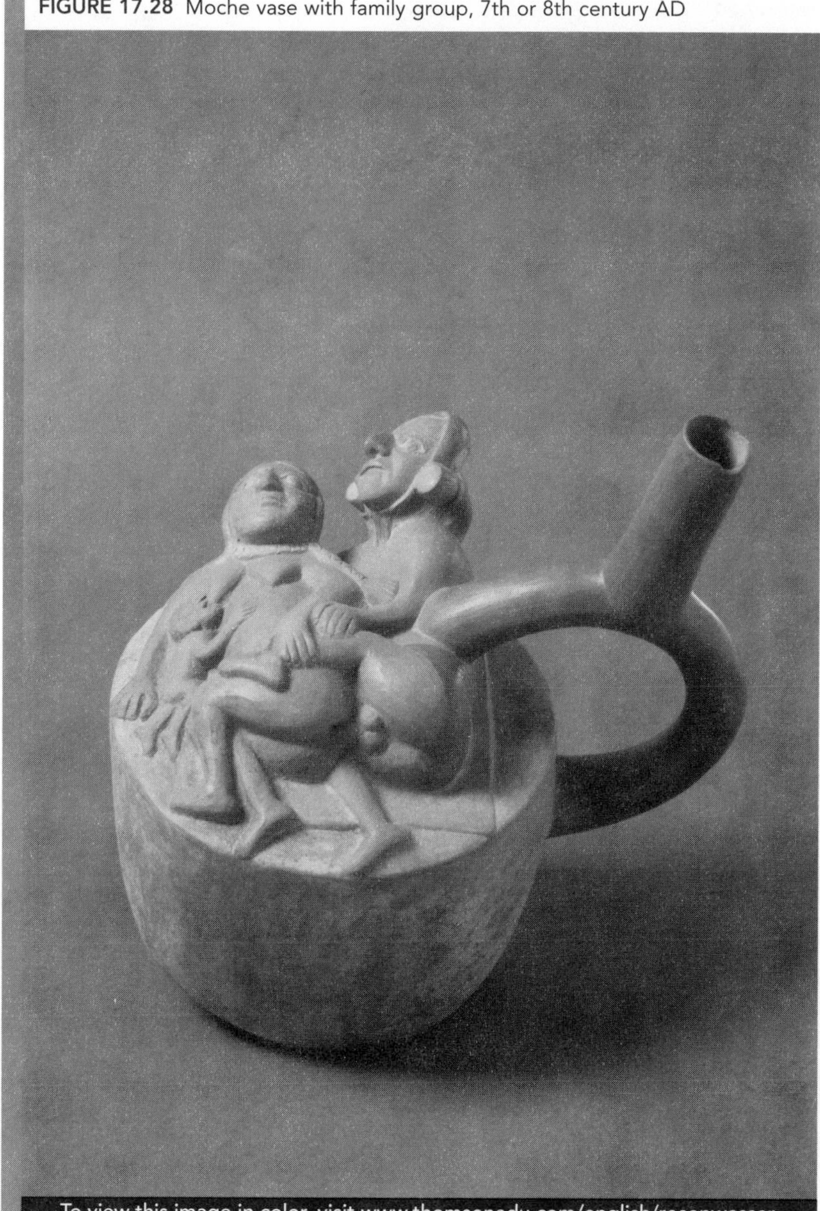

To view this image in color, visit www.thomsonedu.com/english/rosenwasser

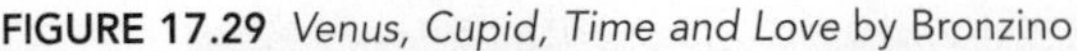

FIGURE 17.29 *Venus, Cupid, Time and Love* by Bronzino

To view this image in color, visit www.thomsonedu.com/english/rosenwasser

Almost all post-Renaissance European sexual imagery is frontal—either literally or metaphorically—because the sexual protagonist is the spectator-owner looking at it. 40

The absurdity of this male flattery reached its peak in the public academic art of the nineteenth century.

Men of state, of business, discussed under paintings like this. When one of them felt he had been outwitted, he looked up for consolation. What he saw reminded him that he was a man.

FIGURE 17.30 *Bacchus, Ceres and Amor*. Canvas by Hans von Aachen.

To view this image in color, visit www.thomsonedu.com/english/rosenwasser

There are a few exceptional nudes in the European tradition of oil painting to which very little of what has been said above applies. Indeed they are no longer nudes—they break the norms of the art form; they are paintings of loved women, more or less naked. Among the hundreds of thousands of nudes which make up the tradition, there are perhaps a hundred of these exceptions. In each case the painter's personal vision of the particular woman he is painting is so strong that it makes no allowance for the spectator. The painter's vision binds the woman to him so that they become as inseparable as couples in stone. The spectator can witness their relationship—but he can do no more: He is forced to recognize himself as the outsider he is. He cannot deceive himself into believing that she is naked for him. He cannot turn her into a nude. The way the painter has painted her includes her will and her intentions in the very structure of the image, in the very expression of her body and her face.

The typical and the exceptional in the tradition can be defined by the simple naked/nude antinomy, but the problem of painting nakedness is not as simple as it might at first appear.

What is the sexual function of nakedness in reality? Clothes encumber contact 45
and movement. But it would seem that nakedness has a positive visual value in its own right: we want to *see* the other naked: The other delivers to us the sight of themselves, and we seize upon it—sometimes quite regardless of whether it is for the first time or the hundredth. What does this sight of the other mean to us, how does it, at that instant of total disclosure, affect our desire?

Their nakedness acts as a confirmation and provokes a very strong sense of relief. She is a woman like any other: or he is a man like any other: we are overwhelmed by the marvellous simplicity of the familiar sexual mechanism.

We did not, of course, consciously expect this to be otherwise: Unconscious homosexual desires (or unconscious heterosexual desires if the couple concerned are homosexual) may have led each to half expect something different. But the "relief" can be explained without recourse to the unconscious.

We did not expect them to be otherwise, but the urgency and complexity of our feelings bred a sense of uniqueness which the sight of the other, as she is or as he is, now dispels. They are more like the rest of their sex than they are different. In this revelation lies the warm and friendly—as opposed to cold and impersonal—anonymity of nakedness.

One could express this differently: At the moment of nakedness first perceived, an element of banality enters: an element that exists only because we need it.

Up to that instant the other was more or less mysterious. Etiquettes of 50
modesty are not merely puritan or sentimental: It is reasonable to recognize a loss of mystery. And the explanation of this loss of mystery may be largely visual. The focus of perception shifts from eyes, mouth, shoulders, hands—all of which are capable of such subtleties of expression that the personality expressed by them is manifold—it shifts from these to the sexual parts, whose formation suggests an utterly compelling but single process. The other is reduced or elevated—whichever you prefer—to their primary sexual category: male or female. Our relief is the relief of finding an unquestionable reality to whose direct demands our earlier, highly complex awareness must now yield.

We need the banality which we find in the first instant of disclosure because it grounds us in reality. But it does more than that. This reality, by promising the familiar, proverbial mechanism of sex, offers, at the same time, the possibility of the shared subjectivity of sex.

FIGURE 17.31 *The Oreads*, 1902 by William-Adolphe Bourguereau

To view this image in color, visit www.thomsonedu.com/english/rosenwasser

The loss of mystery occurs simultaneously with the offering of the means for creating a shared mystery. The sequence is: subjective—objective—subjective to the power of two.

We can now understand the difficulty of creating a static image of sexual nakedness. In lived sexual experience nakedness is a process rather than a state. If one moment of that process is isolated, its image will seem banal, and its banality, instead of serving as a bridge between two intense imaginative states, will be chilling. This is one reason why expressive photographs of the naked are even rarer than paintings. The easy solution for the photographer is to turn the figure into a nude, which, by generalizing both sight and viewer and making sexuality unspecific, turns desire into fantasy.

FIGURE 17.32 *Danae*, 1643 by Rembrandt van Rijn

To view this image in color, visit www.thomsonedu.com/english/rosenwasser

Let us examine an exceptional painted image of nakedness. It is a painting by Rubens of his young second wife, whom he married when he himself was relatively old.

We see her in the act of turning, her fur about to slip off her shoulders. 55
Clearly she will not remain as she is for more than a second. In a superficial sense her image is as instantaneous as a photograph's. But, in a more profound sense, the painting "contains" time and its experience. It is easy to imagine that a moment ago, before she pulled the fur round her shoulders, she was entirely naked. The consecutive stages up to and away from the moment of total disclosure have been transcended. She can belong to any or all of them simultaneously.

Her body confronts us, not as an immediate sight but as experience—the painter's experience. Why? There are superficial anecdotal reasons: her dishevelled hair, the expression of her eyes directed toward him, the tenderness with which the exaggerated susceptibility of her skin has been painted. But the profound reason is a formal one. Her appearance has been literally re-cast by the painter's subjectivity. Beneath the fur that she holds across herself, the upper part of her body and her legs can never meet. There is a displacement sideways of about nine inches: her thighs, in order to join onto her hips, are at least nine inches too far to the left.

Rubens probably did not plan this: The spectator may not consciously notice it. In itself it is unimportant. What matters is what it permits. It permits the body to become impossibly dynamic. Its coherence is no longer within itself but within the experience of the painter. More precisely, it permits the upper and lower halves of the body to rotate separately, and in opposite directions, round the sexual center which is hidden: the torso turning to the right, the legs to the left. At the same time this hidden sexual center is connected by means of the dark fur coat to all the surrounding darkness in the picture, so that she is turning both around and within the dark, which has been made a metaphor for her sex.

Apart from the necessity of transcending the single instant and of admitting subjectivity, there is, as we have seen, one further element which is essential for any great sexual image of the naked. This is the element of banality which must be undisguised but not chilling. It is this which distinguishes between voyeur and lover. Here such banality is to be found in Rubens's compulsive painting of the fat softness of Hélène Fourment's flesh, which continually breaks every ideal convention of form and (to him) continually offers the promise of her extraordinary particularity.

The nude in European oil painting is usually presented as an admirable expression of the European humanist spirit. This spirit was inseparable from individualism. And without the development of a highly conscious individualism, the exceptions to the tradition (extremely personal images of the naked), would never have been painted. Yet the tradition contained a contradiction which it could not itself resolve. A few individual artists intuitively recognized this and resolved the contradiction in their own terms, but their solutions could never enter the tradition's *cultural* terms.

The contradiction can be stated simply. On the one hand the individualism of 60
the artist, the thinker, the patron, the owner: on the other hand, the person who is the object of their activities—the woman—treated as a thing or an abstraction.

Dürer believed that the ideal nude ought to be constructed by taking the face of one body, the breasts of another, the legs of a third, the shoulders of a fourth, the hands of a fifth—and so on.

The result would glorify Man. But the exercise presumed a remarkable indifference to who any one person really was.

In the art form of the European nude, the painters and spectator-owners were usually men and the persons treated as objects, usually women. This unequal relationship is so deeply embedded in our culture that it still structures the consciousness of many women. They do to themselves what men do to them. They survey, like men, their own femininity.

In modern art the category of the nude has become less important. Artists themselves began to question it. In this, as in many other respects, Manet represented a turning point. If one compares his *Olympia* with Titian's original, one sees a woman, cast in the traditional role, beginning to question that role, somewhat defiantly. [See Figures 17.36 and 17.37.]

FIGURE 17.33 Peter Paul Rubens, *Helene Fourment in a Fur Coat*

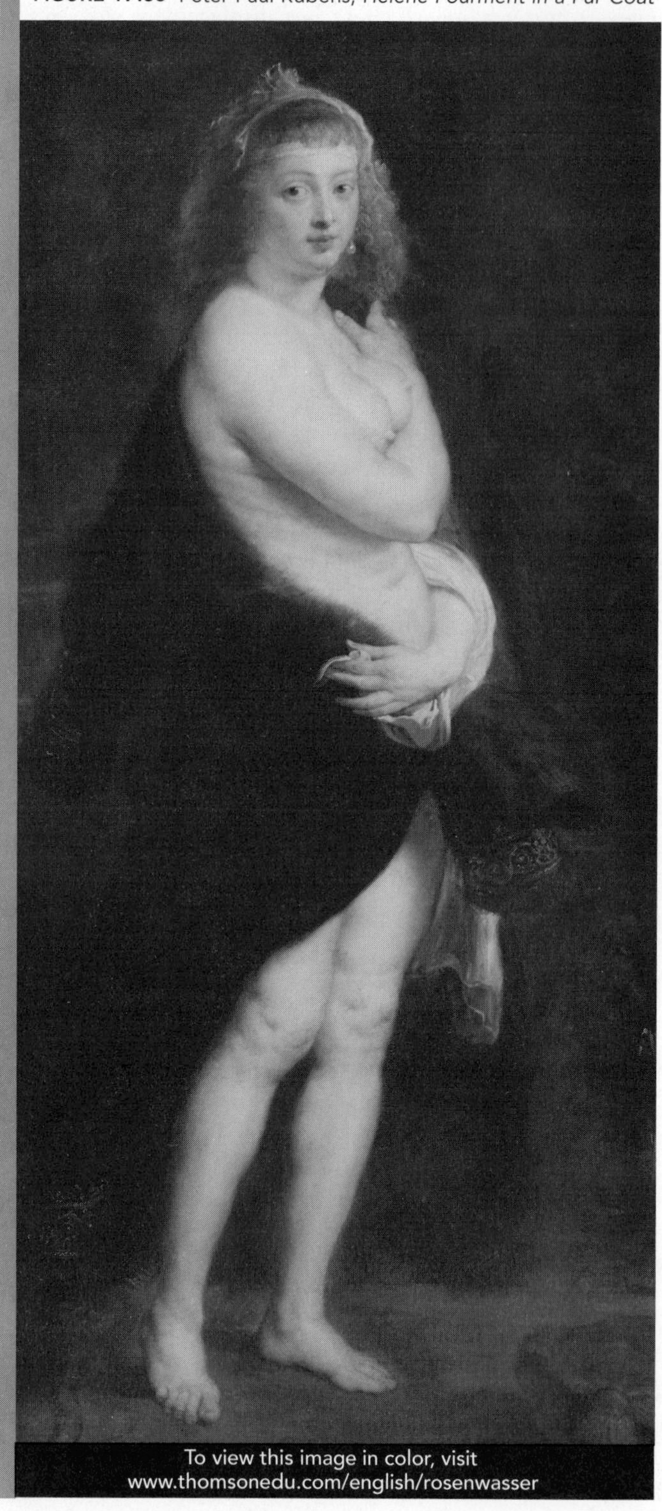

To view this image in color, visit
www.thomsonedu.com/english/rosenwasser

FIGURE 17.34 Artist drawing a model in foreshortening through a frame using a grid system. Woodcut from *Unterweysung der Messung* Nuremberg, 1527 by Albrecht Dürer

FIGURE 17.35 Woodcut of woman from *Four Books on the Human Proportions* by Albrecht Dürer

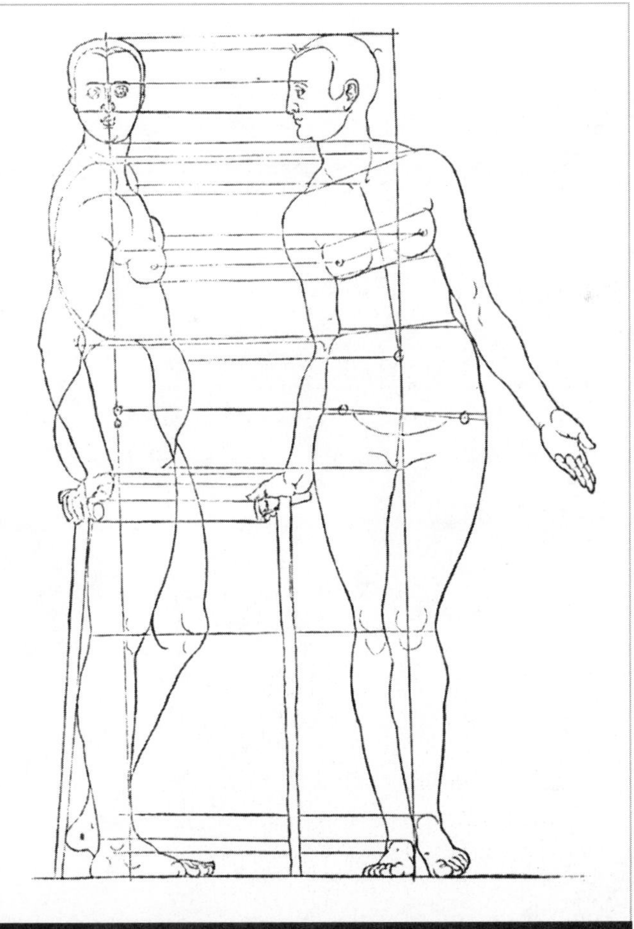

FIGURE 17.36 *The Venus of Urbino* by Titian

To view this image in color, visit www.thomsonedu.com/english/rosenwasser

FIGURE 17.37 *Olympia* by Edouard Manet

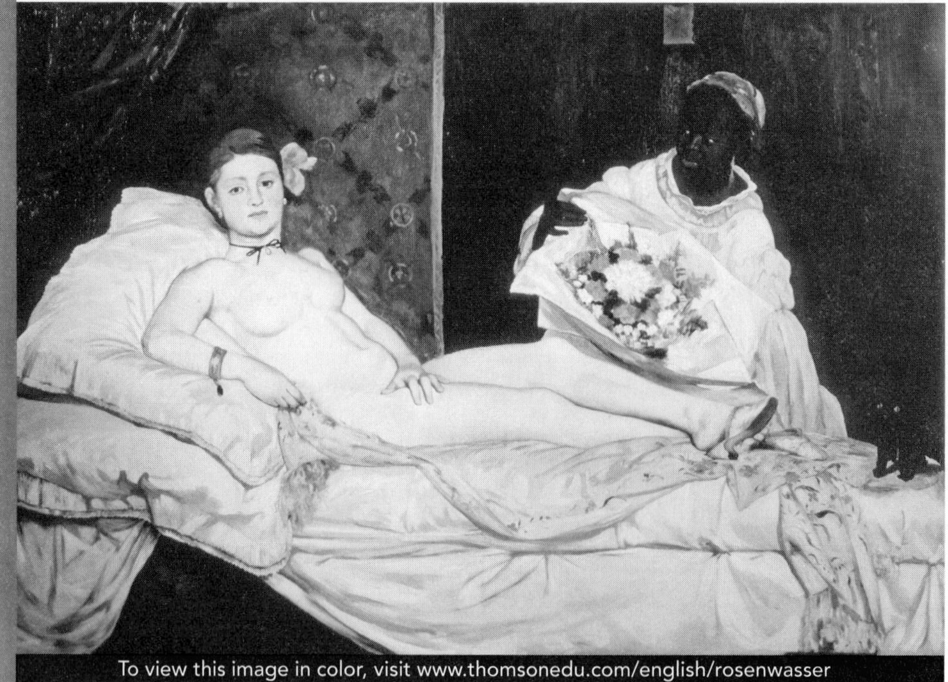

To view this image in color, visit www.thomsonedu.com/english/rosenwasser

The ideal was broken. But there was little to replace it except the “realism” of 65
the prostitute—who became the quintessential woman of early avant-garde twentieth-century painting. (Toulouse-Lautrec, Picasso, Rouault, German Expressionism, etc.) In academic painting the tradition continued.

Today the attitudes and values which informed that tradition are expressed through other, more widely diffused media—advertising, journalism, television.

But the essential way of seeing women, the essential use to which their images are put, has not changed. Women are depicted in a quite different way from men—not because the feminine is different from the masculine—but because the “ideal” spectator is always assumed to be male, and the image of the woman is designed to flatter him. If you have any doubt that this is so, make the following experiment. Choose [...] an image of a traditional nude. Transform the woman into a man, either in your mind's eye or by drawing on the reproduction. Then notice the violence which that transformation does-not to the image, but to the assumptions of a likely viewer.

FIGURE 17.38 *Self-Portrait*, 1980 by Alice Neel. Oil on canvas, 54" × 40"

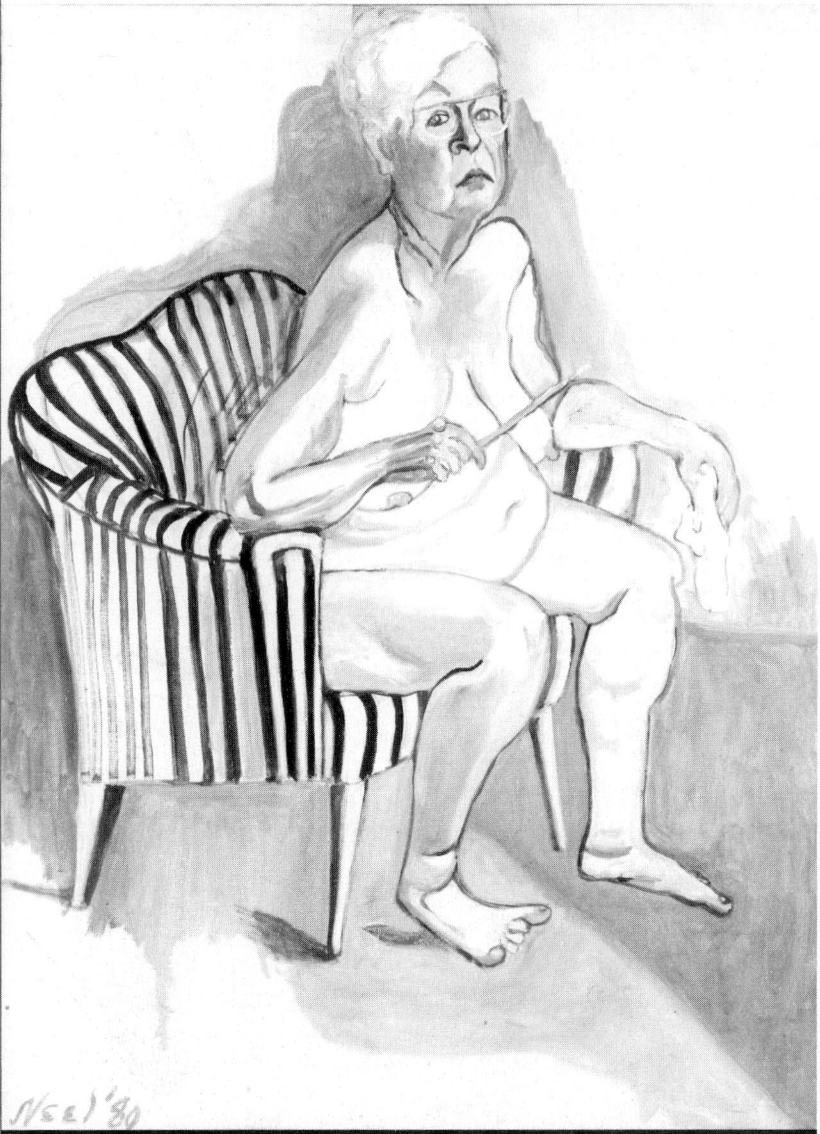

Neel '80

To view this image in color, visit www.thomsonedu.com/english/rosenwasser

FIGURE 17.39 Alice Neel, *Hartley*, 1965, oil on canvas, 50" × 36"

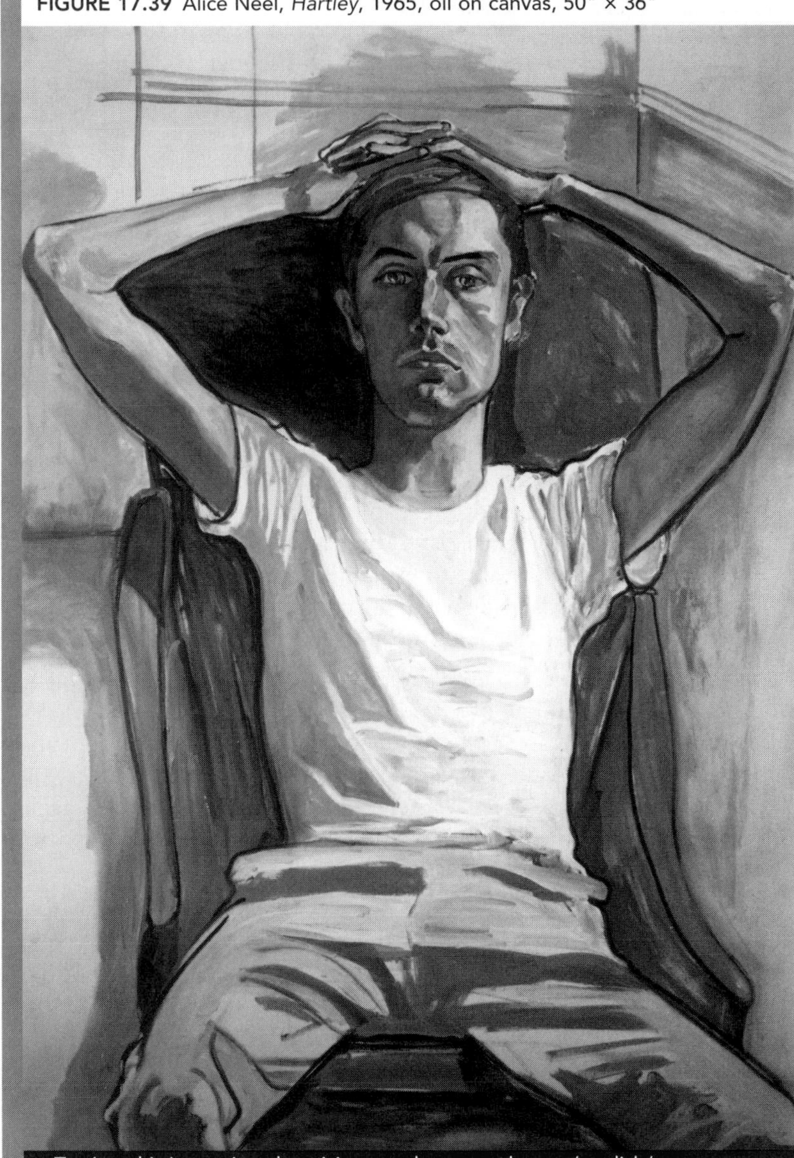

To view this image in color, visit www.thomsonedu.com/english/rosenwasser

THINGS TO DO WITH THE READING

1. Throughout this book we promote a discovery-oriented model of writing in which writers start with a distinct data-gathering stage before allowing themselves to move to claims. The guiding question is not "What do I think?" but "What do I notice?" (see pages 29–31). The observation heuristic that we call the Method aids the noticing phase by focusing attention on pattern—on things that repeat (see pages 44–49). At the end of this deliberately prolonged data-gathering (observation) stage, we use the question "So what?" to push observations to conclusions, to push from data to its implications and possible significance (see, for example, page 32).

   It is interesting to think about Berger's essay in this way—to watch him record his observations (features of the paintings that he has noticed) and then reason to implications and conclusions. Make a list of features of the paintings that Berger has noticed. You might start with his observations about the two paintings of Susannah and the Elders and about the painting of Bacchus, Ceres, and Cupid by Von Aachen. What did Berger notice? Then make a list of the various answers he offers to the "So what?" question. Be able to explain Berger's reasoning process, how he reasoned from his evidence to his conclusions. Find places in the essay where this reasoning process is explicit.

2. Throughout this book we promote paraphrase-based freewriting as a tactic for deepening understanding of a reading (see pages 13 and 116–117). We recommend building an analytical summary from close paraphrase of an especially telling, interesting, and perhaps knotty (complex and thus difficult) sentence. Choose such a sentence from the Berger essay, perhaps one having to do with the effect on women of the tradition in European art that Berger is analyzing. Rather than generalize about Berger's essay, write about it by working with the key words in your chosen sentence. Consider, for example, the sentence, "And so she comes to consider the surveyor and the surveyed within her as the two constituent yet always distinct elements of her identity as a woman." Whatever sentence you choose as your starting point, do *not* write about whether you agree or disagree with Berger. Write to deepen your understanding of Berger's ideas and make them your own to the extent that you might begin to use the Berger essay as a lens for thinking about representations of women in, for example, fashion photography or on magazine covers aimed at either male or female audiences.

3. An important part of observation is training yourself to notice not just what seems to fit with an evolving theory of yours, but also what seems not to fit—anomalies (see page 47). Explain how Berger uses anomaly in his essay.

4. **Link:** Several of the photographers discussed in the interview with Joseph Elliott have made a project of photographing women—Lauren Greenfield's "Girl Culture," for example. What might Berger notice about the Greenfield photograph we have included in this book, the one of the girl on the scale? (See Figure 17.15, page 539.) How might we see the gender

of the photographer (female) having a shaping effect in this photograph? Write an essay in which you explore this question as well as analyze the photograph in light of insights you have gained from the Berger essay. There is a mirror in the Greenfield photograph, for example. So what? For that matter, how do the female figures captured by Greenfield (and/or Sally Mann) compare with the photograph of the young woman on the porch by Alfred Stieglitz?

5. **Link Across Chapters**: In the final chapter of this anthology, we assemble reviews of various things (a book, a film, a television show, an ad campaign) and talk about how reviews operate as a form of cultural analysis. The essay/review by Malcolm Gladwell from *The New Yorker* magazine on the ad campaign for Dockers trousers ("Listening to Khakis: What America's Most Popular Pants Tell Us About the Ways Guys Think") is interesting in the context of Berger's essay because it analyzes the ways these ads seek to appeal to their assumed audience of male viewers. Apply Berger's way of thinking to this essay as a means both of understanding the essay and extending its thinking. Locate some Dockers ads on the web. What might Berger notice about the conventions of Dockers ads in terms of how they are designed to appeal to males?

6. **Application**: Berger's essay offers not just an interpretation of selected paintings but a rhetorical analysis of a set of conventions in European art. As in all rhetorical analyses, Berger focuses on how the paintings are designed to appeal to an assumed audience—in this case, an audience of male viewers. This kind of rhetorical analysis has come to be housed under the concept of the "gaze"—a word taken from French (Lacanian) psychology and developed by cultural analysts such as Teresa de Lauretis, who writes about women in film. In this mode of analysis, attention is focused on the ways in which assumptions about the values and interests of particular viewers have shaped the painting, photograph, advertisement, or building (etc.) under consideration. One of the reasons writing teachers so often ask students to write about the visual images in advertising is that the makers of such images can be assumed to be more conscious about their selection of a particular target audience and about the desire to win over that audience.

   Experiment with this analytical approach by studying something for what it seems to assume about its audience. You might study commercials for products typically aimed at men—beer, for example. It would be interesting to see what is different if you could find a beer commercial (or commercial for some other product typically associated with men) that seems aimed at women.

7. **Application**: Look for some kind of depiction of men that is apparently aimed at female viewers, such as pictures of men in women's fashion magazines or in magazines aimed at (mostly female) teenagers. What assumptions about this female audience does the visual language of the thing you are studying suggest? How, conceivably, have these assumptions shaped the image?

8. **Application**: Using the Berger essay as a lens, write about one or both of the paintings by Alice Neel—the nude self-portrait and the painting of her

son, Hartley. How might we interpret Neel's self-portrait in the context of the conventions governing the representation of women as nudes in European art? How does the painting speak to some of the conventions noted by Berger in his essay? What features of Neel's painting of her son Hartley read interestingly in the context of portraits of female nudes in European art? Hartley is neither naked nor nude, and yet he is clearly being put on display. What does the painting arguably reveal about Neel's assumptions about her audience? Which features of the painting might be designed to negotiate the possible anxiety among male viewers being invited to gaze at another male? Which features of the painting might reveal that it is the product of the gaze of a female viewer (the painter herself)? ◗

FOR FURTHER RESEARCH: SEEING

By Kelly Cannon, Reference Librarian

The readings and activities below invite you to further explore the theme of Seeing. WARNING: Some essays are polemical; they are intended to promote insight and discussion (or a starting point for your next paper). To access the online readings, visit the *Writing Analytically with Readings* website at www.thomsonedu.com/english/rosenwasser.

Online

***Artcyclopedia*. 2005. 30 December 2005.**
The premier art search engine on the web. Search by artist, title, or museum.
Explore: Search on the artist Andrew Wyeth. How would one or more of the authors in this chapter talk about Wyeth's ways of seeing?

"Documenting America: Photographic Series." *American Memory*. 1998. Library of Congress. 30 December 2005.
Some of the more renowned photographs and photographers from the Depression-era documentary project associated with the Farm Security Administration.
Explore: Find out more about the Farm Security Administration. What was the reason these photographs were taken? Given that the photos' original aim was documentary, how do they seem nonetheless in some ways staged?

Johnston, Mike. "Evidence, Not Proof." *The Luminous Landscape*. 7 March 2004. 3 January 2006.
Discusses the practical and much-debated matter of how photographers enlist cooperation from their subjects.
Explore: Click on the "discussion" link embedded in the essay. What question is at the center of this discussion?

"Edward S. Curtis's The North American Indian." *American Memory*. 2001. Northwestern University Library and Library of Congress. 30 December 2005.
Renowned collection of photographs of North American Indians taken in the early 1900s. This collection has exerted tremendous influence on pop culture's perception of American Indians.
Explore: To what extent do you think Curtis accomplished his goal to accurately document "the old time Indian, his dress, his ceremonies, his life and manners"? How so? What elements of the photograph speak to why Elliott lists him as a stager?

Kipnis, Laura. "The Eloquence of Pornography." *Frontline*. 2002. PBS. 1 January 2006.
Eloquent essay proposing that pornography "insists on a sanctioned space for fantasy."
Explore: How would Berger respond to Kipnis's argument?

Rosen, Christine. "The Image Culture." *The New Atlantis: A Journal of Technology and Society*. Number 10, Fall 2005, 27–46.
Historical survey of the technology of the image, beginning with the daguerreotype, and then chronicling the rise of photography and film, up to "the MTV effect" (the discontinuous barrage). Along the way, dispassionate history begins to give way to jeremiad.
Explore: How does Rosen's point of view resemble but also differ from that of Susan Sontag in the essay included in this chapter? Note: For purposes of comparison, there is another essay by Christine Rosen in Chapter 15 of this book.

***SandLotScience.com*. 2005. 30 December 2005.**
Click on any of the links to the "Optical Illusion Tours." Contains over 100 optical illusions.
Explore: Go to the website's "reading room" to find some of the most recent scientific research on what constitutes an optical illusion.

In Print

(Ask your librarian about possible online access to items marked with **.)

Barthes, Roland. (Chapters 25–29.) *Camera Lucida: Reflections on Photography*. New York: Hill and Wang, 1981. 63–72.
In this somewhat difficult piece, the author sorts through old photographs, trying to find one that captures the essence of his memory of his mother.

> **Explore:** Look through Barthes's entire book, *Camera Lucida*. Find the image that most appeals to you. What is it specifically about the image that draws you in, what Barthes calls its punctum?

Colbert, Charles. *Seeing What I Like & Liking What I See*. Pendaya Publications, 1991.
Contains 120 "mind-eye" photographs, mostly landscapes, taken by the author, representing a stunning visual feast.

> **Explore:** What pattern or patterns run through the images that reveal the photographer's interests and aims?

Elkins, James. "How to Look at a Postage Stamp." *How to Use Your Eyes*. New York: Routledge, 2000. 2–11.
Looks back to old postage stamps designed by people who "knew that there is no reason to make everything easy to see." These old stamps are "tiny worlds" in themselves.

> **Explore:** Visit the online stamp collection (the URL is located at www.thomsonedu.com/english/rosenwasser). Click on each stamp to make it as large as possible. In what ways do these old postage stamps support Elkins's contention that stamps are "tiny worlds"?

Frisby, John P. "Pictures in Our Heads." *Seeing: Illusion, Brain and Mind*. New York: Oxford, 1980. 8–25.
A psychologist scientifically examines what goes on inside our heads when we see.

> **Explore:** What does the author think of the "inner screen" theory—and how do you know?

****Lisle, Debbie. "Gazing at Ground Zero: Tourism, Voyeurism and Spectacle." *Journal for Cultural Research* 8.1 (January 2004): 3–21.**
Discusses how Ground Zero at the site of the World Trade Center has become a tourist attraction, illustrating the public's "voyeuristic" fascination with violence, conflict, and disaster.

> **Explore:** Have you been to see Ground Zero, or would you go? Why or why not?

CHAPTER 18

Race, Ethnicity, and the "Melting Pot"

Quick Take

At the heart of this chapter is the contested concept of the "melting pot"—a phrase that belongs inside quotations as a mark of its uncertain status. To what extent does it actually exist, some merging of diverse peoples into an undifferentiated national whole? To what extent is it a utopian dream? More troublingly, might it be a sham that serves entrenched interests and oppresses others—those to be "melted"?

It is probably accurate to say that matters of race and ethnicity in American history have been powder kegs. They have often found homes in the vitriol of diatribes and jeremiads rather than in more dispassionate and subtle reflection. The writers assembled in this chapter offer a kind of tonic response to the usual clamoring. They comprise a community of voices who occupy very different positions but all, in one way or another, see the questions raised by the prospect of assimilation as anything but easy and clear.

ABOUT THE READINGS IN THIS CHAPTER

Over half of the selections in the chapter are first-person narratives: people who chronicle their own divided allegiance to the expectations of their more local ethnic neighborhood on the one hand, and to the lures of a denatured—but really "whiter"?—American dream of assimilation on the other. These narratives are framed by three more discursive essays, which treat matters of race and assimilation from a broader social scientific perspective.

The chapter opens with Peter Salins's brief history of the "melting pot," seen in the context of the tension between assimilation and multiculturalism. His essay serves to contextualize the four memoirs that follow—analyses that spring from personal experience but do not remain there. Richard Rodriguez invites us to imagine a nation transformed by the marriage of Latin culture with the Protestant individualism that has been our country's past. Then Henry Louis Gates, Jr., recalls his childhood experience with African-American hairstyles: a platform for thinking about the "permanent, irredeemable, irresistible kink" at the back of the neck that black folks called "the kitchen."

Next, there are two narratives about neighborhoods. Ishmael Reed focuses on the implications of moving into the kind of African-American neighborhood in Oakland, California, that his parents had "spent about a third of their lives trying to escape." By contrast, in Marianna Torgovnick's homecoming to her Italian-American neighborhood in Brooklyn, the comforts of the neighborhood and the past are undercut by the claustrophobia and potential for violence in the present.

The next two essays in the chapter supply more overtly theoretical lenses. In a trenchant analysis of interracial buddy films, Benjamin DeMott indicts the attempts of modern America to forget about white guilt and affirmative action. The long-term historical effects of institutionalized racial oppression also concern Peggy McIntosh, who catalogues the nearly invisible privileges that accrue to white folks on the basis of race. What might these two writers think of the four memoirists, and vice versa? That analytical project is built into the chapter.

Finally, the Belfastian Robert McLiam Wilson, the only writer speaking of ethnicity outside the United States, brings matters to a close by challenging many of the assumptions the other writers share. To what extent, he wonders, are national and even some racial identities inevitably fabrications?

Peter Salins

Assimilation, American Style

This essay offers a brief history of that influential American myth, the "melting pot." It provides a useful frame for this chapter by locating the melting pot in relation to such key terms in thinking about race as "assimilation" and "multiculturalism." The piece was written in 1997 by the urban planning scholar Peter Salins, who is Provost and Vice Chancellor for Academic Affairs of the State University of New York system. Salins is also a fellow of a think tank known as the Manhattan Institute for Policy Research, and under its banner, he has published a number of articles in the popular press on the housing crisis in urban areas.

> California Chinese, Boston Irish, Wisconsin Germans, yes, and Alabama Negroes, have more in common than they have apart. … It is a fact that Americans from all sections and of all racial extractions are more alike than the Welsh are like the English, the Lancashireman like the Cockney, or for that matter the Lowland Scot like the Highlander.
>
> —John Steinbeck, 1962

Most Americans, both those who favor and those who oppose assimilation, believe that for immigrants to assimilate, they must abandon their original cultural attributes and conform entirely to the behaviors and customs of the majority of the native-born population. In the terminology of the armed forces, this represents a model of "up or out": Either immigrants bring themselves "up" to native cultural standards or they are doomed to live "out" of the charmed circle of the national culture. 1

The notion is not entirely far-fetched because this is exactly what assimilation demands in other societies. North African immigrants to France are, for example, expected to assimilate by abandoning their native folkways with alacrity. Official French policy has been zealous in making North African and other Muslim women give up wearing their *chador*[1] and, in the schools, instilling a disdain for North African and Muslim culture in their children. To varying degrees, most European countries that have had to absorb large numbers of immigrants since World War II interpret assimilation this way—an interpretation that has promoted national and ethnic disunity.

In America, however, assimilation has not meant repudiating immigrant culture. Assimilation, American style has always been much more flexible and accommodating and, consequently, much more effective in achieving its purpose—to allow the United States to preserve its "national unity in the face of the influx of hordes of persons of scores of different nationalities," in the words of the sociologist Henry Fairchild.

A popular way of getting hold of the assimilation idea has been to use a metaphor, and by far the most popular metaphor has been that of the "melting

[1] *Chadors* are the long black veils worn by Muslim women.

pot," a term introduced in Israel Zangwill's 1908 play of that name: "There she lies, the great Melting-Pot—Listen! Can't you hear the roaring and the bubbling? ... Ah, what a stirring and a seething! Celt and Latin, Slav and Teuton, Greek and Syrian, black and yellow ... Jew and Gentile. ... East and West, and North and South, the palm and the pine, the pole and the equator, the crescent and the cross—how the great Alchemist melts and fuses them with his purifying flame! Here shall they all unite to build the Republic of Man and the Kingdom of God."

For all its somewhat ahistorical idealism, the melting-pot metaphor still rep- 5
resents the standard around which fervent proponents of assimilation have rallied over the years. According to the melting-pot metaphor, assimilation involved the fine-grained intermingling of diverse ethnicities and cultures into a single national "alloy." If taken literally, this metaphor implied two things. The point most commonly taken is that the new human products of the melting pot would, of necessity, be culturally indistinguishable. Presumably every piece of metal taken from a melting pot should have the same chemical composition. Less frequently understood is the metaphor's implication that natives and their indigenous cultural characteristics would also be irreversibly changed—blended beyond recognition—because they constituted the base material of the melting pot.

These two corollaries of the melting-pot metaphor have long invited criticism by those who thought they were inconsistent with the ethnic realities of American society. Critics of the metaphor have spanned the ideological spectrum and mounted several different lines of attack on it. Empiricists submitted evidence that the melting pot wasn't working as predicted and concluded, as did Nathan Glazer and Daniel Patrick Moynihan in *Beyond the Melting Pot* (1963), "The point about the melting pot—is that it did not happen." Other critics rejected the second corollary of the metaphor—that natives were changed by it, too—and saw no reason that native Americans should give up any part of their cultural attributes to "melt" into the alloy. If true assimilation were to occur, the criticism went, immigrants would have to abandon all their cultural baggage and conform to American ways. It is the immigrant, said Fairchild, representing the views of many Americans, "who must undergo the entire transformation; the true member of the American nationality is not called upon to change in the least."

A third strain of criticism was first voiced by sociologist Horace Kallen in the early part of this century. Among the most prolific American scholars of ethnicity, Kallen argued that it was not only unrealistic but cruel and harmful to force new immigrants to shed their familiar, lifelong cultural attributes as the price of admission to American society. In place of the melting pot, he called for "cultural pluralism." In Kallen's words, national policy should "seek to provide conditions under which each [group] might attain the cultural perfection that is proper to its kind."

Kallen introduced the concept in 1916, only eight years after publication of Zangwill's *The Melting Pot*, determined to challenge that work's premises. Cultural pluralism rejects melting-pot assimilationism not on empirical grounds but on ideological ones. Kallen and his followers believed that immigrants to the United States should not "melt" into a common national ethnic alloy but, rather, should steadfastly hang on to their cultural ethnicity and band together for social and political purposes even after generations of residence in the United States. As such, cultural pluralism is not an alternative theory of assimilation; it is a theory opposed to assimilation.

Cultural pluralism is, in fact, the philosophical antecedent of modern multiculturalism—what I call "ethnic federalism": official recognition of distinct, essentially fixed ethnic groups and the doling out of resources based on membership in an ethnic group. Ethnic federalism explicitly rejects the notion of a transcendent American identity, the old idea that out of ethnic diversity there would emerge a single, culturally unified people. Instead, the United States is to be viewed as a vast ethnic federation—Canada's Anglo-French arrangement, raised to the *n*th power. Viewing ethnic Americans as members of a federation rather than a union, ethnic federalism, a.k.a. multiculturalism, asserts that ethnic Americans have the right to proportional representation in matters of power and privilege, the right to demand that their "native" culture and putative ethnic ancestors be accorded recognition and respect, and the right to function in their "native" language (even if it is not the language of their birth or they never learned to speak it), not just at home but in the public realm.

10 Ethnic federalism is at all times an ideology of ethnic grievance and inevitably leads to and justifies ethnic conflict. All the nations that have ever embraced it, from Yugoslavia to Lebanon, from Belgium to Canada, have had to live with perpetual ethnic discord.

Kallen's views, however, stop significantly short of contemporary multiculturalism in their demands on the larger "native" American society. For Kallen, cultural pluralism was a defensive strategy for "unassimilable" immigrant ethnic groups that required no accommodation by the larger society. Contemporary multiculturalists, on the other hand, by making cultural pluralism the basis of ethnic federalism, demand certain ethnic rights and concessions. By emphasizing the failure of assimilation, multiculturalists hope to provide intellectual and political support for their policies.

The multiculturalists' rejection of the melting pot idea is seen in the metaphors they propose in its place. Civil rights activist Jesse Jackson suggested that Americans are members of a "rainbow coalition." Former New York Mayor David Dinkins saw his constituents constituting a "gorgeous mosaic." Former Congresswoman Shirley Chisholm characterized America's ethnic groups as being like ingredients in a "salad bowl." Barbara Jordan, recent chairperson of the U.S. Commission on Immigration Reform, said: "We are more than a melting-pot; we are a kaleidoscope."

These counter-metaphors all share a common premise: that ethnic groups in the United States may live side by side harmoniously, but on two conditions that overturn both assumptions of the melting-pot metaphor. First, immigrants (and black Americans) should never have to (or maybe should not even want to) give up any of their original cultural attributes. And second, there never can or will be a single unified national identity that all Americans can relate to. These two principles are the foundations of cultural pluralism, the antithesis of assimilationism.

While all these metaphors—including the melting pot—are colorful ways of representing assimilation, they don't go far in giving one an accurate understanding of what assimilation is really about. For example, across the ideological spectrum, they all invoke some external, impersonal assimilating agent. Who, exactly, is the "great alchemist" of the melting pot? What force tosses the salad or pieces together the mosaic? By picturing assimilation as an impersonal, automatic process and thus placing it beyond analysis, the metaphors fail to illuminate its most important secrets. Assimilation, if it is to succeed, must be a voluntary process, by both the assimilating immigrants and the assimilated-to natives. Assimilation is a human accommodation, not a mechanical production.

15 The metaphors also mislead as to the purposes of assimilation. The melting pot is supposed to turn out an undifferentiated alloy—a uniform, ethnically neutral, American protoperson. Critics have long pointed out that this idea is far-fetched. But is it even desirable? And if it is desirable, does it really foster a shared national identity? The greatest failing of the melting-pot metaphor is that it overreaches. It exaggerates the degree to which immigrants' ethnicity is likely to be extinguished by exposure to American society and it exaggerates the need to extinguish ethnicity. By being too compelling, too idealistic, the melting-pot idea has inadvertently helped to discredit the very assimilation paradigm it was meant to celebrate.

On the other hand, behind their unexceptionable blandness, the antithetical cultural pluralist metaphors are profoundly insidious. By suggesting that the product of assimilation is mere ethnic coexistence without integration, they undermine the objectives of assimilation, even if they appear more realistic. Is assimilation only about diverse ethnic groups sharing the same national space? That much can be said for any multiethnic society. If the ethnic greens of the salad or the fragments of the mosaic do not interact and identify with each other, no meaningful assimilation is taking place.

Perhaps a new assimilation metaphor should be introduced—one that depends not on a mechanical process like the melting pot but on human dynamics. Assimilation might be viewed as more akin to religious conversion than anything else. In the terms of this metaphor, the immigrant is the convert, American society is the religious order being joined, and assimilation is the process by which the conversion takes place. Just as there are many motives for people to immigrate, so are there many motives for them to change their religion: spiritual, practical (marrying a person of another faith), and materialistic (joining some churches can lead to jobs or subsidized housing). But whatever the motivation, conversion usually involves the consistent application of certain principles. Conversion is a mutual decision requiring affirmation by both the convert and the religious order he or she wishes to join. Converts are expected in most (but not all) cases to renounce their old religions. But converts do not have to change their behavior in any respects other than those that relate to the new religion. They are expected only to believe in its theological principles, observe its rituals and holidays, and live by its moral precepts. Beyond that, they can be rich or poor, practice any trade, pursue any avocational interests, and have any racial or other personal attributes. Once they undergo conversion, they are eagerly welcomed into the fellowship of believers. They have become part of "us" rather than "them." This is undoubtedly what writer G. K. Chesterton had in mind when he said: "America is a nation with the soul of a church."

THINGS TO DO WITH THE READING

1. Salins's essay is good at making the implicit explicit and at uncovering assumptions (reasoning back to premises). (See "Make the Implicit Explicit" on pages 57–59 and "Uncovering Assumptions" on pages 97–100.) He is especially interested in the implications of the metaphors that have been used to talk about cultural identity and assimilation in America: melting pot, rainbow coalition, and so on. Using Salins's method as a model, draw out the implications of Jesse Jackson's metaphor—the rainbow coalition. How is the rainbow metaphor like and unlike the melting pot metaphor? Next, draw out the implications of Salins's proposed religious conversion metaphor as defined in the last paragraph of the essay. How is this metaphor like and unlike the rainbow and the melting pot?
2. Salins is also good at distinguishing ideas that seem the same or similar, which is to say that he employs the strategy called "Looking for Difference within Similarity" (see pages 158–159). Locate the difference between cultural pluralism, as defined by Kallen, and "contemporary multiculturalism" as defined by Salins in paragraph 11. To what extent does Salins's proposal, as articulated in the last paragraph of the essay, address the problem his essay raises in its critique of multiculturalism?
3. Though Salins's piece is a historical analysis, it also is a problem/solution piece with a point of view. This point of view emerges gradually but becomes evident when you notice that the critique offered of each idea on assimilation, starting with the melting pot, is essentially the same critique. Compare the end of paragraph 6 beginning "These two corollaries" with paragraph 11 beginning "Kallen's views" and locate the common element.
4. A metaphor is a comparison, a way of thinking by analogy. Arguments made by analogy are persuasive and fair only when the two things being compared have enough in common to justify the comparison. (See the explanation of common logical errors and analogy and false analogy on pages 212–215.) What is compared to what in Salins's conversion metaphor? What does this analogy suggest about Salins's way of thinking about being (and becoming) American?
5. Do a rhetorical analysis (see pages 69–70) of the Salins essay. Locate a word choice that seems to reveal something about Salins's target audience and the kind of relationship he wishes to establish with these readers. What, for example, does the phrase "native folkways" (in the essay's second paragraph) reveal in this regard?
6. **Link:** See the Link (question 2) following the next essay, "The Fear of Losing a Culture," which asks you to use the Salins essay as a lens.
7. **Link Across Chapters:** First visit the website for the Manhattan Institute for Policy Research, of which Salins is a fellow (a link to this site can be found at www.thomsonedu.com/english/rosenwasser.) Then apply the lexicon contained in Christopher Borick's "On Political Labels" in Chapter 19 to the key words in the website's articulation of its mission.

Where does the website fit in terms of the political categories discussed in Borick's essay? Find language in Salins's essay that would make its point of view identifiable among the categories that Borick discusses.

8. **Application:** The issues and questions raised in Salins's essay are far from dead. Based on the historical definitions Salins provides, spend some time (perhaps a week) observing and making note of the language used in the media (newspapers, websites, television) in talking about issues of assimilation and cultural identity. What metaphors do you find, and what do these reveal about contemporary thinking on this issue?

Richard Rodriguez

The Fear of Losing a Culture

Richard Rodriguez provides a distinctively Latin American spin on the concept of the melting pot. He argues that Latin America was "formed by a rape that became a marriage" and goes on to tell his North American audience, "Expect marriage." A teacher, journalist (on PBS), and award-winning essayist, Rodriguez, the child of Mexican-American immigrants, earned degrees at Stanford and University of California-Berkeley. This piece is taken from his 1982 memoir, *Hunger of Memory*.

What is culture? 1

The immigrant shrugs. Latin American immigrants come to the United States with only the things they need in mind—not abstractions like culture. Money. They need dollars. They need food. Maybe they need to get out of the way of bullets.

Most of us who concern ourselves with Hispanic-American culture, as painters, musicians, writers—or as sons and daughters—are the children of immigrants. We have grown up on this side of the border, in the land of Elvis Presley and Thomas Edison; our lives are prescribed by the mall, by the DMV and the Chinese restaurant. Our imaginations yet vascillate between an Edenic Latin America (the blue door)—which nevertheless betrayed our parents—and the repellent plate glass of a real American city—which has been good to us.

Hispanic-American culture is where the past meets the future. Hispanic-American culture is not a Hispanic milestone only, not simply a celebration at the crossroads. America transforms into pleasure what America cannot avoid. Is it any coincidence that at a time when Americans are troubled by the encroachment of the Mexican desert, Americans discover a chic in cactus, in the decorator colors of the Southwest? In sand?

Hispanic-American culture of the sort that is now showing (the teen movie, 5
the rock songs) may exist in an hourglass; may in fact be irrelevant to the epic. The U.S. Border Patrol works through the night to arrest the flow of illegal immigrants over the border, even as Americans wait in line to get into "La Bamba." Even as Americans vote to declare, once and for all, that English shall be the official language of the United States, Madonna starts recording in Spanish.

But then so is Bill Cosby's show irrelevant to the 10 o'clock news, where families huddle together in fear on porches, pointing at the body of the slain boy bagged in tarpaulin. Which is not to say that Bill Cosby or Michael Jackson are irrelevant to the future or without neo-Platonic influence. Like players within the play, they prefigure, they resolve. They make black and white audiences aware of a bond that may not yet exist.

Before a national TV audience, Rita Moreno tells Geraldo Rivera that her dream as an actress is to play a character rather like herself: "I speak English perfectly well … I'm not dying from poverty … I want to play *that* kind of Hispanic woman, which is to say, an American citizen." This is an actress talking, these are show-biz pieties. But Moreno expresses as well the general Hispanic-American predicament. Hispanics want to belong to America without betraying the past.

Hispanics fear losing ground in any negotiation with the American city. We come from an expansive, an intimate culture that has been judged second-rate by the United States of America. For reasons of pride, therefore, as much as of affection, we are reluctant to give up our past. Hispanics often express a fear of "losing" culture. Our fame in the United States has been our resistance to assimilation.

The symbol of Hispanic culture has been the tongue of flame—Spanish. But the remarkable legacy Hispanics carry from Latin America is not language—an inflatable skin—but breath itself, capacity of soul, an inclination to live. The genius of Latin America is the habit of synthesis.

We assimilate. Just over the border there is the example of Mexico, the coun- 10
try from which the majority of U.S. Hispanics come. Mexico is *mestizo*—Indian and Spanish. Within a single family, Mexicans are light-skinned and dark. It is impossible for the Mexican to say, in the scheme of things, where the Indian begins and the Spaniard surrenders.

In culture as in blood, Latin America was formed by a rape that became a marriage. Due to the absorbing generosity of the Indian, European culture took on new soil. What Latin America knows is that people create one another as they marry. In the music of Latin America you will hear the litany of bloodlines—the African drum, the German accordion, the cry from the minaret.

The United States stands as the opposing New World experiment. In North America the Indian and the European stood apace. Whereas Latin America was formed by a medieval Catholic dream of one world—of meltdown conversion—the United States was built up from Protestant individualism. The American melting pot washes away only embarrassment; it is the necessary initiation into public life. The American faith is that our national strength derives from separateness, from "diversity." The glamour of the United States is a carnival promise: You can lose weight, get rich as Rockefeller, tough up your roots, get a divorce.

Immigrants still come for the promise. But the United States wavers in its faith. As long as there was space enough, sky enough, as long as economic success validated individualism, loneliness was not too high a price to pay. (The cabin on the prairie or the Sony Walkman.)

As we near the end of the American century, two alternative cultures beckon the American imagination—both highly communal cultures—the Asian and the Latin American. The United States is a literal culture. Americans devour what we might otherwise fear to become. Sushi will make us corporate warriors. Combination Plate #3, smothered in *mestizo* gravy, will burn a hole in our hearts.

Latin America offers passion. Latin America has a life—I mean *life*—big 15
clouds, unambiguous themes, death, birth, faith, that the United States, for all its quality of life, seems without now. Latin America offers communal riches: an undistressed leisure, a kitchen table, even a full sorrow. Such is the solitude of America, such is the urgency of American need, Americans reach right past a fledgling, homegrown Hispanic-American culture for the real thing—the darker bottle of Mexican beer; the denser novel of a Latin American master.

For a long time, Hispanics in the United States withheld from the United States our Latin American gift. We denied the value of assimilation. But as our presence is judged less foreign in America, we will produce a more generous art, less timid, less parochial. Carlos Santana, Luis Valdez, Linda Ronstadt—Hispanic Americans do not have a "pure" Latin American art to offer. Expect bastard themes, expect ironies, comic conclusions. For we live on this side of the border, where Kraft manufactures bricks of "Mexican style" Velveeta, and where Jack in the Box serves "Fajita Pita."

The flame-red Chevy floats a song down the Pan American Highway: From a rolled-down window, the grizzled voice of Willie Nelson rises in disembodied harmony with the voice of Julio Iglesias. Gabby Hayes and Cisco are thus resolved.

Expect marriage. We will change America even as we will be changed. We will disappear with you into a new miscegenation.

Along the border, real conflicts remain. But the ancient tear separating Europe from itself—the Catholic Mediterranean from the Protestant north—may yet heal itself in the New World. For generations, Latin America has been the place—the bed—of a confluence of so many races and cultures that Protestant North America shuddered to imagine it.

Imagine it. 20

THINGS TO DO WITH THE READING

1. Rodriguez has an interesting fix on the way that Americans react to other cultures. He says that "America transforms into pleasure what America cannot avoid" (see paragraph 4) and that "Americans devour what we might otherwise fear to become" (see paragraph 14). Try paraphrasing these remarks in their given context, as a way of uncovering their implications. Be alert to figurative language—why, for example, "devour"?
2. **Link:** In an interview conducted 15 years after the publication of *Hunger of Memory*, Rodriguez said, "I am no more in favor of assimilation than I am in favor of the Pacific Ocean. Assimilation is not something to oppose or favor—it just happens." How does this point of view, beyond "good or bad," connect to particular claims articulated in "The Fear of Losing a Culture"? And how does it conflict with the view of assimilation offered by Peter Salins in "Assimilation, American Style"? How might we account for the difference in the two writers' points of view? What are the assumptions that underlie each of their essays? (For an explanation of how to uncover assumptions, see pages 97–100; for a discussion of what's bad about the terms "good" and "bad," see page 267.)
3. Take the passage at the end of paragraph 16, which reads "Expect bastard themes, expect ironies, comic conclusions. For we live on this side of the border where Kraft manufactures bricks of 'Mexican style' Velveeta, and where Jack in the Box serves 'Fajita Pita.'" How does the essay condition us to respond to this passage? In what verbal strands (see the Method, pages 44–49) does this language participate?

Henry Louis Gates, Jr.

In the Kitchen

In this carefully crafted and subtly inflected memoir, Henry Louis Gates, Jr., uses his own memories of African-American hairstyling figuratively—as a way of thinking about more than just hair. Neither an apology nor a diatribe, the piece offers a complex and affectionate parable of assimilation. Henry Louis "Skip" Gates, Jr., is the W.E.B. Du Bois Professor of Humanities at Harvard and director of the W.E.B. Du Bois Institute for African-American Research. In 1997, Gates was voted one of *TIME* magazine's "25 Most Influential Americans." Like a number of other authors included in this book, he too was a winner of a MacArthur "genius" Fellowship.

We always had a gas stove in the kitchen, in our house in Piedmont, West Virginia, where I grew up. Never electric, though using electric became fashionable in Piedmont in the sixties, like using Crest toothpaste rather than Colgate, or watching Huntley and Brinkley rather than Walter Cronkite. But not us: gas, Colgate, and good ole Walter Cronkite, come what may. We used gas partly out of loyalty to Big Mom, Mama's Mama, because she was mostly blind and still loved to cook, and could feel her way more easily with gas than with electric. But the most important thing about our gas-equipped kitchen was that Mama used to do hair there. The "hot comb" was a fine-toothed iron instrument with a long wooden handle and a pair of iron curlers that opened and closed like scissors. Mama would put it in the gas fire until it glowed. You could smell those prongs heating up. 1

I liked that smell. Not the smell so much, I guess, as what the smell meant for the shape of my day. There was an intimate warmth in the women's tones as they talked with my Mama, doing their hair. I knew what the women had been through to get their hair ready to be "done," because I would watch Mama do it to herself. How that kink could be transformed through grease and fire into that magnificent head of wavy hair was a miracle to me, and still is.

Mama would wash her hair over the sink, a towel wrapped around her shoulders, wearing just her slip and her white bra. (We had no shower—just a galvanized tub that we stored in the kitchen—until we moved down Rat Tail Road into Doc Wolverton's house, in 1954.) After she dried it, she would grease her scalp thoroughly with blue Bergamot hair grease, which came in a short, fat jar with a picture of a beautiful colored lady on it. It's important to grease your scalp real good, my Mama would explain, to keep from burning yourself. Of course, her hair would return to its natural kink almost as soon as the hot water and shampoo hit it. To me, it was another miracle how hair so "straight" would so quickly become kinky again the second it even approached some water.

My Mama had only a few "clients" whose heads she "did"—did, I think, because she enjoyed it, rather than for the few pennies it brought in. They would sit on one of our red plastic kitchen chairs, the kind with the shiny metal legs, and brace themselves for the process. Mama would stroke that red-hot iron—which by this time had been in the gas fire for half an hour or more—slowly but firmly through their hair, from scalp to strand's end. It made a scorching, crinkly sound, the hot iron did, as it burned its way through kink, leaving in its wake straight strands of hair, standing long and tall but drooping over at the ends, their shape like the top of a heavy willow tree. Slowly, steadily, Mama's hands would transform a round mound of Odetta kink into a darkened swamp of everglades. The Bergamot made the hair shiny; the heat of the hot iron gave it a brownish-red cast. Once all the hair was as straight as God allows kink to get, Mama would take the well-heated curling iron and twirl the straightened strands into more or less loosely wrapped curls. She claimed that she owed her skill as a hairdresser to the strength in her wrists, and as she worked her little finger would poke out, the way it did when she sipped tea. Mama was a southpaw, and wrote upside down and backward to produce the cleanest, roundest letters you've ever seen.

The "kitchen" she would all but remove from sight with a handheld pair of 5
shears, bought just for this purpose. Now, the kitchen was the room in which we were sitting—the room where Mama did hair and washed clothes, and where we all took a bath in that galvanized tub. But the word has another meaning, and the kitchen that I'm speaking of is the very kinky bit of hair at the back of your head, where your neck meets your shirt collar. If there was ever a part of our African past that resisted assimilation, it was the kitchen. No matter how hot the iron, no matter how powerful the chemical, no matter how stringent the mashed-potatoes-and-lye formula of a man's "process," neither God nor woman nor Sammy Davis, Jr., could straighten the kitchen. The kitchen was permanent, irredeemable; irresistible kink. Unassimilably African. No matter what you did, no matter how hard you tried, you couldn't de-kink a person's kitchen. So you trimmed it off as best you could.

When hair had begun to "turn," as they'd say—to return to its natural kinky glory—it was the kitchen that turned first (the kitchen around the back, and nappy edges at the temples). When the kitchen started creeping up the back of the neck, it was time to get your hair done again.

Sometimes, after dark, a man would come to have his hair done. It was Mr. Charlie Carroll. He was very light-complected and had a ruddy nose—it made me think of Edmund Gwenn, who played Kris Kringle in "Miracle on 34th Street." At first, Mama did him after my brother, Rocky, and I had gone to sleep. It was only later that we found out that he had come to our house so Mama could iron his hair—not with a hot comb or a curling iron but with our very own Proctor-Silex steam iron. For some reason I never understood, Mr. Charlie would conceal his Frederick Douglass-like mane under a big white Stetson hat. I never saw him take it off except when he came to our house, at night, to have his hair pressed. (Later, Daddy would tell us about Mr. Charlie's most prized piece of knowledge, something that the man would only confide after his hair had been pressed, as a token of intimacy. "Not many people know this," he'd say, in a tone of circumspection, "but George Washington was Abraham Lincoln's daddy." Nodding solemnly, he'd add the clincher: "A white man told me." Though he was in dead earnest, this became a humorous refrain around our house—"a white man told me"—which we used to punctuate especially preposterous assertions.)

My mother examined my daughters' kitchens whenever we went home to visit, in the early eighties. It became a game between us. I had told her not to do it, because I didn't like the politics it suggested—the notion of "good" and "bad" hair.

"Good" hair was "straight," "bad" hair kinky. Even in the late sixties, at the height of Black Power, almost nobody could bring themselves to say "bad" for good and "good" for bad. People still said that hair like white people's hair was "good," even if they encapsulated it in a disclaimer, like "what we used to call 'good.'"

Maggie would be seated in her high chair, throwing food this way and that, and Mama would be cooing about how cute it all was, how I used to do just like Maggie was doing, and wondering whether her flinging her food with her left hand meant that she was going to be left-handed like Mama. When my daughter was just about covered with Chef Boyardee Spaghetti-O's, Mama would seize the opportunity: wiping her clean, she would tilt Maggie's head to one side and reach down the back of her neck. Sometimes Mama would even rub a curl between her fingers, just to make sure that her bifocals had not deceived her. Then she'd sigh with satisfaction and relief: No kink ... yet. Mama! I'd shout, pretending to be angry. Every once in a while, if no one was looking, I'd peek, too.

I say "yet" because most black babies are born with soft, silken hair. But after 10
a few months it begins to turn, as inevitably as do the seasons or the leaves on a tree. People once thought baby oil would stop it. They were wrong.

Everybody I knew as a child wanted to have good hair. You could be as ugly as homemade sin dipped in misery and still be thought attractive if you had good hair. "Jesus moss," the girls at Camp Lee, Virginia, had called Daddy's naturally "good" hair during the war. I know that he played that thick head of hair for all it was worth, too.

My own hair was "not a bad grade," as barbers would tell me when they cut it for the first time. It was like a doctor reporting the results of the first full physical he has given you. Like "You're in good shape" or "Blood pressure's kind of high—better cut down on salt."

I spent most of my childhood and adolescence messing with my hair. I definitely wanted straight hair. Like Pop's. When I was about three, I tried to stick a wad of Bazooka bubble gum to that straight hair of his. I suppose what fixed that memory for me is the spanking I got for doing so: he turned me upside down, holding me by my feet, the better to paddle my behind. Little *nigger*, he had shouted, walloping away. I started to laugh about it two days later, when my behind stopped hurting.

When black people say "straight," of course, they don't usually mean literally straight—they're not describing hair like, say, Peggy Lipton's (she was the white girl on "The Mod Squad"), or like Mary's of Peter, Paul & Mary fame; black people call that "stringy" hair. No, "straight" just means not kinky, no matter what contours the curl may take. I would have done *anything* to have straight hair—and I used to try everything, short of getting a process.

Of the wide variety of techniques and methods I came to master in the chal- 15
lenging prestidigitation of the follicle, almost all had two things in common: a heavy grease and the application of pressure. It's not an accident that some of the biggest black-owned companies in the fifties and sixties made hair products. And I tried them all, in search of that certain silken touch, the one that would leave neither the hand nor the pillow sullied by grease.

I always wondered what Frederick Douglass put on *his* hair, or what Phillis Wheatley put on hers. Or why Wheatley has that rag on her head in the little engraving in the frontispiece of her book. One thing is for sure: you can bet that when Phillis Wheatley went to England and saw the Countess of Huntingdon she did not stop by the Queen's coiffeur on her way there. So many black people still get their hair straightened that it's a wonder we don't have a national holiday for Madame C. J. Walker, the woman who invented the process of straightening kinky hair. Call it Jheri-Kurled or call it "relaxed," it's still fried hair.

I used all the greases, from sea-blue Bergamot and creamy vanilla Duke (in its clear jar with the orange-white-and-green label) to the godfather of grease, the formidable Murray's. Now, Murray's was some *serious* grease. Whereas Bergamot was like oily jello, and Duke was viscous and sickly sweet, Murray's was light brown and *hard.* Hard as lard and twice as greasy, Daddy used to say. Murray's came in an orange can with a press-on top. It was so hard that some people would put a match to the can, just to soften the stuff and make it more manageable. Then, in the late sixties, when Afros came into style, I used Afro Sheen. From Murray's to Duke to Afro Sheen: that was my progression in black consciousness.

We used to put hot towels or wash-rags over our Murray-coated heads, in order to melt the wax into the scalp and the follicles. Unfortunately, the wax also had the habit of running down your neck, ears, and forehead. Not to mention your pillowcase. Another problem was that if you put two palmfuls of Murray's on your head your hair turned white. (Duke did the same thing.) The challenge was to get rid of that white color. Because if you got rid of the white stuff you had a magnificent head of wavy hair. That was the beauty of it: Murray's was so hard that it froze your hair into the wavy style you brushed it into. It looked really good if you wore a part. A lot of guys had parts *cut* into their hair by a barber, either with the clippers or with a straightedged razor. Especially if you had kinky hair—then you'd generally wear a short razorcut, or what we called a Quo Vadis.

We tried to be as innovative as possible. Everyone knew about using a stocking cap, because your father or your uncle wore one whenever something really big was about to happen, whether sacred or secular: a funeral or a dance, a wedding or a trip in which you confronted official white people. Any time you were trying to look really sharp, you wore a stocking cap in preparation. And if the event was really a big one, you made a new cap. You asked your mother for a pair of her hose, and cut it with scissors about six inches or so from the open end—the end with the elastic that goes up to the top of the thigh. Then you knotted the cut end, and it became a beehive-shaped hat, with an elastic band that you pulled down low on your forehead and down around your neck in the back. To work well, the cap had to fit tightly and snugly, like a press. And it had to fit that tightly because it *was* a press: it pressed your hair with the force of the hose's elastic. If you greased your hair down real good, and left the stocking cap on long enough, voila: you got a head of pressed-against-the-scalp waves. (You also got a ring around your forehead when you woke up, but it went away.) And then you could enjoy your concrete do. Swore we were bad, too, with all that grease and those flat heads. My brother and I would brush it out a bit in the mornings, so that it looked—well, "natural." Grown men still wear stocking caps—especially older men, who generally keep their stocking caps in their top drawers, along with their cufflinks and their see-through silk socks, their "Maverick" ties, their silk handkerchiefs, and whatever else they prize the most.

A Murrayed-down stocking cap was the respectable version of the process, 20
which, by contrast, was most definitely not a cool thing to have unless you

were an entertainer by trade. Zeke and Keith and Poochie and a few other stars of the high-school basketball team all used to get a process once or twice a year. It was expensive, and you had to go somewhere like Pittsburgh or D.C. or Union-town—somewhere where there were enough colored people to support a trade. The guys would disappear, then reappear a day or two later, strutting like peacocks, their hair burned slightly red from the lye base. They'd also wear "rags"—cloths or handkerchiefs—around their heads when they slept or played basketball. Do-rags, they were called. But the result was straight hair, with just a hint of wave. No curl. Do-it-yourselfers took their chances at home with a concoction of mashed potatoes and lye.

The most famous process of all, however, outside of the process Malcolm X describes in his "Autobiography," and maybe the process of Sammy Davis, Jr., was Nat King Cole's process. Nat King Cole had patent-leather hair. That man's got the finest process money can buy, or so Daddy said the night we saw Cole's TV show on NBC. It was November 5, 1956. I remember the date because everyone came to our house to watch it and to celebrate one of Daddy's buddies' birthdays. Yeah, Uncle Joe chimed in, they can do shit to his hair that the average Negro can't even *think* about—secret shit.

Nat King Cole was *clean*. I've had an ongoing argument with a Nigerian friend about Nat King Cole for twenty years now. Not about whether he could sing—any fool knows that he could—but about whether or not he was a handkerchief head for wearing that patent-leather process.

Sammy Davis, Jr.,'s process was the one I detested. It didn't look good on him. Worse still, he liked to have a fried strand dangling down the middle of his forehead, so he could shake it out from the crown when he sang. But Nat King Cole's hair was a thing unto itself, a beautifully sculpted work of art that he and he alone had the right to wear. The only difference between a process and a stocking cap, really, was taste; but Nat King Cole, unlike, say, Michael Jackson, looked *good* in his. His head looked like Valentino's head in the twenties, and some say it was Valentino the process was imitating. But Nat King Cole wore a process because it suited his face, his demeanor, his name, his style. He was as clean as he wanted to be.

I had forgotten all about that patent-leather look until one day in 1971, when I was sitting in an Arab restaurant on the island of Zanzibar surrounded by men in fezzes and white caftans, trying to learn how to eat curried goat and rice with the fingers of my right hand and feeling two million miles from home. All of a sudden, an old transistor radio sitting on top of a china cupboard stopped blaring out its Swahili music and started playing "Fly Me to the Moon," by Nat King Cole. The restaurant's din was not affected at all, but in my mind's eye I saw it: the King's magnificent sleek black tiara. I managed, barely, to blink back the tears.

THINGS TO DO WITH THE READING

1. What is the attitude in this piece toward the way that the America in which the author grew up dealt with the "problem" of kinky hair? What sentences in the piece seem most revealing of the point of the view that Gates wishes us to take? How in particular does the piece make use of the various meanings of the word "kitchen"?
2. The subject of assimilation is a primary thread of this chapter. How does Gates's outlook compare with Salins's and Rodriguez's outlooks on assimilation? Consider especially the impact of the essay's final paragraph in this regard.

Ishmael Reed

My Neighborhood

In this piece, Ishmael Reed takes the reader on a meditative tour through the various neighborhoods in which he has dwelled as an adult, using these places as sites for thinking about race and matters of assimilation. Reed has been nominated for the Pulitzer Prize and twice shortlisted for the National Book Award. The musician Max Roach has called him the Charlie Parker of American fiction, and in the biographical sketch of him in the august *Dictionary of Literary Biography*, Henry Louis Gates, Jr., (author of the previous selection) argued that Reed has "no true predecessor or counterpart" in American letters.

My stepfather is an evolutionist. He worked for many years at the Chevrolet division of General Motors in Buffalo, a working-class auto and steel town in upstate New York, and was able to rise from relative poverty to the middle class. He believes that each succeeding generation of Afro-Americans will have it better than its predecessor. In 1979 I moved into the kind of neighborhood that he and my mother spent about a third of their lives trying to escape. According to the evolutionist integrationist ethic, this was surely a step backward, since "success" was seen as being able to live in a neighborhood in which you were the only black and joined your neighbors in trying to keep out "them." 1

My neighborhood, bordered by Genoa, Market Street, and 48th and 55th streets in North Oakland, is what the media refer to as a "predominantly black neighborhood." It's the kind of neighborhood I grew up in before leaving for New York City in 1962. My last New York residence was an apartment in a brownstone, next door to the building in which poet W. H. Auden lived. There were trees in the backyard, and I thought it was a swell neighborhood until I read in Robert Craft's biography of [the composer] Stravinsky that "when Stravinsky sent his chauffeur to pick up his friend Auden, the chauffeur would ask, 'Are you sure Mr. Auden lives in this neighborhood?' " By 1968 my wife and I were able to live six months of the year in New York and the other six in California. This came to an end when one of the people I sublet the apartment to abandoned it. He had fled to England to pursue a romance. He didn't pay the rent, and so we were evicted long distance.

My first residence in California was an apartment on Santa Ynez Street, near Echo Park Lake in Los Angeles, where I lived for about six months in 1967. I was working on my second novel, and Carla Blank, my wife, a dancer, was teaching physical education at one of Eddie Rickenbacker's camps, located on an old movie set in the San Bernardino Mountains. Carla's employers were always offering me a cabin where they promised I could write without interruption. I never took them up on the offer, but for years I've wondered about what kind of reception I would have received had they discovered that I am black.

During my breaks from writing I would walk through the shopping areas near Santa Ynez, strolling by vending machines holding newspapers whose headlines screamed about riots in Detroit. On some weekends we'd visit novelist Robert

Gover (*The One Hundred Dollar Misunderstanding*) and his friends in Malibu. I remember one of Gover's friends, a scriptwriter for the *Donna Reed Show*, looking me in the eye and telling me that if he were black he'd be "on a Detroit rooftop, sniping at cops," as he reclined, glass of scotch in hand, in a comfortable chair whose position gave him a good view of the rolling Pacific.

My Santa Ynez neighbors were whites from Alabama and Mississippi, and we 5
got along fine. Most of them were elderly, left behind by white flight to the suburbs, and on weekends the street would be lined with cars belonging to relatives who were visiting. While living here I observed a uniquely Californian phenomenon. Retired men would leave their houses in the morning, enter their cars, and remain there for a good part of the day, snoozing, reading newspapers, or listening to the radio.

I didn't experience a single racial incident during my stay in this Los Angeles neighborhood of ex-southerners. Once, however, I had a strange encounter with the police. I was walking through a black working-class neighborhood on my way to the downtown Los Angeles library. Some cops drove up and rushed me. A crowd gathered. The cops snatched my briefcase and removed its contents: books and notebooks having to do with my research of voodoo. The crowd laughed when the cops said they thought I was carrying a purse.

In 1968 my wife and I moved to Berkeley, where we lived in one Bauhaus box after another until about 1971, when I received a three-book contract from Doubleday. Then we moved into the Berkeley Hills, where we lived in the downstairs apartment of a very grand-looking house on Bret Harte Way. There was a Zen garden with streams, waterfalls, and bridges outside, along with many varieties of flowers and plants. I didn't drive, and Carla was away at Mills College each day, earning a master's degree in dance. I stayed holed up in that apartment for two years, during which time I completed my third novel, *Mumbo Jumbo*.

During this period I became exposed to some of the racism I hadn't detected on Santa Ynez or in the Berkeley flats. As a black male working at home, I was regarded with suspicion. Neighbors would come over and warn me about a heroin salesman they said was burglarizing the neighborhood, all the while looking over my shoulder in an attempt to pry into what I was up to. Once, while I was eating breakfast, a policeman entered through the garden door, gun drawn. "What on earth is the problem, officer?" I asked. He said they got word that a homicide had been committed in my apartment, which I recognized as an old police tactic used to gain entry into somebody's house. Walking through the Berkeley Hills on Sundays, I was greeted by unfriendly stares and growling, snarling dogs. I remember one pest who always poked her head out of her window whenever I'd walk down Bret Harte Way. She was always hassling me about parking my car in front of her house. She resembled Miss Piggy. I came to think of this section of Berkeley as "Whitetown."

Around 1974 the landlord raised the rent on the house in the hills, and we found ourselves again in the Berkeley flats. We spent a couple of peaceful years on Edith Street, and then moved to Jayne Street, where we encountered another next-door family of nosy, middle-class progressives. I understand that much time at North Berkeley white neighborhood association meetings is taken up with discussion of and fascination with blacks who move through the neighborhoods, with special concern given those who tarry, or who wear dreadlocks. Since before the Civil War, vagrancy laws have been used as political weapons against blacks. Appropriately, there has been talk of making Havana—where I understand a woman can get turned in by her neighbors for having too many boyfriends over—Berkeley's sister city.

10 In 1976 our landlady announced that she was going to reoccupy the Jayne Street house. I facetiously told a friend that I wanted to move to the most right-wing neighborhood he could think of. He mentioned El Cerrito. There, he said, your next-door neighbor might even be a cop. We moved to El Cerrito. Instead of the patronizing nosiness blacks complain about in Berkeley, I found the opposite on Terrace Drive in El Cerrito. The people were cold, impersonal, remote. But the neighborhood was quiet, serene even—the view was Olympian, and our rented house was secluded by eucalyptus trees. The annoyances were minor. Occasionally a car would careen down Terrace Drive full of white teenagers, and one or two would shout, "Hey, nigger!" Sometimes as I walked down The Arlington toward Kensington Market, the curious would stare at me from their cars, and women I encountered would give me nervous, frightened looks. Once, as I was walking to the market to buy magazines, a white child was sitting directly in my path. We were the only two people on the street. Two or three cars actually stopped, and their drivers observed the scene through their rearview mirrors until they were assured I wasn't going to abduct the child.

At night the Kensington Market area was lit with a yellow light, especially eerie during a fog. I always thought that this section of Kensington would be a swell place to make a horror movie—the residents would make great extras—but whatever discomfort I felt about traveling through this area at 2 A.M. was mixed with the relief that I had just navigated safely through Albany, where the police seemed always to be lurking in the shadows, prepared to ensnare blacks, hippies, and others they didn't deem suitable for such a neighborhood.

In 1979 our landlord, a decent enough fellow in comparison to some of the others we had had (who made you understand why the communists shoot the landlords first when they take over a country), announced he was going to sell the house on Terrace Drive. This was the third rented house to be sold out from under us. The asking price was way beyond our means, and so we started to search for another home, only to find that the ones within our price range were located in North Oakland, in a "predominantly black neighborhood." We finally found a huge Queen Anne Victorian, which seemed to be about a month away from the wrecker's ball if the termites and the precarious foundation didn't do it in first, but I decided that I had to have it. The oldest house on the block, it was built in 1906, the year the big earthquake hit Northern California, but left Oakland unscathed because, according to Bret Harte, "there are some things even the earth can't swallow." If I was apprehensive about moving into this neighborhood—on television all black neighborhoods resemble the commotion of the station house on *Hill Street Blues*—I was later to learn that our neighbors were just as apprehensive about us. Were we hippies? Did I have a job? Were we going to pay as much attention to maintaining our property as they did to theirs? Neglected, the dilapidated monstrosity I'd got myself into would blight the entire block.

While I was going to college I worked as an orderly in a psychiatric hospital, and I remember a case in which a man was signed into the institution, after complaints from his neighbors that he mowed the lawn at four in the morning. My neighbors aren't that finicky, but they keep very busy pruning, gardening, and mowing their laws. Novelist Toni Cade Bambara wrote of the spirit women in Atlanta who plant by moonlight and use conjure to reap gorgeous vegetables and flowers. A woman on this block grows roses the size of cantaloupes.

On New Year's Eve, famed landscape architect John Roberts accompanied me on my nightly walk, which takes me from 53rd Street to Aileen, Shattuck, and back to 53rd Street. He was able to identify plants and trees that had been imported from Asia, the Middle East, and Australia. On Aileen Street he discovered a banana tree! And Arthur Monroe, a painter and art historian, traces the "Tabby" garden design—in which seashells and plates are mixed with lime, sand, and water to form decorative borders, found in this Oakland neighborhood, and others—to the influence of Islamic slaves brought to the Gulf Coast.

15 I won over my neighbors, I think, after I triumphed over a dozen generations of pigeons that had been roosting in the crevices of this house for many years. It was a long and angry war, and my five year old constantly complained to her mother about Daddy's bad words about the birds. I used everything I could get my hands on, including chicken wire and mothballs, and I would have tried the clay owls if the only manufacturer hadn't gone out of business. I also learned never to underestimate the intelligence of pigeons; just when you think you've got them whipped, you'll notice that they've regrouped on some strategic rooftop to prepare for another invasion. When the house was free of pigeons and their droppings, which had spread to the adjoining properties, the lady next door said, "Thank you."

Every New Year's Day since then our neighbors have invited us to join them and their fellow Louisianans for the traditional Afro-American good luck meal called Hoppin' John. This year the menu included black-eyed peas, ham, corn bread, potato salad, chitterlings, greens, fried chicken, yams, head cheese, macaroni, rolls, sweet potato pie, and fruitcake. I got up that morning weighing 214 pounds and came home from the party weighing 220.

We've lived on 53rd Street for three years now. Carla's dance and theater school, which she operates with her partner, Jody Roberts—Roberts and Blank Dance/Drama—is already five years old. I am working on my seventh novel and a television production of my play *Mother Hubbard.* The house has yet to be restored to its 1906 glory, but we're working on it.

I've grown accustomed to the common sights here—teenagers moving through the neighborhood carrying radios blasting music by Grandmaster Flash and Prince, men hovering over cars with tools and rags in hand, decked-out female church delegations visiting the sick. Unemployment up, one sees more men drinking from sacks as they walk through Market Street or gather in Helen McGregor Plaza, on Shattuck and 52nd Street, near a bench where mothers sit with their children, waiting for buses. It may be because the bus stop is across the street from Children's Hospital (exhibiting a brand-new antihuman, postmodern wing), but there seem to be a lot of sick black children these days. The criminal courts and emergency rooms of Oakland hospitals, both medical and psychiatric, are also filled with blacks.

White men go from door to door trying to unload spoiled meat. Incredibly sleazy white contractors and hustlers try to entangle people into shady deals that sometimes lead to the loss of a home. Everybody knows of someone, usually a widow, who has been gypped into paying thousands of dollars more than the standard cost for, say, adding a room to a house. It sure ain't El Cerrito. In El Cerrito the representatives from the utilities were very courteous. If they realize they're speaking to someone in a black neighborhood, however, they become curt and sarcastic. I was trying to arrange for the gas company to come out to fix a stove when the woman from Pacific Gas and Electric gave me some snide lip. I told her, "Lady, if you think what you're going through is an inconvenience, you can imagine my inconvenience paying the bills every month." Even she had to laugh.

The clerks in the stores are also curt, regarding blacks the way the media 20
regard them, as criminal suspects. Over in El Cerrito the cops were professional, respectful—in Oakland they swagger about like candidates for a rodeo. In El Cerrito and the Berkeley Hills you could take your time paying some bills, but in this black neighborhood if you miss paying a bill by one day, "reminders" printed in glaring and violent typefaces are sent to you, or you're threatened with discontinuance of this or that service. Los Angeles police victim Eulia Love, who was shot in the aftermath of an argument over an overdue gas bill, would still be alive if she had lived in El Cerrito or the Berkeley Hills.

I went to a bank a few weeks ago that advertised easy loans on television, only to be told that I would have to wait six months after opening an account to be eligible for a loan. I went home and called the same bank, this time putting on my Clark Kent voice, and was informed that I could come in and get the loan the same day. Other credit unions and banks, too, have different lending practices for black and white neighborhoods, but when I try to tell white intellectuals that blacks are prevented from developing industries because the banks find it easier to lend money to communist countries than to American citizens, they call me paranoid. Sometimes when I know I am going to be inconvenienced by merchants or creditors because of my 53rd Street address, I give the address of my Berkeley studio instead. Others are not so fortunate.

Despite the inconveniences and antagonism from the outside world one has to endure for having a 53rd Street address, life in this neighborhood is more pleasant than grim. Casually dressed, well-groomed elderly men gather at the intersections to look after the small children as they walk to and from school, or just to keep an eye on the neighborhood. My next-door neighbor keeps me in stitches with his informed commentary on any number of political comedies emanating from Washington and Sacramento. Once we were discussing pesticides, and the man who was repairing his porch told us that he had a great garden and didn't have to pay all that much attention to it. As for pesticides, he said, the bugs have to eat, too.

There are people on this block who still know the subsistence skills many Americans have forgotten. They can hunt and fish (and if you don't fish, there is a man who covers the neighborhood selling fresh fish and yelling, "Fishman," recalling a period of ancient American commerce when you didn't have to pay the middleman). They are also loyal Americans—they vote, they pay taxes—but you don't find the extreme patriots here that you find in white neighborhoods.

Although Christmas, Thanksgiving, New Year's, and Easter are celebrated with all get-out, I've never seen a flag flying on Memorial Day, or on any holiday that calls for the showing of the flag. Blacks express their loyalty in concrete ways. For example, you rarely see a foreign car in this neighborhood. And this 53rd Street neighborhood, as well as black neighborhoods like it from coast to coast, will supply the male children who will bear the brunt of future jungle wars, just as they did in Vietnam.

We do our shopping on a strip called Temescal, which stretches from 46th to 51st streets. Temescal, according to Oakland librarian William Sturm, is an Aztec word for "hothouse," or "bathhouse." The word was borrowed from the Mexicans by the Spanish to describe similar hothouses, early saunas, built by the California Indians in what is now North Oakland. Some say the hothouses were used to sweat out demons; others claim the Indians used them for medicinal purposes. Most agree that after a period of time in the steam, the Indians would rush en masse into the streams that flowed through the area. One still runs underneath my backyard—I have to mow the grass there almost every other day.

Within these five blocks are the famous Italian restaurant Bertola's, "Since 25
1932"; Siam restaurant; La Belle Creole, a French-Caribbean restaurant; Asmara, an Ethiopian restaurant; and Ben's Hof Brau, where white and black senior citizens, dressed in the elegance of a former time, congregate to talk or to have an inexpensive though quality breakfast provided by Ben's hardworking and courteous staff.

The Hof Brau shares its space with Vern's market, where you can shop to the music of DeBarge. To the front of Vern's is the Temescal Delicatessen, where a young Korean man makes the best po' boy sandwiches north of Louisiana, and near the side entrance is Ed Fraga's Automotive. The owner is always advising his customers to avoid stress, and he says goodbye with a "God bless you." The rest of the strip is taken up by the Temescal Pharmacy, which has a resident health advisor and a small library of health literature; the Aikido Institute; an African bookstore; and the internationally known Genova deli, to which people from the surrounding cities travel to shop. The strip also includes the Clausen House thrift shop, which sells used clothes and furniture. Here you can buy novels by J.D. Salinger and John O'Hara for ten cents each.

Space that was recently occupied by the Buon Gusto Bakery is now for rent. Before the bakery left, an Italian lady who worked there introduced me to a crunchy, cookie-like treat called "bones," which she said went well with Italian wine. The Buon Gusto had been a landmark since the 1940s, when, according to a guest at the New Year's Day Hoppin' John supper, North Oakland was populated by Italians and Portuguese. In those days a five-room house could be rented for $45 a month, she said.

The neighborhood is still in transition. The East Bay Negro Historical Society, which was located around the corner on Grove Street, included in its collection letters written by nineteenth-century macho man Jack London to his black nurse. They were signed, "Your little white pickaninny." It's been replaced by the New Israelite Delight restaurant, part of the Israelite Church, which also operates a day care center. The restaurant offers homemade Louisiana gumbo and a breakfast that includes grits.

Unlike the other California neighborhoods I've lived in, I know most of the people on this block by name. They are friendly and cooperative, always offering to watch your house while you're away. The day after one of the few whites who lives on the block—a brilliant muckraking journalist and former student of mine—was robbed, neighbors gathered in front of his house to offer assistance.

30 In El Cerrito my neighbor was indeed a cop. He used pomade on his curly hair, sported a mustache, and there was a grayish tint in his brown eyes. He was a handsome man, with a smile like a movie star's. His was the only house on the block I entered during my three-year stay in that neighborhood, and that was one afternoon when we shared some brandy. I wanted to get to know him better. I didn't know he was dead until I saw people in black gathered on his doorstep.

I can't imagine that happening on 53rd Street. In a time when dour thinkers view alienation and insensitivity toward the plight of others as characteristics of the modern condition, I think I'm lucky to live in a neighborhood where people look out for one another.

A human neighborhood.

THINGS TO DO WITH THE READING

1. Reed has made a career out of being provocative and hard to peg, and so the issue of tone in his essay is crucial. (For further discussion of tone—the implicit point of view (POV) in a piece toward its subject—see pages 260–263.) This is clearly an essay interested in race and matters of assimilation, but what is its POV on these matters? Make a list of indirect references and apparent throw-away lines about race in the piece. Then make inferences about these lines—"close read" them—to bring out Reed's POV toward race and assimilation. (See page 211 on close reading.)
2. Track and analyze the ways that the police function as a strand (see page 48). See especially paragraphs 6, 8, and 20, and the essay's last four paragraphs.
3. Irony is a complex verbal gesture that generally acknowledges the relative validity of both sides of an issue, as well as the limitations of both positions. The famous critic William Empson once described irony with a phrase from Romeo and Juliet, "a plague on both your houses." Ishmael Reed is fond of irony, and it provides an interesting way into his essay. How does the concept of evolution function ironically (and unironically) in the piece? How does the fact that Reed is African-American and is writing about race and racism add to this irony? See especially the essay's first paragraph, paragraphs 12–15, and paragraph 23.
4. **Link:** Consider paragraphs 25–28 wherein Reed catalogues the names and ethnic origins of shops—mostly shops selling food in his neighborhood. Use Rodriguez's essay as a lens for thinking about Reed's essay, starting

with this point of contact between the two essays: food. How does Reed's thinking about assimilation fit and not fit with Rodriguez's? Would Salins see Reed as an "ethnic federalist"?

Note: See the Link and Application on writing about neighborhoods following the end of the next selection.

Marianna Torgovnick

On Being White, Female, and Born in Bensonhurst

A visit to her old neighborhood in Brooklyn shortly after a racially motivated killing provides the occasion for Marianna Torgovnick to re-evaluate her conflicted attitudes toward her own past. Wandering the neighborhood, she reflects on the legacy of ethnic and gender prejudice in her own family, on the desire it bore in her not only to escape her upbringing but to obscure it, and ultimately, on the cost of doing so. Torgovnick is a professor of English at Duke University with a special interest in cultural studies. A version of this essay appeared in her 1994 book *Crossing Ocean Parkway: Readings by an Italian American Daughter*, which won the American Book Award.

The mafia protects the neighborhood, our fathers say, with that peculiar satisfied pride with which law-abiding Italian Americans refer to the Mafia: the Mafia protects the neighborhood from "the coloreds." In the fifties and sixties, I heard that information repeated, in whispers, in neighborhood parks and in the yard at school in Bensonhurst. The same information probably passes today in the parks (the word now "blacks," not "coloreds") but perhaps no longer in the schoolyards. From buses each morning, from neighborhoods outside Bensonhurst, spill children of all colors and backgrounds—American black, West Indian black, Hispanic, and Asian. But the blacks are the only ones especially marked for notice. Bensonhurst is no longer entirely protected from "the coloreds." But in a deeper sense, at least for Italian Americans, Bensonhurst never changes. 1

Italian-American life continues pretty much as I remember it. Families with young children live side by side with older couples whose children are long gone to the suburbs. Many of those families live "down the block" from the last generation or, sometimes still, live together with parents or grandparents. When a young family leaves, as sometimes happens, for Long Island or New Jersey or (very common now) for Staten Island, another arrives, without any special effort being required, from Italy or a poorer neighborhood in New York. They fill the neat but anonymous houses that make up the mostly tree-lined streets: two-, three-, or four-family houses for the most part (this is a working, lower to middle-middle class area, and people need rents to pay mortgages), with a few single family or small apartment houses tossed in at random. Tomato plants, fig trees, and plaster madonnas often decorate small but well-tended yards which face out onto the street; the grassy front lawn, like the grassy back yard, is relatively uncommon.

Crisscrossing the neighborhood and making out ethnic zones—Italian, Irish, and Jewish, for the most part, though there are some Asian Americans and some people (usually Protestants) called simply Americans—are the great shopping streets: Eighty-sixth Street, Kings Highway, Bay Parkway, Eighteenth Avenue, each with its own distinctive character. On Eighty-sixth Street, crowds bustle along sidewalks lined with ample, packed fruit stands. Women wheeling shopping carts or baby strollers check the fruit carefully, piece by piece, and often bargain with the dealer, cajoling for a better price or letting him know that the vegetables, this time, aren't up to snuff. A few blocks down, the fruit stands are gone and the streets are lined with clothing and record shops, mobbed by teenagers. Occasionally, the el rumbles overhead, a few stops out of Coney Island on its way to the city, a trip of around one hour.

On summer nights, neighbors congregate on stoops which during the day serve as play yards for children. Air conditioning exists everywhere in Bensonhurst, but people still sit outside in the summer—to supervise children, to gossip, to stare at strangers. "*Buona sera*," I say, or "*Buona notte*," as I am ritually presented to Sal and Lily and Louie, the neighbors sitting on the stoop. "*Grazie*," I say when they praise my children or my appearance. It's the only time I use Italian, which I learned at high school, although my parents (both second-generation Italian Americans, my father Sicilian, my mother Calabrian) speak it at home to each other but never to me or my brother. My accent is the Tuscan accent taught at school, not the southern Italian accents of my parents and the neighbors.

5 It's important to greet and please the neighbors, any break in this decorum would seriously offend and aggrieve my parents. For the neighbors are the stern arbiters of conduct in Bensonhurst. Does Mary keep a clean house? Did Gina wear black long enough after her mother's death? Was the food good at Tony's wedding? The neighbors know and pass judgment. Any news of family scandal (my brother's divorce, for example) provokes from my mother the agonized words: "But what will I *tell* people?" I sometimes collaborate in devising a plausible script.

A large sign on the church I attended as a child sums up for me the ethos of Bensonhurst. The sign urges contributions to the church building fund with the message, in huge letters: "EACH YEAR ST. SIMON AND JUDE SAVES THIS NEIGHBORHOOD ONE MILLION DOLLARS IN TAXES." Passing the church on the way from largely Jewish and middle-class Sheepshead Bay (where my in-laws live) to Bensonhurst, year after year, my husband and I look for the sign and laugh at the crass level of its pitch, its utter lack of attention to things spiritual. But we also understand exactly the values it represents.

In the summer of 1989, my parents were visiting me at my house in Durham, North Carolina, from the apartment in Bensonhurst where they have lived since 1942: three small rooms, rent-controlled, floor clean enough to eat off, every corner and crevice known and organized. My parents' longevity in a single apartment is unusual even for Bensonhurst, but not that unusual; many people live for decades in the same place or move within a ten-block radius. When I lived in this apartment, there were four rooms; one has since been ceded to a demanding landlord, one of the various landlords who have haunted my parents' life and must always be appeased lest the ultimate threat—removal from the rent-controlled apartment—be brought into play. That summer, during their visit, on August 23 (my younger daughter's birthday) a shocking, disturbing, news report issued from the neighborhood: it had become another Howard Beach.

Three black men, walking casually through the streets at night, were attacked by a group of whites. One was shot dead, mistaken, as it turned out, for another black youth who was dating a white, although part-Hispanic, girl in the neighborhood. It all made sense: the crudely protective men, expecting to see a black arriving at the girl's house and overreacting; the rebellious girl dating the outsider boy; the black dead as a sacrifice to the feelings of the neighborhood.

I might have felt outrage, I might have felt guilt or shame, I might have despised the people among whom I grew up. In a way I felt all four emotions when I heard the news. I expect that there were many people in Bensonhurst who felt the same rush of emotions. But mostly I felt that, given the set-up, this was the only way things could have happened. I detested the racial killing, but I also understood it. Those streets, which should be public property available to all, belong to the neighborhood. All the people sitting on the stoops on August 23 knew that as well as they knew their own names. The black men walking through probably knew it too—though their casual walk sought to deny the fact that, for the neighbors, even the simple act of blacks walking through the neighborhood would be seen as invasion.

10 Italian Americans in Bensonhurst are notable for their cohesiveness and provinciality; the slightest pressure turns those qualities into prejudice and racism. Their cohesiveness is based on the stable economic and ethical level that links generation to generation, keeping Italian Americans in Bensonhurst and the Italian-American community alive as the Jewish-American community of my youth is no longer alive. (Its young people routinely moved to the suburbs or beyond and were never replaced, so that Jews in Bensonhurst today are almost all very old people.) Their provinciality results from the Italian Americans' devotion to jealous distinctions and discriminations. Jews are suspect, but (the old Italian women admit) "they make good husbands." The Irish are okay, fellow Catholics, but not really "like us"; they make bad husbands because they drink and gamble. Even Italians come in varieties, by region (Sicilian, Calabrian, Neapolitan, very rarely any region further north) and by history in this country (the newly arrived and ridiculed "gaffoon" versus the second or third generation).

Bensonhurst is a neighborhood dedicated to believing that its values are the only values; it tends toward certain forms of inertia. When my parents visit me in Durham, they routinely take chairs from the kitchen and sit out on the lawn in front of the house, not on the chairs on the back deck; then they complain that the streets are too quiet. When they walk around my, neighborhood (these De Marcos who have friends named Travaglianti and Occhipinti), they look at the mailboxes and report that my neighbors have strange names. Prices at my local supermarket are compared, in unbelievable detail, with prices on Eighty-sixth Street. Any rearrangement of my kitchen since their last visit is registered and criticized. Difference is not only unwelcome, it is unacceptable. One of the most characteristic things my mother ever said was in response to my plans for renovating my house in Durham. When she heard my plans, she looked around, crossed her arms, and said, "If it was me, I wouldn't change nothing." My father once asked me to level with him about a Jewish boyfriend who lived in a different part of the neighborhood, reacting to his Jewishness, but even more to the fact that he often wore Bermuda shorts: "Tell me something, Marianna. Is he a Communist?" Such are the standards of normality and political thinking in Bensonhurst.

I often think that one important difference between Italian Americans in New York neighborhoods like Bensonhurst and Italian Americans elsewhere is that the others moved on—to upstate New York, to Pennsylvania, to the Midwest. Though they frequently settled in communities of fellow Italians, they did move on. Bensonhurst Italian Americans seem to have felt that one large move, over the ocean, was enough. Future moves could be only local: from the Lower East Side, for example, to Brooklyn, or from one part of Brooklyn to another. Bensonhurst was for many of these people the summa of expectations. If their America were to be drawn as a *New Yorker* cover, Manhattan itself would be tiny in proportion to Bensonhurst and to its satellites, Staten Island, New Jersey, and Long Island.

"Oh, no," my father says when he hears the news about the shooting. Though he still refers to blacks as "coloreds," he's not really a racist and is upset that this innocent youth was shot in his neighborhood. He has no trouble acknowledging the wrongness of the death. But then, like all the news accounts, he turns to the fact, repeated over and over, that the blacks had been on their way to look at a used car when they encountered the hostile mob of whites. The explanation is right before him but, "Yeah," he says, still shaking his head, "yeah, but what were they *doing* there? They didn't belong."

Over the next few days, the television news is even more disturbing. Rows of screaming Italians lining the streets, most of them looking like my relatives. I focus especially on one woman who resembles almost completely my mother: stocky but not fat, mid-seventies but well preserved, full face showing only minimal wrinkles, ample steel-gray hair neatly if rigidly coiffed in a modified beehive hairdo left over from the sixties. She shakes her fist at the camera, protesting the arrest of the Italian-American youths in the neighborhood and the incursion of more blacks into the neighborhood, protesting the shooting. I look a little nervously at my mother (the parent I resemble), but she has not even noticed the woman and stares impassively at the television.

15 What has Bensonhurst to do with what I teach today and write? Why did I need to write about this killing in Bensonhurst, but not in the manner of a news account or a statistical sociological analysis? Within days of hearing the news, I began to plan this essay, to tell the world what I knew, even though I was aware that I could publish the piece only someplace my parents or their neighbors would never see or hear about it. I sometimes think that I looked around from my baby carriage and decided that someday, the sooner the better, I would get out of Bensonhurst. Now, much to my surprise, Bensonhurst—the antipode of the intellectual life I sought, the least interesting of places—had become a respectable intellectual topic. People would be willing to hear about Bensonhurst—and all by the dubious virtue of a racial killing in the streets.

The story as I would have to tell it would be to some extent a class narrative: about the difference between working class and upper middle class, dependence and a profession, Bensonhurst and a posh suburb. But I need to make it clear that I do not imagine myself as writing from a position of enormous self-satisfaction, or even enormous distance. You can take the girl out of Bensonhurst (that much is clear), but you may not be able to take Bensonhurst out of the girl. And upward mobility is not the essence of the story, though it is an important marker and symbol.

In Durham today, I live in a twelve-room house surrounded by an acre of trees. When I sit on my back deck on summer evenings, no houses are visible through the trees. I have a guaranteed income, teaching English at an excellent university, removed by my years of education from the fundamental economic and social conditions of Bensonhurst. The one time my mother ever expressed pleasure at my work was when I got tenure, what my father still calls, with no irony intended, "ten years." "What does that mean?" my mother asked when she heard the news. Then she reached back into her experience as a garment worker, subject to periodic layoffs. "Does it mean they can't fire you just for nothing and can't lay you off?" When I said that was exactly what it means, she said, "Very good. Congratulations. That's *wonderful.*" I was free from the *padrones*, from the network of petty anxieties that had formed, in large part, her very existence. Of course, I wasn't really free of petty anxieties: would my salary increase keep pace with my colleagues', how would my office compare, would this essay be accepted for publication, am I happy? The line between these worries and my mother's is the line between the working class and the upper middle class.

But getting out of Bensonhurst never meant to me a big house, or nice clothes, or a large income. And it never meant feeling good about looking down on what I left behind or hiding my background. Getting out of Bensonhurst meant freedom—to experiment, to grow, to change. It also meant knowledge in some grand, abstract way. All the material possessions I have acquired, I acquired simply along the way—and for the first twelve years after I left Bensonhurst, I chose to acquire almost nothing at all. Now, as I write about the neighborhood, I recognize that although I've come far in physical and material distance, the emotional distance is harder to gauge. Bensonhurst has everything to do with who I am and even with what I write. Occasionally I get reminded of my roots, of their simultaneously choking and nutritive power.

Scene one: It's after a lecture at Duke, given by a visiting professor from Princeton. The lecture was long and a little dull and—bad luck—I had agreed to be one of the people having dinner with the lecturer afterward. We settle into our table at the restaurant: this man, me, the head of the comparative literature program (also a professor of German), and a couple I like who teach French, the husband at my university, the wife at one nearby. The conversation is sluggish, as it often is when a stranger, like the visiting professor, has to be assimilated into a group, so I ask the visitor from Princeton a question to personalize things a bit. "How did you get interested in what you do? What made you become a professor of German?" The man gets going and begins talking about how it was really unlikely that he, a nice Jewish boy from Bensonhurst, would have chosen, in the mid-fifties, to study German. Unlikely indeed.

20 I remember seeing *Judgment at Nuremberg* in a local movie theater and having a woman in the row in back of me get hysterical when some clips of a concentration camp were shown. "My God," she screamed in a European accent, "look at what they did. Murderers, MURDERERS!"—and she had to be supported out by her family. I couldn't see, in the dark, whether her arm bore the neatly tattooed numbers that the arms of some of my classmates' parents did—and that always affected me with a thrill of horror. Ten years older than me, this man had lived more directly through those feelings, lived with and *among* those feelings. The first chance he got, he raced to study in Germany. I myself have twice chosen not to visit Germany, but I understand his impulse to identify with the Other as a way of getting out of the neighborhood.

At the dinner, the memory about the movie pops into my mind but I pick up instead on the Bensonhurst—I'm also from there, but Italian American. Like a flash, he asks something I haven't been asked in years: Where did I go to high school and (a more common question) what was my maiden name? I went to Lafayette High School, I say, and my name was De Marco. Everything changes: his facial expression, his posture, his! accent, his voice. "Soo, Dee Maw-ko," he says, "dun anything wrong at school today—got enny pink slips? Wanna meet me later at the park on maybe bye the Baye?" When I laugh, recognizing the stereotype that Italians get pink slips for misconduct at school and the notorious chemistry between Italian women and Jewish men, he says, back in his Princetonian voice: "My God, for a minute I felt like I was turning into a werewolf."

It's odd that although I can remember almost nothing else about this man—his face, his body type, even his name—I remember this lapse into his "real self" with enormous vividness. I am especially struck by how easily he was able to slip into the old, generic Brooklyn accent. I myself have no memory of ever speaking in that accent, though I also have no memory of trying not to speak it, except for teaching myself, carefully, to say "oil" rather than "earl."

But the surprises aren't over. The female French professor, whom I have known for at least five years, reveals for the first time that she is also from the neighborhood, though she lived across the other side of Kings Highway, went to a different, more elite high school, and was Irish American. Three of six professors, sitting at an eclectic vegetarian restaurant in Durham, all from Bensonhurst—a neighborhood where (I swear) you couldn't get the *New York Times* at any of the local stores.

Scene two: I still live in Bensonhurst. I'm waiting for my parents to return from a conference at my school, where they've been summoned to discuss my transition from elementary to junior high school. I am already a full year younger than any of my classmates, having skipped a grade, a not uncommon occurrence for "gifted" youngsters. Now the school is worried about putting me in an accelerated track through junior high, since that would make me two years younger. A compromise was reached: I would be put in a special program for gifted children, but one that took three, not two, years. It sounds okay.

Three years later, another wait. My parents have gone to school this time to 25
make another decision. Lafayette High School has three tracks: academic, for potentially college-bound kids; secretarial, mostly for Italian-American girls or girls with low aptitude-test scores (the high school is de facto segregated, so none of the tracks is as yet racially coded, though they are coded by ethnic group and gender); and vocational, mostly for boys with the same attributes, ethnic or intellectual. Although my scores are superb, the guidance counselor has recommended the secretarial track; when I protested, the conference with my parents was arranged. My mother's preference is clear: the secretarial track—college is for boys; I will need to make a "good living" until I marry and have children. My father also prefers the secretarial track, but he wavers, half proud of my aberrantly high scores, half worried. I press the attack, saying that if I were Jewish I would have been placed, without question, in the academic track. I tell him I have sneaked a peek at my files and know that my IQ is at genius level. I am allowed to insist on the change into the academic track.

What I did, and I was ashamed of it even then, was to play upon my father's competitive feelings with Jews: his daughter could and should be as good as theirs. In the bank where he was a messenger, and at the insurance company where he worked in the mailroom, my father worked with Jews, who were almost always his immediate supervisors. Several times, my father was offered the supervisory job but turned it down after long conversations with my mother about the dangers of making a change, the difficulty of giving orders to friends. After her work in a local garment shop, after cooking dinner and washing the floor each night, my mother often did piecework making bows; sometimes I would help her for fun, but it *wasn't* fun, and I was free to stop while she continued for long, tedious hours to increase the family income. Once a week, her part-time boss, Dave, would come by to pick up the boxes of bows. Short, round, with his shirttails sloppily tucked into his pants and a cigar almost always dangling from his lips, Dave was a stereotyped Jew but also, my parents always said, a nice guy, a decent man.

Years after, similar choices come up, and I show the same assertiveness I showed with my father, the same ability to deal for survival, but tinged with Bensonhurst caution. Where will I go to college? Not to Brooklyn College, the flagship of the city system—I know that, but don't press the invitations I have received to apply to prestigious schools outside of New York. The choice comes down to two: Barnard, which gives me a full scholarship, minus five hundred dollars a year that all scholarship students are expected to contribute from summer earnings, or New York University, which offers me one thousand dollars above tuition as a bribe. I waver. My parents stand firm: they are already losing money by letting me go to college; I owe it to the family to contribute the extra thousand dollars plus my summer earnings. Besides, my mother adds, harping on a favorite theme, there are no boys at Barnard; at NYU I'm more likely to meet someone to marry. I go to NYU and do marry in my senior year, but he is someone I didn't meet at college. I was secretly relieved, I now think (though at the time I thought I was just placating my parents' conventionality), to be out of the marriage sweepstakes.

The first boy who ever asked me for a date was Robert Lubitz, in eighth grade: tall and skinny to my average height and teenage chubbiness. I turned him down, thinking we would make a ridiculous couple. Day after day, I cast my eyes at stylish Juliano, the class cutup; day after day, I captivated Robert Lubitz. Occasionally, one of my brother's Italian-American friends would ask me out, and I would go, often to ROTC dances. My specialty was making political remarks so shocking that the guys rarely asked me again. After a while I recognized destiny: the Jewish man was a passport out of Bensonhurst. I of course did marry a Jewish man, who gave me my freedom and, very important, helped remove me from the expectations of Bensonhurst. Though raised in a largely Jewish section of Brooklyn, he had gone to college in Ohio and knew how important it was, as he put it, "to get past the Brooklyn Bridge." We met on neutral ground, in Central Park, at a performance of Shakespeare. The Jewish-Italian marriage is a common enough catastrophe in Bensonhurst for my parents to have accepted, even welcomed, mine—though my parents continued to treat my husband like an outsider for the first twenty years ("Now Marianna. Here's what's going on with you brother. But don't tell-a you husband").

Along the way I make other choices, more fully marked by Bensonhurst cautiousness. I am attracted to journalism or the arts as careers, but the prospects for income seem iffy. I choose instead to imagine myself as a teacher. Only the availability of NDEA fellowships when I graduate, with their generous terms, propels me from high school teaching (a thought I never much relished) to college teaching (which seems like a brave new world). Within the college teaching profession, I choose offbeat specializations: the novel, interdisciplinary approaches (not something clear and clubby like Milton or the eighteenth century). Eventually I write the book I like best about primitive others as they figure within Western obsessions: my identification with "the Other," my sense of being "Other," surfaces at last. I avoid all mentoring structures for a long time but accept aid when it comes to me on the basis of what I perceive to be merit. I'm still, deep down, Italian-American Bensonhurst, though by this time I'm a lot of other things as well.

Scene three: In the summer of 1988, a little more than a year before the shoot- 30
ing in Bensonhurst, my father woke up trembling and in what appeared to be a fit. Hospitalization revealed that he had a pocket of blood on his brain, a frequent consequence of falls for older people. About a year earlier, I had stayed home, using my children as an excuse, when my aunt, my father's much loved sister, died, missing her funeral; only now does my mother tell me how much my father resented my taking his suggestion that I stay home. Now, confronted with what is described as brain surgery but turns out to be less dramatic than it sounds, I fly home immediately.

My brother drives three hours back and forth from New Jersey every day to chauffeur me and my mother to the hospital: he is being a fine Italian-American son. For the first time in years, we have long conversations alone. He is two years older than I am, a chemical engineer who has also left the neighborhood but has remained closer to its values, with a suburban, Republican inflection. He talks a lot about New York, saying that (except for neighborhoods like Bensonhurst) it's a "third-world city now." It's the summer of the Tawana Brawley incident, when Brawley accused white men of abducting her and smearing racial slurs on her body with her own excrement. My brother is filled with dislike for Al Sharpton and Brawley's other vocal supporters in the black community—not because they're black, he says, but because they're troublemakers, stirring things up. The city is drenched in racial hatred that makes itself felt in the halls of the hospital: Italians and Jews in the beds and as doctors; blacks as nurses and orderlies.

This is the first time since I left New York in 1975 that I have visited Brooklyn without once getting into Manhattan. It's the first time I have spent several days alone with my mother, living in her apartment in Bensonhurst. My every move is scrutinized and commented on. I feel like I am going to go crazy.

Finally, it's clear that my father is going to be fine, and I can go home. She insists on accompanying me to the travel agent to get my ticket for home, even though I really want to be alone. The agency (a Mafia front?) has no one who knows how to ticket me for the exotic destination of North Carolina and no computer for doing so. The one person who can perform this feat by hand is out. I have to kill time for an hour and suggest to my mother that she go home, to be there for my brother when he arrives from Jersey. We stop in a Pork Store, where I buy a stash of cheeses, sausages, and other delicacies unavailable in Durham. My mother walks home with the shopping bags, and I'm on my own.

More than anything I want a kind of *sorbetto* or ice I remember from my childhood, a *cremolata*, almond-vanilla-flavored with large chunks of nuts. I pop into the local bakery (at the unlikely hour of 11 A.M.) and ask for a *cremolata*, usually eaten after dinner. The woman—a younger version of my mother—refuses: they haven't made a fresh ice yet, and what's left from the day before is too icy, no good. I explain that I'm about to get on a plane for North Carolina and want that ice, good or not. But she has her standards and holds her ground, even though North Carolina has about the same status in her mind as Timbuktoo and she knows I will be banished, perhaps forever, from the land of *cremolata*.

Then, while I'm taking a walk, enjoying my solitude, I have another idea. On 35
the block behind my parents' house, there's a club for men, for men from a particular town or region in Italy: six or seven tables, some on the sidewalk beneath a garish red, green, and white sign; no women allowed or welcome unless they're with men, and no women at all during the day when the real business of the club—a game of cards for old men—is in progress. Still, I know that inside the club would be coffee and a *cremolata* ice. I'm thirty-eight, well-dressed, very respectable looking; I know what I want. I also know I'm not supposed to enter that club. I enter anyway, asking the teenage boy behind the counter firmly, in my most professional tones, for a *cremolata* ice. Dazzled, he complies immediately. The old men at the card table have been staring at this scene, unable to place me exactly, though my facial type is familiar. Finally, a few old men's hisses pierce the air. "*Strega*," I hear as I leave, "*mala strega*"—"witch," or "brazen whore." I have been in Bensonhurst less than a week, but I have managed to reproduce, on my final day there for this visit, the conditions of my youth. Knowing the rules, I have broken them. I shake hands with my discreetly rebellious past, still an outsider walking through the neighborhood, marked and insulted—though unlikely to be shot.

THINGS TO DO WITH THE READING

1. It's a paradox of effective reading that sometimes you can see more out of the corner of your eye than by staring straight ahead. That is, looking at issues aslant, from one side, rather than directly, can be especially revealing. What functions do Torgovnick's brother, husband, high school boyfriends, and the female French professor who has been her friend for five years serve in her larger discussion of ethnicity and the melting pot?

2. A key word in this essay is the often-capitalized "Other." It is used in reference to the visiting lecturer at the end of paragraph 20, for example: "I myself have twice chosen not to visit Germany, but I understand his impulse to identify with the Other as a way of getting out of the

neighborhood." Find other references in the essay to the Other, or situations of Otherness, and consider how this concept operates in Torgovnick's struggle to understand assimilation American style.

3. With what Other did Torgovnick identify in order to get out of the neighborhood? At what places in the essay do we see anxiety about this identification of hers, and how is it (or is it) resolved?

4. Torgovnick explicitly names social class as a barrier between, for example, herself and her parents. In paragraph 16, Torgovnick asserts, "The story as I would have to tell it would be *to some extent* a class narrative" (our italics). To what extent? As you answer this question, take care to look for ways that her thinking about class—and about her parents—changes as the essay progresses.

5. **Link:** How does Torgovnick's Bensonhurst compare and contrast with Reed's El Cerrito? What features of El Cerrito might Reed point to as preventing it from having the kind of provinciality that Torgovnick shows us leads to racism and violence in Bensonhurst? To what extent do Reed and Torgovnick find similar things to celebrate in their largely unassimilated neighborhoods?

6. **Link:** The essay ends with a brief scene in which Torgovnick is treated as an outsider by a group of Italian-American men. In this case, they have verbally insulted her primarily for her gender. Where else does gender discrimination appear in the essay? How does it compare as a lens—seeing as a woman—with the lens of race adopted by Reed and Gates in their essays? What are the biggest similarities? And given those similarities, what's the biggest difference? (See page 158 on difference within similarity.)

7. **Link Across Chapters:** Torgovnick's essay begins with the issue of neighborhood safety as seen by her Italian-American parents and neighbors, wherein safety and racism are directly connected. Put Torgovnick's essay into conversation with Jane Jacobs's essay, "Uses of Sidewalks: Safety" in Chapter 16. What might Jacobs find to praise about Bensonhurst, and why? What's different about the neighborhoods that Jacobs describes that apparently make them safer for strangers and outsiders? How is Bensonhurst different from the neighborhood around the White Horse Tavern that Jacobs describes, and so what?

8. **Application:** Equipped with a notebook or laptop, spend an afternoon wandering around your old neighborhood. Make a point of stopping every half hour or so to freewrite on the question, "How has my neighborhood shaped me?" Obviously, the readings in this chapter should have enriched the implications of that question for you, to include such matters as

   - the marks of social class
   - the elements in yourself you have wished to conceal or make over
   - your tastes to this day, but also (gulp) your "local" prejudices
   - your own ambivalence to your past, that strange mix of reverence and dread that neighborhoods specialize in inspiring

Make at least three entries of 20 minutes or more. Then return to these—type them if you have handwritten them—and revise and expand them. If you carried this project through to some sort of completion, one or more of them might open out into your personal essay about the complex hold that a neighborhood can claim on who and what we become. See the sections on writing the self (see pages 10–11) and freewriting (see pages 15–16) for more advice on this kind of writing.

Benjamin DeMott

Put On a Happy Face: Masking the Differences Between Blacks and Whites

Focusing on the "romance" of black-white friendship represented in popular American film, this piece argues, with angry irony, that "the cleansing social force" of friendship has been embraced by mainstream white culture as an easy out from the responsibility for historically produced and institutionalized racism. "People forget the theoretically unforgettable—the caste history of American blacks, the connection between no schools for longer than a century and bad school performance now," declares Benjamin DeMott. This essay, which first appeared in *Harper's* magazine in 1995, seeks to make us remember.

At the movies these days, questions about racial injustice have been amicably resolved. Watch *Pulp Fiction* or *Congo* or *A Little Princess* or any other recent film in which both blacks and whites are primary characters and you can, if you want, forget about race. Whites and blacks greet one another on the screen with loving candor, revealing their common humanity. In *Pulp Fiction*, an armed black mobster (played by Samuel L. Jackson) looks deep into the eyes of an armed white thief in the middle of a holdup (played by Tim Roth) and shares his version of God's word in Ezekiel, whereupon the two men lay aside their weapons, both more or less redeemed. The moment inverts an earlier scene in which a white boxer (played by Bruce Willis) risks his life to save another black mobster (played by Ving Rhames), who is being sexually tortured as a prelude to his execution. 1

Pulp Fiction (gross through July [1995]: $107 million) is one of a series of films suggesting that the beast of American racism is tamed and harmless. Close to the start of *Die Hard with a Vengeance* (gross through July [1995]: $95 million) the camera finds a white man wearing sandwich boards on the corner of Amsterdam Avenue and 138th Street in Harlem. The boards carry a horrific legend: I HATE NIGGERS. A group of young blacks approach the man with murderous intent, bearing guns and knives. They are figures straight out of a national nightmare—ugly, enraged, terrifying. No problem. A black man, again played by Jackson, appears and rescues the white man, played by Willis. The black man and white man come to know each other well. In time the white man declares flatly to the black, "I need you more than you need me." A moment later he charges the black with being a racist—with not liking whites as much as the white man likes blacks—and the two talk frankly about their racial prejudices. Near the end of the film, the men have grown so close that each volunteers to die for the other.

Pulp Fiction and *Die Hard with a Vengeance* follow the pattern of *Lethal Weapon 1, 2,* and *3*, the Danny Glover/Mel Gibson buddy vehicles that collectively grossed $357 million, and *White Men Can't Jump*, which, in the year of the L.A. riots, grossed $76 million. In *White Men Can't Jump*, a white dropout, played by Woody Harrelson, ekes out a living on black-dominated basketball courts in Los Angeles. He's arrogant and aggressive but never in danger because he has a black protector and friend, played by Wesley Snipes. At the movie's end, the white, flying above the hoop like a stereotypical black player, scores the winning basket in a two-on-two pickup game on an alley-oop pass from his black chum, whereupon the two men fall into each other's arms in joy. Later, the black friend agrees to find work for the white at the store he manages.

WHITE (helpless): I gotta get a job. Can you get me a job?
BLACK (affectionately teasing): Got any references?
WHITE (shy grin): You.

Such dialogue is the stuff of romance. What's dreamed of and gained is a place where whites are unafraid of blacks, where blacks ask for and need nothing from whites, and where the sameness of the races creates a common fund of sweet content.[1] The details of the dream matter less than the force that makes it come true for both races, eliminating the constraints of objective reality and redistributing resources, status, and capabilities. That cleansing social force supersedes political and economic fact or policy; that force, improbably enough, is friendship.

5 Watching the beaming white men who know how to jump, we do well to remind ourselves of what the camera shot leaves out. Black infants die in America at twice the rate of white infants. (Despite the increased numbers of middle-class blacks, the rates are diverging, with black rates actually rising.) One out of every two black children lives below the poverty line (as compared with one out of seven white children). Nearly four times as many black families exist below the poverty line as white families. More than 50 percent of African American families have incomes below $25,000. Among black youths under age twenty, death by murder occurs nearly ten times as often as among whites. Over 60 percent of births to black mothers occur out of wedlock, more than four times the rate for white mothers. The net worth of the typical white household is ten times that of the typical black household. In many states, five to ten times as many blacks as whites age eighteen to thirty are in prison.

The good news at the movies obscures the bad news in the streets and confirms the Supreme Court's recent decisions on busing, affirmative action, and redistricting. Like the plot of *White Men Can't Jump*, the Court postulates the existence of a society no longer troubled by racism. Because black-white friendship is now understood to be the rule, there is no need for integrated schools or a congressional Black Caucus or affirmative action. The Congress and state governors can guiltlessly cut welfare, food assistance, fuel assistance, Head Start, housing money, fellowship money, vaccine money. Justice Anthony Kennedy can declare, speaking for the Supreme Court majority last June, that creating a world of genuine equality and sameness requires only that "our political system and our society cleanse themselves … of discrimination."

[1] I could go on with examples of movies that deliver the good news of friendship: *Regarding Henry, Driving Miss Daisy, Forrest Gump, The Shawshank Redemption, Philadelphia, The Last Boy Scout, 48 Hours I–II, Rising Sun, Iron Eagle I–II, Rudy, Sister Act, Hearts of Dixie, Betrayed, The Power of One, White Nights, Clara's Heart, Doc Hollywood, Cool Runnings, Places in the Heart, Trading Places, Fried Green Tomatoes, Q & A, Platoon, A Mother's Courage: The Mary Thomas Story, The Unforgiven, The Air Up There, The Pelican Brief, Losing Isaiah, Smoke, Searching for Bobby Fischer, An Officer and a Gentleman, Speed*, etc.

The deep logic runs as follows: *Yesterday white people didn't like black people, and accordingly suffered guilt, knowing that the dislike was racist and knowing also that as moral persons they would have to atone for the guilt. They would have to ante up for welfare and Head Start and halfway houses and free vaccine and midnight basketball and summer jobs for schoolkids and graduate fellowships for promising scholars and craft-union apprenticeships and so on, endlessly. A considerable and wasteful expense. But at length came the realization that by ending dislike or hatred it would be possible to end guilt, which in turn would mean an end to redress: no more wasteful ransom money. There would be but one requirement: the regular production and continuous showing forth of evidence indisputably proving that hatred has totally vanished from the land.*

I cannot tell the reader how much I would like to believe in this sunshine world. After the theater lights brighten and I've found coins for a black beggar on the way to my car and am driving home through downtown Springfield, Massachusetts, the world invented by *Die Hard with a Vengeance* and America's highest court gives way only slowly to the familiar urban vision in my windshield—homeless blacks on trash-strewn streets, black prostitutes staked out on a corner, and signs of a not very furtive drug trade. I know perfectly well that most African Americans don't commit crimes or live in alleys. I also know that for somebody like myself, downtown Springfield in the late evening is not a good place to be.

The movies reflect the larger dynamic of wish and dream. Day after day the nation's corporate ministries of culture churn out images of racial harmony. Millions awaken each morning to the friendly sight of Katie Couric nudging a perky elbow into good buddy Bryant Gumbel's side. My mailbox and millions of demographically similar others are choked with flyers from companies (Wal-Mart, Victoria's Secret) bent on publicizing both their wares and their social bona fides by displaying black and white models at cordial ease with one another. A torrent of goodwill messages about race arrives daily—revelations of corporate largesse, commercials, news features, TV specials, all proclaiming that whites like me feel strongly positive impulses of friendship for blacks and that those same admirable impulses are effectively eradicating racial differences, rendering blacks and whites the same. BellSouth TV commerciais present children singing "I am the keeper of the world"—first a white child, then a black child, then a white child, then a black child. Because Dow Chemical likes black America, it recruits young black college grads for its research division and dramatizes, in TV commercials, their tearful-joyful partings from home. ("Son, show 'em what you got," says a black lad's father.) American Express shows an elegant black couple and an elegant white couple sitting together in a theater, happy in one another's company. (The couples share the box with an oversized Gold Card.) During the evening news I watch a black mom offer Robitussin to a miserably coughing white mom. Here's *People* magazine promoting itself under a photo of John Lee Hooker, the black bluesman. "We're these kinds of people, too," *People* claims in the caption. In [a recent] production of *Hamlet* on Broadway, Horatio [was] played by a black actor. On *The 700 Club*, Pat Robertson joshes Ben Kinchlow, his black sidekick, about Ben's far-out ties.

What counts here is not the saccharine clumsiness of the interchanges but the 10
bulk of them—the ceaseless, self-validating gestures of friendship, the humming,

buzzing background theme: *All decent Americans extend the hand of friendship to African Americans; nothing but nothing is more auspicious for the African American future than this extended hand.* Faith in the miracle cure of racism by change-of-heart turns out to be so familiar as to have become unnoticeable. And yes, the faith has its benign aspect. Even as they nudge me and others toward belief in magic (instant pals and no-money-down equality), the images and messages of devoted relationships between blacks and whites do exert a humanizing influence.

Nonetheless, through these same images and messages the comfortable majority tells itself a fatuous untruth. Promoting the fantasy of painless answers, inspiring groundless self-approval among whites, joining the Supreme Court in treating "cleansing" as *inevitable*, the new orthodoxy of friendship incites culture-wide evasion, justifies one political step backward after another, and greases the skids along which, tomorrow, welfare block grants will slide into state highway-resurfacing budgets. Whites are part of the solution, says this orthodoxy, if we break out of the prison of our skin color, say hello, as equals, one-on-one, to a black stranger, and make a black friend. We're part of the problem if we have an aversion to black people or are frightened of them, or if we feel that the more distance we put between them and us the better, or if we're in the habit of asserting our superiority rather than acknowledging our common humanity. Thus we shift the problem away from politics—from black experience and the history of slavery—and perceive it as a matter of the suspicion and fear found within the white heart; solving the problem asks no more of us than that we work on ourselves, scrubbing off the dirt of ill will.

The approach miniaturizes, personalizes, and moralizes; it removes the large and complex dilemmas of race from the public sphere. It tempts audiences to see history as irrelevant and to regard feelings as decisive—to believe that the fate of black Americans is shaped mainly by events occurring in the hearts and minds of the privileged. And let's be frank: the orthodoxy of friendship feels *nice*. It practically *consecrates* self-flattery. The "good" Bill Clinton who attends black churches and talks with likable ease to fellow worshipers was campaigning when Los Angeles rioted in '92. "White Americans," he said, "are gripped by the isolation of their own experience. Too many still simply have no friends of other races and do not know any differently." Few black youths of working age in South-Central L.A. had been near enough to the idea of a job even to think of looking for work before the Rodney King verdict, but the problem, according to Clinton, was that whites need black friends.

Most of the country's leading voices of journalistic conscience (editorial writers, television anchorpersons, syndicated columnists) roundly endorse the doctrine of black-white friendship as a means of redressing the inequalities between the races. Roger Rosenblatt, editor of the *Columbia Journalism Review* and an especially deft supplier of warm and fuzzy sentiment, published an essay in *Family Circle* arguing that white friendship and sympathy for blacks simultaneously make power differentials vanish and create interracial identity between us, one by one. The author finds his *exemplum* in an episode revealing the personal sensitivity, to injured blacks, of one of his children.

"When our oldest child, Carl, was in high school," he writes, "he and two black friends were standing on a street corner in New York City one spring evening, trying to hail a taxi. The three boys were dressed decently and were doing nothing wild or threatening. Still, no taxi would pick them up. If a driver spotted Carl first, he might slow down, but he would take off again when he saw the others. Carl's two companions were familiar with this sort of abuse. Carl, who had never observed it firsthand before, burned with anger and embarrassment that he was the color of a world that would so mistreat his friends."

Rosenblatt notes that when his son "was applying to colleges, he wrote his 15
essay on that taxi incident with his two black friends. ... He was able to articulate what he could not say at the time—how ashamed and impotent he felt. He also wrote of the power of their friendship, which has lasted to this day and has carried all three young men into the country that belongs to them. To all of us."

In this homily white sympathy begets interracial sameness in several ways. The three classmates are said to react identically to the cabdrivers' snub; i.e., they feel humiliated. "[Carl] could not find the words to express his humiliation and his friends *would* not express theirs."

The anger that inspires the younger Rosenblatt's college-admission essay on racism is seen as identical with black anger. Friendship brings the classmates together as joint, equal owners of the land of their birth ("the country that belongs to [all of] them"). And Rosenblatt supplies a still larger vision of essential black-white sameness near the end of his essay: "Our proper hearts tell the truth," he declares, "which is that we are all in the same boat, rich and poor, black and white. We are helpless, wicked, heroic, terrified, and we need one another. We need to give rides to one another."

Thus do acts of private piety substitute for public policy while the possibility of urgent political action disappears into a sentimental haze. "If we're looking for a formula to ease the tensions between the races," Rosenblatt observes, then we should "attack the disintegration of the black community" and "the desperation of the poor." Without overtly mocking civil rights activists who look toward the political arena "to erase the tensions," Rosenblatt alludes to them in a throwaway manner, implying that properly adjusted whites look elsewhere, that there was a time for politicking for "equal rights" but we've passed through it. Now is a time in which we should listen to our hearts at moments of epiphany and allow sympathy to work its wizardry, cleansing and floating us, blacks and whites "all in the same boat," on a mystical undercurrent of the New Age.

Blacks themselves aren't necessarily proof against this theme, as witness a recent essay by James Alan McPherson in the Harvard journal *Reconstruction*. McPherson, who received the 1977 Pulitzer Prize for fiction for his collection of stories *Elbow Room*, says that "the only possible steps, the safest steps ... small ones" in the movement "toward a universal culture" will be those built not on "ideologies and formulas and programs" but on experiences of personal connectedness.

"Just this past spring," he writes, "when I was leaving a restaurant after taking a 20
[white] former student to dinner, a black [woman on the sidewalk] said to my friend, in a rasping voice, 'Hello, girlfriend. Have you got anything to spare?'" The person speaking was a female crack addict with a child who was also addicted. "But," writes McPherson, when the addict made her pitch to his dinner companion, "I saw in my friend's face an understanding and sympathy and a shining which transcended

race and class. Her face reflected one human soul's connection with another. The magnetic field between the two women was charged with spiritual energy."

The writer points the path to progress through interpersonal gestures by people who "insist on remaining human, and having human responses. ... Perhaps the best that can be done, now, is the offering of understanding and support to the few out of many who are capable of such gestures, rather than devising another plan to engineer the many into one."

The elevated vocabulary ("soul," "spiritual") beatifies the impulse to turn away from the real-life agenda of actions capable of reducing racial injustice. Wherever that impulse dominates, the rhetoric of racial sameness thrives, diminishing historical catastrophes affecting millions over centuries and inflating the significance of tremors of tenderness briefly troubling the heart or conscience of a single individual—the boy waiting for a cab, the woman leaving the restaurant. People forget the theoretically unforgettable—the caste history of American blacks, the connection between no schools for longer than a century and bad school performance now, between hateful social attitudes and zero employment opportunities, between minority anguish and majority fear.

How could this way of seeing have become conventional so swiftly? How did the dogmas of instant equality insinuate themselves so effortlessly into courts and mass audiences alike? How can a white man like myself, who taught Southern blacks in the 1960s, find himself seduced—as I have been more than once—by the orthodoxy of friendship? In the civil rights era, the experience for many millions of Americans was one of discovery. A hitherto unimagined continent of human reality and history came into view, inducing genuine concern and at least a temporary setting aside of self-importance. I remember with utter clarity what I felt at Mary Holmes College in West Point, Mississippi, when a black student of mine was killed by tailgating rednecks; my fellow tutors and I were overwhelmed with how shamefully wrong a wrong could be. For a time, we were released from the prisons of moral weakness and ambiguity. In the year or two that followed—the mid-Sixties—the notion that some humans are more human than others, whites more human than blacks, appeared to have been overturned. The next step seemed obvious: society would have to admit that when one race deprives another of its humanity for centuries, those who have done the depriving are obligated to do what they can to restore the humanity of the deprived. The obligation clearly entailed the mounting of comprehensive *long-term* programs of developmental assistance—not guilt-money handouts—for nearly the entire black population. The path forward was unavoidable.

It was avoided. Shortly after the award of civil rights and the institution, in 1966, of limited preferential treatment to remedy employment and educational discrimination against African Americans, a measure of economic progress for blacks did appear in census reports. Not much, but enough to stimulate glowing tales of universal black advance and to launch the good-news barrage that continues to this day (headline in the *New York Times*, June 18, 1995: "Moving On Up: The Greening of America's Black Middle Class").

After Ronald Reagan was elected to his first term, the new dogma of black- 25
white sameness found ideological support in the form of criticism of so-called

coddling. Liberal activists of both races were berated by critics of both races for fostering an allegedly enfeebling psychology of dependency that discouraged African Americans from committing themselves to individual self-development. In 1988, the charge was passionately voiced in an essay in these pages, "I'm Black, You're White, Who's Innocent?" by Shelby Steele, who attributed the difference between black rates of advance and those of other minority groups to white folks' pampering. Most blacks, Steele claimed, could make it on their own—as voluntary immigrants have done—were they not held back by devitalizing programs that presented them, to themselves and others, as somehow dissimilar to and weaker than other Americans. This argument was all-in-the-same-boatism in a different key; the claim remained that progress depends upon recognition of black-white sameness. Let us see through superficial differences to the underlying, equally distributed gift for success. Let us teach ourselves—in the words of the Garth Brooks tune—to ignore "the color of skin" and "look for … the beauty within."

Still further support for the policy once known as "do-nothingism" came from points-of-light barkers, who held that a little something might perhaps be done *if* accompanied by enough publicity. Nearly every broadcaster and publisher in America moves a bale of reportage on pro bono efforts by white Americans to speed the advance of black Americans. Example: McDonald's and the National Basketball Association distribute balloons when they announce they are addressing the dropout problem with an annual "Stay in School" scheme that gives schoolkids who don't miss a January school day a ticket to an all-star exhibition. The publicity strengthens the idea that these initiatives will nullify the social context—the city I see through my windshield. Reports of white philanthropy suggest that the troubles of this block and the next should be understood as phenomena in transition. The condition of American blacks need not be read as the fixed, unchanging consequence of generations of bottom-caste existence. Edging discreetly past a beggar posted near the entrance to Zabar's or H&H Bagels, or, while walking the dog, stepping politely around black men asleep on the sidewalk, we need not see ourselves and our fellows as uncaring accomplices in the acts of social injustice.

Yet more powerful has been the ceaseless assault, over the past generation, on our knowledge of the historical situation of black Americans. On the face of things it seems improbable that the cumulative weight of documented historical injury to African Americans could ever be lightly assessed. Gifted black writers continue to show, in scene after scene—in their studies of middle-class blacks interacting with whites—how historical realities shape the lives of their black characters. In *Killer of Sheep*, the brilliant black filmmaker Charles Burnett dramatizes the daily encounters that suck poor blacks into will-lessness and contempt for white fairy tales of interracial harmony; he quickens his historical themes with images of faceless black meat processors gutting undifferentiated, unchoosing animal life. Here, say these images, as though talking back to Clarence Thomas, here is a basic level of black life unchanged over generations. Where there's work, it's miserably paid and ugly. Space allotments at home and at work cramp body and mind. Positive expectation withers in infancy. People fall into the habit of jeering at aspiration as though at the bidding of physical law.

Obstacles at every hand prevent people from loving and being loved in decent ways, prevent children from believing their parents, prevent parents from believing they themselves know anything worth knowing. The only true self, now as in the long past, is the one mocked by one's own race. "Shit on you, nigger," says a voice in *Killer of Sheep*. "Nothing you say matters a good goddamn."

For whites, these words produce guilt, and for blacks, I can only assume, pain and despair. The audience for tragedy remains small, while at the multiplex the popular enthusiasm for historical romance remains constant and vast. During the last two decades, the entertainment industry has conducted a siege on the pertinent past, systematically excising knowledge of the consequences of the historical exploitation of African Americans. Factitious renderings of the American past blur the outlines of black-white conflict, redefine the ground of black grievances for the purpose of diminishing the grievances, restage black life in accordance with the illusory conventions of American success mythology, and present the operative influences on race history as the same as those implied to be pivotal in *White Men Can't Jump* or a BellSouth advertisement.

Although there was scant popular awareness of it at the time (1977), the television miniseries *Roots* introduced the figure of the Unscathed Slave. To an enthralled audience of more than 80 million the series intimated that the damage resulting from generations of birth-ascribed, semi-animal status was largely temporary, that slavery was a product of motiveless malignity on the social margins rather than of respectable rationality, and that the ultimate significance of the institution lay in the demonstration, by freed slaves, that no force on earth can best the energies of American Individualism. ("Much like the Waltons confronting the depression," writes historian Eric Foner, a widely respected authority on American slavery, "the family in 'Roots' neither seeks nor requires outside help; individual or family effort is always sufficient.") Ken Burns's much applauded PBS documentary *The Civil War* (1990) went even further than *Roots* in downscaling black injury; the series treated slavery, birth-ascribed inferiority, and the centuries-old denial of dignity as matters of slight consequence. (By "implicitly denying the brutal reality of slavery," writes historian Jeanie Attie, Burns's programs crossed "a dangerous moral threshold." To a group of historians who asked him why slavery had been so slighted, Burns said that any discussion of slavery "would have been lengthy and boring.")

Mass media treatments of the civil rights protest years carried forward the process, contributing to the "positive" erasure of difference. Big-budget films like *Mississippi Burning*, together with an array of TV biographical specials on Dr. Martin Luther King and others, presented the long-running struggle between disenfranchised blacks and the majority white culture as a heartwarming episode of interracial unity; the speed and caringness of white response to the oppression of blacks demonstrated that broadscale race conflict or race difference was inconceivable. 30

A consciousness that ingests either a part or the whole of this revisionism loses touch with the two fundamental truths of race in America; namely, that because of what happened in the past, blacks and whites cannot yet be the same; and that because what happened in the past was no mere matter of ill will or insult but the outcome of an established caste structure that has only very recently begun to be dismantled, it is not reparable by one-on-one goodwill. The word "slavery" comes to induce stock responses with no vital sense of a grinding devastation of mind visited upon generation after generation. Hoodwinked by the orthodoxy of friendship, the nation either ignores the past, summons for it a detached, correct "compassion," or gazes at it as though it were a set of aesthetic conventions, like twisted trees and fragmented rocks in nineteenth-century picturesque painting—lifeless phenomena without bearing on the present. The chance of striking through the mask of corporate-underwritten, feel-good, ahistorical racism grows daily more remote. The trade-off—whites promise friendship, blacks accept the status quo—begins to seem like a good deal.

Cosseted by Hollywood's magic lantern and soothed by press releases from Washington and the American Enterprise Institute, we should never forget what we see and hear for ourselves. Broken out by race, the results of every social tabulation from unemployment to life expectancy add up to a chronicle of atrocity. The history of black America fully explains—to anyone who approaches it honestly—how the disaster happened and why neither guilt money nor lectures on personal responsibility can, in and of themselves, repair the damage. The vision of friendship and sympathy placing blacks and whites "all in the same boat," rendering them equally able to do each other favors, "to give rides to one another," is a smiling but monstrous lie.

THINGS TO DO WITH THE READING

1. How does this essay use references to time? Look for mention of dates, of terms such as "history" and "long-term" and "centuries-old," as well as various aspects of the present, the contemporary scene. What is the piece saying about historical consciousness in America?
2. What is DeMott's answer to the idea that blacks in America don't need government aid because they should be able to harness "the energies of American individualism" to improve their condition? So what that DeMott holds both blacks and whites responsible for projecting these "'positive' erasure(s) of difference" (see paragraph 30)? Consider, for example, the message that DeMott says the African-American made miniseries *Roots* sent about the situation of blacks in America and their best hope for the future.
3. **Link:** Use DeMott as a lens for analyzing the representation of black-white relationships and black-black relationships in Ishmael Reed's essay "My Neighborhood." What are the chances DeMott would find Reed unduly "rosy" about black-black relationships?
4. **Link Across Chapters:** Notice how James Peck defines melodrama against tragedy in his analysis, "September 11th: A National Tragedy" (included in Chapter 19). In what ways are Peck's anxieties about representations of 9/11 on the same ground (sharing assumptions) with DeMott? Find sentences in each essay to put into conversation with each other. To what extent does DeMott's use of the term "romance" mean the same thing as Peck's use of the term "melodrama?"

Alternatively, study Kera Bolonik's analysis of *Will & Grace* in her review entitled "Oy Gay!" (in Chapter 20). To what extent does the deception Bolonik sees in the television show resemble the one DeMott observes in his list of films?

5. **Application:** DeMott cites at least two dozen films (see the footnote after paragraph 6) that he says present "the long-running struggle between disenfranchised blacks and the majority white culture as a heartwarming episode of interracial unity" (see paragraph 30). Using the black-white buddy film *White Men Can't Jump* as a primary example of what he calls the "good will messages about race," DeMott argues that the effect of this cultural trend is to create the illusion that blacks and whites are "all in the same boat" so that all that is needed to solve centuries of disaster for blacks is displays of warmhearted sympathy.

   DeMott's essay was published in 1995. Your task is to update it, in one of the following ways:

   - Consider the extent to which the trend he describes in movies and other media is still alive and well today. Locate one or more current films or other media that seem to you to send the message of black-white friendship as an indication of sameness and as evidence that one-on-one compassion can solve the problems of race in America.

   - Locate one or more films or other media that seem to be representative of a different trend in the way that black-white relationships are being represented now. Determine what you think this new trend offers as a message about the state of black-white relations in America, the situation of blacks in America, and what does or does not need to be done about it.

   - Use DeMott's analysis as a model for looking at representational trends depicting marginalized groups besides blacks in contemporary films or other media. Does the trend that you locate seem to fall into DeMott's category of "deceptive romances"? Or, does the trend represent the group in a way that DeMott might be more optimistic about? In either case, what does this representation "say" about the situation of this group in America? ◗

Peggy McIntosh

White Privilege and Male Privilege: [... Unpacking the Invisible Knapsack]

In this classic analysis, Peggy McIntosh takes a look at her own "overprivilege" by virtue of her skin color and asks the question, what do I take for granted as a white person in ways that I am blind to? To answer, she inventories herself, arriving at a list of "unacknowledged privileges" that express "unconscious oppressiveness" as she imagines it can be perceived by persons of color. For many years the associate director of the Wellesley College Center for Research on Women, McIntosh now co-directs the National S.E.E.D. (Seeking Educational Equity and Diversity) Project on Inclusive Curriculum.

Through work to bring materials and perspectives from Women's Studies into 1
the rest of the curriculum, I have often noticed men's unwillingness to grant that they are overprivileged in the curriculum, even though they may grant that women are disadvantaged. Denials that amount to taboos surround the subject of advantages that men gain from women's disadvantages. These denials protect male privilege from being fully recognized, acknowledged, lessened, or ended.

Thinking through unacknowledged male privilege as a phenomenon with a life of its own, I realized that since hierarchies in our society are interlocking, there was most likely a phenomenon of white privilege that was similarly denied and protected, but alive and real in its effects. As a white person, I realized I had been taught about racism as something that puts others at a disadvantage, but had been taught not to see one of its corollary aspects, white privilege, which puts me at an advantage.

I think whites are carefully taught not to recognize white privilege, as males are taught not to recognize male privilege. So I have begun in an untutored way to ask what it is like to have white privilege. This paper is a partial record of my personal observations and not a scholarly analysis. It is based on my daily experiences within my particular circumstances.

I have come to see white privilege as an invisible package of unearned assets that I can count on cashing in each day, but about which I was "meant" to remain oblivious. White privilege is like an invisible weightless knapsack of special provisions, assurances, tools, maps, guides, codebooks, passports, visas, clothes, compass, emergency gear, and blank checks.

Since I have had trouble facing white privilege, and describing its results in my 5
life, I saw parallels here with men's reluctance to acknowledge male privilege. Only rarely will a man go beyond acknowledging that women are disadvantaged to acknowledging that men have unearned advantage, or that unearned privilege has not been good for men's development as human beings, or for society's development, or that privilege systems might ever be challenged and *changed.*

I will review here several types or layers of denial that I see at work protecting, and preventing awareness about, entrenched male privilege. Then I will draw parallels, from my own experience, with the denials that veil the facts of white privilege. Finally, I will list forty-six ordinary and daily ways in which I experience having white privilege, by contrast with my African American colleagues in the same building. This list is not intended to be generalizable. Others can make their own lists from within their own life circumstances.

Writing this paper has been difficult, despite warm receptions for the talks on which it is based.[1] For describing white privilege makes one newly accountable. As we in Women's Studies work reveal male privilege and ask men to give up some of their power, so one who writes about having white privilege must ask, "Having described it, what will I do to lessen or end it?"

The denial of men's overprivileged state takes many forms in discussions of curriculum change work. Some claim that men must be central in the curriculum because they have done most of what is important or distinctive in life or in civilization. Some recognize sexism in the curriculum but deny that it makes male students seem unduly important in life. Others agree that certain *individual* thinkers are male oriented but deny that there is any *systemic* tendency in disciplinary frameworks or epistemology to overempower men as a group. Those men who do grant that male privilege takes institutionalized and embedded forms are still likely to deny that male hegemony has opened doors for them personally. Virtually all men deny that male overreward alone can explain men's centrality in all the inner sanctums of our most powerful institutions. Moreover, those few who will acknowledge that male privilege systems have overempowered them usually end up doubting that we could dismantle these privilege systems. They may say they will work to improve women's status, in the society or in the university, but they can't or won't support the idea of lessening men's. In curricular terms, this is the point at which they say that they regret they cannot use any of the interesting new scholarship on women because the syllabus is full. When the talk turns to giving men less cultural room, even the most thoughtful and fair-minded of the men I know will tend to reflect, or fall back on, conservative assumptions about the inevitability of present gender relations and distributions of power, calling on precedent or sociobiology and psychobiology to demonstrate that male domination is natural and follows inevitably from evolutionary pressures. Others resort to arguments from "experience" or religion or social responsibility or wishing and dreaming.

After I realized, through faculty development work in Women's Studies, the extent to which men work from a base of unacknowledged privilege, I understood that much of their oppressiveness was unconscious. Then I remembered the frequent charges from women of color that white women whom they encounter are oppressive. I began to understand why we are justly seen as oppressive, even when we don't see ourselves that way. At the very least, obliviousness of one's privileged state can make a person or group irritating to be with. I began to count the ways in which I enjoy unearned skin privilege and have been conditioned into oblivion about its existence, unable to see that it put me "ahead"

[1]This paper was presented at the Virginia Women's Studies Association conference in Richmond in April, 1986, and the American Educational Research Association conference in Boston in October, 1986, and discussed with two groups of participants in the Dodge seminars for Secondary School Teachers in New York and Boston in the spring of 1987.

in any way, or put my people ahead, overrewarding us and yet also paradoxically damaging us, or that it could or should be changed.

My schooling gave me no training in seeing myself as an oppressor, as an 10
unfairly advantaged person, or as a participant in a damaged culture. I was taught to see myself as an individual whose moral state depended on her individual moral will. At school, we are not taught about slavery in any depth; we are not taught to see slaveholders as damaged people. Slaves were seen as the only group at risk of being dehumanized. My schooling followed the pattern which Elizabeth Minnich has pointed out: whites are taught to think of their lives as morally neutral, normative, and average, and also ideal, so that when we work to benefit others, this is seen as work that will allow "them" to be more like "us." I think many of us know how obnoxious this attitude can be in men.

After frustration with men who would not recognize male privilege, I decided to try to work on myself at least by identifying some of the daily effects of white privilege in my life. It is crude work, at this stage, but I will give here a list of special circumstances and conditions I experience that I did not earn but that I have been made to feel are mine by birth, by citizenship, and by virtue of being a conscientious law-abiding "normal" person of goodwill. I have chosen those conditions that I think in my case *attach somewhat more to skin-color privilege* than to class, religion, ethnic status, or geographical location, though these other privileging factors are intricately intertwined. As far as I can see, my Afro-American co-workers, friends, and acquaintances with whom I come into daily or frequent contact in this particular time, place, and line of work cannot count on most of these conditions.

1. I can, if I wish, arrange to be in the company of people of my race most of the time.
2. I can avoid spending time with people whom I was trained to mistrust and who have learned to mistrust my kind or me.
3. If I should need to move, I can be pretty sure of renting or purchasing housing in an area which I can afford and in which I would want to live.
4. I can be reasonably sure that my neighbors in such a location will be neutral or pleasant to me.
5. I can go shopping alone most of the time, fairly well assured that I will not be followed or harassed by store detectives.
6. I can turn on the television or open to the front page of the paper and see people of my race widely and positively represented.
7. When I am told about our national heritage or about "civilization," I am shown that people of my color made it what it is.
8. I can be sure that my children will be given curricular materials that testify to the existence of their race.
9. If I want to, I can be pretty sure of finding a publisher for this piece on white privilege.
10. I can be fairly sure of having my voice heard in a group in which I am the only member of my race.
11. I can be casual about whether or not to listen to another woman's voice in a group in which she is the only member of her race.

12. I can go into a book shop and count on finding the writing of my race represented, into a supermarket and find the staple foods that fit with my cultural traditions, into a hairdresser's shop and find someone who can deal with my hair.
13. Whether I use checks, credit cards, or cash, I can count on my skin color not to work against the appearance that I am financially reliable.
14. I could arrange to protect our young children most of the time from people who might not like them.
15. I did not have to educate our children to be aware of systemic racism for their own daily physical protection.
16. I can be pretty sure that my children's teachers and employers will tolerate them if they fit school and workplace norms; my chief worries about them do not concern others' attitudes toward their race.
17. I can talk with my mouth full and not have people put this down to my color.
18. I can swear, or dress in secondhand clothes, or not answer letters, without having people attribute these choices to the bad morals, the poverty, or the illiteracy of my race.
19. I can speak in public to a powerful male group without putting my race on trial.
20. I can do well in a challenging situation without being called a credit to my race.
21. I am never asked to speak for all the people of my racial group.
22. I can remain oblivious to the language and customs of persons of color who constitute the world's majority without feeling in my culture any penalty for such oblivion.
23. I can criticize our government and talk about how much I fear its policies and behavior without being seen as a cultural outsider.
24. I can be reasonably sure that if I ask to talk to "the person in charge," I will be facing a person of my race.
25. If a traffic cop pulls me over or if the IRS audits my tax return, I can be sure I haven't been singled out because of my race.
26. I can easily buy posters, postcards, picture books, greeting cards, dolls, toys, and children's magazines featuring people of my race.
27. I can go home from most meetings of organizations I belong to feeling somewhat tied in, rather than isolated, out of place, outnumbered, unheard, held at a distance, or feared.
28. I can be pretty sure that an argument with a colleague of another race is more likely to jeopardize her chances for advancement than to jeopardize mine.
29. I can be fairly sure that if I argue for the promotion of a person of another race, or a program centering on race, this is not likely to cost me heavily within my present setting, even if my colleagues disagree with me.
30. If I declare there is a racial issue at hand, or there isn't a racial issue at hand, my race will lend me more credibility for either position than a person of color will have.

31. I can choose to ignore developments in minority writing and minority activist programs, or disparage them, or learn from them, but in any case, I can find ways to be more or less protected from negative consequences of any of these choices.
32. My culture gives me little fear about ignoring the perspectives and powers of people of other races.
33. I am not made acutely aware that my shape, bearing, or body odor will be taken as a reflection on my race.
34. I can worry about racism without being seen as self-interested or self-seeking.
35. I can take a job with an affirmative action employer without having my co-workers on the job suspect that I got it because of my race.
36. If my day, week, or year is going badly, I need not ask of each negative episode or situation whether it has racial overtones.
37. I can be pretty sure of finding people who would be willing to talk with me and advise me about my next steps, professionally.
38. I can think over many options, social, political, imaginative, or professional, without asking whether a person of my race would be accepted or allowed to do what I want to do.
39. I can be late to a meeting without having the lateness reflect on my race.
40. I can choose public accommodation without fearing that people of my race cannot get in or will be mistreated in the places I have chosen.
41. I can be sure that if I need legal or medical help, my race will not work against me.
42. I can arrange my activities so that I will never have to experience feelings of rejection owing to my race.
43. If I have low credibility as a leader, I can be sure that my race is not the problem.
44. I can easily find academic courses and institutions that give attention only to people of my race.
45. I can expect figurative language and imagery in all of the arts to testify to experiences of my race.
46. I can choose blemish cover or bandages in "flesh" color and have them more or less match my skin.

I repeatedly forgot each of the realizations on this list until I wrote it down. For me, white privilege has turned out to be an elusive and fugitive subject. The pressure to avoid it is great, for in facing it I must give up the myth of meritocracy. If these things are true, this is not such a free country; one's life is not what one makes it; many doors open for certain people through no virtues of their own. These perceptions mean also that my moral condition is not what I had been led to believe. The appearance of being a good citizen rather than a troublemaker comes in large part from having all sorts of doors open automatically because of my color.

A further paralysis of nerve comes from literary silence protecting privilege. My clearest memories of finding such analysis are in Lillian Smith's unparalleled

Killers of the Dream and Margaret Andersen's review of Karen and Mamie Field's *Lemon Swamp.* Smith, for example, wrote about walking toward black children on the street and knowing they would step into the gutter; Andersen contrasted the pleasure that she, as a white child, took on summer driving trips to the south with Karen Fields' memories of driving in a closed car stocked with all necessities lest, in stopping, her black family should suffer "insult, or worse." Adrienne Rich also recognizes and writes about daily experiences of privilege, but in my observation, white women's writing in this area is far more often on systemic racism than on our daily lives as light-skinned women.[2]

In unpacking this invisible knapsack of white privilege, I have listed conditions of daily experience that I once took for granted, as neutral, normal, and universally available to everybody, just as I once thought of a male-focused curriculum as the neutral or accurate account that can speak for all. Nor did I think of any of these perquisites as bad for the holder. I now think that we need a more finely differentiated taxonomy of privilege, for some of these varieties are only what one would want for everyone in a just society, and others give license to be ignorant, oblivious, arrogant, and destructive. Before proposing some more finely tuned categorization, I will make some observations about the general effects of these conditions on my life and expectations.

In this potpourri of examples, some privileges make me feel at home in the 15
world. Others allow me to escape penalties or dangers that others suffer. Through some, I escape fear, anxiety, insult, injury, or a sense of not being welcome, not being real. Some keep me from having to hide, to be in disguise, to feel sick or crazy, to negotiate each transaction from the position of being an outsider or, within my group, a person who is suspected of having too close links with a dominant culture. Most keep me from having to be angry.

I see a pattern running through the matrix of white privilege, a pattern of assumptions that were passed on to me as a white person. There was one main piece of cultural turf; it was my own turf, and I was among those who could control the turf. I could measure up to the cultural standards and take advantage of the many options I saw around me to make what the culture would call a success of my life. *My skin color was an asset for any move I was educated to want to make.* I could think of myself as "belonging" in major ways and of making social systems work for me. I could freely disparage, fear, neglect, or be oblivious to anything outside of the dominant cultural forms. Being of the main culture, I could also criticize it fairly freely. My life was reflected back to me frequently enough so that I felt, with regard to my race, if not to my sex, like one of the real people.

Whether through the curriculum or in the newspaper, the television, the economic system, or the general look of people in the streets, I received daily signals and indications that my people counted and that others *either didn't exist or must be trying, not very successfully, to be like people of my race.* I was given cultural permission not to hear voices of people of other races or a tepid cultural tolerance for hearing or acting on such voices. I was also raised not to suffer seriously from anything that darker-skinned people might say about my group, "protected,"

[2] Andersen, Margaret, "Race and the Social Science Curriculum: A Teaching and Learning Discussion." *Radical Teacher*, November, 1984, pp. 17–20. Smith, Lillian, *Killers of the Dream*, New York: W. W. Norton, 1949.

though perhaps I should more accurately say *prohibited*, through the habits of my economic class and social group, from living in racially mixed groups or being reflective about interactions between people or differing races.

In proportion as my racial group was being made confident, comfortable, and oblivious, other groups were likely being made unconfident, uncomfortable, and alienated. Whiteness protected me from many kinds of hostility, distress, and violence, which I was being subtly trained to visit in turn upon people of color.

For this reason, the word "privilege" now seems to me misleading. Its connotations are too positive to fit the conditions and behaviors which "privilege systems" produce. We usually think of privilege as being a favored state, whether earned, or conferred by birth or luck. School graduates are reminded they are privileged and urged to use their (enviable) assets well. The word "privilege" carries the connotation of being something everyone must want. Yet some of the conditions I have described here work to systematically overempower certain groups. Such privilege simply *confers dominance*, gives permission to control, because of one's race or sex. The kind of privilege that gives license to some people to be, at best, thoughtless and, at worst, murderous should not continue to be referred to as a desirable attribute. Such "privilege" may be widely desired without being in any way beneficial to the whole society.

Moreover, though "privilege" may confer power, it does not confer moral 20
strength. Those who do not depend on conferred dominance have traits and qualities that may never develop in those who do. Just as Women's Studies courses indicate that women survive their political circumstances to lead lives that hold the human race together, so "underprivileged" people of color who are the world's majority have survived their oppression and lived survivors' lives from which the white global minority can and must learn. In some groups, those dominated have actually become strong through *not* having all of these unearned advantages, and this gives them a great deal to teach the others. Members of so-called privileged groups can seem foolish, ridiculous, infantile, or dangerous by contrast.

I want, then, to distinguish between earned strength and unearned power conferred systemically. Power from unearned privilege can look like strength when it is, in fact, permission to escape or to dominate. But not all of the privileges on my list are inevitably damaging. Some, like the expectation that neighbors will be decent to you, or that your race will not count against you in court, should be the norm in a just society and should be considered as the entitlement of everyone. Others, like the privilege not to listen to less powerful people, distort the humanity of the holders as well as the ignored groups. Still others, like finding one's staple foods everywhere, may be a function of being a member of a numerical majority in the population. Others have to do with not having to labor under pervasive negative stereotyping and mythology.

We might at least start by distinguishing between positive advantages that we can work to spread, to the point where they are not advantages at all but simply part of the normal civic and social fabric, and negative types of advantage that unless rejected will always reinforce our present hierarchies. For example, the positive "privilege" of belonging, the feeling that one belongs within the human circle, as Native Americans say, fosters development and should not be seen as privilege for a few. It is, let us say, an entitlement that none of us should have to earn; ideally it is an *unearned entitlement.* At present, since only a few have it, it is an *unearned advantage* for them. The negative "privilege" that gave me cultural permission not to take darker-skinned Others seriously can be seen as arbitrarily conferred dominance and should not be desirable for anyone. This paper results from a process of coming to see that some of the power that I originally saw as attendant on being a human being in the United States consisted in *unearned advantage* and *conferred dominance,* as well as other kinds of special circumstance not universally taken for granted.

In writing this paper I have also realized that white identity and status (as well as class identity and status) give me considerable power to choose whether to broach this subject and its trouble. I can pretty well decide whether to disappear and avoid and not listen and escape the dislike I may engender in other people through this essay, or interrupt, answer, interpret, preach, correct, criticize, and control to some extent what goes on in reaction to it. Being white, I am given considerable power to escape many kinds of danger or penalty as well as to choose which risks I want to take.

There is an analogy here, once again with Women's Studies. Our male colleagues do not have a great deal to lose in supporting Women's Studies, but they do not have a great deal to lose if they oppose it either. They simply have the power to decide whether to commit themselves to more equitable distributions of power. They will probably feel few penalties whatever choice they make; they do not seem, in any obvious short-term sense, the ones at risk, though they are, we are all at risk because of the behaviors that have been rewarded in them.

25 Through Women's Studies work I have met very few men who are truly distressed about systemic, unearned male advantage and conferred dominance. And so one question for me and others like me is whether we will be like them, or whether we will get truly distressed, even outraged, about unearned race advantage and conferred dominance and if so, what we will do to lessen them. In any case, we need to do more work in identifying how they actually affect our daily lives. We need more down-to-earth writing by people about these taboo subjects. We need more understanding of the ways in which white "privilege" damages white people, for these are not the same ways in which it damages the victimized. Skewed white psyches are an inseparable part of the picture, though I do not want to confuse the kinds of damage done to the holders of special assets and to those who suffer the deficits. Many, perhaps most, of our white students in the United States think that racism doesn't affect them because they are not people of color; they do not see "whiteness" as a racial identity. Many men likewise think that Women's Studies does not bear on their own existences because they are not female; they do not see themselves as having gendered identities. Insisting on the universal "effects" of "privilege" systems, then, becomes one of our chief tasks, and being more explicit about the *particular* effects in particular contexts is another. Men need to join us in this work.

In addition, since race and sex are not the only advantaging systems at work, we need to similarly examine the daily experience of having age advantage, or ethnic advantage, or physical ability, or advantage related to nationality, religion, or sexual orientation. Professor Marnie Evans suggested to me that in many ways the list I made also applies directly to heterosexual privilege. This is a still more taboo subject than race privilege: the daily ways in which heterosexual privilege makes some persons comfortable or powerful, providing supports, assets, approvals, and rewards to those who live or expect to live in heterosexual pairs. Unpacking that content is still more difficult, owing to the deeper imbeddedness of heterosexual advantage and dominance and stricter taboos surrounding these.

But to start such an analysis I would put this observation from my own experience: The fact that I live under the same roof with a man triggers all kinds of societal assumptions about my worth, politics, life, and value and triggers a host of unearned advantages and powers. After recasting many elements from the original list I would add further observations like these:

1. My children do not have to answer questions about why I live with my partner (my husband).
2. I have no difficulty finding neighborhoods where people approve of our household.
3. Our children are given texts and classes that implicitly support our kind of family unit and do not turn them against my choice of domestic partnership.
4. I can travel alone or with my husband without expecting embarrassment or hostility in those who deal with us.
5. Most people I meet will see my marital arrangements as an asset to my life or as a favorable comment on my likability, my competence, or my mental health.
6. I can talk about the social events of a weekend without fearing most listeners' reactions.
7. I will feel welcomed and "normal" in the usual walks of public life, institutional and social.
8. In many contexts, I am seen as "all right" in daily work on women because I do not live chiefly with women.

Difficulties and dangers surrounding the tasks of finding parallels are many. Since racism, sexism, and heterosexism are not the same, the advantages associated with them should not be seen as the same. In addition, it is hard to isolate aspects of unearned advantage that derive chiefly from social class, economic class, race, religion, region, sex, or ethnic identity. The oppressions are both distinct and interlocking, as the Combahee River Collective statement of 1977 continues to remind us eloquently.[3]

One factor seems clear about all of the interlocking oppressions. They take both active forms that we can see and embedded forms that members of the dominant group are taught not to see. In my class and place, I did not see myself as racist because I was taught to recognize racism only in individual acts of meanness by members of my group, never in invisible systems conferring racial dominance on my group from birth. Likewise, we are taught to think that sexism or heterosexism is carried on only through intentional, individual acts of discrimination, meanness, or cruelty, rather than in invisible systems conferring

[3] "A Black Feminist Statement," The Combahee River Collective, pp. 13–22 in G. Hull, P. Scott, B. Smith, Eds., *All the Women Are White, All the Blacks Are Men, But Some of Us Are Brave: Black Women's Studies*, Old Westbury, NY: The Feminist Press, 1982.

unsought dominance on certain groups. Disapproving of the systems won't be enough to change them. I was taught to think that racism could end if white individuals changed their attitudes; many men think sexism can be ended by individual changes in daily behavior toward women. But a man's sex provides advantage for him whether or not he approves of the way in which dominance has been conferred on his group. A "white" skin in the United States opens many doors for whites whether or not we approve of the way dominance has been conferred on us. Individual acts can palliate, but cannot end, these problems. To redesign social systems, we need first to acknowledge their colossal unseen dimensions. The silences and denials surrounding privilege are the key political tool here. They keep the thinking about equality or equity incomplete, protecting unearned advantage and conferred dominance by making these taboo subjects. Most talk by whites about equal opportunity seems to me now to be about equal opportunity to try to get into a position of dominance while denying that *systems* of dominance exist.

30 Obliviousness about white advantage, like obliviousness about male advantage, is kept strongly inculturated in the United States so as to maintain the myth of meritocracy, the myth that democratic choice is equally available to all. Keeping most people unaware that freedom of confident action is there for just a small number of people props up those in power and serves to keep power in the hands of the same groups that have most of it already. Though systemic change takes many decades, there are pressing questions for me and I imagine for some others like me if we raise our daily consciousness on the perquisites of being light-skinned. What will we do with such knowledge? As we know from watching men, it is an open question whether we will choose to use unearned advantage to weaken invisible privilege systems and whether we will use any of our arbitrarily awarded power to try to reconstruct power-systems on a broader base.

THINGS TO DO WITH THE READING

1. McIntosh organizes her essay around a single simile (comparison): "White privilege is like an invisible weightless knapsack of special provisions, assurances, tools, maps, guides, codebooks, passports, visas, clothes, compass, emergency gear, and blank checks." Find and discuss single sentences and short passages in the essay that explain some of the word choice in this simile—"invisible," for example, and "weightless."
2. As is the case in much good analytical writing, the key terms in McIntosh's essay evolve in their meaning rather than remaining inert and unchanging. Trace McIntosh's thinking on the word "privilege," for example. How does McIntosh define this key term early in the essay? What has it come to mean at the end? Locate the various synonyms or alternate terms that McIntosh proposes and explain why she proposes these.
3. McIntosh presents this essay (originally given as a paper at a women's studies conference) as a personal reflection: "This paper is a partial record

of my personal observations and not a scholarly analysis. It is based on my daily experiences within my particular circumstances." Even though the piece is written in the first-person and includes the author's personal experience, it also employs language characteristic of academic discourse in the social sciences. The more specialized, more academic language allows McIntosh to give her argument greater specificity.

Do Paraphrase × 3 (see page 13) with the following sentences from the essay and then explain what these add to the essay's way of defining white privilege.

- "Others agree that certain *individual* thinkers are male oriented but deny that there is any *systemic* tendency in disciplinary frameworks or epistemology to overempower men as a group" (see paragraph 8).
- "The negative 'privilege' that gave me cultural permission not to take darker-skinned Others seriously can be seen as arbitrarily conferred dominance and should not be desirable for anyone" (see paragraph 22).

4. How does McIntosh explain the analogy she draws between male privilege and white privilege? What features of her experience—as a white woman—does McIntosh posit as analogous to those of white males?
5. **Link:** Use the following two sentences, one from McIntosh's essay and one from DeMott's, to put these two writers' thinking into conversation. Which key words in each quote are the best indications of common ground between McIntosh and DeMott? (See pages 303–305 on putting sources into conversation.)
   - McIntosh: "Obliviousness about white advantage, like obliviousness about male advantage, is kept strongly inculturated in the United States so as to maintain the myth of meritocracy, the myth that democratic choice is equally available to all" (see paragraph 30).
   - DeMott: "Factitious renderings of the American past blur the outlines of black-white conflict, redefine the ground of black grievances for the purpose of diminishing those grievances, [and] restage black life in accordance with the illusory conventions of American success mythology" (see paragraph 28).
6. **Application:** Before she offers her list of privileges, McIntosh offers a somewhat disingenuous disclaimer—"This list is not intended to be generalizable"—and then proceeds to invite her readers to undergo the same self-scrutiny she has undertaken: "Others can make their own lists from within their own life circumstances."

   This challenge brings to mind two obvious applications: to expand McIntosh's list and/or to corroborate it (that is, find confirming evidence) with your own experience.

   Obviously, it could prove very challenging to expand McIntosh's already capacious list, but nonetheless, if you can restrict yourself to your own "life circumstances," who knows what you might discover about the privileges you have heretofore unconsciously enjoyed (or, if you are a person of color, observed others enjoy)?

And quite possibly, if you seek primarily not to expand but just to become more conscious of and observe the ways in which you exercise white privilege or see others doing so—establishing a match between her list and your experience—you may find yourself gradually beginning to evolve your own subtly different instances anyway.

It will take time and attention to do this expansion/corroboration project. Give yourself at least a week. Carry around a special notebook for the purpose. Keep the idea of unacknowledged privilege alive in the back of your mind (see page 38 on the "back burner") but also visit sites where people congregate—a square, a shopping district, a lunchroom—with the conscious project of conducting observation.

At the end of the week, write your results. Start with a list, but then you might take the most vivid instances and expand them into brief narratives (of a paragraph or two).

Robert McLiam Wilson

Sticks and Stones: The Irish Identity

In this salty, iconoclastic piece, the Northern Irish novelist Robert McLiam Wilson offers a broadly subversive response to many of the assumptions about both national identity and racial identity shared by the other contributors to this chapter. "Our racial authenticity," Wilson says of the Irish, "is an extremely negotiable commodity"—a flabby myth, prone to marketing and mistruth.

1 I am five foot eleven. I weigh around 170 pounds. I have brown hair, green eyes, and no real distinguishing marks. I'm heterosexual, atheist, liberal, and white. I don't shave as often as I should and I have pale, Irish skin. I smoke and I always wear a suit. I drive a small black car and I don't drink much alcohol. I prefer cats to dogs.

I don't know what that makes me, but I suspect that it makes me what I am.

When I was seventeen, I decided that I wanted to be Jewish. Like most Roman Catholics, I had only the vaguest notion of what this might entail. I stopped being good at sports and frequented the only kosher butcher in the city. (How he blushed for me, the poor man). I could never understand why no one took me seriously. I could never understand why I should not simply decide such questions for myself. Why was I such a goy? Who had decided that this should be so?

Like that of most citizens of Belfast, my identity is the subject of some local dispute. Some say I'm British, some say I'm Irish, some even say that there's no way I'm five foot eleven and that I'm five ten at best. In many ways I'm not permitted to contribute to this debate. If the controversy is ever satisfactorily concluded, I will be whatever the majority of people tell me I am.

5 As a quotidian absolute, nationality is almost meaningless. For an Italian living in Italy, Italinness is patently not much of a distinction. What really gives nationality its chiaroscuro, its flavor, is a little dash of hatred and fear. Nobody really knows or cares what they are until they meet what they don't want to be. Then it's time for the flags and guns to come out.

So when the airport cops ask me what I am, how do I explain that I live in the northeastern segment of an island sliced like a cheap pizza and with as many titles as a bar full of yuppie cocktails—Ireland, Northern Ireland, Britain, Eire, Ulster, etc. How do I explain how little that would tell them?

I suppose I could tell them that I live in a place where people have killed and died in an interminable fight over the names they should call themselves and each other. (In Belfast, sticks and stones may break your bones but names will blow you to pieces on a regular basis.) I could tell them about the self-defeating eugenic templates of racial purity by which no human being still living on the island can be properly deemed Irish. That the English and the Scottish have been here a long time and that we're all smudged by now—café au lait, mulattoes, half-breeds, spicks, wops, and dagos. I could tell them that I don't really understand the question.

Irishness is unique amongst the self-conscious nationalisms. A self-conscious Frenchman bores everyone. A self-conscious American is a nightmare. And a self-conscious Englishman makes you want to lie down in a darkened room. But a self-conscious Irishman is a friend to the world and the world listens attentively. The reviews are always good. There's a global appetite for Irishness that is almost without parallel.

Nationalistic self-obsession is corrupt, corrosive, and bogus enough without this extra angle. When well-received, this fake concoction of myth and bullshit is reflected in the mirror of imprecise good will and sentimental foolishness. This in itself produces further distortions which are then seamlessly incorporated into the "genuine" article. Over the years I've watched the fundamental concepts of what it is to be Irish being altered by common-currency American errors. Here in the "old country," when we hear that New Yorkers are marching in green-kilted bagpipe bands (an entirely Scottish phenomenon) on St. Patrick's Day, we immediately look around for somewhere to buy green kilts and bagpipes. Our racial authenticity is an extremely negotiable commodity.

Yet I've always believed that such Americans have it just about right. Their 10
ideas of Irishness are as fake as a hooker's tit, but then so are ours.

To understand all things Irish, you must understand something fundamental. Everyone knows that Ireland is the land of myth. And myth is a beautiful and resonant word. It sounds so profound, so spiritual. There is something visceral in it. Our mythmaking is vital to the self-imposed standardized norms of nationality that are current here at home. Catholics are Irish, so Irish, and Protestants are British, poor things. The common assumption that the Irish language, Irish music, and Irish history are pure Catholic monoliths, and the oft-suppressed expression of the indigenous culture, ignores the truth that the Irish linguistic, musical, and cultural revivals were the product of nineteenth-century Protestant historicism. Everything we say is myth. The lies are old and dusty. The waters are muddy and the truth long gone.

Even our understanding of our own history—you know the kind of thing, perfidious Albion, eight hundred years of oppression, etc.—teems with bullshit. King William of Orange waged war in seventeenth-century Ireland and is still a Catholic-baiting Protestant icon who causes trouble here. No one remembers that he was blessed by the Pope. Wolfe Tone is a much-loved historical rebel leader who sailed with a French army to liberate Catholic Ireland. No one mentions that he was defeated by a Catholic militia. The President of Ireland called on a German minister to express his official condolences after Hitler's suicide at the end of World War II. Nobody wrote any songs about that.

In some ways, the Irish tendency for romancing can be seen as harmless, almost charming. It is, after all, what produces our leprechauns, our fairy rings, all our beguiling fakery. But it also produces people who will murder for lies they only half-believe and certainly never understand—for the Irish have always armed their ideas. We don't have any white lies here anymore. We only have the deadly barbaric type.

Given the wildest differences in latitude and climate, it is remarkable how countries can remind you of one another. In cold March Manhattan, the air is as thick, dark, and injurious as any Berlin winter. In Paris, the rain falls and stains the pale stone with the same dispiriting grace you find in Cambridge on most days of the year. London can look and feel like everywhere.

If true of the places, how much truer of the people. *Quod erat demonstrandum* 15
and then some.

We are a pretty poor species. Even the most gifted of us, the wisest and most studious of us, are weak-minded. We toss aside our Pushkin and read Judith Krantz. We watch goofy TV shows and asinine movies. We can't help liking big noises, colored lights, and pictures of naked people.

Our beliefs are often fantastic alloys of fear, self-interest, prejudice, and ignorance. As Tolstoy gloriously demonstrates, our finest moments of heroism, selflessness, and grandeur are usually founded on the meanest egotisms and vanities. Our notion of the sublime is laughable. In acts of worship, many of us pay homage to some form of invisible man who mimics us in the pettiest detail. Apart from our uncharacteristic capacity for love (a mistake, a design flaw), we're a shambles.

It is the things we say that most prove what monkeys we still are. We are driven to generalize, to sweep on through, to prognosticate, to diagnose. Typically male, we say, typically female. That's the problem with rich people, we opine. The poor were ever so. Gentlemen prefer blondes. Fuck right off, I can't help thinking.

Our most outrageous banalities are reserved for questions of race and nationality. This is how the French behave, we say. How do we know? Have we met them all? Have we asked any of them? Millions of people are summoned and dismissed in a few moments of robust fatuousness.

I'm five foot eleven. I weigh around 170 pounds. I have brown hair, green 20
eyes, and so on. Irish or British is very far down on my list—somewhere below my favorite color. Nonetheless, I must concede that nationality is tenacious. People have real stamina when it comes to this business. I must further concede that Irishness is a great arena for disquisitions on national identity. Because the Irish conflict is internecine (it has nothing to do with the English anymore), definitions of Irishness have particular charm. Nationalities primarily define themselves by what they're not. The Swiss are not German, the Scottish are not English, and the Canadians are definitely not American. But the Irish make internal distinctions as well. Some of the Irish aren't properly Irish. Some of the Irish aren't even vaguely Irish. In pursuit of the mantle of absolute Irishness, brother kills brother and sisters look on and applaud.

A few years ago I had an apartment on a leafy South Belfast street called Adelaide Park. A police station was being rebuilt across the street from my building (the original had been flattened by a bomb a few years before). It was a controversial building site, naturally. Apart from their well-known attacks on the policemen, soldiers, prison officers, and almost everyone else, the IRA liked to target construction workers who helped build police stations. Thus, the site was guarded round the clock by the police. For nearly six months there were always a couple of cops standing in my driveway, all peaked caps, submachine guns, and high anxiety. This was okay in the spring. It was fine in the summer, and manageable in the fall. But as winter set in, the position of these guys became more and more unpleasant. It was windy and cold, and it rained for months. As night fell, I would look out my apartment window and watch the damp rozzers. It was obviously not a good gig.

For weeks I debated whether or not I should take them cups of coffee. It was more complicated than it might sound. Policemen and soldiers here are very unlikely to accept such things from the public now. Twenty-five years of ground glass, rat poison, and Drano in friendly cups of tea discouraged them from accepting such largesse. Not long before, a woman had handed some soldiers a bomb in a biscuit tin in a charming incident near Derry. Additionally, of course, there might have been swathes of people willing to do me grief for being nice to the police.

Policemen are usually Protestant and I myself am customarily Catholic. They couldn't have known that I was a Catholic, but they would have been suspicious. (In this country, the big haters can't really tell each other apart. How we envy those who hate black or white people—that obvious difference, that demonstrable objection.)

It was a small thing, a minor transaction, an unimportant detail. The weeks passed, the wind blew, and the rain rained. I didn't hand out any coffee.

—July 1997

THINGS TO DO WITH THE READING

1. Wilson's essay is the kind of writing that sometimes gets called a *tour de force* (a feat of strength, power or skill, according to the *OED*). In writing of this sort, authors often deliberately overstate their points, using exaggeration and an aggressively assertive tone to jolt people into seeing absurdity in what they might otherwise wish to guard as cherished positions. There is strategy in this. If the writer tries to take a mile, we might be cajoled by his sheer audacity into giving him an inch, which is perhaps all that he really wanted in the first place. What do you think Wilson actually hoped to accomplish with this essay, given that it is unlikely to cause the Irish (or any other group) to completely give up on "Irishness"? Start with paragraphs 16 and 17 and analyze the rhetoric of Wilson's piece. What do these two paragraphs reveal about Wilson's aims and his means of achieving those aims through style? (See pages 69–70 on rhetorical analysis.)

2. **Link:** We chose to end our chapter on Race, Ethnicity, and the "Melting Pot" with Wilson's essay because it challenges and interestingly undercuts many of the assumptions about cultural identity that inform previous essays. For reasons particular to his own circumstances as a citizen of Belfast (Northern Ireland), Wilson is extremely dubious about the concept of national identity. "Nationalistic self-obsession," writes Wilson, "is corrupt, corrosive, and bogus. … When well-received, this fake concoction of myth and bullshit is reflected in the mirror of imprecise good will and sentimental foolishness. This in itself produces further distortions which

are then seamlessly incorporated into the 'genuine' article" (see paragraph 9). A repeated word in the essay is "bullshit," part of a strand including "fake," "fake concoction," "myth," "beguiling fakery," "bogus," and "lies." The word "genuine" is placed emphatically in quotes.

Write an essay in which you reflect backward from Wilson's essay to others in this chapter that you think it interestingly illuminates. What might Wilson say, for example, about Salins's position on the importance of people choosing to "convert" to being American? Alternatively, how might he respond to Jesse Jackson's rainbow metaphor or to what Salins has to say about ethnic federalism or to Torgovnick's mixed emotions about the cohesiveness and tenacity of Italian-American neighborhoods?

3. **Link:** Because of the long-standing civil war in Northern Ireland between Catholics and Protestants—between proponents of a United Ireland and those supporting Northern Ireland remaining under English rule—Wilson worries about the potential of nationalism and cultural identities to fuel violence. "In pursuit of the mantle of absolute Irishness," he writes, "brother kills brother and sisters look on and applaud." In the second to last paragraph of his essay, however, he writes, "In this country, the big haters can't really tell each other apart. How we envy those who hate black or white people—that obvious difference, that demonstrable objection."

   What is one to do about racial identities—whether the product of mythologizing and stereotyping or not—where physical difference and long histories of struggle and oppression come more starkly into play? To what extent can these be willed out of existence? Write a paper in which you bring Wilson, Reed, and Rodriguez into conversation on the issue of cultural and racial difference. To what extent would Rodriguez agree with Wilson on the phoniness and foolishness and even the potential danger of so valuing distinct national identities? What sort of conversation do you imagine Reed would have with Wilson on the same issue?

4. **Application:** It is interesting to consider which of our personal tendencies and traits each of us would choose to include if asked to identify ourselves to others. This is especially interesting to think about in America, which contains so many different racial, national, and ethnic groups, and so many different religions, customs, and regions. Write your own version of Wilson's opening paragraph as a means of generating some thinking about the markers of particular identities in America. After you have written your paragraph of identifying traits, write a second paragraph in which you try to explain how the information you chose to include in your first paragraph makes you who you are.

FOR FURTHER RESEARCH: RACE, ETHNICITY, AND THE "MELTING POT"

By Kelly Cannon, Reference Librarian

The readings and activities below invite you to further explore the theme of Race, Ethnicity, and the "Melting Pot." WARNING: Some essays are polemical; they are intended to promote insight and discussion (or a starting point for your next paper). To access the online readings, visit the *Writing Analytically with Readings* website at www.thomsonedu.com/english/rosenwasser.

Online

Chavez, Linda. "One Nation, One Common Language." ***Center for Equal Opportunity*****. August 1995. 6 January 2006.**
A leading member of an organization "devoted exclusively to the promotion of colorblind equal opportunity and racial harmony" contends that bilingual education hampers assimilation efforts.

Explore: Click on the "About CEO: General Info" link. How does this essay support the CEO's mission?

Current Population Reports**. 19 December 2005. United States Census Bureau. 6 January 2006.**
Current in-depth statistical reports from the Census Bureau on Asian and Pacific Islander, black, foreign-born, and Hispanic populations in the United States.

Explore: Compare one variable such as "family size" across the various ethnic groups. What differences and similarities do you notice?

Fasenfest, David, et al. "Living Together: A New Look at Racial and Ethnic Integration in Metropolitan Neighborhoods, 1990–2000." ***The Brookings Institution*****. April 2004. 6 January 2006.**
Argues that mixed-race/ethnic neighborhoods are on the rise, especially for Asian and Hispanic populations. This calls for creating policies that foster racial and ethnic integration with positive social outcomes.

Explore: Where do blacks fit into this changing racial/ethnic mix?

Le, C. N. "Assimilation and Ethnic Identity." ***Asian-Nation: The Landscape of Asian America*****. 2006. 4 January 2006.**
Looks succinctly yet eloquently at assimilation and the melting pot through the lens of Asian America.

Explore: How important is it that an essay on this topic be written by someone from that community, in this case Asian American?

In Print

(Ask your librarian about possible online access to items marked with **.)

****De Rienzo, Harold. "Beyond the Melting Pot."** ***National Civic Review*** **84.1 (Winter/Spring 1995): 5–15.**
Argues against assimilation, in favor of "intercultural co-existence."

Explore: As succinctly as you can, define the alternative De Rienzo offers to assimilation. What does De Rienzo think of the "melting pot"?

****Firmat, Gustavo Perez. "On Bilingualism and Its Discontents."** ***Daedalus*** **134.3 (Summer 2005): 89–92.**

A Spanish professor whose native language is Spanish but who teaches in the United States reveals some discontent over his bilingual existence.

Explore: What is at the heart of Firmat's discontent? If you speak a second language, how does this affect your "language loyalty"?

Kopp, Achim. "Of the Most Ignorant Stupid Sort of Their Own Nation: Perceptions of the Pennsylvania Germans in the Eighteenth and Twentieth Centuries." ***Yearbook of German American Studies*** **35 (2000): 41–55.**

Shows the twists and turns of assimilation of German immigrant culture in early and present-day Pennsylvania. German immigrants initially resisted speaking their native tongue because of negative stereotypes about Germans. This contrasts with current-day efforts by their descendents to revive German language and culture.

Explore: How might this bit of history help us understand current debates over assimilation?

****Utkin, Anatolii. "The Future of the West."** ***Russian Social Science Review*** **45.4 (July/August 2004): 4–27.**

A thought-provoking, peer-reviewed article forecasting the apocalyptic effect that changing demographics will have on world powers. Europe is losing population rapidly. In the United States, non-European minorities will soon be the majority.

Explore: What does Utkin think of the "melting pot" idea? How important is immigrant assimilation in determining the future? If you find Utkin's prediction extreme, what in particular makes it so?

****Wilkes, Rima, and John Iceland. "Hypersegregation in the Twenty-First Century."** ***Demography*** **41.1 (2004): 23–36.**

A population study that indicates startling differences in segregation geographically and among different minority groups.

Explore: Reflect on how your own community is and is not racially segregated. To what extent does it reflect the trends in this article?

CHAPTER 19

The Language of Politics and the Politics of Language

Quick Take

This is a chapter about a particular kind of rhetoric—political rhetoric. Its aim is to equip you to analyze political language, attuning you to the characteristic vocabularies of different political orientations, and sensitizing you to the politics of spin. The writers sampled here share the assumption that we inhabit a world of competing voices telling us what to believe and whom to support. And they share the conviction that political language is always partisan: it's never just the facts, though that is the position it most often claims to be presenting.

And so as citizens of a democratic society, we are faced with the challenge of figuring out what others who have political designs upon us "really" believe, or at least what they are "really" saying. This challenge has been rendered more difficult by the rise in the last few decades of increasingly subtle methods of crafting and wording political positions, methods that build upon what political rhetoricians glean from focus groups and public opinion polls. In this context, the selections in this chapter offer a primer in decoding the language of politics that surrounds us.

ABOUT THE READINGS IN THIS CHAPTER

The opening selection, Christopher Borick's "On Political Labels," offers the primary lens through which to read subsequent pieces in this chapter, and for that matter, to interpret examples of political speeches wherever you find them. Borick provides a brief history of key terms such as liberal, conservative, and libertarian, charts the ways they overlap, and then offers readers a simple test to measure the gap between the labels they embrace and their actual beliefs. At the end of the essay Borick includes a "vocabulary of contemporary ideological positions" that can be used to smoke out the political leanings of articles and speeches one is likely to encounter in the popular press. Following this piece are four editorials that readers can use to test out the tools that Borick has provided. What are the key words and phrases, we ask, that enable you to identify each piece as primarily liberal or conservative?

Next comes a classic essay in the field: George Orwell's "Politics and the English Language." His analysis of the strategies by which political language tends to "defend the indefensible" concludes with a list of prescriptions for writing politically responsible prose. This discussion serves as a frame for the next three pieces, all of which examine the contemporary politics of spin. First comes a profile of the conservative pollster Frank Luntz by Dante Chinni, entitled "Why Should We Trust This Man?" Chinni examines the ethics of Luntz's procedures (his use of polls and focus groups) as a way of inviting us to think more resonantly about the representation of pubic opinion in American politics today. This subject is taken up overtly by Luntz himself in the next piece, an extensive interview conducted on PBS's *Frontline* series. His comments invite us to contemplate how Borick and Orwell might interpret his views on the language of politics. Following the interview, Matt Bai's "The Framing Wars" focuses on political consultant (and linguist) George Lakoff, the Democratic counterpart to the Republican Luntz. The two figures, Luntz and Lakoff, offer intriguing opportunities for comparison and contrast.

At the end of the chapter, as is frequently the case in this text, is a piece with a different slant, designed to get readers to test the limits of the lenses they have been offered. James Peck's "September 11th: A National Tragedy?" suggests that although most politicians and members of the press labeled the terrorist attacks as a tragedy, they actually treated the event as a melodrama. He concludes by inviting us to interpret the event as tragedy, but to take that label seriously. Drawing on the history of theater and dramatic theory, Peck argues that tragedy is not only about loss but also about painful self-assessments.

Christopher Borick

On Political Labels

Written specifically for this book, "On Political Labels" is a primer for decoding the spin doctors now employed by both political parties. The author, Christopher P. Borick, is a professor of political science and the director of the Muhlenberg College Institute of Public Opinion, which has conducted over 100 large-scale surveys during the past decade, which have appeared in the *Wall Street Journal, Los Angeles Times, London Guardian,* and *Washington Post.* He has also provided analysis for the BBC, National Public Radio's *Morning Edition, CBS News,* and *NBC Nightly News.* This piece offers a history of the key terms "liberal" and "conservative." Borick charts the ways that each of these terms is connected to a set of assumptions about what government should be and do. "On Political Labels" provides a lens for analyzing the rest of the readings in this chapter.

Note: Respond to the questionnaires in Boxes 19.1 and 19.2 of this essay as you are reading it for the first time. Do so before you get to the interpretation and the statistics that Borick subsequently provides about them.

In the world of politics labels are a currency. Labels allow politicians to set the public's image of themselves and their opponents and help advance and destroy plans and policies. Even though history shows us that labels are as much a part of politics as waving flags or kissing babies, the meaning of labels remains quite elusive. What does it really mean to call oneself a libertarian, a compassionate conservative, a progressive? Is there actually such a thing as a "Massachusetts Liberal" or "Blue Dog Democrat"? While there are no easy answers to those questions, the legendary Humpty Dumpty of Alice in Wonderland fame offers some insight on the matter. When Humpty tells Alice that there is "glory for you" on your birthday, Alice replies, "I don't know what you mean by glory." Humpty answers, "of course you don't until I tell you … when I use a word it means what I choose it to mean—neither more or less!" This wisdom, while emanating from a fictional egg-shaped character, is used regularly by today's real world political consultants. Wordsmiths such as the Republican political consultant Frank Luntz have crafted careers out of making words mean just what they want them to. Luntz advises his politician clients to change the name of the "estate tax" to the "death tax" and to switch the word "privatize" to "personalize" in an attempt to sway public perceptions. There is evidence that Luntz and others have been successful in making the public believe that words mean what they want them to, and that this success is changing the way politics is done in the United States. But just what changes are taking place and what can you do as a citizen to better understand the use of labels in our political discourse? 1

To answer this question, it is essential to realize that political labels are often more about emotion than reason. Politicians have long made the assumption that the public lacks the interest and attention to critically analyze government affairs. Constitutional architect James Madison went to great measures to try to limit public control over government because he viewed the public as prone to emotional reactions that lacked insight into the complexities of governance. Fearful that public opinion could be shaped through the linguistic trickery of a demagogue, Madison tried to insulate government from direct public pressure through institutions such as the Electoral College and Supreme Court. In the end, Madison simply was not confident enough that the general public had the tools necessary to critically engage the debates pertinent to governing.

In contrast, Madison's counterpart Thomas Jefferson did not share his skepticism about the public's ability to analyze political matters. Instead, Jefferson believed citizens could be educated in a manner that could enhance their ability to make political judgments. In essence, he thought regular citizens, given proper training, could get beyond the emotional trickery of political language and discern broader meaning. While strong arguments can be made for both the Madisonian and Jeffersonian positions, I believe that Jefferson's approach to this matter must be the framework for how we are to think about political labels today. Simply accepting that the public will act on emotion rather than reason, and therefore the government should be insulated from public pressures, is not a very attractive proposition. This approach undermines the central role of the citizen in a democratic system of government, and in some ways creates a self-fulfilling prophecy where citizens have limited need to think analytically about politics. Such an approach to democratic discourse also plays into the hands of political consultants and strategists who want the public to act on emotion rather than reason because emotion is often easier to manipulate.

Thus, I suggest that we take some time to think about political labels in a manner that allows for critical reflection—especially given the threat posed by today's spin doctors. Since in all likelihood you will encounter thousands of political labels over the course of your lifetime as a citizen, it is important to develop a lens that will allow for a productive analysis of a label's use and effects. It is not my purpose to contend that labels have no place in politics or political discourse. Quite the contrary, labels help us organize our thoughts and provide meaningful reference points from which citizens can engage in thoughtful political discussions. But while labels are completely necessary for productive discourse, they can also be used to confuse and control the voting public. Therefore, in the remainder of this article I offer a number of suggestions for you (in your capacity as one of Jefferson's informed citizens) to consider when you are confronted with a label. In particular much of my attention will be directed to the most commonly used political labels in the United States: liberal and conservative. While my suggestions are by no means inclusive, the following list offers some perspective on how you might think about political labels.

1. Think About the Historical Background of the Label

One of the first things you should think about when you see or hear a political 5
label is where it came from. Common political labels such as "liberal" or "conservative" have long histories that shed light on their contemporary use. It's important to recognize that a label's meaning differs from place to place and over time. A conservative in Texas may believe much differently from a conservative in New York, just as an American conservative varies in view points from a conservative in Norway. Similarly, someone calling herself a conservative in 2005 would significantly differ from someone calling himself a conservative in 1905 or even 1975.

You may wonder, with such variation over time and place, how can we attach meaning to key political terms at all? While not always easy to see, at least part of the answer can be discovered through an examination of the history of the terms.

Let's look at liberalism for a start. The term liberal can be traced at least back to 17th-Century England, where it evolved from debates dealing with the voting franchise among English citizens. Proponents of including greater numbers of Englishmen in elections came to be known as liberals, thanks in part to the writings of John Locke, whose ideas about the social contract helped to build the philosophical underpinnings of this political ideology. Over time liberalism has maintained its focus on public control over government actions, but there have been splits that have led to its current manifestation. In the 18th and 19th centuries, liberalism began to stress the importance of individual freedom and broader rights of the citizenry in terms of limits on government. In essence, this type of liberalism focused on "negative rights" or the restrictions on what government could do to its citizens. The First Amendment of the Constitution includes numerous examples of negative rights. The granting of the right to freedom of speech or the press is achieved through the prohibition of government from creating laws that abridge such freedoms. Thus negating an action of government creates rights for the people.

In the 20th Century however, liberalism became synonymous with the view that government had to be much more active in helping citizens get to the point where they would be able to truly live a free life. In this expanding view of liberalism, government intervention in society is necessary to create a more level playing field on which individuals can then use their freedom to achieve desired goals. Such beliefs have been at the roots of government expansion into social welfare policies such as public housing, food stamps and affirmative action, and have formed the core of government agendas such as Franklin Roosevelt's New Deal and Lyndon Johnson's Great Society.

It is also this focus on active government that has helped transform the term liberal into a derogatory term in contemporary political dialogue. For example, let's look at the title of the recent best selling book *Treason: Liberal Treachery from the Cold War to the War on Terrorism.* As can be seen, author Ann Coulter equates a liberal philosophy with treason against the nation itself. She finds liberalism's focus on protecting individual rights to be detrimental to the security of the United States and a threat to the very survival of the republic. Thus Coulter attaches a scarlet "L" to anyone and anything that places high value on civil rights or civil liberties if those rights and liberties can be seen as undermining national security.

While Coulter uses the term liberal to slam those who believe government is a positive force in society, conservative author Sean Hannity tries to disentangle contemporary liberalism from its historical focus on individual liberty. In his book, *Let Freedom Ring: Winning the War of Liberty Over Liberalism*, Hannity contends that it's conservatism that is really interested in liberty, while it's liberalism that creates an environment where government activity limits individual freedom and autonomy. He sees the regulations and programs that are designed to create level playing fields for citizens as counterproductive to democracy and the vitality of the country. Hannity is reflecting the beliefs of modern conservative thinkers such as Russel Kirk who equate government efforts to achieve equality with severely limiting individualism. Kirk famously stated, "men are created different; and a government which ignores this law becomes an unjust government, for it sacrifices nobility to mediocrity; it pulls down the aspiring natures to gratify the inferior natures." In other words, for conservatives, government is not a force for improving the human condition; rather it's an anchor on the driving force of individual motivation.

10 While someone identifying herself or himself as a liberal may take great exception to the arguments and reasoning of writers like Coulter and Hannity, the core belief that government can be a force for positive social change is a fundamental element of modern liberalism. Liberalism's interest in the equality of citizens may indeed come at the expense of individual liberties. For example, in trying to create a fair playing field for candidates in elections, contemporary liberalism embraces strong government regulations on campaign contributions and spending. The "liberal" defense of such restrictions rests in the notion that the compelling public interest in having elections that are not controlled by those with the greatest financial resources trumps any individual's claim to spend as one chooses. So aspects of freedom are sometimes reduced in the name of equality—in this case, the freedom to spend as much as one wants on a political campaign. Similarly, liberals tend to believe that government should limit the freedom of businesses when such freedom comes into conflict with the public good—such as the right to clean air and clean water.

Unlike liberalism's evolution to the point where authors like Hannity and Coulter use it as a negative label, the history of the term conservative is one of increasing political value. Like liberalism, conservatism has a long history that can be traced back to the 18th Century. The Anglo-Irish philosopher Edmund Burke is generally credited with developing the core ideas associated with conservative thought. In particular, Burke espoused a philosophy that rested on individual control of property and small and limited government. These tenets of conservatism are in large part the cornerstone of contemporary conservatism in the United States. In essence, government is often more of the problem than the answer. Here is an example of these beliefs coming out in a famous quote by Ronald Reagan during his presidency. Reagan claimed that "The most terrifying words in the English language are: I'm from the government and I'm here to help." The clear animosity to government intervention in Reagan's words symbolizes the core conservative belief that the best government is the smallest government. As we shall see, this conviction is not always upheld, as in the case of defense spending for national security.

While conservatism has consistently focused on the role of limited government and private property rights, self-identified American conservatives are increasingly interested in using government to limit individual behaviors that are considered counter to the traditional values of the nation. In particular, behaviors such as homosexuality and choosing abortion are seen as direct threats to the order of society and thus require government intervention in the lives of individuals. This tendency to embrace government intervention as a means of protecting values has become an accepted principle for many in the United States, but also a persistent point of tension among individuals identifying themselves as conservative. In particular, many contemporary conservatives who have found a home in the Republican Party are uneasy with the inconsistency of endorsing government intervention in some aspects of an individual's life such as reproductive rights, while excoriating government intervention in other areas such as property rights. For some, these inconsistencies in contemporary American conservatism are too great to accept; thus, many individuals identify themselves more as libertarian rather than conservative.

A libertarian generally agrees with the conservative focus on limited government, but can't accept exceptions where government limits freedoms to preserve traditional values. A libertarian stresses the minimal role of government, with functions such as public safety and defense the only necessary roles of government. A quote from the 2004 United States Libertarian Party platform nicely summarizes this philosophy:

> We, the members of the libertarian party challenge the cult of the omnipresent state and defend the rights of the individual. We hold that all individuals have the right to exercise sole dominion over their own lives, and have the right to live in whatever manner they choose, so long as they do not forcibly interfere with the equal right of others to live in whatever manner they choose."

Thus, a libertarian would likely agree with a contemporary conservative on issues like low taxes and fewer government programs, but disagree with policies that might limit individual freedom such as restrictions on marijuana use and abortion. Similarly, libertarians and liberals share a belief in free expression even in controversial areas such as flag burning, yet libertarians would split with their liberal counterparts on topics such as government restrictions on the ownership and use of firearms. In Figure 19.1 below you can see that while the ideologies of liberalism, conservatism, and libertarianism may have distinctive qualities, they also can have areas of commonality.

FIGURE 19.1

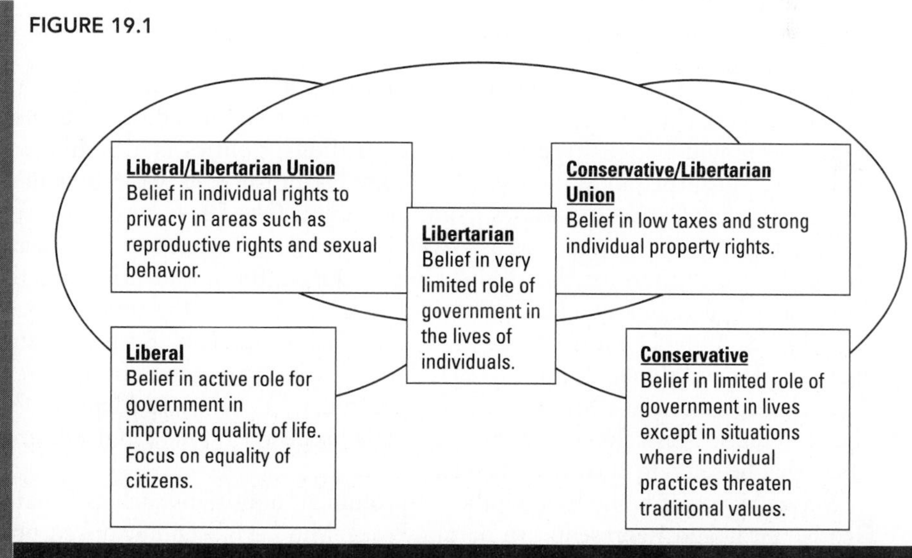

The shared positions of various ideological positions are often obscured by 15
their differences. Therefore it is essential to dig deeper beneath broad ideological labels to discern important nuances of thought.

2. Labels Can Exaggerate Difference

While labels can be used to demonstrate real differences among individuals and political parties, they may mask similarities that cut across ideologies in the United States. It is important to note that American liberals and conservatives have more in common than one might anticipate. For foreign observers of politics in the United States there is often a belief that there is very little difference between Democrats and Republicans and liberals and conservatives. Let's look in particular at the role of government in the area of the economy and taxes. Among conservatives and liberals in the United States there is general agreement that government control of the economy should be limited. While there may be some argument about how government should regulate businesses, there is almost no discussion about government ownership or control of companies. Conversely, in Sweden the government owns 25% of businesses in the country.

Similarly, while it may appear that liberals and conservatives in the United States vehemently disagree on the issue of taxation, the scope of the debate is fairly limited. The highly debated 2003 tax cuts in the United States lowered tax rates in the top bracket from 39.6% to 35%. Compare these tax rates to those in Sweden where the top rate is 47% or France where the richest are taxed at 49% of their income.

Thus while the American liberal and conservative may have real differences, the divide may be exaggerated when labels are being applied in the heat of political debate. It serves the interest of politicians to distinguish differences between themselves and their opponents for voters. It would be a bad political strategy to campaign on the platform that "my opponent and I are in agreement on most issues." Nevertheless, the reality of American politics is that the differences between liberalism and conservatism may not be as great as we are led to believe.

3. The Source of the Label Matters

When a label is applied to something or someone, it's rarely a spontaneous off the cuff remark. In a world where political campaigns are priced in the billions and government budgets are measured in trillions, politics is a high stakes endeavor. Not surprisingly, then, each word used is measured very carefully in an attempt to elicit desired responses from the public. Take for example the term "Massachusetts Liberal" that was used against presidential candidate John Kerry in the 2004 campaign for the White House. During the presidential race the Bush campaign regularly added a Massachusetts qualifier to the time honored liberal label. A good example of the use of this label is a quote by Bush campaign manager Ken Mellman, who, in regard to John Kerry's nomination, stated, "America doesn't need a Massachusetts liberal today." Why would Mellman feel the need to use Massachusetts in this context? The answer is found in the desired effect that he seeks to elicit from voters.

Massachusetts is home to a number of prominent politicians such as Senator 20
Ted Kennedy and Representative Barney Frank who have been outspoken proponents of policies that are considered both liberal and contentious. Among these polices are equal rights for homosexuals and preferential treatment for

minority individuals in the areas of education and employment. Furthermore, in a well publicized 2003 decision the Massachusetts Supreme Court ruled to allow gay and lesbian couples to legally marry. With a history of controversial officials and legal precedents, the term *Massachusetts* carried with it a degree of political baggage. By applying the term to John Kerry, Mellman and the rest of the Bush campaign were hoping to attach the polarizing aspects of Massachusetts politics to their Democratic opponent, even if Kerry himself did not support the positions that were synonymous with his home state. Given the number of times that this label was used, we can be confident that at least the Bush campaign thought the label was scoring political points for the conservatives.

Sometimes a politician gives himself or herself a label as part of a broader goal of shaping public perceptions. Such was the case with George W. Bush's self-identification as a "compassionate conservative." While long referring to himself as a conservative, Bush began adding the term compassionate as he began to pursue the White House in the late 1990s. What was the reason for including this new term with the time honored conservative moniker? It seems to me that Bush is using compassionate as a qualifier for conservative. The term conservative, while generally regarded more positively than liberal, has been associated with a cold-heartedness in the past. Conservatives in their zest to keep government out of the public's business were accused of neglecting the needs of the poor and minorities, and being out of touch with the struggles facing the common person. Thus, in packaging himself as a viable presidential candidate, Bush and his handlers sought to qualify conservative with a term that displayed caring and understanding for all Americans.

But what are we to do with labels that are applied by politicians themselves? Just as you probably would question the validity of someone at your college who gave himself his own nickname, you should always question the names that politicians give themselves. When a guy calls himself "Romeo" or "Stud," you would probably think twice before accepting the accuracy of the tag. So, shouldn't you think twice when you come across the "compassionate conservatives" and "new Democrats" of the world?

4. Does the Label Hold Up to Facts?

Another thing to think about regarding labels is their ability to measure reality. Earlier I discussed some of the general tenets of conservatives and liberals in the United States. For example, liberals are generally considered to favor government activity to level the playing field in society. Therefore such policies as affirmative action and a high minimum wage are often thought of as core liberal beliefs. If one's overall ideological stance guides his or her positions on particular issues, we might reasonably expect an individual who self-identifies as a "liberal" to support government policies that are consistent with an active government approach. These expectations can actually be tested fairly easily by looking at public opinion data from surveys of the American public. By asking individuals to state their opinion on key issues that are indicative of broader political philosophies such as liberalism and conservatism, it's possible to measure how consistent their beliefs may be. For example, let's look at the relationship between what label you use to identify your political beliefs and your views on a number of specific political issues. Start by answering the question in Box 19.1.

BOX 19.1 Which of the following best describes your overall political beliefs?

Very Liberal

Somewhat Liberal

Moderate

Somewhat Conservative

Very Conservative

Next, take the survey in Box 19.2 regarding key issues in contemporary American politics. Mark the box that best describes your position on each of the statements that is given:

BOX 19.2 Survey of Political Attitudes

Statement	**Agree**	**Disagree**
It should be more difficult for a woman to get an abortion in the United States.	☐	☐
Prayer should be allowed in public schools.	☐	☐
Burning the American flag should be made illegal.	☐	☐
There should be a national law prohibiting marriage between members of the same sex.	☐	☐
Citizens should be allowed to own assault weapons.	☐	☐
The 10 Commandments should be allowed to be displayed in government buildings.	☐	☐
Affirmative Action policies should be abolished in the United States.	☐	☐
The minimum wage in the United States should not be increased.	☐	☐

Now, add up the total number of times that you agreed with the statements 25
given. Each check mark in the "agree" column signifies that you support a position that is generally perceived as conservative in the United States. Thus, if you

identified yourself as very conservative and agreed with 8 out of 8 statements presented, your policy positions appear consistent with your self-identified political ideology. However if you call yourself very conservative and only agree with a few of the statements presented, there appears to be a disconnect between your perception of your ideological standing and the issue positions that define one as conservative. Similarly, if you agreed with most of the statements presented, and call yourself a liberal, then the label might be misplaced.

While the previous exercise may have demonstrated an inconsistency between the label you used to describe yourself and your beliefs on specific issues, many surveys have found that the American public as a whole demonstrates similar inconsistencies. For example, each year I survey hundreds of students at Muhlenberg College to see if the labels they use to describe themselves are consistent with their positions on particular issues. What I have regularly found is that while our self-identified ideological labels may paint a generally accurate picture of our political views, these labels mask key inconsistencies that are common among individuals. In Box 19.3 the responses of self-identified conservative students to the policy questions are presented.

BOX 19.3 Policy Positions of Self-Identified Conservative Students

Statement	Agree	Disagree
The practice of abortion should be made illegal.	43%	57%
Prayer should be allowed in public schools.	63%	37%
Burning the American flag should be made illegal.	77%	23%
There should be a national law prohibiting marriage between members of the same sex.	62%	38%
Citizens should be allowed to own assault weapons.	23%	77%
The 10 Commandments should be allowed to be displayed in government buildings.	60%	40%
Affirmative Action policies should be abolished in the United States.	79%	21%
The minimum wage should not be increased.	24%	76%

Survey results drawn from surveys of Muhlenberg College students conducted between 2002 and 2005. Survey conducted by the Muhlenberg College Institute of Public Opinion. The respondents were drawn randomly from the student body and completed the survey via telephone. Sample sizes ranged from 350 to 400 respondents.

As can be seen in Box 19.3, there is by no means consensus among self-identified conservatives regarding the array of issues that were presented to them. While all of the positions presented in the table are considered conservative viewpoints, many of those students who view themselves as conservative disagree with the conservative stances. For example, the issue of same sex marriage in the United States has been seen as divisive between liberals and conservatives, with conservative Americans supporting bans on marriages between individuals of the same sex. In our surveys we find that while about 2 out of 3 conservatives support a ban on same sex marriage, 1 out of 3 oppose such action. Similarly, while allowing prayer in public schools is seen as a conservative position, about 4 in 10 self-identified conservatives in our surveys oppose such policies.

Clearly, the conservative and liberal labels that are so commonly used in the United States often mask important details about the individuals that the labels are applied to. Public opinion researchers have recognized the inconsistencies that are associated with broad labels, and have thus tried to come up with labels that capture patterns. Labels such as "Reagan Democrat," "Christian Conservative," "Limousine Liberal," and "Country Club Republican," are used to describe individuals who share some of the characteristics of the core label (e.g., conservative, liberal) but differ on other key factors. For example, the term "Country Club Republican" is commonly used to describe individuals who vote Republican because of the party's pro-business and anti-tax positions, yet oppose the party's increasing emphasis on socially conservative issuessuch as banning abortion or restricting same-sex marriage. In contrast, the label "Christian Conservative" is used to describe individuals whose major goal is for government to intervene in social matters to preserve traditional values (e.g., marriage between a man and a woman). While both "Country Club Republicans" and "Christian Conservatives" would likely identify themselves as conservative when asked in a survey question such as the example from Box 19.1, they by no means share identical ideological perspectives.

5. An Alternative Vocabulary of Ideology

Finally, while labels such as liberal and conservative can be used by political figures to elicit desired reactions from the public, there are other terms to look for when reading literature related to political affairs. There are times when a commentator, speechwriter, or politician does not want to use labels such as liberal or conservative for fear of losing credibility with the general public. Thus, it becomes useful to adopt a language that captures ideological leanings without sounding partisan. For example, if the term *liberal* has indeed taken on a negative connotation for many Americans, it becomes necessary for advocates of liberal policies to adopt other terms in an attempt to persuade the public. Similarly, while politicians don't run from the term conservative like they run from the liberal moniker, there are times when it's better to avoid explicit use of any politically charged label.

Without using terms that are considered too partisan or controversial, how 30
can individuals still make arguments that rest on strong ideological beliefs? The answer lies in an alternate vocabulary that helps to transmit ideological beliefs without the partisan baggage. This vocabulary includes terms that capture elements of partisanship without sounding overly divisive, and are thus attractive forms of language for those engaging in political persuasion.

Political language guru Frank Luntz, whom you will read about later in this unit of the book, has regularly advised his Republican clients to avoid words that may sound overtly partisan, and instead embrace language that resonates as more neutral. By no means are Luntz and other political linguists advocating that political figures should abandon partisan positions, but simply that they embrace language that most effectively shapes public perceptions in a way that helps them advance their agenda in a more effective way.

Not only is the choice of words important in shaping public opinion, but also the number of times the words are used. You may have heard the expression, "if you say something enough times people will start to believe it." For political consultants this adage is a guiding principle that permeates their communication strategies. Repetition of key words is seen as essential to conveying a message that people will remember. This repetition is commonly referred to as staying "on message." Political party leaders regularly encourage their members to uniformly employ language that is considered effective in shaping public perceptions. One of the most prominent examples of staying on message is the use of the term "war on terror." When President Bush was making his case for going to war in Iraq, he framed the military campaign as part of a broader war on terror. While Saddam Hussein and the Iraqi regime had clearly committed atrocities during its tenure, there was no compelling evidence that Iraq had any substantial role in the attacks of 9/11. Nevertheless, in almost every speech where he discussed the invasion of Iraq, the president included the military endeavor as part of the war on terror, often mentioning 9/11 and Saddam Hussein in the same sentence. While never going so far as pinning the attacks directly on the Iraqi dictator, the linguistic connection of the terrorist threat with Iraq helped reinforce the impression that the two were linked. It appears from looking at public opinion polls conducted as the invasion began in 2003 that the White House's framing strategy had paid dividends, with almost half of the American population indicating a belief that Hussein was "personally involved" in the attacks of September 11, 2001. Once again, if you say something enough times, people will believe it.

As with the selection of "war on terror," many other words are regularly employed to achieve partisan ends through less overtly partisan language. Box 19.4 includes a selection of terms that are commonly used by individuals to make ideological arguments. These terms are directly related to the underlying roots of liberalism and conservatism, but may be perceived as more politically neutral. For example, the word ownership has become popular in many speeches and articles from self-described conservatives, often in the form of a call to create an "ownership society." The principle of ownership usually resonates among Americans who have come to strive for the day when they can buy that first new car or house. The idea of owning a piece of property can hardly be viewed as a highly ideological or partisan notion when an overwhelming majority of Americans make such action a life goal. The safety of the word helps explain why it has been regularly employed in debates on one of the most controversial topics of the day—Social Security reform. When President Bush advocates allowing Americans to invest part of their Social Security savings in individual retirement accounts, he claims his plan is part of the broader "ownership society" that benefits all Americans. The safety and acceptance of the ownership concept helps him to sell an idea that regularly draws high levels of concern and suspicion from a public that has become very attached to Social Security as a key source of retirement income.

BOX 19.4 Vocabulary of Contemporary Ideological Positions

Conservative	**Liberal**
Individualism	Community
Ownership	Equality
Traditional	Progressive
Free market	Social Justice
Property Rights	Human Rights

Conclusion

As I noted earlier in this article, labels permeate the political discourse in the United States. It has not been my intent to have you believe that labels are necessarily a negative part of politics, but to empower you to better control the effects of labels on your own thoughts about politics and government. I have tried to provide you with a list of things to consider when you are confronted with a political label that can be applied when you are listening to a speech, watching the news or reading an editorial in a newspaper. It is through the process of evaluating political language that you can limit the control that politicians and consultants believe they have over the political discourse in the nation. When Frank Luntz says that most of politics is about emotion he assumes a public that does not reflect upon political language, but instead one that simply responds to feelings. While I don't disagree with his appraisal, I take great offense at the arrogance that it demonstrates. Luntz is practically flaunting the fact that he can consistently trick the public into reacting in ways that he desires by simply changing language to induce emotional rather than reasoned reactions.

Luntz assumes a laziness in the electorate that is indeed all too present. 35
However, the control that he wields is very tenuous. By simply looking more closely at political labels, you and your counterparts can diminish the control that Luntz and other language gurus claim over the public. Remember the fate of another character who claimed that he could make words mean just what he wanted to. The arrogant Humpty Dumpty met his end during a fateful fall, with all the king's horses and all the king's men unable to put him together again. A more careful and thoughtful consideration of political language may crack the control that today's masters of the word believe they have.

THINGS TO DO WITH THE READING

1. In paragraph 31 of his essay, Borick tells us that politicians of both parties are advised by their language experts to "avoid words that may sound overtly partisan, and instead embrace language that resonates as more neutral." Earlier in the essay he tells us, "Luntz advises his politician clients to change the name of the 'estate tax' to the 'death tax' and to switch the word 'privatize' to 'personalize' in an attempt to sway public perceptions" (see paragraph 1; also see Luntz, paragraphs 34 and 57). Obviously, these paired terms have different associations. What are these different associations? And why might renaming in this way enable Republicans to attract a wider range of voters?
2. Using Borick's discussion of the questionnaires in paragraphs 26–29 as a model, interpret the results of your answers to the questionnaires in Boxes 19.1 and 19.2. Where (if at all) does your self-identification (on the continuum from "Very Liberal" to "Very Conservative" in Box 19.1) diverge from your stance on political attitudes, as ascertained by Box 19.2? How (if at all) do you account for these divergences? How do you "fit" relative to the statistical profile offered in Box 19.3?
3. One source of possible confusion for most people about the terms "liberal," "conservative," and "libertarian" is that each political orientation seems to cherish individual rights, but each defines these rights differently and has different ideas about how these can best be guaranteed. Summarize how each group, according to Borick, thinks about the concept of individual rights, and attend as well to how they differ from one another. (See pages 117–120 on summary and pages 123–125 on comparing and contrasting.)
4. Borick lists "individualism" as the first term under "Conservative" in his chart on the Vocabulary of Contemporary Ideological Positions (see Box 19.4). He lists "community" as the opposing value under "Liberal." Use Borick's essay to explain his choice of this binary as a defining one between liberals and conservatives (see pages 53–57 on using binaries).
5. The essay seeks to sensitize you to the keywords used by different political orientations (conservative, libertarian, and liberal) by seeing them in historical context. Consider the following list of terms. What would a conservative think of each term? What would a liberal think? What would a libertarian think? Why?
   - Level playing field
   - National security
   - Negative rights
   - Property rights
6. Borick's is a particularly good essay for studying logic—moving forward to inference (this follows from that) and backward to premise (this underlies

that). (See pages 212–216, "Common Logical Errors in Constructing a Thesis.") Consider in this context the logic of the quote from modern conservative thinker Russell Kirk:

> "men are created different; and a government which ignores this law becomes an unjust government, for it sacrifices nobility to mediocrity; it pulls down the aspiring natures to gratify the inferior natures" (see paragraph 9).

Clearly, Kirk is alluding to the Declaration of Independence: "We hold these truths to be self-evident, that all men are created equal" (which goes on to say "that they are endowed by their Creator with certain inalienable rights; that among these, are life, liberty, and the pursuit of happiness").

What spin has Kirk done on this famous assertion? (See "Equivocation" on page 215—does Kirk equivocate?) Also trace the chain of reasoning by which Kirk moves from his modified language of the Declaration to his claim about sacrificing "nobility to mediocrity." To what extent does this claim (an inference) follow logically from his opening move?

7. Look at the quote from the 2004 United States Libertarian Party platform in paragraph 13 of the essay. How might this philosophy play out (in both theory and practice) if one property owner chooses to erect a fast food restaurant on his or her land next to the property of another individual who wants to preserve quiet, clean air, and privacy?
8. **Link Across Chapters:** Once you have become comfortable with the essay's terminology, use "On Political Labels" as a tool for indexing the political orientation of any other chapter in this book. Arrange the writers that you have read in that chapter from most conservative to most liberal, briefly citing the telltale sentences and word choice that allow you to make this kind of discrimination. Chapter 18 might be a good place to start. (Consider Salins versus Rodriguez.) The public versus private language in Chapters 15 and 16 could also yield interesting political analysis.
9. **Application:** Use Borick's essay as a lens for analyzing news articles and editorials on matters such as Social Security, the war in Iraq, tax cuts, and Medicare. See especially Box 19.4 on the Vocabulary of Contemporary Ideological Positions. *Resist the urge to take a position on any of these issues.* Instead, locate the key terms in your article or editorial that reveal political orientation and explain what they reveal. Once you have "decoded" it, explain what makes it essentially liberal, conservative, or libertarian (or some combination of these) in its orientation?

Note: There will be links inviting you to apply "On Political Labels" to most of the succeeding selections in this chapter. For example, next up you will find a set of editorials that you might decode using tools from Borick's essay.

Four Editorials

What follows are four newspaper editorials to which you can apply Borick's essay on political labels. Three of the editorials are about Supreme Court decisions because the make-up of the Supreme Court has been a tumultuous issue in the second term of the Bush presidency. The fourth is a *New York Times* opinion piece on the status of the middle class in early twenty-first-century America. As you read the editorials, circle words that seem to indicate the writer's political orientation. Be able to state the positions in each piece that identify it as liberal or conservative.

Note: The editorials refer to two eras in twentieth-century America—the New Deal, which was President Franklin Roosevelt's response to the Depression of the 1930s, and the Robber Baron era—a reference to the pre-taxation open market years early in the century when there were few limits on the methods industrial entrepreneurs could use to amass wealth.

James J. Kilpatrick

Justices Amended Constitution on Their Own ...

The Supreme Court ended its current term on Monday with more of a whimper 1
than a bang. In the Ten Commandments cases, the justices further muddied the muddy waters of the First Amendment. In a Colorado case, they found no way to compensate a victim of grossly incompetent cops. They refused even to hear the appeal of two reporters who face prison for doing their job. Then they doffed their robes and departed for the summer.

One is reminded of Oliver Cromwell's farewell to the Rump Parliament of 1653: "You have sat too long for any good you have done. Let us have done with you! In the name of God, go!"

The most regrettable decision of a regrettable term came a week ago, in the eminent domain case of *Kelo v. City of New London.* Speaking through Justice John Paul Stevens, the court applied the law according to Humpty Dumpty. To that eminent jurist, words meant only what he chose them to mean, and neither more nor less. Until last week, the words "public use" meant "public use." Now they mean "public purpose or private benefit."

To be sure, this was not the first time the court has effectively amended the Constitution by judicial interpretation. The subtle process dates from the days of John Marshall. Only a few weeks ago the court rewrote the 21st Amendment in order to nullify the liquor laws of Michigan and New York. Last week's plastic surgery on the Fifth was surgery at a more critical level.

Every sixth-grader can identify a public "use." The indispensable power of 5
eminent domain permits governments to build roads, establish parks, erect public buildings and establish public schools. These are *public uses.*

Nothing of the sort was at the heart of last week's decision. The city now may proceed to seize the unoffending home of Susette Kelo, smash it to bits, haul away the debris, and sell the vacant land to the highest bidder. A few doors away, the redevelopers will evict Wilhelmina Dery from the home she has occupied for more than 80 years.

Will the owners receive "just compensation"? Of course, but for Kelo and other owners, the modifying "just" mocks the noun. Their property will not be put to a "public use." It will pass unjustly to private developers. If all goes well, the developers can go to their banks with a bundle. Ms. Kelo and her neighbors can go to—they can go to some other neighborhood, somewhere else.

In his majority opinion for the court, Justice John Paul Stevens smiled upon the city's rose-petaled justification. The city has been slowly losing jobs and population. What to do? Get rid of the owners! Then land could be cleared for the Pfizer corporation to build a $300 million research facility. The city fathers licked their chops. Their eyes rolled around like Mr. Toad's when he saw the motorcar. They saw classy restaurants, retail stores, a marina! There would be 80 new residences, none of which Susette Kelo could afford. What a deal!

To Stevens and his four colleagues, the "narrow view" that "use" means "use" is a view that has steadily eroded over time. A literal interpretation has proved to be "impractical" and "difficult to administer." Mrs. Kelo's eviction must be viewed "in light of the entire plan." This plan "unquestionably serves a public purpose, and the takings satisfy the public use requirement of the Fifth Amendment."

Justice Sandra Day O'Connor filed a powerful dissent: "Today the court aban- 10
dons a long-held, basic limitation on government power. Under the banner of economic development, all private property is now vulnerable to being taken and transferred to another private owner, so long as it might be upgraded—i.e., given to an owner who will use it in a way that the legislature deems more beneficial to the public."

She asked rhetorically: "Are economic development takings constitutional?" She answered without equivocation: "I would hold that they are not."

In a separate dissenting opinion, Justice Clarence Thomas agreed with O'Connor: "If 'economic development' takings are for a 'public use,' any taking is, and the court has erased the Public Use Clause from our Constitution. ... Once one permits takings for public *purposes* in addition to public *uses*, no coherent principle limits what could constitute a valid public use ... "

So ends the court's term. It should have ended when it began nine months ago.

Richard A. Epstein

... By Letting Redevelopers Take Little Guy's Property

The dreadful decision of the U.S. Supreme Court in Kelo v. City of New 1
London recently held that New London, Conn., could take the homes of ordinary citizens in the name of urban planning. It didn't seem to matter to the five-member majority that the city's porous redevelopment plan did not evince any intelligible purpose, let alone the public use that the Constitution requires.

The good news in the aftermath of Kelo is that it has forced people, especially on the political left, to rethink their views on the place of private property. Ever since the decisive and wrongheaded New Deal decisions in the mid-1930s, the Supreme Court has by and large held that the constitutional protections of private property should be read weakly so as to allow governments to act in ways that advance some notion of the common or public good. The underlying liberal vision was that private property was the instrument of individuals of privilege and power, which had to be cut down to size by an alert legislature that had the interests of the little man at heart. The liberal justices on the Supreme Court have accordingly done everything to give their blessing to local land use condemnation and regulation.

Kelo shows the utter fatuity in that position. There is of course every reason to believe that people with great wealth will use their power and influence to turn legislative decisions in their direction. But it hardly follows that private property is the villain of the piece. In many cases, the system of strong property rights works to protect people of limited wealth from the machinations of others. This defensive use of private property was evident to such philosophers as John Locke and such economists as Adam Smith. It impressed itself on this nation's Founders, who understood the risk that political factions put to the stability of our social order.

Here is one telltale sign of the massive amounts of political favoritism in Kelo. One common argument in favor of a broad use of the eminent domain power is that it is necessary to allow developers to assemble large parcels of land for major developments. But in Kelo the New London planners were quite happy to slate private homes for destruction while allowing the Italian Dramatic Club (a watering hole for local politicians) to remain untouched, even though it abutted one of the private homes that was taken.

Last year, the Michigan Supreme Court held that its state constitution 5
blocked the use of the eminent domain power for so-called economic development. Other states are now falling into line. With a little bit of hard work, the instinctive revulsion toward the Kelo decision could lead to a groundswell of public action. But whatever the future brings, remember that the four dissenters —Rehnquist, O'Connor, Scalia and Thomas—all so-called conservatives, were the defenders of the Constitution and the little man.

John F. Grim

More than Abortion Is at Stake in Supreme Court Picks

Far-right Republicans were incensed that 14 U.S. senators brokered a deal to 1
avoid the "nuclear option" to bar a filibuster on judicial nominations, news reports said. And a Republican activist wrote an op-ed column on June 18 that said 14 "centrist" senators may hold the key to confirming Supreme Court nominees who would overturn Roe v. Wade.

Again, the foes of a woman's right to choose show tunnel vision, because a court with just one or two more members who share the aggressive and ideologically extreme philosophy of Justices Antonin Scalia and Clarence Thomas could overturn not only Roe v. Wade but also more than 100 high court precedents protecting civil rights, privacy and reproductive choice, the environment, worker rights, consumer rights, religious liberty and much more.

"Courting Disaster 2005," a report by the liberal People for the American Way Foundation, documents how President Bush has picked lawyers and judges who favor a pre-New Deal approach to the Constitution: An era when property rights and states rights were given greater weight than protecting individual rights, and when the courts forbade Congress to address urgent issues of poverty and health care.

Examining the concurring and sometimes angry dissenting opinions of Scalia and Thomas, the report (www.pfaw.org) lists decisions that could be overturned by more justices with the same philosophy. Some of those cases, their dates and what a reversal would do are:

5 Ferguson v. Charleston (2001): Hospitals would be allowed to test pregnant women without their knowledge and consent for drug use and give results to police.

Hill v. Colorado (2000): States would be forbidden to pass laws to protect people approaching health care facilities from harassment.

City of Indianapolis v. Edmond (2000): Police would be free to set up roadblocks and randomly stop motorists to look for drugs.

Lawrence v. Texas (2003): Criminal prosecution of private sexual conduct by consenting adults would be allowed.

Grutter v. Bollinger (2003): Affirmative action in higher education would be forbidden.

10 Jackson v. Birmingham Bd. of Educ. (2005): Retaliation against those who complain about illegal sex discrimination in education under federal law would be allowed.

Johnson v. Transportation Agency (1987): Affirmative action for women under Title VII of the 1964 Civil Rights Act would be eliminated.

J.E.B. v. Alabama (1994): Sex discrimination in jury selection would be allowed.

Olmstead v. L.C. (1999): Improper and unnecessary institutionalization of disabled persons would no longer violate the Americans With Disabilities Act.

Hibbs v. Winn (2004): Federal courts would be forbidden to decide challenges to discriminatory and unconstitutional state tax laws.

15 Zadvydas v. Davis (2001): The government would be allowed to keep an immigrant who is under a final order of removal in jail indefinitely, even though no other country will accept that person.

Rasul v. Bush (2004): It would be impossible to challenge the indefinite imprisonment of foreign nationals on U.S. territory in Guantanamo, even if they contend they have been tortured or are not combatants.

Chavez v. Martinez (2003) and Hope v. Pelzer (2002): The ability to sue law enforcement officials for violating constitutional rights would be severely limited.

Lee v. Weisman (1992) and Santa Fe Independent School Dist. v. Doe (2000): True government neutrality toward religion would be eliminated, and government-sponsored prayer at graduation and at other public school events would be allowed.

Kiryas Joel Village School District v. Grumet (1994): School district lines could be drawn to permit one religious sect to predominate.

Rutan v. Republican Party of Illinois (1990): Government employees could be 20
fired for belonging to the wrong political party.

Alaska Department of Conservation v. EPA (2004): EPA would be stripped of the authority to prevent damaging air pollution by industries when state agencies improperly fail to do so.

Americans deserve high court justices who are fair to all sides, who guard against abuses of power by the executive and legislative branches, and who protect our rights and liberties. Returning the nation to the early 20th century and the days of the robber barons is an exorbitant price to pay to satisfy people who were characterized by U.S. Rep. Barney Frank on the House floor as believing life begins at conception and ends at birth.

Paul Krugman

Losing Our Country

Baby boomers like me grew up in a relatively equal society. In the 1960's America 1
was a place in which very few people were extremely wealthy, many blue-collar workers earned wages that placed them comfortably in the middle class, and working families could expect steadily rising living standards and a reasonable degree of economic security.

But as *The Times*'s series on class in America reminds us, that was another country. The middle-class society I grew up in no longer exists.

Working families have seen little if any progress over the past 30 years. Adjusted for inflation, the income of the median family doubled between 1947 and 1973. But it rose only 22 percent from 1973 to 2003, and much of that gain was the result of wives' entering the paid labor force or working longer hours, not rising wages.

Meanwhile, economic security is a thing of the past: year-to-year fluctuations in the incomes of working families are far larger than they were a generation ago. All it takes is a bit of bad luck in employment or health to plunge a family that seems solidly middle-class into poverty.

But the wealthy have done very well indeed. Since 1973 the average income of 5
the top 1 percent of Americans has doubled, and the income of the top 0.1 percent has tripled.

Why is this happening? I'll have more to say on that another day, but for now let me just point out that middle-class America didn't emerge by accident. It was created by what has been called the Great Compression of incomes that took place during World War II, and sustained for a generation by social norms that favored equality, strong labor unions and progressive taxation. Since the 1970's, all of those sustaining forces have lost their power.

Since 1980 in particular, U.S. government policies have consistently favored the wealthy at the expense of working families—and under the current administration, that favoritism has become extreme and relentless. From tax cuts that favor the rich to bankruptcy "reform" that punishes the unlucky, almost every domestic policy seems intended to accelerate our march back to the robber baron era.

It's not a pretty picture—which is why right-wing partisans try so hard to discredit anyone who tries to explain to the public what's going on.

These partisans rely in part on obfuscation: shaping, slicing and selectively presenting data in an attempt to mislead. For example, it's a plain fact that the Bush tax cuts heavily favor the rich, especially those who derive most of their income from inherited wealth. Yet this year's Economic Report of the President, in a bravura demonstration of how to lie with statistics, claimed that the cuts "increased the overall progressivity of the federal tax system."

The partisans also rely in part on scare tactics, insisting that any attempt to 10
limit inequality would undermine economic incentives and reduce all of us to shared misery. That claim ignores the fact of U.S. economic success after World War II. It also ignores the lesson we should have learned from recent corporate scandals: sometimes the prospect of great wealth for those who succeed provides an incentive not for high performance, but for fraud.

Above all, the partisans engage in name-calling. To suggest that sustaining programs like Social Security, which protects working Americans from economic risk, should have priority over tax cuts for the rich is to practice "class warfare." To show concern over the growing inequality is to engage in the "politics of envy."

But the real reasons to worry about the explosion of inequality since the 1970's have nothing to do with envy. The fact is that working families aren't sharing in the economy's growth, and face growing economic insecurity. And there's good reason to believe that a society in which most people can reasonably be considered middle class is a better society—and more likely to be a functioning democracy—than one in which there are great extremes of wealth and poverty.

Reversing the rise in inequality and economic insecurity won't be easy: the middle-class society we have lost emerged only after the country was shaken by depression and war. But we can make a start by calling attention to the politicians who systematically make things worse in catering to their contributors. Never mind that straw man, the politics of envy. Let's try to do something about the politics of greed.

THINGS TO DO WITH THE READING

1. For each of these editorials, state the position that most clearly enables readers to identify it as primarily liberal or conservative. Which key words and phrases are most useful in making this identification?
2. As Borick makes evident in his piece, a major element of the politics of language involves having the power to define what words mean. Interestingly, both Borick and Kilpatrick quote Humpty Dumpty on this subject. What is the keyword in "Justices Amended Constitution on Their Own ..." that the Supreme Court has (re)defined? How has it redefined this term? How would Kilpatrick prefer to see it defined?

3. Kilpatrick's editorial takes an interesting stance on the rights of individuals. Locate its position. What individual right is the editorial defending, and on what grounds?
4. Epstein's " ... By Letting Redevelopers Take Little Guy's Property" is more overtly partisan than Kilpatrick's editorial. It wishes to use the same case discussed by Kilpatrick, *Kelo v. City of New London*, to argue for the shortcomings of the political left. In the editorial's final sentence, the writer says "the so-called conservatives were the defenders of the Constitution and the little man." Again using Borick's essay as a lens, determine which aspects of liberal thinking the editorial writer wishes to contest. What language best identifies these aspects?
5. Use the reading strategy in Chapter 4 called finding "the pitch, the complaint, and the moment" (see pages 111–113) as a means of figuring out what Epstein is trying to accomplish in this editorial. Against which positions (the complaint) is he arguing? One of these is fairly explicit, but another is handled more subtly. What potential attack on conservatives is the writer somewhat worried about, and how does he defend against it?
6. In "More than Abortion Is at Stake in Supreme Court Picks" John F. Grim reveals himself from the beginning as an opponent of what he calls "far-right Republicans." He then offers a list of relatively recent high court decisions that he claims could be reversed by a more decidedly Republican (conservative) Supreme Court. The reader is left to decide why a Republican court would make the decisions the writer says it would make. Using Borick's article as a lens, articulate for each legal decision (or the three that you find most interesting) the political philosophy that might cause conservative Supreme Court judges to rule in the way the writer fears (see the explanation of uncovering assumptions on pages 93–100).
7. Paul Krugman's "Losing Our Country" is filled not only with the key words of the liberal political orientation but with some dire predictions about the direction in which the country is heading. What attacks does the writer make on the policies of the Bush administration and its Republican predecessors? How do these attacks reveal both the writer's liberal orientation and the conservative orientation of the Bush government?
8. Krugman's editorial anticipates an issue that will occupy many of the subsequent readings in this chapter: the politics of spin, which Krugman attacks as "name-calling." He cites two phrases: "class warfare" and "the politics of envy." Why does he find these labels not only objectionable but essentially inaccurate? ◗

George Orwell

Politics and the English Language

The British writer George Orwell has left so emphatic a mark on modern thinking about politics and language that the adjective "Orwellian" has arisen to characterize forms of political oppression, especially those involving the manipulation of language. The dystopian vision of the future in his novel *1984* is probably the source of the adjective that bears his name, but in the influential essay "Politics and The English Language" (1946), Orwell first gives voice to the ominous tendency of modern public prose to obscure its aims.

Most people who bother with the matter at all would admit that the English language is in a bad way, but it is generally assumed that we cannot by conscious action do anything about it. Our civilization is decadent and our language—so the argument runs—must inevitably share in the general collapse. It follows that any struggle against the abuse of language is a sentimental archaism, like preferring candles to electric light or hansom cabs to aeroplanes. Underneath this lies the half-conscious belief that language is a natural growth and not an instrument which we shape for our own purposes. 1

Now, it is clear that the decline of a language must ultimately have political and economic causes: it is not due simply to the bad influence of this or that individual writer. But an effect can become a cause, reinforcing the original cause and producing the same effect in an intensified form, and so on indefinitely. A man may take to drink because he feels himself to be a failure, and then fail all the more completely because he drinks. It is rather the same thing that is happening to the English language. It becomes ugly and inaccurate because our thoughts are foolish, but the slovenliness of our language makes it easier for us to have foolish thoughts. The point is that the process is reversible. Modern English, especially written English, is full of bad habits which spread by imitation and which can be avoided if one is willing to take the necessary trouble. If one gets rid of these habits one can think more clearly, and to think clearly is a necessary first step towards political regeneration: so that the fight against bad English is not frivolous and is not the exclusive concern of professional writers. I will come back to this presently, and I hope that by that time the meaning of what I have said here will have become clearer. Meanwhile, here are five specimens of the English language as it is now habitually written.

These five passages have not been picked out because they are especially bad—I could have quoted far worse if I had chosen—but because they illustrate various of the mental vices from which we now suffer. They are a little below the average, but are fairly representative samples. I number them so that I can refer back to them when necessary:

> "(1) I am not, indeed, sure whether it is not true to say that the Milton who once seemed not unlike a seventeenth-century Shelley had not become, out of an experience ever more bitter in each year, more alien [*sic*] to the founder of that Jesuit sect which nothing could induce him to tolerate."
>
> Professor Harold Laski (Essay in *Freedom of Expression*)

"(2) Above all, we cannot play ducks and drakes with a native battery of idioms which prescribes such egregious collocations of vocables as the Basic *put up with* for *tolerate* or *put at a loss* for *bewilder.*"

Professor Lancelot Hogben (*Interglossa*)

"(3) On the one side we have the free personality: by definition it is not neurotic, for it has neither conflict nor dream. Its desires, such as they are, are transparent, for they are just what institutional approval keeps in the forefront of consciousness; another institutional pattern would alter their number and intensity; there is little in them that is natural, irreducible, or culturally dangerous. But *on the other* side, the social bond itself is nothing but the mutual reflection of these self-secure integrities. Recall the definition of love. Is not this the very picture of a small academic? Where is there a place in this hall of mirrors for either personality or fraternity?"

Essay on psychology in *Politics* (New York)

"(4) All the 'best people' from the gentlemen's clubs, and all the frantic fascist captains, united in common hatred of Socialism and bestial horror of the rising tide of the mass revolutionary movement, have turned to acts of provocation, to foul incendiarism, to medieval legends of poisoned wells, to legalize their own destruction of proletarian organizations, and rouse the agitated petty-bourgeoisie to chauvinistic fervour on behalf of the fight against the revolutionary way out of the crisis."

Communist pamphlet

"(5) If a new spirit *is* to be infused into this old country, there is one thorny and contentious reform which must be tackled, and that is the humanization and galvanization of the B.B.C. Timidity here will be-speak cancer and atrophy of the soul. The heart of Britain may be sound and of strong beat, for instance, but the British lion's roar at present is like that of Bottom in Shakespeare's *Midsummer Night's Dream*—as gentle as any sucking dove. A virile new Britain cannot continue indefinitely to be traduced in the eyes or rather ears, of the world by the effete languors of Langham Place, brazenly masquerading as 'standard English.' When the Voice of Britain is heard at nine o'clock, better far and infinitely less ludicrous to hear aitches honestly dropped than the present priggish, inflated, inhibited, school-ma'amish arch braying of blameless bashful mewing maidens!"

Letter in *Tribune*

Each of these passages has faults of its own, but, quite apart from avoidable ugliness, two qualities are common to all of them. The first is staleness of imagery: the other is lack of precision. The writer either has a meaning and cannot express it, or he inadvertently says something else, or he is almost indifferent as to whether his words mean anything or not. This mixture of vagueness and sheer incompetence is the most marked characteristic of modern English prose, and especially of any kind of political writing. As soon as certain topics are raised, the concrete melts into the abstract and no one seems able to think of turns of speech that are not hackneyed: prose consists less and less of *words* chosen for the sake of their meaning, and more and more of *phrases* tacked together like the sections of a prefabricated hen-house. I list below, with notes and examples, various of the tricks by means of which the work of prose-construction is habitually dodged:

Dying Metaphors

5 A newly invented metaphor assists thought by evoking a visual image, while on the other hand a metaphor which is technically "dead" (e.g. *iron resolution*) has in effect reverted to being an ordinary word and can generally be used without loss of vividness. But in between these two classes there is a huge dump of worn-out metaphors which have lost all evocative power and are merely used because they save people the trouble of inventing phrases for themselves. Examples are: *Ring the changes on, take up the cudgels for, toe the line, ride roughshod over, stand shoulder to shoulder with, play into the hands of, no axe to grind, grist to the mill, fishing in troubled waters, on the order of the day, Achilles' heel, swan song, hotbed.* Many of these are used without knowledge of their meaning (what is a "rift," for instance?), and incompatible metaphors are frequently mixed, a sure sign that the writer is not interested in what he is saying. Some metaphors now current have been twisted out of their original meaning without those who use them even being aware of the fact. For example, *toe the line* is sometimes written *tow the line.* Another example is *the hammer and the anvil,* now always used with the implication that the anvil gets the worst of it. In real life it is always the anvil that breaks the hammer, never the other way about: a writer who stopped to think what he was saying would be aware of this, and would avoid perverting the original phrase.

Operators or Verbal False Limbs

These save the trouble of picking out appropriate verbs and nouns, and at the same time pad each sentence with extra syllables which give it an appearance of symmetry. Characteristic phrases are: *render inoperative, militate against, make contact with, be subjected to, give rise to, give grounds for, have the effect of, play a leading part (role) in, make itself felt, take effect, exhibit a tendency to, serve the purpose of, etc., etc.* The keynote is the elimination of simple verbs. Instead of being a single word, such as *break, stop, spoil, mend, kill,* a verb becomes a *phrase,* made up of a noun or adjective tacked on to some general-purposes verb such as *prove, serve, form, play, render.* In addition, the passive voice is wherever possible used in preference to the active, and noun constructions are used instead of gerunds (*by examination of* instead of *by examining*). The range of verbs is further cut down by means of the *-ize* and *de-* formation, and the banal statements are given an appearance of profundity by means of the *not un-* formation. Simple conjunctions and prepositions are replaced by such phrases as *with respect to, having regard to, the fact that, by dint of, in view of, in the interests of, on the hypothesis that;* and the ends of sentences are saved from anticlimax by such resounding commonplaces as *greatly to be desired, cannot be left out of account, a development to be expected in the near future, deserving of serious consideration, brought to a satisfactory conclusion,* and so on and so forth.

Pretentious Diction

Words like *phenomenon, element, individual* (as noun), *objective, categorical, effective, virtual, basic, primary, promote, constitute, exhibit, exploit, utilize, eliminate, liquidate,* are used to dress up simple statements and give an air of scientific impartiality to biased judgments. Adjectives like *epoch-making*, *epic*, *historic*, *unforgettable*, *triumphant*, *age-old*, *inevitable*, *inexorable*, *veritable*, are used to dignify the sordid processes of international politics, while writing that aims at glorifying war usually takes on an archaic color, its characteristic words being: *realm*, *throne*, *chariot*, *mailed fist*, *trident*, *sword*, *shield*, *buckler*, *banner*, *jackboot*, *clarion*. Foreign words and expressions such as *cul de sac*, *ancien régime*, *deus ex machina*, *mutatis mutandis*, *status quo*, *gleichschaltung*, *weltanschauung*, are used to give an air of culture and elegance. Except for the useful abbreviations *i.e.*, *e.g.*, and *etc.*, there is no real need for any of the hundreds of foreign phrases now current in English. Bad writers, and especially scientific, political and sociological writers, are nearly always haunted by the notion that Latin or Greek words are grander than Saxon ones, and unnecessary words like *expedite*, *ameliorate*, *predict*, *extraneous*, *deracinated*, *clandestine*, *subaqueous* and hundreds of others constantly gain ground from their Anglo-Saxon opposite numbers.[1] The jargon peculiar to Marxist writing (*hyena*, *hangman*, *cannibal*, *petty bourgeois*, *these gentry*, *lackey*, *flunky*, *mad dog*, *White Guard*, etc.) consists largely of words and phrases translated from Russian, German or French; but the normal way of coining a new word is to use a Latin or Greek root with the appropriate affix and, where necessary, the *-ize* formation. It is often easier to make up words of this kind (*deregionalize*, *impermissible*, *extra-marital*, *nonfragmentatory* and so forth) than to think up the English words that will cover one's meaning. The result, in general, is an increase in slovenliness and vagueness.

Meaningless Words

In certain kinds of writing, particularly in art criticism and literary criticism, it is normal to come across long passages which are almost completely lacking in meaning.[2] Words like *romantic*, *plastic*, *values*, *human*, *dead*, *sentimental*, *natural*, *vitality*, as used in art criticism, are strictly meaningless in the sense that they not only do not point to any discoverable object, but are hardly ever expected to do so by the reader. When one critic writes, "The outstanding feature of Mr. X's work is its living quality," while another writes, "The immediately striking thing about Mr. X's work is its peculiar deadness," the reader accepts this as a simple

[1] An interesting illustration of this is the way in which the English flower names which were in use till very recently are being ousted by Greek ones, *snapdragon* becoming *antirrhinum*, *forget-me-not* becoming *myosotis*, etc. It is hard to see any practical reason for this change of fashion: it is probably due to an instinctive turning-away from the more homely word and a vague feeling that the Greek word is scientific.

[2] Example: "Comfort's catholicity of perception and image, strangely Whitmanesque in range, almost the exact opposite in aesthetic compulsion, continues to evoke that trembling atmospheric accumulative hinting at a cruel, an inexorably serene timelessness … Wrey Gardiner scores by aiming at simple bull's-eyes with precision. Only they are not so simple, and through this contented sadness runs more than the surface bittersweet of resignation" (*Poetry Quarterly*).

difference of opinion. If words like *black* and *white* were involved, instead of the jargon words *dead* and *living*, he would see at once that language was being used in an improper way. Many political words are similarly abused. The word *Fascism* has now no meaning except in so far as it signifies "something not desirable." The words *democracy, socialism, freedom, patriotic, realistic, justice*, have each of them several different meanings which cannot be reconciled with one another. In the case of a word like *democracy*, not only is there no agreed definition, but the attempt to make one is resisted from all sides. It is almost universally felt that when we call a country democratic we are praising it: consequently the defenders of every kind of régime claim that it is a democracy, and fear that they might have to stop using the word if it were tied down to any one meaning. Words of this kind are often used in a consciously dishonest way. That is, the person who uses them has his own private definition, but allows his hearer to think he means something quite different. Statements like *Marshal Pétain was a true patriot, The Soviet Press is the freest in the world, The Catholic Church is opposed to persecution*, are almost always made with intent to deceive. Other words used in variable meanings, in most cases more or less dishonestly, are: *class, totalitarian, science, progressive, reactionary, bourgeois, equality*.

Now that I have made this catalog of swindles and perversions, let me give another example of the kind of writing that they lead to. This time it must of its nature be an imaginary one. I am going to translate a passage of good English into modern English of the worst sort. Here is a well-known verse from *Ecclesiastes:*

> "I returned and saw under the sun, that the race is not to the swift, nor the battle to the strong, neither yet bread to the wise, nor yet riches to men of understanding, nor yet favor to men of skill; but time and chance happeneth to them all."

Here it is in modern English: 10

> "Objective consideration of contemporary phenomena compels the conclusion that success or failure in competitive activities exhibits no tendency to be commensurate with innate capacity, but that a considerable element of the unpredictable must invariably be taken into account."

This is a parody, but not a very gross one. Exhibit (3), above, for instance, contains several patches of the same kind of English. It will be seen that I have not made a full translation. The beginning and ending of the sentence follow the original meaning fairly closely, but in the middle the concrete illustrations—race, battle, bread—dissolve into the vague phrase "success or failure in competitive activities." This had to be so, because no modern writer of the kind I am discussing—no one capable of using phrases like "objective consideration of contemporary phenomena"—would ever tabulate his thoughts in that precise and detailed way. The whole tendency of modern prose is away from concreteness. Now analyse these two sentences a little more closely. The first contains forty-nine words but only sixty syllables, and all its words are those of everyday life. The second contains thirty-eight words of ninety syllables: eighteen of its words are from

Latin roots, and one from Greek. The first sentence contains six vivid images, and only one phrase ("time and chance") that could be called vague. The second contains not a single fresh, arresting phrase, and in spite of its ninety syllables it gives only a shortened version of the meaning contained in the first. Yet without a doubt it is the second kind of sentence that is gaining ground in modern English. I do not want to exaggerate. This kind of writing is not yet universal, and outcrops of simplicity will occur here and there in the worst-written page. Still, if you or I were told to write a few lines on the uncertainty of human fortunes, we should probably come much nearer to my imaginary sentence than to the one from *Ecclesiastes.*

As I have tried to show, modern writing at its worst does not consist in picking out words for the sake of their meaning and inventing images in order to make the meaning clearer. It consists in gumming together long strips of words which have already been set in order by someone else, and making the results presentable by sheer humbug. The attraction of this way of writing is that it is easy. It is easier—even quicker, once you have the habit—to say *In my opinion it is a not unjustifiable assumption that* than to say *I think.* If you use ready made phrases, you not only don't have to hunt about for words; you also don't have to bother with the rhythms of your sentences, since these phrases are generally so arranged as to be more or less euphonious. When you are composing in a hurry—when you are dictating to a stenographer, for instance, or making a public speech—it is natural to fall into a pretentious, Latinized style. Tags like *a consideration which we should do well to bear in mind* or *a conclusion to which all of us would readily assent* will save many a sentence from coming down with a bump. By using stale metaphors, similes and idioms, you save much mental effort, at the cost of leaving your meaning vague, not only for your reader but for yourself. This is the significance of mixed metaphors. The sole aim of a metaphor is to call up a visual image. When these images clash—as in *The Fascist octopus has sung its swan song, the jackboot is thrown into the melting pot*—it can be taken as certain that the writer is not seeing a mental image of the objects he is naming; in other words he is not really thinking. Look again at the examples I gave at the beginning of this essay. Professor Laski (1) uses five negatives in fifty-three words. One of these is superfluous, making nonsense of the whole passage, and in addition there is the slip *alien* for akin, making further nonsense, and several avoidable pieces of clumsiness which increase the general vagueness. Professor Hogben (2) plays ducks and drakes with a battery which is able to write prescriptions, and, while disapproving of the everyday phrase *put up with,* is unwilling to look *egregious* up in the dictionary and see what it means. (3), if one takes an uncharitable attitude towards it, is simply meaningless: probably one could work out its intended meaning by reading the whole of the article in which it occurs. In (4), the writer knows more or less what he wants to say, but an accumulation of stale phrases chokes him like tea leaves blocking a sink. In (5), words and meaning have almost parted company. People who write in this manner usually have a general emotional meaning—they dislike one thing and want to express solidarity with another—but they are not interested in the detail of what they are saying. A scrupulous writer, in every sentence that he writes, will ask himself at least four questions, thus: What am I trying to say? What words will express it? What image or idiom will make it clearer? Is this image fresh enough to have an effect? And he will probably ask himself two more: Could I put it more shortly? Have I said anything that is avoidably ugly? But you are not obliged to go to all this trouble. You can shirk it by simply throwing your mind open and letting the ready-made phrases come crowding in. They will construct your sentences for you—even think your thoughts for you, to a certain extent—and at need they will perform the important service of partially concealing your meaning even from yourself. It is at this point that the special connection between politics and the debasement of language becomes clear.

In our time it is broadly true that political writing is bad writing. Where it is not true, it will generally be found that the writer is some kind of rebel, expressing his private opinions and not a "party line." Orthodoxy, of whatever color, seems to demand a lifeless, imitative style. The political dialects to be found in pamphlets, leading articles, manifestos, White Papers and the speeches of under-secretaries do, of course, vary from party to party, but they are all alike in that one almost never finds in them a fresh, vivid, home-made turn of speech. When one watches some tired hack on the platform mechanically repeating the familiar phrases—*bestial atrocities, iron heel, bloodstained tyranny, free peoples of the world, stand shoulder to shoulder*—one often has a curious feeling that one is not watching a live human being but some kind of dummy: a feeling which suddenly becomes stronger at moments when the light catches the speaker's spectacles and turns them into blank discs which seem to have no eyes behind them. And this is not altogether fanciful. A speaker who uses that kind of phraseology has gone some distance towards turning himself into a machine. The appropriate noises are coming out of his larynx, but his brain is not involved as it would be if he were choosing his words for himself. If the speech he is making is one that he is accustomed to make over and over again, he may be almost unconscious of what he is saying, as one is when one utters the responses in church. And this reduced state of consciousness, if not indispensable, is at any rate favorable to political conformity.

In our time, political speech and writing are largely the defense of the indefensible. Things like the continuance of British rule in India, the Russian purges and deportations, the dropping of the atom bombs on Japan, can indeed be defended, but only by arguments which are too brutal for most people to face, and which do not square with the professed aims of political parties. Thus political language has to consist largely of euphemism, question-begging and sheer cloudy vagueness. Defenseless villages are bombarded from the air, the inhabitants driven out into the countryside, the cattle machine-gunned, the huts set on fire with incendiary bullets: this is called *pacification*. Millions of peasants are robbed of their farms and sent trudging along the roads with no more than they can carry: this is called *transfer of population* or *rectification of frontiers*. People are imprisoned for years without trial, or shot in the back of the neck or sent to die of scurvy in Arctic lumber camps: this is called *elimination of unreliable elements*. Such phraseology is needed if one wants to name things without calling up mental pictures of them. Consider for instance some comfortable English professor defending Russian totalitarianism. He cannot say outright, "I believe in killing off your opponents when you can get good results by doing so." Probably, therefore, he will say something like this:

“While freely conceding that the Soviet régime exhibits certain features 15
which the humanitarian may be inclined to deplore, we must, I think, agree that a certain curtailment of the right to political opposition is an unavoidable concomitant of transitional periods, and that the rigors which the Russian people have been called upon to undergo have been amply justified in the sphere of concrete achievement.”

The inflated style is itself a kind of euphemism. A mass of Latin words falls upon the facts like soft snow, blurring the outlines and covering up all the details. The great enemy of clear language is insincerity. When there is a gap between one's real and one's declared aims, one turns as it were instinctively to long words and exhausted idioms, like a cuttlefish squirting out ink. In our age there is no such thing as “keeping out of politics.” All issues are political issues, and politics itself is a mass of lies, evasions, folly, hatred and schizophrenia. When the general atmosphere is bad, language must suffer. I should expect to find—this is a guess which I have not sufficient knowledge to verify—that the German, Russian and Italian languages have all deteriorated in the last ten or fifteen years, as a result of dictatorship.

But if thought corrupts language, language can also corrupt thought. A bad usage can spread by tradition and imitation, even among people who should and do know better. The debased language that I have been discussing is in some ways very convenient. Phrases like *a not unjustifiable assumption*, *leaves much to be desired*, *would serve no good purpose*, *a consideration which we should do well to bear in mind*, are a continuous temptation, a packet of aspirins always at one's elbow. Look back through this essay, and for certain you will find that I have again and again committed the very faults I am protesting against. By this morning's post I have received a pamphlet dealing with conditions in Germany. The author tells me that he “felt impelled” to write it. I open it at random, and here is almost the first sentence that I see: “(The Allies) have an opportunity not only of achieving a radical transformation of Germany's social and political structure in such a way as to avoid a nationalistic reaction in Germany itself, but at the same time of laying the foundations of a cooperative and unified Europe.” You see, he “feels impelled” to write—feels, presumably, that he has something new to say—and yet his words, like cavalry horses answering the bugle, group themselves automatically into the familiar dreary pattern. This invasion of one's mind by ready-made phrases (*lay the foundations*, *achieve a radical transformation*) can only be prevented if one is constantly on guard against them, and every such phrase anaesthetizes a portion of one's brain.

I said earlier that the decadence of our language is probably curable. Those who deny this would argue, if they produced an argument at all, that language merely reflects existing social conditions, and that we cannot influence its development by any direct tinkering with words and constructions. So far as the general tone or spirit of a language goes, this may be true, but it is not true in detail. Silly words and expressions have often disappeared, not through any evolutionary process but owing to the conscious action of a minority. Two recent examples were *explore every avenue* and *leave no stone unturned*, which were killed by the jeers of a few journalists. There is a long list of flyblown metaphors which could similarly be got rid of if enough people would interest themselves in the job; and it should also be possible to laugh the *not un*-formation out of existence,[3] to reduce the amount of Latin and Greek in the average sentence, to drive out foreign phrases and strayed scientific words, and, in general, to make pretentiousness unfashionable. But all these are minor points. The defense of the English language implies more than this, and perhaps it is best to start by saying what it does *not* imply.

To begin with it has nothing to do with archaism, with the salvaging of obsolete words and turns of speech, or with the setting up of a "standard English" which must never be departed from. On the contrary, it is especially concerned with the scrapping of every word or idiom which has outworn its usefulness. It has nothing to do with correct grammar and syntax, which are of no importance so long as one makes one's meaning clear, or with the avoidance of Americanisms, or with having what is called a "good prose style." On the other hand it is not concerned with fake simplicity and the attempt to make written English colloquial. Nor does it even imply in every case preferring the Saxon word to the Latin one, though it does imply using the fewest and shortest words that will cover one's meaning. What is above all needed is to let the meaning choose the word, and not the other way about. In prose, the worst thing one can do with words is to surrender to them. When you think of a concrete object, you think wordlessly, and then, if you want to describe the thing you have been visualizing you probably hunt about till you find the exact words that seem to fit. When you think of something abstract you are more inclined to use words from the start, and unless you make a conscious effort to prevent it, the existing dialect will come rushing in and do the job for you, at the expense of blurring or even changing your meaning. Probably it is better to put off using words as long as possible and get one's meaning as clear as one can through pictures or sensations. Afterwards one can choose—not simply *accept*—the phrases that will best cover the meaning, and then switch round and decide what impression one's words are likely to make on another person. This last effort of the mind cuts out all stale or mixed images, all prefabricated phrases, needless repetitions, and humbug and vagueness generally. But one can often be in doubt about the effect of a word or a phrase, and one needs rules that one can rely on when instinct fails. I think the following rules will cover most cases:

(i) Never use a metaphor, simile or other figure of speech which you are used to seeing in print.

(ii) Never use a long word where a short one will do.

(iii) If it is possible to cut a word out, always cut it out.

(iv) Never use the passive where you can use the active.

(v) Never use a foreign phrase, a scientific word or a jargon word if you can think of an everyday English equivalent.

(vi) Break any of these rules sooner than say anything outright barbarous.

These rules sound elementary, and so they are, but they demand a deep change 20
of attitude in anyone who has grown used to writing in the style now fashionable. One could keep all of them and still write bad English, but one could not

[3] One can cure oneself of the *not un*- formation by memorizing this sentence: A *not unblack dog was chasing a not unsmall rabbit across a not ungreen field.*

write the kind of stuff that I quoted in those five specimens at the beginning of this article.

I have not here been considering the literary use of language, but merely language as an instrument for expressing and not for concealing or preventing thought. Stuart Chase and others have come near to claiming that all abstract words are meaningless, and have used this as a pretext for advocating a kind of political quietism. Since you don't know what Fascism is, how can you struggle against Fascism? One need not swallow such absurdities as this, but one ought to recognize that the present political chaos is connected with the decay of language, and that one can probably bring about some improvement by starting at the verbal end. If you simplify your English, you are freed from the worst follies of orthodoxy. You cannot speak any of the necessary dialects, and when you make a stupid remark its stupidity will be obvious, even to yourself. Political language—and with variations this is true of all political parties, from Conservatives to Anarchists—is designed to make lies sound truthful and murder respectable, and to give an appearance of solidity to pure wind. One cannot change this all in a moment, but one can at least change one's own habits, and from time to time one can even, if one jeers loudly enough, send some wornout and useless phrase—some *jackboot*, *Achilles' heel*, *hotbed*, *melting pot*, *acid test*, *veritable inferno* or other lump of verbal refuse—into the dustbin where it belongs.

THINGS TO DO WITH THE READING

1. In two different sites earlier in the rhetoric section of this book—pages 13–14 and pages 272–273—reference is made to "Politics and the English Language." If you review these discussions, you will see that an important *subtext* of Orwell's essay is that language is never neutral: it cannot simply reflect a pre-existent reality in some objective way. Rather, language constitutes reality: the way we talk about reality shapes it. With this notion in mind, do Try this 1.9 (see pages 13–14), focusing on collecting and analyzing clichés.
2. Orwell's discussions of the ways that presentation can affect meaning correlate well with the discussions of style in Chapters 10 and 11 of this book. Virtually all of the "Try this" sections in those two chapters might help you to understand and apply concepts that Orwell raises to both your own writing and your analysis of others'. Sample, for example, Try this 10.4 or 10.5 (see page 269) to sensitize yourself to concrete and abstract words. Or do Try this 10.6 (see page 270) on "Distinguishing Latinate from Anglo-Saxon Diction." A current political speech might provide an interesting test case (a selection is available at the American Rhetoric website mentioned in question 4).
3. In the section "Operators or Verbal False Limbs" (see paragraph 6) and again in the "rules" offered at the end of the essay (see paragraph 19), Orwell articulates (and justifies) his preference for cutting unnecessary

words and avoiding the passive voice. With these notions in mind, read the last section of Chapter 11, "Cutting the Fat" (see pages 286–292). As you do so, experiment with Try this exercises 11.7, 11.8, and 11.9 (see pages 289–292) to sharpen your ability to distinguish active voice from passive voice and to refine your understanding of what each of these options offers a writer.

4. **Application:** Near the end of his essay, Orwell delivers its most famous sentence, "In our time political speech and writing are largely the defense of the indefensible" (see paragraph 14). He illustrates this declaration with a series of examples of "euphemism, question-begging, and sheer cloudy vagueness," such as use of the term "pacification" to describe "defenseless villages bombarded from the air, inhabitants driven out into the countryside, the cattle machine-gunned, the huts set on fire with incendiary bullets" (see paragraph 14).

   That was a half-century ago. How about now? Visit a wonderful website for its collection of speeches, American Rhetoric, using the link at www.thomsonedu.com/english/rosenwasser. Find a speech that you think Orwell would condemn for defending the indefensible, and offer examples of its methods of doing so.

5. **Application:** Orwell's essay also conveys, both explicitly and by implication, a set of traits that characterize politically responsible language. Review the essay to extract a list of those traits Orwell approves of in political speech. Then go to the American Rhetoric website (cited in the previous Application question) and locate an example of a speech he would like. Point out specific features he would like about it to explain the reasoning behind your judgment. You might want to start by looking at speeches by Barbara Jordan, the first African-American woman to be elected to the House of Representatives in Texas. She went on to a high-profile career in Congress where she came to be recognized as one of America's great orators. Try to find the speech she gave in Congress on the occasion of the House Judiciary Committee, of which she was a member, being asked to speak about their deliberations on the question of impeaching a president (Richard Nixon). This speech made Jordan a nationally known and admired speaker. Why?

6. **Application:** In paragraph 7, Orwell makes an interesting observation about language that is used to justify and even to glorify war. He says that such language "usually takes on an archaic color." The word "archaic" means old-fashioned or ancient, language that belongs to an earlier period but is still used, often for poetic purposes (*OED*). There is much passionate language in the press these days—and on various political websites, including those from countries in the Middle East. Find some examples of language that is justifying war. You might, for example, take some passages from speeches by George W. Bush on the war in Iraq and then some communications from militant groups in the Middle East. Use these to see the extent to which the verbal phenomenon Orwell notes is

still the case. What else do you notice that might illuminate and extend the thinking of the Orwell piece on the language of war?

Note: Some of the "Things to Do with the Reading" sections following the remaining readings in this chapter will offer links for using Orwell's essay as a lens for thinking about contemporary trends in the language of politics. ◗

Dante Chinni

Why Should We Trust This Man?

This profile of the pollster Frank Luntz first appeared online at Salon.com. on May 26, 2000. In it Dante Chinni, a columnist for the *Christian Science Monitor*, focuses on Luntz's controversial methods of gathering information, but he is also interested in thinking about Luntz as, in his words, "part of a new class of media personality, the celebrity pollster." This piece is interesting in its own right, but it also serves the purpose of framing the interview with Luntz about his methods (which follows as the next selection).

Whatever it is about the pollster Frank Luntz—the baby face, the unctuous 1 charm, the ever-changing hairdo—no one seems to be able to get enough of him. Even since last week, when his sole candidate, Rudy Giuliani, made a tortured exit from the campaign trail, Luntz still makes the media rounds, from CNBC's "Rivera Live" to the New York Times.

He's possibly the best example of what we could call the pollster pundit: someone who both purports to scientifically poll the opinions of the public, and then also interpret that data to support his own—in Luntz's case, conservative—point of view. This is what allows Luntz to face a room full of journalists and, in all seriousness, proclaim George W. Bush's jittery, time-delayed appearance on David Letterman—the one which prompted boos from the audience—a total success.

It's what allows Luntz to proclaim that Giuliani would've been no more hurt from his admission of marital difficulties than his admission that he has cancer. "He beat crime, he beat drugs, he beat unemployment, he beat welfare, he beat trash in the streets, he beat the squeegee guy," Luntz said. "He's like a mayor machine."

What's more, it's what allows Luntz to do this without citing a single polling result, a single number, and yet still be taken quite seriously as a pollster.

In a city full of cynical, number-hungry journalists who pride themselves for 5 taking no one at their word, this would seem to fall under the category of a neat trick. Then again, Luntz is a special case. Since about 1994, he has been a rising star in politics (Time listed him that year among "50 with the requisite ambition, vision and community spirit to help guide us in the new millennium"), part of a new class of media personality, the celebrity pollster. Along with fellow Republican darling Kellyanne Fitzpatrick, he's regularly called upon to explain candidate strategies and voter reaction.

But while the media can be disdainful of Fitzpatrick (through the occasional referring to her as a "pundette"), Luntz gets the heavy-hitter treatment, frequently getting called in by the networks to offer color commentary on politics even when he has no poll to cite.

The day Luntz spoke of W's Letterman appearance, he wasn't just beguiling an uncombative TV audience. He was addressing the Sperling Breakfast, the long-held meeting of powerful journalists organized by Godfrey Sperling of the Christian Science Monitor. (Full disclosure: I'm a Monitor political columnist.) These breakfasts can certainly be stuffy, but there's no denying that an invitation to speak at one is tantamount to a stamp of approval by Washington's establishment press, with previous invitees including Al Gore and Ken Starr.

The morning of the breakfast, Luntz showed up ready to talk about politics armed with nothing more than a tape of himself conducting a focus group on MSNBC. He spun fast and furiously, and then told everyone in the room the reason he was giving them his information (the less-than-shocking revelation that Bush needs a good chunk of McCain's supporters to win the presidency) is that he wanted the press to pass along the news to Bush. He would have told the Bush campaign himself, he said, but his commitment to his job as a media pollster—with occasional gigs for outlets like MSNBC and U.S. News & World Report—forbids it. The crowd chuckled, nodding knowingly and kept writing.

Of course it's hard to know how seriously to take Luntz. His "polling" and "analysis" always seems half-serious and half performance art. Whatever he really means, however, the media generally seems to take him at his word. Much of the polling industry, however, has been more circumspect.

10 In 1997, Luntz was formally reprimanded by the American Association for Public Opinion Research for his work polling on the GOP's 1994 "Contract with America" campaign document.

Luntz told the media that everything in the contract had the support of at least 60 percent of the general public. Considering the elementary phrasing of that document (stop violent criminals, protect our kids, strong national defense), it seems almost laughably uncontroversial. But one of AAPOR's 1,400 members wasn't so amused, and filed a complaint requesting to see Luntz's research and a verification of the figure.

Luntz's response? He couldn't reveal the information because of client confidentiality.

"None of those people have ever worked for a private client," Luntz says now. When told that some members of AAPOR do actually work in the private sector, he replied: "Then they should understand about confidentiality."

In fact, Luntz says, the AAPOR slap had a surprising effect. "Look, I shouldn't say this," he says, "but I made money off that incident. People basically said, 'If you're willing to go through that to honor your commitment, I want to work with you.'"

15 But what about AAPOR's claim that when you make results public, you owe it to people to release all the data. "I don't agree," he says. "Say you poll on an environmental issue, and on eight of the 10 questions the numbers are in your favor. Why release the other two? It's like being a lawyer … This is my case, and these are the strong arguments and these are the weak ones. You go with your strongest case."

There are a few problems with this analogy. First, pollsters aren't lawyers; they are (in theory) researchers and are treated by journalists as such. Second, in a trial there are prosecutors and defense lawyers and everyone is working off the same page. There is an established pool of evidence that either side can argue over. What Luntz proposes is a trial in which a lawyer makes his case with no opposition and no opportunity for a jury to consider the source.

"These are not complicated questions," says Diane Colasanto, who was president of the AAPOR when it reprimanded Luntz. "It is simply wanting to know: 'How many people did you question? What were the questions?' He did finally give us some information, but it wasn't enough. It didn't really explain what the figures were based on. All we could tell was it seemed like there might have been some survey done.

"We understand the need for confidentiality, but once a pollster makes results public, the information needs to be public. People need to be able to evaluate whether it was sound research."

Warren Mitofsky, the current standards chair at AAPOR, says the complaint against Luntz was a rarity. There are only one or two complaints filed against pollsters each year and they hardly ever go as far as Luntz's.

Of course, critics of the AAPOR complaint note that the group is not really 20
the domain of political pollsters. The group's membership mostly includes academic pollsters and commercial research firms. But even in the world of political pollsters, Luntz is a special case, says David W. Moore, author of the book "The Super Pollsters."

"And it's not just a question of being a political pollster," Moore says. "Both Peter Hart and Bob Teeter are political pollsters and both are very solid. When you hear them talk, they genuinely try to analyze the data." (Hart, a Democratic pollster, and Teeter, a Republican, work together to poll for NBC and The Wall Street Journal.)

Luntz's work and that of other celebrity pollsters, such as Fitzpatrick, is nothing more than "propaganda" masked as research, Moore says.

"What bothers me is they are given so much prominence. One of the reasons media organizations started doing their own polling was to make sure they wouldn't get biased data." Now, the media pay these people to poll, he says. "The whole trend is really a backward step."

Luntz has risen to media stardom on the strength of his work with focus groups, typically gatherings of a dozen or so people, carefully screened to be representative of a larger population. A moderator leads the group in a discussion, and carefully chooses questions to elicit the participants' deep feelings about candidates or issues.

And Luntz is an able moderator. Watching him work a room is like watching 25
a good politician: He's bright, funny, amiable and connects with his subjects. He speaks in simple, direct sentences, and asks questions like "Is Bush a smart guy?" or "Does he have what it takes to be president?" He's a first-rate empathizer, all grins and furrowed brows.

This has undoubtedly helped the media pine for him, but it's also fallen in love with those wonderful little gizmos he often gives his groups that allow voters to instantly make their opinion known during a speech or debate—a little dial that they can turn one way for approval and the other for disapproval.

As an event unfolds, he sits back and watches a constantly shifting fever-line that shows which statements people favor or dislike. If you have ever wondered about the fickleness of the American public, just watch one of Luntz's dial tapes as I did during the 1996 presidential debate in Hartford, Conn. It's an experience in terror. One line may elicit a negative response, while a different line meaning basically the same thing is all positive.

Of course, political focus groups aren't new. Their use dates back to World War II. They allow the moderator to dig into specific questions more deeply than "Do you support abortion rights?" or "Do you use Clorox?" and check for emotional responses.

They are not, however, substitutes for polling data. They create no hard numbers, and since the groups are usually small, it's hard to extrapolate any definitive results. "You cannot generalize from the results of a focus group, period," says Mitofsky. "You can get results you can explore in a real survey, but that's all. A lot of people do research on the cheap and that's a good way to get in trouble."

But Luntz argues that regular polling often misses what's really going on with voters. "Human behavior studies have consistently proven that people will reveal their innermost thoughts only to those [with whom] they believe they share a common bond," he wrote in a 1994 polling-report article called "Voices of Victory." "If conventional wisdom and telephone polls were accurate, Ross Perot should have barely scraped into double digits in 1992."

Luntz's reasoning is thought-provoking, and sounds kind of sensible—except that the polls leading up to the 1992 election were actually pretty on target. Just days before the voters went to the polls, ABC had Perot with 18 percent. A Harris Poll had Perot at 17 percent. He wound up with 19 percent.

Some days after his appearance at the Sperling Breakfast, I ran into another journalist who was at the table that morning. Didn't it bother him, I wondered, that Luntz offered no numbers to back up his assertions and that he said he was using the press to pass a message to Bush, regardless of how silly that message was?

"Luntz is different," he told me. "He's not a regular pollster. He's more interpretive."

But the whole point of polling is to collect data. It is not a perfect science but, done properly and explained well, polls yield hard numbers that can be discussed.

What Luntz does is something else: scientific man-on-the-street interviews. And regardless of how scientific the samples are, how serious can one take the results when there are no numbers to point to and the moderator happily admits he's doing what he can to aid a specific party?

"We call people pollsters when they poll," Moore says. "Why don't we all call Luntz a focus-groupster?" Probably because that wouldn't sound nearly as good on TV.

THINGS TO DO WITH THE READING

1. This short piece "opens up" analytically once you have tracked its organizing contrasts (see pages 45 and 52–53). One of these contrasts is between focus groups and polls as methods of acquiring information. How does Chinni explain each of these—with what advantages and limitations?
2. The title of Chinni's piece on Luntz is a question—"Why should we trust this man?" The piece cites relatively authoritative sources (the American Association for Public Opinion, the author of a book on pollsters, and a journalist in attendance at a breakfast for "powerful journalists") that question Luntz's trustworthiness. It is clear, however, that Chinni is genuinely interested in Luntz, his strategies, and what the emergence of

celebrity pollsters like Luntz might mean. What does he concede to, or perhaps even grudgingly admire, about Luntz's point of view? And what finally does he find most troubling about Luntz's practice, the grounds upon which he indicts Luntz most fully? Locate specific passages in which Chinni offers concessions and refutations (see page 247 for a discussion of these terms).

3. Chinni gives us an instructive example of how to argue by questioning the appropriateness and accuracy of an analogy (see page 213, "Analogy and false analogy"). Trace the logic of Chinni's critique of Luntz comparing his use of data with what lawyers do.
4. Dante Chinni says that we might call Frank Luntz a "pollster pundit." Look up (preferably in the *OED*) "pundit," which is a Hindi word. In what ways does Luntz, as described in Chinni's online article, conform to this definition? On what grounds does Chinni worry about pollsters also being pundits?

Interview with Frank Luntz

This interview with the controversial pollster Frank Luntz first appeared on PBS's *Frontline* on December 15, 2003, as part of a series of interviews entitled *The Persuaders*. The series explored the broader influence that the cultures of marketing and advertising have had on American life. In the interview, Luntz discusses his central role in crafting the Contract of America that the Republican Party presented to voters in 1994, as well as his theories about the construction and presentation of messages in political language. A graduate of the University of Pennsylvania with a PhD from Oxford, Luntz is currently the chairman of a strategic research consulting group. He made headlines when his memo prepared to help the Republican Party win "the environmental communications battle" was leaked to the press, and again when MSNBC bowed to pressure to remove him from the station's presidential debate coverage because of his partisan stands.

What are you measuring with the dial technology? [A mechanism Luntz uses whereby people in a focus group register their moment by moment responses to a speech or presentation.] 1

It's like an X-ray that gets inside your head, and it picks out every single word, every single phrase [that you hear], and you know what works and what doesn't. And you do it without the bias of a focus group. People are quiet as they're listening, and they're reacting anonymously. The key to dial technology is that it's immediate, it's specific, and it's anonymous.

It's so immediate, it feels instantaneous.

But it is, because politics is instantaneous. Politics is gut; commercials are gut. You're watching a great show on TV, you now come to that middle break, you decide in a matter of three seconds whether or not you're going to a) flip the channel; b) get up; or c) keep watching. It's not intellectual; it is gut.

Is it the same for political decisions about power companies and politicians, though? 5

We decide based on how people look; we decide based on how people sound; we decide based on how people are dressed. We decide based on their passion. If I respond to you quietly, the viewer at home is going to have a different reaction than if I respond to you with emotion and with passion and I wave my arms around. Somebody like this is an intellectual; somebody like this is a freak. But that's how we make up our minds. Look, this is about the real-life decisions of real-life Americans, who to vote for, what to buy, what to agree with, what to think, how to act. This is the way it is.

You think emotions are more revelatory than the intellect for predicting these decisions?

80 percent of our life is emotion, and only 20 percent is intellect. I am much more interested in how you feel than how you think. I can change how you think,

but how you feel is something deeper and stronger, and it's something that's inside you. How you think is on the outside, how you feel is on the inside, so that's what I need to understand.

And this technology can get at that?

The great thing about dial technology is you can get a small response on the 10
dial, or you can get a huge jump. You watch with your own eyes: At some points, the lines are way up at the top of the screen or even out beyond. People were practically breaking their dials in agreement at certain points, and at other points, they were flat. It measures intensity. And if you want to understand public opinion, if you want to understand public behavior, if you want to understand the way we operate as Americans and as humans, you've got to understand that one word: intensity.

It can be anything, then, that you're selling.

I'm not going to let you twist the words, because if I say to you that you can sell a politician the way you sell soap—and it may even look that way from the outside—that says to Americans that they shouldn't respect politicians or soap. It really isn't that way. The way you communicate an idea is different than the way you communicate a product. However, the way you measure [the response of the public in both instances] is quite similar. And the principles behind explaining and educating the product or the elected official is similar, even though the actual execution of it is very, very different.

Are there different techniques you use when working with politics versus corporations?

The technique is a little bit different because politics and corporations are a little bit different. But in the end you're still using the same focus groups; you're still using the same dial technology; you're still using the same quantitative data; you're still doing split samples where you ask half a sample one way and the other half a different way. You're still asking and re-asking the questions. You're still showing them visuals to see what they like the best, and you're still showing them or having them listen to audio track to see how they respond. So the actual techniques are the same, but how they are applied is different. And that really is the separation; that's the differentiation between politics and the corporate world.

Was there a eureka moment, watching the responses of these people to the 15
power company's ideas, where you figured out what really worked?

The eureka moment is two reasons why the output-based standard should be adopted: common sense and accountability. Input-based standards don't encourage energy diversity; they don't create any incentives; they don't produce solar, hydro, nuclear. As a result, companies are actually penalized if they use the cleanest fuels, and it doesn't make sense. It's not substance; it's language. And when they heard the language that they wanted to hear and they were able to apply it to an idea that at least they were open to, you watched a marriage of good communication and good policy. That was the eureka moment: I watched people nod their heads; I watched them look to each other, and they were willing at this point to fight for this position. Now I'll be able to walk to this electricity company on Monday and be able to say to them, "Your policy makes sense, and here's the language to explain it."

And the amazing thing was, it explained a very complicated policy. That's the job of language; that's the job of English. This is not about politics; this is not about selling soap. This is taking very traditional, simple, clear-cut words of the English language and figuring out which words, which phrases to apply at which opportunities, which times.

So what will you say at that Monday meeting?

On Monday I will sit down with a Washington representative of Florida Power & Light and I will tell him that what he wants to do, his goal for his company, is the goal of America; that if he uses this language to explain his principles and his policies, not only will the company benefit, but the public will be appreciative of what they're trying to do. This is a good company, this is a clean company, but it's got all the baggage of every other electric company, of every other power company. We as Americans assume that big companies are bad, and big power companies are even worse. This language, what we saw tonight, is a demonstration that a single company can differentiate itself, can improve its public image.

You believe language can change a paradigm. 20

I don't believe it—I know it. I've seen it with my own eyes. I have seen how effective language attached to policies that are mainstream and delivered by people who are passionate and effective can change the course of history. I watched in 1994 when the group of Republicans got together and said: "We're going to do this completely differently than it's ever been done before. We are going to prove to the American people that we are different." And so instead of a platform, instead of a policy, instead of a mass of different issues and policies, they came up with a "contract," because a contract is different. A contract says that it is a legal document. It says that you put your name on it, and it says that there is enforcement if you don't do it. The word "contract" means something different than "platform." Every politician and every political party issues a platform, but only these people signed a contract.

Was that your idea?

The concept of it was hatched in Salisbury, MD, at a Republican retreat. I was fortunate enough to have been invited to do a presentation about how the American people didn't trust politicians in general and, quite frankly, didn't trust Republicans in particular. And Newt Gingrich was there, and he listened to the presentation, and he said: "We have to do it differently in this election. We have to find a way to communicate that takes all of these policies that we believe in, that the Democrats don't, and articulates that difference. How can we do it?" I presented at that presentation a proclamation. I got the idea from a Massachusetts campaign I was involved with. Gingrich saw that, and he came up with the phrase "contract."

I didn't create the "Contract with America;" I was the pollster for it. I said, "If you're going to do a contract, you've got to make it a contract." For example, "Keep this page to hold us accountable"—that did not exist in the original document. I insisted that that be added, because they wanted to know that you could actually hold these guys accountable. One of the things that you have trouble with politicians, particularly in Washington, is when you get mad at them and you can't touch them; you can't punch them; you can't yell at them. This accountability says, "I can really demand that they do what they promise."

This sentence was the one that I had the most trouble keeping in this final 25
document: "If we break this contract, throw us out. We mean it." When has a politician ever said, "If I don't come through with what I promise, boot me"? I said: "You need that sentence in there, and you need it at the very bottom of the document. People will read the top, and they read the bottom, and only if they believe in the top and the bottom will they actually read the text, will they read the substance." This is the enforcement clause, and this is what told people that this was for real.

It's not the "Republican Contract with America," because in 1994, as it is today, Americans don't want partisanship. So you will notice that there are mentions of the word "Republican," but I did not want it in red; I did not want it as the lead line that people would see because it was too overtly partisan. Part of my job is to teach subtlety. I may not be a subtle person—I'm pretty loud and outspoken—but so often subtlety, the quiet voice, actually communicates.

"We listen to your concerns, and we hear you loud and clear." [The contract] is responsive. That's what the public was looking for back in 1994: a politician who was responsive and responding to them. And all of this language was all tested to make sure it would be effective. The whole document is filled with listening, with responsiveness, with accountability.

Who hired you?

The Republican National Committee hired me, and they hired me because they wanted someone who could look members straight in the eye and tell them the truth. There's a problem with political polling in that you have so much pressure to do what your client wants you to do and say what your client wants you to say. I've never felt that pressure. I am independent of the political parties. I came up outside that structure so that I could tell these members: "This document is going to work. People are going to believe you." And they would believe me because they knew that I was not making money from it.

You must admit that language can cloud as well as clarify. 30

If it doesn't describe what it's selling, then it is a very poor descriptor. If you've got a bad product, you shouldn't be selling it. And people like me have to have the discipline only to work for clients, corporations, political people, products, services, networks that we believe in and want to see succeed. I don't believe that good language can obscure a bad product.

What about replacing "global warming" with "climate change?"

What is the difference? It is climate change. Some people call it global warming; some people call it climate change. What is the difference?

Look, for years, political people and lawyers—who, by the way, are the worst communicators—used the phrase "estate tax." And for years they couldn't eliminate it. The public wouldn't support it because the word "estate" sounds wealthy. Someone like me comes around and realizes that it's not an estate tax, it's a death tax, because you're taxed at death. And suddenly something that isn't viable achieves the support of 75 percent of the American people. It's the same tax, but nobody really knows what an estate is. But they certainly know what it means to be taxed when you die. I argue that is a clarification; that's not an obfuscation.

The language of America changed with the election of Bill Clinton, because with all due respect to my friends on the Republican side, Bill Clinton is the best communicator of the last 50 years. He felt your pain. Now, I'd argue that he caused your pain, but at least he felt it while he was causing it. When Bill Clinton spoke, his words were so good, and they were spoken with such passion. And that biting of the lower lip and the squinching of the eyes—you just couldn't turn away. Bill Clinton made Frank Luntz because Bill Clinton discovered the power and the influence of words. Now, I'd like to think that I apply them to clients, to philosophies, to products and services and corporations that I believe in, that are good. I don't argue with you that words can sometimes be used to confuse, but it's up to the practitioners of the study of language to apply them for good and not for evil. It is just like fire; fire can heat your house or burn it down.

There are words that work, that are meant to explain and educate on policies that work, on products that work, on services that work. I'm not going to ever try to sell a lemon. I don't do that. I work for pharmaceutical companies because my dad was kept alive for a long time on medications thanks to companies like Pfizer. I work for a company like Federal Express because it allows me to get my packages there the next morning. It's a wonderful, innovative corporation. I work for a company like Merrill Lynch because I believe in the financial services and the quality of the product.

I believe in the people who work at the corporations that I work for, and the political people. The best example is Rudy Giuliani. What have I done that's wrong if I provide someone like a Rudy Giuliani or a corporation like a Pfizer language that helps them explain or educate? I've simplified the process for them which allows them to explain. What did they say in there [in the focus group]? They kept coming back to it again and again: What they want from their elected officials, from the CEOs, from the elite of America is clarity. They said it again and again: "Be clear with us. Be straight with us. Common sense; clarity; down the road, look us straight in the eye." That's exactly what I do. I help them do that.

Talk to me about the Healthy Forests Initiative of President Bush. Isn't calling it "Healthy Forests" obfuscating the fact that it entails keeping the forests healthy with widespread logging?

Yes, the Bush administration benefited from the phrase "healthy forest." But what do we know as a fact? If you allow this underbrush to subsume the forest, to get so thick that you can't walk through it, you can't get through it, if you don't touch a twig or a tree and you say, "Oh, let Mother Nature deal with it," then you get these catastrophic forest fires that we saw in Arizona, Colorado and in California. The Native Americans, they know how to thin a forest, and yes, they do take trees out, and what happens? A fire burns, and it stops right where that thinning process took place. But thanks to environmentalists who are extreme and radical in their approach, who say that we must not touch anything at any time in any way, we lose thousands, thousands, hundreds of thousands of acres of forests and all the wildlife that was inside it. And they don't come back again. It takes generations for it to regenerate. So don't tell me about language, because "healthy forests" actually is what it means. And you have to understand the policy, and you've got to understand the product if you want to be able to communicate it. You can't just approach it naively.

Is there a line you won't cross in the creative use of language? 40

You cannot lie ever, because a lie destroys the credibility of the product, and credibility is more important than anything. Credibility's even more important than clarity. They have to believe you before they will listen to you. So you can't lie. This is an interesting line, because in my own life, in some of the things I've worked for, I get angry. I am a proponent of the pharmaceutical industry. I believe in these heart medications and these anti-cancer drugs. I'm a supporter of a very famous medication right now, OxyContin, because I think that this is a miracle drug which allows people to get through the day. And this is a medication that some people want to see taken off the market. There are all sorts of lawsuits. I believe that there are things worth fighting for. I believe that there are things worth explaining and educating, even if it takes months or years. The only thing I don't believe in is lying. Beyond that, you can use almost anything. You can use emotion. It is acceptable to bring someone to tears if it explains to them in an emotional way why a product, a service, or a candidate is the right person, is the right thing to do.

Do facts matter?

Of course facts matter. And what we do—and you watched it here—is to give them accurate facts and see which facts matter. My point is that when you're talking issues like the environment, a straight recitation of facts is going to fall on deaf ears, and that industry has been very ineffective. Even by using that word "industry," people think of smokestacks. So often corporate America, business America, are the worst communicators because all they understand are facts, and they cannot tell a story. They know how to explain their quarterly results, but they don't know how to explain what they mean.

I don't understand why people whose entire lives or their corporate success depends on communication, and yet they are led on occasion by CEOs who cannot talk their way out of a paper bag and don't care to. I know some CEOs who are outstanding communicators, and those individuals have a much better time with shareholders, have a much better time with the media, and, most importantly, with their consumers and the general public, because they know how to explain the benefits; they know how to put things in context. But there are so many CEOs that only know how to talk about numbers. Numbers don't mean anything. You talk about billions and tax procedures and all sorts of acronyms, and the only people who understand that are government bureaucrats and accountants. Americans don't want to hear the language of accountants; they want to hear the language of teachers and social workers.

Do you think Republicans do this better than Democrats? 45

That is brand new. When I started in this business, everybody said the Democrats were the better communicators because they sounded like social workers, and

Republicans were awful because they sounded like morticians. In some cases. they actually dressed like morticians. That has changed over the last 10 years. Bill Clinton brought the change in the Democratic Party, and George W. Bush brought a significant change in the Republican Party: that it was not enough to have a superior policy, or it was not enough to have all the facts at your fingertips; it became essential that you be able to communicate that on a one-to-one basis, as individuals on a personal level rather than a philosophical or ideological level.

There are people still in the Republican Party that I believe practice the communication of anger, of disappointment, of regret, of pain, of sorrow, of suffering. That's not what the American people want to hear. For 20 years, the Democrats were effective at the communication of hope and things that are positive. I asked Republicans at one point to do this little test, to turn down the television set in a debate between Republicans and Democrats, just look at the two individuals—which one would you want to hang out with? Which one would you want to have a beer with? Which one would you want as your uncle, or who would you want to hang out with at Thanksgiving? For years the Democratic candidate was the one that smiled; the Republican candidate was the one that was angry. Now, there are always exceptions to this, and I'm sure you can come up with 10 of them. But basically, Republicans practiced the politics of anger, and Democrats practiced the politics of hope. And all that began to change in 1994, and it finally came to fruition in 2000. And now it's the Democrats who are angry and the Republicans who are hopeful.

Who else were the visionaries?

The change in Republican language began with Newt Gingrich in 1994, and while much of his communication still came across as angry and partisan, when Newt was speaking about policy and not talking about those who opposed him, there was none better, and there has been none better. Newt Gingrich had the ability to explain a very complicated process in very clear-cut, common-sense ways, unlike anyone I've ever seen. He explained the difference between taxing and spending. He explained the difference between investment and savings. He explained the difference between a weak foreign policy and a strong one. This is a guy who knew how to articulate a philosophical point of view in a way that just made sense. And if it wasn't coming from Newt Gingrich, you believed it; you absolutely supported it. The problem with Gingrich was he was too angry in some of his communication.

So what we needed was someone with that level of explanatory ability with a gentle heart and a gentle soul, and that's where George W. Bush came in. The Bush that we know now is not the Bush that ran for election in 2000. The one who ran in 2000 talked about education; talked about Social Security; talked about a kinder, gentler conservatism; talked about an inclusive conservatism. And it's exactly what the public wanted.

And you compare that with Al Gore. The Democrats became the party of the cold and the aloof. And in 2004, you look at Howard Dean and John Kerry and to a lesser extent Dick Gephardt; the Democratic Party is now the party of anger. I know that this is what happens when you're an opposition party, but that's not what Republicans did in 1994 or 2000. In '94 they offered a "contract." They offered something positive, and people voted for it. And in 2000 they offered a change, an alternative to Bill Clinton; people voted for it. George Bush attacked Al Gore a lot less than Gore attacked Bush. And now in 2004 the Democrats are making the same mistakes. We don't want our messages screamed at us. We don't want to be yelled at.

How important is keeping the consistency of the message in political language?

The advantage of working for a corporation is that it has only one message, because a product or a service doesn't speak; it's just there, and you can advertise it. The challenge in working in politics, particularly if you're working for a political party, is that everyone's a messenger. I think the best example of this, frankly, is Israel, where you can have 20 members of the Cabinet, and they've got 68 messages between them, because among the 20, all of them think that they're prime minister or will be prime minister or should be prime minister or hate the person who is prime minister. And when you have all these people saying things in a different way, nobody hears anything.

I've got a certain rule that I always teach my staff: It's not what you say; it's what people hear that matters. I may respond to you effectively, but if you edit it in such a way that they only hear the negativity of what I do, then that's all they're going to know. And so they're going to conclude that my profession isn't an honorable profession. And that's why how I say it has as much of an impact on what people think of me as what I say.

55 [Regarding consistency,] there's a simple rule: You say it again, and you say it again, and you say it again, and you say it again, and you say it again, and then again and again and again and again, and about the time that you're absolutely sick of saying it is about the time that your target audience has heard it for the first time. And it is so hard, but you've just got to keep repeating, because we hear so many different things—the noises from outside, the sounds, all the things that are coming into our head, the 200 cable channels and the satellite versus cable, and what we hear from our friends. We as Americans and as humans have very selective hearing and very selective memory. We only hear what we want to hear and disregard the rest.

Republicans use think tanks to come up with a lot of their messages.

The think tanks are the single worst, most undisciplined example of communication I've ever seen. Cato [Institute] still calls it the "privatization of Social Security." Heritage [Foundation] did so until a couple of years ago. Every time you use the words "privatization" and "Social Security" in the same sentence, you frighten seniors, and more of them turn against you. This is a specific and perfect example of the intellectual goo-goo heads who are more interested in policy than they were in success. Changing the word from "privatize" to "personalize," which is the work that we had done, they wouldn't accept it, because to them it was selling an idea short.

They would rather communicate their way and lose the issue than communicate in a sensible way and win. The fact is, ideology and communication more often than not run into each other rather than complement each other. Principle and communication work together. Ideology and communication often work apart.

Tell me about your work for Rudy Giuliani.

Rudy Giuliani hired me because I was recommended by his political consultant 60
and because I love baseball. I hate to admit this, but I brought my baseball card collection to show him, because I'd heard he was a fanatic Yankee fan, and I figured this would be a way that we could bond. We ended up talking for 22 minutes. My whole interview with Rudy Giuliani in 1993 lasted for 22 minutes, and at least 19 of the 22 minutes was focused on baseball. So I don't know if he got it right or wrong; all I know is that this was a guy who understood the value of words and understood the value of language, but even more than that, it's the power of personality. You know, you have asked me what matters in research and how do you apply different components. What matters most in politics is personality. It's not issues; it's not image. It's who you are and what you represent. And this guy, from the very beginning of his administration, even if people disagreed with what he was doing, they trusted him to do it, and even if they didn't like him, they respected him.

My job as a pollster is to understand what really matters. Those levers of importance—sometimes they're called levers; sometimes they're called triggers. What causes people to buy a product? What causes someone to pull a lever and get them to vote? I need to know the specifics of that. And in politics, more often than not, it's about the personality and the character of the individual rather than where they stand, and that's exactly the opposite of what your viewers will think.

Did you help him?

Part of the task is using language and using speeches and using photo ops and using the power of campaign to convey a specific message. And my job in '93 and '97 was to explain to the campaign what the public wanted and to help explain to the public that that's exactly what he was offering. A pollster, a marketer, someone who is the explainer of public opinion, has the ability to inform somebody like Rudy Giuliani [of] what really matters to the public, and so that makes Rudy Giuliani an even better candidate.

Can you talk about how you've applied your approach to the use of language to corporate America?

I've done reasonably well over the last 10 years because I took the strategy of lan- 65
guage and politics and applied it to the corporate world, which has never been done before. Up to this point, the only people who ever communicated were those little 30-second characters, the little Alka-Seltzer guy or the StaPuf, whatever his name is.

And were your ideas well received in corporate America?

Oh, you have no idea. I am amazed at how eager the CEOs of the biggest companies are today to communicate as effectively as possible, to employ the skills and the language of what you saw right here earlier. They want to know that they can talk to a shareholder one-on-one, not just through their head but also through their heart. They want to know that they can reach their consumer not just on an intellectual basis, but on an emotional basis. In fact, I'd argue that CEOs, with all the corporate scandals that have taken place, are more interested in effective communication than even political people, because corporate people are interested in the bottom line, and so for them good words, good phrases, good presentation matter more than anything.

If we're getting information from 200 cable channels, if we're talking to 200 people a day, there are so many different messages that are cluttering our heads. It's the same way in corporate America. If a CEO speaks and no one hears it, it doesn't matter. And so they're looking for people like me to help them cut through the clutter, to help them explain and educate why their product or their service or their company is better. And the challenge for CEOs is that they generally came up through the ranks by being good numbers people. And I have seen 99 out of 100 cases, if you're a good numbers person, you're a bad language person.

What kind of reception do you get from their marketing departments?

There are two people that tend to beat up on me. One are the ideologues, particularly in the far left or the far right, who don't want to communicate to everybody; they don't want to be loved; they don't even want to be respected. They want to say it their own way, and they don't like people like me who challenge the way they communicate their policies, their platforms or their principles. The other people who beat me up are the market research people in some of these big companies, because they don't understand language.

The problem with the job and the service that I provide is that I have to be involved in it. I can't write a memo from somebody else's focus group. I can't do this from traditional polling of 1,000 people on the telephone. I have to be able to hear it. Traditional market researchers are cold and calculating and scientific. In this business of language, you have to have a heart, and you have to have emotion, and you have to be willing to become what you are studying, no matter what it puts you through.

So the main point is emotion.

It's all emotion. But there's nothing wrong with emotion. When we are in love, we are not rational; we are emotional. When we are on vacation, we are not rational; we are emotional. When we are happy, we are not [rational]. In fact, in more cases than not, when we are rational, we're actually unhappy. Emotion is good; passion is good. Being into what we're into, provided that it's a healthy pursuit, it's a good thing.

But if emotion is the main point, why go for the words?

Because the words provide the emotions.

Words are keys to the emotions?

Yeah. You call it keys, but my job is to look for the words that trigger the emotion. Words alone can be found in a dictionary or a telephone book, but words with emotion can change destiny, can change life as we know it. We know it has changed history; we know it has changed behavior; we know that it can start a war or stop it. We know that words and emotion together are the most powerful force known to mankind.

What new directions do you see for market research like yours?

Part of what market research and the understanding of language that has not been exploited sufficiently is actually in the courtroom. There are jury consultants and there are message consultants for trials, but not to the degree that it's been applied to politics and the corporate world. This is where people are going next, and frankly, this is where I'm going next. There's a lot of money with a lot of big law firms that have a tremendous amount at stake by getting the right language to convince the right jury that my client is either innocent or that the opposition is guilty.

THINGS TO DO WITH THE READING

1. Another of "the persuaders" interviewed in the PBS series from which this interview was taken commented that the influx of marketing and advertising into politics has created an environment in which "the principle of democracy yields to the practice of demography." How would you paraphrase that remark? (See Paraphrase × 3, pages 116–117.) And how would Luntz respond to that charge? As you think about this question, review Borick's discussion at the beginning of "On Political Labels" on Madisonian versus Jeffersonian views on democracy. Whose point of view is Luntz closer to and so what? (See page 32 on the "So what?" question.)

2. If you were to do the Method (see pages 44–49) on Luntz's interview, you would undoubtedly discover repetitions of such terms as *the heart*, *emotion*, and *passion*, which comprise a strand we might label "Emotion" (including as well *enthusiasm*, *empathy*, *feeling*, etc.) and which constitute half of an organizing contrast opposed to what Luntz names "Intellect" (see paragraph 8, "80 percent of our life is emotion, and only 20 percent is intellect").

   How do you account for the emphasis Luntz places on emotion? How does the language of emotion figure in the way that Luntz thinks about politics, and more, about winning in the political arena? What, in short, is the logic of his argument about emotion?

3. **Link:** Chinni cites David W. Moore, author of a book called *The Super Pollsters*, saying that "Luntz's work and that of other celebrity pollsters, such as Fitzpatrick, is nothing more than 'propaganda' masked as research" (see Chinni, paragraph 22). This suggests that Luntz's practices and the current debate about the framing wars could be usefully informed by existing rhetorical studies of propaganda—whether or not one decides to agree with Moore that Luntz is primarily a propagandist. Look up any of the items in the following list of standard propaganda methods and consider the extent to which Luntz's way of talking, as represented by this interview, reveals him as inclined toward propaganda techniques: name-calling, glittering generalities, bandwagon, transfer or association, testimonial, red herring, card-stacking, "plain folks," and slanted word.

   Note: Negotiating websites that deal with propaganda definitions is itself very interesting from the point of view of the politics of language and the language of politics. Google the phrase "propaganda devices" and then make sure to track the pages back to their sources. See the discussion of finding quality websites by librarian Kelly Cannon starting on page 326 for advice on how to backtrack.

4. Luntz's self-described practice—"figuring out which words, which phrases to apply at which opportunities, which times" (see paragraph 17)—locates him as a rhetorician, or, as Luntz calls himself, "a communicator." And so it should prove revealing to look at Luntz's rhetoric in the PBS interview with him.

   You will notice, for example, that Luntz is fond of certain forms of repetition, especially the one that rhetoricians call *anaphora*. Here is an example of anaphora in a sentence of Luntz's (about ex-New York mayor, Rudy Giuliani, cited by Chinni in "Why Should We Trust this Man?": "He beat crime, he beat drugs, he beat unemployment, he beat welfare, he beat trash in the streets, he beat the squeegee guy" (see Chinni, paragraph 3). For another example, check out the American Rhetoric website linked to the site for this book, www.thomsonedu.com/english/rosenwasser. (Note: This is part of an excellent glossary of rhetorical figures with audio clips.)

   Find as many examples as you can of this rhetorical figure of anaphora in the Luntz interview and come up with a total count. Consider, for example, Luntz's repetition of "to understand" in paragraph 10 and repetition of the phrase "that work" in paragraph 36. How does Luntz's attraction to this rhetorical figure fit with his way of thinking on how people make up their minds?

5. Toward the end of the interview, in response to a question about working for Rudy Giuliani, Luntz says, "What matters most in politics is personality. It's not the issues; it's not image. It's who you are and what

you represent" (see paragraph 60). Rhetoricians study the role that a speaker's character plays in his or her ability to persuade others under the category "ethos," a word that comes from the Greek for "character, a person's nature or disposition" (*OED*). (See page 246 for a fuller discussion of ethos.)

Track what we might call the "ethos strand" in the Luntz interview, noting places where Luntz seems to be supplying language or information (especially biographical information) designed to win readers and listeners through winning their support for his character and personality. Consider, for example, what Luntz says in response to the question "Who hired you?" (see paragraph 29). See also the personal information he offers when explaining why he works for pharmaceutical companies (see paragraph 41). What kind of ethos is Luntz trying to establish? What possible criticisms of Luntz might this ethos help him to deflect? Given that Luntz has a PhD in political science from Oxford, why do you think he refers to intellectuals as "goo-goo heads" in his response to a question about Republican think tanks?

6. **Link:** See question 2 above. Along these lines, note that in his essay, "On Political Labels," Christopher Borick overtly converses with the positions that Luntz has adopted. (See paragraphs 1, 31, and 34 of Borick's essay.) How does Borick view Luntz, and how might Luntz respond to Borick's remarks? You might also find it useful to consider Borick's discussion of the term "compassionate conservatives" in paragraph 21. As you write about this intersection of viewpoints, "find your own role in the conversation," as that activity is discussed on pages 306–307 of Chapter 12.

7. **Link:** Put Orwell's arguments in "Politics and the English Language" into conversation with Luntz's arguments. Consider, for example, what Orwell might say to Luntz on Luntz's assertion, "I don't believe that good language can obscure a bad product."

   Luntz does not here define what he means by "good language," but elsewhere in the piece he talks about using "traditional, simple, clear-cut words of the English language." He says that what Americans want is clarity: "Be clear with us. Be straight with us." He also says that his job is "to look for the words that trigger emotion." Presumably, Orwell would agree with these criteria for good language because he is opposed to language that hides its real intent and that seeks to soften people's response to what is being talked about—the brutality of war, for example. But Orwell also speaks of language "as an instrument for expressing and not for concealing or preventing thought." Luntz says that changing the phrase "estate tax" to "death tax" is a clarification and does not obscure. Would Orwell agree with Luntz that this change is a clarification and that it does not, in Orwell's terms, conceal and prevent thought? Why or why not?

8. **Application:** Click on the link to the Luntzspeak website at www.thomsonedu.com/english/rosenwasser.

   Then locate some political language anywhere on the web or in the newspapers and subject it to the same kind of translation. What is the politician "really" saying? How might this be translated, without the euphemism? Perform your own decodings. ◗

Matt Bai

The Framing Wars

This article, originally a cover story of the *New York Times Magazine*, focuses on the Democrats' answer to the Republicans' Frank Luntz, the linguist George Lakoff, a professor at the University of California, Berkeley, who specializes in metaphor. Political reporter Matt Bai offers an analysis of how the Democrats have regrouped since the defeat of John Kerry by attempting to construct a more coherent party narrative and stick to it with reinforced party discipline.

After last November's defeat, Democrats were like aviation investigators sifting through twisted metal in a cornfield, struggling to posit theories about the disaster all around them. Some put the onus on John Kerry, saying he had never found an easily discernable message. Others, including Kerry himself, wrote off the defeat to the unshakable realities of wartime, when voters were supposedly less inclined to jettison a sitting president. Liberal activists blamed mushy centrists. Mushy centrists blamed Michael Moore. As the weeks passed, however, at Washington dinner parties and in public post-mortems, one explanation took hold not just among Washington insiders but among far-flung contributors, activists and bloggers too: the problem wasn't the substance of the party's agenda or its messenger as much as it was the Democrats' inability to communicate coherently. They had allowed Republicans to control the language of the debate, and that had been their undoing. 1

Even in their weakened state, Democrats resolved not to let it happen again. And improbably, given their post-election gloom, they managed twice in the months that followed to make good on that pledge. The first instance was the skirmish over the plan that the president called Social Security reform and that everybody else, by spring, was calling a legislative disaster. The second test for Democrats was their defense of the filibuster (the time-honored stalling tactic that prevents the majority in the Senate from ending debate), which seemed at the start a hopeless cause but ended in an unlikely stalemate. These victories weren't easy to account for, coming as they did at a time when Republicans seem to own just about everything in Washington but the first-place Nationals. (And they're working on that.) During the first four years of the Bush administration, after all, Democrats had railed just as loudly against giveaways to the wealthy and energy lobbyists, and all they had gotten for their trouble were more tax cuts and more drilling. Something had changed in Washington—but what?

Democrats thought they knew the answer. Even before the election, a new political word had begun to take hold of the party, beginning on the West Coast and spreading like a virus all the way to the inner offices of the Capitol. That word was "framing." Exactly what it means to "frame" issues seems to depend on which Democrat you are talking to, but everyone agrees that it has to do with choosing the language to define a debate and, more important, with fitting individual issues into the contexts of broader story lines. In the months after the election, Democratic consultants and elected officials came to sound like creative-writing teachers, holding forth on the importance of metaphor and narrative.

Republicans, of course, were the ones who had always excelled at framing controversial issues, having invented and popularized loaded phrases like "tax relief" and "partial-birth abortion" and having achieved a kind of Pravda-esque discipline for disseminating them. But now Democrats said that they had learned to fight back. "The Democrats have finally reached a level of outrage with what Republicans were doing to them with language," Geoff Garin, a leading Democratic pollster, told me in May.

In January, Geoff Garin conducted a confidential poll on judicial nominations, 5
paid for by a coalition of liberal advocacy groups. He was looking for a story—a frame—for the filibuster that would persuade voters that it should be preserved, and he tested four possible narratives. Democratic politicians assumed that voters saw the filibuster fight primarily as a campaign to stop radically conservative judges, as they themselves did. But to their surprise, Garin found that making the case on ideological grounds—that is, that the filibuster prevented the appointment of judges who would roll back civil rights—was the least effective approach. When, however, you told voters that the filibuster had been around for over 200 years, that Republicans were "changing rules in the middle of the game" and dismantling the "checks and balances" that protected us against one-party rule, almost half the voters strongly agreed, and 7 out of 10 were basically persuaded. It became, for them, an issue of fairness.

Garin then convened focus groups and listened for clues about how to make this case. He heard voters call the majority party "arrogant." They said they feared "abuse of power." This phrase struck Garin. He realized many people had already developed deep suspicions about Republicans in Washington. Garin shared his polling with a group of Democratic senators that included Harry Reid, the minority leader. Reid, in turn, assigned Stephanie Cutter, who was Kerry's spokeswoman last year, to put together a campaign-style "war room" on the filibuster. Cutter set up a strategy group, which included senior Senate aides, Garin, the pollster Mark Mellman and Jim Margolis, one of the party's top ad makers. She used Garin's research to create a series of talking points intended to cast the filibuster as an American birthright every bit as central to the Republic as Fourth of July fireworks. The talking points began like this: "Republicans are waging an unprecedented power grab. They are changing the rules in the middle of the game and attacking our historic system of checks and balances." They concluded, "Democrats are committed to fighting this abuse of power."

Cutter's war room began churning out mountains of news releases hammering daily at the G.O.P.'s "abuse of power." In an unusual show of discipline, Democrats in the Senate and House carried laminated, pocket-size message cards—"DEMOCRATS FIGHTING FOR DEMOCRACY, AGAINST ABUSE OF POWER," blared the headline at the top—with the talking points on one side and some helpful factoids about Bush's nominees on the other. During an appearance on "This Week With George Stephanopoulos" in April, Senator Charles Schumer of New York needed all of 30 seconds to invoke the "abuse of power" theme—twice.

By the time Reid took to the airwaves in late May, on the eve of what looked to be a final showdown on the filibuster ("This abuse of power is not what our founders intended," he told the camera solemnly), the issue seemed pretty well defined in the public mind. In a typical poll conducted by Time magazine, 59 percent of voters said they thought the G.O.P. should be stopped from eliminating the filibuster.

Perhaps feeling the pressure, a group of seven Republicans joined with seven Democrats in a last-minute compromise. Bill Frist, the Senate majority leader, and his team, smarting from crucial defections, had no choice but to back down from a vote. The truce meant that several of Bush's judges would be confirmed quickly, but it marked a rare retreat for Republicans and infuriated conservative activists, who knew that a Supreme Court battle would now be messier than they had hoped.

For their part, Democrats were euphoric at having played the G.O.P. to a 10
draw. The facts of the filibuster fight hadn't necessarily favored them; in reality, the constitutional principle of "checks and balances" on which the Democrats' case was based refers to the three branches of government, not to some parliamentary procedure, and it was actually the Democrats who had broken with Senate tradition by using the filibuster to block an entire slate of judges. ("An irrelevancy beyond the pay grade of the American voter," Garin retorted when I pointed this out.) And yet it was their theory of the case, and not the Republicans', that had won the argument. As Garin explained it, Republicans had become ensnared in a faulty frame of their own making. The phrase "nuclear option"—a term Frist and his colleagues had tried gamely, but unsuccessfully, to lose—had made Dr. Frist sound more like Dr. Strangelove. "It's a very evocative phrase," Garin said. "It's blowing up the Senate. It's having your finger on the button."

Garin was gloating, but it was hard to blame him. On the eve of what promises to be a historic debate over the direction of the nation's highest court, Democrats on Capitol Hill seemed to have starkly reversed the dynamic of last fall's election. Then, they had watched helplessly as George W. Bush and his strategists methodically twisted John Kerry into a hopeless tangle of contradictions and equivocations, using words and imagery to bend him into a shape that hardly resembled the war hero he had been. Now, Democrats believed, they had deciphered the hieroglyphics of modern political debate that had so eluded them in the campaign, and in doing so they had exacted some small measure of revenge. As one of the party's senior Senate aides told me a few days after the filibuster compromise was reached, "We framed them the way they framed Kerry."

The father of framing is a man named George Lakoff, and his spectacular ascent over the last eight months in many ways tells the story of where Democrats have been since the election. A year ago, Lakoff was an obscure linguistics professor at Berkeley, renowned as one of the great, if controversial, minds in cognitive science but largely unknown outside of it. When he, like many liberals, became exasperated over the drift of the Kerry campaign last summer—"I went to bed angry every night," he told me—Lakoff decided to bang out a short book about politics and language, based on theories he had already published with academic presses, that could serve as a kind of handbook for Democratic activists. His agent couldn't find a publishing house that wanted it. Lakoff ended up more or less giving it away to Chelsea Green, a tiny liberal publisher in Vermont.

That book, "Don't Think of an Elephant!" is now in its eighth printing, having sold nearly 200,000 copies, first through liberal word of mouth and the blogosphere and then through reviews and the lecture circuit. (On the eve of last fall's election, I came across a Democratic volunteer in Ohio who was handing out a boxful of copies to her friends.) Lakoff has emerged as one of the country's most coveted speakers among liberal groups, up there with Howard Dean, who, as it happens, wrote the foreword to "Don't Think of an Elephant!" Lakoff has a DVD titled "How Democrats and Progressives Can Win: Solutions From George Lakoff," and he recently set up his own consulting company.

In the 1970's, Lakoff, verging into philosophy, became obsessed with metaphors. As he explained it to me one day over lunch at a Berkeley cafe, students of the mind, going back to Aristotle, had always viewed metaphor simply as a device of language, a facile way of making a point. Lakoff argued instead that metaphors were actually embedded in the recesses of the mind, giving the brain a way to process abstract ideas. In other words, a bad relationship reminds you on an unconscious level of a cul-de-sac, because both are leading nowhere. This results from what might be called a "love as journey" frame in the neural pathways of your brain—that is, you are more likely to relate to the story of, say, a breakup if it is described to you with the imagery of a journey. This might seem intuitive, but in 1980, when Lakoff wrote "Metaphors We Live By," it was considered fairly radical.

15 Through his work on metaphors, Lakoff found an avenue into political discourse. In a seminal 1996 book, "Moral Politics," he asserted that people relate to political ideologies, on an unconscious level, through the metaphorical frame of a family. Conservative politicians, Lakoff suggests, operate under the frame of a strict father, who lays down inflexible rules and imbues his family with a strong moral order. Liberals, on the other hand, are best understood through a frame of the nurturant parent, who teaches his child to pursue personal happiness and care for those around him. (The two models, Lakoff has said, are personified by Arnold Schwarzenegger on one side and Oprah Winfrey on the other.) Most voters, Lakoff suggests, carry some part of both parental frames in the synapses of their brains; which model is "activated"—that is, which they can better relate to—depends on the language that politicians use and the story that they tell.

The most compelling part of Lakoff's hypothesis is the notion that in order to reach voters, all the individual issues of a political debate must be tied together by some larger frame that feels familiar to us. Lakoff suggests that voters respond to grand metaphors—whether it is the metaphor of a strict father or something else entirely—as opposed to specific arguments, and that specific arguments only resonate if they reinforce some grander metaphor. The best evidence to support this idea can be found in the history of the 2004 presidential campaign. From Day 1, Republicans tagged Kerry with a larger metaphor: he was a flip-flopper, a Ted Kennedy-style liberal who tried to seem centrist, forever bouncing erratically from one position to the other. They made sure that virtually every comment they uttered about Kerry during the campaign reminded voters, subtly or not, of this one central theme. (The smartest ad of the campaign may have been the one that showed Kerry windsurfing, expertly gliding back and forth, back and forth.) Democrats, on the other hand, presented a litany of different complaints about

Bush, depending on the day and the backdrop; he was a liar, a corporate stooge, a spoiled rich kid, a reckless warmonger. But they never managed to tie them all into a single, unifying image that voters could associate with the president. As a result, none of them stuck. Bush was attacked. Kerry was framed.

According to Lakoff, Republicans are skilled at using loaded language, along with constant repetition, to play into the frames in our unconscious minds. Take one of his favorite examples, the phrase "tax relief." It presumes, Lakoff points out, that we are being oppressed by taxes and that we need to be liberated from them. It fits into a familiar frame of persecution, and when such a phrase, repeated over time, enters the everyday lexicon, it biases the debate in favor of conservatives. If Democrats start to talk about their own "tax relief" plan, Lakoff says, they have conceded the point that taxes are somehow an unfair burden rather than making the case that they are an investment in the common good. The argument is lost before it begins.

Lakoff informed his political theories by studying the work of Frank Luntz, the Republican pollster who helped Newt Gingrich formulate the Contract With America in 1994. To Lakoff and his followers, Luntz is the very embodiment of Republican deception. His private memos, many of which fell into the hands of Democrats, explain why. In one recent memo, titled "The 14 Words Never to Use," Luntz urged conservatives to restrict themselves to phrases from what he calls, grandly, the "New American Lexicon." Thus, a smart Republican, in Luntz's view, never advocates "drilling for oil"; he prefers "exploring for energy." He should never criticize the "government," which cleans our streets and pays our firemen; he should attack "Washington," with its ceaseless thirst for taxes and regulations. "We should never use the word outsourcing," Luntz wrote, "because we will then be asked to defend or end the practice of allowing companies to ship American jobs overseas."

In Lakoff's view, not only does Luntz's language twist the facts of his agenda but it also renders facts meaningless by actually reprogramming, through long-term repetition, the neural networks inside our brains. And this is where Lakoff's vision gets a little disturbing. According to Lakoff, Democrats have been wrong to assume that people are rational actors who make their decisions based on facts; in reality, he says, cognitive science has proved that all of us are programmed to respond to the frames that have been embedded deep in our unconscious minds, and if the facts don't fit the frame, our brains simply reject them. Lakoff explained to me that the frames in our brains can be "activated" by the right combination of words and imagery, and only then, once the brain has been unlocked, can we process the facts being thrown at us.

This notion of "activating" unconscious thought sounded like something out 20
of "The Manchurian Candidate" ("Raymond, why don't you pass the time by playing a little solitaire?"), and I asked Lakoff if he was suggesting that Americans voted for conservatives because they had been brainwashed.

"Absolutely not," he answered, shaking his head.

But hadn't he just said that Republicans had somehow managed to rewire people's brains?

"That's true, but that's different from brainwashing, and it's a very important thing," he said. "Brainwashing has to do with physical control, capturing people and giving them messages over and over under conditions of physical deprivation or torture. What conservatives have done is not brainwashing in this way. They've done something that's perfectly legal. What they've done is find ways to set their frames into words over many years and have them repeated over and over again and have everybody say it the same way and get their journalists to repeat them, until they became part of normal English."

I asked Lakoff how he himself had avoided being reprogrammed by these stealth Republican words. "Because I'm a linguist, I recognize them," he said. Even to him, this sounded a little too neat, and a moment later he admitted that he, too, had fallen prey to conservative frames now and then. "Occasionally," he said with a shrug, "I've caught myself."

In May 2003, Senator Byron Dorgan, the North Dakota Democrat, read 25
"Moral Politics" and took Lakoff to a Democratic Senate retreat in Cambridge, Md. Lakoff had never met a senator before. "I knew what they were up against, even if they didn't know what they were up against," Lakoff says. "They were just besieged. My heart went out to them."

Lakoff gave a presentation, and in the parlance of comedians, he killed. Hillary Clinton invited him to dinner. Tom Daschle, then the minority leader, asked Lakoff if he would rejoin the senators a few days later, during their next caucus meeting at the Capitol, so that he could offer advice about the tax plan they were working on. Lakoff readily agreed, even though he had come East without so much as a jacket or tie. "I went in there, and it was just this beautiful thing," he told me, recalling the caucus meeting. "All these people I'd just met applauded. They gave me hugs. It was the most amazing thing."

Of course, the idea that language and narrative matter in politics shouldn't really have come as a revelation to Washington Democrats. Bill Clinton had been an intuitive master of framing. As far back as 1992, Clinton's image of Americans who "worked hard and played by the rules," for instance, had perfectly evoked the metaphor of society as a contest that relied on fairness. And yet despite this, Democrats in Congress were remarkably slow to grasp this dimension of political combat. Having ruled Capitol Hill pretty comfortably for most of the past 60 years, Democrats had never had much reason to think about calibrating their language in order to sell their ideas.

"I can describe, and I've always been able to describe, what Republicans stand for in eight words, and the eight words are lower taxes, less government, strong defense and family values," Dorgan, who runs the Democratic Policy Committee in the Senate, told me recently. "We Democrats, if you ask us about one piece of that, we can meander for 5 or 10 minutes in order to describe who we are and what we stand for. And frankly, it just doesn't compete very well. I'm not talking about the policies. I'm talking about the language."

Dorgan has become the caucus's chief proponent of framing theory. "I think getting some help from some people who really understand how to frame some of these issues is long overdue," he says, which is why he invited Lakoff back to talk to his colleagues after the 2004 election. Meanwhile, over on the House side, George Miller, a Democrat from the San Francisco area, met Lakoff through a contributor and offered to distribute copies of "Don't Think of an Elephant!" to every member of the caucus. The thin paperback became as ubiquitous among

Democrats in the Capitol as Mao's Little Red Book once was in the Forbidden City. "The framing was perfect for us, because we were just arriving in an unscientific way at what Lakoff was arriving at in a scientific way," says Representative Nancy Pelosi, the minority leader in the House.

30 In fact, though Lakoff started the framing discussion, he was by no means the only outside expert whom Democrats were consulting about language. To the contrary, a small industry had blossomed. Even before the 2004 election, Pelosi had enlisted John Cullinane, a software entrepreneur in Boston, to help the caucus develop the wording for a vision statement. Cullinane spent an hour and a half with members of the caucus one afternoon, while his aide scrawled suggestions on a white board. Among his recommendations was that they come up with a list that had six parts—either six principles or six values or six ideas. When we spoke, I asked Cullinane why it had to be six. "Seven's too many," he replied. "Five's too few."

Then there was Richard Yanowitch, a Silicon Valley executive and party donor, who worked with Senate Democrats, providing what he calls "private-sector type marketing." Last December, at Dorgan's request, Reid put Yanowitch in charge of a "messaging project" to help devise new language for the party. Another adviser who became a frequent guest on the Hill after the election was Jim Wallis, a left-leaning evangelical minister who wrote "God's Politics: Why the Right Gets It Wrong and the Left Doesn't Get it." In January, after addressing a Senate caucus retreat at the Kennedy Center, Wallis wrote a memo to the Democratic Policy Committee titled "Budgets Are Moral Documents," in which he laid out his argument that Democrats needed to "reframe" the budget in spiritual terms.

What all of these new advisers meant by "framing," exactly, and whether their concepts bore much resemblance to Lakoff's complex cognitive theories wasn't really clear. The word had quickly become something of a catchall, a handy term to describe anything having to do with changing the party's image through some new combination of language. So admired were these outside experts that they could hardly be counted as outsiders anymore. In May, for instance, Roger Altman, Clinton's former deputy treasury secretary, held a dinner for the former president to discuss the party's message with about 15 of its most elite and influential thinkers, including James Carville, Paul Begala, the pollster Mark J. Penn and John Podesta, president of the Center for American Progress, the liberal think tank. Lakoff sat at Clinton's table; Wallis, at the next one over.

Bush's plan to reform Social Security provided, last winter, the first test of the Democrats' new focus on language and narrative. In retrospect, it shows both the limits of framing and, perhaps, the real reason that Democrats have managed to stymie critical pieces of the Bush agenda.

Almost as soon as Bush signaled his intention to overhaul the existing program, Democrats in Congress, enamored of Lakoff's theories, embarked on a search for a compelling story line. Yanowitch's highly secretive messaging group met for months on the topic and came up with two "sample narratives" that Democrats might use. The first, titled "Privatization: A Gamble You Can't Afford to Take," stressed the insecurity of middle-class families and compared Bush's plan to a roll of the dice. The second, "The Magical World of Privatization," spun out a metaphor that centered on Bush as "an old-fashioned traveling salesman, with a cart full of magic elixirs and cure-all tonics." Some of this imagery found its way into the dialogue, for better or worse; Pelosi and other House members, never too proud to put their dignity above the greater good, held an outdoor news conference standing next to a stack of giant dice.

As they would later with the filibuster fight and with the Supreme Court, 35
Senate Democrats, under Reid's direction, set up a war room and a strategy group, this one run by Jim Messina, chief of staff for Senator Max Baucus of Montana. Eschewing all the lofty metaphors, the war room stuck to two simple ideas: Bush's plan relied on privatizing the most popular government benefit in America, and it amounted to benefit cuts coupled with long-term borrowing. In addition to keeping members focused on their talking points, Messina's team and its allies—led by two liberal interest groups, MoveOn.org and Campaign for America's Future, with help from the all-powerful AARP—also had to stop senators and congressmen from offering compromise plans that might drive a wedge into the caucus. In this way, Democrats had decided to follow the example of Bill Kristol, the Republican strategist who had urged his party (shrewdly, as it turned out) to refrain from proposing any alternatives to Clinton's doomed health-care plan in 1993. "The minute we introduce a plan, we have to solve the problem" is how one senior Democratic aide explained it to me. "We are the minority party. It's not our job to fix things."

As it happened, this was where Lakoff himself proved most helpful. In a meeting with House Democrats, some of whom were considering their own versions of private accounts, he urged them to hold firm against Bush's plan. "I pointed out that as soon as you allow them to get a privatization frame in people's minds about retirement and Social Security, it becomes an unintelligible difference," he recalled. "People will not be able to tell the difference between your plan and the other guy's." Referring to Pelosi, he added, "Nancy was saying the same thing, and so they stopped." As Democrats stood firm, Bush's idea for private accounts, which was never all that popular with voters to begin with, seemed to slowly lose altitude. A Gallup tracking poll conducted for CNN and USA Today showed the president's plan losing support, from 40 percent of voters in January to 33 percent in April.

Bush had tried to recast his proposed "private accounts" as "personal accounts" after it became clear to both sides that privatization, as a concept, frightened voters. But as they did on the filibuster, Democrats had managed to trap the president in his own linguistic box. "We branded them with privatization, and they can't sell that brand anywhere," Pelosi bragged when I spoke with her in May. "It's down to, like, 29 percent or something. At the beginning of this debate, voters were saying that the president was a *president* who had new ideas. Now he's a *guy* who wants to cut my benefits." At this, Pelosi laughed loudly.

What had Democrats learned about framing? In the end, the success of the Social Security effort—and, for that matter, the filibuster campaign—may have had something to do with language or metaphor, but it probably had more to do with the elusive virtue of party discipline. Pelosi explained it to me this way: for years, the party's leaders had tried to get restless Democrats to stay "on message," to stop freelancing their own rogue proposals and to continue reading from the designated talking points even after it got excruciatingly boring to do so. Consultants like Garin and Margolis had been saying the same thing, but Democratic congressmen, skeptical of the in-crowd of D.C. strategists, had begun to tune them out. "Listening to people inside Washington did not produce any victories," Pelosi said.

But now there were people from outside Washington—experts from the worlds of academia and Silicon Valley—who were making the same case. What the framing experts had been telling Democrats on the Hill, aside from all this arcane stuff about narratives and neural science, was that they needed to stay unified and repeat the same few words and phrases over and over again. And these "outsiders" had what Reid and Pelosi and their legion of highly paid consultants did not: the patina of scientific credibility. Culturally, this made perfect sense. If you wanted Republican lawmakers to buy into a program, you brought in a guy like Frank Luntz, an unapologetically partisan pollster who dressed like the head of the College Republicans. If you wanted Democrats to pay attention, who better to do the job than an egghead from Berkeley with an armful of impenetrable journal studies on the workings of the brain?

You might say that Lakoff and the others managed to give the old concept of 40
message discipline a new, more persuasive frame—and that frame was called "framing." "The framing validates what we're trying to say to them," Pelosi said. "You have a Berkeley professor saying, 'This is how the mind works; this is how people perceive language; this is how you have to be organized in your presentation.' It gives me much more leverage with my members."

On a recent morning in his Virginia office, seated next to one of those one-way glass walls that you find only in the offices of cops and pollsters, Frank Luntz explained why George Lakoff and his framing theory were leading the Democratic Party astray. In recent years, Luntz's penchant for publicity—he is a frequent commentator on cable television—has earned him no small amount of scorn and ridicule from fellow Republicans; that Lakoff's little book had suddenly elevated Luntz to a kind of mythic villain seemed to amuse him. "In some ways, the Democrats appreciate me more than the Republicans do," Luntz, 43, told me with a trace of self-pity.

The problem with Lakoff, Luntz said, is that the professor's ideology seemed to be driving his science. Luntz, after all, has never made for a terribly convincing conservative ideologue. (During our conversation, he volunteered that the man he admired most was the actor Peter Sellers, for his ability to disappear into whatever role he was given.) Luntz sees Lakoff, by contrast, as a doctrinaire liberal who believes viscerally that if Democrats are losing, it has to be because of the words they use rather than the substance of the argument they make. What Lakoff didn't realize, Luntz said, was that poll-tested phrases like "tax relief" were successful only because they reflected the values of voters to begin with; no one could sell ideas like higher taxes and more government to the American voter, no matter how they were framed. To prove it, Luntz, as part of his recent polling for the U.S. Chamber of Commerce, specifically tested some of Lakoff's proposed language on taxation. He said he found that even when voters were reminded of the government's need to invest in education, health care, national security and retirement security, 66 percent of them said the United States overtaxed its citizenry and only 14 percent said we were undertaxed. Luntz presented this data to chamber officials on a slide with the headline "George Lakoff Is Wrong!!"

"He deserves a lot of credit," Luntz said of Lakoff. "He's one of the very few guys who understands the limits of liberal language. What he doesn't understand is that there are also limits on liberal philosophy. They think that if they change all the words, it'll make a difference. Won't happen."

Luntz's dismissiveness is what you might expect to hear about Lakoff from a Republican, of course. But the same complaint has surfaced with growing ferocity among skeptical Democrats and in magazines like The Atlantic Monthly and The New Republic. An antiframing backlash has emerged, and while it is, on the surface, an argument about Lakoff and his theories, it is clearly also a debate about whether the party lacks only for language or whether it needs a fresher agenda. Lakoff's detractors say that it is he who resembles the traveling elixir salesman, peddling comforting answers at a time when desperate Democrats should be admitting some hard truths about their failure to generate new ideas. "Every election defeat has a charlatan, some guy who shows up and says, 'Hey, I marketed the lava lamp, and I can market Democratic politics,' " says Kenneth Baer, a former White House speechwriter who wrote an early article attacking Lakoff's ideas in The Washington Monthly. "At its most basic, it represents the Democratic desire to find a messiah."

In a devastating critique in The Atlantic's April issue, Marc Cooper, a contributing editor at The Nation, skillfully ridiculed Lakoff as the new progressive icon. "Much more than an offering of serious political strategy, 'Don't Think of an Elephant!' is a feel-good, self-help book for a stratum of despairing liberals who just can't believe how their common-sense message has been misunderstood by eternally deceived masses," Cooper wrote. In Lakoff's view, he continued, American voters are "redneck, chain-smoking, baby-slapping Christers desperately in need of some gender-free nurturing and political counseling by organic-gardening enthusiasts from Berkeley." 45

Lakoff doesn't have much patience for criticism (he's a tenured professor, after all), and he keeps at his disposal a seemingly bottomless arsenal of linguistic and philosophical theories with which to refute such attacks. In response to Cooper's article and another in The Atlantic, by Joshua Green, Lakoff fired off a nine-page draft response to a long e-mail list of friends and journalists in which he accused Cooper and Green of living in the "rationalist-materialist paradigm" (that's RAM for short), an outdated belief system that mistakenly assumes the rationality of other human beings. He also pointed out that they had cleverly, but unsuccessfully, tried to trap him in the "guru frame," a story line about one individual who passes himself off as having all the answers to other people's problems.

Lakoff has some valid points. In his writing, at least, he explains framing in a way that is more intellectually complex than his critics have admitted. His essential insight into politics—that voters make their decisions based on larger frames rather than on the sum of a candidate's positions—is hard to refute. And Lakoff does say in "Don't Think of an Elephant!" albeit very briefly, that Democrats need not just new language but also new thought; he told me the party suffers from "hypocognition," or a lack of ideas. What's more, when it comes to the language itself, Lakoff has repeatedly written that the process of reframing American political thought will take years, if not decades, to achieve. He does not suggest in his writing that a few catchy slogans can turn the political order on its head by the next election.

The message Lakoff's adherents seem to take away from their personal meetings with him, however, is decidedly more simplistic. When I asked Senator Richard Durbin of Illinois, the minority whip and one of Lakoff's strongest supporters, whether Lakoff had talked to the caucus about this void of new ideas in the party, Durbin didn't hesitate. "He doesn't ask us to change our views or change our philosophy," Durbin said. "He tells us that we have to recommunicate." In fact, Durbin said he now understood, as a result of Lakoff's work, that the Republicans have triumphed "by repackaging old ideas in all new wrapping," the implication being that this was not a war of ideas at all, but a contest of language.

The question here is whether Lakoff purposely twists his own academic theories to better suit his partisan audience or whether his followers are simply hearing what they want to hear and ignoring the rest. When I first met Lakoff in Los Angeles, he made it clear, without any prompting from me, that he was exasperated by the dumbing down of his intricate ideas. He had just been the main attraction at a dinner with Hollywood liberals, and he despaired that all they had wanted from him were quick fixes to long-term problems. "They all just want to know the magic words," he told me. "I say: 'You don't understand, there aren't any magic words. It's about ideas.' But all everyone wants to know is: 'What three words can we use? How do we win the next election?' They don't get it."

Peter Teague, who oversees environmental programs at the liberal Nathan 50
Cummings Foundation, was Lakoff's most important patron in the days after he wrote "Moral Politics." When I spoke with Teague about Lakoff a few months ago, he sounded a little depressed. "There's a cartoon version of Lakoff out there, and everyone's responding to the cartoon," Teague said. "It's not particularly useful. As much as we talk about having a real dialogue and a deeper discussion, we really end up having a very superficial conversation.

"I keep saying to George, 'You're reinforcing the very things you're fighting against.' "

I asked Lakoff, during an afternoon walk across the Berkeley campus, if he felt at all complicit in the superficiality that Teague was describing. "I do," he said thoughtfully. "It's a complicated problem. Of course it bothers me. But this is just Stage I, and there are stages of misunderstanding. People have to travel a path of understanding."

His celebrity may yet prove to be his undoing. When I visited him in Berkeley in April, Lakoff, who until then had done all his work with Washington Democrats on a volunteer basis, had submitted a proposal to leaders in the House for a consulting contract. Although the details were closely guarded, it had something to do with a project to use focus groups to study narrative. In May, House Democrats decided not to finalize the deal after some members and senior aides wondered out loud if Lakoff mania had gotten out of hand. Lakoff, it seemed, was experiencing a common Washington phenomenon to which Frank Luntz could easily relate: the more famous an adviser gets, the more politicians begin to suspect him of trying to further himself at their expense. A friend of Lakoff's suggested to me that we were witnessing the beginning of an all-too-familiar frame: the meteoric rise and dizzying fall of a political sensation.

If that were true, it seemed, then the whole notion of framing might just be a passing craze, like some post-election macarena. It certainly sounded like that might be the case when I visited Harry Reid just before Memorial Day. Reid waved away the suggestion that language had much to do with the party's recent successes. "If you want my honest opinion, and I know you do, I think people make too much out of that," he said. "I'm not a person who dwells on all these people getting together and spending hours and days coming up with the right words. I know that my staff thinks, 'Oh, why don't you tell him about all this great work we've done on framing?' But honestly, that's not it."

55 Reid credited the "team effort" and message discipline of the caucus for its victory on the filibuster issue. At one point, when I asked Reid, a former boxer, about Lakoff's theories, he seemed to equate them with psychotherapy. "I'm not going to waste a lot of time sitting in a room talking about how my parents weren't good to me or something like that," Reid said firmly. "I'm not involved in any of that gimmickry."

After leaving Reid, I walked across the Capitol to see Nancy Pelosi, who told a different story. She assured me that Lakoff's ideas had "forever changed" the way Democratic House members thought about politics. "He has taken people here to a place, whether you agree or disagree with his particular frame, where they know there has to be a frame," she told me. "They all agree without any question that you don't speak on Republican terms. You don't think of an elephant."

I suggested that maybe she and Reid had different views on the value of framing as a strategy. "Oh, no," she said emphatically, drawing out the last word. "He's been a leader on it! The two of us know better than anyone what's at stake here. In fact, he sort of initiated our abuse-of-power frame."

It was hard to know what to make of these conflicting conversations. Perhaps Reid feared that if he admitted to caring about framing, he would be framed as one of those clueless Democrats seeking easy answers. Perhaps Pelosi was covering for him by suggesting they were unified when in fact they weren't. But it seemed more likely that the disconnect between the party's two elected leaders reflected a broader confusion among Democrats about what they actually mean by framing. There is no doubt that having a central theme and repeating it like robots has made Democrats a respectable opposition force in Congress. To Pelosi and a lot of other Democrats, that is the miracle of this thing called framing. To Reid, it is just an intuitive part of politics, and he doesn't need some professor to give it a name or tell him that Democrats haven't been very good at it.

Whatever you call it, this kind of message discipline will be a crucial piece of what will most likely become, in the weeks ahead, a Democratic push to block Bush's designs on the Supreme Court. In order to stop a nominee, Democrats will have to frame the filibuster battle in the public arena all over again, and this time, they will have to convince voters that it is Bush's specific choice for the nation's highest court—and not simply a slate of faceless judges—who represents the reckless arrogance of Republican rule. Even in the hours after

O'Connor made her announcement, you could see in Democratic responses the first stirrings of this new campaign. "If the president abuses his power and nominates someone who threatens to roll back the rights and freedoms of the American people," said Ted Kennedy, lifting lines directly from Garin's latest polling memo, "then the American people will insist that we oppose that nominee, and we intend to do so." Meanwhile, Susan McCue, Reid's powerful chief of staff, offered me a preview of the theory to come: "It goes beyond 'abuse of power.' It's about arrogance, irresponsibility, being out of touch and catering to a narrow, narrow slice of their ideological constituency at the expense of the vast majority of Americans."

It is not inconceivable that such an argument could sway public opinion; 60
Americans are congenitally disposed to distrust whichever party holds power. The larger question—too large, perhaps, for most Democrats to want to consider at the moment—is whether they can do more with language and narrative than simply snipe at Bush's latest initiative or sink his nominees. Here, the Republican example may be instructive. In 1994, Republican lawmakers, having heeded Bill Kristol's advice and refused to engage in the health-care debate, found themselves in a position similar to where Democrats are now; they had weakened the president and spiked his trademark proposal, and they knew from Luntz's polling that the public harbored serious reservations about the Democratic majority in Congress. What they did next changed the course of American politics. Rather than continue merely to deflect Clinton's agenda, Republicans came up with their own, the Contract With America, which promised 10 major legislative acts that were, at the time, quite provocative. They included reforming welfare, slashing budget deficits, imposing harsher criminal penalties and cutting taxes on small businesses. Those 10 items, taken as a whole, encapsulated a rigid conservative philosophy that had been taking shape for 30 years—and that would define politics at the end of the 20th century.

By contrast, consider the declaration that House Democrats produced after their session with John Cullinane, the branding expert, last fall. The pamphlet is titled "The House Democrats' New Partnership for America's Future: Six Core Values for a Strong and Secure Middle Class." Under each of the six values—"prosperity, national security, fairness, opportunity, community and accountability"—is a wish list of vague notions and familiar policy ideas. ("Make health care affordable for every American," "Invest in a fully funded education system that gives every child the skills to succeed" and so on.) Pelosi is proud of the document, which—to be fair—she notes is just a first step toward repackaging the party's agenda. But if you had to pick an unconscious metaphor to attach to it, it would probably be a cotton ball.

Consider, too, George Lakoff's own answer to the Republican mantra. He sums up the Republican message as "strong defense, free markets, lower taxes, smaller government and family values," and in "Don't Think of an Elephant!" he proposes some Democratic alternatives: "Stronger America, broad prosperity, better future, effective government and mutual responsibility." Look at the differences between the two. The Republican version is an argument, a series of philosophical assertions that require voters to make concrete choices about the direction of the country. Should we spend more or less on the military? Should government regulate industry or leave it unfettered? Lakoff's formulation, on the other hand, amounts to a vague collection of the least objectionable ideas in American life. Who out there wants to make the case against prosperity and a better future? Who doesn't want an effective government?

What all these middling generalities suggest, perhaps, is that Democrats are still unwilling to put their more concrete convictions about the country into words, either because they don't know what those convictions are or because they lack confidence in the notion that voters can be persuaded to embrace them. Either way, this is where the power of language meets its outer limit. The right words can frame an argument, but they will never stand in its place.

Matt Bai, a contributing writer, covers national politics for the magazine. He is working on a book about the future of the Democrats.

THINGS TO DO WITH THE READING

1. Apply the heuristic "Looking for Difference within Similarity" (pages 158–159) to a comparison of George Lakoff and Frank Luntz. Aside from being resident language gurus for their respective parties, what do the two have in common? What assumptions about political language do they share? Then, crucially, what are the most significant differences between them, and so what? (See pages 32–33 on asking "So what?")
2. In the questions following the Luntz interview, we noted the strand of "emotion" words in Luntz's language, suggesting that this orientation was a revealing (and complicating) aspect of his approach. What is the status of emotion (and similar words) in Lakoff's program? Luntz opposes the emotional to the intellectual: what is Lakoff's position on this binary? And how does he value each side of it?
3. **Link:** Lakoff argues that people tend to think about political ideologies in terms of what he calls "the metaphorical frame of a family": "Conservative politicians, Lakoff suggests, operate under the frame of a strict father, who lays down inflexible rules and imbues his family with a strong moral order. Liberals, on the other hand, are best understood through a frame of the nurturant parent, who teaches his child to pursue personal happiness and care for those around him" (see paragraph 15). What links do you see between these two parental metaphors (and the terms associated with each of them) and the way that Christopher Borick characterizes conservatism and liberalism in "On Political Labels"? How, for example, might the histories of the two parties, as traced by Borick, have inclined them toward these roles?

   Note: Language in the Application question that follows provides further key terms for considering these parental metaphorical frames in light of liberal and conservative values as defined by Borick.
4. **Application:** Use the language of "The Framing Wars" to interpret any political conflict or campaign in your immediate environment. Bai defines framing as having "to do with choosing the language to define a debate

and, more important, with fitting individual issues into the contexts of broader story lines" (see paragraph 3). Locate some "individual issue" in your town or on your campus within the story lines implicit in Lakoff's parenting metaphors. (The front page of college newspapers customarily teems with such issues.) In what ways does one side of the issue or campaign resemble the strict father who, in the words of columnist Michael Erard "protects moral dependents, punishes moral inferiors, and aims to raise independent children to fend for themselves in a dangerous world"? Where do you see the other side resembling "the nurturing parent who encourages children's inherent goodness so that they will treat others with fairness and equality"? (Michael Erard, "Frame Wars," *The Texas Observer*, November 5, 2004.) Try, in short, to discern how each side is framing the issue. ◗

James Peck

September 11th: A National Tragedy?

A director and Professor of Theater, James Peck feels troubled by the label so casually attached by the press, the politicians, and the rest of us to the September 11th attacks: "a national tragedy." In applying tragic theory to American response to the attack, Peck calls upon us to distinguish tragic events from just bad stuff happening, and reminds us that "we have our own hubris to face." Beyond that, this piece helps us to see how much the label can matter when we talk about what things mean.

It is not the grave we mourn, but the dead.
Clytemnestra, in Euripides' *Iphigenia at Aulis*

1 Since the events of September 11th, I've been pursued by thoughts and images of tragedy. Frequently, I hear the terrorist attacks called "tragic" or "a national tragedy." The lead article in the *New York Times Magazine* the following Sunday, for example, was a collection of short pieces by prominent writers called "Elements of Tragedy." The title alludes to a key passage of Aristotle's *Poetics*, the canonical treatment of Greek tragedy and the most influential book of dramatic theory in the Western world. Subsequently, I've heard the tragic evoked by Sunday morning pundits, politicians of the left, right, and center, rock stars, talk-show hosts, the mayor of New York, professional athletes, my friends and colleagues, preachers, and members of my family. Probably others, too. As a lifelong theater person, this use of the language always triggers specific associations in me. Tragedy, of course is a theatrical genre dating in its origins from the fifth-century B.C. in Athens. The idea of the tragic recalls a long, vexed history in my art form. For many centuries, tragedy was the gold standard of drama, and debates about the definition and meaning of tragedy constitute some of the most vital episodes in the history of the theater. People in my field still make their reputations arguing the grounds or even the possibility of tragedy. Given my intellectual context, I confess to a certain proprietary interest in the way the concept of tragedy is deployed. Usually when I hear current events called tragic, I privately roll my eyes and lament the abuse of a term that is, if not exacting, at least rich, complicated, and possessed of a distinctive critical lineage. A voluminous literature theorizes the limits of tragic form, and I admit it rankles me to hear the word "tragic" used as a generic modifier for anything really bad that happens.

With the events of September 11th, however, I have found myself using the language of tragedy pretty indiscriminately. My immediate reaction to the attacks was precise and striking. Right after learning that the Twin Towers had collapsed, I wanted to read Euripides. I had an urge to go get *Iphigenia at Aulis* from the library and read it. Like scripture—for metaphors, sustenance, moral compass. I had not read this play in several years and still don't know it especially well, but it seemed at the time like my best hope for some kind of framework to apprehend what I was experiencing. I shuffled numbly around my office for a while feeling like this was kind of a silly notion till something else took over and I went about trying to make it through the day. But the impulse persisted, and eventually I found my way to the bottom floor of Trexler to browse the Greeks. I can't say and won't boast that reading a few tragedies has clarified much about the socio-political, ethical, and spiritual crisis in which we find ourselves. But I am coming to the conviction that tragedy offers a demanding, stark paradigm that at least accounts for some of the emotional force of these events and may even suggest some generative ways to think about them. Beyond simply capturing a bit of the devastation wrought by the attacks, can the form of tragedy help us narrate, image, or otherwise represent these horrors?

I acknowledge that it may seem frivolous, even blasphemous, to discuss these overwhelming and all too real events in a matrix borrowed from the relatively rarified topic of dramatic form. I do know that life is life and theater is theater. And though I have faith that theater is enormously important, I recognize that it is not quite life. The suffering of the thousands of people who died, lost their loved ones, or lost their livelihoods is quite real. Retaliatory air strikes and civilian casualties in Afghanistan are quite real. It's essential to mark the distance between aesthetic forms and world events. At the same time, it is also the case that we have no choice but to narrate September 11th. In fact, the story is being told all the time—on news reports, in snappily edited video clips, in press conferences, in office conversations while the xeroxing goes on. A truism of contemporary narrative theory states that humans order their world by telling stories about it. We innately turn people into characters and assemble incidents into narratives. We are hardwired to do this. But an array of incidents can be strung together in an endless variety of ways. Who's in our cast of characters? What's the plot? Whose point of view predominates? The choices we make matter because they articulate our perspective on how the world works. They matter, too, because narratives often function as guides for action. Stories are, among many other things, templates of behavior. They propose options and suggest outcomes; they mediate relations between people. What kind of a person can I be? Given the sort of person I am, how might I act? With what likely consequences? What should I expeot from people seemingly unlike myself? In the end, the stories we experience collapse back onto the material world because they shape our deeds. If we are to assimilate the events of September 11th into a meaningful context (or allow them to alter our sense of what a meaningful context might be), we have no choice but to hear them as stories.

I'm suggesting that the form of tragedy might accommodate some of the affective power of September 11th, and even point towards some of its moral claims. It seems fitting to me that the rhetoric of the tragic is so frequently invoked of late. Tragedy is above all a genre of suffering and witness. A form of lamentation, it facilitates mourning and generates memory. In its classical form, tragedy oscillates between a protagonist caught in an unlivable situation and a chorus who collectively responds to his or her anguish. While it does not celebrate or fetishize pain, it places hope in the belief that pain can catalyze insight. Above all, tragedy investigates contradiction. Tragedy stages moments when the systems people live by fall apart and fail them. It examines the inadequacy of familiar categories to provide meaningful accounts of catastrophic experiences. It resists easy resolution, preferring a difficult, even agonizing process of self-recognition to the reassuring comforts of self-deception. It is both analytic and empathetic. It defers closure in quest of revelation. Tragedy recognizes tensions between individual ambitions and group solidarity, and it often turns its self-scrutinizing impulse to the struggles of civic life. In fact, tragedy has flourished in epochs (Classical Athens, Renaissance England, Absolutist France, Romantic Germany) endeavoring to remake the social order or authorize a social order recently remade. It speaks to adversities faced on the cusp of history; considered historically, it often gives testament to the death of one era as another labors to be born. Tragedy admits the seemingly arbitrary nature of so much human suffering, even as it finds the will to go on living through communal rites that grieve the persistence of this condition.

5 I think this ought to be the tenor of our discourse in the wake of September 11th. As a nation, I believe we would benefit from seeking out the tragic potential in the destruction of the Twin Towers, the attack on the Pentagon, and the crash of a plane in southwestern Pennsylvania destined for an undetermined Washington landmark. A tragic response to September 11th, a tragic witnessing of it, would try to hold at least three contradictory impulses together. First, we need to mourn, and stories of loss seem fundamental. Many people died and many more have seen their lives irrevocably altered. The ripples are endless, from the unremitting absence of dead friends and family members to the slow burn of a faltering economy to the muscle tension that arises at the sight of camouflaged military personnel patrolling the airport with M-16s, to the permanent gap in the Manhattan skyline. I suspect most Americans feel a level of anxiety for their personal safety that they did not experience prior to September 11th. I admit that I do. Degrees of loss differ widely and are by no means commensurate. But loss is widespread and deserves to be marked.

A tragic witnessing of September 11th must also preserve outrage at these callous acts. "Terror is theater," said the leader of the terrorists who kidnapped and murdered Israeli athletes at the Munich Olympics. Human carnage for the sake of good video is indisputably evil. It may turn out to be the greatest, most characteristically postmodern of evils. The attackers need to be (as they have been) resoundingly and unequivocally condemned. A tragic perspective particularly rejects the murder of innocents in the service of signification. Deeply invested in a politics of empathy, tragedy asserts that insight into the order of things arises only through compassion. It demands the imaginative leap of trying to see the world from someone else's position in it, and insists that we act based on these imaginative identifications. Tragedy deals harshly with those who inflict suffering, in order to hold to or advance an idea. It names this unfeeling form of arrogance *hubris*, and punishes it.

Finally, a tragic witnessing of these events should squarely face some awful truths, dwell in the full weight of those truths, and try to see ourselves anew as a result of doing so. The terrorists staged September 11th for maximum semiotic impact. Their message was clear. In their rhetoric, the World Trade Center figures America's global economic power and a certain modernist insouciance; the Pentagon figures America's military power. The attacks construct America as the wealthy superpower it is, and dramatize its destruction. Clearly, these attacks were a despicable criminal act. The perpetrators must be brought to justice through appropriate processes of national and international law. However, they do articulate some partial truths about the United States. We are the principal agents and beneficiaries of globalization. We have the most powerful military in the world and often deploy it in bellicose ways. I think we need to hear that much of the world perceives us in this manner and accept that this perception, while not the whole story, has its basis in US actions. Since becoming the world's lone superpower in 1989, we have moved toward a dangerous and arrogant isolationism in foreign affairs. We have tended toward self-congratulatory smugness, representing ourselves as the victors of history, the champions of an economic system that will inevitably bring peace and prosperity to the entire planet. We have not adequately appreciated other peoples' fears for their material and cultural autonomy, nor have we done enough to temper the material and cultural inequities that have thus far accompanied globalization. We have our own hubris to face.

The cornerstone of Aristotle's theory of tragedy is the dual principle of *peripety* and *recognition.* A peripety is a reversal, a moment when the plot shifts powerfully for better or worse. In tragedies, peripeties are catastrophic, often unbearable. But terrible events do not alone make for tragedy. For Aristotle, the defining feature of tragedy is that peripety leads to recognition. As a result of their bad fortune, tragic characters see themselves in a new light. They recognize some unfortunate, painful, even devastating truth about themselves. From suffering comes insight. Nationally, we have endured peripety but are refusing recognition. We ought to take seriously the view of the United States that generated these evil acts. How did it arise? How is it justified? What can we do to change it? I do not stand with those who believe that if we change, "the terrorists will have won." We have already changed, and inevitably so given the magnitude of events and the levels of loss endured. But how will we change? Will we take up the moral rigor of tragedy and examine ourselves anew? Will we question and alter those policies and practices that inhibit reciprocity in our material and cultural relations with other nations? It is a sad truth that the rest of the world knows much more of us than we know of it. Let us consider the discomfiting possibility that it may also know something of us that we do not yet know of ourselves.

I worry that my discussion may seem tasteless, or worse, coy. Who cares whether we witness September 11th in the spirit of tragedy? I actually think the stakes of the genre are concrete, the consequences of it utterly material. In point of fact, since September 11th, our national policy has been determined by a narrative borrowed from a dramatic form. That form is melodrama. Melodrama is a genre of moral absolutes. It traffics in heroes and villains, white hats and black hats. It dates from the early nineteenth-century and dominated American theater into the early twentieth-century. It remains powerfully with us in film, television, and to some lesser degree theater. Luke Skywalker and Darth Vader are its progeny, as are Buffy and Angel, Rambo, professional wrestling, and soap opera. To its credit, melodrama cares about questions of morality and takes seriously the evil that men do. But it also divides the world into stark, simplistic categories. It thrives on a politics of us and them. Since September 11th, I believe we've been living out a national melodrama. The defining moment of this melodrama came when President Bush cast Osama bin Laden as the villain in a movie Western: "Wanted: Dead or Alive," he announced. I've since seen bin Laden's visage in a mock Old

West poster many times in many places. I am not so much concerned with the representation of bin Laden here as I am with the implicit representation of the United States. In this scenario, the US is a hero without blemish crusading for a rugged, frontier justice. I share the President's view that the people involved in planning these attacks should be pursued, captured, and prosecuted. All signs point to al Qaeda. However, our intervention into Afghanistan has come perilously close to state-sponsored vigilantism. We have not acted within the most relevant and authoritative legal framework, seeking an international tribunal under the authority of the United Nations to apprehend these criminals and to prosecute their crimes. We have opted instead to proclaim the post-September 11th world a new place, the rule of law obsolete, and invent new rules of engagement to fight "a new kind of war." To me, this seems more like the plot of a John Ford film than a considered, far-seeing approach to international leadership.

10 I don't want to live in a melodrama. Melodrama is pleasing like a Twinkie is pleasing, but like a Twinkie it's a lie. Melodrama makes for dissatisfying theater. More gravely, it makes for disastrous foreign policy. I do not believe that in the long term the "war on terrorism" as we are currently waging it will make us safer. If anything, it will harden the resolve of people sufficiently desperate to kill themselves and murder massive numbers of innocent civilians to voice their opinions. Even more pragmatically, most of the foreign policy analysis I've read since September 11th suggests that a bombing campaign is a grossly ineffective way to combat terrorism. Human intelligence (spying), combined with cross-national cooperation between domestic law enforcement agencies (states the consensus), is far more effective. To defeat terrorism, we need to cultivate friends, not make more enemies. We need to place ourselves within the norms and constraints of international law to demonstrate our genuine desire to be a leader within the community of nations rather than the boss country that unilaterally determines its agenda. Nor do I believe that the war on terrorism as we are currently waging it will lead to a lasting peace. Everything I've ever read on the subject of terrorism suggests that terrorist violence correlates most consistently and most strongly with poverty. The experience of abjection powerfully nurtures feelings of resentment that easily grow into hatred. People turn to terrorism when they believe they have no other means of influencing public affairs. Ultimately, the solution is economic. The best assurance that the US will not again be the object of a comparably horrific terrorist attack is an equitable distribution of global capital that moves wealth more evenly throughout the world and generates genuinely reciprocal forms of cultural encounter. In the wake of September 11th, we should be as powerfully concerned to work toward this goal as we are urgently resolved to bring to justice the perpetrators of these terrible crimes.

It deeply worries me that the dominant national discourse in the aftermath of September 11th is melodramatic. As I write this, it looks like the Northern Alliance, aided by the US bombing campaign, will win the war in Afghanistan and preside over a broad-based coalition government. I hope this brings some stability to the people of Afghanistan and relieves the poverty and repression that, by all reports, they have endured under the Taliban. When this happens, the melodramatic narrative put in motion by the Bush administration will reach at least a temporary denouement. However, I fear that by donning the white hat we are refusing to hear some necessary lessons of September 11th. I fear we are failing to recognize our role in creating the circumstances that led to such intense hatred of the United States. I fear that by acting above the community of nations we are confirming our enemies' worst view of us. I fear that in turning tragedy into melodrama, we are inviting more terror onto our shores.

I'd like to close by evoking the function of tragedy in Athenian democracy. Throughout the fifth-century B.C. tragedies were performed every spring at the City Dionysia, an annual theater festival sponsored by the state. The City Dionysia was a competition—five comic writers competed for one prize, three tragedians for the other. The tragic writers each staged a tragic cycle comprised of three tragedies and a satyr play. The festival lasted several days (between five and eight, depending upon how you read the evidence), with prizes awarded at the end. Most recent work on Greek theater emphasizes the civic character of theater-going in classical Athens. Theater-going was a privilege of citizenship and the theater a significant institution of political life. Approximately half the voting population of Athens attended the City Dionysia each year. Audience members sat with their tribes, a distribution of spectators that echoed the city's political structure. The judges were similarly appointed, one from each tribe. Wealthy citizens could pay their taxes by sponsoring a production. The performers were not professionals, but were themselves citizens. Rituals performed on the first day framed the festival within Athenian civic discourse. These rituals particularly emphasized Athens' military prowess: generals from each tribe poured libations; the children of those who had died in war were brought on stage; tribute from subject nations was paraded in the arena; names of men who had greatly benefited the city were read aloud.

Given this avowedly patriotic context, the most remarkable thing about the City Dionysia was its frank criticism of Athenian public life. The City Dionysia consistently and ferociously scrutinized the *polis.* Comedy specialized in scurrilous mockery of leading public figures. Tragedy placed local questions into contexts of ultimate concern. Tragedies especially investigated the fissures of civic ideology—the relationships, impulses, and desires that the dominant discourse could not accommodate. I don't want to totally romanticize Athenians; they were, in many ways, a belligerent, exclusionary society. However, I do find it inspiring that they gathered on a yearly basis to collectively consider the contradictions, failures, and inadequacies of their political system. Doing so was in fact an expression of their loyalty to and love of their homeland. It quite literally constituted them as democratic subjects. In this moment of national crisis, I think we would benefit from bringing the same questioning, restless, self-critical spirit to our own national conversation.

I hope we take seriously our casual language, and witness September 11th as a tragedy. Remember the dead. Pursue their killers. Interrogate ourselves.

THINGS TO DO WITH THE READING

1. Which features of tragedy does Peck offer as particularly useful for assimilating the events of September 11th, using and understanding them in what Peck calls a "generative" way?
2. Chapter 4 talks about a number of subjects in interpretation, one of which is interpretive context (see pages 90–93). Peck's essay is a good example of arguing carefully for the appropriateness and usefulness of an interpretive context. Peck invites us to view the events of September 11th in two contexts: tragedy and melodrama. Locate the places in the essay where Peck defends his choice of interpretive contexts. On what grounds does he defend his choice of tragedy as a productive lens?
3. The essay reveals its awareness of, and indeed anxiety about, seeming to trivialize a very real event by locating it in the context of dramatic and narrative theory. Look at the shape of Peck's argument to see where it locates its concessions (and what these are) and where and how it introduces its more challenging points. How, for example, would the essay differ if Peck rearranged the order of the "three contradictory impulses" announced in paragraph 5? (See pages 247–248 on concessions.)
4. **Link:** How does Peck's notion of story (narrative) compare with Luntz's and Lakoff's? Apply the heuristic of "Looking for Difference within Similarity," in which you start by noting similarities, accounting for the significance of these shared features, and then move on to consider within that context the significance of the most important differences (see pages 158–159). One feature of Peck's essay is the depth and quality of his definitions. Dwell for a while on paragraph 3: what is at stake in the way we choose, in Peck's words, "to turn people into characters and assemble incidents into narratives"?
5. **Link:** Find the keywords in Peck's piece that locate him politically as defined by Borick. How would the thinking and value system in his piece fit in the categories that Borick lays out?
6. **Application:** Where do you see evidence of melodrama in the national or international news? And what would a rescripting of melodrama into tragedy for this particular event entail? For example, what would the melodramatic and then the tragic readings of Hurricane Katrina be?

FOR FURTHER RESEARCH: THE LANGUAGE OF POLITICS AND THE POLITICS OF LANGUAGE

By Kelly Cannon, Reference Librarian

The readings and activities below invite you to further explore the theme of The Language of Politics and the Politics of Language. WARNING: Some essays are polemical; they are intended to promote insight and discussion (or a starting point for your next paper). To access the online readings, visit the *Writing Analytically with Readings* website at www.thomsonedu.com/english/rosenwasser.

Online

***American Rhetoric Online Speech Bank*. Ed. Michael E. Eidenmuller. 2006. 7 January 2006.**

A searchable collection of thousands of public speeches, with a preponderance of political voices. Speech categories include "Rhetoric of 9/11," "Christian Rhetoric," and "Iraq War Speeches."

Explore: Try out the "Cool Exercises" to test your rhetorical savvy.

"Claim vs. Fact." *American Progress Action Fund*. 7 January 2006.

A database charting "conservatives' dishonesty" and comparing it with "the truth."

Explore: What sources does this website pull its information from to refute conservatives' claims? To what extent are these sources more reliable than the ones they refute?

***FactCheck.org*. 2006. Annenberg Public Policy Center, University of Pennsylvania. 7 January 2006.**

"A nonpartisan, nonprofit, 'consumer advocate' for voters that aims to reduce the level of deception and confusion in U.S. politics."

Explore: Examine the "About us" portion of the website. Then look at a number of entries. To what extent does this website live up to its claim of nonpartisanship? How so?

***PollingReport.com*. 2006. Polling Report, Inc. 10 January 2006.**

Selections from the major public opinion polls on a wide variety of topics.

Explore: Examine the language from a number of different opinion polls on a given topic, like "Hillary Clinton." How does the way questions are asked matter? Be as specific as you can.

In Print

(Ask your librarian about possible online access to items marked with **.)

****Hardisty, Jean, and Deepak Bhargava. "Wrong About the Right." *Nation* (7 November 2005): 22–26.**

Contends that the conservative rise to power is not just about rhetoric and framing, but about such things as ideas and organization.

Explore: To what extent is the political orientation of these authors evident? What are the clues?

****Jerit, Jennifer. "Survival of the Fittest: Rhetoric During the Course of an Election Campaign."** ***Political Psychology*** **25.4 (August 2004): 563–575.**
A psychological study of the role of rhetoric in political campaigns. Discusses the types of emotional appeals that are likely to prove most effective in a political campaign.

Explore: Look closely at the conclusion of the article. To what extent does it offer more questions than answers? How does this reflect on what you know about writing in the social sciences?

****Kolbert, Elizabeth. "Firebrand: Phyllis Schlafly and the Conservative Revolution."** ***New Yorker*** **(7 November 2005): 134–138.**
"Schlafly's denunciatory tone, more than any of her actual campaigns, probably represents her most lasting contribution to American life. While Ann Coulter and Laura Ingraham were still playing tea party, she recognized that deliberation was no match for diatribe, and logic no equal to contempt. She was, in this way, a woman ahead of her time."

Explore: What is the tone of this essay (its attitude toward Schlafly)? To what extent is it condemnatory? To what extent admiring? Find evidence for both positions.

****Nankani, Sandhya. "Spin and Substance: How Words Win Elections."** ***Writing*** **27.2 (October 2004): 8–11.**
Nankani offers a brief overview of the power of rhetoric in presidential campaigns.

Explore: How important is metaphor in political rhetoric? Why?

****Rubin, Lillian B. "Why Don't They Listen to Us?"** ***Dissent*** **52.1 (Winter 2005): 86–91.**
This article from the liberal press explains why liberals have lost out to conservatives. Conclusion: It's all about rhetoric.

Explore: What aspect of liberal rhetoric does Rubin find most counterproductive?

CHAPTER 20

The Review as Cultural Analysis

Quick Take

Unlike the previous chapters of this book, this final chapter is organized around genre rather than topic. A genre is a category of composition characterized by a particular style, form, or content. Poetry is one; so is fiction, and so too is the review. As a genre, a review is a report or commentary on some kind of cultural product such as a film or a book or a musical or theatrical performance.

This chapter is not labeled "How to Write a Review"—though encouraging you to do so is one of its primary aims—but rather, The Review as Cultural Analysis. This title contains two key premises:

- That cultural products do more than simply entertain: they comment, intentionally or not, on the state of the culture. They have something to say beyond the literal words and images that they offer. There is *a vision* to be communicated—of where we are or have been or are heading.
- That the purpose of the review is to bring out this vision. The purpose is not simply to vote yea or nay on the cultural product under review with the judgmental thumbs up/thumbs down made popular by some critics.

Reviewers suggest contexts within which a piece might be most profitably viewed, so that it can be understood more richly. (For more on cultural meanings and interpretive contexts, see pages 82–86.)

ABOUT THE READINGS IN THIS CHAPTER

All of the readings in this chapter are reviews—of films, a book, TV shows, and an ad campaign. And the majority of the writing opportunities in the "Things to Do with the Reading" sections that follow these selections invite you to write your own reviews. In closing with a focus on more specialized kinds of writing projects, however, the book is also attempting to culminate. Writing reviews of cultural phenomena calls upon skills that previous chapters have sought to develop: how to interpret the culture, how to read its words and images and spaces and prejudices.

The chapter opens with two essays by Adam Gopnik. We have chosen to include two (along with his earlier piece on Times Square in Chapter 16) to provide the opportunity for you to experiment with *reading across* a writer's works. To do so, discerning what carries over from piece to piece, is to observe what characterizes a writer's rhetoric, style, and mode of perception. In his analyses of the sequel to *The Matrix* and a new biography of Ben Franklin, Gopnik models primary skills of effective review writing. For one, he chooses subjects that are representative of larger cultural trends. He also demonstrates how to use interpretive contexts and how to incorporate research. Additionally, both of his reviews illustrate clearly how a reviewer distinguishes between the point of view that the film or book offers and the reviewer's own point of view—in other words, between what the work thinks and what he or she thinks about what the work thinks. This distinction lies at the heart of the best review writing.

Following Gopnik are two brief reviews of television shows. Matt Bai offers an offbeat discussion of the animated series *King of the Hill*, relying on American party politics to provide an interpretive context. (Another piece of his has been included in this book as well—an analysis of a political spin doctor in Chapter 19—to enable further "reading across" of an author.) In "Oy Gay!" Kera Bolonik provides a revelatory way of thinking about *Will & Grace*, less as a show about gays (as it is usually seen) than about Jews and Gentiles. Both of these reviews have the advantage of being adaptable: a writer could apply the lenses they provide to other TV shows (or films or plays or ads or ...).

Malcolm Gladwell's "Listening to Khakis" takes the representation of gender from TV into the realm of men's clothing. His interviews give voice to a range of resonant cultural commentators about how we live now. Some of these voices address how men, as opposed to women, see—an issue that takes us back to Berger and other writers in Chapter 17. What Gladwell discovers about how those who make ads theorize gender and perception provides rich matter for both analysis and application.

The chapter concludes, as most of them have, with something a little different from what has gone before, something to test the flexibility of the chapter's analytical project. X.J. Kennedy's "Who Killed King Kong?" is a review that is nearly a half-century old, and one that focuses on *reception*—that is, on how some segment of the culture responds to ("receives") a particular cultural product. Kennedy is interested in how African Americans responded during the heyday of the Civil Rights Movement to the original 1933 film of *King Kong*. His review not only allows us to see how reviews are bounded by their own historical moment; it also invites us to update the review's vision of the culture by contemplating how our own moment has re-envisioned *King Kong* (in Peter Jackson's 2005 remake) and the volatile issues of race, class, and gender that burble just below the surface in the original film.

SOME GUIDELINES FOR WRITING REVIEWS

As you will see in the reviews that follow, there is no single model of organization. There are, however, shared assumptions about the work that a review should accomplish and the features that reviews conventionally contain. The following guidelines suggest these common elements.

1. A reviewer tells his or her audience that the object under analysis is not just a book (say) or kind of book but a **cultural phenomenon**, part of a trend. This is a primary move by which a review becomes a form of cultural analysis.
2. The opening paragraphs of the review commonly raise the issue of the **appeal** or popularity of the phenomenon. For example, the review may question why books about American heroes are popular as a way into querying why the hero of this particular book is appealing.
3. The reviewer typically presents his or her point of view after, and in the context of, **prevailing views**. Reviewers don't just tell us what they think; they tell us how their thinking fits with (is in conversation with) what others think.
4. The review usually arrives at one or more moments in which the reviewer uses the subject of his or her review as **an occasion to comment more broadly** on the culture. The review provides a means for the reviewer to comment not just on (for example) a film, but on the subject that the film itself is implicitly commenting upon.
5. An effective review usually involves some kind of **research** beyond what is found in the book (or film, etc.) under consideration. A good review doesn't just tell us what is praiseworthy (and blameworthy) about the thing being reviewed. A good review teaches readers things that they need to know in order to better understand, and thus evaluate for themselves, the cultural product under scrutiny.
6. A good review extends the range of its reflection—broadens its scope into informative cultural analysis—through various forms of **comparison**.
7. A reviewer makes careful rhetorical decisions about the **views of his or her assumed readers**, what they need to know and probably already know.

Adam Gopnik

The Unreal Thing: What's wrong with the Matrix?

Adam Gopnik is a frequent contributor to *The New Yorker,* where this piece first appeared in May, 2003. Here he reviews *The Matrix Reloaded,* the sequel to the wildly popular Wachowski Brothers's film *The Matrix.* While lauding the first film and reporting more acerbically about the second, Gopnik offers a series of illuminating interpretive contexts within which to locate *The Matrix.* These include an intellectual history of the idea that the material world is a delusion—also known as the "brain-in-the-vat problem," as well as a discussion of this notion as it appears in science fiction novels. (See pages 68 and 82–86 for a discussion of the concept of interpretive contexts.) His review of books about the revitalization of Times Square is included in Chapter 16. The selection that follows this one offers yet another of his reviews.

For the past four years, a lot of people have been obsessed with the movie "The Matrix." As the sequel, "The Matrix Reloaded," arrived in theatres this week, it was obvious that the strange, violent science-fiction film, by the previously more or less unknown Wachowski brothers, had already inspired both a cult and a craze. (And had made a lot of money into the bargain, enough to fuel two sequels; "Matrix Revolutions" is supposed to be out in November.) There hasn't been anything quite like it since "2001: A Space Odyssey," which had a similar mix of mysticism, solemnity, and mega-effects. Shortly after its mostly unheralded release, in 1999, "The Matrix" became an egghead *extase.* The Slovenian philosopher Slavoj Zizek's latest work, "Welcome to the Desert of the Real," took its title from a bit of dialogue in the film; college courses on epistemology have used "The Matrix" as a chief point of reference; and there are at least three books devoted to teasing out its meanings. ("Taking the Red Pill: Science, Philosophy and Religion in 'The Matrix'" is a typical title.) If the French philosopher Jean Baudrillard, whose books—"The Gulf War Did Not Take Place" is one—popularized the view that reality itself has become a simulation, has not yet embraced the film it may be because he is thinking of suing for a screen credit. (The "desert of the real" line came from him.) The movie, it seemed, dramatized a host of doubts and fears and fascinations, some half as old as time, some with a decent claim to be postmodern. To a lot of people, it looked like a fable: *our* fable. 1

The first "Matrix"—for anyone who has been living in Antarctica for the past four years—depended on a neatly knotted marriage between a spectacle and a speculation. The spectacle has by now become part of the common language of action movies: the amazing "balletic" fight scenes and the slow-motion aerial display of destruction. The speculation, more peculiar, and even, in its way, esoteric, is that reality is a fiction, programmed into the heads of sleeping millions by evil computers. When we meet the hero of the "Matrix" saga, he's a computer programmer—online name Neo—who works in a generic office building in a present-day, Chicago-like metropolis. Revelation arrives when he's recruited by a mysterious guerrilla figure named Morpheus, played by Laurence Fishburne with a baritone aplomb worthy of Orson Welles. Morpheus offers Neo a choice between two pills, one blue and one red: "You take the blue pill, the story ends, you wake up in your bed and believe whatever you want to believe. You take the red pill … and I show you how deep the rabbit hole goes." Neo takes the red pill and wakes up as he really is: a comatose body in a cocoon, his brain penetrated by a cable that inserts the Matrix, an interactive virtual-reality program, directly into his consciousness. All the people he has ever known, he realizes, are recumbent in incubators, stacks of identical clear pods, piled in high towers; the cocooned sleepers have the simulation piped into their heads by the machines as music is piped into headphones. What they take to be experiences is simply the effect of brain impulses interacting with the virtual-reality program. Guerrilla warriors who have been unplugged from the Matrix survive in an underground city called Zion, and travel in hovercraft to unplug promising humans. Morpheus has chosen to unplug Neo, it turns out, because he believes Neo is the One—the Messiah figure who will see through the Matrix and help free mankind. The first film, which told of Neo's education by Morpheus and his pursuit of the awesomely cute and Matrix-defying Trinity (the rubber-suited Carrie-Anne Moss), ends with Neo seeing the Matrix for what it is: a row of green digits, which he has learned to alter as easily as a skilled player can alter the levels of a video game.

What made the spectacle work was the ingenuity and the attention to detail with which it was rendered. The faintly greenish cast and the curious sterility of life within the Matrix; the reddish grungy reality of Morpheus's ship; the bizarre and convincing interlude with the elderly Oracle; and, of course, those action sequences, the weightless midair battles—few movies have had so much faith in their own mythology. And the actors rose to it, Laurence Fishburne managing to anchor the whole thing in a grandiloquent theatricality. Even Keanu Reeves, bless him, played his part with a stolidity that made him the only possible hero of the film, so slow in his reactions that he seemed perfect for virtual reality, his expressions changing with the finger-drumming time lag of a digital image loading online.

If it was the spectacle that made the movie work, though, it was the speculations that made it last in people's heads. It spoke to an old nightmare. The basic conceit of "The Matrix"—the notion that the material world is a malevolent delusion, designed by the forces of evil with the purpose of keeping people in a state of slavery, has a history. It is most famous as the belief for which the medieval Christian sect known as the Cathars fought and died, and in great numbers, too. The Cathars were sure that the material world was a phantasm created by Satan, and that Jesus of Nazareth—their Neo—had shown mankind a way beyond that matrix by standing outside it and seeing through it. The Cathars were fighting a losing battle, but the interesting thing was that they were fighting at all. It is not unusual to take up a sword and die for a belief. It is unusual to take up a sword to die for the belief that swords do not exist.

5 The Cathars, like the heroes of "The Matrix," had an especially handy rationale for violence: if it ain't real, it can't really bleed. One reason that the violence in "The Matrix"—those floating fistfights, the annihilation of entire squads of soldiers by cartwheeling guerrillas—can fairly be called balletic is that, according

to the rules of the movie, what is being destroyed is not real in the first place: the action has the safety of play and the excitement of the apocalyptic. Of course, the destruction of a blank, featureless, mirrored skyscraper by a helicopter, and the massacre of the soldiers who protect it, has a different resonance now than it did in 1999. The notion that some human beings are not really human but, rather, mere slaves, nonhuman ciphers, and therefore expendable, is exactly the vision of the revolutionary hero—and also of the mass terrorist. The Matrix is where all violent fanatics insist that they are living, even when they are not.

It would have been nice if some of that complexity, or any complexity, had made its way into the sequel. But—to get to the bad news—"Matrix Reloaded" is, unlike the first film, a conventional comic-book movie, in places a campy conventional comic-book movie, and in places a ludicrously campy conventional comic-book movie. It feels not so much like "Matrix II" as like "Matrix XIV"—a franchise film made after a decade of increasing grosses and thinning material. The thing that made the Matrix so creepy—the idea of a sleeping human population with a secondary life in a simulated world—is barely referred to in the new movie; in fact, if you hadn't seen the first film, not just the action but the basic premise would be pretty much unintelligible. The first forty-five minutes—set mainly in Zion, that human city buried deep in the earth—are particularly excruciating. Zion seems to be modelled on the parking garage of a giant indoor mall, with nested levels clustered around an atrium. Like every good-guy citadel in every science-fiction movie ever made, Zion is peopled by stern-jawed uniformed men who say things like "And what if you're wrong, God damn it, what then?" and "Are you doubting my command, Captain?" and by short-haired and surprisingly powerful women whose eyes moisten but don't overflow as they watch the men prepare to go off to war. Everybody wears earth tones and burlap and silk, and there are craggy perches from which speeches can be made while the courageous citizens hold torches. (The stuccoed, soft-contour interiors of Zion look like the most interesting fusion restaurant in Santa Fe.)

The only thing setting Zion apart from the good-guy planets in "The Phantom Menace" or "Star Trek" is that it seems to have been redlined at some moment in the mythic past and is heavily populated by people of color. They are all, like Morpheus, grave, orotund, and articulate to the point of prosiness, so that official exchanges in Zion put one in mind of what it must have been like at a meeting at the Afro-American Studies department at Harvard before Larry Summers got to it. (And no sooner has this thought crossed one's mind when—lo! there is Professor Cornel West himself, playing one of the Councillors.) Morpheus, winningly laconic in the first film, here tends to speechify, and, in a sequence that passes so far into the mystically absurd that it is almost witty, leads the inhabitants of Zion in a torchlit orgy, presumably meant to show the machines what humans can do that they can't; the humans heave and slam well-toned bodies in a giant rave—Plato's Retreat to the last leaping shadow. Neo and Trinity make love while this is going on, and we can see the cable holes up and down Neo's back, like a fashion-forward appliqué. (Soon, everyone will want them.) No cliché goes unresisted; there is an annoying street kid who wants Neo's attention, and a wise Councillor with swept-back silver hair (he is played by Anthony Zerbe, Hal Holbrook presumably having been unavailable) who twinkles benignly and creases up his eyes as he wanders the city at night by Neo's side. Smiles gather at the corner of his mouth. He's that kind of wise.

More damagingly, once Zion has been realized and mundanely inhabited, most of the magic disappears from the fable; it becomes a cartoon battle between more or less equally opposed forces, and the sense of a desperately uneven contest between man and machine is gone. The Matrix, far from being a rigorously imposed program, turns out to be as porous as good old-fashioned reality, letting in all kinds of James Bond villains. (They are explained as defunct programs that refused to die, but they seem more like character ideas that refused to be edited.) Lambert Wilson appears as a sort of digital Dominique de Villepin—even virtual Frenchmen are now amoral, the mark of Cain imprinted on their foreheads, so to speak, like a spot of chocolate mousse. He is called the Merovingian ("Holy Blood, Holy Grail" having apparently been added to the reading list) and announces that "choice is an illusion created between zose wis power and zose wisout" as he constructs a virtual dessert with which he inflames the passion of a virtual woman. The stunning Monica Bellucci appears as his wife, who sells out his secrets in exchange for a remarkably chaste kiss from Neo, while Trinity looks on, smoldering like Betty in an "Archie" comic. (But then Monica is Italian, a member of the coalition of the willing.) Then, there are his twin dreadlocked henchmen, dressed entirely in white, who have all the smirking conviction of Siegfried and Roy. Even the action sequences, which must have been quite hard to make, remind one of those in the later Bond films; interesting to describe, they are so unbound by any rules except the rule of Now He'll Jump Off That Fast-Moving Thing Onto the Next Fast-Moving Thing that they are tedious to watch. A long freeway sequence has the buzzing predictability of the video game it will doubtless become. In the first film, the rules of reality were bendable, and that was what gave the action its surprises; in the new one there are hardly any rules at all. The idea of a fight between Neo and a hundred identical evil "agents" sounds cool but is unintentionally comic. Dressed in identical black suits and ties, like the staff of MCA in the Lew Wasserman era (is that why they're called agents?), they simultaneously rush Neo and leap on him in a giant scrum; it's like watching a football team made up of ten-year-olds attempt to tackle Bronko Nagurski—you know he's going to rise up and shake them off. Neo has become a superhuman power within the Matrix and nothing threatens him. He fights the identical agents for fifteen minutes, practically yawning while he does, and then flies away, and you wonder—why didn't he fly away to start with? As he chops and jabs at his enemies, there isn't the slightest doubt about the outcome, and Keanu Reeves seems merely preoccupied, as though ready to get on his cell phone for a few sage words with Slavoj Zizek. There are a few arresting moments at the conclusion when Neo meets the architect of the Matrix. But by then the spectacle has swept right over the speculation, leaving a lot of vinyl and rubber shreds on the incoming tide.

For anyone who was transfixed by the first movie, watching the new one is a little like being unplugged from the Matrix: What was I experiencing all that time? Could it have been ... *all a dream?* A reassuring viewing of the old movie suggests that its appeal had less to do with its accessories than with its premise. Could it be that what you took to be your life was merely piped into your brain like experiential Muzak? The question casts a spell even when the spell casters turn out to be more merchandisers than magi.

10 Long before the first "Matrix" was released, of course, there was a lot of fictional life in the idea that life is a fiction. The finest of American speculators, Philip K. Dick, whose writing has served as the basis of some of the more ambitious science-fiction movies of the past couple of decades ("Blade Runner," "Total Recall," "Minority Report"), was preoccupied with two questions: how do we know that a robot doesn't have consciousness, and how do we know that we can trust our own memories and perceptions? "Blade Runner" dramatized the first of these two problems, and "The Matrix" was an extremely and probably self-consciously Dickian dramatization of the second. In one of Dick's most famous novels, for instance, "The Three Stigmata of Palmer Erdrich," a colony of earth-men on Mars, trapped in a miserable life, take an illegal drug that transports them into "Perky Pat Layouts"—miniature Ken and Barbie doll houses, where they live out their lives in an idealized Southern California. Like Poe, Dick took the science of his time, gave it a paranoid twist, and then became truly paranoid himself. In a long, half-crazy book called "Valis," he proposed that the world we live in is a weird scramble of information, that a wicked empire has produced thousands of years of fake history, and that the fabric of reality is being ripped by a battle between good and evil. The Dick scholar Erik Davis points out that, in a sequel to "Valis," Dick even used the term "matrix" in something like a Wachowskian context.

In the academy, too, the age-old topic of radical doubt has acquired renewed life in recent years. In fact, what's often called the "brain-in-the-vat problem" has practically become its own academic discipline. The philosopher Daniel Dennett invoked it to probe the paradoxes of identity. Robert Nozick, famous as a theorist of the minimal state, used it to ask whether you would agree to plug into an "experience machine" that would give you any experience you desired—writing a great book, making a friend—even though you'd really just be floating in a vat with electrodes attached to your brain. Nozick's perhaps too hasty assumption was that you wouldn't want to plug in. His point was that usually something has to happen in the world, not just in our heads, for our desires to be satisfied. The guerrilla warriors in "The Matrix," confirming the point, are persuaded that the Matrix is wrong because it isn't "real," and we intuitively side with them. Yet, unlike Nozick, we also recognize that it might be a lot more comfortable to remain within the virtual universe. That's the decision made by a turncoat among the guerrillas, Cypher. (Agents of the "machine world" seal the pact with him over dinner at a posh restaurant: "I know this steak doesn't exist," Cypher tells them, enjoying every calorie-free bite. "I know that when I put it in my mouth the Matrix is telling my brain that it is juicy and delicious. After nine years, you know what I realize? Ignorance is bliss.")

A key feature of "The Matrix" is that all those brains are wired together—that they really can interact with one another. And it was, improbably, the Harvard philosopher and mathematician Hilary Putnam who, a couple of decades back, proposed the essential Matrixian setup: a bunch of brains in a vat hooked up to a machine that was "programmed to give [them] all a *collective* hallucination, rather than a number of separate unrelated hallucinations." Putnam used his Matrix to make a tricky argument about meaning: since words mean what they normally refer to within a community, a member of the vatted-brain community might be telling the truth if it said it was looking at a tree, or, for that matter, at Monica Bellucci. That's because the brains in that vat aren't really speaking our language. What they are speaking, he said, is "vat-English," because by "a tree" they don't mean a tree; they mean, roughly, a tree image. Presumably, by "Monica Bellucci" they mean "the image of Monica Bellucci in 'Malèna,'" rather than the image of Monica Bellucci in "Matrix Reloaded," brains-in-vats having taste and large DVD collections.

Like most thought experiments, the brain-in-the-vat scenario was intended to sharpen our intuitions. But recurrent philosophical examples tend to have a little symbolic halo around them, a touch of their time—those angels dancing on the head of a pin were dancing to a thirteenth-century rhythm. The fact that the brain-in-a-vat literature has grown so abundant, the vat so vast, suggests that it has a grip on our imagination as a story in itself.

And there, in retrospect, might lie the secret of the first "Matrix": beyond the balletic violence, beyond the cool stunts, the idea that the world we live in isn't real is one that speaks right now to a general condition. For the curious thing about the movie was that everybody could grasp the basic setup instantly. Whether it occurs in cult science fiction or academic philosophy, we seem to be fascinated by the possibility that our world might not exist. We're not strangers to the feeling that, for much of our lives, we might just as well *be* brains-in-vats, floating in an amniotic fluid of simulations. It doesn't just strike us as plausibly weird. It strikes us as weirdly plausible.

15 When, in the first film, Neo sees the Matrix for what it is, a stream of green glowing digits, and thus is able to stop bullets by looking at them, the moment of vision is not simply liberating. It is also spooky and, in a Dickian way, chilling. This moment is the opposite of the equivalent scene in "Star Wars," a quarter century ago, when Luke Skywalker refuses to wear the helmet that will put him in contact with his targeting machinery, and decides instead to bliss out and trust the Force, the benevolent vital energy of the universe. Neo's epiphany is the reverse: the world around him is a cascade of cold digital algorithms, unfeeling and lifeless. His charge is not to turn on and tune in but to turn off and tune out.

This moment of discovery—that the world is not merely evil but fake—has become a familiar turn in American entertainment. ("The Truman Show" does it with stage sets, but the virtual-reality versions are played out in "Dark City" and "eXistenZ" and, especially, the fine, frightening film noir "The Thirteenth Floor," in which the hero drives to the edge of Los Angeles and discovers that the landscape beyond is made of the glowing green lines and honeycombs of a computer graphic—that he has been living his life within someone else's program.) Even if we don't remotely buy the notion that reality has been drowned by its simulations, we accept it as the melodramatic expression of a kind of truth. The Grand Guignol is possible only because the Petit Guignol exists.

There are so many brains in vats around, in fact, that we need to remind ourselves why we don't want to be one. In a long article on the first "Matrix" film, the Princeton philosopher James Pryor posed the question "What's so bad about living in the Matrix?," and, after sorting through some possible answers, he concluded that the real problem probably has to do with freedom, or the lack of it. "If your ambitions in the Matrix are relatively small-scale, like opening a restaurant or becoming a famous actor, then you may very well be able to achieve them," Pryor says. "But if your ambitions are larger—e.g., introducing some long-term social change—then whatever progress you make toward that goal will be wiped out when the simulation gets reset. ... One thing we place a lot of value on is being in charge of our own lives, not being someone else's slave or plaything. We want to be *politically free*."

Here's where the first "Matrix" pushed beyond the fun of seeing a richly painted dystopia. Although the movie was made in 1999, its strength as a metaphor has only increased in the years since. The monopolization of information by vast corporations; the substitution of an agreed-on fiction, imposed from above, for anything that corresponds to our own reality; the sense that we have lost control not only of our fate but of our small sense of what's real—all these things can seem part of ordinary life now. ("More Like 'The Matrix' Every Day" was the title of a recent political column by Farai Chideya.) In a mood of Dickian paranoia, one can even start to wonder whether the language we hear constantly on television and talk radio ("the war on terror," "homeland security," etc.) is a sort of vat-English—a language from which all earthly reference has been bled away. This isn't to say that any of us yet exist within an entirely fictive universe created by the forces of evil for the purpose of deluding a benumbed population—not unless you work for Fox News, anyway. But we know what it's like to be captive to representations of the world that have, well, a faintly greenish cast.

Especially in view of the conventionality of the second film, it's clear that the first film struck so deep not because it showed us a new world but because it reminded us of this one, and dramatized a simple, memorable choice between the plugged and the unplugged life. It reminded us that the idea of free lives is inseparable from the idea of the real thing. Apparently, we needed the reminder. "Free your mind!," the sixties-ish slogan of the new film, is too ambitious to be convincing, and betrays the darkness that made the first film so unusual. "Unplug thy neighbor!," though, still sounds *just* possible.

THINGS TO DO WITH THE READING

1. As noted in the introduction to this chapter, the arts do more than simply entertain; they offer us a vision of the culture—where it has been, where it is, and where it is heading. One function of the review as cultural analysis is to excavate this largely implicit vision and make it explicit. In addition to revealing the novel's, film's, or CD's point of view, the best reviews will also offer a point of view on that point of view. The review's point of view will do more than simply agree or disagree with what it takes the work of art to be "saying": it will contemplate and assess what the work of art is saying, guiding the way we might interpret it.

As a prelude to writing your own review, use Gopnik's "The Unreal Thing" as a way of identifying both how a reviewer (1) conveys an artwork's point of view, and (2) offers a point of view on that point of view.

Locate two or three key passages in the review where Gopnik offers what he takes to be the Wachowski Brothers's point of view on cultural issues. Summarize these, giving both the data and the implications that Gopnik provides his readers. In effect, you will be summarizing the way that Gopnik is "reading with the grain" of the film. [See the discussions of summary (pages 117–120) and of reading with and against the grain (pages 133–135).]

Then locate several passages in which Gopnik moves beyond the reach of the film to comment more broadly on the larger questions he has used the film to raise—what, at its most searching, this review is about. Might it be Fox News, mentioned in paragraph 18, for example?

2. The last two sentences of the introduction set up some key words that will function both as trial thesis (opening hypothesis) and organizational devices. One of these is the word "fable." Find at least two definitions of "fable," from more than one source (such as the *OED* and, perhaps, some kind of glossary of literary terms). Later in the review, Gopnik contrasts *The Matrix* with its first sequel, *The Matrix Reloaded* by characterizing the sequel as a cartoon. What is the difference between a cartoon and a fable as Gopnik uses the terms? Follow this strand in Gopnik's review and analyze how he uses it to make his argument about *The Matrix Reloaded.*

3. As with most good reviews, this one clearly required some research. Gopnik refers to a number of people (scholars, actors, authors, cartoon characters, show business people) and places/concepts in order to establish a rich cultural context for understanding both the popular appeal and the argument of the two *Matrix* films. Do some research of your own on the following words and names from the review and explain how at least two of these function in Gopnik's argument: redlining, Zion, Cornell West, Siegfried and Roy, Grand and Petit Guignol, Philip K. Dick, and Morpheus—the word as opposed to just the film character.

4. Central to the review are comparisons of the *Matrix* films to earlier films in the same or similar genre—speculative science fiction films such as *Star Wars* and the films based on American "speculator" (as Gopnik calls him) Philip K. Dick: *Blade Runner*, *Total Recall*, and *Minority Report*. (To this might be added a number of other films such as *I, Robot*, which is based on an Isaac Asimov story.) Rather than simply summarizing these other films, Gopnik identifies what he calls their questions and premises. What does he say are the questions that concerned Philip K. Dick? What does he cite as the culminating moment/point of *Star Wars*? Then explain how Gopnik uses *Star Wars* and Philip K. Dick to define what he finds admirable and interesting about *The Matrix* and considerably less compelling about *The Matrix Reloaded*. Various of Gopnik's organizing contrasts (binaries) should come into play in your

discussion, including spectacle versus speculation, plugged versus unplugged, and turn on and tune in versus turn off and tune out.

5. **Links:** Consider what the introductory paragraph does in Gopnik's review and how it might be typical of the way writers set up and frame a review as a form of cultural analysis. In addition to sparking readers' interest in a particular film, the opening paragraph typically (1) locates the subject in question (in this case, the second *Matrix* film) in a larger cultural context and (2) positions the writer to speculate about what factors might be responsible for the film's popularity. Notice the repetition of the phrase "a lot of people" in the first and last sentences of the paragraph. How does this phrase help to frame the review, and what other language in the paragraph does it fit with? (See pages 219–221 on introductions.)

   In this context, study the ways that all of the selections in this chapter craft their introductions and take some notes about what you notice. This observation exercise should enable you to see how most effective reviews perform the following opening gambits—moves that you might profitably include in your review:

   - How does the writer establish a context for the review—a frame larger than the particular item being reviewed?
   - What comparisons does the reviewer point to as a means of contextualizing the review?
   - How does the writer make a case for the significance of the subject? (Does the writer say, for example, that the review is part of a major trend, an overlooked or yet-to-break contemporary phenomenon, unexpectedly popular?)
   - What if anything does the writer tell us about prevailing views on the topic?

6. **Application:** One of the best lessons you can learn from studying Gopnik's reviews is the value of doing background research. His reviews are always learned: more than just reporting on the film or novel under question, they offer a broader setting within which to view it. And so in this review, Gopnik has clearly researched the Cathars religious sect (see paragraphs 4–5), the novels of Philip K. Dick (see paragraph 10), and various philosophers of the brain-in-the vat problem, such as Daniel Dennett, Robert Nozick, and Hilary Putnam (see paragraphs 11–12).

   Choose any film that you might conceivably review, and look for research openings. What might you identify as likely contexts for background research in order to understand the film more resonantly, to locate it in one or preferably two different interpretive contexts? Then try to write about the film in these contexts, using Gopnik as a model.

7. **Application:** The primary claim Gopnik makes to get his article started is that "the first 'Matrix' […] depended on a neatly knotted marriage between spectacle and speculation." Spectacle he attaches to "the common language of action movies," and speculation he attaches to the philosophical idea that "reality is a fiction" (see paragraph 2).

How does this organizing contrast (see pages 45 and 52–55) of spectacle and speculation provide a lens for looking at other science fiction films? Note that for Gopnik both the spectacle (special effects) and the speculation have political implications for us here now, as in the ways that the film represents the control of information (see paragraph 18) and the terroristic struggle against that control (see paragraph 5).

So don't simply look for moments of spectacle and speculation in the final *Star Wars* film, for example. Instead ponder how the film of your choice marries the two, and what ideas are implicit in its way of presenting this marriage. At the end of paragraph 8, Gopnik comments that in *The Matrix Reloaded* the spectacle has overwhelmed the speculation. In what way does the film you have chosen have difficulty keeping the two in harmony, and with what consequences?

8. **Application:** In its generic function of providing an occasion for cultural analysis, the review consistently gestures at the world beyond film, the one we inhabit. It follows that a related function of the review is to discern cultural trends—in effect, using films as a kind of cultural barometer of how we see ourselves, and what we are worried about.

At the end of paragraph 13, Gopnik states, "The fact that the brain-in-a-vat literature has grown so abundant, the vat so vast, suggests that it has a grip on our imagination as a story in itself." He subsequently names some of these films: *The Truman Show*, *Dark City*, *eXistenZ*, and *The Thirteenth Floor*.

Use Gopnik's review as a model and a lens for reviewing any of these films or another one in the brain-in-a-vat genre. As you write your review, converse with Gopnik's viewpoints, but don't simply apply what he has said to your film. Instead, apply the heuristic of "Looking for Difference within Similarity" (see page 125) as you analyze your chosen film.

Adam Gopnik

American Electric: Did Franklin fly that kite?

In this, the third review by Adam Gopnik included in this anthology, the author takes on a controversial biography of that American icon, Ben Franklin. Along the way, Gopnik employs a range of reviewing practices that less experienced writers might emulate:

- He uses the review to educate his readers about the subject, not just to convince them to share his like or dislike. His review is not, in other words, fundamentally concerned with whether the book is good or bad, or whether readers should or shouldn't purchase it.
- He doesn't try to cover everything from the book inside his review; instead he focuses on a question that he finds both primary and suggestive—whether Franklin really flew that kite and whether it matters if he did or not.
- He locates his discussion in a context enriched by additional research beyond that offered by the text he is reviewing, so that neither he nor his readers are limited solely to a single account.

The review originally appeared in *The New Yorker* on June 30, 2003.

We are said to be living in an icon-smashing age, but the odd thing is how few shards can be found on the floor. Joe DiMaggio may now be chilly and Bing Crosby charmless, but the essential pantheon of heroes remains in place. Lincoln, John Adams, Lewis and Clark, Seabiscuit—those who matter most to us are intact, and the common activity is not to smash their images but to trace on them, as though with a diamond pen, the signature of our own favored flaws, allowing their heroism to shine through more brightly. The thrust of popular history has been to remake old heroes as more like us than we knew, and better than us than we could imagine. (Even John Kennedy, if sicker than we recognized, was braver, too.) The Founding Fathers have been remade as Founding Brothers, our superior siblings. 1

Of them all, Benjamin Franklin seems the most secure, since he has always been the most "human," the one Founding Father who has no trace of asceticism, neither Massachusetts Puritan nor Virginia Neo-Roman. He is all godless materialist Pennsylvania merchant (although he borrowed some simplicity from the Quakers from time to time, as the need suited him). You could swing a baseball bat of propriety at him, and he would bounce back, beaming. This gives him, and his legend, endless vitality. If you were a child growing up in Philadelphia in the nineteen-sixties, Franklin was still alive, everywhere you looked. At night, his electric profile, wattles outlined in neon, hovered above the city in the sign for the Benjamin Franklin Hotel. He was known in Philadelphia the way St. Francis was known in Assisi, as both presiding deity and local boy.

Central to his myth was the story of the Kite and Key. (An honors society at the University of Pennsylvania still has that name.) He went out to a field in a thunderstorm, flew his kite, saw it struck by lightning, and then watched the lightning sparkle around a key held in a jar at the end of the kite twine. If he put his knuckle on the twine, he could feel the spark. What this accomplished, exactly, was something that schoolboys were vague about: "He discovered electricity" was the usual formula. In fact, he had shown that lightning was a form of electricity, and that ingenuity could hold its own against book learning. In one of the two greatest editorial emendations in American letters (the other is Maxwell Perkins keeping Fitzgerald from calling "Gatsby" "Trimalchio in West Egg"), Franklin changed Jefferson's "We hold these truths to be sacred and undeniable" to the modest, conclusive "We hold these truths to be self-evident"—and Franklin could make that change because he was known as the master of self-evidence, with all the authority of a man willing to face down lightning with a kite while everyone else was safe inside arguing about ideas. "He Took Lightning from the Sky and the Scepter from the Tyrant's Hand" was the (originally Latin) inscription that a French poet would later offer, conclusively.

Now, however, a new book argues that the legend on which Franklin's reputation rests is dubious. There was no kite, no key, no bolt, no knuckle, no charge. He let people believe that he had been places he never went, done things he never did, and seen things that never happened. No wonder he's been called the father of American journalism.

The new book, "Bolt of Fate," by Tom Tucker (Public Affairs; $25), is part of 5
an apparently unstoppable wave of Franklin biography. In the past three years, we have had Edmund S. Morgan's short, loving "Benjamin Franklin" (Yale; $24.95) and H. W. Brands's "The First American" (Doubleday; $35), and this month Walter Isaacson's energetic, entertaining, and worldly "Benjamin Franklin: An American Life" (Simon & Schuster; $30) joins them. Two more Franklin biographies are supposedly on the way. Tucker's book, it should be said, is not so much a wet blanket cast over the party as an "Aw, nuts" uttered at it: his evidence is far from conclusive, but neither does his book have any of the usual telltale signs of overreaching, special pleading, paranoia, or conspiracy-mongering. This is Franklin unmasked, but not, so to speak, Franklin dressed up in women's clothing. True or false, Tucker's argument touches on the heart of who Franklin was, who we want him to be, and who he might have been. "*Eripuit coelo fulmen*"—he snatched the lightning from the sky. What if, just conceivably, he didn't?

There are no bad biographies of Franklin for the same reason that there are no bad Three Stooges movies, or, for that matter, demolition derbies: *something* always happens. Just when Franklin is getting becalmed in diplomatic squabbles, say, or running a tedious printing business in a provincial city, he writes about farts or invents bifocals. Yet there is, even in Isaacson's genial book and Morgan's almost hagiographic one, a sense that this figure is seen at a distance, and remains hard to know. Where John Adams comes before us in all his bad-tempered intelligence, and Washington in his thin-lipped realism, Franklin is elusive: he can at times be Santa Claus or William James, bubbly and intelligent, and at times he is Franklin Roosevelt, with a carefully composed affability overlaying a character essentially calculating and remote.

In part, this is because he had to adapt to two different times, one of which, at least, he helped to make. His career, as Isaacson suggests, bridges two centuries of sensibility: in the first half of his life, up until the seventeen-fifties, we are in a largely seventeenth-century world of nascent capitalism and virtuous upward mobility. Franklin is an ambitious early capitalist operator at the edge of the empire, a provincial Pepys. He starts a business from scratch and chases women, and both the culture and the science around him feel skin-thin. By the end of the Franklin biographies, we are in a late-Enlightenment world of fully fledged science and sensibility—where the reign of violence and feeling is beginning. This is partly a question of place, Philadelphia traded for Paris, but it is also an effect of growing knowledge and an expanded universe, and science is the crossing point. The electrical experiments are the link between the early Franklin and the later Franklin—between the young striver and the Papa Savant.

Franklin was born in Boston in 1706, to a family of freethinking artisans, and was apprenticed as a boy to his half brother James, a printer. A printer in those Colonial days often had his own newspaper, and James's was the *New England Courant*, America's first independent paper. Benjamin picked up the newspapering habit—for a brief period, still an adolescent, he ran the paper while his brother was in jail over a censorship dispute. But he disliked his brother ("I fancy his harsh and tyrannical treatment of me might be a means of impressing me with that aversion to arbitrary power that has stuck to me through my whole life," he wrote years later) and, at seventeen, ran away to Philadelphia, a village of two thousand people that nonetheless dreamed of itself as a metropolis of tolerance. Compared with Mathered Boston, it was.

Franklin, tall and physically formidable—he was a terrific swimmer and runner—almost immediately brought himself to the center of Philadelphia life. He earned a reputation as the publisher and editor of the *Pennsylvania Gazette*, a newspaper begun by a printer whom he helped drive out of business. Like Dr. Johnson, his almost exact contemporary, he made his way by sheer force of talent as a miscellaneous journalist; unlike the bulldoggish Dr. Johnson, he understood, and pioneered, the American principle that it pays to be liked. "The consummate networker," as Isaacson calls him, he turned a little circle of fellow-apprentices and small tradesmen, the Junto, into a kind of freewheeling all-purpose civic association. He was a funny writer, with a dry, pawky prose style, modelled on Addison's, and a taste for pseudonymous pranks; he hid his most acerbic opinions behind the masks of made-up characters. But he had world-class ambitions, and he understood that those ambitions were probably best served by achievement in natural philosophy—the sciences. No one in London gave a damn about Philadelphia politics, but they cared about Philadelphia lightning. Distance lends authority to experiments: if it can be done out there, it can be done anywhere.

10 Franklin had just given up his career as a printer when he began his work as an "electrician," fascinated by the small shocks you could make out of amber rods and glass jars. Electricity was not yet a serious science. Though everyone agreed that it was a phenomenon, no one was sure at first if it was a phenomenon like the hula hoop or a phenomenon like gravity. People played with it for fun. Then, in the seventeen-forties, the Leyden jar, an early capacitor, showed that an electrical charge could be held in place and made to pass through glass. Essentially, you could collect and store electricity; and in 1749 Franklin reported to the Royal Academy in London that he had created the first electric battery.

In his correspondence with the academy, he understood that he would inevitably be viewed as a provincial, and that it paid to play the clown a little. In the midst of his serious submissions, he also wrote to the academy, apropos the state of "American electricity," that "a turkey is to be killed for our dinners by the electrical shock, and roasted by the electrical jack, before a fire kindled by the electrified bottle, when the healths of all the famous electricians in England, France and Germany, are to be drank in electrified bumpers, under the discharge of guns from the electrical battery." The metropolis, while it mistrusts an upstart, forgives a lovable provincial eccentric. (Though he was being funny about the American enthusiasm for electricity, he wasn't entirely joking. He electrocuted at least one turkey, and boasted of how tender it was, a thing typical of the way he could turn a joke into a fact.)

Previously, it had been proposed that there were two different kinds of electricity, both fluid: one generated by glass and one generated by resin. Franklin, experimenting with varieties of electric shock, swiftly arrived at a fundamental insight: that electricity was a single fluid, and that what he was the first to call "positive" and "negative" charges came from having too much or too little of it. The importance of Franklin's theory, as the great historian of science I. Bernard Cohen has shown, was not only that it insisted on the conservation of charge but that it accepted "action at a distance": there didn't have to be holes for the charge to pass through, or invisible levers in the sky to send it along; electricity was just there, like gravity.

Many people, whatever theory they held, had noticed that lightning in the sky looked a lot like electricity in a jar, only there was more of it. In 1749, it seems, Franklin himself made a list of the resemblances, a list that reveals the tenor of his scientific mind, at once disarmingly particular and searching for unity: "Electrical fluid agrees with lightning in these particulars. 1. Giving light. 2. Color of the light. 3. Crooked direction. 4. Swift motion. 5. Being conducted by metals. 6. Crack or noise in exploding. 7. Subsisting in water or ice. ... Since they agree in all particulars wherein we can already compare them, is it not probable they agree likewise in this? Let the experiment be made." The lightning experiment would be suggestive about the centrality of electricity in an essentially Newtonian world picture. The simpler the world picture, the less intricate the celestial mechanics, and the greater the play of universal forces, however bizarre their action. *E pluribus unum* applied—a motto that Franklin, once again running from the absurd to the solemn, took from a classical recipe for salad dressing.

Did he really do it? There were actually two experiments. In 1750, Franklin proposed that if you could get up high enough to be above trees and other natural obstacles, on a steeple or a spire, safely insulated in a sentry box (about the size of a telephone booth), you might be able to draw electricity from a thundercloud through a long iron rod, and "determine whether the clouds that contain lightning are electrified or not." A group of French scientists who read the proposal—for all that it took six weeks for mail to cross the Atlantic, there was a constant and meaningful exchange of ideas and data—tried it, in a town called Marly, outside Paris, and found that it worked. (Significantly, the apparatus didn't function right away—no experiment ever really works the first time you try it, for the same reason that no child's toy ever works on Christmas morning, the first time you assemble it—and it was a fairly lowly assistant who eventually made the discovery.)

Well, if you didn't have a steeple or a spire, you could use a kite to make the same 15
experiment, with a key attached at a silk ribbon to the twine on the kite; the key and the twine would conduct the electricity. Franklin published an account of this experiment—which took place, if it did, sometime in 1752—in the *Pennsylvania Gazette*, and it is worth quoting, for its clarity and for its odd future tenses. After some details about the construction of the kite, which is to be made of a "large thin silk handkerchief," Franklin explains:

> The kite is to be raised, when a thunder-gust appears to be coming on, (which is very frequent in this country) and the person, who holds the string, must stand within a door, or window, or under some cover, so that the silk riband may not be wet. ... As soon as any of the thunder-clouds come over the kite, the pointed wire will draw the electric fire from them; and the kite, with all the twine, will be electrified; and the loose filaments of the twine will stand out every way, and be attracted by the approaching finger. When the rain has wet the kite and twine, so that it can conduct the electric fire freely, you will find it stream out plentifully from the key on the approach of your knuckle. ... All the other electrical experiments [can] be performed, which are usually done by the help of a rubbed glass globe or tube, and thereby the sameness of the electric matter with that of lightning completely demonstrated.

The first thing to note is that there is no bolt of lightning. Lightning, as Tucker points out, is a weird phenomenon. You won't find it by waiting in a field, and, if you did, it might fry you like a turkey; it would certainly vaporize the twine. What Franklin was trying to get was the electrostatic energy in clouds, which is usually there.

The next thing to note is the conditional spirit in which Franklin tells the story: he doesn't say he did it; he says that it can be done. This, Tucker notes, is not the era's usual scientific style, and in other cases Franklin is very careful, to the fetishistic degree beloved of eighteenth-century science, to say exactly what, when, and how. Tucker writes, "In his letter to George Whatley, an old London friend, describing the invention of bifocal glasses and in his 'Description of an Instrument for Taking Down Books from High Shelves' Franklin is unambiguous: he invented both items, he writes at length, he gives specifics, he uses active voice, he offers diagrams, *he says he did it.*" In this first account, anyway, he doesn't.

The third thing to note is how hard it is to do. Tucker argues that a kite made of the kind of handkerchief that would have been available (a thirty-inch square of lingerie-thin silk), dragging a standard chunky key of the time (a quarter-pound brass latchkey), would have been nearly impossible to fly in the first place, especially if you were trying to keep it aloft from inside a shed—you can't get the key out and up. (Tucker notes that the job of keeping the key from falling to the ground while you're still flying the kite—and doing both from inside some kind of box—is one that has defeated the imagination of every illustrator, including Currier & Ives, who put Franklin's hand above the key, on the electrified twine, to support the weight.) He says that he himself tried the experiment and couldn't get the kite off the ground: "My wife held a large picture frame as a stand-in for a window frame. When I tried to keep the key safely on my side of the picture frame and 'dry' and not let the line brush against the frame, especially with the reduced handling caused by the dangling key, there came the sudden realization: *He-really-didn't-do-this.*" Which may have been a good thing. Tucker says that the experiment was also fantastically dangerous, and Franklin was lucky not to get killed trying to do it, if he did it.

Isaacson, for his part, rejects Tucker, and sensibly directs us toward Cohen's books on Franklin's science. Cohen notes that other people claimed to have reproduced the experiment not long afterward, but for Cohen perhaps the most important consideration in its favor is the simple fact that Franklin said that he did it. The idea that Franklin might have made up his account is simply alien to his conception of Franklin.

20 Who is to decide when doctors disagree? It is, finally, as conservatives like to say, all about character. And here one approaches an area of subtle gradations, easy to misinterpret. Tucker points to evidence of Franklin's series of hoaxes as conclusive, or anyway highly suggestive. He offers a long list and shows how they often advanced Franklin's career; for instance, when he was just starting out as a printer he wrote a pseudonymous essay in favor of paper currency and then, after the legislature had been persuaded, got the government contract to print money. As Tucker recognizes, the majority of these impostures are closer to deadpan satiric jokes than they are to self-seeking lies. Franklin liked to write letters claiming to be from other people—a "famous Jesuit," or a Scottish Presbyterian—in order to dramatize some political point through obvious overload. The last thing he wrote was a letter purportedly from a Muslim slaver, "Sidi Mehemet Ibrahim," whose lust for slavery was intended to hold a mirror up to the American slaveholder's own, and shame him.

This is the reason for Franklin's opacity and, perhaps, for the doubts about the kite, which do not begin with Tucker. Franklin was an instinctive ironist. That is not to make him contemporary; it was Enlightenment irony, not Duchampian irony—begun as a way of getting past censorship. But it was his natural mode, as in the joke about the electrocuted turkeys: which *was* a joke, and had a serious point, and was something he actually did, and the whole thing depended on being reported with an absolutely straight face. It was not that he did not value honesty. He did. It is that he did not value sincerity, a different thing. He would have been reluctant to say something that he believed to be a lie. But, as a businessman and a writer and a diplomat, he might very well have been willing to dramatize, or even overdramatize, something he believed to be essentially the truth.

Everyone, doubters and believers, meets in Paris, for what all can agree on is that the image of Franklin, the American electrician, was more essential to his success as a diplomat in France than any other element of his legend. By 1776, Franklin was, of course, a very senior American, and his tastes and allegiances, which throughout his life had been almost passionately English and imperial, seemed fully formed. He came home from a long posting to London as a representative of the Pennsylvania legislature, and was immediately asked to join the first Congress. He was, at the start, suspected by the more radical patriots of being a "wet," if not actually a spy. (His son William, with whom he was said to have done the kite-flying, was then the loyal Tory governor of New Jersey.) But he soon proved to be as ardently in favor of unilateral independence as Adams or

Jefferson. ("He does not hesitate at our boldest Measures, but rather seems to think us too irresolute," John wrote to Abigail, perpetually annoyed at Franklin's gift for arriving late at a party and then lighting all the candles on the cake.) And, when it became plain that the war for independence would live or die on French aid, he was the obvious candidate to go to France and ask for it. "There can be no question that when Franklin arrived in France on that grave mission he was already a public figure," Cohen writes. "And this was so because of his stature as a scientist and because of the spectacular nature of his work on lightning." We may have thought we were sending over Will Rogers; they thought they were getting Richard Feynman.

Franklin's essentially ironic, distancing turn of mind, which was often so baffling to his literal-minded American colleagues—Isaacson's funniest pages are supplied by John Adams's stunned and alarmed accounts of Franklin's nonchalant diplomacy on the Paris mission—gave him a kind of second sight into the minds of his hosts. There is little sham in French life, but a lot of show, a lot of rhetorical gesturing. Franklin understood the style instantly. He was pretending to be a naïf (he left his wig and powder, which he normally wore, back home in Philadelphia), which the French knew to be faux, and they were pretending to be worldly, which he knew to be an illusion.

Franklin was not just shrewder than he seemed, having the measure of his host very well down. He was also politically far more skillful. As Morgan points out, there was no necessity for the French to side with the Americans, whose cause looked like the longest of long shots and involved making league with a frankly king-hating new republic. Adams and the ornery Arthur Lee, another member of the French mission, were exasperated by Franklin's attention to social trivia. Why didn't he just bluntly insist on the power political formula that stared them in the face? America is the enemy of England, England is the enemy of France. Franklin understood that the "realistic" formula was essentially empty, and that there was, and is, no more maddeningly fatuous cliché than that nations have interests rather than affections. It was in France's interest to supplant the British, against its interest to support a republic, in its interest to form an alliance with the Spanish and leave the Americans alone, and on and on. But the logic of power depends largely on the perceptions, and feelings, of the people who have it. Franklin understood that, above all, the good opinion of the French mattered. It paid to be liked and admired, and he made sure that he was. He knew that he could not make his country, and its needs, inescapable if he did not make himself, and his cause, irresistible.

Was Franklin, because he was calculating and clear-eyed, a fraud? Nothing 25
seems more false. Might he have, in the American, or, for that matter, the electrical, cause, massaged the data in what he thought was the pursuit of truth, or told a half-truth and then been enclosed within it? Nothing seems more human.

One need not have a pragmatic or skeptical vision of truth to have a charitable view of the frailty of those who pursue it. The electrical kite could never have really been a hoax, because it was never really a claim. Even if the experiment did take place, it would not, on its own, have counted as scientific data by any standard, Enlightenment or modern. There was no specification, no replication by the experimenter, no protocol. It was, really, a thought experiment: if you did this, then what might happen? Despite all the rhetoric, much of it self-created, of

Franklin as natural man, pragmatic man, empirical man, man with a kite, the plain truth is that his genius was, in every realm, for airy abstraction brought to earth, the single-fluid theory of life.

Franklin the political theorist was not drawing on his own experience, either, which consisted entirely of more or less slavish negotiations with colonial powers and absolute monarchs. He was, in the end, proposing a system of governance that no one had experienced at all. It was a pure thought experiment, a kite that might fly.

The moral of the kite is not that truth is relative. It is that nothing is really self-evident. Scientific truths, like political beliefs, are guesses and arguments, not certainties. Dr. Johnson's great, comforting gloss on the Christian funeral service comes to mind: "In the sure and certain hope of a resurrection" did not mean that the resurrection was certain, only that the hope was certain. "We hold these truths to be self-evident," similarly, means that we hold them to be so. We hold these truths as we hold the twine, believing, without being sure, that the tugs and shocks are what we think they are. We hold the string, and hope for the best. Often, there is no lightning. Sometimes, there is no kite.

THINGS TO DO WITH THE READING

1. Like other reviewers in this chapter, Gopnik, in his review of current Benjamin Franklin biographies, tells us that he is analyzing not just a book or kind of book but a cultural phenomenon or trend. This is one of the primary ways in which a review becomes a form of cultural analysis. "The new book" on Franklin, Gopnik tells us, "is part of an apparently unstoppable wave of Franklin biography" (see paragraph 5)—four within a period of three years, with two more on the way. The opening paragraphs of the essay frame the review by speaking not to the particular books, but to the appeal of books about American heroes (in general) and one American hero (in particular)—Benjamin Franklin. Locate the sentences in Gopnik's opening frame (the first three paragraphs of the essay) where Gopnik theorizes (offers an explanation for) the popularity of books that "remake old heroes." In what way is the binary in the last sentence of paragraph 2—"presiding deity and local boy"—similar to the binaries stated in the last two sentences of paragraph one?
2. One responsibility of reviewers is, typically, to locate the treatment of a subject in the context of prevailing views. Reviewers don't just tell us what they think—they tell us how their thinking fits with what others think. The fifth and sixth paragraphs of the review are especially interesting in this regard. How do these paragraphs locate Tom Tucker's Franklin biography relative to other Franklin biographies and to tendencies in biography writing, such as conspiracy mongering? Consider, for example, how Gopnik locates Tucker's approach to Franklin by saying what it isn't. Look up the word "hagiography" in this regard.

3. A good review doesn't just tell us what is praiseworthy (and potentially less so) about the thing being reviewed. A good review teaches readers things that they need to know in order to better understand and thus evaluate for themselves both the review and the thing being reviewed. Thus, review writing usually involves some kind of research, beyond what is found in the book (or film, etc.) under consideration. Notice, for example, the information that Gopnik provides on the history of electricity throughout the review. Which pieces of this information are most important to support Gopnik's ultimate conclusion that Franklin was not guilty of fraud?
4. Gopnik extends the range of his review through various forms of comparison, which broaden its scope into informative cultural analysis. Although many of Gopnik's comparisons (and contrasts) between Franklin and other people are humorous (and thus serve to lighten the tone of the review), they are also central to the review's goal of teaching us how best to understand both Franklin and Tucker's book on him. Start by finding some of the humorous comparisons and contrasts that Gopnik makes between Franklin and others, such as the one at the beginning of paragraph 6 involving Three Stooges movies and demolition derbies.

   More generally, Gopnik's comparisons often take the form of "not this but that." See, for example, the one at the end of paragraph 22, beginning "Everyone, doubters and believers, meets in Paris," about Franklin's manipulation of his own reception by the French. Which of these "not this but that" comparison/contrasts do you think are most important to the impression of Franklin that Gopnik wishes to leave readers with? What potential misreadings does this format seek to counter?
5. A related question: in his 2001 memoir entitled *Paris to the Moon*, Gopnik reflects on a year spent in Paris with his parents during his boyhood, and then a return to live there as an adult for several years before returning to New York City. Clearly, one reason Franklin's ambassadorial experience interests Gopnik is that it touches a chord in him on the Parisian response to Americans. What is this response, as defined in the review, and what does Franklin do about it?
6. Like all writers, but perhaps especially writers of reviews, Gopnik clearly had to make decisions about the views and background of his readers. He chooses to assume, for example, that his readers are fairly knowledgeable about history because he refers to historical figures like Samuel Johnson and Addison (of Addison and Steele) and Marcel Duchamp and John Adams and Richard Feynman, among others, without explaining who they are. To counteract the impression of highbrow or academic snobbery, Gopnik often includes more popular, contemporary references in the same sentence: "Lincoln, John Adams, Lewis and Clark, Seabiscuit." Similarly, he shares the interesting and crowd-pleasing information that Franklin took the Latin phrase "*E. pluribus unum*," the motto carried by the eagle on the United States great seal, "from a classical recipe for salad dressing" (see paragraph 13). (Note: If you Google this phrase you will find other origins for it, which are illuminating in terms of Gopnik's, and probably Franklin's, rhetorical choices.) Write on the various ways that

Gopnik uses comparison in the essay to create a particular understanding of both Franklin and Tucker's book on Franklin.

7. Gopnik is especially careful in the ways that he qualifies for his readers the idea that he—and the book he is reviewing—are attacking Franklin and debunking his American hero status. Analyze the way that Gopnik's review treats the question of whether or not Franklin was a liar and a fraud—not just what Gopnik says but how he says it. What words in the review are particularly important in the way that Gopnik wishes to shape our thinking in the context of these charges? How does the concluding paragraph, wherein the famous kite experiment gets converted into metaphor, work in this regard?

8. **Link Across Chapters:** All writers have characteristic rhetorical moves—ways that they typically approach a subject, negotiate with their assumed readers, and present themselves (see page 246 on logos, pathos, and ethos). Much can be learned, both about how to write and about a particular writer, by reading a number of pieces by him or her—what we call "reading across" an author. Adam Gopnik is a featured author in this anthology, having penned three different selections: the reviews of the Franklin biography and the *Matrix* films included in this chapter and the review of books on Times Square, which is included in Chapter 16.

   Read across these three pieces. What shared features of the writing do you notice—favorite words, favorite rhetorical moves, typical ways of beginning and ending, etc.? After you have compiled this list of observations, attempt to formulate some generalizations about Gopnik as a reviewer. What trends does he seem to value most about contemporary culture? What trends is he most worried about? What does he typically find funny?

   You might extend this kind of "reading across" exercise to other reviewers—either those we have included here or some of your favorites.

9. **Application:** One link between "American Electric" and "The Unreal Thing" is that both reviews focus on narratives that feature a larger-than-life hero engaged in revolutionary activity: the historical Ben and the fictional Neo are both the stuff of legend. In "American Electric," Gopnik repeatedly contemplates the sources of Franklin's success. This is a common gambit in reviews that offer cultural analysis—to ask what it says about contemporary culture that this phenomenon, of which the particular work is an example, is so popular.

   Using Gopnik's reviews as models, review some cultural product—a celebrity (or legendary hero of the moment), book, film, CD, or TV show—that is a representative of some peaking cultural trend, asking and answering the question, "What is the source of its appeal?" What does its appeal tell us about our cultural moment? If you are writing about a popular performer as legend, you should incorporate into your review an account of prevailing views of that figure, which you would find by reading other reviews. You will also need to choose a context. See the template at the head of this chapter on page 751.

Matt Bai

King of the Hill Democrats?

This essay, which first appeared in the *New York Times Magazine*, June 26, 2005, in the "Way We Live Now" section, analyzes one of the few TV shows in recent history that doesn't make fun of Southerners. The author, whose analysis of political spin doctors is included in the Politics of Language chapter, specializes in examining the state of the Democratic Party today. In this piece, Bai explores the possibility, advanced by the Governor of North Carolina, that *King of the Hill* offers privileged insight into the thinking of small town American conservatives, and that "understanding the show's viewers might resolve some of the mysteries confronting [the Democratic] party about the vast swaths of red on the electoral map."

If you watch a lot of cable news, by now you've probably heard someone refer to a bloc of voters known as "'South Park' conservatives." The term comes from the title of a new book by Brian C. Anderson, a conservative pundit who adapted it from the writer Andrew Sullivan, and it refers to the notion that Comedy Central's obscene spoof of life in small-town America, with its hilarious skewering of liberal snobbery, is somehow the perfect crucible for understanding a new breed of brash and irreverent Republican voters. In truth, aside from its title, Anderson's book has very little to say about "South Park" itself; it's really just a retread of the argument that the mainstream media is losing its grip on world domination, marketed rather cynically to appeal to the same red-state radio hosts and book clubs that make so many right-wing polemics best sellers. 1

If politicians and pundits are really so desperate to understand the values of conservative America without leaving their living rooms, then they should start setting the TiVo to record another animated sitcom, which Anderson mentions only in passing and which, despite its general policy of eschewing politics, somehow continues to offer the most subtle and complex portrayal of small-town voters on television: "King of the Hill," on Fox. North Carolina's two-term Democratic governor, Mike Easley, is so obsessed with the show that he instructs his pollster to separate the state's voters into those who watch "King of the Hill" and those who don't so he can find out whether his arguments on social and economic issues are making sense to the sitcom's fans.

For those who have somehow missed "King of the Hill" during its nine-year run, here's a lightning-quick primer: It revolves around a classic American everyman, the earnest Hank Hill, who sells "propane and propane accessories" in the small town of Arlen, Tex. Hank lives with his wife, Peggy, a substitute Spanish teacher who can't really speak Spanish, and his son, Bobby, a sensitive class clown who exhibits none of his father's manliness. ("This is a carburetor," Hank tells his son. "Take it apart, put it back together; repeat until you're normal.")

The important thing here is that Hank Hill may be a Texan, but he and his friends could live in any of the fast-developing rural and exurban areas around Columbus or Phoenix or Atlanta that are bound to become the political weathervanes of the new century. The families in Arlen buy American-made pickups, eat at chain restaurants, maniacally water their lawns and do their shopping at the huge Mega Lo Mart. This could easily be the setup for a mean parody about rural life in America, in the same vein as "South Park," but "King of the Hill," which was created by Mike Judge (who is the voice of Hank and who also created "Beavis and Butt-head"), has never been so crass. The show's central theme has always been transformation—economic, demographic and cultural. Hank embodies all the traditional conservative values of those Americans who, as Bill Clinton famously put it, "work hard and play by the rules." He's a proud gun owner and a Nascar fan. When Bobby announces that he has landed a job selling soda at the track, Hank solemnly responds, "If you weren't my son, I'd hug you."

As Arlen becomes more built up and more diverse, however, Hank finds himself 5
struggling to adapt to new phenomena: art galleries and yoga studios, latte-sipping parents who ask their kids to call them by their first names and encourage them to drink responsibly. The show gently pokes fun at liberal and conservative stereotypes, but the real point is not to eviscerate so much as to watch Hank struggle mightily to adapt to a world of political correctness and moral ambiguity. When Peggy tells him he'll look like a racist for snubbing his Laotian neighbor, Hank replies, "What the hell kind of country is this where I can only hate a man if he's white?" And yet, like a lot of the basically conservative voters you meet in rural America—and here's where Democrats should pay close attention—Hank never professes an explicit party loyalty, and he and his buddies who sip beer in the alley don't talk like their fellow Texan Tom DeLay. If Hank votes Republican, it's because, as a voter who cares about religious and rural values, he probably doesn't see much choice. But Hank and his neighbors resemble many independent voters, open to proposals that challenge their assumptions about the world, as long as those ideas don't come from someone who seems to disrespect what they believe.

The composition of the audience for "King of the Hill" is telling. You might expect that a spoof of a small-town propane salesman and his beer-drinking buddies would attract mostly urban intellectuals, with their highly developed sense of irony. In fact, as Governor Easley long ago realized, the show's primary viewer looks a lot like Hank Hill. According to Nielsen Media Research, the largest group of "King of the Hill" viewers is made up of men between the ages of 18 and 49, and almost a quarter of those men own pickup trucks. "This is only the second show that's a comedy about the South—this and 'Andy Griffith'—that doesn't make fun of Southerners," Easley told me recently, adding that Hank and his neighbors remind him of the people he grew up with in the hills near Greenville. (Which is probably why Easley does startlingly good impressions of the various characters, including the verbally challenged Boomhauer.)

Easley polls surprisingly well for a Democrat among these voters, and he says he thinks that understanding the show's viewers might resolve some of the mysteries confronting his party about the vast swaths of red on the electoral map. Easley is reasonably progressive—he raised taxes during his first term to protect education spending—but he's also known as a guy who cracked up a race car during a spin on a Nascar course. When the governor, a former prosecutor, prepares to make his case on a partisan issue, he likes to imagine that he's explaining his position to Hank—an exercise that might be useful for his colleagues in Washington too. For instance, Easley told me that Hank would never support a budget like the one North Carolina's Senate recently passed, which would drop some 65,000 mostly elderly citizens from the Medicaid rolls; Hank, after all, has pitched in to support his own father, a brutish war veteran, and he would never condone a community's walking away from its ailing parents. Similarly, Hank may be a lover of the environment—he was furious when kids trashed the local campground—but he resents self-righteous environmentalists like the ones who forced Arlen to install those annoying low-flow toilets. Voters like Hank, if they had heard about it on the evening news, would have supported Easley's "Clean Smokestacks" law, which forced North Carolina's coal-powered electric plants to burn cleaner, but only because industry was a partner in the final bill, rather than its target.

If other Democrats want to learn from "King of the Hill," they may need to act fast. John Altschuler, one of the show's executive producers, fears that the show's 10th season next year could be its last; despite decent ratings, Fox has been buying fewer episodes and shifting its time slot, and there are rumors that the network may want to substitute yet another new reality show in its place. This is odd: after all, there is more reality about American life in five minutes of "King of the Hill" than in a full season of watching Paris Hilton prance around a farm in high heels. But none of this would come as much of a surprise to Hank Hill and his neighbors, who realized long ago that, as a nation, we often discard the things we once cherished in favor of a more synthetic modernity. "The only place you can find a Main Street these days is in Disneyland," Hank once said. "And just try to buy a gun there."

THINGS TO DO WITH THE READING

1. Rather than telling us primarily how he responds to the show, the author, Matt Bai, mostly tells us how the Democratic governor of North Carolina responds to it. What does Bai gain by filtering his response to the show through Governor Easley's? What, for example, are the rhetorical advantages of this approach?
2. Bai frames his analysis of *King of the Hill* by defining it against another animated TV show, *South Park*. How does this framing work? What does it allow us to see about *King of the Hill* that we otherwise might have been less likely to notice? What does Bai cause us, his readers, to see through his description of *South Park*? Which sentences and words in the essay best define the differences that Bai sees between the two shows?
3. **Link Across Chapters:** Bai offers *King of the Hill* as a useful guide to the values and beliefs of people who live in "red states"—those that voted Republican in the last two presidential elections. Bai also sees the show as a "subtle and complex portrayal of small town voters" (see paragraph 2). He notes that the show's main character never expresses an explicit political party loyalty. Using the chart at the end of Christopher Borick's essay on political labels (in Chapter 19), locate the features of Hank Hill's values and assumptions that would identify him as a conservative. Also locate features that complicate this categorization of Hank.

4. **Application:** Bai claims that Democrats could usefully educate themselves about Red State Americans by watching *King of the Hill.* He notes that the show does more than poke "fun at liberal and conservative stereotypes" (see paragraph 5). It also allows us to "watch Hank struggle mightily to adapt to a world of political correctness and moral ambiguity" (see paragraph 5). Find another TV program that you think deals intelligently with political party stereotypes and the struggle to adapt to moral ambiguity. What might Bai notice about Homer Simpson, for example, or President Mackenzie Allen on *Commander-in-Chief*? Write a review that uses the show of your choice as a platform for cultural analysis. Remember that there are other forms of politics, such as gender politics. So you might analyze a show that sends up stereotypes of women or men and reveals them to be struggling with difficult questions in a changing culture.

Kera Bolonik

Oy Gay!

In this piece Kera Bolonik, who reviews books for the *Village Voice* and writes for Salon.com, *The Nation*, the *New York Times*, and many other publications, uses a review of the TV sitcom *Will & Grace* to anchor a cultural analysis of the representation of Jews and gays on television. Along the way she manages to survey the formulaic "neurotic Levites and their sane-to-a-fault bemused Protestant spouses"—a formula she praises *Will & Grace* for challenging.

Without baring flesh, exchanging fluids or even shedding blood, *Will & Grace* has become the craftiest, if not the most radical, show in the history of network television—though not merely for its unabashed depiction of gay existence, or the risqué, multi-entendre-filled dialogue its writers slyly sneak under the censors' radar. 1

Will & Grace is revolutionary for something so utterly conventional it would warm the hearts of *bubbes* and *zeydes* across America's urban landscapes: sliding a portrait of a twenty-first-century Jewish American's life into a sitcom about a gay man and his best gal pal. Who in America would want to watch a show explicitly about a Jewish woman living in New York? Sounds like *Rhoda Redux*. But pair a single woman with a gay man and suddenly, you've got a winning formula.

Actually, it's downright brilliant. There hasn't been a program this overtly Jewish since *The Goldbergs*, a popular show from 1949 to 1955 that depicted the travails of a hard-working Jewish family of Bronx tenement-dwellers. For starters, the show's name is taken from the "I-Thou" treatise by twentieth-century Jewish philosopher Martin Buber, which described the ongoing dialogue between man and God. And *Will & Grace* is the first prime-time sitcom *ever* to feature a wedding between a Jewish woman and a Jewish man. When American viewers watched the nuptials between interior decorator Grace Adler (Debra Messing) and Southern Jewish doctor Marvin "Leo" Markus (Harry Connick Jr.) last year, they were bearing witness to more than just a sweeps ploy. Those "I do's" doubled as "I don'ts" to decades' worth of assimilationist portrayals of Jews. Two simple words in that context spoke volumes: More than upholding an age-old tradition that would make parents *kvell*, they communicated to Middle America that a Jewish main character does not need a gentile foil to validate his or her presence on television.

It could've been so easy for the redheaded Manhattan transplant from Schenectady to live out her boob-tube destiny in sexless wedded bliss with her *goyishe* gay best friend, Will Truman (Eric McCormack). They're symbiotic, they love and respect each other, they share man problems and they even considered having a baby together. But co-creators Max Mutchnick and David Kohan decided to thumb their collective nose at television's love affair with interfaith marriage—which, by the way, is *so* 1990s—and delivered Grace a Hebraic knight on a white horse in Central Park just as she was en route to the obstetrician's office to be inseminated with Will's sperm. A few short months later, there stood bride and groom under a *chuppah* amid a sea of white *kippot* for the entire nation to behold.

5 Until Leo galloped into Grace's life that fateful afternoon, couch potatoes had been barraged with neurotic Levites and their sane-to-a-fault, bemused Protestant spouses for more than ten years. There was nice Jewish boy Paul Buchman and his wispy WASP wife, Jamie Stemple, on *Mad About You;* nasal nanny Fran Fine, the Barbra Streisand-loving borough girl, and her haughty English boss, Maxwell Sheffield, on *The Nanny;* and hippie-dippy Dharma Finkelstein and her buttoned-up blue-blooded hubby, Greg Montgomery, in *Dharma & Greg*. On *Friends*, Ross and Monica Geller and the children of a couple who married outside the faith, are both brother and sister follow suit (Ross does so again and again). Jerry never married on *Seinfeld*, but neither did he date Jewish women in a city that boasts a surplus of eligible *madelach*. And to think, back in 1972 Jews and Catholics protested the Meredith Baxter and David Birney comic vehicle *Bridget Loves Bernie* for its depiction of a marriage between an Irish Catholic woman and a Jewish man (it was subsequently canceled). This is what you call progress?

Apparently, it *was* a step up. Before the 1990s, the Jew was relegated to a secondary character, at best—Juan Epstein (*Welcome Back, Kotter*), Natalie Green (*The Facts of Life*), Abner and Gladys Kravitz (*Bewitched*), Alex Rieger (*Taxi*)—if their Jewishness was even explicitly articulated. They were the nosy neighbors, the class clowns, the voice of reason and the best friends, and were frequently asexual or spectacular failures in the love department. Rhoda Morgenstern was a rare case, her popularity as a sidekick allowing her to spin off from *The Mary Tyler Moore Show* in 1974 to have her very own sitcom.

Still, a Jew cast as a sitcom lead was usually stuck playing the quirky partner of a straitlaced gentile, the fact of a character's Judaism almost always serving as shorthand for "neurotic," "funny" or "eccentric." (Perhaps the sole, and remarkable, exception is the case of *Seinfeld*, where the show's namesake was both the Jew and the straight man, while his "non-Jewish" friends were the oddballs.) Yet even as Jews vacated the minor-character role, another group was waiting to be typecast. Gays and lesbians (and the occasional transgendered person) turned up all over the tube: Roseanne's gay boss Leon in *Roseanne;* bed-and-breakfast owners Ron and Erick in *Northern Exposure;* Paul's lesbian sister Debbie in *Mad About You;* Ross's lesbian ex-wife Carol on *Friends*, to name just a few.

Will & Grace is the antidote to this long legacy of marginalizing and stereotyping of Jews and gays. Grace Adler and Will Truman are *both* nutty—the two are as competitive as they are insecure and self-deprecating—and enjoy their vanity as much as they do their geeky qualities (Will has a penchant for puns, Grace loves to sing badly). Yet neither Will nor Grace has anything on secondary characters like Jack McFarland (Sean Hayes), a manic Himbo with huge theatrical aspirations, pop-celebrity obsessions and delusions of grandeur, who recognizes little outside his microcosmic world of bad cabaret and gym bunnies; and Grace's gin-soaked assistant, Karen Walker (Megan Mullally), a rich bitch who knows the boldfaced names in all the New York society pages, but most days can barely remember her own. These two, along with Karen's devoted, acid-tongued maid, Rosario Salazar (Shelley Morrison), set the comedy in motion with their outrageous dysfunctions and interactions as Karen and Jack affectionately grope each other, "charge themselves some happy" at Barney's and Hermes, prank-call Marlo Thomas and torture Karen's fleet of servants.

All four friends, plus the deadpan Rosario, are fluent in queerspeak, trading bawdy quips, wicked in-jokes and pop-cultural references. But only the Upper West Side-dwelling Will understands Grace's self-referential humor, which is largely shaped by her Jewish experience. She dubs Will "Uncle Hachel" when he's being a jerk, drops casual mentions of her summers at Camp Ramah and has been known to intone a self-pitying prayer "*Borchu et adonai*, I'm gonna die alone." Jack and Karen would seem to have encountered only one Jew in their life—Grace—so they are often puzzled by her comical asides. But Grace does not become the butt of the joke; rather, we laugh at Karen and Jack for their ignorance about things Jewish. These two *über*-gentiles are the eccentrics for a change.

10 It would be so simple for Mutchnick and Kohan to posit the "straight" pair against the wacky duo. But there is one crucial difference between Will and Grace—one steeped in cultural mores—that threatens to propel one forward in life and leave the other behind. Will cleaves to his WASP reserve out of fear, preferring denial and decorum to confrontation, which can prove paralytic for him. He is out to his parents, for example, but can't bring himself to acknowledge his father's infidelities, even as he meets the mistress. Grace is the product of a theatrical Jewish mother who knows no bounds (or boundaries), and if it isn't confidence that allows it, she at least has the chutzpah to take leaps of faith.

Last year's season finale of *Will & Grace* intimated that the honeymoon between the newlywed Markuses might have been drawing to a close, though the new season shows the couple negotiating their new life together. But the survival of Grace's marriage hardly even matters. The fact that she did it at all demonstrated to her gang that she was ready to reconfigure her friendship with Will so that she could pursue sexual and emotional fulfillment through a marriage built on romance. More so, it conveyed to millions of viewers that, as *Will & Grace* blazes trails by offering fully realized, nonstereotypical gay characters, it is simultaneously an extremely entertaining sitcom about a Jewish gal from Schenectady who is as American as (the Big) Apple Pie.

THINGS TO DO WITH THE READING

1. "Oy Gay!" appeared in the November 17, 2003 issue of *The Nation*. As those of you who are *Will & Grace* fans know, the show continued for another three years. How would Bolonik read the later history of the show, in light of her interpretation of the marriage plot that she focuses on here? To what extent, for example, does the show eventually succumb to some of the sitcom conventions that threaten virtually any show on network television? In other words, update Bolonik's review: to what extent does *Will & Grace* remain "the antidote to this long legacy of marginalizing and stereotyping of Jews and gays" (see paragraph 8)?
2. **Application:** This review is a classic example of the analytical heuristic that this text calls "Seems to be about *x*, but could also be (or is 'really') about *y*." See pages 86–88 for an extended discussion of how to apply this strategy to formulating ideas, and then study how Bolonik uses it in her

analysis of *Will & Grace*. Apply this analysis to some show you know well, looking for the overt social agenda (the representation of gays in *Will & Grace*) and the covert one that lurks alongside it (the representation of Jews). Bring out the implications of the latter in your review.

3. **Application:** "Oy Gay!" offers an excellent model of focused analysis within a broader context. This is the model that this text calls "10 on 1," which is shorthand for analyzing evidence in depth. See pages 148–154, which explains the central idea behind 10 on 1: that it is better to make 10 points about a single *representative* example than to make the same basic point about 10 related examples.

   Bolonik endows her review with cultural resonance by looking at *Will & Grace* as representative of a genre—an example of a kind of television show that has long been popular. This TV show, and more, a particular episode of the show, functions as the "1" of her 10-on-1 analysis. Note the range of other shows she includes in her review and the economical way that she characterizes them (see paragraph 5 in particular). The inclusion of these other shows as comparative context is a sign that Bolonik is doing what is known as genre criticism in her review.

   Write a review of some show you know well. Use "Oy Gay!" as a model and/or use the model offered at the end of Chapter 5 in the section entitled "A Template for Organizing Papers Using 10 on 1" (pages 160–161). Locate your show in the context of other shows in the same genre and, focusing on a particular episode or two as representative of the genre, explore how the show comments on contemporary culture.

Malcolm Gladwell

Listening to Khakis: What America's Most Popular Pants Tell Us About the Way Guys Think

Named one of the "100 most influential people" by *Time* magazine in 2005, Malcolm Gladwell is the author of two best-selling books on trends, *The Tipping Point: How Little Things Can Make a Big Difference* (2000) and *Blink: The Power of Thinking Without Thinking* (2006). Originally trained as a historian, Gladwell entered journalism as a science writer (for the *Washington Post*) but has become, to use one of the terms that *The Tipping Point* made famous, "a connector"—one who bridges different fields of knowledge. In "Listening to Khakis," which was first published in 1997 in *The New Yorker*, Gladwell explores the success of the ad campaign for Dockers pants, talking with ad designers and social psychologists on the challenges of producing successful fashion advertising for men.

In the fall of 1987, Levi Strauss & Co. began running a series of national television commercials to promote Dockers, its new brand of men's khakis. All the spots—and there were twenty-eight—had the same basic structure. A handheld camera would follow a group of men as they sat around a living room or office or bar. The men were in their late thirties, but it was hard to tell, because the camera caught faces only fleetingly. It was trained instead on the men from the waist down—on the seats of their pants, on the pleats of their khakis, on their hands going in and out of their pockets. As the camera jumped in quick cuts from Docker to Docker, the men chatted in loose, overlapping non sequiturs—guy-talk fragments that, when they are rendered on the page, achieve a certain Dadaist poetry. Here is the entire transcript of "Poolman," one of the first—and, perhaps, best—ads in the series: 1

"She was a redhead about five foot six inches tall."

"And all of a sudden this thing starts spinning, and it's going round and round."

"Is that Nelson?"

"And that makes me safe, because with my wife, I'll never be that way."

"It's like your career, and you're frustrated. I mean that—that's—what you want."

"Of course, that's just my opinion."

"So money's no object."

"Yeah, money's no object."

"What are we going to do with our lives, now?"

* * *

"Well ..."

"Best of all ..."

[Voice-over] "*Levi's one-hundred-percent-cotton Dockers. If you're not wearing Dockers, you're just wearing pants.*"

"And I'm still paying the loans off."

"You've got all the money in the world."

"I'd like to at least be your poolman."

By the time the campaign was over, at the beginning of the nineties, Dockers had grown into a six-hundred-million-dollar business—a brand that if it had spun off from Levi's would have been (and would still be) the fourth-largest clothing brand in the world. Today, seventy per cent of American men between the ages of twenty-five and forty-five own a pair of Dockers, and khakis are expected to be as popular as bluejeans by the beginning of the next century. It is no exaggeration to call the original Dockers ads one of the most successful fashion-advertising campaigns in history.

This is a remarkable fact for a number of reasons, not the least of which is that the Dockers campaign was aimed at men, and no one had ever thought you could hit a home run like that by trying to sell fashion to the American male. Not long ago, two psychologists at York University, in Toronto—Irwin Silverman and Marion Eals—conducted an experiment in which they had men and women sit in an office for two minutes, without any reading material or distraction, while they ostensibly waited to take part in some kind of academic study. Then they were taken from the office and given the real reason for the experiment: to find out how many of the objects in the office they could remember. This was not a test of memory so much as it was a test of awareness—of the kind and quality of unconscious attention that people pay to the particulars of their environment. If you think about it, it was really a test of fashion sense, because, at its root, this is what fashion sense really is—the ability to register and appreciate and *remember* the details of the way those around you look and dress, and then reinterpret those details and memories yourself.

When the results of the experiment were tabulated, it was found that the women were able to recall the name and the placement of seventy per cent more objects than the men, which makes perfect sense. Women's fashion, after all, consists of an endless number of subtle combinations and variations—of skirt, dress, pants, blouse, T-shirt, hose, pumps, flats, heels, necklace, bracelet, cleavage, collar, curl, and on and on—all driven by the fact that when a woman walks down the street she knows that other women, consciously or otherwise, will notice the name and the placement of what she is wearing. Fashion works for women because women can appreciate its complexity. But when it comes to men what's the point? How on earth do you sell fashion to someone who has no appreciation for detail whatsoever?

5 The Dockers campaign, however, proved that you could sell fashion to men. But that was only the first of its remarkable implications. The second—which remains as weird and mysterious and relevant to the fashion business today as it was ten years ago—was that you could do this by training a camera on a man's butt and having him talk in yuppie gibberish.

* * *

I watched "Poolman" with three members of the new team handling the Dockers account at Foote, Cone & Belding (F.C.B.), Levi's ad agency. We were in a conference room at Levi's Plaza, in downtown San Francisco, a redbrick building decorated (appropriately enough) in khakilike earth tones, with the team members—Chris Shipman, Iwan Thomis, and Tanyia Kandohla—forming an impromptu critical panel. Shipman, who had thick black glasses and spoke in an almost inaudible laid-back drawl, put a videocassette of the first campaign into a VCR—stopping, starting, and rewinding—as the group analyzed what made the spots so special.

"Remember, this is from 1987," he said, pointing to the screen, as the camera began its jerky dance. "Although this style of filmmaking looks everyday now, that kind of handheld stuff was very fresh when these were made."

"They taped real conversations," Kandohla chimed in. "Then the footage was cut together afterward. They were thrown areas to talk about. It was very natural, not at all scripted. People were encouraged to go off on tangents."

After "Poolman," we watched several of the other spots in the original group—"Scorekeeper" and "Dad's Chair," "Flag Football," and "The Meaning of Life"—and I asked about the headlessness of the commercials, because if you watch too many in a row all those anonymous body parts begin to get annoying. But Thomis maintained that the headlessness was crucial, because it was the absence of faces that gave the dialogue its freedom. "They didn't show anyone's head because if they did the message would have too much weight," he said. "It would be too pretentious. You know, people talking about their hopes and dreams. It seems more genuine, as opposed to something stylized."

The most striking aspect of the spots is how different they are from typical 10
fashion advertising. If you look at men's fashion magazines, for example, at the advertisements for the suits of Ralph Lauren or Valentino or Hugo Boss, they almost always consist of a beautiful man, with something interesting done to his hair, wearing a gorgeous outfit. At the most, the man may be gesturing discreetly, or smiling in the demure way that a man like that might smile after, say, telling the supermodel at the next table no thanks he has to catch an early-morning flight to Milan. But that's all. The beautiful face and the clothes tell the whole story. The Dockers ads, though, are almost exactly the opposite. There's no face. The camera is jumping around so much that it's tough to concentrate on the clothes. And instead of stark simplicity, the fashion image is overlaid with a constant, confusing patter. It's almost as if the Dockers ads weren't primarily concerned with clothes at all—and in fact that's exactly what Levi's intended. What the company had discovered, in its research, was that baby-boomer men felt that the chief thing missing from their lives was male friendship. Caught between the demands of the families that many of them had started in the eighties and career considerations that had grown more onerous, they felt they had lost touch with other men. The purpose of the ads—the chatter, the lounging around, the quick cuts—was simply to conjure up a place where men could put on one-hundred-percent-cotton khakis and reconnect with one another. In the original advertising brief, that imaginary place was dubbed Dockers World.

This may seem like an awfully roundabout way to sell a man a pair of pants. But that was the genius of the campaign. One of the truisms of advertising is that it's always easier to sell at the extremes than in the middle, which is why the advertisements for Valentino and Hugo Boss are so simple. The man in the market for a thousand-dollar suit doesn't need to be convinced of the value of nice clothes. The man in the middle, though—the man in the market for a forty-dollar pair of khakis—does. In fact, he probably isn't comfortable buying clothes at all. To sell him a pair of pants you have to take him somewhere he *is* comfortable, and that was the point of Dockers World. Even the apparent gibberish of lines like "'She was a redhead about five foot six inches tall.' / 'And all of a sudden this thing starts spinning, and it's going round and round.'/'Is that Nelson?" have, if you listen closely enough, a certain quintessentially guy-friendly feel. It's the narrative equivalent of the sports-highlight reel—the sequence of five-second film clips of the best plays from the day's basketball or football or baseball games, which millions of American men watch every night on television. This nifty couplet from "Score-keeper," for instance—"'Who remembers their actual first girlfriend?'/'I would have done better, but I was bald then, too'"—is not nonsense but a twenty-minute conversation edited down to two lines. A man schooled in the highlight reel no more needs the other nineteen minutes and fifty-eight seconds of that exchange than he needs to see the intervening catch and throw to make sense of a sinking liner to left and a close play at the plate.

"Men connected to the underpinnings of what was being said," Robert Hanson, the vice-president of marketing for Dockers, told me. "These guys were really being honest and genuine and real with each other, and talking about their lives. It may not have been the truth, but it was the fantasy of what a lot of customers wanted, which was not just to be work-focussed but to have the opportunity to express how you feel about your family and friends and lives. The content was very important. The thing that built this brand was that we absolutely nailed the emotional underpinnings of what motivates baby boomers."

Hanson is a tall, striking man in his early thirties. He's what Jeff Bridges would look like if he had gone to finishing school. Hanson said that when he goes out on research trips to the focus groups that Dockers holds around the country he often deliberately stays in the background, because if the men in the group see him "they won't necessarily respond as positively or as openly." When he said this, he was wearing a pair of stone-white Dockers, a deep-blue shirt, a navy blazer, and a brilliant-orange patterned tie, and these worked so well together that it was obvious what he meant. When someone like Hanson dresses up that fabulously in Dockers, he makes it clear just how many variations and combinations are possible with a pair of khakis—but that, of course, defeats the purpose of the carefully crafted Dockers World message, which is to appeal to the man who wants nothing to do with fashion's variations and combinations. It's no coincidence that every man in every one of the group settings profiled in each commercial is wearing—albeit in different shades—*exactly the same kind of pants.* Most fashion advertising sells distinctiveness. (Can you imagine, say, an Ann Taylor commercial where a bunch of thirtyish girlfriends are lounging around chatting, all decked out in matching sweater sets?) Dockers was selling conformity.

"We would never do anything with our pants that would frighten anyone away," Gareth Morris, a senior designer for the brand, told me. "We'd never do too many belt loops, or an unusual base cloth. Our customers like one-hundred-per-cent-cotton fabrics. We would never do a synthetic. That's definitely in the market, but it's not where we need to be. Styling-wise, we would never do a wide, wide leg. We would never do a peg-legged style. Our customers seem to have a definite idea of what they want. They don't like tricky openings or zips or a lot of pocket flaps and details on the back. We've done button-through flaps, to push it a little bit. But we usually do a welt pocket—that's a pocket with a button-through. It's funny. We have focus groups in New York, Chicago, and San Francisco, and whenever we show them a pocket with a flap—it's a simple thing—they hate it. They won't buy the pants. They complain, 'How do I get my wallet?' So we compromise and do a welt. That's as far as they'll go. And there's another thing. They go, 'My butt's big enough. I don't want flaps hanging off of it, too.' They like inseam pockets. They like to know where they put their hands." He gestured to the pair of experimental prototype Dockers he was wearing, which had pockets that ran almost parallel to the waistband of the pants. "This is a stretch for us," he said. "If you start putting more stuff on than we have on our product, you're asking for trouble."

15 The apotheosis of the notion of khakis as nonfashion-guy fashion came several years after the original Dockers campaign, when Haggar Clothing Co. hired the Goodby, Silverstein & Partners ad agency, in San Francisco, to challenge Dockers' khaki dominance. In retrospect, it was an inspired choice since Goodby, Silverstein is Guy Central. It does Porsche ("Kills Bugs Fast") and Isuzu and the recent "Got Milk?" campaign and a big chunk of the Nike business, and it operates out of a gutted turn-of-the-century building down-town, refurbished in what is best described as neo-Erector set. The campaign that it came up with featured voice-overs by Roseanne's television husband, John Goodman. In the best of the ads, entitled "I Am," a thirtyish man wakes up, his hair all mussed, pulls on a pair of white khakis, and half sleepwalks outside to get the paper. "*I am not what I wear. I'm not a pair of pants, or a shirt.*" Goodman intones. The man walks by his wife, handing her the front sections of the paper. "*I'm not in touch with my inner child. I don't read poetry, and I'm not politically correct.*" He heads away from the kitchen, down a hallway, and his kid grabs the comics from him. "*I'm just a guy, and I don't have time to think about what I wear, because I've got a lot of important guy things to do.*" All he has left now is the sports section and, gripping it purposefully, he heads for the bathroom. "*One-hundred-per-cent-cotton wrinkle-free khaki pants that don't require a lot of thought. Haggar. Stuff you can wear.*"

"We softened it," Richard Silverstein told me as we chatted in his office, perched on chairs in the midst of—among other things—a lacrosse stick, a bike stand, a gym bag full of yesterday's clothing, three toy Porsches, and a giant model of a Second World War Spitfire hanging from the ceiling. "We didn't say 'Haggar Apparel' or 'Haggar Clothing.' We said, 'Hey, listen, guys, don't worry. It's just *stuff.* Don't worry about it.' The concept was 'Make it approachable.' " The difference between this and the Dockers ad is humor. F.C.B. assiduously documented men's inner lives. Goodby, Silverstein made fun of them. But it's essentially the same message. It's instructive, in this light, to think about the Casual Friday phenomenon of the past decade, the loosening of corporate dress codes that was spawned by the rise of khakis. Casual Fridays are commonly thought to be about men rejecting the uniform of the suit. But surely that's backward. Men started wearing khakis to work because Dockers and Haggar made it sound as if khakis were going to be even easier than a suit. The khaki-makers realized that men didn't want to get rid of uniforms; they just wanted a better uniform.

The irony, of course, is that this idea of nonfashion—of khakis as the choice that diminishes, rather than enhances, the demands of fashion—turned out to be a white lie. Once you buy even the plainest pair of khakis, you invariably also buy a sports jacket and a belt and a whole series of shirts to go with it—maybe a polo knit for the weekends, something in plaid for casual, and a button-down for a dressier look—and before long your closet is thick with just the kinds of details and options that you thought you were avoiding. You may not add these details as brilliantly or as consciously as say, Hanson does, but you end up doing it nonetheless. In the past seven years, sales of men's clothing in the United States have risen an astonishing twenty-one per cent, in large part because of this very fact—that khakis, even as they have simplified the bottom half of the male wardrobe, have forced a steady revision of the top. At the same time, even khakis themselves—within the narrow constraints of khakidom—have quietly expanded their range. When Dockers were launched, in the fall of 1986, there were just three basic styles: the double-pleated Docker in khaki, olive, navy, and black; the Steamer, in cotton canvas; and the more casual flat-fronted Docker. Now there are twenty-four Dockers and Haggar and everyone else has been playing a game of bait and switch: lure men in with the promise of a uniform and then slip them, bit by bit, fashion. Put them in an empty room and then, ever so slowly, so as not to scare them, fill the room with objects.

* * *

There is a puzzle in psychology known as the canned-laughter problem, which has a deeper and more complex set of implications about men and women and fashion and why the dockers ads were so successful. Over the years, several studies have been devoted to this problem, but perhaps the most instructive was done by two psychologists at the University of Wisconsin, Gerald Cupchik and Howard Leventhal. Cupchik and Leventhal took a stack of cartoons (including many from *The New Yorker*), half of which an independent panel had rated as very funny and half of which it had rated as mediocre. They put the cartoons on slides, had a voice-over read the captions, and presented the slide show to groups of men and women. As you might expect, both sexes reacted pretty much the same way. Then Cupchik and Leventhal added a laugh track to the voice-over—the subjects were told that it was actual laughter from people who were in the room during the taping—and repeated the experiment. This time, however, things got strange. The canned laughter made the women laugh a little harder and rate the cartoons as a little funnier than they had before. But not the men. They laughed a bit more at the good cartoons but much more at the bad cartoons. The canned laughter also made them rate the bad cartoons as much funnier than they had rated them before, but it had little or no effect on their ratings of the good cartoons. In fact, the men found a bad cartoon with a laugh track to be almost as funny as a good cartoon without one. What was going on?

The guru of male-female differences in the ad world is Joan Meyers-Levy, a professor at the University of Chicago business school. In a groundbreaking series of articles written over the past decade, Meyers-Levy has explained the canned-laughter problem and other gender anomalies by arguing that men and women use fundamentally different methods of processing information. Given two pieces of evidence about how funny something is—their own opinion and the opinion of others (the laugh track)—the women came up with a higher score than before because they added the two clues together: they integrated the information before them. The men, on the other hand, picked one piece of evidence and ignored the other. For the bad cartoons, they got carried away by the laugh track and gave out hugely generous scores for funniness. For the good cartoons, however, they were so wedded to their own opinion that suddenly the laugh track didn't matter at all.

20 This idea—that men eliminate and women integrate—is called by Meyers-Levy the "selectivity hypothesis." Men are looking for a way to simplify the route to a conclusion, so they seize on the most obvious evidence and ignore the rest, while women, by contrast, try to process information comprehensively. So-called bandwidth research, for example, has consistently shown that if you ask a group of people to sort a series of objects or ideas into categories, the men will create fewer and larger categories than the women will. They use bigger mental bandwidths. Why? Because the bigger the bandwidth the less time and attention you have to pay to each individual object. Or consider what is called the invisibility question. If a woman is being asked a series of personal questions by another woman, she'll say more if she's facing the woman she's talking to than she will if her listener is invisible. With men, it's the opposite. When they can't see the person who's asking them questions, they suddenly and substantially open up. This, of course, is a condition of male communication which has been remarked on by women for millennia. But the selectivity hypothesis suggests that the cause of it has been misdiagnosed. It's not that men necessarily have trouble expressing their feelings; it's that in a face-to-face conversation they experience emotional overload. A man can't process nonverbal information (the expression and body language of the person asking him questions) and verbal information (the personal question being asked) at the same time any better than he can process other people's laughter and his own laughter at the same time. He has to select, and it is Meyers-Levy's contention that this pattern of behavior suggests significant differences in the way men and women respond to advertising.

Joan Meyers-Levy is a petite woman in her late thirties, with a dark pageboy haircut and a soft voice. She met me in the downtown office of the University of Chicago with three large folders full of magazine advertisements under one arm, and after chatting about the origins and the implications of her research she handed me an ad from several years ago for Evian bottled water. It has a beautiful picture of the French Alps and, below that, in large type, "Our factory." The text ran for several paragraphs, beginning:

> You're not just looking at the French Alps. You're looking at one of the most pristine places on earth. And the origin of Evian Natural Spring Water.
>
> Here, it takes no less than 15 years for nature to purify every drop of Evian as it flows through mineral-rich glacial formations deep within the mountains. And it is here that Evian acquires its unique balance of minerals.

"Now, is that a male or a female ad?" she asked. I looked at it again. The picture baffled me. But the word "factory" seemed masculine, so I guessed male.

She shook her head. "It's female. Look at the picture. It's just the Alps, and then they label it 'Our factory.' They're using a metaphor. To understand this, you're going to have to engage in a fair amount of processing. And look at all the imagery they're encouraging you to build up. You're not just looking at the

French Alps. It's 'one of the most pristine places on earth' and it will take nature 'no less than fifteen years' to purify." Her point was that this is an ad that works only if the viewer appreciates all its elements—if the viewer integrates, not selects. A man, for example, glancing at the ad for a fraction of a second, might focus only on the words "Our factory" and screen out the picture of the Alps entirely, the same way he might have screened out the canned laughter. Then he wouldn't get the visual metaphor. In fact, he might end up equating Evian with a factory, and that would be a disaster. Anyway, why bother going into such detail about the glaciers if it's just going to get lost in the big male bandwidth?

Meyers-Levy handed me another Evian advertisement. It showed a man—the Olympic Gold Medal swimmer Matt Biondi—by a pool drinking Evian, with the caption "Revival of the fittest." The women's ad had a hundred and nineteen words of text. This ad had just twenty-nine words: "No other water has the unique, natural balance of minerals that Evian achieves during its 15-year journey deep within the French Alps. To be the best takes time." Needless to say, it came from a men's magazine. "With men, you don't want the fluff," she said. "Women, though, participate a lot more in whatever they are processing. By giving them more cues, you give them something to work with. You don't have to be so literal. With women you can be more allusive, so you can draw them in. They will engage in elaboration, and the more associations they make the easier it is to remember and retrieve later on."

Meyers-Levy took a third ad from her pile, this one for the 1997 Mercury 25
Mountaineer four-wheel-drive sport-utility vehicle. It covers two pages, has the heading "Take the Rough with the Smooth," and shows four pictures—one of the vehicle itself, one of a mother and her child, one of a city skyline, and a large one of the interior of the car, over which the ad's text is superimposed. Around the border of the ad are forty-four separate, tiny photographs of roadways and buildings and construction sites and manhole covers. *Female.* Next to it on the table she put another ad—this one a single page, with a picture of the Mountaineer's interior, fifteen lines of text, a picture of the car's exterior, and, at the top, the heading: "When the Going Gets Tough, the Tough Get Comfortable." *Male.* "It's details, details. They're saying lots of different stuff," she said, pointing to the female version. "With men, instead of trying to cover everything in a single execution, you'd probably want to have a whole series of ads, each making a different point."

After a while, the game got very easy—if a bit humiliating. Meyers-Levy said that her observations were not anti-male—that both the male and the female strategies have their strengths and their weaknesses—and, of course, she's right. On the other hand, reading the gender of ads makes it painfully obvious how much the advertising world—consciously or not—talks down to men. Before I met Meyers-Levy, I thought that the genius of the famous first set of Dockers ads was their psychological complexity, their ability to capture the many layers of eighties guyness. But when I thought about them again after meeting Meyers-Levy, I began to think that their real genius lay in their heroic simplicity—in the fact that F.C.B. had the self-discipline to fill the allotted thirty seconds with as *little* as possible. Why no heads? The invisibility rule. Guys would never listen to that

Dadaist extemporizing if they had to process nonverbal cues, too. Why were the ads set in people's living rooms *and* at the office? Bandwidth. The message was that khakis were wide-bandwidth pants. And why were all the ads shot in almost exactly the same way, and why did all the dialogue run together in one genial, faux-philosophical stretch of highlight reel? Because of canned laughter. Because if there were more than one message to be extracted men would get confused.

* * *

In the early nineties, Dockers began to falter. In 1992, the company sold sixty-six million pairs of khakis, but in 1993, as competition from Haggar and the Gap and other brands grew fiercer, that number slipped to fifty-nine million six hundred thousand, and by 1994 it had fallen to forty-seven million. In marketing-speak, user reality was encroaching on brand personality; that is, Dockers were being defined by the kind of middle-aged men who wore them, and not by the hipper, younger men in the original advertisements. The brand needed a fresh image, and the result was the "Nice Pants" campaign currently being shown on national television—a campaign widely credited with the resurgence of Dockers' fortunes.

In one of the spots, "Vive la France," a scruffy young man in his early twenties, wearing Dockers, is sitting in a café in Paris. He's obviously a tourist. He glances up and sees a beautiful woman (actually, the supermodel Tatjana Patitz) looking right at him. He's in heaven. She starts walking directly toward him, and as she passes by she says, "*Beau pantalon.*" As he looks frantically through his French phrase book for a translation, the waiter comes by and cuffs him on the head: "Hey, she says, 'Nice pants.' " Another spot in the series, "Subway Love," takes place on a subway car in Chicago. He (a nice young man wearing Dockers) spots her (a total babe), and their eyes lock. Romantic music swells. He moves toward her, but somehow, in a sudden burst of pushing and shoving, they get separated. Last shot: she's inside the car, her face pushed up against the glass. He's outside the car, his face pushed up against the glass. As the train slowly pulls away, she mouths two words: "Nice pants."

It may not seem like it, but "Nice Pants" is as radical a campaign as the original Dockers series. If you look back at the way that Sansabelt pants, say, were sold in the sixties, each ad was what advertisers would call a pure "head" message: the pants were comfortable, durable, good value. The genius of the first Dockers campaign was the way it combined head and heart: these were all-purpose, no-nonsense pants that connected to the emotional needs of baby boomers. What happened to Dockers in the nineties, though, was that everyone started to do head and heart for khakis. Haggar pants were wrinkle-free (head) and John Goodman-guy (heart). The Gap, with its brilliant billboard campaign of the early nineties—"James Dean wore khakis," "Frank Lloyd Wright wore khakis"—perfected the heart message by forging an emotional connection between khakis and a particular nostalgic, glamorous all-Americanness. To reassert itself, Dockers needed to go an extra step. Hence "Nice Pants," a campaign that for the first time in Dockers history raises the subject of sex.

"It's always been acceptable for a man to be a success in business," Hanson 30
said, explaining the rationale behind "Nice Pants." "It's always been expected of a

man to be a good provider. The new thing that men are dealing with is that it's O.K. for men to have a sense of personal style, and that it's O.K. to be seen as sexy. It's less about the head than about the combination of the head, the heart, and the groin. It's those three things. That's the complete man."

The radical part about this, about adding the groin to the list, is that almost no other subject for men is as perilous as the issue of sexuality and fashion. What "Nice Pants" had to do was talk about sex the same way that "Poolman" talked about fashion, which was to talk about it by not talking about it—or, at least, to talk about it in such a coded, cautious way that no man would ever think Dockers was suggesting that he wear khakis in order to look *pretty*. When I took a videotape of the "Nice Pants" campaign to several of the top agencies in New York and Los Angeles, virtually everyone agreed that the spots were superb, meaning that somehow F.C.B. had managed to pull off this balancing act.

What David Altschiller, at Hill, Holiday/Altschiller, in Manhattan, liked about the spots, for example, was that the hero was naïve: in neither case did he know that he had on nice pants until a gorgeous woman told him so. Naïveté, Altschiller stressed, is critical. Several years ago, he did a spot for Claiborne for Men cologne in which a great-looking guy in a bar, wearing a gorgeous suit, was obsessing neurotically about a beautiful woman at the other end of the room: "*I see this woman. She's perfect. She's looking at me. She's smiling. But wait. Is she smiling at me? Or laughing at me? … Or looking at someone else?*" You'd never do this in an ad for women's cologne. Can you imagine? "I see this guy. He's perfect. Ohmigod. Is he looking at me?" In women's advertising, self-confidence is sexy. But if a man is self-confident—if he knows he is attractive and is beautifully dressed—then he's not a man anymore. He's a fop. He's effeminate. The cologne guy had to be neurotic or the ad wouldn't work. "Men are still abashed about acknowledging that clothing is important," Altschiller said. "Fashion can't be important to me as a man. Even when, in the first commercial, the waiter says 'Nice pants,' it doesn't compute to the guy wearing the nice pants. He's thinking. What do you mean, 'Nice pants'?" Altschiller was looking at a videotape of the Dockers ad as he talked—standing at a forty-five-degree angle to the screen, with one hand on the top of the monitor, one hand on his hip, and a small, bemused smile on his lips. "The world may think they are nice, but so long as he doesn't think so he doesn't have to be self-conscious about it, and the lack of self-consciousness is very important to men. Because '*I don't care.*' Or 'Maybe I care, but I can't be *seen* to care.' " For the same reason, Altschiller liked the relative understatement of the phrase "nice pants," as opposed to something like "great pants," since somewhere between "nice" and "great" a guy goes from just happening to look good to the unacceptable position of actually trying to look good. "In focus groups, men said that to be told you had 'nice pants' was one of the highest compliments a man could wish for, "Tanyia Kandohla told me later, when I asked about the slogan. "They wouldn't want more attention drawn to them than that."

In many ways, the "Nice Pants" campaign is a direct descendant of the hugely successful campaign that Rubin-Postaer & Associates, in Santa Monica, did for Bugle Boy Jeans in the early nineties. In the most famous of those spots, the camera opens on an attractive but slightly goofy-looking man in a pair of jeans who is hitchhiking by the side of a desert highway. Then a black Ferrari with a fabulous babe at the wheel drives by, stops, and backs up. The babe rolls down the window and says, "Excuse me. Are those Bugle Boy Jeans that you're wearing?" The goofy guy leans over and pokes his head in the window, a surprised half smile on his face: "Why, yes, they *are* Bugle Boy Jeans."

"Thank you," the babe says, and she rolls up the window and drives away.

This is really the same ad as "Nice Pants"—the babe, the naïve hero, the 35
punch line. The two ads have something else in common. In the Bugle Boy spot, the hero wasn't some stunning male model. "I think he was actually a boxboy at Vons in Huntington Beach," Larry Postaer, the creative director of Rubin-Postaer & Associates, told me. "I guess someone"—at Bugle Boy—"liked him." He's O.K.-looking, but not nearly in the same class as the babe in the Ferrari. In "Subway Love," by the same token, the Dockers man is medium-sized, almost small, and gets pushed around by much tougher people in the tussle on the train. He's cute, but he's a little bit of a wimp. Kandohla says that F.C.B. tried very hard to find someone with that look—someone who was, in her words, "aspirational real," not some "buff, muscle-bound jock." In a fashion ad for women, you can use Claudia Schiffer to sell a cheap pair of pants. But not in a fashion ad for men. The guy has to be *believable.* "A woman cannot be too gorgeous," Postaer explained. A man, however, can be too gorgeous, because then he's not a man anymore. It's pretty rudimentary. Yet there are people who don't buy that, and have gorgeous men in their ads. I don't get it. Talk to Barneys about how well that's working. It couldn't stay in business trying to sell that high-end swagger to a mass market. The general public wouldn't accept it. Look at beer commercials. They always have these gorgeous girls—even now, after all the heat—and the guys are always just guys. That's the way it is. We only reflect what's happening out there, we're not creating it. Those guys who run the real high-end fashion ads—they don't understand that. They're trying to remold how people think about gender. I can't explain it, though I have my theories. It's like a Grecian ideal. But you can't be successful at advertising by trying to re-create the human condition. You can't alter men's minds, particularly on subjects like sexuality. It'll never happen."

Postaer is a gruff, rangy guy, with a Midwestern accent and a gravelly voice, who did Budweiser commercials in Chicago before moving West fifteen years ago. When he wasn't making fun of the pretentious style of East Coast fashion advertising, he was making fun of the pretentious questions of East Coast writers. When, for example, I earnestly asked him to explain the logic behind having the goofy guy screw up his face in such a—well, goofy—way when he says, "Why, yes, they *are* Bugle Boy Jeans," Postaer took his tennis shoes off his desk, leaned forward bemusedly in his chair, and looked at me as if my head came to a small point. "Because that's the only way he could say it," he said. "I suppose we might have had him say it a little differently if he could actually *act.*"

Incredibly, Postaer said, the people at Bugle Boy wanted the babe to invite the goofy guy into the car, despite the fact that this would have violated the most important rule that governs this new style of groin messages in men's-fashion advertising, which is that the guy absolutely cannot ever get the girl. It's not just that if he got the girl the joke wouldn't work anymore; it's that if he got the girl it might look as if he had deliberately dressed to get the girl, and although at the back of every man's mind as he's dressing in the morning there is the thought of getting the girl, any open admission that that's what he's actually trying to do would undermine the whole unself-conscious, antifashion statement that men's advertising is about. If Tatjana Patitz were to say "*Beau garçon*" to the guy in "Vive Ia France," or the babe on the subway were to give the wimp her number, Dockers would suddenly become terrifyingly conspicuous—the long-pants equivalent of wearing a tight little Speedo to the beach. And if the Vons boxboy should actually get a ride from the Ferrari babe, the ad would suddenly become believable only to that thin stratum of manhood which thinks that women in Ferraris find twenty-four-dollar jeans irresistible. "We fought that tooth and nail," Postaer said. "And it more or less cost us the account, even though the ad was wildly successful." He put his tennis shoes back up on the desk. "But that's what makes this business fun—trying to prove to clients how wrong they are."

* * *

The one ad in the "Nice Pants" campaign which isn't like the Bugle Boy spots is called "Motorcycle." In it a nice young man happens upon a gleaming Harley on a dark back street of what looks like downtown Manhattan. He strokes the seat and then, unable to contain himself, climbs aboard the bike and bounces up and down, showing off his Dockers (the "product shot") but accidentally breaking a mirror on the handlebar. He looks up. The Harley's owner—a huge, leather-clad biker—is looking down at him. The biker glowers, looking him up and down, and says, "Nice pants." Last shot: the biker rides away, leaving the guy standing on the sidewalk in just his underwear.

What's surprising about this ad is that, unlike "Vive la France" and "Subway Love," it *does* seem to cross the boundaries of acceptable sex talk. The rules of guy advertising so carefully observed in those spots—the fact that the hero has to be naïve, that he can't be too good-looking, that he can't get the girl, and that he can't be told anything stronger than. "Nice pants"—are all, in some sense, reactions to the male fear of appearing too concerned with fashion, of being too pretty, of not being masculine. But what is "Motorcycle"? It's an ad about a sweet-looking guy down in the Village somewhere who loses his pants to a butch-looking biker in leather. "I got so much feedback at the time of 'Well, God, that's kind of *gay*, don't you think?'" Robert Hanson said. "People were saying, 'This buff guy comes along and he rides off with the guy's pants. I mean, what the hell were they doing?' It came from so many different people within the industry. It came from some of our most conservative retailers. But do you know what? If you put these three spots up—'Vive La France,' 'Subway Love,' and 'Motorcycle'—which one do you think men will talk about ad nauseam? 'Motorcycle.' It's No. 1. It's because he's really cool. He's in a really cool environment, and it's every guy's fantasy to have a really cool, tricked-out fancy motorcycle."

Hanson paused, as if he recognized that what he was saying was quite sensi- 40
tive. He didn't want to say that men failed to pick up the gay implications of the ad because they're stupid, because they aren't stupid. And he didn't want to sound condescending, because Dockers didn't build a six-hundred-million-dollar business in five years by sounding condescending. All he was trying to do was point out the fundamental exegetical error in calling this a gay ad, because the only way for a Dockers man to be offended by "Motorcycle" would be if he thought about it with a little imagination, if he picked up on some fairly subtle

cues, if he integrated an awful lot of detail. In other words, a Dockers man could only be offended if he did precisely what, according to Meyers-Levy, men don't do. It's not a gay ad because it's a guy ad. "The fact is," Hanson said, "that most men's interpretation of that spot is: You know what? Those pants must be really cool, because they prevented him from getting the shit kicked out of him."

THINGS TO DO WITH THE READING

1. What reasons does the essay offer for the differences between men and women in the two experiments it describes—one testing men's and women's ability to remember detail and the other testing the response of men versus women to canned laughter when assessing the humor of cartoons?
2. Gladwell concludes his analysis of male-oriented fashion advertising campaigns not with summary but with a final and culminating example. Inclusion of the word "integrating" makes the link with a binary (selective versus integrating) that advertisers consider when designing ads for either gender. Explain how the essay's final paragraph (about response to the ad "Motorcycle") ties together and culminates the essay's main ideas. According to the essay, why was the ad successful with male viewers?
3. **Link Across Chapters:** Throughout this book we have argued that interpretation always takes place inside particular interpretive contexts and that more than one plausible interpretive context may apply to the same data (see pages 88–93). Compare the conclusions Gladwell arrives at about headlessness in the early Dockers ad campaign with the conclusions that Berger (author of the last essay in Chapter 17) might arrive at about the same feature. Berger, in his essay on the nude in European art, theorized that the image of the female nude in European paintings was designed to flatter a presumed male viewer. He argues that as a result of this tradition women come to see themselves in a divided way—as both spectacle and spectator. Use this interpretive context to offer an alternative explanation of headlessness in the early Docker ads and of the importance of guy fashion being represented as "non-fashion." What might Berger say to the claim from Gladwell's essay that "A woman cannot be too gorgeous. A man, however, can be too gorgeous, because then he's not a man anymore" (see paragraph 35)?
4. **Application:** Gladwell's analysis offers interesting ideas about ad design—about how ad makers act on theories about gender and perception ("processing") in order to target male or female audiences. Do your own primary research with advertisements in order to illustrate, test, and possibly extend Gladwell's analysis. Look for ads for the same product or kind of product in magazines (mainstream) aimed primarily at women and in magazines aimed primarily at men. Locate what seem to be significant differences and then determine the extent to which the "selectivity" and

"integration" hypotheses presented in Gladwell's essay could account for the differences.

Alternatively, test one of the following assertions by surveying current fashion ads aimed at men: (1) "Most fashion advertising sells distinctness. ... Dockers was selling conformity" (see paragraph 13). (2) "What 'Nice Pants' had to do was talk about sex the same way that 'Poolman' talked about fashion, which was to talk about it by not talking about it ..." (see paragraph 31). ◗

X.J. Kennedy

Who Killed King Kong?

This essay, originally published in *Dissent* in Spring 1960, offers an analysis of the causes for the continued popularity of the original 1933 film of *King Kong* with African-American audiences. Reviews of more recent versions of the film might have been included in this book, but this one offers readers a chance to think about how reviews function historically. The piece also illustrates an important context for thinking about review writing: reception theory. Reception theory is an analytical mode that looks less at the work itself than at the way the work was received by its audiences. It is provocative to see the context in which the poet and essayist X.J. Kennedy published his views of the reception of *King Kong* in 1960 in a leftist journal. And it is similarly provocative now to compare that reading to the ones that might be produced post-9/11 about a destructive force unleashed in New York City.

The ordeal and spectacular death of King Kong, the giant ape, undoubtedly have been witnessed by more Americans than have ever seen a performance of *Hamlet*, *Iphigenia at Aulis*, or even *Tobacco Road*. Since RKO-Radio Pictures first released *King Kong* a quarter-century has gone by; yet year after year, from prints that grow more rain-beaten, from sound tracks that grow more tinny ticket-buyers by thousands still pursue Kong's luckless fight against the forces of technology, tabloid journalism, and the DAR. They see him chloroformed to sleep, see him whisked from his jungle isle to New York and placed on show, see him burst his chains to roam the city (lugging a frightened blonde), at last to plunge from the spire of the Empire State Building, machine-gunned by model airplanes. 1

Though Kong may die, one begins to think his legend unkillable. No clearer proof of his hold upon the popular imagination may be seen than what emerged one catastrophic week in March 1955, when New York WOR-TV programmed *Kong* for seven evenings in a row (a total of sixteen showings). Many a rival network vice-president must have scowled when surveys showed that *Kong*—the 1933 B-picture—had lured away fat segments of the viewing populace from such powerful competitors as Ed Sullivan, Groucho Marx and Bishop Sheen.

But even television has failed to run *King Kong* into oblivion. Coffee-in-the-lobby cinemas still show the old hunk of hokum, with the apology that in its use of composite shots and animated models the film remains technically interesting. And no other monster in movie history has won so devoted a popular audience. None of the plodding mummies, the stultified draculas, the white-coated Lugosis[1] with their shiny pinball-machine laboratories, none of the invisible stranglers, berserk robots, or menaces from Mars has ever enjoyed so many resurrections.

Why does the American public refuse to let King Kong rest in peace? It is true, I'll admit, that *Kong* outdid every monster movie before or since in sheer carnage. Producers Cooper and Schoedsack crammed into it dinosaurs, headhunters, riots, aerial battles, bullets, bombs, bloodletting. Heroine Fay Wray, whose function is mainly to scream, shuts her mouth for hardly one uninterrupted minute from first

[1] Bela Lugosi, an actor in many horror movies.

reel to last. It is also true that *Kong* is larded with good healthy sadism, for those whose joy it is to see the frantic girl dangled from cliffs and harried by pterodactyls. But it seems to me that the abiding appeal of the giant ape rests on other foundations.

Kong has, first of all, the attraction of being manlike. His simian nature gives 5
him one huge advantage over giant ants and walking vegetables in that an audience may conceivably identify with him. Kong's appeal has the quality that established the Tarzan series as American myth—for what man doesn't secretly image himself a huge hairy howler against whom no other monster has a chance? If Tarzan recalls the ape in us, then Kong may well appeal to that great-granddaddy primordial brute from whose tribe we have all deteriorated.

Intentionally or not, the producers of *King Kong* encourage this identification by etching the character of Kong with keen sympathy. For the ape is a figure in a tradition familiar to moviegoers: the tradition of the pitiable monster. We think of Lon Chaney in the role of Quasimodo, of Karloff in the original *Frankenstein.* As we watch the Frankenstein monster's fumbling and disastrous attempts to befriend a flower-picking child, our sympathies are enlisted with the monster in his impenetrable loneliness. And so with Kong. As he roars in his chains, while barkers sell tickets to boobs who gape at him, we perhaps feel something more deep than pathos. We begin to sense something of the problem that engaged Eugene O'Neill in *The Hairy Ape:* the dilemma of a displaced animal spirit forced to live in a jungle built by machines.

King Kong, it is true, had special relevance in 1933. Landscapes of the depression are glimpsed early in the film when an impresario, seeking some desperate pretty girl to play the lead in a jungle movie, visits souplines and a Woman's Home Mission. In Fay Wray—who's been caught snitching an apple from a fruitstand—his search is ended. When he gives her a big feed and a movie contract, the girl is magic-carpeted out of the world of the National Recovery Act. And when, in the film's climax, Kong smashes that very Third Avenue landscape in which Fay had wandered hungry, audiences of 1933 may well have felt a personal satisfaction.

What is curious is that audiences of 1960 remain hooked. For in the heart of urban man, one suspects, lurks the impulse to fling a bomb. Though machines speed him to the scene of his daily grind, though IBM comptometers ("freeing the human mind from drudgery") enable him to drudge more efficiently once he arrives, there comes a moment when he wishes to turn upon his machines and kick hell out of them. He wants to hurl his combination radio-alarmclock out the bedroom window and listen to its smash. What subway commuter wouldn't love—just for once—to see the down-town express smack head-on into the uptown local? Such a wish is gratified in that memorable scene in *Kong* that opens with a wide-angle shot: interior of a railway car on the Third Avenue El. Straphangers are nodding, the literate refold their newspapers. Unknown to them, Kong has torn away a section of trestle toward which the train now speeds. The motorman spies Kong up ahead, jams on the brakes. Passengers hurtle together like so many peas in a pail. In a window of the car appear Kong's bloodshot eyes. Women shriek. Kong picks up the railway car as if it were a rat, flips it to the street and ties knots in it, or something. To any commuter the scene must appear one of the most satisfactory pieces of celluloid ever exposed.

Yet however violent his acts, Kong remains a gentleman. Remarkable is his sense of chivalry. Whenever a fresh boa constrictor threatens Fay, Kong first sees that the lady is safely parked, then manfully thrashes her attacker. (And she, the ingrate, runs away every time his back is turned.) Atop the Empire State Building, ignoring his pursuers, Kong places Fay on a ledge as tenderly as it she were a dozen eggs. He fondles her, then turns to face the Army Air Force. And Kong is perhaps the most disinterested lover since Cyrano: his attentions to the lady are utterly without hope of reward. After all, between a five-foot blonde and a fifty-foot ape, love can hardly be more than an intellectual flirtation. In his simian way King Kong is the hopelessly yearning lover of Petrarchan convention. His forced exit from his jungle, in chains, results directly from his single-minded pursuit of Fay. He smashes a Broadway theater when the notion enters his dull brain that the flashbulbs of photographers somehow endanger the lady. His perilous shinnying up a skyscraper to pluck Fay from her boudoir is an act of the kindliest of hearts. He's impossible to discourage even though the love of his life can't lay eyes on him without shrieking murder.

10 The tragedy of King Kong then, is to be the beast who at the end of the fable fails to turn into the handsome prince. This is the conviction that the scriptwriters would leave with us in the film's closing line. As Kong's corpse lies blocking traffic in the street, the enterpreneur who brought Kong to New York turns to the assembled reporters and proclaims: "That's your story, boys—it was Beauty killed the Beast!" But greater forces than those of the screaming Lady have combined to lay Kong low, if you ask me. Kong lives for a time as one of those persecuted near-animal souls bewildered in the middle of an industrial order, whose simple desires are thwarted at every turn. He climbs the Empire. State Building because in all New York it's the closest thing he can find to the clifftop of his jungle isle. He dies, a pitiful dolt, and the army brass and publicity-men cackle over him. His death is the only possible outcome to as neat a tragic dilemma as you can ask for. The machine-guns do him in, while the manicured human hero (a nice clean Dartmouth boy) carries away Kong's sweetheart to the altar, O, the misery of it all. There's far more truth about upper-middle-class. American life in *King Kong* than in the last seven dozen novels of John P. Marquand.

A Negro friend from Atlanta tells me that in movie houses in colored neighborhoods throughout the South, *Kong* does a constant business. They show the thing in Atlanta at least every year, presumably to the same audiences. Perhaps this popularity may simply be due to the fact that Kong is one of the most watchable movies ever constructed, but I wonder whether Negro audiences may not find some archetypical appeal in this serio-comic tale of a huge black powerful free spirit whom all the hardworking white policemen are out to kill.

Every day in the week on a screen somewhere in the world, King Kong relives his agony. Again and again he expires on the Empire State Building, as audiences of the devout assist his sacrifice. We watch him die, and by extension kill the ape within our bones, but these little deaths of ours occur in prosaic surroundings. We do not die on a tower, New York before our feet, nor do we give our lives to smash a few flying machines. It is not for us to bring to a momentary standstill the civilization in which we move. King Kong does this for us. And so we kill him again and again, in much-spliced celluloid; while the ape in us expires from day to day, obscure, in desperation.

THINGS TO DO WITH THE READING

1. Get a copy of the 1933 version of *King Kong* and watch it. From today's perspective, which of the claims that Kennedy makes from his contemporary perspective—one that is now nearly 50 years old—seem least credible, and why? And which arguably are still pertinent interpretations of the original *Kong*? In short, which features of our current cultural climate would require a writer to update and adjust the 1960 lens?

2. The Kennedy essay offers the opportunity to think about how all research needs to be conditioned by a sense of history. In other words, to some extent, "Who Killed King Kong?" is a piece that tells us at least as much about 1960, when it was written, as it does about 1933, when the film was produced. What does the review tell us about 1960—or at least about political attitudes on the left in 1960? (See pages 111–113 on "the pitch, the complaint, and the moment.")

3. **Link:** For Kennedy, Kong is a kind of avenging hero figure, at least in the eyes of African Americans, circa 1960. For Gopnik in "The Unreal Thing," Neo is a similarly avenging hero. What common denominators do you find between Gopnik's way of explaining the attraction of heroic figures and Kennedy's? (For that matter, Kong's heroism might be viewed in terms of the lens Gopnik offers for viewing the heroic Ben Franklin in "American Electric.")

4. **Application:** One interesting analytical project is to study several versions of a film—the original and its remake(s). The fact that the film gets remade speaks to something enduring in its vision of things, something that might be called mythic or transhistorical. But the remake also suggests the desire to update that vision, or at least it suggests that a new version of the vision might prove newly marketable.

   There are at least three full-fledged versions of *King Kong*: Merian C. Cooper's 1933 original, John Guillerman's 1976 version, and Peter Jackson's 2005 remake. For more data on these, see the links at www.thomsonedu.com/english/rosenwasser. How do contemporary reviews of these films interpret them as cultural statements? Explore a range of reviews, focusing on how the films are being received. Clearly, you could study just one of these films in this context, or you could look at two or three. Surely Kennedy's remarks about the "impulse to fling a bomb" lurking "in the heart of urban man" (see paragraph 8) sound differently to post-9/11 ears. But his is a Civil Rights era review, not a post-9/11 review. Is Peter Jackson's version of *King Kong* a post-9/11 one? What do the reviews think?

5. **Application:** Rather than focusing on remakes, choose a film and its sequel. Here you might use Gopnik's review as a model. Look at the kinds of comparisons he offers between the first and the second *Matrix* films to guide the ways you assess the sequel in relation to the original. Once again, compile a reception history of the films in question.

6. **Application:** Select a film that has enjoyed significant popularity and, using Kennedy's essay as a model, analyze the reasons for the film's popularity with a particular audience. After you have drafted a version of your review, you may find it useful to compile a reception history of the film. (First, though, produce your own analysis, to avoid losing your point of view to what others have written.) ◗

FOR FURTHER RESEARCH: THE REVIEW AS CULTURAL ANALYSIS

By Kelly Cannon, Reference Librarian

The readings and activities below invite you to further explore the theme of The Review as Cultural Analysis. WARNING: Some essays are polemical; they are intended to promote insight and discussion (or a starting point for your next paper). To access the online readings, visit the *Writing Analytically with Readings* website at www.thomsonedu.com/english/rosenwasser.

Online

***Common Sense Media Reviews*. 2006. Common Sense Media, Inc. 26 March 2006.**
Family-friendly reviews of movies and television.

Explore: Search for a favorite television program or movie. How would you characterize the politics of this site? (Borick's article "On Political Labels" in Chapter 19 might be of help here.) What particular language in the review you have selected indicates how the website itself is a comment on American culture?

"*King Kong*." *IMDb*. 2006. Internet Movie Database, Inc. 26 March 2006.
A well-known movie review website, linking to nearly 300 reviews of the 2005 *King Kong*, all from recognized film review sites.

Explore: Choose the link to "external reviews" and to "user ratings." What makes someone an authority on film?

***KongisKing.net*. 2006. 26 March 2006.**
A blog devoted to *King Kong*.

Explore: Who is this blog for? Click on the link to "Boards." What did *King Kong* devotees tend to like and dislike about the new version—and culturally speaking, so what?

In Print

(Ask your librarian about possible online access to items marked with **.)

****Adalian, Josef. "'King' Ascends to Fox Crown: Toon Comedy Gets Payback for Years of Blue-Collar Slogging." *Variety* (12 August 2002): 15.**
An article that attempts to explain why the television cartoon *King of the Hill* has survived but not necessarily thrived.

Explore: Watch an episode of *King of the Hill*. Then, reflect on this article, comparing it with Matt Bai's essay on the show. Why do you think *King of the Hill* appeals to rather than offends its Middle America audience?

****Carlson, Shawn. "Benjamin Franklin's Science." *Scientific American* 92.1 (January/February 2003): 77–79.**
A different take from that of Gopnik on the book *Bolt of Fate: Benjamin Franklin and His Electric Kite Hoax* by Tom Tucker.

Explore: What is it about this book review that is so different from Gopnik's review of the same book? To what extent can the difference be attributed to the subject area of the journal in which this review was published?

****"Classroom Reviews of *The Matrix*." *Journal of Adolescent and Adult Literacy* 44.5 (February 2001): 483–485.**
Australian high school students review the film *The Matrix*.

Explore: How are these reviews similar to or different from each other? Taken as a group (and with the idea of reception theory in mind), how do they illuminate elements of the *Matrix* phenomenon?

****"Man vs. Man." *Advertising Age* (13 June 2005): 2+.**
Probes the future of men, looking at where masculinity is headed.

Explore: Compare this essay with the Malcolm Gladwell essay on men wearing khakis. What does men's fashion say about masculinity today?

****Marranca, Bonnie. "The Solace of Chocolate Squares: Wallace Shawn in Mourning." *PAJ: A Journal of Performance and Art* 22.3 (2000): 38–46.**
A review of a Wallace Shawn play that also analyzes the cultural significance of *The New Yorker*, a magazine that has employed such fine essayists as Adam Gopnik and Malcolm Gladwell.

Explore: Consider Gopnik's *New Yorker* pieces about Ben Franklin and about *The Matrix* in light of this essay, or Gladwell's on the Dockers ads.

CREDITS

This page constitutes an extension of the copyright page. We have made every effort to trace the ownership of all copyrighted material and to secure permission from copyright holders. In the event of any question arising as to the use of any material, we will be pleased to make the necessary corrections in future printings. Thanks are due to the following authors, publishers, and agents for permission to use the material indicated.

Chapter 1. Page 34: Freewrite on a scene from the film *Good Bye Lenin!* by Sarah Kersh. Reprinted by permission of the author.

Chapter 2. Page 49: "Brooklyn Heights, 4:00 A.M." by Dana Ferrelli. Reprinted by permission of the author. **Page 66:** *Hua dan*: The Dance of Values in the Beijing Opera, reprinted by permission of the author. **Page 71:** Marketing the Girl Next Door: A Declaration of Independence? reprinted by permission of the author.

Chapter 3. Page 84: *The Dancers*, by Sarah Kersh. Pen and ink drawing, 6" × 13.75." Used by permission of Sarah Kersh. **Page 100:** "Playing by the Antioch Rules?" by Eric Fassin, *The New York Times*, December 26, 1993, p. 11. Copyright © 1993 by The New York Times Co. Reprinted by permission.

Chapter 4. Page 122: Excerpt from student paper on *The Tempest*, reprinted by permission of the author.

Chapter 15. Page 389: Christine Rosen, "Our Cell Phones, Ourselves," *The New Atlantis*, Number 6, Summer 2004, pp. 26–45. Reprinted with permission. For more information, visit www.TheNewAtlantis.com. **Page 405:** *Disconnected Urbanism*, Paul Goldberger. Reprinted with permission of the author. **Page 408:** *The Naked Crowd*, Jeffrey Rosen. © Jeffrey Rosen. This essay, which appeared in Spiked.com, is an excerpt from the Naked Crowd: Reclaiming Security and Freedom in an Anxious Age, (Random House, 2004), and is reprinted by permission. **Page 421:** *Blogging in the Global Lunchroom*, Geoffrey Nunberg, Center for the Study of Language and Information. Reprinted with permission of the author. **Page 425:** Ritual (pp. 17–27) from *The Rituals of Dinner: The Origins, Evolutions, Eccentricities, and Meaning of Table Manners*, Margaret Visser. Reprinted with permission of Grove/Atlantic, Inc. **Page 441:** "Imperial Bedroom" from HOW TO BE ALONE by Jonathan Franzen. Copyright © 2003 by Jonathan Franzen. Reprinted by permission of Farrar, Straus and Giroux, LLC. **Page 451:** Reprinted by permission, from Edward R. Tufte, *The Cognitive Style of PowerPoint* (Cheshire, Connecticut, Graphics Press, 2003), as appeared in *Wired* Magazine, September 2003. Originally published in Wired.

Chapter 16. Page 459: Reprinted with the permission of Simon & Schuster Adult Publishing Group, from HOME FROM NOWHERE: Remaking Our Everyday World for the Twenty-First Century by James Howard Kunstler. Copyright © James Howard Kunstler. All rights reserved. **Page 471:** Demolition Zones, Jack Gambino. Reprinted with permission of the author. **Page 484:** Times Regained: First published in The New Yorker, March 2004 © 2004 by Adam Gopnik, permission of The Wylie Agency. **Page 493:** From THE DEATH AND LIFE OF GREAT AMERICAN CITIES by Jane Jacobs, copyright © 1961, 1989 by Jane Jacobs. Used by permission of Random House, Inc. **Page 506:** *Fortress Los Angeles*, Mike Davis from Mike Sorkin's *Variations on a Theme Park* (Hill & Wang, 1992). Reprinted with permission of Verso Books.

Chapter 17. Page 517: Looking at Photographs: Stagers and Recorders, Joseph Elliott. Interviewed by David Rosenwasser and Jill Stephen. Reprinted with permission. **Page 551:** "In Plato's Cave" from ON PHOTOGRAPHY by Susan Sontag. Copyright © 1977 by Susan Sontag. Reprinted by permission of Farrar, Straus and Giroux, LLC. **Page 565:** "Learning to See," from ABOUT THIS LIFE by Barry Lopez, copyright © 1998 by Barry Holstun Lopez. Used by permission of Alfred A. Knopf, a division of Random House, Inc. **Page 577:** "Chapter 3: Images of Women in European Art", from WAYS OF SEEING by John Berger, copyright © 1972 by John Berger. Used by permission of Viking Penguin, a division of Penguin Group (USA) Inc.

Chapter 18. Page 607: *Assimilation, American Style*, Peter Salins. REASON MAGAZINE. Reprinted with permission of The Burr Media Group. **Page 613:** "The Fear of Losing a Culture" from *Hunger of Memory* by Richard Rodriguez. Reprinted by permission of David R. Godine, Publisher, Inc. Copyright © 1982 by Richard Rodriguez. **Page 616:** "In the Kitchen" from COLORED PEOPLE: A MEMOIR by Henry Louis Gates, Jr., copyright © 1994 by Henry Louis Gates, Jr. Used by permission of Alfred A. Knopf, a division of Random House, Inc. **Page 622:** *My Neighborhood*, Ishmael Reed, Originally titled, "My Oakland, There Is a There There." Excerpted from the book, Writin' is Fightin' by Ishmael Reed. Copyright © 1988 by Ishmael Reed. Permission granted by Lowenstein-Yost Associates, Inc. **Page 630:** Reprinted with permission. "On Being White, Female, and Born in Bensonhurt," from Crossing Ocean Parkway, by Marianna De Marco Torgovnick. The University of Chicago Press. **Page 641:** *Put On a Happy Face: Masking the Differences Between Blacks and Whites*, by Benjamin DeMott, 9/1/95. Copyright © 1995 by Harper's Magazine. All rights reserved. Reproduced from the September issue by special permission. **Page 651:** *White Privilege: Unpacking the Invisible Knapsack*, by Peggy McIntosh, from White Privilege and Male Privilege. Reprinted with permission. **Page 663:** *Sticks and Stones: The Irish Identity* by Robert McLiam Wilson. Reprinted with permission of Antony Harwood, Ltd., Agent for Robert McLiam Wilson.

Chapter 19. Page 673: *On Political Labels*, Christopher Borick. Reprinted with permission of the author. **Page 687:** *Justices Amended Constitution on Their Own …*, by James J. Kilpatrick. © 2005. Reprinted by special permission from Universal Press Syndicate and the author. **Page 688:** *… by letting redevelopers take little guy's property*, Richard A. Epstein, *The Morning Call*, July 6, 2005. Reprinted with permission of the author. **Page 689:** *More than Abortion is at Stake in Supreme Court Picks*, John F. Grim, The Morning Call, July 27, 2005. Reprinted with permission of the author. **Page 691:** *Losing Our Country*, Paul Krugman. Copyright © 2005 by The New York Times Co. Reprinted with permission. **Page 694:** "Politics and the English Language" by George Orwell. First published in *Horizon*, April 1946. **Page 706:** *Why Should We Trust This Man?* By Dante Chinni. Reprinted with permission of the author. **Page 711:** *Interview with Frank Luntz*, Online Frontline Piece, 11/9/04. From Frontline and WGBH Educational Foundation Copyright (2) 2005 WBGH/Boston. **Page 725:** Matt Bai, "The Framing Wars" The New York Times Magazine, July 17, 2005. Copyright © The New York Times Magazine. Reprinted by permission. **Page 740:** September 11th: A National Tragedy? James Peck, from Aftermath: Thinking After September 11th: Occasional Papers of the Center for Ethics and Leadership. Reprinted with permission of the author.

Chapter 20. Page 752: The Unreal Thing: First published in The New Yorker, May 19, 2003 © 2003 by Adam Gopnik, permission of The Wylie Agency. **Page 762:** American Electric: First Published in The New Yorker, June 30, 2003 © 2003 by Adam Gopnik, permission of The Wylie Agency. **Page 772:** Matt Bai, The Way We Live Now. "King of the Hill Democrats?" *The New York Times Magazine*, June 26, 2005. Copyright © The New

York Times Magazine. Reprinted by permission. **Page 776:** *Oy Gay!* Kera Bolonik. Reprinted with permission from the November 17, 2003 issue of *The Nation.* For subscription information, call 1-800-333-8536. Portions of each week's Nation magazine can be accessed at http://www.thenation.com **Page 780:** Malcolm Gladwell, "Listening to Khakis: What America's Most Popular Pants Tell Us About the Way Guys Think," The New Yorker. Reprinted with permission of the author. **Page 794:** *Who Killed King Kong?* X.J. Kennedy. Originally published in Dissent Magazine in 1961. Reprinted with permission of the author.

IMAGE CREDITS

Chapter 3. Page 78: Figure 3.1. REUNION DES MUSEES NATIONAUX, ART RESOURCE, NY. James Abbott McNeil Whistler. *Arrangement in Gray and Black No 1: Portrait of the Artist's Mother*, 1871.

Chapter 5. Page 151: Figure 5.4. © Jeff Widener/AP

Chapter 6. Page 179: Figure 6.5. SCALA/ART RESOURCE, NY. Diego Rodrigues Velazquez. *Las Meninas*. 1656.

Chapter 15. Page 452: AP/Wide World Photos.

Chapter 16. Page 472: Figure 16.1. Images Courtesy: Charles Cowles Gallery, New York - Robert Koch Gallery, San Francisco - Nicholas Metivier, Toronto - Galeria Toni Tapies - Barcelona. **Page 474:** Figure 16.2. Images Courtesy: Charles Cowles Gallery, New York - Robert Koch Gallery, San Francisco - Nicholas Metivier, Toronto - Galeria Toni Tapies - Barcelona. **Page 475:** Figure 16.3. Images Courtesy: Charles Cowles Gallery, New York - Robert Koch Gallery, San Francisco - Nicholas Metivier, Toronto, Galeria Toni Tapies - Barcelona. **Page 478:** Figure 16.4. Photographs by Camilo Jose Vergara. **Page 480:** Figure 16.5. Photo by Camilo Jose Vergara. **Page 482:** Figure 16.6. Photo by Camilo Jose Vergara.

Chapter 17. Page 519: Figure 17.1. Photograph © 2006 Museum Associates/LACMA. **Page 520:** Figure 17.2. Courtesy of the artist and Luhring Augustine, New York. **Page 520:** Figure 17.3. Courtesy of the artist and Luhring Augustine, New York. **Page 521:** Figure 17.4. Courtesy of the artist and Luhring Augustine, New York. **Page 522:** Figure 17.5. Hulton Archive/Getty Images. **Page 524:** Figure 17.6. International Center for Photography/Getty Images. **Page 524:** Figure 17.7. © Copyright 2006 Eggleston Artistic Trust, courtesy Cheim and Read, New York. Used with permission. All rights reserved. **Page 527:** Figure 17.8. MOMA, NY/Art Resource, NY. **Page 530:** Figure 17.9. Philadelphia Museum of Art/Corbis © Estate of Marcel Duchamp/ADAGP, Paris. **Page 532:** Figure 17.10. Loretta Lux/Yossi Milo Gallery. **Page 533:** Figure 17.11. Loretta Lux/Yossi Milo Gallery. **Page 534:** Figure 17.12. Time-Life Pictures/Getty Images. **Page 536:** Figure 17.13. © 2004 Andreas Gursky/ARS, NY/VG Bildekunst, Bonn. Courtesy of the artist and Matthew Marks Gallery, NY. **Page 538:** Figure 17.14. Sebastiao Salgado/Contact Press Images. **Page 539:** Figure 17.15. Lauren Greenfield/VII Photo Agency LLC. **Page 540:** Figure 17.16. Sally Mann/Gagosian Gallery, New York. **Page 542:** Figure 17.17. Ed Ruscha/Gagosian Gallery, Beverly Hills. **Page 543:** Figure 17.18. Silver print by Joseph Elliott. **Page 544:** Figure 17.19. Gelatin silver print by Joseph Elliott. **Page 580:**

Figure 17.20. © Musee Conde, Chantilly/Bridgeman Art Library. **Page 581:** Figure 17.21. Bildarchiv Preussischer Kulturbesitz/Art Resource, NY. Gemaeldegalerie, Staatliche Museen zu Berlin, Germany. **Page 582:** Figure 17.22. Erich Lessing/Art Resource, NY. Louvre, Paris, France. **Page 583:** Figure 17.23. Erich Lessing/Art Resource, NY. Kunsthistorisches Museum, Vienna, Austria. **Page 584:** Figure 17.24. © Musee des Beaux-Arts, Strasbourg France/Bridgeman Art Library. **Page 585:** Figure 17.25. © Prado, Madrid, Spain/Bridgeman Art Library. **Page 585:** Figure 17.26. © Army and Navy Club, London, UK/Bridgeman Art Library. **Page 586:** Figure 17.27. Robert Harding/Getty Images. **Page 587:** Figure 17.28. Scala/Art Resource, NY. Museo Etnografico di Castello d'Albertis, Genoa, Italy. **Page 588:** Figure 17.29. National Gallery, London/Corbis. **Page 589:** Figure 17.30. Erich Lessing/Art Resource, NY. **Page 591:** Figure 17.31. Private Collection/Giraudon/Bridgeman Art Library. **Page 592:** Figure 17.32. © Hermitage, St. Petersburg, Russia/Bridgeman Art Library. **Page 594:** Figure 17.33. Kunsthistorisches Museum, Vienna/Bridgeman Art Library. **Page 595:** Figure 17.34. Foto Marburg/Art Resource, NY. **Page 595:** Figure 17.35. Getty Images. **Page 596:** Figure 17.36. Uffizi, Florence/Corbis. **Page 596:** Figure 17.37. Louvre, Paris/Art Archive. **Page 598:** Figure 17.38. The National Portrait Gallery, Smithsonian Institution, Washington, D.C./Art Resource, NY. **Page 599:** Figure 17.39. National Gallery of Art, Washington, D.C.

INDEX